Community Care and the Law

fourth edition

Luke Clements is a consultant solicitor with Scott-Moncrieff Harbour & Sinclair, London and a recognised authority on community care law. He is a Professor at Cardiff Law School (University of Wales) and a member of the Law Society's Mental Health and Disability Committee. He is a consulting editor to the *Journal of Community Care Law and Practice* and *Social Care Law Today* (Arden Davies Publishing) and on the editorial board of the *Community Care Law Reports* (Legal Action Group). He has written widely and his recent publications include *Disabled Children and the Law* (Jessica Kingsley Publishers, 2006) and *Disabled People and European Human Rights* (Policy Press, 2003) – both co-written with Janet Read.

Pauline Thompson is a policy adviser on care finance for Age Concern England. Her background is in social work and welfare rights advice. For many years she wrote the chapters on community care in the *Disability Rights Handbook* (Disability Alliance), and was one of the original authors of the *Paying for Care Handbook* (CPAG). She is a member of the Law Society's Mental Health and Disability Committee and is on the editorial board of the *Community Care Law Reports* (Legal Action Group). She has written this book in a private capacity and the views expressed are not necessarily those of Age Concern England.

Luke Clements and **Pauline Thompson** can be contacted by e-mail at **clementslj@cf.ac.uk**

Community Care and the Law

FOURTH EDITION

Luke Clements and Pauline Thompson

LAG Legal Action Group
2007

This edition published in Great Britain 2007
by LAG Education and Service Trust Limited
242 Pentonville Road, London N1 9UN
www.lag.org.uk

First edition 1996
Reprinted with revisions 1997
Second edition 2000
Third edition 2004

British Library Cataloguing in Publication Data
A CIP catalogue record for this book is available from the British Library

Crown copyright material is produced with the permission of the Controller of HMSO and the Queen's Printer for Scotland.

ISBN 978 1 903307 47 2

Typeset by Refinecatch Ltd, Bungay, Suffolk.
Printed by Hobbs the Printer, Totton, Hants.

Preface

Community care law results from a hotchpotch of statutes, many of which originated as private members' bills (and are all the better for it). Although there are a number of general rules which can be applied to the subject, the most important appears to be that for every general rule there is at least one exception.

As with the previous editions, it has been difficult to decide what to exclude. How can any text do justice to the subject and yet exclude detailed consideration of welfare benefits or special education? And so on. These subjects, however, are not covered in detail. We have tried to keep to the central community care statutes as listed in section 46 of the National Health Service and Community Care Act 1990. Welfare benefits are not covered for two reasons: the first is that they change so frequently and the second is that the Child Poverty Action Group and the Disability Alliance already publish comprehensive and indispensable annual guides. The same can also be said for the excellent *Education Law and Practice* published by Jordans.

We have tried to keep to a minimum the use of abbreviations, but have had to shorten references to the commonly used statutes. Likewise we have referred throughout to the early and important general policy guidance, *Community Care in the Next Decade and Beyond: policy guidance* (1990) as the '1990 Policy Guidance'. In several chapters or sections a particular piece of policy or practice guidance is important and in that section we have given it a shortened title, having of course explained what the shortened title refers to.

A terminological difficulty arises in England concerning references to social services departments. As a result of the Children Act 2004 local authority children's services responsibilities have been effectively merged with their education responsibilities and new Children's Services Departments created – and in due course these may transform themselves into 'children's trusts'. These organisational reconfigurations do not apply in Wales, and in England the change only affects children: on reaching 18, social care responsibility shifts to the relevant Adult Social Services Department. For the sake of simplicity we continue to refer to social services departments in this text, although depending upon the context, this may be a reference to a Children's Services Department or and Adult Services Department – or indeed to both.

In writing this book very special thanks are due to Melanie Lee of Turpin & Miller solicitors, Oxford who took primary charge for chapter 22 on Asylum seekers and persons who are destitute.

Special thanks are also due to:

- Kiran Dattani Pitt on behalf of Values into Action of Oxford House, Derbyshire Street, London E2 6HG and the authors Andrew Holman and Catherine Bewley for the kind permission to use the precedent Independent Living Trust Deed – that appears in Appendix 3. The precedent is extracted from their indispensable guide to Independent Living Trusts 'Trusting Independence: a practical guide to independent living trusts' (2001).
- Paul Bowen for the kind permission to use extracts from his article (jointly written with Luke Clements) 'NHS Continuing Care and independent living' that appears in the *Community Care Law Reports*, (2007) 10 CCLR 343 (Legal Action Group).
- The Welsh Assembly officers who have helped us try and understand the distinct community care regime in Wales and in doing so shown considerable patience.
- Those officials at the Department of Health who have shown no less patience as we have pestered them concerning the many and on-going changes which were likely to have been published by the time of this new edition.

Special apologies and thanks are due to our publisher, Esther Pilger for all the missed deadlines and the support in getting this latest edition into print.

In writing this book we have received enormous assistance from countless kind and wise people. Many important concepts have been explained to us by social workers in particular, and our clients and members of the public raising their many and varied questions have taught us far more than (we hope) they will ever realise. Special thanks are due to: Karen Ashton, John Bangs, Richard Bartholomew, Caroline Bielanska, Steve Brett, Simon Bull, Caroline Ellis, Jean Gould, Nigel Godfrey, Francis Hasler, Carolyn James, Nicola Mackintosh, Michael Mandelstam, Jim McKenny, Camilla Parker, Phil Fennell, Stephen Knafler, Jenny McGhie, Jenny McCabe, Ed Mitchell, Mark Partridge, Janet Read, Cathy Score, Wendy Smart, Patricia Southern, Helen Winfield and Radoslaw Stech. We have almost certainly omitted from this list many who have also assisted us and to them we apologise.

What is wrong in this text is entirely our own doing and we would welcome any critical feedback.

Luke Clements
Pauline Thompson
August 2007

Contents

APPENDICES

Table of cases

Table of statutes

Table of statutory instruments

Table of circulars and guidance

CIRCULARS

DFES Circulars

1/93	9.83

DHSS Circulars

12/70 para 5	2.12, 2.39
19/7	11.39, 20.15
para 3	20.15
para 4	9.53, 20.20, 20.21
para 5(b)	20.21
para 6(a)	20.24
para 6(b)	20.24
para 7	20.17, 20.21
para 10	20.22, 20.28, 20.29
para 11 *et seq*	20.21

Department of Health Circulars

11/50	14.10
HC (90)23: LASSL (90)11	21.7, 27.2

Department of the Environment Circulars

10/90	9.100, 15.30
10/92. See *Housing and Community Care*	
17/96	9.100, 9.103, 15.74, 15.85
para 5	9.103
para 6	9.103
para 7.5.4	15.85
para 7.6.1	15.74
para 7.6.2	15.75
Annex I	15.29
Annex I para 7	15.75
Annex I para 8	15.75
Annex I para 9	15.75
Annex I para 45	15.85
4/98	9.100, 15.30
para 6	1.67

Health Service Circulars

HSC 1998/048	7.124, 7.139
HSC 1998/158	1.54
HSC 1999/180	14.24
para 2	14.24

Health Service Circulars *continued*

HSC 2000/003: LAC (2000)3 *After-care under the Mental Health Act 1983: section 117 after-care services*	6.40, 6.50, 6.74, 21.34, 21.41, 21.44
HSC 2000/010	13.124
HSC 2001/15	14.25, 14.32, 14.35, 14.36, 14.37, 14.44, 14.67, 14.69, 14.71, 14.92, 14.110, 14.111
Annex C	14.86
Annex E para 8	5.58
HSC 2001/17	5.55, 5.56, 5.57, 6.65, 13.67, 13.72, 13.98
para 8	13.92
para 9	13.92
HSC 2003/006	6.65, 13.98
para 30	13.93

Local Authority Circulars

LAC 13/74	
para 11(i)	9.24, 9.28, 9.32
para 11(ii)	9.41
LAC (87)6	16.28
para 3	3.9
para 4	3.9
LAC (90)7	9.102, 9.106, 15.30
para 14	9.101
para 15	9.100
paras 15–17	9.102
para 19	9.115
para 58	9.102
LAC (91)6	2.13
LAC (92)17	13.125, 14.102, 14.103
Annex A para 10	13.127
LAC 92(24)	13.88
Annex A para 7	14.110
para 2	13.75, 13.86
LAC(93)2	3.53, 4.77, 23.12, 23.16, 23.30, 23.35
para 10	23.35

Welsh Guidance

Table of local government ombudsman complaints

Table of European conventions

Abbreviations

AD	Advance decision
ADD	Attention deficit disorder
ADHD	Attention deficit hyperactivity disorder
ADSS	Association of Directors of Social Services
CA	Children Act
CAF	Common assessment framework
CC(DD)A	Community Care (Delayed Discharges etc) Act
CC(DP)A	Community Care (Direct Payments) Act
CCLR	Community Care Law Reports
CDCA	Carers and Disabled Children Act
CHC	Community health council
CRAG	Charging for Residential Accommodation Guide
CRB	Criminal Records Bureau
C(RS)A	Carers (Recognition and Services) Act
CSA	Care Standards Act
CSCI	Commission for Social Care Inspection
CSDPA	Chronically Sick and Disabled Persons Act
CSSIW	Care and Social Services Inspectorate Wales
CVI	Certificate of vision impairment
DAT	Drug action team
DDA	Disability Discrimination Act
DFG	Disable facilities grant
DHSS	Department of Health and Social Security
DLA	Disability living allowance
DP(SCR)A	Disabled Persons (Services, Consultation and Representation) Act
DWP	Department for Work and Pensions
EHB	Enhanced housing benefit
EMI	Elderly mentally ill
EPA	Enduring power of attorney
EPIOC	Electric powered indoor/oudoor wheelchair
FACS	Fair access to care services
FSS	Formula spending share
GP	General practitioner
HA	Housing Act/Health Act
HASSASSAA	Health and Social Services and Social Security Adjudications Act
HGCRA	Housing Grants, Construction and Regeneration Act

HSCA	Health and Social Care Act
HSC(CHS)A	Health and Social Care (Community Health and Standards) Act
HSCWB	Health, social care and well-being
HSPHA	Health Services and Public Health Act
IAA	Immigration and Asylum Act
IMCA	Independent mental capacity advocate
IRP	Independent review panel
JIP	Joint investment plan
LAA	Local area agreement
LASSA	Local Authority Social Services Act
LASSL	Local authority social services letter
LDIAG	Learning Disability Implementation Advisory Group
LGA	Local Government Act
LHB	Local health board
LPA	Lasting power of attorney
LRR	Local reference rent
MCA	Mental Capacity Act
MHA	Mental Health Act
NAA	National Assistance Act
NAM	New Asylum Model
NASS	National Asylum Support Service
NCSC	National Care Standards Commission
NHS	National Health Service
NHSA	National Health Service Act
NHSCCA	National Health Service and Community Care Act
NIAA	Nationality, Immigration and Asylum Act
NMS	National minimum standard
NSF	National service framework
NTA	National Treatment Agency for Substance Misuse
OFT	Office of Fair Trading
OT	Occupational therapist
PALS	Patient advice and liaison service
PCT	Primary care trust
PSSRU	Personal Social Services Research Unit
PTS	Patient transport services
RAP	Referrals, assessments and packages of care
RHA	Registered Homes Act
RNCC	Registered nursing care contribution
RRO	Regulatory Reform (Housing Assistance) (England and Wales) Order 2002
SAP	Single assessment process
SCIE	Social Care Institute for Excellence
SHA	Strategic health authority
SVGA	Safeguarding Vulnerable Groups Act
UFSAMC	Unified and fair system for assessing and managing care
WRS	Worker Registration Scheme

Flowcharts contained in this text

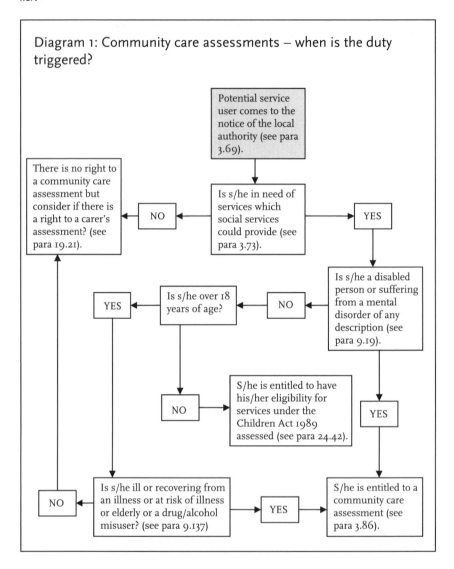

Diagram 1: Community care assessments – when is the duty triggered?

Potential service user comes to the notice of the local authority (see para 3.69).

Is s/he in need of services which social services could provide (see para 3.73).

NO → There is no right to a community care assessment but consider if there is a right to a carer's assessment? (see para 19.21).

YES → Is s/he a disabled person or suffering from a mental disorder of any description (see para 9.19).

NO → Is s/he over 18 years of age?

YES →

NO → S/he is entitled to have his/her eligibility for services under the Children Act 1989 assessed (see para 24.42).

YES → S/he is entitled to a community care assessment (see para 3.86).

Is s/he ill or recovering from an illness or at risk of illness or elderly or a drug/alcohol misuser? (see para 9.137)

NO →

YES → S/he is entitled to a community care assessment (see para 3.86).

Diagram 2: Department of Health Guidance concerning the assessment process
For the Welsh Assembly equivalent guidance see para 3.26 and footnotes 26 and 35.

General Assessment Guidance Adults with community care needs

- *Fair Access to Care Services – Policy Guidance*, 2002 [FACS 2002 policy guidance]* (see para 3.27)
- *Fair Access to Care Services – Practice Guidance*, 2003 [FACS 2003 practice guidance] (see para 3.27)
- *Community Care – Community Care in the Next Decade and Beyond: policy guidance*, 1990 [1990 Policy Guidance] (see para 3.24) *Care Management And Assessment:*
- *Practitioners' Guide*, 1991 (see para 3.24)

Carers

Guidance on carers' assessments is in *The Carers and Disabled Children Act 2000: a practitioners guide to carers' assessments*, 2001 (see para 16.7) and general guidance is in the practice guide to the Carers (Equal Opportunities) Act 2004 (see para 16.8)

Disabled children

FACS guidance is not of direct relevance. Specific guidance exists as *The Framework for the Assessment of Children in Need and their Families*, 2000, policy and practice guidance (see para 24.15)

Specific user group assessment guidance

Older people

- NSF for Older People (see para 3.29)
- Single assessment process, 2002 (see para 3.30)

Mental health service users

- NSF for Mental Health, 1999 (see para 3.35)
- *Effective Care Co-ordination in Mental Health Services – Modernising the Care Programme Approach*, 1999.

People with learning disabilities

- *Valuing people: White Paper*, 2001 (see para 3.36)
- *Valuing people: implementation policy guidance*, LAC (2001)23

Diagram 3: The three stages in assessment and care planning

Information Gathering

The social services department obtain sufficient information in order to make a decision about the most appropriate way of meeting the person's community care needs (see para 3.86).

Note

Note
Depending on the extent of the person's care needs, this may be a brief process, or more complex, potentially requiring input from carers (see para 16.17), and others with relevant information such as health (see para 3.126) and housing (see para 3.130). It may also require consideration of factors such as the person's emotional, cultural and psychological needs and preferences (see para 3.89).

Service provision decision

The social services department decides which of the 'needs' and 'requirements' that have been identified in the assessment 'call for the provision of services' (see para 3.134).

Note

Note
The social services department may not consider that it is 'necessary' to provide everything which is identified in the assessment as being of potential benefit to the person. In general it will only provide services which are essential or for which the assessed need meets its 'eligibility criteria' (see para 3.143).

Care plan

The social services department now prepares a 'care plan' which explains what 'care needs' must be met and details the services that are to be provided in order to do this (see para 4.1). The care plan also explains what health or housing services are to be provided by the housing or health authority (if any). The plan will take account of the user's preferences and also identify those 'unmet needs' which do not qualify for services (see para 4.14).

Diagram 6: Common service provision problems

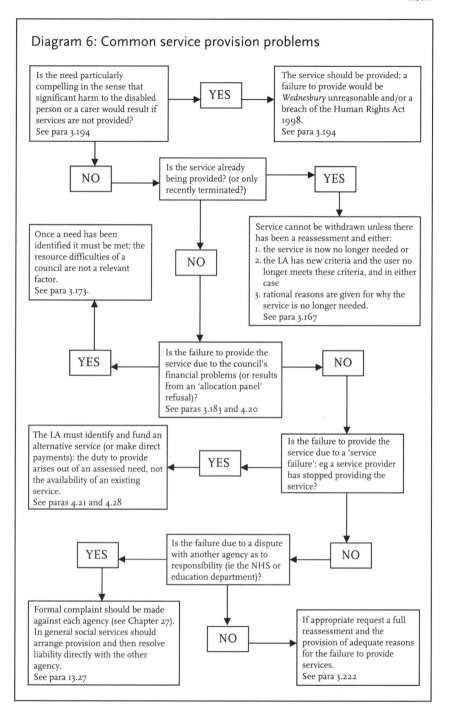

Is the need particularly compelling in the sense that significant harm to the disabled person or a carer would result if services are not provided?
See para 3.194

YES

The service should be provided; a failure to provide would be *Wednesbury* unreasonable and/or a breach of the Human Rights Act 1998.
See para 3.194

NO

Is the service already being provided? (or only recently terminated?)

YES

Service cannot be withdrawn unless there has been a reassessment and either:
1. the service is now no longer needed or
2. the LA has new criteria and the user no longer meets these criteria, and in either case
3. rational reasons are given for why the service is no longer needed.
See para 3.167

Once a need has been identified it must be met; the resource difficulties of a council are not a relevant factor.
See para 3.173.

NO

YES

Is the failure to provide the service due to the council's financial problems (or results from an 'allocation panel' refusal)?
See paras 3.183 and 4.20

NO

The LA must identify and fund an alternative service (or make direct payments): the duty to provide arises out of an assessed need, not the availability of an existing service.
See paras 4.21 and 4.28

YES

Is the failure to provide the service due to a 'service failure': eg a service provider has stopped providing the service?

YES

Is the failure due to a dispute with another agency as to responsibility (ie the NHS or education department)?

NO

Formal complaint should be made against each agency (see Chapter 27). In general social services should arrange provision and then resolve liability directly with the other agency.
See para 13.27

NO

If appropriate request a full reassessment and the provision of adequate reasons for the failure to provide services.
See para 3.222

Diagram 10: Care home entitlement

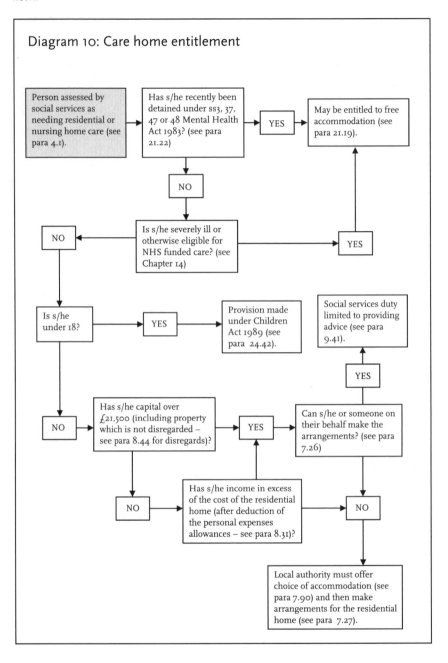

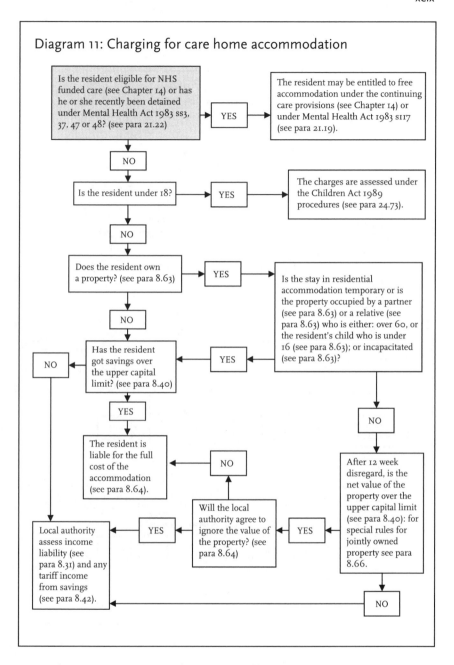

Diagram 11: Charging for care home accommodation

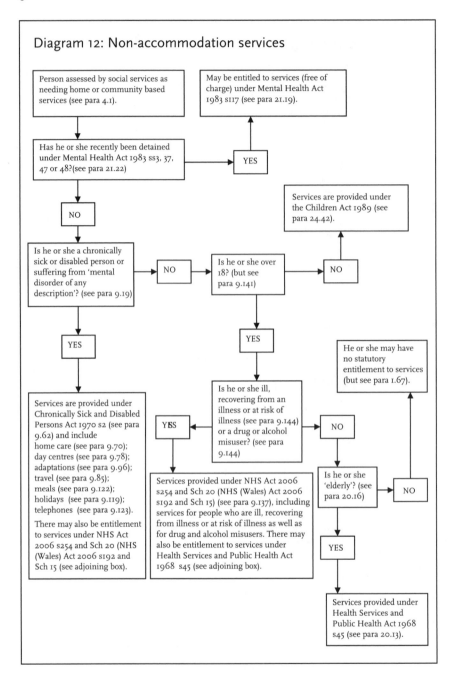

Diagram 12: Non-accommodation services

Person assessed by social services as needing home or community based services (see para 4.1).

May be entitled to services (free of charge) under Mental Health Act 1983 s117 (see para 21.19).

Has he or she recently been detained under Mental Health Act 1983 ss3, 37, 47 or 48?(see para 21.22)

YES

NO

Services are provided under the Children Act 1989 (see para 24.42).

Is he or she a chronically sick or disabled person or suffering from 'mental disorder of any description'? (see para 9.19)

NO

Is he or she over 18? (but see para 9.141)

NO

YES

YES

He or she may have no statutory entitlement to services (but see para 1.67).

Services are provided under Chronically Sick and Disabled Persons Act 1970 s2 (see para 9.62) and include
home care (see para 9.70);
day centres (see para 9.78);
adaptations (see para 9.96);
travel (see para 9.85);
meals (see para 9.122);
holidays (see para 9.119);
telephones (see para 9.123).

There may also be entitlement to services under NHS Act 2006 s254 and Sch 20 (NHS (Wales) Act 2006 s192 and Sch 15 (see adjoining box).

Is he or she ill, recovering from an illness or at risk of illness (see para 9.144) or a drug or alcohol misuser? (see para 9.144)

YES

NO

Is he or she 'elderly'? (see para 20.16)

NO

Services provided under NHS Act 2006 s254 and Sch 20 (NHS (Wales) Act 2006 s192 and Sch 15) (see para 9.137), including services for people who are ill, recovering from illness or at risk of illness as well as for drug and alcohol misusers. There may also be entitlement to services under Health Services and Public Health Act 1968 s45 (see adjoining box).

YES

Services provided under Health Services and Public Health Act 1968 s45 (see para 20.13).

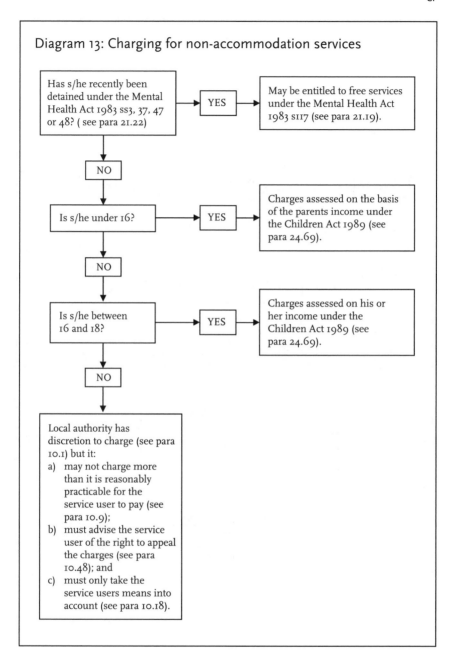

Diagram 13: Charging for non-accommodation services

Has s/he recently been detained under the Mental Health Act 1983 ss3, 37, 47 or 48? (see para 21.22)

YES → May be entitled to free services under the Mental Health Act 1983 s117 (see para 21.19).

NO

Is s/he under 16?

YES → Charges assessed on the basis of the parents income under the Children Act 1989 (see para 24.69).

NO

Is s/he between 16 and 18?

YES → Charges assessed on his or her income under the Children Act 1989 (see para 24.69).

NO

Local authority has discretion to charge (see para 10.1) but it:
a) may not charge more than it is reasonably practicable for the service user to pay (see para 10.9);
b) must advise the service user of the right to appeal the charges (see para 10.48); and
c) must only take the service users means into account (see para 10.18).

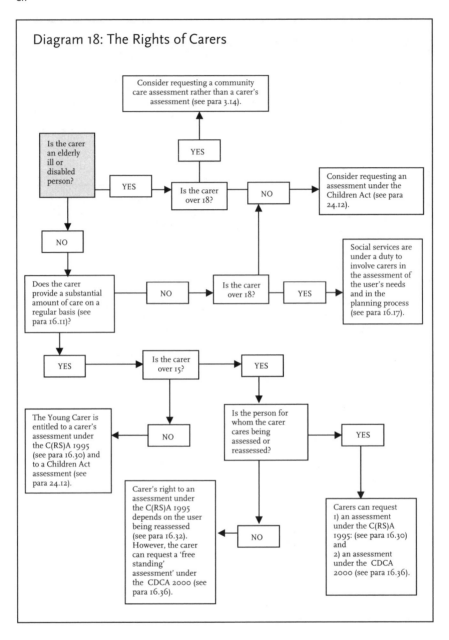

Diagram 18: The Rights of Carers

Consider requesting a community care assessment rather than a carer's assessment (see para 3.14).

YES

Is the carer an elderly ill or disabled person?

YES

Is the carer over 18?

NO

Consider requesting an assessment under the Children Act (see para 24.12).

NO

Does the carer provide a substantial amount of care on a regular basis (see para 16.11)?

NO

Is the carer over 18?

YES

Social services are under a duty to involve carers in the assessment of the user's needs and in the planning process (see para 16.17).

YES

Is the carer over 15?

YES

The Young Carer is entitled to a carer's assessment under the C(RS)A 1995 (see para 16.30) and to a Children Act assessment (see para 24.12).

NO

Is the person for whom the carer cares being assessed or reassessed?

YES

Carer's right to an assessment under the C(RS)A 1995 depends on the user being reassessed (see para 16.32). However, the carer can request a 'free standing' assessment' under the CDCA 2000 (see para 16.36).

NO

Carers can request
1) an assessment under the C(RS)A 1995: (see para 16.30) and
2) an assessment under the CDCA 2000 (see para 16.36).

Diagram 20: Complaints

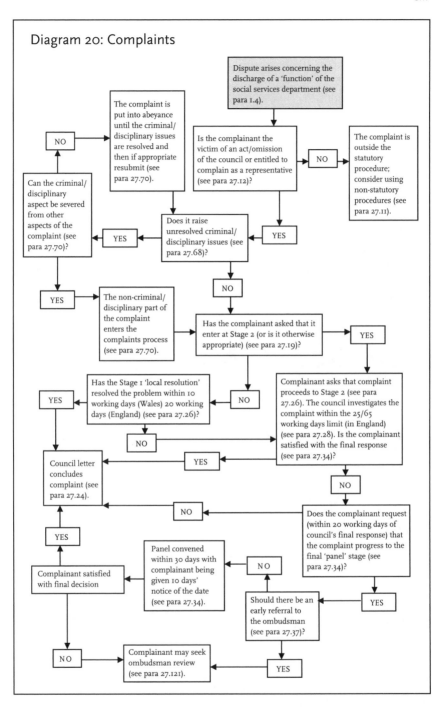

Dispute arises concerning the discharge of a 'function' of the social services department (see para 1.4).

Is the complainant the victim of an act/omission of the council or entitled to complain as a representative (see para 27.12)?

NO → The complaint is outside the statutory procedure; consider using non-statutory procedures (see para 27.11).

YES

Does it raise unresolved criminal/disciplinary issues (see para 27.68)?

YES → The complaint is put into abeyance until the criminal/disciplinary issues are resolved and then if appropriate resubmit (see para 27.70).

NO → Can the criminal/disciplinary aspect be severed from other aspects of the complaint (see para 27.70)?

NO

YES → The non-criminal/disciplinary part of the complaint enters the complaints process (see para 27.70).

Has the complainant asked that it enter at Stage 2 (or is it otherwise appropriate) (see para 27.19)?

YES → Complainant asks that complaint proceeds to Stage 2 (see para 27.26). The council investigates the complaint within the 25/65 working days limit (in England) (see para 27.28). Is the complainant satisfied with the final response (see para 27.34)?

NO → Has the Stage 1 'local resolution' resolved the problem within 10 working days (Wales) 20 working days (England) (see para 27.26)?

YES → Council letter concludes complaint (see para 27.24).

NO → YES → Council letter concludes complaint

Does the complainant request (within 20 working days of council's final response) that the complaint progress to the final 'panel' stage (see para 27.34)?

NO → Council letter concludes complaint (see para 27.24).

YES → Should there be an early referral to the ombudsman (see para 27.37)?

NO → Panel convened within 30 days with complainant being given 10 days' notice of the date (see para 27.34).

Complainant satisfied with final decision

YES → Council letter concludes complaint

NO → Complainant may seek ombudsman review (see para 27.121).

YES → Complainant may seek ombudsman review (see para 27.121).

Introduction

I.1   When Sir William Beveridge declared war on the five giant evils in society he had in mind Giant Want; Giant Disease; Giant Ignorance; Giant Squalor and Giant Idleness. At the end of the Second World War legislation was brought forward with the purpose of slaying some of these monsters: the Education Act 1944, the NHS Act 1946 and the National Assistance Act (NAA) 1948. Giant Squalor was to be slain by a concerted programme of slum clearance and the building, within ten years, of three million new houses.[1]

I.2   The neglect of disabled, elderly and ill people living in the community was in many respects the forgotten sixth Giant. NAA 1948 Part III did however contain the means by which Giant Neglect was to be slain, namely the provision of 'community care services for ill, elderly and disabled people' and indeed accommodation for anyone else who was 'in need of care and attention which is not otherwise available'.[2]

I.3   It is difficult to lay down strict rules as to the nature of these 'services'. In general they are provided by social services departments, although the NHS also has community care responsibilities (see Chapter 14); in general they are personal care services although social services departments may now provide the disabled person with cash by a direct payment (see Chapter 12). While the service is primarily concerned with personal care rather than health care, on occasions it will involve the provision of nursing (see para 14.20). Likewise, while community care is not primarily concerned with the provision of housing or education services, at its margins it does embrace obligations in both these areas (see paras 7.51 and 9.82). At its heart community care is about the provision of accommodation in residential care homes and the provision 'in the community' of home helps, adaptations, day centres and meals on wheels. As an arm of the welfare state it commands £12 billion per annum of public resources in services.[3]

I.4   The state's assumption of responsibility for the provision of community care services predates Beveridge, however, by almost 400 years

---

1   N Timmins, *The Five Giants*, Fontana, 1996.
2   NAA 1948 s21.
3   HC Debates col 332W, 16 April 2007, Ms Rosie Winterton in response to question by Mr Laws: Community Care Expenditure – the gross current expenditure on residential care, home care and other community-based services for adults, England 2005–06 (in 000s) being (a) £7,042,900, (b) £2,486,400 and (c) £2,258,600.

and although NAA 1948 s1 boldly proclaims that the 'Poor Law is abolished', the present scheme bears many traits of its infamous forebear.

1.5   Sir William Holdsworth[4] considered that the poor law system commenced with a Statute of 1535–36 (27 Henry VIII c 25), the preamble to which declared that the former Acts were defective because no provision was made in them for providing work for the unemployed. Sir William listed six principles, which he considered as underlying the early poor law development, namely:

1) the duty to contribute to the support of the poor was a legal duty of the state;
2) the parish (via the justices) was the administrative unit for assessing need and payments;
3) the impotent poor were to be supported in the places in which they were settled (but not necessarily where they were born – previously they would have been directed to return to their birth place);
4) the children of people who could not work had to be taught a trade to enable them to support themselves;
5) the able bodied vagrant and beggar should be suppressed by criminal law;
6) the able bodied should have work provided for them and it be compulsory for them to do that work.

1.6   We see, particularly in 1–3, signs of this parentage today. The obligation still rests with local councils (albeit social services authorities rather than the parish). The concept of ordinary residence persists, as do the liable relative rules and the importance of the inter-relationship between community care and education, housing and employment. While categories 5 and 6 are of relevance to our present welfare benefits system, they too have echoes in the concept of work fare, claimants' availability for work and indeed under NAA 1948 s51 it still remains a criminal offence to 'neglect to maintain oneself'.

1.7   With the abolition of the 'Poor Law' by NAA 1948 Part I, local resources (principally the workhouses) had to be redistributed. The best of these were absorbed into the fledgling NHS and the remainder were put to use in meeting the new obligations created by Part III of the 1948 Act.[5]

1.8   Part II replaced the poor law system with a national means tested benefits system known as national assistance administered by the National Assistance Board, rather than by local councils. In due course Part II was repealed and national assistance replaced by supplementary benefit, which itself has been replaced by income support. Income support and pension credit is, however, based upon essentially the same means tested national principles which characterised national assistance.

1.9   Part III of the Act tackled the needs of vulnerable people for residential accommodation and community or home-based (domiciliary) care

---

4   Sir William Holdsworth, *A History of English Law* vol IV, 3rd impression, 1977, pp390 et seq.
5   For an excellent account of the evolution of 'community care' see R Means and R Smith, *Community Care*, Macmillan, 1994.

services. Section 21 obliged authorities to provide residential accommodation for elderly and disabled people as well as temporary residential accommodation for homeless people where their homelessness had arisen through unforeseen circumstances. The accommodation obligations were met by the use of workhouses: as hostels for the homeless and as 'homes' for the disabled and elderly. The residential accommodation obligations under section 21 have changed little since 1948; it is still the statutory basis for the vast majority of local authority residential accommodation placements. In 1977 the primary duty to accommodate homeless people was transferred to housing authorities via Stephen Ross MP's private member's bill which became the Housing (Homeless Persons) Act 1977: its enactment addressing many of the appalling problems highlighted in the film 'Cathy Come Home'.

I.10 The only other significant change to section 21 resulted from the National Health Service and Community Care Act (NHSCCA) 1990. The 1990 Act repealed a provision under NHS Act 1977 Sch 8 which enabled social services authorities to provide residential accommodation for people who needed it through illness, and by amendment this accommodation obligation was transferred to section 21. The 1990 Act also amended section 21 so as to enable social services authorities to purchase nursing home accommodation in addition to residential care accommodation.

I.11 Despite the rationing and general shortages present in 1948, section 21 placed a duty on authorities to provide residential accommodation for such persons who were ordinarily resident in their area and who were in need of care and attention which was not otherwise available to them. This obligation, in addition to the other social welfare duties – the house building programme, the creation of the new NHS and the education reforms – represented a huge public spending commitment. Perhaps not surprisingly therefore, when it came to the provision of community or domiciliary care services, authorities were not obliged to provide these services, although they were given discretion to do so if they were able.

I.12 NAA 1948 s29 empowered[6] authorities to provide four general types of service:

- advice and guidance;[7]
- the preparation of a register of disabled people;
- the provision of 'occupational activities' (such as workshops) for disabled people; and
- facilities which assist disabled people to overcome limitations of communication or mobility.

I.13 The power to provide such services was limited to disabled people. This represented the concern in 1948 to ensure that those people who had sacrificed their health for peace should be given priority when it came to

---

6   These discretionary powers were subsequently converted to 'target duties' (see para 1.26) by directions issued as LAC (93)10.
7   It is pursuant to this provision that most social services welfare rights units are still provided.

the provision of scarce resources.[8] In 1948 there was in relative terms a greater number of younger disabled people – in the form of wounded soldiers returning home and those injured in the bombing. This legislative prioritisation of the needs of disabled people (as opposed to those of the temporarily ill or elderly) remains anachronistically today, albeit to a lesser extent.

I.14 Given the enormous obligations placed on authorities in the post-war austerity years, the community care services provided under section 29 were in general modest. Authorities were not under a statutory duty to provide them and in any event the community care services available under section 29 were vaguely expressed, eg, 'assistance in overcoming limitations of mobility or communication'. What was required therefore was a statutory provision (similar in nature to section 21) which provided, as of right, specific community care services for all those in need.

I.15 Although the post-war austerity years gave way to the increasingly prosperous 1950s and the relatively affluent 1960s, the provision of community care services remained a Cinderella area in social welfare terms. The mid and late 1960s were also characterised by a change in social philosophical attitudes – with, for instance, the enactment of the Family Law Reform Act 1969, the Children and Young Persons Act 1969 and the creation of social services departments in 1971 consequent upon the Seebohm report. This attitude was at considerable variance with that which promoted NAA 1948 s29; the cross-heading to which section blandly states 'services for blind, deaf, dumb and crippled persons, etc'. While therefore the pressure for a change in the statutory framework of community care services was present by the mid-1960s, reform was slow in coming.

I.16 We will never again see major social welfare legislation of the type enacted during the period 1945–51. Since that time, beneficial social welfare legislation has generally originated from one of two sources. The first is the European Court of Human Rights; into this category one might place the Mental Health Act (MHA) 1983 and the Children Act 1989. In terms of community care, questions concerning physical or learning difficulties, age and (non-mental) ill health have attracted hardly any complaints to Strasbourg. The second source is Acts of Parliament which started life as private members' bills, such as the Housing (Homeless Persons) Act 1977.

I.17 On 6 November 1969 it was announced that Alf Morris MP had won first place in the annual ballot for private members' bills. He chose to promote his own bill (which he himself drafted), the Chronically Sick and Disabled Persons Bill. The Act received Royal Assent on 29 May 1970, the day that parliament was dissolved for the 1970 general election.[9] The most important section of that Act has proved to be section 2. It is drafted so as to make the provision of services under NAA 1948 s29 obligatory (rather

8 H Bolderson, *Social Security, Disability and Rehabilitation*, Jessica Kingsley Publishers, 1991, p115.
9 For an account of the passing of the Act, see RADAR, *Be it enacted . . .*, 1995.

than discretionary) and in place of section 29's vague wording, to spell out precisely what services are to be provided. The 1970 Act remains the finest community care statute, providing disabled people with private law rights to specific services. Despite the significance of section 2, however, history has shown it to have three defects.

I.18   The first is that its services are only available to disabled people (as with NAA 1948 s29). Other statutory provisions are therefore required to cater for people who need such services not because they are 'permanently and substantially handicapped',[10] but because they are either frail elderly or ill (but not permanently ill). The second defect concerns two particular drafting imperfections with this section, which are considered below. The third is that the section has proved to be simply too generous – from the perspective of social services authorities. On any reasonable interpretation it entitles disabled people to receive high quality services 'as of right'. In 1970, at the end of the 'Golden Phase' of the 20th century,[11] such rights were perhaps seen as a logical next step in the development of the welfare state. The subsequent turmoil in the west, precipitated by the oil crisis in the early 1970s, led to a general retreat from such specific and (in budgetary terms) open-ended welfare rights. As a consequence, subsequent community care legislation has been cloth of a duller weave; generally 'resource' rather than 'rights' oriented. Section 2 is, sadly, out of step with all the other community care legislation and this incongruity is becoming ever more obvious.

I.19   Section 2 provided disabled people with the right to good quality community care services. The need for elderly people to have such services (when they were not themselves 'permanently and substantially handicapped') was satisfied by the enactment of Health Services and Public Health Act 1968 s45 which enabled authorities to make similar arrangements for 'promoting the welfare of old people'.[12] Likewise authorities were empowered to provide such services for ill people (ie, those not 'chronically sick') by virtue of NHS Act 1977 Sch 8. Thus by 1977 social services authorities were under varying degrees of obligation to provide an array of community care services to the three main client groups: ill, elderly and disabled people.

I.20   During the late 1970s and in the 1980s the closure of long-stay mental hospitals gathered pace, such that community care became linked in the public mind with the care of people with mental health difficulties in the community rather than by incarceration in isolated hospitals. MHA 1983 s117 accordingly made particular provision for community care services to be provided for certain patients on their discharge from hospital. Section 117 services are only available to a restricted number of people.[13] Most people with a mental health difficulty receive their community care services under CSDPA 1970 s2.

10   The definition applied under the 1948 Act, see para 9.19.
11   See E Hobsbawm, *Age of Extremes*, Michael Joseph, 1994.
12   Sections 2 and 45 came into force on the same date, 29 August 1970.
13   People who are discharged after detention under section 3 or one of the criminal provisions of the MHA 1983, see para 21.19.

1.21   When the term 'community care services' is used today in its generic legal sense, it means (as defined by NHSCCA 1990 s46):

> ... services which a local authority may provide or arrange to be provided under any of the following provisions –
> (a) Part III of the National Assistance Act 1948;
> (b) section 45 of the Health Services and Public Health Act 1968;
> (c) section 254 and Sch 20 NHS Act 2006 and section 192 and Sch 15 NHS (Wales) Act 2006;
> (d) section 117 of the Mental Health Act 1983;

1.22   Although section 46 does not mention services under CSDPA 1970 s2 as being 'community care services', this is because the Department of Health has always considered section 2 to be part of section 29 of the 1948 Act. This somewhat confusing statement is explained at para <?> below. The question of the status of CSDPA 1970 s2 constitutes the first of its two drafting problems. The second concerns the question of when the duty under the Act crystallises in favour of a disabled person. Section 2 services are only owed to an individual when the authority is 'satisfied' that the services are necessary in order to meet his or her needs. What happens if the authority simply fails to decide whether or not it is 'satisfied' as to the person's need? In essence the duty to provide services requires a collateral duty to 'assess' a person's eligibility for that service. While Tom Clarke MP endeavoured (unsuccessfully) to fill this lacuna via his private member's bill in 1986,[14] it was only as a result of NHSCCA 1990 s47 that a comprehensive duty to assess potential service users for their possible need for services under the community care statutes was created.

1.23   A significant motivation for the 1990 Act was the soaring social security expenditure on private residential care and nursing home accommodation; this had increased from about £10 million per annum in 1979 to £2.5 billion per annum in 1993. Hospitals were closing long-stay geriatric and psychiatric wards and discharging the patients into private nursing homes where the cost could be funded by the Department of Health and Social Security (DHSS), essentially, therefore, transferring the cost from one central government department's budget (the NHS) to another (Social Security). At the same time social services authorities were doing much the same, by closing their own residential care homes and transferring the residents to independent-sector homes, which again were capable of being funded via the DHSS, thus transferring the cost from local to central government.

1.24   The 1990 Act sought to cap this expenditure by transferring most of the funding responsibility to social services authorities and restricting access to residential and nursing homes if the person was to be supported by public funds. Access in such care was to be conditional on the authority being satisfied that such a placement was appropriate. Social services authorities were provided with a 'Special Transitional Grant' to compensate them for their extra costs in implementing the community care reforms and in particular for assuming responsibility for funding such

14   Disabled Persons (Services, Consultation and Representation) Act 1986 s4.

accommodation. In the first full year of the reforms (1994–95) the Grant amounted to £735.9 million of which 85 per cent was ring-fenced to the extent that it had to be spent on independent sector care services.[15]

I.25　　The Act also endeavoured to bring together the disparate statutes which governed individual entitlement to community care services and, by various amendments, create a degree of coherence in this field of law. It was preceded by a white paper, *Caring for People*,[16] which owed much to a report prepared in 1998 by Sir Roy Griffiths for the Secretary of State for Social Services, *Community Care: Agenda for Action*. The NHSCCA 1990 does not, however, convert into law many of the themes which infuse the white paper, the Griffiths report and many of the subsequent practice guides issued by the Department of Health. These documents received considerable publicity and a number of myths have arisen therefore about the legal entitlement of service users.

I.26　　The white paper set out six key objectives in relation to the community care reforms (at para 1.11), namely:

- **to promote the development of domiciliary, day and respite services to enable people to live in their own homes wherever feasible and sensible.**
  Existing funding structures have worked against the development of such services. In future, the Government will encourage the targeting of home-based services on those people whose need for them is greatest;
- **to ensure that service providers make practical support for carers a high priority.**
  Assessment of care needs should always take account of the needs of caring family, friends and neighbours;
- **to make proper assessment of need and good case management the corner stone of high quality care.**
  Packages of care should then be designed in line with individual needs and preferences;
- **to promote the development of a flourishing independent sector alongside good quality public services.**
  The Government has endorsed Sir Roy Griffiths' recommendation that social services authorities should be 'enabling' agencies. It will be their responsibility to make maximum possible use of private and voluntary providers, and so increase the available range of options and widen consumer choice;
- **to clarify the responsibilities of agencies and so make it easier to hold them to account for their performance.**
  The Government recognises that the present confusion has contributed to poor overall performance;
- **to secure better value for taxpayers' money by introducing a new funding structure for social care.**
  The Government's aim is that social security provisions should not, as

15　For further details see B Meredith, *The Community Care Handbook*, Age Concern England, 1995, p165.
16　Cm 849, 1989.

they do now, provide any incentive in favour of residential and nursing home care.

I.27   The NHSCCA 1990 was however largely silent on these themes. It provided no practical support for carers – this was left to Malcolm Wicks MP and his private member's bill which became the Carers (Recognition and Services) Act 1995. As to the emphasis on individual choice (or 'preferences'), this concept appears nowhere in any of the legislation, with the exception of the NAA 1948 (Choice of Accommodation) Directions 1992.

I.28   The reforms of the 1990s coincided with the emergence, at a national political level, of the disability rights movements. Many disabled people viewed the community care regime as disabling and disempowering and sought greater control, by way of direct payments and involvement at a strategic planning level. On the positive side, the Disability Discrimination Act 1995, the Community Care (Direct Payments) Act 1996 and the Human Rights Act 1998 have begun to address – directly or indirectly – some of these issues.

I.29   The last ten years have not, however, seen any radical new thinking by the governments in England and Wales. The Royal Commission on Long Term Care's 1999 report *With Respect to old age* recommending a fundamental change in the funding arrangements was rejected (or more accurately, in Wales 'not implemented'). Instead the focus has been on structural/administrative reform with the Health and Social Care Act 2001 providing for the effective merger of social and health care bodies. During this period of organisational turbulence, health and social care staff have additionally been subjected to a plethora of targets, performance indicators, auditing regimes, National Service Frameworks and central government micro-guidance. As Onora O'Neill observed in the 2002 Reith lecture, 'central planning may have failed in the Soviet Union but it is alive and well in Britain today'.[17]

I.30   At the beginning of the 21st century, there appears to be no prospect of a fundamental reappraisal of the role of the law in relation to the provision of community care services. Community care law remains a hotchpotch of conflicting statutes, which have been enacted over a period of 50 years; each statute reflects the different philosophical attitudes of its time. Community care law is in much the same state as was the law relating to children in the 1980s. The law was in a mess; there were no unifying principles underlying the statutes; there were many different procedures for essentially similar problems (for instance, the umpteen different ways a child could end up in local authority care or a custody or maintenance order could be made, and so on). A great deal of this confusion and nonsense was swept away by the Children Act 1989, which repealed many statutes, in full or in part, and replaced them with a unified procedure underscored by a set of widely accepted basic principles. It takes no great genius to realise that community care law is crying out for similar treatment.

17   O O'Neill, *A Question of Trust*, Cambridge University Press, 2002.

CHAPTER 1

The regulatory regimes of social services and the NHS

Introduction

1.1   Primary responsibility for the delivery of community care services rests with local authorities. In a number of instances, however, responsibility is shared with the NHS and in certain situations it may be the NHS's exclusive responsibility.

1.2   Since both local authorities and the NHS are the creatures of statute, they are obliged to restrict their activities to actions specifically authorised by statute. This chapter commences with an outline of the statutory regimes regulating these two bodies in relation to the discharge of their community care responsibilities. It then considers the nature of their public law obligations and concludes by considering Part I of the Local Government Act (LGA) 2000 which has significantly widened the powers of local authorities to promote the economic, social or environmental well-being of their area (see para 1.67 below). Although there has been no similar general relaxation of the NHS powers, the courts have generally found that the wording of the NHS Acts provides substantial latitude to accommodate the commissioning ambitions of health bodies (see for instance para 13.10).

1.3   In its encouragement of greater joint commissioning by the NHS and local authorities in preventing ill health, the government has recently reminded primary care trusts (PCTs) and practice based commissioners that:

> . . . it is not normally reasonable for PCTs and therefore practice based commissioners, to use NHS funds and resources on community care services that fall within the legal remit of local authorities. Such community care services are defined in Section 46(3) of the NHS and Community Care Act 1990 and include the provision of residential accommodation and domiciliary care services. However PCTs (and therefore practice based commissioners) **can** spend money in this way where they are satisfied that the provision of such services is necessary to meet a health need, or where the PCT has entered into a formal partnership arrangement with a local authority under Section 31of the Health Act 1999.[1]

Local authority social services functions

The structure of social services authorities

1.4   The community care obligations created by the National Assistance Act (NAA) 1948 were initially discharged by the welfare departments of county and county borough councils. Concern over the effectiveness of these local arrangements culminated in a critical report – the 'Seebohm report'[2] – that led to the enactment of the Local Authority Social

---

1   Department of Health, *Commissioning Framework for Health and Well Being*, consultation document, March 2007.
2   *Report of the Committee on Local Authority and Allied Personal Social Services* Cmnd 3703, 1968.

Services Act (LASSA) 1970 which required major reform of the way councils discharged their social care responsibilities and resulted in the creation of 'social services departments'. The 1970 Act remains the primary statute governing authorities that discharge social services functions (the material parts of the Act are in Appendix 1 below). These permitted 'functions' are listed in the first schedule to LASSA 1970. The list is regularly updated and comprises a familiar (and long) list of statutory provisions, such as the NAA 1948, the Children Act (CA) 1989, the Carers (Equal Opportunities) Act 2004 and so on. The local authorities concerned are county councils, the London and metropolitan boroughs and other unitary authorities as well as the Common Council of the City of London and the Council of the Isles of Scilly (section 1).

1.5   LASSA 1970 s6 required all social services authorities to appoint a director of social services and this requirement remains in Wales. However, since the enactment of the CA 2004 (itself listed in Schedule 1 to the 1970 Act) social services in England are obliged to appoint a Director of Children's Services (section 18). CA 2004 amends LASSA 1970 s6 requiring the appointment of an officer who fulfils the functions of a Director of Adult Social Services.[3] Accordingly social services in England are now the responsibility of two departments, namely an adult social services department (not uncommonly combining other functions – eg housing and 'well-being' in some unitary authorities) and a children's services department (incorporating education and children's social services functions).

1.6   As a consequence of LGA 2000 s102, social services authorities now have considerable flexibility as to how their elected members supervise the discharge of their social services responsibilities: this may be by way of a traditional social services committee, or by way of the new executive arrangements (sometimes called the 'cabinet system').

1.7   The Department of Health has issued two guidance documents concerning the role of the Director of Adult Social Services in England,[4] one being policy guidance under LASSA 1970 s7(1) (see para 1.46 below) and the other being best practice guidance.

1.8   The policy guidance requires among other things that local authorities ensure that the director is responsible/accountable for:

- the authority's delivery of social services for adults;
- promoting social inclusion and wellbeing with a view to (among other things) developing sustainable services that promote independence and minimise the need for intensive home care and residential services;

---

3   It is expected that this amendment will take effect on 1 January 2008 and accordingly this section is based on the law as it will then be.

4   Department of Health, *Guidance on the Statutory Chief Officer Post of Director of Adult Social Services issued under s7(1) Local Authority Social Services Act 1970*, 2006; Department of Health, *Best Practice Guidance on the role of the Director of Adult Social Services*, 2006.

- maintaining clear and effective arrangements to support the joint planning, monitoring and delivery of local authority social services with the NHS, housing authorities, Supporting People programme and other statutory agencies;
- ensuring (with the director of children's services) 'adequate arrangements' are in place 'to ensure that all young people with long-term social care needs have been assessed and, where eligible, receive a service which meets their needs throughout their transition to becoming adults' (see para 24.59 below).

1.9   By LASSA 1970 s6(6) it is the authority's duty to 'secure the provision of adequate staff[5] for assisting' in the exercise of the director's functions. Whilst authorities will be given a wide discretion by the courts in deciding what is an 'adequate' staff (for the purposes of section 6(6)), the question may be raised in judicial review proceedings, particularly where the applicant is challenging the non-provision of a service dependent upon 'human resources'.[6] In *R v Hereford and Worcester CC ex p Chandler*,[7] for instance, leave to seek judicial review was granted on several grounds, including the argument that the applicant had not received the service he needed (a one-to-one carer) because the authority had inadequate staff, in breach of its statutory duty under section 6(6). Judicial review is, however, unlikely to be appropriate where the complaint concerns the interruption of services due to unpredictable staff absences,[8] although where the complaint concerns a repeated failure of the service due to predictable interruptions, this would seem at least a matter of maladministration and amenable to remedy via the complaints system.

1.10   LASSA 1970 (as amended) sets out the broad framework as to how social services departments are to be organised. As with many social welfare statutes, reserve powers were retained by the secretary of state to enable 'orders', 'directions' and 'guidance' to be issued; however, in the early years of the Act, central government exercised a lightness of touch over these levers of control:

> ... there was no notion of a direct line of command from central government dictating either the organisational structure of social work at the local level or the detailed policies to be implemented within and through that structure in response to legislation. Within loose overall financial controls there was room for local authority social services departments to shape structures and policies within the framework of central government's legislation and general policy guidance.[9]

5   As well as the parallel duty, under the National Health Service Act (NHSA) 2006 s254 and Sch 20, to provide 'sufficient' approved social workers for the purposes of the Mental Health Act 1983, see para 9.158.
6   To establish a case under this ground, useful evidence can be obtained from social services committee minutes, which not infrequently record unsuccessful requests by the director for extra staff.
7   Unreported but see September 1992 *Legal Action* 15: settled on terms that the applicant receive the assessed service.
8   *R v Islington LBC ex p McMillan* (1995) 1 CCLR 7 at 10.
9   J Harris, *The Social Work Business* Routledge, 2003, p18.

1.11   This is no longer the case. Through the provisions of LASSA 1970 s7 (see below), and array of performance indicators,[10] performance ratings[11] and inspection regimes the Department of Health (in England) and the Assembly (in Wales) exercise a degree of control over the actions of social services departments — which is at times best characterised as micromanagement.

NHS community care functions

1.12   At the beginning of the 20th century the majority of institutional health and social care services were provided via the poor law boards. Gradually as the century progressed, local authorities assumed greater responsibilities for both functions. The 1929[12] poor law reforms led to the creation of local authority health committees, which took control of the better poor law hospitals (then known as public health hospitals). The remaining poor law institutions, workhouses and basic poor law hospitals were also transferred from the poor law boards, becoming the responsibility of the county and county borough councils.

1.13   The creation of the NHS in 1948 did not initially wrest responsibility for health services from local authorities. Although today it is convenient to see the National Health Service Act (NHSA) 1946 and the NAA 1948 as demarcating the responsibilities of what we now call social services departments and the NHS, this separation of responsibilities has in fact developed largely as a consequence of subsequent legislation. The NHSA 1946 stipulated that many services we would today label as 'health services', such as ambulances (section 27), midwifery (section 23), health visitors (section 24), were to be the responsibility of local authority health committees (called 'local health authorities').[13] Indeed NAA 1948 s21(7)(b), as originally enacted, authorised the provision by local authorities of 'health services,[14] not being specialist services or services of a kind normally provided only on admission to hospital'.

1.14   While minor changes to the health/social care responsibilities of NHS/local authorities occurred over the next 25 years,[15] major reform did

---

10   As at June 2007 there were 27 performance assessment indicators measuring, for instance, local authority delivery of intensive home care services; the number of adults with learning disabilities helped to live at home; the number of assessments of adults and older people leading to provision of services; the number of carers receiving 'carer's breaks'; the waiting time for care packages; the ethnicity of older people receiving assessment, etc. For details full details see http://www.csci.org.uk/care_professional/councils/paf/performance_indicator_definiti/2006–07_pis.aspx.

11   See eg Commission for Social Care Inspection, *Adult Performance Indicators For 2006–07*, 2006, at http://www.csci.gov.uk/docs/adult_PIs_2006–07.doc.

12   LGA 1929.

13   NHSA 1946 Part II Sch 4.

14   Including nursing services by virtue of NHSA 1946 s25.

15   Most notably the Health Services and Public Health Act 1968 which transferred to local health authorities responsibility for health visitors and nursing other than in a person's home; and the LASSA 1970 which in its first schedule sought to delineate the responsibilities of local authority social services departments.

not take place until 1974, when the LGA 1972 and the NHS Reorganisation Act 1973 came into force. The 1973 Act sought to transfer all nursing functions (whether in hospital, at home or elsewhere) to the NHS. It abolished local health authorities (ie local authority health committees) and in their place created free standing regional, area and district health authorities.

1.15   Since the early 1970s the NHS has been the subject of continual reform – a process that shows no evidence of abating. In 1977, the 1946 Act was repealed and replaced by a consolidating Act, the NHSA 1977, and in 2006 this itself was repealed and consolidated – into three Acts, the NHSA 2006, the NHS (Wales) Act (NHS(W)A) 2006 and the NHS (Consequential Provisions) Act (NHS(CP)A) 2006, of which the former is the principal Act (see para 13.5 below).

Primary care trusts, care trusts and local health boards

1.16   The reforms, which have been described elsewhere,[16] have culminated with the current configuration, namely that services are primarily commissioned in England by approximately 150 PCTs[17] or care trusts whose performance is assessed and directed by ten strategic health authorities[18] (SHAs). Within the PCTs there can be practice-based commissioning. In Wales, services are primarily commissioned by 22 local health boards[19] (LHBs) whose performance is assessed and directed by the National Assembly.

1.17   In England, PCTs, once they have established partnership working arrangements with a local authority (see para 13.122) and undertaken consultations, may effectively 'merge' with the social services arm of that authority[20] and create a 'care trust'.[21] As at May 2007 ten care trusts had been established in England. Care trusts are separate entities and legally responsible for the discharge of their health and social care functions (which should be compared with the situation in relation to partnership working arrangements – see para 13.122 below). Some concern has been expressed that care trusts tend to prioritise health services over social care.[22]

NHS trusts and foundation trusts

1.18   PCTs, LHBs and care trusts have the primary responsibility for commissioning services to ensure, so far as is possible, that there is a 'comprehensive' health service (see para 13.13). They discharge this obliga-

---

16   See eg the third edition of this text at paras 10.3–10.11.
17   NHSA 2006 ss18–24.
18   Ibid s13.
19   NHS(W)A 2006 ss11–17.
20   Care Trusts (Applications and Consultation) Regulations 2001 SI No 3788.
21   NHSA 2006 s77.
22   See eg Commission for Social Care Inspection, *Inspection of social care services for older people Northumberland County Council June 2006*, 2006, para 9.12.

tion by providing and commissioning primary care services, and by contracting with NHS trusts[23] and NHS foundation trusts (ie hospitals).

1.19   NHS trusts are semi-autonomous bodies which came into being as a result of the National Health Service and Community Care Act (NHSCCA) 1990 reforms and are responsible for the ownership and management of hospitals or other NHS facilities.

1.20   As a result of Health and Social Care (Community and Health Standards) Act 2003 s1, NHS trusts in England are able to achieve semi-independence from the Department of Health and greater financial flexibilities by becoming an NHS foundation trust. There were (at May 2007) 54 such trusts, which are now governed by NHSA 2006 s30.

1.21   NHS trusts and foundation trusts do not receive funding in the way that PCTs, LHBs and care trusts do, but rather through the contracts they conclude with these bodies.[24]

Statutory duties and powers

1.22   Social services and NHS functions are normally expressed as being obligatory (ie a statutory duty) or discretionary (ie a statutory power). Accordingly the use of the words 'can' and 'may' in a statute are interpreted as conferring a permissive power rather than a duty. Conversely, the appearance of the words 'shall' or 'must' are in general construed as creating a duty – an obligation to do or refrain from doing something. This is not, however, always the case. As *de Smith* points out,[25] a local authority empowered to approve building plans has been held to be obliged to approve plans that were in conformity with its bylaws,[26] whereas a local authority required by statute to provide suitable alternative accommodation for those displaced by a closing order has been held not to be obliged to place them at the top of the housing waiting list.[27]

Powers

1.23   Where an authority has a power to act, but not a duty, it must (when the possible use of that power arises) exercise its discretion in each case. Authorities are generally free to refuse to use a power, provided they reach such a decision in accordance with the principles of administrative law (and the refusal does not result in a breach of the European Convention

---

23 NHSA 2006 ss25–27; NHS(W)A 2006 ss18–21.

24 Under NHSA 2006 s9 and NHS(W)A 2006 s7, 'NHS contracts' are not legally enforceable but are subject to arbitration by the secretary of state/Welsh Assembly. For details of the contracting and commissioning responsibilities of PCTs, see generally *The NHS Contractors' Companion*, available from the Department of Health website at http://www.dh.gov.uk.

25 De Smith, Woolf and Jowell, *Judicial Review of Administrative Action*, 5th edn, Sweet & Maxwell, 1995, p301.

26 *R v Newcastle-upon-Tyne Corporation* (1889) 60 LT 963.

27 *R v Bristol Corporation ex p Hendy* [1974] 1 WLR 498.

on Human Rights[28]). They must not, for instance, ignore circular guidance,[29] operate a perverse policy which (in practice) fetters its discretion[30] or in certain situations fail to consult before reaching certain decisions.[31]

Duties

1.24   Statutory duties owed by public bodies can be divided into two categories, general public law duties (known as 'target' duties) and specific duties owed to individuals. Specific duties are worded in precise and personal terms, so that it is clear that they are intended to confer enforceable rights upon individuals, and also make clear when these rights arise. Accordingly a failure to comply with a specific law duty may entitle an aggrieved party to a court order compelling the authority to carry out its duty (for instance an order requiring it to provide a specific community care service).

1.25   In *R v Gloucestershire CC ex p Mahfood*[32] McCowan LJ held that Chronically Sick and Disabled Persons Act 1970 s2 created specific public law duties. In his opinion, once an authority had decided that it was under a duty to make arrangements under s2, it was 'under an absolute duty to make them. It is a duty owed to a specific individual and not a target duty.'[33] The duty under Mental Health Act 1983 s117 has also been held to be capable of being an individual public law duty.[34]

1.26   In contrast, general public law (or 'target') duties are worded in broad and impersonal terms, and contain a 'degree of elasticity'[35] in their interpretation – such that it is generally left to the authority in question to decide when (and to what extent) the duty comes into being. Callaghan[36] argues that target duties are essentially aspirational in nature, requiring an authority to 'do its best',[37] and that 'courts will permit public authorities to take into account practical realities, including budgetary and resource considerations, in determining how best to fulfil the target duty'.

1.27   A notable example of such a general duty is to be found in NHSA 2006 s1[38] which places a duty on the secretary of state 'to continue the promotion in England of a comprehensive health service'. The duty is not expressed as being owed to any specific individual and it is particularly

---

28   See para 27.207 below.
29   *R v North Derbyshire Health Authority ex p Fisher* (1998) 1 CCLR 150 (see para 1.41 below).
30   *R v North West Lancashire Health Authority ex p A* [2000] 1 WLR 977; (1999) 2 CCLR 419 and see para 13.16 below generally.
31   See eg *R v North West Lancashire Health Authority ex p A* [2000] 1 WLR 977; (1999) 2 CCLR 419 and *R (Morris) v Trafford Healthcare NHS Trust* [2006] EWHC 2334 (Admin); (2006) 9 CCLR 648.
32   (1997) 1 CCLR 7.
33   Ibid at 16G.
34   *R (IH) v Secretary of State for the Home Department and others* [2003] UKHL 59; [2003] 3 WLR 1278; (2004) 7 CCLR 147.
35   Per Woolf LJ in *R v Inner London Education Authority ex p Ali* (1990) 2 Admin LR 822, p828D.
36   C Callaghan, 'What is a "target duty"?' (2000) 5(3) *Judicial Review* 184–187.
37   *R v Radio Authority ex p Bull* [1998] QB 294 at 309, CA.
38   In Wales, NHS(W)A 2006 s1.

difficult for a court to decide when it has been breached. To mount a successful action, an aggrieved patient would have to show, not only that he or she failed to receive a health service due to the service not being 'comprehensive' (whatever that may mean) but also that the secretary of state had effectively abandoned any intention of 'promoting' such a service. As the Court of Appeal held in *R v North and East Devon Health Authority ex p Coughlan*:[39]

> 25. When exercising his judgment [the secretary of state] has to bear in mind the comprehensive service which he is under a duty to promote as set out in section 1. However, as long as he pays due regard to that duty, the fact that the service will not be comprehensive does not mean that he is necessarily contravening either section 1 or section 3

The section 1 duty is considered further at para 13.6 below.

1.28   It is not always clear whether a particular obligation falls into the specific or target category. As Scott-Baker J observed in *R (A) v Lambeth LBC*:[40]

> Community care legislation has grown up piecemeal through numerous statutes over the past half century. There are many statutes aimed at different targets whose provisions are drawn in differing language. Each Act contains its own duties and powers. Specific duties have to be distinguished from target or general duties and duties from discretions. Sometimes a local authority has several ways in which it can meet an obligation. Some provisions overlap with others and the inter-relationship is not always easy.

1.29   A number of community care duties can be characterised as hybrid in nature; that is to say that although drafted in general terms, they can 'crystallise'[41] during the assessment process (see para 3.135) into specific public law duties owed to individual service users. Thus the general duty under NAA 1948 s21(1)(a) to provide residential accommodation for adults in need of care and attention (see para 3.172) may be converted by a community care assessment into a specific public law duty.[42] In *R (T, D and B) v Haringey LBC*[43] Ouseley J accepted that, in principle, obligations under the Human Rights Act 1998 could 'crystallise' target duties into specific law duties.

1.30   Arguments concerning the enforceability of such statutory provisions are becoming increasing rarefied and difficult to follow.[44] In *R (W) v*

---

39 [2000] 2 WLR 622; (1999) 2 CCLR 285.

40 [2001] EWHC 376 (Admin); [2001] 2 FLR 1201; the quotation also appears in the subsequent Court of Appeal judgment, *R (A) v Lambeth LBC* [2001] EWCA Civ 1624; (2001) 4 CCLR 486 at 499–450.

41 See the comments of Laws LJ in *R (A) v Lambeth LBC* [2001] EWCA Civ 1624; (2001) 4 CCLR 486, p499D where he adopted Richard Gordon QC's use of this phrasing.

42 See eg *R v Sefton MBC ex p Help the Aged and Blanchard* [1997] 4 All ER 532; (1997) 1 CCLR 57, and *R v Kensington and Chelsea RLBC ex p Kujtim* [1999] 4 All ER 161; (1999) 2 CCLR 340.

43 [2005] EWHC 2235 (Admin); (2006) 9 CCLR 58 at [142].

44 See eg the comments of Potter LJ in *R v Kensington and Chelsea RLBC ex p Kujtim* [1999] 4 All ER 161; (1999) 2 CCLR 340, p353J where he admitted to finding difficulty in following the arguments of Sedley J (concerning a parallel set of target duties) in *R v Islington LBC ex p Rixon* (1997) 1 CCLR 119.

Lambeth LBC[45] and *R (G) v Barnet LBC*,[46] for example, the Court of Appeal and the House of Lords grappled with the differing phrasing of the obligations to provide care services for disabled children and disabled adults. They concluded that although the assessment process for adults (under NHSCCA 1990 s47) could result in specific public law duties, this was not the case in relation to children (whose assessment process was governed by CA 1989 s17). Not only is it difficult to follow the logic of the court's analysis in reaching this conclusion, but it is particularly difficult to see the sense in (effectively) prioritising the rights of disabled adults to services over the rights of disabled children.

1.31   It has been argued that what we are seeing in such cases is an 'attempt to shore up the increasingly questionable public policy approach towards the state delivery of community care services'.[47] In effect, that the artificial distinction between target and specific public law duties stems from the judiciary's anxiety over the resource implications of their judgments,[48] and that this entirely artificial construct is proving to be insufficiently flexible to mediate between the complexities of state responsibilities (in a post Human Rights Act 1998 era) and individual need. Increasingly the courts appear to be using the imperative (if not the logic) of the European Convention on Human Rights in determining the enforceability of statutory obligations – and this approach is considered in greater detail at para 3.194 below.

Regulations

1.32   In common with many other Acts, NHS and local authority statutes empower the secretary of state/Welsh Assembly to issue various forms of delegated legislation – most commonly as regulations, rules and orders. These flesh out the bare bones of the duty or power imposed by the primary statute. In relation to residential accommodation, for instance, NAA 1948 s22(1) requires authorities to charge for such accommodation and section 22(5) authorises the secretary of state to issue regulations detailing how this shall be done. These were subsequently issued as the National Assistance (Assessment of Resources) Regulations 1992.[49]

1.33   Such delegated legislation has the force of law, and the procedure by which it is promulgated is set out in the Statutory Instruments Act 1946, as modified in relation to Wales by the Government of Wales Act 1998. These Acts detail the requirements for publication and the various types

---

45   [2002] EWCA Civ 613; [2002] 2 All ER 901; (2002) 5 CCLR 203.
46   [2003] UKHL 57; [2003] 3 WLR 1194; (2003) 6 CCLR 500 (see para 24.45 below).
47   L Clements, 'The collapsing duty: a sideways look at community care and public law' [1997] *Judicial Review Journal* 162.
48   Lord Hoffman put the position frankly when delivering the 2001 Commercial Bar Lecture ('The Separation of Powers', unpublished) commenting 'even when a case appears to involve no more than the construction of a statute or interpretation of a common law rule, the courts are very circumspect about giving an answer which would materially affect the distribution of public expenditure'.
49   SI No 2977; see para 8.10.

of procedures by which the legislation is laid before Parliament/the Assembly. Delegated legislation must not, therefore, stray outside the ambit of its enabling statutory provision. Accordingly, in the example of the 1948 Act above, the regulations issued under section 22(5) could only lawfully address the question of the assessment of charges for residential accommodation. Judicial review will lie where the statutory instrument exceeds such limits.[50] In similar terms, delegated legislation must not derogate from provisions in the enabling legislation; thus where rights are conferred by a statute, any subsequent regulations must not detract from those rights[51] (see para 27.187 where this question is further considered).

Directions and guidance

1.34   LASSA 1970 ss7(1) and 7A require social services authorities to be administered under the general supervision of the secretary of state/ Welsh Assembly. The provisions state as follows:

> *Local authorities to exercise social services functions under guidance of Secretary of State*
> 7(1)   Local authorities shall, in the exercise of their social services functions, including the exercise of any discretion conferred by any relevant enactment, act under the general guidance of the Secretary of State.
>
> *Directions by the Secretary of State as to exercise of social services functions*
> 7A(1)   Without prejudice to section 7 of this Act, every local authority shall exercise their social services functions in accordance with such directions as may be given to them under this section by the Secretary of State.
> (2)   Directions under this section –
> (a) shall be given in writing; and
> (b) may be given to a particular authority, or to authorities of a particular class, or to authorities generally.

1.35   The distinction between 'directions' and 'guidance' is therefore a distinction between having to act 'in accordance with' directions as opposed to having to act 'under' guidance.

Directions

1.36   Directions are mandatory, and are phrased as such. The power of the secretary of state/Welsh Assembly to issue directions, contained in LASSA 1970 s7A (above), are replicated in the NHS Acts 2006. NHSA 2006 s8 empowers the secretary of state to issue directions to NHS bodies in England and NHS(W)A 2006 ss12 and 19 give the corresponding power to the Assembly in Wales. NHSA 2006 s20 empowers SHAs in England to issue directions to PCTs.

---

50   See eg *Re Ripon* [1939] 2 KB 838 and *Dunkley v Evans* [1981] 1 WLR 1522.
51   See eg *King v Henderson* [1898] AC 720.

1.37   In relation to social services functions, examples of such directions include the National Assistance Act (Choice of Accommodation) Directions 1992 (see para 7.90 below) and the Community Care Assessment Directions 2004 (see para 3.20 below). Examples of NHS directions are the NHS Continuing Healthcare (Responsibilities) Directions 2007 (see para 14.38 below) and the Directions Concerning Dowry Payments HSG (95)45 (see para 13.125 below). These have the force of law and are set out as would be any statutory instrument.

1.38   Directions are problematical constitutional instruments. Many of them are not issued as statutory instruments.[52] This results in them avoiding any possibility of parliamentary scrutiny (contrary to the constitutional convention that it is Parliament which makes law rather than the executive) and being difficult (sometimes impossible) to obtain. In England the Department of Health website has a list – by no means exhaustive – of some relevant directions, whereas in Wales the situation is lamentable. The Assembly site (itself woeful) lists some of the directions issued after 2005 but it appears that there is no central register of those that were issued prior to this date. The Assembly puts this down to the difficulty 'in defining what amounts to non-statutory instrument subordinate legislation' and (in 2006) indicated that it was undertaking a 'feasibility study to consider the issue of indexing non-statutory instrument subordinate legislation made between 1999 and 2005'.[53] It is highly questionable whether such a policy complies with the Assembly's publication scheme under the Freedom of Information Act 2000 and indeed whether any of the inaccessible directions can be deemed to be 'law' – given that it is a 'fundamental requisite of the rule of law that the law should be made known'.[54]

1.39   To add to the confusion, directions are not always published separately: they may appear as appendices to guidance issued by the Department of Health or Welsh Assembly. In this context important directions were issued as appendices to local authority circular LAC (93)10/Welsh Office Circular WOC 35/93 (concerning NAA 1948 Part III and the then NHSA 1977 Sch 8[55]), and DHSS Circular 19/71 (concerning Health Services and Public Health Act 1968 s45[56]).

1.40   In *Godbold v Mahmood*,[57] Mitting J noted that leading counsel had been unable to trace a direction (in this case LAC(93)10 – see para 7.29 below) and that he (Mitting J) had come across it 'by chance' whilst hearing a separate judicial review. The judge himself commented on the unusual

---

52   Directions are only published in the form of a statutory instrument if this requirement is stipulated in the primary Act: see eg NHSA 2006 s273(4) and NHS(W)A 2006 s204(3).

53   Letter, First Minister for Wales to Lord Evans of Temple Guiting, 22 June 2006.

54   *R (Salih) v SSHD* [2003] EWHC 2273 (Admin) at [45], per Stanley-Burnton J where he held that this requirement extended to certain extra-statutory policy documents issued by the government.

55   See paras 7.29 and 9.39 where these directions are considered further.

56   See paras 7.09, 9.13 and 9.142 where this direction is considered in detail.

57   [2005] EWHC 1002 (QB); [2005] Lloyd's Rep Med 379 at [24]–[26].

nature and effect of such instruments since 'the duty is imposed not by primary legislation or even by secondary legislation, but by a combination of primary legislation and ministerial direction. The ministerial direction can be changed or withdrawn at any time without recourse to Parliament.'

1.41   Given the uncertain nature of directions, it will not always be clear if a departmental instruction to a local authority or the NHS is a direction or guidance. Such a question arose in *R v North Derbyshire Health Authority ex p Fisher*[58] where Dyson J had to decide whether an executive letter[59] was a 'direction' under the then NHSA 1977,[60] and if not, how much weight a health authority was required to afford it. He held that directions could be contained in such a circular, but that the wording of the circular was not sufficiently mandatory to be a 'direction'.

> If it is the intention of the Secretary of State to give directions which attract a statutory duty of compliance, then he should make it clear that this is what he is doing. The difference between a policy which provides mere guidance and one which the . . . authority is obliged to implement is critical. Policy which is in the form of guidance can be expressed in strong terms and yet fall short of amounting to directions.

1.42   Accordingly it was to be construed as 'strong guidance'. This meant that the health authority, although not obliged to follow the circular, could only depart from it by giving clear reasons for so doing and that those reasons would be susceptible to a *Wednesbury* challenge (see para 27.172). In finding against the health authority the judge held that it had failed to understand the circular properly and therefore its actions were defective (as if it had had no regard to the circular at all).

1.43   Many of the directions that concern NHS responsibilities were issued in relation to the (now repealed) NHSA 1977. These continue to apply, notwithstanding the 1977 Act's repeal and its replacement by the NHS Acts 2006, by virtue of NHS(CP)A 2006 s4 and Sch 2 para 1(2) which provide that directions issued in relation to the 1977 Act continue and apply with equal effect to the consequent provisions in the NHS Acts 2006.

Guidance

1.44   As noted above (see para 1.10), the original scheme for health and social care legislation was for a loose legislative framework within which there was room for local bodies to shape structures and policies. The enabling Acts, however, provided central government with the powers to exert control if needs be, by (for example) issuing regulations, directions and guidance. Over the last 50 years these powers have been used with increasing frequency to the point today that it could be argued that the mass of detailed guidance that now exists – particularly in relation to social

---

58 (1998) 1 CCLR 150.
59 EL(95)97, concerning the prescribing of Beta-Interferon drugs to people with MS.
60 At that time the relevant section was s13.

services activities – is itself a major problem, inhibiting innovation and undermining local initiative (see para 3.43).

Social services guidance

1.45   There are two basic types of social services guidance:

- *formal guidance* (often referred to as 'policy guidance') issued by the secretary of state specifically declaring that it is issued under LASSA 1970 s7(1) (ie 's7(1) guidance');
- *general guidance* (often called 'practice guidance') of the classic form, ie advice to which an authority should have regard when reaching a decision, but which it is not required to follow slavishly.

Social services policy guidance

1.46   Social services policy guidance is a higher-status form of guidance and is generally labelled as such: frequently it commences with the statement 'this guidance is issued under s7(1) Local Authority Social Services Act 1970'.

1.47   The wording of section 7(1) is such that local authorities (and care trusts)[61] are not merely required to bear such advice in mind when making decisions; they must 'act under' it, which is a significantly more powerful obligation.

1.48   Examples include guidance issued concerning the charging for residential accommodation rules, generally known as CRAG (see para 8.10) and guidance concerning the community care assessment process, such as the 'Fair Access to Care Services' issued as LAC (2002)13 (see para 3.26). Such guidance covers the breadth of social services responsibilities; thus a series of volumes of section 7(1) guidance have been issued concerning the implementation of the CA 1989.

1.49   The question of how far policy guidance must be followed has been the subject of a number of court judgments. In *R v Islington LBC ex p Rixon*[62] Sedley J held:

> In my judgment Parliament in enacting s7(1) did not intend local authorities to whom ministerial guidance was given to be free, having considered it, to take it or leave it. Such a construction would put this kind of statutory guidance on a par with the many forms of non-statutory guidance issued by departments of state. While guidance and directions are semantically and legally different things, and while 'guidance does not compel any particular decision' (*Laker Airways Ltd v Department of Trade* [1967] QB 643, 714 per Roskill LJ), especially when prefaced by the word 'general', in my view Parliament by s7(1) has required local authorities to follow the path charted by the Secretary of State's guidance, with liberty to deviate from it where the local authority judges on admissible grounds that there is good reason to do so, but without freedom to take a substantially different course.

61   NHSA 2006 s77(11).
62   (1998) 1 CCLR 119 at 123.

1.50   This view was reiterated in *R v Gloucestershire CC ex p Barry and others*[63] where Hirst LJ contrasted the binding nature of policy guidance with other social services guidance which he considered to be merely of 'persuasive authority on the proper construction of the legislation'.[64]

1.51   Accompanying the enactment of the NHSCCA 1990, the government issued a substantial volume of general policy guidance, entitled *Community Care in the Next Decade and Beyond: policy guidance*.[65] In many publications this is simply referred to as 'the Policy Guidance' (and in this book is referred to as the '1990 policy guidance') since it represents the first and still the most definitive general statement of the key policy objectives underpinning the 1990 community care reforms.

1.52   The consequences of failing to take into account section 7(1) policy guidance were spelt out by Sedley J in *ex p Rixon* (above):

> . . . if this statutory guidance is to be departed from it must be with good reason, articulated in the course of some identifiable decision-making process even if not in the care plan itself. In the absence of any such considered decision, the deviation from statutory guidance is in my judgment a breach of law . . .

1.53   It follows that if a local authority decides not to follow policy guidance it must give clear and adequate reasons for its decision and its departure from the guidance must be as limited as is possible in the particular circumstances.

1.54   Although policy guidance has quasi-legal characteristics, it cannot amend or frustrate primary or subordinate legislation, and can of course be the subject of judicial review if it contains an error of law.[66] It can, in addition be struck down if its purpose is to circumvent or frustrate a statutory provision.[67] In *R v Secretary of State for Health ex p Pfizer Ltd*[68] Collins J held that HSC 1998/158, which suggested that GPs should not prescribe Viagra, was unlawful in that it (among other things) sought to restrict the GP's statutory duty to provide patients with all necessary and appropriate personal medical services.[69]

1.55   In *R (B and H) v Hackney LBC*[70] Keith J held that policy guidance might not be 'strong guidance' if it concerned a process for which the statute provided that guidance could be issued by way of directions (see para 3.19).

63 [1996] 4 All ER 421; (1998) 1 CCLR 19 at 24, CA.
64 Hirst LJ's dissenting opinion was approved by the majority in the House of Lords: [1997] 2 WLR 459; (1998) 1 CCLR 40.
65 HMSO, 1990.
66 See eg *R v North and East Devon Health Authority ex p Coughlan* [2000] 2 WLR 622; (2000) 2 CCLR 285 and *Gillick v West Norfolk Area Health Authority* [1986] AC 112.
67 *R v Secretary of State for Health ex p Pfizer Ltd* (1999) 2 CCLR 270 and *R v Worthing BC ex p Birch* (1985) 50 P & CR 53.
68 (1999) 2 CCLR 270.
69 Under NHS (General Medical Services) Regulations 1992 SI No 635, Sch 2 para 12(1).
70 [2003] EWHC 1654 (Admin).

Codes of practice

1.56   Codes of practice are another example of 'guidance'. Many (but not all) codes of practice are 'statutory' in the sense that they are prepared as a result of a statutory requirement. For example, Mental Capacity Act 2005 s42 requires that a code of practice be prepared and obliges certain persons (see para 18.4 below) to have regard to it when discharging their functions and for courts/tribunals to take notice of any material failures in this respect. It follows that the extent to which such guidance is binding will depend upon the specific context of any decision, but in many cases it is likely to have equivalent force to policy guidance. Guidance of similar effect is to be found in relation to local authorities' duties to house homeless people (see para 15.19) and in relation to general obligations under the Disability Discrimination Act 1995. The code of practice issued under Mental Health Act 1983 s118 is guidance to which all professionals working in the mental health field must have regard. In *R (Munjaz) v Mersey Care NHS Trust*[71] the House of Lords (by a majority of 3:2) concluded that the code was not absolutely binding, but, like policy guidance, could be departed from where justification for the departure was explained in very considerable detail.

Social services practice guidance

1.57   The majority of guidance issued by the Department of Health/Welsh Assembly concerning community care issues is not issued under section 7(1), but is general guidance. Such guidance is advice as to how an authority might go about implementing or interpreting a particular statutory responsibility. It is often said that policy guidance tells an authority what it must do, whereas practice guidance suggests how it might go about doing it. Such guidance is common to other areas of social welfare law – for instance in relation to children, CA 2004 s10(8) requires children's services authorities to 'have regard to any guidance given to them' by the secretary of state, and Housing Act 1996 s182(1) places a similar obligation on housing authorities when exercising their homelessness functions.[72]

1.58   Although authorities (including care trusts)[73] are not therefore required to 'act under' such guidance, they are required to have regard to it when reaching a decision in respect of which it may be material (see para 27.182). It follows that a failure to have regard to it (rather than a failure to follow it) may result in the subsequent decision being quashed by the courts or condemned by the ombudsman. In *ex p Rixon*[74] Sedley J referred to practice guidance in the following terms:

> While such guidance lacks the status accorded by s7(1) of Local Authority Social Services Act 1970, it is, as I have said, something to which regard

71   [2005] UKHL 58; [2005] 3 WLR 793.
72   See eg *R (Khatun, Zeb and Iqbal) v Newham LBC* [2004] EWCA Civ 55; [2004] 3 WLR 417 at [23].
73   NHSA 2006 s77(11).
74   *R v Islington LBC ex p Rixon* (1998) 1 CCLR 119, QBD.

must be had in carrying out the statutory functions. While the occasional lacuna would not furnish evidence of such a disregard, the series of lacunae which I have mentioned does . . .[75]

1.59　Practice guidance takes many forms. Previously Department of Health guidance was given a sequential reference number and a status – for instance some were labelled 'LAC' (local authority circular) which had a higher standing than those identified as 'LASSL' (local authority social services letter). This system has now been abandoned[76] as a result of a 2002 Department of Health led initiative 'Shifting the Balance of Power'.[77] The change was designed to increase local autonomy with the central government adopting a 'a less hands-on approach': no longer issuing 'detailed guidance with many milestones and targets' but instead setting 'clear long term outcomes' and leaving the process by which these outcomes are reached to local bodies. Whether this lofty aim has been achieved is debatable – the amount of guidance from the centre does not appear to have abated, although it is now much more difficult to ascertain its precise status.[78]

Cancelled guidance

1.60　Some guidance issued by the Department of Health has a self-destruct date – frequently containing a statement that 'this guidance will be cancelled on' a specified date. This does not of course mean that it ceases thereafter to be of relevance, since it will generally remain a statement of good practice (unless specifically contradicted by subsequent guidance). Some guidance expresses this proposition in explicit terms: for example the circular LAC (2001)8 concerning social care arrangements for 'deafblind people' states 'The circular . . . will be cancelled on 28 February 2006. Though the Department will not be reissuing this document, councils are reminded that the principles of good practice the Guidance contains continue to be valid.'

National Minimum Standards and National Service Frameworks

1.61　Certain guidance issued by the Department of Health and Welsh Assembly is entitled a 'National Minimum Standards' or a 'National Service Framework' document.

1.62　Care Standards Act 2000 s23 authorises the secretary of state/Welsh Assembly to publish 'national minimum standards'. National minimum standards have been published on a wide variety of subjects and although not legally binding they must be taken into account by the Commission

---

75　(1998) 1 CCLR 119, p131E, QBD.
76　For an explanation as to this now discarded system, see the third edition of this text at para 1.43.
77　Department of Health, *Shifting the Balance of Power: The Next Steps*, 2002, paras 1.3.1 and 1.5.3.
78　Or indeed to locate it – guidance lacks an easily identifiable reference, and can appear on a range of websites, as the many and varied footnotes to this book testify.

for Social Care Inspection in England and the Care Standards Inspector-ate for Wales when making decisions about whether or not the regulations have been complied with. These are considered further at para 17.21.

1.63   National service frameworks (NSFs) are non-statutory in origin and are essentially aspirational – setting out the Department of Health's and the Welsh Assembly's long term strategies for improving specific areas of care. They are NHS led but define both health and social services obliga-tions and detail measurable goals within set time frames, generally being ten-year programmes. They cover a wide variety of subjects including services for older people (see para 20.2), for children (see para 24.57;), for people with long term conditions (see para 13.46) and for mental health services (see para 21.3).

NHS guidance

1.64   While the NHS Acts 2006 authorise the issuing of directions (see para 1.36 above) in much the same way as authorised under the LASSA 1970, there is no specific provision in the 2006 Acts concerning the issuing of guid-ance.[79] Under section 2(1)(b) of both the English and Welsh NHS Acts 2006 however, the Secretary of State/Welsh Assembly have power to do 'anything whatsoever which is calculated to facilitate or is conducive or incidental to, the discharge of' the duty to promote a comprehensive health service. Such a power clearly authorises the issuing of guidance. In all other respects, though, the Acts are silent on the effect of such guidance.

1.65   The extent to which NHS guidance is binding on local NHS bodies is therefore a contextual question that will depend in most cases on the wording of the guidance, the nature of the process in question and the particular facts of an individual case. In some situations it would appear that guidance will have the same coercive effect as social services 'policy guidance' – as indeed Dyson J so concluded in *R v North Derbyshire Health Authority ex p Fisher*[80] (para 1.41 above). In similar vein it would appear that where joint policy guidance is issued to social services and NHS bodies – but is primarily aimed at the latter – it is not unreasonable to assume that its legal force is no less in relation to the NHS than it is for social services.

Accessing guidance

1.66   Guidance is generally only accessible via the internet. The Department of Health website[81] has an archive of 'circulars and letters' and an efficient search engine that generally makes accessing these documents a straight forward exercise. Accessing guidance issued by the Welsh Assembly

---

79 Although by virtue of NHSA 2006 s77(11), care trusts (see para 1.17) are subject to such s7 guidance and s75(6) of the same Act empowers the secretary of state to issue guidance concerning consultation processes.
80 (1998) 1 CCLR 150.
81 http://www.dh.gov.uk.

(or the predecessor Welsh Office) can however be an extremely difficult exercise. The website[82] is lamentable although on occasions the search engine can be of assistance. Given our criticisms concerning the lack of access to directions (see para 1.38 above) and the fact that policy guidance may have the force of law, it is arguable that the Assembly failings in this respect are vulnerable to a maladministration complaint not least for its apparent failure to even comply with its own publication scheme under the Freedom of Information Act 2000.

Local Government Act 2000 Part I

1.67 As outlined above (para 1.6), LGA 2000 s2 provides local authorities with considerable flexibility in that it empowers them to do anything they consider likely to promote or improve the economic, social or environmental well-being of their area (whether for the benefit of all or part of it; or for all or any persons resident in it). In exercising these new powers councils are required to have regard to guidance issued by the secretary of state (section 3(5)). Such guidance was issued in March 2001[83] and at para 6 stresses that the 'purpose in introducing the well-being power is to reverse that traditionally cautious approach, and to encourage innovation and closer joint working between local authorities and their partners to improve communities'.

1.68 By virtue of LGA 2000 s3, local authorities are unable to use the power to do anything which is specifically prohibited, or limited by other statutory provisions, nor can it be used to raise money (whether by precepts, borrowing or otherwise).

1.69 The prohibition on using the power as a money raising device does not prevent a local authority charging for any services provided under section 2, nor does it prevent companies established by local authorities under the section 2 power from raising money. This power has been further widened by LGA 2003 s93 which specifically enables local authorities to charge for discretionary services (but not services the authority is 'required' to provide). Guidance on the use of the LGA 2003 charging power[84] advises that there is some flexibility in the amounts raised by charging, provided that, taking one financial year with another, the income from charges does not exceed the costs of provision. This means therefore that (for instance) when establishing a new service it would be lawful for the authority initially to accumulate a small surplus – provided that at the end of the year this is no longer the case.

---

82 http://new.wales.gov.uk/topics/health/?lang=en.
83 Department of the Environment, Transport and the Regions, *Power to promote or improve economic, social or environmental well-being*, 2001, available from the website of the Department for Communities and Local Government at http://www.communities.gov.uk.
84 Office of the Deputy Prime Minister, *General Power for Best Value Authorities to Charge for Discretionary Services – Guidance on the Power in the Local Government Act 2003*, 2003, para 21.

1.70   An evaluation of the use by local authorities of their section 2 powers[85] shows that it has been patchy, but that in relation to councils' health and social care responsibilities they had been used to:

- charge for topping-up packages of day care where clients would like assistance beyond that for which they have been assessed but for which they are willing to pay;
- fill perceived gaps in the legislation for housing with care schemes;
- provide assistance to vulnerable young people and families in the home;
- support elderly residents leaving hospital;
- take a charge on property and pay contributions to the costs of housing to allow families to remain in their own home rather than incur extra costs of care and new accommodation;
- provide grants (in most cases, relatively small grants);
- charge for providing 'community alarm systems', ie personal alarms for older people if they fall/get attacked, which could previously be done for council tenants, but is now provided more widely.

1.71   Although general empowering provisions of this nature are not new,[86] Part I of the 2000 Act provides considerably more freedom for councils than was previously the case – and the extent of this freedom to fund community care services has been the subject of analysis in a number of recent cases.[87]

1.72   *R (Khan) v Oxfordshire CC*[88] concerned an applicant to whom Immigration and Asylum Act 1999 s115 applied,[89] such that she was not eligible for any assistance unless she was able to obtain accommodation under NAA 1948 s21 or LGA 2000 s2. The local authority had concluded that she was excluded from assistance under the 1948 Act, by virtue of section 21(1A) which provides (in sum) that a person to whom section 115 of the 1999 Act applies may not be provided with residential accommodation if her need for care and attention has arisen solely because of destitution (see para 22.12 where this provision is further considered). On the basis that the local authority was correct, Moses J had to decide whether there remained a power to provide assistance under LGA 2000 s2, the problem

---

85   Office of the Deputy Prime Minister, *Formative Evaluation of the Take-Up and Implementation of the Well Being Power, 2003–2006*, 2005, available from the website of the Department for Communities and Local Government at http://www. communities.gov.uk.

86   LGA 1972 s111, for instance, empowers authorities to 'do anything (whether or not involving the expenditure, borrowing or lending of money or the acquisition or disposal of any property or rights) which is calculated to facilitate, or is conducive to, the discharge of any of their functions'; see eg *R (A and B) v East Sussex CC* [2002] EWHC 2771 (Admin); (2003) 6 CCLR 117, where the use of this power in relation to community care services was considered.

87   See also *R (Theophilus) v Lewisham LBC* [2002] EWHC 1371 (Admin); [2002] 3 All ER 851 which concerned further education funding

88   [2002] EWHC 2211 (Admin); (2002) 5 CCLR 611.

89   Being a person subject to 'immigration control' who had leave to enter the UK subject to a condition that she did not have recourse to public funds.

being that (by virtue of LGA 2000 s3) the power could not used to provide anything which was otherwise prohibited, or limited by another statutory provision. Having considered Elias J's judgment in *R (J) v Enfield LBC and Secretary of State for Health (intervener)*,[90] Moses J concluded:

> 33. I take the view that, unlike the absence of power under s17 of the Children's Act 1989, the prohibition under s21(1A) is a prohibition within the meaning of section 3. Thus, it is not open to the local authority to provide finance under the Local Government Act 2000. [91]

1.73   *R (J) v Enfield LBC and Secretary of State for Health (intervener)*[92] concerned an applicant and her baby daughter who sought accommodation assistance from the local authority. The applicant, who was HIV positive, was unlawfully within the UK having overstayed her visa. At the time of the hearing it was considered that there was no power under CA 1989 s17 to provide accommodation.[93] Elias J concluded that in the absence of any express statutory power to provide for the applicant and her daughter, such a power existed under LGA 2000 s2. He further held that if the use of this power were 'the only way in which [the local authority] could avoid a breach of the claimant's article 8 rights, then . . . it would be obliged to exercise its discretion in that way'.[94] This analysis was accepted in *R (Grant) v Lambeth LBC*[95] which concerned a family who were unlawfully within the UK and who had no right to be accommodated. The council concluded that to avoid a breach of the family's convention rights (within the provisions of Nationality, Immigration and Asylum Act 2002 Sch 3 para 3 – see para 22.38 below) it would offer to pay for their travel back to their country of origin. The Court of Appeal held that once an authority had reached this conclusion it was obliged to consider 'whether there was some other power by the exercise of which a breach of Mrs Grant's Convention rights could be avoided' and, in that context, the use of the power conferred by section 2.

90 [2002] EWHC 432 (Admin); (2002) 5 CCLR 434.
91 [2002] EWHC 2211 (Admin); (2002) 5 CCLR 611 at [33]. This aspect of the judgment was upheld on appeal – see *R (Khan) v Oxfordshire CC* [2004] EWCA Civ 309; (2004) 7 CCLR 215.
92 [2002] EWHC 432 (Admin); (2002) 5 CCLR 434.
93 The Court of Appeal having held in *R (A) v Lambeth LBC* [2001] EWCA Civ 1624; (2001) 4 CCLR 486, that no such power existed: this finding was set aside by a differently constituted Court of Appeal in *R (W) v Lambeth LBC* [2002] EWCA Civ 613; [2002] 2 All ER 901; (2002) 5 CCLR 203.
94 [2002] EWHC 432 (Admin); (2002) 5 CCLR 434 at [72]: a view affirmed by the Court of Appeal in *R (W) v Lambeth LBC* [2002] EWCA Civ 613; [2002] 2 All ER 901; (2002) 5 CCLR 203 at [74]–[75], and in *R (A and B) v East Sussex CC* [2002] EWHC 2771 (Admin); (2003) 6 CCLR 117 (but see *R (G) v Barnet LBC* [2003] UKHL 57; [2003] 3 WLR 1194; (2003) 6 CCLR 500 and see also *Anufrijeva v Southwark LBC* [2003] EWCA Civ 1406; [2004] 2 WLR 603; (2003) 6 CCLR 415.
95 [2004] EWCA Civ 1711; [2005] 1 WLR 1781 at [50].

CHAPTER 2

Strategic planning and information to the public

2.1   This chapter considers the wider public health and social care planning functions of social services authorities and NHS bodies, including the obligation of social services departments to prepare registers of disabled people. It also considers the obligations to provide information about the services offered locally, and other non-confidential recorded information held by public authorities under the Freedom of Information Act 2000. Individual care planning is considered separately in chapter 3 and the data protection and confidentiality obligations of public authorities in chapter 26.

Social services strategic planning obligations

2.2   The duties upon social services authorities to plan can be subdivided into a specific obligation to compile registers about the needs of disabled people in their area, and a more general duty to prepare strategic plans as to how best to deliver services to those 'in need' within their area, and generally to promote 'well being'.

Registers of disabled people

2.3   National Assistance Act (NAA) 1948 s29(4)(g) and the directions made under that section[1] oblige social services authorities to maintain a register of disabled adults ordinarily resident in their area.[2] The purpose of such registers is to facilitate the obligation on social services authorities to inform 'persons to whom [section 29] relates of the services available for them [under section 29]'.[3]

2.4   The guidance accompanying the directions (LAC (93)10 Appendix 4, para 2) explains that, for certain statutory purposes (ie to establish a right to certain social security and tax benefits[4]) unconnected with NAA 1948 s29, there is a need to keep a register of the persons who come within the section's client group. The guidance points out that in addition the registers serve an important community care planning role – by helping to ascertain the demand and potential demand for domiciliary care services. Although the form of the registers is not prescribed, the guidance requires that they contain sufficient information to produce the annual statistical returns required by the Department of Health.[5] The register

---

1   LAC (93)10 Appendix 2 para 2(2). The material parts of which are to be found in Appendix B below: for a discussion concerning this Direction, see para 9.39.
2   See Chapter 6 for the definition of 'ordinary residence'.
3   LAC (93)10 Appendix 2 para 2(1)(2) and s29(4)(g).
4   Various benefits for blind people remain dependent upon registration – most notably an extra income tax allowance; in addition such persons are exempt from the 'personal capability assessment' for incapacity benefit together with other miscellaneous benefits such as certain income support premiums and relief from non-dependent deductions for housing benefit and council tax benefit, certain car parking concessions, a small reduction in the TV licence and access to free NHS eye examinations
5   LAC (93)10 Appendix 4.

aims at recording all persons who come within the NAA 1948 s29 client group – including 'mentally disordered persons'.

2.5   Information on the numbers of people with visual and hearing impairments who fall within the scope of s29 and are recorded on the registers, is collected every three years in England using two separate statistical returns – SSDA 902 (Registration of blind persons and partially sighted persons) and SSDA 910 (Registers of people who are deaf or hard of hearing).[6]

2.6   In many authorities the maintenance of a register of disabled people is seen as an administrative chore of little practical value. Potentially however these registers could be used for strategic planning purposes and as important proactive tools for disseminating information about new services and resources and as databases to facilitate consultation exercises, mail-shots and so on.

2.7   For community care purposes, however, the register is purely a planning tool; where a person comes within the NAA 1948 s29 client group and is assessed as requiring domiciliary services, those services must be provided irrespective of whether he or she is registered. Indeed, the guidance makes clear that an individual has the right not to have his or her name included on the formal register if he or she so chooses.[7]

2.8   The NAA 1948 s29 client group comprises 'persons aged eighteen or over who are blind, deaf or dumb or who suffer from mental disorder of any description, and other persons aged eighteen or over who are substantially and permanently handicapped by illness, injury, or congenital deformity'. The meaning of these terms is considered in detail at para 9.19 below.

2.9   The Department of Health guidance requires social services authorities to divide their registers of 'substantially and permanently handicapped' persons into three categories,[8] namely:

1) *Very severe handicap*
    This category includes those persons who:

    a) need help going to or using the WC practically every night. In addition, most of those in this group need to be fed and dressed or, if they can feed and/or dress themselves, they need a lot of help during the day with washing and the WC, or are incontinent; or
    b) need help with the WC during the night but not quite so much help with feeding, washing, dressing, or, while not needing night-time help with the WC, need a great deal of daytime help with feeding and/or washing and the WC; or
    c) are permanently bedridden or confined to a chair and need help to get in and out, or are senile or mentally impaired, or are not able to care for themselves as far as normal everyday functions are

---

6   See eg Department of Health, *People Registered as Deaf or Hard of Hearing Year ending 31 March 2004, England,* December 2004; Department of Health, *Registered Blind and Partially Sighted People Year ending 31 March 2003, England,* December 2003.
7   LAC (93)10 Appendix 4 para 3.
8   LAC (93)10 Appendix 4 para 9c and annex 1.

concerned, but who do not need as much help as categories a) and b) above.

2) *Severe or appreciable handicap*
This category includes those persons who:

a) either have difficulty doing everything, or find most things difficult and some impossible; or
b) find most things difficult, or three or four items difficult and some impossible; or
c) can do a fair amount for themselves but have difficulty with some items, or have to have help with one or two minor items.

3) *Other persons*
This category is not defined, save only that it includes such persons as those suffering from a less severe heart or chest condition or from epilepsy.

2.10   An equivalent registration duty in relation to disabled children is found in Children Act (CA) 1989 Sch 2 Part I para 2 – see para 24.10.

The social services duty to prepare strategic plans

2.11   Chronically Sick and Disabled Persons Act (CSDPA) 1970 s1(1) sought to increase the planning obligation on social services authorities by making them take a more proactive role. The section requires the authority to 'inform themselves' of the number of disabled people in its area (rather than passively waiting for people to register themselves as disabled). CSDPA 1970 s1(1) is, however, restricted in its ambit to disabled people. It provides as follows:

> It shall be the duty of every local authority having functions under section 29 of the National Assistance Act 1948 to inform themselves of the number of persons to whom that section applies within their area and of the need for the making by the authority of arrangements under that section for such persons.

2.12   DHSS circular 12/70[9] explained the planning purpose underlying CSDPA 1970 s1(1) thus:

> . . . it requires the authorities concerned to secure that they are adequately informed of the numbers and needs of substantially and permanently handicapped persons in order that they can formulate satisfactory plans for developing their services. . . . It is not a requirement of the Section that authorities should attempt 100% identification and registration of the handicapped. This would be a difficult, expensive and time-consuming exercise, diverting excessive resources from effective work with those who are already known, involving a restrictive and artificial definition and likely to be counter-productive.

2.13   The need for a more effective planning obligation was highlighted by the

9   Para 5.

white paper *Caring for People*[10] which stated the government's intention that authorities would be required to draw up and publish plans for community care services, in consultation with health authorities and other interested agencies.[11] The intention was realised via National Health Service and Community Care Act (NHSCCA) 1990 s46 which gives to the secretary of state powers to direct local authorities to prepare annual plans concerning the provision in their area of community care services. In 1991, detailed directions and guidance gave effect to this legislative intention:[12] namely that community care plans were to be the main vehicle for the strategic planning of adult care services by social services authorities.

2.14   Since 1991 the frequency with which the Department of Health has changed its requirements for local strategic plans is indicative of a central strategic planning failure. In the last ten years these planning obligations have included: the preparation of community care charters; community care plans; local action plans and local strategic partnerships; health improvement programmes; local health partnership and modernisation board plans; health and modernisation plans; joint investment plans (JIPs); Better Care, Higher Standards charters; local community strategy initiatives; carers strategies, and Best Value plans.

2.15   The NHSCCA 1990 envisaged that the key strategic planning tool for adult care services would be community care plans (s46), but the increased emphasis on joint health and social services collaboration marginalised their importance[13] such that in 2002 the duty to prepare such plans in England was repealed.[14] Since that time, as noted above, new strategic planning requirements have arisen with considerable frequency, only to be eclipsed by the next obligation – such that it is difficult to know at any one time which plan is in vogue and which is passé. With the demise of community care plans, for instance, it appeared that their central function would be addressed in health and modernisation plans, but these were then discarded in favour of JIPs (see para 2.27 below) and Better Care, Higher Standards charters[15] (see para 2.41 below). These now appear to have been sidelined (without being formally abandoned) by the requirement for local area agreements (LAAs). In future these will be informed by statutory strategic needs assessments.[16]

---

10 CM 849, HMSO, November 1989.
11 At para 5.3.
12 The Community Care Plans Direction 1991 and its accompanying guidance LAC (91)6. This was followed by Community Care Plans (Consultation) Directions 1993 and accompanying guidance in LAC (93)4.
13 There is additionally evidence to suggest that the increasing requirements of Whitehall for performance management data through the Performance Assessment Framework, which leads directly to the star-rating of social services departments, is to have a significant influence on the shape of individual strategic plans.
14 Care Plans (England) Directions 2003.
15 LAC (2001)6: HSC 2001/006, issued under LASSA 1970 s7(1). The 'Charters are for anyone 18 or over in England who has difficulties associated with old age, long term illness or disability and for carers who support people in these circumstances' (p1).
16 Department of Health, *Commissioning Framework for Health and Well-being*, March 2007.

Performance indicators and star ratings

2.16   In practice, it is arguable that councils have concentrated not so much on meeting their strategic goals (or indeed their legal obligations) but on meeting non-statutory targets: primarily targets set (in England) by the Commission for Social Care Inspection (CSCI).[17] Authorities are required to submit statistical returns on their performance in meeting these targets and on the basis of these and an inspection by the CSCI they are awarded a star rating. In political and managerial terms these star ratings have assumed great importance. Although targets have the potential to improve performance, there are concerns that they have become a distraction which has undermined good practice. Harris,[18] for instance, has described how those being audited, 'adapt their behaviour to the audit process, distorting reality so that it conforms to an auditable reality', and how councils have engaged in fabricating impression management and performing to the audience of regulation. Acknowledging the validity of these concerns the CSCI has announced its intention[19] to reduce the number of performance indicators and to replace the existing National Standards and Criteria with the seven social care outcomes, for which the scoring system will be weighted to reflect activity and expenditure considerations for five separate client groups, namely: older people 40 per cent; carers 15 per cent; people with learning disabilities 15 per cent; mental health 15 per cent; and physical and sensory disability 15 per cent.

Local area agreements

2.17   The English local government white paper *Strong and prosperous communities* (2006)[20] announced that LAAs would become the key planning tool and 'delivery contract' between central and local government in England. LAAs, which incorporate earlier local public service agreements, are seen as part of the English government's attempt to reduce the number of centrally set targets for local authorities and to encourage them to act 'strategically', to use their Local Government Act (LGA) 2000 s2 powers (see para 1.67 above) and co-ordinate local service delivery by working together with 'partner authorities' which include, for instance, primary care trusts (PCTs), district councils, police authorities, Learning and Skills Councils[21]). In relation to the reduction in centrally generated targets, the white paper (at p11) stated:

---

17   See eg CSCI, *Adult Performance Indicators for 2006–07* at http://www.csci.gov.uk/docs/ adult_PIs_2006–07.doc.

18   J Harris, *The Social Work Business* Routledge, 2003, p94.

19   CSCI consultation document, *A New Outcomes Framework for Performance Assessment of Adult Social Care 2006–07*, August 2006

20   Department for Communities and Local Government, *Strong and prosperous communities – The Local Government White Paper*, Cm 6939-I, HMSO, 2006, see in particular para 5.34.

21   Currently listed in the Local Government and Public Involvement in Health Bill (2007) at clause 80.

We propose a radical simplification of the performance framework. There will be around 35 priorities [ie targets] for each area, tailored to local needs through the Local Area Agreement. Instead of the many hundreds of indicators currently required by central government there will be a single set of about 200 outcome based indicators covering all important national priorities like climate change, social exclusion and anti-social behaviour.

2.18   LAAs are structured around four blocks (or policy fields): children and young people; safer and stronger communities; healthier communities and older people; and economic development and enterprise. They are drawn up by local authorities with their partners who (it is claimed by the Department for Communities and Local Government) identify their own priorities and targets, and are negotiated with the relevant government regional office. Once agreement has been reached, it is sent to the various ministers of central departments for approval as well as the Secretary of State for Health. As at 2007 relatively small sums of central government funding were determined by LAAs (approximately £500 million). It is proposed, however, that they will become a key factor in future funding, and regulate in the region of £4.7 billion government funding.

2.19   These proposals will be given statutory force as and when the Local Government and Public Involvement in Health Bill (introduced into Parliament on 12 December 2006) becomes law, via Part 5 Chapter 1 (currently clauses 79–92). It is anticipated that the relevant duty will commence in April 2008.

The NHS duty to prepare strategic plans

2.20   National Health Service Act (NHSA) 2006 s24[22] requires every PCT (in partnership with the local authorities it covers) to prepare and keep under review (in accordance with directions issued by the secretary of state) a plan which sets out a strategy for improving:

(a)   the health of the people for whom they are responsible, and
(b)   the provision of health care to such people.

2.21   The key role of the local authority in the development and implementation of such plans was initially underscored by the creation of a new duty under Health Act 1999 s27 requiring co-operation between health bodies and local authorities and now by NHSA 2006 s242,[23] which places a duty on NHS organisations to have arrangements for involving patients and the public in planning development and provision of services. In England this duty was augmented by the obligation under NHSA 2006 s237 to establish patients' forums.

22   Under NHS (Wales) Act (NHS(W)A) 2006 s17, local health boards have equivalent obligations.
23   NHS(W)A 2006 s183.

Local delivery plans

2.22   As for local authorities, local health bodies have been required to prepare a plethora of different plans over the last decade. With the emergence of strategic health authorities, the Department of Health announced in May 2003 that local delivery plans (LDPs)[24] – which 'focussed on the health and social care priorities set out in the PPF'[25] – would be the only plan that PCTs were obliged to prepare. In future it is proposed that there will be a legal duty on PCTs along with local authorities to produce a strategic needs assessment.

2.23   LDPs must put in place a programme by which the government's priorities for the NHS (eg waiting list and other performance targets) are translated into concrete local action. The initial priorities were detailed in a three year programme announced in guidance issued to strategic health authorities in 2002 as *Planning and Priorities Framework (PPF) guidance.*[26] In 2004 the English government announced an intention to reduce the number of targets for PCTs.[27] More recently it has stated a wish to move away from setting new priorities and place greater emphasis on continuity and the need for PCTs 'to work with local authorities to improve health and well-being, reduce inequalities and achieve a shift towards prevention' and to align the NHS planning timetable with the local authority planning cycle 'to facilitate effective joint working' and in particular to ensure that PCTs 'play their full part in the local area agreement process and to agree with local authorities those aspects of LDPs that require joint work'.[28]

⊕ NHS/social services joint planning

2.24   The need for collaboration between the NHS and local authority welfare agencies has been the subject of discussion since the formation of the modern welfare state in 1948. With the inexorable trend towards structural reconfigurations (if not mergers) between social services and NHS bodies (see para 1.17) the importance of joint planning has assumed greater importance.

2.25   Chapter 2 of the 1990 Policy Guidance[29] gave general advice on what authorities were expected to achieve through planning, and throughout it placed considerable emphasis on the need for partnership and collaboration between authorities and the NHS:

24 Guidance on these is to be found at http://www.doh.gov.uk/himp.
25 *Planning and Priorities Framework guidance,* October 2002.
26 The 2007–08 targets are detailed in Department of Health, *The NHS in England: operating framework for 2007–08,* 2006, which sets out amongst other things, the health and service priorities for the specified period and details the national targets and local delivery plan requirements.
27 Department of Health, *National Standards, Local Action: Health and Social Care Standards and Planning Framework 2005/06–2007/08,* 2004.
28 Department of Health, *The NHS in England: operating framework for 2007/08,* 2006, para 1.13.
29 *Community Care in the Next Decade and Beyond: policy guidance,* HMSO, 1990.

2.3 Joint planning will be essential if the new planning agreements are to work. Many authorities believe there should be joint plans by LAs, [*health authorities and primary care trusts*] as this would most effectively ensure the 'seamless' service which they wish to achieve. The Department recommends that where ever possible joint plans are produced but recognises that in some areas problems exist (not least where authorities do not have coterminous boundaries) which mean that this objective would not be realistic at least in the short term. However, all authorities are expected to take a joint approach to planning and ensure their plans are complementary. Plans will be monitored to ensure this joint approach.

And at para 2.11 the point is again emphasised:

At an early stage [*social services and health authorities/primary care trusts*] should draw up joint resource inventories and analyses of need which enable them to reach agreement on key issues of 'who does what' for whom, when, at what cost and who pays.

2.26   The crucial importance of social services and local NHS bodies developing common procedures for recording information and 'mapping' the needs of their service users has been emphasised on many occasions, including in the highly influential Audit Commission Report *The Coming of Age* (1997)[30] which stressed that 'Health authorities, trusts and social services departments must map needs and the services available to meet them. They should share this information with each other as the basis for joint planning and commissioning.'

2.27   These messages were taken forward in 1997 guidance issued to both health and social services authorities as *Better Services for Vulnerable People* in 1997[31] which required them to prepare JIPs for older people including those with mental illness. Initially the requirement was little more than a joint mapping exercise, but it required 'a joint analysis' of such matters as local population needs, current resources, current investment and agreed service outcomes – with a view to agreeing gaps in service provision and 'present and future commissioning priorities'. Follow-up guidance added detail to the requirements of JIPs and their scope (being extended to cover all adults with mental health needs and subsequently 'all other care groups').[32]

2.28   By 2001 JIPs had (as noted above) subsumed the social services function of preparing 'community care plans' and became the main strategic planning tool for the provision of health and social care services for vulnerable people. 2002 guidance outlined the aims of the JIP as follows:

6. The aim of the JIP process is to enable the delivery of better services and therefore improved outcomes for service users. The emphasis must be on:

---

30 (1997) Recommendation 1 p77.
31 EL (97)62/CI (97)24.
32 See *Better Services for Vulnerable People – Maintaining the Momentum*, letter issued by NHS and Social Care Regions in August 1998 which can be accessed at http://www.dh.gov.uk/en/Publicationsandstatistics/Lettersandcirculars/Dearcolleagueletters/DH_4082495.

- promoting the independence of adults
- using the plan to determine local targets and enabling the development of responsive services to meet the needs of the local population
- improving the use of resources to meet joint objectives for health and social care, and
- transparency about current and planned investment.

7. In broad terms, the JIP process involves participating agencies setting out jointly to answer the following questions:
- what are the needs to be met?
- what is the prevalence of each need?
- what services are required to meet the needs?
- what is the provision actually made at this stage?
- what action is required to move services closer to what is required and so close the gaps that have been demonstrated?
- what are the agreed service outcomes?
- what outcomes are expected for the particular need being addressed at both a patient/user level and at a population level?

2.29   Whilst JIPs are no longer referred to in current Department of Health guidance, it appears that the future vehicle for joint planning will be an obligation on local authorities and their partner PCTs to produce a 15-year joint strategic needs assessments of population health and social care need. This duty is currently proposed in the Local Government and Public Involvement in Health Bill.[34] The priorities identified in the joint assessment will then form part of the overarching community strategy for the area and would be supported by funding from, amongst other sources, LAAs (see para 2.17 above) or other sources.

Wales

2.30   The NHSCCA 1990 s46(1)[35] obligation to prepare community care plans continues in Wales although it has been updated to take account of the new statutory functions, including those under the LGA 2000. The relevant guidance is contained in circular NAFWC 36/00 and a policy document which accompanied it, *Social Services Guidance on Planning.*[36] The guidance includes a requirement to produce five-year strategies monitored by annual reviews or business plans; a clear role for best value and performance management in setting targets and implementing service plans; and the need to produce and implement a strategy for informing the public of intentions included within plans.

---

34 Currently listed in the Local Government and Public Involvement in Health Bill (2007) at clause 118 and being consulted upon in Department of Health, *Commissioning Framework for Health and Well-being*, March 2007.

35 As detailed in WOC 55/91 Secretary of State's directions – NHSCCA 1990 s46(1): Community Care Plans; WOC 20/93 Community Care Plans (Consultation) Directions 1993; and WOC 29/94 Social Care Plans (Independent Sector Non-Residential Care) Direction 1994.

36 Accessible at http://www.joint-reviews.gov.uk/money/commissioning/ files%5Cguidonplan_e.pdf.

2.31   The relevant regulations[37] require the section 46(1) plans to be integrated with the health, social care and well-being (HSCWB) strategies that are required to be produced by local authorities and local health boards under these regulations.

2.32   Guidance on HSCWB strategies was issued in 2003[38] and is likely to be reviewed in 2007 as a result of consultation[39] which proposes that local authorities, local health boards and their partners be required to develop a revised three-year HSCWB strategy by April 2008 which must be capable of delivering 'demonstrable improvements in health and well-being, and streamlined and effective health services and social services'.

2.33   The Welsh Assembly monitors all social services authority and local health board plans in Wales.[40] Ultimately, if a plan were out of line with national policies and priorities then the Assembly's powers under Local Authority Social Services Act 1970 s7A could be invoked.[41]

The general duty to inform

2.34   The duty to prepare strategic plans and the duty to disseminate information about available services are complimentary obligations. Information derived from assessments,[42] complaints and user group representations should inform the strategic planning process. In turn information should be disseminated to service users, their carers and user groups as to what services are available, how they can be accessed and all other relevant factors – including for instance the charges that will accompany them and how complaints can be made concerning service deficiencies.

2.35   The following section reviews the obligations that local authorities and health bodies have to inform community care service users (and potential service users) of their rights. It is essentially a proactive obligation – to disseminate information regardless of an individual request. In paras 2.49 and 2.64 we consider the obligations these bodies have to provide specific information when asked – the reactive obligation.

2.36   Although the duty on social services to provide general information is

---

37   Health, Social Care and Well-Being Strategies (Wales) Regulations 2003 SI No 154 (W24).

38   Welsh Assembly, *Health, Social Care and Well-being Strategies Policy Guidance*, 2003, accessible at http://www.wales.nhs.uk/documents/prepare-strat-e.pdf.

39   The draft revised HSCWB guidance was issued for consultation in November 2006 and is accessible at http://new.wales.gov.uk/consultations/currentconsultation/ healandsoccarecurrcons/?lang=en.

40   *Social Services Guidance on Planning*, 2000, para 2.4.

41   See para 1.36 above.

42   See eg *R v Bristol CC ex p Penfold* (1998) 1 CCLR 315 where Scott Baker J held that community care assessments were of importance in relation to strategic planning 'even if there is no hope' of the disabled person being deemed to be in need of services since they 'serve a useful purpose in identifying for the local authority unmet needs which will help it to plan for the future. Without assessment this could not be done.'

primarily statutory (and in particular under CSDPA 1970 s1) all public
bodies have general public law obligations to provide information in certain situations. As discussed in chapter 27 there is a developing duty to
provide reasons for certain decisions (see para 27.200). In addition the
European Court of Human Rights has held that article 8 of the Convention may oblige state authorities to provide information – particularly
when that information will enable individuals to make crucial decisions
about the extent of a physical risk they may face.[43]

2.37   NAA 1948 s29(1)(a)[44] empowers authorities to make arrangements 'for
informing' disabled adults 'of the services available for them' under that
section.

2.38   CSDPA 1970 s1(2) converts this discretionary power into an obligation
and spells out in greater detail the nature of that duty. The duty only
applies to disabled people and leaves considerable discretion as to the way
in which the information is published. It remains, however, the most
important statutory provision in relation to the duty to provide general
information. It provides as follows:

> (2) Every such local authority –
> (a) shall cause to be published from time to time at such times and in such
>   manner as they consider appropriate general information as to the
>   services provided under arrangements made by the authority under
>   the said section 29 which are for the time being available in the area;
>   and
> (b) shall ensure that any such person as aforesaid who uses any of those
>   services is informed of any other service provided by the authority
>   (whether under any such arrangements or not) which in the opinion
>   of the authority is relevant to his needs and of any service provided by
>   any other authority or organisation which in the opinion of the
>   authority is so relevant and of which particulars are in the authority's
>   possession.

2.39   DHSS circular 12/70, para 5 explains the purpose of CSDPA 1970
s1(2) as ensuring that 'those who might benefit by help, and their families, should know what help is available to them and this is to be secured
both by general publicity and by personal explanations'. Whilst the duty to
provide information to an individual service user is an essential part of
the assessment process under NHSCCA 1990 s47, the general duty to
publicise services is not specifically addressed by the 1990 Act. The 1990
policy guidance[45] only deals with this issue as an aspect of community care
planning, requiring that plans include details of what arrangements
authorities intend to make to inform service users and their carers about
services.

---

43   See *Guerra v Italy* (1998) 26 EHRR 357; *McGinley and Egan v UK* (1998) 27 EHRR 1;
     and *LCB v UK* (1998) 27 EHRR 212.
44   As authorised by the secretary of state's directions – LAC (93)10 Appendix 2 para 2(1)
     (see para 9.44).
45   *Community Care in the Next Decade and Beyond: policy guidance*, HMSO, 1990,
     para 2.25.

2.40   *Care Management and Assessment, A Practitioners' Guide*[46] states (at para 1.2) that 'a greatly increased emphasis on the sharing of information' is 'an essential feature' of community care planning and that this should include the publishing of information on the resources/services available and the assessment and review procedures. In this context it advises:

> 1.3 It is the responsibility of the practitioner to ensure that this published information reaches potential users and carers who are considering seeking assistance. The availability of such material should help practitioners in their task but will also mean that they will be more open to public challenge on the quality of service they provide.

2.41   Although the 1991 guidance remains in force, it has been updated such that the principal non-statutory obligation on social services and the NHS in England to publicise the availability of their services for adults now derives from the Better Care, Higher Standards policy guidance issued in March 2001.[47] Relevant extracts from the guidance include:

> 2. Social services with their partners in housing and health should: –
>
> - . . .
> - Have a dissemination strategy for the charter which ensures all those in need of long term care can readily obtain a copy of the charter or summary which is accessible to people with sight, hearing, learning or other disabilities;
> - . . .
> - Develop a jointly agreed strategy for the provision of information about long term care services across health, social services and housing for inclusion in charters for 2002/03;
>
> 10. It is strongly re-emphasised that charters must be accessible to people with sight, hearing, learning or other disabilities (this means authorities considering the availability of information in a range of formats including Braille, Moon, Maketon, audio tape and video tape) and for people whom English is not their first language.
>
> **The importance of developing an information strategy**
>
> 19. A strategy for the provision of information should be developed including:
>
> - A. Training of front-line staff in basic information about long term care services across health, social services, and housing and benefits as well as knowledge of where to refer for more detailed information. To support the charter authorities also need to continue to build the charter into their training programmes for all staff.

---

46 *Care Management and Assessment – A Practitioners' Guide*, HMSO, 1991.
47 LAC (2001)6: HSC 2001/006, issued under LASSA 1970 s7(1). The 'Charters are for anyone 18 or over in England who has difficulties associated with old age, long term illness or disability and for carers who support people in these circumstances' (p1).

- B. Using the views expressed by users and carers to improve the accessibility of information. This would include making available accessible and user-friendly written information, including local BCHS charters. It should also include using and working with information/ advice points such as libraries, Citizens' Advice Bureaux, local voluntary agencies and community groups; considering the use of electronic media, including terminals at publicly accessible points and times, and the use of the Internet.
- C. 'One stop shops' providing comprehensive information about long term care across health, social services, and housing and benefits. These may take different forms, including public enquiry offices open to personal callers, telephone help lines open through extended hours and outreach facilities to suit the environment and local population. In all cases, they require a high level of knowledge of local services for staff to answer enquiries with comprehensive, consistent and accurate information.

20. Care Direct will involve a 'one stop shop' service, covering the same services as Better Care, Higher Standards charters. Subject to the evaluation of the pilots, it will eventually offer a single national telephone help line number, linked to local help desks. Further, it will aim to go beyond the provision of information and will provide a service arranging appointments for assessment or access to services.[48]

2.42   In addition to the Better Care, Higher Standards policy guidance in England, there is an abundance of references to the duty to inform service users of their rights, in departmental guidance aimed at specific client groups. These include advice in the Single Assessment Process guidance[49] (Annex E), advice in the Valuing People initiative[50] and the Fair Access to Care Services Guidance[51] which at para 29 advises that:

> . . . councils should help individuals who may wish to approach them for support by publishing and disseminating information about access, eligibility and services, in a range of languages and formats. The information should also say what usually happens during assessment and care management processes, related time-scales, and how individuals might access direct payments.

2.43   The practice guidance issued under the Carers and Disabled Children Act 2000[52] provides a useful overview of other government information

---

48   Care Direct has now been subsumed into Linkage *Plus* which is a one stop shop initiative for giving information to people aged 50 and over.

49   Annex E HSC 2002/001/LAC (2002)1, *Guidance on the Single Assessment Process for Older People* – see para 3.29 below where this guidance is considered further.

50   See Department of Health white paper, *Valuing People – A New Strategy for Learning Disability for the 21st Century*, Cm 5086, 2001, para 4.30 and the policy guidance, *Valuing People: A New Strategy for Learning Disability for the 21st Century: Implementation Guidance*: HSC 2001/016: LAC(2001)23, at Annex D and see also para 3.36 below where this initiative is considered further.

51   LAC (2002)13, *Fair Access to Care Services – guidance on eligibility for adult car services* – see para 3.26 below where this guidance is considered further.

52   Paras 15–20.

dissemination initiatives, including reference to the strategy document *A framework for improving quality in social care through better use of information and information technology* (2001)[53] and the government's internet strategy *e-government: a strategic framework for public services in the information age* (2000).[54]

2.44 The requirement that NHS bodies and local authorities have information dissemination strategies is a public law, rather than a private law obligation. In essence this means that a failure properly to discharge this duty could result in criticism by the ombudsman or censure in a judicial review. It cannot, however, in general form the basis for a private law claim for damages. In *Qazi v Waltham Forest LBC*[55] the applicants sought to argue that a failure by a local authority to provide accurate information concerning the processing of disabled facilities grants could found an action based upon negligent misstatement in accordance with the principles established in *Hedley Byrne & Co Ltd v Heller & Partners Ltd.*[56] Rejecting this approach, Richards J observed:

> It was a normal and legitimate incident of the defendant's statutory functions to provide information and advice about the system to those making inquiries about the availability of grants or applying for grants. I do not see how, by providing such information or advice, the defendant could be said to have assumed a responsibility in private law towards would-be or actual applicants.

Wales

2.45 There is no equivalent of Better Care, Higher Standards in Wales. The principal guidance stems from the policy guidance *Health and Social Care for Adults: Creating a Unified and Fair System for Assessing and Managing Care* at paras 2.17 et seq and in Annex 10, which requires agencies to 'work together to publish and disseminate a coordinated set of information about services and eligibility in a range of languages and accessible formats. The information should also say what usually happens during assessment and care management processes, related time-scales, and how individuals might access direct payments.' In relation to the NHS, *Improving Health in Wales – A Plan for the NHS and its Partners* (January 2001),[57] chapter 3, made a commitment to publish improved information on accessing health and social care services[58] and required NHS trusts and local health groups to publish an annual prospectus providing information on available services.

53 http://www.dh.gov.uk/en/Publicationsandstatistics/Publications/PublicationsPolicy AndGuidance/DH_4008239.
54 http://archive.cabinetoffice.gov.uk/e-envoy/ukonline-estrategy/$file/contents.htm.
55 (2000) 32 HLR 689.
56 [1964] AC 465.
57 http://www.rcgp.org.uk/pdf/ISS_SUMM01_01.pdf.
58 Now published as the *Health and Social Care Guide for Wales*, accessible at http:// www.wales.nhs.uk/documents/4decH&SCareGuide.pdf.

Children

2.46   The obligations under the 1948 and 1970 Acts in relation to the provision of information relate only to persons aged 18 or over. The concomitant duty to inform in relation to services for disabled children and other children in need exists in CA 1989 Sch 2 Part I para 1. This duty is considered in volume 6 of the *Children Act 1989 Guidance (Children with Disabilities)*, which makes the following observations:

> 3.6 ... SSD's should build on their existing links with community groups, voluntary organisations and ethnic minority groups to involve them in planning services and as a sounding board when formulating policies. The publicity required must include information about services provided both by the SSD and, to the extent they consider it appropriate, about such provision by others (eg voluntary organisations). Publicity should be clearly presented and accessible to all groups in the community, taking account of linguistic and cultural factors and the needs of people with communication difficulties. SSD's should take reasonable steps to ensure that all those who might benefit from such services receive the relevant information.

2.47   The Children Act guidance additionally deals with the need for professionals to communicate with disabled children in the assessment process and this aspect is considered at para 24.27 below.

2.48   A parallel duty to prepare plans in relation to services for disabled children and other children in need also exists in CA 1989 Sch 2 Part I para 1.

The specific duty to inform

2.49   Access to non-confidential publicly-held information is presently regulated by a variety of statutory and non-statutory provisions, including:

Local Government Act 1972

2.50   Prior to the coming into force of the Freedom of Information Act 2000 (below) the principal statute governing access to local authority information was the LGA 1972 (as amended), ss100A–100K of which primarily concerned the public's right of access to meetings, and the papers considered at these meetings, including 'background papers' relating to reports considered at the meetings. Papers, agendas and minutes of meetings must generally be available three clear days prior to the date of the meeting. With the advent of the internet, many authorities (and government bodies) argue that they comply with this obligation by placing the information on their websites: given the problems in navigating such sites (the Welsh Assembly site is a prime example) this assertion may be open to challenge.

Freedom of Information Act 2000

2.51   The Freedom of Information Act 2000 gives any person (which includes not only individuals but also companies, other organisations and other public authorities) the general right of access to all types of 'recorded' information[59] held by public authorities (and those providing services for them), sets out exemptions from that right, and places a number of obligations on public authorities. A 'public authority' is widely defined and includes parliament, government departments and local authorities, NHS bodies, GPs etc (although not independent care homes). Authorities must comply with a request within 20 working days – although if a 'conditional exemption' (see below) applies – the timescale is then such period as is reasonable in the circumstances.

2.52   The Act places two main responsibilities on public authorities, namely:

1) the adoption and maintenance of a 'Publication Scheme', and
2) the provision of information in response to requests from the public.

2.53   A publication scheme must specify the types of information the authority publishes, the form in which that information is published, and details of any charges for accessing that information. The scheme must be approved by the Information Commissioner[60] who is additionally responsible for enforcing and overseeing the Data Protection Act 1998.

2.54   The 2000 Act provides that anyone requesting information from a public authority is entitled to be informed in writing whether it holds information, and if so to have that information communicated to him or her. The application must, however, (1) be in writing, (2) state the applicant's name and address, and (3) describe the information requested. There is therefore no special form or precedent to use for such requests, although it is wise to describe as precisely as possible what information is sought (as otherwise the authority might refuse to provide it on costs grounds) and to state that the request is being made under 'the Freedom of Information Act 2000'.

2.55   Regulations[61] made under the Act stipulate that requests for information below a ceiling of £600 staff time for central government (eg Department of Health[62] or Welsh Assembly) or £450 for other authorities must be provided free of charge: it has been suggested that this equates to two days of staff time. Where the fee would exceed this limit, the public body can refuse to supply the information, or decide to supply subject to payment of the full costs of doing so. Authorities are however entitled to be paid for disbursements, such as the cost of photocopying/printing and postage etc.

59 This is widely defined: there is no time limit for when the material was compiled and it may include photos, plans etc.
60 See http://www.ico.gov.uk.
61 Freedom of Information and Data Protection (Appropriate Limit and Fees) Regulations 2004 SI No 3244.
62 The Freedom of Information releases are accessible at http://www.dh.gov.uk/en/ Publicationsandstatistics/Freedomofinformationpublicationschemefeedback/ FOIreleases/index.htm.

2.56   Authorities are exempted from providing the information in certain situations – depending upon whether an 'absolute' or 'conditional' exemption applies. Where an absolute exemption applies, the authority is not even under a duty to confirm or deny the existence of the information. All that is required is a letter, within 20 working days, explaining that the exemption is being invoked and advising the applicant of his or her right to appeal or complain about the decision. Absolute exemptions include information otherwise accessible; information concerning security matters; information in court records; parliamentary privileged material; personal information (that relates to the applicant – see para 2.58 below); information provided in confidence; and information whose disclosure is restricted by law.

2.57   Conditional exemptions apply where it may be in the public interest not to have disclosure. In some cases there is a presumption that disclosure will be against the public interest, whereas in others the authority is required to provide credible evidence of the particular prejudice, before it can use the ground as a reason for withholding disclosure. Those cases where no prejudice need be established include information that is intended for future publication as well as information that concerns public inquiries, government policy formulation, and legal professional privilege. Those cases where prejudice needs to be established include such matters as: national security; law enforcement; audit functions; effective conduct of public affairs; and health and safety.

2.58   Where a request concerns personal information, the 2000 Act defers to the Data Protection Act 1998 and in general the information should be sought under the 1998 Act. Sometimes, it will not be clear which Act is relevant – for instance a request for information concerning the salary paid to a public officer. The Information Commissioner has advised that in general, where information is sought concerning someone acting in an official capacity, it should be provided under the 2000 Act.[63] The data protection regime regulating the retention and accessibility of personal information is considered further at chapter 26 below.

2.59   Anyone dissatisfied with a response to their request has a number of options, including a right to have the refusal reviewed by the authority, and a right of appeal to the Information Commissioner and to the Information Tribunal.

Code of Practice on Access to Government Information

2.60   Under the Code of Practice on Access to Government Information (first published in 1994 and revised in 1997) most central government departments are under a general obligation to provide information to the public. The Code is policed by the Central Government Ombudsman.[64]

---

63   See the Information Commissioner's guidance, *Freedom of Information: access to information about public authorities' employees*, 2005.
64   Whose proper title is the Parliamentary and Health Service Ombudsman, see http://www.ombudsman.org.uk.

The potential scope of the Code is wide, although certain information is exempted – such as information whose disclosure might harm national security or the administration of justice, personal information about a third party, commercial confidences, information which is requested in an unreasonably general way, or which would demand an unreasonable diversion of resources to supply it.

2.61   The procedure is for the request to be made initially in writing to the public authority (referring to the Code) and then making a complaint via a sympathetic MP, if the information has not been provided, or is incomplete or has been unduly delayed (the Code states that simple requests should be answered within 20 working days) or if the authority is imposing excessive charges for the disclosure.

Code of Practice on Openness in the NHS

2.62   The Health Service Commissioner was given responsibility for over-seeing the Code of Practice on Openness in the NHS in England[65] in 1995; the Code was subsequently revised and reissued in 2003. The underlying principle of the Code is that information (not necessarily the documents from which the information derives) should be made available unless it can be shown to fall into one of the exempt categories (which largely parallel those for the above Code of Practice on Access to Government).

2.63   The Code requires that (i) each health body must publish the name of an individual in their employ responsible for the operation of the Code, and (ii) the method for requesting information through that individual should be publicised locally. Complaints about non-disclosure, or about delays in disclosure, or charges for information, should be made to that individual. The Code provides that if complainants are dissatisfied with the response they receive they should write to the Chief Executive of the health body concerned. Time limits are set for each stage. Complainants still dissatisfied after receiving a reply from the Chief Executive are then entitled to complain to the Health Service Commissioner.

2.64   The Health Service Commissioner issued a special report on the work-ings of the scheme in 1996[66] in which he stated that, unlike his practice with other complaints (where individuals must show some prima facie reason for their claim and have suffered some hardship or injustice), in relation to complaints about non-disclosure he regarded the refusal as of itself a ground on which to claim injustice or hardship. To date, the Ombudsman has taken a robust approach to the enforcement of the Codes and required the health body to establish with precision the specific exemption relied upon, in order to justify any refusal to disclose information.

65   A similar but separate code was issued in respect of Wales.
66   Health Service Commissioner, *First Report for Session 1996–97: Selected Investigations – Access to Official Information in the NHS*, HC 6, HMSO, 1996.

Community care assessments

continued

continued

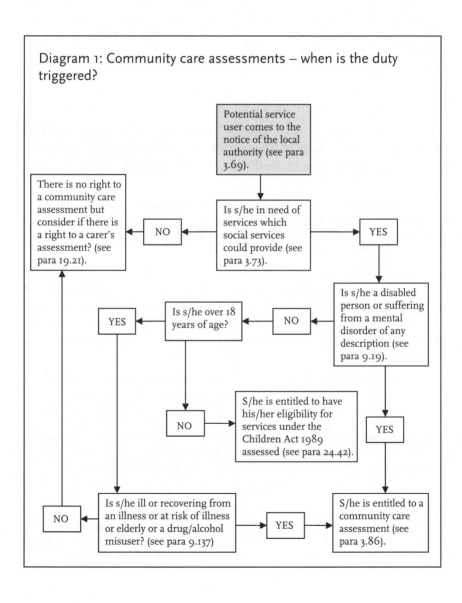

Diagram 1: Community care assessments – when is the duty triggered?

Introduction

3.1   The public provision of community care services is dependent in each case on a public authority making an administrative decision that the particular individual could not only benefit from the service, but also that the service should be provided. The decision-making procedure is known as the assessment process. The assessment process commences with the potential service user coming to the notice of the social services authority and ends with a decision as to whether or not he or she is entitled to services. If services are required, the next stage is the preparation of a care plan which describes and quantifies the services and specifies how (and by whom) they are to be delivered. This chapter is concerned with social services assessments and the following chapter with the care plans. The duty to assess carers is considered separately in chapter 16. The NHS duty to assess for continuing NHS health care is considered in chapter 14.

The theoretical framework

3.2   Assessment and care planning are central to community care law. They are the legislative response to the social services 'resource problem'. As Phyllida Parsloe commented when the key community care reforms took effect in 1993:[1]

> The NHS & Community Care Act backs a whole field of horses, with the two front-runners being user choice and scarce resources. Local authorities are apparently expected to give equal weight to empowering users and keeping within their own budget.

3.3   The assessment process therefore seeks to reconcile the demand for services with the resources available. This is not a new problem, or one unique to community care. Over 25 years ago in his seminal analysis, Michael Lipsky[2] charted the growth of street-level bureaucracies (legal aid lawyers, social workers, health care workers and so on). In his view their essential role is:

> . . . to make decisions about other people. Street-level bureaucrats have discretion because the nature of service provision calls for human judgment that cannot be programmed and for which machines cannot substitute . . . It is the nature of what we call human services that the unique aspects of people and their situations will be apprehended by public service workers and translated into courses of action responsive to each case within (more or less broad) limits imposed by their agencies.[3]

---

1   'Making a bid for fair play', *Community Care*, 5 August 1993.
2   Michael Lipsky, *Street-Level Bureaucracy*, Russell Sage Foundation, 1980: the term 'street-level bureaucracies' encompasses 'schools, police and welfare departments, lower courts, legal services officers, and other agencies whose workers interact with and have wide discretion over the dispensation of benefits or the allocation of public sanctions' (p xi).
3   Ibid, p162.

3.4 Lipsky argued that for this function to be exercised effectively, such employees had to be accountable both to their employers' preferences and to their clients' claims and that in order to maintain client confidence (given these twin roles) it was essential that the exercise of discretion was perceived as being independent: this in turn necessitated that street-level bureaucrats be seen to act as 'professionals'.[4] The organisational response to this quasi-independence has been to make:

> . . . street-level bureaucrats more accountable by reducing their discretion and constraining their alternatives. [To] write manuals to cover contingencies. [To] audit performance of workers to provide retrospective sanctions in anticipation of which it is hoped future behaviour will be modified.[5]

3.5 Many community care practitioners would identify with this analysis. Increasingly they are subject to micromanagement by unrealistically detailed central and local guidance (discussed below) and all pervasive performance indicators and targets. The development of 'managerialism'[6] within social services has unquestionably undermined the ability of social workers to carry out 'needs led' assessments. Increasingly they are budget or audit led exercises whose primary purpose is to conform to internal administrative imperatives, rather than the empowerment of service users and their carers.

3.6 At the heart of this dilemma is the issue of resources, and the extent to which the courts are prepared to defer to the problems of government (central and local) in ensuring that the state's finite resources are applied equitably. An analysis of the courts' approach to this question is provided at para 3.163 below.

The duty to assess – the legislative and administrative framework

3.7 The community care assessment obligation, although underpinned by statute, is fleshed out by directions and considerable volumes of guidance.

The statutory framework

3.8 Arguably social services authorities have always been under a public law obligation to assess potential community care service users. Where a council has a duty to provide services for people if 'satisfied' they are 'necessary',[7] there must be a concomitant obligation on that council to have a procedure for making determinations as to when, in any given case, the duty crystallises.

---

4 See Note 2 above.
5 Ibid.
6 See in particular, J Harris, *The Social Work Business*, Routledge, 2003.
7 Chronically Sick and Disabled Persons Act (CSDPA) 1970 s2(1).

Disabled Persons (Services, Consultation and Representation)
Act 1986 s4

3.9   Because of doubt about the extent of this obligation, in relation to the provision of services under Chronically Sick and Disabled Persons Act (CSDPA) 1970 s2, the Disabled Persons (Services, Consultation and Representation) Act (DP(SCR)A) 1986 s4 gave to disabled people (and their carers) the right to request an assessment. The circular accompanying the 1986 Act (LAC (87)6) explained the position thus:

> 3. However, s2(1) does not make it explicit whether a local authority has a duty to determine the needs of a disabled person. It was suggested in the course of debates in Parliament on the Disabled Persons (Services, Consultation and Representation) Bill that as the duty to 'make arrangements' could be interpreted as applying only after the local authority are satisfied that such arrangements are necessary in order to meet particular needs, local authorities might refuse to come to a view as to what are those needs as a means of avoiding the obligation to make arrangements. It has never been the Government's view that subsection 2(1) should be interpreted in that way, and it is clear that this is shared by the vast majority of local authorities. However, it was agreed that the matter should be put beyond doubt.

> 4. Section 4 of the 1986 Act accordingly makes it clear that local authorities have a duty to decide whether the needs of a disabled person call for the provision of services under section 2 of the 1970 Act, if they are requested to do so by a disabled person (section 4(a)) or by anyone who provides care for him or her (section 4(c)) in the circumstances mentioned in section 8 of the 1986 Act.

3.10 Section 4 of the 1986 Act provides:

> When requested to do so by–
> (a) a disabled person,
> (b) . . .[8]
> (c) any person who provides care for him in the circumstances mentioned in section 8,[9] a local authority shall decide whether the needs of the disabled person call for the provision by the authority of any services in accordance with section 2(1) of the 1970 Act (provision of welfare services).

3.11 Although the section 4 duty remains, it is largely a historical curiosity: now effectively subsumed by the subsequent legislation. The right to request an assessment proved to be an unsatisfactory mechanism to access services under the CSDPA 1970, as it required people to know of the existence of their right to services before they could access those services. As most people did not know of their rights under that Act, they were unable to make the necessary request under DP(SCR)A 1986 s4. What was required, therefore, was a duty to assess regardless of any

---

8   This provision, which related to requests by 'authorised representatives', has not been brought into force.

9   That is, someone 'who provides regular and substantial care for the disabled person – see para 16.11.

request from the potential service user: a duty that extended not only to services under CSDPA 1970 s2, but to all services under all the community care statutes.

3.12 The intention to create such a general duty to assess was announced in the 1989 white paper *Caring for People* (Cm 849) which at para 3.1.3 stated that social services authorities would be responsible for:

> . . . carrying out an appropriate assessment of an individual's need for social care (including residential and nursing home care), in collaboration as necessary with medical, nursing and other agencies, before deciding what services should be provided.

3.13 The effect of the changes has been to make social services departments the 'gate-keepers', controlling access to state-supported community care services. Such services can only be provided at public expense after an assessment of need has occurred[10] and a decision has been made by the social services authority that, having regard to the assessment of need, services should be provided. More recently however government rhetoric has been to distance itself from this gatekeeping role, and the executive summary to the green paper of 2005 said:

> For too long social work has been perceived as a gatekeeper or rationer of services and has been accused, sometimes unfairly, of fostering dependence rather than independence. We want to create a different environment, which reinforces the core social work values of supporting individuals to take control of their own lives, and to make the choices which matter to them.[11]

However no new resources have been forthcoming, and so within a finite budget, it is difficult to see how social work can avoid being a rationer of services.

The assessment obligation under NHS and Community Care Act 1993 s 47(1)

3.14 National Health Service and Community Care Act (NHSCCA) 1990 s47(1) is the general assessment duty presaged by the white paper. It provides:

> (1) Subject to subsections (5) and (6) below, where it appears to a local authority that any person for whom they may provide or arrange for the provision of community care services may be in need of any such services, the authority–
> (a) shall carry out an assessment of his needs for those services; and
> (b) having regard to the results of that assessment, shall decide whether his needs call for the provision by them of any such services.

3.15 Section 47(1) obliges social services authorities to carry out an assessment of an individual's needs for community care services even where the individual has made no request for an assessment. All that is required in order to trigger the assessment obligation is that:

10 Except in emergencies – NHSCCA 1990 s47(5), see para 4.76.
11 Department of Health, *Independence, Well-being and Choice*, 2005.

   a) the individual's circumstances have come to the knowledge of the
      authority;
   b) he or she may be in need of community care services.

3.16   The NHSCCA 1990 s47(1) duty lies at the very centre of all community
        care law – it is central to virtually all social services community care
        responsibilities and the nature of this obligation is considered in detail at
        para 3.86 and in the succeeding sections of this chapter.

The assessment obligation under NHS and Community Care Act 1993 s47(2)

3.17   In addition to the section 47(1) assessment obligation, section 47(2) states:

> If at any time during the assessment of the needs of any person under
> subsection (1)(a) above it appears to a local authority that he is a disabled
> person, the authority –
> (a) shall proceed to make such a decision as to the services he requires as is
>   mentioned in section 4 of the Disabled Persons (Services, Consultation
>   and Representation) Act 1986 without his requesting them to do so
>   under that section; and
> (b) shall inform him that they will be doing so and of his rights under that
>   Act.

3.18   Detailed practice guidance issued by the Department of Health in its *Care
        Management and Assessment: A Practitioners Guide*[12] (referred to in this
        chapter as the 1991 practice guidance) advised that NHSCCA 1990 s47(2)
        entitled all disabled people to a 'comprehensive assessment' regardless of
        the complexity of their needs. This was, however, incorrect, as Carnwath J
        explained in *R v Gloucestershire CC ex p RADAR*.[13] In his opinion the
        Department of Health had misunderstood the effect of section 47(2).
        The subsection is, in effect, merely a modest provision aimed at flagging
        up the duty to provide services under CSDPA 1970 s2 as Lord Clyde
        explained in *R v Gloucestershire CC ex p Barry*:[14]

> So far as the twofold provision in s47(1) and (2) is concerned the
> obligation on the local authority introduced by s47(1) was to carry out an
> assessment on its own initiative and the separate provision made in sub-s
> (2) cannot have been intended merely to achieve that purpose. It seems to
> me that there is sufficient reason for the making of a distinctive provision
> in sub-s (2) in the desire to recognise the distinctive procedural situation
> relative to the disabled. But it does not follow that any distinction exists in
> the considerations which may or may not be taken into account in making
> an assessment in the case of the disabled as compared with any other
> case.

---

12 Department of Health Social Services Inspectorate, HMSO, 1991.
13 (1998) 1 CCLR 476 at 484.
14 [1997] 2 WLR 459; (1997) 1 CCLR 40.

Directions

3.19   NHSCCA 1990 s47(4) empowers the secretary of state to give directions as to the form community care assessments should take.[15] As noted in para 1.55 below, in *R (B and H) v Hackney LBC*[16] the judge suggested that the terms of section 47(4) had the effect of limiting the binding nature of the policy guidance issued in respect of the section 47(1) assessment obligation. This interesting argument has not however been adopted by any other court and is at variance with a number of Court of Appeal decisions.

England

3.20   Directions have been issued in England by the Department of Health, namely the Community Care Assessment Directions 2004,[17] Direction 2 of which requires social services authorities, when undertaking a community care assessment, to:

- consult the person to be assessed;
- consider whether the person has any carers and, if so, also consult them if the authority 'thinks it appropriate';
- take all reasonable steps to reach agreement with the person and, where they think it appropriate, any carers of that person, on the community care services which they are considering providing to meet his or her needs;
- provide information to the person and, where they think it appropriate, any carers of that person, about the amount of the payment (if any) which the person will be liable to make in respect of the community care services which they are considering providing to him or her.

3.21   The circular that accompanies the Directions (LAC (2004)24)[18] provides further information about the intended effect of the Directions.

Wales

3.22   It appears[19] that no equivalent directions have been issued in Wales. In the absence of directions NHSCCA 1990 s47(4) provides that assessments are to be carried out in such manner and take such form as the local authority considers appropriate. It follows that the adequacy of an assessment in any given case will depend upon its compliance with the relevant principles of public law, including:

1) that the aim of the process adopted by the social services department must be to determine the section 47(1)(b) question, ie, which of the

---

15   See also Carers (Recognition and Services) Act 1995 s1(4), where a similar provision applies.
16   [2003] EWHC 1654 (Admin).
17   26 August 2004; accessible at http://www.dh.gov.uk/en/Publicationsandstatistics/ Lettersandcirculars/LocalAuthorityCirculars/AllLocalAuthority/DH_4088369.
18   Accessible at the above link.
19   The Assembly has failed to keep track of what directions it has issued prior to 2005 – see para 1.38 above.

applicant's needs 'call for' the provision of services. This therefore requires the local authority to:

(a) gather sufficient data about the applicant in order to make an informed decision about what his or her needs are; and

(b) have some general standard or formula by which it can make consistent decisions as to when needs do and do not 'call for' services;

2) that the process must be conducted fairly – ie, ensuring the individual understands what is occurring and has a full opportunity to contribute and respond to any third party evidence; that the process be non-discriminatory and completed within a reasonable period of time, etc;

3) that all relevant matters are taken into account – ie, central and local government guidance; the views of important persons (the service user, relevant professionals, carers and friends, etc) who have relevant information to the section 47(1)(b) judgment.

Policy and practice guidance

3.23   A plethora of guidance exists concerning the assessment process: some of it of general application and some of it specific to certain user groups.

3.24   The original policy guidance accompanying the community care reforms contained only six paragraphs concerning the assessment process.[20] Although this was buttressed by the 1991 practice guidance, the lack of firm policy guidance, combined with severe financial pressures on local authorities, led to a fragmented system which was, in the opinion of an influential 1996 Audit Commission report, unfair and extremely confusing for service users. The report commented:

> The effect of all this is to produce a maze of different criteria which are complex and difficult for people to understand. People who qualify for care in one authority may not qualify in another. The price of freedom of local decision-making is considerable variation in access to services between areas. Authorities may be able to reduce the worst effects of the inequities that result by comparing approaches and, here again, guidance may be useful.[21]

3.25   The government in England, in its 1998 white paper *Modernising Social Services*[22] accepted these criticisms and committed itself to setting national standards and define service models for specific services or care groups (para 2.34). The product of this commitment in England and Wales has been a series of national service frameworks (NSFs)[23] and (particularly in England) other guidance concerning the assessment of various care groups. The relationship between the various guidance documents is depicted in Diagram 2 below.

20 *Community Care in the Next Decade and Beyond: Policy Guidance*, HMSO, 1990, paras 3.15–3.20.
21 *Balancing the Care Equation: Progress with Community Care*, HMSO, 1996, para 32.
22 Cm 4169, TSO, 1998.
23 The principle NSFs of direct relevance to social services are those that relate to (1) older people (see para 20.2 below), (2) mental health (see para 21.3 below) and (3) children (see para 24.57 below).

Diagram 2: Department of Health Guidance concerning the assessment process
For the Welsh Assembly equivalent guidance see para 3.26 and footnotes 26 and 35.

General Assessment Guidance Adults with community care needs	Carers	Disabled children
• *Fair Access to Care Services – Policy Guidance*, 2002 [FACS 2002 policy guidance]* (see para 3.27) • *Fair Access to Care Services – Practice Guidance*, 2003 [FACS 2003 practice guidance] (see para 3.27) • *Community Care – Community Care in the Next Decade and Beyond: policy guidance*, 1990 [1990 Policy Guidance] (see para 3.24) *Care Management And Assessment: Practitioners' Guide*, 1991 (see para 3.24)	Guidance on carers' assessments is in *The Carers and Disabled Children Act 2000: a practitioners guide to carers' assessments*, 2001 (see para 16.7) and general guidance is in the practice guide to the Carers (Equal Opportunities) Act 2004 (see para 16.8)	FACS guidance is not of direct relevance. Specific guidance exists as *The Framework for the Assessment of Children in Need and their Families*, 2000, policy and practice guidance (see para 24.15)

Specific user group assessment guidance

Older people	Mental health service users	People with learning disabilities
• NSF for Older People (see para 3.29) • Single assessment process, 2002 (see para 3.30)	• NSF for Mental Health, 1999 (see para 3.35) • *Effective Care Co-ordination in Mental Health Services – Modernising the Care Programme Approach*, 1999.	• *Valuing people: White Paper*, 2001 (see para 3.36) • *Valuing people: implementation policy guidance*, LAC (2001)23

3.26 Additionally the government undertook to 'introduce greater consistency in the system for deciding who qualifies' for community care services by developing generic policy and practice guidance on 'Fair Access to Care Services' (FACS) (para 2.36). A similar approach was taken by the Assembly in Wales, where the equivalent guidance to FACS is known as the 'Unified and Fair System for Assessing and Managing Care' (UFSAMC) 2002.

3.27 All community care assessments should be undertaken in accordance with the FACS guidance[24] in England and the UFSAMC guidance in

24 The FACS guidance comprises policy guidance (which was first published on 28 May 2002, under cover of a local authority circular, LAC (2002)13) published in January 2003 and practice guidance. It is intended that the practice guidance be regularly updated – the most recent, at the time of writing (April 2007) was issued on

Wales. This guidance does not replace the earlier guidance (for instance the 1991 practice guidance) but 'builds on' it.[25] In the FACS 2003 practice guidance (which is in a questions and answers format) at Q8.1. it is stated that:

> In general, councils should in the first instance refer to the FACS guidance, and to the recent guidance on assessment and care planning for specific groups. They can usefully refer to the 1991 practice guidance for fuller information, where appropriate.

Specific user group assessment guidance

3.28   The 'user group specific' guidance can be broken down into the various categories listed below. The guidance relating to the assessment of older people is considered in this chapter, whereas the guidance specifically relating to people with mental health problems, learning disabilities, disabled children and carers is dealt with in the subsequent chapters that deal with these client groups.

Older people

- *NSF for Older People*, March 2001[26]
- *Single Assessment Process (SAP) Policy Guidance*, 2002[27]

3.29   This guidance is considered at para 20.9 below.

3.30   Standard Two of the English NSF[28] outlined the SAP which had been first proposed in *The NHS Plan*.[29] The SAP for older people would (the NSF stated at para 2.27) ensure that:

- a more standardised assessment process is in place across all areas and agencies;
- standards of assessment practice are raised;
- older people's needs are assessed in the round.

3.31   Guidance[30] on the SAP was issued to health and social services bodies and required that they had fully integrated commissioning arrangements and integrated provision of services including community services and

6 March 2003. The guidance can be found at http://www.dh.gov.uk/en/ Publicationsandstatistics/Publications/PublicationsPolicyAndGuidance/DH_4009653. UFSAMC guidance in Wales was published in April 2005 (NAfWC 09/2002 and 09A/ 2002) and can be found at http://new.wales.gov.uk/publications/circular/ circulars2002/NAFWC092002?lang=en.

25   FACS 2002 policy guidance, para 31.
26   *Strategy for Older People in Wales* (January 2003).
27   UFSAMC (Wales) 2002 incorporates the key elements of both FACS and SAP.
28   *Strategy for Older People in Wales* (January 2003) para 33 confirmed that the NSF for older people in Wales would build upon the unified assessment guidance already issued.
29   Department of Health white paper, *The NHS Plan* Cm 4818-I, 2000, para 7.3.
30   In particular HSC 2002/001 and LAC (2002)1, *Guidance on the Single Assessment Process for Older People*, January 2002.

continence services by April 2004.[31] In Wales the UFSAMC 2002 policy guidance constitutes the equivalent guidance (ie effectively a combined FACS and SAP document).

3.32   The raison d'être of the process is both organisational – in compelling health and social services bodies to work together in assessing and providing care services – and cultural – to provide what the guidance calls a 'person-centred approach'. The aim is to ensure that older people are not subjected to ineffective (and inefficient) multiple assessments. As the guidance explains:[32]

> . . . many frail older people will have numerous separate assessments per year with the majority of the information being repeated on each assessment. The single assessment process will help to minimise this unnecessary duplication, while allowing a full assessment to be built up over time. It will also reduce paperwork by providing a single assessment summary (preferably based on electronic records) for health and social care.

3.33   Apart from the insistence on a joint health/social services assessment process, the SAP guidance is in many respects a gloss on the FACS guidance and reference should be made to chapter 20 where this guidance is further considered. Such assessments cannot in fact be 'unified' in the legal sense, unless the agencies have entered into formal partnership arrangements under NHSA 2006 ss 75–76 and 256–257 (see para 13.120 below).

3.34   The SAP does not seek to impose a single prescribed assessment tool: individual authorities are free to develop their own processes. However these must satisfy rigorous criteria laid down in the policy guidance,[33] against which they will be evaluated. It is expected however that there will be, over time, a convergence of the assessment methods used.[34]

Mental health service users

- *NSF for Mental Health,* September 1999[35]
- *Effective Care Co-ordination in Mental Health Services – Modernising the Care Programme Approach,*[36] 1999.

3.35   This guidance is considered at paras 21.3 and 21.7 below.

---

31 Updated implementation guidance and advice on 'off the shelf' assessment tools continues to be provided by the Department of Health, accessible at http://www.dh.gov.uk/PolicyAndGuidance/HealthandSocialCareTopics/ SocialCare/SingleAssessmentProcess/fs/en.
32 *The Single Assessment Process: Guidance for Local Implementation* policy guidance, para 12.
33 HSC 2002/001: LAC (2002)1 Annex C.
34 *The Single Assessment Process: Guidance for Local Implementation* policy guidance, para 12(IX).
35 *Adult Mental Health Services: A National Service Framework for Wales,* April 2002.
36 *Adult Mental Health Services in Wales: Equity, Empowerment, Effectiveness, Efficiency. A Strategy Document,* 2001.

People with learning disabilities

- *Valuing people: a new strategy for learning disability for the 21st century,* 2001
- *Valuing people: a new strategy for learning disability for the 21st century: implementation,* LAC (2001)23.

3.36   This guidance is considered at chapter 19 para 19.4 below.

Disabled children

3.37   The right of disabled children to be assessed stems primarily from the Children Act (CA) 1989, although they also have certain rights under the community care regime (see para 24.55 below). However FACS is not of direct application: the specific guidance of relevance being:

- *Framework for the Assessment of Children in Need and their Families,* 2000 policy guidance[37]
- *Assessing Children in Need and their Families,* 2000 practice guidance.

3.38   This guidance is considered at chapter 24 para 24.15 below.

Disabled parents

3.39   The 'presenting needs' of a disabled parent will include the need to discharge his or her parental responsibilities. Accordingly if, for instance, as a result of an impairment a parent is unable to get his or her child to school, this 'need' should, prima facie, be seen as a 'presenting need' of the parent and not a need of the child under the CA 1989. Disabled parents are specifically identified as being entitled to direct payments,[38] and their needs are addressed by the FACS guidance.[39] The 2002 policy guidance states that 'in the course of assessing an individual's needs, councils should recognise that adults, who have parenting responsibilities for a child under 18 years, may require help with these responsibilities' (para 9): the 2003 practice guidance (see para 3.27 above) provides additional detail on the social services obligation, including that the assessment process must cover the assistance required to carry out 'family and other social roles and responsibilities' and that 'family responsibilities' include 'parenting roles and responsibilities' (Q4.1 onwards).

3.40   The particular needs of disabled parents for support have been highlighted in specific reports, such as a 2000 Social Services Inspectorate report *A Jigsaw of Services,* a 2006 Norah Fry Research Centre report[40]

---

37 In Wales, *Framework for the Assessment of Children in Need and their Families,* 2001 policy guidance.
38 Health and Social Care Act 2001 s58 inserted a new s17A(2)(b) into the CA 1998 which provides for direct payments for disabled persons with parental responsibility for a child.
39 In Wales see in particular UFSAMC 2002 p65 which contains equivalent guidance.
40 B Tarleton, L Ward and J Howarth, *Finding the Right Support: A Review of Issues and Positive Practice to Support Parents with Learning Disabilities and their Children,* The Baring Foundation, 2006.

concerning the challenges faced by parents with learning disabilities, and a 2005 research report by the Joseph Rowntree Foundation/National Family and Parenting Institute (2004):[41] this latter report advises that professionals should 'think parent' and view disabled parents in the same way as non-disabled parents.

Carers

3.41   Carers' assessments are not governed by NHSCCA 1990 s47 and accordingly the FACS guidance is not of direct relevance. Guidance on carers' assessments is provided in both England and Wales as *The Carers and Disabled Children Act 2000: a practitioner's guide to carers' assessments* (2001) and additionally in England by a practice guide issued by the Social Care Institute for Excellence (SCIE).[42] These are considered at para 16.7 below.

Guidance and s47(4)

3.42   As has been noted (para 1.55), in *R (B and H) v Hackney LBC*[43] Keith J held that policy guidance issued under Local Authority Social Services Act (LASSA) 1970 s7(1) was not 'strong guidance' in relation to the assessment process under NHSCCA 1990 s47. In his view, since section 47(4) states that in the absence of directions local authorities are entitled to conduct assessments as they deem appropriate – it then logically follows that it is only a direction that can materially restrict this latitude. If this controversial view is correct, it conflicts with other High Court decisions and the Court of Appeal in the *Gloucestershire* judgment (albeit that this argument was not considered in these cases). It would also downgrade the force of the key FACS, SAP and UFSAMC guidance (see para 3.26 above) – although only so far as this guidance relates to the actual assessment process under NHSCCA 1990 s47 (ie information gathering and the service provision decision): the guidance would remain strong 'policy guidance' in so far as it relates to care planning and service provision.

Guidance as overly prescriptive

3.43   Valuable as well drafted guidance undoubtedly is, in ensuring assessments are properly conducted and decisions on 'need' taken rationally and fairly, such guidance has the potential to create not insignificant difficulties. This is particularly the case if (as is arguably the case with elements of the assessment guidance) it is overly prescriptive, overly voluminous,[44] ambiguous and contradictory. By way of example, an older person in

41   R Olsen and H Tyers, *Supporting disabled adults as parents*, November 2004 – Ref N34 accessible at http://www.jrf.org.uk/knowledge/findings/socialcare/n34.asp.
42   SCIE practice guide to the Carers (Equal Opportunities) Act 2004, accessible at http://www.carers.gov.uk/whatsnew.htm.
43   [2003] EWHC 1654 (Admin).
44   The plethora of material emanating from central government has been referred to as 'hyperactive policy-making' – see A Coote, *Community Care*, 17 February 2005, p18.

England will need to be assessed in accordance with two separate regimes – the SAP and FACS guidance. Both change over time and interface with other assessment procedures (for instance) if the older person has learning disabilities or mental health problems. SAP and FACS each comprise several different documents, some of which are policy and some of which are practice guidance. These require the assessor (amongst other things) to opt for one of four different types of assessment, which may necessitate consideration of nine domains of need (broken down into 34 sub-sets) each of which 'need' to be placed into one of four categories of 'presenting need', which are themselves divided into a minimum of 19 descriptors. Such a process, by requiring practitioners to focus on the micro level, can obscure the macro reality – such that the wood is not seen for the trees. This is especially so when the development of panels (see para 3.183) has the effect of divorcing the 'service provision decision' from the information gathering – with different professionals undertaking these two processes. In such situations the element of genuine discretion may be lost since it assumes that the totality of a person's situation can be expressed in the bureaucratic language of a pro forma assessment spreadsheet: in effect, the human element is simply lost.

Delegation of duty to assess

3.44   The duty to assess under NHSCCA 1990 s47[45] is a social services function (for the purposes of LASSA 1970 Sch 1, see para 1.4). There is no general power for social services authorities to delegate this function to other bodies.[46] The only situation in which it can be legally delegated, is where the social services authority has entered into a formal partnership arrangement with an NHS body (either a primary care trust (PCT) or an NHS trust under the National Health Service Act (NHSA) 2006 ss75–76 and ss256–257[47] (see para 13.122).

3.45   In the absence of such partnership arrangements, there is no express power for the authority to delegate the function to another agency. In practice authorities often request third parties to carry out key tasks in the assessment – for instance, an occupational therapist employed by a PCT in assessing the need for home adaptations. In such cases, an authority may be, to all intents and purposes, bound by that third party's view on need – especially if it has expertise which the social services authority lacks.[48]

3.46   A not uncommon situation where key assessment functions are in effect delegated, concerns the assessment of detained drug and alcohol misusers wishing to attend community rehabilitation facilities: frequently key aspects of such assessments are carried out by expert probation

45   Or indeed, under the Carers Acts – see para 16.44 below.
46   *R v Kirklees MBC ex p Daykin* (1996) 1 CCLR 512, p525D.
47   National Health Services (Wales) Act (NHS(W)A) 2006 ss33–34 and 194–196.
48   This will not invariably be the case, particularly if the opinion only addresses one particular aspect of an individual's circumstances – see eg *R (Goldsmith) v Wandsworth LBC* [2004] EWCA Civ 1170; (2004) 7 CCLR 472.

officers on behalf of social services (see para 23.13 where this is further considered).

3.47   An argument could be made that the SAP guidance, with its emphasis on integrated assessment and commissioning arrangements (see para 20.6 below) fails to express with sufficient emphasis the non-delegable nature[49] of the community care assessment process.

3.48   It has been suggested that local authorities might be able to delegate their assessment functions by virtue of Local Government (Contracts) Act 1997 s1 which empowers councils to contract with third parties to discharge certain of their functions. Section 4(3) of the Act however places a significant limitation on such delegation, restricting its application to contracts 'for the provision or making available of services'. In the context of the 1997 Act, which in section 1 refers to 'assets or services, or both, (whether or not together with goods)' it seems unlikely that an assessment could be deemed a 'service'. It is also doubtful that an assessment could be described as the 'making available of services': it is a qualitatively different function – namely the decision as to whether or not there is any need to make any such arrangements. Such an interpretation is strongly supported by the relevant policy guidance.[50]

Timescale for assessments

3.49   There is no general statutory timescale for the completion of community care assessments – although such timescales have been prescribed in policy guidance for assessments under the CA 1989 (see para 24.18) and in directions under the Community Care (Delayed Discharge etc) Act 2003 (see para 5.31).

3.50   A significant factor concerning the speed with which assessments are undertaken and services provided, stems from the pressure on English local authorities to meet a variety of Department of Health imposed 'Social Services Performance Assessment Framework Indicators'.[51] Since December 2004 it has been a performance indicator, for instance, that all assessments of older people under the SAP should begin within 48 hours and be completed within a month.[52] Another indicator[53] measures delay by requiring authorities to record '[f]or new older clients, the percentage for

49 Except if accompanied by formal partnership arrangements.
50 See eg SAP 2002 policy guidance, p16; the UFSAMC 2002 policy guidance, p10 fn 2 and the combined policy guidance under the 2000 and 2004 Carers Acts, para 45.
51 Details of the performance assessment framework indicators can be accessed at http://www.csci.org.uk/docs/adult_PIs_2006–07.doc, and for a critique of the pressure these targets creates within social services authorities, see J Harris, *The Social Work Business*, Routledge, 2003.
52 Commission for Social Care Inspection (CSCI), *Adult Performance Indicators for 2006–07*, 2006, Indicator AO/D55 'Acceptable waiting times for assessments' (BVPI 195) (KT): 'For new older clients, the average of (i) the percentage where the time from first contact to contact with the client is less than or equal to 48 hours (that is, 2 calendar days), and (ii) the percentage where the time from first contact to completion of assessment is less than or equal to four weeks (that is, 28 calendar days)'.
53 Ibid, Indicator AO/D56 'Acceptable waiting times for care packages' (BVPI 196) (KT).

whom the time from completion of assessment to provision of all services in the care package is less than or equal to 4 weeks'. Local authorities are required to report their performance on these measures to the Department of Health under a process known as RAP (Referrals, Assessments and Packages of Care[54]) and these results are collated and published by the department.

3.51   As a matter of statutory interpretation, where a provision is silent on the time for compliance, the law implies that it be done within a reasonable time, and that what is a 'reasonable time' is a question of fact, depending on the nature of the obligation and the purpose for which the computation is to be made.[55]

3.52   The FACS guidance[56] requires that local Better Care, Higher Standards charters (see para 2.15) contain information about the authority's timescales for assessments and that individuals will be told how long they have to wait for assessment, and how long the assessment process will take. When considering complaints about delayed assessments, the local government ombudsman has regard to the timescales set out in the relevant local authorities charter[57] – and this would appear to be an appropriate starting point for any such review. In a 2006 complaint, for instance, he held that a three-month delay in assessing for adaptations was 'simply unacceptable – (the Council's own targets for assessments were one month for urgent cases and two months for others)'.[58]

3.53   Authorities frequently adopt a grading scheme for assessments – with a view to prioritising the most urgent. The arrangements for these schemes are detailed in the authority's Better Care, Higher Standards charter. While the idea of a scheme setting priorities for assessment is to a degree anomalous (given that in general the object of assessment is to identify the extent and urgency of need), the local government ombudsman has accepted that such a system 'does not seem unreasonable'.[59] LAC (93)2 (although primarily aimed at the particular needs of persons who misuse alcohol and/or drugs) makes a number of observations of more general application to assessments.[60] It supports the idea of some assessments being carried out faster than others, stating that authorities 'should have criteria for determining the level of assessment that is appropriate to the severity or complexity of the need' (at para 14). It further advocates the need for authorities to develop 'fast-track assess-

---

54   Details of the RAP process can be accessed from the Department of Health website under the heading, 'Referrals, Assessments and Packages of Care'.
55   See eg *Re North ex p Hasluck* [1895] 2 QB 264; *Charnock v Liverpool Corporation* [1968] 3 All ER 473.
56   FACS 2002 policy guidance, para 29 and FACS 2003 practice guidance, para 8.7.
57   See eg complaint no 01/C/15434 against South Tyneside Metropolitan BC, 20 January 2003, where the Charter stipulated 21 days for the completion of community care assessments.
58   Complaint no 05/C/07195 against Northumberland CC, 18 April 2006, paras 7, 29 and 30.
59   Para 33, Complaint no 00/B/00599 against Essex, 3 September 2001.
60   See eg paras 26–27 concerning the applicability of its observations to the needs of homeless people.

ment' procedures (at paras 16–20). The circular is considered in detail in chapter 23.

3.54 The local government ombudsman has investigated a considerable number of complaints concerning delayed assessments relating to home adaptations (see para 9.108). By way of example, in a 1996 report[61] a delay of six months in assessing a disabled person's needs was held to be maladministration, and another 1996 report found seven months for an assessment and a further four months' delay by the authority in processing the disabled facilities grant approval to be maladministration.[62] In this complaint the local ombudsman reiterated her view that if the authority has a shortage of occupational therapists, it should not use them for assessment purposes if this will result in unreasonable delay, stating, '[i]f such expertise is not available, councils need to find an alternative way of meeting their statutory responsibilities'. While the local government ombudsman has approved in principle the idea of prioritising certain assessments, she has criticised the way such a scheme is administered. In a 1995 complaint[63] she stated:

> The Council's system of priorities is over-simple. Within the category of 'complex' cases there is no provision for relatively simple solutions to tide people over until a full assessment can be made. Also, there will be cases which cannot be described as 'emergencies' but need to be dealt with more urgently within the 'complex' category than others. The Council's over-simple system of priorities resulted in a failure to meet [the complainants' disabled daughter's] needs promptly and I consider that to be an injustice resulting in maladministration.

3.55 Where there is unreasonable delay in assessing (or an intimation that there will be), the complaints process may be invoked (see para 27.4 below). The effect of this,[64] is that some element of a fixed timescale is introduced into the process. The complainant should emphasise (if it be the case) that the duty to assess commenced when his or her potential needs first came to the notice of the authority, rather than at the time of any later request being made for an assessment.

3.56 In cases of urgency councils have power to provide services before completing the assessment (see para 4.76 below) and such an obligation will have particular force if the urgent need has been exacerbated by the authority's delay.

---

61 Complaints nos 93/B/3111 and 94/B/3146 against South Bedfordshire DC and Bedfordshire CC .
62 Complaints nos 94/C/0964 and 94/C/0965 against Middlesbrough DC and Cleveland CC.
63 Complaint no 93/C/3660 against Rochdale Metropolitan BC.
64 See para 27.15.

Urgent need

3.57   NHSCCA 1990 s47(5) makes provision for a local authority to provide care services for a person without an assessment 'if in the opinion of the authority, the condition of that person is such that he requires those services as a matter of urgency'. Section 47(6) provides that if such services are provided without an assessment, 'as soon as practicable there-after, an assessment of his needs shall be made in accordance with the preceding provision of this section'. The provision support pursuant to the section 47(5) power is further considered at para 4.76 below.

Reform – a common assessment framework

3.58   There is considerable anecdotal evidence to suggest that the proliferation of different assessment regimes for different client groups has created a complex and confusing assessment bureaucracy, dramatically increasing the time spent by care managers in 'form filling', significantly reducing their face to face contact with service users and doing little or nothing to improve the quality of services or decision making. Arguably, much of the bureaucracy that now accompanies assessments is driven by a need to satisfy statistical returns to the Department of Health or Welsh Assembly rather than to maximise the quality of the support provided for individual service users.

3.59   The SAP and UFSAMC appear to have had particular problems in this respect, but given the substantial political and financial investment in these procedures, a direct acknowledgement of their relative failure seems unlikely. Tangential acceptance of this fact, however, is emerging in England with a proposal in the white paper, *Our Health, Our Care, Our Say* (January 2006) to develop a new assessment process, to be known as the Common Assessment Framework (CAF) for Adults. The Department of Health in its statements concerning CAF[65] accepts that having different assessment regimes for different client groups causes 'difficulties . . . particularly for individuals with multiple needs who have to negotiate the different systems'. It suggests that a CAF would overcome many of these problems, particularly if 'geared towards self-determination and planning for independence'. The statement acknowledges that 'there has been significant investment in SAP' and that 'this investment must not go to waste'. It proposes to satisfy this objective by ensuring that 'the momentum behind the implementation of SAP, including developing and implementing e-SAP solutions, continues in local communities' – presumably being harnessed by the new CAF. The proposals also include a commitment to allow people to self-assess wherever possible, and the department is undertaking research on the 'feasibility of people with health and social care needs to self assess for support from a range of

---

65   See eg Department of Health Care Services Improvement Partnership, *Common Assessment Framework*, 2006, at http://www.socialcare.csip.org.uk/index.cfm?pid=7.

services, including equipment/aids, home care, housing adaptations and low level preventative services'.[66]

3.60   It is probably unrealistic to expect an acknowledgement by the Department of Health or the Assembly that their attempt to micromanage the care planning process – through the multiplicity of excessively detailed assessment regimes – has proved to be a profound mistake. The evidence suggests that any new assessment regime needs to be simpler, considerably less prescriptive than the existing systems, and substantially more 'user' sensitive. If the CAF delivers this with a minimum of bureaucratic upheaval, it may prove to be a positive development.

The duty to assess: when does it arise?

Social services authority awareness of the individual

3.61   The first requirement for the triggering of the duty to assess is that the person in need comes to the knowledge of the social services authority. It is the authority that must have the requisite knowledge, rather than the individual social services department. By way of example, in the case of a unitary authority (which has responsibility for both housing and social services) the duty to assess will in general be triggered when a 'vulnerable'[67] person presents him/herself as homeless (see para 15.16 below).

3.62   In *R (Patrick) v Newham LBC*[68] the applicant, who had physical and mental health difficulties was living rough after the authority had determined that she was intentionally homeless. Lawyers acting on her behalf wrote to the authority, enclosing a doctor's letter confirming her significant psychiatric problems and requested urgent accommodation. In the subsequent judicial review proceedings it was argued (among other things) that this should have triggered an assessment under NHSCCA 1990 s47. Henriques J held:[69]

> I am wholly unable to accept any suggestion that the respondent has discharged its duty under section 47. The authority has not carried out any assessment of the applicant's needs for community care services. There is no record of any consideration of the applicant's individual circumstances at all . . .
>
> An assessment of needs is a formal task to be carried out in accordance with Central Government Guidance and involves collation of medical evidence, psychiatric evidence, etc, with a view thereafter to matching accommodation to needs. 1 am satisfied that the Council have not complied with their duty under section 47. That duty plainly accrued [on the date when] the applicant's solicitors wrote to the respondent describing the applicant's circumstances and requesting urgent accommodation.

66 See eg Department of Health Care Services Improvement Partnership, *Self Assessment Project*, 2006, at http://www.socialcare.csip.org.uk/index.cfm?pid=81.
67 Under Housing Act 1996 s189.
68 (2000) 4 CCLR 48.
69 (2000) 4 CCLR 48, pp51–52.

3.63   It follows that authorities should ensure that they have the necessary internal organisational networks so that the needs of vulnerable individuals are automatically referred to the relevant community care team irrespective of the point at which first local authority contact with that individual occurs.[70] A failure to make such arrangements may amount to maladministration.

Individuals who 'may be in need' of community care services

3.64   The second requirement for the triggering of the duty to assess is that the authority have knowledge[71] that the person may be in need of services. In *R v Bristol CC ex p Penfold*[72] the court held that this was 'a very low threshold test'. The FACS 2002 policy guidance, para 30[73] stresses this point, namely that in deciding whether a person appears to be in need of community care services, local authorities should 'set a low threshold, and avoid screening individuals out of the assessment process before sufficient information is known about them'.

What of a 'future need' for services?

3.65   NHSCCA 1990 s47(1) speaks of a possible – rather than a present – need: it must appear that the individual '*may*' be in need'. Since everyone 'may' at some future time be in need of community care services, the courts and the guidance have adopted a pragmatic approach to the interpretation of the provision. If a person seeks an assessment on the basis of a future need, the key questions appear to be (1) how likely and (2) how imminent?

3.66   In relation to patients expected to be discharged from hospital, the guidance is phrased in mandatory terms[74] even though they will not be in need of community care services until their actual discharge. For such patients, however, the predictability and imminence of need is a given. The hospital discharge assessment duty is now reinforced by legislation – Community Care (Delayed Discharges etc) Act 2003 s2 (see para 5.7 below).

3.67   In *R (B) v Camden LBC*[75] the court was required to consider the interpretation of the provision in the context of a patient detained under the Mental Health Act 1983, who was seeking discharge. Stanley Burnton J

---

70   See FACS 2002 policy guidance, para 68, which states (among other things) 'if individuals need other services, officers of the council should help them to find the right person to talk to in the relevant agency or organisation, and make contact on their behalf (see Better Care, Higher Standards)'.
71   Presumably this may include constructive knowledge.
72   (1998) 1 CCLR 315.
73   In Wales, UFSAMC 2002 policy guidance, para 2.23.
74   The English guidance (see para 5.22) for instance states that 'planning for hospital discharge' (and by implication the section 47 community care assessment process) 'should start prior to admission (for planned admissions) and as soon as possible for all other admissions'.
75   [2005] EWHC 1366 (Admin); (2005) 8 CCLR 422 at [66]–[67].

held that the phrase 'a person ... may be in need of such services' referred:

> ... to a person who may be in need at the time, or who may be about to be in need. A detained patient who is the subject of a deferred conditional discharge decision of a tribunal, which envisages his conditional discharge once section 117 after-care services are in place, is a person who 'may be in need of such services', since if such services are available to him he will be discharged and immediately need them. Whether a patient who may reasonably be considered to be liable to have such an order made in an impending tribunal hearing is an issue I do not have to decide in the instant case, but I incline to the view that he is.

> 67. However, the duty under section 47 does not arise until it 'appears' to the local authority that a person may be in need, and it cannot appear to it that he may be in need unless it knows of his possible need. It is presumably for this reason that the Community Care (Delayed Discharges etc) Act 2003 was enacted. ...

3.68   *R v Mid-Glamorgan CC ex p Miles*[76] concerned a similar problem: a prisoner whose only hope of parole was dependent upon a prior confirmation that the local authority would fund a drug rehabilitation hostel for him. The authority was not prepared to assess him until parole was granted. The case was settled on terms that the local authority undertook the assessment.

No need to 'request' an assessment

3.69   As has been noted above, NHSCCA 1990 s47(1) marked a major advance on the previous assessment obligation (under DP(SCR)A 1986 s4) by dispensing with the need for a 'request' in order to activate the obligation. In *R v Gloucestershire CC ex p RADAR*[77] it was held that the local authority could not discharge its obligation to potential service users (who had previously received services) simply by writing to them, asking them to reply if they wanted to be considered for assessment. Carnwath J stated:

> The obligation to make an assessment for community care services does not depend on a request, but on the 'appearance of need' .... Of course, the authority cannot carry out an effective reassessment without some degree of co-operation from the service user or his helpers. However, that is a very different thing from saying that they can simply rest on having sent a letter of the type to which I have referred.

3.70   In reaching this decision the court emphasised the essential frailty of many of the potential service users:

> In some areas of law that might be an adequate response, where those affected can be assumed to be capable of looking after their own interests, and where silence in response to an offer can be treated as acceptance or

---

76   Unreported, January 1994 *Legal Action* 21.
77   (1998) 1 CCLR 476.

acquiescence. However, that approach cannot be and is not valid in the present context.[78]

3.71   Clearly it will be a question of fact and degree, whether a local authority has, in any particular situation, sufficient knowledge of a potential service user, so as to trigger the duty to assess. In *R v Bexley LBC ex p B*[79] for instance the court held that:

> Authorities are, however, under an obligation to make provision . . . whenever they are satisfied that the relevant conditions have been met. A request by or on behalf of a disabled person is not one of those conditions. It seems to me that the Court should look at the reality of the situation. In the present case, although no formal request was made by the applicant's mother for an assessment of the applicant's needs, that was the effect of what happened in the early months of 1994.

3.72   Not only is the duty to assess independent of any request from the potential service user, it also arises irrespective of:

a) there being any prospect of the potential service user actually qualifying for any services;[80]
b) the financial circumstances of the service user;[81] or
c) the service user being ordinarily resident[82] in the local authority's area.[83]

Entitlement to services is not relevant

3.73   The duty to assess is triggered when the authority is aware of an 'appearance of need', and not the likelihood of entitlement to services. *R v Bristol CC ex p Penfold*[84] concerned a 52-year-old person who suffered from anxiety and depression. She was accepted as being homeless by the respondent council and offered two properties, although she refused both as neither were in the part of the city where her relations (and support network) lived. Her solicitors then asked the authority to carry out a community care assessment of her needs, on the basis that she either be offered accommodation under National Assistance Act 1948 s21[85] or, if she moved elsewhere, that she would need support to replace her family.

3.74   The authority refused to carry out a community care assessment on

---

78   (1998) 1 CCLR 476 at 482D.
79   (2002) 3 CCLR 15 at 22J.
80   See *R v Bristol CC ex p Penfold* (1998) 1 CCLR 315 (discussed below) although in such cases the assessment may be rudimentary.
81   LAC (98)19 [WOC 27/98 in Wales] para 8 and FACS 2002 policy guidance, para 70 [UFSAMC 2002, para 2.33 in Wales].
82   See chapter 6 where 'ordinary residence' is considered further.
83   See *R v Berkshire CC ex p P* (1996) 1 CCLR 141 (discussed below), although in general this will only be necessary for a local authority to carry out an assessment of someone who is not ordinarily resident in its area, if the person's residence is disputed or he or she has no settled residence.
84   (1998) 1 CCLR 315.
85   See also para 7.8.

the grounds (among others) that there was no prospect of meeting any needs that might have emerged in the course of the assessment (because their eligibility criteria were so tightly drawn, that only people at considerable risk were likely to be offered services). In relation to this argument, Scott Baker J held:

1) where there is an apparent need for community care services which a local authority is empowered to provide, the authority must undertake an assessment under NHSCCA 1990 s47(1)(a) (and this duty is not a 'resource dependent' duty);

2) even if it were the case that a service user has no sensible prospect of being awarded services because of constraints upon resources, that does not absolve the local authority from conducting a section 47(1)(a) assessment;

3) the discharge by a housing authority of its obligations under the homelessness legislation does not preclude the need for a community care assessment.

3.75   Of particular relevance, the judgment states as follows:[86]

> I do not, therefore accept [the] submission that Parliament cannot have intended expenditure to a pointless end when it was clear that any established need could not be met. Even if there is no hope from the resource point of view of meeting any needs identified in the assessment, the assessment may serve a useful purpose in identifying for the local authority unmet needs which will help it to plan for the future. Without assessment this could not be done.

> If the Respondent's argument on construction is accepted, the consequence will be that not only can authorities set wholly disparate eligibility criteria for services they intend top provide but they may also utilise such criteria as a basis for whether they will undertake a community care assessment at all. This cannot be right. The mere fact of unavailability of resources to meet a need does not mean that there is no need to be met. Resource implications in my view play no part in the decision whether to carry out an assessment.

The duty to assess arises where entitlement exists to NHS continuing care

3.76   As noted at para 14.113 below, the fact that it is the policy of the Department of Health and the Welsh Assembly that individuals eligible for NHS continuing healthcare should have all their care needs met by the NHS, does not in itself displace the statutory duties owed to them under the community care legislation – most importantly under NHSA 2006 s254 and Sch 20 (NHS (Wales) Act (NHS(W)A) 2006 s192 and Sch 15). Such people may still remain 'in need' of such services and as a consequence the duty to assess under the 1990 Act is triggered. The Department of Health has expressed its view on this question (following the abuse

---

86 (1998) 1 CCLR 315 at 322.

inquiry concerning people with learning disabilities accommodated by the Cornwall Partnership NHS Trust[87]) in the following terms:[88]

> One of the key contributing factors identified in Cornwall was a clear absence of person-centred planning together with a failure to provide comprehensive, local authority-led assessments for people living in NHS accommodation. Assessments and person-centred planning – a fundamental tenet of *Valuing People* – are essential in ensuring that services meet an individual's needs and are in their best interests.
>
> It is a matter of significant concern that this was allowed to happen and I am writing to remind you of your duty to ensure that such assessments are provided under section 47(1) of the NHS and Community Care Act (1990).

The duty to assess arises even when services are discretionary

3.77   The duty to assess is not dependent upon a collateral statutory duty 'to provide' or upon the person being ordinarily resident in the local authority's area. In *R v Berkshire CC ex p P*[89] the respondent local authority refused to assess the applicant, because it claimed that he was not 'ordinarily resident' within its area. Laws J held:[90]

> I reject the respondent's submission that s47(1) imports a condition requiring the physical availability of services to a person before the duty of assessment arises in relation to that person. The word 'may' in the subordinate clause in question means, in the context of the subsection as a whole, that the duty to assess arises where the local authority possesses the legal power[91] to provide or arrange for the provision of community care services to the individual in question.

3.78   Accordingly the duty to assess is not conditional upon whether the service user is resident in the authority's area or indeed whether the local authority is prepared to exercise its discretion to make any such services available. The rationale behind this decision (in relation to the ordinary residence question) must be that without such a duty, persons whose residence was disputed by two or more authorities would effectively be in limbo until their residence was resolved. However in *R (J) v Southend BC*[92] Newman J held that where the 'ordinarily resident' authority accepts responsibility to assess, the authority in whose area the service user is actually physically present, cannot (absent unusual factors) be compelled to undertake an assessment.

87   See in particular the joint investigation by the CSCI and the Commission for Healthcare Audit and Inspection into allegations of abuse suffered by people with learning disabilities in accommodation provided by the Cornwall Partnership NHS Trust, July 2006.
88   Letter from the Director General for Social Care dated 2 November 2006 sent to all social services authorities.
89   (1998) 1 CCLR 141.
90   (1998) 1 CCLR 141, p147F.
91   Social services authorities have the power under National Assistance Act (NAA) 1948 s29 to provide services for people who are not ordinarily resident in their area, see para 9.49.
92   [2005] EWHC 3547 (Admin).

Returning UK nationals

3.79 The principle established in *R v Berkshire CC ex p P* is of relevance in relation to returning UK nationals who may have been living for an extended period abroad. If on arrival they present with community care needs, it may be that they have no settled residence (see para 6.23) or at least their ordinary residence is disputed. The receiving authority will therefore have a duty to assess their community care needs – even if an ordinary residence determination is being sought (see para 6.42): UK nationals (unlike other EEA nationals or non-European nationals) are not disentitled to community care services (see para 22.51). Any such assessment may have to rely (initially at least) to a greater or lesser extent upon information provided by the overseas authorities.

Financial circumstances are not relevant

3.80 The financial circumstances of a person are irrelevant for the purposes of assessment. This point is made explicit by policy guidance in relation to residential care LAC (98)19[93] which states:

> 8. Local authorities are under a legal duty under the NHS and Community Care Act 1990 to assess the care needs of anyone who, in the authority's view, may be in need of community care services. It is the Department's view that the law does not allow authorities to refuse to undertake an assessment of care needs for anyone on the grounds of the person's financial resources, eg because they have capital in excess of the capital limit for residential accommodation. Even if someone may be able to pay the full cost of an services, or make their own arrangements independently . . . they should be advised about what type of care they require, and informed about what services are available.[94]

3.81 This view is reinforced by the FACS guidance. The 2002 policy guidance states at para 70:[95]

> An individual's financial circumstances should have no bearing on whether a council carries out a community care assessment or not. Neither should the individual's finances affect the level or detail of the assessment process. Once an individual's care needs have been assessed and a decision made about the care to be provided, an assessment of their ability to pay charges should be carried out promptly, and written information about any

---

93 WOC 27/98, para 8 in Wales.
94 The circular is expressed as being issued under LASSA 1970 s7(1); see also para 7.26 below where it is further considered. See also the statement of Liam Byrne, Parliamentary Under Secretary of State for Care Services, in response to a written question from Paul Burstow MP, HC Debates col 1799W, 12 December 2005, that 'an individual's financial circumstances should have no bearing on whether a LA carries out a community care assessment or not. Once an individual's care needs have been assessed and a decision made about the care to be provided, an assessment of his/her ability to pay charges should be carried out promptly. Written information about any charges payable, and how they have been calculated, should be communicated to the individual.'
95 UFSAMC 2002, para 2.33 in Wales makes the same point, but more briefly.

charges payable, and how they have been calculated, should be communicated to the individual.

3.82   Importantly, this approach is amplified in the FACS 2003 practice guidance (at Q8.5):

> The carrying out and completion of a community care assessment should not be contingent on whether or not an individual can pay for care services, be they provided in a care home or the individual's own home.

> Following assessment, arranging residential care on behalf of service users is dealt with in paragraphs 71 and 72 of the FACS policy guidance. With respect to individuals receiving services at home, a council should arrange those services irrespective of the resources or capacity of the service user, if that is what the service user wants the council to do. Where an individual is to receive services under section 29 of the National Assistance Act 1948 and is ordinarily resident in a council area, that council has a duty to arrange services on his/her behalf

3.83   Once a section 47 assessment has been undertaken, a duty to provide care home accommodation may crystallise even where the subsequent financial assessment reveals that the person has capital in excess of the upper capital limit. This is considered further at para 7.26.

The nature of an assessment

3.84   Despite the central importance of the assessment in community care law, there is no effective legislative description of the process. DP(SCR)A s3 described with some precision the procedure to be followed in an assessment, but this section has not been brought into force and previous secretaries of state have indicated that it will be long delayed (if indeed ever brought into force) because of its 'resource and administrative implications'. However, given that such procedures have received royal assent, it may be difficult for the executive to issue directions that are radically different to the scheme prescribed by the 1986 Act.[96]

3.85   The only provisions in the NHSCCA 1990 in relation to how local authorities should carry out assessments are:

s47(3) which specifies when the NHS and the housing authority should be invited to be involved (see para 3.124 below); and

s47(4) which requires assessments to be carried out in accordance with any directions issued by the secretary of state. As noted above (para 3.20), directions have been issued in England.[97] But other than requiring that the person to be assessed and 'where appropriate' carers are

---

96   See eg *R v SSHD ex p Fire Brigades Union* [1995] 2 All ER 244, where 'the Secretary of State could not validly . . . resolve to give up his statutory duty to consider from time to time whether or not to bring the statutory scheme into force' (per Lord Browne-Wilkinson at p256b) and so could not introduce a conflicting non-statutory criminal injuries compensation scheme.

97   26 August 2004; accessible at http://www.dh.gov.uk/assetRoot/04/08/84/77/ 04088477.pdf.

consulted, and that reasonable steps are taken to reach agreement about the care plan, the directions are remarkably short on the procedure to be followed in an assessment.

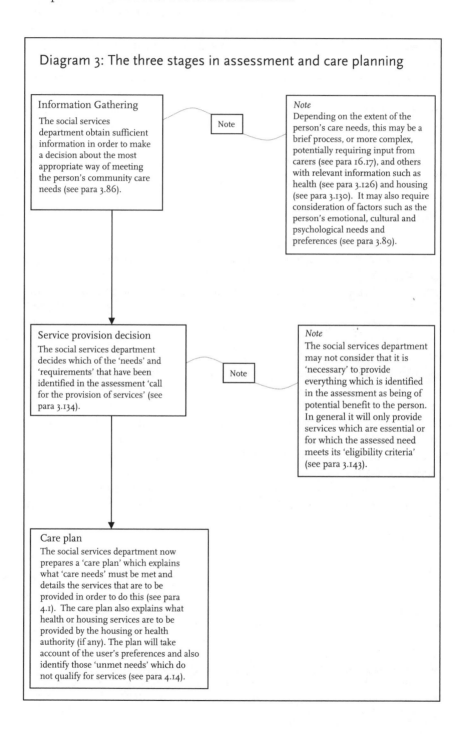

Diagram 3: The three stages in assessment and care planning

Information Gathering

The social services department obtain sufficient information in order to make a decision about the most appropriate way of meeting the person's community care needs (see para 3.86).

Note

Note

Depending on the extent of the person's care needs, this may be a brief process, or more complex, potentially requiring input from carers (see para 16.17), and others with relevant information such as health (see para 3.126) and housing (see para 3.130). It may also require consideration of factors such as the person's emotional, cultural and psychological needs and preferences (see para 3.89).

Service provision decision

The social services department decides which of the 'needs' and 'requirements' that have been identified in the assessment 'call for the provision of services' (see para 3.134).

Note

Note

The social services department may not consider that it is 'necessary' to provide everything which is identified in the assessment as being of potential benefit to the person. In general it will only provide services which are essential or for which the assessed need meets its 'eligibility criteria' (see para 3.143).

Care plan

The social services department now prepares a 'care plan' which explains what 'care needs' must be met and details the services that are to be provided in order to do this (see para 4.1). The care plan also explains what health or housing services are to be provided by the housing or health authority (if any). The plan will take account of the user's preferences and also identify those 'unmet needs' which do not qualify for services (see para 4.14).

The assessment and 'presenting needs'

3.86   The first stage of the NHSCCA 1990 s47(1) assessment process obliges authorities to identify those needs which could potentially be satisfied by the provision of a community care service. In the terminology of the Department of Health, these are now known as 'presenting needs'.[98] The assessor is required to collect sufficient data concerning these 'presenting needs' (under section 47(1)(a)) in order to determine the section 47(1)(b) question, namely: 'which of the applicant's presenting needs call for the provision of community care services?'. As Hale LJ observed in *R v Tower Hamlets LBC ex p Wahid*,[99] 'need is a relative concept, which trained and experienced social workers are much better equipped to assess than are lawyers and courts, provided that they act rationally'.

Relevant information

3.87   The assessment process must ensure that – so far as is practicable – all relevant information is collected and taken into account when the 'service provision decision' is made. It follows that a failure to collect such information and to take it into account in the decision-making process could invalidate the assessment. What is 'relevant' and what is 'practicable' will depend upon the circumstances of a person's situation, and so the scope and depth of the assessment process will vary from case to case. Thus, if the principal purpose of the assessment is to decide whether a disabled person's parking badge should be awarded, the assessment will be materially different to one assessing the needs of a frail elderly person awaiting discharge from hospital. What authorities cannot do, however, is to restrict the scope of assessments for policy or financial reasons. By way of example, *R v Haringey LBC ex p Norton*[100] concerned the adequacy of the local authority's assessment, undertaken in response to his complaint about a decision to reduce his community care services. In the assessment the council only considered its obligation to provide 'personal care needs' rather than other needs such as social, recreational and leisure needs. The court held this to be unlawful; the assessment had to investigate all potential needs.

Assessments prepared by other social services authorities

3.88   Relevant information will also include any assessments and associated evidence prepared by other authorities, the opinions of experts and other

---

98   FACS 2002 policy guidance, para 13: 'presenting needs' mean 'the issues and problems that are identified when individuals contact, or are referred to, councils seeking social care support': UFSAMC 2002 (Wales) does not use this term or any other specific tem of art.
99   [2001] EWHC 641 (Admin); (2001) 4 CCLR 455.
100   (1998) 1 CCLR 168, QBD.

professionals and other people with knowledge of the person being assessed. In this respect the FACS 2002 policy guidance states:[101]

> When a service user permanently moves from one council area to another, the 'receiving' council should, pending an assessment, take account of the services that were previously received and the effect of any substantial changes on the service user when reaching an interim decision about what services to provide. The 'receiving' council should have regard to these factors, as well as the outcomes that were previously pursued, when carrying out the assessment and reaching longer-term decisions about what services will be provided. Where 'receiving' councils intend to pursue significantly different outcomes, or provide significantly different services, they should produce clear and written explanations for service users.

Presenting needs

3.89   The FACS guidance distinguishes between 'presenting needs' and eligible (or 'assessed') needs. A presenting need is a need that is identified by the person being assessed or some other on his or her behalf. It is not however a 'need' that the local authority is under a duty to meet: such a duty only arises when the authority decides that the need is sufficiently important that it is 'eligible' for services – ie that the result of the assessment is that the 'need' should be met.

3.90   Early (1991) practice guidance on the assessment process[102] described the concept of 'presenting needs' (without using the term) as follows:

> 11. Need is a complex concept which has been analysed in a variety of different ways. In this guidance, the term is used as a shorthand for the requirements of individuals to enable them to achieve, maintain or restore an acceptable level of social independence or quality of life, as defined by the particular care agency or authority.

> 16 . . . Need is a multi-faceted concept which, for the purposes of this guidance, is sub-divided into six broad categories, each of which should be covered in a comprehensive assessment of need:
> * Personal/social care
> * health care
> * accommodation
> * finance
> * education/employment/leisure
> * transport/access.

3.91   Some presenting needs (such as those listed above) tend to suggest specific services, for instance a need for accommodation, whereas some will condition the way a service is delivered, for instance a person might have a need for 'a rigid routine'.[103] In *R v Avon CC ex p M*[104] the applicant had Down's syndrome, a symptom of which was that he had formed an

---

101 Para 56; UFSAMC 2002, para 5.43 in Wales.
102 Department of Health Social Services Inspectorate, *Care Management and Assessment, A Practitioners' Guide*, HMSO, 1991.
103 See eg complaint no 03/C/16371 against Stockton-on-Tees BC, 18 January 2005.
104 (1999) 2 CCLR 185; [1994] 2 FLR 1006.

entrenched view that he wanted to go to a particular residential home even though an alternative, cheaper home objectively catered for all his other needs. The authority, in deciding what accommodation he needed, had regard to a psychologist's report which stated that M's entrenched position was attributable to his Down's syndrome. The authority refused to fund the more expensive home on the ground that it would set a precedent by accepting psychological need as being part of an individual's needs which could force it to pay more than it would usually expect to pay in such cases. Rejecting this argument, Henry J held:[105]

> The [local authority's report] . . . proceeds on the basis that the psychological need can simply be 'excluded': . . . M's needs are thus arbitrarily restricted to the remainder of his needs, which are then described as 'usual'. Meeting his psychological needs is then treated as mere 'preference', a preference involving payments greater than usual.
>
> The law is clear. The council have to provide for the applicant's needs. Those needs may properly include psychological needs.

3.92   The SAP policy guidance (2002)[106] gives a table outlining the range of the more common and specific 'presenting needs' for older people (the table is reproduced as Diagram below). For younger disabled people, additional factors might need greater emphasis, for instance the need to discharge one's obligations as a parent (see para 3.39 above).

Diagram 4: Single assessment process (SAP) Annex F

The domains and sub-domains of the single assessment process

User's perspective

- Needs and issues in the users' own words
- Users' expectations, strengths, abilities and motivation

Clinical background

- History of medical conditions and diagnoses
- History of falls
- Medication use and ability to self-medicate

Disease prevention

- History of blood pressure monitoring
- Nutrition, diet and fluids
- Vaccination history
- Drinking and smoking history
- Exercise pattern
- History of cervical and breast screening

---

105 (1999) 2 CCLR 185, pp195–196.
106 At Annex F. A similar list for Wales appears at UFSAMC 2002, para 4.24.

Personal care and physical well-being

- Personal hygiene, including washing, bathing, toileting and grooming
- Dressing
- Pain
- Oral health
- Foot-care
- Tissue viability
- Mobility
- Continence and other aspects of elimination
- Sleeping patterns

Senses

- Sight
- Hearing
- Communication

Mental health

- Cognition and dementia, including orientation and memory
- Mental health including depression, reactions to loss, and emotional difficulties

Relationships

- Social contacts, relationships, and involvement in leisure, hobbies, work, and learning
- Carer support and strength of caring arrangements, including the carer's perspective

Safety

- Abuse and neglect
- Other aspects of personal safety
- Public safety

Immediate environment and resources

- Care of the home and managing daily tasks such as food preparation, cleaning and shopping
- Housing – location, access, amenities and heating
- Level and management of finances
- Access to local facilities and services

The assessment process

The scope of the assessment

3.93   The scope and depth of an assessment will be determined in large measure by the complexity of the person's needs. The assessment may consist of little more than a single conversation with a social worker or may involve complex analysis of data, protracted interviews and multi-disciplinary meetings spanning many months. For older people the process has been standardised, to a degree, by the SAP guidance. Although SAP is specific rather than generic guidance, its categorisation of assessments into four types is of wider relevance.[107] The four are:

- contact assessment;
- overview assessment;
- specialist assessments; and
- comprehensive assessment.

Contact assessment

3.94   This refers to a contact between an older person and health and social services where significant needs are first described or suspected. The assessment consists of recoding relevant (but limited) information and then deciding whether the person's needs are straightforward and can be dealt with there and then (eg provision of a blue parking badge, or a grab rail or other equipment, etc). If this is not possible, there may be a need for a more in-depth assessment (eg of a type below). The collection/verification of the data for a contact assessment may be 'by trained, but not professionally qualified, staff. The exploration of the presenting and other needs should be undertaken by a trained and competent single professional, qualified or not, in any of the settings to which this guidance applies.'[108]

Overview assessment

3.95   Assessment of this type occurs when the 'individual's needs are such that a more rounded assessment should be undertaken'. It will involve consideration of 'all or some of the domains of the single assessment process, such as "personal care and physical well-being", "senses" and "mental health"'. The guidance explains that such an assessment may be completed by a 'single professional from either the NHS or social services'. This person need not be a 'qualified professional' but must have competence to carry out the assessment.[109]

Specialist assessments

3.96   Whereas the overview assessment looks at a broad range of a person's needs, a specialist assessment focuses on specific needs – such as a health condition or problem or a social care need. Such assessments should be administered by the appropriate qualified professional.[110]

---

107 *The Single Assessment Process Guidance for Local Implementation* policy guidance, para 12(IX).
108 UFSAMC 2002 policy guidance in Wales, Annex E p14; paras 4.15–4.25.
109 Ibid pp14–16; paras 4.25–4.31.
110 Ibid p18; paras 4.32–4.35.

Comprehensive assessment

3.97 This arises when the individual's needs are such that all or most of the SAP domains need consideration and some (or all) require specialist assessment in addition. Such assessments should be carried out 'where the level of support and treatment likely to be offered is intensive or prolonged, including permanent admission to a care home, intermediate care services, or substantial packages of care at home'. Such assessments will involve a range of different professionals or specialist teams.[111]

3.98 In reality, however, the division into four types of assessment merely describes arbitrary points on a line between the very simple and the highly complex. The 1991 practice guidance advice (at para 3.3) expressed this point thus:

> ... the scope of an assessment should be related to its purpose. Simple needs will require less investigation than more complex ones. In the interests of both efficiency and consumer satisfaction, the assessment process should be as simple, speedy and informal as possible.[112]

3.99 The FACS 2002 policy guidance reiterated this advice, stating (at para 34):

> ... councils should not operate eligibility criteria to determine the complexity of the assessment offered; rather the depth and breadth of the assessment should be proportionate to individuals' presenting needs and circumstances. Based on their judgment, professionals may wish to carry out initial assessments, or assessments to take stock of wider needs, or specialist assessments of particular needs, or comprehensive assessment across all potential needs. In many cases, combinations of these assessment types may be used.

3.100 The courts have been unenthusiastic about guidance that dictates an overly prescriptive approach to the assessment process. The 1991 practice guidance, for instance, put forward six models of assessment, from simple to comprehensive and then stated that all disabled people had the right to a comprehensive assessment (regardless of how complex their needs might be). This advice was considered by Carnwath J in *R v Gloucestershire CC ex p RADAR*,[113] where (referring to the 1991 practice guidance) he held:

> I have some sympathy with those trying to write these sort of guides since the complexity of the legislative chain, combined with the length of the titles of most of the Acts, makes short and accurate exposition particularly difficult. However, if what is intended is to define the legal obligation in respect of the disabled, then it can only be intended as a reference to the decision referred to in s4 Disabled Persons (Services, Consultation and Representation) Act 1986, that is, as to the range of services required under s2 of the 1970 Act. I take that to be the intended meaning of the word 'comprehensive'. If it is intended to mean anything else, it is misleading.

---

111 Ibid pp18–19; paras 4.36–4.42.
112 FACS 2002 policy guidance, para 35 advises that they be 'as simple and timely as possible'.
113 (1998) 1 CCLR 476, p484.

Screening assessments

3.101   As noted above, the FACS 2002 policy guidance, para 30,[114] cautions against individuals being screened out of the assessment process before sufficient information is known about them. This is amplified in the FACS 2003 practice guidance at para 8.2, where it is stated:

> There is considerable evidence that screening systems operated by councils can turn people away without their needs being identified. Some councils go further by declaring that they do not help particular groups of individuals, such as those with higher functioning autism/Asperger Syndrome, and make no attempt to assess needs as they should do. This is unacceptable. Often these screening systems are not connected to assessment and care management systems, which cannot be helpful. Councils should always bear in mind that almost all adults approach social services for support only when they feel they need to.

3.102   Certain basic matters must be considered in even the most rudimentary interview for it to amount to an assessment. In *R v Bristol City Council ex p Penfold*[115] the respondent sought to argue that a mere consideration by the council of an applicant's request for an assessment, was itself an assessment. Rejecting this, Scott Baker J held that an assessment 'cannot be said to have been carried out unless the authority concerned has fully explored the need in relation to the services it has the power to supply. In some cases the exercise will be very simple; in others more complex.'[116]

3.103   Notwithstanding the reservations in statutory guidance concerning screening assessments, many authorities have such a process as a way of weeding out potential service users. Effectively such applicants are advised, after a telephone conversation, that they are not entitled to services. In principle there is nothing wrong with such an approach provided the screening assessment complies with certain minimum criteria. Indeed such procedures enable authorities to conserve their limited human resources and target scarce officer time on more detailed assessments of those in most need.

Steps in data gathering

3.104   The data gathering element of an assessment must, at the very minimum, be structured in such a way that it seeks to obtain/provide the following information:

1) The applicant's name and contact details.
2) The applicant's choice of the setting for the assessment. If the applicant is content, the assessment may take place over the telephone but it is essential that the person being assessed has a real choice over the setting of the assessment and (if it be the case) freely chooses the telephone option.
3) Whether there is a need for an interpreter or other facilitator (such as

114 UFSAMC 2002, para 2.23 in Wales. See also para 3.20 of the 1990 policy guidance.
115 (1998) 1 CCLR 315.
116 (1998) 1 CCLR 315 at 321C.

an advocate) or indeed if there is a duty on the authority to involve an Independent Mental Capacity Advocate (see para 18.67).

4) The applicant's care needs – this requires (in the absence of good reasons):
   a) the user's involvement and (with his or her consent) the involvement of any carer;
   b) the applicant's opinion as to what his or her needs are;
   c) that the full spectrum of potential needs be considered (see *R v Haringey LBC ex p Norton* at para 3.87 above);
   d) the particular risk factors that the applicant faces as well as his or her aptitudes, abilities and access to existing social support networks;
   e) what services the applicant wants, and his or her preferences as to any service that may be offered as a result of the assessment.

5) Whether there is any carer who may potentially be entitled to an assessment under the Carers (Recognition and Services) Act 1995 or the Carers and Disabled Children Act 2000.[117]

6) Any associated health or housing difficulties the applicant may have. If such exist then there must be a referral to the health or housing authority and it would seem therefore that the assessment cannot be finally concluded until a response has been received to that referral and the contents of that response fully considered.

7) The applicant should also be advised of his or her right to:
   a) have a written copy of the assessment; and
   b) make representations/use the complaints procedures if he or she believes that services have been unreasonably refused.

The setting of an assessment

3.105   The 1991 practice guidance (at paras 3.12–3.15) emphasises the importance of the assessment being conducted in an appropriate location, as this may have a material effect on its outcome. It points out that office interviews, whilst administratively convenient and less costly than domiciliary assessments, may give false results if the interviewee is not at ease, and that the applicant is more likely to relax in the home setting. The following important points are also made:

> 3.13 Where the assessment is concerned with the maintenance of a person at home, the assessment should take place in that setting. If users are considering admission to residential or nursing home care, involving irreversible loss of their home, they should always be given the opportunity of experiencing that setting before making their final decision.

> 3.14 There may be advantages to some part of the assessment being undertaken in settings external to the home, for example, day or residential care settings, so that staff have longer contact with the individual. In such circumstances, assessors will be working in close collaboration with service providers.

117 Community Care (Assessment) Directions 2004, direction 2.

3.15 In considering such options, care should be taken to avoid exposing individuals to unnecessary disruption. In addition, it is necessary to avoid assuming that behaviour will be replicated in other settings. Such considerations may, occasionally, affect assessment arrangements for hospital discharges.

User involvement

3.106 The Community Care (Assessment) Directions (see para 3.20 above) requirement to consult the user is amplified in the FACS 2002 policy guidance which advises that assessments should be 'rounded and person-centred' and that (at para 35):

> Councils should recognise that individuals are the experts on their own situation and encourage a partnership approach to assessment. They should help them prepare for the assessment process and find the best way for each individual to state their views. The use of interpreters, translators, advocates or supporters can be critical in this regard.

3.107 The 1991 policy guidance also stressed the importance of involving users in the assessment process so that the resulting services fully take into account their preferences (and so far as possible those of their carers).[118] It highlighted the need for the assessor to establish a relationship of trust and to clarify what the assessment will entail. The FACS 2002 policy guidance at para 36 states that assessments should be carried out in such a way, and be sufficiently transparent, for individuals to:

- gain a better understanding of their situation;
- identify the options that are available for managing their own lives;
- identify the outcomes required from any help that is provided;
- understand the basis on which decisions are reached.

3.108 The SAP guidance gives similar advice. In relation to the 'user's perspective' domain (Annex F) the person being assessed should be asked:

> . . . to describe their needs and expectations, and the strengths and abilities they can bring to addressing their needs, in their own words and on their own terms. This person-centred beginning should set the tone for the rest of the assessment and subsequent care planning, and due account of the user's perspective should remain to the fore throughout.[119]

3.109 In *R v North Yorkshire CC ex p Hargreaves*[120] the social services authority came to a service provision decision without taking into account the preferences of the disabled person – largely because (in Dyson J's opinion) her carer was very protective and probably considered by the social services authority as obstructing its ability to communicate with the disabled person. Nevertheless this did not discharge the authority's obligation to discover what her preferences were, and accordingly the decision was quashed.

118 At paras 3.16 and 3.25.
119 SAP Policy Guidance Annex E p19.
120 (1997) 1 CCLR 104.

3.110   As we note above (see paras 3.59 and 12.76), the Department of Health is currently evaluating the potential for self assessment by service users.

Persons unable to participate fully in the assessment process

3.111   Individual involvement in the assessment process becomes a more difficult question where the potential service user is unable to participate fully due to lack of ability to communicate or mental capacity (see also chapter 18 where questions of mental capacity are further considered). The Code of Practice for the Mental Capacity Act 2005 gives detailed guidance on good practice for assessing capacity and much of it is in general good practice regarding assessment.

3.112   Much of the general and specific user group assessment guidance stresses the importance of endeavouring to communicate with service users, no matter how severe their impairments, and of the particular importance of advocacy services in this respect.[121]

3.113   The 1990 policy guidance states that 'where a user is unable to participate actively [in the assessment] it is even more important that he or she should be helped to understand what is involved and the intended outcome'.[122] The 1991 practice guidance elaborates on this advice, stating that where it is clear that a user or carer would benefit from independent advocacy, he or she should be given information about any schemes funded by the authority or run locally. It goes on to state that it is consistent with the aims of basing service provision on the needs and wishes of users that those who are unable to express their views – for example, those with severe learning disabilities or dementia – or those who have been previously disadvantaged – for example, those from minority ethnic groups – should, as a matter of priority, be supported in securing independent representation.[123]

3.114   In *R (A and B) v East Sussex CC (No 2)*,[124] a case concerning the appropriate way to lift and move two young women (X and Y) with profound physical and learning difficulties, Munby J stressed the importance of ascertaining their views on the process:

> 132. I have said that the assessment must take account of the disabled person's wishes, feelings and preferences. How are these to be ascertained?
>
> 133. In a case where the disabled person is, by reason of their disability, prevented, whether completely or in part, from communicating their wishes and feelings it will be necessary for the assessors to facilitate the ascertainment of the person's wishes and feelings, so far as they may be deduced, by whatever means, including seeking and receiving advice – advice, not instructions – from appropriate interested persons such as X and Y involved in the care of the disabled person.

---

121 See para 19.19 for further considerations of the role of advocacy services.
122 At para 3.16.
123 See paras 3.25–3.27.
124 [2003] EWHC 167 (Admin); (2003) 6 CCLR 194.

134. Good practice, Miss Foster suggests, would indicate, and I am inclined to agree that:

i)   A rough 'dictionary' should be drawn up, stating what the closest carers (in a case such as this, parents and family, here X and Y) understand by the various non verbal communications, based on their intimate long term experience of the person. Thus with familiarisation and 'interpretation' the carers can accustom themselves to the variety of feelings and modes of expression and learn to recognise what is being communicated.

ii) Where the relatives are present with the carers and an occasion of 'interpretation' arises, great weight must be accorded to the relatives' 'translation'.

iii) As I commented in *Re S* (2003)[125]
     'the devoted parent who . . . has spent years caring for a disabled child is likely to be much better able than any social worker, however skilled, or any judge, however compassionate, to "read" his child, to understand his personality and to interpret the wishes and feeling's which he lacks the ability to express.'

iv) That said, in the final analysis the task of deciding whether, in truth, there is a refusal or fear or other negative reaction to being lifted must . . . fall on the carer, for the duty to act within the framework given by the employer falls upon the employee. Were the patient not incapacitated, there could be no suggestion that the relative's views are other than a factor to be considered. Because of the lack of capacity and the extraordinary circumstances in a case such as this, the views of the relatives are of very great importance, but they are not determinative.

Persons unwilling to be involved in the assessment process

3.115   The issue of user involvement becomes controversial where the potential service user chooses not to participate in (or actively objects to) the assessment.

3.116   A literal interpretation of the section 47(1) duty suggests that the assessment duty is activated even when the potential service user objects to being assessed: strictly speaking, his or her consent is not required.[126] While he or she can refuse to take part in an assessment, he or she cannot stop the assessment taking place. Of course, in practice, an objection would generally be an end of the matter, provided the person has full mental capacity to make an informed decision on the question[127] – since, as Carnwath J observed, without some degree of co-operation the effectiveness of any assessment will be significantly impaired.[128]

---

125 [2002] EWHC 2278; [2003] 1 FLR 292 at [49] – see para 25.67 below.

126 Para 11.2 of the practice guidance to the Carers (Recognition and Services) Act 1995 suggests that users can refuse an assessment; while this may be a statement of practice, as a matter of law it appears incorrect. All an individual can do, is not co-operate and if needs be, refuse any services which are offered.

127 Presumably the mental capacity required would need to encompass an understanding of the potential consequences of that refusal – which may for instance be an exposure to significant direct and indirect risk of harm.

128 *R v Gloucestershire CC ex p RADAR* (1995) 1 CCLR 476 at 282F.

3.117   The 1991 practice guidance accepts that an individual's involvement in the assessment process may be involuntary (at para 3.17) and that any individual can withdraw at any stage from active involvement. The effect of such 'wilful lack of co-operation' may be that the social services authority finds it impossible to ascertain the preferences of the user and/or carer.[129] In this respect the local government ombudsman has observed that 'before a council can conclude that it is unable to carry out an assessment due to user non-cooperation, it must try and explain to him/her the potential advantages of the process (generally in writing)'.[130] The 1991 practice guidance makes a number of further and important observations:

> 3.17 Individuals who enter voluntarily into the assessment process should also be made aware of their entitlement to withdraw at any stage. Where the assessment is on an involuntary basis, for example as a prelude to possible compulsory admission to psychiatric hospital, it is even more important that the individuals are helped to understand, as far as they are able, the nature of the process in which they are engaged. It is less clear cut where practitioners are dealing with someone, with failing capacities, for example, relapse of a psychotic illness, where intervention has been on a voluntary basis but, at a certain threshold of risk or vulnerability, it is likely to tip over into compulsory admission. That threshold should be clearly defined in policy terms and agreed with other relevant agencies, for example, police and health authorities. All practitioners should be clear on the distinction between using assessment as an instrument of social support as opposed to social control. The former offers choices to the user while the latter imposes solutions. The one should not be allowed to shade into the other without all parties appreciating the full implications of that change.

3.118   The local government ombudsman has criticised a local authority for accepting a service user's refusal to be assessed – even though it was clear he was in considerable need and placing an unsustainable burden on his main carer. Although she accepted that a council 'cannot force services upon an unwilling person', in her opinion, such a refusal does not absolve it of all responsibility. She criticised a council for accepting the refusal at face value, instead of questioning whether the disabled person was in fact making an informed decision in his refusal or considering the implications for his carer. In her report she stated that the council needed to find a way to work through such a problem and referred to the fact that an intervention by the community nurse, the psychologist, and the worker from the voluntary caring organisation had proved successful in overcoming many of the problems that had led to the initial rejection of the care services.[131]

3.119   The obligation on councils not to take a refusal to be assessed as an end of the matter has been emphasised in a number of different cases and

129 Per Dyson J in *R v North Yorkshire CC ex p Hargreaves* (1997) 1 CCLR 104, p111J.
130 Report no 02/B/03191 against Buckinghamshire, 5 November 2003.
131 Complaint no 02/C/08690 against Sheffield City Council, 9 August 2004.

contexts.[132] *R (J) v Caerphilly CBC*[133] contains a clear expression of the public law obligation underlying the courts' approach to this question – ie the requirement for the assessor to be persistent – even though it concerns a materially different statutory regime (the CA 1989). Munby J (at para 56) stated:

> The fact that a child is uncooperative and unwilling to engage, or even refuses to engage, is no reason for the local authority not to carry out its obligations under the Act and the Regulations. After all, a disturbed child's unwillingness to engage with those who are trying to help is often merely a part of the overall problems which justified the local authority's statutory intervention in the first place. The local authority must do its best.

3.120   This important point was further emphasised in *R (M) v Hammersmith and Fulham LBC*,[134] a case that also concerned the CA 1989 duty, where the court observed that 'any system can deal with the compliant' and pointed out (at para 74) that people being assessed (like the applicant) who may have had:

> . . . wretched childhoods, or who have been otherwise abused or neglected as children, and who have gone on to commit criminal offences, may well, like M, fail to co-operate with any investigation by the council into their circumstances. This fact does not, in my judgment, either of itself and as a matter of law, absolve local authorities of their duty both to investigate, and to put in place the services which children such as M require.

3.121   The public law duty to persist in the endeavour of delivering community care support services for vulnerable people even when confronted by unco-operative behaviour, is little different to that described in the above cited *Caerphilly* and *Hammersmith* cases. People eligible for community care services will frequently have mental health or leaning difficulties and their refusals of support may be due to misconceptions, miscomprehensions, temporary lapses and/or be contrary to their best interests. In such cases the public law duty demands perseverance. The specific issue of service refusals is considered further at para 4.36 below.

3.122   A problem that used to arise, if a disabled person refused an assessment, was that it disentitled their carer to an assessment since the obligation under Carers (Recognition and Services) Act 1995 s1 was only activated when a community care assessment was being undertaken. This problem has been rectified by Carers and Disabled Children Act 2000 s1 (see para 16.36) which provides for 'free-standing' carers' assessments. In such cases the relevant guidance advises:[135]

---

132 See eg *R v Kensington and Chelsea RLBC ex p Kujtim* [1999] 4 All ER 161; (1999) 2 CCLR 340, p354I and *R (Patrick) v Newham LBC* (2000) 4 CCLR 48, considered further at paras 4.36 and 7.34 below.
133 [2005] EWHC 586 (Admin); (2005) 8 CCLR 255.
134 [2006] EWCA Civ 917; (2006) 9 CCLR 418.
135 Department of Health, *Carers and Disabled Children Act 2000 and Carers (Equal Opportunities) Act 2004 Combined Policy Guidance*, 2005, para 39.

Where the cared for person is unwilling to be assessed, local authorities should use the Contact Assessment on either the cared for person or the carer themselves to make a reasoned judgement about the need to conduct a carer's assessment.

3.123 The Community Care (Delayed Discharges etc) Act 2003 obliges local authorities to complete certain assessments within set timescales (see para 5.32). Department of Health guidance addresses the question of where liability rests if a patient refuses to co-operate with an assessment:[136]

If the patient is clear that they do not want the involvement of social services and that they will not accept the services put in place for them, at this stage they become responsible for themselves. Up to that point social services must use their best endeavours to perform an assessment and prepare a care plan, however limited that might be . . .

The section 47(3) referral duty in relation to health and housing needs

3.124 Where the assessment discloses a possible housing or medical need, NHSCCA 1990 s47(3) obliges the authority to notify the relevant housing or health authority.[137] Section 47(3) provides:

If at any time during the assessment of the needs of any person under subsection (1)(a) above, it appears to a local authority –
(a) that there may be a need for the provision to that person by such Primary Care Trust or Health Authority[138] as may be determined in accordance with regulations of any services under the National Health Service Act 1977, or
(b) that there may be a need for the provision to him of any services which fall within the functions of a local housing authority (within the meaning of the Housing Act 1985) which is not the local authority carrying out the assessment,
the local authority shall notify that Primary Care Trust, Health Authority or local housing authority and invite them to assist, to such extent as is

---

136 *Community Care (Delayed Discharges etc.) Act: Frequently asked questions on reimbursement*, 2004, Q & A 32, at http://www.dh.gov.uk/assetRoot/04/07/19/26/04071926.pdf.
137 The consequent obligations on the health and housing authorities are considered below at para 13.28 and 15.10 respectively. Although there is no duty on the notified authority to respond following notification, the service user will benefit where parallel duties are triggered.
138 Although the section has been amended (as a result of the demise of health authorities in England and Wales) to insert 'Primary Care Trusts' (National Health Service Reform and Health Care Professions Act 2002 Sch 2(2) para 56), no equivalent amendment has occurred in Wales to refer to 'Local Health Boards'. It appears however that this is not strictly necessary, as a result of a combination of the Health Authorities (Transfer of Functions, Staff, Property, Rights and Liabilities and Abolition) (Wales) Order 2003 SI No 813 (W98) – which transfers all functions of health authorities in Wales to the Assembly – and the Local Health Boards (Functions) (Wales) Regulations 2003 SI No 150 (W20) which provides (subject to exceptions) that functions that were exercised by health authorities and were transferred to the Assembly by SI No 2003/813 are to be exercised by local health boards.

reasonable in the circumstances, in the making of the assessment; and, in making their decision as to the provision of the services needed for the person in question, the local authority shall take into account any services which are likely to be made available for him by that Primary Care Trust, Health Authority or local housing authority.

3.125   A social service failure to make a referral to the appropriate body may undermine the legality of the assessment process. In general, however, the courts have considered such cases from the public law perspective as a failure to take into account a relevant consideration (see para 17.182) rather than a breach of statutory duty. The greater the likelihood that a referral could have resulted in a different decision being reached, the more probable is it that the courts will conclude that such a failure is material. Thus in *R v Birmingham CC ex p Killigrew*[139] the point relied upon was a failure to follow the 1990 policy guidance quoted below. The applicant was a profoundly disabled person and a reassessment of her needs failed to seek up-to-date medical evidence. Given the severity of her condition, Hooper J considered this to be a fundamental breach of the assessment obligation and accordingly quashed the resulting care plan.[140]

The NHS referral obligation

3.126   In relation to the s47(3) obligation, the 1990 policy guidance advised as follows:

> 3.47   It is expected that, as a matter of good practice, GPs will wish to make a full contribution to assessment. It is part of the GP's terms of service to give advice to enable patients to avail themselves of services provided by a local authority.[141]
>
> 3.48   Where advice is needed by the local authority in the course of assessment, this should be obtained from the GP orally (eg by telephone) as far as possible. A record should be kept of the advice given. In addition to the information that only the patient's own GP can provide, local authorities may, on occasion, also require a clinical examination or an interpretation of the medical report provided by the GP. Local authorities should, therefore, be aware that GPs have a personal duty to and a relationship with their patients, and may not be best placed to act in addition as an assessor on the authority's behalf. In such circumstances local authorities may wish other practitioners to act in, this capacity.

3.127   It follows that where during the assessment process an NHS need is disclosed, the assessing authority is obliged to notify the PCT or local

---

139 (2000) 3 CCLR 109.

140 See also local government ombudsman complaint no 99/A/00988 against Southwark, 12 March 2001, further considered at para 3.218 below.

141 This obligation continues: the current GMS contract (as with the previous) requires GPs to refer (as appropriate) a 'patient for other services under [what is now the NHSA 2006/NHS(W)A 2006]' (National Health Service (General Medical Services) Contracts) Regulations 2004 SI No 291, reg 15(5)(b) – see para 13.35). NHSA 2006 s254 and Sch 20 and NHS(W)A 2006 s192 and Sch 15 place substantial duties on social services for the provision of community care services – see para 9.137 below.

health board and at the same time to specify what assistance it is that the authority is requested to provide in order to facilitate the assessment. The health authority is not, however, under any statutory duty to respond or co-operate.[142] A failure to respond – or failure to respond within a reasonable time or in a reasonable manner – would however be vulnerable to challenge as maladministration.

3.128   During the passage of the Health Act 1999 through parliament, an attempt was made to insert an amendment which would have required a positive response from health authorities to any request for assistance by a local authority (of a similar nature to that required under CA 1989 s27). On the amendment being withdrawn, the government gave an assurance that guidance would be issued requiring health and local authorities to publish details as to how they will work together to ensure that all the assessment needs of individuals are met.[143]

3.129   Where the NHS responds to a s47(3) referral, the local authority will be required to give this information substantial weight in reaching its service provision decision and in general to evidence the fact.[144] Ultimately the decision on need will be for the social services authority to make and not the health body: a local authority is required to exercise independence and a misplaced belief that it is bound by a medical opinion will be vulnerable to a public law challenge.[145]

The housing authority referral obligation

3.130   Section 47(3) requires that if, during the assessment process, a housing need is disclosed, the assessing authority is obliged to notify the housing authority and at the same time to specify what assistance that authority is requested to provide in order to facilitate the assessment.

3.131   It follows that the s47(3) duty only applies if the housing authority is a different authority – ie is not a department within the same council. Nevertheless, there is substantial guidance exhorting housing and social services departments to co-operate[146] and an administrative obligation must exist, even within unitary authorities, for such departments to work together. In *R (Wahid) v Tower Hamlets LBC*,[147] for example, Hale LJ observed that it was 'obviously good practice ... to involve the housing department where this is part of the same local authority'. However in *R v*

---

142 Unlike the equivalent duty under CA 1989 s27. Adult care guidance places a positive obligation on the NHS in certain situations, eg SAP policy guidance (2002) and UFSAMC 2002 (Wales).

143 Lord Hunt of Kings Heath, HL Debates col 851, 18 March 1999. Lord Hunt confirmed that this guidance would 'set out the requirement for health and local authorities to develop a framework for multi-disciplinary assessment in their first joint investment plans'. Although the obligation on the NHS to co-operate now exists in the SAP guidance (see para 20.3) there remains no equivalent guidance binding on the NHS for younger disabled people.

144 But see *R (Ireneschild) v Lambeth LBC* [2007] EWCA Civ 2354; (2006) 9 CCLR 686.

145 *R (Goldsmith) v Wandsworth LBC* [2004] EWCA Civ 1170; (2004) 7 CCLR 472.

146 See para 15.10.

147 [2002] EWCA Civ 287; (2002) 5 CCLR 239.

Lewisham LBC ex p Pinzon and Patino[148] Laws J held that the recommendations in the circular guidance that housing and social services authorities work together does not in itself convert that obligation into a legally enforceable duty

3.132   Although the housing authority is not under any statutory duty to respond to or co-operate with a section 47(3) request,[149] separate, parallel duties under the Housing Act (HA) 1996 may well be triggered. The housing authority will be under a duty to receive applications[150] and to make enquiries under HA 1996 s184 in cases of homelessness and apparent priority need. As the application need not be in any particular form,[151] it may be argued in appropriate cases that notification of housing need amounts in itself to an application made on behalf of the assessed person.[152]

3.133   As noted above, a failure to respond to a section 47(3) referral, or failure to respond within a reasonable time or in a reasonable manner, would be vulnerable to challenge as maladministration.

The service provision decision: what needs must be satisfied by the provision of services?

3.134   Once the authority has complied with its obligations under NHSCCA 1990 s47(1)(a) – ie it has gathered together all the data it considers necessary (reports, interviews etc) – section 47(1)(b) requires it to make a decision: to decide which of the individual's presenting 'needs' 'call for' the provision of community care services. 'Community care services' are defined by NHSCCA 1990 s46 as services which a local authority may provide or arrange to be provided under:

(a)   Part III of the National Assistance Act 1948;
(b)   section 45 of the Health Services and Public Health Act 1968;
(c)   section 254 of, and Schedule 20 to, the National Health Service Act 2006, and section 192 of, and Schedule 15 to, the National Health Service (Wales) Act 2006;
(d)   section 117 of the Mental Health Act 1983.

3.135   NHSCCA 1990 s47(1)(b) obliges the authority to 'have regard to' the results of the section 47(1)(a) assessment, rather than obliging it to provide services to meet all the presenting needs. It is this decision that is generally referred to as the 'service provision decision'. It is of consider-

148 (1999) 2 CCLR 152.
149 Unlike under CA 1989 s27: see *R v Northavon DC ex p Smith* [1994] 3 WLR 403, HL.
150 *R v Camden LBC ex p Gillan* (1989) 21 HLR 114, DC.
151 *R v Chiltern DC ex p Roberts* (1990) 23 HLR 387, DC.
152 Disabled adults with insufficient mental capacity to make an application or authorise someone else to do so are not entitled to apply under Part VII of the 1996 Act – see *R v Tower Hamlets LBC ex p Begum* [1993] 2 WLR 609; (1993) 25 HLR 319, HL; however see also *R (Patrick) v Newham LBC* (2000) 4 CCLR 48 – considered at para 7.35 above.

able importance, since it determines which community care services an individual is legally entitled to receive. It is the point at which the individual's needs are reconciled with the local resources that are available to meet such needs. As Swinton-Thomas LJ observed in the Court of Appeal decision in *R v Gloucestershire CC ex p Barry*:[153]

> Section 47(1)(a) provides for the provision of Community Care Services generally, the need for such services, the carrying out of an assessment and then, section 47(1)(b) gives the Local Authority a discretion as to whether to provide those services. The discretion in making the decision under section 47(1)(b) arises by reason of the words 'having regard to the results of that assessment'. In making that decision they will be entitled to take into account resources.

3.136 When a decision has to be made concerning the need for services under CSDPA 1970 s2, the service provision decision under section 47(1)(b) is deemed to chime with the inherent assessment obligation under section 2. Although in theory it appears that a council deciding whether a person's 'needs call for the provision of community care services' is materially different from it 'deciding whether it is 'satisfied' it is 'necessary to meet' that person's needs, in practice the courts determined that they are the same.

The scope of the local authority's discretion

3.137 Although NHSCCA 1990 places responsibility on the social services authority for making the service provision decision, this does not of course mean that it is free to reach whatever decision it chooses. Social services decisions, like any public law decision, must be lawful, be reasonable, be in accordance with the evidence, must take into account all relevant factors and ignore all irrelevant ones (see para 27.182 where these principles are further considered).

3.138 Frequently the local authority's decision is heavily influenced by the views of third parties – for instance as consultants, community nurses and occupational therapists. In such cases local authorities are generally unable to reject a clear opinion by such a professional on a matter within their area of expertise – unless of course the authority has an equally authoritative and conflicting report. The point being that there are limits to local authorities' expertise and outside these areas they may have little choice but to accept the conclusions of third parties (but see in this respect para 3.45 above). This will also be the case in relation to certain statements by non-professionals. Carers, for instance, are experts as to what they can and cannot do – or more usually, what they are and are not prepared to do (see para 16.56). Likewise many of the statements made by the person being assessed will have to be accepted by social services; in some cases because these described preferences, but not always. For example, the

---

153 [1996] 4 All ER 421; 1 CCLR 19, CA. Although reversed by the House of Lords ([1997] 2 WLR 459; (1997) 1 CCLR 40) these observations concerning the effect of NHSCCA 1990 s47(1) were in no way contradicted by the Lords.

extent of pain an individual experiences is not capable of objective calibration:

> . . . medical professionals who are expert in pain do not recognise a direct link between clinical findings and pain . . . As there is no direct causal link between disease or injury and pain, the only direct evidence of pain can come from the claimant.[154]

3.139   Even in those areas where a local authority is entitled to rely on its own expertise, it may still be under a duty to give reasons for rejecting the evidence or opinions of another – particularly where that evidence or opinion is well informed and of central relevance to the assessment.

Individual financial circumstances and the service provision decision

3.140   In making a service provision decision, in general an individual's financial circumstances will only be relevant to the extent that he or she may be required to contribute towards the cost of the service.[155] As a general rule, however, it is important that the assessment of need precedes the financial assessment. In this respect the 2003 practice guidance states (at Q8.5):

> The carrying out and completion of a community care assessment should not be contingent on whether or not an individual can pay for care services, be they provided in a care home or the individual's own home.

> Following assessment, arranging residential care on behalf of service users is dealt with in paragraphs 71 and 72 of the FACS policy guidance. With respect to individuals receiving services at home, a council should arrange those services irrespective of the resources or capacity of the service user, if that is what the service user wants the council to do. Where an individual is to receive services under section 29 of the National Assistance Act 1948 and is ordinarily resident in a council area, that council has a duty to arrange services on his/her behalf.

3.141   In limited circumstances the authority is permitted to have general regard to the service user's financial circumstances in determining whether it is 'necessary' to meet a presenting need. Most commonly this occurs in relation to residential care placements under National Assistance Act (NAA) 1948, s21. For the duty to be triggered under this section, the person must be in need of care and attention which is 'not otherwise' available. The courts have accepted that if a person has assets above the limits specified in the legislation, then it may be reasonable for a local authority to conclude that the support is 'otherwise available'. However, a duty to provide care home accommodation may subsist even where the subsequent financial assessment reveals that the person has capital in excess of the upper capital limit if the individual lacks the capacity to make his or her own arrangements and has no one else willing and able to make the arrangements on his or her behalf (see para 7.26).

---

154 Social Security Commissioner's Decision CDLA 902 2004, 18 June 2004, para 15.
155 Some services and certain persons are exempt from charges – considered in chapters 8 and 10 below.

3.142   In the unusual fact case of *R (Spink) v Wandsworth LBC*[156] the Court of Appeal held that where an application for a disabled facilities grant failed due to the applicants declining to provide details of their financial circumstances, the authority could decide that the adaptations were not 'necessary' under the CSDPA 1970 (see para 9.105).

Eligibility criteria and 'eligible needs'

3.143 Social workers need some external scale, formula or criteria in order to make consistent and sensible service provision decisions. Council treasuries also require standardised criteria in order to control overall expenditure: they have finite resources and need to ensure that these are applied equitably – to those whose needs (however this concept is defined) are greatest.

3.144   Early guidance on eligibility criteria was provided in 1994, in what was termed the 'Laming Letter'[157]. It was this guidance that was considered in a number of early community care cases.[158] The guidance suggested that:

> 14. Authorities can be helped in this process by defining eligibility criteria, ie a system of banding which assigns individuals to particular categories, depending on the extent of the difficulties they encounter in carrying out everyday tasks and relating the level of response to the degree of such difficulties. Any 'banding' should not, however, be rigidly applied, as account needs to be taken of individual circumstances. Such eligibility criteria should be phrased in terms of the factors identified in the assessment process.

3.145 The guidance was considered in the *Gloucestershire* proceedings,[159] Lord Clyde stating as follows:[160]

> In deciding whether there is a necessity to meet the needs of the individual some criteria have to be provided. Such criteria are required both to determine whether there is a necessity at all or only, for example, a desirability, and also to assess the degree of necessity. Counsel for the respondent suggested that a criterion could be found in the values of a civilised society. But I am not persuaded that that is sufficiently precise to be of any real assistance. It is possible to draw up categories of disabilities, reflecting the variations in the gravity of such disabilities which could be experienced. Such a classification might enable comparisons to be made between persons with differing kinds and degrees of disability. But in determining the question whether in a given case the making of particular arrangements is necessary in order to meet the needs of a given individual

---

156 [2005] EWCA Civ 302; [2005] 1 WLR 2884; (2005) 8 CCLR 272.
157 CI (92) 34; although the guidance was expressed as being cancelled on 1 April 1994, Sedley J accepted that 'in the sense that it gives plainly sensible advice' its content is still relevant although not mandatory – see *R v Islington LBC ex p Rixon* (1996) 1 CCLR 119 at 127B.
158 [1997] 2 WLR 459; (1997) 1 CCLR 40.
159 *R v Gloucestershire CC ex p Barry* [1997] 2 WLR 459; (1997) 1 CCLR 40 at 54.
160 In relation to an assessment of a person's need for services under CSDPA 1970 s2.

it seems to me that a mere list of disabling conditions graded in order of severity will still leave unanswered the question at what level of disability is the stage of necessity reached. The determination of eligibility for the purposes of the statutory provision requires guidance not only on the assessment of the severity of the condition or the seriousness of the need but also on the level at which there is to be satisfaction of the necessity to make arrangements. In the framing of the criteria to be applied it seems to me that the severity of a condition may have to be to be matched against the availability of resources.

3.146   Although there are many theoretical models by which such criteria may be constructed, the Department of Health and Welsh Assembly have now issued detailed (and prescriptive) policy guidance that has standard-ised individual local authority eligibility criteria for community care ser-vices. These are the FACS 2002 policy guidance in England, and the UFSAMC 2002 policy guidance in Wales. The eligibility criteria sections of these two documents differ in only minor respects and both base their criteria on the issue of 'independence'. As the FACS 2002 policy guidance states (at para 15):[161]

> Councils should use the following eligibility framework to specify their eligibility criteria. In other words, they should use the framework to describe those circumstances that make individuals, with the disabilities, impairments and difficulties described in paragraph 14, eligible for help. The eligibility framework is based on the impact of needs on factors that are key to maintaining an individual's independence over time. The framework makes no reference to age, gender, ethnic group, religion, disabilities, impairments or similar difficulties, personal relationships, location, living and caring arrangements, and similar factors. In themselves, these factors do not threaten independence; however, they may need to be taken into account as needs are assessed and services considered.

3.147   The evidence suggests that the introduction of FACS has resulted in (or coincided with) a reduction in the number of service users who qualify for community care services.[162]

3.148   The framework detailed in the FACS 2002 policy guidance (at para 16) is reproduced as Diagram 5 below. The equivalent framework in the Welsh guidance[163] adopts similar, though generally less demanding, phrasing. By way of example, the first descriptor of the critical band in Wales states 'life is, or could be, threatened' (as opposed to the English requirement that it 'is, or will be'); the Welsh guidance places 'abuse or neglect (self or other) have occurred or are likely to occur' in the critical band, whereas the English requires 'serious abuse or neglect has occurred or will occur'.

---

161 UFSAMC 2002, paras 5.16–5.17 in Wales.
162 See eg L Browne and J Newton, *How fair is Fair Access to Care?*, London Metropolitan University, 2006, unpublished.
163 UFSAMC 2002, para 5.16 in Wales.

Diagram 5: FACS policy guidance para 16

Critical[164] – when

- life is, or will be, threatened; and/or
- significant health problems have developed or will develop;[165] and/or
- there is, or will be, little or no choice and control over vital aspects of the immediate environment; and/or
- serious abuse or neglect has occurred or will occur; and/or
- there is, or will be, an inability to carry out vital personal care or domestic routines; and/or
- vital[166] involvement in work, education or learning cannot or will not be sustained; and/or
- vital social support systems and relationships cannot or will not be sustained; and/or
- vital family and other social roles and responsibilities cannot or will not be undertaken.

Substantial – when

- there is, or will be, only partial choice and control over the immediate environment; and/or
- abuse or neglect has occurred or will occur; and/or
- there is, or will be, an inability to carry out the majority of personal care or domestic routines; and/or
- involvement in many aspects of work, education or learning cannot or will not be sustained; and/or
- the majority of social support systems and relationships cannot or will not be sustained; and/or
- the majority of family and other social roles and responsibilities cannot or will not be undertaken.

Moderate – when

- there is, or will be, an inability to carry out several personal care or domestic routines; and/or
- involvement in several aspects of work, education or learning cannot or will not be sustained; and/or
- several social support systems and relationships cannot or will not be sustained; and/or *Continued*

164 Critical means that life is threatened or individuals are at great risk of serious illness or harm (Q3.6 of the FACS 2003 practice guidance).
165 See *R (Heffernan) v Sheffield City Council* [2004] EWHC 1377 (Admin); (2004) 7 CCLR 350 considered at para 3.161 below.
166 Vital 'means that without help, individuals are at great risk of *either* losing their independence, possibly necessitating admission to institutional care *or* making very little, damaging or inappropriate contributions to family and wider community life with serious consequences for the individual and others . . . [however] what may be "vital" to one individual may not be "vital" to another' (Q3.6 of the FACS 2003 practice guidance).

> - several family and other social roles and responsibilities cannot or will not be undertaken.
>
> **Low – when**
>
> - there is, or will be, an inability to carry out one or two personal care or domestic routines; and/or
> - involvement in one or two aspects of work, education or learning cannot or will not be sustained; and/or
> - one or two social support systems and relationships cannot or will not be sustained; and/or
> - one or two family and other social roles and responsibilities cannot or will not be undertaken.

3.149   Every social services authority in England must use the above framework and must use the exact wording. However they are permitted to 'add additional risk factors as extra bullet points within a band'.[167]

3.150   Although all social services authority eligibility criteria must adopt the above framework, this does not mean that they must all come to the same service provision decisions. The guidance allows individual local authorities to decide how high on the scale an individual must be, before he or she qualifies for services. Effectively therefore the guidance sanctions a continuation of the existing local variations in eligibility for services: the so called 'postcode lottery'.[168]

3.151   Arguments concerning the need for local authorities to have flexibility over their eligibility criteria are not wholly convincing. The justification for such variations is based on the proposition that criteria must accommodate local financial and demographic variables: for instance that an area might be relatively poor, or have a relatively high population of elderly people or relatively high morbidity etc. However, these are the very factors that the government seeks to iron out, by its sophisticated Local Government Finance Formula Grant.

3.152   In order to determine the annual grant for each local authority, the government calculates a formula spending share (FSS)[169] which is based on formulae that include detailed information on the population profile, social structure and other characteristics of each authority. The FSS therefore allocates the central government grant according to authorities' relative circumstances. In theory therefore it puts each authority – so far as the funding of social welfare services is concerned – in the same financial situation.

3.153   Notwithstanding this criticism, the guidance, advises as follows:[170]

167 FACS 2003 practice guidance, Q3.1.
168 Audit Commission, *Balancing the Care Equation: Progress with Community Care*, HMSO, 1996, para 32 considered above at para 3.24.
169 In April 2003 the FSS replaced the previous formula grant system, known as standard spending assessment. This change took place in order to ensure that the formula was as responsive as possible to local variations in need: see the local government white paper, *Strong Local Leadership – Quality Public Services*, CM 5237, 2001.
170 FACS 2003 practice guidance, Q3.9.

For any given planning period . . . a council should estimate the numbers of adults currently receiving services, and who potentially may be referred to it. The council should attempt to categorise these individuals' needs into the four bands of the eligibility framework. The council should then estimate the kinds of services that typically would be required to meet the needs arising in each band, including immediate needs and developing needs. It should cost this service provision with respect to prices typically faced when commissioning and purchasing services. (A council should also reflect on the longer-term costs of not meeting low level needs that would considerably worsen for the lack of timely help.) The council should then add up the costs of meeting needs falling into each eligibility band. Starting with the critical band, if the estimated costs of providing services to individuals with needs in this band equals the resources locally available to adult social care, then the council's eligibility framework would simply comprise the critical band. If a council's resources could cover the cost of services for individuals whose needs fall within the critical or substantial bands, then the council's eligibility criteria should comprise the critical and substantial bands; and so on.

3.154   In the English guidance, therefore, it is explicit (whereas in the Welsh it is merely implicit) that if a council considers that it only has resources to fund service users whose eligible needs fall into the critical category, that would be acceptable.[171] Both English and Welsh guidance, however, contain caveats: the UFSAMC 2002 policy guidance, at para 5.21 comments 'any set of criteria must also allow for exceptional cases . . . . [and] . . . must remain in line with the implications of case law'. The FACS 2003 practice guidance contains the somewhat curious statement (in response to Q3.9) that in deciding where to draw the eligibility line a council should be 'observant of its statutory duties under community care legislation'. The legality of this approach is considered at para 3.200 below.

3.155   The guidance[172] emphasises that (with the exception of life threatening circumstances in the critical band) there is no hierarchy of needs and related risks within an eligibility band. It also explains what should happen where a council considers that it has sufficient resources to meet all the eligible needs in (for instance) both the critical and substantial bands, and can extend into the moderate band without being able to meet all needs that would fall into the moderate band. The guidance[173] advises that in such cases local authorities have a discretion as to how to proceed, and suggests two possible alternatives; the first being:

. . . to separate the moderate band into two sub-bands termed, 'moderate – greater' and 'moderate – lesser'. In doing the separation the council should regard each of the current four elements of the band as having equal weight, and split each element up into risks of greater or lesser importance. The costs of meeting the greater risks should be equal to the resources that

171 According to latest statistics from the CSCI three (2%) authorities now only provide services for those in critical need and 87 (58%) provide services only for those in substantial and critical need. CSCI, December 2006.
172 FACS 2003 practice guidance, Q3.3.
173 Ibid, Q3.10.

are left over once needs falling into the critical and substantial bands are met. The council's eligibility criteria comprise the critical and substantial bands and the 'moderate – greater' sub-band.

3.156   The second being to:

> . . . take a less formal approach. Instead of reclassifying the moderate band, they could ask their professionals to make judgments as to whether risks, arising from an individuals' needs, lean more to substantial than 'mainstream' moderate. In doing so the council should again regard each of the current four elements of the moderate band as having equal weight. Councils would need to monitor professionals' judgments to ensure both consistency and that they stay within budget.

3.157   The process prescribed in the English and Welsh guidance accordingly follows the following sequence:

1) the local authority ascertains the extent of the individual's 'presenting needs';
2) these presenting needs are subjected to a risk analysis (risk of harm to the user and others and risks to independence);
3) these risks are then compared to the above framework categories 'critical, substantial, medium or low';
4) if the individual's 'presenting needs' fall into one or more of the categories of risk that the local authority has decided that it will provide services to meet, then the local authority must meet those needs: such needs being termed 'eligible needs'.[174]

3.158   To assist in the second stage of the above analysis, the FACS 2002 policy guidance, states at para 40:

> As presenting needs are fully described and explored, the individual and professional should consider and evaluate the risks to independence that result from the needs both in the immediate and longer-term. This evaluation should take full account of how needs and risks might change over time and the likely outcome if help were not to be provided. The evaluation of risks should focus on the following aspects that are central to an individual's independence:
> - Autonomy and freedom to make choices.
> - Health and safety including freedom from harm, abuse and neglect, and taking wider issues of housing and community safety into account.
> - The ability to manage personal and other daily routines.
> - Involvement in family and wider community life, including leisure, hobbies, unpaid and paid work, learning, and volunteering.

3.159   Thus in each case the assessor should ask 'what are the risks to a person's (autonomy or health and safety, etc) if no services are provided'; or put another way, what would be the consequences for the individual, if services are not provided? The answer is then categorised in terms of critical, substantial, medium or low.

---

174 FACS 2002 policy guidance, para 13; UFSAMC 2002 policy guidance, para 5.14.

3.160   The key paragraphs[175] in the FACS 2002 policy guidance, which explain how the various elements of the assessment process culminate in a service provision decision, are as follows:

> 42. Eligibility for an individual is determined following assessment. As part of the assessment, information about an individual's presenting needs and related circumstances is established, and should be recorded. This information is then evaluated against the risks to his/her autonomy, health and safety, ability to manage daily routines, and involvement in family and wider community life. Councils may wish to facilitate the risk evaluation by asking their professionals to identify risks using the framework in paragraph 16 above. These identified risks to independence will then be compared to the council's eligibility criteria. Through identifying the risks that fall within the eligibility criteria, professionals should identify eligible needs.

> 43. Once eligible needs are identified, councils should meet them. However, services may also be provided to meet some presenting needs as a consequence of, or to facilitate, eligible needs being met.

3.161   The community care reforms sought to challenge procrustean attitudes towards service provision – pigeon-holing disabled people into one of a dozen or so existing services. At times, however, (as above) the FACS guidance seems to be suggesting that this can be replaced by pre-service provision pigeon-holing into only four defined categories. Local authorities should not therefore regard the FACS guidance simply as a quasi-scientific auditing exercise whereby the totality of a person's 'needs' can be so compartmentalised. Whilst it is of course desirable to attempt some objective measure of 'presenting' need, the subjective element is also important, as is the ability to stand back from the assessment process and look at the overall picture – ie balance the micro assessment process with a macro overview (see para 3.43 above). The importance of a wider perspective was identified in *R (Heffernan) v Sheffield City Council*[176] where Collins J expressed concern about the compartmentalisation of needs based upon a significant health problem – commenting that 'the existence of significant . . . health problems will not of itself result in any particular need, although the need to prevent development of such problems may'. Although this judgment has been the subject of criticism,[177] it is perhaps best viewed as a difficult fact case where the judge found the FACS assessment approach to be severely limited.

Revising eligibility criteria

3.162   The formulation of eligibility criteria is a core policy function of social services authorities. The FACS 2002 policy guidance directs that, once determined, the criteria 'should be published in local "Better Care, Higher

175 Q3.12 of the FACS 2003 practice guidance describes para 42 of the policy guidance as the paragraph 'which spells out the logic of how to go from the assessment to a determination of eligibility'.
176 [2004] EWHC 1377 (Admin) at [16]; (2004) 7 CCLR 350.
177 See eg (2004) 14 *Journal of Community Care Law* 2.

Standards" charters [see para 2.41 above], and made readily available and accessible to service users, the public more generally, and other relevant local bodies'.[178] The clear implication of this requirement is that eligibility criteria should be set for a reasonable period – presumably for the duration of the relevant Better Care, Higher Standards charter. Obviously if an unforeseen financial crisis arises (for instance of the type that resulted in the *Gloucestershire* proceedings), emergency changes to the criteria may have to be instigated,[179] but in the absence of such situations, criteria should not be the subject of frequent amendments. If this were otherwise, and criteria were changed frequently (to reflect the annual cycle of local authority economic woes[180]), service users would have no idea from day to day where their entitlements lay – effectively comparing their need against a moving target. Such a situation would give pre-eminence to short term financial issues – if not make them determinative.

Resources and the limits of eligibility criteria

3.163   In *R v Gloucestershire CC ex p Barry*[181] the House of Lords considered the legality of eligibility criteria. The case arose because the authority had its resources for community care drastically cut by an unexpected change in the size of the grant made by the Department of Health. The authority wrote to those people (about 1,500) on its lowest priority level advising them it had decided that their home care service would be reduced or withdrawn. Some of the people who were affected, who were receiving their services under CSDPA 1970 s2, sought a judicial review of the decision. Their basic argument was straightforward; their condition had not changed and so their need for services remained. How could the state of an authority's finances make their individual need no longer a 'need'? The solution adopted by the House of Lords (a majority 3:2 judgment) was that authorities can (within limits) change their eligibility criteria and if they then become more austere, they can reassess existing service users against these new criteria. If on such a reassessment it is found that they are no longer eligible for assistance, the service can be withdrawn. Accordingly it had been lawful for Gloucestershire to take into account its resources when framing its eligibility criteria, but unlawful for it to withdraw services without a prior reassessment.

3.164   The majority decision, in relation to the resource argument, has been criticised[182] and the Lords themselves have sought to restrict the impact of the decision. Subsequently, in *Re T (A Minor)*,[183] a differently constituted

178 FACS 2002 policy guidance, para 20, and UFSAMC 2002 policy guidance, para 2.17.
179 FACS 2002 policy guidance, para 19 and UFSAMC 2002 policy guidance, para 5.22.
180 As the 2003 practice guidance concedes (Q11.3), local authority budgeting 'is not a science'.
181 [1997] 2 WLR 459; (1997) 1 CCLR 40.
182 See eg B Rayment, 'Ex p. Barry in the House of Lords' (1997) 2 *Judicial Review* 158 and L Clements, 'The collapsing duty' (1997) 2 *Judicial Review* 162.
183 Sub nom *R v East Sussex CC ex p Tandy* [1998] 2 WLR 884; (1998) 1 CCLR 352.

House of Lords held that 'resource arguments' in the *ex p Barry* decision were in large measure restricted to cases concerning CSDPA 1970 s2, the statutory construction of which the Lords held to be a 'strange one'.[184] Indeed the court found certain aspects of the majority's reasoning in *ex p Barry* to be 'with respect . . . very doubtful . . .'.[185] A similar line was taken by the Court of Appeal in *R v Sefton MBC ex p Help the Aged*[186] where the Master of the Rolls felt 'compelled' to follow the reasoning of the majority in the *ex p Barry* decision, but only to a limited degree. The Court of Appeal effectively distinguished the *ex p Barry* decision, as one peculiar to the situation under CSDPA 1970 s2. This line was also adopted by Scott Baker J in *R v Bristol City Council ex p Penfold*[187] when he rejected the respondent's argument that its resource problems justified its refusal to carry out a community care assessment. It was also adopted by Dyson J in *R v Birmingham CC ex p Mohammed*[188] where he held that housing authorities were not entitled to take resources into account when deciding whether or not to approve a disabled facilities grant.

3.165 The courts have further restricted the ability of local authorities to make blanket 'shortage of resources' assertions, by requiring that in appropriate cases contentions of this nature be buttressed by cogent evidence.[189]

3.166 The effect of the *Gloucestershire* and subsequent judgments is that social services authorities are entitled to take their available resources into account, when framing their general eligibility criteria. This principle is, however, subject to four significant constraints. These can be summarised as:

1) the reassessment obligation;
2) resources shape eligibility criteria not assessments;
3) resources cannot be the sole criterion;
4) the Human Rights Act (HRA) 1998 obligation.

The reassessment obligation

3.167 As noted, local authorities are entitled (within limits) to change their eligibility criteria (for instance when they have a budgetary problem – as occurred in the *Gloucestershire* case). However when criteria are revised and made more severe, existing service users must be the subject of a full individual community care reassessment before any decision can be taken on the withdrawal of services. The logic for this requirement is two-fold: first, that the service users' circumstances may have altered since their previous assessment and so they may be eligible under the new, more austere criteria; and second, even if their needs do not satisfy the revised

---

184 (1998) 1 CCLR 352 at 359I.
185 (1998) 1 CCLR 352 at 360G.
186 [1997] 4 All ER 532; (1997) 1 CCLR 57 at 67H.
187 (1998) 1 CCLR 315.
188 [1999] 1 WLR 33; (1998) 1 CCLR 441.
189 See para 4.58 below.

criteria, the criteria are not 'determinative' and so there may be special reasons why the services should continue notwithstanding.

3.168   McCowan LJ highlighted this requirement in the first instance hearing of the *Gloucestershire* case[190] when he held:

> It would certainly have been open to the Gloucestershire County Council to reassess the individual applicants as individuals, judging their current needs and taking into account all relevant factors including the resources now available and the competing needs of other disabled persons. What they were not entitled to do, but what in my judgment they in fact did, was not to re-assess at all but simply to cut the services they were providing because their resources in turn had been cut. This amounted to treating the cut in resources as the sole factor to be taken into account, and that was, in my judgment, unlawful.

Resources shape eligibility criteria not assessments

3.169   The 1992 'Laming Letter'[191] stated as follows:

> 13. An authority may take into account the resources available when deciding how to respond to an individual's assessment. However, once the authority has indicated that a service should be provided to meet an individual's needs and the authority is under a legal obligation to provide it or arrange for its provision, then the service must be provided. It will not be possible for an authority to use budgeting difficulties as a basis for refusing to provide the service.

3.170   The legality of the Laming Letter advice on resources was in issue (and upheld) in the *Gloucestershire* case. McCowan LJ in the first instance hearing expressed the legal position thus:[192]

> . . . once they have decided that it is necessary to make the arrangements, they are under an absolute duty to make them. It is a duty owed to a specific individual and not a target duty. No term is to be implied that the local authority are obliged to comply with the duty only if they have the revenue to do so. In fact, once under that duty resources do not come into it.

3.171   In the House of Lords Lord Clyde reiterated this point in the following terms:[193]

---

190 *R v Gloucestershire CC ex p Mahfood* (1997) 1 CCLR 7, DC.
191 CI (92) 34; although the guidance was expressed as being cancelled on 1 April 1994, Sedley J accepted that 'in the sense that it gives plainly sensible advice' its content is still relevant although not mandatory – see *R v Islington LBC ex p Rixon* (1997) 1 CCLR 119, p127B.
192 *R v Gloucestershire CCex p Mahfood* [1997] 1 CCLR 7, DC; and see also *R v Kirklees MBC ex p Daykin* (1998) 1 CCLR 512 at 525D, where Collins J expressed the proposition in the following terms, 'once needs have been established, then they must be met and cost cannot be an excuse for failing to meet them. The manner in which they are met does not have to be the most expensive. The Council is perfectly entitled to look to see what cheapest way for them to meet the needs which are specified.'
193 [1997] 2 WLR 459 at 474G; (1997) 1 CCLR 40 at 54F.

The right given to the person by section 2(1) of the Act of 1970 was a right to have the arrangements made which the local authority was satisfied were necessary to meet his needs. The duty only arises if or when the local authority is so satisfied. But when it does arise then it is clear that a shortage of resources will not excuse a failure in the performance of the duty.

3.172 Lord Clyde's approach was followed by Lord Woolf MR in *R v Sefton MBC ex p Help the Aged*[194] in relation to the duties under the NAA 1948 and is expressed by the FACS 2002 policy guidance (at para 52)[195] as follows:

Councils are also reminded that they may take their resources into account when drawing up their eligibility criteria against which they assess individuals' needs, and when deciding which services will be provided to meet those needs. However, this does not mean that councils can take decisions on the basis of resources alone. Once a council has decided it is necessary to provide services to meet the eligible needs of an individual, it is under a duty to provide those services.

3.173 The principle underlying this formulation is of fundamental importance. All local authorities have limited resources and all are required to fulfil a variety of statutory obligations. If a council could assert resource shortages as a reason for not complying with a statutory duty, this would effectively result in these duties being 'collapsed into powers' (as Richard Gordon QC argued in the *Gloucestershire* case). The resolution of this problem is achieved in the *Gloucestershire* judgment by the court holding that the duty to provide community care services only arises once a service provision decision under NHSCCA 1990 s47(1)(b) has occurred. However once a local authority has decided that a person has 'eligible needs', these must be met irrespective of resource arguments. In *Re T (A Minor)*,[196] Lord Browne-Wilkinson dealt with this issue as follows:

There remains the suggestion that, given the control which central Government now exercises over local authority spending, the court cannot, or at least should not, require performance of a statutory duty by a local authority which it is unable to afford . . . My Lords I believe your Lordships should resist this approach to statutory duties.

. . . The argument is not one of insufficient resources to discharge the duty but of a preference for using the money for other purposes. To permit a local authority to avoid performing a statutory duty on the grounds that it prefers to spend the money in other ways is to downgrade a statutory duty to a discretionary power. A similar argument was put forward in the *Barry* case but dismissed by Lord Nicholls (at p470F–G) apparently on the ground that the complainant could control the failure of a local authority to carry out its statutory duty by showing that it was acting in a way which was *Wednesbury* unreasonable in failing to allocate the necessary resources. But with respect this is a very doubtful form of protection. Once the reasonableness of the actions of a local authority depends upon its decision how to apply scarce financial resources, the local authority's decision

194 [1997] 4 All ER 532; (1997) 1 CCLR 57 at 67I.
195 UFSAMC 2002 policy guidance, para 5.32.
196 [1998] 2 WLR 884; (1998) 1 CCLR 352 at 360.

becomes extremely difficult to review. The court cannot second-guess the local authority in the way in which it spends its limited resources: see also *R v Cambridge District Health Authority ex parte B* [1995] 1 WLR 898, especially at p906D–F. Parliament has chosen to impose a statutory duty, as opposed to a power, requiring the local authority to do certain things. In my judgment the courts should be slow to downgrade such duties into what are, in effect, mere discretions over which the court would have very little real control. If Parliament wishes to reduce public expenditure on meeting the needs of sick children then it is up to Parliament so to provide. It is not for the courts to adjust the order of priorities as between statutory duties and statutory discretions.

Failure to meet an assessed need

3.174   It follows that once a local authority has assessed an individual as having 'eligible needs' then any failure to provide services to meet those needs will be open to legal challenge. In *R v Wigan MBC ex p Tammadge*,[197] for example, the applicant lived with her four children, three of whom had severe learning disabilities. Over a considerable period of time she sought a larger property in order to be able to better provide for their needs. In due course a complaints panel concluded that the family needed a larger property and asked the director of social services to investigate the possibility of one being found. Following the hearing a social worker visited the applicant on 22 October and made it clear that the social services department accepted the panel's recommendations. Subsequently on 15 November a multi-disciplinary meeting was convened where it was again agreed that a larger property was needed. The matter was then referred to a meeting of senior officers and councillors. This meeting decided however that 'it was not appropriate to commit the authority to the purchase or adaptation of a larger property'. In quashing that decision, Forbes J held that by 22 September at the latest Wigan's 'own professionally qualified staff and advisors' had concluded that that her need for larger accommodation had been established.

3.175   Once the duty had arisen in this way, it was not lawful of Wigan to refuse to perform that duty because of shortage of or limits upon its financial resources.

3.176   Many cases concerning inadequate service provision arrangements have been considered by the local government ombudsman, and are cited in the following paragraphs (see also para 3.186 below and para 4.2). In some cases the ombudsman recommends not insignificant sums in compensation.[198] By way of example, in a 2005 report[199] the authority agreed to pay a total of £35,000 in compensation to a family, where it had delayed for over two years in providing adequate services for the applicant's adult son who had learning and behavioural disabilities.

197 (1998) 1 CCLR 581.
198 See para 27.57 where the ombudsman's approach to compensation is considered further.
199 Report no 04/A/10159 (Southend on Sea BC), 1 September 2005.

Waiting lists and delayed service provision decision

3.177   Rather than refusing to provide a service to meet an eligible need, councils may merely delay their decision: for instance by simple prevarication or by adopting unnecessary processes (eg continually referring the case back for further information, reports etc) or by the use of a lengthy waiting list.

3.178   In *R v South Lanarkshire Council ex p MacGregor*[200] the applicant was one of 199 people in the council's area who (due to the local authority's limited resources) were on a waiting list for a place in a nursing home, of whom 106 were in hospitals. The court (the Outer House of the Court of Session) held that the policy was unlawful, and that:

> . . . once a local authority determines that an individual's needs call for a particular provision the local authority is obliged to make that provision. In particular having decided that an individual requires the provision of a permanent place in a nursing home . . . a local authority could not . . . refuse to make such a provision simply because it did not have the necessary resources.

3.179   The local government ombudsman has made similar findings. For instance in 2001 the ombudsman upheld a complaint against Cambridgeshire that a resource-led policy that delayed the provision of residential care (once the person had been assessed as needing it) was maladministration,[201] and in a complaint against Essex[202] stated:

> The Council believes it does not have to provide a care service or funding for care immediately it has decided that it is necessary to provide the service to meet a person's assessed needs. It considers that it is acting correctly by having a waiting list on which the time a person may have to wait for resources to become available is indeterminate and depends to a significant extent on the needs and priority of other people on the waiting list and those who may come on to the list. That cannot, in my view, be correct.

Physical resource shortages

3.180   The courts have reacted differently where the shortage concerns physical or human resources as opposed to financial. In such cases the courts have generally been more sympathetic to the local authority position – provided it is taking reasonable steps to resolve the problem. Thus in *R v Lambeth LBC ex p A1 and A2*[203] the Court of Appeal held that provided the authority was making a 'sincere and determined' effort to resolve the physical resource problem, it would not intervene.

3.181   However where an authority makes no such effort, the situation will be otherwise. In *R v Islington LBC ex p Rixon*,[204] for instance, Sedley J

200 (2000) 4 CCLR 188.
201 Complaint no 99/B/04621 against Cambridgeshire, 29 January 2001.
202 Complaint no 00/B/00599 against Essex, 3 September 2001.
203 (1998) 1 CCLR 336 and see also *R v Islington BC ex p McMillan* (1997) 1 CCLR 7 at 17.
204 (1998) 1 CCLR 119 at 130F.

considered that a local authority could not assess someone as needing a service (for instance a day centre placement) and then fail to provide it, merely because none was available. This reason, alone would be insufficient:

> There are two points at which, in my judgment, the respondent local authority has fallen below the requirements of the law. The first concerns the relationship of need to availability . . . [T]he local authority has, it appears, simply taken the existing unavailability of further facilities as an insuperable obstacle to any further attempt to make provision . . .

3.182　It also follows that where the first choice service is not available, in addition to demonstrating that it is taking purposeful steps to resolve the service supply problem (including if needs be, commissioning an independent specialist to help identify and secure a suitable provider or placement[205]) the local authority will be required to make alternative interim arrangements – as the FACS 2002 policy guidance[206] states:

> Councils should provide services promptly once they have agreed to do so, but where waiting is unavoidable they should ensure alternative services are in place to meet eligible needs.

Allocation and funding panels

3.183　Many local authorities use 'panels' of various types (sometimes termed 'allocation panels', 'funding panels' or 'purchasing panels') as a means of rationing services. In effect they constitute a non-statutory 'post service provision decision' hurdle that applicants must traverse. *R v Wigan MBC ex p Tammadge*[207] (para 3.174 above) is an example: objectively the authority had made a decision that the applicant's presenting needs called for the provision of services. However, the individual officers were unable to progress this, since the local authority's procedures stated that only a panel meeting was able to make a formal decision on resource allocation; a meeting at which the assessing social worker had little or no role. This is not untypical of the procedures adopted by many local authorities. In response to judicial and ombudsmen doubts concerning the legality of these panels, some authorities have endeavoured to project these panels as 'quality control' mechanisms – namely to ensure that their social workers have completed the assessment correctly.[208] Not infrequently the panel will refer a funding application back for further analysis or paperwork to be completed. The effect of this is to create delay, which arguably is the whole point of the exercise: the protection of resources by (among other

---

205 Complaint no 02/B/10226: against Cambridgeshire, 6 July 2004.
206 Para 53; UFSAMC 2002 policy guidance, para 5.35.
207 (1998) 1 CCLR 581.
208 Many of those authorities that suggest their panels are quality control mechanisms commonly have difficulty in sustaining this argument, when their council's minutes are reviewed. Not unusually it can be shown that the panel was created as a response to a budgetary problem – rather than as a response to a concern about the quality of social workers' assessments. Indeed if this were the problem one would assume that the logical response would be to improve the quality of their training.

things) deferring service provision. Occasionally however, as in *R v South Lanarkshire Council ex p MacGregor*,[209] the panel is more blatant: in that case it openly restricted access to residential care solely on the basis of the authority's budget.

3.184 Commenting upon this 'unfortunately commonplace' and 'unlawful practice' in evidence to the Joint Committee on Human Rights,[210] Help the Aged explained that it persisted because:

> Individual cases are settled to avoid threatened litigation, but the widespread use of funding panels to ration care continues. Individuals then find themselves unable to access essential services they have been assessed as needing, thus forcing them to live in conditions which, in some cases, may be sufficiently severe as to constitute inhuman and degrading treatment within the meaning of Article 3 and potentially put their lives at risk. There is, as far as we know, no monitoring of how many people die in their homes or following emergency admission to hospital because they have been denied a service they were assessed as needing.

3.185 Panels create a fault line between the data collection phase of the assessment process and the service provision decision. In so doing they reduce a person's needs to the bare words of the assessment paperwork or to scores on a spreadsheet: they sideline (or remove completely) the assessing social worker from the decision making process and with him or her the element of discretion that is essential to any informed decision on such personal questions as the extent of human need. In effect they represent the end game in Michael Lipsky's analysis of street-level bureaucracy (see para 3.3 above), where without the knowledge of the disabled person the 'human judgment that cannot be programmed and for which machines cannot substitute' is in fact removed from the process.

3.186 The local government ombudsmen have considered many complaints concerning panel decisions. A frequent scenario concerns disabled people with complex needs which require potentially expensive care packages and in relation to which a social worker will have undertaken considerable research and recommended a particular care plan. The care plan is then considered by a panel and rejected – essentially the social worker being required to trim the assessment of need to fit the budget (to paraphrase Sedley J[211]) – even though no suitable alternative exists.

3.187 A 2005 ombudsman's report[212] is illustrative in this respect. It concerned the placement of a learning disabled adult in a series of inappropriate care homes. His social worker had undertaken a detailed assessment of needs and identified a suitable placement 'after a long, careful process over many months'. However her plan was rejected by the council's Care Purchasing Panel relying on advice from an acting

---

209 (2001) 4 CCLR 188.
210 Memorandum from Help the Aged contained in the Appendices to the Sixth Report of the Joint Committee on Human Rights, *The Case for a Human Rights Commission*, 19 March 2003. Report together with Proceedings of the Committee HL 67-I; HC 489-I.
211 Sedley J referred to 'trimming the assessment of need to fit available provision' in *R v Islington LBC ex p Rixon* (1996) 1 CCLR 119 at 129B.
212 Complaint no 04/A/10159 against Southend on Sea BC, 1 September 2005.

manager who 'barely knew' the service user (he had observed him at most on three occasions in a day centre). The alternative care package proposed proved to be unsuitable and ultimately – once the ombudsman had become involved – a suitable placement was secured. In the ombudsman's opinion:

> Having correctly prepared a detailed assessment in accordance with the statutory guidance, it was wrong for the Council to dismiss all the information gathered in that process, and make a decision on the basis of [the acting manager's] assurance. The decision flew in the face of the assessment.

3.188   A similar finding occurred in another 2005 ombudsman's report.[213] It concerned a teenager whose placement in a specialist residential school became unsustainable due to his autism, severe learning disabilities and complex challenging behaviour. The local authority had a provisional indication from a care provider that an appropriate residential place would become available and accordingly decided that, pending this, he should move back with his parents with a substantial package of support. The social worker identified a suitable home support package – costing about £4,600 per week – but this was vetoed by her area manager because it was 'too expensive'. An alternative support arrangement was put in place (costing £2,000 per week) but this foundered as did the provisional place with the residential care provider. Accordingly the parents were left holding the fort without adequate day to day support and no immediate hope of a stable residential placement. The ombudsman found maladministration. In his opinion (para 65):

> The only provision identified at the outset was that provided by a specialist agency. That was rejected because it was expensive but nothing suitable was put in its stead. I do not consider that this was proper. The Council had a duty to meet [the disabled person's] needs. If there were two options available that could meet his needs, the Council could take resources into account when deciding which to use. But the option chosen by the Council did not meet his needs. There was another option available which might have met them (we will never know for sure), and the Council was at fault in refusing to consider that option because of the expense.

3.189   Even where a panel accepts that a specific care plan is required, it not infrequently defers funding, essentially to address the authority's cash flow demands (as occurred in *R v South Lanarkshire Council ex p MacGregor*[214]). A 2001 complaint against Essex[215] concerned such a practice. A council social worker had assessed the complainant's mother as in need of residential care and prepared a care plan naming an appropriate care home. This came before the 'purchasing panel' which accepted the plan, but decided that the need was not of sufficient priority to justify immediate funding and so her name was placed on a waiting list. The local

213 Complaint nos 04/A/00818 and 04/A/00819 against Surrey CC, 29 September 2005 – the ombudsman recommended a total of £60,000 compensation in this case.
214 (2001) 4 CCLR 188 – see para 3.178 above.
215 Complaint no 00/B/00599, 3 September 2001.

government ombudsman considered that this amounted to maladministration; that there was 'no justification for the council's use of a waiting list for funding care which is otherwise available and which only comes into operation *after* the council has decided that it will provide a service to meet particular needs'.

3.190 A similar process was described in a 2003 complaint against East Sussex[216] which concerned a young man with learning disabilities due to leave college. His parents wanted him to move to an independent residential provider for his post college needs (as many of his co-pupils were moving to this provider). The local authority assessed his needs and concluded that (1) this provider would meet his needs and (2) there was no suitable alternative local provision available. The provider indicated that the council should make a speedy decision as other students were also seeking the place identified. The council's internal policies however required that the placement be approved by a series of funding panels which met throughout the year. The funding panel initially refused funding and placed the request on a 'service pending list'. As a consequence the placement ceased to be available and although the council made temporary arrangements, the young man's placement in the independent facility was delayed by two years. In finding maladministration (and recommending over £30,000 compensation) the ombudsman held:

> ... clearly the council's Social Services budget is under heavy pressure ... however, the council knew of [the disabled person's] needs, has accepted its duty to fund the provision and was happy that the provision offered by [the independent provider] was suitable. Therefore it was unacceptable for it not to have made specific budgetary provision that would enable it to respond more quickly once a placement was offered.

3.191 Whilst the widespread use by local authorities of funding panels has attracted criticism, this is not to say that all 'panels' are unlawful. There is of course nothing objectionable about a panel of social care experts being called upon to make a decision concerning the necessary elements of a complex care package (where of course it has the necessary expertise to discharge such a role). Thus in *R (Rodriguez-Bannister) v Somerset Partnership NHS and Social Care Trust*[217] the court found not unreasonable the role of a panel whose primary task was to determine the kind of accommodation that was required, 'whether residential, supported living or other', and not to make recommendations about the necessary levels of support in any particular setting.

---

216 Complaint no 00/B/18600 against East Sussex CC, 29 January 2003: and see also the not dissimilar report on complaint no 02/C/17068 against Bolton MBC, November 2004 where the ombudsman found that the service user was not in any way properly prepared for his return to the community on leaving school and that 'there is overwhelming evidence that' the council's reluctance to fund the parents' preferred option was because of the impact this would have 'on the Social Services agency budget' (see also para 24.67 below).
217 [2003] EWHC 2184 (Admin); (2004) 7 CCLR 385.

Resources cannot be the sole criterion

3.192   Although councils are entitled to take into account the extent of their available resources when they frame their eligibility criteria, they cannot make resource availability the sole criterion: resource availability alone cannot be 'determinative'. In many situations it appears that this is precisely what allocation or funding panels do (see para 3.183 above). Likewise the application by an authority of a rigid 'costs ceiling' would have the same effect (see para 4.65 below).

3.193   In the *Gloucestershire* decision Hirst LJ (in the Court of Appeal) held that resources were 'no more than one factor in an overall assessment, where no doubt the objective needs of the individual disabled person will always be the paramount consideration'.[218] In the first instance decision McCowan LJ – when quashing the decision of the county council (to withdraw services without reassessment) – stated that this 'amounted to treating the cut in resources as the sole factor to be taken into account, and that was, in my judgment, unlawful'.[219]

The Human Rights Act 1998 obligation[220]

3.194   There is a point at which resource availability ceases to be a legitimate reason for refusing to provide services; or, put another way, there is a level of austerity beyond which eligibility criteria cannot venture. This aspect of the argument was articulated by McCowan LJ in the first instance *Gloucestershire* judgment,[221] when he observed:

> I should stress, however, that there will, in my judgment, be situations where a reasonable authority could only conclude that some arrangements were necessary to meet the needs of a particular disabled person and in which they could not reasonably conclude that a lack of resources provided an answer. Certain persons would be at severe physical risk if they were unable to have some practical assistance in their homes. In those situations, I cannot conceive that an authority would be held to have acted reasonably if they used shortage of resources as a reason for not being satisfied that some arrangement should be made to meet those persons' needs.

3.195   The *Gloucestershire* proceedings took place prior to the enactment of the Human Rights Act (HRA) 1998; using the language of the European Convention on Human Rights (the 'Convention') McCowan LJ was, in effect, stating that limited resources could not be used as a reason for allowing a violation of article 3 to take place. There can be little doubt that domestic law recognises a core set of 'positive' justiciable, non-resource dependent rights – the uncertainty relates to their scope. As Lord Hoffman has commented:[222]

218 *R v Gloucestershire CC ex p Barry* [1996] 4 All ER 421; (1997) 1 CCLR 19 at 31G.
219 *R v Gloucestershire CC ex p Mahfood* (1997) 1 CCLR 7 at 16I, DC.
220 For a brief review of the relevant provisions of the European Convention on Human Rights see para 27.207.
221 *R v Gloucestershire CC ex p Mahfood* (1997) 1 CCLR 7, DC.
222 L Hoffman, *The 'Separation of Powers'*, Annual Commercial Bar Lecture, COMBAR, 2001, unpublished transcript.

Human rights probably include not only freedom from certain forms of state interference but also a positive obligation upon the State to provide every citizen with certain basic necessities which he requires in order to be able to function as a human being.

3.196   Arguably, therefore, there is a point at which simple decisions about the provision of community care services cross over from the realm of socio-economic rights and into the domain of those civil and political rights protected by the Convention. Although this may be an overly simplistic reading of these two categories of rights, it nevertheless serves as a useful device for considering the 'austerity' limits of eligibility criteria.

3.197   In relation to social care services, it is perhaps self evident that services could not be denied (on resource grounds) if the consequence were that the disabled person's life was at risk, or that significant health problems would develop or that there was a risk of serious abuse or neglect occurring. In effect, therefore, the core set of social care rights are at least those detailed in the 'critical' category of the prescribed eligibility framework (see para 3.148 above); these being risks associated with articles 2 and 3 of the Convention.

3.198   The same could be argued in relation to article 5. *R v Manchester City Council ex p Stennett*,[223] for instance, concerned the right of detained patients to 'free' aftercare services under Mental Health Act 1983 s117. The court accepted that in many cases patients were only discharged from their detention in psychiatric wards if they 'agreed' to move into a specialist care home. It was argued, therefore, that to require payment for this service would, in effect, be requiring a patient to pay for his or her freedom. Lord Steyn found such a proposition compelling, stating:

> It can hardly be said that the mentally ill patient freely chooses such accommodation. Charging them in these circumstances may be surprising . . . If the argument of the authorities is accepted that there is a power to charge these patients such a view of the law would not be testimony to our society attaching a high value to the need to care after the exceptionally vulnerable.

3.199   It follows that a resource argument alone will seldom dispose of a claim to respect for a Convention right. In relation to the articles 2, 3 and 5 rights, financial resource arguments will rarely if ever be relevant. Even in relation to qualified rights, such as article 8, where the state can legitimately play the resource card, it cannot expect it to trump all others – particularly where the consequences of inaction for the applicant are serious. We separately discuss at para 4.43 below the extent to which the resource card can be played in relation to the independent living obligation and the provision of 'minimum' services – the 'dignity' principle.

223 [2002] UKHL 34; [2002] 3 WLR 584; (2002) 5 CCLR 500.

The critical/substantial bands

3.200   The FACS guidance advises that local authorities are entitled (subject to being 'observant of [their] statutory duties under community care legislation'[224]) to restrict community care services to the critical band of need (see para 3.148 above). Since a few authorities have restricted their services to those in the critical band (and the evidence suggests an increasing number are considering such a move[225]) it is legitimate to consider the legality of such a policy in the context of the HRA 1998.

3.201   Any analysis of this question must first acknowledge the latitude provided by some of the critical band descriptors. Local authorities may, for instance, vary widely in how they interpret:

- significant health problems;
- little or no choice and control over vital aspects of the immediate environment;
- serious abuse or neglect;
- an inability to carry out vital personal care or domestic routines.

3.202   However, some of the criteria in the 'substantial' band give a steer as to the meaning of the 'critical' band descriptions, and suggest that the bar to be crossed in order to register a critical need is a high one. For instance abuse or neglect (apart from when it is 'serious') only scores a substantial rating – as does a person who is unable 'to carry out the majority of [his or her] personal care or domestic routines' or to sustain 'the majority of [his or her] social support systems and relationships'. Such an analysis suggests that the Department of Health considers it acceptable to deny support to people who are being abused and neglected, and who are unable to attend to most of their personal care needs. Such a criticism is less easily levied against the Welsh Assembly guidance, which (for instance) requires all abuse (not merely 'serious abuse) to be recorded as 'critical'. The acceptance of 'non-serious' abuse flies in the face of SCIE guidance that requires commissioners of services to have a 'a zero tolerance of all forms of abuse'.[226]

3.203   Although the courts have not been called upon to adjudicate upon the acceptability of a council only catering for 'critical needs', consideration of the general case law would tend to suggest that they might look unfavourably on the English policy. In *R (A and B, X and Y) v East Sussex*

---

224 By this it is presumably meant (among other things) that authorities cannot adopt a rigid policy of only meeting need that has been assessed as 'critical' since the eligibility criteria are merely 'guidance' and must therefore admit exceptions – and that any policy that failed to make this point clear could amount to a fettering of its duties under the community care legislation.

225 The CSCI noted in 2006 that 'the thresholds for accessing services are high'; that nearly two thirds of councils' threshold for services was set at 'substantial' and that a number of these councils are expecting to raise their eligibility thresholds: CSCI, *Performance Ratings for Adults' Social Services (England)*, 2006, p1 – accessible at http://www.csci.org.uk/PDF/star_ratings_report_2006.pdf.

226 SCIE, *Dignity in care: Adults' Services Practice Guide 09*, 2006, p8, accessible at http://www.scie.org.uk/publications/practiceguides/practiceguide09/files/pg09.pdf.

CC[227] Munby J dwelt at length on the 'core value' of 'human dignity' as a component of articles 3 and 8 of the Convention. In his opinion 'thoughtless, uncaring and uncharitable' behaviour[228] was a relevant factor in assessing the threshold at which action (or inaction) engaged article 3. His judgment suggests that the threshold is not an excessively high one when the basic care and support needs of disabled people are being considered. In assessing whether article 3 is engaged he considered it relevant to consider (amongst other things) 'the duration of the [lack of suitable care], its physical and mental effects . . . the sex, age and state of health of the victim'.[229]

3.204   In *R (Bernard) v Enfield LBC*[230] Sullivan J accepted that not every breach of a community care obligation would result in a breach of the Convention. However, in view of the vulnerability of the client group, he considered that article 8 obliged councils to take positive measures 'to enable them to enjoy, so far as possible, a normal private and family life'. In the particular case he held that the council's failure to provide services had left the applicant 'housebound, confined to a shower chair for most of the day, [and] lacking privacy in the most undignified of circumstances'. It had effectively isolated her and made her a 'burden, wholly dependent upon the rest of her family' and in his opinion unquestionably violated article 8.

> An ordinary interpretation of Mrs Bernard's needs suggests that they are more likely to fall into the 'substantial' band' than the 'critical'. If correct, this means that either the critical band descriptors are too severe, or that the FACS guidance on this issue is mistaken.

3.205   It seems therefore that there is a disparity between the guidance issued by the Department of Health and the approach taken by the courts on this question. The disparity is not solely in the dimension of 'severity' although the critical band described by the guidance appears well above the level of severity generally identified by the courts (and ombudsman – see below) to trigger the service provision obligation. The disparity is also to be found in the language used by the courts and ombudsmen – in that they place reliance upon the multi dimensional concept of 'human dignity', a phrase that does not appear in the FACS eligibility criteria scale. Human dignity addresses not only the question of whether a need should be provided for (eg to avoid neglect or abuse) but also the way that need should be met, and this question is further explored at para 4.69 below.

Family separation and 'locational' need

3.206   The assessment and care planning process may result in the separation of couples and/or other family members. In evidence to the Joint Committee on Human Rights, Help the Aged referred to this situation in the following terms:

227 [2003] EWHC 167; (2003) 6 CCLR 194 at [88].
228 Ibid at [89].
229 Here citing from the judgment of the European Court of Human Rights in *Price v UK* (2001) 34 EHRR 1285 at [24].
230 [2002] EWHC 2282 (Admin); (2002) 5 CCLR 577 at [32].

It is not uncommon for older couples to be separated against their will when the local authority says that it cannot provide sufficient care to one of them to enable them to continue living at home, and he or she must instead go into residential care . . . This flagrant disregard for the Article 8 rights of older people indicates the lack of any systematic, conscious application of human rights in this area and underlines the need for a change in the culture of care planning.[231]

3.207   In what circumstances is it lawful for a local authority to conclude a care plan that has or would have the effect of separating close family members?

3.208   Before any such care plan can be proposed, an assessment must have been undertaken which considered (amongst other things) the person's important relationships. The various presenting needs would then have been graded against the four eligibility categories. Both the English and Welsh criteria describe as 'critical' a situation where 'vital social support systems and relationships cannot or will not be sustained'. An ordinary interpretation of the word 'vital'[232] in this context would encompass the preservation of a marriage or common law relationship. The same may also be true for other relationships – with the factual context of each such case being crucial. Any assessment of these matters would have to ensure that full regard was had to the positive obligation under article 8[233] of the Convention to have respect for the private and family life of the person being assessed as well as those affected by any separation. The argument may have an added dimension in relation to married partners, since article 12 most probably enshrines a right to cohabit.[234]

3.209   By way of example, if an elderly husband has a progressive condition that means it is no longer possible for him to be cared for in his home, it may be necessary for the local authority to secure a nursing home placement for him. This in itself would not amount to a violation of article 8 – in the sense that the authority is not actually interfering with the relationship (ie by forcibly removing the husband from the home). Whether the placement discharges the authority's positive obligations will depend upon the proportionality of the response. Assuming that it is not feasible for him to remain at home with support, the assessment must

---

231 Memorandum from Help the Aged contained in the Appendices to the Sixth Report of the Joint Committee on Human Rights, *The Case for a Human Rights Commission*, 19 March 2003. Report together with Proceedings of the Committee HL 67-I; HC 489-I.

232 Vital 'means that without help, individuals are at great risk of *either* losing their independence, possibly necessitating admission to institutional care *or* making very little, damaging or inappropriate contributions to family and wider community life with serious consequences for the individual and others . . . [however] what may be "vital" to one individual may not be "vital" to another' (Q3.6 of the FACS 2003 practice guidance).

233 Although there appear to be no directly relevant Strasbourg judgments, *Kutzner v Germany* (2002) 35 EHRR 35 at [76] stressed the positive duty to take measures to facilitate family reunification, and *Tuquabo-Tekle v Netherlands* [2006] 1 FLR 798 at [42] accepted that in such cases the boundaries between the state's positive and negative obligations under article 8 do not lend themselves to precise definition.

234 See eg *Re Jennifer Connor* [2004] NICA 45 at [23], accessible at http://www.bailii.org/nie/cases/NICA/2004/45.html.

address whether there is a need for the husband and wife to see each other regularly – and in normal circumstances the conclusion would be that this is a 'critical' need. In determining what is an acceptable distance between the wife's home and the care home placement, regard will have to be paid to her mobility and access to transport. If there is no suitable care home within easy reach of the wife, the local authority may have to make arrangements for the wife's transport. If however a suitable care home is available close by, but above the local authority's normal fees ceiling, this home may have to be funded, without top up, since the authority is merely meeting the disabled person's assessed need (and not paying for something more than is required – see para 7.98).

3.210   The importance of locational factors is not confined to assessments of married or cohabiting persons. In *R v Sutton LBC ex p Tucker*[235] the Rubella impaired applicant's fundamental relationships were with her close family who lived in London. The local authority proposed a care home placement in Birmingham, but the family, clinicians and other experts considered that this would not be viable since she needed to be close to her family. In this case, location was therefore an assessed need and had to be met. On occasions a local authority may be unable to meet such a need, not because of resource difficulties (which would not be an acceptable reason – see para 3.172) but because there is no suitable facility in the area. In such cases, the authority will have to show that it is taking purposeful steps to address this problem and doing its best in the meantime to meet the person's needs (see para 3.182).

The written record of the assessment

3.211   There is no statutory requirement that assessments be recorded in writing, although in practice all social services authorities have pro forma assessment forms. These are generally completed in manuscript and then keyed into the authority's IT system. The FACS 2002 policy guidance is silent on the right of service users to a copy of their assessments, although it states that service users should receive a copy of their care plan.[236] The 1991 practice guidance however states (at para 3.54) that a 'copy of the assessment of needs should normally be shared with the potential service user, any representative of that user and all other people who have agreed to provide a service. Except where no intervention is deemed necessary, this record will normally be combined with a written care plan.'[237] The SAP guidance[238] is specific in this respect, stating:

> All key decisions and issues relating to assessment, eligibility and service provision should be put in writing, or other appropriate formats, and a copy

235 (1998) 1 CCLR 251.
236 Para 49; UFSAMC 2002 policy guidance, para 2.49.
237 See also para 17.18 which concerns the obligation to ensure the care plan is copied to the care home.
238 SAP 2003 policy guidance Annex E p19.

given to the older person. For older people who go on to receive services, these decisions and issues will be summarised in their care plan or statement of service delivery.

3.212   Where a service user has difficulty obtaining a copy of his or her assessment and/or care plan, a formal request can be made under the Data Protection Act 1998 (see para 0.00), although in practice it will generally be more effective to make a formal complaint.

Disputed service provision decisions

3.213   The 1990 community care reforms made social services the 'gate keepers' of the community care regime: ultimately it is the local authority that decides what a person's 'eligible needs' are and what they are not. Judges are not expert in the practice of social work and so must defer to their professional expertise – even when the decisions they reach appear harsh.

3.214   As has been noted above (see para 3.5), social workers are subjected to intense scrutiny – primarily to ensure that their decisions do not place undue pressure on local authority budgets, notwithstanding the rhetoric that 'counsels against trimming the assessment of need to fit available provision'.[239] On one level this is entirely reasonable, and on another it can lead to assessments being 'service' or 'budget' driven – in effect social workers being so constrained by organisational pressures that they do not assess individuals as needing services which are not available or which might exceed the available budget.

3.215   Given that judicial review is a blunt legal instrument and that courts are seldom prepared to consider a service provision decision '*Wednesbury*'[240] unreasonable[241] (see para 27.172 below), the question arises as to how errant authorities can be called to account – particularly if their complaints panels are insufficiently robust or well informed to address such problems.

3.216   The evidence suggests that the courts and ombudsmen adopt a variety of public law mechanisms to find fault with the decision-making process when they apprehend an improbably austere service provision decision. In general, the harsher the apparent service provision decision, the greater the courts/ombudsmen's insistence on 'due process' – particularly on compliance with policy and practice guidance. This approach is sometimes referred to as the anxious scrutiny test[242] (see para 27.173) – the more a decision engages fundamental rights, the 'more anxiously' will the courts scrutinise the procedure by which it was reached.

---

239 *R v Islington LBC ex p Rixon* (1996) 1 CCLR 119, p129B per Sedley J.
240 *Associated Provincial Picture Houses v Wednesbury Corporation* [1948] 1 KB 223, CA.
241 Although not invariably – see eg *R v Sutton LBC ex p Tucker* (1998) 1 CCLR 251, p275J.
242 See eg *R v Ministry of Defence ex p Smith* [1996] QB 517, p554.

3.217   By way of example, *R v Birmingham CC ex p Killigrew*[243] concerned an applicant with severe disabilities whose condition (multiple sclerosis) was deteriorating. Her husband and main carer was also a disabled person. At the end of 1997 she was assessed as requiring 12 hours' continuous care each day seven days a week. The council undertook a manual handling assessment in 1998 and decided that she required two care assistants to move her, rather than the one that had previously done this. A community care reassessment then occurred, as a result of which the council proposed to reduce the day care from 12 to 3.5 hours. Hooper J held that no such reduction could occur without compliance with the 1990 policy guidance which in his view required (1) detailed reasons as to why 12 hours were no longer required and (2) up-to-date medical evidence – which the local authority had failed to obtain (1990 policy guidance, paras 3.47 onwards).

3.218   The local government ombudsman has adopted a similar approach to what appear to be 'resource led' reassessments. A 2001 complaint[244] concerned what appeared to be a particularly harsh decision. He held that although the final decision on what was the appropriate care plan lay with social services, in the specific case any proposed reductions should be communicated to the other professionals that were involved (ie physiotherapists, voluntary organisations that provided volunteers, occupational therapists, district nurses etc) and their views on its suitability obtained, before deciding on its adoption.

3.219   Although the decision in *R v Ealing LBC ex p C*[245] involved an assessment under the CA 1989 (see chapter 24), the principles in issue are identical. The case concerned a profoundly disabled nine-year-old boy who lived with his mother and 15-year-old brother in a two bedroomed council flat. An assessment in 1998 stated that 'the family would benefit from provision for aids and adaptations. Transfer to a larger property.' The council however asserted that the property was suitable if sufficient adaptations/aids were provided.

3.220   The High Court (Scott-Baker J) considered the decision harsh as it meant that the mother was sharing a bed with the child who was incontinent and whose sleep was very disturbed; nevertheless applying the classic *Wednesbury* formulation he did not feel that the decision was one which 'no reasonable authority' could have reached. His judgment was overruled by the Court of Appeal, although the logic of its decision is difficult to follow: the local authority had failed 'to ask itself the right question, and take reasonable steps to acquaint itself with the relevant information to enable it to answer it correctly'. It could be argued that the reality of this case is that the Court of Appeal conjured up 'due process' reasons to quash what it considered an excessively harsh decision.

243 (2000) 3 CCLR 109: see also, eg, *R v Lambeth LBC ex p K* (2000) 3 CCLR 141 where the court quashed a budget driven harsh service provision decision on the basis that the council had not followed the 1990 policy guidance and had confused 'needs' and 'services'.
244 Complaint no 99/A/00988 against Southwark, 12 March 2001.
245 (2000) 3 CCLR 122.

3.221   Where a local authority seeks to defend what appears to be a harsh or inequitable decision, the reasons it gives for the decision, as well as the process, will scrutinised. In *R (Goldsmith) v Wandsworth LBC*[246] the court found it almost impossible to understand who in the authority had made the various decisions in issue or how they had been reached. It concluded that virtually every aspect of the council's decision making process was flawed – including its failure to share information with the applicant's daughter, its denial of her right to attend a hearing and make submissions, its failure to keep minutes at that hearing and its mistaken belief as to the evidential value of a medical opinion.

Reassessment and reviews

3.222   Councils have a general public law duty to ensure that the community care needs of service users are kept under review. As the local government ombudsman has observed:

> As an individual's need for community care services will vary over time, the duties placed on councils are continuous. Councils should therefore provide for the review of assessments and service delivery decisions.[247]

3.223   This obligation is underpinned by the FACS 2002 policy guidance[248] which requires that:

> There should be an initial review within three months of help first being provided or major changes made to current services. Thereafter, reviews should be scheduled at least annually or more often if individuals' circumstances appear to warrant it. Reviews may be considered on request from service users, providers of services and other appropriate individuals or agencies.

3.224   Reviews should:[249]

- establish how far the services provided have achieved the outcomes set out in the care plan;
- reassess the needs and circumstances of individual service users;
- help determine individuals' continued eligibility for support;
- confirm or amend the current care plan, or lead to closure;
- comment on the effectiveness of direct payments, where appropriate.

3.225   Reviews should (except in exceptional circumstances) consist of a face to face meeting between the user and 'council professional responsible for the review'[250] and should generally involve all relevant parties: for instance,

---

246 [2004] EWCA Civ 1170; (2004) 7 CCLR 472.
247 Complaint no 02/B/10226 against Cambridgeshire CC, July 6 2004.
248 FACS 2002 policy guidance, para 60; UFSAMC 2002 policy guidance, paras 2.54 onwards.
249 FACS 2002 policy guidance, paras 47–67; UFSAMC 2002 policy guidance, paras 2.44–2.51.
250 That is an officer of the authority that commissions and purchases the care services – but not in general an officer actually responsible for the provision of the services (FACS 2002 policy guidance, para 61).

carers; the service user's advocate; the purchasers and the providers of the care services. The outcome of reviews should be recorded in writing and care plans updated accordingly.[251]

3.226   The local government ombudsman has stressed the importance of reviews being 'proactive and frequent' and that it will be maladministration to stick rigidly to a predetermined review cycle when changed circumstances demand an earlier review.[252] She has also stressed the need for councils to devote 'adequate resources' to this function to ensure that they adequately monitor contract performance.[253]

3.227   Councils should only withdraw services after a review if satisfied that the person's needs will not significantly worsen or increase in the foreseeable future for the lack of help (and this includes involvement in employment, training and education, and parenting responsibilities). In making such decisions, councils should not make assumptions about the capacity of family members or close friends to offer support. Service users must have such decisions fully explained to them – and interpreters, translators, advocates and supporters will be required in this process where appropriate. All decisions must be in writing and individuals must be advised of their right to use the complaints procedures.[254] A failure to inform carers by letter of a material change to a service user's care plan will generally constitute maladministration.[255]

3.228   Where a local authority decides to reduce significantly the level of services provided as a result of a reassessment, it must provide rational and cogent reasons for this alteration[256] and before making any reduction it must provide the service user with an opportunity for the decision to be reviewed.[257] The ombudsman has commented that a social services justification for the withdrawal of services – namely the 'need to prioritise' – suggested that 'a comparative judgment was being made rather than a consideration of whether the individual's need had changed'.[258]

3.229   Where a local authority settles a complaint by agreeing to reassess, the reassessment should do more than 'go through the motions'. In *Banks v Secretary of State for the Environment*[259] Sullivan J gave guidance on what such a review should entail, advising that one of the functions of a review

---

251 FACS 2002 policy guidance, para 61.
252 Complaint no 05/A/00880 against Essex CC, 16 January 2006, para 56 and see also complaint no 02/B/10226 against Cambridgeshire CC, 6 July 2004.
253 Complaint no 03/C/17141 against Blackpool BC, 23 February 2006 and see also complaint no 01/B/00305 against Cambridgeshire CC, 9 July 2002 complaint no 05/A/00880 against Essex CC, 16 January 2006 and complaint no 05/C/6420 against Sheffield City Council, 20 February 2007.
254 FACS 2002 policy guidance, para 61.
255 Complaint no 02/B/03622 against Harrow LBC, 22 June 2004.
256 *R (LB) v Newham LBC* [2004] EWHC 2503.
257 Complaint nos 02/C/14235, 02/C/15396, 02/C/15397 & 02/C/15503 against Derbyshire CC, 24 June 2004.
258 Complaint nos 02/C/14235, 02/C/15396, 02/C/15397 & 02/C/15503 against Derbyshire CC, 24 June 2004 reported at p99 of Local Government Ombudsman Digest of Cases 2004/05.
259 [2004] EWHC 416 (Admin) a non-community care case.

procedure must be to 'give some degree of assurance' that there will be a genuine reconsideration: and that in order to dispel user suspicion, it should as far as possible involve review by another (and preferably more senior) official who has not been connected with the decision under review or given an opportunity to comment upon it.

CHAPTER 4

The care planning process and the delivery of services

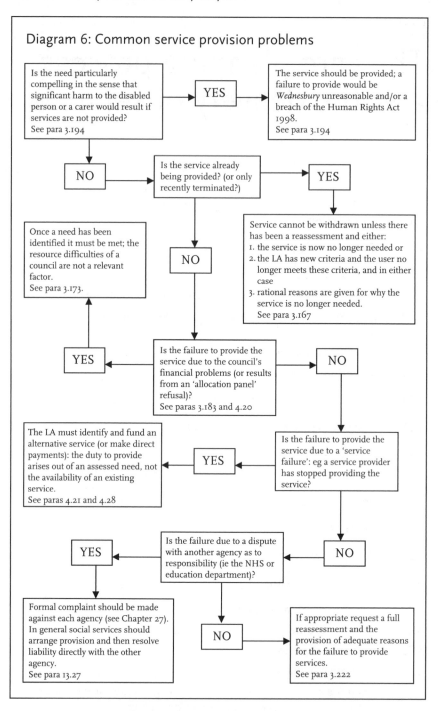

Diagram 6: Common service provision problems

Is the need particularly compelling in the sense that significant harm to the disabled person or a carer would result if services are not provided?
See para 3.194

YES → The service should be provided; a failure to provide would be *Wednesbury* unreasonable and/or a breach of the Human Rights Act 1998.
See para 3.194

NO

Is the service already being provided? (or only recently terminated?)

YES → Service cannot be withdrawn unless there has been a reassessment and either:
1. the service is now no longer needed or
2. the LA has new criteria and the user no longer meets these criteria, and in either case
3. rational reasons are given for why the service is no longer needed.
See para 3.167

NO

Once a need has been identified it must be met; the resource difficulties of a council are not a relevant factor.
See para 3.173.

YES ← Is the failure to provide the service due to the council's financial problems (or results from an 'allocation panel' refusal)?
See paras 3.183 and 4.20 → **NO**

The LA must identify and fund an alternative service (or make direct payments): the duty to provide arises out of an assessed need, not the availability of an existing service.
See paras 4.21 and 4.28

YES ← Is the failure to provide the service due to a 'service failure': eg a service provider has stopped providing the service?

NO

YES ← Is the failure due to a dispute with another agency as to responsibility (ie the NHS or education department)? ← **NO**

Formal complaint should be made against each agency (see Chapter 27). In general social services should arrange provision and then resolve liability directly with the other agency.
See para 13.27

NO → If appropriate request a full reassessment and the provision of adequate reasons for the failure to provide services.
See para 3.222

Introduction

4.1 Once an authority has made a decision under National Health Service and Community Care Act (NHSCCA) 1990 s47(1)(b) that a person's presenting needs are such that community care services are called for, then the authority must make arrangements for those services to be provided. This process is generally referred to as 'care planning'. Good practice requires that the authority specify in a written care plan what services the individual is entitled to receive and all other salient information connected with the delivery of those services. Likewise where a direct payment (see chapter 12) or individual budget (see para 12.72) is to be the outcome of the assessment, the authority should provide a statement specifying the amount of the direct payment or the resources that will be allocated, and how that figure has been calculated.

4.2 Although there is no statutory reference to care plans, they are essential to the community care process and the subject of detailed policy and practice guidance. This guidance addresses two key issues: (1) the format and content of care plans and (2) the principles and aims that they should embody – a division that is also adopted in this chapter, which initially considers the format and content of care plans and then their underpinning principles and aims.

4.3 The problems caused by the excessive volume of guidance concerning the assessment process (see para 3.5) are also evident in relation to the final care planning phase. Practitioners must adhere to the 1990 policy guidance (even though this is no longer in print) as well as the 2002 FACS policy guidance: they must then follow, so far as is reasonable, the FACS practice guidance and the original 1991 practice guidance as well as the condition specific practice guidance that relates to older people and/or people with learning difficulties and/or people with mental health problems (see page 53 above). In this section we attempt to provide a coherent overview of the care planning phase and selectively cite this myriad guidance.

Care plan – format and content

4.4 The original 1990 policy guidance[1] requires that:

> Once needs have been assessed, the services to be provided or arranged and the objectives of any intervention should be agreed in the form of a care plan (at para 3.24).

and that:

> Decisions on service provision should include clear agreement about what is going to be done, by whom and by when, with clearly identified points of access to each of the relevant agencies for the service user, carers and for the care manager (at para 3.26).

---

1   *Community Care in the Next Decade and Beyond: policy guidance*, HMSO, 1990.

4.5   The 2002 Fair Access to Care (FACS) policy guidance (at para 47) provides greater detail, requiring care plans to be structured in such a way that they address the following six key requirements:

The written record of the care plan should include as a minimum:

- A note of the eligible needs and associated risks.
- The preferred outcomes of service provision.
- Contingency plans to manage emergency changes.
- Details of services to be provided, and any charges the individual is assessed to pay, or if direct payments have been agreed.
- Contributions which carers and others are willing and able to make.
- A review date.

4.6   The 1991 practice guidance provides further detail, para 4.37 stating:[2]

> Care plans should be set out in concise written form, linked with the assessment of need. The document should be accessible to the user, for example, in Braille of translated into the user's own language. A copy should be given to the user but it should also, subject to constraints of confidentiality, be shared with other contributors to the plan . . .

A care plan should contain:

- the overall objectives
- the specific objectives
- users
- carers
- service providers
- the criteria for measuring the achievement of these objectives
- the services to be provided by which personnel/agency
- the cost to the user and the contributing agencies
- the other options considered
- any point of difference between the user, carer, care planning practitioner or other agency
- any unmet needs with reasons – to be separately notified to the service planning system
- the named person(s) responsible for implementing, monitoring and reviewing the care plan
- the first date of the first planned review.

4.7   The single assessment process guidance (SAP) guidance[3] gives yet further advice on the content of care plans. Although the guidance is directed at older people's care needs it can be seen as providing a useful checklist for the categories of information that plans should contain. The guidance

---

2   *Care Management and Assessment – A Practitioners' Guide*, HMSO, 1991, para 4.37.
3   HSC 2002/001 and LAC (2002)1, *Guidance on the Single Assessment Process for Older People*, 2002 Annex E pp24–25 (accessible at http://www.dh.gov.uk/en/Publicationsandstatistics/Lettersandcirculars/Healthservicecirculars/DH_4003995); in Wales broadly similar wording is adopted – the Unified and Fair System for Assessing and Managing Care (in Wales) (UFSAMC) 2002 policy guidance, para 2.44.

stresses, however that not all care plans need contain such detailed information, advising that:

> The detail of the care plan should be in proportion to the assessed/eligible needs and service provision. For people who receive one-off support or treatment of a very basic nature, a simple statement of service delivery and purpose is all that is needed. Service users should be given their own copy of the care plan or statement of service delivery, in the most appropriate format.

4.8   Where, however, on-going services are provided, the SAP guidance[4] requires 'an appropriate single care plan' that 'should include':

- A summary of identified/eligible needs indicating the intensity, instability, predictability, and complexity of needs, the associated risks to independence, and the potential for rehabilitation.
- A note on whether or not the service user has agreed the care plan, and a reason where this was not possible.
- A note on whether or not the user has consented for care plan information to be shared among relevant agencies, and a reason where this was not possible.
- The objectives of providing help and anticipated outcomes for users.
- A summary of how services will impact on identified/eligible need and associated risks.
- The part the user will play in addressing needs, including the strengths and abilities s/he will bring to this.
- Details on managing risk as appropriate. Where it has been agreed that users will accept a certain degree of risk, this must be written in the care plan.
- Details of what carers are willing to do, and related needs and support.
- A description of the level and frequency of the help that is to be provided, stating which agency is responsible for what service.[5]
- Details of any contributions to care costs that users are asked to make.
- A nursing plan (integrated not attached) where appropriate.
- The level of Registered Nurse Care Contribution for admissions to care homes which provide nursing care.
- The name of the person co-ordinating the care plan and their contact number.
- A contact number or office in case of emergencies, and a contingency plan if things go wrong.
- Monitoring arrangements and a date for review.

4.9   In addition to complying with practice and policy guidance, care plans must also satisfy the demands of public law and sound administrative practice. Service users need to know, for instance, what it is that they are entitled to receive and how this decision has been reached. It follows that

---

4   HSC 2002/001 and LAC (2002)1.
5   The local government ombudsman has held that care plans should specify the frequency of services, for instance of respite care: Complaint no 03/C/16371 against Stockton-on-Tees BC, 18 January 2005.

care plans must spell out with sufficient detail all the relevant aspects of the care arrangements that are to be made – not unlike a schedule of works – such as the frequency of services,[6] the actual services that will be provided[7] and so on. Where services are not directly provided by the social services department, the details of the care plan should be spelt out in the contract with the provider as part of the service user specification. It is this detail that should be monitored as part of contract compliance in order to ensure the user receives the services that are in the care plan.[8]

4.10   The demands of public law were highlighted in *R v Islington LBC ex p Rixon*[9] where Sedley J accepted the respondent's submission that 'nowhere in the legislation is a care plan, by that or any other name required' and that 'a care plan is nothing more than a clerical record of what has been decided and what is planned'. In his view, however, this state of affairs:

> . . . far from marginalising the care plan, places it at the centre of any scrutiny of the local authority's due discharge of its functions. As paragraph 3.24 of the [1990] policy guidance indicates, a care plan is the means by which the local authority assembles the relevant information and applies it to the statutory ends, and hence affords good evidence to any inquirer of the due discharge of its statutory duties. It cannot, however, be quashed as if it were a self-implementing document.

4.11   In assessing whether the care plan produced by the authority was fit for purpose, Sedley J paid particular regard to the local authority's obligation to 'act under'[10] the relevant policy guidance and to take into account the relevant practice guidance. When subjected to such an analysis, the care plan was deficient: in his opinion:

> The care plan . . . does not comply either with the [1990] policy guidance or the [1991] practice guidance issued by central government. There has been a failure to comply with the guidance contained in paragraph 3.24 of the [1990] policy document[11] to the effect that following assessment of need, the objectives of social services intervention as well as the services to be provided or arranged should be agreed in the form of a care plan.
> . . .
>
> The care plan also fails at a number of points to comply with the [1991] practice guidance[12] on, for example, the contents of a care plan, the specification of its objectives, the achievement of agreement on implementation on all those involved, leeway for contingencies and the identification and feeding back of assessed but still unmet need.

---

6 Complaint no 03/C/16371 against Stockton-on-Tees BC, 18 January 2005.
7 *R (LH and MH) v Lambeth LBC* [2006] EWHC 1190 (Admin); (2006) 9 CCLR 515.
8 The ombudsman has criticised councils for not ensuring that services specified in the contract have actually been provided (in two of the cases the service user died). Complaint nos 05/C/06420 against Sheffield City Council, 20 February 2007; 05/C/08592 against Liverpool City Council, 17 January 2007 and 03/C/17141 against Blackpool, 23 February 2006.
9 (1998) 1 CCLR 119, p128.
10 See para 1.49 above.
11 Cited at para 4.44 below.
12 Cited at para 4.6 above.

In such a situation I am unable to [agree] that the failures to follow the policy guidance and practice guidance are beyond the purview of the court.

4.12 In *R v Sutton LBC ex p Tucker*[13] Hidden J was equally critical of the council's care plan, stating:

There are no stated overall objectives in terms of long term obligations, carers' obligations or service providers, there are no criteria for the measurement of objectives because the objectives themselves are not recorded in any care plan. There are no costings, no long term options, no residential care options considered, there are no recorded points of difference, there is no reference to unmet need and there is no reference to a next date of review.

4.13 The importance that the courts attach to policy and practice guidance in this area is illustrated by the relief ordered in the *Tucker* case, which included:

[First] an order of Mandamus to provide within 21 days a care plan which complies, as far as possible, with the [1991] practitioners' guide and with paragraph 3.25 of the [1990] policy guidance. Secondly, a declaration that the respondent has acted unlawfully and in breach of paragraphs 3.24 and 3.41[14] of the policy guidance in failing to make a service provision decision under section 47(1)(b) of the National Health Service and Community Care Act 1990, as to the long term placement of the applicant. Thirdly, a declaration that the respondent has acted unlawfully and contrary to paragraph 3.25 of the policy guidance in failing to produce a lawful care plan.

Care plans and 'unmet need'

4.14 The 1991 practice guidance advised that unmet need be recorded in a care plan and at the time some controversy arose as to whether the concept of 'unmet need' was lawful. Its legality (as a concept) depends however upon how it is defined. The Welsh guidance[15] does this as follows:

. . . presented needs that are not evaluated as eligible needs or where eligible needs are met but an alternative more appropriate/desirable service should ideally be available.

4.15 This explanation illustrates the difficulty, since it incorporates two distinct categories of need, namely (1) presenting needs that are not assessed as eligible needs; and (2) eligible needs that cannot be meet in the most appropriate way. These are considered separately below.

---

13 (1998) 1 CCLR 251.
14 Which provides (among other things) that 'it is most undesirable that anyone should be admitted to, or remain in, hospital when their care could be more appropriately provided elsewhere'.
15 UFSAMC 2002 policy guidance Annex 9 p101.

Presenting needs that are not assessed as eligible needs

4.16   As detailed above (see para 3.89) a person may express the view that he or she has a 'need' for a variety of community care services, but on assessment the local authority may decide that these needs are not sufficiently substantial to entitle the person to such support. These are needs that do not meet the authority's eligibility criteria. On this definition therefore, unmet needs are those needs which the individual (or others) consider of relevance (ie 'presenting needs') but which on assessment are not deemed sufficiently important to be 'eligible needs'.

4.17   Although there can be nothing unlawful with 'unmet need' if defined this way, the reason why a person may not be entitled to services requires further analysis since it should have a bearing on the way an assessment/ care plan is expressed. In simple terms, a person may not have a need for community care services, because, either:

- he or she would not suffer harm of the required level, if the support were not provided at all; or
- he or she would suffer harm of the required level, if the support was not provided, but the support is not required from the local authority because some third party is already providing the support (ie a carer[16]).

4.18   In these situations a 'need' exists, but in both cases it does not 'call for' a response from the authority: in the first case, because it is not sufficiently serious and in the second case, because someone else is attending to it. The second category requires careful treatment in the care plan record. Ideally the care plan should record it as an assessed need rather than an unmet need, because (a) this is the case, and (b) if for some reason the third party ceased to provide the service, there needs to be a record that this need is a 'need' that would then 'call for' a local authority service response.

Eligible needs the authority cannot meet in the most appropriate way

4.19   Where a presenting need is assessed as an 'eligible need' (see para 3.143 above), the authority is obliged to provide services to meet that need. If, for one reason or another, the authority finds itself unable to provide services to meet that need, it could be categorised as 'unmet' need. In certain situations this will be unlawful, but not always, since there may be a variety of reasons why the need is not being met. These include:

Budgetary difficulties

4.20   Once a need has been assessed as an eligible need, services must be provided to address that need. If such services are not provided because

---

16   In such cases, a local authority could only so decide if it had offered a carer an assessment and, if one has been undertaken, had concluded that the caring role is sustainable without such a need being met – see para 16.53 below.

the local authority has a budgetary difficulty, this is unlawful: accordingly unmet need in this context is not permissible (see para 3.171 above). The same principle applies to direct payments and individual budgets.

Physical or human resource difficulties

4.21 In certain situations, an assessed need will not be capable of being met, not because the local authority lacks the financial resources, but simply because there is no readily available service to meet that need. Typically this will be because such a service does not exist. In such cases the court will accept that an assessed need is 'unmet' provided determined steps are being taken to resolve the problem: in essence that the local authority is doing the best that it can do.[17] Thus in *R v Sutton LBC ex p Tucker*[18] the applicant was assessed as needing a specialist facility in or around the Sutton area of London – which at that time did not exist. The local authority was not held to have acted unlawfully by not meeting the need immediately: its unlawful action lay in its failure to take prompt steps to commission the necessary services.

4.22 A similar finding occurred in *R v Islington LBC ex p Rixon*[19] where the applicant was assessed as needing (amongst other things) specialist day-care support outside his home. Because no such facilities were immediately available, the authority did nothing other than place his name on a waiting list, which the court held to be unlawful:

> . . . the local authority has, it appears, simply taken the existing unavailability of further facilities as an insuperable obstacle to any further attempt to make provision. The lack of a day care centre has been treated, however reluctantly, as a complete answer to the question of provision for Jonathan's recreational needs.'

Recording unmet need

4.23 The FACS 2003 practice guidance[20] (unlike the Welsh guidance[21] and the 1991 practice guidance[22]) is coy about the requirement to record 'unmet need' on individual assessments – merely requiring that the information on the user's presenting needs be recorded and placed on his or her file. This is particularly unhelpful. In effect it means that in order to assess what 'presenting' needs are not being met, the individual (or someone on his or her behalf) will have to gain access to the file and find the relevant statement. This will then have to be compared against the care plan and a list prepared of those needs that the local authority has decided can be

---

17 See eg *R v Exeter City Council ex p Gliddon and Draper* [1985] 1 All ER 493 (a housing case) where the court held that what is suitable in the short term might not be suitable in the long term.
18 (1998) 1 CCLR 251.
19 (1998) 1 CCLR 119 at 128.
20 At Q.11.1–Q11.3: see also UFSAMC 2002 policy guidance, paras 2.45, 6.22, 8.8, fn 4 p16, Annex 9 p101.
21 UFSAMC 2002 policy guidance, paras 2.45, 6.22, 8.8, fn 4 p16, Annex 9 p101.
22 At para 4.32.

'unmet'. Given that the Welsh policy guidance and the 1991 practice guidance specifically advise that unmet need should be recorded; that this is not specifically contradicted by the FACS guidance (which is merely oblique on the question); that recording unmet need will be relatively straight forward (if done during the assessment process) and given the bureaucratic run around that service users may have to pursue if it is not recorded – the balance of administrative fairness strongly favours it being recorded on the care plan. The recording of unmet need is also an essential component of a local authority's strategic planning obligations.[23]

Confusing needs and services

4.24   Commonly there may be several possible services that may address an eligible need. For example, an assessment might reveal that a person who lives alone needs to be helped with many activities, such as dressing, bathing, feeding, and that there is a general need for someone to keep a watchful eye on the person to ensure there are no falls or other neglectful acts. These are all likely to be 'eligible needs' since a failure to address them could have serious consequences. The services that could meet these needs are many: home help, day centre, meals on wheels, a residential home, and so on. The care plan determines which services most appropriately meet the eligible needs. Thus, in care planning terminology, no one has a 'need' for a place in a day centre: what they might have is a need to be kept occupied or in a safe environment during the day. This could be met in a variety of different ways depending on the user's preference, which might be for a sitting service at home, or a direct payment or individual budget.

4.25   In *R v Kirklees MBC ex p Daykin*[24] Collins J observed that it was 'not always easy to differentiate between what is a need and what is merely the means by which such need can be met'. The case concerned a disabled person who had been assessed as unable to manage the stairs to his council flat. Collins J considered the 'need' in this case was to be able to get into and out of his dwelling. In his opinion 'the means by which this need could be met included, among other things, the provision of a stairlift or re-housing'. The 1991 practice guidance mirrors the statutory requirements of NHSCCA 1990 s47(1) by emphasising the importance of

---

23   See eg *R v Bristol CC ex p Penfold* (1998) 1 CCLR 315 at 322 where Scott Baker J held that the duty to assess was not predicated upon the likelihood of a service being provided and the FACS 2003 practice guidance (Q.11.1–Q11.3) and UFSAMC 2002 policy guidance (paras 2.45, 6.22, 8.8, fn 4 p16, Annex 9 p101) which adopt the same approach, stating that the difference between presenting needs and eligible needs should be monitored, and the results used to inform service delivery, planning and commissioning.

24   (1998) 1 CCLR 512: see also, eg, *R v Lambeth LBC ex p K* (2000) 3 CCLR 149 where the court quashed a service provision decision on the basis that the council had not followed the 1990 policy guidance and the care plan had confused 'needs' and 'services'.

treating the assessment of need as a separate exercise from consideration of service response, stating (at para 3.1):

> It is easy to slip out of thinking 'what does this person need?' into 'what have we got that he/she could have?' The focus on need is most clearly achieved where practitioners responsible for assessment do not also carry responsibility for the delivery or management of services arising from that assessment (at para 22 of the guide's summary).[25]

4.26   The local government ombudsman has also been critical of councils that are 'service led' – in the sense that they allow existing service arrangements to dictate how an individual's needs will be met – rather than seeking to meet the identified need by (if necessary) an individually crafted care package. In a 2004 complaint he noted:[26]

> The impression I am given is that [the disabled person] was fitted into activities that might be available, rather than a programme based on her assessed needs.

Delayed and/or defective care plans

4.27   Once an assessment has been completed, a care plan should follow without delay. If the eligible needs cannot be met immediately (because for instance there are no suitable services available), the care plan should explain how these services will be identified and procured: the drafting of the care plan should not be delayed whilst services are sought. In *R v Sutton LBC ex p Tucker*[27] the applicant had been waiting in hospital for two years without a care plan, while the local authority took inadequate steps to identify an appropriate care package. In this case the court ordered that the local authority produce a care plan within 21 days – essentially spelling out how it would ensure that the applicant's care needs would be addressed without further delay. The courts have been called upon to consider very many cases of local authorities failing to provide adequate services to meet assessed needs – sometimes through delay and sometimes because the care package proved to be inappropriate. The courts' and ombudsmen's approach to such cases is considered at para 3.174 para 3.213 above and para 4.28.

Care plan breakdowns

4.28   Where a care plan is not meeting a disabled person's needs, the authority is under a duty to address the problem – the urgency of the remedial action depending in part on the severity of the problem. Where complex

---

25 In *R v Islington LBC ex p Rixon* (1996) 1 CCLR 119 at 129B Sedley J put it thus: 'The practice guidance . . . counsels against trimming the assessment of need to fit the available provision'.

26 Report on complaint no 03/B/18884 against Bromley LBC, 9 December 2004.

27 (1998) 1 CCLR 251.

care packages are involved, authorities may have difficulty in making rapid and effective changes to restore the position: nevertheless a failure to take prompt and, if necessary, urgent action in such cases may amount to maladministration.[28] Where a care package is breaking down, generally this can be explained in terms of the authority failing to provide appropriate services to meet the disabled person's needs.

4.29   Not infrequently, a care plan breakdown can occur because an existing service ceases to be available. This problem is illustrated by a 2002 local government ombudsman's report[29] concerning the care plan for a young adult with multiple and profound mental and physical disabilities. In 1994 her needs were assessed and provision made for her to have one weekend per month respite care in a residential unit, paid by the local authority, but provided by a charitable organisation. In 2000 the family were notified that owing to funding problems the unit was closed at weekends. Although the council had no record of their assessment, it argued that the need was for three days' respite care a week, not necessarily at weekends. The family made a formal complaint arguing that weekend respite was essential as it gave them a substantial break (as during the week their daughter was at a residential special school). The complaints panel noted that the 1994 assessment was 'not as sophisticated as current assessments' but concluded that since it did not specify an entitlement to weekend respite there was no obligation to provide this. The ombudsman found it 'astonishing that the Council acknowledges managing . . . regular periods of respite care for six years with neither a proper assessment nor a care plan'. However, having regard to the records of the service provider (and the history of weekend service provision) she was satisfied that weekend respite had been agreed. She then stated:

> The council says that because it was not responsible for the closure of [the respite facility] it cannot be held responsible for the withdrawal of [the complainant's] provision. I do not accept this. It is the council, not [the charitable provider] which has statutory responsibility for providing for [the complainant's] needs. If [the respite facility] could not, for whatever reason, meet those needs, the council had a duty to find, in the locality, somewhere else where [the complainant] would feel equally settled and in which her parents would have confidence.

4.30   The ombudsman reached the same conclusion in a complaint concerning adult care respite arrangements that broke down because of problems with the centre providing the care (which included an allegation of abuse during a respite period). The ombudsman noted:[30]

28 See eg report on complaint no 04/C/12489 against Oldham MBC, 7 September 2006.
29 Complaint no 01/C/03521 against North Yorkshire, 19 August 2002.
30 Complaint no 02/B/16654 against Bedfordshire CC, 16 October 2003: see also Complaint no 03/B/18884 against Bromley LBC, 9 December 2004, which concerned a service user who was no longer able to attend a day centre because it was likely that she would come into contact with her alleged abuser. The council's response was so inadequate that her carer, the complainant, had no choice but to make alternative arrangements herself. The ombudsman upheld the complaint.

I understand why the Council found it difficult to identify alternative opportunities for respite care. And I appreciate the fact that the solution proposed [by the parents] requires resources that the department did not necessarily have. But there is case law to say that a want of resources in a particular budget does not excuse the council from carrying out its statutory duty.

4.31   A further ombudsman's report[31] on the question of service delivery difficulties concerned a severely disabled person and his main carer, both aged over 90. He was assessed as needing help getting up and going to bed; the weekend and evening cover being provided by an agency. Because of recruitment problems the agency gave notice to the council that it proposed to withdraw its service and the council was unable to find another agency willing to provide this service unless the council would pay travel costs to the staff, above the flat rate fee for the service, and the council refused as this was against its policy. In finding a fettering of discretion and maladministration the ombudsman commented:

It cannot be easy to arrange for home care in the rural parts of the county's area, and even the best contractual agreements must fail from time to time. But it seems to me that when a service failure occurs, the council might well have to seize any realistic opportunity to make the service good. Here it had such an opportunity. Another home care contractor offered to provide the . . . service but only if the council would pay its staff travel costs over and above the flat rate fee for providing home care. Doubtless there are many tussles between the council and its providers over such arrangements and I can understand why the council might have considered this a precedent and the thin end of the wedge, but what was that to Mr and Mrs Derwent?[32] It seems to me that Mr Derwent's home care was entirely sacrificed to maintain the purity of the council's contractual arrangements. . . . This was a classic case of the council fettering its discretion, and was maladministration.

4.32   In a 2003 report,[33] the ombudsman reviewed a complaint concerning the failure of a social services authority to respond to a breakdown in care arrangements. The complainant's adult daughter (who had severe physical and visual disabilities and learning disabilities) decided that she wished to return home from a specialist residential care placement in which she had been living for some time. Her father made interim arrangements and requested an urgent reassessment by the council with a view to producing a new care plan – potentially funded by direct payments and the Independent Living Fund. The council delayed such that the complainant had little or no choice but to make the support arrangements himself.

4.33   The ombudsman concluded that the council should have produced a final care plan within three months and the failure to do this amounted to maladministration. The ombudsman accepted that the complainant had spent £70,000 in supporting his daughter during the two-year period of council inaction – and in his view the council itself had probably saved

31   Complaint no 99/B/00799 against Essex, 29 March 2001.
32   The names used are not the real names.
33   Complaint no 01/B/09360 against Hertfordshire CC, 22 September 2003.

about £100,000 by not making any services available. Accordingly an award of £80,000 was recommended.

Breakdowns in care packages due to service user behaviour

4.34 Many service users will have behavioural difficulties which are an inextricable part of their condition. Their care plan should therefore take into account these characteristics and in general it would be inappropriate to withdraw a service from such person because of his or her behaviour. Accordingly, the local government ombudsman has criticised a council for withdrawing respite care services from a young adult with severe learning disabilities and autistic tendencies – because of a challenging outburst.[34] Although she accepted that 'sometimes brief withdrawal of provision is unavoidable in situations like this', she found that the prolonged exclusion was primarily the consequence of inadequate respite care provision services – and accordingly a failure to meet his assessed need. She recommended 'the council to adopt as a top priority the provision of a new local facility or facilities for [this client group]'.

4.35   Where, for example, a disabled person behaves offensively to home care assistants or refuses to comply with the reasonable requirements of a day centre etc, it might reach a point where the local authority cannot continue to provide a service and considers that it has discharged its duty. In deciding whether to withdraw the service, the applicant's mental health and its treatability may be relevant factors.[35]

Rejection of a care package

4.36 Disabled people are entitled to refuse services,[36] either explicitly or by their behaviour. In *R v Kensington and Chelsea RLBC ex p Kujtim*,[37] for instance, Potter LJ held that the duty to provide accommodation (under National Assistance Act (NAA) 1948 s21; see paras 3.121 above and 7.34 below) can be treated as discharged if the applicant 'either unreasonably refuses to accept the accommodation provided or if, following its provision, by his conduct he manifests a persistent and unequivocal refusal to observe the reasonable requirements of the local authority in relation to the occupation of such accommodation'.

4.37   In *R v Southwark LBC ex p Khana and Karim*[38] it was alleged that Mrs Khana (the disabled party subject to the community care assessment) refused to accept the offer of a residential care home placement proposed by the local authority – and insisted upon the provision of a community

---

34 Complaint no 03/C/16371 against Stockton-on-Tees BC, 18 January 2005.
35 See *Croydon LBC v Moody* (1998) 2 CCLR 92.
36 See also para 3.115 above and para 5.44 below.
37 [1999] 4 All ER 161; (1999) 2 CCLR 340 at 354I.
38 [2001] EWCA Civ 999; (2001) 4 CCLR 267.

based care package. In finding that the local authority had acted appropriately, Mance LJ commented:

> . . . although I do not consider that the case requires analysis in these terms, I would, if necessary, also treat Mrs Khana's refusal of the offer of residential home accommodation – the only course that would meet her assessed needs – as unreasonable in the sense intended by Potter LJ, when he was considering in *ex p Kujtim* what would discharge a local authority from any further duty for so long as such refusal was maintained.

Challenging care plans

4.38   The appropriate procedure for disputing the content of a care plan will generally be via the local authority complaints procedures (see para 27.4 below). This may additionally include a complaint concerning the adequacy of the assessment – and particularly the needs that have been identified as 'eligible needs'. In *R (Lloyd) v Barking and Dagenham LBC*[39] the Court of Appeal held that it was not an appropriate organ to prescribe the degree of detail that should go into a care plan.

Care plan reviews

4.39   Councils must not only take all reasonable steps to ensure that appropriate services are provided to satisfy the eligible needs a person is assessed as having, they must also ensure that care plans are monitored so that any problems are picked up and addressed. The FACS 2002 policy guidance[40] requires that there should be an initial review of all care plans:

> . . . within three months of help first being provided or major changes made to current services. Thereafter, reviews should be scheduled at least annually or more often if individuals' circumstances appear to warrant it. Reviews may be considered on request from service users, providers of services and other appropriate individuals or agencies.

4.40   Since review of a care plan, is at law, a 'reassessment', this question is considered at para 3.222 above.

Copies of care plans

4.41   As noted above, the 1991 practice guidance,[41] the FACS 2002 policy guidance[42] and the SAP guidance[43] require service users to be given copies of their care plans (in the most appropriate format).

---

39   [2001] EWCA Civ 533; (2001) 4 CCLR 196 at 205G.
40   FACS 2002 policy guidance, para 60; UFSAMC 2002 policy guidance, paras 2.54–2.51.
41   Para 4.37.
42   Para 49; UFSAMC 2002 policy guidance, para 2.49.
43   SAP Policy Guidance 2003 Annex E p24.

Key care planning principles

4.42   Unlike modern social welfare statutes,[44] the community care legislation contains no express statement of core principles.[45] Such principles can however be discerned from the government's broad policy documents and from the English and Welsh community care policy guidance. These principles are uncontroversial and have varied hardly at all over the last 20 years. The declaration in the 1989 community care white paper *'Caring for People'*[46] (at para 1.8) that 'promoting choice and independence underlies all the Government's proposals' remains true today. Neither devolution[47] nor electoral changes have altered these objectives, a point manifest in the title of the 2005 English green paper *'Independence, Well-being and Choice: our vision for the future of social care for adults in England'*.[48] The 2006 white paper[49] that followed sought to encapsulate this 'vision' in three key 'themes', namely:

- putting people more in control of their own health and care;
- enabling and supporting health, independence and well-being;
- rapid and convenient access to high-quality, cost-effective care.

4.43   While the promotion of independent living and user choice are long standing and core principles underpinning the legislation, there is a third that has received less political air-time, but is nevertheless central to any analysis such as this: the issue of cost effectiveness. A final 'principle' that has come more clearly into focus over the last ten years is that of 'dignity'.[50] Although implicit in the concept of independent living, with the enactment of the Human Rights Act 1998 it is a principle that now warrants analysis in its own right. Of these four 'principles' – independent living, dignity, 'choice and control' and cost effectiveness – the first two are (in jurisprudential theory at least) accorded the greater weight; however in practice the scales appear most affected by 'cost effectiveness' (or in reality, merely 'cost'). These four principles are considered separately below.

---

44   See eg Children Act 1989 s1 or Mental Capacity Act 2005 s1.
45   For an indication of what these principles might look like in a statutory format, see the Disabled Persons (Independent Living) Bill [HL] introduced into the House of Lords by Lord Ashley of Stoke on 27 November 2006.
46   Secretaries of State for Health, Social Security, Wales and Scotland, *Caring for People: community care in the next decade and beyond*, Cm 849, HMSO, 1989.
47   See eg the UFSAMC 2002 policy guidance which at p6 gives as the first two 'key aims' social inclusion and independence.
48   Department of Health, March 2005: which at p9 gave as its vision the promotion of certain principles, of which the first was the development of services 'to help maintain the independence of the individual by giving them greater choice and control over the way in which their needs are met'.
49   Secretary of State for Health, *Our health, our care, our say: a new direction for community services*, Cm 6737, 2006, p13; see also Cabinet Office, *Improving the Life Chances for Disabled People*, 2005.
50   Most recently explicitly taken up by ministers with the launch of the *Dignity in Care* initiative in November 2006.

The promotion of independent living

4.44 The promotion of independent living is a core – perhaps the core – principle underpinning the community care legislation. References to independence litter the policy documents of the last 20 years and have been given quasi-statutory force by the policy guidance. The 1990 policy guidance[51] states:

> **CARE PLANS**
>
> 3.24. Once needs have been assessed, the services to be provided or arranged and the objectives of any intervention should be agreed in the form of a care plan. The objective of ensuring that service provision should, as far as possible, preserve or restore normal living implies the following order of preference in constructing care packages which may include health provision, both primary and specialist, housing provision and social services provision:
>
> - support for the user in his or her own home including day and domiciliary care, respite care, the provision of disability equipment and adaptations to accommodation as necessary;
> - a move to more suitable accommodation, which might be sheltered or very sheltered housing, together with the provision of social services support;
> - a move to another private household ie, to live with relatives or friends or as part of an adult fostering scheme;
> - residential care;
> - nursing home care;
> - long-stay care in hospital.

4.45 The courts have placed very considerable reliance upon this requirement:[52] thus in *R v Sutton LBC ex p Tucker*[53] the fact that there was an 'effective option' for the service user's discharge from long-stay care in hospital was treated as creating an obligation to act purposefully to progress this objective.

4.46 The duty to promote independent living has developed to the stage that it can be seen as a core domestic and international human rights obligation. Domestically, Disability Discrimination Act (DDA) 1995 s49A[54] places a duty on all public bodies to have due regard to the need to promote equality of opportunity between disabled persons and other persons. In furtherance of this duty public bodies must develop Disability Equality Schemes[55] that (among other things) encourage participation by disabled

---

51 *Community Care in the Next Decade and Beyond: policy guidance*, HMSO, 1990; and see also the 2002 FACS policy guidance which at para 15 provides further emphasis, stressing the importance of maintaining an individual's independence over time; and the UFSAMC 2002 policy guidance in Wales which lists at p6 as a key aim social inclusion and independence.

52 See eg *R v Islington LBC ex p Rixon* (1998) 1 CCLR 119 at 128.

53 (1998) 1 CCLR 251, pp255H and 274H.

54 Inserted by DDA 2005 s3.

55 Disability Discrimination (Public Authorities)(Statutory Duties) Regulations 2005 SI No 2966.

people in public life. Disability Rights Commission Guidance for social services authorities concerning such schemes[56] gives as its first 'Action Point' (p30) the objective of increasing 'the proportion of disabled people who are enabled to live independently'.

4.47   Internationally, the UN Convention on the Rights of Persons with Disabilities, article 19 declares:

> States Parties to this Convention recognize the equal right of all persons with disabilities to live in the community, with choices equal to others, and shall take effective and appropriate measures to facilitate full enjoyment by persons with disabilities of this right and their full inclusion and participation in the community, including by ensuring that:
> a. Persons with disabilities have the opportunity to choose their place of residence and where and with whom they live on an equal basis with others and are not obliged to live in a particular living arrangement;
> b. Persons with disabilities have access to a range of in-home, residential and other community support services, including personal assistance necessary to support living and inclusion in the community, and to prevent isolation or segregation from the community;
> c. Community services and facilities for the general population are available on an equal basis to persons with disabilities and are responsive to their needs.

4.48   A powerful argument can be made that the inappropriate institutionalisation of elderly and disabled people may be contrary to the European Convention on Human Rights ('the Convention') – contrary to article 8 alone or in combination with article 14. This is particularly the case given that the UK has accepted the right in the UN Convention on the Rights of Persons with Disabilities, article 19 (which it signed in March 2007) and is effectively estopped from denying that such a right can be read into analogous binding conventions such as the European Convention on Human Rights (article 8).[57]

4.49   As yet there is no decided case that addresses this question directly, although there is relevant authority for this proposition in the form of a US Supreme Court decision, *Olmstead v LC*.[58] *Olmstead* concerned the Americans with Disabilities Act 1990 which (amongst other things) proscribes discrimination in the provision of public services. Whilst there is no exactly equivalent legislation in England and Wales, Part III of the DDA 1995 (goods, facilities and services) is sufficiently similar to permit comparison. *Olmstead* concerned a care planning regime in the state of Georgia, which skewed funding arrangements to favour institutional placements, rather than community based independent living placements.

56 *The Social Care sector and the Disability Equality Duty: A guide to the Disability Equality Duty and Disability Discrimination Act 2005 for social care organisations*, accessible at http://www.drc-gb.org/docs/Social_Care_Guidance_September06(England).doc; see also Dame Denise Platt, 'It's about more than handrails', *Community Care*, 30 November 2006, pp34–35.

57 For an analysis of the enhancement effect of such interconnected Convention provisions, see L Clements and J Read, *Disabled People and the Right to Life*, Routledge, 2007, forthcoming, and see article 53 of the Convention .

58 527 US 581 (1999).

4.50   The applicants alleged that this constituted unlawful discrimination and the majority of the Supreme Court agreed. Whilst the court emphasised that the financial resources of States' were relevant factors in determining their policies, it stressed the importance of policies being rational and fair and of the basic principle that 'unnecessary institutionalization' should be avoided if possible. In the view of the majority:

> The identification of unjustified segregation as discrimination reflects two evident judgments: Institutional placement of persons who can handle and benefit from community settings perpetuates unwarranted assumptions that persons so isolated are incapable or unworthy of participating in community life . . .;

and

> confinement in an institution severely diminishes the everyday life activities of individuals, including family relations, social contacts, work options, economic independence, educational advancement, and cultural enrichment.

4.51   The Supreme Court's acknowledgement that financial resources were of relevance in determining the extent of the independent living obligation raises the question of how these two community care principles, 'independence' and 'cost effectiveness', should be balanced. The issue was addressed tangentially by the court of Appeal in *R v Southwark LBC ex p Khana and Karim*[59] where the applicants, an elderly couple, sought judicial review of the council's decision to meet their care needs by provision of a placement in a residential care home. The applicants wanted, for personal and cultural reasons, to live in the community independently in a home of their own with the support of their relatives and the statutory services. Mance LJ, giving judgment of the Court of Appeal, held that:

> . . . section 47 of the 1990 Act contemplate[s] an assessment by the local authority of a person's accommodation needs, which takes very full account of their wishes, including the very fundamental aim of preserving the independence of elderly people in the community and in their own homes for as long and as fully as possible. A certain degree of risk-taking is often acceptable, rather than compromise independence and break family or home links. But, where a local authority concludes, as Southwark did here, that 'the only way in which Mrs Khana's needs can properly be met is for her to go into a full time residential home', and makes a corresponding offer, and where this assessment and the reasonableness of the offer made cannot be challenged as such, then the local authority has in my judgment satisfied its duties under the legislation.[60]

4.52   The judgment confirms that the default position for any care plan is the promotion of independent living and that only where the social care authority concludes for professional (ie not solely financial) reasons that independent living is not viable, is it reasonable for it to propound an institutional care plan. The strong presumption in favour of independent

59   [2001] EWCA Civ 999; (2001) 4 CCLR 267.
60   Ibid at 281K.

living (over and above financial considerations) comes additionally from the positive obligations imposed by article 8 of the Convention:[61] to take action to 'the greatest extent feasible to ensure that they have access to essential economic and social activities and to an appropriate range of recreational and cultural activities' to ensure that their lives are not 'so circumscribed and so isolated as to be deprived of the possibility of developing [their] personality'.[62] Such compensatory measures, as Judge Greve observed in *Price v UK*,[63] are fundamental to disabled people's article 8 rights.

Choice and control

4.53   Respect for service user preferences is central to the rhetoric accompanying all major community care policy initiatives of the last 20 years. As already noted, increased service user 'choice' was one of the three key changes that the 1989 reforms sought to promote:[64] 'to give people a greater individual say in how they live their lives and the serves they need to help them to do so'. This core value remains – as evidenced by the 2005 English green paper '*Independence, Well-being and Choice: our vision for the future of social care for adults in England'*.[65]

4.54   Only once, however, has 'choice' been given statutory expression – in the Choice of Accommodation Directions (see para 7.90 below): all things being equal these provide a service user with the right to choose his or her care home.

4.55   The courts have distinguished between 'preferences' and 'needs'. In *R v Avon CC ex p M*[66] the applicant, because of his learning disabilities, had formed a fixed psychological attachment to a particular home which was more expensive than the alternative proposed by the local authority. A complaints panel heard uncontroverted evidence concerning his psychological needs and unanimously recommended the placement in the more expensive home. The local authority refused. Henry J, in finding for the applicant, stated as follows:

> Here, there was a clear finding by a body set up for detailed fact finding that M's needs included his psychological needs and, unless that finding could be disposed of, the authority was liable to meet those needs. Without that

---

61   See, eg, the observations made by Collins J in *Gunter v South West Staffordshire PCT* [2005] EWHC 1894 (Admin); (2006) 9 CCCLR 121 at [20].
62   Per Commissioner Bratza (as he then was) in *Botta v Italy* (1998) 26 EHRR 241 and cited by Munby J in *R (A, B, X & Y) v East Sussex CC* [2003] EWHC 167; (2003) 6 CCLR 194 at [102] and see also *R (T, D & B) v Haringey LBC* [2005] EWHC 2235 (Admin); (2006) 9 CCLR 58.
63   (2002) 34 EHRR 53.
64   Secretaries of State for Health, Social Security, Wales and Scotland, *Caring for People: community care in the next decade and beyond*, Cm 849, HMSO, 1989, para 1.8.
65   Department of Health, March 2005: which at p9 gave as its vision the promotion of certain principles, the first of which was the development of services 'to help maintain the independence of the individual by giving them greater choice and control over the way in which their needs are met'.
66   (1999) 2 CCLR 185.

finding being overthrown, there were not two options before the social services committee, as the paper suggests, there was only one: to meet M's needs, including his psychological needs.

4.56 M's attachment to the particular home was a 'need' not a 'choice'. This point was picked up in *R v Southwark LBC ex p Khana and Karim*[67] where the applicants were demanding a care plan that the local authority considered inappropriate. The Court of Appeal dealt with the claim in the following terms:

> In some circumstances, instanced by *R v Avon CC ex p M*[68] . . . a person may have a need . . . as distinct from a preference, to reside in a particular place. Here, it seems to me that Mrs Khana . . . is in reality seeking to insist, as against Southwark, on the – no doubt strongly held – preferences or beliefs of Mrs Khana and her family as to what community services should be provided to Mrs Khana and in what way. Under the relevant legislation and guidance, Southwark must take into account Mrs Khana's and Mr Karim's beliefs and preferences, but the assessment of any needs regarding, *inter alia*, accommodation and how to provide for them rests ultimately with Southwark.[69]

4.57 The courts, therefore, treat the principle of 'user choice', not as a fundamental right, but as a relevant consideration that must be taken into account by the authority. It follows that the preferences of service user in relation to his or her care plan should (except in relation to residential care placements – for which see para 7.90 below):

1) be fully taken into account by the authority; and
2) be accommodated in the care plan, so long as the local authority does not consider it inappropriate.

However if an authority considers it inappropriate to propound a care plan that complies with the service user's preferences, the authority must:

3) give cogent reasons for so deciding and highlight those parts of the care plan where there is disagreement.[70]

Cost effectiveness

Choosing between alternative care packages

4.58 While *ex p Khana and Karim* suggests that the promotion of 'independent living' is the principle generally to be accorded greatest weight, it is less clear as to how the balance is to be struck between 'cost effectiveness' and 'user preferences'. In general, however, if an authority is asserting

67 [2001] EWCA Civ 999; (2001) 4 CCLR 267.
68 See para 3.91 above.
69 [2001] EWCA Civ 999; (2001) 4 CCLR 267 at 281H.
70 See eg *Care Management and Assessment – A Practitioners' Guide*, HMSO, 1991, para 4.37 which requires that the care plan identify any point of difference between the user, carer and care planning practitioner, and the SAP guidance (2002) Annex E pp24–25 which requires that the care plan include a note on whether or not the service user has agreed the care plan, and a reason where this was not possible – the UFSAMC 2002 policy guidance contains similar obligations at para 2.44.

resource constraints as a reason for rejecting a user's preferred option, it cannot assume that the court or ombudsman will accept these as self-evident: in such cases, as Mance LJ has observed,[71] 'any problem of resources would require to be made out by evidence, and cannot be assumed to be present'.

4.59   The assessment process may identify needs which are capable of being met by two or more alternative care packages. In such situations it is not unreasonable for the authority to consider the relative cost of each option – as the above quoted 1990 policy guidance (at para 3.25) so advises – to 'secure the most cost-effective package of services that meets the user's care needs, taking account of the user's and carers' own preferences'.

4.60   Authorities are not obliged to opt for the cheapest care plan, although if the less expensive plan is favoured, a number of factors must be considered. First, if the choice concerns a care home placement, the choice of accommodation provisions may apply (see para 7.90). Secondly, if the cheaper option is within an institutional setting, it may be trumped by the 'independent living' obligation (see para 4.44 above). Finally, if in so deciding the authority rejects a user's preferred care package, it is obliged to (a) give cogent reasons for its decision (not least because the authority may have misunderstood the costing implications[72]), and (b) be able to identify its preferred care package – in the sense that such a package must actually exist, rather than being a hypothetical alternative.[73] In constructing a care plan, the issue of resources (the 'cheaper option') only arises if there is objectively a real and present choice of care packages available – which was not the case in *R v Avon CC ex p M*[74] (considered above) or indeed in *R v Sutton LBC ex p Tucker*[75] which concerned a Rubella impaired applicant. The local authority favoured a home in Birmingham run by the specialist charity SENSE, but the applicant's family, clinicians and indeed the SENSE staff considered that this would not be viable since she needed to be close to her family in Sutton, where unfortunately no such facility existed. The authority balked at the cost of commissioning a purpose created unit solely for the applicant; the net result being that nothing concrete happened and she remained inappropriately placed in short term NHS accommodation. In the judicial review proceedings, the authority sought to explain their inaction by reference to the family's unreasonable refusal of a care option – namely the placement in Birmingham. Hidden J disagreed. This was not a situation where there was a choice of care plans; indeed this was a case where there was no care plan at all. In his view, the authority preference for the Birmingham placement was untenable and

---

71   *R v Southwark LBC ex p Khana and Karim* [2001] EWCA Civ 999; (2001) 4 CCLR 267, p282I; see also *Sabah Mohamoud v Greenwich LBC* January 2003 *Legal Action* 23 where impatience was expressed concerning unspecified and 'general assertions' of a similar nature (albeit in a housing context).
72   *R (Alloway) v Bromley LBC* [2004] EWHC 2108 (Admin); (2005) 8 CCLR 61.
73   Ibid.
74   (1999) 2 CCLR 185.
75   (1998) 1 CCLR 251.

local placement the only option. Since there was no 'choice of care plan' the issue of resources was not relevant and the local authority had to prepare a plan to this effect.

4.61 Although the question has not as yet been fully litigated, it is not always obvious how one can compare the real cost of two alternative services. Not infrequently, for example, an authority will reject on financial grounds a package that has been the subject of detailed costing in favour of a package that is (at best) a theoretical option.[76] Such a situation arose in *R (Alloway) v Bromley LBC*[77] where the court expressed concern over the authority's relative costs analysis, without having to reach a final decision on whether it was indeed flawed.

4.62 Another difficulty may concern the question of net versus gross costs. A care option that is more expensive in gross terms (ie to UK Plc) may be less expensive in net cost terms to the authority (because for example part of the cost is met by another state funding stream, or by the individuals themselves). This difficulty was identified by the Audit Commission in 1996:

> The financial incentive for authorities to use residential care remains strong. In nearly all situations it is substantially cheaper for local authorities to place people in residential care, even where there is no difference between the gross cost of residential care and care at home.[78]

4.63 In such an analysis it would presumably be unreasonable for an authority to take into account the service user's likely financial contribution. Although there appears to be no authority on this point, to permit this could have a seriously distorting influence: for instance, the net cost to an authority of placing a person with capital into residential accommodation could in many situations be nil. In similar fashion, a care plan may only be a cheaper option in the short term: as the 1990 policy guidance observes (at para 3.25), '[f]ailure to satisfy particular needs can result in even greater burdens on particular services for example where a person becomes homeless as a result of leaving inappropriate accommodation which has been provided following discharge from hospital'.

Cost disputes and independent charitable providers

4.64 While the cost of a care package may be ascertained at its outset, over time it is likely to change – if only to take account of inflation. At the outset, the bargaining power of the local authority and the care provider are relatively equal – it being a simple purchaser/provider relationship. Over time this equality of arms may change, particularly in relation to a charitable provider. What for instance can such a provider do, if a local authority unreasonably refuses to make payments that keep track with the real cost

76 See eg *R (LH and MH) v Lambeth LBC* [2006] EWHC 1190 (Admin); (2006) 9 CCLR 622 where the local authority rejected a plan put forward by the disabled person on the basis that its hypothetical alternative arrangement was to be preferred.

77 [2004] EWHC 2108 (Admin); (2005) 8 CCLR 61.

78 *Balancing the Care Equation*, HMSO, 1996, para 40.

increases it is experiencing?[79] Whilst some commercial care providers might simply serve notice to terminate the contract, for the charitable provider the problem is less straightforward: it either accommodates an unreasonable council and undermines its viability by using its charitable resources to subsidise a public authority or it abandons the service user (even when there may be no viable or cheaper alternative care plan for him or her). As part of the negotiations such a provider would not normally feel able to serve a contract termination notice, since the very issuing of such a notice could cause untold distress to the service user and his or her carers.[80] Unreasonable refusals (or delays) by a council to consider real costs increases born by such a provider may amount to maladministration[81] (see also para 7.73 below).

Cost ceilings

4.65   The formal or informal community care policies of many authorities include reference to a 'costs ceiling'. Not uncommonly this will take the form of a financial limit on the total weekly cost of home care services that can be put into any one household, or a maximum permitted sum on any domiciliary care package (the implication being that if the package costs more, then a residential care plan will be preferred). If the costs ceiling relates to a package of residential care, this may offend the Choice of Accommodation Directions – see para 7.90 below.

4.66   As noted, blanket policies of this nature are likely to be unlawful, in that they would amount to a fettering of a duty (see para 27.184) and make resource questions determinative, rather than being 'no more than one factor in an overall assessment, where . . . the individual disabled person will always be the paramount consideration'.[82] Where such a policy would promote institutional care over non-institutional options, it would also offend the legal presumption in favour of independent living (see para 4.44 above).

4.67   Subject to these caveats, a council policy that refers to a particular costs figure as a 'guideline' rather than a fixed 'ceiling' will generally be lawful (unless perhaps the figure is entirely arbitrary). In this context the FACS 2003 practice guidance (Q6.4) gives the following advice:

> Cost-ceilings may be used as a guide, but they should not be used rigidly. Councils should always base their decisions on their assessment of a particular individual's needs, and if spending above a cost-ceiling can make

---

79   ie in relation to such costs attributable to above inflation increases in pay and staff conditions, changed legislative and practice requirements, particularly compliance with care standards and so on.

80   In complaint no 04/C/16195 against Birmingham City Council, 23 March 2006 the authority had advised a care provider in such a situation that she should simply abandon the service user if she was not prepared to accept the authority's payment rate – an attitude that the ombudsman considered 'extraordinary'.

81   Given the reluctance of the courts to become involved in such disputes (see para 7.70) the local government ombudsman would appear to provide the more appropriate remedy.

82   Per Hirst LJ in *R v Gloucestershire CC ex p Barry* (1997) 1 CCLR 19 at 31G.

a significant difference to an individual, then the council should consider doing so. . . . Cost-ceilings used in this sensible way can ensure fairness to both individuals whose needs might call for extra help or for whom the costs of services are higher and other service users.

4.68   This above extract is open to criticism. It fails to explain the importance of ensuring that any cost guideline is the product of a rational and practical process that has taken into account all relevant factors – and is not an arbitrary figure dreamt up in the fog of a council meeting.[83] In her 1998 report concerning a complaint against Liverpool City Council[84] the local government ombudsman considered a council imposed financial ceiling (of £110.00 per week) on the level of domiciliary care provided, which reflected the average cost to the council for an older person in residential care. She found that in setting the limit the council had fettered its discretion since there was no evidence that it had ever exceeded the limit and that such a fees policy was unfair and unreasonably discriminated against elderly people (as opposed to other service users).

Minimum services and respect/dignity

4.69   Commonly, a local authority may be able to satisfy a person's assessed needs in a variety of ways. Given that how it decides to meet the need is primarily its decision,[85] the question arises as to how austere a care package will have to be, before the courts or ombudsmen will intervene. This in turn raises the question as to the standard by which the court or ombudsman would judge 'austerity' or 'disagreeability' or whatever the measure may be.

4.70   By way of example, a local authority might assess as an 'eligible need' the person's need to access the toilet. If the problem is that the existing toilet is upstairs, and the person has mobility difficulties, this 'need' could be addressed by the provision of a stair lift, or the construction of a downstairs toilet or merely by the provision of a commode. Likewise a person who is unable to use their bath due to mobility problems may be assessed as needing to have help to keep clean – and this could be addressed by the provision of a wheelchair accessible shower, or a specially adapted bath or merely by an occasional 'strip /blanket' wash.

4.71   In assessing the adequacy of the service provision response, the courts and ombudsmen have sought to develop the concept of 'dignity' in the context of a state's positive obligations under article 8 of the Convention – the duty to ensure 'respect' for individual privacy (see para 27.225). Accordingly the local government ombudsman has held that the ability properly to manage bathing/washing with dignity is the entitlement of everybody.[86] By this measure a policy of only doing strip washes would fail

---

83   Complaint nos 90/A/2675, 2075, 1705, 1228 and 1172 against Essex.
84   Complaint no 96/C/4315, 20 August 1998; (1999) 2 CCLR 128. A sum of £10,000 compensation was recommended by the ombudsman.
85   *R v Southwark LBC ex p Khana and Karim* [2001] EWCA Civ 999; (2001) 4 CCLR 267.
86   Complaint nos 02/C/8679, 8681 and 10389 against Bolsover DC, 30 September 2003.

the 'dignity threshold' and amount to maladministration. Likewise, although the provision of a commode might (in the short term) be a lawful response to an urgent need, it is unlikely that in the medium term this would be acceptable – against the 'dignity' measure.[87] In *R (Burke) v General Medical Council and Disability Rights Commission (Interested Party)*[88] Munby J gave an extended review of the extent to which it could be argued that the concept of human dignity is now protected by domestic law. In the analysis he cited from *Price v UK*,[89] where in her concurring opinion Judge Greve stated:

> In a civilised country like the United Kingdom, society considers it not only appropriate but a basic humane concern to try to improve and compensate for the disabilities faced by a person in the applicant's situation. In my opinion, these compensatory measures come to form part of the disabled person's physical integrity.

4.72   In his earlier judgment in *R (A, B, X and Y) v East Sussex CC and the Disability Rights Commission (No 2)*[90] Munby J had observed that the 'protection of human dignity' was a core value that the courts would protect and that in so doing this amounted to a 'solemn affirmation of the law's and of society's recognition of our humanity and of human dignity as something fundamental'.

4.73   Baroness Hale of Richmond has made much the same point:[91]

> . . . human dignity is all the more important for people whose freedom of action and choice is curtailed, whether by law or by circumstances such as disability. The Convention is a living instrument . . . We need to be able to use it to promote respect for the inherent dignity of all human beings but especially those who are most vulnerable to having that dignity ignored. In reality, the niceties and technicalities with which we have to be involved in the courts should be less important than the core values which underpin the whole Convention.

4.74   In November 2006 the government in England launched a 'dignity in care' campaign endorsing the courts and ombudsmen's approach in this area.[92] Coinciding with the launch, guidance was published by the Commission

---

87 See eg *R (Bernard) v Enfield LBC* [2002] EWHC 2282 (Admin); (2002) 5 CCLR 577 where Sullivan J found a violation of article 8 for a delayed provision of proper toileting for the applicant – holding that it 'would have restored her dignity as a human being' (at [33]). Commodes will also be questionable on health and safety, and indeed economic, grounds.

88 [2004] EWHC 1879 (Admin); [2005] 2 WLR 431; (2004) 7 CCLR 609.

89 (2002) 34 EHRR 1285, p1296.

90 [2003] EWHC 167 (Admin); (2003) 6 CCLR 194 at [86].

91 'What can the human rights act do for my mental health?', the 2004 Paul Sieghart Memorial Lecture, accessible at http://www.bihr.org/downloads/transcipt_hale.doc. Baroness Hale used a 2002 British Institute of Human Rights report as the inspiration for her lecture – namely J Watson, *Something for Everyone: The impact of the Human Rights Act and the need for a Human Rights Commission*, British Institute of Human Rights, 2002.

92 See press release accessible at http://www.gnn.gov.uk/environment/ fullDetail.asp?ReleaseID=241940&NewsAreaID=2&NavigatedFrom Department= False.

for Social Care Inspection[93] containing ten standards, No 3 of which requires authorities to 'treat each person as an individual by offering a personalised service' and in the explanatory text, states that this requires that the care and support provided should 'consider individual physical, cultural, spiritual, psychological and social needs and preferences' and should 'respect individual needs, preferences and choices, and protect human rights'.

4.75   The requirement to treat all patients with 'dignity and respect' is now assessed as part of the annual health check against the Department of Health's core standard on patient focus.[94]

Urgent cases

4.76   Where an individual's need is so pressing that there is not time even to carry out a 'fast-track' assessment (see para 3.53), a service can be provided without an assessment. NHSCCA 1990 s47(5) provides:

> Nothing in this section shall prevent a local authority from temporarily providing or arranging for the provision of community care services for any person without carrying out a prior assessment of his needs in accordance with the preceding provisions of this section if, in the opinion of the authority, the condition of that person is such that he requires those services as a matter of urgency.

4.77   While an authority is not obliged by NHSCCA 1990 s47(5) to make such provision, it would be an unlawful fettering of discretion for it to reach a policy decision prohibiting the provision of any community care service without a prior assessment. 1993 guidance suggested that the power under NHSCCA 1990 s47(5) should be used sparingly[95] and the FACS 2002 policy guidance advises:[96]

> Councils should provide an immediate response to those individuals who approach them, or are referred, for social care support in emergencies and crises. After this initial response, they should inform the individual that a fuller assessment will follow, and services may be withdrawn or changed as a result of this assessment.

4.78   In *R (Alloway) v Bromley LBC*[97] the applicant's urgent need for a care home placement had been delayed by the local authority's flawed assessment process. In his judgment, Crane J suggested that pending the outcome of a further reassessment, the authority could use its powers under section 47(5) to conclude a temporary placement of the applicant in order to avoid the likely hardship that would result from further delay.

---

93 CSCI, *Dignity in Care: Adults' Services Practice Guide No 9*, accessible at http://www.scie.org.uk/publications/practiceguides/practiceguide09/files/pg09.pdf.

94 Commission for Healthcare Audit and Inspection, *Living well in later life: A review of progress against the National Service Framework for Older People*, 2006, p14.

95 See eg LAC (93)2, para 17 but compare paras 21–22.

96 Para 69; UFSAMC 2002 policy guidance, para 5.36.

97 [2004] EWHC 2108 (Admin); (2005) 8 CCLR 61.

It follows that where an authority's delay in completing an assessment is causing hardship, it should consider using its powers under section 47(5), and a failure so to do might, in an appropriate case, amount to maladministration.

Health and safety

4.79   On occasions, manual handling arrangements can radically affect a care plan to the detriment of service users. The legal principles that regulate health and safety considerations in this field – including manual handling – are considered at para 17.29 below.

CHAPTER 5

Assessment and planning for discharge from hospital

Introduction

5.1   The law that regulates the hospital discharge responsibilities of the NHS and social services authorities is an amalgam of statute and tort. The patient is owed a duty of care (in the tort of negligence) by both the social services authority and the relevant NHS body. The NHS has a statutory responsibility to provide care under the National Health Service Act (NHSA) 2006 – albeit that this is a weak duty (see para 13.13) – and social services have responsibilities under the community care legislation to assess and provide services. Patients have in general[1] no right to remain in an NHS facility and can be discharged against their wishes – provided that the NHS and social services authorities consider that it is safe (ie have satisfied themselves that it would not be negligent – by exposing the patient to an unnecessary or involuntary risk of harm). In this respect the two bodies are subject to considerable Department of Health and Welsh Assembly guidance.

5.2   As a consequence of the current fixation with waiting lists, the introduction of 'payment by results'[2] and the dramatic decline in the number of NHS beds (see para 14.15), there is considerable pressure on hospitals to move patients from acute facilities as soon as it is safe to do so. NHS trusts are subject therefore to a number of performance indicators that require them to record a variety of delayed discharge statistics.[3]

5.3   In England, the introduction of the Community Care (Delayed Discharges etc) Act (CC(DD)A) 2003 has seen a significant decline in the number of people in hospital recorded as subject to a 'delayed discharge'.[4]

5.4   Concern has however been expressed about the rise in readmission rates. Official figures show that emergency readmission rates increased by 29 per cent between 1998/99–2005/06 with half a million patients being readmitted to hospital within 28 days of being discharged in 2005/06.[5] Mindful of this problem, the Healthcare Commission in its *State of Health Care Report 2004* emphasised the importance of ensuring that health staff

---

1   Unless they are entitled to continuing health care support, detained under the Mental Health Act (MHA) 1983 or have been in NHS accommodation for a prolonged period – such that it might be deemed their 'home' for the purposes of European Convention on Human Rights article 8 (see para 27.225).
2   Under the 'Payment by Results' reforms, instead of being commissioned through block agreements, hospitals are paid for work they do – the intention being to encourage activity which should help reduce waiting lists. Since the payments are based on fixed tariffs this is also expected to reward the more efficient providers.
3   See eg the Healthcare Commission National Targets 2006/2007 at http://ratings2007.healthcarecommission.org.uk/Indicators_2007/home.asp.
4   The records indicate that these fell from 4,147 (of whom 3,025 were over 75) in the last quarter of 2002–03 to 2,175 (of whom 1,604 were over 75) in the last quarter of 2005–06. However some of the success of the policy may be tempered with the knowledge that in the same quarters the number of people who were readmitted as an emergency within 28 days of discharge rose from 138,773 to 198,777 – a rise from 5.5% to 7.1% of all patients discharged: see *Report of the Chief Executive to the NHS*, June 2006.
5   Quoted in *Public Finance* magazine, 8 June 2007.

discussed discharge arrangements with patients *before* the decision to discharge took place. The report cited:

> (1) a 2001/02 National Acute Inpatient Survey[6] which found that while nearly two thirds (64%) of hospital patients aged 70 and over felt that there should have been a discussion with staff about the health and social care they would receive after leaving hospital, in almost a quarter (23.8%) of these cases the patient said that these arrangements had not been discussed with them; and
>
> (2) a National Sentinel Stroke Audit has also highlighted circumstances in which communication about discharge could be improved. In 43% of cases examined, patients (the great majority being 60 and over) were discharged before their GP was informed that they would be leaving hospital. Furthermore, in 39% of the cases, the information supplied to the GP on discharge did not include details of the patients' ability to look after themselves on leaving hospital.[7]

5.5 In order to address this failure of communication with patients the Commission reminded health and social care authorities of their obligations under the National Service Framework for Older People and in particular the single assessment process which requires, amongst other things, that 'individuals are placed at the heart of assessment and care planning'.[8] Two years later in its latest report, the Healthcare Commission found that in a survey of stroke patients some found the experience of hospital discharge distressing and 54 per cent of those who reported they needed home care did not get any.[9]

5.6 In most instances patients are keen to move on from a hospital ward. When a patient requires ongoing assistance either in the form of NHS or social care, establishing whether it is safe to discharge the patient, and assessing what services are needed following a hospital stay, are key to a smooth transition. In this respect the Health Select Committee's 2002 report on delayed discharges stated that the key objective was to ensure 'the right care in the right place at the right time'.[10]

The discharge process

5.7 The relationship between the NHS and social services in the discharge process is shaped by statute – the CC(DD)A 2003, subordinate legislation

---

6 Healthcare Commission, *Analysis of national inpatient survey data*, accessible at http://www.dh.gov.uk/PublicationsAndStatistics/PublishedSurvey/NationalSurveyOfNHSPatients/NationalSurveyInpatients/fs/en.

7 Clinical Effectiveness and Evaluation Unit, Royal College of Physicians on behalf of the Intercollegiate Stroke Working Party, *Concise report on the National sentinel audit of stroke 2001/02*, 2002, accessible at http://www.rcplondon.ac.uk/college/ceeu/strokeconciseauditreport.pdf.

8 Department of Health, *SAP Implementation Guidance for April 2004*.

9 Healthcare Commission, *State of Healthcare 2006*, p57.

10 House of Commons Health Committee, *Delayed discharges*, HC 671–1, 2002. Accessible at http://www.publications.parliament.uk/pa/cm200102/cmselect/cmhealth/617/617.pdf.

and central government guidance.[11] The regulations and guidance accompanying the 2003 Act[12] contain significant material relating to the rights of patients and their carers in the discharge process. It was the coming into force of this Act in England that spurred the secretary of state, in 2004, to issue directions for the first time under National Health Service and Community Care Act (NHSCCA) 1990 s47(4) on the assessment process (see para 3.20 above).[13] In the same year directions were also issued (now replaced by directions issued in 2007 to the same effect) which require the NHS to satisfy itself that a patient was not entitled to continuing NHS health care funding before it issued a notification under CC(DD)A 2003 s2 to social services (see para 14.49 below).[14] Both sets of directions reinforce the duty on authorities to consult with patients (and, where appropriate, their carers) and to give them information about the outcome of the assessment.

5.8   The legal obligations that arise on hospital discharge are activated by the discharge of the patient from NHS care – not his or her transfer to another NHS facility. Patients do not have the right to choose the place at which they receive NHS care.[15] The decision that they are safe to be transferred to another NHS facility is therefore primarily that of the responsible consultant and the NHS team on the receiving ward. It follows that when discussing hospital discharge, the issue is not of internal transfer but discharge from an NHS setting. A consultant's decision that a patient is medically fit to be transferred is the *sine qua non* – the key triggering event – in the discharge planning process.[16]

5.9   When such a decision has been made, and the patient has (or may have) a need for community care services, a safe discharge cannot occur until the NHS and social services are satisfied that the patient is not only (1) ready for discharge, but also (2) safe to be discharged. In essence this is

11 There is no present intention to bring the reimbursement provisions of the 2003 Act into force in Wales.

12 Delayed Discharges (England) Regulations 2003 SI No 2277 (the '2003 Regulations') and guidance as HSC 2003/009: LAC (2003)21 on 24 September 2003. In addition a host of other materials (directions, protocols, forms, question and answer statements etc) have been issued and are accessible at http://www.dh.gov.uk/en/Policyandguidance/Organisationpolicy/IntegratedCare/Delayeddischarges/index.htm.

13 Community Care Assessment Directions 2004 LAC (2004)24.

14 Delayed Discharges (Continuing Care) Directions 2007. The 2007 Directions virtually replicate the 2004 Directions with additional paragraphs, added in relation to the requirements contained in the NHS Continuing Healthcare (Responsibilities) Directions 2007, see para 14.39, which comes into effect on 1 October 2007.

15 See para 7.119.

16 The NHS/social services cannot (without invoking their powers under the MHA 1983) prevent patients from discharging themselves – provided they have sufficient mental capacity to make the decision (see para 18.13). Para 5.4.3 of the pathways guidance (see para 5.10) explains that 'self-discharge or discharge against medical advice may fall into one of the following categories. The patient (1) understands the risks he or she are taking in discharging him/herself; (2) is not competent to understand the risks associated with discharge due to his or her medical condition; (3) is not competent to understand the risks associated with discharge due to mental health problems. The discharge policy must set out the procedure to be followed by the ward-based care co-ordinator in such circumstances.

therefore a twin key process. Once the consultant activates the system, the discharge conveyor belt only starts to move when two keys have been turned; the first is primarily the responsibility of the NHS and the second, primarily the responsibility of social services. Once the two keys have been turned and the belt is in motion, then (if the process is regulated by the CC(DD)A 2003) social services are generally unable to stop the system without incurring the possibility of reimbursing the NHS if they are the cause of any delay in the patient's discharge from hospital.

Key guidance

5.10   In England three central documents give key guidance on the process that should be followed to ensure a 'non-simple' discharge is safe. These are *Discharge from hospital: pathway, process and practice*;[17] the safe discharge protocol *Definitions – Medical Stability and 'Safe to Transfer'*[18] and the *CC(DD)A 2003 Guidance for Implementation*[19] (referred to in the following section as the 'pathways guidance', the 'discharge protocol' and the 'delayed discharge guidance' respectively). In terms of good practice, the pathways guidance should be viewed as the core guidance shaping the basic structure, processes and the collaborations that are essential to a sympathetic and effective hospital discharge system. The provisions of the CC(DD)A 2003 are designed to synchronise with the good practice guidance; thus the service of a notice under the Act should not be seen as an event that dominates or in any way undermines the operation of the system.

5.11   In Wales the guidance on hospital discharge is to be found in the relatively brief Assembly document *Hospital Discharge Planning Guidance.*[20]

5.12   In England, good practice guidance has additionally been issued in relation to people in mental health settings[21] and regarding hospital admission and discharge of people who are homeless.[22]

---

17   Department of Health, 2003, accessible at http://www.dh.gov.uk/en/ Publicationsandstatistics/Publications/PublicationsPolicyAndGuidance/ DH_4003252.

18   Department of Health, 2003, accessible at http://www.dh.gov.uk/en/ Publicationsandstatistics/Publications/PublicationsPolicyAndGuidance/ DH_4071847.

19   *The Community Care (Delayed Discharges etc.) Act 2003 Guidance for Implementation*, September 2003, HSC 2003/009: LAC (2003)21.

20   WHC (2005)35: NAFWC 17/2005 available at http://www.wales.nhs.uk/documents/ WHC_2005_035.pdf.

21   Care Services Improvement Partnership, *A Positive Outlook – a good practice toolkit to improve discharge from inpatient mental health care*, April 2007, available at http:// www.cat.csip.org.uk/_library/A%20Positive%20Outlook.pdf.

22   Department for Communities and Local Government and Department of Health, *Hospital Admission and Discharge: People who are homeless or living in temporary or insecure accommodation*, December 2006, available at http://www.dh.gov.uk/en/ Publicationsandstatistics/Publications/PublicationsPolicyAndGuidance/DH_063736.

Simple hospital discharges

5.13   A 'toolkit' has been issued by the Department of Health concerning 'simple' discharge procedures. The guidance *Achieving timely 'simple' discharge from hospital*[23] ('the 2004 guidance') applies to patients classified as simple discharges – which it is thought make up 'at least 80% of all discharges'. These are discharges in which the patient is returned to his or her own home and which do not require social services involvement to the extent of requiring a community care assessment. For non-simple (classified as 'complex') discharges, the pathways guidance remains the relevant document.

5.14   The idea behind the 2004 guidance is to implement relatively simple procedures which it appears can have a dramatic impact on freeing up beds – including discharging patients earlier in the day before the peak demand for admissions (the build up starts in general at 7am and reaches its peak at 12.30pm); having discharge procedures operating on the same basis seven days a week; and authorising less senior medical/nursing staff to implement the process. The 2004 guidance stresses that 'patients and carers are at the centre of care and should be involved in discharge plans early in the patient's stay' and that 'discharge decisions are made following senior assessment of the patient on admission and patients and carers are informed about the expected date of discharge early in their stay'.[24]

Patient and carer involvement

5.15   Directions issued in 2004 have given added weight to earlier guidance regarding involving patients and carers. The Assessment Directions state that 'The local authority must consult the person, consider whether the person has any carers, and, where they think it appropriate, consult those carers.' Further they must provide information to the person and if appropriate any carers about the costs of any services they are considering providing.[25] Directions on the assessment for NHS continuing health care, place the same duties on the NHS to consult patients and carers, and to notify the patient in writing of the outcome of the assessment, giving reasons and to make a record on the patient's notes. The NHS body must further, if the person is not considered eligible for NHS continuing healthcare, inform the person (or where relevant someone acting on the person's behalf) of their right to request a review of the decision.[26]

5.16   The pathways guidance states that 'the engagement and active participation of individuals and their carers as equal partners is central to the delivery of care and in the planning of a successful discharge' (para 1.4)[27]

23   2004, available at http://www.dh.gov.uk/prod_consum_dh/groups/dh_digitalassets/ @dh/@en/documents/digitalasset/dh_4088367.pdf.
24   *Achieving Timely 'Simple' Discharges from Hospital*, 2004, p9.
25   Community Care Assessment Directions 2004, paras 2 and 4.
26   Delayed Discharges (Continuing Care) Directions 2007.
27   An equivalent statement is found at paras 22 and 24 of the Welsh Assembly circular *Hospital Discharge Planning Guidance*, 13 May 2005, WHC (2005) 035.

and stresses the importance of them being 'kept fully informed by regular reviews and updates of the care plan'.[28] The pathways guidance acknowledges that carers have often considered themselves marginalised by discharge arrangements, particularly with patients being sent home too early (para 4.1), leaving their carers to cope with unacceptable caring situations.[29] Working with carers is a responsibility of discharge co-ordinators – and it should not be seen merely as a social services function. If patients refuse permission to allow their carer to be involved in decisions about their future care, carers should be informed of this and their right to an assessment reinforced. Carers should be should be given time to consider their options 'in making what are often life changing decisions' and they should be 'informed about the support networks and services that may be available to them' (para 4.3).

5.17   At para 4.3 the pathways guidance makes the following points:

> The need of the carer should be under constant review to take account of their personal health and social care needs as well as the caring role they are undertaking. The assessment and review process should consider the need for a short-term break from caring.
>
> Patients may also have responsibilities such as being the parent of young children or as a carer of someone who has a disability and who is unable to live independently. It is important to identify whether an adult has dependent children and to ensure that arrangements are in place for their care during the period of admission. If the child is the carer of an adult with a chronic illness or disability, the child's own needs for support must be addressed. It is vital that every effort is made to ensure that the family has sufficient services to ensure that children are not left with unacceptable caring responsibilities that affect their welfare, education or development. In addition, patients can also be carers, and it is important to ensure that if they are caring for someone that they have the right services upon discharge, to ensure that they can look after their own needs, as well as the person they are caring for.

Mental capacity

5.18   In relation to patients with limited mental capacity the pathways guidance (at para 5.3) states that 'where patients cannot represent themselves, the next of kin, and/or an advocate, should be involved'; that 'advocates might enable views that differ from the carers' views to be heard' and that it is necessary therefore for staff to have access to interpreting and advocacy services. The Mental Capacity Act 2005 reinforces the importance of health and social care authorities' awareness of the situations when carers, health and welfare attorneys and deputies (if any) should be consulted as part of establishing the patient's best interests, and the situations when an Independent Mental Capacity Advocate is required (see para 18.67 where these questions are further considered).

28 Pathways guidance, para 1.2. And para 4.5.1 provides a detailed 'carer's checklist' of relevant factors to be considered.
29 *Hospital discharge practice briefing*, Carers UK, 2002, which reported that 43% of carers considered they were not given adequate support when the person returned home. See also J Mather et al, *Carers 2000*, Office of National Statistics.

Information/communication

5.19   In a number of investigations the Health Service Ombudsman has been critical of trusts which have failed to communicate properly with (and provide adequate information to) patients and their carers.[30] She has stressed that where the obligation to inform is a joint one (ie shared with the social services) this does not excuse a failure by the trust to provide the information (ie it cannot assume that social services will discharge its duty).[31] The ombudsman has also criticised as inadequate the provision of general brochures to patients and situations where staff provided patients with only limited advice on their possible options.[32]

5.20   The pathways guidance stresses the importance of patients and their carers being 'provided with information, both verbal and written, and in a range of media formats (to take into account any sensory or spoken language needs) on what to expect and their contribution to the process'. This should include details of arrangements, contact details and any relevant information regarding their future treatment and care (para 3.4), and para 4.2 advises that:

> Any form of communication must take account of the individual's ability to understand and absorb information. The same information will need to be available in plain language and in a variety of appropriate forms. This should include, for example, appropriate minority and ethnic languages and presentations in large print, Braille and British Sign Language. Other formats might also be appropriate including audiotapes and visual formats such as interactive CD-rom. For some patients it will be necessary to involve an advocate or interpreter to provide further assistance. Every effort must be made to ensure consistency and continuity of information from different personnel.[33]

Ward-based care/discharge co-ordinator

5.21   Central to the operation of an effective and sympathetic discharge process is the presence of a 'ward care co-ordinator or discharge co-ordinator'. This 'important' and 'highly skilled role' requires an 'experienced practitioner who has a good understanding of discharge planning' and although usually undertaken by nurses 'it may be appropriate in a transitional or rehabilitation service for a therapist or social worker to be the care co-ordinator' (pathways guidance at para 5.4.1). The guidance additionally observes (at para 5.4):

> On admission to the ward a named individual from the ward staff should be identified to coordinate all stages of the patient journey to proactively

---

30 Complaint nos E 1631/03–04 and E 2050/02–03, both in Selected Cases for October 2003 – March 2004 which contains five cases on the question of hospital discharge. Available at http://www.ombudsman.org.uk/improving_services/selected_cases/HSC/ic0403/index.html.

31 Fifth report for session 1995–96, *Investigations of Complaints about Long-Term NHS Care*, HMSO; Complaint E.685/94–95

32 Complaint E.672/94–95.

33 Department of Health, *Patient and public involvement in the new NHS*, 2000.

support and facilitate the work of the multidisciplinary team in delivering the best outcomes for the patient and guide them through the system to receive what they need, when they need it.[34] This role, henceforth referred to as the ward-based care co-ordinator, should focus on the needs of patients who have been identified as requiring additional support in discharge planning . . . If the patient is transferred to another ward it is the responsibility of the ward-based care co-ordinator to provide a formal transfer of responsibility.

Safe discharge

5.22   The pathways guidance stresses that 'planning for hospital discharge is part of an ongoing process that should start prior to admission (for planned admissions) and as soon as possible for all other admissions' (para 1.2). It explains the nature of the shared responsibility of the NHS and social services in the discharge decision in the following terms (para 5.4.3):

> A decision that a patient is medically fit for discharge can only be made by the patient's consultant (or by someone to whom the consultant has delegated his/her authority) or by another doctor who is responsible for the care of the patient. Patients, who have both health and social care needs, must only be discharged when they are clinically fit. This is a decision made by the multidisciplinary team when considering all the factors, which will include the relative safety of remaining in hospital or being elsewhere and the patient's and carer's view of these risks. It is also important to include the carer as part of the team as they will have expertise regarding the patient's home environment.

5.23   The *Hospital Discharge Workbook*[35] expressed this responsibility in a rather more direct way, namely:

> The decision that a patient is medically fit for discharge can only be made by a consultant (or by someone to whom the consultant has delegated his authority), or by another doctor who is responsible for the care of an individual patient (such as a general practitioner responsible for GP beds). However, the decision to discharge a patient should be the result of a jointly agreed, multi-disciplinary process in which social services are responsible for assessing the needs of people for social care.

5.24   The discharge protocol lists three key criteria for the making of the discharge decision and emphasises that they 'are not separate or sequential stages; all three should be addressed at the same time whenever possible':

1) a clinical decision has been made that the patient is ready for transfer;
2) a multi-disciplinary team decision has been made that the patient is ready for transfer; and
3) the patient is safe to discharge/transfer.

---

34   House of Commons Health Committee, *Delayed Discharges (2001–02)* vol 1, TSO.
35   Department of Health, 1994, p1: para 1 of the pathways guidance explains that it 'builds on the very successful *Hospital discharge workbook* first published by the Department of Health in 1994'.

5.25   The discharge protocol comments that:

> In some cases we are told the process consists almost entirely of the consultant deciding a patient is medically fit for discharge, followed by referral to social services. Hence the multi-disciplinary input to the decision making process is minimal and – in extreme cases – non-existent. In addition this does not fulfil the, now legal, requirement to begin planning for discharge as soon as possible during the hospital stay.

5.26   The discharge protocol goes on to analyse the critical questions in relation to each of the three steps:

1) The clinical decision (ready to transfer/discharge)
   - Does the patient need to remain in an acute bed to receive intensive medical input from a consultant team?
   - Does the patient need intensive or specialist nursing, therapy or other clinical support only available in an acute setting, such as the administration of specialist drugs or intensive monitoring through the use of specialist equipment?
   - Has the patient's condition been monitored within an agreed period?
   - Is the patient's health likely to deteriorate significantly if moved elsewhere?
   - Has the patient recovered from the acute episode sufficiently to be able to return home or move to another setting?
   - Could the patient be managed at home by primary care or in a nurse or therapy led unit?
2) The multi-disciplinary team decision (ready to transfer/discharge)
   - Will the patient benefit from further acute treatment and/or rehabilitation?
   - Can rehabilitation or recuperation be provided in an alternative setting, including the patient's own home and has the team come to a decision about where the patient should be managed?
   - What are the risks of remaining in the acute bed?
   - Has the patient (and have any carers) been involved in the assessment?
3) The objective decision (safe to transfer/discharge)
   - Does the multi-disciplinary team have a clear picture of the patient's living circumstances prior to this episode and know enough to be able to make a decision that the person is safe to discharge/transfer?
   - Can the assessment be continued/completed in another setting, including the person's own home?
   - What does the patient want and expect?
   - Has the carer been consulted and what are his or her views?
   - Has a similar level of need for this patient previously been met by primary and community care services?
   - Does everyone, including the patient and carer, understand the risk of transferring the patient?

5.27 Although the protocol uses the word 'assessment' this does not appear to refer to a 'community care assessment' but merely whether the patient and carer have been involved in the multi-disciplinary decision that he or she is safe to transfer. However CC(DD)A 2003 ss4(9) and (10) clarify that assessments carried out under this Act are to be treated as done under NHSCCA 1990 s47 or, in the case of carers, under the Carers and Disabled Children Act (CDCA) 2000 ss1 or 2 (see para 16.36 below). The delayed discharge guidance at para 36 refers to this as meaning not necessarily all of the assessment and that 'assessment for discharge covers the services needed to allow the patient to move from the acute bed – a further assessment may be needed to put in place a longer term package of care or the next step, eg from intermediate care to home'. Further it specifically states that if a person is discharged to a home care package, social services 'should check the adequacy of the care package within at most two weeks of discharge. This should ensure that the patients are suitably cared for and not, for example, unable to cope and at risk of a deterioration in their condition or of readmission to hospital.'[36]

Delayed discharge payments in England

5.28 The charging arrangements (known as 'reimbursement') apply to local authorities who delay the discharge of adults who are (1) safe to be discharged, (2) have been receiving acute medical care and (3) are in need of community care services. A lack of capacity in a community care service (for instance the absence of any available care home places) does not exempt social services from their liability to make a payment. These provisions do not apply in Wales.[37]

Acute medical care

5.29 The reimbursement rules currently only apply to patients receiving 'acute medical care' – defined as 'intensive NHS funded medical treatment provided by or under the supervision of a consultant which is for a limited time after which the patient no longer benefits from that treatment'. Maternity care, mental health care,[38] palliative care, intermediate care and care provided for recuperation or rehabilitation are excluded from the definition of acute care. CC(DD)A 2003 s14 enables the minister, by order, to extend the scope of the reimbursement provisions to cover NHS patients in care homes. The explanatory notes to CC(DD)A 2003 s14 state that the intention is to include in time 'patients receiving intermediate care in a care home setting . . . as well as those receiving intermediate care

---

36 Hospital Discharge Implementation Guidance 2003, para 107.
37 The Welsh Assembly has indicated that it does not intend to implement Part I of the Act (the fining provisions) – see Health and Social Services Committee Minutes HSS(2)-11–04(p.2) 6 October 2004 at para 3.3.4.
38 As detailed in Delayed Discharges (Mental Health Care) (England) Order 2003 SI No 2276 art 2.

in a hospital'. It appears that support is growing for the extension of the reimbursement provisions to cover mental health inpatient services.[39]

5.30   The Department of Health held a number of preconsultation events during 2005 on whether to extend reimbursement to mental health and non-acute settings, but as yet no final decision has been made. In the meantime good practice guidance has been issued by the Care Services Improvement Partnership in relation to discharge from mental health settings.[40]

The timings of the CC(DD)A 2003 notices

5.31   The NHS is required to give social services two notifications

1) The first, known as an assessment notification (under section 2) gives notice of the patient's possible need for services on discharge. Following this notification, social services have a minimum of three days to carry out an assessment and arrange care.

2) The second, a discharge notification (under section 5) gives notice of the day on which it is proposed that the patient will be discharged.

5.32   Reimbursement liability commences on the day after the minimum period (the third day after an assessment notification) or the day after the proposed discharge date, whichever is the later. A notification after 2pm is counted from the next day.

5.33   The technicalities of the notifications are slightly involved.[41] Notifications sent on Sundays and Bank Holidays are deemed to have been sent on the following days as are notifications sent after 2pm on a Friday or after 5pm on any other day.[42] Originally it was intended that this would change so that all days were treated in the same way and no concessions made for holidays or weekends, however so far no changes have been made.

The CC(DD)A 2003 assessment obligations

The NHS

5.34   Before the NHS can issue the first notification (under section 2) it must:

• take reasonable steps to ensure that an assessment for NHS continuing

39 R Lewis and J Glasby, 'Delayed discharge from mental health hospitals' (2006) 14 *Health & Social Care in the Community* 225–230.

40 Care Services Improvement Partnership, *A Positive Outlook – a good practice toolkit to improve discharge from inpatient mental health care*, April 2007, available at http://www.cat.csip.org.uk/_library/A%20Positive%20Outlook.pdf.

41 Detailed explanations are given in guidance at http://www.dh.gov.uk/ PolicyAndGuidance/OrganisationPolicy/IntegratedCare/ DelayedDischarges/ DH_4126245.

42 2003 Regulations, regs 10 and 11.

health care is carried out in all cases where it appears that the patient may have need for such care;[43]

- consult with the patient about involving social services (and the notification to social services must clarify the outcome of this consultation and provide certain minimum information – detailed in the regulations);
- identify the patient's responsible social services authority.[44]

5.35 Not infrequently it appears that the first time that a social services authority is aware that a trust deems a patient ready for discharge, is the receipt of a section 2 notice. Since service of a section 2 notice starts the discharge conveyor belt moving – a process which the social services authority is unable to delay without paying a fine – this would appear to be questionable practice and contrary to the above guidance.[45] Where community care services are likely to be required on discharge, the duty of care owed by both authorities to the patient would suggest that he or she should not be discharged unless they both deem a discharge within a fixed timescale to be safe and it should not be open to the NHS to act unilaterally in this respect. This approach is reinforced by the above cited Healthcare Commission's *State of Healthcare Report 2004*[46] (see para 5.4) which stressed the importance of ensuring that health staff discussed discharge arrangements with patients *before* the decision to discharge took place.

Social services

Community care assessment obligation

5.36 On receiving the assessment notification, social services are required to undertake an assessment of the patient's needs for community care services – and this 'is to be treated as done' under NHSCCA 1990 s47[47] (see para 3.14 above).

---

43 Delayed Discharge (Continuing Care) Directions 2007, direction 2(2). The 2004 Directions which the 2007 replace stated that before issuing a notification to social services 'The NHS body *must* carry out such an assessment as it considers appropriate of the patient's need for continuing care, in consultation, where it considers it appropriate, with the relevant social services authority.' The 2007 Directions only require the NHS body 'to *take reasonable steps to ensure* that an assessment for NHS Continuing Healthcare is carried out in all cases where it appears to the body that the patient may have a need for such care, in consultation, where it considers it appropriate, with the relevant social services authority.' (Italics added).
44 HSC 2003/009: LAC (2003) 21, para 65.
45 Unless some collateral agreement exists between the two bodies to mitigate this consequence.
46 Accessible at http://www.healthcarecommission.org.uk/_db/_documents/ 04006366.pdf.
47 CC(DD)A 2003 s4(9).

Carer's assessment obligation

5.37 The assessment notification also triggers social services' obligations under the CDCA 2000[48] and in this respect the discharge guidance states:[49]

> Just as assessment for discharge need not be a full community care assessment, a carer's assessment related to a patient discharge may be only part of a full assessment which continues after the patient is discharged. Where the carer will be undertaking lifting, or other tasks that need training to ensure that the carer or patient is not put at risk, staff should ensure that appropriate training is provided.

The CC(DD)A reimbursement liability

5.38 To be liable for reimbursement, it must be social services provision and only social services provision which is not available.[50] The discharge guidance goes into considerable detail as to how responsibility can arise in various situations – for instance when jointly commissioned care services are delayed; where the patient receives direct payments and so on.

5.39 If social services do not have services in place by 11am of the day after the proposed discharge date, such that the discharge cannot take place, they are liable for a charge[51] – provided this is the sole reason for the delay. The charge, which may be increased by regulation,[52] is currently £100 per day for the majority of social services authority areas, but £120 for authorities in the Home Counties, London and the South East.[53] Liability ends when the patient is discharged[54] or the patient needs to remain in hospital for other treatment or dies.[55]

Delays to discharge caused by moving into a care home

5.40 The delayed discharge guidance states that 'it is established good practice that where possible people should not move directly from a hospital to a care home for the first time, but should have a period of time to make personal arrangements and adjust'.[56] However it is not uncommon for patients to move permanently into care homes from an acute ward.[57]

---

48 Ibid s4(3).
49 HSC 2003/009: LAC (2003)21, para 47.
50 CC(DD)A 2003 s6; HSC 2003/009: LAC (2003)21, para 55.
51 CC(DD)A 2003 s6; 2003 Regulations, regs 10 and 11.
52 Currently detailed in the 2003 Regulations, reg 7.
53 Known as 'Higher Rate' authorities and listed in the Schedule to the 2003 Regulations.
54 CC(DD)A 2003 s6(4)(b).
55 2003 Regulations, reg 9.
56 Para 104.
57 In a study investigating the implementation of the reimbursement scheme, CSCI found that in some councils up to a third of older people needing council support on leaving hospital were moving into a care home. CSCI, *Leaving Hospital – the Price of Delays*, October 2004.

5.41   Not inconsiderable numbers of patients considered to be inappropriately occupying NHS beds do so because they have been assessed as
requiring a care home place and either the home of their choice has no
current vacancies or the patient does not wish to move into a care home.
All patients should be able to choose which home they move into.

5.42   In this respect the pathways guidance states (para 2.2):

> Although *patient choice* is considered extremely important, patients who
> have been assessed as not requiring NHS continuing in-patient care, do
> not have the right to occupy, indefinitely, an NHS bed (with the exception of
> a very small number of cases where a patient is being placed under Part 11
> of the Mental Health Act 1983). They do, however, have the right to refuse
> to be discharged from NHS care into a care home.

5.43   Those who will be funding themselves are normally not the responsibility
of social services (unless patients are unable to make their own arrangements and have no one else willing and able to assist them – see para 7.26
below). In such cases the social services authority will have no
reimbursement liability and it will be for the NHS to work out how best to
provide for patients who cannot return home but no longer require acute
medical in hospital. Patients who are the responsibility of social services
come under the Choice of Accommodation Directions and accompanying
guidance (see para 7.92 below). In such cases it will be for social services
to work out interim arrangements in order to avoid liability for
reimbursement.

5.44   The delayed discharge guidance deals with this problem as follows:

> 97. . . . [Local protocols] should make it clear that an acute bed is not an
> appropriate place to wait and the alternatives that will be offered. Where
> social services are responsible for providing services and a person's
> preferred home of choice is not immediately available, they should offer an
> interim package of care. All interim arrangements should be based solely
> on the patients assessed needs and sustain or improve their level of
> independence. If no alternative is provided which can meet the patient's
> needs, social services are liable for reimbursement.
>
> 98. Social services should take all reasonable steps to gain a patient's
> agreement to a care package, that is to provide a care package which the
> patient can be reassured will meet the needs identified and agreed in the
> care plan. . . .
>
> 99. If the patient continues to unreasonably refuse the care package
> offered by social services they cannot stay in a hospital bed indefinitely and
> will need to make their own arrangements so that they can be discharged
> safely. If at a later date further contact is made with social services
> regarding the patient, the council should re-open the care planning
> process, if it is satisfied that the patient's needs remain such to justify the
> provision of services and there is no longer reason to think that the patient
> will persist in refusing such services unreasonably. Councils may wish to
> take their own legal advice in such circumstances.
>
> 100. Where appropriate alternative services, which take account of the
> patient's views, have been offered, and active encouragement given to the
> patient to transfer, but they unreasonably refuse to move to the alternative,
> social services will not be held responsible . . .

5.45   Although the guidance stresses that patients have the right to refuse to move into a care home[58] the trust will, in appropriate cases, be able to evict patients who have no need for NHS care and are merely remaining because they do not wish to move into a care home. In *Barnet Primary Care Trust v X*[59] the patient had been in a hospital ward for a prolonged period and for the previous three years he had not had any medical reason to be there. Although his home was uninhabitable due to ongoing (and very slowly progressing) renovation works, there were several residential homes capable of meeting his social care needs. The patient did not however agree to the trust's repeated attempts to discuss his discharge. Wilkie J held that the patient was not entitled to occupy the bed which he did or any other part of the trust's premises because he was not in need of any ongoing medical or nursing treatment. In his view, the evidence was overwhelming. Since alternative arrangements had been proposed, the court considered that eviction would not violate his article 8 rights.

5.46   The fact that the patient had been in hospital for three years indicates the difficulties experienced by the NHS when patients refuse to move into a care home. Some local NHS acute trusts have produced local guidelines to patients and staff to cover such situations.

Where the preferred care home is full

5.47   A more frequent reason for delay is that the care home of choice is full, and the question arises as to what arrangements should then be made for the service user. The situation is generally of most concern to the statutory agencies, if the patient is in hospital awaiting discharge to such a home. The Choice of Accommodation 2004 guidance states at para 2.5.9 as follows:

> Waiting for the preferred care home should not mean that the person's care needs are not met in the interim or that they wait in a setting unsuitable for their assessed needs, and this includes an acute hospital bed, until the most suitable or preferred accommodation becomes available. In view of the Community Care (Delayed Discharges etc.) Act 2003, councils should have contingency arrangements in place, that address the likelihood that an individual's preferred accommodation will not always be readily available. These arrangements should meet the needs of the individual and sustain or improve their level of independence. For some, the appropriate interim arrangement could be an enhanced care package at home.[60]

5.48   The pathways guidance at para 7.6 gives the following advice in relation to patients who are the responsibility of social services as well as those who will be funding and arranging their own care :

> Because residential placements can be delayed considerably while people wait for a place in their home of choice to become available, transition or

---

58 LAC 2004(20), para 2.5.13.
59 [2006] EWHC 787; [2006] All ER (D) 65 (March) and see further Stephen Cragg, 'Legislation update' (2006) *Times* 11 April.
60 LAC 2004(20).

interim placement should be considered when the first choice of home is not available. If the interim placement meets a person's needs, it is acceptable for a person to move from an acute setting to a transitional placement until a permanent/alternative choice becomes available.

In circumstances where waiting for a care home placement is causing an unacceptable delay in care transfer, the following processes should be put in place:

- Patients and carers should be informed about the possibility of an interim placement as soon as possible. It is important that people understand that it is inappropriate for them to remain on an acute ward indefinitely while they are waiting for admission to a care home.
- The interim or transitional placement must be able to meet the assessed care needs of the patient and they must receive active help to move on to the home of their choice when a place is available.
- There must be support (such as an independent advisory service) to patients and their carers in making important decisions. Self-funders should also be offered support in making such choices.
- Practitioners should be signed up to the use of transitional placements with appropriate protocols.
- Trusts should have in place agreed policies and procedures to address situations in which patients and their families refuse to move from an acute bed to another setting.

5.49   A Department of Health 'questions and answers statement' (on the CC(DD)A 2003) addresses the question of patient choice, by advising:[61]

NHS staff will have to make a judgement about whether the patient will be safe to discharge without any help from social services. If they do not think it will be safe, they will need to explain further to the patient their concerns and this might be helped by contacting social services to discuss options with the patient. If the patient still refuses any help from social services the NHS will need to consider providing NHS services to help the patient go home safely.

Delayed discharge and ordinary residence

5.50   Difficult questions are likely to arise concerning 'ordinary residence' since responsibility for the assessment process (and ultimately the reimbursement liability) depends upon the NHS body serving the correct local authority. The responsible authority is the one in which the patient is ordinarily resident (considered generally in chapter 6 below). The basic duties are detailed in the 2003 Regulations[62] and the delayed discharge guidance which at para 65 advises that if the NHS trust serves the wrong council it will have to withdraw the notice and 'risks causing a delay in the patient's discharge, as the time allowed for the assessment and care planning process starts again for the new council'. At para 67 it then advises:

---

61   *Community Care (Delayed Discharges etc.) Act – Frequently Asked Questions on Reimbursement* (Q29).
62   2003 Regulations, reg 18.

... if a council receives an assessment notification in respect of a patient who it believes is ordinarily resident elsewhere, it should inform the issuing NHS body, which should withdraw the notice if it agrees with the council's opinion. If the NHS body does not agree and the matter cannot be resolved locally and informally, the council receiving the assessment notification must proceed with assessment and care planning as if it were the responsible authority.

5.51   However, after services have been provided or reimbursement has been paid, the council which has been dealing with the case is entitled to reclaim the costs incurred in providing services or any reimbursement payments, if made, from the correct council (delayed discharge guidance, para 69).

5.52   Disputes about ordinary residence will be determined by the department of health unless the dispute involves a Welsh council and an English council – in which case it is the country in which the patient is located which will indicate who has responsibility for determining ordinary residence (ie, either the department of health or the Welsh Assembly) see para 6.45.

Reviews/challenges to discharge decisions

5.53   Strategic health authorities (SHAs) are required to set up disputes panels to arbitrate between social services and the primary care trusts (PCTs) over disputes as to reimbursement. These panels are not for use by patients challenging their discharge (for whom a separate process exists – see para 5.57 for analysis of the review process and para 27.88 where the general NHS complaints process is considered). The panels comprise an independent chair person and two wing members, one from a local authority and the other an NHS representative – both of whom must be from a different local authority/NHS body to the ones involved in the dispute (2003 Regulations, reg 15).

Patient's right to seek a review of a discharge decision

5.54   If patients are unhappy about the assessment of their needs or the pro-posed care package on offer after they leave hospital 'they should have access to the appropriate complaints procedure. But in the meantime they do not have the right to stay in an acute hospital bed if they no longer need that type of care and the NHS and social services will need to consider providing suitable non-acute care.'[63] In such cases it is likely that while the complaint is being dealt with other arrangements will be made; the delayed discharge guidance suggests a number of alternatives at paras 104–106.

5.55   If there is a dispute about whether a patient should have been assessed as needing continuing NHS health care, from 26 June 2007 the guidance contained in *The National Framework for NHS Continuing NHS Healthcare*

---

63   HSC 2003/009: LAC (2003)21, para 96.

and NHS Funded Nursing Care should apply as good practice. From 1 October 2007, when directions will be issued under the NHSA 2006 and under the Local Authority Social Services Act 1970 come into force it will become mandatory guidance. The previous guidance in HSC 2001/17 and LAC (2001)26 has been cancelled.

5.56   The 2007 guidance differs from the 2001 guidance in that it introduces into guidance a practice that has become common, that of using a PCT review panel before taking the review to a SHA panel (see below). The NHS Continuing Healthcare (Responsibilities) Directions 2007 states that a person can apply to the SHA for a review if he or she 'has been unable to resolve the matter through any local dispute resolution procedure where the use of such a procedure would not have caused undue delay.' This appears to be an attempt to try to speed up the often protracted procedures that PCTs can sometimes adopt at the local resolution stage.

5.57   The 2007 guidance (at Annex E) reissued with little change the 2001 guidance concerning the establishment by SHAs of panels to adjudicate where a patient/carer challenges an NHS decision that the patient is not eligible for continuing care funded by the NHS. The review process is considered further at para 14.76.

5.58   The 2007 Directions[64] also largely replicate the previous 2004 directions relating to the setting up of panels. However one change is that the 2004 directions stipulated that the SHA must provide the applicant with its decisions (and reasons) in writing within two weeks of it receiving a request for a review (except in exceptional circumstances). The new guidance issued on 26 June 2007 ('the 2007 guidance') merely states that '[e]ach SHA needs to identify clear timeframes for the process which should be made explicit, especially to individuals and carers'. The 2007 Directions just state that 'notice must be given as soon as is reasonably practicable'. Patients can use the review process if they consider the criteria for continuing NHS health care have not been properly applied. During the period of the review the patient remains the responsibility of the NHS and no delay liability accrues to social services.[65] The 2007 guidance further stipulates that the PCT should continue to fund appropriate care. Any existing care package, whether hospital care or community health services, should not be withdrawn under any circumstances until the outcome of the review is known.[66] The ombudsman found maladministration where a patient was discharged into a care home when it was clear before she left hospital that her husband would wish to use the review procedure.[67]

---

64 The Continuing Care (National Health Service Responsibilities) Directions 2004 (which will be replaced in October 2007 when the new continuing NHS healthcare framework comes into operation).
65 HSC 2003/009: LAC (2003)21, para 42.
66 The National Framework for NHS Continuing Healthcare and NHS-funded Nursing care Annex E para 8.
67 Case no E.33/99–00 against Barnet NHS Healthcare Trust and Barnet Health Authority. Investigations Completed October 1999–March 2000.

Obligations following discharge

5.59   In general the normal obligations to provide services that have been assessed as being required will apply post hospital discharge. In addition the delayed discharge guidance states that if a patient is discharged home either as an interim measure or on a long-term basis, social services 'should check the adequacy of the arrangements within at most two weeks of discharge. This should ensure the patients are suitably cared for and are not, for example, unable to cope and at risk of deterioration of their condition or readmission to hospital' (para 107).

5.60   In other cases where interim arrangements have been made because the person's home of choice has no vacancies, the guidance states that councils:

> . . . should place individuals on the waiting list of their preferred accommodation and aim to move them into that accommodation as soon as possible. Information about how the waiting list is handled should be clear and the individual kept informed of progress. If the duration of the interim arrangement exceeds a reasonable time period, e.g 12 weeks, the individual should be reassessed to ensure that the interim and the preferred accommodation, are still able to meet the individual's assessed needs. . .[68]

68 LAC (2004)20, para 2.5.10.

CHAPTER 6

Ordinary residence

Establishing which geographical area is responsible for providing social care or NHS services

continued

Introduction

6.1 The baffling nature of the 'ordinary residence' provisions originate in the Poor Law. The earliest such laws placed responsibility for the support of the poor on the parishes within which they were 'settled'[1] and there is considerable evidence to suggest that these parishes resorted to 'underhand means to get rid of paupers',[2] including clandestine exporting of the poor into neighbouring parishes.[3] Marshall comments that 'in some cases the law was so complex and obscure that both parishes might have good grounds for thinking themselves right'[4] – with the result that there was considerable litigation between the authorities.[5] The fact that between 2001 and 2006 39 disputes[6] between authorities reached an impasse to the extent that there was an application to the secretary of state for a resolution, indicates that matters have not improved to any great extent in the 21st century.

6.2 Before providing or arranging any services, the local authority or local NHS body will check that it is the body that is responsible for doing so. In the case of local authorities this is generally done by reference to the service user's 'ordinary residence'.[7] The importance of the 'ordinary residence' of the service user varies depending on which statute is used to provide the service. For the NHS it is done by reference to establishing the responsible commissioner as described in paras 6.52 to 6.75 in this chapter.[8]

Ordinary residence – social services

6.3 Not all of the statutes regulating the provision of community care services by local authorities contain specific 'ordinary residence' restrictions: broadly speaking the situation can be summarised as in Table 7 below.

---

1 D Marshall, *The English Poor Law in the Eighteenth Century*, Routledge, 1926, p162, states that this responsibility dates 'back to 43 Eliz C.2 [*An Act for the Relief of the Poor (1601)*] and Vagrancy Laws of Richard II & Tudors' (eg the Statute of Labourers 1351 and 1388).
2 ME Rose, *English Poor Law*, David & Charles, 1971, p191.
3 Sir FM Eden, *The State of the Poor Volume 1*, 1797, Frank Cass & Co, Facsimile edition, 1966, p185.
4 Marshall (note 1 above) p169.
5 PA Fideler, *Social Welfare in Pre-Industrial England*, Palgrave, 2006, p143.
6 HC Debates col 247W, 15 March 2005 and email correspondence between the Department of Health and Age Concern, 31 July 2006.
7 Similar but distinct from the device of local connection used under Housing Act 1996 Part VII; in this respect, see LAC (93)7 paras 16–17.
8 Department of Health, *Establishing the responsible commissioner: guidance for PCT commissioners on the application of the legal framework on PCTs' secondary care commissioning responsibilities*, April 2006, as revised March 2007.

Table 7: Ordinary residence				
Statute	**Ordinary residence**			
	of direct legislative relevance	*of indirect legislative relevance*	*of no legislative relevance*	*For further details see para*
NAA 1948 Part III	√			6.6
HSPHA 1968 s45			√	20.18
CSDPA 1970 s2	√			9.64
HASSASSAA 1983 Sch 9			√	20.33
MHA 1983 s117	√			21.29
CA 1989 Part III	√			6.33
NHSCCA 1990 s47		√		3.77
C(RS)A 1995		√		16.33
CDCA 2000		√		6.41
HSCA 2001, ss57 and 58		√		12.6
CC(DD)A 2003	√			5.50
C(EO)A 2004		√		16.41
NHSA 2006, Sch 20 NHS(W)A 2006 Sch 15			√	9.137

Ordinary residence and the National Assistance Act 1948

6.4   The National Assistance Act (NAA) 1948 places primary responsibility for the provision of its services (under sections 21 and 29) on the authority in which the relevant person is 'ordinarily resident'.

6.5   In relation to the accommodation obligation under section 21, section 24 provides as follows:

Authority liable for provision of accommodation.

24 (1) The local authority empowered under this Part of this Act to provide residential accommodation for any person shall subject to the following provisions of this Part of this Act be the authority in whose area the person is ordinarily resident.

. . .

(3) Where a person in the area of a local authority –
   (a) is a person with no settled residence, or
   (b) not being ordinarily resident in the area of the local authority, is in urgent need of residential accommodation under this Part of this Act,
   the authority shall have the like power to provide residential accommodation for him as if he were ordinarily resident in their area.
(4) Subject to and in accordance with the arrangements under section twenty-one of this Act, a local authority shall have power, as respects a person ordinarily resident in the area of another local authority, with the consent of that other authority to provide residential accommodation for him in any case where the authority would have a

duty to provide such accommodation if he were ordinarily resident in their area.

(5) Where a person is provided with residential accommodation under this Part of this Act, he shall be deemed for the purposes of this Act to continue to be ordinarily resident in the area in which he was ordinarily resident immediately before the residential accommodation was provided for him.

(6) For the purposes of the provision of residential accommodation under this Part of this Act, a patient in a hospital vested in the Secretary of State, a Primary Care Trust, or an NHS trust or an NHS foundation trust shall be deemed to be ordinarily resident in the area, if any, in which he was ordinarily resident immediately before he was admitted as a patient to the hospital, whether or not he in fact continues to be ordinarily resident in that area.

(7) In subsection (6) above 'NHS trust' means a National Health Service trust established under the National Health Service Act 2006, the National Health Service (Wales) Act 2006 or under the National Health Service (Scotland) Act 1978 and 'Primary Care Trust' means a Primary Care Trust established under section 18 of the National Health Service Act 2006.

6.6   Directions issued by the secretary of state in LAC (93)10 place a duty on local authorities to provide accommodation for the categories of person listed in NAA 1948 s21 'who are ordinarily resident in their area and other persons who are in urgent need thereof'.[9] In the other situations in section 24 it remains just a power. The position can be summarised as follows (Table 8 below.)

Table 8: Residential accommodation – NAA 1948 s21			
	Ordinarily resident	**No settled residence**	**Not ordinarily resident**
P O W E R	Expectant or nursing mothers (although they may also come within the ambit of 'any other circumstance' if over 18 – see column below).		Persons aged 18 or over who by reason of age, illness, disability or any other circumstance AND the other authority agrees.
D U T Y	Persons aged 18 or over who by reason of age, illness, disability or any other circumstance (which includes a mental disorder of any description and alcohol or drug dependent persons).	Persons aged 18 or over who by reason of age, illness, disability or any other circumstance AND are living in the authority's area when the need arises.	Persons aged 18 or over who by reason of age, illness, disability or any other circumstance AND who are in urgent need.

9   LAC (93)10 appendix 1 para 2(1)(b).

6.7   The duty to provide NAA 1948 s29 services[10] applies only to persons, who are ordinarily resident in the local authority's area, whereas a power exists to provide services for other persons.[11] There are no exceptions to these two basic requirements (eg, no exception for cases of urgency). Ordinary residence has the same meaning as in relation to NAA 1948 s21 (see para 7.44) with a minor exception under NAA 1948 s29(7) in relation to certain service users who are (or have been) employed in a workshop or an equivalent occupational activity promoted by the social services authority (see para 7.156). In *R v Berkshire CC ex p P*[12] Laws J described the arrangement of the section as follows:

> In my judgment s29(1) confers two distinct functions on local authorities; one permissive, the other mandatory. Within it the duty to make arrangements is confined to cases where the Secretary of State has given a direction relating to persons ordinarily resident in the authority's area. The power to make arrangements is not so confined; it arises where the Secretary of State has given his approval to arrangements being made, and his approval may be given without regard to the place of residence of any potential beneficiary.

6.8   Although it will often be academic to individuals which authority has the responsibility for providing their care services, this will not always be so: most obviously this will be the case where one authority has more generous eligibility criteria than another (see para 3.150). The question was also of importance in *R (J and others) v Southend BC and Essex CC*[13] where a number of service users had in effect become stranded when Southend had become a unitary authority and ceased to be part of Essex County Council. Essex service users continued to attend day centres in the new unitary council area in spite of it no longer being within their council area. When Southend BC decided to close one day centre and restrict the use of the other to its residents only, the court found no duty on Southend to assess an Essex resident prior to closure – that responsibility was for Essex.

Defining ordinary residence

6.9   Although NAA 1948 fails to provide any statutory definition for the term 'ordinary residence', the Department of Health has issued interpretative guidance in circular LAC (93)7, which includes reference to a number of reported decisions in which its meaning has been considered. It also covers the process for dispute resolution. In 2004 the Department of Health committed itself to update and revise LAC (93)7[14] but, as at August 2007, no such revision had been published. In Wales virtually identical guidance (to LAC (93)7) on ordinary residence exists as WOC 41/93,[15]

10   LAC (93)10 appendix 2 para 2(1); albeit that it is only a target duty, see para 9.16.
11   (1996) 1 CCLR 141.
12   Ibid, p148G.
13   [2005] EWHC 3457 (Admin).
14   HSC 2003/009: LAC (2003)21 para 68.
15   *Ordinary Residence – Personal Social Services*, 26 June 1993.

which also contains advice on the process for disputes resolution. In contrast Scotland has consulted on options for change[16] and as a consequence enacted new legislation to clarify and update the ordinary residence provisions.[17]

6.10   The key is in the word 'residence'; it will generally be the place where a person's normal residential address is to be found. The circular states that the phrase involves questions of fact and degree, and factors such as time, intention[18] and continuity.

6.11   The leading case on ordinary residence is the House of Lords' decision in *Shah v Barnet LBC*.[19] In Lord Scarman's judgment a person's long-term future intentions or expectations are not relevant; the test is not what is a person's real home[20] but whether a person can show a regular, habitual mode of life in a particular place, the continuity of which has persisted despite temporary absences.[21] A person's attitude is only relevant in two respects; the residence must be voluntarily adopted, and there must be a settled purpose in living in the particular residence. 'Ordinary residence' is to be given its 'ordinary and natural meaning', namely 'a man's abode in a particular place or country which he had adopted voluntarily and for settled purposes as part of the regular order of his life for the time being, whether of short or long duration'.[22]

6.12   *R v Waltham Forest LBC ex p Vale*[23] concerned a 28-year-old applicant with profound learning disabilities such that she was totally dependent on her parents. In these circumstances the court held that 'concepts of voluntarily adopted residence and settled purpose did not arise'. Importing principles from child care law,[24] it determined that her ordinary residence was that of her parents, not because it was her real home, but because it was her 'base'. The court further held that a person's ordinary residence could result after a stay in one place of only short duration; and that there was no reason why one month should be adjudged too short.

6.13   The *Waltham Forest* decision was tested in *R v Redbridge LBC ex p East Sussex CC*[25] which concerned two adult male autistic twins with profound learning disabilities who were boarded at a school in East Sussex, but whose parents lived in Redbridge. Applying the principles enunciated in the *Waltham Forest* decision, the court held that the twins were at law ordinarily resident in Redbridge. Subsequently, however, the parents went to live in Nigeria. It was held that when this occurred the twins ceased to

16 Consultation on the proposed amendment to the Social Work Scotland Act 1968 issued 5 September 2005, accessible at http://www.scotland.gov.uk/Publications/2005/09/placed-persons/contents.

17 Adult Support and Protection (Scotland) Act 2007 s65.

18 In view of the comments of Lord Scarman in *Shah v Barnet LBC* [1983] 1 All ER 226 intention must be given a restrictive interpretation.

19 Ibid: a case concerning the interpretation of 'ordinary residence' for the purposes of the Education Act 1962.

20 Ibid, p239.

21 Ibid, p236.

22 Ibid, p235.

23 (1985) *Times* 25 February, QBD.

24 See eg *In re P (GE) (an infant)* [1965] Ch 568.

25 (1993) *Times* 3 January; [1993] COD 265, QBD.

have any settled residence and accordingly became the responsibility of East Sussex. LAC (93)7 advises, however, that except in cases involving persons with severe learning difficulties, 'an adult with learning disabilities should be regarded as capable of forming his own intention of where he wishes to live'.[26]

6.14   The question of where residence has been 'voluntarily adopted' has arisen in relation to asylum seekers, who if accommodated by the National Asylum Seekers Support Service (NASS), have no choice as to where they are accommodated. In *R (Mani) v Lambeth LBC*[27] it was held that as the applicant had been living in NASS accommodation for six months, it was sufficiently voluntary.[28]

Residential accommodation

6.15   Where a person is provided with residential accommodation by a social services authority, he or she is deemed to continue to be ordinarily resident in the area in which he or she was ordinarily resident immediately before the residential accommodation was provided.[29] This will be the case even if the person is in effect a 'self funder' (see paras 7.27 and 8.75), but has relied upon the local authority to make the placement and contract with the care home.

6.16   What constitutes 'making a placement' has been considered in two cases determined by the secretary of state. In the first, determined in 1996, the social worker involved in the assessment assisted the resident to the extent of taking her to the home in the other authority. But as the resident had assets over the capital limit, she made her own contract with the home and so was thus considered to be ordinarily resident in the new area. Taking someone to the home did not constitute making the placement.[30]

6.17   In the second determination, the secretary of state[31] found that a young man who lacked capacity and who had residential accommodation arranged for him remained the responsibility of that council after he moved to another authority in spite of an inheritance which meant he could afford to pay for his own care. Although he had a receiver to look

---

26   LAC (93)7 para 12: and see also *R v Kent CC and Salisbury and Pierre* (2000) 3 CCLR 38 (at para 6.47 below).
27   [2002] EWHC 735 (Admin); (2002) 5 CCLR 486.
28   Relying on Lord Slynn's analysis in *Shah v Barnet LBC* [1983] 1 All ER 226, 'so long as that place where he eats and sleeps is voluntarily accepted by him, the reason why he is there rather than somewhere else does not prevent that place from being his normal residence. He may not like it, he may prefer some other place, but that place is for the relevant time the place where he normally resides. If a person, having no other accommodation, takes his few belongings and moves into a barn for a period to work on a farm that is where during that period he is normally resident, however much he might prefer some more permanent or better accommodation.'
29   NAA 1948 s24(5). The situation will generally be otherwise where the person has independently admitted him/herself to the home and without financial assistance from the local authority – see LAC (93)7 paras 10 and 15.
30   Determination dated 8 March 1996 (not published).
31   Determination dated 20 July 1999 (not published).

after his finances, the council had not contacted her with a view to her making the contract with the home and there was no evidence that it expected her to do so. The invoices were sent to the council. The secretary of state found that the authority, by contacting the home in the new area, arranging a visit by the manager to see the young man and his subsequent immediate transfer, and the issuing of invoices to the council by the home, amounted to 'the characteristics of an arrangement for the provision of residential accommodation under Part III of the 1948 Act'.

6.18 Although in the above case the receiver was not asked to make the arrangements, a similar situation could arise if an attorney or receiver refused to contract with a home in another authority area. Guidance makes clear that the duty remains with the authority when people who cannot make their own arrangements have no one who is willing and able to do so (see para 7.27 below).

6.19 The capital disregard rules can have an affect on ordinary residence, for example the 12-week disregard of the property (see para 8.63) and the deferred payments scheme (see para 8.75), as can local authority funding pending a resident's access to funds (for instance if waiting for a house sale to go through). People benefiting from one of these provisions may choose to move into a care home in another authority's area, albeit funded on a temporary basis by their former local authority. As their former local authority in these circumstances will have entered into a contract with the home, it will remain the deemed 'ordinary residence'. However if at any time the home authority ends the contract with the home (for instance because the resident now has access to his or her funds), any request for future assistance required by the resident will need to be addressed to the authority in which the home is situated.[32]

6.20 A further difficulty can arise when a resident, placed by another authority in a care home (and so deemed to be ordinarily resident in the placing authority's area), leaves to take up a tenancy and receives domiciliary care and support. Another not uncommon difficulty results from a care home deregistration, or a change in an adult placement arrangement (in such cases it is now the scheme rather than the individual placement that is registered – see para 15.115). On leaving the care home the person's ordinary residence crystallises in the local authority area in which he or she is actually living. With the greater emphasis on independent living, there is likely to be an increase in the number of such situations. Informal advice from the Department of Health states:

> Where a local authority provides a person with accommodation under Part 3 of the National Assistance Act 1948, then the deeming provision will apply and the person will be deemed to be ordinarily resident in the area in which he or she was ordinarily resident immediately before the accommodation was provided. But the deeming provisions only apply to Part 3 accommodation.
>
> Where a person ceases to be in Part 3 accommodation then the question of where they are ordinarily resident is decided by looking at the facts and the

32 Letter from Department of Health to Age Concern England, 17 April 1998.

relevant case law in each particular case. However, if a person is living in their own home the starting assumption would probably be that they are ordinarily resident in the local authority in which their home is located. The cost of any non-residential care they require will, therefore, usually be the responsibility of the local authority in whose area they have chosen to settle but each case will depend on its particular facts.

Where a person is transferring from Part 3 accommodation to other forms of social care and the responsibility for funding that care moves from one local authority to another, the Department expects the local authorities involved to make any necessary changes to the funding arrangements in a way which ensures continuity of care and appropriate care for the service user.[33]

6.21 The deregistration question has been considered in a secretary of state's determination, in a case concerning a young man with moderate learning disabilities. His care home deregistered and then granted him a tenancy – the rent for which was covered by housing benefit. Upon deregistration he ceased to be accommodated under the NAA 1948 and accordingly the 'deeming provision' in section 24(5) no longer applied. The secretary of state held that the residence had been 'voluntarily' adopted as the young man had made links in the area and had entered into a tenancy agreement. Based on the particular facts, it appears that the decision would have been no different had he lacked the capacity to form an intention as to where he wished to live.[34]

Hospital

6.22 Where a person is in NHS care he or she is deemed to be ordinarily resident in the area in which he or she was ordinarily resident immediately before admission as a patient to the NHS facility.[35] Where a person was not ordinarily resident in any area prior to admission, the responsible social services authority will be the one in whose area he or she is at that time.[36] The guidance suggests that these principles should also be followed when assessing responsibility for people leaving prisons, resettlement units and other similar establishments.[37]

No settled residence

6.23 When a person presents him/herself to a social services authority and claims to have no settled residence or fixed abode, the authority is advised that it should normally accept responsibility.[38] If this were not the case, authorities could argue that they owed no duty to such persons, as the secretary of state's direction in LAC (93)10 appendix 1 (with one

---

33 Correspondence between the Department of Health and Age Concern England, 23 June 2006.
34 Determination 3 of 2006, accessible at http://www.dh.gov.uk/prod_consum_dh/idcplg?IdcService=GET_FILE&dID=29865&Rendition=Web.
35 NAA 1948 s24(6).
36 Ibid, s24(3).
37 LAC (93)7 para 14.
38 Ibid, para 16.

exception)[39] limits their duty to those ordinarily resident in the area, or in urgent need. As a general rule, it would appear that if a person has no settled residence, his or her ordinary residence is the place where he or she is actually living (or perhaps – in extreme cases – the place where the previous night was spent).[40] The guidance makes it clear that the ordinary residence test for housing purposes should not be used for social services.[41] Guidance accompanying the Community Care (Delayed Discharges etc) Act 2003 suggests that the ordinary residence of people of no fixed abode who are admitted to hospital will be determined by the postcode of the place they were at immediately prior to admission.[42]

6.24   Guidance on the special needs of homeless people has been given in LAC (93)2, including the following.

> RESIDENTIAL CARE FOR HOMELESS PEOPLE WITH OTHER NEEDS
> 26. There may be other vulnerable people who are homeless and who are in need of residential care. Many of the above considerations apply to them as much as to alcohol and drug misusers. Like any other section of the population, homeless people may be in need of care because of frailty, physical disability, mental disorder of any description or a combination of any of these. They may have complex needs which also include alcohol and drug misuse. Their needs may be hard to classify by standard client groups.
>
> 27. As with alcohol and drug misusers, LAs should have flexible systems of assessment and care management that allow such people access to the services they need in a way that meets their special circumstances. Their homelessness may in itself mean that an urgent response is called for. LAs will be aware that there are a wide variety of agencies which specialise in providing care for homeless people. As with specialist alcohol and drug providers, these agencies may be in a position to assist in assessment procedures. Some of these homes receive additional support from the Home Office specifically to reserve places for vulnerable offenders and ex-offenders whose care needs require residential support. As above, LAs will need to collaborate with the Probation Service to make best use of these resources.

Urgent need

6.25   The secretary of state's direction places a duty on authorities to make arrangements not only for persons ordinarily resident in their area, but also for 'other persons who are in urgent need [of support services]' (see para 3.57).[43] Urgent need is not defined; in this context, however, it is only

39   Ibid appendix 1 para 2(3).
40   In *R v Eastleigh BC ex p Betts* [1983] 2 AC 613 (which concerned a different phrase, 'normally resident') Lord Brightman suggested that 'in appropriate circumstances a single day's residence may be enough to enable a person to say that he was normally resident in the area in which he had arrived only yesterday'. It has been argued that this finding is capable of being read across into the interpretation of 'ordinary residence': see P Eccles QC, 'Ordinary Residence and Community Care: An Overview' (1999) 2 CCLR 100 at 104.
41   LAC (93)7 para 16
42   HSC 2003/009: LAC (2003)21 para 33.
43   LAC (93)10, para 2(1)(b), and see also NHSCCA 1990 s47(5) concerning the provision of community care services in cases of urgency.

relevant when the person is ordinarily resident in another authority's area. It would appear therefore that the duty to persons in urgent need will almost invariably be a short-term duty, only subsisting during the currency of the urgency, and even then, only until such time as the other authority assumes responsibility. Note though that there is only a duty in relation to NAA 1948 s21 (accommodation); it is merely a power under NAA 1948 s29.

Cross border placements by local authorities

6.26   Cross border placements have the potential to create considerable confusion: a problem not helped by the mismatch between policy and legislation and further complicated by the different residential and nursing care funding systems resulting from devolution (see para 6.30 below).

6.27   The stated policy intention has been for authorities to be free to place service users in any UK nation of their choice (see para 7.94), however the legislation limits the power to make placements to England and Wales. Although both Health and Social Care Act 2001 s56 and Community Care and Health (Scotland) Act 2002 s5 provide for regulations to be made to allow the placement of residents in England, Scotland, Wales, Northern Ireland, Channel Islands and the Isle of Man, as at August 2007, no such UK-wide regulations had been made.[44] In the absence of regulations being issued the relevant guidance is contained in LAC (93)18,[45] although in addition a protocol has been developed between England and Wales regarding the payment of the NHS registered nurse contribution (see para 6.71 below).

6.28   For those moving to Scotland and who are placed in homes in the independent sector under NAA 1948 s26, authorities are advised to arrange for the Scottish authority to contract and pay for the care home with the English authority reimbursing the Scottish authority net of any charges it makes to the resident.[46]

6.29   For those moving from Scotland to England, LAC (93)18 states that Scottish authorities are allowed to make placements directly for those moving into an independent residential care home but not for a nursing home. If a person wishes to move to a nursing home in England, Scottish authorities are advised to arrange for the English authority to contract and pay for the care with the Scottish authority reimbursing the English authority.

6.30   Significant complexities also arise in relation to the reimbursement obligations consequent upon the introduction of free personal care in Scotland and the advent of the NHS paying for registered nursing care in

---

44   Adult Support and Protection (Scotland) Act 2007 s66 makes further provision enabling Scottish ministers to make regulations to amend the Social Work (Scotland) Act 1968 in relation to people who are placed in Scotland by an arrangement made by a local authority in any other part of the UK, Channel Isles or the Isle of Man.
45   SWSG 6/94 in Scotland.
46   LAC (93)18 para 7.

England and Wales[47] (see para 13.96). In summary, Scottish authorities can arrange, but are not allowed to charge for personal and nursing care, and English and Welsh authorities can charge for personal care but are not allowed to arrange or pay for registered nurse care. In practice, however, it appears that authorities endeavour to agree an arrangement whereby residents are in the same position in respect of charges as they would have been had they remained within their home authority.

6.31   Until the legislation is amended local authorities appear to lack the power to place and remain responsible for service users who wish to move to or from Northern Ireland, the Channel Isles or the Isle of Man.

Ordinary residence and the Chronically Sick and Disabled Person's Act 1970

6.32   The definition of ordinary residence in Chronically Sick and Disabled Persons Act (CSDPA) 1970 s2 is identical to that under NAA 1948 s29, and accordingly the same considerations apply. However the process for resolving disputes concerning ordinary residence is materially different to that under the 1948 Act, and this is considered at para 6.47 below.

Ordinary residence and the Children Act 1989

6.33   As a matter of principle, children are presumed to have the ordinary residence of their parents.[48] The Children Act (CA) 1989, however, adopts a different test for determining responsibility for children in need. The duty under CA 1989 s17 (to safeguard and promote the welfare of children in need)[49] and the duty under CA 1989 s20 (to accommodate) are owed by social services authorities to children 'within their area'. However, financial responsibility for certain accommodation services provided under the Act[50] rests with the local authority in whose area the child is 'ordinarily resident'. Thus a child may be ordinarily resident in local authority A but 'within the area' of local authority B. Accordingly provision is made in CA 1989 s20(2) for local authority A to take over the responsibilities of local authority B.

Within the area

6.34   A series of cases have considered the question of which authority is responsible for carrying out an assessment of children in need – and thus the true construction of the phrase 'within their area'. In *R (Stewart) v Wandsworth LBC, Hammersmith and Fulham LBC and Lambeth LBC*[51] the

47   As opposed to Scotland where it is still the local authority that pays for nursing care.
48   See eg *In re P (GE) (an infant)* [1965] Ch 568.
49   See para 24.4.
50   See CA 1989 ss20(2), 21(3), 29(7) and (9).
51   [2001] EWHC 709 (Admin); (2001) 4 CCLR 446.

applicant applied to Hammersmith LBC for housing (under the home-lessness provisions). Hammersmith accommodated her in a hostel in Lambeth and then determined that she was intentionally homeless and obtained a possession order against her. The applicant then requested that Hammersmith assess her children's needs under CA 1989 s17. Hammersmith refused on the basis that this was Lambeth's responsibility. Lambeth refused as did Wandsworth LBC (the children's school being within their area). The court decided that 'within their area' was simply a question of physical presence (even though that might mean that more than one authority could be under the duty to assess). Accordingly it held that Lambeth and Wandsworth were responsible but Hammersmith was not.

6.35   The decision was followed in a similar fact case, *R (M) v Barking and Dagenham LBC and Westminster LBC*[52] where the court agreed that the relevant test was physical presence. It noted that no formal guidance existed to deal with such jurisdictional problems and encouraged inter-authority co-operation in such cases:

> . . . to avoid any impression that local authorities are able to pass responsibility for a child on to another authority . . . To put it shortly, the needs should be met first and the redistribution of resources should, if necessary take place afterwards. It is also important, quite plainly, that the parents of children should not be able to cause inconvenience or extra expense by simply moving on to another local authority . . .

Ordinary residence: the Children Act/National Assistance Act interface

6.36   In *R v Lambeth LBC ex p Caddell*[53] the applicant had been placed by the respondent London borough with paid carers who lived in Kent. When he became 18 Lambeth determined that he had ceased to be their responsibility since he was no longer a child, and accordingly the ordinary residence rules under the NAA 1948 applied. Kent County Council contended, however, that Lambeth was still the responsible authority since CA 1989 s24 allowed for social services authorities to continue to provide advice and assistance to young persons who had been in care once they achieved their majority. Connell J rejected this line of argument, holding that the duty under CA 1989 s24 was owed by the authority in whose area the young person resided, ie Kent.

6.37   CA 1989 s24 (which specifically concerns the needs of looked after children who are leaving care) has since been amended by the Children (Leaving Care) Act 2000. In effect the financial obligations imposed by the 2000 Act (particularly in the substituted sections 24A and 24B of the 1989 Act) are now the responsibility of the local authority which looked after the young person immediately before he or she left care. This responsibility

---

52   [2002] EWHC 2663 (Admin); (2003) 6 CCLR 87.
53   [1998] 1 FLR 235.

extends until the age of 21 (or beyond in the case of certain education and training costs). A 2004 protocol exists for inter-authority arrangements for care leavers outside of their responsible authority.[54]

Ordinary residence and Mental Health Act 1983 s117

6.38   The duty to provide services under Mental Health Act (MHA) 1983 s117 is a joint health and social services responsibility. MHA 1983 s117(3) stipulates that the responsible health bodies are 'the Primary Care Trust[55] or Health Authority' and that these together with the relevant social services authority are those 'for the area in which the person concerned is resident or to which he is sent on discharge by the hospital in which he was detained'.

6.39   It might appear, therefore, that MHA 1983 s117(3) gives a choice of responsible authorities – either the health/social services authorities in whose area the person was resident at the time of admission to hospital[56] or those to which he or she is sent on discharge. In *R v Mental Health Review Tribunal ex p Hall*[57] Scott Baker J considered this question. He noted:

> The word 'or' in sub-section (3) clearly envisages an alternative so that there is always some authority that will be responsible when a patient is discharged; if not that of his residence that of the place to which he is sent. One or the other authority is responsible but not both; otherwise there would be a recipe for disaster with the prospect of endless disagreements and failures to make arrangements. Section 117 does not provide for multi social services department or health authority responsibility. The words 'or to whom he is sent on discharge from Tribunal' are included simply to cater for the situation where a patient does not have a current place of residence. The sub-section does not mean that a placing authority where the patient resides suddenly ceases to be 'the local social services authority' if on discharge the Applicant is sent to a different authority'.

6.40   The Department of Health has issued guidance on the implications of this

---

54   LASSL (2004)20: although the protocol states that it was to be reviewed in 2005, this did not occur and (at August 2007) no new protocol had been published.

55   Inserted by NHS Reform and Health Care Professionals Act 2002 Sch 2(2) para 47. Specific reference to local health boards in Wales appears not to be strictly necessary, as a result of a combination of the Health Authorities (Transfer of Functions, Staff, Property, Rights and Liabilities and Abolition) (Wales) Order 2003 SI No 813 (W98) – which transfers all functions of health authorities in Wales to the Assembly – and the Local Health Boards (Functions) (Wales) Regulations 2003 SI No 150 (W20) which provides (subject to exceptions) that functions that were exercised by health authorities and were transferred to the Assembly by SI No 2003/813 are to be exercised by local health boards.

56   A person does not cease to be resident in the area of an authority by reason only of his or her admission to hospital – *Fox v Stirk* [1970] 2 QB 463.

57   [1999] 3 All ER 132; (1999) 2 CCLR 361, p731I–J. Although the case went to the Court of Appeal – [2000] 1 WLR 1323; (1999) 2 CCLR 383 – the question of the responsible department was not argued in that court.

judgment,[58] reminding authorities that a patient who was resident before admission to hospital does not cease to be a resident because of detention under the Act. It refers local authorities to LAC (93)7 and NHS bodies to the guidance in existence at the time regarding establishing district of residence. The latest guidance on establishing the responsible commissioner (see para 6.47) explicitly states at para 64 that the guidance to be followed for establishing responsibility for MHA 1983 s117 services is HSG 1994/27 and HSC 2000/003.

Ordinary residence and the carers legislation

6.41   In general a carer's assessment under either the Carers (Recognition of Services) Act (C(RS)A) 1995 or Carers and Disabled Children Act (CDCA) 2000 is predicated upon a community care or Children Act assessment being undertaken (see para 16.26). Practice guidance to the CDCA 2000 (para 24–7)[59] advises that where the carer lives some distance away from the user it will be the disabled person's home authority (not the carer's) which will be responsible for the assessment and the provision of any services under the 2000 Act.

Disputed ordinary residence

Disputed 'ordinary residence' and the National Assistance Act 1948

6.42   Where two or more social services authorities are in dispute over a person's ordinary residence, NAA 1948 s32(3) provides that the question is to be determined by the secretary of state. This procedure is however only available for disputes which concern potential services under the NAA 1948. LAC (93)7[60] Part II sets out the procedure to be followed by authorities in such cases, namely:

a)   Before the secretary of state is approached, one of the authorities must provisionally accept responsibility and be providing services.
b)   An agreed written statement of facts, signed by all authorities involved, must be sent, together with the application for determination. The statement should include:
  • full information about the person whose ordinary residence is in dispute;
  • details relating to the prior residence of the person;
  • details of the statutory provisions under which services have been provided.

---

58   HSC 2000/003: LAC (2000)3.
59   Para 4.3 of the Welsh guidance.
60   There is identical Welsh guidance in WOC 41/93.

Copies of all relevant correspondence between the authorities should be annexed to the agreed statement.

c)   In addition each authority may also send separate written representations concerning the agreed statement (ie, a legal submission).

6.43   The guidance requires authorities to use their best endeavours to resolve their dispute – and that seeking a determination by the secretary of state is only an option of last resort. The ombudsman has found maladministration where there was a delay of a year before a determination was sought,[61] and where the dispute meant charges went unpaid, causing the resident considerable anxiety, rather than resolving the matter without involving the client.[62]

6.44   A major failing of this system for resolving disputes between authorities is that until October 2006 the determinations were not published. This meant that authorities had little chance of learning how similar issues have been determined, which might indeed lead to fewer cases having to go to this level of arbitration.[63] Following a Freedom of Information request, 12 cases since 2004 have been anonymised and published on the Department of Health website and a commitment given to publish new cases as they arise.[64]

6.45   A new protocol has been developed to deal with ordinary residence disputes between English and Welsh local authorities.[65] The responsible authority for making the determination is the national authority (ie either the Welsh Minister or the Secretary of State for Health) in whose country the subject of the dispute is currently living: the eventual determination being issued in the name of both the Welsh Ministers and the Secretary of State. It is understood that local authorities in both England and Wales will be notified of this new procedure shortly as an update to the current guidance on ordinary residence.

6.46   The secretary of state's determinations are final, subject only to judicial review. *R (Greenwich LBC) v Secretary of State for Health and Bexley LBC*[66] concerned a resident who lacked capacity who had been moved by Bexley from a residential home in its area to a nursing home in Greenwich. At the time of the move the resident was fully funding her care, but it was known that in a matter of a few weeks she would need help from a local authority as her capital was nearing the limits under which she would fall to be helped under the means test. Charles J upheld the secretary of state's determination that the resident was ordinarily resident in Greenwich since the deeming provisions in NAA 1948 s24(5) had been triggered,

61 Complaint nos 95/C/1472 and 95/C/2543 against Redbridge LBC, 16 June 1998.
62 Reported in 2005/6 Local Government Ombudsman Digest of Cases (case reference confidential).
63 The reason given by the Department of Health for not publishing them was that they contain personal information about the service-user.
64 As at June 2007, of the cases published six concerned children reaching adulthood, two concerned changing to more independent living situations, and two concerned the position following a period of continuing NHS health care.
65 Under Government of Wales Act 1998 s41.
66 [2006] EWHC 2576 (Admin); (2006) 10 CCLR 60.

notwithstanding that no arrangements with the provider under NAA 1948 s26 had been concluded. In the court's opinion the secretary of state had had regard to the correct tests for ordinary residence, had taken into account all the relevant factors – those of particular relevance being that the resident did not have anywhere to live in Bexley and was actually living in Greenwich.

Disputed 'ordinary residence' and the Chronically Sick and Disabled Persons Act 1970

6.47   In *R v Kent CC and Salisbury and Pierre*[67] a dispute arose as to the potential service user's ordinary residence and the council argued that the court could not determine this question since NAA 1948 s32(3) provided for it to be decided by the minister. The services in question, however, were being provided under the CSDPA 1970 and not the NAA 1948. Latham J held:[68]

> The difficulty with this submission is that . . . it is raised not under the National Assistance Act 1948, but under the 1970 Act. There is no equivalent provision in this latter Act. The reference to section 29 of the 1948 Act is not, in my judgment, sufficient to justify the conclusion that the provisions of section 32(3) of that Act apply to the determination of any issue under section 2 of the 1970 Act. The phrase 'are satisfied in the case of any person to whom that section applies' does not involve consideration of ordinary residence. It is a reference to the nature of the disabilities which trigger consideration of the question whether a person is one to whom, the duty under section 2 of the 1970 Act is owed. That is why it was necessary to include the phrase 'who is ordinarily resident in their area' in that section. That being so, it seems to me that the present claim requires me to determine whether or not [the service user] is ordinarily resident in Kent.

6.48   The judge then determined the question of ordinary residence on the basis of the existing legal authorities. The service user had learning difficulties, but these were not so severe as those considered in *ex p Vale* (see para 6.12 above), and accordingly it was held that:

> In the present case, the papers show that [the service user] has expressed a clear and consistent desire to stay with [her paid carers who lived in Kent]. I think that is sufficient to justify the conclusion that she is in her present abode voluntarily, and with a settled intention to remain there for the time being. Her disabilities do not appear to be such as to prevent her from having the requisite understanding for both mental elements. That is sufficient to justify the conclusion that she is ordinarily resident in Kent. If I am wrong, she is nonetheless to be treated, in my view, as if [her paid carers] were her parents, and she were a child. This would produce the same result.

67   (2003) 3 CCLR 38.
68   Ibid at 43J.

Disputed 'ordinary residence' and the Children Act 1989

6.49 Although, as noted above, there is no formal dispute resolution process where authorities are unable to agree on whether or not a child is 'within their area', CA 1989 s30(2) provides a formal process for disputes concerning ordinary residence. This is essentially the same secretary of state process as with NAA 1948 s32(3) (above).

Disputed 'ordinary residence' and Mental Health Act 1983 s117

6.50 Where doubt arises as to a person's area of residence, Department of Health guidance HSC 2000/003: LAC (2000)3 and the judgment in *R v Mental Health Review Tribunal ex p Hall* (see para 6.39 above) confirm that responsibility will fall on the authority where the patient is sent on discharge.

Disputed 'ordinary residence' and the Community Care (Delayed Discharges etc) Act 2003

6.51 Guidance is available on the Department of Health website[69] on the procedure to follow in cases of disputes about ordinary residence in the context of which local authority should reimburse the NHS acute trust for the delay in providing suitable care for patients ready for discharge from hospital (see para 5.38). It essentially tells authorities that in England they should use LAC (93)7 and it is for the secretary of state to determine. Where it is a cross border matter the determination is dealt with by the secretary of state if the person is currently residing in England, and by the Welsh assembly if the person is currently residing in Wales (see para 6.45 above). The main guidance on delayed discharges LAC (2003)21 points out that as Wales has not implemented the Act, if a resident of Wales is delayed in an English hospital, there can be no reimbursement.

Establishing the responsible commissioner for NHS services

6.52 Entitlement to services under the National Health Service Acts 2006 is not in theory a local right but a 'national' one: accordingly the Acts are silent as to a need to establish a local connection or ordinary residence.

6.53 The framework for determining which primary care trust (PCT) or local health board is responsible for commissioning an individual's care is detailed in regulations. In England it is primarily linked to registration

---

69 *Arrangements for determining questions as to the ordinary residence of an individual requested pursuant to section 8(1) Community Care (Delayed Discharges etc) Act 2003*, accessible at http://www.dh.gov.uk/en/Policyandguidance/Organisationpolicy/ IntegratedCare/Delayeddischarges/DH_4126245.

with a GP, and for those who are not registered with a GP it is based on where they are 'usually resident'.[70] The situation is otherwise in Wales, in that the responsible health board is the one where the person is 'usually resident' regardless of the address of their GP. 'Usually resident' is determined by the address the person gives to the body providing the service, or the most recent address he or she can give, or if the usual address cannot be established the patient will be treated as usually resident in the area where the person is present.[71]

6.54   Practice guidance in England was issued in April 2006[72] and reference to the guidance in the rest of this section is to the April 2006 guidance.

6.55   The guidance makes it clear that no treatments should be refused or delayed due to uncertainty as to which PCT is responsible for funding an individual's health care provision. Ministers have specifically asked to be advised of those NHS bodies that fail to reach local resolution of any disputes between themselves or with independent providers.[73]

6.56   PCTs are responsible for commissioning hospital and community health services for patients registered with GPs associated with their PCT, and persons usually resident in their area, or resident outside the UK and present in their area who are not registered with a GP.[74] It follows, that where a patient is registered with a GP the responsible PCT will generally be the one where the GP is situated rather than where the patient lives. Where a GP practice has patients resident in more than one PCT area, the normal rule of thumb is that the practice will be associated with the PCT in which the largest number of registered patients reside.

6.57   It is only therefore for people who are not registered with a GP where 'usual residence' becomes important in establishing the responsible commissioner. Annex A of the 2006 guidance offers definitions of 'usually resident'. It is based on the principle of the patient's perception of where he or she lives. If the patient is unable to give a current address, the address at which he or she was last resident should establish the PCT of residence. If the patient can not give a present or most recent address, the location of the unit providing treatment (ie where the patient is 'present') should be considered as the district where he or she lives.[75]

6.58   If a patient is away from his or her normal area where he or she is registered with a GP, 'Out of Area Treatment' arrangements exist to cover emergency treatments when it is not possible to get prior approval from

---

70   NHS (Functions of Strategic Authorities and Primary Care Trusts and Administration Arrangements) (England) Regulations 2002 SI No 2375 as amended by SI Nos 2002/2548, 2003/1497, 2006/359 and 2007/559; Local Health Board (Functions) (Wales) Regulations 2003 as amended.

71   Local Health Board (Functions) (Wales) Regulations 2003 reg 2(3).

72   *Establishing the Responsible Commissioner: Guidance for PCT commissioners on the application of the legal framework on PCTs' secondary care commissioning responsibilities*, 2006 revision (which was further revised in relation to looked after children in March 2007).

73   2006 guidance, paras 6 and 7.

74   NHS (Functions of Strategic Authorities and Primary Care Trusts and Administration Arrangements) (England) Regulations 2002 reg 3(7).

75   Ibid, reg 3(8).

the patient's PCT. Additionally some services are provided on an 'all-comers' basis such as accident and emergency, family planning, and NHS walk-in centres. These are provided by the host PCT regardless of registration or residence. The full list of such services is provided in the 2006 guidance.

Patients who move

6.59 If a patient moves during a course of treatment, the guidance suggests flexible solutions, which might mean that the originating PCT continues to exercise the functions on behalf of the receiving PCT for a specific time.[76] The respective responsibilities in is summarised in Table 9 below.[77]

Table 9: Patients who move			
Situation	PCT A	PCT B	Responsible commissioner
Patient not yet moved	Registered resident		PCT A
Patient moved	Registered	Resident	PCT A
Patient moved	Deregistered	Resident not yet registered	PCT B
Patient moved		Registered resident	PCT B

Patients who receive fully funded NHS continuing care

6.60 Different rules apply for people who receive continuing NHS health care (see chapter 14) either in care homes or independent hospitals. Although the subject of specific regulations,[78] responsibility is also governed by the same 2006 guidance considered above. In such cases where the placing PCT arranges the care, it remains responsible for the NHS payments for the care of that placement even though the person may change GP (and thus PCT). However if the patient requires other health services not related to the placement (for instance, in patient treatment in hospital) it will be the responsibility of the PCT where the patient is now registered. Annex C of the guidance gives more details of how this should work in practice.[79]

6.61 These new arrangements apply to both fully funded NHS continuing health care and where the NHS contribution is assessed as requiring more than just the registered nurse care contribution (RNCC – see para 13.98) and there is at least one other planned service to bring about a

76 2006 guidance, para 35.
77 Ibid, para 37.
78 National Health Service (Functions of Strategic Health Authorities and Primary Care Trusts and Administrations Arrangements) (England) Regulations 2002 as amended by SI No 359.
79 2006 guidance, para 66.

specific outcome in relation to treatment.[80] Examples given in Annex C of the guidance are physiotherapy, occupational therapy, speech and language therapy, dietetics and podiatry. The list is not exhaustive.

6.62   If the patient recovers sufficiently to no longer require fully funded NHS health care, or extra services other than registered nursing care, the resident will become the responsibility of the new PCT area.[81] The placing authority is responsible for reviews unless and until the person no longer requires the services, although it can make arrangements for the PCT where the home or hospital is to undertake reviews on its behalf.[82] It is also responsible for any increases in the care needed in the home or independent hospital if the patient's condition worsens. If the patient needs to move to another care home or independent hospital, the placing PCT remains responsible. The arrangements do not apply where a person has either independently chosen to move to a different part of the country or if the arrangement is made by social services only.

6.63   Where patients receive fully funded NHS continuing health care in their own home and decides to move house, they come under the normal rules for establishing the responsible commissioner (ie the PCT area where they are now registered with a GP). The guidance suggests[83] that there might be flexible solutions such as whether patient care should be provided by another PCT exercising functions on its behalf. Presumably this means that if any nursing service is already visiting the patient, this can continue rather than subject the patient to the upheaval of staff changes.

Responsibility for registered nurse care contributions

6.64   If the person is moving into a nursing home which is out of the PCT area where the GP is, the RNCC will become the responsibility of the PCT on whose GP list the resident is included (ie normally where the home is). This is of course unless there is some other NHS service planned for the resident (see para 6.61 above).

6.65   The April 2006 guidance refers back to earlier guidance produced when the NHS assumed responsibility for registered nursing care. This guidance advises[84] that:

> In some cases, for instance where care homes are close to the boundary of a neighbouring PCT, it may be sensible for responsibility for the management of the contract with the care home to be transferred to a neighbouring PCT if the majority of residents are registered in that PCT.[85]

80   Ibid, para 67.
81   ie the PCT area within which the patient's present GP is situated.
82   NHS (Functions of Strategic Health Authorities and Primary Care Trusts and Administrations Arrangements) (England) Regulations 2002 as amended by SI No 2006/359.
83   At para 70.
84   See HSC 2003/006: LAC (2003)7 paras 66–68 and HSC 2001/17: LAC (2001)26.
85   HSC 2003/006: LAC (2003)7 para 67.

6.66 Advice has been issued by the Department of Health regarding respite care in specialist facilities run by the Multiple Sclerosis Society and Vitalise (formerly known as the Winged Fellowship). As these centres take residents from all parts of the country for short periods, funding has been reallocated so that the PCTs in which the homes are situated pay for the respite care rather than the PCT where the person is registered with a GP.[86]

Cross border arrangements

6.67 England is the only country of the UK which places the responsibility on the PCT where the GP is registered, rather than where the patient is usually resident. In the case of a person living Scotland but registered with a GP in England, responsibility falls on the Scottish NHS body. For patients who are resident in England but who are registered with a GP in Wales, Northern Ireland or Scotland, responsibility lies with the English PCT where the patient is resident.[87]

6.68 In 2005 a protocol was agreed between Wales and England for those who live in specified PCT areas in England or in a specified health board in Wales. Originally planned to last until 2006, it has been extended to 2008. In these cases the health board where the GP is situated is responsible for the patient who is resident in an English PCT area. The English PCT where the person is registered with a GP is responsible for the person who is resident in the Welsh health board area. It had been planned that there would be a new system set up in 2006 based on the residency of the patient.[88] However this has not yet occurred and the guidance issued in 2005 will still stand until April 2008.[89] The specified health boards and PCTs are limited to those that directly border each other and are listed in the protocol.

6.69 If a patient is resident in Wales (in an area not covered by the above protocol) or Northern Ireland and registered with a GP in England, both Wales/Northern Ireland and England could be deemed to be responsible. At this point, perhaps not surprisingly, the towel is thrown in and the guidance just encourages health organisations to agree locally appropriate arrangements.[90]

6.70 An agreement exists, however, between the four devolved administrations about cross border emergency treatment, when patients need immediate treatment when they are away from home.[91]

86 This is from April 2005: http://www.dh.gov.uk/PolicyAndGuidance/ OrganisationPolicy/IntegratedCare/NHSFundedNursingCare/NHSFundedNursing-CareArticle/fs/en?CONTENT_ID=4106715&chk=Q%2BZGaA.
87 2006 guidance, para 39 and see SI 2003/1497 which amended the 2002 regulations.
88 This is issued as guidance in Wales – WHC (2005)12, and a 'Dear colleague' letter in England which was sent to the Chief Executives of SHAs in February 2005, accessible at http://www.dh.gov.uk/en/Publicationsandstatistics/Lettersandcirculars/ Dearcolleagueletters/DH_4103332.
89 WHC (2007)036.
90 2006 guidance, para 40.
91 Department of Health, *Cross Border Emergency Treatment* September 2006; WOC (2006)066.

6.71   A protocol also exists between England and Wales regarding the payment of the registered nurse contribution. The English PCT where the home is based pays the appropriate level of RNCC if the home is in England. The Welsh health board pays a single level of payment if the home is in Wales. The April 2006 guidance points out that it is based on the default position of usual residence to ensure all patients receive the services they are assessed as needing, and it does not override the regulations.[92] From 1 October 2007 England is moving to having one band for nursing, but as the proposed figure of £101 is less than the amount for registered nursing paid in Wales (£114.90) it seems likely that a protocol will remain in order to establish the level of payment due from the NHS.

People not ordinarily resident in the UK and overseas visitors

6.72   Although PCTs rely on usual residence to establish whether they are responsible for commissioning services, the test for whether the NHS should provide free services for those from abroad is based on the ordinary residence test used in local authorities (see para 6.5). Asylum seekers who have made a formal application for refugee status are considered to be resident and so the responsible PCT is based on their GP or where they are usually resident. If a person is detained because of his or her immigration status, the responsible commissioner should be determined by the address of the unit providing treatment.

Prisoners

6.73   New arrangements have been made for prisoners so that currently the PCT in which the prison is situated commissions the majority of the care services for the prison population.[93]

People detained under the Mental Health Act

6.74   If a person is detained for treatment under the Mental Health Act 1983, commissioning responsibility will lie with the PCT where the person is registered with a GP or where the person is usually resident prior to admission. If these cannot be established, responsibility lies with area where the unit is providing treatment. Although the 2006 guidance points out that responsibility for section 117 services does not fall under the normal arrangements for establishing the responsible commissioner, it refers back to previous guidance (HSC 2000/003) which in turn refers back to earlier guidance on establishing the district of residence.

---

92 The protocol can be found at http://www.dh.gov.uk/PolicyAndGuidance/
OrganisationPolicy/IntegratedCare/NHSFundedNursingCare/fs/en.

93 NHS (Functions of Strategic Health Authorities and Primary Care Trusts and Administration Arrangements) (England) (Amendment) Regulations 2003 SI No 1497.

Children

6.75   If a local authority is accommodating a child it should contact the PCT where the child will be residing, and the normal rules will apply based on either where the child is registered with a GP or where the child is now residing. The originating PCT might continue to exercise functions on behalf of the receiving PCT if this is in the best interests of the child. New regulations came into force in April 2007 and apply to arrangements made after this date.[94] In summary the changes mean that where a PCT or a local authority, or a PCT and a local authority acting jointly, arrange accommodation in an area of another PCT, the originating PCT remains responsible even where the child changes GP. When a young person who has been placed in another PCT area to meet his or her continuing health care needs reaches 18 years, the arrangement can be treated as being made under adult continuing care provisions. The relevant guidance notes that since the threshold for providing continuing NHS health care may be higher for adults than children, arrangements for a reassessment will be required, but that young people should continue to receive their health care on an unchanged basis pending this assessment.[95]

Resolving disputes about who is the responsible commissioner

6.76   In cases that cannot be resolved locally the strategic health authority (SHA) should be consulted as it has the responsibility to resolve disputes that threaten the delivery of services in its geographical area.

6.77   Ultimately the resolution of such disputes is the function of the secretary of state. Where SHAs have not been able to settle a dispute, the guidance requires that they submit a report to the Department of Health together with the proposed solution.[96] The department however expects that all disputes should be resolved locally.

94   NHS (Functions of Strategic Health Authorities and Primary Care Trusts and Administration Arrangements) (England) (Amendment) Regulations 2007 SI No 559.
95   March 2007 amendment to the 2006 guidance, para 83.
96   April 2006 guidance, paras 87 and 88.

CHAPTER 7

Care home accommodation

continued

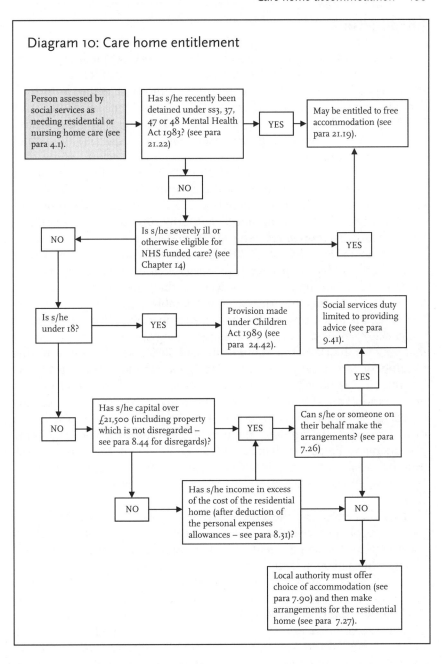

Diagram 10: Care home entitlement

Introduction

7.1   It is estimated that there are approximately 421,000 people living in care homes in the UK (as at April 2006.) Of these, 60 per cent of residents in the independent sector are estimated to be funded or helped with their funding by local authorities; 32 per cent of UK care home residents (some 118,000) fund their own care; and some 30,000 residents are funded by the NHS, representing 19 per cent of residents in homes providing nursing care.[1]

7.2   According to Department of Health statistics for England, of the 259,000 residents supported by local authorities in March 2006, 61 per cent were in independent residential care, 28 per cent in homes providing nursing care and 19 per cent in local authority run homes. 78 per cent of local authority supported residents are 65 or over.

7.3   With an average fee of £570 per week for care homes providing nursing care and £398 per week for residential care homes in the UK, moving into a care home is not a decision that most people would take lightly. In some areas the prices are considerably higher than the average.

7.4   One of the major reasons for the community care reforms in 1993 was the concern about the amount of money being spent by government (at that time via the Department of Health and Social Security) on providing funding for care in care homes. By placing local authorities in a gatekeeping role, it was hoped to cap the amount spent, and free money up to provide more care at home. Undoubtedly many more people are receiving a package of care at home who would in the past have been placed in a care home, but the amount spent by local authorities for care home placements in England still accounts for 42 per cent of the gross expenditure by social services at some £8.2 billion (£7.0 billion excluding children's residential care). Of this some £1.6 billion is recouped through charges.[2]

7.5   This chapter covers the various duties of local authorities to accommodate people in care homes and also looks at the provisions that are in place to protect to some extent those who fund their own care, normally because they fall outside the local authority means test.

7.6   The powers and duties of social services departments to provide residential accommodation are primarily dealt with in Part III of the National Assistance Act (NAA) 1948, and in particular in section 21. In addition accommodation services can be provided under NAA 1948 s29(4), Mental Health Act (MHA) 1983 s117, Children Act (CA) 1989 s17 and Local Government Act (LGA) 2000 s2; these are separately considered at paras 7.156, 7.154, 7.158 and 1.73 respectively.

---

1   Figures from Laing & Buisson, *Care of Elderly People UK Market Survey*, London, 2006. More recent figures published by the Department of Health which accompanied the *National Framework for Continuing NHS Healthcare* in June 2007, gave the numbers receiving continuing NHS care in England alone as being 30,975 at March 2007.

2   Department of Health, *Personal Social Services Expenditure and Unit Costs 2005–6*, 2007.

Residential accommodation services and the NHS overlap

7.7   There is a duty on the NHS to accommodate people in care homes under continuing NHS health care and this responsibility is considered separately in chapter 14. The NHS also has certain duties to people in care homes regardless of whether they are the responsibility of the social services or funding their own care, namely:

- the duty on the NHS to deliver specific services to persons in care homes (eg district nursing services). This responsibility is considered at para 13.85 below.
- the duty on the NHS to make 'registered nursing care' contributions (Health and Social Care Act (HSCA) 2001 s49). This responsibility is considered at para 13.95 below.

Accommodation under National Assistance Act 1948 s21

7.8   NAA 1948 s21(1) as amended reads as follows:

(1)   Subject to and in accordance with the provisions of this Part of this Act, a local authority may with the approval of the Secretary of State, and to such extent as he may direct shall, make arrangements for providing–
(a)   residential accommodation for persons aged eighteen or over who by reason of age, illness, disability or any other circumstances are in need of care and attention which is not otherwise available to them; and
(aa)   residential accommodation for expectant and nursing mothers who are in need of care and attention which is not otherwise available to them.
(1A)   A person to whom section 115 of the Immigration and Asylum Act 1999 (exclusion from benefits) applies may not be provided with residential accommodation under subsection (1)(a) if his need for care and attention has arisen solely–
(a)   because he is destitute; or
(b)   because of the physical effects, or anticipated physical effects, of his being destitute.
(1B)   Subsections (3) and (5) to (8) of section 95 of the Immigration and Asylum Act 1999, and paragraph 2 of Schedule 8 to that Act, apply for the purposes of subsection (1A) as they apply for the purposes of that section, but for the references in subsections (5) and (7) of that section and in that paragraph to the Secretary of State substitute references to a local authority.

Chapter 22 considers persons to whom Immigration and Asylum Act 1999 s115 applies.

7.9   As is evident from the text of section 21(1), social services authorities have no power to make any arrangements under section 21 unless and until the secretary of state has issued a direction specifying the arrangements which may be made (are 'approved') and those which must be made (are 'directed' to be made).³ The secretary of state's most recent direction in England is found at appendix 1 to LAC (93)10⁴ and came into force on 1 April 1993 (see appendix B for the full text of the direction).

7.10   NAA 1948 s21 specifies two hurdles which a person must (with one exception) surmount before being considered by a social services authority for residential accommodation under this section: the exception relates to expectant and nursing mothers, for whom the age requirement does not apply (see below). The two requirements are:

a)   the person must be 18 or over and have certain characteristics (see 'client group' below), and

b)   the person must be in need of care and attention which is not otherwise available.

Client group

7.11   NAA 1948 s21 lists the criteria which may cause a person to be considered in need of the necessary care and attention, namely:

Age   This is usually taken as a reference to those who have become frail as a result of the ageing process. Age is, of course, frequently accompanied by disabling conditions or illness, which are alternative qualifying conditions for the purpose of section 21.⁵

Illness   This is not defined by the NAA 1948 although by National Health Service Act (NHSA) 2006 s275/ National Health Service (Wales) Act (NHS(W)A) 2006 s206 it is defined as including mental disorder within the meaning of the MHA 1983 and any injury or disability requiring medical or dental treatment or nursing. The care and attention may be required not merely because the person is ill; it may arise in order to prevent that person becoming ill, or by way of aftercare.⁶ The residential accommodation duties parallel the obligations under NHSA 2006 Sch 20 para 2/ NHS(W)A 2006 Sch 15 para 2 which enable social services authorities to provide domiciliary services for people who are or have been ill (or for the prevention of illness – see para 9.137).⁷

---

3   Authority to provide accommodation may however derive from other provisions – eg MHA 1983 s117 (see para 7.154 below) and LGA 2000 s2 (para 1.73 above).

4   WOC 35/93 in Wales; since the texts are virtually identical the English direction is referred to henceforth.

5   The NHS has responsibilities for very frail elderly people (particularly for respite and rehabilitation services) and this obligation is considered in greater detail at paras 13.42 and 13.49 below.

6   LAC (93)10 appendix 1 para 2(5).

7   The criterion of 'illness' was inserted into section 21 by National Health Service and Community Care Act (NHSCCA) 1990 s42(1)(a). Prior to this amendment a parallel

Disability	This is not qualified in NAA 1948 s21. It follows that the condition need not necessarily be substantial or permanent (ie unlike under section 29 – see para 7.12 below).
Expectant or nursing mothers	The secretary of state's direction specifically states that residential accommodation can be provided for expectant and nursing mothers of any age, ie irrespective of whether or not they are over 18.[8]
Any other circumstances	The secretary of state's direction[9] does not limit the potential client group entitled to services under NAA 1948 s21 (as the direction also refers to persons whose need arises as a result of any other circumstance). The direction nevertheless specifically refers to two categories of condition:
Mental disorder	Residential accommodation can be provided for persons who are or have been suffering from mental disorder, as well as for the purpose of the prevention of mental disorder – see below.[10]
Alcohol or drug dependency	In this case however the residential accommodation is for those actually dependent (rather than for prevention).[11] The provision of accommodation for persons who are alcohol or drug-dependent is considered in greater detail in chapter 23.

7.12 The list should be contrasted with that under NAA 1948 s29 (which deals with domiciliary services – see para 9.14). The section 29 list does not include age as a qualifying criterion and is generally more restrictive in its requirements (for instance, an impairment must substantially and permanently 'handicap' the person before he or she qualifies).

Care and attention

7.13 Accommodation under NAA 1948 s21 is only available to persons who (among other things) are in need of 'care and attention'; a phrase which is not defined in the legislation. The courts have adopted a reasonably generous approach to its interpretation – based on the supposition that this too is the intention of the secretary of state[12] – thus in *R v Hammersmith*

social services accommodation obligation existed under NHSA 1977 Sch 8 para 2 which was repealed by NHSCCA 1990 Sch 10. This power to accommodate was generally used to provide accommodation for people who were able to live more independently than those accommodated under section 21, but who nevertheless required some degree of care and support. These were mostly (but not always) people under pension age (see para 8.111).

8 LAC (93)10 appendix 1 para 3.
9 LAC (93)10 appendix 1.
10 Ibid, para 2(3).
11 Ibid, para 2(6).
12 *R v Westminster City Council ex p M, P, A and X* (1997) 1 CCLR 85, p92D, CA.

LBC ex p M[13] the Court of Appeal observed that '[t]hose who needed assistance because they lacked care and attention have always remained the subject of s21(1)(a) . . .'.

7.14   The *Hammersmith* case, as with many others, concerned an asylum seeker. The respondent local authorities denied responsibility, claiming that for the purposes of section 21, a need of accommodation alone was insufficient – there had also to be a need for care and attention. The Court of Appeal summarised a key part of the local authority argument as follows:[14]

> . . . [counsel for the local authority] submitted that the effect of the legislation was to provide three separate solutions for three different problems. The problems; lack of resources which had originally been dealt with under Part II of the 1948 Act;[15] lack of care and attention which alone continued to be dealt with by Part III of the 1948 Act and finally lack of accommodation which initially had been dealt with by section 21(1)(b) of the 1948 Act.[16]

> Basing their submissions upon this division, the appellants argue that the purpose of section 21(1)(a) was not to provide money for those in need of money or to provide accommodation for those who need 'accommodation *per se*' but to provide accommodation for those who required care and attention. Such persons could be rich and own their own homes but still could need the local authority's assistance under section 21(1)(a). The accommodation was not in itself an end but a means whereby the required care and attention can be provided.

7.15   Although the court accepted that there were 'three paths of legislative provision', this did not mean that their 'paths could not overlap making an applicant *prima facie* eligible for more than one form of assistance'.

7.16   In *R (Mani) v Lambeth LBC and SSHD*[17] the Court of Appeal also rejected a subtly different argument, namely that the need for care and attention had to be an 'accommodation related need'.

7.17   'Care and attention', for the purposes of NAA 1948 s21, does not therefore suggest care services of an intrusive nature – for instance attention with bodily functions, or care of an intimate or of a specifically personal character. It can be precautionary – and primarily related to external factors (sleeping rough and going without food). The courts however insist that the construction that they have given to section 21 does not undermine the importance of there being a need for care and attention in addition to the provision of accommodation: a need that can only be addressed if residential accommodation is provided. As Hale LJ held in *Wahid v Tower Hamlets LBC*:[18]

13   This being a consolidated appeal, comprising *R v Hammersmith LBC ex p M; R v Lambeth LBC ex p P and X; and R v Westminster City Council ex p A* (1997) 1 CCLR 85.
14   (1997)1 CCLR 85 at 92K–93C.
15   This provided for 'National Assistance', a means tested benefit – see para 1.6.
16   This provided for the temporary accommodation of homeless people, and was repealed by the Housing (Homeless Persons) Act 1977 – see para 15.16.
17   [2003] EWCA Civ 836; (2003) 6 CCLR 376.
18   [2002] EWCA Civ 287; (2002) 5 CCLR 239 at 248G–J; The judgment was cited with approval by Lord Hoffman in *Westminster City Council v National Asylum Support Service* [2002] UKHL 38; [2002] 1 WLR 2956; (2002) 5 CCLR 511 at 518H.

The duty under s21(1)] is premised on an unmet need for 'care and attention' (a 'condition precedent', as this Court put it in the *Westminster* case, at p93E[19]). These words must be given their full weight. Their natural and ordinary meaning in this context is 'looking after': this can obviously include feeding the starving, as with the destitute asylum-seekers in the *Westminster* case. Ordinary housing is not in itself 'care and attention'. It is simply the means whereby the necessary care and attention can be made available if otherwise it will not (I do not understand this Court to have rejected that part of the local authority's argument in the *Westminster* case, at p93B–D). The destitute asylum-seekers in the *Westminster* case had a claim because their destitution would reduce then to a situation in which they required such care and attention and it could not be made available to them in any other way because of the restrictions placed upon their ability to seek other forms of support buy the Asylum and Immigration Act 1996.

7.18   In spite of the court's insistence on the importance of a need existing for 'care and attention' it is difficult to see what the phrase adds in any given situation. Without materially changing the outcome of the various cases, NAA 1948 s21(1) could have been worded to direct that accommodation can only be provided if (1) the person is in imminent risk of significant harm and (2) absent the provision of residential accommodation there is no other way of avoiding this harm. Section 21 is not however so framed: although the second factor exists ('not otherwise available'), the first does not – it speaks instead of a 'need for care and attention'. Nevertheless (and notwithstanding judicial protestations to the contrary) the present interpretation of NAA 1948 s21 conforms more closely to the former 'risk assessment' wording than to the latter 'care assessment' wording – and although linked, these are different concepts. This point is illustrated by Hale LJ's observation (above) that 'care and attention' means 'looking after' or merely 'feeding the starving'. The problem with this approach is that feeding the hungry also amounts to 'looking after' or 'care and attention'. It is therefore questionable whether the requirement materially affects the legal determination of need in any particular case.

7.19   If in practice the key test is the establishment of a risk of harmful consequences, this element is already addressed in the assessment process under National Health Service and Community Care Act (NHSCA) 1990 s47(1); namely that the need for accommodation must be sufficiently pressing to 'call for' the provision of accommodation. Pill LJ in *Wahid* accepted that the section 47(1) process envelops (if not makes redundant) the NAA 1948 s21 requirement for 'care and attention', observing:

> The material available in the section 47(1) assessment was relevant to an assessment under the 1948 Act. There was no need for the judge to make a specific reference to the fact that two statutory provisions were engaged in the exercise.[20]

19   This being a consolidated appeal, comprising *R v Hammersmith LBC ex p M; R v Lambeth LBC ex p P and X; and R v Westminster City Council ex p A* (1997) 1 CCLR 85.
20   (2002) 5 CCLR 239 at 245I.

7.20   More recently Collins J[21] commented that in cases other than asylum seekers, individuals may be in need of care and attention, but because their needs can be met other than in residential accommodation, section 21 does not always have to apply:

> It is not necessary, as all the authorities under section 21 show, for the need for care and attention to be for care and attention provided by the local authority. It is a general need for care and attention and, as it seems to me, a person who is chronically ill and who, therefore, needs continual medical care and continual provision of medicines is, by that very fact, properly to be said to be in need of care and attention. Whether that need for care and attention will in a particular case mean that he is required to have accommodation is a wholly different question and it may well be that in cases not involving asylum-seekers, where there are other means whereby these matters can be provided for, section 21 will not come into play at all.

7.21   Thus although the courts have given a wide interpretation of the meaning of 'care and attention', the second step of whether the need for care and attention calls for the provision by the local authority of residential accommodation, has still to be met.

'Not otherwise available to them'

7.22   The social services' obligation to provide residential accommodation only arises when the care and attention that a person needs is 'not otherwise available'. Other options may of course include a package of domiciliary care services to enable the person to remain in his or her own home, and/or the provision of accommodation under the Housing Act 1996[22] or assistance from the NHS under its continuing care responsibilities.[23]

7.23   The interpretation of this phrase has been considered by the House of Lords in *Steane v Chief Adjudication Officer*[24] which concerned the payment of attendance allowance to persons placed in independent residential accommodation by social services authorities but whose residential home fees were not being funded by the authority.[25] The effect of this decision was to confirm that accommodation is not being provided under NAA 1948 s21 if the resident is a 'self funder', ie is paying for the accommodation without any support from the local authority *and* making direct pay-

---

21   *R (M) v Slough BC* [2004] EWHC 1109 (Admin) following *R (H) v Kingston upon Thames RLBC* [2002] EWHC 3158 (Admin); (2003) 6 CCLR 240.

22   See chapter 15 and also para 7.64 below where this point is discussed in *R (Mooney) v Southwark LBC* [2006] EWHC 1912 (Admin); (2006) 9 CCLR 670.

23   See chapter 14.

24   [1995] 1 WLR 1195; (1998) 1 CCLR 538, HL and see also *Chief Adjudication Officer v Quinn and Gibbon* [1995] 1 WLR 1184; (1998) 1 CCLR 529, HL.

25   Social Security (Attendance Allowance) Amendment (No 3) Regulations 1983 SI No 1741 reg 4(1)(c) provided that attendance allowance was not payable for any period during which a person is living in accommodation provided in circumstances in which the cost of the accommodation may be borne wholly or partly out of public funds: now with minor amendment to be found in the Social Security (Attendance Allowance) Regulations 1991 SI No 2740. These regulations were further amended by SI No 2259 when the 'may be borne' provisions were deleted.

ment to the home owner (see para 7.81). In effect, therefore, the duty on the social services authority to provide residential accommodation is one of last resort.[26]

7.24   The proposition that local authorities did not owe a duty to provide residential accommodation for 'self funders'[27] was tested in *R v Sefton MBC ex p Help the Aged.*[28] Here the authority decided that it would not accept responsibility for any person already in residential care or nursing home accommodation until such time as his or her capital fell below £1,500 (notwithstanding that the charging rules at that time required capital below £10,000 to be disregarded, and that residents could be helped by the local authority once their capital fell to £16,000 or below). The Court of Appeal held such a policy to be unlawful, and that 'care and attention is not to be regarded as "otherwise available" if the person concerned is unable to pay for it according to' the charging rules (see para 8.7).

7.25   The matter has now been put beyond question via NAA 1948 s 21(2A)[29] which stipulates that for the purposes of deciding whether care and attention are otherwise available to a person, a local authority shall disregard so much of the person's capital as does not exceed the capital limit for the purposes of NAA 1948 s22.[30] The guidance produced to accompany this statutory clarification[31] makes it clear that even if a person's capital exceeds the statutory limit, there will nevertheless be situations where the authority cannot decide that care and attention is not required (for instance because of lack of mental capacity).[32]

7.26   Once a community care assessment has been undertaken, and it is decided that care in a care home is required, a duty to provide care home accommodation may subsist even where the subsequent financial assessment reveals that the person has capital in excess of the upper capital limit. In this respect LAC (98)19 advises (at para 10):

> It is the Department's view that having capital in excess of the upper limit . . . does not in itself constitute adequate access to alternative care and attention. Local authorities will wish to consider the position of those who have capital in excess of the upper limit . . . and must satisfy themselves that the individual is able to make their own arrangements, or has others who are willing and able to make arrangements for them, for appropriate care. Where there is a suitable advocate or representative (in most cases a

---

26 As stated in *Adjudication Officers Guidance* para 11 (DSS 1994) concerning the payment of attendance allowance and disability living allowance. Because of the changes to the regulations since that date, this term is no longer required in the Decision Maker's Guide, but the general recognition that the duty of social services is one of 'last resort' still applies because of the requirement in NAA 1948 s21 that care and attention is 'not otherwise available' to the person.

27 That is persons already in such accommodation who were paying their own fees.

28 (1997) 1 CCLR 57.

29 Section 21(2A) was initially inserted by Community Care (Residential Accommodation) Act 1998 s1 and now derives from HSCA 2001 s53.

30 See para 8.40.

31 LAC (98)19; WOC 27/98 in Wales (both being 'policy guidance').

32 LAC (98)19; WOC 27/98 para 9.

close relative) it is the Department's view that local authorities should provide guidance and advice on the availability and appropriate level of services to meet the individual's needs. Where there is no identifiable advocate or representative to act on the individual's behalf it must be the responsibility of the LA to make the arrangements and to contract for the person's care.

7.27   This latter point can sometimes be a fall back for individuals who are acting on behalf of a person who lacks capacity to make their own arrangements. If they wish to make use of the local authority negotiating position in relation to care fees (which in some cases are considerably lower than the home would charge for the same services for a person making their own arrangements), they can refuse to make the contract with the home. In such a situation, the care and attention is not 'otherwise available' as there is no one both 'willing and able' to make the contract with the home on the individual's behalf (see para 8.16 below). Accordingly the duty reverts to the local authority to provide the accommodation.

Powers and duties

7.28   Certain of the accommodation obligations placed on authorities by NAA 1948 s21 are discretionary (ie, powers), whereas the majority are mandatory (ie, duties); these two categories are dealt with separately below (see para 1.22 for analysis of the nature of statutory powers and duties).

Duty

7.29   As a result of the secretary of state's direction contained in appendix 1 to circular LAC (93)10,[33] social services authorities are under a duty to provide residential accommodation for all of the categories of persons described in NAA s21(1)(a), namely persons aged 18 or over who by reason of age, illness, disability or any other circumstance are in need of care and attention not otherwise available to them (but subject to the asylum and immigration exceptions discussed in chapter 22).

7.30   The duty does not therefore extend to expectant or nursing mothers per se (although presumably they may nevertheless come within the ambit of 'any other circumstance'). The secretary of state's direction restricts the general duty to such persons who are either:

a)   ordinarily resident in the social services authority's area, or
b)   in urgent need of residential accommodation.

These terms are considered in greater detail in chapter 6.

7.31   Originally section 21 obliged authorities to provide temporary accommodation for persons who were homeless in circumstances that could not have been foreseen. Although the power was repealed by the Housing (Homeless Persons) Act 1977, the relic duty to provide residential

---

33   The full text of the directions is in appendix B

accommodation for persons 'in urgent need' remains under NAA 1948 s21(1)(a). Common examples are where a person is staying with relatives outside his or her home area and the caring situation suddenly breaks down, or where a UK national returns from living abroad because he or she needs care and attention. It could also include disasters where large numbers of people might not be able to go back to their authority area. Guidance[34] states that councils should provide an immediate response in emergencies or crises to those who need social care support, but that this might be withdrawn or changed following an assessment.

Mental disorder

7.32 In relation to persons who are or who have been suffering from mental disorder (or for the purpose of the prevention of mental disorder) the duty to provide residential accommodation is specifically stated as including those with no settled residence who are in the authority's area.[35]

Alcoholic or drug-dependent

7.33 The secretary of state's direction specifically refers to persons who are alcoholic or drug-dependent as being persons for whom a social services authority is empowered to provide residential accommodation.[36] It would appear to follow that there is therefore a duty to provide residential accommodation for such persons when they are ordinarily resident in the authority's area and have been assessed as needing care and attention not otherwise available to them. NAA 1948 s21 sets out the full extent of the potential client group. The secretary of state cannot add new categories to the list; he or she can merely select who from this group is to qualify. As the direction states that social services authorities have a potential to accommodate all of the categories of persons specified in NAA 1948 s21(1)(a), it must therefore follow that this includes persons who are alcoholic or drug dependent.

Discharge of the duty to accommodate

7.34 In *R v Kensington and Chelsea RLBC ex p Kujtim*[37] the Court of Appeal held that the duty can be treated as discharged if the applicant 'either unreasonably refuses to accept the accommodation provided if, following its provision, by his conduct he manifests a persistent and unequivocal refusal to observe the reasonable requirements of the local authority in relation to the occupation of such accommodation'.

7.35 In *R (Patrick) v Newham LBC*[38] the applicant, who had mental health difficulties, was evicted on the grounds of neighbour nuisance. The respondent authority from whom she sought assistance decided that she

---

34 Department of Health, *Fair Access to Care Services*, 2003, para 69.
35 LAC (93)10 appendix 1 para 2(3).
36 Ibid, para 2(6).
37 (1999) 2 CCLR 340 at 354I and see para 7.55 below.
38 (2001) 4 CCLR 48.

was intentionally homeless and in due course evicted her from the temporary accommodation it had provided. Shortly afterwards she started sleeping rough. Lawyers wrote on her behalf, enclosing a doctor's letter confirming her significant psychiatric problems and requested urgent accommodation. The authority refused, stating that it had offered the applicant accommodation in a charitable hostel for people with mental health problems, but that she had refused this offer.

7.36   The authority sought to rely on the judgment in *Kujtim* – namely that she had unreasonably refused the accommodation offered. In rejecting this argument, Henriques J held:

> I do not myself consider that an apparent refusal of accommodation by a psychiatrically ill applicant puts an end to the respondent's continuing duty to provide Part III accommodation when she may well have been labouring under a complete misapprehension as to the nature of the accommodation.[39]

and

> If the respondent sought to put an end to its section 21 duties to provide accommodation, they ought in my judgment at the very least to have ensured that the applicant was legally represented when the offer was made to her ensure not only that she understood what the offer was, both in terms of location and services offered, but also that she understood the legal consequences or potential legal consequences of refusing the offer.[40]

7.37   For the purposes of the Community Care (Delayed Discharges etc) Act 2003 the responsibility of the local authority ceases (for reimbursement purposes) where appropriate services have been offered to the patient, and despite the authority's 'active encouragement' the patient has unreasonably refused to move to take up these services (see para 8.44).[41]

Out of area accommodation

7.38   Not infrequently the accommodation offered by an authority in discharge of its section 21 duty is at some distance from the resident's family or home locality. Indeed, some 19 per cent of residents supported by local authorities are in care homes outside the funding authority. Over half of these are adults with physical disabilities. There is also a distinct geographical pattern with inner and outer London placing 55 per cent and 37 per cent of their residents respectively in care homes outside their boundaries.[42]

7.39   There are many reasons why such an 'out of area' care home may be proposed by an authority. It may be because suitable accommodation to meet the person's needs is not available locally. It may however be that accommodation at a price the local authority is prepared to pay is not

39 (2001) 4 CCLR 48 at 53D.
40 Ibid at 53H.
41 LAC (2003)21 Annex A, *Reasonableness and adequacy of care plans.*
42 *Statistical Bulletin Community Care Statistics 2006 Supported Residents (Adults), England,* accessible at http://www.ic.nhs.uk/pubs/ccs06suppres.

available (see para 7.99 regarding choice) within a reasonable distance to enable visits from friends and family. Much will come down to questions of fact as to whether it is part of an individual's assessed need to be near family and friends (see para 7.102). In some cases a placement will be out of area through the individual's choice to move to live near family who are some distance away.

7.40   The law is silent on where individuals should be placed other than that they should be given choice as to where they live. This is in contrast with housing legislation where Housing Act 1996 s208 obliges housing authorities (as far as possible) to provide accommodation in the district where the applicant resides.[43]

Delayed discharge and 'out of area' placements

7.41   The Department of Health guidance on delayed discharges gives as an example of unreasonable practice, a decision by a London council to move frail older people to care homes on the south coast unless the individuals in question wished to move there.[44]

Power

7.42   Social services authorities have the power (but not the duty) to provide residential accommodation for persons described in NAA 1948 s21(1)(a) and (aa) who are ordinarily resident in the area of another local authority, provided that the other authority agrees.[45]

7.43   The secretary of state's direction empowers (but does not direct) social services authorities to provide residential accommodation for expectant and nursing mothers.[46] There is not therefore a duty to accommodate such persons, although if the woman is over 17, being an 'expectant or nursing mother' would appear to be an 'other circumstance' that would therefore bring her within the ambit of NAA 1948 s21(1)(a) rather than NAA s21(1)(aa).

Ordinary residence

7.44   Section 21 is silent as to ordinary residence (unlike section 29 – see para 9.14). However the secretary of state's direction limits the duty to provide accommodation to those persons who are 'ordinarily resident' in the authority, unless the need is urgent or the individual has no settled residence. If a local authority places a resident in a care home in another authority area he or she is deemed to remain ordinarily resident in the placing authority's area unless the responsibility comes to an end

43 This obligation is however limited, see *R (Calgin) v Enfield LBC* [2005] EWHC 1716 (Admin); [2006] 1 All ER 112.
44 LAC (2003)21: HSC 2003/009 Annex A.
45 LAC (93)10 appendix 1 para 2(1)(a) and see NAA 1948 s24(4).
46 Ibid, para 3.

(normally because the resident has sold his or her property and so is able to fund him/herself so that the accommodation is now 'otherwise available' to him or her). Ordinary residence is considered at para 6.15.

National Assistance Act 1948 s47: local authority's removal powers

7.45   Very occasionally local authorities use their powers to remove people to accommodation against their will. Environmental health departments have power under NAA 1948 s47 to apply to a magistrates' court for an order removing chronically sick, disabled or elderly persons to more suitable accommodation.[47]

7.46   The application for removal requires that the vulnerable person or 'some person in charge of him' be given seven days' notice of the intended application, unless the case is urgent, in which case an ex parte application is permitted to a single justice.[48]

7.47   The requirements for a removal order to be made are:

1) that the respondent is either suffering from grave, chronic disease or, being aged, infirm or physically incapacitated, is living in unsanitary conditions. Thus the 'unsanitary conditions' requirement does not apply to persons suffering from grave or chronic disease;
2) is 'unable to devote to himself and is not receiving from other persons proper care and attention'; and
3) the community physician has provided an appropriate certificate.[49]

7.48   Where the court is satisfied it can order the removal of the person concerned to a suitable hospital or other place[50] for a period of up to three months and the order can be renewed indefinitely. Inappropriate use of the provision has clear potential to violate the European Convention on Human Rights ('the Convention') (see para 27.219 below): its scope extends beyond the categories of persons specified in article 5(1)(e) of the Convention, and of particular concern is the possibility of removal for a lengthy period as a result of a hearing at which the person may not be present based on the authority of limited medical evidence.

---

47   NAA 1948 s47 (as amended) enables a person to be detained for up to three weeks on the authority of only the most limited of medical evidence without having any prior notice of the application or right to be heard. The certifying doctors need have no particular knowledge of the detained person.
48   National Assistance (Amendment) Act 1951.
49   Essentially that he or she is satisfied that it is either in the interests of the person concerned; or for the prevention of injury to the health of, or serious nuisance to other persons; and that it is necessary to remove the person concerned from the premises in which he or she is residing. In addition, if the application is made ex parte, that it is in the interests of the person concerned that he or she be removed without delay.
50   Which hospital or other place (usually a residential or nursing home) has also been given seven days' notice of the intended application.

National Assistance Act 1948 s48: duty to protect property

7.49   Where a person is provided with accommodation under NAA 1948 s21 or removed from his or her home by the local authority using its powers under NAA 1948 s47, section 48 obliges the authority to take steps to protect that person's property, if there is a danger of loss or damage to it and no other suitable arrangements have been made to protect it. Authorities are empowered to enter premises in order to take steps to protect property and to recover from the resident[51] any reasonable expenses incurred in taking such action.

The nature of residential accommodation

7.50   The duty under NAA 1948 s21 is to make arrangements for providing 'residential accommodation'. While typically this will be in a care home, the duty is not limited to the provision of such accommodation. As Hale LJ observed in *Wahid v Tower Hamlets LBC:*[52]

> It can no longer be assumed that a need for care and attention can only be properly met in an institutional setting. There are people who are undoubtedly in need of care and attention for whom local authority social services authorities which to provide residential accommodation in ordinary housing.

Ordinary housing

7.51   In *R v Newham LBC ex p Medical Foundation for the Care of Victims of Torture and others*[53] the respondent argued that under NAA 1948 s21 it was unlawful to provide residential accommodation in the form of simple bed and breakfast accommodation, or indeed ordinary private sector flats or houses. In rejecting this assertion, Moses J held that the word 'residential' meant no more than 'accommodation where a person lives'. In his judgment, an authority might be obliged to provide accommodation under NAA 1948 s21 notwithstanding that it had decided that the person did not need board or any other services. A similar local authority submission was rejected by Scott Baker J in *R v Bristol City Council ex p Penfold*[54] where he held that NAA 1948 s21 can:

> In appropriate circumstances extend to the provision of 'normal' accommodation. 'Normal' housing can be provided . . . when it is the

---

51 NAA 1948 s48(3). Any money owed as a result of protecting the person's property is recoverable as a civil debt under NAA 1948 s56.
52 (2002) 5 CCLR 239 at 248D.
53 (1998) 1 CCLR 227.
54 (1998) 1 CCLR 315; see also *R v Wigan MBC ex p Tammadge* (1998) 1 CCLR 581 at 584A, where the respondent did not dispute that NAA 1948 s21 permitted the provision of 'normal' or 'bare' accommodation, ie without any board or services.

answer to a need which would otherwise have to be met by other community care services.

7.52   In *ex p Penfold*, the court further held that discharge by a housing authority of its obligations under the homelessness legislation does not preclude the need for a community care assessment. It follows therefore that a person may be entitled to housing under the community care legislation notwithstanding that he or she has been refused such accommodation under the homelessness legislation. In general however (as was the case in *ex p Penfold*), the mere fact that a person is entitled to a community care assessment is no guarantee that his or her 'assessed need' will be sufficiently substantial to warrant such a service.

7.53   A series of subsequent cases (notably *R v Wigan MDC ex p Tammadge*,[55] *R v Kensington and Chelsea RLBC ex p Kujtim*[56] and the 'asylum seeker' cases – referred to above and in chapter 22) confirmed the view of the High Court that ordinary housing was capable of being provided under NAA 1948 s21. This acceptance may have been seen by some as a way of circumventing the traditional route of obtaining publicly provided housing accommodation – most notably under the Housing Act 1996. Thus an increasing number of applicants argued that they were entitled to more appropriate accommodation, because this need had been referred to in their community care assessments. Thus, by way of example in *R v Richmond LBC ex p H*[57] the applicant was assessed as ready to return from supported (mental health) lodgings to ordinary housing in the community. His doctor wrote: 'He is requesting to get accommodation in a street house in a residential area which I believe is entirely justified considering his mental health needs'. The council failed to offer a suitable property. Newman J held that the description of the accommodation put forward was not mere preference but part of the individual applicant's needs. He accordingly made a mandatory order that the council (ie social services) provide the 'accommodation in accordance with his lawfully assessed needs, including his psychological needs, within three months'.

7.54   A similar outcome was reached in *R (Batantu) v Islington LBC*[58] where the social services department had assessed the applicant (who lived in a 12th floor property) as needing (1) a ground floor property with enough space to house him and his family; and (2) safe, secure and easily accessible accommodation. It then referred him to the housing department. Henriques J held that the duty to accommodate lay with social services, not the housing department; that since nine months had elapsed since the assessment and the case was an emergency, the court made a mandatory order to provide the accommodation.

7.55   Judicial disquiet about this trend was however expressed in *R (Wahid) v Tower Hamlets LBC*.[59] The case concerned a claimant who suffered from

---

55   (1998) 1 CCLR 581.
56   (1998) 2 CCLR 340.
57   (2000) 20 July, Admin Ct, unreported. Referred to in *R (Batantu) v Islington LBC* (2000) 4 CCLR 445 and *R v Richmond LBC ex p T* January 2001 *Legal Action* 28.
58   (2001) 4 CCLR 445.
59   (2001) 4 CCLR 455.

schizophrenia and lived in a two-bedroomed house with his wife and eight children. His community care assessment stated that 'mental stability can only be maintained by his transfer to a more congenial and relaxed environment'. Mr Wahid sought a judicial review to compel the provision of appropriate accommodation. In finding that there was no duty to provide this alternative accommodation under NAA 1948 s21 (and when giving leave) Stanley Burnton J was quoted as saying that this area of law cried out for 'comprehensive analysis and clarification by the Court of Appeal'.[60] This analysis and clarification was provided by the Court of Appeal judgement which upheld Stanley Burnton J's first instance decision.[61]

7.56   Hale LJ confirmed that ordinary housing could be provided under NAA 1948 s21 without the provision of any ancillary services, even though when originally enacted 'the kind of accommodation originally envisaged was in a residential home or hostel'. She gave as an example:

> ... small groups of people with learning disabilities who are able to live in ordinary houses with intensive social services support; or single people with severe mental illnesses who will not receive the regular medication and community psychiatric nursing they need unless they have somewhere to live.[62]

7.57   However the court held that the mere fact that ordinary housing could be provided under NAA 1948 s21 and that the applicant was in need of this did not mean that a duty arose under NAA 1948 s21. In the opinion of Hale LJ:

> Such care and attention as the claimant did need as a result of his illness was being met by his wife and other members of the family together with the community mental health team. He was free of hallucinations and happier than he had been for a long time. The family does have a housing problem, alleviation of which would have a beneficial effect upon the claimant's mental health. But the housing problem is the family's rather than the claimant's alone. The claimant's problem is his fragile mental health. While together they might sometimes give rise to a need for care and attention, [the social services authority] was entitled to conclude that this was not so in this case.[63]

7.58   In the court's opinion (and that of the first instance judge) the case could be distinguished from *Batantu* (above) since in that case it had been accepted that the family's unsatisfactory housing situation was likely to have been one of the factors which maintained the applicant's psychiatric illness;[64] and that the local authority had actually assessed the need for accommodation and the situation was urgent – whereas in *Wahid* the local authority had not assessed accommodation as being an eligible need and in the court's opinion the need was not urgent.[65]

60 October 2001 *Legal Action* 17.
61 *R (Wahid) v Tower Hamlets LBC* [2002] EWCA Civ 287; (2002) 5 CCLR 239.
62 (2002) 5 CCLR 239 at 248C.
63 (2002) 5 CCLR 239 at 249B.
64 Ibid at 246K per Pill J.
65 *R (Wahid) v Tower Hamlets LBC* (2001) 4 CCLR 455 at 465D.

Overlapping provisions of the National Assistance Act 1948 and the Housing Act 1996

7.59   The fact that NAA 1948 s21 duties can be met by providing ordinary housing inevitably brings some overlap with the provisions of the Housing Act 1996 (see para 15.4 for more details of the housing provisions). If an individual's need for care and attention can be met by a combination of housing and a suitable package of care it might be 'otherwise available' and so section 21 does not come into play.

7.60   A further and significant additional hurdle identified by Hale LJ in *Wahid* concerned NAA 1948 s21(8), which in her opinion meant that:

> Nothing in section 21 allows, let alone requires, a local social services authority to make any provision authorised or required to be made, whether by them or by any other authority, by or under any enactment other than Part Ill of the 1948 Act. The asylum-seekers succeeded because there was no other power, let alone duty, to provide them with the care needed to sustain life and health. There is power to meet ordinary housing needs, either through the procedures for allocating social housing under Part VI of the Housing Act 1996, or through the provisions for assisting and accommodating the homeless under Part VII of that Act.

7.61   On one reading, NAA 1948 s21(8) could be interpreted as prohibiting the provision of ordinary housing (under NAA 1948 s21(1)) to anyone not specifically excluded from accessing housing under the Housing Act 1996. It is clear that this was not the Court of Appeal's interpretation (for otherwise it would pose an insuperable barrier rather than mere 'hurdle'). In other contexts the exclusory impact of section 21(8) has been given a limited and pragmatic interpretation.[66] In *R v North and East Devon Health Authority ex p Coughlan*,[67] for example, the Court of Appeal considered NAA 1948 s21(8) from the perspective of the provision of local authority funded nursing care (see para 14.20 below) and concluded that the section 'should not be regarded as preventing a local authority from providing any health services' – albeit that the court considered that NAA 1948 s21(8) made a material distinction between NHS services and other services (such as housing).

7.62   The applicability of section 21(8) in relation to housing was considered in *R (Hughes) v Liverpool City Council*.[68] The case concerned a young man with severe mental and physical disabilities who lived with his mother in accommodation unsuitable to his needs. The property was incapable of being adapted and the local authority accepted that since 'the housing

---

66   See eg *R (AW) v Croydon LBC* [2005] EWHC 2950 (Admin); (2006) 9 CCLR 252 at [37] where (in relation to failed 'infirm destitute' asylum seekers) it was argued that section 21(8) was a bar to the provision of accommodation by a local authority since the secretary of state was empowered to provide support under Immigration and Asylum Act 1999 s4(2). However, having regard to the wording of the secretary of state's regulatory making powers under Immigration and Asylum Act 1999 s95(12) and Sch 8 paras 1 and 2(1)(b) the court determined that section 21(8) was of no relevance in such cases.

67   [2000] 2 WLR 622; (1999) 2 CCLR 285, CA.

68   [2005] EWHC 428 (Admin); (2005) 8 CCLR 243.

issues have remained unaddressed for a number of years ... it has now become a crisis situation'.[69] The applicant sought a judicial review arguing that appropriate accommodation be provided under NAA 1948 s21. The local authority contended that in view of section 21(8) this was not possible. Mitting J rejected this argument, holding that the homelessness legislation was 'not directed to cases in which a person has a requirement for specially adapted accommodation' and accordingly accommodation of this nature was not 'authorised or required' to be provided under that legislation.

7.63   While reservations have been expressed concerning the broad reasoning in the judgment,[70] the finding suggests a two stage approach, namely: (1) if the local authority secures suitably adapted accommodation for the disabled person through the use of its Housing Act 1996 powers, then section 21 is not relevant – the need for care and attention is 'otherwise available' since it can be provided via services under Chronically Sick and Disabled Persons Act (CSDPA) 1970 s2 (see para 9.62) below); (2) if however suitable accommodation is not so secured, then the NAA 1948 s21 duty to provide accommodation is engaged.

7.64   This reasoning was adopted in *R (Mooney) v Southwark LBC* where the court found six reasons why in this case the NAA 1948 s21 did not apply:[71]

a)   There is a substantial gap between establishing a need for housing and triggering a duty under section 21(1). The one does not automatically follow from the other.

b)   The needs of children (which in this case were considered to be 'real and obvious') cannot trigger any duty under section 21 of the 1948 Act.

c)   The claimant's need for better accommodation was assessed as 'significant' (the penultimate category of need a scale of one to four).

d)   Nowhere in the various assessments was it suggested that the claimant had a need for care and attention by reason of her disability and that such care and attention was not available to her otherwise than by the provision of accommodation under section 21.

e)   In fact the assessments concluded that there was a need for the social services (i) to provide additional support for the family, and (ii) to make a priority housing nomination under the council's housing allocation policy – which would enable her to access suitable accommodation under Part VI of the Housing Act 1996. In taking this course, social services were acting in a manner envisaged by section 47(3) of the 1990 Act.

f)   Since in this case suitable accommodation could be provided under the Housing Act 1996 this meant that section 21(8) was engaged and so the section 21 duty did not arise.

The interface between local authorities' community care and housing obligations is further considered at chapter 15 below.

69   Ibid, at [19].
70   See eg (2005) 21 *Journal of Community Care Law* 6–8.
71   *R (Mooney) v Southwark LBC* [2006] EWHC 1912; (2006) 9 CCLR 670 at [51]–[56].

Accommodation in care homes

7.65   As noted above, the duty under NAA 1948 s21 is generally discharged by social services authorities making arrangements for the provision accommodation in care homes. This accommodation may be provided by:

- the social services authority itself;[72] or
- another social services authority;[73] or
- a voluntary organisation;[74] or
- a private for reward provider.[75]

7.66   A key aim of the community care reforms was the promotion of a flourishing independent sector (providing services such as residential accommodation) alongside good quality public services.[76] Given this policy objective the question arose as to whether a mix of all four types of provision was essential.

7.67   In *R v Wandsworth LBC ex p Beckwith*[77] a proposal by the respondent council to close all its residential care homes for elderly people was challenged by an elderly resident on the ground that the council was under a legal duty under NAA 1948 ss21 and 26 to maintain some accommodation for the elderly under its own management. The House of Lords rejected the argument. Provided there is sufficient residential accommodation in the local authority's area, there is no requirement that any be actually provided by the authority; it can consist entirely of arrangements made with voluntary organisations or other persons. Although LAC (93)10 para 4 states that authorities are required to maintain some public provision, this was, in the Lords' judgment 'simply wrong'.

7.68   Since the *Beckwith* judgment there has been a rapid move away from direct provision of care homes in some areas. Currently only some 10 per cent of local authority supported residents are in local authority homes.[78] There were 38,600 local authority care home beds in the UK in 2006 compared to 136,900 in 1986.[79] The decline in numbers has been achieved by a combination of closures and transferring the homes to the independent sector. Both aspects have resulted in considerable concern in relation to the Human Rights Act 1998 and have been subject to numerous court cases which are considered at para 7.120.

---

72 NAA 1948 s21(3).
73 Ibid, s21(3).
74 Ibid, s26(1).
75 Ibid, s26(1).
76 White Paper, *Caring for People*, Cm 849, 1989, para 1.11.
77 [1996] 1 WLR 60, HL.
78 Department of Health, *Community Care Statistics 2006 Supported Residents (Adult) England*, October 2006.
79 Laing & Buisson, *Care of Elderly People UK Market Survey*, London, 2006.

Commissioning care from the independent sector

7.69 It follows from the above figures that the vast majority of local authority arranged placements in care homes are made under the provisions of NAA 1948 s26(1). In such cases the authority's commissioners negotiate with the care homes in relation to the fees and terms and conditions. Over the years there has been a plethora of guidance to local authorities on commissioning practice,[80] including regular exhortations for providers and commissioners to work in partnership and develop trust. Guidance on Fairer Contracting issued by the Care Services Improvement Partnership (CSIP)[81] acknowledges that in practice relationships between providers and commissioners are not always mature and mutually sustaining, stating:

> In some instances the absence of close working relationship has lead to providers cutting costs in unsustainable ways or by failing to adequately invest in their staff or by trying to be unrealistically price-attractive and competitive. Providers may also have been complicit in bad practice in order to keep prices down and maintain contracts in order to stay in business. Conversely, local authorities have felt that some providers have sought to increase margins without fully explaining the rationale behind this, or the size or purpose of their profit. This has raised suspicions among purchasers that public money has not been well spent.

Disputes about fee levels and contract issues

7.70 The courts have proved resistant to care home proprietors' claims concerning the inadequate fees they receive from local authorities[82] – suggesting that these are not so much public law issues as 'fiercely contested private law' actions.[83] Thus in *R v Cumbria CC ex p Cumbria Professional Care Ltd*[84] it was held that the council's preference for its own in-house care services and its failure to enter into block contracts with private sector respite care providers was not unlawful; did not breach its obligations under the Public Service Contract Regulations 1993[85] or EEC Directive

---

80 Department of Health, *Building Capacity and Partnership in Care*, 2001, and following on from this a Better Commissioning Learning Improvement Network was set up in 2004 (see http://icn.csip.org.uk/betterCommissioning) and more recently an outcome based commissioning podcast has been produced by the CSIP. Most recently still a joint commissioning framework for the NHS and local authorities has been published for consultation, see http://www.dh.gov.uk/en/Publicationsandstatistics/Publications/PublicationsPolicyAndGuidance/DH_072604.

81 CSIP, *A Guide to Fairer Contracting Part 1*, 2005.

82 In *Douce v Staffordshire CC* [2002] EWCA Civ 506; (2002) 5 CCLR 347 the court was prepared to consider 'arguable' that the authority's (then) regulatory functions under the Registered Homes Act 1984 could give rise to a duty of care to care home proprietors – but on the facts the claim (in tort) was rejected: see also *Yorkshire Care Developments Ltd v North Yorkshire CC* (2004) 6 August, Newcastle County Ct, Lawtel.

83 In *R v Cumbria CC ex p Cumbria Professional Care Ltd* (2000) 3 CCLR 79, p97K per Turner J and see also *Hampshire CC v Supportways Community Services Ltd* [2006] EWCA Civ 1035; (2006) 9 CCLR 484.

84 (2000) 3 CCLR 79.

85 SI No 3228.

92/50 article 1 or its general duty to promote a 'mixed economy' of care. In *R (Birmingham Care Consortium) v Birmingham City Council*[86] a challenge that home care fees were insufficiently high to enable residents to exercise a reasonable choice of accommodation under the NAA 1948 (Choice of Accommodation) Directions 1992 was likewise dismissed – so too was a generalised public law claim in *R v Coventry City Council ex p Coventry Heads of Independent Care Establishments and others*.[87]

7.71   Care homes have also looked to consumer law to address their concerns about local authority pricing, but so far this too has proved unsuccessful. Likewise organisations representing residents of care homes have made attempts to test the strength of consumer law, alleging that local authorities are abusing their dominant position in the care home market. Given that some 60 per cent of care home places are purchased via or provided by local authorities (with a significantly higher percentage than this in some areas[88]) there is general concern that local authorities are, in relation to pricing, unreasonably exploiting the benefit of their position in this market. This concern resulted in 2003 in an informal super-complaint under the Enterprise Act 2000.[89] Although the Office of Fair Trading (OFT) agreed to investigate some of the areas of the complaint, most notably consumer information, contracts and redress, it declined to investigate the position of local authorities. Its reasoning was that the fact that care homes are not obliged to accept the rate local authorities are prepared to pay, in combination with the duties of local authorities to provide residential care under NAA 1948, would mean that 'public authorities are unlikely to persist in setting excessively low prices for care homes residents over the medium to long term, because care homes will refuse to accept older people at such rates'.[90] Such reasoning is open to question – in that it fails to address a third possibility, namely that contract prices can be kept low and still satisfy local authority and private provider expenditure/profit objectives. This can be done by reducing the quality of care or by charging those funding their own care considerably more in order to remain viable.[91]

7.72   If, as a result of a contractual dispute between a local authority and independent provider, notice is to be given to a resident who lacks mental capacity to decide where he or she wishes to live and is unbefriended, there is a requirement to involve an independent mental capacity advocate (IMCA) (see para 18.67). It is indeed arguable that authorities should refer such a case to an IMCA at an earlier stage – namely when negotiations

86 [2002] EWHC 2188 (Admin); (2002) 5 CCLR 600.
87 (1998) 1 CCLR 379.
88 Laing & Buisson,*Care of Elderly People UK Market Survey*, London, 2006.
89 'Informal super-complaint on care home sector', *Which?*, December 2003. Available at http://www.which.co.uk/files/application/pdf/0312carehomes_ scomplaint-445–55754.pdf .
90 *Response to the supercomplaint on care homes made by the Consumers Association*, OFT 703, March 2004, available at http://www.dti.gov.uk/files/file17611.pdf.
91 As guidance from the CSIP (*A Guide to Fairer Contracting: Part 1*, 2005) observes (at p4), 'Providers may also have been complicit with bad practice in order to keep costs down and maintain contracts in order to stay in business'.

have become deadlocked: Mental Capacity Act 2005 ss35 and 39 require that an IMCA be engaged where the authority 'proposes to make arrangements' for a change in such a resident's residential accommodation.

Cost disputes and independent charitable providers

7.73   Whilst the cost of a care package may be ascertained at its outset, over time it is likely to change – if only to take into account of inflation. At the outset, the bargaining power of the local authority and the care provider are relatively equal – it being a simple purchaser/provider relationship. Over time this equality of arms may change, particularly in relation to a charitable provider. What for instance can such a provider do, if a local authority unreasonably refuses to make payments that keep track with the real cost increases it is experiencing?[92] A commercial care provider could simply serve notice to terminate the contract (although in practice few are prepared to take this step), or opt to take only residents who can make a third party top up, or only take those funding their own care. For the charitable provider the problem is less straightforward: it either accommodates an unreasonable council and undermines its viability by using its charitable resources to subsidise a public authority or it abandons the service user (even when there may be no viable or cheaper alternative care plan for him or her). As part of the negotiations such a provider would not normally feel able to serve a contract termination notice, since the very issuing of such a notice could cause untold distress to the service user and his or her carers.[93] Unreasonable refusals (or delays) by a council to consider real costs increases born by such a provider may amount to maladministration.[94]

7.74   The view of the government is that charitable providers are entitled to full cost recovery and that statutory funders should have implemented a contractual policy of accepting the principle of full cost recovery by April 2006.[95] The Charity Commission has however expressed grave concern about the failure of statutory funders to implement full cost recovery contracts[96] – particularly in relation to contracts lasting over three years where research suggests that full costs recovery is less

---

92   ie in relation to such costs attributable to the above inflation increases in pay and staff conditions, changed legislative and practice requirements, particularly compliance with care standards and so on.

93   In complaint no 04/C/16195 against Birmingham City Council, 23 March 2006 the authority had advised a care provider in such a situation that she should simply abandon the service user if she was not prepared to accept the authority's payment rate – an attitude that the ombudsman considered 'extraordinary'.

94   Given the reluctance of the courts to become involved in such disputes (see para 7.70) the local government ombudsman would appear to provide the more appropriate remedy.

95   HM Treasury, *The Role of the Voluntary and Community Sector in Service Delivery: A Cross Cutting Review*, 2002, paras 6.3 and 8.1.

96   Charity Commission, *Stand and Deliver; The future for charities providing public services*, RS15, 2007.

likely to occur. In 2007 advice the Commission reinforced this view, stating:[97]

> In those circumstances where a public authority has an absolute legal duty to provide a service and no discretion over the level of service, there would have to be very clear justification in the interests of the charity for subsidising the service.

Local authority consortia and the Competition Act 1998

7.75   The Department of Health has encouraged local authorities to co-operate and form purchasing consortia to improve the effectiveness of their commissioning role.[98] By way of example, in its advice relating to the purchase of care for drug misusers[99] it encouraged, whenever possible, joint commissioning between health, social services and other agencies, such as probation. It also advised on the benefits of forming consortia which could share information about needs, costs and quality, and which could pool specialist skills such as working with the prison service (para 5.3). From the purchasers' perspective, membership of a consortium enables them to impose agreed service standards and prices. From a provider perspective the benefits are that they do not have to meet different service standards from the separate purchasers. Large consortia (such as the 29 local authority London consortia), however, have such a dominant position in the market place that they can, in effect, create an unhealthy unbalanced market where they effectively dictate all the contractual terms (particularly price). The guidance cautions therefore that:

> Where purchasing intentions of health and local authorities change and funding is shifted from one service provider to another, purchasers should consult with other purchasers and funders of that service, and the service provider before a decision is made, to ensure that the impact of such shifts in funding is minimised for both provider and purchaser.[100]

7.76   It is possible that unfair action by such consortia might constitute oppressive trade practices contrary to articles 81 and 82 of the EC Treaty (formerly articles 85 and 86) and more importantly, domestically contrary to Competition Act 1998 s18. Action by 'undertakings' which have the effect of distorting competition or amount to an abuse of a dominant position in the market place may violate s18 of the 1998 Act and articles 81 and 82 of the Treaty.

---

97 Charity Commission, *Charities and Public Service Delivery: An introduction and overview*, CC37, 2007, para 14.
98 CSIP, *A Guide to Fairer Contracting: Part 1*, 2005.
99 Department of Health,*Purchasing Effective Treatment and Care for Drug Misusers*, March 1997, para 5.1.
100 Ibid, para 5.5 and see also CSIP, *A Guide to Fairer Contracting: Part 1*, 2005, p20 where similar cautionary advice is provided.

7.77   The crucial issue is whether consortia members constitute 'undertakings' within the meaning of the Treaty. It has been held that in general member states and local authorities, when exercising public law powers, do not constitute undertakings for the purpose of the Treaty,[101] although if the local authority or other public body is involved in a quasi-commercial activity it may come within the definition.[102] The question may become of increasing relevance if primary care trusts become significant members of such consortia.

7.78   The judgment of the Competition Commission Appeal Tribunal in the *Bettercare* case in 2004[103] suggested that the ambit of an 'undertaking' was wider than had hitherto been considered, but this has been called into question by a Court of First Instance decision[104] which, at the time of writing, is pending before the European Court of Justice on appeal. In view of the uncertainty the OFT has issued a guidance note[105] which advises that:

> . . . even if an entity is in a position to generate anti-competitive effects, it will not be an undertaking for the purposes of the competition rules if the subsequent related supply of the goods or services (for which the purchases are made) do not themselves constitute economic activities and the entity does not itself directly provide the services.

7.79   In the meantime, in spite of some improvements in relationships between providers and some authorities, negotiations about pricing can result in virtual stand-offs in some areas. For instance fee increases in the majority of authorities for 2005/06 were less than the 3.5 per cent level required on average to maintain margins for 2006/07. In response to this the chief executive of the English Community Care Association (a body representing a large number of care home providers) was quoted as saying: 'All too often local authorities behave in a bullying and totally unacceptable way when negotiating fee increases. The take it or leave it approach is not helpful . . .'[106]

7.80   The unreasonable exploitation by local authorities or health bodies of their dominant position may of course violate public law principles even if it is held not to offend the 1998 Act.

---

101 Cases C-159 and 160/91 *Poucet v Assurances Generales de France* [1993] ECR I-637.

102 *Höfner & Elser v Macroton* [1991] ECR I-1079.

103 *Bettercare Group Limited v Director of the Office of Fair Trading* (2004) 7 CCLR 194, CCAT.

104 Case T-319/99 *Federacion Nacional de Empresas de Instrumentacion Cientifica, Medicina, Tecnica y Dental (FENIN) v Commission* [2003] ECR II-357 and Case C-264/01 *AOK Bundesverband v Ichthyol Gesellschaft Cordes* [2004] ECR I-2493.

105 Policy note 1/2004,*The Competition Act 1998 and public bodies*, OFT443, August 2004, accessible at http://oft.gov.uk/shared_oft/business_leaflets/ca98_mini_guides/oft443.pdf.

106 Laing & Buisson, *Community Care Market News*, July 2006 vol 13 issue 4. The latest figure for 2007/8 show that again the majority of authorities increased their fees below inflation rate *Community Care Market News*, July 2007 Vol 14 issue 4.

Individuals who contract directly with care homes (self funders)

7.81   Currently some 32 per cent of residents contract directly for their residential care. This may not be through choice but because their resources make them ineligible for local authority support (see para 7.24). Although such residents may have care and attention 'otherwise available' to them, guidance makes clear that there is still a duty to assess their needs and to offer advice about the type of care they require and information as to what services are available.[107] Welsh guidance takes this further by stating that individuals funding their own care 'should be provided with the same advice, guidance and assistance on choice as fully or partly funded individuals'.[108]

7.82   The ombudsman has found maladministration where a local authority had failed properly to assess and advise a resident of the type of care that was needed. A place in a nursing home was found but consequently it was discovered that the resident did not need nursing care and could have received the requisite level of care in a residential care home. As the resident had been self funding this involved excess payments of almost £7,000 being paid in nursing home fees.[109]

7.83   Lack of information to self funders was the cause of maladministration in another local government ombudsman's finding, where a relative was merely told that social services would contribute towards a resident's care if a private care insurance plan which did not fully meet the fees was purchased. The authority did not explain that this would only be up to a maximum rate. As the nursing home chosen by the family was more expensive than the local authority was prepared to meet, the family were asked to make a top-up. Had they been advised of this at the outset, they might have chosen a different investment plan. The ombudsman considered that the information given was 'too general to be of use, and the council should have told him clearly and in writing the approximate level of support he would receive'.[110]

7.84   Local authorities are not alone in failing to provide self funders with appropriate support and information. The 2005 OFT report of its Market Study[111] made a number of recommendations regarding the need for better information and redress for residents as consumers.[112] The study found in a mystery shopping exercise that it was difficult to get fee information even with prompting, and 66 per cent of the 152 contracts scrutin-

---

107   LAC (1998)19 para 8 and also LAC (2002)13 *Fair Access to care services* para 72.
108   NAFWC 46 (2004) para 8.1.
109   Complaint nos 00/C/03176 and 00/C/05525, against Nottingham CC and Nottingham City Council, 22 January 2002: in addition the ombudsman recommended a further £16,584 be paid to cover the expenses of the attorney in dealing with the complaint.
110   Complaint no 05/B/12629 against Wiltshire CC, 30 April 2007.
111   In response to a supercomplaint brought by *Which?* (see footnote 89).
112   *Care homes for older people: a market study*, OFT, May 2005, accessible at http://www.oft.gov.uk/shared_oft/reports/consumer_protection/oft780.pdf.

ised had more than one fee related term that the OFT considered was potentially unfair and 6 per cent had no fee related terms. In a separate earlier exercise the OFT had already scrutinised the contracts of ten of the larger providers and received undertakings that they would change their contracts to comply with the Unfair Terms in Consumer Contracts Regulations 1999.[113] The OFT has also issued guidance to advisers and the public on what might constitute an unfair term in care homes.[114]

7.85   In response to the OFT report the government amended the Care Standard Regulations[115] to ensure that the service user's guide (issued by care homes) provides information about the fees payable[116] for the provision for standard services offered by the home and the arrangements for paying such fees; the arrangements for charging and paying for any additional services; and a statement of whether services, terms and conditions and fees vary according to the source of funding for a person's care. Homes have five working days to provide this information if it is requested. The Commission for Social Care Inspection is, at the time of writing, undertaking its own in depth survey to see if matters have improved since the OFT report and in the light of the new regulations.[117] A *Which?* magazine survey in March 2007 covering 50 homes found that two in five packs sent by homes failed to mention fees, only two out of 43 packs received included the latest inspection report, and only eight homes sent an example of their contract.[118]

The nature of care homes

7.86   Where care is arranged in a care home which provides personal or nursing care it must be registered under the Care Standards Act (CSA) 2000. Personal care is not defined, although CSA 2000 s121(3) states that the expression 'does not include any prescribed activity' and section 121(9) states that the care that is provided must include 'assistance with bodily functions (eg toileting, eating) where such assistance is required'. The Department of Health[119] and Welsh Assembly[120] guidance on the 2000 Act currently define personal care as care requiring:

- assistance with bodily functions such as feeding, bathing, and toileting;

---

113 Details about the homes can be found in a press release issued in March 2005 at http://www.oft.gov.uk/news/press/2005/51–05.
114 *Guidance on unfair terms in care home contracts*, OFT, October 2003.
115 Care Standards Act 2000 (Establishments and Agencies) (Miscellaneous Amendments) Regulations 2006 SI No 1493.
116 In the case of nursing homes, the information about the total fees payable must relate to the fee before any contribution from the NHS is taken into account.
117 Details of this study can be found at http://www.csci.gov.uk/about_csci/news/our_oft_response.aspx.
118 'Care essentials', *Which?* June 2007.
119 *Supported Housing and Care Homes Guidance on Regulation*, August 2002.
120 *Clarification of the Registration Requirements for Supported Housing and Extra Care Schemes under the Care Standards Act 2000 Guidance*, August 2002.

- care which falls just short of assistance with bodily functions, but still involving physical and intimate touching, including activities such as helping a person get out of a bath and helping him or her to get dressed.

7.87   If a home is planning to offer nursing care under the CSA 2000 (and the regulations thereto) the regulatory body has power when issuing a certificate of registration to impose conditions, including the categories of person the home can accommodate – for instance authorising the accommodation of people requiring nursing care.[121] The current terminology therefore for what formerly was called a nursing home is a 'care home with nursing'.

7.88   It is of course legally possible for nursing to be provided at a care home that is not registered to provide nursing (by, for instance, the NHS district nursing services providing this care).[122]

7.89   See chapter 17 for a more detailed discussion on the regulation of care homes.

Choice of accommodation

7.90   The NAA 1948 (Choice of Accommodation) Directions 1992 constitute one of the few examples of genuine choice that individuals have in relation to their community care services. In general service users' wishes and preferences must be taken into account – but not necessarily satisfied. However, when they are engaged, the directions give service users a legal right to choose the setting of their residential care.

7.91   The 1992 directions have been amended[123] as a result of the deferred payments scheme[124] (see para 8.75) and new guidance on the amended directions was issued in 2004 (referred to in the following section as the '2004 guidance'[125]): a copy of the directions and guidance is at appendix 2 of this text.

7.92   Once a social services authority has assessed a person as eligible for accommodation under NAA 1948 s21, it is then obliged to make arrangements to accommodate that person in a care home of his or her

---

121   National Care Standards Commission (Registration) Regulations 2001 SI No 3969 reg 9(f).

122   *R (Goldsmith) v Wandsworth LBC* [2004] EWCA Civ 1170; (2004) 7 CCLR 472.

123   LAC (2004)20, accessible at http://www.dh.gov.uk/assetRoot/04/09/09/87/ 04090987.pdf, and NAFWC 46/2004 for Wales, accessible at http://wales.gov.uk/ publications/circular/circulars04/NAFWC462004?lang=en.

124   Direction 4 of the 1992 Directions was repealed by the NAA 1948 (Choice of Accommodation) (Amendment) (England) Directions 2001. The revised text of relevance to 'Preferred accommodation outside local authority's usual limit' is now found in the National Assistance (Residential Accommodation) (Additional Payments and Assessment of Resources) (Amendment) (England) Regulations 2001 SI No 3441. The guidance accompanying the 1992 Directions was revised as a result of LAC (2001)29. The revised directions, the 2001 Regulations and the revised guidance is contained in appendix B below.

125   LAC (2004)20; NAFWC 46/2004.

choice provided that the conditions specified in direction 3 of the NAA 1948 (Choice of Accommodation) Directions 1992 (as amended) are satisfied. The conditions which need to be satisfied are:

- the preferred accommodation appears to the authority to be suitable[126] in relation to the person's needs as assessed by it;
- the cost of making the arrangements at the preferred accommodation would not require the authority to pay more than it would usually expect to pay having regard to the assessed needs (in this context, however, a local authority cannot reject a care home on cost grounds before a viable alternative has been identified[127]);
- the preferred accommodation is available; and
- the persons in charge of the preferred accommodation will provide it subject to the authority's usual terms and conditions, having regard to the nature of the accommodation, for providing accommodation for such a person under NAA 1948 Part III.

7.93   In *R (S) v Leicester City Council*[128] it was held that the Choice of Accommodation Directions do not require a service user to live in the most suitable accommodation that is available. So long as the service user's preferred accommodation is suitable to meet his or her needs, it should not matter that another residential placement would provide a better range of services – and a residential placement is not unsuitable merely because it is located some distance from the funding authority.

7.94   The preferred accommodation must be in England, Wales or Scotland.[129] Health and Social Care Act 2001 (HSCA) s56 provides regulatory powers to the secretary of state to make provision for cross border placements by local authorities in Scotland, Northern Ireland, the Channel Islands and the Isle of Man, however at the time of writing (August 2007) no such regulations had been made. It is possible that the restriction of funded accommodation to Great Britain could be vulnerable to an EC law challenge, since, on the face of it, it appears to be an unreasonable restriction on the free movement of services.[130]

---

126 Accommodation will not necessarily be unsuitable simply because it fails to conform with the authority's preferred model of provision – see 2004 guidance para 3.5.2.

127 *R (Alloway) v Bromley LBC* [2004] EWHC 2108 (Admin); (2004) 8 CCLR 61.

128 *R (S) v Leicester City Council* [2004] EWHC 533 (Admin); (2004) 7 CCLR 254.

129 NAA 1948 (Choice of Accommodation) Directions 1992 direction 2, extended to Scotland by NAA 1948 (Choice of Accommodation) (Amendment) Directions 1993. See LAC (93)18 and WOC 47/93 in relation to the 1993 Scottish amendment. See also para 6.26 for more details about cross border placements and 'ordinary residence'.

130 See eg article 49 (ex article 59) of the Treaty establishing the European Community which prohibits restrictions on the freedom to provide services within the Community. A reported case challenging the discriminatory impact of the restriction in Great Britain on access to care home accommodation ((1996) *Independent* 4 March) was – it appears – withdrawn as a result of the death of the applicant. The position may (or may not) be clarified by the eventual adoption of the EU Directive on Services in the Internal Market: and by analogy, see *R (Watts) v Bedford PCT* [2004] EWCA Civ 166; (2004) 77 BMLR 26.

7.95   There is a duty on social services authorities to explain to residents and prospective residents (and their carers) their rights under the direction.[131] Any failure in this regard would amount to maladministration as would be a policy of requiring service users or their carers to find accommodation at an acceptable cost to the authority.[132]

More expensive accommodation

7.96   Where a person's preferred accommodation is more expensive than the accommodation proposed by the authority, then he or she may nevertheless require the authority to support him or her in that accommodation, provided either:

a)   a third party agrees to top up the difference *and* that third party can reasonably be expected to pay the sum for the duration of the proposed placement[133] (in this category the directions exclude residents from topping up their own fees[134] and also residents' spouses if a liable relative payment has been sought[135]);

b)   the resident is subject to the 12-weeks property disregard – during which the resident can top up his or her own fees (see para 8.63); or

c)   the resident has entered into a deferred payment scheme with the local authority under HSCA 2001 s53 — in which case the resident can top up his/her own fees (see para 8.75).

7.97   The amount of top-up is calculated as the difference between:

a)   the cost which the authority would usually expect to pay for the accommodation having regard to the person's assessed need; and

b)   the full standard rate for the accommodation.[136]

7.98   The 2004 guidance emphasises that it is the cost the council would usually have expected to pay for someone with the individual's assessed need that must be used for comparative purposes.[137] While the Choice of Accommodation Directions enable an individual to opt for more expensive accommodation (and to enter into a topping up agreement) this only applies if the usual cost figure used by the authority would genuinely secure the person a placement in a less expensive home which met his or her assessed needs (including in certain situations psychological needs).[138]

---

131   2004 guidance para 7.1 (9.1 in Welsh guidance).
132   Complaint no 97/A/3218 against Merton LBC, 25 October 1999.
133   2004 guidance para 3.5.4 (4.2 in Welsh guidance).
134   This exclusion was confirmed in *R v East Sussex CC ex p Ward* (2000) 3 CCLR 132.
135   Since 1 October 2001 a resident's spouse making a payment cannot enter into a topping up agreement (National Assistance (Residential Accommodation) (Additional Payments and Assessment of Resources) (Amendment) (England) Regulations 2001 SI No 3441 reg 4 and 2004 guidance para 3.5.10). In practice this has very little effect given the commitment to abolish the liable relative rules – see para 8.117. Note this provision regarding spouses topping up is absent in Wales.
136   LAC (2001)29 Annex 1 para 10; as specified in NAA 1948 s22(2) or pursuant to section 26(2) and (4) of that Act.
137   2004 guidance para 3.5.5 (this is not made so explicit in the Welsh guidance which merely refers to being more than it would 'expect to pay').
138   *R v Avon CC ex p M* [1994] 2 FCR 259, QBD.

The English 2004 guidance gives detail as to how councils should set their prices including having due regard to the actual costs of providing care and other local factors. They must not set arbitrary ceilings on the amount they would pay, and residents and relatives should not routinely be required to make up the difference between what the local authority will pay and the actual cost of the home. It further reminds councils that costs may vary depending on the type of care.[139]

7.99   The English guidance[140] makes clear that if an individual wishes to exercise choice and the home is more expensive, this has to be a genuine choice:

> Individual residents should not be asked to pay more towards their accommodation because of market inadequacies or commissioning failures. Where an individual has not expressed a preference for more expensive accommodation, but there are not, for whatever reason, sufficient places available at a given time at the council's usual costs to meet the assessed care needs of supported residents, the council should make a placement in more expensive accommodation. In these circumstances neither the resident nor a third party should be asked to contribute more than the resident would normally be expected to contribute and councils should make up the cost difference between the resident's assessed contribution and the accommodation's fees. Only when an individual has expressed a preference for more expensive accommodation than a council would usually expect to pay, can a third party or the resident be asked for a top up (see paragraph 3.1).[141]

7.100   Both the English and Welsh 2004 guidance reflect that the preferred accommodation may be outside the council's area and that 'because costs vary from area to area, if in order to meet a resident's assessed needs it is necessary to place an individual in another area at a higher rate than the funding council's usual costs, the placing council should meet the additional costs itself'.[142]

7.101   In spite of the guidance clearly explaining the responsibilities of local authorities in relation to enabling genuine choice there is concern about widespread disregard by councils of the directions and guidance. The 2005 OFT Market Study report[143] found that between 30 and 35 per cent of local authority residents were relying on top-ups, and that 40 per cent of the authorities surveyed suspected that more top-ups were being paid than they knew about. The report found a general lack of information in local authority leaflets about top-ups, and also found that some could lead residents and their relatives to believe, mistakenly, that top-ups were required before a care home place could be found. The OFT recommended that local authority leaflets should make it clear that third party top-ups do not need to be secured in order to find a care home place suitable to the person's needs.

139 2004 guidance paras 2.5.4–2.5.8.
140 The Welsh guidance is far less expansive on this subject.
141 2004 guidance para 2.5.5.
142 Ibid, para 2.4 (para 3.3 in Welsh guidance).
143 *Care Homes for Older People in the UK: A Market Study*, OFT, 2005.

Challenging top-up payments

7.102 The need for a third party top-up payment can be challenged in two ways. The first route is via the assessment. The local government ombudsman has stressed that since councils have discretion to exceed the normal amount that they are willing to contribute to the costs of residential care, they must have regard to the particular circumstances of each case.[144] If the prospective resident has needs which can only be met in homes that are more expensive than the local authority is prepared to pay, this should be met by the local authority. In assessing such needs the authority must take into account the psychological and social needs of the resident. It might thus be unreasonable to expect a resident to move a long way from his or her home if this is going to interfere with the ability to visit of close relatives and friends (see para 7.118). Or if the prospective resident has religious or cultural beliefs which can only be met in certain homes this should be taken into account as part of the person's assessed needs. In some cases the local authority price might mean that the prospective resident would have to share a room – again, if this is not appropriate for the individual, a single room should be considered as part of the assessed need.

7.103 The second way a top-up payment can be challenged arises where the authority has imposed an arbitrary costs ceiling. In such cases the authority must be able to show that there are homes in the area with vacancies at the designated price. In this respect the press release which accompanied the guidance contains the government's view in forceful language:

> Councils should not request top-up payments from either residents or their families simply because they have failed to agree fees that reflect the actual costs of care with providers. It is totally unacceptable for residents or their relatives to pick up the tab, week in, week out, as a result of poor commissioning practice by councils.

7.104 It follows that if local authorities are not able to show a choice of homes at their normal price they could be open to challenge for setting arbitrary ceilings. The Welsh guidance implies there should be at least three homes to choose from.[145]

Where the preferred care home is full

7.105 Not infrequently the care home of choice will be full, and the question arises as to what arrangements should then be made for the service user. The situation is generally of most concern to the statutory agencies, if the patient is in hospital awaiting discharge. Detailed guidance has been issued in relation to choice of accommodation and hospital discharge (see para 5.40). The 2004 guidance states at para 2.5.9 as follows:

> Waiting for the preferred care home should not mean that the person's care needs are not met in the interim or that they wait in a setting unsuitable for

---

144 Complaint no 97/A/3218 against Merton LBC, 25 October 1999.
145 Welsh 2004 guidance para 3.12.

their assessed needs, and this includes an acute hospital bed, until the most suitable or preferred accommodation becomes available. In view of the Community Care (Delayed Discharges etc.) Act 2003, councils should have contingency arrangements in place, that address the likelihood that an individual's preferred accommodation will not always be readily available. These arrangements should meet the needs of the individual and sustain or improve their level of independence. For some, the appropriate interim arrangement could be an enhanced care package at home.[146]

7.106　If interim arrangements in another care home are made, councils should place the individual on the waiting list of their preferred home and they should be kept informed of progress. If the temporary accommodation is more expensive than the authority would normally pay, councils should make up the cost difference.[147] If a person later chooses to remain at a home even if a place at his or her preferred home becomes available, 'upon making the choice to remain in that home, a third party or the resident could be approached for the total difference between the two rates'.[148] It is arguable that any top-up should not apply until the person has expressly stated that he or she chooses to stay in the interim home and not move to the preferred accommodation.

Residents already in care homes

7.107　The right to exercise choice over accommodation extends not only to prospective residents, but also to existing residents who wish to move to different or more expensive accommodation.[149]

7.108　　Conversely (and more frequently) residents may wish to stay in the home in which they have lived for some time. However residents who were funding their own care but now have to apply to the local authority for help towards the fees, may be requested to move if it is more expensive than the local authority will pay for that level of assessed need. The wording in the guidance on this subject is significantly different in England and Wales. The English guidance states at para 4.1:

> Should a self-funder who is resident in a care home that is more expensive than a council would usually expect to pay later becomes the responsibility of the council due to diminishing funds, this may result in the resident having to move to other accommodation, unless after an assessment of need, it is shown that the assessed needs can only be met in the current accommodation.

7.109　The Welsh guidance in contrast states at para 5.1:

> Their needs should be assessed using the Unified Assessment Process. Any such individual who wishes to remain in more expensive

---

146　Similar wording is in the Welsh 2004 guidance at para 3.11.
147　2004 guidance paras 2.5.10 and 2.5.11 (Welsh guidance has similar wording).
148　2004 guidance para 2.5.14. The Welsh 2004 guidance para 3.19 states that the 'local authority would need to require the resident or third party to agree to pay the difference in the costs'.
149　2004 guidance para 4.1 (England) and 5.1 (Wales).

accommodation than that usually funded by the local authority may seek to do so on the same basis as anyone about to enter residential care for the first time. The individual should not be asked for a top-up or be expected to move from the care home if the assessment process has identified that a move to alternative accommodation poses a risk to the individual's care and well being.

7.110   The Welsh guidance makes it clear (unlike the English guidance) that a risk assessment of moving the person should be part of the assessment. Where residents have lived in a home for some time, both the risk of moving them and whether this would be detrimental to their social and psychological needs should be taken into account. In addition the local authority would need to be able to show that there are other homes in the area that would be able to meet the person's needs at the price the authority is prepared to pay. These questions should all be satisfied before any question is raised either about the person moving or a third party top-up being requested. All too often this does not happen and the individual and his or her family are just informed that a top-up will be needed if the resident wishes to stay in the home.

7.111   Not infrequently top-ups start to be required from existing residents because local authority fee ceilings increase at a lower rate than the fees of the care homes. In such cases the resident has not chosen to move into more expensive accommodation; instead the home has become more expensive than the local authority is prepared to pay. The guidance is silent on this matter, dealing only with cases where third party top-ups were agreed when the resident moved in. Such residents or their families who are asked to find a third party to top up the fees would appear to be able to rely upon the same arguments as above – namely that there should be (a) a proper assessment of the risk of moving and (b) alternative suitable homes available to meet the needs of the resident at the local authority price.

7.112   If, as frequently happens, the home approaches the family directly for the additional top-up sum, the local authority should be informed so it is aware that this is happening, since local authority contracts with care homes should prohibit such approaches. If, however, any top up is agreed, the contract should in general be made via the local authority even if the third party pays the home directly, so that full liability remains with the local authority.

Payments of top-ups

7.113   Councils are advised that persons making top-up payments will need to demonstrate that they will be able to meet the payment for the duration of the arrangements.[150] In *R (Daniel) v Leeds City Council*[151] Richards J held (when refusing permission for a judicial review) that a local authority was

---

150   2004 guidance para 3.5.4; Welsh guidance para 4.9.
151   [2004] EWHC 562 (Admin).

entitled to refuse to enter into a top-up arrangement because it had doubts as to whether the third party would, in fact, pay the top-ups.[152]

7.114   Authorities are advised to have a written agreement with the resident, third party and the person providing the accommodation when they seek to exercise their right to use more expensive accommodation. In particular it should be made clear from the outset that:[153]

- failure to keep up top-up payments may result in the resident having to move to other accommodation, unless, after an assessment of need, it is shown that assessed needs can only be met in the current accommodation. In these circumstances councils should make up the cost difference between the resident's assessed contribution and the accommodation's fees. Where resident's top-ups are being made against the value of property subject to a deferred payments agreement, a council will have assured itself from the outset that top-up payments are viable and recoverable when the home is sold;
- an increase in the resident's income will not necessarily lessen the need for a top-up contribution, since the resident's own income will be subject to charging by the council in the normal way;[154]
- a rise in the accommodation's fees will not automatically be shared equally between council, resident (if making a top-up), and third party.

7.115   The local government ombudsman has stressed the importance of councils having a consistent charging policy for top-ups and criticised a top-up scheme whereby the amount by which a relative had to supplement a home care fee varied depending upon the year in which the person became a resident (because the council had adopted differing 'standard' care home rates for differing years).[155]

More expensive accommodation and Mental Health Act 1983 s117

7.116   Although the choice of accommodation rules do not apply to accommodation provided under MHA 1983 s 117 (see para 21.19), there appears to be nothing in principle to suggest topping up is not permitted by service users (or third parties on their behalf) in relation to section 117 services.

7.117   In many cases a care home placement under section 117 will be one that a resident must accept or risk not being discharged from formal detention under the 1983 Act. It follows that any interference with a person's choice in such a situation would engage article 8 of the Convention (private and family life) and require justification. Put in the alternative, any interpretation of what is permitted under section 117 in terms of service provision should, so far as possible, avoid an interference with the article 8 right. Given that section 117 is capable of being interpreted so as

---

152 (2004) 12 *Community Care Law* 8.
153 LAC (2001)29 Annex 1 para 13.
154 See chapter 8.
155 Complaint no 03/C/02451 against Bolton MBC, 10 March 2004.

to allow top-ups, this interpretation would seem to be preferred in the absence of compelling statutory prohibitions to the contrary. In practice what might occur is that the after care meeting would agree that a residential home package (with certain specified facilities) would meet the detained patient's needs. If however he or she wished to have more than this, there would seem no reason why he or she could not contract directly with the home to pay for the additional facilities.

7.118   The local government ombudsman has seen nothing obviously wrong with such an arrangement.[156] In the case of section 117 placements, usually the person has particular needs for residential care linked to his or her mental health problems. It is therefore important to establish that the local authority price offered to the care home reflects in full the assessed needs of that particular person, rather than the general price it is prepared to pay for people with mental health problems. In a recent case the local government ombudsman found maladministration where the local authority did not take into account the need for frequent contact with family members.[157]

NHS-funded care home placements

7.119   Patients in NHS-funded care homes do not have a statutory right of choice; the government expects however that before any placement there will be 'considerable consultation with the patient and his or her family and [hospitals should] take account of the patient's wishes'.[158] The problem of patients having to move care home once they are funded by the NHS was mentioned in the Health Select Committee report on continuing care. In its response the government stated that:

> . . . the risks (both physical and emotional) of moving that resident should be fully considered before the decision is made to move him/her. However the Department cannot say that continuing care should always be provided in the care home where the individual is currently resident, since this would constrain the NHS's responsibility to provide appropriate care (the care home may not be able to provide the type of care needed) and manage its finances.[159]

Closure of care homes

7.120   The closure of care homes, in particular for older people, has proved to be one of the more controversial effects of the community care changes. The period 1990–95 saw a 25 per cent reduction in the number of local authority homes in England (amounting to almost 40,000 fewer residents).

156 Complaint no 04/B/01280 against York City Council, 31 January 2006, and see also Complaint No 05/C/13158 against N. Yorkshire County Council.
157 Complaint no 05/C/13158 against N. Yorkshire County Council.
158 Statement of the Minister for Health, John Bowis, to Health Committee, recorded at para 79 of *First Report into Long-Term Care*, HMSO, 1995.
159 *Response to the Health Select Committee Report on Continuing Care*, Cm 6650, June 2005.

There has been a further 20 per cent fall in the number of residents in local authority care homes since 2002 with a 9 per cent fall in 2006.[160] In some cases this is due to care homes being transferred to the independent sector rather than closed. In other cases, due to reconfiguring services, some local authority homes have closed in order to concentrate resources on sheltered or extra care housing.

7.121 The decline in the NHS provision of long term geriatric beds has been no less dramatic, with the loss of 38 per cent of such beds between 1983 and 1999.[161] On top of this dramatic fall in the numbers of state run care homes and hospitals there has been both an extension of independent sector homes largely during the 1980s and 1990s, and some recent decline caused by a number of factors.

7.122 Care homes can close or alter for a number of reasons, but whatever the reason, it is likely to mean anxiety and distress for the resident particularly if as a result he or she has to move.

7.123 In relation to the closure of long-stay NHS accommodation, there is an obligation on health bodies to consult with patients and their representative bodies (including overview and scrutiny committees),[162] and (in Wales) the community health council.[163] Registered social landlords are also subject to a duty to consult when contemplating the closure of a supported living scheme, as well as ensuring that suitable alternative accommodation is secured for tenants.[164]

Guidance

7.124 There is no national guidance for local authorities on the process of managing home closures. However, in response to an particular incident regarding the closure of an NHS facility, health service guidance on the 'transfer of frail elderly patients to other long stay settings' (HSC 1998/048) was issued in 1998. Although primarily aimed at NHS bodies, the circular was copied to all directors of social services in England, and has formed the basis of many protocols developed by local authorities.[165]

160 *Community Care Statistics 2006*, Department of Health, 2006.
161 *With Respect to Old Age*, Royal Commission for Long Term Care, 1999.
162 NHSA 2006 s242/NHS(W)A s183 and subsequent Department of Health guidance, *Strengthening Accountability Involving Patients and the Public*, February 2003 and *Overview and Scrutiny of Health – guidance*, July 2003.
163 Community Health Council Regulations 1996 SI No 640 and see also EL (90)185. See also *R v North East Devon Health Authority ex p Pow* (1997) 1 CCLR 280 and *R v North East Devon Health Authority ex p Coughlan* (1999) 2 CCLR 285 considered at paras 13.16 and 27.231 below.
164 Under the Housing Act 1985 landlords must consult secure tenants and take account of their views in 'matters of housing management' and the Housing Corporation (in its Regulatory Code) requires all registered landlords to meet similar requirements and offers good practice advice.
165 Many local authorities do however have protocols – see J Williams and A Netten, *Guidelines for the Closure of Care Homes: Prevalence and Content of Local Government Protocols*, PSSRU discussion paper 1861/2, 2003, available at http://www.pssru.ac.uk/pdf/dp1861_2.pdf.

7.125   The guidance provides checklists of steps to be taken during the closure process and emphasises the importance of consultation at all stages. A key part of any strategy should be a 'project plan . . . which is flexible enough to adapt to changing circumstances'. Authorities should set up a steering group to see the whole project through, with a project manager, a patient transfer co-ordinator, a key worker who works at the hospital and knows the patient and his or her needs and will liaise with the patient and relatives or carers as well as with staff in the receiving care setting. Contingency plans must be prepared for all aspects of the project and the vital importance of information sharing (both between all professionals and with patients and carers) is stressed.

7.126   The guidance advises against winter and weekend transfers and suggests that whenever possible groups of friends should be moved together. There should be a named staff member authorised to postpone or cancel the transfer of any individual should this become necessary – even if this means that the patient has to be moved within the hospital.

Challenging home closures

7.127   The courts have indicated that they consider home closure decisions to be an area where litigation should be avoided if at all possible. In *Cowl and others v Plymouth City Council*[166] the Court of Appeal spoke of the heavy obligation on lawyers in such disputes to resort to litigation only it is really unavoidable, and in *R v Barking and Dagenham LBC ex p Lloyd*[167] the Court of Appeal held that it was not an appropriate organ to prescribe the amount of consultation to be carried out with a resident's advisers. Courts are similarly reluctant to investigate the closure of community care facilities – see *R (Bishop) v Bromley LBC*[168] (a case concerning a day centre) where the court reaffirmed the Court of Appeal's view in *Coughlan* that it was only in exceptional circumstances that a comprehensive multidisciplinary assessment would be required before a decision could be taken to close such a facility.

7.128   Increasingly it appears that judicial review challenges to care home closures are being rejected at the permission stage (see for instance *R (Lindley) v Tameside MBC*[169] and *R (Grabham and others) v Northamptonshire CC*.[170]

7.129   The numerous challenges that have been mounted to local authority and NHS decisions to close care homes have raised many different public law arguments which can be broadly categorised under the following five general headings.

166 [2001] EWCA Civ 1935; [2002] 1 WLR 803; (2002) 5 CCLR 42 at 49B. Views reiterated by Maurice Kay J in *R (Dudley, Whitbread and others) v East Sussex CC* [2003] EWHC 1093 (Admin).

167 [2001] EWCA Civ 533; (2001) 4 CCLR 196 at 205G.

168 [2006] EWHC 2148 (Admin); (2006) 9 CCLR 635.

169 [2006] EWHC 2296 (Admin).

170 [2006] EWHC 3292 (Admin).

Promises for life

7.130   Not infrequently existing residents assert that they were given a promise – or at least formal or informal assurances – that on moving to the particular home, they would be able to remain there for the rest of their lives. Moving into a care home is a very major step for many people, and often taken at a time when they are frail and uncertain about the wisdom of giving up their independence. Such explicit or implicit assurances can be pivotal in the making of these crucial decisions.

7.131   *R v North and East Devon Health Authority ex p Coughlan*[171] concerned such a promise. The Court of Appeal took as its starting point that the health authority could break its promise 'if, and only if, an overriding public interest required it' (at para 52). Having considered the reasons advanced by the health authority (essentially budgetary) the court undertook an extensive review of the public law principles underlying the concept of legitimate expectation (see para 27.192) and considered that such expectations can fall into three broad categories:

1)   where the public authority need only bear in mind its assurance when reaching a decision;

2)   where the assurance was such as to require the authority to follow a particular procedural course in its decision making process (for instance consulting the relevant parties);

3)   where the assurance was so specific that it gave rise to substantive rights – in which case the court must determine 'whether to frustrate the expectation is so unfair that to take a new and different course will amount to an abuse of power'.

7.132   The court considered that the *Coughlan* case fell into the third category, and after weighing up the competing questions it held:

> 89. We have no hesitation in concluding that the decision to move Miss Coughlan against her will and in breach of the Health Authority's own promise was in the circumstances unfair. It was unfair because it frustrated her legitimate expectation of having a home for life in Mardon House. There was no overriding public interest which justified it. In drawing the balance of conflicting interests the court will not only accept the policy change without demur but will pay the closest attention to the assessment made by the public body itself. Here, however, as we have already indicated, the Health Authority failed to weigh the conflicting interests correctly . . .

7.133   What counts as overriding public interest justifying closure where home for life promises have been made was the main issue in *CH and MH v Sutton and Merton PCT*.[172] A previous judicial review on the promise for life had been successful in 2000 but in 2004 it was proposed again that the hospital be closed as it was considered to be in the residents' 'best interests . . . to re-provide services that enable residents to live in small groups in everyday settings'. Evidence from the assessments

---

171   [2000] 2 WLR 622; (1999) 2 CCLR 285.
172   [2004] EWHC 2984 (Admin); (2005) 8 CCLR 5.

indicated raised questions about whether a move would be in the best interests of a number of patients. The court found that the question as to whether there is an overriding public interest is one the court needs to resolve actively rather than measure from a distance, and patients were entitled to challenge whether the closure was in their best interests and the court must determine this for itself on the evidence.[173]

7.134   The courts will in general only accept that a promise for life has been made when 'convincing' evidence is advanced by the applicant of a 'clear and unequivocal assurance'.[174] The assurance should however be viewed from the perspective of the resident – the test being 'what would the ordinary resident think that the [statement in question] was trying to convey'.

Failure to consult properly

7.135   *R v Devon CC ex p Baker and Durham CC ex p Curtis and others*[176] concerned the proposed closure of residential homes in Devon and in Durham. The Court of Appeal held that (in respect of the procedure followed by Durham County Council) the decision to close a particular home was unlawful; the council had failed to consult the residents properly. The court approved the proposition that consultation contained four elements,[177] namely:

> First, that consultation must be at a time when proposals are still at a formative stage. Second, that the proposer must give sufficient reasons for any proposal to permit of intelligent consideration and response. Third, that adequate time must be given for consideration and response and, finally, fourth, that the product of consultation must be conscientiously taken into account in finalising any statutory proposals.

7.136   The consultation process must include a statement setting out the relevant context for the proposals under consideration – for instance that some residents may have been promised a home for life. Although a failure to refer to such key topics may not vitiate the consultation process, it may render the decision making process vulnerable to challenge on the basis of having omitted a relevant consideration.[178] Consultation will be

173 The difficulty in assessing whether or not closure of such facilities is in the best interests of the applicants who are seeking to stop the closure was brought into sharp relief in this case. The facility concerned was subsequently the subject of a report by the Healthcare Commission (*Investigation into the service for people with learning disabilities provided by Sutton and Merton Primary Care Trust*, January 2007) which was requested after a series of serious incidents including allegations of physical and sexual abuse.

174 *R (Phillips and Rowe) v Walsall MBC* [2001] EWHC 789 (Admin); (2001) 5 CCLR 383 at 387D; and see also *R (Lloyd) v Barking* (2000) 4 CCLR 27.

177 *R (Bodimeade) v Camden LBC* [2001] EWHC 271 (Admin); (2001) 4 CCLR 246 at 255H.

176 [1995] 1 All ER 72, p91, CA.

177 These elements were first propounded in *R v Brent LBC ex p Gunning* (1986) 84 LGR 168 and adopted by the Court of Appeal in *R v North and East Devon Health Authority ex p Coughlan* [2000] 2 WLR 622; (1999) 2 CCLR 285.

178 *Merton, Sutton and Wandsworth Health Authority ex p Perry and others* (2000) 3 CCLR 378.

held to be inadequate if the residents are not given the true reason for the closure, and for why one home was favoured to remain open rather than another.[179]

7.137   The court also approved the proposition that if a resident is to be transferred from one home to another (for whatever reason), he or she must be consulted over his or her removal from the existing home as well as over the home to which he or she is to be transferred.[180]

7.138   Provided the key stages of the consultation process are followed and the product of the consultation 'conscientiously taken into account',[181] the court will 'not strain to find technical defects which will make the obligations imposed on local authorities unworkable'.[182] The courts will also be slow to add additional obligations, for instance that a proposal could only be adopted (after consultation) if it enjoyed 'consensus or the agreement or consensus of the consultees'.[183] Whether or not there is a duty to 're-consult' if new issues emerge during the consultation process will depend upon the facts of a given case,[184] but in general there is 'no duty to consult further on [an] amended proposal which had itself emerged from the consultation process'.[185] Even if in the early stages the consultation process is problematic, and the process of consultation 'challenging', such flaws may not, when viewed as part of the overall process, inevitably invalidate the consultation.[186]

Failure properly to assess existing residents

7.139   In *Coughlan* it was argued that prior to consulting on the closure of her nursing facility there should have been a multi-disciplinary assessment of her individual needs and a risk assessment of the effects of moving her to new accommodation;[187] the argument being that if her needs were incapable of being met elsewhere then closure of the facility would not have been possible.

7.140   The health authority denied that such an obligation existed, arguing that under the relevant guidance (HSG 1998/048 – see para 7.124) it was only after a closure decision that the detailed transfer procedures (set out in the 1998 guidance) applied and that it was:

---

179 *R (Madden) v Bury MBC* [2002] EWHC 1882 (Admin); (2002) 5 CCLR 622.
180 [1995] 1 All ER 72, p86.
181 *R v North and East Devon Health Authority ex p Coughlan* [2000] 2 WLR 622; (1999) 2 CCLR 285 at [108].
182 *R (Smith) v East Kent NHS Hospital Trust* [2002] EWHC 2640 (Admin); (2003) 6 CCLR 251 at 276C.
183 Ibid at 267C.
184 Ibid at 271F.
185 *R v Islington LBC ex p East* [1996] ELR 74, p88 cited with approval by Silber in *Smith v East Kent NHS Hospital Trust* [2002] EWHC 2640 (Admin); (2002) 6 CCLR 251 at 266H.
186 *R (Grabham) v Northamptonshire CC* [2006] EWHC 3292 (Admin).
187 *R v North and East Devon Health Authority ex p Coughlan* [2000] 2 WLR 622; (1999) 2 CCLR 285 at [94]: 'as required both by the Guidance in both HSG(95)8 (paras 17–20) and HSC 1998/048 and also by the general obligation to take all relevant factors into account in making the closure decision'.

. . . impracticable and unrealistic in the vast majority of cases to carry out the assessments and to identify alternative placements prior to a closure decision, let alone prior to consultation on a proposed closure. Funds for the development of alternative facilities might only become available after the closure decision is taken; only then would the range of alternative available placements become clear; large closure programmes might take years to implement, in which case assessments and alternative facilities considered at the time of consultation or closure would change over time; and in practice the necessary co-operation of individual patients for effective assessments and alternative placements might be more difficult to obtain before rather than after a final decision has been taken on closure.[188]

7.141   On the facts of this particular case (and in view of its other findings against the health authority) the court considered that it was unnecessary to rule separately in the legality of the health authorities' actions in this regard.

7.142   However, *Merton, Sutton and Wandsworth Health Authority ex p Perry and others*[189] concerned a decision to close a long stay hospital and provide alternative community-based replacement services for over a hundred long stay residents who had profound learning disabilities, and physical impairments such as lack of mobility, incontinence and eating problems. Some of the residents who challenged the closure decision had been at the facility for almost 30 years. They argued (among other things) that they had not had a full assessment of their needs prior to the consultation on closure, and the health authority responded by citing the Court of Appeal's judgment in *Coughlan* that a failure to undertake such an assessment did not necessarily render the process unlawful. Jackson J found in favour of the residents, stating:[190]

It should be remembered that Miss Coughlan was not a person with learning disabilities. The government guidance which is applicable in the present case, but which was not applicable in Coughlan, is HSG(92)42. This circular states on page 2 as follows:

The large majority of people with learning disabilities not living with their families can be cared for in residential accommodation arranged through the relevant social services authority. There are, however, likely to be a small number of people with severe or profound learning disabilities and physical, sensory or psychiatric conditions who need long term residential care in a health setting. Where this seems to be the case a multi-professional assessment and consultation with parents or carers are necessary to determine whether the services they need can only be provided by the NHS or whether other alternatives would be more appropriate and cost effective.

The residents of Orchard Hill, whose problems are far greater than those of the average person with learning disability, require a detailed assessment of the kind set out in HSG(92)42 before any decision can be taken about moving them out of NHS care.

---

188   HSG 1998/048, para 98.
189   (2003) 3 CCLR 378.
190   Ibid, at [91]–[93].

7.143 In the absence of special factors, such as existed in the *Merton, Sutton and Wandsworth* proceedings, it would appear that as a general principle specialist assessments (such as specifically addressing the psychological and risk impacts of a relocation) are 'not necessary or appropriate when making decision on closure'.[191]

Failure to consider relevant matters

7.144 In *R (Dudley, Whitbread and others) v East Sussex CC*[192] the claimant argued that the authority had reached its closure decision without considering relevant guidance, including (1) a report prepared at the request of Plymouth City Council[193] following *Cowl and others v Plymouth City Council*[193] and (2) Department of Health guidance concerning *The transfer of frail older NHS patients to other long stay settings*, HSG 1998/048 (see para 7.124). In relation to the former the court held that notwithstanding the eminence of the report's author, Plymouth did not have the authority to promulgate guidelines for the world at large and so the material was not something to which East Sussex had to have regard. In relation to HSG 1998/048, since it was specifically NHS guidance and not addressed to social services (although it had been copied to them) it was again not something to which the authority had to have regard. If there was a best interests declaration that it would be a risk to move the person, this would need to be a relevant consideration in relation to closure.

Human Rights Act 1998

7.145 Many home closure cases, involving local authority care homes, have invoked the provisions of the Human Rights Act (HRA) 1998. However independent sector care homes have been held in the House of Lords[195] not to be exercising functions of a public nature within the meaning of section 6(3)(b) of the 1998 Act and therefore not directly subject to the Act's provisions. This is discussed further at para 27.209 below.

---

191 *R (Phillips and Rowe) v Walsall MBC* [2001] EWHC 789 (Admin); (2001) 5 CCLR 383 at 387J.
192 [2003] EWHC 1093 (Admin).
193 *Report and Findings of the Extraordinary Complaints Panel – Closure of Granby Way Residential Care Home for Older People, Plymouth – November 2002* (2002) 6 CCLR 393 and see also *Scrutiny Inquiry into Care Homes, Gloucestershire County Council*, June 2003, D Latham, accessible at http://www.gloucestershire.gov.uk/index.cfm?articleid=4397; *Guidelines for the Closure of Care Homes for Older People* (note 164 above).
194 [2001] EWCA Civ 1935; [2002] 1 WLR 803; (2002) 5 CCLR 42.
195 *YL v Birmingham City Council and others* [2007] UKHL 27.

Article 2

7.146   The relocation of institutionalised older people to a new residence may have a dramatic effect on their mental health and life expectancy.[196] Although the research evidence is mixed,[197] adverse publicity concerning the deaths of older people following such relocations add to the general concern about the consequences of home closures.

7.147   In *R (Dudley, Whitbread and others) v East Sussex CC*[199] a closure decision was challenged on (among others) human rights grounds. Maurice Kay J accepted that article 2 of the Convention (the right to life) had been given 'an extended meaning', observing:

> As was said by the Strasbourg Court in *Osman v UK* (1998) 29 EHRR 245 at paragraph 115:
>
>> Article 2 of the Convention may also imply in certain well-defined circumstances a positive obligation on the authorities to take preventative operational measures to protect an individual whose life is at risk.
>
> Although the risk in that case was of criminal acts, the principle is not so limited. However, the evidence does not point to a breach of Article 2 in this case. No particularised medical evidence has been filed showing that the life of any particular resident is seriously at risk. What the claimant needs to establish is that 'the authorities did not do all that could reasonably be expected of them to avoid a real and immediate risk to life of which they have or ought to have knowledge' – see *Osman*. The claimants have not established that in this case.

Article 3

7.148   Again in *R (Dudley, Whitbread and others) v East Sussex CC*[200] Maurice Kay J assessed the submissions concerning a violation of article 3 of the Convention in the following terms:

> The issue here is whether the closure decision crosses the threshold of the minimum level of severity required which depends on the circumstances of the particular case . . . the threshold is simply not reached in this case – see for example *R v North West Lancashire Health Authority ex parte A* [2000] 1 WLR 977 at pages 1000 to 1001, per Buxton LJ:
>
>> Article 3 of the ECHR addresses positive conduct by public officials of a high degree of seriousness and opprobrium. It has never been applied

---

196   See eg (1994) *Times* 7 July, 'Elderly patients die within weeks of transfer'; JM Mallick and TW Whipple, 'Validity of the nursing diagnosis of relocation stress syndrome' (2000) 49(2) *Nursing Research* 97–100; JA Thorson and RE Davis, 'Relocation of the institutionalized aged' (2000) 56(1) *Journal of Clinical Psychology* 131–138; AA McKinney and V Melby, 'Relocation stress in critical care: a review of the literature' *Journal of Clinical Nursing* 149–157.

197   *Guidelines for the Closure of Care Homes for Older People* (note 164 above).

197   Violet Townsend, 10 June 2003, http://news.bbc.co.uk/1/hi/england/ gloucestershire/2978234.stm and Winifred Humphrey, 8 July 2003, http:// news.bbc.co.uk/1/hi/england/kent/3054264.stm.

199   [2003] EWHC 1093 (Admin) at [27]–[33].

200   Ibid.

to merely policy decisions on the allocation of resources, such as the present case is concerned with. That is clear not only from the terms of Article 3 itself, and the lack of any suggestion in any of the authorities that it could apply in a case even remotely like the present, but also from the explanation of the breach of article 3 that has been given by the Convention organs. Thus in *Tyrer v UK* (1978) 2 EHHR 1, a case concerned with corporal punishment, the Strasbourg Court held, at paragraphs 30 and 35 of its judgment that:

> in order for a punishment to be 'degrading' and in breach of article 3, the humiliation or debasement involved must attain a particular level . . . the court finds that the applicant was subjected to a punishment in which the element of humiliation attained the level inherent in the notion of 'degrading' punishment.

More generally, the Strasbourg Commission has on a number of occasions stressed the degree of seriousness of the conduct that article 3 addresses. For instance, the Commission said in *East African Asian v United Kingdom* (1973) 3 EHRR 76, 81, paragraph 195:

> The Commission finally recalls its own statement in the first *Greek* case (1969) 12 YB Eur Conv HR 1 that treatment of an individual may be said to be degrading in the sense of article 3 'if it grossly humiliates him before others or drives him to act against his will or conscience' . . . the word 'grossly' indicates that article 3 is only concerned with 'degrading treatment' which reaches a certain level of severity.

These strong statements clearly demonstrate, if demonstration were needed, that to attempt to bring the present case under article 3 not only strains language and common sense, but also, and even more seriously, trivialises that Article in relation to the very important values that it in truth protects.

In my judgment, the same considerations apply to the present case.

Article 8

7.149　The Court of Appeal in *ex p Coughlan*[201] considered the finding of the first instance judge that Miss Coughlan's rights under article 8 of the Convention had been violated, in the following terms:[202]

> Miss Coughlan views the possible loss of her accommodation in Mardon House as life-threatening. While this may be putting the reality too high, we can readily see why it seems so to her; and we accept, on what is effectively uncontested evidence, that an enforced move of this kind will be emotionally devastating and seriously anti-therapeutic.

> The judge was entitled to treat this as a case where the Health Authority's conduct was in breach of article 8 and was not justified by the provisions of article 8(2). Mardon House is, in the circumstances described, Miss Coughlan's home. It has been that since 1993. It was promised to be just that for the rest of her life. It is not suggested that it is not her home or that she has a home elsewhere or that she has done anything to justify depriving her of her home at Mardon House.

201　[2000] 2 WLR 622; (1999) 2 CCLR 285, CA.
202　Ibid, at [92]–[93].

7.150   In *R (Madden) v Bury MBC*[203] Richards J held that in such cases article 8 was engaged and in consequence there needed to be:

> . . . a clear recognition of the interests at stake under article 8 and of the matters relied on by way of justification of an interference with those interests, with an appropriate balancing exercise to ensure that the principle of proportionality is observed. This can be done on a relatively generalised basis looking at the interests of residents as a whole and does not, in the absence of special circumstances, require an individualised balancing exercise by reference to an assessment of the needs of each individual resident. The detailed individual assessment can follow. It may well be that in a situation of this kind, the balancing exercise does not need to be elaborate, and that its outcome is reasonably predictable, especially given the existence of what are plainly substantial public interest considerations in favour of closure.

> The fact remains that the point needs to be addresses. There is no evidence in this case that is was addressed . . . Thus there was a failure to consider article 8; a failure to reach a proper assessment that the admitted interference with the rights of residents under article 8 was justified. In my judgment that amounts to a further and independent reason for upholding the decision to be unlawful.

7.151   In *R (Dudley, Whitbread and others) v East Sussex CC*,[204] however, Maurice Kay J was satisfied (on the facts of this case) that any interference with article 8 could be justified,[205] stating:

> I am prepared to assume, without deciding, that article 8 is engaged. That may be a generous assumption in a case which does not have the *Coughlan* element of a particular home for life, and when the Council will be finding alternative accommodation for the residents. The issue then becomes justification under article 8(2). In my judgment, the Council has clearly established justification. It is relevant that the East Sussex area contains a higher proportion of residents aged 65-plus than any other local authority. It has also been 'zero' rated by the Audit Commission which restricts the level of finance available. That is not a matter for congratulation, but it highlights the circumstances in which the Council was carrying out its review of residential care homes. These are plainly relevant considerations as the Council seeks the most effective ways of fulfilling its various statutory responsibilities within existing financial constraints. It is hardly surprising that it was anxious not to lose the prospect of a £1 million grant from central government. The court is slow to interfere with decisions which 'involve a balance of competing claims on the public purse in the allocation of economic resources', see Neill LJ in *R v CICB ex parte P* [1995] 1 WLR 845 at 857. This has been reaffirmed in home closure cases since the coming into force of the Human Rights Act. In *R (Phillips & Rowe) v Walsall MBC* [2001] ECHR Admin 789, Lightman J said, paragraph 11:

>> I may add that if (contrary to my view) a move such as is presently contemplated could possibly constitute an interference with a

203   [2002] EWHC 1882 (Admin); (2002) 5 CCLR 622 at 636–637.
204   [2003] EWHC 1093 (Admin) at [27]–[33].
205   See also *R (Lloyd) v Barking* (2001) 4 CCLR 27, another disputed home closure case where the Court of Appeal upheld the first instance judge's finding that arguments under article 8 added 'nothing to the case'.

fundamental right under article 8, it would surely be justified as required for the economic wellbeing of the Council and of those in need of its services. Resources of public authorities are notoriously limited and it must be a matter for elected authorities such as the Council to have leeway in how they are husbanded and applied.

7.152 In *R (Goldsmith) v Wandsworth LBC*[206] the Court of Appeal noted:

It is not in dispute that a change to a strange environment for a person of the Appellant's frailty could have serious if not fatal consequences. The proportionality of the response is, therefore, of the utmost importance. In my judgment it is not good enough for Wandsworth, after the institution of proceedings, to produce evidence that this was a factor in its mind when it made the decision (whenever that was). In my judgment, the court has to look at the decision at the time it was made and at the manner in which it was communicated to the person or persons affected by it.

Residential accommodation services and the NHS overlap

7.153 Both social services authorities and the NHS have obligations to care for people who are disabled, ill or who have learning difficulties. In the context of care home accommodation, however, the overlap takes three forms:

1) the duty on the NHS to deliver specific services to persons in care homes (both private residents and those where the accommodation is secured by the local authority (this issue is considered at para 13.85 below);

2) the duty on the NHS to make nursing care contributions under HSCA 2001 s49, which is considered at para 13.95 below;

3) the duty on the NHS to pay for the care home fees in full – continuing NHS health care – which is considered in chapter 14.

Accommodation under Mental Health Act 1983 s117

7.154 The duty to provide accommodation (and other community care services) under MHA 1983 s117 is a quite separate community care service to the duty under NAA 1948 s21.[207] The duty only arises in respect of persons who have been detained under MHA 1983 s3,[208] or admitted to a hospital under one of the criminal provisions (ie section 37[209] or transferred to a hospital under a transfer direction made under section 47 or 48[210] – see para 21.22 below) and then cease to be detained and leave hospital.

206 [2004] EWCA Civ 1170; (2004) 7 CCLR 472.
207 NHSCCA 1990 s46(3).
208 Admission to hospital for treatment of a mental disorder.
209 A hospital order made in criminal proceedings.
210 Transfer to hospital of a prisoner suffering from a mental disorder.

7.155   The duty to provide accommodation under MHA 1983 s117 only arises after the patient has been assessed as requiring this service. Accommodation provided under MHA 1983 s117 differs from the service under NAA 1948 s21 in that authorities are not permitted to charge for this service. MHA 1983 s117 services are considered at para 21.19.

Accommodation under National Assistance Act 1948 s29(4)(c)

7.156   NAA 1948 s29(4) empowers social services authorities (subject to direction by the secretary of state) to provide hostel accommodation for disabled people engaged in workshops provided by the authority under that section. The secretary of state's direction empowers (but does not oblige) authorities to provide such facilities.[211]

7.157   The provision of workshop activities is considered at para 9.47. The effect of NAA 1948 s29(4A) is to make the hostel accommodation so provided subject to the same charging provisions as apply to residential accommodation services under NAA 1948 s21 (see para 8.7 below).

Accommodation under Children Act 1989 s17

7.158   Children Act 1989 s17 requires social services authorities to safeguard and promote the welfare of children in need in their area; this includes the provision of an almost unlimited range of services, of which accommodation (in a care home or ordinary rented dwelling) may be one. The duties owed to children in need (including disabled children) are considered at para 24.4 below.

---

211 LAC (93)10 appendix 2 para 2(4).

CHAPTER 8

Local authority charges for accommodation

continued

Diagram 11: Charging for care home accommodation

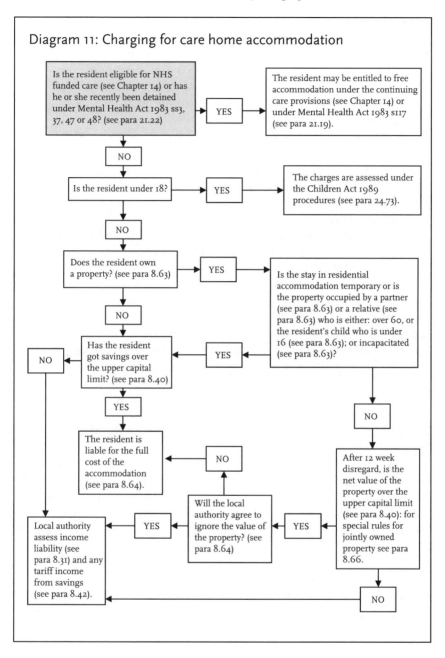

Is the resident eligible for NHS funded care (see Chapter 14) or has he or she recently been detained under Mental Health Act 1983 ss3, 37, 47 or 48? (see para 21.22)

YES → The resident may be entitled to free accommodation under the continuing care provisions (see Chapter 14) or under Mental Health Act 1983 s117 (see para 21.19).

NO ↓

Is the resident under 18?

YES → The charges are assessed under the Children Act 1989 procedures (see para 24.73).

NO ↓

Does the resident own a property? (see para 8.63)

YES → Is the stay in residential accommodation temporary or is the property occupied by a partner (see para 8.63) or a relative (see para 8.63) who is either: over 60, or the resident's child who is under 16 (see para 8.63); or incapacitated (see para 8.63)?

NO ↓

Has the resident got savings over the upper capital limit? (see para 8.40)

NO ←

YES (from property box) → Has the resident got savings...

YES ↓

The resident is liable for the full cost of the accommodation (see para 8.64).

NO ← Will the local authority agree to ignore the value of the property? (see para 8.64)

YES ← (from property NO box)

After 12 week disregard, is the net value of the property over the upper capital limit (see para 8.40): for special rules for jointly owned property see para 8.66.

Local authority assess income liability (see para 8.31) and any tariff income from savings (see para 8.42).

YES → Will the local authority agree to ignore the value of the property?

NO (from 12 week box) ↓

Introduction

8.1   When social services authorities arrange the care for an individual in a care home, either by providing the care in a registered home owned and managed by the local authority, or (more often) in a registered home owned and managed by an independent provider, they are under a general duty to charge that individual.

8.2   As diagram 11 on page 245 illustrates, social services authorities are able to provide accommodation in registered care homes under various statutory provisions. The majority of residents are accommodated by social services under National Assistance Act (NAA) 1948 Part III although residents under 18 are generally placed using powers under the Children Act (CA) 1989.

8.3   The charging rules relating to accommodation provided under NAA 1948 Part III are considered below. The charging rules under the CA 1989 are considered at paras 24.73.

8.4   In certain situations, where the resident was formerly a detained patient under the Mental Health Act (MHA) 1983, the accommodation is provided under MHA 1983 s117. In such cases there is no provision to charge the individual. See para 21.41 for more detail.

8.5   Local authorities should only subject a person to the means test if it is required because the accommodation is to be provided or arranged under the NAA 1948. The local authority role in ensuring that they do not take responsibility for (and thus means-test) individuals who should be funded in full by the NHS is explored in chapter 14. At April 2006 some 30,000 residents in care homes in the UK were the responsibility of the NHS (see para 7.1).[1]

8.6   This chapter details the charging regime for the some 275,000 residents in England and Wales whose accommodation is provided by the local authority under NAA 1948 ss21 and 26. The situation of those who fund their own care (in most cases because they have more than the upper capital limit used in the local authority means test) is considered at para 7.81.

Charges for accommodation provided under National Assistance Act 1948 Part III

8.7   NAA 1948 s22(1) places a general obligation on social services authorities to charge for accommodation in registered care homes which they provide under NAA 1948 Part III. Section 22(1) refers to NAA 1948 s26, which deals with the charging situation where the authority has provided residential accommodation in an independent home. The only exceptions to

---

1   Laing & Buisson, *Care of Elderly People Market Study*, 2006, p154. However most recent figures state that nearly 31,000 are funded by the NHS in England alone – *Final Regulatory Impact Assessment for the National Framework for NHS Continuing Care*, June 2007. The vast majority of these will be funded in care homes.

the obligation to charge are where the accommodation is temporary, or it is part of a package of intermediate care (see chapter 11).[2]

8.8   NAA 1948 s22(2) stipulates that the maximum charge for such accommodation shall be fixed by the local authority but that this must be the full cost to the authority of providing that accommodation.

8.9   Section 22(3) requires that the charging provisions be means-tested, and section 22(4) directs that every resident must be allowed to retain (or receive) a minimum weekly personal allowance. The amount is laid down each year by the National Assistance (Sums for Personal Expenses) Regulations and is the same for each resident whether in a social services authority-run home or an independent sector home (see para 8.24 for details of the allowance).

8.10   Most importantly, however, NAA 1948 s22(5) stipulates that the way the means-tested charging system operates is to be specified in separate regulations made by the secretary of state. The principal regulations in this respect are the National Assistance (Assessment of Resources) Regulations 1992,[3] although they are the subject of regular amendments. Detailed guidance has been issued on the interpretation of the Assessment of Resources Regulations (subsequently referred to in this section as 'the Regulations'). The guidance, known as CRAG (Charging for Residential Accommodation Guide), is issued separately by the Department of Health and the Welsh Assembly.[4]

8.11   Where a resident is unable to pay the standard rate care home charges or the actual cost incurred by the local authority (either for a local authority or independent home)[5] the authority is obliged to assess that person's ability to pay by reference to the Regulations and to CRAG. If, having carried out such an assessment, the authority is satisfied that the resident is unable to pay the standard rate (or in the case of an independent home, make a full refund of the fees) the authority must decide on the basis of the assessment what the person's contribution should be. If the resident refuses to co-operate with the financial assessment, the authority will charge the full standard rate.

---

2   Local authorities are not obliged to charge for temporary periods of accommodation of less than eight weeks, NAA 1948 s22(5A), see para 8.114 below. As a result of Community Care (Delayed Discharges etc) Act (CC(DD)A) 2003 ss15 and 16 and the Community Care (Delayed Discharges etc) Act (Qualifying Services) (England) Regulations 2003 SI No 1196 intermediate care services are to be provided free of charge.

3   SI No 2977 as amended.

4   Up to date versions of CRAG are available on the Department of Health website at http://www.dh.gov.uk/en/Publicationsandstatistics/Lettersandcirculars/Local AuthorityCirculars/DH_073648. The latest version is with LAC(DH) (2007)4. The Welsh circular is NAFWC 19/2007. However the latest Welsh version of CRAG had not been produced at the time of writing. The 2006 version is at http:// new.wales.gov.uk/publications/circular/circulars2006/1552923/?lang=en.

5   The standard rate for local authority homes is the 'full cost' to the authority of providing the accommodation (NAA 1948 s22(2)); the standard rate for accommodation in homes not managed by the local authority is the full cost to the authority of providing or purchasing the accommodation under contract with the independent sector home (NAA 1948 s26(2)).

8.12   References in the following sections of this chapter to paragraph numbers are to paragraphs in the English CRAG unless otherwise stated. The Department of Health might review CRAG in which case the paragraph numbers could alter before the next edition. The details given below are those applying as at April 2007. The CRAG guidance specifically states that it is 'policy guidance' for the purposes of Local Authority Social Services Act 1970 s7(1). It is therefore guidance which local authorities must follow in all but the most exceptional of circumstances.[6]

8.13   Much of the National Assistance (Assessment of Resources) 1992 Regulations directly refers to the Income Support (General) Regulations 1987. Reference should be made to specialist texts for an analysis of the interplay between these differing regimes.[7]

Paying the assessed charge

8.14   Residents can pay their assessed charge direct to the local authority. However under NAA 1948 s26(3A), where residents have been placed by local authorities in independent sector homes (and where the resident, the authority and the organisation or person managing the home *all* agree), the resident may pay the assessed charge direct to the home with the authority paying the remainder. This provision was introduced in 1993 as an administrative easement at a time when many local authority supported residents received benefit income via an order book. It therefore avoided the situation of residents having to cash their order book and then send the money to the local authority. The need for this arrangement has largely disappeared, since benefits are now paid into bank accounts, and most people can arrange standing orders and direct debits.

8.15   CRAG suggests that the advantage of such an arrangement is not only administrative convenience; it may also enable the resident to have a direct contractual relationship with the home owner (rather than having to rely on the authority's agreement). However such a relationship can be problematical if care homes use it as a device to claim top-ups directly from the resident or their relatives without the local authority being aware of this.[8] It is arguable that local authorities, as part of their duty of care, should have a clause in their contract in order to protect residents and relatives from being approached directly for top-ups in such a way.

8.16   In the current situation of some homes charging those who make their own contracts (self funders) more than the amount agreed with local authorities, it can be of benefit for individuals to have the local authority contract with the home, and for the authority to pay the home the gross amount. Such residents can then take advantage of the negotiating power

---

6   See para 1.48 above for consideration of 'policy guidance'.
7   See Child Poverty Action Group, *Paying for Care Handbook* and Disability Alliance, *Disability Rights Handbook*. Both are updated regularly.
8   The Office of Fair Trading, in its study of the care home market (see para 7.101) found that 40% of local authorities responding to the survey suspected top-ups were requested which they did not know about outside of the local authority contract.

of the local authority in setting the fee to be paid, although of course the resident will pay a full contribution to the local authority. Such arrangements will most commonly arise where residents lack the capacity to make their own contract with the home and no one else is willing and able to do so on their behalf. In such cases the responsibility for providing accommodation remains with the local authority (see para 7.26). The general obligation on local authorities to maintain client confidentiality would mean that councils should not disclose a resident's' contributions (or the absence of them) to a care home without the resident's' permission.

8.17　　Other advantages of the local authority paying the gross fees, are that defaults in contributions can be speedily picked up and investigated. Where a three way arrangement exists the authority still remains liable to the home owner for any arrears, should the resident fail to pay the home as agreed (CRAG paras 1.023–1.024). Nevertheless there can be delays where the home is being paid directly either by the resident or his or her representative, as commonly the home tries to resolve the problem itself first, such that significant arrears may accrue.

8.18　　There is evidence that care homes and residents are not being given the choice of entering into a three way arrangement and the government has undertaken to regularise the position.[9]

Preliminary financial advice

8.19　　CRAG obliges authorities to ensure that residents are given a clear explanation (usually in writing) of how their assessed contribution has been calculated and why this figure may fluctuate, particularly where a new resident's charge may vary in the first few weeks of admission because, for instance, of the effect of benefit pay-days on income support/ pension credit or the withdrawal of attendance allowance (CRAG para 1.015). The local government ombudsman found maladministration in a case where no mention was made by the local authority that the resident would need to make a contribution, in addition to the son who had agreed to make a third party top-up of £75 per week.[10]

8.20　　Guidance issued under the Community Care (Residential Accommodation) Act 1998[11] – LAC (98)19 – required local authorities to have in place procedures to ensure that when the net capital of a resident (who is self-funding) reduces below the upper capital limit (see para 8.40), they undertake an assessment and if necessary step in and take over funding arrangements to ensure that the resident is not forced to use capital below the upper capital limit (other than the tariff income from that capital). It follows that a failure to provide appropriate advice in such cases could amount to maladministration and may render the authority liable to reimburse the 'spent down' monies.

9　*Government response to the Office of Fair Trading (OFT) Care Homes Study 2005.* Available at http://www.dti.gov.uk/files/file17611.pdf.

10　Case H3 in Digest of Cases 2005–06 (case reference confidential): as part of the settlement the council agreed to waive the care home charges of nearly £3,000 and pay the legal costs incurred.

11　Repealed and re-enacted by Health and Social Care Act (HSCA) 2001 s53 and Sch 6.

8.21   Similar advice is provided in LAC (2000)11 and LAC (2001)25 which states (para 25):

> ... once a council is aware of the resident's circumstances, any undue delay in undertaking an assessment and providing accommodation if necessary would mean that the council has not met its statutory obligations. Consequently, the council could be liable to reimburse the resident for any payment he has made for the accommodation which should have been met by the council pursuant to its duties.

8.22   There is no requirement to specify the assessed charge in the contract with the home. As stated above, if the local authority has the contract with the home, and is paying the gross fee, it is not a relevant matter for the home. If in such a situation the authority gave information about the assessed charge to the home without the consent of the resident, it would be a breach of the duty of confidentiality.

The treatment of income

8.23   Part II of the Regulations contains the procedure by which a resident's income (earned and unearned) is assessed for charging purposes; the provisions adopt many of the same rules used in the assessment of income for income support[12] and are the subject of detailed guidance in sections 8 and 9 of CRAG. A major difference between the two assessment regimes is that the income taken into account for CRAG purposes is that of the resident' alone. Under the NAA 1948 authorities have no power to assess a couple (whether or not married) according to their joint resources. Each person entering residential care should be assessed according to his or her individual means (CRAG para 4.001). There are rules relating to contributions from spouses (see para 8.117 for more details).

Personal expenses allowance

8.24   The basis of the charging provisions is that residents are required to pay all of their assessed income (above the personal expense allowance) towards the charge for the residential accommodation: 'The personal expense allowance is intended to enable residents to have money to spend as they wish, for example on stationery, personal toiletries, treats and small presents for friends and relatives' (CRAG para 5.001). The minimum amount of the personal expenses allowance is stipulated each year in the National Assistance (Sums for Personal Expenses) Regulations,[13]

---

12   Under the Income Support (General) Regulations 1987 SI No 1967.
13   National Assistance (Sums for Personal Requirements and Assessment of Resources) (Amendment) (England) Regulations 2007 SI No 725. The equivalent Welsh Regulations are SI 2007 No 1041 (W101).

although by virtue of NAA 1948 s22(4) there is power to allow a different amount from that prescribed for personal expenses in special circumstances (see below).

8.25   LAC (2003)8 reminds local authorities that the personal expense allowance must not be spent on aspects of care which have been assessed as necessary to meet the individual's needs by the council and the NHS. 'In this regard councils should ensure that an individual resident's need for continence supplies or chiropody is fully reflected in their care plan.'

8.26   The same advice was repeated in LAC (2004)9, and councils and providers were reminded that they could not require residents to use their personal expense allowance in particular ways, and that pressure of any kind to the contrary is 'extremely poor practice'. LAC 2007(4) again repeated the advice of the previous circulars. NAFWC 19/2007 reflects the same advice for Welsh authorities.

8.27   The weekly allowance for the period April 2007–March 2008 was £20.45 in England and in Wales was £20.88.

Discretion to allow different amounts of personal expense allowance

8.28   Under NAA 1948 s22(4) authorities have the power in 'special circumstances' to allow a different amount from that prescribed for personal expenses. CRAG gives various examples at para 5.005 where it may be appropriate for an authority to allow a resident to retain a higher amount, including:

- where a person in residential accommodation has a dependent child, the authority should consider the needs of the child in setting the personal allowance;
- where a person temporarily in residential accommodation receives income support/pension credit including an amount for a partner who remains at home;
- where the resident is the main recipient of an unmarried couple's overall income, the authority can use its discretion to increase the resident's personal expenses allowance in special circumstances to enable the resident to pass some of that income to the partner remaining at home (see also para 8.36 below);
- where someone does not qualify as a 'less dependent' resident solely because his or her care home accommodation provides board and so cannot be assessed under the rules relating to 'less dependent' residents (see para 8.111 below). In such cases the local authority can increase the personal expenses allowance if it considers that this could enable the resident to lead a more independent life, for example if he or she is working;
- where the resident is responsible for a property that has been disregarded, for example because the stay is temporary (see para 8.114 below), the local authority should consider increasing the allowance

to meet any resultant costs. In such cases the authority should disregard any reasonable housing related expenditure (CRAG para 3.012).

8.29   The above examples are illustrative, not exhaustive. Accordingly in any case where a resident is experiencing hardship, an application can be made for an increase in the allowance. This may be because the lack of income means that he or she is unable to live as independent life as possible (for instance being unable to take part in community activities or attend family gatherings etc) or for any other reason. Such a claim would be made by way of a request for a review (see para 8.120 below). Presumably in any such complaint it would be relevant for the local authority to have regard to its 'anti-poverty' and any well-being strategy: on the basis that this must apply to all people within its area, including care home residents.

8.30   A number of organisations are calling on the government to increase the personal expense allowance to a more realistic amount for the items it is supposed to cover, and most have set this at about double the current rate.

Income disregards

8.31   In general all income is taken into account in full. The situation can however be briefly summarised as follows:

Income taken into account in full

8.32   Most income is taken into account in full. This includes, for instance, net earnings,[14] most social security benefits,[15] annuity income, pensions, trust income etc (CRAG paras 8.005–8.020). Attendance allowance/disability living allowance (care component) is taken into account in full if the resident is a permanent resident, but disregarded if the stay is temporary. However these benefits normally cease to be paid after four weeks if a resident is funded by the local authority.

Income partly disregarded

8.33   Some income is partly ignored, for instance £10 of certain war pensions, half of occupational and private pensions in certain circumstances (see para 8.36 below) and modest amounts of the income from lodgers/sub-letting are ignored (CRAG paras 8.031–8.032).

8.34   A specific disregard of income exists for people aged 65 and over called a 'savings disregard'. It was introduced in October 2003 when pension credit replaced income support for people aged 60 and over. The pension credit scheme provides a minimum income guarantee for people aged

---

14   Subject to a £5 or £20 disregard; see CRAG paras 9.018–9.020.
15   Provision exists however to disregard housing benefit that continues to be paid during a 'notice period' in certain situations – see http://www.dwp.gov.uk/hbctb/circulars/2004/a18–2004.pdf.

over 60. In addition, people aged 65 and over can benefit from 'savings credit' which is designed to reward those who have made provision for their old age through second-tier pensions or similar savings. In order to reflect in part the rules that are in the pension credit scheme, a new 'savings disregard' was introduced for people aged 65 and over. The disregard applies to income and savings that count, within the pension credit scheme, towards the 'savings credit'. A resident who actually receives the 'savings credit' within his or her pension credit receives up to a maximum 'savings disregard' of (for April 2007–March 2008) £5.25 for a single person and £7.85 for a couple. So, for example, if the resident receives only £4.45 actual 'savings credit' it would be this figure that is disregarded. If he or she happens to receive a 'savings credit' above £5.25 (as a single person) he or she would still only have £5.25 of this figure disregarded. Individuals whose income is such that it takes them above the pension credit 'savings credit' level are still entitled to have £5.25 of their income disregarded (CRAG para 8.024).

8.35 Temporary residents who continue to have commitments for their home are allowed such disregards on their income as appear reasonable. CRAG suggests that this would include interest charges on loans for repairs for improvements to the dwelling, services charges, insurance premiums, and water rates. The list is not exhaustive (para 3.012).

Occupational and personal pensions

8.36 Where the resident has an occupational, personal pension or payment from a retirement annuity contract and has a spouse or civil partner who is not living in the same residential home, 50 per cent of the amount should be disregarded, providing the resident is actually paying such a sum over to the spouse or civil partner. In all other cases the use of the 'discretion' to increase the personal expenses allowance detailed above should be considered (CRAG para 8.024A–C). State pensions including SERPS are not disregarded in this way but are counted in full.

Income fully disregarded

8.37 Some income is fully disregarded. Some examples include disability living allowance mobility component (and mobility supplement), disability living allowance care/attendance allowance for temporary residents (these cease in any event after four weeks if a resident is helped with funding by the local authority and is not going to be paying the funding back), Christmas bonus payments, income from the independent living funds and social fund payments (including the winter fuel payment), and war widows' and widowers' special payments (CRAG para 8.038 gives the full list).

8.38 As a consequence of changes to the income support regulations introduced in October 2006 it was proposed that income from charitable and voluntary payments and from personal injury trusts funds and annuities should be fully disregarded (see para 8.55). Following the consultation, due to concerns by some local authorities as to the financial effects of such changes, they are still being reviewed.[16] Such receipts are at present fully disregarded if intended or used for any item not taken into account when the standard rate was fixed for the accommodation provided. Otherwise only £20 is disregarded (CRAG paras 8.051–8.054 and 10.026).

The treatment of capital

8.39   Part III of the Regulations deals with the ways a resident's capital is calculated for charging purposes. These differ in a number of respects from those that apply for income support and pension credit purposes, particularly in respect of the maximum permissible sums and the disregards. Capital is widely defined for care home charging purposes, and includes all land and buildings (unless disregarded – see below). It also includes savings, shares, bonds and the like (CRAG para 6.002 provides a list that is not exhaustive).

Capital limits

8.40   The capital limits are generally increased each year; the limits for the period April 2007–March 2008 are as follows (with the Welsh figures in brackets):

Lower limit	£13,000	(£17,250)
Upper limit	£21,500	(£22,000)

8.41   For so long as the resident's assessed capital exceeds the upper limit, he or she is not entitled to receive financial assistance from the local authority in respect of the payment of care home fees. In most cases this means that the resident will make his or her own arrangements with the care home. If the resident moves into a local authority home or lacks the capacity to contract with a care home (see para 7.26), the local authority will be responsible for providing the accommodation. In such cases however, the resident will be liable to pay the full cost to the local authority. (See para 8.75 below for situations where the local authority funds on an interim basis until funds are accessed.)

8.42   Capital between the upper and lower limits is taken into account by attributing a 'tariff income' of £1.00 per week for each £250 (or part of £250) above the lower limit. Thus if a resident in England has £13,630 capital, a tariff income of £3.00 per week is taken into account as income.

8.43   Capital below £13,000 (or £17,250 in Wales) is not assumed to accrue any income, although if unspent interest on capital takes the resident's savings above these figures, tariff income will be counted.

---

16   LAC (2007)4 – a further consultation has been issued asking local authorities for more detail about the financial effects the proposals would have.

Capital disregards

8.44 Some capital is taken into account in full and some is disregarded indefinitely or for a fixed period. The treatment of the former home is covered at paras 8.63 to 8.78.

8.45 Full details of the disregards are contained in Sch 4 to the Regulations and at chapter 6 of CRAG.

Capital taken into account in full

8.46 Most capital is taken into account including capital held abroad (where the transfer is not prohibited, in which case it may have a lower value). Capital that is not immediately realisable – such as premium bonds; National Savings Certificates and the surrender value of investment bonds (unless there is a life assurance element) is also taken into account. Where capital (other than land) is held jointly it is divided equally by the number of joint owners. If the account is split so that the resident is in possession of his or her actual share, that amount is then used in the calculation.

Capital disregarded indefinitely

8.47 This includes the surrender value of an insurance policy or annuity; the value of any payment made from the social fund; personal possessions (as long as they were not purchased with the intention of reducing capital to avoid charges); payments 'in kind' from a charity; student loans; the value of funds held in trust or administered by a court which derive from a personal injury payment (see para 8.55 below); payments from the Macfarlane trust; and any payments to people who have been infected with hepatitis C as a result of NHS treatment with blood products.[17]

Capital disregarded for 26 weeks or longer

8.48 This includes business assets where the resident intends to take up work again (if the resident is planning to dispose of the business asset it will be disregarded for a 'reasonable period'); money acquired for repairs to the resident's home; and capital from the former home if it is intended to buy another property.

Capital disregarded for 52 weeks

8.49 This includes arrears of most benefits (although as they cover specific periods they are normally treated as income) and payments and refunds for dental or optical treatment and travel expenses.

Capital disregarded for two years

8.50 This includes payments made to relatives of CJD victims.

17 This was added to CRAG in April 2004 although the accompanying circular LAC (2004)9 stated that the date of the scheme starting had yet to be finalised.

Couples

8.51   As with income, the authority is only permitted to take into account the capital of the resident. CRAG is explicit on this point, stating:

> The LA has no power to assess a couple, or civil partners according to their joint resources. Each person entering residential care should be assessed according to their individual means, although liability of a married person to maintain their spouse [see para 8.117 below] should be considered in each case (para 4.001).

8.52   Where a resident is one of a couple, the resident is liable to pay the standard rate or full contracted fee if he or she has more than the upper capital limit, or, in respect of jointly held capital, his or her share exceeds the upper capital limit (reg 20 and CRAG para 6.003). If the capital is in a joint account,[18] there will be a presumption that it is owned in equal shares, thus if the account is held by the resident and his or her partner it will be presumed that half of it is owned by the resident (CRAG para 6.010). For some couples it is advisable to split the account in order to avoid spending down more than necessary. For example if a couple jointly own £50,000, if they leave it in a joint account they would need to spend down to £43,000 in England (ie spend £7,000) before the resident qualifies for help. Whereas if they split their account to £25,000 in each account, the resident will receive help after spending £4,500.

Trust funds

8.53   Section 10 of CRAG advises on the question of the assessment of trust funds from which a resident may benefit. In general the capital value of a discretionary trust is disregarded – whereas payments from the trust to the resident may be taken into account as income under the rules for voluntary payments (see para 8.38 above). CRAG advises that certain minimum information be obtained in all such cases, and accordingly parties should ensure this is made available – even if satisfied that the trust monies ought ultimately be disregarded for means testing purposes.

Personal injury trusts

8.54   In respect of personal injury trusts, Sch 4 para 10 to the Regulations stipulates that their capital value and any right to receive income be fully disregarded (CRAG para 10.25). In relation to actual income derived from such trusts, CRAG advises (para 10.026) that:

> The following periodical payments are disregarded:
> - Payments from a trust whose funds are derived from a payment made in consequence of any personal injury.
> - Payments under an annuity purchased pursuant to any agreement or court order to make payments, or from funds derived from such a payment, in consequence of any personal injury.

---

18   Different rules apply in relation to jointly owned interests in land – see para 8.66 below.

- Payments received by virtue of any agreement or court order to make payments to the resident in consequence of any personal injury. (The agreements mentioned above include out-of-court settlements.)

[Such payments] are fully disregarded if intended and used to pay for any item which was not taken into account when the standard rate was fixed for the accommodation provided. Otherwise, £20 is disregarded.

8.55 In October 2006 the social security rules were changed and from that date (for means-tested benefits) payments of income from personal trust funds should be fully disregarded; any capital payment for personal injury should be disregarded for up to 52 weeks; and any personal injury award should be disregarded not only where those awards are held in court but also where they are subject to an order or direction of the court. In order to be consistent with the social security regulations the Department of Health would need to make changes to its' regulations. It has not yet done so, wishing to give the matter further consideration.[19] This suggests a greater willingness on behalf of the Department of Health to move away from automatically following changes to the rules relating to social security which has largely been the case in the past.[20]

8.56 There is, not surprisingly, a general concern by local authorities that generally no charges can be made for the local authority provision of care against personal injury awards. In effect the insurers gain where residential care is required, as they can reduce the amount they pay because the care is provided by the local authority.

8.57 This issue has been the subject of considerable litigation. The cases concern the difficulty of predicting the future care needs of an individual as well as the suitability of the care arrangements that would be made by a local authority. The Court of Appeal in *Sowden v Lodge and Crookdake v Drury*[21] has held that *if* the statutory provision of care and accommodation is capable of meeting the reasonable requirements of the individuals, the liability for this element does not fall on the insurers. In this case Pill LJ stressed the importance of:

> ... placing before the court cogent evidence as to how the regimes proposed by the parties for the care and accommodation of claimants will operate ... Whatever is proposed should be particularised and costed in the schedule, or counter-schedule, of damages. (para 85)

8.58 The sense of injustice about public subsidy of such settlements was expressed by Longmore LJ in the same case, in the following terms:

---

19 LAC (2007)4. For a detailed explanation of the effect of the changes to income related benefits regarding personal injury awards see 'Personal Injury Damages and Means Tested Benefits' on the Public Guardianship Office website at http://www.guardianship.gov.uk/news/newsforprofessionals_945.htm.

20 See LAC (98)8 and LAC (2002)15.

21 [2004] EWCA Civ 1370; [2005] 1 WLR 2129. In relation to *Sowden*, the Court of Appeal held that the claimant should remain in residential care funded by her local authority but that the personal injuries award should include an element to top up the provision. In relation to *Crookdake*, the state provision could not be said to meet the claimant's reasonable requirements and so the personal injury award was made to include the private provision of care costs.

It might be thought that it would be more appropriate for legislation to provide that both National Health Trusts and local authorities could recover the costs of medical expenses and care respectively from the tortfeasor as the Law Commission recommended (at any rate in relation to medical expenses) in 1999. (para 89)

Some judges also have an instinctive feeling that if no award for care is made at all, on the basis that it will be provided free by local authorities, the defendant and his insurers will have received an undeserved windfall. (para 92)

8.59   Given the recent trend towards greater rights for disabled people to have their care needs in a more independent living situation, it might be considered dangerous to make assumptions that a disabled person will remain in a care home setting for the rest of his or her life, or that the charging regimes will remain unaltered: a point made by the Court of Appeal in *Crofton v NHS Litigation Authority*[22] in the following terms:

It is by no means far-fetched to suggest that, at some time in the future, the ministerial policy of ring-fencing personal injury damages and/or the Council's approach to that policy will change. (para 108)

8.60   In relation to persons living in non-residential care settings, the prospect of accurately predicating future funding and charging regimes would appear to be no less daunting – given that these may change as a result of both national and local policy decisions[23] (see para 10.28 where this issue is considered).

8.61   As with other cases regarding the interplay between the awards of damages and local authority responsibilities to provide care and their charging regimes, the Court of Appeal in *Crofton* expressed 'dismay at the complexity and labyrinthine nature of the relevant legislation and guidance, as well as (in some respects) its obscurity' (para 111).

8.62   It should be noted that in the case of personal injury awards, there is a specific exception to the deprivation rules (see para 8.79) in the case of the award being placed in a trust for the benefit of the resident.[24]

The treatment of property

8.63   In general the capital value of a property or former home is taken into account in full (less 10 per cent for disposal costs – CRAG para 6.011); there are however a number of circumstances in which it must be disregarded. These are:

a)   The value of a resident's home is disregarded for the first 12 weeks of a permanent admission to a care home. CRAG clarifies this provision as follows (at para 7.003B):

Where a person leaves residential care (where they have been living on permanent basis), before the end of the 12 weeks and then re-enters on

---

22   [2007] EWCA Civ 71; [2007] 1 WLR 923; (2007) 10 CCLR 123.
23   A point accepted by Tomlinson J in *Freeman v Lockett* [2006] EWHC 102 (QB).
24   Regulations, reg 25(1)a.

a permanent basis within 52 weeks they will be entitled to the remaining balance of the 12 week disregard. If a resident leaves permanent care and then re-enters more than 52 weeks later, they will qualify for the disregard again.

If a resident enters a home and funds him/herself for 12 weeks or more, the disregard does not apply if at a later stage the resident needs local authority support as it is based on the date the person moves into the home on a permanent basis.

b) The value of a dwelling normally occupied by a resident as his or her home should be ignored if his or her stay in a care home is temporary; and

- he or she intends to return to that dwelling, and the dwelling is still available to him or her; or
- he or she is taking reasonable steps to dispose of the property in order to acquire another more suitable property for the resident to return to.

If the resident's stay is initially thought to be permanent but turns out to be only temporary, the dwelling should be treated as if the stay had been temporary from the outset (CRAG para 7.002; Regulations Sch 4 para 1). Regulation 2(1) allows an authority to regard a person's stay as temporary if it is likely to last for any period not exceeding 52 weeks, or, in exceptional circumstances, is unlikely to exceed that period substantially.

c) Where the resident no longer occupies a dwelling as his or her home, its value should be disregarded where it is occupied in whole or in part by:

- the resident's partner or former partner or civil partner[25] (except where the resident is estranged or divorced from the former partner – unless a lone parent);[26] or
- a relative[27] of the resident or member of his or her family (ie, another person for whom the resident is treated as responsible) who:

---

25 This need not therefore be a 'spouse' but could include an unmarried couple living together as husband and wife. It follows (although it is not clear in CRAG) that if a same sex couple are living together as if they were civil partners, the property would have to be disregarded. For instance if a same sex couple have either decided not to register as civil partners, or have not done so because by the time the legislation came into force one of the partners was no longer, through lack of capacity, able to consent to registration, they should be in no worse position than heterosexual partners who never married.

26 See para 8.81 for what happens if a spouse or civil partner wishes to move from the disregarded property, but still needs funds from the proceeds to buy somewhere else.

27 'Relative' is specified as including: parents, parents-in-law, sons, sons-in-law, daughters, daughters-in-law, step-parents, step-sons, step-daughters, brothers, sisters, grandparents, grandchildren, uncles, aunts, nephews, nieces and the spouse, civil partner or unmarried partner of any except the last five (CRAG para 7.004). The relevant point here is that this is an *inclusive* definition rather than an exclusive one.

    i) is aged 60 or over, or

    ii) is aged under 16 and is a child whom the resident is liable to maintain, or

    iii) is incapacitated.[28]

The ombudsman found maladministration in a case where a property was not disregarded in spite of the mental health problems of the daughter who lived in it, and considered that in all likelihood being told the house had to be sold played a key part in her breakdown.[29]

In cases where the relative was living in the property at the time the resident moved into a care home, and later reaches the age of 60, or becomes incapacitated, the mandatory disregard should apply from the date the relative reached 60 or became incapacitated (if the property has not already been disregarded under the discretionary provisions described below).

More difficult is the situation where a relative in the above categories moves into the property as his or her home after the resident has moved into a care home. It is likely that a court determining a case concerning such a situation would be heavily influenced by its particular facts, although its interpretation may well be guided by principles of public policy – namely that the aim of the Regulations appears to be to protect from homelessness, certain people living in the property when the owner is institutionalised and not to protect people who use the exemption as a means of acquiring a benefit at the local authority's expense. It may be that in certain situations, where there is a perceived exploitation of the exemption, the question of a deprivation of assets may be considered[30] (see para 8.79 below).

d) Where the resident has acquired property which he or she intends eventually to occupy as his or her home, the value should be disregarded for up to 26 weeks from the date the resident first takes steps to take up occupation, or such longer period as is considered reasonable (CRAG para 7.006; Regulations Sch 4 para 16).

---

28 The meaning of 'incapacitated' is not defined by the Regulations, but CRAG suggests that it includes a person receiving (or whose incapacity is sufficient to that required to qualify for) one of the following: 'incapacity benefit, severe disablement allowance, disability living allowance, attendance allowance, constant attendance allowance, or an analogous benefit'. Again this is an inclusive rather than an exclusive definition (CRAG para 7.005).

29 Case H1 2005–06 Digest of cases (case reference confidential).

30 It is uncertain how far such an argument could be taken. First the resident still owns the property, thus raising the question of whether he has 'deprived' himself of it. Second, the Regulations merely state that capital is disregarded if 'it is occupied in whole or in part' by the relatives specified 'as their home'. They do not specify 'continuing to occupy' which by implication would mean that they were living in the home before the resident moved to residential care. The discretionary disregard in the Regulations specifically states that the disregard can be applied where a third party 'continues to live' in the resident's home (see para 8.64). Absent the word 'continue' and given the present tense of the words 'is occupied' it is thus arguable that where a relative moves into the resident's home with the resident's permission, the property should be disregarded from that date if the relative is in one of the above categories.

8.64   In addition local authorities have an overall discretion to disregard the capital value of premises, not covered by the above exceptions, in which a third party continues to live.[31] Paragraph 7.007 of CRAG suggests that:

> LAs will have to balance the use of this discretion with the need to ensure that residents with assets are not maintained at public expense. It may be reasonable, for example, to disregard a dwelling's value where it is the sole residence of someone who has given up their own home in order to care for the resident, or someone who is an elderly companion of the resident particularly if they have given up their own home.

8.65   The above example is illustrative and in no way restricts the scope of the local authority discretion in this area. It appears that local authorities vary widely in their use of this power to disregard property.

Joint beneficial ownership of property

8.66   CRAG and the Regulations[32] deal with the approach to be adopted in order to value property which is the subject of joint beneficial ownership. The general rule is that where a resident jointly owns property (ie, he or she has the right to receive some of the proceeds of a sale) the resident's share is valued at the amount that that interest would realise if it were sold to a willing buyer. From this figure a further 10 per cent and the amount of any encumbrance secured solely on the resident's share should be deducted.

8.67   Establishing beneficial interest in property has been the subject of several cases. In *Kelly v Hammersmith and Fulham LBC*[33] the resident had purchased her council house (exercising her right to buy) but her daughter had funded the entire purchase costs and mortgage repayments. The court nevertheless held that the local authority was entitled to maintain a caution on the property in the mother's name for outstanding residential home fees because the daughter was unable to adduce sufficient evidence to show that her mother had no beneficial interest in the property. In another case, *Campbell v Griffin*,[34] the Court of Appeal found that a long term lodger, who had provided care over a number of years to an elderly couple prior to their moving into a care home, had as a consequence acquired an equitable interest in the property. Rather than the right to remain in the property, the court found entitlement to £35,000 from the proceeds of sale of the property, albeit that this claim ranked above the charge on the property placed by the council for unpaid care home fees

8.68   CRAG points out that the value of the resident's interest in a jointly owned property will be governed by:

a)   the resident's ability to reassign the beneficial interest to somebody else; and

---

31 Regulations Sch 4 para 18.
32 Ibid, reg 27(2) and CRAG paras 7.012–7.016.
33 [2004] EWHC 435 (Admin); (2004) 7 CCLR 542.
34 [2001] EWCA Civ 990, http://www.bailii.org/ew/cases/EWCA/Civ/2001/990.html.

b)   there being a market, ie, the interest being such as to attract a willing buyer for the interest.

8.69   CRAG suggests that in most cases there is unlikely to be any legal impediment preventing a joint beneficial interest in a property being reassigned. But the likelihood of there being a willing buyer will depend on the conditions in which the joint beneficial interest has arisen. It goes on to advise (at paras 7.012 *et seq*) that where an interest in property is beneficially shared between relatives:

> . . . the value of the resident's interest will be heavily influenced by the possibility of a market amongst his or her fellow beneficiaries. If no other relative is willing to buy the resident's interest, it is highly unlikely that any 'outsider' would be willing to buy into the property unless the financial advantages far outweighed the risks and limitations involved. The value of the interest, even to a willing buyer, could in such circumstances effectively be nil. If the local authority is unsure about the resident's share, or their valuation is disputed by the resident, again professional valuation should be obtained.

8.70   CRAG provides local authorities with further advice (including the 'example' below) as to what action they should take in such situations (at para 7.014A):

> If ownership is disputed and a resident's interest is alleged to be less than seems apparent from the initial information, the local authority will need written evidence on any beneficial interest the resident, or other parties possess. Such evidence may include the person's understanding of events, including why and how the property came to be in the resident's name or possession. Where it is contended that the interest in the property is held for someone else, the local authority should require evidence of the arrangement, the origin of the arrangement and the intentions for its future use. The law of equity may operate to resolve doubts about beneficial ownership, by deciding what is reasonable by reference to the original intentions behind a person's action, rather than applying the strict letter of the law.

> **Example**
> The resident has a beneficial interest in a property worth £60,000. He shares the interest with two relatives. After deductions for an outstanding mortgage, the residual value is £30,000. One relative would be willing to buy the resident's interest for £5,000. Although the value of the resident's share of the property may be £10,000, if the property as a whole had been sold, the value of just his share is £5,000 as this is the sum he could obtain from a willing buyer. The resident's actual capital would be £4,500 because a further 10 per cent would be deducted from the value of his share to cover the cost of transferring the interest to the buyer.

8.71   If a local authority disputes a valuation in such a case, CRAG advises that a professional valuation be obtained (para 7.011). A failure to do this may constitute maladministration.[35]

8.72   A number of authorities have argued that almost invariably there will

---

35 Complaint no 03/C/09384 against Lincolnshire CC, 28 June 2004.

be a willing buyer (especially in cases where the jointly owned property is not lived in by the joint owner), on the grounds that a reasonably informed buyer would be aware that after purchase he or she will have rights as a co-owner, which include the right to apply to the court for a sale. Under Trust of Land and Appointment of Trustees Act 1996 s15 the court has to consider amongst other things the intentions of the persons who created the trust, and the purposes for which the property is held in trust.

8.73   Such an argument is conjectural and ultimately will depend upon the opinion of a sufficiently experienced/specialist valuer who knows the state of the local market. It is far from clear why someone would buy a property which has a co-owner who does not wish to sell – particularly if there are similar properties for sale with no problems attached.

8.74   Although the Regulations relating to jointly owned property in the Income Support (General) Regulations 1987 are slightly different to Assessment of Resources Regulations 1992 reg 27(2), there is nevertheless useful advice in the *Decision Maker's Guide* on the questions that a valuation officer should take into account when reaching a valuation of a resident's share in jointly owned property.[36]

Charges to enable the sale of property to be deferred

8.75   Health and Social Care Act (HSCA) 2001 ss53–55 introduced a 'deferred payments' scheme which enables a resident to enter into an agreement with the local authority whereby the value of his or her main home is disregarded when deciding whether or not that person needs 'care and attention which is not otherwise available'. In effect the council then pays the resident's care home fees (including any top-up' – see para 7.90) and recovers these payments from the sale of the property, normally after the resident's death. In some cases where there is likely to be a delay on the sale of the property these provisions are used. The scheme was implemented in England in 2001 and in Wales in 2003[37] and is the subject of guidance[38] that explains that its aim is to:

> . . . allow people with property, but without income and other assets sufficient to meet their full assessed contribution, to have a legal charge placed on their property to meet any shortfall. Hence people will be able to keep their homes on admission to residential care and for the duration of the deferred payments agreement.

8.76   The Department of Health was sufficiently concerned about the low take up of deferred payments by local authorities that in LAC (2002)15 it drew

---

36   Vol 5 chapter 29 paras 29642–20647, available at http://www.dwp.gov.uk/publications/dwp/dmg.

37   National Assistance (Residential Accommodation) (Relevant Contributions) (England) Regulations 2001 SI No 3069; National Assistance (Residential Accommodation) (Additional Payments, Relevant Contributions and Assessment of Resources) (Wales) Regulations 2003 SI No 931 (W121); National Assistance (Residential Accommodation) (Disregarding of Resources) (Wales) Regulations 2003 SI No 969 (W131).

38   LAC (2001)25 and LAC (2001)29 in England; NAFWC 21/2003 in Wales.

attention to CI (2002)12 in which the Chief Inspector of Social Services reminded them that they are expected to have a deferred payments scheme in place and that they 'could be challenged if they did not consider exercising their discretion to offer deferred payments in individual cases'. The local government ombudsman held that it was maladministration for a local authority not to have introduced a deferred payment scheme.[39] More recently maladministration was found where a council did not offer a deferred payment. Had it done so it would have been possible to avoid selling the resident's house until after he had died, which would have increased in value by £20,000. This amount was paid to the claimant.[40]

8.77   The procedure for implementing a deferred payment arrangement is described by CRAG at para 7.018 which includes reference to a pro forma legal agreement (in respect of the legal charge – revised to take account of the Land Registration Act 2002) that councils may wish to use in such cases.[41] At para 7.019 it contrasts such agreements with charges imposed under Health and Social Services and Social Security Adjudications Act (HASSASSAA) 1983 s22 (see para 8.107 below) in the following terms:

> Councils should bear in mind that deferred payments under section 55 of the Health and Social Care Act 2001 are distinct from the pursuit of debt through section 22 of HASSASSAA 1983 . . . Deferred payments should be offered when individuals are willing to pay their assessed contribution but do not wish to do so immediately. Section 22 of HASSASSAA applies to situations where residents are unwilling to pay their assessed contribution, either now or in the future, and a debt arises

Property owned but rented to tenants

8.78   CRAG provides (para 7.017) that where a resident owns property, the value of which takes the resident's total capital above the upper capital limit, and the property is rented to tenants, the resident will be assessed as able to pay the standard charge for the accommodation (because of the level of capital). In such a situation the local authority may deem the resident to be a 'self funder' or require him or her to pay the rental income (along with any other income) to it in order to reduce the accruing debt. In cases where no deferred payment arrangement has been agreed (as above) authorities may choose to place a legal charge on the property and wait until the tenant dies before enforcing payment of the accrued debt (plus

---

39   Complaint no 04/C/04804 against Manchester City Council, 31 March 2005.
40   See Health Service and Parliamentary Ombudsman, *Report on retrospective continuing care funding and redress*, 2007, Annex A (see para 14.189). The complainants had already referred the matter to the local government ombudsman. They were pursing a claim for fully funded NHS care, but needed help with funding. The local authority did not tell the family about the possibility of having a charge placed on the property under the deferred payment scheme. As Greenwich LBC settled during the investigation it did not reach report stage. It is also mentioned in the annual letter which the local government ombudsman sends to each council – which in 2006, for the first time, has been made public on the LGO website.
41   However it appears that this document is no longer available on the website.

interest from the date of death) against the estate,[42] but they are not obliged to take this course (see para 8.107 below).

Deprivation of capital

8.79   Regulation 25(1) of the Regulations provides that:

> A resident may be treated as possessing actual capital of which he has deprived himself for the purpose of decreasing the amount that he may be liable to pay for his accommodation except –
> (a) where that capital is derived from a payment made in consequence of any personal injury and is placed on trust for the benefit of the resident; or
> (b) to the extent that the capital which he is treated as possessing is reduced in accordance with regulation 26 [the diminishing notional capital rule – see below]; or
> (c) any sum to which paragraph 44(a) or 45(a) of Schedule 10 to the Income Support Regulations[43] (disregard of compensation for personal injuries which is administered by the Court) refers (see para 8.62).

8.80   In seeking to determine whether a deprivation has occurred, para 10 of LAC (98)8 advised as follows:

> Much information can be verified by reference to recent documentation provided by the client such as bank statements and building society account books. Authorities should also make use of information available to them from other departments within the authority or District Councils to verify client details, for example council tax benefit and housing records. They should also, as appropriate and with the consent of the client, undertake checks with other agencies such as the Social security office, banks and private pension firms. Obviously it is not necessary for all information to be verified, and it is for authorities themselves to determine the extent and circumstances for verifying information.

Notional capital

8.81   CRAG explains (at paras 6.057 et seq) the impact of the rule in regulation 25(1) – that where an authority feels that a resident has deliberately deprived him/herself of a capital asset in order to reduce the accommodation charge it may treat the resident as still possessing the asset. CRAG provides further guidance in the following terms:

---

42 See HASSASSAA 1983 ss22 and 24.
43 The Income Support (General) Regulations 1987 SI No 1967 which provide for the disregard of capital administered on behalf of a person by the High Court or the county court under Civil Procedure Rules 1998 SI No 3132 r21.11(1) or the Court of Protection, where such sum derives from (a) an award of damages for a personal injury to that person; or (b) compensation for the death of one or both parents where the person concerned is under the age of 18. Note however that since October 2006 changes to the income support regulations mean that regs 44(a) and 45(a) have been altered and are now contained in regs 44(1)(a) and 45(1)(a).

6.062 There may be more than one purpose for disposing of a capital asset, only one of which is to avoid a charge for accommodation. Avoiding the charge need not be the resident's main motive but it must be a significant one.

6.063 If, for example, a person has used capital to repay a debt, careful consideration should be given to whether there was a need for the debt to be repaid at that time. If it seems unreasonable for the resident to have repaid that debt at that time, it may be that the purpose was to avoid a charge for accommodation.

Examples [CRAG para 6.063]

[1] A person moves into residential accommodation and has a 50% interest in property which continues to be occupied by his spouse or civil partner. The LA ignore the value of the resident's share in property while the spouse or civil partner lives there but the spouse or civil partner decides to move to smaller accommodation and so sells the former home. At the time the property is sold, the resident's 50% share of the proceeds could be taken into account in the charging assessment but, in order to enable the spouse or civil partner to purchase the smaller property, the resident makes part of his share of the proceeds from the sale available to the spouse or civil partner. In these circumstances, in the Department's view, it would not be reasonable to treat the resident as having deprived himself of capital in order to reduce his residential accommodation charge.

[2] A person has £24,000 in the bank. He is about to move permanently to a residential care home, and before doing so, pays off £3,500 outstanding on a loan for home improvements. It would be reasonable in these circumstances not to treat him as having deprived himself of the £3,500 deliberately in order to reduce his residential accommodation charge.

[3] A resident has £18,000 in a building society. Two weeks before entering the home, he bought a car for £10,500, which he gave to his son on entering the home. If the resident knew he was to be admitted permanently to a residential care home at the time he bought the car, it would be reasonable to treat this as deliberate deprivation. However, all the circumstances must be taken into account. If he was admitted as an emergency and had no reason to think he would not be in a position to drive the car at the time he bought it, it would not be reasonable to treat it as deliberate deprivation.

Timing of the disposal

8.82 The length of time between the disposal and the application for financial assistance will generally be relevant; the longer the time between the disposal of an asset and a person's liability for accommodation charges, the less likely it is that the obtaining of the financial advantage was a foreseeable consequence of the transaction. CRAG states (para 6.064):

> The timing of the disposal should be taken into account when considering the purpose of the disposal. It would be unreasonable to decide that a resident had disposed of an asset in order to reduce his charge for accommodation when the disposal took place at a time when he was fit and healthy and could not have foreseen the need for a move to residential accommodation.

8.83 The leading judgment concerning a deprivation under regulation 25 is that of the Scottish Court of Session (Extra Division) in *Yule v South Lanarkshire Council*[44] where it was held that a local authority was entitled to take account of the value of an elderly woman's home transferred to her daughter over 18 months before the woman entered residential care. The court held that there was no time limit on local authorities when deciding whether a person had deprived him/herself of assets for the purposes of avoiding residential care fees.

8.84 Richards J relied upon the following extract from the *Yule* judgment in the subsequent case of *R (Beeson) v Dorset CC*:[45]

> The process of assessment, therefore begins with the requirement for the resident or prospective resident to provide information to the local authority from which the local authority can be satisfied that he is unable to pay the standard charge for the accommodation. The local authority cannot be so satisfied if the capital, both actual and notional, exceeds the specified sum. In determining the matter of notional capital, the local authority can only proceed upon the material which is available to them either from their own sources or upon that material as supplemented by material from the applicant and from such other sources as the local authority can reasonably be expected to apply to. We agree with counsel for the petitioner that in considering whether there is notional capital to be added to the actual capital of an applicant, the local authority must look to the information before them to determine whether a purpose to the effect specified in the regulations can be deduced. But in our opinion, this is not a matter of onus of proof. Rather, before the local authority can reach such a view, it must have material before it from which it can be reasonably inferred that the deprivation of capital took place deliberately and with a purpose of the nature specified. The local authority cannot look into the mind of the person making the disposition of capital or of others who may be concerned in the transaction. It can only look at the nature of the disposal within the context of the time at which and the circumstances in which that disposal took place.

> . . . [W]e do not consider . . . that it is necessary that the claimant should know of 'the' capital limit above which, in terms of the relevant regulations applicable at the time, the local authority is bound to refuse the application, if it is a reasonable inference, looking to the transaction in the whole surrounding circumstances relating to the applicant, that it must have been a purpose of the transaction to avoid having to pay any charges in the event of becoming a resident in residential accommodation provided by the local authority. In this respect we consider that the 1992 Regulations have to be looked at in a different light to those concerned with provision for income related benefits, not least because the purpose of the individual may have formed possibly some time ahead of the prospect that he or she might require to enter such residential accommodation . . .

8.85 The *Beeson* proceedings concerned a challenge to a decision that the resident had deprived himself of his house for the purpose of decreasing his

---

44 (2001) 4 CCLR 383.
45 The extract from the *Yule* judgment is at (2001) 4 CCLR 383 at 395–396 and is cited in the *Beeson* judgment at [2001] EWHC 986 (Admin); (2002) 5 CCLR 5 at [9].

liability for residential care fees. Mr Beeson senior transferred his house to his son by deed of gift, his stated reason being that he wished to ensure his son had a home if he needed it following the breakdown of his marriage. He then continued to live in the house for two years before finally being assessed by the council as being in need of residential care. His wish had been to live at home as long as possible and to die there. He returned home after several spells in hospital and received home care. At the time of the transfer, social services had not mentioned the possibility of residential care being required, but the council took the view that residential care was an inevitability and that this was the motive in making the transfer and accordingly it treated the house as notional capital for the purposes of regulation 25.

8.86   The Court of Appeal[46] upheld the first instance decision of Richards J concerning the relevant test for disposals of assets, as stated in *Yule v South Lanarkshire*. Richards J held that the local authority had shown no evidence that Mr Beeson had transferred the property with the intention of reducing his potential liability for care home charges – indeed the evidence was the other way. The council's decision was therefore quashed and had to be reconsidered.

Diminishing notional capital rule

8.87   Where a resident is deemed to possess notional capital (such that he or she is deemed liable to pay some or all of the standard rate for the residential accommodation), the diminishing notional capital rule means that over time he or she may nevertheless qualify for financial assistance from the authority in meeting the accommodation charges. Regulation 26 provides that where a resident has been assessed as having notional capital, that capital will have to be reduced each week by the difference between the rate which the resident is paying for the accommodation and the rate he or she would have paid if he or she was not treated as possessing the notional capital. CRAG gives the following example of the workings of such a calculation (albeit based on out of date capital and income thresholds) (para 6.068):

> A resident is assessed as having notional capital of £15,750 plus actual capital of £6,000. This results in him having to pay the standard charge for the cost of the accommodation eg £250. If he did not possess the notional capital, his capital would not affect his ability to pay for the accommodation so, based on an income of £86 and a personal allowance of, for example, £16 he would be assessed as paying a charge of £70. The notional capital should be reduced by £180.00 per week ie the difference between the sum he has to pay because of the notional capital (£750.00) and the charge he would have had to pay if the notional capital did not exist (£70.00).

46   *R (Beeson) v Dorset CC* [2002] EWCA Civ 1812; (2003) 6 CCLR 5.

Local authority responses to deliberate deprivations

8.88   If an authority believes that a resident has disposed of capital in order to reduce the charge payable, it will have to decide whether to treat the resident as having the capital (notional capital) and assess the charge payable accordingly. It will then have to decide what if any action it should take. Although few cases come to the courts, there is considerable evidence that local authorities are taking a more robust approach when deprivation is considered to have taken place.

8.89   CRAG advises that there are two options, namely (para 6.067):

a)   to recover the assessed charge from the resident; or

b)   if the resident is unable to pay the assessed charge, to use the provisions of HASSASSAA 1983 s21 to transfer liability to the recipient of the asset for that part of the charges assessed as a result of the notional capital (see para 8.97 below).

8.90   In addition to their enforcement powers under HASSASSAA 1983 s21 authorities are able in certain situations to use powers provided by the Insolvency Act 1986. These options are considered below.

8.91   Local authorities would also appear to have a further response where it is believed that a deliberate deprivation has occurred. If the authority believes that in consequence the resident has notional capital in excess of the upper capital limit it may decide that it need not provide or fund the accommodation at all. Whether this is a lawful response will almost certainly depend upon the context of any particular case – although if the resident has sufficient mental capacity to make the arrangement, then it may well be that the local authority has no continuing obligation (see in this respect para 7.24 above). However if he or she lacks the necessary capacity the situation may be otherwise. In *Robertson v Fife Council*[47] the House of Lords had to construe the Scottish legislation on this issue – which although similar is in key respects materially different from that in England.[48] Fife Council had assessed an applicant as having notional capital above the upper limit and then had refused to provide assistance on

---

47 [2002] UKHL 35 at [53]; (2002) 5 CCLR 543 at 558G.

48 The material difference between the two legislative frameworks being that unlike the situation in England and Wales – where the duty to assess is separate from the 'community care service' provision obligation – in Scotland the two functions are combined (in the Social Work (Scotland) Act 1968). The key provisions of the 1968 Act are (1) section 12(1) (which is broadly equivalent to a hybrid version of NAA 1948 ss21–s29 and CA 1989 s17) which places a general duty on local authorities to promote social welfare by making a variety of services available including residential (but not nursing care); (2) section 12A (which in broadly the same wording as National Health Service Community Care Act (NHSCCA) 1990 s47(1) creates the assessment obligation); and (3) section 13A which has no English/Welsh equivalent, and which creates a specific duty to provide nursing home accommodation, where a person has been assessed as needing it. Neither this obligation (nor that under section 12(1) above) is subject to a proviso (as in England/Wales under section 21) that the duty only arises 'if the need for care and attention is not otherwise available'. Mrs Robertson was in need of nursing home accommodation.

the above basis (that no continuing obligation existed under NAA 1948 s21). The House of Lords rejected this, holding:

> The assessment of need and decisions as to whether they call for the provision of any of the community care services comes first. The assessment of means, and the requirement to pay what a person can afford, comes afterwards.

8.92   A persuasive argument exists that the opposite conclusion would have been reached had the case been determined according to the legislative regime in England/Wales: namely that a person with full capacity who had notional capital above the upper limit might be owed no duty under NAA 1948 s21. This was referred to by the Court of Appeal in the *Beeson* judgment, where it was noted (but the question not determined) that it had been argued:

> That different amendments to the 1948 Act as between England and Scotland made all the difference; and if it had been an English appeal *Robertson* would gave been decided the other way.[49]

8.93   However if a person no longer has access to the amount assessed as notional capital (perhaps because the person to whom the funds have been transferred has spent them) and has been assessed as in need of care in a care home, it is arguable that a duty will still arise to provide accommodation.

Enforcement powers

8.94   If the local authority decides to take action to recover the disposed property (or the proceeds of sale) it has a number of statutory provisions available to assist.

8.95   The Court of Appeal has held that in any enforcement proceedings the respondent is, as a general principle, entitled to plead a public law breach by the local authority as one of its grounds for resisting a claim (for instance a failure to follow CRAG or other guidance etc).[50]

8.96   Where the resident has transferred assets to other parties with the purpose of avoiding or reducing his or her liability for charges, the options available to the authority will depend, in part, on when the transfer occurred.

Transfers within six months requiring local authority help with funding in a care home

8.97   HASSASSAA 1983 s21(1) provides:

> (1) Subject to the following provisions of this section, where –
>   (a) a person avails himself of Part III accommodation; and

---

49   *R (Beeson) v Dorset CC* [2001] EWHC 986 (Admin); (2002) 5 CCLR 5 at 22D; see also in this respect *Ellis v Chief Adjudication Officer* [1998] FLR 184.

50   *Derbyshire CC v Akrill* [2005] EWCA Civ 308; (2005) 8 CCLR 173 and see also *Rhondda Cynon Taff CBC v Watkins* [2003] EWCA Civ 129; [2003] 1 WLR 1864.

(b) that person knowingly and with the intention of avoiding charges for the accommodation –

    (i) has transferred any asset to which this section applies to some other person or persons not more than six months before the date on which he begins to reside in such accommodation; or

    (ii) transfers any such asset to some other person or persons while residing in the accommodation; and

(c) either –

    (i) the consideration for the transfer is less than the value of the asset; or

    (ii) there is no consideration for the transfer,

the person or persons to whom the asset is transferred by the person availing himself of the accommodation shall be liable to pay the local authority providing the accommodation or arranging for its provision the difference between the amount assessed as due to be paid for the accommodation by the person availing himself of it and the amount which the local authority receive from him for it.

8.98 The effect of HASSASSAA 1983 s21 is that where a resident has transferred any asset to a third party at less than its full value, the authority can take enforcement proceedings against the third party if:

a) the transfer took place no more than six months before the resident entered local authority funded care home accommodation, and

b) the authority can establish that the transfer was effected 'knowingly and with the intention of avoiding charges for the accommodation'.

8.99 Although section 21 is differently worded to the notional capital rule under regulation 25 of the Regulations ('knowingly and with the intention of' rather than 'for the purpose of'), it is doubtful whether any practical differences of interpretation emerge from the two phrases; where a deprivation of capital is assessed as having occurred, it would seem that this is also sufficient for the purposes of section 21.

Transfers over six months before entering residential accommodation

8.100 If an authority has determined that:

a) a resident has notional capital; and

b) the notional capital asset was transferred to a third party more than six months before the resident took up residence in the residential home; and

c) in order to recover its charges (or payments made on the resident's behalf) it needs to take proceedings to set aside the disposition of the notional capital asset,

the authority has the option of using the enforcement procedures under the Insolvency Act 1986 by which the court is empowered in certain situations to set aside such transfers and restore the position to what it would have been if the resident had not entered into the transaction.

8.101 By virtue of Insolvency Act 1986 s339, where an individual is adjudged bankrupt and he or she has entered into a transaction at an undervalue, the trustee in bankruptcy may (subject to the following time limits) apply to the court for an order restoring the position to what it would have been had the transaction not occurred.[51] The relevant time limits are computed backwards from the day of presentation of the bankruptcy petition and are, in general:

5 years	if the individual was insolvent[52] at the time of the transaction, or became insolvent in consequence of the transaction; or
2 years	if the above criteria do not apply.

8.102   By virtue of Insolvency Act 1986 s423, where the court is satisfied that an individual entered into a transaction (amongst other things) at an undervalue for the purpose of putting assets beyond the reach of a creditor or future creditor, it may make such order as it thinks fit (including an order restoring the position to what it would have been had the transaction not been entered into).

8.103   The powers available to the court under section 423 are without time limit and are exercisable without the need for bankruptcy proceedings[53] (or for the individual in question to be insolvent). In *Midland Bank v Wyatt*[54] the court held that for the purposes of section 423 proof of dishonesty was not a requirement, 'merely proof of avoidance of creditors whether they be existing or future creditors'; that the judge had to be 'fully satisfied as to the true nature or object of the transaction'; and that:

> . . . if the purpose of the transaction can be shown to put assets beyond the reach of future creditors, s423 will apply whether or not the transferor was about to enter into a hazardous business . . . It is a question of proof of intention or purpose underlying the transaction. Clearly, the more hazardous the business being contemplated is, the more readily the court will be satisfied of the intention of the settlor or transferor.

8.104   The breadth of section 423 has been explained thus:

> While the burden of proof remains on the applicant, establishing the necessary purpose should be less difficult to achieve than proving intent to defraud under the previous law . . . The inclusion of persons who 'may at some time claim' against the debtor envisages potential future creditors who, individually unknown to the debtor at the time of the transaction, become victims of a risky business enterprise against the consequences of failure of which the debtor seeks to protect himself at the outset. In

---

51   The details given here are a simplified account of the actual provisions; 'transactions at an undervalue' are defined by Insolvency Act 1986 s339 and are contrasted with 'preferences' (section 340), for which slightly different rules apply.

52   Insolvency Act 1986 s341(3) states that an individual is insolvent if he or she is unable to pay his or her debts as they fall due, or the value of his or her assets is less than the amount of his or her liabilities, taking into account contingent and prospective liabilities. Section 341(2) creates a rebuttable presumption that an individual is insolvent where he or she enters into a transaction at an undervalue with an associate – see section 435.

53   See generally *Midland Bank v Wyatt* [1995] 1 FLR 697.

54   [1995] 1 FLR 697.

extending the purposes of present or future claimants, the ambit of the section is made very wide . . .[55]

8.105 Where the resident has transferred the capital asset using a firm or business which specifically markets schemes designed to avoid the value of the asset being taken into account for residential fee purposes, this may, perversely, be used as evidence to establish the purpose behind the transaction.[56]

8.106 In *Derbyshire CC v Akrill*[57] the local authority's claim included a claim under Insolvency Act 1986 s423 for an order that the house be retransferred to the deceased's estate. In this case the deceased had completed various transactions including a gift and leaseback of the house in which he had been living, and a declaration of solvency whilst in hospital following several strokes and a few weeks before moving into a care home. Although the case was remitted back to the county court to resolve, it was held that section 423 could be used to set aside a gift of property in such situations, where the purpose was to put property beyond the reach of the authority.

Registering of a charge or caution on any interest in land which the resident may have (under HASSASSAA 1983 s22)[58]

8.107 Where a resident fails to pay an assessed charge for accommodation and has a beneficial interest in land, HASSASSAA1983 s22 enables the local authority to create a charge in its favour on that land.[59] CRAG advises that where a local authority is contemplating taking such a step, it should advise the resident to consult a solicitor about the procedure. Any charge so registered does not carry interest until the resident's death, when section 24 of the 1983 Act provides for interest from that date 'at a reasonable rate' (determined by the local authority). Whilst local authorities have no statutory power to charge interest[60] there would appear to be nothing to prevent them suing on the accumulated arrears since such a judgment debt would normally then carry interest at the statutory rate.

8.108 Section 22 empowers, but does not oblige, local authorities to place charges on property. In certain situations authorities may consider that the possession of a valuable asset (such as a house) is such that the resident has no need of assistance. The basis for this view being that the resident has capital in excess of the upper capital limit (ie the value of the house) and accordingly is able to pay his or her own way (by for instance, raising a commercial loan secured on the property, pending its sale). The

55 Berry et al, *Personal Insolvency*, Butterworths, 1993.
56 See paras 3 and 12 in particular of the Law Society guidelines, *Gifts of Property: Guidelines for Solicitors*, 2000 and see also *Barclays Bank v Eustice* [1995] 1 WLR 1238.
57 *Derbyshire CC v Akrill* [2005] EWCA Civ 308; (2005) 8 CCLR 173.
58 For guidance on the application of s22 see CRAG Annex D.
59 If the land is jointly owned, the local authority cannot create a charge, but can register a caution (CRAG Annex D para 3.5).
60 CRAG Annex D para 3A specifically states that the general powers under Local Government Act 1972 s111 cannot be used for this purpose.

authority could then determine that the care and attention is 'otherwise available' and refuse to provide temporary financial support and to register a charge under HASSASSAA 1983 s22.

8.109   As section 22 is phrased in discretionary terms, authorities are in principle entitled, where the circumstances allow, to take such a course. Whether such a decision is reasonable in any particular situation will depend upon the relevant facts. In general, a suggestion that a person take out a commercial loan (or obtain a home's agreement to defer payment until the sale of a property) assumes (at a minimum);

- the need for accommodation does not arise in an emergency (ie there is sufficient time to arrange a loan); and
- that the person has sufficient mental capacity and experience to arrange such a loan; and
- that in all the circumstances, the taking of a commercial loan is something that it would be reasonable for the resident to do.

8.110   The ombudsman held that it was maladministration for a local authority to fail to inform the home owner properly when it imposes such a charge.[61]

Less dependent residents

8.111   For the purposes of the charging rules[62] 'less dependent' means:

> . . . a resident who is in, or for whom accommodation is proposed to be provided in, premises which are not an establishment which is carried on or managed by a person who is registered under Part II of the Care Standards Act 2000.

8.112   Regulation 5 allows local authorities not to apply the rules for calculating income and capital if they consider it reasonable in the circumstance not to do so. It is recognised that, for some people, leaving just the personal expenses allowance (ie for 2007–08, £20.45) would hamper the acquisition of independent living skills (such as purchasing their own food and paying for their expenses or travel to work), often with a view to eventually living independently in the community. Where ordinary housing (see para 7.51) is provided under NAA 1948 s21 it would of course make little sense to apply the charging rules as if the person were in a care home.

8.113   Regulation 5 accordingly enables authorities to continue to treat 'less dependent' residents differently where they consider it reasonable in the circumstances to do so. It enables authorities to disregard the resources of such residents, taking into account:

- the resident's commitments, ie, costs of necessities such as food, fuel, and clothing,

---

61   Complaint no 04/C/04804 against Manchester City Council, 31 March 2005.
62   Regulation 2(1).

- the degree of the resident's independence, ie, the extent to which he or she should be encouraged to take on expenditure commitments, and
- whether he or she needs a greater incentive to become more independent, eg, he or she may be encouraged to take on paid employment if most or all of the earnings are disregarded.

Temporary residents

8.114 As noted above (para 8.7) residents placed in care home accommodation as part of a programme of intermediate care are entitled to that service free of charge. Additionally, NAA 1948 s22(5A) stipulates that authorities are not obliged to apply the charging rules to other temporary residents. The subsection provides:

> If they think fit, an authority managing premises in which accommodation is provided for a person shall have power on each occasion when they provide accommodation for him, irrespective of his means, to limit to such amount as appears to them reasonable for him to pay the payments required from him for his accommodation during a period commencing when they begin to provide the accommodation for him and ending not more than eight weeks after that.

8.115 CRAG advises that where the authority decides to make an assessment of ability to pay, it should do so on the normal charging basis. Where it decides not to make such an assessment, it is able to charge such amount as it considers reasonable for the resident to pay (CRAG para 3.005).

8.116 Additional disregards are allowed for temporary residents (including the disregard of the home) in order to enable them to keep more income to carry on running the home. These are explained at paras 3.009–3.015, the main ones being for a range of housing costs and a disregard on attendance allowance and disability living allowance.

Liable relatives

8.117 The Department of Health and the Welsh Assembly have, since 2003, stated their intention to repeal the rules in NAA 1948 ss42 and 43, under which local authorities can pursue spouses of residents for payments towards care costs.[63] In 2006 the Department of Health made an extra payment to local authorities of £4 million for each of 2006–07 and 2007–08 in order to compensate them for the costs that they might incur. At that time it was hoped that the rules would be repealed by April 2007. However as it requires primary legislation a suitable Bill is still awaited. In the meantime in both England and Wales, local authorities are strongly encouraged to use their discretion not to apply the liable relatives rules.[64]

---

63 Such was the confidence that the rules would be repealed, there has been no extension to these rules when civil partnership provisions were introduced.
64 LAC 2007(4) and NAFWC 10/2007.

8.118   Guidance on the application of the liable relative rules remains in section 11 of CRAG. However, given the exhortations not to use the rules (and the compensation they have been paid) it would appear inappropriate for a local authority to seek such payments.

Liable relative payments

8.119   If a spouse or former (divorced) spouse voluntarily makes payments, CRAG provides procedures for deciding whether these payments are to be treated as capital or income. The possible permutations for such payments are many, and the detailed guidance in CRAG should be referred to if such a problem is encountered (see paras 11.007–11.025).

Challenging charges

8.120   Complaints about the level of charges levied by an authority are subject to the usual social services complaints procedures; see chapter 27. However many local authorities have a separate procedure for appeals against the amount being charged. While such a process may be sensible, it cannot of course disqualify or limit a service user's right to make a complaint under the standard local authority's complaints procedure.

Domiciliary and community based services

continued

Diagram 12: Non-accommodation services

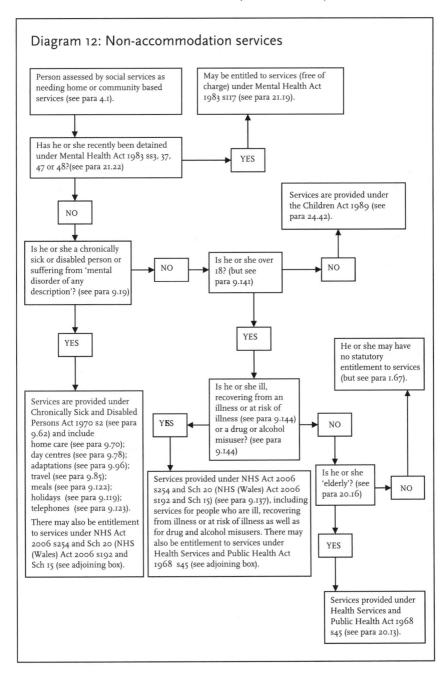

Person assessed by social services as needing home or community based services (see para 4.1).

May be entitled to services (free of charge) under Mental Health Act 1983 s117 (see para 21.19).

Has he or she recently been detained under Mental Health Act 1983 ss3, 37, 47 or 48?(see para 21.22)

YES

NO

Services are provided under the Children Act 1989 (see para 24.42).

Is he or she a chronically sick or disabled person or suffering from 'mental disorder of any description'? (see para 9.19)

NO

Is he or she over 18? (but see para 9.141)

NO

YES

YES

He or she may have no statutory entitlement to services (but see para 1.67).

Services are provided under Chronically Sick and Disabled Persons Act 1970 s2 (see para 9.62) and include home care (see para 9.70); day centres (see para 9.78); adaptations (see para 9.96); travel (see para 9.85); meals (see para 9.122); holidays (see para 9.119); telephones (see para 9.123).

There may also be entitlement to services under NHS Act 2006 s254 and Sch 20 (NHS (Wales) Act 2006 s192 and Sch 15 (see adjoining box).

Is he or she ill, recovering from an illness or at risk of illness (see para 9.144) or a drug or alcohol misuser? (see para 9.144)

YES

NO

Services provided under NHS Act 2006 s254 and Sch 20 (NHS (Wales) Act 2006 s192 and Sch 15) (see para 9.137), including services for people who are ill, recovering from illness or at risk of illness as well as for drug and alcohol misusers. There may also be entitlement to services under Health Services and Public Health Act 1968 s45 (see adjoining box).

Is he or she 'elderly'? (see para 20.16)

NO

YES

Services provided under Health Services and Public Health Act 1968 s45 (see para 20.13).

Introduction

9.1   Domiciliary and day care services constitute a range of services which are generally provided or secured by social services authorities with the aim of enabling those people who receive them to continue to live in the community (rather than in residential care or nursing homes). The services available include help in the home (personal care and domestic assistance); transport; disability equipment; home adaptations; day care (in day centres or workshops); leisure facilities; and other services aimed at providing support for individuals and carers.[1] Where such services are delivered to a person's home they are referred to collectively as 'domiciliary' services, whereas services provided in a community setting are generally termed 'community based services', although in this text, unless the contrary intention is made clear, the phrase 'community care services' is generally used to embrace all non-accommodation services (ie, including domiciliary services).

9.2   The governments in England and Wales are encouraging councils to make (in appropriate cases) cash payments in lieu of community care services – ie direct payments. The 2006 English white paper concerning health and social care[2] made a commitment to 'increase the take-up of direct payments' and to introduce 'new legislation to extend their availability to currently excluded groups and will pilot the introduction of individual budgets'. Such arrangements are considered separately at chapter 12 below.

Statutes governing domiciliary care provision

9.3   The statutory regime governing community based services is founded on National Assistance Act (NAA) 1948 s29 which lists, in general terms, the range of services that local authorities are empowered to provide. The statutory shortcomings of NAA 1948 s29 eventually led to the enactment of the Chronically Sick and Disabled Persons Act (CSDPA) 1970 which spells out in greater detail some of the services that must be provided.

9.4   The persons entitled to receive services under the CSDPA 1970 and under NAA 1948 s29 are broadly the same. Certain vulnerable groups are not, however, covered by these provisions (for instance, frail older people and those recovering from an illness). Such groups are nevertheless entitled to receive various community care services as a result of separate legislative provisions (namely the Health Services and Public Health Act (HSPHA) 1968, the National Health Service Act (NHSA) 2006, the National Health Service (Wales) Act (NHS(W)A) 2006 and the Mental Health Act (MHA) 1983).

---

1   See white paper *Caring for People: Community Care in the Next Decade and Beyond*, Cm 849, 1990, para 3.61.
2   Department of Health, Our health, our care, our say: a new direction for community services, Cm 6737, 2006, HMSO, para 17, and see also paras 4.21 et seq.

9.5   In addition, as noted above (see para 1.67), local authorities have extensive powers to provide services under Local Government Act (LGA) 2000 s2 to promote (amongst other things) 'social well being' and, under the 'Supporting People' programme (see para 15.96 below), to provide housing-related support services. The NHS too, has power to provide a range of community based services, for persons eligible for continuing care funding and for reducing the risks of a person becoming unwell[3] – this responsibility is considered at chapter 14 below.

9.6   Although limited steps have been taken to harmonise these disparate statutory provisions, they still retain distinctive features – often incongruous and frequently overlapping.

9.7   With the enactment of the Children Act (CA) 1989, an attempt was made to make separate provision for disabled children; accordingly community based services for children are now primarily governed by CA 1989 Part III and CSDPA 1970 s2. The CA 1989 amended NAA 1948 ss21 and 29 so that in general services under these sections are not available to children. Accordingly the community care statutes are often considered to be restricted to providing services for adults. There are, however, exceptions to this rule (most significantly, services under NHSA 2006 Sch 20 para 3 are available for adult or child alike).

9.8   The National Health Service and Community Care Act (NHSCCA) 1990 Part III made a further attempt to introduce some logical structure into the various community care statutes; section 46(3) defining (for the purposes of the Act) 'community care services' as being services under:

- NAA 1948 Part III;
- HSPHA 1968 s45;
- NHSA 2006 s254 and Sch 20;
- NHS(W)A s192 and Sch 15;
- MHA 1983 s117.

9.9   While the NHSCCA 1990 s46 makes no direct reference to services provided under CSDPA 1970 s2, the Court of Appeal has however determined that services under s2 are 'community care services' notwithstanding this omission. The particular difficulties caused by the wording of CSDPA 1970 s2 in this respect are considered in detail at para 9.124. Contradictions and inconsistencies of this kind run like fault lines through the community care legislation, which has been well described as a set of sometimes incomprehensible and frequently incompatible principles. Nowhere is this statement truer than in relation to domiciliary and community based services; these services have developed erratically since the war, first by way of cautious general provisions (eg, NAA 1948 s29), and subsequently by way of more idealistic and specific rights (such as those provided by CSDPA 1970 s2). Fundamental contradictions have emerged between these statutes, as a result of both poor and hurried drafting and

---

3   See eg the Commissioning Framework for Health and Well-being which offers a number of suggestions as to the flexibility with which NHS funds can be used to avoid hospital admission or prevent illness.

the absence of any coherent policy underlying the provision of community care. Put plainly, this is an area of law in need of radical codification and updating to reflect current thinking.

> **NAA 1948 s29** (see para 9.14 below) ⎫
> **CSDPA 1970 s2** (see para 9.62 below) ⎬ Major provisions
> **HSPHA 1968 s45** (see para 20.13 below) ⎫
> **NHSA 2006 Sch 20 and NHS(W)A 2006 Sch 15** ⎬
> (see para 9.137 below) ⎭ Minor provisions
> **MHA 1983 s117** (see para 21.19 below)

9.10   Each of the various community care statutes entitles similar (but not identical) client groups to similar (but not identical) services. An analysis of these statutory provisions could therefore either focus on client groups or the services they deliver. Given the substantial overlap between the client groups covered by each statute and the overwhelming legal and practical importance of NAA 1948 s29 and CSDPA 1970 s2, this chapter will focus on the legal entitlements that derive from these two so called 'major provisions'. These two provisions apply to people who are disabled, or chronically sick or who have a mental disorder (including a learning disability) of any description. The final section of this chapter will consider NHSA 2006 Sch 20/NHS(W)A 2006 Sch 15. Although the social care obligations created by the NHS Acts 2006 are in practice of primary legal relevance to drug and alcohol misusers, these provisions encompass many other potential service users (including disabled people and expectant and nursing mothers) and accordingly more conveniently fall to be considered in this general chapter.

9.11   The remaining minor community care statutory provisions (namely HSPHA 1968 s45 – which applies only to frail older people and MHA 1983 s117 which applies only to certain formerly detained psychiatric patients) are considered separately in the chapters addressing these specific client groups (namely chapter 20 and chapter 21).

9.12   In general the statutory provisions that authorise or require councils to provide community care services, do so in such a way that the authority has the power to provide the services itself or to make arrangements for the service to be provided by a third party. By way of example, a local authority may provide services under NAA 1948 s29 via 'any voluntary organisation[4] or any person carrying on, professionally or by way of trade or business, activities which consist of or include the provision of services'. In addition Local Government (Contracts) Act 1997 s1 in general terms permits councils to contract with third parties to discharge functions of this nature.

9.13   The mere fact that the local authority has commissioned such a third party to provide care to meet the assessed needs of a person, does not absolve the council of its duties to ensure that the care is actually

---

4   NAA 1948 s64 defines a voluntary organisation as 'a body the activities of which are carried on otherwise than for profit, but does not include any public or local authority' – see *R (A and B) v East Sussex CC* [2002] EWHC 2771 (Admin); (2003) 6 CCLR 177.

delivered, and it will be maladministration for it not to have mechanisms to monitor effectively contracts with care agencies[5] and resolve promptly the problem of poor service provided by its agency.[6] In general, organisations providing community care services will need to be registered under the Care Standards Act 2000 as domiciliary care agencies (including those run by local authorities) and this obligation is considered at para 17.25 below.

Services under National Assistance Act 1948 s29

9.14   The cross-heading to NAA 1948 s29 reveals the profound change in terminology (if not social attitude) that has occurred in the last 60 years – describing the content of the section as 'Welfare arrangements for blind, deaf, dumb and crippled persons, etc'. The amended text of NAA 1948 s29(1) now reads as follows:

> **29.**—(1) A local authority may, with the approval of the Secretary of State, and to such extent as he may direct in relation to persons ordinarily resident in the area of the local authority shall, make arrangements for promoting the welfare of persons to whom this section applies, that is to say persons aged eighteen or over who are blind, deaf or dumb or who suffer from mental disorder of any description, and other persons aged eighteen or over who are substantially and permanently handicapped by illness, injury, or congenital deformity or such other disabilities as may be prescribed by the Minister.

9.15   As with NAA 1948 s21 (see para 7.9), it follows that social services authorities have no power to make any arrangements for the promotion of anyone's welfare under this section unless and until the secretary of state has issued a direction specifying the arrangements which may be made (are 'approved') and those which must be made (are 'directed' to be made). The secretary of state's most recent direction in respect of NAA 1948 s29 is found at Appendix 2 to LAC (93)10[7] and came into force on 1 April 1993 (the full text of the direction is in appendix B below).

9.16   The nature of the duty created by s29 is uncertain. It was suggested in *R v Islington LBC ex p Rixon*[8] that these duties were 'target' duties rather than duties owed to a specific individual (see para 1.24). However in *R v Kensington and Chelsea RLBC ex p Kujtim*[9] the Court of Appeal indicated that it had difficulty in following the logic of this particular argument. More recently, in *R (Hughes) v Liverpool City Council*[10] Mitting J held that the s29 duty crystallised into a specific law duty subsequent to an

---

5   Complaint no 05/C/06420 against Sheffield City Council, 20 February 2007.
6   Complaint no 05/C/08592 against Liverpool City Council, 17 January 2007.
7   WOC 35/93 in Wales.
8   (1997) 1 CCLR 119, p131H.
9   [1999] 4 All ER 161; (1999) 2 CCLR 340 at 353J – where Potter LJ admitted to finding difficulty in following the arguments of Sedley J.
10 [2005] EWHC 428 (Admin); (2005) 8 CCLR 243 at [26].

assessment under section 47 of the 1990 Act and in this respect was indistinguishable from the duty created by NAA 1948 s21:

> Section 29 imposes a duty to make arrangements for promoting the welfare of relevant persons to such an extent as the Secretary of State may direct. He has so directed in local authority circular 93/10 appendix 2 to provide 'such support as may be needed for people in their own home'. Section 7 of the Local Authority Social Services Act 1970 provides that the Secretary of State may give guidance to local authorities in the exercise of their functions under section 29. Liverpool accept that they are obliged to follow the guidance of the Secretary of State in making those arrangements. The Secretary of State's Guidance[11] provide that they should identify eligible needs and meet them; see paragraphs 3 and 43 of the Guidance.

9.17   Whilst the analysis of Mitting J would appear to be the most authoritative, in practice this problem (from the service user's perspective) will generally be academic, since in most cases the section 29 functions are duplicated by those in CSDPA s2: and the section 2 duties are universally accepted as being specific law duties.

18 or over and ordinarily resident

9.18   Section 29 services are only available if they promote the welfare[12] of persons who are 18 or over. The duty to provide section 29 services[13] applies only to persons who are ordinarily resident in the local authority's area, whereas a power exists to provide services for other persons[14] (ordinary residence is considered in chapter 6 above).

Disabled people – statutory definition

9.19   The definition provided in NAA 1948 s29 of the persons who may potentially qualify for its services, is generally considered to be the principal definition of a 'disabled person' for the purposes of the community care legislation, namely:

> persons . . . who are blind, deaf or dumb or who suffer from mental disorder of any description, and other persons aged eighteen or over who are substantially and permanently handicapped by illness, injury, or congenital deformity . . .

9.20   People who fall within this definition are entitled to services, not only under NAA 1948 s29 but also under CSDPA 1970 s2. It is this definition (with amendment as to age alone) that was also adopted in CA 1989 s17(11) (see para 24.6). NAA 1948 s29 does not, however, permit the provision

---

11 LAC (2003)13 *Fair Access to Care Services Guidance on Eligibility Criteria for Adult Social Care* (see para 3.26 above).
12 It would appear from the wording of NAA 1948 s29(1) that the service need not be provided *to* the disabled person. It is at least arguable that a service provided to a carer may be an 'arrangement which promotes the welfare of the disabled person'.
13 LAC (93)10 appendix 2 para 2(1); albeit that it is only a target duty, see para 1.24 above.
14 *R v Berkshire CC ex p P* (1997) 1 CCLR 141.

of services to people whose need arises by virtue of age alone – ie because their age has made them frail. The social care needs of this group are addressed by HSPHA 1968 s45 which is considered at para 20.13 below.

9.21 In order to be eligible for any of the services available under NAA 1948 s29, a person must be:

- blind, or
- deaf, or
- dumb, or
- suffering from mental disorder of any description, or
- substantially and permanently handicapped by 'illness, injury, congenital deformity or such other disabilities as may be prescribed by the Minister'.

9.22 The list should be contrasted with that under NAA 1948 s21 (see para 7.11) which is less restrictive, including such groups as frail elderly people, expectant mothers and disabled persons (without having to establish that their 'handicap' is either permanent or substantial.

9.23 As already noted, NAA 1948 s29 places a duty on social services authorities to maintain registers of people in their area who may be entitled to its services (at para 2.3 above). The test, however, of whether a person qualifies for services under NAA 1948 s29 is independent of whether or not he or she is on a particular authority's register – ie registration is not a prerequisite to obtaining assistance.[15]

Blind

9.24 Although NAA 1948 s29 makes no reference to partially sighted persons, previous guidance[16] confirms that the phrase 'other persons who are substantially and permanently handicapped' covers persons who are partially sighted.

9.25 Social services authorities have well established procedures for determining whether a visually impaired person is blind or partially sighted and thus whether the terms of NAA 1948 s29(1) – and registration – apply. The procedure is initiated by a hospital eye clinic completing the relevant form – a certificate of vision impairment (CVI)[17] – which certifies that the person is severely sight impaired or sight impaired. When signed by a consultant ophthalmologist, the CVI is the formal notification required for section 29 registration purposes. Circular guidance advises that the effective date of registration should be the same as that of certification.[18] The guidance further recommends that social services authorities have separate sections in their register for each of the groups of persons to

---

15 LAC (93)10 appendix 4 para 3.
16 LAC 13/74 para 11(i).
17 Details of the arrangements are provided on the Department of Health website under the heading 'Identification and notification of sight loss'.
18 LAC (93)10 appendix 4 para 6.

whom NAA 1948 s29 applies (ie, that blind and partially sighted persons be separately recorded).[19]

9.26   Concern has been expressed by the local government ombudsman about delays in the assessment of people who have suffered sight loss – and of inadequate referral arrangements between the NHS and social services.[20] The Department of Health has however sought to improve the co-ordination of services for such persons, with the development of a website containing key information on service arrangements[21] and the distribution of a joint Chief Inspector Social Services Inspectorate/NHS Executive letter 'Identifying and Assessing People With Sensory Impairment' in October 2000.[22] In addition the Association of Directors of Social Services has sought to establish a national standard for services in this field, namely *Progress in Sight: National standards of social care for visually impaired adults.*[23] Amongst other things this states that 'the waiting time for an assessment should be closely monitored to ensure that it is not more than four weeks from the date of referral'.[24]

9.27   Concern has also been voiced about the failure of some social services authorities properly to assess the needs of people with visual impairments, such that they 'slip into ill-health and premature dependency'.[25]

Deaf

9.28   Although NAA 1948 s29 makes no specific reference to people with impaired hearing, previous guidance[26] confirms that the phrase 'other persons who are substantially and permanently handicapped' covers persons who are hard of hearing.

9.29   There are no formal examination procedures for determining whether a person is deaf for the purposes of NAA 1948 s29.[27] Social services authorities are advised that all persons who suffer from a disabling loss of hearing should be regarded as being deaf for the purposes of section 29.[28] The guidance suggests, however, that this single class should be sub-divided into three categories:[29]

19   Ibid, para 9.
20   Complaint no 02/C/03831 against Stockport MBC, 28 August 2003.
21   Accessible at http://www.dh.gov.uk/PolicyandGuidance/HealthandSocialCareTopics/Optical/fs/en.
22   http://www.dh.gov.uk/en/Publicationsandstatistics/Lettersandcirculars/Dearcolleagueletters/DH_4008252.
23   Association of Directors of Social Services, October 2002, accessible at http://www.adss.org.uk/eyes/progress.pdf.
24   *Progress in Sight: National standards of social care for visually impaired adults*, para 11.2 – the four week period being the limit recommended by the Social Services Inspectorate in its report *A sharper focus: Inspection of services for adults who are visually impaired or blind*, Department of Health, 1998.
25   See in this respect Royal National Institute for the Blind (RNIB), *Facing FACS: Applying the eligibility criteria in 'Fair access to care services' to adults with sight problems*, 2005 – a report concerning good practice in this area, accessible at http://www.rnib.org.uk/xpedio/groups/public/documents/publicwebsite/public_ilcff.hcsp.
26   LAC 13/74 para 11(i); see also LAC (93)10 appendix 4 para 7.
27   LAC (93)10 appendix 4 para 7.
28   Ibid, annex 2 para 2.
29   Ibid, annex 2 para 2.

Deaf without speech: Those who have no useful hearing and those whose normal method of communication is by signs, finger spelling or writing.

Deaf with speech: Those who (even with a hearing aid) have little or no useful hearing but whose normal method of communication is by speech and lip-reading.

Hard-of-hearing: Those who (with or without a hearing aid) have some useful hearing and whose normal method of communication is by speech, listening and lip-reading.

9.30 The guidance in LAC (93)10 appendix 4 annex 2 makes a number of general statements concerning the importance the government attaches to services for deaf people; these statements are directed principally at the training and duties of specialist social workers in this field rather than being specific statements about the type of services to be provided.

Deafblind

9.31 The Department of Health website has general advice concerning the needs of people who are deafblind[30] and in particular has issued policy guidance concerning the arrangements that individual local authorities must make to cater for the needs of people who are deafblind: LAC (2001)8 *Social Care for Deafblind Children and Adults*. Amongst other things it requires authorities to:

- ensure that assessments are carried out by a specifically trained persons and in particular to assess need for one-to-one human contact, assistive technology and rehabilitation;
- ensure services provided to deafblind people are appropriate;
- ensure that one member of senior management includes, within his or her responsibilities, overall responsibility for deafblind services.

Dumb

9.32 The guidance gives no advice as to the criteria for determining whether or not a person with limited speech comes within the scope of NAA 1948 s29 (other than by reference to persons who are 'deaf without speech' – see above). By implication, however, persons who have little or no useful speech must come within the scope of the phrase 'substantially and permanently handicapped'.[31]

Suffering from a mental disorder of any description

9.33 Persons suffering from a mental disorder of any description (ie, within the ambit of MHA 1983 s1) are included in the NAA 1948 s29 client

---

30 Under the heading of 'sensory impairment'.
31 See LAC 13/74 para 11(i) and LAC (93)10 appendix 4 annex 2 para 2.

group.[32] However, as is detailed below, NAA 1948 s29 services cannot be provided to a person if the same service has been ' required' to be provided under the NHSA 2006 or the NHS(W)A 2006.[33] The relevant part of the NHS Acts 2006 (and the secretary of state's direction issued under them) has been so drafted that NAA 1948 s29 services are generally of little relevance to persons suffering from a mental disorder. The importance, however, of including such persons within section 29 is that they are thereby included and eligible for services under CSDPA 1970 s2. Persons who suffer from a mental disorder are entitled to community care services under NHSA 2006 Sch 20 and NHS(W)A 2006 Sch 15 and/or under MHA 1983 s117 (see para 9.156 and para 21.19 respectively) in addition to CSDPA 1970 s2.[34]

9.34   Whereas all the other potential service users under NAA 1948 s29 (and/or CSDPA 1970 s2) are persons whose 'handicap' is permanent and substantial, this is not however a requirement for persons suffering from a mental disorder.

Substantially and permanently handicapped

9.35   Circular guidance[35] states:

> It has not proved possible to give precise guidance on the interpretation of the phrase 'substantially and permanently handicapped'. However, as hitherto, authorities are asked to give a wide interpretation to the term 'substantial', which the Department fully recognises must always take full account of individual circumstances. With regard to the term 'permanent', authorities will also wish to interpret this sufficiently flexibly to ensure that they do not feel inhibited from giving help under s29 in cases where they are uncertain of the likely duration of the condition.

'Illness, injury, or congenital deformity or such other disabilities as may be prescribed by the Minister'

9.36   To qualify for services under NAA 1948 s29 a person who is substantially and permanently handicapped must be so by virtue of an illness, an injury, or congenital deformity; no further disabilities have been prescribed by the minister. Furthermore, persons who are disabled as a result of an illness or congenital deformity will not be entitled to receive NAA 1948 s29 services where those services are required under the NHS Acts 2006.[36] It is undecided as to whether substantial and permanent handicap resulting from drug or alcohol misuse can be defined as arising out of

---

32 LAC (93)10 appendix 4 para 14.

33 NAA 1948 s29(6); see para 9.58.

34 LAC (93)10 appendix 4 para 13 incorrectly states that such services are generally provided under HSPHA 1968 s12 – this section had been repealed and reference should have been made to the then NHSA 1977 Sch 8 (although since CSDPA 1970 s2 applies to persons suffering from a mental disorder of any description, arguably this section is of greater importance).

35 LAC (93)10 appendix 4 para 8.

36 NAA 1948 s29(6).

illness or injury so as to qualify the person for NAA 1948 s29 services; in practice domiciliary services to such persons will generally be delivered under the NHS Acts 2006 (and are considered at para 9.137).

Services

9.37 NAA 1948 s29 leaves to the secretary of state the power to determine the type of domiciliary services which can be provided; the only limitations being:

a) that the purpose of the services must be the promotion of the welfare of the NAA 1948 s29 client group;[37]

b) by virtue of NAA 1948 s29(6)(a) that the direct payment of money to service users is not permitted under section 29 (except if a payment for their work or produce). However the impact of this restriction has been neutered by the direct payments legislation see chapter 12 below); and

c) by virtue of NAA 1948 s29(6)(b) that no accommodation or services can be provided under section 29 if the accommodation or services have been 'required' to be provided under the NHS Acts 2006.[38]

9.38 Although NAA 1948 s29(4) contains an illustrative list of the type of services that may be made available, the Act leaves to the secretary of state the power to decide what services must and what services may be provided. The services referred to by section 29(4) are:

(a) for informing persons to whom arrangements under that subsection relate of the services available for them thereunder;

(b) for giving persons instruction in their own homes or elsewhere in methods of overcoming the effects of their disabilities;

(c) for providing workshops where such persons may be engaged (whether under a contract of service or otherwise) in suitable work, and hostels where persons engaged in the workshops, and others to whom arrangements under subsection (1) of this section relate and for whom work or training is being provided in pursuance of the Disabled Persons (Employment) Act 1944, or the Employment and Training Act 1973 may live;

(d) for providing persons to whom arrangements under subsection (1) of this section relate with suitable work (whether under a contract of service or otherwise) in their own homes or elsewhere;

(e) for helping such persons in disposing of the produce of their work;

(f) for providing such persons with recreational facilities in their own homes or elsewhere

(g) for compiling and maintaining classified registers of the persons to whom arrangements under subsection (1) of this section relate.

37 A person's welfare may however be promoted by providing a service to a third party (eg, a carer).

38 The provision of accommodation is however specifically excluded from NHSA 2006 Sch 20 para 2(11) and NHS(W)A 2006 Sch 15 para 2(11).

9.39   The secretary of state's most recent directions in respect of section 29 services were issued as Appendix 2 to LAC (93)10[39] in March 1993. The directions distinguish between services[40] which a social services department *may* provide (ie, has a power to provide – generally known as an 'approval') and those which it *must* provide (ie, is under a duty to provide).

Services which social services departments have a duty to provide

9.40   As noted above, the duty on social services departments to provide services under NAA 1948 s29 is restricted to persons who are ordinarily resident in the authority's area. The services being:

Social work service, advice and support

9.41   Social services authorities are required to 'provide a social work service and such advice and support as may be needed for people in their own homes or elsewhere'.[41] This duty is complemented by Local Authority Social Services Act 1970 s6(6) which obliges local authorities to provide 'adequate staff for assisting' the director of social services in the exercise of his or her functions.[42] 'Advice and support' would cover such services as welfare rights advice and counselling.[43] Previous circular guidance[44] advised that the provision of advice and support would frequently necessitate offering advice and other help to the families of the disabled person; and that authorities should bear in mind the part which voluntary workers can play in delivering this service. Welfare rights advice is increasingly seen as a core local authority activity, working in joint teams with the Department for Work and Pensions or other advice agencies. Thus guidance requires this advice when charges are being assessed for non-residential care services (see para 10.14). The NHS is also empowered to provide advice and assistance in relation to access to state benefits for its service users, under section 3(1)(e) of the NHS Acts 2006.[45]

Social rehabilitation or adjustment to disability

9.42   Social services authorities are required 'to provide, whether at centres or elsewhere, facilities for social rehabilitation and adjustment to disability

---

39   The full text of which is at appendix B below. The directions were issued in Wales as WOC 35/93.
40   The local authority may provide the services alone, or in conjunction with another authority or by employing an independent or private provider: see NAA 1948 s30 and LAC (93)10 appendix 2 paras 3 and 4.
41   LAC (93)10 appendix 2 para 2(1)(a).
42   See para 1.9 above.
43   Complaint no 05/A/00880 against Essex CC, 16 January 2006.
44   DHSS circular 13/74 para 11(ii) – cancelled by LAC (93)10.
45   *R (Keating) v Cardiff Local Health Board* [2005] EWCA Civ 847; [2006] 1 WLR 159; (2005) 8 CCLR 504 – see para 13.10 below.

including assistance in overcoming limitations of mobility or communication'.[46] These services will generally be provided for a short or medium-term period covering the disabled person's rehabilitation or adjustment to his or her disability. The reference to 'social' rehabilitation makes the point that medical rehabilitation is either a service to be provided under NHSA 2006 Sch 20/NHS(W)A 2006 Sch 15 (and thus excluded from provision under NAA 1948 s29)[47] or is one which should be provided by the NHS. The bundle of services referred to in this category covers, in many cases, services for which there is an overlapping responsibility between the NHS and the social services authority – and particularly 'intermediate care' (see chapter 11).

9.43   The direction, in respect of these services, subsumes (and extends) the services referred to in NAA 1948 s29(4)(b), which merely refers to arrangements for 'giving persons instruction in their own homes or elsewhere in methods of overcoming the effects of their disabilities'.

Information for disabled people

9.44   Social services authorities are required to make arrangements 'for informing persons to whom [section 29] relates of the services available for them [under section 29]'.[48] The extent and nature of this duty is considered at para 2.37 above.

Day centres and other facilities

9.45   Social services authorities are required 'to provide, whether at centres or elsewhere, facilities for occupational, social, cultural and recreational activities and, where appropriate, the making of payments to persons for work undertaken by them'.[49] These services include the day centre in its various forms, workshops, recreational and educational activities, as well as art, sport, drama sessions and so on. In relation to people with learning disabilities (in particular) the government is seeking to reduce reliance on these services.[50] Accordingly in *R (J and others) v Southend BC and Essex CC*[51] (a case challenging the closure of a day centre) Newman J observed:

> It is plain that the underlying reason for the closure of the M Centre is to comply with Government policy and that policy itself is designed to foster the autonomy of the learning disabled, to ensure services are provided to them and that they are not set apart from the community. It is a situation in which the policy itself is driving towards what could be regarded as an aspect of private life which it is seen will be enhanced by these measures.

---

46 LAC (93)10 appendix 2 para 2(1)(a).
47 NAA 1948 s29(6)(b).
48 LAC (93)10 appendix 2 para 2(1)(2) and s29(4)(g).
49 Ibid, para 2(1)(c).
50 Secretary of State for Health, *Valuing People: A New Strategy for Learning Disability for the 21st Century*, Cm 5086, March 2001, paras 4.7 and 7.21.
51 *R (J and others) v Southend BC and Essex CC* [2005] EWHC 3457 (Admin); (2007) 10 CCLR 407.

9.46   The direction, in respect of these services, overlaps with the workshop services referred to in NAA 1948 s29(4)(c) and subsumes (and extends) the services referred to in section 29(4)(f) which merely refers to arrangements for 'providing such persons with recreational facilities in their own homes or elsewhere'. In most cases services of this nature will in fact be provided to the eligible NAA 1948 s29 service user via CSDPA 1970 s2(1)(c) (see para 9.77 below).

Workshop and workshop hostel services

9.47   The provision of facilities for occupational activities often takes the form of a local authority workshop which provides employment (paid or otherwise) for particular user groups – frequently people with learning disabilities. In addition to the power to pay users employed in the workshops,[52] social services authorities are specifically empowered to help such persons dispose of the products of their work. The use of workshops continues the tradition of the segregated workhouse of the pre-welfare state. In the early post-war years many such workshops were former poor-law workhouses which continued to be devoted to menial mechanical tasks – and hence a few are still to be found located on the old industrial estates.

9.48   The social services authorities' duty to provide workshops is coupled with the power to provide hostel accommodation (including board and other services, amenities and requisites)[53] for those engaged in the workshop or other occupational activity under NAA 1948 s29(4). Section 29(4A) applies the same charging rules for the provision of such accommodation as apply to residential accommodation provided under NAA 1948 s21 (see para 8.7).

Services which social services departments have power to provide

9.49   The directions[54] give social services authorities the discretion to provide the following services (regardless of the potential service user's ordinary residence).

Holiday homes

9.50   The discretion to provide holiday homes under NAA 1948 s29 should be contrasted with the duty under CSDPA 1970 s2(1)(f) to facilitate the taking of a holiday (see para 9.119).

---

52   LAC (93)10 appendix 2 para 2(1)(c) contains an express power for local authorities to pay disabled persons who undertake work in workshops.
53   NAA 1948 s29(4)(c) and LAC (93)10 appendix 2 para 2(4).
54   LAC (93)10 appendix 2 paras 2(3) and (4).

Free or subsidised travel

9.51 'Provide free or subsidised travel for all or any persons who do not other-wise qualify for travel concessions, but only in respect of travel arrangements for which concessions are available.' Travel concessions are dealt with under the Transport Act 1985,[55] section 93(7) and is more fully considered below at para 9.85. Under the 1985 Act as amended the persons concerned must be:

a) over 60;[56] or
b) under 16; or
c) aged 16–18 undergoing full-time education; or
d) blind; or
e) suffering from any disability or injury which, in the opinion of the authority, seriously impairs their ability to walk.

9.52 All disabled people and pensioners are entitled to free off peak bus travel in their local areas. The government intends that this be extended (in April 2008) to cover all such travel in England (ie 'cross-border' travel).[57]

Assistance in finding accommodation

9.53 'Assist a person in finding accommodation which will enable him or her to take advantage of any arrangements made under s29(1) of the Act.' The power to provide such assistance (see also paras 9.54 and 9.55 below) mirrors that approved for older people under DHSS circular 19/71 para 4 (see para 20.20).

Subsidy of warden costs

9.54 'Contribute to the cost of employing a warden on welfare functions in warden assisted housing schemes.' See the note to para 9.53 above.

Warden services

9.55 'Provide warden services for occupiers of private housing.' See the note to para 9.53 above. This power complements the payment arrangements available under the Supporting People scheme – see para 9.5 below.

---

55 See also Greater London Authority Act 1999 s151, the Travel Concessions (Eligibility) Act 2002 and the Transport for London (Consequential Provisions) Order 2003 SI No 1615.
56 Travel Concessions (Eligibility) Act 2002.
57 HM Treasury, *Budget 2006 – A Strong and Strengthening Economy: Investing in Britain's Future*, 2006, para 5.50.

Information on disability services

9.56   The power under section 29 to provide information services for disabled people[58] has been subsumed into the wider duty set out in CSDPA 1970 s1 (see para 2.38).

Direct payments to service users under NAA 1948 s29

9.57   Although section 29(6)(a) prohibits authorities from making cash payments (under section 29) to service users to enable them to procure their own care,[59] its impact has been largely neutralised by Health and Social Care Act 2001 s57 which is considered at para 12.6 below.

Section 29(6)(b) and the NHS overlap

9.58   NAA 1948 s29(6)(b) excludes services being provided under section 29 where such services 'are required to be provided' under the NHS Acts 2006.

9.59   The use of the word 'required' suggests that it is only where there is a duty to provide the service under the 2006 Acts that the provision must be under those statutes rather than under NAA 1948 s29. A consideration of the similar exclusionary provision which exists in relation to accommodation services under NAA 1948 s21[60] supports this interpretation. The section 21(8) prohibition is more severe, since it proscribes services that are 'authorised or required' to be provided under the 2006 Acts and was considered by the Court of Appeal in *R v North East Devon Health Authority ex p Coughlan*[61] (see also para 7.60 above and 14.7 below). Amending the relevant judgment to accommodate the slightly different wording of NAA 1948 s29(6)(b),[62] the court's interpretation would appear to be as follows:

> The subsection should not be regarded as preventing a local authority from providing any health services. The subsection's prohibitive effect is limited to those health services which, in fact, [been] . . . required to be provided under the [NHS Acts 2006]. Such health services would not therefore include services which the Secretary of State legitimately decided under section 3(1) of the [NHS Acts 2006] it was not necessary for the NHS to provide . . . The true effect is to emphasise that [the NAA 1948] provision, . . . is secondary to [the NHS Acts 2006] provision.

9.60   The fact that NAA 1948 s29(6)(b) may require certain services to be provided under the NHS Acts 2006, does not in itself exclude social services responsibility for the provision of such services, since such authorities also have functions under the NHS Acts 2006 – see para 14.7 below.

---

58 NAA 1948 s29(4)(a) and LAC (93)10 appendix 2 para 2(4).
59 This provision is mirrored in NHSA 2006 Sch 20 para 2(2) and NHS(W)A 2006 Sch 15 para 2(2) (see para 9.155).
60 NAA 1948 s21(8); although this subsection prohibits social services from providing any services which are '*authorised or* required' to be provided under the NHSA 1977.
61 [2000] 2 WLR 622; (1999) 2 CCLR 285 at [29].
62 That is by excluding reference to the phrase '*authorised or*'.

9.61   In *R v Gloucestershire CC ex p Mahfood*[63] the council sought to argue that a further consequence flowed from NAA 1948 s29(6)(b). The argument hinged on whether or not services provided by virtue of CSDPA 1970 s2 are NAA 1948 s29 services or free-standing CSDPA 1970 s2 services.[64] This general question is considered in greater detail at para 9.124. In the context of NAA 1948 s29(6)(b), McCowan LJ disposed of the respondent counsel's submissions as follows:

> His argument was that it is a pre-condition of the duty under section 2 of the 1970 Act that the local authority has power to provide the service under section 29 of the 1948 Act. If there is no power under section 29 there can be no duty under section 2. But section 29(6) of the 1948 Act positively provides that there is no power to exercise certain functions, in particular those which involve services which have to be provided under the National Health Service Act 1977.[65] There is a duty to provide home helps for the aged and handicapped, but it is a duty under the 1977 Act. Therefore, the power to provide the service is excluded and home help services could not lawfully have been provided to Mr Mahfood and Mr Barry under section 2 of the 1970 Act.

> The submission is an unattractive one because it would follow that if the local authority was satisfied by reason of the fact that general arrangements had not been made for the home help, it would have no power and thus no duty to make these arrangements. The short answer to the point, however, is that section 29(6) of the 1948 Act merely states 'nothing in the foregoing provisions of this section shall authorise or require'. What is authorising the local authority to make arrangements under section 2 is section 2. Thus the provisions which authorise the local authority to meet the needs of a disabled person if those needs are not being otherwise met are section 2 itself.[66]

Services under Chronically Sick and Disabled Persons Act 1970 s2

9.62   The CSDPA 1970, sponsored by Alf Morris MP, was the first of a distinguished line of private members' bills in this field[67] and represents an early marker in the continuing struggle by disabled people for full civil rights. Writing 25 years after its enactment, Alf Morris commented:

> It seems incredible and outrageous now, but from 1945–1964, there was not one debate in the Commons on disability. Westminster and Whitehall

---

63   (1997) 1 CCLR 7.
64   The respondent did not pursue this argument in the Court of Appeal or the House of Lords.
65   The material provisions in the 1977 Act have been transposed in identical terms into the NHS Acts 2006 – see para 13.5.
66   (1997) 1 CCLR 7 at 16K.
67   The Disabled Persons (Services, Consultation and Representation) Act 1986 was promoted by Tom Clarke MP, the Carers (Recognition and Services) Act 1995 was promoted by Malcolm Wicks MP and the Carers (Equal Opportunities) Act 2004 was promoted by Dr Hywel Francis MP.

always had more pressing things to do than respond to the claims of people with disabilities. No-one even knew how many disabled people there were in Britain. They were treated not so much as second-class citizens, more as non-people: seen or heard only by families or, if they were in institutions, by those who controlled their lives.[68]

9.63   The speed with which the Act was drafted resulted in ambiguities which have frustrated its interpretation, most significantly the extent to which CSDPA 1970 s2 is distinct from NAA 1948 s29; this question is considered in greater detail below. The underlying purpose of section 2 was undoubtedly to convert the vaguely worded, generally discretionary services under section 29 into a set of specific services to which individual disabled people had an enforceable right. CSDPA 1970 s2(1) provides:

> (1) Where a local authority having functions under section 29 of the National Assistance Act 1948 are satisfied in the case of any person to whom that section applies who is ordinarily resident in their area that it is necessary in order to meet the needs of that person for that authority to make arrangements for all or any of the following matters, namely—
>
> (a) the provision of practical assistance for that person in his home;
> (b) the provision for that person of, or assistance to that person in obtaining, wireless, television, library or similar recreational facilities;
> (c) the provision for that person of lectures, games, outings or other recreational facilities outside his home or assistance to that person in taking advantage of educational facilities available to him;
> (d) the provision for that person of facilities for, or assistance in, travelling to and from his home for the purpose of participating in any services provided under any arrangements made by the authority under the said section 29 or, with the approval of the authority, in any services provided otherwise than as aforesaid which are similar to services which could be provided under such arrangements;
> (e) the provision of assistance for that person in arranging for the carrying out of any works of adaptation in his home or the provision of any additional facilities designed to secure his greater safety, comfort or convenience;
> (f) facilitating the taking of holidays by that person, whether at holiday homes or otherwise and whether provided under arrangements made by the authority or otherwise;
> (g) the provision of meals for that person whether in his home or elsewhere;
> (h) the provision for that person of, or assistance to that person in obtaining, a telephone and any special equipment necessary to enable him to use a telephone,
>
> then, [subject to the provisions of section 7(1) of the Local Authority Social Services Act 1970 (which requires local authorities in the exercise of certain functions, including functions under the said

---

68   DW Issues, June 1995.

section 29, to act under the general guidance of the Secretary of State)], it shall be the duty of that authority to make those arrangements in exercise of their functions under the said section 29.

'Ordinarily resident'

9.64 Section 2 services are only available to persons who are ordinarily resident in the local authority's area. Ordinary residence has the same meaning as it does under NAA 1948 s24, although the statutory procedure for resolving inter-authority disputes on this question (under NAA 1948 s32(3)) is not available where the disagreement concerns services under CSDPA 1970 s2[69] – see para 6.47 above.

Client group

9.65 CSDPA 1970 s2 services are available to both disabled children and disabled adults (unlike services under NAA 1948 s29, which are only available to disabled adults). Section 2 requires social services authorities to make arrangements 'for that person' – whereas NAA 1948 s29 speaks of the need to make arrangements to 'promote the welfare' of a class of people. It follows therefore that services under CSDPA 1970 s2 must only be provided to the disabled person, whereas it is arguable that NAA 1948 s29 services can be provided to third parties so long as they thereby 'promote the welfare' of the person in question.[70]

Disabled adults

9.66 Section 2 services are available to the same group of adult persons as specified in NAA 1948 s29, namely persons aged 18 or over who are blind, deaf, dumb or who suffer from mental disorder of any description, and other persons aged 18 or over who are substantially and permanently handicapped by illness, injury, or congenital deformity (see para 9.19 where these terms are considered).

Disabled children

9.67 By virtue of CSDPA 1970 s28A, section 2 services are additionally available to disabled children within the meaning of CA 1989 s17(11), namely a child who is 'blind, deaf, dumb or suffers from mental disorder of any kind or is substantially and permanently handicapped by illness, injury or congenital deformity'. It will be seen that the CA 1989 follows the wording used in NAA 1948 s29, and accordingly the comments made in this following section in respect of the adult client group apply equally to disabled children.

---

69 *R v Kent CC ex p Salisbury and Pierre* (2000) 3 CCLR 38.
70 See note 37 above.

9.68   While the CA 1989 itself makes provision for a wide range of services for disabled children (considered at para 24.42 below), in general, if the service is capable of being provided under both Acts, then it will (as a matter of law) be provided under the CSDPA 1970.[71]

Services

9.69   As already noted (see para 3.171), once a social services authority has carried out an assessment of the needs of a disabled person and decided that the provision of services under CSDPA 1970 s2 is necessary in order to meet that person's needs, the authority is under an specific duty to provide that service.[72] The services detailed in section 2 are described below.

Practical assistance in the home

9.70   A wide range of services could be interpreted as providing 'practical assistance' to a person in his or her home under CSDPA 1970 s2(1)(a). It has for instance been suggested that the phrase encompasses the provision of some disabled facilities[73] although these are traditionally considered to be covered by section 2(1)(e) (see para 9.93 below). Although it is possible to divide such services into two broad categories – those primarily concerned with the maintenance of the home (eg, house cleaning, ironing, decorating etc) and those primarily concerned with the personal care of the disabled person (eg, help with getting out of and into bed, dressing, cooking, laundry, a sitting service etc), it would be a mistake to suggest that the first category is of less importance than the second. Nevertheless many (if not most) social services departments operate a rigid policy of not providing the former services under CSDPA 1970 s2. Such a policy is not merely a fettering of their duty; it is also contrary to good practice, in that it is 'needs' that are prioritised under the community care regime, not services. While it may follow that a need for personal care will generally be of higher priority than a need to live in a clean and safe environment, this will not always be the case.

9.71   The local government ombudsman has held it to be maladministration for a council to have criteria which stipulate that no domestic assistance can be provided – unless accompanied by a need for personal care,[74] and guidance to the Carers and Disabled Children Act 2000 emphasises this point: [75]

---

71 *R v Bexley LBC ex p B* (1995) 3 CCLR 15, see para 9.131 below where this question is considered further.

72 *R v Gloucestershire CC ex p Mahfood* (1995) 1 CCLR 7.

73 Department for Communities and Local Government, Department for Education and Skills and the Department of Health, *Delivering Housing Adaptations for Disabled People: A Good Practice Guide*, June 2006, para 2.6.

74 Complaint no 01/C/17519 against Salford CC, 11 December 2003.

75 Department of Health, *Practitioners Guide to Carers' Assessments under the Carers and Disabled Children Act 2000*, March 2001, para 80.

. . . local authorities that have decided not to provide or commission certain services as community care services – such as shopping only, cleaning only, or other low-level services – should review their positions. Such services, if targeted purposively, can be of genuine assistance in sustaining the caring relationship, and be cost effective.

9.72 Not only have authorities adopted arbitrary and unlawful policies of not providing domestic assistance, many (if not most) have also restricted their bathing support services assistance to cases where there is an identified medical need – essentially requiring the disabled person to produce a doctor's letter verifying that such a medical need exists. The local government ombudsman has also declared it to be maladministration for a local authority to have such a policy – to suggest that bathing is not an essential activity. Some authorities have attempted to circumvent their duty to provide bathing assistance by suggesting that the 'service response' to a person's 'need to clean' might be a strip wash rather than a bath. Indeed a number of social services authorities have adopted such a policy as a cost saving measure. In this respect, the ombudsman has further held that the ability properly to manage bathing/washing with dignity is the entitlement of everybody[76] – see also para 4.69 above.

9.73 There is appreciable overlap between the duty under CSDPA 1970 s2(1)(a) and that under NHSA 2006 Sch 20 para 3, which places a duty on social services authorities to provide home help for households where such help is required owing to the presence of a person who is suffering from illness, lying in, an expectant mother, aged, or 'handicapped' as a result of having suffered from illness or by congenital deformity (see para 9.161 below).The main differences between these two provisions are:

a) The NHS Acts 2006 service is available to a wider client group (ie, the 'handicap' need not be permanent or substantial: expectant mothers, the temporarily ill and the elderly are covered), but it does not cover persons 'handicapped' as a result of injury.

b) The service under the NHS Acts 2006 is generally regarded as a target duty, whereas the duty under CSDPA 1970 s2 can create an individual right to the service (see para 1.25).

c) The NHS Acts 2006 service is provided to 'households' (ie, a direct beneficiary might be the carer), whereas the CSDPA 1970 s2 service can only be provided to the disabled person (ie, a carer could only be an indirect beneficiary).

d) The NHS Acts 2006 use the phrase 'home help' whereas CSDPA 1970 s2(1)(a) refers to 'practical assistance' in the home – although it is difficult to see whether anything of significance can be discerned from this difference.

9.74 In *R v Islington LBC ex p McMillan*[77] the applicant complained that, amongst other things, although he had been assessed as needing regular

---

76 Complaint no 02/C/8679, 8681 and 10389 against Bolsover DC, 30 September 2003.
77 (1997)1 CCLR 7 at 17.

home care assistance, this had on occasions not materialised (because of staff being on leave or ill). The court held that this did not amount to a breach of duty since the applicant had been notified in the care plan that the service might suffer from such interruptions and, given his comparative need, that this was not unreasonable.

9.75   In *R (T, D and B) v Haringey LBC*[79] the court held that the concept of 'practical assistance' within the meaning of section 2 could not cover the provision of services akin to medical treatment (in this case the replacement of oesophageal feeding tubes (see para 14.29 below) even where this service was not being undertaken by a qualified nurse.

The provision of a wireless, television, library, etc

9.76   The service described by CSDPA 1970 s2(1)(b) consists of the social services authority actually providing (or helping with the acquisition of) equipment to satisfy a recreational need. The items referred to (ie wireless, television, library or similar recreational facilities) are illustrative not exhaustive, and presumably equipment such as a personal computer or hi-fi system could also be provided under section 2(1)(b). Whether or not this provision enables a local authority also to provide aids that facilitate the use of such equipment (such as a sound loop or audio-headphone for people with impaired hearing) would appear questionable, since (unlike section 2(1)(h)) there is no additional reference to 'special equipment necessary to enable him to use' the wireless, TV library etc. Such equipment could however be provided pursuant to the duty under NAA 1948 s29 (see para 9.42 above), namely the duty to provide 'facilities for social rehabilitation and adjustment to disability including assistance in overcoming limitations of mobility or communication'.[80]

The provision of recreational/educational facilities

9.77   CSDPA 1970 s2(1)(c) requires social services authorities to provide two separate types of service, namely:

Recreational facilities

9.78   This service is complementary to the home-based service detailed in CSDPA 1970 s2(1)(a) above, and must be provided outside the person's home. Included within this provision are traditional day centres and 'drop-in' clubs as well as such recreational activities as outings and so on.

9.79   It is government policy to require local authorities to develop more positive activities for disabled people (particularly people with learning disabilities) than those traditionally provided by day centres. This policy initiative (which is considered at para 19.15 below) has resulted in a number of challenges to the closure of such centres and these actions (in the context of care homes) are considered at para 7.120 above.

---

79 [2005] EWHC 2235 (Admin); (2006) 9 CCLR 58.
80 LAC (93)10 appendix 2 para 2(1)(b).

9.80   In *R v Haringey LBC ex p Norton*[81] the council, when carrying out its assessment, only considered its obligation to provide 'personal care needs' rather than other needs such as social, recreational and leisure needs (such as those available under section 2(1)(c)). The court held this to be unlawful; the assessment had to investigate all potential needs (see para 3.87 above).

9.81   Where a person's assessment identifies a need that could be met by services under section 2(1)(c)) – for instance in a day centre –that need must be met. If the appropriate centre is full, merely placing that person's name on the waiting list is likely to be an inadequate response (unless the wait is known to be reasonably short). This situation was considered by Sedley J in *R v Islington LBC ex p Rixon*[82] where he held:

> The duty owed to the applicant personally by virtue of section 2(1) of the Chronically Sick and Disabled Persons Act 1970 includes the provision of recreational facilities outside the home to an extent which Islington accepts is greater than the care plan provides for. But the local authority has, it appears, simply taken existing unavailability of further facilities as an insuperable obstacle to any further attempt to make provision. The lack of a day care centre has been treated, however reluctantly, as a complete answer to the question of provision for Jonathan's needs. As McCowan LJ explained in the *Gloucestershire* case, the section 2(1) exercise is needs-led and not resource-led. To say this is not to ignore the existing resources either in terms of regular voluntary care in the home or in budgetary terms. These, however, are balancing and not blocking factors.

For further consideration of waiting lists, see para 3.177 above.

Educational facilities

9.82   The educational service required in this case may be either home-based or otherwise. The wording of section 2(1)(c) suggests that the service provided by the authority consists of enabling the disabled person to have access to an (already existing) educational facility – rather than the provision of the educational facility itself. Potentially the scope of the educational obligation is wide. In particular the subsection appears to enable the provision of:

a)   services for which there is an overlapping NHS responsibility (eg, communication assistance via speech synthesisers, speech therapy, hearing and writing aids etc); and

b)   services to support disabled (adult) students. LAC (93)12[83] gives specific guidance on the these responsibilities, and in particular stresses that CSDPA 1970 s2(1)(c) covers funding the personal care requirements of such students so as to enable them to pursue their studies (even if those studies are undertaken outside the local authority's area). The relevant part of the circular states as follows:

---

81   (1998) 1 CCLR 168.
82   (1996) 1 CCLR 119 at 126D.
83   See paras 9–11.

9. Social services departments have been reminded of their duty under s2(1)(c) of the Chronically Sick & Disabled Persons Act 1970 to make arrangements for assisting a disabled person who is ordinarily resident in their area in taking advantage of educational facilities available to him/her, (even where provision is made outside that local authority's area), if they are satisfied that it is necessary in order to meet that person's needs. Such assistance might, in appropriate cases include the funding by the local authority of the personal care required to enable the student in question to pursue his/her studies. It is, of course, for the authority to decide, in each case, what the individual's needs are, and how they are to be met.

10. Disabled students attending higher education courses may be eligible to receive up to three Disabled Students Allowances from the local education authority, as part of their mandatory award. These allowances are for a non-medical helper, major items of special equipment, or minor items such as tapes or braille paper. They are aimed at helping students with costs related to their course, and are not intended to meet other costs arising from their disability which would have to be met irrespective of whether or not they were in a course. For those attending further education courses, similar support may be provided at the discretion of the LEA.

11 There may be occasions where the social services department is asked to consider the provision of additional care support for an individual who will receive a Disabled Students Allowance or discretionary support from the LEA. It will, therefore, be appropriate in some circumstances for the support for an individual's personal care needs to be provided jointly by the SSD and the LEA.

9.83   The *ex p Rixon* judgment (above) also considered the interplay between the duties owed under CSDPA 1970 s2(1)(c) and the general duty under Education Act 1944 s41[84] which obliges education authorities to secure adequate further education facilities for (amongst others) adults who have learning difficulties. Sedley J considered that for persons with the gravest learning difficulties the section 41 duty might be met by the provision of facilities under CSDPA 1970 s2. He suggested however, that if this was the case, the appropriate remedy for an alleged breach of the section 41 duty was (in the first instance) via the secretary of state's default powers under the Act (default powers are further considered at para 27.201 below).

9.84   *R v Further Education Funding Council and Bradford MBC ex p Parkinson*[85] concerned a 20-year-old applicant with severe mental and physical impairments. He was unable to take advantage of a place at a further education college without first being able to communicate to the required standard. He sought to compel the respondents to provide the necessary facilities under either Education Act 1944 s41 or Higher Education Act

84   As substituted by Further and Higher Education Act 1992 s11. See also DFE circular 1/93 *The Further and Higher Education Act 1992 Guidance* (WOC 15/93 in Wales) and *Duties and Powers: The Law Governing the Provision of Further Education to Students with Learning Difficulties and/or Disabilities*, HMSO, 1996.
85   (1996) *Times* 31 October.

1992 Sch 2. In dismissing the application, Jowitt J observed that although 'purely education facilities' could not be provided under the community care legislation, the applicant might be eligible for services under CSDPA 1970 s2(1)(c) 'as providing assistance to take advantage of education facilities which are available to him'.

Travel and other assistance

9.85 Travel assistance under NAA 1948 s29 is considered at para 9.51 above. CSDPA 1970 s2(1)(d) concerns the provision of travel assistance or facilities to enable a disabled person to travel from his or her home in order to participate in any community based services provided under CSDPA 1970 s2 and NAA 1948 s29. In relation to services not provided under section 29, but which are of a similar nature, the local authority has a discretion to provide assistance under section 2(1)(d) ('with the approval of the authority'). While social services authorities are empowered (but not obliged) to charge for such transport services (see para 10.37), in assessing a person's ability to pay, his or her mobility component of disability living allowance (DLA) (if received) must be ignored.[86] It remains, however, a moot point as to whether a local authority could determine that a person did not have a need for transport under section 2(1)(d) because he or she was in receipt of the DLA mobility component. A blanket policy of this nature would, of course, amount to a fettering of the council's duty. Even in individual cases, such a decision may be unreasonable, since a person's need to be compensated for limitations of mobility covers a wide range of situations and expenses (eg additional car use expenses, taxi costs, wheelchair servicing and repair costs, the travel costs of an escort and so on): in such circumstances, for a council to expect a disabled person to use his or her mobility allowance solely (or predominantly) to offset its liability under section 2(1)(d) would seem unreasonable.

9.86 The Welsh Ombudsman has found maladministration where a local authority refused to provide transport to a day centre for a new service user because she was in receipt of the DLA mobility component. This did not apply to existing service users. Systematic maladministration was found on the basis there was an absence of any policy framework and no written guidelines on the eligibility of clients who could use local authority run transport.[87]

9.87 In general, where transport is required in order that a disabled child attend a school specified in a special educational needs statement, it will be for the education department to provide this.[88] Occasionally a disabled parent may be unable get a non-disabled child to school – or to some other location – because the parent's impairment renders him or her unable to undertake this task. In such cases, there is often agreement as to the need

---

86 Social Security Contributions and Benefits Act 1992 s73(14).
87 Case no B2004/0180 against Newport City Council, 31 August 2006.
88 This may even be the case where the statement provides that 'the mother [is] to be responsible for transport to and from the school at her own expense', see *R v Havering LBC ex p K* (1997) *Times* 18 November.

for transport, but a dispute as to whether this is the responsibility of the adult social services or of the children's services department. This question is considered at para 3.39 below – however as a general rule the need should be deemed to be a need of the disabled adult (a need to discharge a usual parenting role) and accordingly addressed in the parent's community care assessment.

Blue Badge Scheme

9.88   CSDPA 1970 s21 (as subsequently amended) requires motor vehicle badges to be made available for the benefit of disabled people and for regulations to be issued concerning the operation of this scheme, now known as the Blue Badge Scheme.[89] As at March 2005 there were 2.1 million such badges across England.[90]

9.89   Persons who meet at least one of the following criteria have a statutory right to a badge:

- receive the higher rate of the mobility component of the disability living allowance;
- are registered blind;
- use a vehicle supplied by a government department;
- receive a grant from a government department for their vehicle;
- receive a war pensioners' mobility supplement; or
- have a severe disability in both upper limbs, regularly drive a motor vehicle but cannot turn the steering wheel of a motor vehicle by hand, even if that wheel is fitted with a turning knob.

9.90   An additional ground exists (at the discretion of the local authority) under which a disabled person may be issued with a badge if he or she has a permanent and substantial disability that means he or she is unable to walk or has very considerable difficulty in walking.

9.91   Although local authorities are entitled to charge £2 for processing Blue Badge applications, they are advised[91] not to claim it, since it costs substantially more than this to collect and process this sum.

Reform

9.92   The Department of Transport in England proposes to modify the Blue Badge Scheme and introduce in 2007 amending Regulations – the Disabled Persons (Badges for Motor Vehicles) (England) (Amendment) Regulations 2007.[92] The changes will include:

---

89 The Disabled Persons (Badges for Motor Vehicles) (England) Regulations 2000 SI No 682, as amended by the Disabled Persons (Badges for Motor Vehicles) (England) (Amendment) Regulations 2000 SI No 1507 and see also the Disabled Persons (Badges For Motor Vehicles) (Wales) Regulations 2000 WSI No 1786.
90 See Department of Health, *Care Services Efficiency Programme 'Blue Badge Initiative' Report*, 2006, accessible at http://www.rcoe.gov.uk/rce/aio/20055.
91 Ibid.
92 See 'Consultation on the Blue Badge disabled parking scheme' at http://www.dft.gov.uk/consultations/closed/bluebadgescheme.

- a new category of eligibility for children under the age of two;
- allowing badges to be issued for a period of less than three years to people who are awarded DLA higher rate mobility component for less than three years;
- changes to the criteria which apply for disabled people who have difficulty operating parking meters etc.

Home adaptations and disabled facilities

9.93   CSDPA 1970 s2 (1)(e) reads as follows:

> The provision of assistance for that person in arranging for the carrying out of any works of adaptation in his home or the provision of any additional facilities designed to secure his greater safety, comfort or convenience.

9.94   Section 2(1)(e) is in two parts; one concerned with adaptations (ie, significant works, possibly of a structural nature) and the other with the provision of additional facilities (ie, works involving the provision of fixtures and fittings and equipment). As noted above (para 9.70) it has been suggested that section 2(1)(a) may also require the provision of certain disabled facilities.

9.95   In relation to 'additional facilities' the duty on the authority is to provide these ('the provision of'), whereas in relation to adaptations the duty is stated as being the 'provision of assistance . . . in arranging for the carrying out of'. Whether the difference in wording is legally significant is not clear. The subsection does not oblige social services authorities to carry out (or otherwise provide) the adaptations, merely to provide assistance for that person in arranging for the carrying out of the works. Arguably this might be no more than assistance in finding a suitable architect or builder or assistance with a grant application form. The guidance in relation to disabled facilities grants suggests, however, that the duty is more substantial, namely a duty to ensure that appropriate works are carried out including, for instance, the provision of financial assistance.

Adaptations

9.96   The social services obligation under CSDPA 1970 s2(1)(e) to assist in arranging works of adaptation is a specific duty and arises once an assessment has concluded that it is necessary for this service to be provided. In legislative terms it is distinct from the responsibility born by the housing authority[93] under Housing Grants, Construction and Regeneration Act (HGCRA) 1996 Part I to provide (subject to a means test[94]) disabled facilities grants (DFGs) for such works. The procedures for securing such grants are considered in detail at para 15.22 below. Unfortunately, however, the manner in which authorities discharge these

---

93 Notwithstanding that the two authorities will frequently be one and the same.
94 The means test for DFGs depends upon the financial resources of the disabled person and his or her partner.

two responsibilities often results in considerable confusion and delay and has resulted in numerous complaints to the local government ombudsman.

Interface with the disabled facilities grant obligation

9.97   The suggestion has been made that since the duty under the 1970 Act only arises where the authority is satisfied its assistance is 'necessary', it is arguable that this duty does not in general arise (if at all) until after a DFG application has been determined.[95] This is an unattractive argument for a number of reasons, not least the very different nature of the two obligations. By way of example, the HGCRA 1996 permits a delay of six months in the payment of a grant (see para 15.83). Given that the need for adaptations is often urgent and the fact that the section 2(1)(e) duty has no such deferment proviso, it would arguably be unlawful for a social services authority to refuse to assess a person's needs for an adaptation under the 1970 Act on the ground that it was possible that at some distant time in the future he or she would be awarded a DFG.

9.98   Although the relationship between the duties under the 1996 and 1970 Acts is best characterised as one of overlapping and complementary responsibilities, the existence of the two provisions has in practice created a pretext for considerable administrative delay.

9.99   In general, social services in assessing a need for assistance under section 2(1)(e) will require that an application be made to the housing authority for a DFG. At this stage, the applicant is likely to be told that an occupational therapist will have to undertake an assessment of the need and that there is a waiting list of very many months for such an assessment. The problem of chronic delay in this context is well documented and, notwithstanding many critical reports from the local government ombudsman, persists.[96]

9.100   When such delay occurs and the grant is being processed by a separate council (ie a district council) the appropriate response from the social services authority will be to assist the disabled person in resolving the problem – by actively intervening in the process if needs be. Such delay, however, does not of itself absolve the social services authority of its separate responsibility under CSDPA 1970 s2(1)(e). This point is emphasised in circular LAC (90)7,[97] which refers to the social services department as the 'lead body', and (as noted below) states that its duty to act remains regardless of the housing authority's actions.[98]

---

95   See *R (Fay) v Essex CC* [2004] EWHC 879 (Admin) at [28].

96   See paras 9.108 and 15.92 for a general analysis of the ombudsman's comments on such delay.

97   At para 14. LAC (90)7 was issued jointly as Department of the Environment circular 10/90. While DoE circular 10/90 has been withdrawn (and superseded by new guidance circular 17/96), LAC (90)7 remains in force (see DoE 4/98 and LASSL (99)21).

98   LAC (90)7 para 15.

9.101   Typically home adaptations concern such matters as stair lifts, ground-floor extensions, doorway widening, ramps and wheelchair accessible showers. Unlike under HGCRA 1996 Part I (considered at para 15.49 below), the 1970 Act imposes no requirement that work be either 'appropriate' or 'reasonable and practicable'. All the 1970 statute requires is that the social services authority be satisfied that the works are necessary in order to meet the needs of the disabled person (by securing his or her greater safety, comfort or convenience).

9.102   Department of Health guidance, LAC (90)7, illustrates this difference of approach (at paras 15–17 and also at para 58):

> 15. The existing responsibilities of [social service's authorities] under s2 of the CSDP Act are unchanged. In cases of their duty to make arrangements for home adaptations, under s2(1)(e), the responsibility will, in many instances, be effectively discharged on their behalf by the housing authority, by the giving of a disabled facilities grant. However the [social services authority's] duty to act remains, and they may be called upon to meet this duty in two ways. The first is where the needs as assessed by the [social services] authority exceed the scope for provision by the housing authority under s114(3) of the 1989 [Local Government and Housing] Act[99] and where the authority decline to use their discretionary powers under s114(4). If the [social services] authority deem the need to be established, then it will be their responsibility in these circumstances to make arrangements for this need to be met under s2 of the CSDP Act.
>
> 16. Such a responsibility might arise when for instance the [social services] authority considers there is need related to the individual's social needs that demands a greater level of provision than is required for the disability alone, and where the housing authority chooses not to exercise its discretionary powers. This may occur, for example, where the size of a bedroom for a disabled child is required to be greater than is necessary for sleeping, because it needs to fulfil the role of bed/sitting room to provide more independent social space.
>
> 17. The second instance where *the [social services] authority may find they have a continuing duty to provide assistance concerns cases where a disabled person asks the [social services] authority for financial assistance, under section 2(1)(e) of the CSDP Act, with that part of the costs of an adaptation which he is expected to finance himself in the light of the test of resources for the disabled facilities grant. On occasion, this could be as much as the total costs of the adaptation. In such cases, the [social services] authority still has a duty to assist.*[100] However, in order to maintain consistency with the new arrangements for disabled facilities grants, the [social services] authority may wish to use their existing powers to charge for their services (under section 17 of the [Health and Social Services and Social Security Adjudications] Act 1983) to recover the full cost of any assistance given, provided that they consider that the client is able to afford to repay this. In examining the question of financial assistance, [social services] authorities are recommended to bear in mind that the amount of grant approved will

99 Now Housing Grants, Construction and Regeneration Act 1996 Part 1 – see para 15.25 below.

100 This section in italics (emphasis added) has been the subject of adverse comment by Richards J – see para 15.86 below.

have been calculated on the basis of a test of resources (described in more detail in paragraphs 64 and 65 and Appendix II below). [Social services] authorities should not try to make their own separate assessment of what a grant applicant is expected to pay; but they might consider whether, in their opinion, the meeting of those costs would cause hardship.[101] The method of charging or of recovery of costs is for the [social services] authority to decide; but alternatives which might be considered include loans, with or without interest, possibly secured in either case by a charge on the property[102] or the placing of a charge on the property for a set period.

9.103   Similar advice was given in now revoked circular guidance 17/96 issued by the Department of the Environment (see para 15.29), namely:

Role of the social services authority to assist with adaptations
5. Social services authorities' responsibilities under s2 Chronically Sick & Disabled Persons Act 1970 to make arrangements for home adaptations are not affected by the grants legislation. Where an application for DFG has been made, those authorities may be called upon to meet this duty in two ways:
(a) where the assessed needs of a disabled person exceeds the scope for provision by the housing authority under section 23 of the 1996 Act; and
(b) where an applicant for DFG has difficulty in meeting is assessed contribution determined by the means test and seeks financial assistance from the authority.

6. In such cases, where the social services authority determine that the need has been established, it remains their duty to assist even where the local housing authority either refuse or are unable to approve the application. Social services authorities may also consider using their powers under section 17 of the Health and Social Services and Social Security Adjudications Act 1983 to charge for their services where appropriate.

9.104   Where a DFG is inadequate to cover the full cost of the necessary works, the social services authority can make up the shortfall by way support under section 2(1)(e) and/or the housing authority can assist using its powers under the Regulatory Reform (Housing Assistance) (England and Wales) Order 2002 (see para 15.66 below). In either situation the relevant council can impose conditions on such a 'top-up' payment. In *R (BG) v Medway Council*[103] the High Court held that it was not unreasonable for a local authority in a case such as this to make the payment by way of a loan secured as a 20 year legal charge on the home which would not be repayable, unless the disabled person ceased to reside at the property during

---

101 Charging for domiciliary services is considered in detail at chapter 10. The reference to 'hardship' in the circular is unhelpful: Health and Social Services and Social Security Adjudications Act (HASSASSAA) 1983 s17 merely requires that the disabled person satisfy the authority that his or her means are insufficient for it to be reasonably practicable for him or her to pay for the service – in this respect see in particular para 10..10 below.
102 Such a charge could presumably only be secured on the property with the owner's consent as HASSASSAA 1983 s17 does not empower authorities to create such charges (unlike section 22).
103 [2005] EWHC 1932 (Admin); (2005) 8 CCLR 448.

that period and that any amount repayable would be subject to interest. In this case the authority had agreed that in the event of repayment being required it would have regard to the family's personal and financial circumstances and would not act unreasonably by insisting repayment immediately or on terms that would result in financial hardship.

9.105 Where a DFG application is not completed or fails on financial grounds and it is not unreasonable for the authority to believe that the applicant may have sufficient resources to fund the adaptations, the authority may be entitled to refuse to provide support under the 1970 Act on the ground that its support was not 'necessary'. *R (Spink) v Wandsworth BC*[104] is such a case and concerned two disabled children for whom an occupational therapists' report concluded that adaptations to their parents' home were required. At that time DFGs for disabled children's needs were subject to a parental means test (this is no longer the case – see para 15.77) and the local authority was not satisfied, on financial grounds, that the parents' qualified for a DFG. The parents argued that having decided that the adaptations were required, the authority was obliged to provide them under the 1970 Act. Richards J, in the High Court (with whom the Court of Appeal agreed) held that in deciding whether it was *necessary* to provide a service to meet an assessed need a local authority could have regard to a disabled child's parents' resources 'when deciding under section 2 of the 1970 Act whether it is necessary for it to make arrangements to meet the claimant children's needs' (at para 50). In his opinion:

> 52. Given that the authority has to decide whether it is necessary *for that authority* to make arrangements to meet the needs, it would be surprising if the authority were not entitled to consider the possibility of the needs being met instead by a third party. The example . . . of a case where the local housing authority (which may be a different council from the local social services authority) has accepted that a DFG is available to meet the needs, is in my view a good one. It would be entirely reasonable for the local social services authority to decide in those circumstances that it was not *necessary* for *it* to make arrangements to meet the needs. I cannot see any sensible reason for reading the section as precluding a reasonable exercise of judgment of that kind.

> 54. If it is accepted that an authority is entitled to look at the possibility of the needs being met by a third party, it follows that it is entitled to look at the possibility of their being met by the parents or another relative of a disabled child. Just as an authority might reasonably conclude that it was not necessary for it to make arrangements where a local housing authority had stated that a DFG was available for the purpose, so it might reasonably conclude that it was not necessary for it to make arrangements where the parents had expressed a willingness to make funds available to meet the needs. I see no difference in principle between the situations. In neither case are the needs currently being met, but in neither case would it be unreasonable to decide that it was not necessary for the authority to make arrangements to meet them.

104 [2004] EWHC 2314 (Admin); [2005] 1 WLR 258.

9.106   Accordingly, Wandsworth was entitled to take into account the parents' financial resources when deciding whether it was necessary for them to fund the works of adaptation. This interpretation differed to a limited degree from guidance in LAC (90)7 which advised:

> . . . the welfare authority may find they have a continuing duty to provide assistance concerns cases where a disabled person asks the welfare authority for financial assistance, under section 2(e) of the CSDP Act, with that part of the costs of an adaptation which he is expected to finance himself in the light of the test of resources for the disabled facilities grant. On occasion, this could be as much as the total costs of the adaptation. In such cases, the welfare authority still has a duty to assist.

The judge held that to a limited degree this advice was incorrect, stating:

> It pays insufficient attention to the second stage of the analysis under section 2, namely the decision whether it is 'necessary' for the local social services authority to make arrangements to meet the relevant needs. In any event, in so far as it states that an authority is under a duty to make such arrangements irrespective of whether the disabled person (or, by implication, the parent of a disabled child) has the resources to meet the needs, I take the view that the circular is wrong.

9.107   The approach adopted by the courts in *Spink* was followed in *Freeman v Lockett*[105] where Tomlinson J stated (in the context of a personal injuries damages assessment) that it 'might be said that it is unnecessary [for a local authority to provide adaptations for] . . . a person who has received an award of damages calculated so as to cater for all his or her foreseeable needs in a reasonable manner, at any rate for so long as the award can be seen to be fulfilling that purpose'.

Delay

9.108   As noted above, unreasonable delay characterises the manner with which many, if not most, local authorities discharge their obligations to facilitate the provision of adaptations for disabled people. In assessing whether the delay is unlawful or constitutes maladministration, it is necessary to consider separately the statutory obligations under CSDPA 1970 s2 and HGCRA 1996 Part I. In relation to the duty under CSDPA 1970 s2, the general principles relevant to the assessment and provision of services timetable (under NHSCCA 1990 s47) apply. The assessment will generally require specialist involvement and this may result in delay. The local government ombudsman has produced a number of reports on this issue.[106] In a 1991[107] report she dealt with a situation where the complainant had (among other things) waited nine months for an occupational therapist's (OT) assessment. In finding maladministration, she commented:

---

105   [2006] EWHC 102 (QB).
106   See para 27.121 below where the ombudsman's role is considered.
107   Complaint no 90/C/0336 against Redbridge LBC, 3 October 1991.

The Council say that they suffered from a shortage of OTs during 1989; while I recognise that this is a national problem, nevertheless the Council still retain their responsibility to assess their client's needs. If sufficient OTs are not available, they may need to find another way of assessing those needs.

9.109 Her finding in this case does not of course mean that delays of less than nine months are acceptable. Her finding means that any council, knowing that the use of OTs for an assessment will cause a substantial delay, is guilty of maladministration when it opts to use OTs nevertheless (ie, it is maladministration the moment such a procedure is adopted).

9.110 Unlike the CSDPA 1970, HGCRA 1996 s36 allows for the delayed payment of a DFG – up to a maximum of 12 months following the date of the application. The issue of delay in relation to DFGs is considered further at para 15.92 below.

Equipment and additional facilities

9.111 CSDPA 1970 s2(1)(e) also covers the provision of 'additional facilities' designed to secure the disabled person's greater safety, comfort or convenience. This includes all manner of fittings and gadgets such as handrails, alarm systems, hoists, movable baths, adapted switches and handles, and so on.

9.112 The importance of the provision of appropriate equipment in promoting the independence and quality of disabled peoples' lives has been emphasised in much guidance and its speedy provision is an England performance indicator.[108] The *National Service Framework for Older People*,[109] for instance, at para 2.48 advises that:

- services should take a preventive approach, recognising that effective equipment provision (including for people with moderate disabilities) is likely to:
  - help older people to maintain their independence and live at home
  - slow down deterioration in function and consequent loss of confidence and self-esteem
  - prevent accidents
  - prevent pressure sore damage
  - support and better protect the health of carers
- services should be timely and resolve the frequently long delays which inhibit older people's discharge from hospital, or their safety and confidence in coping at home.[110]

---

108 Indicator AO/D54 (2006–07): the percentage of items of equipment and adaptations delivered within seven working days – see para 2.16 above.
109 See para 20.2 below.
110 This final point is given considerable emphasis in the NHS hospital discharge guidance, *Discharge from hospital: pathway, process and practice*, Department of Health, February 2003, appendix 5.3.1 pp71–72 (see also para 5.10 below).

9.113   In 2000 and 2002 the Audit Commission published highly critical reports on the state of public provision of equipment for disabled people.[111] The 2002 report found that equipment services were in a parlous state; that users reported 'long delays for equipment of dubious quality'. Its recommendation of a substantial overhaul of the service led to a government initiative to establish integrated 'community equipment services' where both NHS and social services equipment could be accessed at a single point.[112] Each integrated community equipment service is required to meet the following criteria:[113]

- Revenue funding from pooled health and social services contributions using Health Act 1999 flexibilities.
- A single operational manager for the service.
- A board to advise the manager, whose members include representatives of stakeholder organisations.
- Unified stock.

9.114   The guidance accompanying this initiative[114] defined community equipment as follows:

> Community equipment is equipment for home nursing usually provided by the NHS, such as pressure relief mattresses and commodes, and equipment for daily living such as shower chairs and raised toilet seats, usually provided by local authorities. It also includes, but is not limited to:
> - Minor adaptations, such as grab rails, lever taps and improved domestic lighting.
> - Ancillary equipment for people with sensory impairments, such as liquid level indicators, hearing loops, assistive listening devices and flashing doorbells.
> - Communication aids for people with speech impairments.
> - Wheelchairs for short term loan, but not those for permanent wheelchair users, as these are prescribed and funded by different NHS services.[115]
> - Telecare equipment such as fall alarms, gas escape alarms and health state monitoring for people who are vulnerable.

9.115   The above guidance makes plain that the provision of some forms of equipment may be construed as joint social services/NHS responsibility. Similarly, some forms of equipment can be viewed as a joint social services/housing authority responsibility. Circular LAC (90)7 seeks to clarify this question (at para 19):

> ... equipment which can be installed and removed with little or no structural modification to the dwelling should usually be considered the responsibility of the [social services] authority. However, items such as stair

---

111   *Fully Equipped: The Provision of Equipment to Older or Disabled People by the NHS and Social Services in England and Wales*, 29 March 2000 and *Fully Equipped 2002 – Assisting Independence*, 27 June 2002, accessible at http://www.audit-commission.gov.uk.
112   For general information on this initiative see http://www.icesdoh.org/about.asp.
113   *Community Equipment Services* HSC 2001/008; LAC (2001)13 para 8.
114   Ibid, para 7.
115   See para 13.65 below concerning the provision of permanent wheelchairs.

lifts and through-floor lifts, which are designed to facilitate access into or around the dwelling would, in the view of the Secretaries of State, be eligible for disabled facilities grant. With items such as electric hoists, it is suggested that any structural modification of the property – such as strengthened joists or modified lintels – could be grant aidable under the disabled facilities grant, but that the hoisting equipment itself should be the responsibility of the [social services] authority.

Minor adaptations under £1,000

9.116   In England, minor adaptations costing less than £1,000 should be provided free of charge by virtue of regulations made under the Community Care (Delayed Discharges etc) Act (CC(DD)A) 2003 ss15 and 16.[116]

9.117   Many minor adaptations are relatively routine and straightforward and do not, therefore, require the input of an occupational therapist before being approved and provided. The College of Occupational Therapists has produced an excellent two volume guide which identifies a range of minor adaptations for which there is a clear consensus that initial assessment by an OT is generally not required (such as grab and hand rails, threshold ramps and drop kerbs, kitchen and bathroom taps and handles).[117]

Reform

9.118   The government in England is proposing a reform of the way equipment is provided, and is proposing a 'retail solution'[118] – essentially that social services and the NHS will issue users with a 'prescription' that can be exchanged for free equipment at an approved/accredited retailer. Assessments could additionally be undertaken by independent needs assessors who would 'assess an individual to determine not only what equipment may help, but who can also provide other skills eg, additional therapeutic intervention or other supportive services and advice'. It is proposed that the assessors would normally be 'professionally qualified people, probably, occupational therapists or physiotherapists who will be able to offer an independent assessment of equipment need to those individuals who are unable to or choose not to access state provision'.

116 Community Care (Delayed Discharges etc) Act (Qualifying Services) (England) Regulations 2003 S1 No 1196.
117 College of Occupational Therapists, *Minor Adaptations Without Delay: A Practical Guide and Technical Specifications for Housing Associations*, 2002, accessible at http://www.housingcorp.gov.uk/server/show/ConWebDoc.7502.
118 Transforming Community Equipment and Wheelchair Services programme, *Community Equipment – a vision for the future*, Care Services Improvement Partnership's Care Services Efficiency Delivery workstream, 2007, accessible at http://www.csip.org.uk/~csed/workstreams/transforming-community-equipment–wheelchair-services/community-equipment.html.

Holidays

> Facilitating the taking of holidays by that person, whether at holiday homes or otherwise and whether provided under arrangements made by the authority or otherwise.

9.119   The power of social services authorities to provide holiday homes under NAA 1948 s29 (see para 9.50) is complemented by the duty under CSDPA 1970 s2(1)(f) to facilitate the taking of holidays by disabled persons. In *R v Ealing LBC ex p Leaman*[119] the council refused to consider a request made by the applicant for financial assistance in taking a privately arranged holiday – on the ground that it would only grant such assistance which it itself had arranged or sponsored. In quashing the council's decision Mann J held that:

> The effect of the general policy adumbrated by the council is, in my judgement, to excise the words 'or otherwise' where they second occur in section 2(1)(f). Accordingly, the London Borough were wrong in declining to consider any application which the Applicant might have made for assistance with his private holiday. Whether, having regard to a proper consideration of a person's needs, those needs required the making of a grant to a private holiday is an entirely different question. It is a question wholly within the province of the local authority. However, it was quite wrong for them to deprive themselves of the opportunity of asking that question.[120]

9.120   Holidays can amount to a form of respite care for carers – where they have a need for a break and it is not possible or desirable for the disabled person not to accompany them. In such cases, the local authority may be able to fund the carer's holiday costs as a carers service under the Carers and Disabled Children Act 2000 (see para 16.87 below). In some cases however, an authority will have to fund the full cost of the holiday under the 1970 Act (and not merely the additional costs attributable to the user's impairment), where for instance the carer's attendance is necessary (for instance as an escort) as was the case in *R v North Yorkshire CC ex p Hargreaves (No 2)*.[121]

9.121   It is arguable that most community care assessments should identify a need for an annual holiday – it is something recognised as a 'need' by the large majority of the population. Such a need may be all the more important for disabled people to give them a break from the drudgery and exhaustion of living and caring for themselves. The presumption that, in appropriate cases, a care plan will have a holiday component must be strong, since for care home residents this is explicitly stated as an expectation in the relevant national minimum standard,[122] namely Standard 14, para 14.4 of which states:

119   (1984) *Times* 10 February, QBD.
120   From pp4–5 of the transcript of the judgment.
121   (1998) 1 CCLR 331.
122   Department of Health, *Care Homes for Adults (18–65) and Supplementary Standards for Care Homes Accommodating Young People Aged 16 and 17: National Minimum Standards Care Homes Regulations*, 2003, TSO, accessible at http://www.csci.org.uk/ PDF/care_homes_for_adults_18_65.pdf;in Wales the Care Standards Inspectorate

Service users in long-term placements have as part of the basic contract price the option of a minimum seven-day annual holiday outside the home, which they help choose and plan.

Meals

The provision of meals for that person whether in his home or elsewhere.

9.122 CSDPA 1970 s2(1)(g) covers the provision of meals at day centres (or indeed anywhere) as well as meals in the disabled person's home such as meals-on-wheels. The equivalent service for the elderly is governed by HSPHA 1968 s45 (see para 20.13).

Telephone and ancillary equipment

The provision for that person of, or assistance to that person in obtaining, a telephone and any special equipment necessary to enable him to use a telephone.

9.123 CSDPA 1970 s2(1)(h) may cover the installation of a telephone line as well as the provision of an appropriate handset, loud telephone bell (or a flashing visual or vibrating signal), amplifiers, inductive couplers for personal hearing aids and visual transmission machines such as minicoms, faxes and possibly modems for computer email transmission etc.

Chronically Sick and Disabled Persons Act 1970 s2 and National Assistance Act 1948 s29

9.124 The rapid drafting[123] of CSDPA 1970 s2 has led to considerable confusion as to its status. The section commences with the clause '[w]here a local authority having functions under section 29 of the National Assistance Act 1948 are satisfied . . .' and concludes 'it shall be the duty of that authority to make those arrangements in exercise of their functions under the said section 29'. It is not surprising therefore that CSDPA 1970 s2 has been considered as an extension to NAA 1948 s29 – to the extent that services identified under CSDPA 1970 s2 are in fact NAA 1948 s29 services: ie delivered as 'arrangements in exercise of . . . s29'.

9.125 In the courts' view it is for this reason that CSDPA 1970 s2 services are not specifically listed as 'community care services' in National Health Service and Community Care Act (NHSCCA) 1990 s46 – since the reference in section 46 to services under NAA 1948 Part III includes CSDPA 1970 s2 services.[124] However, and conversely, when statutory provisions

---

for Wales, National Minimum Standards for Care Homes for younger adults, 2002, accessible at http://www.csiw.wales.gov.uk/docs/yng_adult_stands_e.pdf.

123 For a description of the speed with which the bill was drafted see *Be it Enacted*, RADAR, 1995 and see also the Introduction paras I.17–I.19 above. Unfortunately there is nothing in the *Hansard* reports on the passage of the bill through Parliament to elucidate the confusing references to section 29.

124 *Hansard* (HC) Standing Committee E, cols 1055 et seq, 15 February 1990.

make specific reference to section 2 in addition to section 29, the courts have generally explained this in terms of *ex abundante cautela*[125] (from an abundance of caution).

9.126　　It follows that the assessment duty under NHSCCA 1990 s47(1) will require consideration of whether services under CSDPA 1970 s2 are 'called' for (see para 3.134 above), notwithstanding the absence of specific reference to this provision. This requirement was explained by Collins J in *R v Kirklees MBC ex p Daykin*[126] in the following terms:

> . . . section 47 and section 2 go hand in hand. Parliament may in other Acts have specifically mentioned section 2 but that was for the purposes of those Acts and no doubt for the avoidance of any doubt. It seems to me quite clear that in the context of section 2 and section 47 the definition of 'community care services' is apt to include the services provided under section 2.

9.127　This interpretation of the status of CSDPA 1970 s2 adult care services must now be considered as settled law. It is probably the 'best fix' that can be achieved in terms of reconciling these two radically different statutes – both in terms of their origins and their philosophical outlook – and in terms of their relations with the other community care statutes.

9.128　　However, having accepted that CSDPA 1970 s2 services are essentially a specifically enforceable species of services provided under the generic umbrella of NAA 1948 s29, certain collateral interpretative difficulties arise. For example NHSCCA 1990 s47(2) appears to create a different assessment procedure for CSDPA 1970 s2 services to those under the NHSCCA 1990 s46 community care statutes. As noted above (see para 3.17) the explanation advanced for this difference of treatment by the Department of Health (namely that section 47(2) assessments are required to be 'comprehensive') was rejected by Carnwath J in *R v Gloucestershire CC ex p RADAR.*[127]

9.129　　A similar incongruity was exposed in *R v Gloucestershire CC ex p Mahfood.*[128] Here the respondent argued that if CSDPA 1970 s2 services were provided under NAA 1948 s29 it followed that a home help service could not be provided under CSDPA 1970 s2 notwithstanding that section 2(1)(a) is concerned with precisely such a service. The argument turned upon NAA 1948 s29(6), which prohibits services being provided under section 29 if they can be provided under the NHS Acts 2006. The 2006 Acts make provision for a home help service.[129] The argument, as already noted (para 9.61), was described as 'unattractive' by McCowan LJ.[130]

9.130　　In *R v Powys CC ex p Hambidge*[131] the point in issue was the ability of local authorities to charge for services provided under CSDPA 1970 s2 notwithstanding that the provision that authorises charges to be levied for

125 *R v Powys CC ex p Hambidge* (1978) 1 CCLR 182 at 189D, QBD, per Popplewell J.
126 (1998) 1 CCLR 512 at 525A.
127 (1998) 1 CCLR 476.
128 (1997) 1 CCLR 7.
129 This aspect is also considered at para 9.161.
130 (1997) 1 CCLR 7 at 17C.
131 (1997) 1 CCLR 458, CA.

non-accommodation services (Health and Social Services and Social Security Adjudication Act (HASSASSAA) 1983 s17 – see para 10.8 below) made no reference to services under CSDPA 1970 s2. The Court of Appeal accepted the view of the Department of Health that section 2 services 'are arranged by local authorities in exercise of their functions under s29 of the 1948 Act'[132] – and since HASSASSAA 1983 s17 refers to NAA 1948 s29 services, that was sufficient authority for charges to be levied.

Chronically Sick and Disabled Persons Act 1970 s2 and the Children Act 1989

9.131 An additional difficulty stems from the differences between the CSDPA 1970 s2 and NAA 1948 s29 client groups. CSDPA 1970 s28A[133] provides that:

> This Act applies with respect to disabled children in relation to whom the local authority have functions under Part III of the Children Act 1989 as it applies in relation to persons to whom section 29 of the National Assistance Act 1948 applies.

9.132 Accordingly the CSDPA 1970 s2 client group includes all disabled people, whereas NAA 1948 s29 applies only to disabled people over 18 years of age. It follows that children's services provided under CSDPA 1970 s2 cannot be provided 'in exercise of ... functions under ... s29'.

9.133 In *R v Bexley LBC ex p B*[134] (see para 24.40 below) the respondent council sought to argue (amongst other things) that home care services provided to a disabled child were provided under the CA 1989 rather than under CSDPA 1970 s2. Latham J rejected the argument, holding that such services were provided under section 2 itself.[135]

9.134 Although the *Bexley* decision is authority for the fact that community based services provided to disabled children are generally provided under CSDPA 1970 s2, it did not address the question of whether or not they were delivered under the generic CA 1989 Part III umbrella. The question is of importance since, if they are, it would entitle local authorities to charge for such services (in pursuance of their powers under CA 1989 s29 – see para 24.68 below). The provenance of the section 2 duty in relation to disabled children was settled by the Court of Appeal in *R (Spink) v Wandsworth LBC*.[136] In the court's opinion:

> 34. .... section 2 of the 1970 Act expressly provided that local authorities were to comply with their obligations under that section in the exercise of their functions under section 29 of the 1948 Act '*notwithstanding anything in any scheme made by the authority under section 29*'. Just as the Secretary of State might be able to impose a duty on local authorities, enforceable by

---

132 Footnote 2 to the SSI advice note on non-accommodation charges, January 1994.
133 Inserted by CA 1989 s108(5), Sch 13 para 27.
134 (2000) 3 CCLR 15.
135 (2000) 3 CCLR 15 at 23C.
136 [2004] EWHC 2314 (Admin); [2005] 1 WLR 258 at [34]–[35].

individuals, to exercise their functions under section 29, so section 2 of the 1970 Act could impose a similar duty.

35.   Once this is appreciated, there is no difficulty in interpreting sections 2 and 28A of the 1970 Act as requiring local authorities to comply with the requirements of section 2, in so far as these apply to children, by the exercise of their functions under Part III of the Children Act, of which section 17 is particularly relevant.

9.135   It follows, that in relation to disabled children, section 2 should be read as follows:

Where a local authority having functions under Part III Children Act 1989 are satisfied in the case of a disabled child . . . it shall be the duty of that authority to make those arrangements in exercise of their functions under the said Part III.

9.136   Statutory recognition of the distinctiveness of CSDPA 1970 s2 services and services under the CA 1989 is found in Carers (Recognition and Services) Act 1989 s1(2)(a). This provision only applies when 'a local authority assess the needs of a disabled child for the purposes of the CA 1989 Part III or s2 of the CSDPA 1970'.

Services under the National Health Services Acts 2006

9.137   Most disabled people receive their domiciliary/community based services from social services authorities under CSDPA 1970 s2. These services, however, are only available to people who are 'substantially and permanently handicapped'[137] or who 'suffer from a mental disorder of any description'. Section 2 services are not therefore available to persons whose impairment is not 'permanent,' notwithstanding that it may be substantial. Domiciliary and community based services for such persons are generally provided by social services pursuant to duties under NHSA 2006 s254 and Sch 20 and NHS(W)A 2006 s192 and Sch 15. Frequently the persons covered by these provisions are referred to as 'ill people'; ie people who have a substantial impairment as a result of an accident or severe illness, but whose prognosis is that they will make a full recovery (and will not therefore be 'permanently handicapped'). The Acts, however, also cover services for a wider client group including older people, expectant mothers, drug and alcohol misusers as well as disabled people.

9.138   In discussing the provision of care services for ill people, one enters the minefield that marks the medical/social divide; a subject considered further in chapter 14. The NHS Acts 2006 attempt to demarcate the duties of the NHS and the social services authorities. Sections 1–3 of these Acts spell out the general nature of the NHS obligation in relation to disease prevention, the care and after-care of ill people. NHSA 2006 s254 (NHS(W)A 2006 s192) then outlines the services which are the responsibility of the social services authorities – these being amplified in

137   See para 9.19 above.

NHSA 2006 Sch 20 (NHS(W)A 2006 Sch 15). NHSA 2006 s82 contains a requirement of co-operation between health and social care service providers (see para 13.25 below).

9.139   The text of NHSA 2006 s254(1) and Sch 20 paras 1–3[138] is set out below:

254(1) Subject to paragraphs (d) and (e) of section 3(1), the services described in Schedule 20 in relation to –

(a) care of mothers,

(b) prevention, care and after-care,

(c) home help and laundry facilities,

are functions exercisable by local social services authorities.

Schedule 20: Local Social Services Authorities

Care of mothers and young children

1   A local social services authority may, with the Secretary of State's approval, and to such extent as he may direct must, make arrangements for the care of pregnant women and women who are breast feeding (other than for the provision of residential accommodation for them).

Prevention, care and after-care

2(1) A local social services authority may, with the Secretary of State's approval, and to such extent as he may direct must, make the arrangements mentioned in sub-paragraph (2).

(2)   The arrangements are for the purpose of the prevention of illness, for the care of persons suffering from illness and for the after-care of persons who have been suffering from illness and in particular for –

(a) the provision, for persons whose care is undertaken with a view to preventing them from becoming ill, persons suffering from illness and persons who have been suffering from illness, of centres or other facilities for training them or keeping them suitably occupied and the equipment and maintenance of such centres,

(b) the provision, for the benefit of such persons as are mentioned in paragraph (a), of ancillary or supplemental services, and

(c) the exercise of the functions of the local social services authority in respect of persons suffering from mental disorder who are received into guardianship under Part 2 or 3 of the Mental Health Act 1983 (c. 20) (whether the guardianship of the authority or of other persons).

(3)   A local social services authority may not, and is not under a duty to, make under this paragraph arrangements to provide facilities for any of the purposes mentioned in section 15(1) of the Disabled Persons (Employment) Act 1944 (c. 10).

(4)   No arrangements under this paragraph may provide for the payment of money to persons for whose benefit they are made, except in so far as they fall within sub-paragraph (5).

(5)   Arrangements fall within this sub-paragraph if –

(a) they provide for the remuneration of such persons engaged in suitable work in accordance with the arrangements of such

---

138 The text of NHS(W)A 2006 s192 and Sch 15 is in all material terms the same save only that it contains no equivalent of Sch 15 para 3.

amounts as the local social services authority considers appropriate in respect of their occasional personal expenses, and

(b) it appears to the authority that no such payment would otherwise be made.

(6) No arrangements under this paragraph may be given effect to in relation to a person to whom section 115 of the Immigration and Asylum Act 1999 (c. 33) (exclusion from benefits) applies solely –

(a) because he is destitute, or

(b) because of the physical effects, or anticipated physical effects, of his being destitute.

(7) Section 95(2) to (7) of that Act apply for the purposes of sub-paragraph (6); and for that purpose a reference to the Secretary of State in section 95(4) or (5) is a reference to a local social services authority.

(8) The Secretary of State may make regulations as to the conduct of premises in which facilities are provided in pursuance of arrangements made under this paragraph for persons –

(a) who are or have been suffering from mental disorder within the meaning of the Mental Health Act 1983, or

(b) whose care is undertaken with a view to preventing them from becoming sufferers from mental disorder.

(9) 'Facilities' means facilities for training such persons or keeping them suitably occupied.

(10) This paragraph does not apply in relation to persons under the age of 18.

(11) No authority is authorised or may be required under this paragraph to provide residential accommodation for any person.

Home help and laundry facilities

3(1) Each local social services authority –

(a) must provide or arrange for the provision of, on such a scale as is adequate for the needs of its area, of home help for households where such help is required owing to the presence of a person to whom sub-paragraph (2) applies, and

(b) may provide or arrange for the provision of laundry facilities for households for which home help is being, or can be, provided under paragraph (a).

(2) This sub-paragraph applies to any person who –

(a) is suffering from illness,

(b) is pregnant or has recently given birth,

(c) is aged, or

(d) handicapped as a result of having suffered from illness or by congenital deformity.

Client group

9.140   The Act requires social services authorities to provide a variety of services for a diverse client group, certain services being restricted to particular client groups. There is no requirement that the persons be ordinarily resident within the social services authority's area.

9.141   The potential client group is wide, in that services can be provided for any adult in order to prevent illness – to which everyone is, of course, vulnerable. The provision of home help under NHSA 2006 Sch 20 para 3 has no age restriction on the person whose need triggers the service (ie, it applies to children as well as adults). It should also be noted that the provision of home helps is specified as being for the benefit of the 'household', rather than merely for the qualifying individual within the home.

9.142 NHSA 2006 Sch 20 (NHS(W)A 2006 Sch 15) paras 1 and 2 are subject to directions issued by the secretary of state (presently LAC (93)10 appendix 3[139] – see appendix 2 below where the full text of the directions is provided).

Mothers

9.143 The client group is restricted to 'expectant and nursing mothers (of any age)'.[140] The services available are without restriction, save only that the provision of accommodation is not permitted. The accommodation needs of such mothers are covered by NAA 1948 s21(1)(aa) (see para 0.00). It is difficult, however, to view this category (and that below of 'mothers lying in') as anything other than a historical anomaly. Either deriving from a 1948 concern about the dangers of child birth and the need for mothers to 'lie in' and rest prior to the birth – or perhaps more probably a throwback to Poor Law Amendment Act 1834 s62 which led to the prohibition of 'outdoor relief' for able-bodied persons and their families, and for whom relief would only be available in harsh workhouses. It has been argued that this put women in particular in an impossible position – forcing them to decide whether they were women or workers[141] – and hence the importance of being classified as an expectant or nursing mother for relief purposes.

The ill

9.144 NHSA 2006 s275(1) (NHS(W)A 2006 s206(1)) defines illness as including mental disorder within the meaning of the MHA 1983 and any injury or disability requiring medical or dental treatment or nursing. Persons who are alcoholic or drug-dependent are specifically included.[142] Services can also be provided for the purpose of preventing illness and for the after-care of persons who have been so suffering; the client group is therefore limited only by the size of the adult population.

9.145 The client group is generally restricted to persons aged 18 or over.[143] The exception to this general rule is that home help and laundry services (under para 3) are available to ill adults or children alike.

139 WOC 35/93 in Wales: by virtue of National Health Service (Consequential Provisions) Act 2006 s4 and Sch 2 para 1(2), directions issued in relation to the NHSA 1977 continue and apply with equal effect to the consequent provisions in the NHS Acts 2006.

140 LAC (93)10 appendix 3.

141 See M Levine-Clark, 'Engendering relief: women, ablebodiedness, and the new poor law in early Victorian England' (2000) 11(4) *Journal of Women's History* 107–130.

142 LAC (93)10 appendix 3 para 3(g); see chapter 23 below where services for alcohol and drug misusers are considered in greater detail.

143 NHSA 2006 Sch 20 (NHS(W)A 2006 Sch 15) para 2(10).

Mothers lying-in

9.146   At first sight it might appear incongruous that separate reference be made to mothers 'lying-in' (literally, 'being in childbed'), when nursing mothers are already included as a category (see above). The reason for this is related to the different services available. Where the need exists, there is a duty to provide home help for mothers lying in, whereas the other services available to expectant and nursing mothers are discretionary. The mother may be of any age (ie, over or under 18).

The aged

9.147   No definition is provided for 'aged'.[144] The overlap with the corresponding provision under HSPHA 1968 s45 (see para 20.16) is presumably explained on the basis that (where need for home help is assessed) section 45 services are discretionary whereas the NHS provision is obligatory.

The handicapped

9.148   The 'handicapped' person may be of any age (ie, over or under 18) and there is no requirement that the 'handicap' be either substantial or permanent (unlike the requirement in NAA 1948 s29 – see para 9.35 above); it must, however, result from either illness or congenital deformity. Those whose impairment results from injury are therefore excluded (NAA 1948 s29 covers this category if the consequent impairment is both permanent and substantial). The apparent lacuna is however largely academic – the definition of illness in the NHS Acts 2006 (as detailed above) includes an injury which requires medical or dental treatment or nursing – and the Acts cover the provision of services for the after-care of such persons.

Excluded groups

9.149   The effect of NHSA 2006 Sch 20 (NHS(W)A 2006 Sch 15) para 2(6) is to exclude from services people who are asylum seekers and are in need of community care services solely on account of being 'destitute' (see para 22.11 above).

Services

9.150   Before the implementation of the NHSCCA 1990, the services that could be provided under NHSA 1977 Sch 8 included the provision of accommodation. The NHSCCA 1990 by amendment[145] removed this power, and all social services authority community care accommodation obligations

---

144   See NAA 1948 s21, where no definition is given of 'age' and likewise HSPHA 1968 s45, which uses the phrase 'old people' – dealt with at paras 7.11 and 20.16 respectively.
145   NHSCCA 1990 Sch 9 para 18(4).

for adults (with the exception of their joint MHA 1983 s 117 obligations, see para 21.19) are now dealt with under the NAA 1948.[146]

9.151   NHSA 2006 Sch 20 paras 1–3 (NHS(W)A 2006 Sch 15 paras 1–2) deal with three separate services:

Paragraph 1   Services for expectant and nursing mothers;

Paragraph 2   Services for the prevention of illness, and the care and after-care of sufferers;

Paragraph 3   Home help and laundry services. This provision does not appear in the Welsh Act.

9.152   Paragraphs 1 and 2 follow the traditional community care drafting convention; they do not authorise the provision of any services but leave to the secretary of state the power to specify in directions what services may and what services must be provided. The most recent directions in this respect were issued on 17 March 1993 as LAC (93)10 appendix 3.[147] Although these pre-date the NHS Acts 2006, by virtue of National Health Service (Consequential Provisions) Act 2006 s4 and Sch 2 para 1(2) they apply with equal effect to the consequent provisions in the NHS Acts 2006.

9.153   Paragraph 3 is not however subject to directions, being a free-standing statutory provision. These three categories of services are dealt with separately below.

Services for expectant and nursing mothers

9.154   The directions merely state[148] that 'the Secretary of State approves the making of arrangements ... for the care of expectant and nursing mothers (of any age) other than the provision of accommodation for them'.[149] For mothers under the age of 18 there is of course an overlapping responsibility under CA 1989 Part III (if the mother or child are considered to be 'in need' – see para 24.4). No circular or other guidance has been issued concerning the nature or extent of these services – they remain at the discretion of the social services authority. There is no reason why the service provided by the social services authority should not include the giving of assistance in kind or, in exceptional circumstances, in cash.[150] The only restrictions (which follow from the actual wording of the direction) are that the service must be a 'care' service and that the service must be for the care of the mother (ie, not for the infant or anyone else in the household).

---

146 NAA 1948 s21 as amended by NHSCCA 1990 s42 (see LAC (93)10 para 6) – and the provision of certain hostel accommodation under NAA 1948 s29 – see para 7.156.

147 WOC 35/93 in Wales.

148 LAC (93)10 appendix 3 para 2.

149 Accommodation services being covered by NAA 1948 s21(1)(aa).

150 The general prohibition on making payment to service users under the community care legislation does not apply in this case; compare NAA 1948 s29(6)(a) and NHSA 2006 Sch 20 (NHS(W)A 2006 Sch 15) para 2(4) and also compare CA 1989 s17(6).

Services for the prevention of illness etc

9.155 Detailed directions have been issued in relation to the range of services that can be provided for the prevention of illness and the care and after-care of those who have been ill (see appendix B for the full text). While the directions oblige social services authorities to provide services for the prevention of mental disorder (or for the care of persons who have been suffering from mental disorder) they leave the provision of services for the alleviation of 'non-mental disorder' to the discretion of the social services authority. These two services are therefore dealt with separately below. The services are, in both cases, only available to adults and (subject to the specific exceptions detailed below) may not include the payment of money to the service user (although the availability of direct payments for such services, under the Health and Social Care Act 2001, has in large measure neutered this prohibition – see chapter 12 below).

The duty to provide services to alleviate mental disorder

9.156 The secretary of state's directions oblige social services authorities to make domiciliary care arrangements (detailed in items a) and b) below) for the purpose of preventing mental disorder, as well as for persons who are or who have been suffering from mental disorder[151] (see appendix B for full text). The directed services are the provision of:

a) centres (including training centres and day centres) or other facilities (including domiciliary facilities), whether in premises managed by the local authority or otherwise, for training or occupation of such persons, including the payment of persons engaged in suitable work at the 'centres or other facilities';[152]

b) social work and related services to help in the identification, diagnosis, assessment and social treatment of mental disorder and to provide social work support and other domiciliary and care services to people living in their own homes and elsewhere.

9.157 The directions would appear to be so widely drafted as to cover most of the commonly encountered domiciliary care services, ie, day centres, drop-in centres, educational, occupational and recreational facilities, transport, meals, home helps and so on. Accommodation services are, however, specifically excluded by NHSA 2006 Sch 20 (NHS(W)A 2006 Sch 15) para 2(11).

9.158 The directions additionally require local authorities to appoint sufficient social workers in their area to act as approved social workers for the purposes of the MHA 1983 and to make arrangements to enable them to exercise their guardianship functions under that Act.

---

151 LAC (93)10 appendix 3 para 3(2).

152 Ibid, para 3(3)(b) – but subject to NHSA 2006 Sch 20 (NHS(W)A 2006 Sch 15) para 2(5), which provides that the amount of such remuneration shall be limited to payment of such persons' occasional personal expenses if their work would not normally be remunerated.

9.159   As has been noted above (see para 9.58), NAA 1948 s29(6)(b) excludes services being provided under section 29 where such services are 'required to be provided' under the NHS Acts 2006. The inclusion of the phrase 'mental disorder of any description' within NAA 1948 s29 and in the secretary of state's direction relating to services under NHSA 2006 Sch 20 (NHS(W)A 2006 Sch 15) would tend to suggest that NAA 1948 s29 is of limited relevance to persons suffering from a mental disorder. It is, however, unlikely that this exclusion applies to services under CSDPA 1970 s2 (for the reasons stated by McCowan LJ noted at para 9.61 above). The tortuous relationship between the almost irreconcilable provisions in these Acts is so unsatisfactory, that only primary legislation can lead to a rational resolution.

The power to provide services to alleviate 'illness'

9.160   The secretary of state's direction empowers (but does not oblige) social services authorities to make the domiciliary care arrangements detailed below. In each case the service can only be provided for the purpose of either preventing illness, or for the care or after-care of a person suffering or recovering from an illness. The directed services are the provision of:

a)   Centres or other facilities for training such persons or for keeping them suitably occupied (and the equipment and maintenance of such centres), together with any other ancillary or supplemental services for such persons.[153] The services provided by a social services authority may include the payment of 'persons engaged in suitable work at the centres or other facilities'.[154] The equivalent services for disabled people (under CSDPA 1970 s2) are considered at para 9.77 and for elderly people (under HSPHA 1968 s45) at para 20.22.

b)   Meals at the centres referred to in a) above, or at other facilities (including domiciliary facilities) and meals-on-wheels for housebound people, provided they are not available under HSPHA 1968 s45(1)[155] or from a district council under HASSASSAA 1983 Sch 9 Part II para 1.[156] The equivalent services for disabled people (under the CSDPA 1970) are considered at para 9.122 and for elderly people (under the HSPHA 1968) at para 20.22.

c)   Social services (including advice and support) for the purposes of preventing the impairment of physical or mental health of adults in families where such impairment is likely, and for the purposes of preventing the break-up of such families, or for assisting in their rehabilitation; the equivalent services for disabled people (under NAA 1948 s29) are considered at para 9.41.

d)   Night-sitter services. Such a service is a specific form of 'practical

---

153   LAC (93)10 appendix 3 paras 3(1)(a) and (b).
154   See note 52 above.
155   See para 20.22.
156   The paragraph empowers a district council to make arrangements (or to employ a suitable voluntary organisation to make these arrangements) for providing meals and recreation for old people in their homes or elsewhere, see para 20.33 below.

assistance within the home' (as covered by CSDPA 1970 s2(1)(a)) and 'home help' (as covered by NHSA 2006 Sch 20 para 3 – see below). The inclusion of specific reference to this service is therefore probably unnecessary.

e)   Recuperative holidays. CSDPA 1970 s2(1)(f) covers holidays for disabled people (see para 9.119) and NAA 1948 s29 enables authorities to provide holiday homes (see para 9.50).

f)   Facilities for social and recreational activities; this is an equivalent power to the duty under CSDPA 1970 s2(1)(c) (see para 9.77) and under HSPHA 1968 s45 (see para 20.22).

g)   Services specifically for persons who are alcoholic or drug-dependent. Such services are considered separately in chapter 23.

Home help and laundry services

Home help

9.161   NHSA 2006 Sch 20 para 3 requires social services authorities to provide[157] a home help service for households where such help is required owing to the presence of a person who is suffering from illness, lying-in, or is an expectant mother, aged, or handicapped as a result of having suffered from illness or by congenital deformity.[158] The potential extent of the service, as well as the overlap (and differences) between this provision and that under CSDPA 1970 s2(1)(a) has been noted above. The NHSA 2006 home help service, unlike the 1970 Act service, can be provided for the benefit of 'the household' rather being restricted to the disabled service user's needs.

Laundry service

9.162   Social services authorities are empowered (but not obliged) to provide[159] a laundry service for households where they assess it as being required owing to the presence of a person who is suffering from illness, or lying-in, an expectant mother, aged, or handicapped as a result of having suffered from illness or by congenital deformity. Laundry services can therefore be provided in any situation where the Act enables the provision of home help; they are not, however, dependent on the household actually receiving that home help service.

9.163   The NHS has overlapping responsibilities for laundry services, particularly as a consequence of incontinence (see para 13.71) or the involvement of the district nursing services or as part of a continuing care package (see para 14.109).

---

157   Although the provision is not found in NHS(W)A 2006 this is because the definition of 'local authority' in NHSA 2006 s275 encompasses Welsh as well as English authorities. The services may either be provided by the authority or arranged by the authority but provided by another authority, a voluntary organisation or private person – see LAC (93)10 appendix 3 para 4.

158   NHSA 2006 Sch 20 para 3.

159   See para 9.2 above.

Charges for non-accommodation services

continued

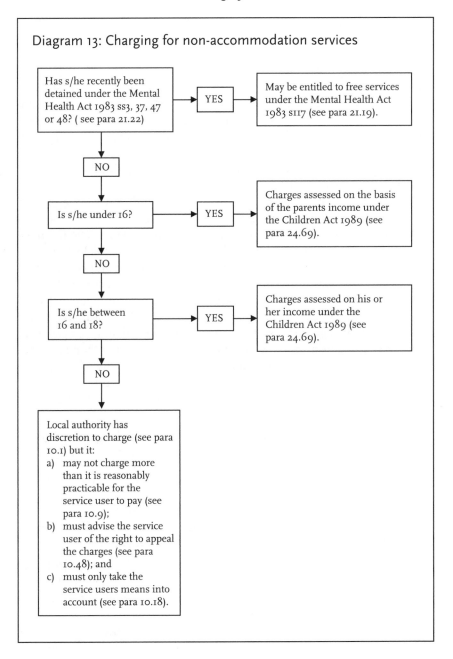

Diagram 13: Charging for non-accommodation services

Has s/he recently been detained under the Mental Health Act 1983 ss3, 37, 47 or 48? (see para 21.22)

YES

May be entitled to free services under the Mental Health Act 1983 s117 (see para 21.19).

NO

Is s/he under 16?

YES

Charges assessed on the basis of the parents income under the Children Act 1989 (see para 24.69).

NO

Is s/he between 16 and 18?

YES

Charges assessed on his or her income under the Children Act 1989 (see para 24.69).

NO

Local authority has discretion to charge (see para 10.1) but it:

a) may not charge more than it is reasonably practicable for the service user to pay (see para 10.9);

b) must advise the service user of the right to appeal the charges (see para 10.48); and

c) must only take the service users means into account (see para 10.18).

Introduction

10.1   The charging provisions for adult non-accommodation services are discretionary. Unlike the situation for residential accommodation, (1) local authorities are under no legal obligation to charge for these services and (2) there is no statutorily defined procedure for assessing non-accommodation charges. The discretionary power to charge for certain non-accommodation services derives from Health and Social Services and Social Security Adjudications Act (HASSASSAA) 1983 s17. Separate charging provisions relate to services provided under Children Act (CA) 1989 Part III, and these are considered at para 24.68.

10.2   The power to charge is one that most local authorities have chosen (albeit often with some reluctance) to employ. There are few authorities that do not make charges for non-accommodation services. The rationale for not charging is varied; it may be the political stance of the local authority, or a pragmatic decision that the costs of assessment and collection of the charges are likely to outweigh the amount collected. Local authorities are under considerable pressure from successive governments to charge. The 1990 policy guidance[1] states that it 'is expected that local authorities will institute arrangements so that users of services of all types pay what they can reasonably afford towards their costs', although it then adds that the provision of services should 'not be related to the ability of the user or their families to meet the costs'. The pressure on authorities to levy charges is also evident from LAC (94)1, which explained the position thus:

> 17. . . . The Government's view . . . has consistently been that users who can pay for such services should be expected to do so taking account of their ability to pay. The White Paper and Policy Guidance also make it clear that ability to pay should not influence decisions on the services to be provided, and the assessment of financial means should therefore follow the care assessment.
>
> 18. Authorities are locally accountable for making sensible and constructive use of the discretionary powers they have, in order to prevent avoidable burdens falling on council and national taxpayers.

10.3   Although the Welsh Assembly had sought to phase out charges for home care in a manifesto commitment in 2003, these plans were dropped in 2006 on the grounds that currently the plans could not be put in place 'equitably and affordably'.

10.4   Those authorities that charge have discretion as to how they set their charging policies, even though guidance issued in 2001[2] was aimed at bringing greater consistency in the way that local authorities charged for their services. Research undertaken on behalf of Age Concern in 2004[3] found:

1   *Community Care in the Next Decade and Beyond: Policy Guidance*, 1990, para 3.31.
2   *Fairer Charging Policies for Home Care and other Non-Residential Social Services*, issued by the Department of Health in 2001, and the National Assembly for Wales in 2002 (see para 10.13).
3   P Thompson and D Mathew, *Fair Enough?* Age Concern England, April 2004. Accessible at http://www.ageconcern.org.uk/AgeConcern/16B4C4516347460CB8D39EEAB4D50B6A.asp.

- 71 per cent of responding authorities set a maximum weekly charge, some charged the full cost and others had a banding system. The range of the maximum weekly charge was £23.50 to £400. Two authorities which responded did not charge.
- Hourly charges varied from £3.50 to £15.50 an hour: 35 per cent did not have any subsidy for hourly charges. For those that did, the subsidy varied from 4 per cent to 72 per cent. Some authorities had a variable hourly charge.
- Most followed the capital limits suggested in the guidance. Ten did not have an upper capital limit and four had a higher capital limit. Some offered more generous tariff income rates.
- Most counted the severe disability premium and attendance allowance or disability living allowance (care) as assessable income.
- A minority allowed extra additions or only charged against a percentage of income on top of the sum below which they could not charge (£131.81 at that time in the case of older people).
- 60 per cent undertook individual assessments of disability-related expenditure; 9 per cent ignored part or all of disability benefits instead; 18 per cent gave a standard allowance ranging from £10 to £40 a week.

10.5   Most striking was a hypothetical case study whereby 65 of the responding local authorities calculated a charge for a person needing ten hours of care and two sessions at day care. The charges varied from £0–£103. The variation was mainly due to the way disability related costs were calculated or whether there was a maximum charge.

10.6   A more recent survey in 2006 found similar variations in charges.[4] But whatever the variations, there is a general trend for rates to increase for those who have to pay the full cost or the maximum charge. A *Public Finance* survey in 2007 found that English councils were proposing to increase their fees for home care by an average of 23 per cent and for day centres by 31 per cent.[5]

10.7   There is general disquiet about the current system[6] and the perverse incentives it can produce, either for authorities to place people in residential care if they can then access funds through sale of the resident's former home, or where charges act as a disincentive for people to get the care they need until they reach a crisis. This latter point was made in a joint report by the All Party Parliamentary Groups on Primary Care and Public Health and Social Care[7] which concluded that 'the level of charges for domiciliary social care is very unpopular with service users and acts as a deterrent

---

4   *Care Contradictions: Higher Charges Fewer Services*, Counsel and Care, 2006. Accessible at http://www.counselandcare.org.uk/influence/publications.
5   Public Finance Magazine, 27 April 2007, accessible at http://www.publicfinance.co.uk/features_details.cfm?News_id=30450.
6   See eg *Securing Good Care for Older People – Wanless Social Care Review*, King's Fund, March 2006.
7   Report of Joint Inquiry by the Primary Care and Public Health and Social Care All Party Parliamentary Groups, *Our health, our care, our say*, November 2006, p33.

from using such services for those with income above entitlement to free provision. This often leads to earlier use of more expensive institutional care.'

The statutory framework for charges

10.8   HASSASSAA 1983 s17[8] provides as follows:

(1) Subject to subsection (3) below, an authority providing a service to which this section applies may recover such charge (if any) for it as they consider reasonable.

(2) This section applies to services provided under the following enactments:

(a) section 29 of the National Assistance Act 1948 (welfare arrangements for disabled persons);

(b) section 45(1) of the Health Services and Public Health Act 1968 (welfare of old people);

(c) schedule 20 to the National Health Service Act 2006 or Schedule 15 to the National Health Service (Wales) Act 2006.

(d) section 8 of the Residential Homes Act 1980[9] (meals and recreation for old people); and

(e) paragraph 1 of Part II of Schedule 9 to this Act, other than the provision of services for which payment may be required under section 22 or 26 of the National Assistance Act 1948.

(f) section 2 of the Carers and Disabled Children Act 2000.

(3) If a person –

(a) avails himself of a service to which this section applies, and

(b) satisfies the authority providing the service that his means are insufficient for it to be reasonably practicable for him to pay for the service the amount which he would otherwise be obliged to pay for it,

the authority shall not require him to pay more for it than it appears to them that it is reasonably practicable for him to pay.

(4) Any charge under this section may, without prejudice to any other method of recovery, be recovered summarily as a civil debt.

Not reasonably practicable

10.9   HASSASSAA 1983 s17 enables local authorities to make reasonable charges for non-residential services, but also requires that they have procedures for reducing or waiving the charge where it is not *'reasonably practicable'* for the user to pay the full charge. The framework to help local authorities decide what is reasonable is now contained in policy and practice guidance – see para 10.13.

---

8   The power was formerly to be found under NAA 1948 s29(5) which provided that '[a] local authority may recover from persons availing themselves of any service provided under this Section such charges (if any) as, having regard to the cost of the service, the authority may determine, whether generally or in the circumstances of any particular case'.

9   Repealed by HASSASSAA 1983 s30, Sch 10 Part I.

10.10   The local government ombudsman has held that it was maladministration for an authority to adopt a charging policy which only permitted
exceptions if users provided 'proof of hardship'[10] since this was a materially more severe criterion than 'not reasonably practicable'. Likewise in *R
v Calderdale DC ex p Houghton*[11] the local authority conceded that its procedures for assessing the reasonableness of its charges were unreasonably
demanding: they required that applicants establish that their expenditure
was so exceptional that it was not reasonable for the authority to charge
the full amount.

10.11   The ombudsman has further held that where a claimant had produced
evidence that her expenditure exceeds her income, the authority cannot
insist on her paying the full charge without providing cogent reasons why
it considers her able to pay the amount claimed.[12]

10.12   In *Avon CC v Hooper*[13] (an unusual fact case) the Court of Appeal considered the interpretation of 'reasonably practicable to pay'. Hobhouse LJ
considered the interpretation of section 17(3) in the following terms:[14]

> If the local authority decides to charge and is acting reasonably [under
> section 17(1)] . . . the person availing himself of the service has . . . to satisfy
> the authority under subsection (3) that his means are insufficient for it to
> be reasonably practicable for him to pay the amount which he would
> otherwise be obliged to pay. It is for the recipient of the service to discharge
> this burden of persuasion. He must show that he has insufficient means.
> The time at which he has to do this is the time when the local authority is
> seeking to charge him for the services. If his means have been reduced, as
> might be the case with a business man whose business had run into
> difficulties after his being injured, the reduction in his means is something
> upon which he would be entitled to rely as making it impracticable for him
> to pay, even though at an earlier date he might have been better off. The
> consideration under subsection (3)(b) is the practical one: are his means
> such that it is not reasonably practicable for him to pay?
>
> This also bears on the alternative argument . . . that only cash should be
> taken into account. This is too narrow a reading of subsection (3). As a
> matter of the ordinary use of English, the word 'means' refers to the
> financial resources of a person: his assets, his sources of income, his
> liabilities and expenses. If he has a realisable asset, that is part of his
> means; he has the means to pay. The subject matter of paragraph (b) is the
> practicability of his paying. If he has an asset which he can reasonably be
> expected to realise and which will (after taking into account any other
> relevant factor) enable him to pay, his means make it practicable for him to
> pay.
>
> Where the person has a right to be indemnified by another against the cost
> of the service, he has the means to pay. He can enforce his right and make
> the payment. There is nothing in any part of section 17 which suggests

10 Complaint nos 99/C/02509 and 02624 against Gateshead, 28 February 2001.
11 Unreported but see 1999 2 CCLR 119.
12 Complaint nos 99/C/02509 and 02624 against Gateshead, 28 February 2001.
13 [1997] 1 WLR 1605; (1998) 1 CCLR 366.
14 Ibid at 371E–K.

that it is intended that subsection (3) should have the effect of relieving those liable to indemnify the recipient of the service for the cost of the service from their liability. On the contrary, it is clear that the intention of the section is to enable the local authority to recover the cost save when it is unreasonable that it should do so or impracticable for the recipient to pay.

Policy guidance

10.13   Until 2001 no national policy guidance on non-accommodation charges existed, with the result that very wide disparities existed in the charges levied by social services authorities. In its white paper *Modernising Social Services*[15] the government acknowledged these local variations and committed itself to establish greater consistency and fairness.[16] This was realised in November 2001 with the publication by the Department of Health of *Fairer Charging Policies for Home Care and other non-residential Social Services*[17] and in July 2002 when the Welsh Assembly issued similar guidance[18] (both under Local Authority Social Services Act (LASSA) 1970 s7). The current guidance in England was issued as an update in September 2003 (to reflect the introduction of the pension credit)[19] and is referred to in this chapter as the '2003 policy guidance'. The guidance in Wales was only partially implemented, because of the manifesto commitment to introduce free home care. Since this proposal has now been dropped, new guidance was issued in March 2007 which introduces certain changes to Fairer Charging which came into effect on 9 April 2007.[20] Where the Welsh policy differs from the English policy this will be noted in the text.

10.14   The key principles embodied in the English and Welsh policy guidance can be summarised as follows:

1) Councils are not obliged to charge for non-residential social services.
2) Flat-rate charges are acceptable only in limited circumstances (for instance where they are a substitute for ordinary living costs – such as for meals on wheels or meals at a day centre).
3) Net incomes should not be reduced below basic income support levels or the guarantee credit of pension credit, plus a buffer of 25 per cent; 'basic levels' of income support includes the personal allowance and all premiums, but it 'need not include the Severe Disability Premium' (para 18).[21] The latest Welsh guidance gives a buffer of 'no less than' 35 per cent.

15   Cm 4169, 1998.
16   Ibid, para 2.31.
17   LAC (2001)32.
18   NAFWC 28/2002.
19   Accessible at http://www.dh.gov.uk/en/Publicationsandstatistics/Publications/ PublicationsPolicyAndGuidance/DH_4117930.
20   NAFWC 11/07.
21   Because the buffer is based on benefits which are paid at different rates according to age, it leads to large differences between what younger disabled people and older people are able to keep. A few authorities try to avoid this potential age discrimination by using the more generous pension credit rates for younger people.

4) Councils should consider and specifically consult on the need to set a maximum charge.

5) Where disability benefits are taken into account as income in assessing ability to pay a charge, councils should assess the individual user's disability-related expenditure; councils should specifically consult on the need to assess disability-related expenditure for other users. It is not acceptable to make a charge on disability benefits without assessing the reasonableness of doing so for each user. In Wales councils must ensure that *all* service users have a disability expenditure disregard of 10 per cent of the 'basic' level of income support and appropriate guarantee pension credit level. If service users believe they have expenditure above this amount they can apply for a further disregard based on their individual expenditure.[22]

6) Councils should ensure that comprehensive benefits advice is provided to all users at the time of a charge assessment. Councils have a responsibility to seek to maximise the incomes of users, where they would be entitled to benefits, particularly where the user is asked to pay a charge.

7) As a minimum, the same savings limits as for residential care charges should be applied. Councils are free to operate more generous rules, as with other parts of the guidance.

8) 'To ensure that disabled people and their carers, who wish to do so, are able to enter and progress in work', the guidance requires earnings (including tax credits) to be disregarded in charge assessments.

9) Any savings credit paid under the pension credit arrangements is disregarded.

10.15 Examples of the practical application of these principles were provided in the September 2003 policy guidance.[23] Diagram 14 reproduces one of these examples, although the figures have been updated to show the amount of the charge for 2007–08.

Practice guidance

10.16 In August 2002 practice guidance concerning the home care charging policy was issued by the Department of Health with the Department for Work and Pensions. The notable points in this important guidance include:

- It favours the creation of a specialist service, separating financial assessment from assessment of care needs (para 27); these financial assessments should normally be carried out by personal interview in the user's own home.
- Users who may be entitled to benefits which would bring them within charging, may be given an 'interim assessment' so that the local authority has the option of backdating the charge assessment against

22 NAFWC 11/07 annex A and para 11.
23 2003 policy guidance annex D.

Diagram 14: Examples from the 2003 policy guidance of the application of home care charging rules (updated applicable figures for 2007/08)		
All the examples detailed below relate to a hypothetical 66-year-old single person, with disability-related benefits and £25 disability-related expenditure		
Pension credit only	**Occupational pensioner**	**Occupational pensioner, higher income**
Basic state pension £87.30 + Guarantee credit £31.75 + Additional amount for severe disability £48.45 + AA £43.15	Basic state pension £87.30 + occupational pension £120.00 + AA £43.15	Basic state pension £87.30 + occupational pension £400.00 + AA £43.15 + Savings £15,000, tariff income = £8.00
Assessable income £210.65	Assessable income £250.45	Assessable income £538.45
Deduct £119.05 + (25%) £29.76 £148.81 Deduct: Rent/housing Nil Council tax Nil Disability-related [£25.00] Dietary £6.00 Extra heating £7.00 Cleaner £7.00 Gardening services £5.00	Deduct £119.05 + (25%) £29.76 £148.81 Deduct: Rent/housing £42.00 Council tax £15.00 Disability-related [£25.00] Dietary £6.00 Extra heating £7.00 Cleaner £7.00 Gardening services £5.00	Deduct £119.05 + (25%) £229.76 £148.81 Deduct: Rent/housing Nil Council tax £15.00 Disability-related [£25.00] Dietary £6.00 Extra heating £7.00 Cleaner £7.00 Gardening services £5.00
Total deductions £173.81	Total deductions £230.83	Total deductions £188.81
Assessable income remaining = £36.84 Actual charge depends on hours of care, subject to assessable income remaining.	Assessable income remaining = £19.62 Actual charge depends on hours of care, subject to assessable income remaining.	Assessable income remaining = £349.64 Actual charge depends on hours of care, subject to assessable income remaining and any maximum.

any backdated benefits award: however the guidance notes that this is 'an issue for local policy' (para 35).

- Spending not incurred, as an unmet need, should not be allowed (para 36). However where disability benefit has been newly awarded, an assessment should be capable of review to take account of the likelihood of the disabled person increasing his or her disability related expenditure due to the higher level of income (para 37).

- Research informing the practice guidance (undertaken in Torbay in 1999/2000) showed that 34 per cent of those assessed had disability related expenditure above £40 per week, and 49 per cent above £30 (para 44).
- Para 46 provides a detailed list of typical disability related expenditure, and how local authorities might cost this including:
  - community alarm;
  - private care arrangements, including respite care. In *R (Stephenson) v Stockton-on-Tees BC*[24] the Court of Appeal held that it was unlawful for a local authority to apply inflexibly a general rule that payments made to family members for help with personal care were not deemed to be 'disability related expenditure';
  - specialist washing powders;
  - laundry;
  - specialist diets;
  - clothing/footwear;
  - additional bedding (eg because of incontinence);
  - extra heating or water (standard rates suggested for heating; and councils must ignore winter fuel/cold weather payments);
  - garden maintenance;
  - cleaning or domestic help – the cost of private cleaning services should be allowed when they are not provided through social services, and 'consideration should be given to higher needs for cleaning as a consequence of disability and the needs of carers';
  - purchase, maintenance and repair of disability related equipment;
  - personal assistance costs – eg paying for the meals or transport costs for personal assistants or carers;
  - other transport costs 'over and above the Mobility Component of DLA';
  - it may be reasonable for a council not to allow costs where a reasonable alternative *is available* at lesser cost.
- Information about how to complain should be available as a matter of routine (para 64).

Services that must be provided free

10.17 Certain non-accommodation services must be provided free of charge, and these include:

- services under Mental Health Act (MHA) 1983 s117 (see para 21.41 below);
- intermediate care services[25] (see chapter 11);

---

24 [2005] EWCA Civ 960; (2005) 8 CCLR 517.
25 In England this is established by Community Care (Delayed Discharges etc) Act (CC(DD)A) 2003 s15 and the subsequent Regulations 2003 SI No 1196. In Wales the CC(DD)A 2003 has not been implemented but NAFWC 43/02; WHC (2002)128 para 22 states that intermediate care should not attract charges.

- (in England[26]) community equipment, and in the case of minor adaptations where the cost is £1,000 or less including the cost of buying and fitting.[27] Councils retain the discretion to charge if a minor adaptation costs more than £1,000. The guidance[28] is silent on the position when a number of minor adaptations are required simultaneously which together cost more than £1,000 for the buying and fitting. It is arguable that each should count as a minor adaptation of less than £1,000 and so be free of charge. See para 9.97 for details on the interface between adaptations under Chronically Sick and Disabled Persons Act (CSDPA) 1970 s2 and the housing provisions for disabled facilities grants (DFGs);

- services provided to persons suffering from any form of Creuzfeldt Jacob Disease (CJD);[29]

- advice about the availability of services or assessment including the assessment of community care needs.[30] Councils also cannot include in the cost of the service, the associated costs of the purchasing function or the costs of operating the charging system.[31]

Assessable income and assets

10.18　HASSASSAA 1983 s17(3) directs local authority attention to the question of whether a service user's means are sufficient for it to be reasonably practicable for him or her to pay for the service. It follows that the question concerns the service user's means alone and that 'any means test must be confined to the means of the service user'.[32] The 2003 policy guidance reinforces this advice stating:

> 62. Section 17 of the HASSASSA Act 1983 envisages that councils will have regard only to an individual user's means in assessing ability to pay a charge.

26　The Welsh Assembly has indicated that it has no intention of bringing CC(DD)A 2003 Part 1 into effect in Wales (the part that deals with fines for delayed discharge). It has not however (as yet) indicated whether or not it will bring into effect the 'free service' provisions under Part 2.

27　It is often mistakenly believed that equipment is only free if it is £1,000 or less. However the Community Care (Delayed Discharges etc) Act (Qualifying Services) (England) Regulations 2003 SI No 1196 only define an *adaptation* as minor if the cost of making the adaptation is £1,000 or less.

28　LAC (2003)14.

29　2003 policy guidance para 75 (para 63 in the Welsh guidance). Since this guidance was written provisions have been made for those in residential care to have any payments made in relation to people who have been infected with Hepatitis C as a result of NHS treatment with blood or blood products – see para 8.47. It might therefore be arguable that at the very least such payments should be ignored for the purposes of charging for home care.

30　2003 policy guidance para 8 (para 10 in the Welsh guidance).

31　2003 policy guidance para 77 (para 65 in the Welsh guidance).

32　Social Services Inspectorate Guidance issued in January 1994 (ostensibly as advice to its own officers) para 12.

63. This will mean that parents and other members of an adult user's family cannot be required to pay the charges, except in certain legal circumstances, for example, where a family member may be managing the user's own resources.

10.19 There will of course be situations where assets belonging to the service user are in fact held in the name of a third party, such as under a power of attorney, a receivership order or a simple trust arrangement. In such cases the assets, although administered by a third party, clearly belong to the service user and can be taken into account in the means test. In this respect the 2003 policy guidance advises:

64. Councils may wish to consider in individual cases whether a user's means may include resources not held in that person's name, but to which the user has a legal entitlement. The most likely instances of this kind will arise in relation to married or unmarried couples. In some circumstances, the user may have a legal right to a share in the value of an asset, for example a bank account, even if it is not in his or her name. In some circumstances, statutory provisions provide such a right. In other circumstances, what are known as 'equitable principles' may apply to give such a right, for example where there is an unwritten agreement between partners that they both own a property or an asset, even though the title is in only one of their names. If the council has some reason to believe that the user does have means other than those initially disclosed, a request may reasonably be made for the user to arrange for the partner to disclose his or relevant resources. If there is no such disclosure, the council may consider that it is not satisfied that the user has insufficient means to pay the charge for the service. It will be for the council to consider each case in the light of their own legal advice.

Couples

10.20 The above advice places local authorities in some difficulties. Before a council can ask the user to arrange for the partner to disclose his or her finances if must have some reason for believing the user does have means other than those that have been disclosed. The user might not be in a position to insist that the partner disclose his or her assets. In some cases it will be the service user who owns the majority of the income or assets, and thus a charge based purely on his or her means could leave the couple in financial difficulties. The National Association of Finance Officers has issued its own advice which many local authorities appear to follow which suggests that couples should be given the option of a single or a joint assessment and can then choose the assessment that is most beneficial to them.

10.21 However research undertaken in 2004[33] found that while nearly all authorities did not take the partner's income into account or only did so in order to maximise the couple's income, six authorities stated they would charge the full cost if the partner refused to disclose his or her income and a further 11 authorities said they would in some cases. Some assessment

---

33 P Thompson and D Mathew, *Fair Enough?* Age Concern England, April 2004.

forms (seen as part of the research) asked a partner to give information but gave no reasons as to why this was being requested; others did not ask for partners' resources at all. A hypothetical case study revealed that within those few authorities which charged against the partner there was considerable variation in what aspects of the partners' resources were taken into account. Some took the income only, one took the capital only and some took both.

10.22   It is surprising, given the confusing nature of the guidance, that decisions to charge against a partner's resources have not yet been challenged to any great extent. Anecdote suggests that local authorities will back down if challenged. In only one case (which was an unusual fact case as the couple were estranged but living in the same house) has guidance been sought as to whether a local authority could take into account the resources of a partner when deciding whether adaptations to the partner's property under CSDPA 1970 s2 were necessary. However it left the point open as the judge concluded that the rights to a DFG should be considered, before considering issues under section 2.[34]

Assessment of income

10.23   Certain income is excluded from the charging calculation. This includes any earnings, tax credits, any pension credit savings credit (see para 10.14) and any income received from the Independent Living (1993) Fund.[35] Para 72 of the 2003 policy guidance advises that 'earnings' should have the same meaning as in the Charging for Residential Accommodation Guide (CRAG) – which at para 9.001 defines 'earnings' in terms of 'any remuneration or profit derived from employment' and at para 9.002 specifically excludes as earnings income from (among other things) any occupational pension.

10.24   Although disability living allowance (DLA) (care component) and attendance allowance can be taken into account, this is only in relation to services provided for the time of day for which the allowance is paid. In *R v Coventry City Council ex p Carton*[36] the local authority changed its non-residential care charges so that there was no automatic disregard for the night component of higher rate DLA for service users receiving day care only. The court held that it was irrational, unlawful and unfair for the council to apply a charging policy which treated as income available for day care sums of DLA paid in respect of night care.

10.25   In addition the mobility component of DLA must be disregarded.[37] The Welsh Ombudsman has found maladministration where a new service

---

34 *R (Fay) v Essex CC* [2004] EWHC 879 (Admin). Another case involved an adaptation for a child where the authority was exercising its CA 1989 s17 functions by providing services under CSDPA 1970 s2. In this case it was found that the parent's means were relevant in respect to children: *R (Spink) v Wandsworth LBC* [2005] EWCA Civ 302; (2005) 8 CCLR 272. Cases involving children are less likely to arise under CSDPA 1970 s2 as there is no longer a charge for DFGs for children (see para 15.77).
35 2003 policy guidance para 74.
36 (2001) 4 CCLR 41.
37 Social Security Contributions and Benefits Act 1992 s73(14) requires this benefit to be disregarded in any charging scheme – see the 2003 policy guidance at para 30.

user was told she could not use the transport to a day centre because she was in receipt of DLA mobility component. This did not apply to existing service users. She therefore had to use taxis and found this too expensive. Systematic maladministration was found on the basis there was an absence of any policy framework and no written guidelines on the eligibility of clients who could use local authority run transport.[38]

Assessment of capital

10.26 The 2003 policy guidance (and the Welsh guidance) state that as a minimum councils should use the upper capital limit as set out in CRAG (see para 8.40). The value of the home may not be taken into account, but apart from that councils are told 'other forms of capital may be taken into account as set out in CRAG'.[39] This then begs the question of how far local authorities should follow guidance that operates under a different legislative regime. In *Crofton v NHS Litigation Authority*[40] Dyson LJ held as follows:

> Section VIII 'includes the minimum requirements for treatment of savings' (paragraph 57). There is no difference between 'savings' and 'capital'. That is clear from the first sentence of paragraph 57 viz: 'Councils may take account of a user's savings or *other capital*' (emphasis added). Paragraph 59 states unequivocally that the main residence occupied by the user should not be taken into account. The sentence continues: 'but other forms of capital may be taken into account, as set out in CRAG'. This wording is not happily expressed. But in our view it means that the CRAG rules for determining what capital should be taken into account are imported in their entirety, on the footing that local authorities have a discretion to treat a person's capital more generously. It follows that, if CRAG stipulates that certain items of capital are to be disregarded, then the Fairer Charging Policy requires the local authority to exercise its discretion in the same way.

10.27 This view may be helpful in ensuring that items not mentioned in the 2003 policy guidance are disregarded – for instance disregarding payments made in relation to people who have been infected with Hepatitis C as a result of NHS treatment with blood or blood products. This was introduced into the National Assistance (Assessment of Resources) Regulations in 2004 after the last update of the Fairer Charging guidance. The question must remain about guidance setting a framework for establishing the reasonableness of charges under HASSASSAA 1983 s17, by reference to CRAG which operates under a separate regulatory regime – namely NAA 1948 s22. This could be contentious, for example, if an authority considered that a person had deprived him/herself of capital and sought to argue that he or she had 'notional capital' for the purposes of setting the charge for non-residential care. It is arguable that in the absence of an enabling legislative provision, local authorities have no

38 Case no B2004/0180 against Newport City Council, 31 August 2006.
39 2003 policy guidance para 59 (para 48 in Welsh guidance).
40 [2007] EWCA Civ 71; [2007] 1 WLR 923; (2007) 10 CCLR 123.

power under HASSASSAA 1983 s17 to assume deprivation of capital, and so adopt such a notional capital rule. Local authorities should therefore keep the discretionary nature of the section 17 power at the forefront of their decision processes: in every case ensuring that the decision on charging is based upon whether it is reasonably practicable for the person to pay, and only pray in aid the CRAG guidance when it does not conflict with this overriding requirement.

Personal injury payments and domiciliary care charges

10.28   As for residential care (see para 8.57) there have been a number of cases relating to whether payments for care costs should be included in a personal injury award if local authorities are not able to charge against them. In the Court of Appeal case *Crofton v NHS Litigation Authority*,[41] referring to an earlier case where another claimant wanted to set up care in her own home via a direct payment, May LJ in relation to the capital award commented:

> 93. In *Freeman v Lockett*, Tomlinson J decided that there should be no reduction in the claimant's damages to reflect the possibility of direct payments by the local authority. A sufficient basis for his decision was his finding that, provided that no deduction on account of the possible receipt of state or local authority funding was made from her award of damages, the claimant would withdraw her application for funding; she wanted to rely exclusively on private funding for her care.

> 94. But he would in any event have refused to make any reduction in the claimant's damages on account of direct payments for other reasons. He said that there was no principled basis on which the court could estimate what funding the claimant could reliably expect to receive from the local authority for the rest of her life. The court 'does not speculate unnecessarily or in an unprincipled manner . . . I cannot understand how it can be appropriate to impose upon the Claimant the unnecessary risk that funding from an alternative source may cease or be reduced rather than simply to order the provision of the fund in its entirety' (paragraph 35).

> 95. In making these observations, Tomlinson J was influenced by the fragility of the policy from which the right to receive direct payments derived. He said that 'in the ordinary way, the regime pursuant to which direct payments are made for domiciliary care is very much more vulnerable to adjustment in order to save costs than is the direct provision of residential care' (paragraph 38).

> 96. We would accept that there may be cases where the possibility of a claimant receiving direct payments is so uncertain that they should be disregarded altogether in the assessment of damages. It will depend on the facts of the particular case. But if the court finds that a claimant will receive direct payments for at least a certain period of time and possibly for much longer, it seems to us that this finding must be taken into account in the assessment. In such a case, the correct way to reflect the uncertainties to which Tomlinson J referred is to discount the multiplier.

41   [2007] EWCA Civ 71; [2007] 1 WLR 923; (2007) 10 CCLR 123.

10.29   Although the court was able to be certain that the capital from the award would be disregarded in the case of domiciliary care because of the link in the 2003 policy guidance to CRAG[42] (see para 8.10 above), it was far from clear how income derived from the capital would be treated in the discretionary regime of HASSASSAA 1983 s17. Referring to para 22 of the 2003 policy guidance the court reflected:

> But it seems to us unlikely that the phrase 'other income' is intended to include investment income. The words in brackets 'usually disability-related benefits' and the reference to the explanation in the next section (which is headed 'Treatment of disability-related benefits') strongly suggest that paragraph 22 is not intended to apply to investment income. But whether there is a lacuna or paragraph 22 does apply, the treatment of investment income is a matter for the discretion of the local authority, untrammelled by any guidance in the Fairer Charging Policy as to how it should be exercised. The question arises, therefore, how in the exercise of its discretion the Council would treat income derived from the claimant's damages. (para 84)

10.30   The court concluded that it could not decide whether the income derived from an award of damages would affect the amount of direct payment the council would make to the claimant. The same difficulties would apply to care provided or arranged by the council. The case was remitted back for a further hearing with the comment:

> 110. In view of the difficulty of the relevant legislation and guidance, the size of the care costs and the fact that the claimant will need care for the rest of his life, we think that it would be highly desirable if the Council were joined as a party to the proceedings.
>
> 111. We cannot conclude this judgment without expressing our dismay at the complexity and labyrinthine nature of the relevant legislation and guidance, as well as (in some respects) its obscurity. Social security law should be clear and accessible. The tortuous analysis in the earlier part of this judgment shows that it is neither.

10.31   It would seem that unless the 2003 policy guidance is made clearer as to the treatment of income or, as indicated in this judgment and others, parliament decides whether the cost for care in damages cases should fall on the public purse or the tortfeasor, the question of the treatment of damages awards is likely to remain a thorny matter.

Expenditure and costs

Disability related expenditure

10.32   The 2003 policy guidance is clear that authorities must take account of disability related expenditure if they take disability related benefits into account. It is very much at the discretion of the local authority as to what it

---

42 For a commentary by the Public Guardianship Office on this subject see http://www.guardianship.gov.uk/news/newsforprofessionals_481.htm.

will take into account, and variations are wide.[43] The latest Welsh[44] guidance has to some extent recognised this by allowing a set rate in all cases (see para 10.14 above) with the ability for users to ask for an individual assessment if their expenditure is above this amount. The advantage is that all users will have a token amount recognised without having to face intrusive questions and prove expenditure. Whether this amount has been set high enough to enable the vast majority of user to accept it without a further individual assessment is questionable.

Capital expenditure and equipment repairs

10.33 It is in general not unlawful for a local authority to adopt a policy that purchase of a capital item (for instance an electrical reclining bed) should be amortised over the life of the item – ie if the item costs £1,800 and the local authority consider it to have a life of ten years – then this would equate to a weekly disability related expenditure of £3.46. However it is unlikely that it would be reasonable to adopt the same approach to the repair costs for such equipment.[45]

Housing costs

10.34 The 2003 policy guidance (at para 21) explains that income should be assessed as net of housing costs less any housing benefit or council tax benefit. It adds that some councils might wish to consider other costs such as home insurance and water charges. Thus in a fairly straightforward case of a home owner without a mortgage, variations can exist between authorities.[46]

10.35 The 2003 policy guidance is silent on the position of housing costs where service users are living with their families. Most often this is where disabled adults live with their parents, or older people with adult children. Practice appears to be varied as to whether any housing costs are allowed for either a contribution towards council tax or rent. If the family are charging for housing costs it would be unreasonable for a local authority not to allow these given that housing costs are always considered to be a priority in any debt situation. On the basis that charges should be designed so that they do not undermine the independence and social inclusion of service users[47] it is arguable the amount allowed for rent and other housing costs in such cases should be set at a level based on what the person would pay for equivalent accommodation on a shared basis if it did not happen to be owned or rented by the person's family, along with his or her proportion of council tax.

43 In one of the case studies in *Fair Enough?* the amount allowed by local authorities for a list of disability related expenditure ranged from £4.09–£70.38.
44 NAFWC 11/07 annex A.
45 *R (Stephenson) v Stockton-on-Tees BC* [2004] EWHC 2228 (Admin); (2004) 7 CCLR 459.
46 P Thompson and D Mathew, *Fair Enough?* Age Concern England, April 2004. The case study showed a range from £11.02–£32.55 being allowed as housing costs.
47 2003 policy guidance para 3 (para 6 in the Welsh guidance).

10.36   Even if the family does not charge a specific rent it is arguable that at the very least local authorities should consider making an allowance based on the non-dependent deduction for housing and council tax benefit, in recognition of the fact that adults are expected to contribute towards their housing costs.[48] As a general principle, local authorities should not rely on relatives (who are often the carers) to subsidise service users further, by not leaving the user enough money to make a contribution to household expenses.

Costs of transport to services

10.37   The 2003 policy guidance warns councils against flat rate charges other than for meals where it is argued that the service user would have to pay for food in any case. However it is not uncommon for local authorities to have a similar flat rate charge for transport to and from services such as day care. In part this is to avoid having to conduct lengthy financial assessments on people whose only service is for day care (which in some councils is still free). As transport to the day care service will have been assessed as part of the service user's needs, it should not be charged in isolation, but be part of the whole cost of the care package. Service users should only pay for transport if they can afford to do so according to the local authority policy. Adding a flat rate charge for transport to the service is in effect adding an extra charge to the individual over and above that which he or she has been assessed as being able to pay.

Local charging schemes: the duty to consult

10.38   HASSASSAA 1983 s17(1) requires local authorities to set a rate that they consider 'reasonable'. This necessarily requires the consideration of a variety of factors – including the views of service users.

10.39   The 2003 policy guidance makes several references to consultation including:

- Consultation is one of the guiding principles and '[w]here changes in charging policies would result in significant increases in charges for some users, this should be specifically explained and considered as part of the consultation' (paras 98 and 99);
- Users should be specifically consulted on whether and how to set an overriding maximum charge (para 17);

---

48   Although most service users are not likely to be working, and may well be on the type of benefit that would in reality preclude a non-dependent deduction for housing benefit, it could be argued, for the purposes of an allowance against charges, that housing costs should be set at least to an equivalent of non-dependent deduction amounts based on the earned income levels which increase as income levels rise. For instance individuals with an income of £111–£163.99 per week are expected to contribute £17 towards rent and £2.30 towards council tax rising on a sliding scale to £47.75 (rent) and £6.95 (council tax) if their income is £353 or more per week.

- Consultation should be used to establish what is a reasonable level of charge and the government expects all the issues that the guidance addresses to be explained to users and carers as part of the consultation (para 80(i) and (xi)).

10.40   The 1996 *Good Practice Handbook* (see para 10.50) stressed the importance of consultation with service users concerning the development and piloting of charging procedures and emphasised that a realistic timescale needed to be set for the consultation process before any changes took place. It noted that 'the experience of local authorities suggests that consultation will take months'.[49] Research into the implementation of the Fairer Charging policy found that the time for consultation varied from one week to 65 weeks with over half of the responding authorities reporting that the consultation was between three and eight weeks.[50]

10.41   Prior to the 2003 policy guidance the court criticised the lack of consultation. In *R v Coventry City Council ex p Carton*[51] the local authority changed its non-residential care charges so that (among other things) there was no automatic disregard for the night component of higher rate DLA for service users receiving day care only. The Administrative Court held that before fundamental changes of this nature could be made to a charging structure, there had to be proper consultation with users.

10.42   The local government ombudsman has also been critical of charging schemes that have been introduced with undue haste, ie before the procedures for their implementation were in place.[52] More recently maladministration was found where the council failed to consult with service users prior to the introduction of a policy from scratch which made it 'more of an imperative for it to ensure it consulted those people who were likely to be affected by this'.[53] The manner of consultation has come under severe criticism by the ombudsman in a case where it was found that the consultation was inadequate, extremely difficult to understand, complex and unfocused, and the results were not reported back to the council's cabinet. The changes included large increases (from £1 to £46) to charges for day care which were not made clear in the consultation documents. The ombudsman comments:

> 'There is little point in a consultation exercise unless you tell the consultees what you are consulting them on. To say that it might prejudice the decision if consultees were told the proposals is as absurd as informing neighbours that a planning application has been received but that they cannot know what the application is for as it might prejudice the decision of the Planning Committee.'[54]

49 At pp16, 25–27.
50 P Thompson and D Mathew, *Fair Enough?* Age Concern England, April 2004. Note that the Cabinet Office guidance is that consultation should normally be for three months.
51 (2001) 4 CCLR 41.
52 Complaint no 91A/3782 against Greenwich LBC 20 May 1993.
53 Complaint nos 02/C/14235, 02/C/15396, 02/C/15397 and 02/C/15503 against Derbyshire CC, 24 June 2004.
54 Complaint no 05/C/08648 against Oldham MBC, 29 January 2007.

The assessment process and information about charges

10.43 The 1990 policy guidance makes it clear 'the assessment of financial means should, therefore, follow the assessment of need and decisions about service provision' (at para 3.31). The 'binding' 2003 policy guidance likewise places the assessment of the ability to pay *after* the service needs decision has been made. However it stresses that information about charges should be given to a service user promptly.

> Once a person's care needs have been assessed and a decision has been made about the care to be provided, an assessment of ability to pay charges should be carried out promptly, and written information about any charges assessed as payable, and how they have been calculated, should be communicated promptly. This should normally be done before sending a first bill. Charges should not be made for any period before an assessment of charges has been communicated to the user, although this may be unavoidable where the user has not co-operated with the assessment. A first bill for a charge for a lengthy past period can cause needless anxiety. Any increase in charges should also be notified and no increased charge made for a period before the notification.[55]

10.44 Whilst the onus is on service users to provide the necessary information in order that the amount of the charge can be reviewed,[56] there is a concomitant obligation on the authority to ensure that it gives clients accurate information about the charges they will face and information as to how they can challenge those charges if they believe that they are unreasonable. Guidance issued by the Social Services Inspectorate in January 1994 (ostensibly as advice to its own officers – the '1994 SSI guidance') at para 28 stipulates:

> Good practice requires that users should be given an accurate indication of the charges that they will incur before they are required to commit themselves to a particular care plan. Only exceptional circumstances can justify not doing so. They also should be given a written statement of their financial liability at the earliest opportunity, with access to advice and explanation as required.

10.45 This advice was echoed in a *Good Practice Handbook* issued in 1996 by the Association of County Councils and the Association of Metropolitan Authorities (and endorsed by the local government ombudsman[57]) which states that authorities should ensure that:

- information about their charging policies for service users and carers is accurate; and

---

55 2003 policy guidance para 96 (para 83 in the Welsh 2002 policy guidance).
56 If a service user refuses to co-operate with the financial assessment, the authority will in general be entitled to charge the full standard rate.
57 Complaint nos 98/C/0911, 98/C/1166, 98/C/1975, 98/C/1977 and 98/C/1978 against Stockton-on Tees BC, 29 July 1999, para 153.

- it contains a clear explanation as of the law and the authority's 'discretion' (p18);[58] and
- copies of the financial information that the user has supplied should be made available to the user (p32).

10.46 Local authorities are under great pressure from the government to find efficiencies.[59] A section within the Department of Health tasked with help-ing local authorities in this endeavour has investigated the financial assessment process for domiciliary services. It found that financial assessments were often not completed until services had been in place for about six weeks, and calculated that this might result in a loss to an authority of between £300,000–£500,000 per annum. It considered that the problem is caused by councils 'delaying the financial assessment until the needs assessment is complete' and suggests that this arises because of a desire not to waste a financial staff visit. It fails however to have regard to the binding policy guidance that requires financial assessments to follow needs assessments, and accordingly there must be doubt as to the lawful-ness of its advice: the advice being 'to trigger the financial assessment from the first exchange at the contact centre. Staff will establish that the customer has eligible needs and ask about their financial circumstances, before booking the visit.'[60]

Challenging the assessed charge

10.47 Where a service user wishes to challenge a non-accommodation charge, the usual procedure will be to pursue the matter through the local authori-ty's complaints procedures (see chapter 27).[61]

10.48   The local government ombudsman has emphasised that service users should be given clear information as to the criteria for having charges reduced or waived, and of their right to a hearing before an appeal panel if their initial challenge was unsuccessful. He has also stressed the need for panel decisions to be as consistent as possible and that clear reasons for their decisions should be given so that appellants can then decide whether or not to pursue the matter further.[62]

---

58 The importance of this information being available in appropriate languages was noted by the local government ombudsman in complaint no 91A/3782 against Greenwich LBC, 20 May 1993.

59 Often called Gershon Efficiencies as they followed from a report by Sir Peter Gershon in 2004 which aimed to find £20 billion savings in the English and Welsh public sector.

60 Care Services Efficiency Delivery Programme, *Initiative 003 Effective Financial Assessment*. Available at http://www.csip.org.uk/silo/files/3iii.pdf – the paper makes it clear that it is merely an initiative which councils are not obliged to follow.

61 The omission of HASSASSAA 1983 s17 from the list of social services 'functions' in LASSA 1970 Sch 1 was rectified via Care Standards Act 2000 s112; see also the 1990 policy guidance para 6.5.

62 Complaint nos 90/A/2675, 90/A/2075, 90/A/1705, 90/A/1228 and 90/A/1172 against Essex CC, 10 October 1991.

10.49   At any hearing, the panel will need to bear in mind that an authority's power to reduce or waive charges is not limited to a consideration of the service user's financial means. As the authority has an overall discretion whether or not to levy any charges, it must retain discretion to waive or reduce charges on any ground. Such an overall discretion might be used where, for instance, the service user lacked mental capacity and the services were therefore being put in without consent, or where the service user is at risk of serious and immediate harm if the services are not provided, but refuses to have the services if he or she is charged for them.

10.50   The 2003 policy guidance at para 102 refers councils to the 1996 *Good Practice Handbook* of the former Association of County Councils/ Association of Metropolitan Authorities in relation to making reviews accessible to users and ensuring consistency of decisions. This states (at p29) that 'the principle that service users should be enabled to seek independent advice and advocacy is one which needs to underpin any charging policy or procedure'. The ombudsman has specifically criticised the lack of proper advocacy assistance to appellants during the appeals process.[63] The ombudsman has also been critical of the lack of clear references to a right of appeal in decision letters that are sent to users.[64]

The consequences of non-payment

10.51   Where the community care service is provided by the authority in consequence of a statutory duty (for instance under CSDPA 1970 s2), the service cannot as a matter of law be withdrawn merely because the service user is refusing to pay for it. The ombudsman has held, accordingly, that it is maladministration to allow a person to terminate his or her care services due to an inability to pay for them, without advising that social services cannot withdraw services for non-payment;[65] and for the council to take such action without first informing the service user of his or her right to challenge the charge.[66]

10.52   The 1990 policy guidance extends this principle to all services, stating 'the provision of services, whether or not the local authority is under a duty to make provision, should not be related to the ability of the service user or their families to meet the costs ... The assessment of financial means should, therefore, follow the assessment of need and decisions about service provision' (at para 3.31). In this respect the 1994 SSI guidance states, 'once someone has been assessed as needing a service, that service should not be withdrawn even if he or she refuses to pay the

63 Complaint nos 98/C/0911, 98/C/1166, 98/C/1975, 98/C/1977 and 98/C/1978 against Stockton-on Tees BC, 29 July 1999.
64 Complaint nos 02/C/14235, 02/C/15396, 02/C/15397 and 02/C/15503 against Derbyshire CC, 24 June 2004.
65 Complaint no 99/C/1983 against Durham, 9 October 2000.
66 Complaint nos 02/C/14235, 02/C/15396, 02/C/15397 and 02/C/15503 against Derbyshire CC, 24 June 2004.

charge required. The authority should continue provision of the service while pursuing the debt, if necessary, through the Magistrates' Court' (at para 26).

10.53　　　HASSASSAA 1983 s17(4) states that any charge levied 'may, without prejudice to any other method of recovery, be recovered summarily as a civil debt'. The use of the phrase 'summarily as a civil debt' is a reference to Magistrates' Courts Act 1980 s58(1). In principle it appears undesirable that such a procedure (normally reserved for the collection of overdue local taxes such as council tax) be used to collect such monies. A far more appropriate course would be the use of the small claims system in the county courts. It is unclear whether local authorities are able to use this option, although, as the magistrates' procedure is expressed as being 'without prejudice to any other method', it would in principle appear to be a possibility.[67] The advantage of the county court process is that the case will be considered by a judge familiar with such civil concepts of lack of mental capacity and its legal consequences (a problem which is frequently an issue with frail service users) and the civil courts have greater expertise in determining realistic debt repayment arrangements.

Charging for direct payments

10.54　The policy intention underlying the direct payments scheme (more generally considered at para 12.45 above) is that recipients should be subject to the same charging regime as that which applies to other service users. Accordingly the 2003 policy guidance (at para 87)[68] advises:

> In considering whether, and if so how, to ask an individual to make a financial contribution to the cost of their care package, councils should treat people receiving direct payments as they would have treated them under the council's charging policy, if those people were receiving the equivalent services. Charges should be assessed and made in all respects in accordance with this guidance.

10.55　The legislative framework for direct payments appears therefore to adopt the same phrasing as HASSASSAA 1983 s17. In England[69] the relevant provision is Community Care, Services for Carers and Children's Services (Direct Payments) (England) Regulations 2003[70] reg 5, which provides:

> (1) Subject to paragraphs (3) and (4), a direct payment shall be made as a gross payment unless the responsible authority decide it shall be made as a net payment
>
> (2) For the purpose of making the payment referred to in paragraph (1), the responsible authority shall determine, having regard to the prescribed person's means, what amount or amounts (if any) it is

---

67　In *Avon CC v Hooper* [1997] 1 WLR 1605; (1997) 1 CCLR 366 the proceedings took place in the High Court and the jurisdictional issue does not appear to have been raised.

68　Welsh guidance para 74.

69　In Wales, the Community Care, Services for Carers and Children's Services (Direct Payments) (Wales) Regulations 2004 SI No 1748 (W185) reg 6.

70　SI No 762.

reasonably practicable for him to pay towards securing the provision of the relevant service (whether by way of reimbursement as mentioned in section 57(4) of the 2001 Act or by way of a contribution as mentioned in section 57(5) of that Act).

(3) Where the relevant service is one which, apart from these Regulations, would be provided under section 117 of the 1983 Act (after-care)
(a) the payment shall be made at the rate mentioned in subsection (4)(a) of section 57 of the 2001 Act; and
(b) subsection (4)(b) of that section shall not apply.

(4) Where a direct payment is made to a person falling within section 17A(5) of the 1989 Act –
(a) the payment shall be made at the rate mentioned in subsection (4)(a) of section 57 of the 2001 Act; and
(b) subsection (4)(b) of that section shall not apply.

10.56 Regulation 5(2) however has the effect of creating a materially different regime for direct payments, since it requires the authority to have 'regard to the prescribed person's means': it obliges it, therefore, to undertake a means assessment, which it is not required to do for service users who are not receiving direct payments. It would appear therefore that the English and Welsh governments have (contrary to their stated policy aim) inadvertently applied different charging regimes to direct payment recipients than to non-direct payment recipients.

Services not directly provided by the social services authority

NHS services

10.57 While the principles of charging for community care services are relatively straightforward in relation to services provided by a social services authority, they become relatively complex in the case of jointly supplied services, such as those provided by a jointly funded NHS/social services arrangement.[71] In this respect the 2003 policy guidance advises:[72]

Use of powers to transfer funds
88. Local councils and health authorities may jointly commission social care services under section 28A of the NHS Act 1977.[73] The details of any charges should be devised with advice from the local council's own lawyers. The council may recover from users up to the full cost of the social care service, even though the NHS may have met some or all of the cost of the social care service. Local councils must, however, bear in mind that section 17 of the HASSASSA Act 1983 is not a provision designed to enable them to raise general revenue. If a council purchases social care and a health authority purchases health care services from the same provider, then

---

71 As noted at para 13.123, the Health Act 1999 – now NHSA 2006 s75; NHS(W)A 2006 s33 – enables the social services charging function to be transferred to the NHS as part of a partnership scheme.
72 The same guidance is in the Welsh guidance at paras 76–78.
73 Now NHSA 2006 s256; NHS(W)A 2006 s194.

charges to users may only be made for the social care element. Any services for which the NHS has underlying responsibility are automatically free at the point of use,[74] in whatever setting they are provided and whichever agencies provide or commission the service in practice.

Health Act 1999 Partnerships[75]

89. The Health Act 1999 did not alter the local authority powers to charge in the event of a partnership arrangement. In agreeing partnership arrangements, agencies will have to consider how best to manage charging (where local councils charge for services) and how to clarify the difference between charged-for and non-charged for services. There is no intention to increase or expand charging arrangements through the Partnership Arrangements. In entering into an arrangement, the partners will need to agree on the approach to be taken on charging.

90. Partners will need to bear in mind that, where charging is retained, the arrangements will need to be carefully explained to users of services, to avoid any misunderstanding that NHS services are being charged for, especially when an NHS Trust is providing a service, part of which is being charged for. It will be critical that charging arrangements are properly explained at the outset of the assessment process. See section XIX below. The existing charging review or appeals mechanisms should be made clear to the user.

91. The NHS Plan makes clear (in the Government's response to the Royal Commission on Long Term Care) that community equipment services should be integrated across health and social services by 2004, using the partnership flexibilities in the Health Act, 1999. Local councils will retain the right to charge for providing disability equipment, but will need to consider the cost-effectiveness of doing so within the new integrated community equipment services.

Mental Health Act 1983 services

10.58   Authorities are only empowered to charge for the community care services listed in HASSASSAA 1983 s17(2). This list does not mention the MHA 1983. The 2003 policy guidance reminds authorities that they must not charge for MHA 1983 s117 services.[76] It is however silent on the question of charging for guardianship under MHA 1983 s7. This is considered in detail at para 21.48.

Supporting People services

10.59   Although 'Supporting People' (see para 15.97) services are not community care services, the Supporting People directions include provisions for making charges for such services and the circumstances where there is relief from such charges and the process for making an application for

---

74   Other than services for which specific charging powers exist, such as NHS prescription charges.

75   These provisions are now to be found in NHSA 2006 ss75–76 and 256–257 (NHS(W)A 2006 ss33–34 and 194–196).

76   2003 policy guidance para 7 (para 10 in Welsh guidance).

relief.[77] Local authorities can use the 2003 policy guidance for Fairer Charging to establish the level of charge for people who are not in receipt of housing benefit (see para 15.110).[78]

Charging for Chronically Sick and Disabled Persons Act 1970 s2 services

10.60   Notwithstanding that CSDPA 1970 s2 services are not listed in HAS-SASSAA 1983 s17(2), the 1994 SSI guidance advised that charges could be recovered for services provided under that section, as 'these services are arranged by local authorities in exercise of their functions under s29 of the 1948 Act'. This advice was upheld by the Court of Appeal, in *R v Powys CC ex p Hambidge*.[79] The relationship between CSDPA 1970 s2 and NAA 1948 s29 is however a difficult one. While the Court of Appeal decision confirmed that local authorities are acting lawfully when they charge adults for the services they provide under CSDPA 1970 s2, the judgment did not address the problem of the different client groups covered by the two sections. If services, assessed as being necessary under section 2, are actually provided 'in exercise of functions under section 29', the question arose as to the authority for providing disabled children with such services since section 29 only applies to persons aged 18 or over. This question has now been resolved. In *R (Spink) v Wandsworth LBC*[80] the Court of Appeal held that charges could be recovered for services provided under section 2 for disabled children, as these services were arranged by local authorities in exercise of their functions under CA 1989 s17 (for which charges can be levied – see para 24.68).

77   Supporting People (England) Directions 2007.
78   *Supporting People Guidance*, 2003, para 43, available at http://www.spkweb.org.uk/NR/rdonlyres/C69EF825-A562-4FD9-8DA5-E07306BD2E4D/0/Statutory_Guidance.doc.
79   (1997) 1 CCLR 458.
80   [2004] EWHC 2314 (Admin); [2005] 1 WLR 258.

Intermediate care

Introduction

11.1   Intermediate care is the product of the government response to the Royal Commission for Long Term Care's report *With Respect to Old Age*.[1] Rather than meet the proposal to fund free personal care, the government decided to invest £900 million by 2003/04 into 'new intermediate care and related services to promote independence and improve quality of care for older people'.[2] As such it is not a creature of statute, but a way of using the legislation aimed at joint working between health and social services (see para 13.20) to improve rehabilitation services as well as services that avoid unnecessary hospital admission.

11.2   Henceforth the NHS and social services were to provide such persons with 'intermediate care' – guidance upon which was provided in circular LAC (2001)1/HSC 2001/01 ('the 2001 guidance').[3] The intermediate care initiative is aimed at freeing up acute hospital beds and promoting the independence of older people. Community teams (of social workers, occupational therapists, physiotherapists, community nurses etc) provide intensive short term support services to prevent unnecessary admissions and facilitate earlier discharge, either back home or via 'step-down' community hospital/care home facilities.[4]

11.3   Although the provision of intermediate care services will often satisfy a patient's needs for rehabilitation and recuperation, this will not always be the case. Given the time limited nature of the service, it will frequently be only a first stage of a programme – for which the NHS may have full responsibility.[5]

11.4   Research evaluating the effects of intermediate care[6] found that:

- given that the services relating to intermediate care were not new, although it has been shaped by national policy, it carried local imprints in the way it developed and reflected local tensions;
- the majority of people using intermediate care are older people, with over half of the referrals being people over 85 years;
- while older people with mild to moderate cognitive problems were accepted into intermediate care services, it was not clear whether short

---

1   Cm 4192–01, March 1999.
2   Department of Health, *NHS Plan: The Plan for Investment and Reform*, Cm 4818–1, June 2000, para 7.4.
3   Although it was essentially an English initiative, guidance has been issued in Wales: WHC (2002) 128; NAFWC 43/02.
4   The Department of Health has produced a model contract for use when contracting with independent sector care homes for intermediate care, accessible at http://www.dh.gov.uk/en/Publicationsandstatistics/Publications/PublicationsPolicyAndGuidance/DH_4077016.
5   See in this respect Department of Health, *Discharge from hospital: pathway, process and practice*, 2003, para 6.1, accessible at http://www.dh.gov.uk/en/Publicationsandstatistics/Publications/PublicationsPolicyAndGuidance/DH_4003252, and comments in para 13.48 below.
6   Institute of Health Sciences and Public Health Research, University of Leeds, *An Evaluation of Intermediate Care for Older People Final Report – 2005*, accessible at http://www.leeds.ac.uk/hsphr/hsc/documents/eoic_conclusions.pdf.

term intermediate care meets the need of those with more severe cognitive problems and/or suffering from depression. A Nuffield Foundation Research Report suggests that this failure can be attributed to inadequate assessment, skills shortages, cash limits, inadequate home support and the timescale of six weeks being inappropriate for many people with mental health needs. It appears that because of this skills (or 'attitude') deficit many people with dementia are deteriorating, through inappropriate care, in acute settings such that they are not being enabled to maximise their coping skills and to return to community based situations.[7]

Definition

11.5 Regulations have been issued in England[8] under the Community Care (Delayed Discharges etc) Act (CC(DD)A) 2003 which stipulate that intermediate care and community equipment services (see para 9.111) are to be provided free of charge. The regulations define intermediate care in the following terms:

> . . . a service which consists of a structured programme of care provided for a limited period of time to assist a person to maintain or regain the ability to live in his home, and is required to be provided free of charge to any person to whom it is provided for any period up to and including six weeks.

11.6 Para 7 of the 2001 guidance had already provided a more detailed definition of intermediate care as services that meet all the following criteria:

a. are targeted at people who would otherwise face unnecessarily prolonged hospital stays or inappropriate admission to acute in-patient care, long term residential care, or continuing NHS in-patient care;

b. are provided on the basis of a comprehensive assessment, resulting in a structured individual care plan that involves active therapy, treatment or opportunity for recovery;

c. have a planned outcome of maximising independence and typically enabling patient/users to resume living at home;

d. are time-limited, normally no longer than six weeks and frequently as little as 1–2 weeks or less; and

e. involve cross-professional working, with a single assessment framework, single professional records and shared protocols.[9]

11.7 The guidance states that such services should 'generally be provided in community-based settings or in the patient/user's own home, but may be provided in discrete step-down facilities on acute hospital sites' (para 11) and time limited, para 8 explaining that:

---

7   Nuffield Institute for Health, *Meeting Mental Health Needs in Intermediate Care*,2002.

8   Community Care (Delayed Discharges etc) Act (Qualifying Services) (England) Regulations 2003 SI No 1196.

9   The Welsh guidance is practically identical at para 11.

Based on current practice, an intermediate care episode should typically last no more than six weeks. Many episodes will be much shorter than this, for example 1–2 weeks following acute treatment for pneumonia, or 2–3 weeks following treatment for hip fracture. Exceptionally, for example following a stroke, patients may require intermediate care for slightly longer than six weeks. Nevertheless, all individual care plans for people receiving intermediate care should include a review date within the six-week period. Exceptional extensions beyond six weeks should be subject to a full re-assessment and should be authorised by a senior clinician. Individual care plans should specifically address what care, therapy or support may be needed on discharge from intermediate care.[10]

Service models

11.8   For planning purposes, intermediate care can be categorised into various service models, which are identified in para 14 of the 2001 guidance as:

- *rapid response*: a service designed to prevent avoidable acute admissions by providing rapid assessment/diagnosis for patients referred from GPs, A&E, NHS Direct or social services and (if necessary) rapid access on a 24-hour basis to short-term nursing/ therapy support and personal care in the patient's own home, together with appropriate contributions from community equipment services and/or housing-based support services. . . .
- *'hospital at home'*: intensive support in the patient's own home, including investigations and treatment which are above the level that would normally be provided in primary care but do not necessarily require the resources of an acute hospital. . . .
- *residential rehabilitation*: a short-term programme of therapy and enablement in a residential setting (such as a community hospital, rehabilitation centre, nursing home, or residential care home) for people who are medically stable but need a short period of rehabilitation to enable them to re-gain sufficient physical functioning and confidence to return safely to their own home. This may range from around 1–2 weeks (e.g. for pneumonia) to 4–6 weeks (e.g. following major surgery) or slightly longer (e.g. for frail older people recovering from major trauma). It will typically involve input from nurses, care managers and a range of allied health professions (e.g. physiotherapists, occupational therapists, speech/language therapists, psychologists, dieticians), supported by auxiliary care staff, to maximise patients'/clients' residual functions and equip them with skills for independent living. Residential rehabilitation may be 'step down', i.e. following a stay in an acute hospital; or it may be 'step up', i.e. following a referral by (say) a GP, social services or rapid response team and following full assessment (including medical assessment) in cases which would otherwise necessitate acute admission or admission to longer-term residential care;

---

10   Virtually identical guidance is in the Welsh guidance at para 12.

- *supported discharge*: a short-term period of nursing and/or therapeutic support in a patient's home, typically with a contributory package of home care support and sometimes supported by community equipment and/or housing-based support services, to enable earlier transfer of care from an acute hospital and to allow a patient to complete their rehabilitation and recovery at home . . .
- *day rehabilitation*: a short-term programme of therapeutic support, provided at a day hospital or day centre. This may be used in conjunction with other forms of intermediate care . . .

11.9 The Welsh guidance does not specifically list these as being service models for intermediate care, but lists them in the glossary at Annex 1.

Charging

11.10 Although the guidance advised that intermediate care should be free at the point of use (para 19), a number of authorities nevertheless levied charges. In England regulations made under the CC(DD)A 2003 have put beyond doubt that intermediate care is free for any period up to and including six weeks.[11] Although the Welsh Assembly has not implemented the 2003 Act, and therefore not made regulations under it, its guidance is also that intermediate care should be free of charge.[12]

11.11 A problem, remains, however that different localities describe intermediate care in different ways, and in some areas the care may not be free purely because it is not described as intermediate care. It also appears that on occasions the intermediate care team is unable (due to resource constraints) to take on new work, such that patients may be referred elsewhere. In such cases, the mere fact that the service is not being provided by the intermediate care team, should not be used as a reason for charges to be levied.

---

11 Community Care (Delayed Discharges etc.) Act (Qualifying Services) (England) Regulations 2003 reg 4(2).
12 NAFWC 43/2002 para 22.

CHAPTER 12

Direct payments and the Independent Living Fund

continued

Introduction

12.1   Direct payments are a different way by which local authorities (and possibly the NHS – see para 12.78 above) can discharge their community care responsibilities. Having assessed a need, social services satisfy that need not by the provision of care services but by the payment of cash to the service user or someone on his or her behalf. Historically such an arrangement was not possible: although the principal social care statutes provided social services with flexibility as to how they discharged their obligations, they almost invariably prohibited the payment of cash directly to the service user.[1]

12.2   The inability of service users to make their own care arrangements was frequently seen as disabling and disempowering.[2] In addition research suggested that the making of direct payments could result in much improved user satisfaction, and indeed cost savings to local authorities.[3] Kestenbaum, for instance, drew attention to the high value placed by service users on choice and control and that in general this could not be provided by local authorities:

> It is not simply a matter of resource levels, though these are significant. As important are the qualities that any large-scale service providing organisation would find hard to deliver: – choice of care assistant, flexibility, consistency, control of times and tasks, etc.[4]

12.3   As a consequence of this pressure for reform a number of direct payment options have been developed over the last 15 years. These initially consisted of 'indirect' or 'third party schemes' whereby the local authority paid the cash to an intermediary who then brokered the care arrangements that the service user required. 1988 saw the development of the first 'Independent Living Fund' which specifically allowed for direct payments to a restricted group of disabled people from a fund set up by the Department of Social Security rather than via local authorities. In 1996 the provisions of the Community Care (Direct Payments) Act (CC(DP)A 1996) brought the possibility of direct payments by social services to almost all disabled people. The 1996 Act was augmented by the Carers and Disabled Children Act (CDCA) 2000 which extended[5] direct payments to certain carers and parents of disabled children. These developments have now been superseded by the provisions of Health and Social Care Act (HSCA) 2001 ss57–58.

---

1   See eg National Assistance Act (NAA) 1948 s29(6)(a) and National Health Service Act (NHSA) 2006 Sch 20 para 2(4)/National Health Service (Wales) Act (NHS(W)A) 2006 Sch 15 para 2(4). Although Children Act (CA) 1989 s17(6) (prior to its amendment by the Carers and Disabled Children Act (CDCA) 2000) permitted the payment of cash, this was only in 'in exceptional circumstances'.

2   See eg J Morris, *Independent Lives: Community Care and Disabled People*, Macmillan, 1993.

3   See eg A Kestenbaum, *Independent Living: a Review*, Joseph Rowntree Foundation, 1996.

4   Ibid, p77.

5   By amendment to the CA 1989 – inserting section 17A.

12.4   Notwithstanding the perceived benefits of the direct payments scheme, local authorities incur not inconsiderable costs in providing support for direct payment service users and in the training of staff. A 2006 Audit Commission study suggests that these costs generally out-weigh potential savings in transferring administrative responsibilities to direct payment recipients.[6]

12.5   The Commission for Social Care Inspection (CSCI) in 2006 noted that although there has been a substantial increase in the numbers of people using direct payments (32,000 in March 2006), these remain very small compared to the overall numbers of people using social care services. There were also variations between councils, ranging from a minimum of 30 people using direct payments per 100,000 population aged over 18 years old, and a maximum of 218.[7]

Direct payments and the Health and Social Care Act 2001

12.6   The power to provide direct payments under the CC(DP)A 1996 and those deriving from the CDCA 2000 have now been superseded in England and Wales by the provisions of HSCA 2001 ss57–58.

12.7   The Department of Health has, since the enactment of the 2001 reforms, placed considerable pressure on councils to increase the number of individuals receiving such support. Initially they were deemed to be 'crucial performance indicators' for local authorities in the targets they were set:[8] although the jargon has now changed – they are now described as 'Key Threshold' criteria – their importance in centrally set performance targets remains.

12.8   Section 57 of the 2001 Act provides the secretary of state in England and the Assembly in Wales with regulatory making powers to enable direct payments to persons for whom a local authority has decided to provide services as a result of an assessment under either National Health Service and Community Care Act 1990 s47 or CDCA 2000 s2. Section 58 amends Children Act (CA) 1989 s17A and provides the secretary of state in England and the Assembly in Wales with regulatory making powers to enable direct payments to be made when, as a result of an assessment under CA 1989 s17, the authority has decided that services should be provided. In such a case, the payment may be made either to the person with parental responsibility for a disabled child, or to a disabled person with parental responsibility for a child[9] or to a disabled child aged 16 or 17.

---

6 Audit Commission, *Choosing Well*, 2006.
7 CSCI, *Performance Ratings for Adults' Social Services (England)*, November 2006, p1, accessible at http://www.csci.org.uk/PDF/star_ratings_report_2006.pdf.
8 In England the number of direct payment arrangements in any particular authority has been included as a Key Threshold criterion, see http://www.csci.gov.uk/care_provider/councils/paf/performance_indicator_definiti/2006–07_pis.aspx.
9 See para 3.39 above.

The 2001 Act additionally repealed the relevant parts of the 1996 Act[10] (and those deriving from the CDCA 2000).

12.9 The 2001 Act's delegated powers have been used in England[11] and Wales[12] and regulations issued (the 'regulations') which provide that individuals can insist upon a direct payment in certain situations. The central criteria being:

- that the potential recipient appears to the authority to be capable of managing the direct payment alone or with 'such assistance as may be available to him';
- the person consents to the making of a direct payment;
- the person is entitled to services under the community care legislation or the CDCA 2000 or (in the case of a parent of a child in need) the CA 1989;
- the person is not a proscribed person (effectively someone who is subject to certain court or tribunal orders);
- the local authority is satisfied that the person's needs for the relevant service can be met by securing the provision of it by means of a direct payment (or in the case of a child in need – that his or her welfare will be safeguarded and promoted by securing the provision of it by means of the direct payment).

12.10 In addition to the regulations, detailed practice guidance has been issued by the Department of Health[13] and policy guidance by the Welsh Assembly.[14] This guidance is collectively referred to below as the 'guidance'. In general the English guidance is quoted – but the Welsh guidance is in most cases identical with the only textual difference being that the English guidance refers to 'councils' whereas the Welsh talks of 'local authorities'. The relevant paragraph numbers of the Welsh guidance are cited in the footnotes and where the guidance differs materially, this difference is addressed in the text.

The obligation to make direct payments

12.11 Individuals are not assessed for direct payments. The direct payment scheme is integral to the assessment and care planning process and such payments are not available unless and until the appropriate assessment

---

10 HSCA 2001 s67 and Sch 6.
11 Community Care, Services for Carers and Children's Services (Direct Payments) (England) Regulations 2003 SI No 762 as amended by the Civil Partnership Act 2004 (Amendments to Subordinate Legislation) Order 2005 SI No 2114 ('English regulations').
12 Community Care, Services for Carers and Children's Services (Direct Payments) (Wales) Regulations 2004 SI No 1748 (W185) ('Welsh regulations').
13 *Direct Payment Guidance. Community Care, Services for Carers and Children's Services (Direct Payments) Guidance England 2003*, September 2003, accessible at http://www.dh.gov.uk/prod_consum_dh/groups/dh_digitalassets/@dh/@en/documents/digitalasset/dh_4069262.pdf ('English guidance').
14 Direct Payments Guidance Community Care, Services for Carers and Children's Services (Direct Payments) Guidance Wales 2004, accessible at http://www.wales.nhs.uk/documents/direct-payment-policy-e-merge.pdf ('Welsh guidance').

has been undertaken; ie either a community care assessment or an assessment under the CA 1989 or under the CDCA 2000. However once a local authority has decided that services are to be provided, then (unless one of the below detailed exemptions apply) it can be required to provide direct payments in lieu of services: the relevant regulations being phrased in mandatory terms.[15] It follows that it is unlawful for a local authority to require reasons to be given by a potential recipient of direct payments as to why he or she wishes this facility (para 75).[16]

12.12   In practice, such an obligation can create budgetary difficulties for local authorities – especially where their expenditure on services is committed to block contracts with providers or to the funding of 'in-house' services. In such situations, a requirement by an individual to switch to a direct payment may create additional expenditure, since the authority will remain liable (at least in the short term) to fund the service no longer required. However, given that much of the governmental pressure to increase the number of people receiving direct payments stems from a desire to see a reconfiguration of service provision, both the Department of Health and the Assembly guidance states that internal authority budgeting arrangements cannot be used to stifle such arrangements:[17]

> Problems with internal budget management procedures may not be used by authorities as a reason to refuse or delay the offering or start of a direct payment to a person to whom there is a duty to make a direct payment.

Consent

12.13   HSCA 2001 s57 and CA 1989 s17A require direct payments to be made only where the proposed recipient consents to such an arrangement. The guidance[18] stresses that local authorities should:

> . . . make clear that a person does not have to agree to a direct payment and that it would arrange services in the normal way if someone decides not to accept direct payments. They should also discuss with people who are to receive direct payments what they should do if they no longer wish to receive direct payments.

12.14   There is evidence to suggest that local authorities are using the availability of direct payments as a mechanism to avoid commissioning difficult care packages. Essentially service users are told that the only way their care needs can be met, is if they accept a direct payment and make the arrangement themselves. In such a situation direct payments become disabling rather than enabling, placing a further and unwelcome obligation on the service user. Such an approach would be unlawful since genuine and freely given 'consent' would be absent.

15   English Regulations reg 4; Welsh Regulations reg 5.
16   Public Service Ombudsman (Wales) Complaint no B2004/0707/S/370 against Swansea City Council, 22 February 2007, para 75.
17   English guidance para 23; Welsh guidance para 25.
18   English guidance para 45; Welsh guidance para 47.

The ability to manage the payment – alone or with assistance

12.15 The Regulations[19] (but not the 2001 or 1989 Acts) specify that direct payments can only be made to persons who appear to the authority 'to be capable of managing' the payment by themselves 'or with such assistance as may be available' to them. The need for such capability is however implicit in the requirement for 'consent' since for this to be valid it must be 'informed'.

12.16 Three significant considerations arise out of this requirement.

a) The test is subjective to the extent that it is the local authority's opinion that is determinative. Accordingly the courts will be slow to interfere with their assessment in any particular situation, provided it is based upon evidence and is rational.

b) The test is 'capability', not 'capacity'. Accordingly a person may be deemed incapable by a local authority, not because he or she lacks sufficient mental capacity, but because he or she is not considered sufficiently responsible to ensure that the payments are properly managed. This might arise because of a variety of factors, for instance because of mental health problems, a chaotic lifestyle, drug or other dependency. The regulations require that the authority must additionally be satisfied that that the relevant need can be met by securing the provision of it by means of a direct payment.[20]

c) If there is doubt as to whether the service user is capable of managing the payment, consideration must be given to what assistance may be available to enable the payment to be properly managed.

Mental capacity and direct payments

12.17 An outline of the law concerning mental capacity is provided at chapter 18 below. However whether or not a person has sufficient mental capacity to mange a direct payment alone or with assistance will depend in part on the use to which the direct payment is put. A person may have mental capacity to manage certain direct payments but not others. For instance, a direct payment to pay for meals might require very little capacity, whereas a direct payment used to employ a carer would generally require significantly more capacity – since employment responsibilities bring with them a number of significant legal consequences. Although such a service user might have assistance in managing the PAYE arrangements, the drafting of the employment contract and the overseeing of the care assistant's training needs, ultimately if the arrangement broke down it would be the service user's name on the unfair dismissal complaint. It is difficult to see how it could be argued that a person could have capacity to enter into a contract of employment but lack capacity to represent him/herself in any consequent employment proceedings.

---

19 English Regulations regs 2 and 3; Welsh Regulations regs 3 and 4.
20 English Regulations reg 4(3); Welsh Regulations reg 5(3).

12.18　In *South Lanarkshire Council v Smith and others*[21] the Scottish Employment Appeal Tribunal heard a complaint concerning unfair dismissal by a care assistant ostensibly employed by two service users, one of whom had significant learning disabilities. The employment arrangements were put in train by the local authority and a brokerage intermediary – but the contract of employment specified the two service users as the employer. The care assistant named the local authority as one of her employers and the Appeal Tribunal agreed. It was, however, at pains to emphasise that this was an unusual case. Lord Johnstone in his judgment noted that 'we would not for a moment seek to suggest that disabled persons cannot be an employer, particularly over someone caring for them'.

12.19　The guidance advises that local authorities 'should not make blanket assumptions that whole groups of people will or will not be capable of managing direct payments', stressing that 'many people will be able to do so, in particular, if they have access to help and support'.[22] It continues:[23]

> If an authority is concerned that a person who wishes to receive a direct payment may not be able to manage the payment, the authority should ensure that it takes into account all relevant factors before making a decision not to make a direct payment. These decisions may need to involve professional staff who are trained to assess capacity and to help people make decisions, and who should consider:
> - the person's understanding of direct payments, including the actions required on their part;
> - whether the person understands the implications of taking or not taking on direct payments;
> - what help is available to the person;
> - the nature of the services the person is assessed as needing;
> - what arrangements the person would make to obtain services.

12.20　The guidance further advises:[24]

> Some people may need help with managing the money. The payment may be made to a third party (nominee) for the recipient and day-to-day management of finances may be delegated in this way. However, the person to whom the direct payment is made must have control over how services are delivered. Direct payments may also, in principle, be provided through someone with power of attorney for the individual or a user-controlled trust.[25] Before direct payments begin, authorities should satisfy themselves that the relationship between the individual and the agent will enable and sustain the individual's independence.
>
> Where someone needs assistance to manage direct payments, the authority might wish to explore ways of delivering this so that adequate help is

---

21　Transcript 19 January 2000, unreported.
22　English guidance para 48; Welsh guidance para 50.
23　English guidance para 49; Welsh guidance para 51.
24　English guidance paras 51–54; Welsh guidance paras 53–56.
25　A legal arrangement by which a third party/agent helps the direct payment recipient to manage the direct payment, for example, by receiving and handling the money, but the user's choices and preferences direct the decision-making, and the user retains control of and is accountable for the arrangements.

available over a sustained period, not just for the set-up period. Recipients may choose to ask family or friends, or advocacy or support groups to help them in this way. They might also choose to buy in assistance, for example, with keeping records, management of day-to-day relationships with staff or using a payroll service.

12.21   In England a 2005 green paper[26] proposed that direct payments be extended to cover persons currently excluded, by using an agent for those without the capacity to consent, or who cannot manage their budget even with assistance. The proposed reform would also extend to young disabled people whose parents have managed the direct payment on their behalf but which arrangements currently cease when they reach 18 years, people with dementia and people with profound learning disabilities. This commitment to new legislation has been reiterated in the white paper *Our Health, Our Care, Our Say.*[27]

Enduring powers of attorney and loss of capacity

12.22   Where a person loses mental capacity to manage a direct payment – alone or with assistance – it will generally follow that direct payments are no longer possible. The Welsh guidance states that this problem is not saved by the making of an enduring power of attorney (paras 60–61) and in this respect differs from the English guidance.[28] However as a general principle the Welsh guidance would appear to be the more correct. It must of course be appreciated that the mere fact that a person has an enduring power of attorney registered does not mean that he or she cannot handle any money. A wealthy person might, for instance, have had an enduring power of attorney registered because he or she was unable to manage complex financial affairs, but still have the mental capacity to manage smaller sums.

The provision of assistance in the managing of the direct payment

12.23   It is not only people with limited mental capacity that are likely to benefit from assistance in the managing of the direct payment, and in this respect the guidance[29] places considerable onus on councils to ensure that independent support services are available to recipients of direct payments and that there should be no undue delay in accessing such services. It suggests that:

> 28. Support services might include training and practical assistance in addition to providing information, advice and peer support. Examples of the range of areas in which support might be welcomed are:
> - a list of local provider agencies

---

26 Department of Health, *Independence, Well-being and Choice*, 2005, para 4.25 and appendix C.
27 Cm 6737, 2006, para 7.
28 Which states (at para 58) that if a person receives direct payments, the attorney under the enduring power could continue to receive payments on his or her behalf.
29 English guidance paras 24–28; Welsh guidance paras 26, 30, 32, 34 and 38–41.

- support and advice in setting up and maintaining a direct payments scheme including financial management
- help for people to draft advertisements, job descriptions and contracts
- help in explaining the safeguards needed in the employment of people to work with children or adults
- rooms for interviews and assistance with interviewing
- an address for responses to advertisements
- support and advice about the legal responsibilities of being an employer
- support and advice about being a good manager of staff
- information about income tax and national insurance
- a payroll service
- advice on health and safety issues, including moving and handling
- regular training, for example, on assertiveness, budgeting skills, etc
- some emergency cover support
- signposting to other services such as welfare benefits advocacy
- advice about user-controlled trusts.

12.24　Many councils provide these 'brokerage services' by funding an independent living support scheme or an independent company (of which a number have a national presence). By emphasising the importance of such support, the guidance puts councils on notice that without them direct payment recipients are likely to experience particular difficulties. Given the existence of a duty of care and the foreseeability of difficulties, it may follow that councils who fail to provide adequate support services become vulnerable to a complaint of maladministration, where for instance a direct payment recipient incurs liability (for instance for a payroll error or unfair dismissal problem) which might have been avoided if general assistance of this nature had been available.

The authority must be satisfied that the assessed need will be met

12.25　The Regulations[30] stipulate that a direct payment can only be made where the authority is satisfied that the service user's needs for the relevant service can be met by securing the provision of it by means of a direct payment – or in the case of a disabled child that his or her welfare will be safeguarded and promoted by securing the provision of it by the means of the direct payment.

12.26　Given that the policy underpinning the 2001 reforms was to make mandatory the previous discretionary entitlements to direct payments, it would appear to follow that:

a)　there must be a presumption (most probably a 'strong' presumption):
　　i)　that service users will be able to satisfy their assessed needs if they receive a direct payment;
　　ii)　that persons with parental responsibility will, if they receive direct payments, use them to safeguard and promote the interests of the relevant disabled child(ren); and

---

30　English Regulations reg 4(3); Welsh Regulations reg 5(3).

b) that if a local authority is of a contrary opinion it will be obliged to provide cogent reasons as to why this is not the case.

Excluded service users

12.27 The Regulations list those service users who are prohibited from receiving direct payments.[31] The list comprises persons who are subject to specific court or tribunal controls, the imposition of which is deemed evidence of their unsuitability to manage direct payments. The following list comprises only those persons subject to English statutory orders, although the regulations also list persons subject to orders imposed by Scottish courts/tribunals:[32]

a) persons required to submit to treatment for mental conditions or drug or alcohol dependency by virtue of a requirement of a community rehabilitation order within the meaning of Powers of Criminal Courts (Sentencing) Act 2000 s41 or a community punishment and rehabilitation order within the meaning of section 51 of that Act;

b) persons subject to a drug treatment and testing order within the meaning of Powers of Criminal Courts (Sentencing) Act 2000 s52;

c) persons released on licence under Criminal Justice Act 1991 s37 subject to a mental health or drug or alcohol dependency treatment condition;

d) persons placed under guardianship in pursuance of –
   i) Mental Health Act (MHA) 1983 s7; or
   ii) MHA 1983 s37;

e) persons absent from hospital under MHA 1983 s17 leave;

f) persons subject to after-care under supervision under MHA 1983 s25A;

g) persons subject to a condition imposed under MHA 1983 s42(2) or s73(4) (including one varied under MHA 1983 s73(5) or s75(3));

h) persons subject to a supervision and treatment order under Criminal Procedure (Insanity and Unfitness to Plead) Act 1991 Sch 2 Part 1.

---

31 English Regulations reg 2(2); Welsh Regulations Sch 1.

32 The Scottish orders referred to in reg 2(2) comprise persons: (i) who are patients subject to after-care under a community care order under Mental Health (Scotland) Act 1984 s35A; (j) who are patients absent from hospital on leave under Mental Health (Scotland) Act 1984 s27; (k) are subject to a guardianship order under Adults with Incapacity (Scotland) Act 2000 s57 by reason of, or by reasons which include, incapacity through mental disorder; (l) who are restricted patients within the meaning of Mental Health (Scotland) Act 1984 s63(1) who have been given a conditional discharge under sections 64 or 68 of that Act; (m) are subject to an order under Criminal Procedure (Scotland) Act 1995 ss57(2)(a), (b), (c) or (d), 58 or 59; (n) are required to submit to treatment for their mental condition or drug or alcohol dependency by virtue of a requirement of a probation order within the meaning of Criminal Procedure (Scotland) Act 1995 ss228–230 or subject to a drug treatment and testing order within the meaning of section 234B of that Act; (o) are released on licence under Prisons (Scotland) Act 1989 s22 or s26 or under Prisoners and Criminal Proceedings (Scotland) Act 1993 s1 and are subject to a mental health or drug or alcohol dependency treatment condition.

Excluded service providers

12.28   Recipients of a direct payment are subject to few restrictions as to who they engage in delivering their services. They are, for instance, exempted from the key requirements of the Safeguarding Vulnerable Groups Act 2006, section 6(5) of which excludes from the definition of 'a regulated activity provider' private arrangements made by individuals, although the government is proposing to introduce legislation obliging 'local authorities to inform direct payments recipients about their right to engage with the vetting and barring scheme' under the Act if they so wish.[33]

12.29   The Regulations, however, limit the ability of the recipients of direct payments to use the monies to purchase care services from their close relatives or partners.[34] These restrictions are less onerous than those that applied under the CC(DP)A 1996. They provide that direct payments cannot (subject to the proviso listed below) be used to purchase services from:

a)   the direct payment recipient's spouse or common law partner;
b)   anyone living in the same household as the direct payment recipient who is also his or her:
  i)   parent or parent-in-law (or their spouse or civil partner or common law partner);
  ii)   son or daughter (or their spouse or civil partner or common law partner);[35]
  iii)   son-in-law or daughter-in-law (or their spouse or civil partner or common law partner);[36]
  iv)   stepson or stepdaughter (or their spouse or civil partner or common law partner);
  v)   brother or sister (or their spouse or civil partner or common law partner);
  vi)   aunt or uncle (or their spouse or civil partner or common law partner); or
  vii)   grandparent (or their spouse or civil partner or common law partner).

12.30   The Regulations[37] provide however that a direct payment recipient can purchase services from one of the above excluded service providers if the

---

33   See comments of Baroness Royall of Blaisdon, HL Debates col 870, 24 May 2006.
34   Welsh Regulations reg 7; English Regulations reg 6 – as amended by Civil Partnership Act 2004 (Amendments to Subordinate Legislation) Order 2005 SI No 3470 Sch 4 Part 2 para 5 and Civil Partnership Act 2004 (Consequential Amendments to Subordinate Legislation) (Wales) Order 2005 SI No 3302 (W256) Sch 1 para 28.
35   This exclusion does not apply in the case of a person mentioned in CA 1989 s17A(2)(c), namely 'a disabled child aged 16 or 17, and a local authority ("the responsible authority") have decided for the purposes of section 17 that the child's needs (or, if he is such a disabled child, his needs) call for the provision by them of a service in exercise of functions conferred on them under that section' – English regulations reg 6(3).
36   This exclusion does not apply in the case of a person mentioned in CA 1989 s17A(2)(c) (see footnote above).
37   Welsh Regulations reg 7; English Regulations reg 6.

social services authority 'is satisfied that securing the service from such a person is necessary to meet satisfactorily the prescribed person's need for that service'. There is however no statutory restriction on the direct payment recipient paying any other relation to provide care.

12.31 Where the payment is made to the parent of a disabled child, payments can be made to 'live-in' close relatives provided the social services authority 'is satisfied that securing the service from such a person is necessary for promoting the welfare of the child in need' (regulation 6(1)(b)).

12.32 The guidance explains[38] that the prohibition applies unless an authority:

> . . . is satisfied that it is necessary to meet satisfactorily a person's needs, a local authority may not allow people to use direct payments to secure services from a spouse (husband or wife), from a partner (the other member of an unmarried couple with whom they live), or from a close relative (or their spouse or partner) who live in the same household as the direct payment recipient.

and that:

> This restriction is not intended to prevent people using their direct payments to employ a live-in personal assistant, provided that that person is not someone who would be usually excluded by the Regulations. The restriction is intended to apply where the relationship between the two people is primarily personal rather than contractual, for example, if the people concerned would be living together in any event.

12.33 In England the Department of Health has encouraged the use of direct payments to pay close relatives, with the minister issuing a press release stating:[39]

> . . . some councils say they are confused over the rules governing how individuals can use their direct payments to pay close relatives. We're reminding councils that there is no legal restriction on individuals using their direct payment to pay close relatives who don't live with them . . . [and that] . . . in exceptional circumstances,[40] people can also use their direct payment to pay a relative who lives with them, if they and their local council decide this is the only satisfactory way of meeting their care needs.

12.34 Relatives who are employed under a direct payment arrangement may cease to be entitled to an assessment and services under the carers' legislation (see para 16.19 below), since these rights only relate to carers who do not provide 'the care in question . . . by virtue of a contract of employment . . .'. If, however, the relative provides additional (and substantial) care over and above that to which the payment relates, the entitlement to an assessment/services would remain.

---

38 English guidance paras 94–95; Welsh guidance paras 96–97.
39 Department of Health press release, 26 January 2004, accessible at http://www.dh.gov.uk/en/Publicationsandstatistics/Pressreleases/Pressreleaseslibrary/index.htm.
40 Reference to 'exceptional circumstances' in this context appears to be in error, since the regulations are significantly less onerous – merely a requirement that the authority is satisfied that the arrangement is necessary.

Excluded services

Residential care

12.35   Direct payments cannot be used to purchase prolonged periods of residential care.[41] Regulation 7 of the English Regulations (regulation 8 of the Welsh) caps the amount of residential accommodation that can be funded by direct payments to a maximum of four weeks in any period of 12 months. The English guidance[42] clarifies the scope of this prohibition in the following terms:

> 74. Direct payments may not pay for adults to live for the longterm in a care home. They may be made to enable people to purchase for themselves short stays in care homes, but this cannot be for more than a four-week period in any twelve-months. Where two successive periods of such care are less than four weeks apart, they are added together to make a cumulative total which may not exceed four weeks. If the two periods are more than four weeks apart they are not added together.[43] It is unlikely that direct payments will be appropriate for emergency (unplanned) residential care.

> 75. People can receive additional weeks in a care home once they have reached the four-week maximum. They cannot purchase the stay using their direct payments, but if the council considers that a longer stay is needed, it can still arrange and fund stays for the person itself in the normal way. There is no restriction on the length of time for which the council may arrange such accommodation for someone.

> 76. A direct payment also cannot be made in relation to the provision of residential accommodation for a disabled child or disabled young person for any single period in excess of four weeks, and for more than 120 days in any period of twelve months. The time limit is imposed to avoid inappropriate use of residential accommodation.

12.36   A person living full time in a residential care home is however able to receive direct payments in relation to non-residential care services – for instance a day care service or 'to try out independent living arrangements before making a commitment to moving out of their care home'.[44]

12.37   In *R (M) v Suffolk CC*[45] it was held that the general prohibition on direct payments for prolonged periods of residential care did not mean that a person in residential care could not receive such payments. The case concerned a 17-year-old with learning disabilities at a special school. Charles J considered that anyone in such care had three categories of expense, namely (a) education, (b) social care and practical care, and (c)

---

41   English Regulations reg 7; Welsh Regulations reg 8.
42   Similar advice is provided in the Welsh guidance at paras 76–77.
43   The Welsh guidance at para 76 explains this with the following example: Ms J spends three weeks in a care home in January 2005 funded through direct payments. In March 2005 she wants to spend another three weeks in a care home. She is entitled to direct payments to fund this second spell because it begins more than four weeks after the first. For the rest of the year she can only insist on direct payments funding for one more week in a care home.
44   English guidance para 77; Welsh guidance para 79.
45   [2006] EWHC 2366 (Admin); (2006) 9 CCLR 704, in particular at [23].

basic residence, and that regulation 7 did not in principle preclude direct payments to cover that portion of the overall fees that related to social care and practical care. This is a slightly surprising conclusion and possibly one that should be limited to the particular facts of the case.

Local authority in-house services

12.38 The Welsh guidance (at para 95 – as with previous English guidance[46]) states that direct payments cannot be used to purchase a service from a local authority (ie an in-house local authority provided service) – explaining that this restriction exists because legally local authorities are not permitted to sell their services. The present English guidance is silent on this question although it would appear on balance that such a restriction continues to be valid. There must however be a slight question as to whether this prohibition still remains at law, in view of the wide powers now available to local authorities, for instance under Local Government Act (LGA) 2000 s2[47] (see para 1.69 above).

The amount of the payment

12.39 HSCA 2001 s57(4) requires that direct payments must be calculated on the basis of the 'reasonable cost of securing the provision of the service concerned'. They should (as detailed in the guidance extract below) include reasonable associated costs, including for instance the cost of training the personal assistant. Concern has been expressed however about the failure of some local authorities to pay for this important item.[48] The legislation permits the payments to be paid gross or net of any charge the local authority deems it is reasonably practicable for the service user to pay[49] (see below). In deciding whether to make a direct payment gross or net (ie having deducted the assessed charge), the guidance advises that authorities 'should take into account the views of users ... allowing sufficient flexibility to respond to individual circumstances'.[50]

12.40 In some cases the calculation of the appropriate amount of a direct payment may be complex. Advice on how this should be done is given in the 2004 guidance and in specialist guidelines produced by the Chartered Institute of Public Finance and Accountancy (CIPFA) for local authorities.[51] The guidance comments:

---

46 LAC (2000)1 para 32.
47 While LGA 2000 s3(2) provides that s2 powers cannot be used to 'raise money', it is questionable whether this prohibits councils recouping costs of providing a service – particularly where the authority will have paid the user the necessary monies in the first place.
48 See Skills for Care (formerly the Training Organisation for the Personal Social Services – TOPSS), *Developing the role of personal assistants*, 2005, accessible at http://www.topssengland.net/files/develop%20role%20PAs%20webedn.pdf.
49 HSCA 2001 s57(4) and (5); English Regulations reg 5; Welsh Regulations reg 6.
50 English guidance para 89; Welsh guidance para 91.
51 CIPFA, *Community Care (Direct Payments) Act 1996; accounting and financial management guidelines*, 1998.

84. . . . the direct payment should be sufficient to enable the recipient lawfully to secure a service of a standard that the local authority considers is reasonable to fulfil the needs for the service to which the payment relates. There is no limit on the maximum or minimum amount of a direct payment either in the amount of care it is intended to purchase or on the value of the direct payment.

85. In estimating the reasonable cost of securing the provision of the service concerned, local authorities should include associated costs that are necessarily incurred in securing provision, without which the service could not be provided, or could not lawfully be provided. The particular costs involved will vary depending upon the way in which the service is secured, but such costs might include recruitment costs, National Insurance, statutory holiday pay, sick pay, maternity pay, employers' liability insurance, public liability insurance and VAT.

86. The authority is not obliged to fund the particular costs associated with the individual's preferred method of securing the service if, taking into account the user's assessed contribution, the costs exceed the authority's estimate of the reasonable cost of securing it and the service can in fact be secured more cost effectively (but still to the required standard) in another way. The local authority is also not obliged to fund particular costs that are incurred by the individual on a discretionary basis, for example, non-statutory liabilities such as an ex -gratia bonus payment. The authority might decide that they are able to increase the amount nevertheless so as to enable the person to secure his or her preferred service if it is satisfied that the benefits of doing so outweigh the costs and that it still represents best value. Direct payments recipients can use their own resources to purchase additional, or better quality, services if they wish to do so.

89. A preventive strategy may necessitate a higher investment to achieve long-term benefits and savings. Provision of direct payments that allow a person to remain in their own home may represent long-term savings if that person does not then require hospital or residential care. Similarly the provision of direct payments to a person in need of rehabilitative care may result in a more sensitive and individualised service which may in turn ease a person's recovery.

12.41   The Personal Social Services Research Unit (PSSRU) has expressed concern about the process by which direct payment rates are calculated. This normally results in the authority deducting its direct and indirect overheads such that average direct payment rates 'are almost universally lower than the costs of contracted home care, the main service for which direct payments substitute'. In the PSSRU's opinion, by setting rates at a level below market value for any form of care other than that of recruiting a personal assistant, the opportunities of direct payments are likely to be reduced.[52] Conversely, however, a 2006 Audit Commission study suggests that in order for direct payment schemes to be cost neutral (ie no more expensive than the local authority providing or commissioning the

---

52   V Davey, *Direct Payment Rates in England*, PSSRU, Kent University, 2006, accessible at http://www.pssru.ac.uk/pdf/uc/uc2006/uc2006_directpayments.pdf.

service), councils should reduce the value of payments below the sum they paid for comparable levels of care.[53]

12.42 Most local authorities have standard rates for the more common services for which a direct payment is required, for instance an hourly rate for day care. Occasionally there are alternative rates, depending upon whether the service user employs a care assistant directly or uses an agency: with the agency rate being higher. Such an arrangement would of course address some of the concerns raised by the PSSRU above. It would also enable service users to have direct payments who did not wish to employ a care assistant but preferred to purchase agency services. Provided such an arrangement was no more expensive than the cost that the authority would bear if it was responsible for the service provision arrangements, it would appear that a service user could insist on such an option.

12.43 The rate proposed by the authority may be insufficient to cover the cost of the services required, for instance because no care assistant or agency is prepared to provide the service at that rate. In such cases the service user can challenge the rate through the complaints process. In this respect the CIPFA guidance[54] states:

> 87. There may be cases where an individual thinks that the total value of the direct payment should be greater than the local authority proposes, and/or that his or her contribution or the amount they are asked to pay by way of reimbursement should be less than the council proposes. Where these cases cannot be resolved through discussion, local authorities should advise the individual that he or she can pursue the matter through the authority's complaints procedure.

> 88. A local authority should give individuals as much notice as possible of the value of a direct payment, and the contribution or repayment they will be expected to make to the cost of their care package. This should be done before the payment begins, or its level is changed, to provide the opportunity for any dispute over the level to be resolved before the payment begins or the change takes effect. If that is not possible, whilst any complaint is being considered, individuals may choose either to manage on the amount of direct payments being offered or refuse to accept the direct payments. If a person does not agree to a direct payment, the authority remains responsible for providing or arranging the provision of the services they are assessed as needing.

Frequency of payments

12.44 Local authorities must agree with the service user the frequency of payments – ensuring that they are in a position to pay for services when payment is due. The guidance advises that it may also be necessary to 'set up procedures for making additional payments in emergencies, for example, if needs change or regular payments go astray' and should

---

53 Audit Commission, *Choosing Well*, 2006.
54 CIPFA, *Community Care (Direct Payments) Act 1996; accounting and financial management guidelines*, 1998.

ensure that recipients clearly understand these arrangements.[55] The guidance advises that payments can be made such that the recipient accumulates a reserve, namely:[56]

> The flexibility inherent in direct payments means that individuals can, subject to any conditions placed upon the direct payments. adjust the amount they use week to week and 'bank' any spare money to use as and when extra needs arise. So long as overall the payments are being used to secure the services they are for and the care plan objectives are met, the actual pattern of 'service' does not need to be predetermined.

Charges for direct payments

12.45   Although, as noted above, direct payments can be paid gross, they will in general be paid 'net' – ie after the council has deducted the sum it would have charged the recipient had the service been provided or commissioned by the council. In this context, the regulations require that any charge be an amount (if any) that it is reasonably practicable for the individual to pay[57] and the guidance[58] refers to the relevant non-residential care advice on charging[59] which states:

> . . . councils should treat people receiving direct payments as they would have treated them under the council's charging policy, if those people were receiving the equivalent services.

12.46   Notwithstanding this policy intention, the regulations in fact require (in certain situations) a difference in treatment, since they state that:

> . . . for the purpose of making the payment . . . the Responsible Authority shall determine, having regard to the prescribed persons means, what amount or amounts (if any) it is reasonably practicable for him to pay towards securing the provision of the relevant service.[60]

12.47   Local authorities are compelled therefore to undertake an individual means test in every case – which is not the situation for service users who do not receive direct payments. It would appear that this difference of approach is inadvertent and that equity would demand that the regulations be amended to dispense with the mandatory means test.

Direct payments and social security

12.48   The relevant social security regulations require 'any payment' made under the direct payments legislation to be disregarded for benefits purposes.[61]

---

55   English guidance para 91; Welsh guidance para 93.
56   English guidance para 92; Welsh guidance para 94.
57   English Regulations reg 5(2); Welsh Regulations reg 6(2).
58   English guidance para 88; Welsh guidance para 90.
59   In England, *Fairer Charging Policies for Home Care and Other Non-residential Social Services*, 2003, para 86 and in Wales guidance of the same name, 2002, para 74.
60   English Regulations reg 5(2); Welsh Regulations reg 6(2).
61   Income Support (General) Regulations 1987 SI No 1967 Sch 9 para 58; Jobseeker's Allowance Regulations 1996 SI No 207 Sch 7 para 56; Housing Benefit Regulations 2006 SI No 213 Sch 5 para 57.

This does not, however, apply to carers who are paid using these payments – since the disregard does not apply to 'earnings'.[62]

The obligations upon the recipient of direct payments

12.49 The recipient of the direct payment must ensure that it is spent on services to meet the assessed need. In relation to the monitoring and auditing of the payments the guidance advises that 'monitoring arrangements should be consistent both with the requirement for the authority to be satisfied that the person's needs for the service can and will be met and with the aim of promoting and increasing choice and independence'.[63] It continues:[64]

> 140. Councils should focus on achieving agreed outcomes, rather than on the service being delivered in a certain way. The council should discuss with individuals what steps it intends to take to fulfil its responsibilities, and may also wish to discuss how it might support them in securing adequate quality care. It should be prepared to consider variations to what it proposes.

> 141. Councils should aim to ensure that the information that the direct payment recipient is asked to provide is as straightforward and the least onerous possible, consistent with monitoring requirements.

> 142. Each council will need to establish how it will know if someone is experiencing difficulty with managing their direct payments . . .

> 144. Councils should follow existing guidance on carrying out reviews. The fact that a council is making direct payments rather than arranging services itself does not affect its responsibility to review an individual's care package at regular intervals. As with all services, the projected timing of the first review should be set at the outset. The purpose of the review remains to establish whether the objectives set in the original care plan are being met. It should therefore cover whether the person's needs have changed, whether the use of direct payments is meeting assessed needs, and how he or she is managing direct payments.

12.50 There is some evidence that local authorities are being over zealous in their requirements for user documentary evidence of their expenditure: the CSCI has in this regard been extremely critical – citing as an example a council that wrote a threatening letter to a direct payment recipient 'because they had been unable to provide two KFC receipts'.[65]

12.51 Direct payment users are legally responsible for the services they purchase with the monies they receive from social services. It follows that in respect of any problem they encounter with the service they purchase,

---

62 See Social Security Commissioner decision no CIS 1068 2006 and for an analysis of the decision see (2007) 39 *Journal of Community Care Law* 17.
63 English guidance para 140; Welsh guidance para 139.
64 English guidance paras 141–145; Welsh guidance paras 140–144.
65 See comments of Denise Platt, chair of CSCI in G Carson, 'Dirty hospitals are important, but excuse me!' *Community Care Journal*, 5 January 2006 p5.

they cannot make complaint to social services, although they can seek the authority's assistance. In this context the guidance advises:[66]

> Councils should make people aware that they should plan for the unexpected and discuss with each person what arrangements he or she will make for emergencies, to ensure that the person receives the care he or she needs when the usual arrangements break down (e.g. through sickness of one of the person's personal assistants). The council will need to be prepared to respond in these circumstances just as it would with any other person using a service. It may decide to step in and arrange the services where this is necessary to meet its responsibilities. The council could also explore other ways of providing assistance to enable the person to continue to manage his or her own care by using direct payments, particularly if the difficulty is temporary or unforeseen.

> Difficulties can be minimised by good assessments, clarity (e.g. about what the money can be used for), and monitoring and effective support arrangements. Discussing potential areas of difficulty and how they will be handled with the individual before direct payments begin is important. Reviews should be carried out regularly, not just when difficulties arise.

Financial monitoring

12.52   The guidance[67] stresses the need for auditing arrangements to be 'as simple and easy to understand as possible' and cautions against requiring complicated paperwork which it considers may be 'a significant disincentive for people considering direct payments'. It suggests that recipients should generally be required to open a single bank account into which only direct payment and Independent Living Fund money (and other money related to personal assistance) are paid. It advises that the bank account may have to be in a nominee's name if the service user has problems opening an account (because of, for instance, a bad credit rating). A 2006 exchange of letters between the Department of Health and the British Bankers Association has endeavoured to clarify (and resolve) some common banking problems encountered by service users such as difficulties in proving their identity and being unable through disability to sign cheques.[68]

Repayment and discontinuance

12.53   The Regulations provide authorities with the power to seek repayment of direct payments[69] if they are satisfied that it has not been used to secure the provision of the service to which it relates (or that the person has not met any condition that the council has properly imposed). The guidance advises that:[70]

---

66   English guidance paras 154–155; Welsh guidance paras 153–154.
67   English guidance paras 147–150; Welsh guidance paras 146–149.
68   Accessible at http://www.dh.gov.uk/en/Publicationsandstatistics/Lettersandcirculars/ Dearcolleagueletters/DH_063742.
69   English Regulations reg 9; Welsh Regulations reg 10.
70   English guidance paras 161–162; Welsh guidance paras 160–161.

Councils should bear in mind that repayment should be aimed at recovering money which has been diverted from the purpose for which it was intended, or where services have been obtained from someone who is ineligible to provide them, or which has simply not been spent at all. It should not be used to penalise honest mistakes, nor should repayment be sought where the individual has been the victim of fraud.

Councils should be satisfied before they start to make payments that people who will receive the direct payment understand all of the conditions they will be required to meet. Councils should also discuss with potential recipients of direct payments the circumstances in which the authority might wish to consider seeking repayment. Councils may wish to take into account hardship considerations in deciding whether to seek repayments. Councils should also bear in mind that there might be legitimate reasons for unspent funds. There may be outstanding legal liabilities necessitating a direct payment recipient to build up an apparent surplus (e.g. to pay their employees' quarterly PAYE, or to pay outstanding bills from a care agency).

12.54   The Regulations additionally provide that a council shall cease making direct payments if it considers that the person is no longer capable of managing the direct payment or of managing it with help – unless (1) the 'incapability' is reasonably expected to be temporary, and (2) a third party is prepared to accept and manage the payments, and (3) any care assistant (or other care provider) agrees to accept payment from this third party.[71]

Equipment/adaptations

12.55   Direct payments can be used to purchase equipment or pay for adaptations or fixtures/fittings assessed as being required by the disabled person. Not uncommonly, for instance, a direct payment will cover the cost of purchasing a key safe or other such item. They cannot however be used to pay for services or equipment for which the authority is not responsible, for example services that the NHS provides, and the guidance also makes clear that they are not a substitute for a disabled facilities grant for major property adaptations.[72]

12.56   Local authorities may be reluctant to make direct payments for the purchase of equipment, even though equipment is exempt from charging because of a concern that it might thereby cease to be available for 're-use'. Many authorities recycle the majority of their equipment, recovering and redeploying it when no longer required by a particular service user. The guidance makes clear that direct payments may not conflict with this practice, stating:[73]

81. Where a council makes a direct payment for equipment, it needs to clarify with the individual at the outset (just as it should where it arranges for the provision of equipment itself) where ownership lies as well as who has responsibility for ongoing care and maintenance. As direct payments mean that the individual will secure for themselves the equipment they are

---

71   English Regulations reg 10; Welsh Regulations reg 11.
72   English guidance para 79; Welsh guidance para 81.
73   The equivalent advice is found at paras 82–83 of the Welsh guidance.

assessed as needing, an authority will need to consider what conditions, if any, should be attached to the payment. For example, concerning what will happen to the equipment if the individual no longer requires the services for which the equipment was purchased. Equipment can be purchased as part of making a package cost effective, for example, supplying pagers or mobile phones to personal assistants.

12.57　However there is anecdotal evidence that some authorities encourage the use of such payments for equipment as they count towards the rigorous performance targets they are required to meet in relation to the numbers of direct payments made. Direct payments for equipment figure heavily in the proposed retail model for the future provision of equipment (see para 9.118).

Employment issues

12.58　In general a local authority will not be responsible for the service secured by a recipient of direct payments, and in general the authority will not be responsible for the well-being of any care assistant employed under such an arrangement. In this respect, therefore the guidance gives the following advice:[74]

> **Health & Safety**
> 96. . . . As a general principle, local councils should avoid laying down health and safety policies for individual direct payment recipients. Individuals should accept that they have a responsibility for their own health and safety, including the assessment and management of risk. They should be encouraged to develop strategies on lifting and handling and other tasks both in the home and outside it where lifting equipment, for example, may not be available.
>
> 97. . . . local councils will wish to take appropriate steps to satisfy themselves that recipients and potential recipients are aware of health and safety issues that affect them as individuals, anyone they employ, and anyone else affected by the manner in which their support is delivered.
>
> 98. . . . local councils should give the recipients and potential recipients the results of any risk assessments which were carried out as part of the care assessment. Such risk assessments are necessary so that health and safety issues can be taken into account. This allows the individual to share the assessment with the care agency or the employee who provides the service. They can therefore take reasonable steps to minimise the risks to the health and safety of any staff they employ. (The recipient or potential recipient has a common law duty of care towards the person they employ.)
>
> **Direct payment recipients as employers**[75]
> 100. Individuals should be made aware of their legal responsibilities in terms of providing a statement of employment particulars, meeting the national minimum wage, taxes and statutory benefits such as sick pay and annual leave. If support services are provided, local councils may wish to

---

74　The equivalent advice is found at paras 98–100 of the Welsh guidance.
75　The equivalent advice is found at paras 102–103 of the Welsh guidance.

include a payroll service which will take responsibility for administering wages, tax and National Insurance for the direct payment recipient. A written contract will help ensure that all those involved have the same understanding about the terms of employment.

12.59   The employment obligations of direct payment recipients may be of particular complexity if the employed person is to care for a disabled child or disabled young person. Detailed guidance exists on this process[76] including advice concerning checks under the Protection of Children Act 1999 via the Criminal Records Bureau.

Transition into adulthood

12.60   Direct payments can be paid to persons with parental responsibility for a disabled child until he or she becomes an adult (ie at 18). At that age the payment must either pass to the young person or cease (eg if he or she lacks the ability to manage the payment alone or with assistance). CA 1989 s17A(2) however provides for direct payments to be paid to disabled young persons at the age of 16. This enables them (if they choose) as part of their transition to adulthood, 'to take control of parts or all of the direct payment that has to date been managed by the person with parental responsibility. This can allow them to gain experience of managing direct payments in a gradual way prior to reaching adulthood.'[77]

12.61   The guidance advises[78] on how the process should be managed in terms of 'best practice' to develop the young person's ability to manage the direct payment. However where conflict exists with those with parental responsibility, it advises:[79]

> Where there is a difference of views between parents and disabled young people aged 16 or 17, the duty to make direct payments might mean that local authorities should give precedence to the views of the young person. It follows that there may be situations where it would be right for a young person to receive a direct payment whether the parents agree or not, although. it is important that local councils consider the welfare of the young person in such circumstances.

Carers

12.62   The CDCA 2000 s2(2) makes provision for social services to provide services to carers (aged 16 or over) which in their opinion 'help the carer care for the person cared for'. As a matter of law, however, respite care is not a service under the 2000 Act (see para 16.88 below). The type of assistance available under the 2000 Act includes such services as relaxation therapy/counselling; mobile phones; trips/holidays/special events for carers; driving lessons; travel assistance; training and the like.

---

76   English guidance paras 104–110; Welsh guidance paras 105–111.
77   Para 128 of both the English and Welsh guidance.
78   English guidance paras 127–135; Welsh guidance paras 127–134.
79   English guidance para 38; Welsh guidance para 40.

12.63   Where a local authority has decided that such a service should be made available, the carer can require it to be provided by way of a direct payment.

Independent living trusts and third party payments

12.64   Prior to the implementation of the CC(DP)A 1996 social services departments were (with very minor exceptions) subject to a specific prohibition against making payments of cash to disabled people, in lieu of services.[80] They were however permitted by NAA 1948 s30 to pay third parties (such as independent home care service providers) that had undertaken to deliver the assessed services. A number of authorities accordingly developed 'third party' schemes whereby they made payments to an intermediary (typically a trust fund or brokerage scheme) which then worked closely with the disabled person in the purchasing of his or her care. Such schemes gave the disabled person effective control over the purchasing of care services and also provided assistance with the administrative obligations inherent in any employment situation (recruitment and appointment of carers, employment contracts, grievance procedures, PAYE, etc).

12.65   Although the 1996 and 2001 Acts have materially relaxed the restrictions on direct payments, there remain a number of instances whereby third party schemes are still of value: most notably where the service user lacks the necessary mental capacity to manage the payments – even with assistance.

12.66   With the passing of the 1996 Act, questions were raised as to whether third party schemes continued to be lawful (despite government assurances[81]). This question was settled in *R (A & B) v East Sussex CC (No 1)*[82] which concerned a local authority payment to a specially created independent trust (known as a 'user independent trust') whose sole purpose was then to arrange the care of two young women with profound physical and learning disabilities. The trust in this case was a company limited by guarantee with relatively sophisticated control arrangements designed to ensure that the best arrangements possible were made for the disabled persons.

12.67   The applicants argued, amongst other things, that NAA 1948 s30 permitted such payments, since it provides that:

> A local authority may, in accordance with arrangements made under section 29 of this Act, employ as their agent for the purposes of that section any voluntary organisation or any person carrying on, professionally or by

---

80 See eg NAA 1948 s29(6)(a), NHSA 2006 Sch 20 para 2(2)(a) and NHS(W)A 2006 Sch 15 para 2(2)(a).

81 Asked to confirm that the 'new possibilities created by the' 1996 Act would not affect the status of existing third-party schemes, the minister, John Bowis, stated that 'schemes that are in place now should not be affected. We are not seeking to undermine such schemes', HC Debates col 380, 6 March 1996.

82 [2002] EWHC 2771 (Admin); (2003) 6 CCLR 177, accessible at http://www.bailii.org/ ew/cases/EWHC/Admin/2002/2771.html.

way of trade or business, activities which consist of or include the provision of services for any of the persons to whom section 29 above applies, being an organisation or person appearing to the authority to be capable of providing the service to which the arrangements apply.

12.68 Section 64 defines a 'voluntary organisation' as 'a body the activities of which are carried on otherwise than for profit, but does not include any public or local authority'. Munby J concluded that the trust in question came within this definition and that it followed, therefore, that such a third party scheme was compatible with the legal requirements of NAA 1948 s29. Had this not been the case, he expressed himself satisfied that the scheme would have been lawful in any event by virtue of both the LGA 1972 s111 and LGA 2000 s2.

12.69 The CSCI in England has advised that in general independent living trusts – if set up solely for the support of a specified disabled user (or siblings) – will not require to be registered under the Care Standards Act 2000 since they are not offering a 'service' and do not therefore (in general) 'fall within the definition of an agency ie they are not carrying on a business or trade with or without a view to profit'.[83]

12.70 *Trusting Independence* is an excellent guide to independent living trusts, available from Values into Action.[84] A copy of the trust deed in this guide is reproduced in Appendix 3 to this book.

Reform

12.71 The Department of Health's green paper on the future of adult care services *Independence, Well-being and Choice*[85] proposed reform of the direct payments scheme by (amongst other things) 'extending the benefits of direct payments to those currently excluded, by using an agent for those without the capacity to consent, or unable to manage even with assistance'. The subsequent white paper *Our health, our care, our say: a new direction for community services*[86] noted that due 'to the strong response to this issue . . . we will seek to extend the availability of direct payments to those groups who are excluded under the current legislation'.

Individual budgets

12.72 The Department of Health announced in its 2005 green paper (above) the development of 'individual budgets' that would take direct payments

---

83 See CSCI, *Policy and Guidance: Registration of Direct Payment Support Services*, 2006, para 15, accessible at http://www.csci.org.uk/docs/direct_pay_registration.doc. It is understood that the Care and Social Services Inspectorate Wales adopts a similar position but it has not been possible to obtain confirmation of this point.

84 A Holman and C Bewley, *Trusting Independence: a practical guide to independent living trusts*, 2001, published by Values into Action, Oxford House, Derbyshire Street, London E2 6HG, http://www.viauk.org.

85 Cm 6499,March 2005, para 4.24.

86 Department of Health, Cm 6737, 2006, para 4.23.

forward. These have been proposed by a number of agencies[87] and essentially pool funds from various sources such as social services, community equipment, Access to Work, independent living funds, disabled facilities grants and the Supporting People programme – but not NHS resources.[88] The 2006 white paper[89] outlined its programme, stating:

> Individuals who are eligible for these funds will then have a single transparent sum allocated to them in their name and held on their behalf, rather like a bank account. They can choose to take this money out either in the form of a direct payment in cash, as provision of services, or as a mixture of both cash and services, up to the value of their total budget. This will offer the individual much more flexibility to choose services which are more tailored to their specific needs.

12.73   In 2006 the Department of Health announced[90] the piloting of individual budgets in 13 local authority areas (Manchester, Barnsley, Coventry, Gateshead, Oldham, Kensington and Chelsea, Barking and Dagenham, Essex, Lincolnshire, Norfolk, West Sussex, Bath and North East Somerset, and Leicester). It is understood[91] that these pilots will run for between 18 months and two years and, if successful, national implementation could follow in 2009/10.

12.74   The Department of Health website explains that the aim of individual budgets 'is to enable people needing social care and associated services to design that support and to give them the power to decide the nature of the services they need'. It then identifies the following key features:[92]

- A transparent allocation of resources, giving individuals a clear cash or notional sum for them to use on their care or support package.
- A streamlined assessment process across agencies, meaning less time spent giving information.
- Bringing together a variety of streams of support and/or funding, from more than one agency.
- Giving individuals the ability to use the budget in a way that best suits their own particular requirements.
- Support from a broker or advocate, family or friends, as the individual desires.

12.75   It appears there are, therefore, two key elements to individual budgets, namely: (1) the service user has more control over his or her assessment and care arrangements; and (2) that in addition to the direct payment received from social services, other (existing) income is pooled to enable

87   See *A Mature Policy on Choice* at http://www.ippr.org/ecomm/files/A_mature_policy.pdf.
88   Department of Health, *Our health, our care, our say: a new direction for community services*, Cm 6737, 2006, para 4.39.
89   Ibid, paras 4.32 *et seq.*
90   LAC (2006)8 *Adults' Personal Social Services (PSS) Allocation 2006–07: Individual Budget Pilot Projects.*
91   Department of Health, *Our health, our care, our say: a new direction for community services*, Cm 6737, 2006, para 4.33.
92   Accessible at http://www.dh.gov.uk/en/Policyandguidance/Healthandsocialcaretopics/Socialcare/DH_4125774.

the service user to identify the total resources he or she has available and to plan the most effective way of spending this: a third optional element being an adviser – for instance an independent broker – who assists the service user in making these arrangements.

12.76   User control over the assessment will extend, it appears, not to the decision over how much state money is allocated, but over how this money is to be spent: meaning that prescriptive care plans spelling out precisely what tasks are to be done, when and by whom, give way to the user deciding how it should be used. It is not difficult to see how this approach could have many attractions and lead to improved care 'outcomes' in certain cases. It is however far from clear how pooling different (but existing) incomes can make a radical change in the majority of cases. Indeed there appear to be considerable financial questions over the viability of such schemes. A Social Care Institute for Excellence research paper[93] comments as follows:

> Information about the costs consumer-directed schemes is patchy, and difficult to compare across countries. Virtually every analogous scheme in the EU has been based on an underestimate of costs, at least partly due to unpredicted demand and previously undetected unmet need.[94] The Swedish scheme was on the point of collapse by the end of 2004, because of ballooning costs and perceived fraud. The Flemish scheme was unable to meet even a fraction of demand, and was criticised for lack of transparency, and long waiting lists. In 2005, the possibility of capping the budget for the new Dutch scheme to halt the upward drift of expenditure was under vigorous political debate, and from 1 January 2006, coverage was altered to eliminate much-valued household help (unless part of a package), and transfer responsibility for it to the municipalities. Germany has protected the financial health of its scheme by building in extensive cost-containment mechanisms; and a review of schemes for older people in the Organisation for Economic Cooperation and development (OECD) area has suggested that confronting the need for cost-effectiveness from the start may help to promote their development.[95]

12.77   The individual budget pilots are being extensively evaluated. The initial findings show a wide variety of models being tested. All sites though are developing resource allocation systems to turn the assessments into an amount of money that the person will be paid. There appear to be both winners and losers with this arrangement. Difficulties have been found in integrating the funding streams, especially the disabled facilities grants and the Independent Living Fund monies, and all sites were finding that individual budgets were offering a challenge to financial planning, and difficulties aligning them with the charging process. Interviews conducted with individual budget recipients (14 in total) were positive

---

93   Social Care Institute for Excellence, *Research Briefing 20:Choice, control and individual budgets: emerging themes*, 2007, accessible at http://www.scie.org.uk/publications/briefings/files/scare20.pdf.

94   L Waterplas and E Samoy, 'L'allocation personnalisée: le cas de la Suède, du Royaume-Uni, des Pays-Bas et de la Belgique' (2005) 2 *Revue française des affaires sociales* 61–101.

95   Organisation for Economic Co-operation and Development, *Policy brief: Ensuring quality long-term care for older people*, 2005.

although a strong theme emerging was the importance of support outside the user's own caring networks. Access to free brokerage, professional advocates and/or mentoring was seen as crucial, especially if users did not want to rely on families for support in managing their individual budget.[96]

NHS and direct payments

12.78   HSCA 2001 makes no provision for direct payments to be made in relation to NHS responsibilities – a point emphasised by the Department of Health in an advice note of February 2005:[97]

> Whilst the Department of Health is unable to comment on individual cases, direct payments made under the Health and Social Care Act 2001 relate only to certain local authority social services. This means that where an individual has an identified health need which falls to the NHS, that part of any 'care' package cannot be delivered as a direct payment within the meaning of the legislation, including where a local authority is acting under a partnership arrangement pursuant to section 31 of the Health Act 1999. This statement is not, nor is it intended to be, a comprehensive description of the legal position concerning direct payments, and councils are advised to take their own legal advice on this issue.

12.79   The Department of Health has re-emphasised this view in the following terms:[98]

> NHS services cannot be provided as part of an Individual Budget or through Direct Payments, and *Our Health, Our Care, Our Say: A New Direction for Community Services* makes it clear that these will not be extended to NHS healthcare in the near future. This means that when an individual begins to receive NHS Continuing Healthcare they may experience a loss of control over their care which they had previously exercised through Direct Payments or similar. It should be emphasised that PCTs can commission to maximise continuity of care, i.e. to maintain a similar package of care to that already in place, and in determining whether to maintain an existing package, the PCT should take into account the individual's preferences wherever possible.

12.80   There is an important preliminary point to note in relation to these two advice extracts. The first is clearly correct, namely that direct payments for health needs cannot be made under the 2001 Act. The second (that NHS services cannot be provided 'as part of an Individual Budget or through Direct Payments') is more problematic, although not in relation to individual budgets: since these are presently a non-statutory initiative, their exclusion of NHS monies is clearly a matter of policy for the department. The reference to 'Direct Payments' can, however, be read in one of two ways. If it is intended to be short-hand for a reference to 'Direct Payments under the 2001 Act' (ie as with the first extract), this cannot be faulted.

96   *Individual Budgets Evaluation. A Summary of early findings*, Ibsen, June 2007.
97   See also the Welsh guidance at para 11.
98   Department of Health, *The National Framework for NHS Continuing Healthcare and NHS-funded Nursing Care*, 2007.

This would seem to be the intended meaning, by virtue of the capitalisation of the phrase and the close similarity the advice bears to the first extract. If however it is purporting to say that the NHS cannot make a money payment to a service user, this would appear to be an incorrect statement of the law. While it might be government policy to discourage such payments, it cannot use guidance to amend the law. In *Gunter v SW Staffordshire PCT*[99] Collins J held that there was nothing in principle in the wording of (what is now) NHS Act (NHSA) 2006 s12 and Sch 3 para 15 to preclude a primary care trust (PCT) making direct payments (in that case to an independent user trust). He observed:

> It seems to me that Parliament has deliberately given very wide powers to Primary Care Trusts to enable them to do what in any given circumstances seem to them to achieve the necessary provision of services.

12.81 NHSA 2006 s12[100] empowers PCTs to contract with 'any person or body' to provide health services and NHSA 2006 Sch 3 para 15 permits it to do 'anything which appears to it to be necessary or expedient for the purposes of or in connection with its functions'[101]). As a matter of law there appears therefore to be no impediment to the NHS making direct payments to any person where it is considered expedient.

12.82 The above analysis suggests that the policy position of the Department of Health and Welsh Assembly is that direct payments for health care needs cannot be made under the 2001 Act – and not that they cannot be made under other legislation – for instance NHSA 2006 s12.[102] In any event, whilst PCTs and local health boards (LHBs) must have regard to such policy statements or formal guidance, they are not required to follow it slavishly and the guidance cannot fetter the scope of the statutory power. There may be many situations where a PCT or LHB considers the making of direct payments 'expedient'. It appears that as a result of the 'Pointon' case[103] Cambridgeshire PCT remedied its maladministration by making direct payments to Mrs Pointon,[104] and no criticism has been made of this action. In more extreme cases it might even be argued that a duty to make such payments could rest with the NHS. Take, for example, a person in receipt of direct payments from social services under the 2001 Act, who is then adjudged likely to die in the near future and entitled to NHS continuing care. If the care arrangements could not be sustained without the NHS body taking over the existing direct payments, considerations of dignity and the distress that might be caused to the dying person might demand that such a course be taken.

12.83 It may be that the Department of Health and the Welsh Assembly advice in this respect is imperfect through omission: the failure to explore

---

99 [2005] EWHC 1894 (Admin); (2006) 9 CCLR 121.
100 In Wales the equivalent being NHS(W)A 2006 s10.
101 NHS(W)A 2006 Sch 2 para 13.
102 In Wales, NHS(W)A 2006 s10.
103 Health Service Commission Report Case no E.22/02–03 concerning a complaint against the former Cambridgeshire Health Authority and Cambridgeshire PCT.
104 See the comments of the Public Guardianship Office at http://www.guardianship.gov.uk/news/newsforprofessionals_485.htm.

the potential implications of the social services obligations under the NHS Acts 2006. At para 14.113 below we consider the residual duties of social services authorities in cases where a determination of entitlement to NHS continuing care has been made. If this analysis is correct, it means that as a matter of law such a determination does not disentitle a person to support under the community care regime. If this is so, various options emerge including the possibility of an NHS body making a payment to the social services authority using its powers under NHSA 2006 s256[105] since there are subsisting social services responsibilities and section 256 payments can be used to fund such health-related local authority functions.

The Independent Living Fund

12.84   The Independent Living Fund (ILF) was established by the Department of Health and Social Security in 1988 as an independent trust[106] to provide a weekly payment to approximately 300 severely disabled people who would have suffered significant financial loss as a result of the abolition of supplementary benefits 'additional requirements' payments in that year.[107] Initially the ILF was intended to be temporary but its expenditure grew from £1.1m in 1988–89 to £263.7m in 2006–07.[108] The fund is financed by the government, but administered by seven independent trustees.

Independent Living (Extension) Fund

12.85   The original trust was wound up in 1993 as part of the community care reforms, with the fund monies being transferred to local authorities via the special transitional grant. However the payments that were being made to disabled people at the time it was wound up, have been preserved and are paid from what is known as the Independent Living (Extension) Fund.

12.86   There is provision for payments made from the Independent Living (Extension) Fund to be increased to recipients if they experience a 'significant change in their circumstances'. The current maximum award is £785 per week. Payments are suspended (as with the 1993 fund below) during any period when the disabled person is accommodated in a hospital, residential or nursing home, although they can be reinstated on discharge. If the carer is privately employed a retainer can be paid for up to four weeks in order to avoid potential disruption to care.[109]

---

105   NHS(W)A 2006 s194.
106   The trust deeds for the various funds are held by the solicitor to the Department of Social Security; the original trust deed being dated 8 June 1988 and the Independent Living (Extension) Fund, 25 February 1993.
107   R Means and R Smith, *Community Care Policy and Practice*, Macmillan, 1994.
108   M Henwood and B Hudson, 'Cash for Care Lifts Off' *Community Care* 27 July 2006 pp34–35.
109   http://www.ilf.org.uk/help_and_faqs/faqs/change_in_circumstances/index.html.

Independent Living (1993) Fund

12.87 After the original fund was wound up in 1993, a new fund, known as the Independent Living (1993) Fund, was created for new applicants: the entitlement terms of the 1993 Fund are, however, more stringent and the benefits less generous. The ILF entitlement terms are periodically reviewed and guidance notes on the workings of the ILF schemes are available from the ILF website.[110]

12.88 In order to qualify for a grant from the 1993 fund, an applicant must:

- be at least 16 and under 66 years of age (but payments can continue for those on ILF prior to their 66th birthday); and
- be assessed by the local authority as being at risk of entering residential care, or capable of leaving it to live in the community; and
- receive at least £200 worth of services per week from the local authority (net of any charge) and be assessed as needing additional care; and
- receive the highest rate care component of the disability living allowance and be able to live in the community for at least the next six months; and
- be on income support (or the guarantee pension credit), or income-based job seekers allowance or have an income which is insufficient to cover the cost of the care needed (ie at or around income support levels after care costs are paid); and
- have less than £18,500 capital (although a disregard of capital earmarked for disability related expenditure can apply for up to six months). A tariff income of £1 per week is assumed for every £250 of capital between £11,500. and £18,500; and
- be assessed as needing a package of care whose cost (as funded by the ILF and the local authority) will not exceed £785 per week during the initial six months.

12.89 Local authorities are required to pay a minimum of £200 per week towards any care package supported by the ILF. Where the authority pays this minimum sum, the ILF will top up the package to a maximum sum of £375 (ie making a joint care package of £575). Larger joint packages are possible, where the authority contributes in excess of £200 per week, with the maximum ILF top-up being £455. The guidance notes detail the local authority payments required for different joint packages and include the explanatory table overleaf.

12.90 Applicants are required to contribute towards the overall cost of the care package, including all of their severe disability premium and half of their disability living allowance (DLA) care component. Earnings are however disregarded, and if the applicant is not in receipt of income support, specific charging rules apply. As the guidance notes explain, any monies contributed by the applicant (by way of DLA, severe disability premium, available income or money from savings), or by some other

110 Accessible at http://www.ilf.org.uk

Table 15: Independent Living (1993) Fund		
Min LA input £ pw	Max 93 Fund can offer £ pw	Joint Package £ pw
200	375	575
250	375	625
LA must at least match any Fund's offer over £375 – see examples below		
250 + 0.01	375 + 0.01	625.02
250 + 80	375 + 80 (max*)	785 (max*)
The Fund's maximum offer has been reached, as has the joint package maximum[111]		

contributor (such as a friend or relative) do not count towards this maximum. Likewise, NHS funding is not included within the limit.[112]

12.91 The ILF award is made on the basis that the care package will remain within the £785 per week limit for the first six months. If the applicant's circumstances change within that period the Fund may be prepared to allow the authority to increase its funding – provided that it is satisfied that the change in circumstances was not foreseeable. However, if after the six-month period the authority wishes to increase its contribution taking the joint input to above £785 per week, the award from the Fund will not normally be withdrawn.

12.92 If the local authority contribution is variable, meaning that the combined weekly cost would occasionally exceed £785, the Fund may still be prepared to contribute – for instance where the variation in local authority contribution is part of a regular and established pattern and the overall cost averaged over 52 weeks is £785 a week or less.

12.93 An independent report (for the Department for Work and Pensions) reviewing the ILF[113] has recommended among other things that ILF users who qualify for continuing health care should not automatically lose their ILF eligibility.

12.94 The review concluded that the ILF should remain in its current form until at least 2009/10 with the possibility of being incorporated within the individual budget programme from that time. It also recommended that work should begin immediately to expand the ILF to those aged 66 and over and for those on the lower rate of DLA.

12.95 The government is likely to be announcing its response to the review in the summer of 2007.

---

111 The cost of the package to be considered between the 1993 Fund and the local authority cannot exceed £785pw for the *initial* six months.

112 It appears also that 'Supporting People's' payments are not counted in this sum.

113 Report by independent consultants, Melanie Henwood and Bob Hudson, *Review of the Independent Living Funds*, Department of Work and Pensions, January 2007, p8, accessible at http://www.ilf.org.uk/cms_media/files/full_ilf_report.pdf.

NHS general responsibilities for services

continued

Introduction

13.1   At no time since the formation of the NHS has there been a clear separation between its responsibilities for health services and those of the local authorities for care services. As we note at para 1.13, the creation of the NHS in 1948 did not initially wrest responsibility for health services from local authorities, and the subsequent division of responsibilities between social services and the NHS has developed largely as a consequence of subsequent legislation.

13.2   Until 1990, successive governments sought, by simultaneous amendment[1] of the community care and NHS legislation, to transfer most health functions from local authorities to the NHS. During this period, however, perceptions as to what was a 'health function' changed. In consequence the NHS tended to concentrate upon the provision of acute health care and sought to shed its responsibilities for the long term health care needs of individuals. During the 1980s responsibility for people who would formerly have been resident in a long stay mental hospital or geriatric ward was in large measure transferred to the social security budget, leading to a substantial increase in the number of private residential and nursing homes. Accordingly the legislative changes of the last 25 years have been dominated by the tripartite tension between these three agencies. The NHS and Community Care Act (NHSCCA) 1990 radically altered the respective responsibilities of the Department of Health and Social Security (as the Department for Work and Pensions was then called) and local authorities, but left virtually unchanged the interface between the NHS and local authorities. In contrast, however, the present reforms of the NHS seek to redraw the relationship between the NHS and local authorities: indeed in relation to primary care services these may result in an effective merger of the two bodies' primary care and social services responsibilities in a 'care trust' (see para 1.17 above).

13.3   This chapter concentrates on the non-acute services for which the NHS is responsible: it does not cover the NHS responsibilities for hospital provision for acute care, either directly or through foundation trusts, nor the ever changing structure of the NHS which is outlined in chapter 1 (para 1.14).

13.4   This chapter first considers the legislation, and then the general services which the NHS provides in the community and to care homes. It then covers the specific duties to meet the registered nurse needs for those whose nursing is provided by the care home. The next chapter turns to the vexed question of when the NHS is responsible for the full cost of the patients' needs under continuing NHS health care, and so is responsible for the whole cost of any health and care package. It is that chapter that takes us to the heart of the health and social care divide.

---

1   The NHS Act 1946 and the National Assistance Act (NAA) 1948 came into force on the same day; as did the Health Services and Public Health Act 1968 and the Local Authority Social Services Act (LASSA) 1970; as did the Local Government Act 1972 and the NHS Reorganisation Act 1973.

The National Health Service Acts 2006

13.5　The principle Act governing the NHS was, initially, the NHS Act 1946. This was replaced in 1977 with the NHS Act of that year – a codification of all the changes that had occurred in the intervening years. In 2006 a further codification occurred with the repeal of the 1977 Act. However this has been replaced by two principal Acts, the NHS Act (NHSA) 2006 and the NHS (Wales) Act (NHS(W)A) 2006. A third Act, the NHS (Consequential Provisions) Act 2006, addressed technical drafting requirements that attended the codification. The decision to have two principal Acts is an expression of the extent to which Welsh devolution has created a distinct legal regime for the health service in Wales. However it is a mistake to consider the NHSA 2006 as an English statute. Although it was possible in most places to 'split' the provisions of the 1977 Act into two separate statutes, in drafting terms this was not feasible in relation to obligations which crossed England and Wales. Accordingly by default these common provisions appear in the NHSA 2006 together with 1977 provisions which were not devolved to the Assembly.[2] By way of example, the duty on NHS bodies to co-operate with local authorities (being a duty that could require co-operation between an English local authority and a Welsh NHS body) is not found in the NHS(W)A 2006. Instead it is found in NHSA 2006 s82 which when read with NHS(W)A 2006 ss28(6) and 275(1) makes it clear that the duty encompasses local health boards and Welsh NHS trusts. Likewise NHSA 2006 Sch 20 para 3, which requires social services authorities to provide home help support, has no equivalent in the Welsh Act because the definition of 'local authority' in NHSA 2006 s275 encompasses Welsh as well as English authorities.

The core health service obligation

13.6　The general NHS duty is to be found in section 1 of both the NHSA 2006 and the NHS(W)A 2006. The extent and nature of this duty is dealt with in detail below, however the wording of section 1 in both Acts is identical, save only that the Welsh Act substitutes for the 'Secretary of State' the words 'Welsh Ministers' and for 'England' the word 'Wales'. NHSA 2006 s1 provides:

　　(1) The Secretary of State must continue the promotion in England of a comprehensive health service designed to secure improvement –
　　　　(a) in the physical and mental health of the people of England, and
　　　　(b) in the prevention, diagnosis and treatment of illness.
　　(2) The Secretary of State must for that purpose provide or secure the provision of services in accordance with this Act.
　　(3) The services so provided must be free of charge except in so far as the making and recovery of charges is expressly provided for by or under any enactment, whenever passed.

2　Government of Wales Act 1998 and the National Assembly for Wales (Transfer of Functions) Order 1999 SI No 672.

13.7 NHSA 2006 s2 confers wide ranging powers in England[3] on the secretary of state to provide such services as are appropriate, namely:

> **2. Secretary of State's general power**
> (1) The Secretary of State may –
> > (a) provide such services as he considers appropriate for the purpose of discharging any duty imposed on him by this Act, and
> > (b) do anything else which is calculated to facilitate, or is conducive or incidental to, the discharge of such a duty.

13.8 NHSA 2006 s3 then sets out those general services which it is the secretary of state's duty in England[4] to provide – to such extent as s/he considers necessary – to meet all reasonable requirements. Most of the services that may be described as hospital and community health services are included under this section.[5]

13.9 Section 3(1) provides:

> **3. Secretary of State's duty as to provision of certain services**
> (1) The Secretary of State must provide throughout England, to such extent as he considers necessary to meet all reasonable requirements –
> > (a) hospital accommodation,
> > (b) other accommodation for the purpose of any service provided under this Act,
> > (c) medical, dental, ophthalmic, nursing and ambulance services,
> > (d) such other services or facilities for the care of pregnant women, women who are breastfeeding and young children as he considers are appropriate as part of the health service,
> > (e) such other services or facilities for the prevention of illness, the care of persons suffering from illness and the after-care of persons who have suffered from illness as he considers are appropriate as part of the health service,
> > (f) such other services or facilities as are required for the diagnosis and treatment of illness.

13.10 In *R (Keating) v Cardiff Local Health Board*[6] the Court of Appeal held that the word 'facilities' in section 3(1)(e) included not only the accommodation, plant and other means by which health services were provided, but also the personnel who actually provided the services. Accordingly, a local health board had the power to fund a project providing a service of advice and assistance in relation to access to state benefits for those with mental health problems.

13.11 The responsibility for actual provision of services under the NHS Acts 2006 is in general terms delegated to NHS trusts. Trusts are

---

3 In the NHS(W)A 2006 the text is identical save that 'Welsh Ministers' is substituted for 'Secretary of State' and the word 'they' for 'him'.

4 In the NHS(W)A 2006 the text is identical save that 'Welsh Ministers' is substituted for 'Secretary of State' and the word 'they' for 'he'.

5 By virtue of section 3(1A) there is power to secure these services from outside England and Wales.

6 [2005] EWCA Civ 847; [2006] 1 WLR 159; (2005) 8 CCLR 504.

semi-autonomous bodies set up to assume responsibility for the owner-ship and management of hospitals or other establishments or facilities. NHS trusts do not receive funding in the way that primary care trusts (PCTs) or local health boards (LHBs) do, but rather through obtaining contracts for their services from PCTs/LHBs.[7]

13.12   NHSA 2006 s8 empowers the secretary of state to issue directions to NHS bodies and in turn section 15 empowers strategic health authorities (SHAs) to direct PCTs. In Wales the Welsh ministers' principal powers of direction are found at NHS(W)A 2006 s19. There is no provision in the 2006 NHS Acts concerning the power to issue general guidance[8] akin to that in Local Authority Social Services Act (LASSA) 1970 s7(1) (see para 1.64 for an analysis of the status of directions and guidance).

The duty to promote a 'comprehensive' health service

13.13   In contrast to the detailed legislative duties laid upon social services authorities, the NHS's statutory duties under sections 1 and 3 are general and indeterminate: 'target duties' in the language of public law (see para 1.24 above). Accordingly the courts have been reluctant to disturb NHS administrative decisions where these general public law duties are involved. In *R v Cambridge Health Authority ex p B*[9] the decision in ques-tion concerned 'the life of a young patient'. At first instance Laws J criti-cised the authority's justification for its decision not to fund any further chemotherapy treatment for the child as consisting 'only of grave and well-rounded generalities', stating that:

> . . . where the question is whether the life of a 10-year-old child might be saved, however slim a chance, the responsible authority . . . must do more than toll the bell of tight resources . . . they must explain the priorities that have led them to decline to fund the treatment.

13.14   The Court of Appeal felt unable to sustain this line, holding instead:

> Difficult and agonising judgements have to be made as to how a limited budget is best allocated to the maximum advantage of the maximum number of patients. That is not a judgement which the court can make . . . It is not something that a health authority . . . can be fairly criticised for not advancing before the court . . .

> It would be totally unrealistic to require the authority to come to court with its accounts and seek to demonstrate that if this treatment were provided

---

7   NHS contracts are dealt with in NHSA 2006 s9 and NHS(W)A 2006 s7. Essentially such contracts are not legally enforceable but are subject to arbitration by the secretary of state/Welsh Assembly. For details of the contracting and commissioning responsibilities of PCTs, see generally http://www.primarycarecontracting.nhs.uk/ 1.php and the consultation on the Commissioning Framework for Health and Well Being, accessible at http://www.dh.gov.uk/en/Consultations/Liveconsultations/ DH_072622.
8   NHS(W)A 2006 s40(7) does however contain a general power enabling the Welsh ministers to issue guidance in relation to health and well-being strategies.
9   [1995] 1 WLR 898, CA.

for B then there would be a patient, C, who would have to go without treatment. No major authority could run its financial affairs in a way which would permit such a demonstration.

13.15 The *ex p B* decision should not be seen as an abrogation by the court of its duty to scrutinise 'anxiously' questions which engage fundamental human rights. In the case the court heard evidence of the lengths to which the health authority had gone to weigh up the likelihood of the treatment being successful, the adverse effects of the treatment and had consulted with the family. The court accepted that it was a bona fide decision taken on an individual basis and supported by respected professional opinion. In such cases, where the key consideration is expertise that the court does not possess, even with the enactment of the Human Rights Act 1998,[10] the court will inevitably hesitate to substitute its opinions. The situation will however be otherwise where the issue concerns questions of law or logic, or where an NHS body is seeking to provide a service that does not properly meet the person's needs – or subjects the person to inappropriate institutionalisation.[11]

13.16 Health bodies must, therefore, comply with the law, respect fundamental human rights and ensure that their decisions are reached in accordance with established public law principles. They must not, for instance, ignore circular guidance,[12] operate a perverse policy which (in practice) fetters their discretion to fund the treatment,[13] violate European Union law,[14] or fail to consult before reaching certain decisions. Thus in *R v North West Lancashire Health Authority ex p A*[15] the court ruled unlawful a health authority policy that allowed for the funding of gender reassignment surgery only upon the patient satisfying unattainable conditions. The policy was simply irrational.

13.17 Likewise in *R (Rogers) v Swindon NHS PCT*[16] the Court of Appeal held that a decision by a PCT not to fund the use of the drug Herceptin to treat a patient with early stage breast cancer was irrational.[17] The PCT's policy was that it would only fund the treatment if (1) the patient fell into the eligible group (namely women who would respond to the treatment) and

10 In *R (Watts) v Bedford PCT* [2003] EWHC 2228 (Admin); (2003) 6 CCLR 566 Munby J reviewed the domestic and Strasbourg jurisprudence concerning the public law obligations to provide health care services. He concluded that notwithstanding the enactment of the Human Rights Act 1998, section 1 remained a 'target' duty (see para 1.24); see also *R (Watts) v Bedford PCT* [2004] EWCA Civ 166; (2004) 77 BMLR 26.

11 See eg *Gunter v South Western Staffordshire PCT* [2005] EWHC 1894 (Admin); (2006) 9 CCLR 121 at [19]–[20].

12 *R v North Derbyshire Health Authority ex p Fisher* (1998) 1 CCLR 150 (see below).

13 *R v North West Lancashire Health Authority ex p A* [2000] 1 WLR 977; (1999) 2 CCLR 419.

14 *R (Watts) v Bedford PCT* [2004] EWCA Civ 166; (2004) 77 BMLR 26.

15 [2000] 1 WLR 977; (1999) 2 CCLR 419.

16 [2006] EWCA Civ 392; [2006] 1 WLR 2649; (2006) 9 CCLR 451.

17 The case is unusual since it was not open to the PCT to argue resource constraints since Department of Health guidance stipulated that 'PCTs should not refuse to fund Herceptin solely on the grounds of its cost', Chief Executive Bulletin, Issue 294 week 4, 10 November 2005.

(2) there were 'exceptional clinical circumstances'. The policy was irrational because there was no clinical means of separating women within the eligible group into 'exceptional' and non-exceptional.

13.18   Sections 1 and 3, the 'core NHS provisions', were subjected to considerable scrutiny by the Court of Appeal in *R v North and East Devon Health Authority ex p Coughlan*.[18] There the court noted that:

> Section 1(1) does not place a duty on the Secretary of State to provide a comprehensive health service. His duty is 'to continue to promote' such a service. In addition the services which he is required to provide have to be provided 'in accordance with this Act.'[19]

and

> . . . the Secretary of State's section 3 duty is subject to two different qualifications. First of all there is the initial qualification that his obligation is limited to providing the services identified to the extent that he considers that they are *necessary* to meet *all reasonable requirements* . . .[20]

and

> 24. The first qualification placed on the duty contained in section 3 makes it clear that there is scope for the Secretary of State to exercise a degree of judgment as to the circumstances in which he will provide the services, including nursing services referred to in the section. He does not automatically have to meet *all* nursing requirements. In certain circumstances he can exercise his judgment and legitimately decline to provide nursing services. He need not provide nursing services if he does not consider they are reasonably required or necessary to meet a reasonable requirement.

> 25. When exercising his judgment he has to bear in mind the comprehensive service which he is under a duty to promote as set out in section 1. However, as long as he pays due regard to that duty, the fact that the service will not be comprehensive does not mean that he is necessarily contravening either section 1 or section 3. The truth is that, while he has the duty to continue to promote a comprehensive free health service and he must never, in making a decision under section 3, disregard that duty, a comprehensive health service may never, for human, financial and other resource reasons, be achievable. Recent history has demonstrated that the pace of developments as to what is possible by way of medical treatment, coupled with the ever increasing expectations of the public, mean that the resources of the NHS are and are likely to continue, at least in the foreseeable future, to be insufficient to meet demand.

> 26. In exercising his judgment the Secretary of State is entitled to take into account the resources available to him and the demands on those resources. In *R v Secretary of State for Social Services and Ors ex parte Hincks* [1980] 1 BMLR 93 the Court of Appeal held that section 3(1) of the Health

---

18 [2000] 2 WLR 622; (1999) 2 CCLR 285. The case concerned the NHSA 1977 but the context of sections 1 and 3 in that Act and in the 2006 Acts is identical.
19 (1999) 2 CCLR 285 at [22].
20 Ibid, at [23].

Act does not impose an absolute duty to provide the specified services. The Secretary of State is entitled to have regard to the resources made available to him under current government economic policy.

13.19 Where a health body decides to fund a care package in such a way that it has an adverse impact on a Convention right, that decision will not be immune from court or ombudsman scrutiny. In *Gunter v South Western Staffordshire PCT*[21] the applicant wished to remain in her own home rather than be placed in an institutional setting by the PCT (which accepted continuing care responsibility for her). Collins J considered this to be a 'very important' consideration which had to 'be given due weight in deciding on her future' since to remove her from her home would 'interfere with her right to respect for her family life'.

13.20 In respect of the PCT's argument that it would be less expensive to provide the care in an institutional setting, the judge observed:

> I do not regard evidence of what benefits could accrue from the expenditure of sums which could be saved in providing a less costly package for Rachel as helpful. It is obvious that Health Authorities never have enough money to provide the level of services which would be ideal, but that cannot mean that someone such as Rachel should receive care which does not properly meet her needs.

13.21 In his opinion:

> The interference with family life is obvious and so must be justified as proportionate. Cost is a factor which can properly be taken into account. But the evidence of the improvement in Rachel's condition, the obvious quality of life within her family environment and her expressed views that she does not want to move are all important factors which suggest that to remove her from her home will require clear justification.

The medical/social divide

13.22 The conflict between health and social care is not a new one. What is a social need and what is a medical need is an intractable problem. In general (but see para 14.112) it is only of practical importance to community care service users because a service provided by the NHS is generally free at the point of need, whereas a service provided by the social services department is generally subject to a means-tested charge. Help with bathing is therefore free if provided in a person's home by the district nurse (or NHS auxiliary), whereas if provided by a social services care assistant it may be subject to a charge. The argument is repeated in a hundred different ways with such items and services as walking sticks, hoists, commodes, speech therapy, chiropody and toenail cutting.

13.23 Exhortations to organisations, professionals and other service providers to work together more closely and effectively litter the policy landscape, yet the reality is all too often a jumble of services factionalised by

21 [2005] EWHC 1894 (Admin); (2006) 9 CCLR 121.

professional culture and organisational boundaries and by tiers of governance.[22] The period since 1998 has however been marked by a series of legislative interventions designed to improve joint working in this sector – most notably by strengthening the duty to co-operate (see the Health Act (HA) 1999, para 13.122), the creation of care trusts (via the Health and Social Care Act (HSCA) 2001, para 1.17) and the duty to co-ordinate hospital discharge procedures (via the Community Care (Delayed Discharges etc) Act (CC(DD)A) 2003, para 5.7).

The duty to co-operate

13.24   There are a number of statutory duties on local authorities and health bodies to work together constructively. These fall into three broad categories, namely:

1) the obligation to co-operate at the strategic level, ie in the preparation of plans for the improvement of the health of the general population and in relation to the closure of hospitals or other facilities – these are analysed at para 2.24 above;

2) the obligation on a general day-to-day level requiring co-operation in the delivery of services to individuals who are disabled, elderly or ill – these are considered below;

3) the obligation to co-operate under the Mental Health Act (MHA) 1983 – which is covered at para 21.34.

NHS Act 2006 s82

13.25   NHSA 2006 s82 provides that:

> In exercising their respective functions NHS bodies (on the one hand) and local authorities (on the other) must co-operate with one another in order to secure and advance the health and welfare of the people of England and Wales.

13.26   The section 82 duty is a cross border obligation extending to all English and Welsh health bodies and local authorities. This extensive obligation derives from an amendment made by HA 1999 s27. The notes of guidance to the 1999 Act explained that the purpose of the amendment was to extend the duty of partnership in order to:

> . . . secure and advance the health and welfare of the people of England and Wales, to cover Primary Care Trusts and NHS trusts as well as Health

---

22   Webb, (1991) 19(4) *Policy and Politics* 29; quoted in R Means and R Smith, *Community Care*, Macmillan, 1994. There has been considerable criticism of successive governments' concentration upon creating administrative joint planning structures, on creating coterminosity, and other organisational devices to promote joint working. The research evidence suggested however that 'where mutual trust has existed between senior officers from health and local authorities, the relationship has appeared to be far more important than joint planning machinery', R Davidson and S Hunter, *Community Care in Practice*, Batsford, 1994; see also L Clements and P Smith, *A 'Snapshot' Survey of Social Services' Responses to the Continuing Care Needs of Older People in Wales* (1999).

Authorities and Special Health Authorities. This recognises the need to work in partnership in commissioning and delivering care, as well as at the strategic planning level. Welfare is used in its wide general sense and is designed to cover functions relating to social services, education, housing and the environment.

13.27 Where a community care service user suffers as a result of an inter-agency dispute, it is generally appropriate for complaints to be made against each authority primarily on the basis that they have failed to 'work together' in violation of their specific statutory obligations. The local government ombudsman has repeatedly criticised authorities for failing to provide services whilst they squabbled over their respective obligations. A 1996 ombudsman complaint, for example, concerned the failure of a health authority and social services department to co-operate. Although the ombudsman considered that the health authority's involvement had been 'reluctant, if not unhelpful', she nevertheless found the social services authority guilty of maladministration. In her opinion, having accepted that a need existed, social services should have 'grasped the nettle' and secured the provision, before entering into protracted negotiations with the NHS on liability for the care costs.[23]

Additional specific duties to co-operate

13.28 During the community care assessment process a specific duty to co-operate arises if the assessor considers that there 'may be a need' for NHS input into the process. The duty, under NHSCCA 1990 s47(3) is considered at para 3.126 above. A similar, but more extensive, duty exists in relation to patients detained under section 3 or one of the criminal provisions of the MHA 1983. The aftercare duty, under section 117 of the 1983 Act, is considered at para 21.19 below.

13.29 Certain patients who are being discharged from hospital care in England are the subject of the CC(DD)A 2003 and for them a duty to co-operate between the NHS and social services arises although the obligations are largely one way – on the social services to facilitate a discharge. The duty is considered at para 5.36 above.

13.30 In relation to children's services Children Act (CA) 1989 s27 provides children's services departments with significant powers to request assistance from (among other agencies) the NHS. This power has been augmented by CA 2004 s10 (s25 in Wales).

General duties to provide NHS services in the community and to care homes

13.31 The NHS general duty to promote a comprehensive health service requires a range of services in the community and elsewhere. All people

---

23 Complaint no 96/C/3868 against Calderdale MBC.

within the UK have a right to these services – regardless of where they are living. These services include of course access to primary care such as that provided by GPs and dentists as well as the full range of similar services such as physiotherapy, occupational therapy, chiropody, district nursing and community nursing and general ophthalmic services etc.

13.32   2007 English guidance[24] gives examples of the range of health services which PCTs are expected to provide, stating that the list 'includes but is not limited to':

- primary health care;
- assessment involving doctors and registered nurses;
- rehabilitation and recovery (where this forms part of an overall package of NHS care as distinct from intermediate care);
- respite health care;
- community health services;
- specialist health care support;
- palliative care.

13.33   Earlier 2001 English guidance[25] and existing Welsh guidance[26] lists, in addition to the above, health care equipment and specialist transport services, which are clearly NHS responsibilities, and are considered further below.

General practitioner services

13.34   NHSA 2006 s84 (NHS(W)A 2006 s42) empowers PCTs (LHBs in Wales) to arrange with medical practitioners to provide personal medical services for all persons in their area who wish to take advantage of the arrangements. These services are described as 'general medical services'. As with hospital services, it is not the PCT/LHB itself which provides the service; instead, it enters into separate statutory arrangements with independent practitioners for the provision of those services. GPs are not therefore employees of the PCT/LHB, but independent professionals who undertake to provide general medical services in accordance a general medical services contract, the terms of which are prescribed by regulations – currently the National Health Service (General Medical Services Contracts) Regulations 2004.[27]

13.35   Considerable concern has been expressed about the general performance of GPs in fulfilling their community care obligations, primarily the responsibility of ensuring that people in need of community care services are provided with the necessary assistance to obtain them.[28] Regulation

24 Department of Health, *The National Framework for NHS Continuing Healthcare and NHS Funded Nursing Care*, 2007, para 79 and the NHS Continuing Healthcare (Responsibilites) Directions 2007 – see para 14.39 below.
25 Department of Health guidance LAC (2001)18 *Continuing Care: NHS and Local Councils' responsibilities* para 16, now superseded by the 2007 National Framework.
26 NAFWC 41/2004 annex B para 2.
27 SI No 291; National Health Service (General Medical Services Contracts) (Wales) Regulations 2004 SI No 478 (W48).
28 See eg EL (96)8 para 11.

15(5)(b) of the 2004 Regulations requires that GPs refer (as appropriate) patients 'for other services under [what is now the NHSA 2006 and NHS(W)A 2006]'. As noted at para 9.137 above, NHSA 2006 s254 and Sch 20 (NHS(W)A 2006 s192 and Sch 15) place substantial duties on social services authorities. It follows that GPs are contractually obliged to make appropriate referrals to social services where it appears that a patient may be entitled to community care services. In those cases where the patient lacks mental capacity or it is otherwise unlikely that he or she will respond to such advice or referral, there will frequently be an equivalent duty owed to the patient's carer and this obligation is considered further at para 16.97 below.

13.36   Concern has been expressed about the difficulty of some care home residents accessing GP services[29] and the failure of GPs to make appropriate referrals for NHS continuing care assessments. Guidance in relation to the former has been issued via the department of health website.[30] Although there has been no specific guidance to address the latter, PCTs are required to ensure that an appropriate assessment is carried out in all cases where it appears there may be a need for continuing care services. It should follow therefore that GPs should be expected to be aware of the eligibility criteria for continuing NHS health care and make the appropriate referrals if when visiting patients they consider they meet that criteria.

GPs' obligation to prescribe drugs and appliances

13.37   The obligation on GPs to render general medical services for their patients brings with it a need to prescribe. This requirement is addressed by the NHS (General Medical Services Contracts) Regulations 2004[31] reg 39 which provides:

> Subject to paragraphs 42 and 43, a prescriber shall order any drugs, medicines or appliances which are needed for the treatment of any patient who is receiving treatment under the contract by issuing to that patient a prescription form or a repeatable prescription and such a prescription form or repeatable prescription shall not be used in any other circumstances.

13.38   Regulation 39 additionally enables GPs to prescribe 'appliances'; ie medical aids, dressings, pads etc as well as basic equipment to help overcome the effects of disability. In relation to disability equipment there is frequently an overlap of responsibility with the local social services department's community care duties. It is therefore common practice for health and social services to arrange joint equipment stores which can be accessed by both social services and the relevant NHS trust (see para 9.113).

---

29 C Glendinning *et al*, 'A survey of access to medical services in nursing and residential homes in England' (2002) 52 *British Journal of General Practice* 545.
30 See *NHS-funded nursing care: guide to care home managers on GP services for residents,* accessible at http://www.dh.gov.uk/PolicyAndGuidance/OrganisationPolicy/ IntegratedCare/NHSFundedNursingCare/NHSFundedNursingCareArticle/fs/ en?CONTENT_ID=4000392&chk=9DPYt3.
31 SI No 291; National Health Service (General Medical Services Contracts) (Wales) Regulations 2004 SI No 478 (W48).

However there are proposals to move away from this to a 'retail' model of providing equipment (see para 9.118).

13.39   The appliances which a GP can prescribe are detailed in a list known as the Drug Tariff[32] at Part IX. The lists enable GPs to provide a range of general items. Where more specialist equipment is needed, this may be obtained via a hospital consultant (see below).

13.40   The appliance list in the Drug Tariff includes such items as:

- stoma and some incontinence care equipment (see also para 13.71 below where PCT/LHB responsibility for incontinence supplies is considered);
- equipment for people with diabetes;
- elastic hosiery, dressings, bandages, trusses etc;
- respiratory equipment (including oxygen cylinders and oxygen concentrators);
- chiropody appliances. GPs can refer patients to NHS chiropodists and consultants for more specialist equipment. PCTs/LHBs must also ensure that adequate chiropody services are available to residents placed by social services in nursing home accommodation (see para 8.25 below).

GPs obligation to provide medical certificates

13.41   GPs have an important role in providing certificates for a variety of purposes, including establishing incapacity to work. Accordingly NHS (General Medical Services Contracts) Regulations 2004 reg 21 provides that GPs are required to issue free of charge to their patients (or their personal representatives) any medical certificate which is reasonably required for certain specified purposes; these being set out in column 1 of Schedule 4 to the 2004 Regulations.

Rehabilitation and recovery services

13.42   There is considerable guidance directed at the NHS stressing the import-ance of the provision of after-care services where they help promote independent living. If, with the assistance of rehabilitation or respite ser-vices, a patient can live independently in the community, resources should be devoted towards this end,[33] 1995 guidance[34] suggested that 'the existence of good rehabilitation services and well developed community health services and social care support may lessen, although not eliminate, the need for continuing inpatient care'.[35] The importance of

32 A copy can be viewed on the website of the NHS Prescription Pricing Division at http://www.ppa.org.uk.

33 The Audit Commission noted however that '[r]ehabilitation is currently advocated by many as the "missing factor" in the care of elderly people. What is clear is that many health authorities lack basic knowledge about the rehabilitation services for older people in their area', *Coming of Age*, Audit Commission, 1997.

34 LAC (95)5: HSG (95)8 *NHS Responsibilities for Meeting Continuing Health Care Needs*: WOC 16/95 and WHC (95)7 in Wales.

35 Annex A p14.

developing rehabilitation and recovery services was described as a 'crucial priority' in EL (96)89.[36]

13.43   The 1995 guidance required health authorities to take full account of the need for services:

> . . . to promote the effective recovery and rehabilitation of patients after acute treatment so as to maximise the chances of the successful implementation of long-term care plans. This is particularly important for older people who may need a longer period to reach their full potential for recovery and to regain confidence. Local policies should guard against the risk of premature discharge in terms of poorer experiences for patients and increased levels of readmissions.

13.44   Follow-up guidance in February 1996 on the local eligibility criteria (EL (96)8) expressed concern over certain rehabilitation and recovery criteria, stating (at para 16) that they would be unduly:

> . . . restrictive if they limit NHS responsibility for rehabilitation to post-acute care and do not take account of responsibilities to contribute to longer-term rehabilitative care which is needed as part of a care package for someone in their own home or in a residential care home or nursing home. Some eligibility criteria include time limits for rehabilitation or recovery. While perhaps helpful in ensuring that services are well focused, such limits will be restrictive if applied rigidly. They will usefully act as a trigger for reassessment.

13.45   The reference to 'longer-term' rehabilitative care is of importance and is echoed by the 1995 guidance in relation to respite services (see para 13.49 below). Health bodies were required to provide rehabilitation services for persons with chronic conditions, as well as acute needs. In general this obligation is not fulfilled; while the NHS provides rehabilitation following an acute episode, such as a stroke, hip operation or accident, such services are not commonly available to people with chronic conditions such as Parkinson's disease. 'Active rehabilitation' for such patients can improve their ability to cope with daily living skills and so prolong their ability to live in the community and relieve some of the pressure on their carers.

National Service Framework for Long-term Conditions

13.46   The *National Service Framework (NSF) for Long-term Conditions*[37] places very considerable emphasis on the importance of appropriate rehabilitation support. Although the weight that should be accorded to the NSF is uncertain (see para 1.61), it is clearly a benchmark of service provision and best practice against which the performance of health bodies should be assessed by disabled people and their carers. Para 16 explains what is meant by a long-term condition, namely one that is primarily

---

36   Para 6; and this emphasis was underscored by its inclusion in the NHS Priorities and Planning guidance of 1996/97 and 1997/98.

37   Department of Health, March 2005.

neurological in origin[38] and 'results from disease of, injury or damage to the body's nervous system (ie the brain, spinal cord and/or their peripheral nerve connections) which will affect the individual and their family in one way or another for the rest of their life'. Para 17 then explains:

> 17. Long-term neurological conditions can be broadly categorised as follows:
> - **Sudden onset conditions**, for example acquired brain injury or spinal cord injury, followed by a partial recovery. (Note: stroke for all ages is covered in the NSF for Older People);
> - **intermittent and unpredictable conditions**, for example epilepsy, certain types of headache or early multiple sclerosis, where relapses and remissions lead to marked variation in the care needed;
> - **progressive conditions**, for example motor neurone disease, Parkinson's disease or later stages of multiple sclerosis, where progressive deterioration in neurological function leads to increasing dependence on help and care from others. For some conditions (eg motor neurone disease) deterioration can be rapid. (Note: dementia for all ages is covered in the NSF for Older People);
> - **stable neurological conditions, but with changing needs due to development or ageing**, for example postpolio syndrome or cerebral palsy in adults.

13.47   At the heart of the NSF are the 11 quality requirements which must be fully implemented by 2015, three of which (standards 4, 5 and 6) specifically relate to rehabilitation support, namely:

4: Early and specialist rehabilitation;

5: Community rehabilitation and support;

6: Vocational rehabilitation.

Intermediate care

13.48   The intermediate care initiative is aimed at freeing up acute hospital beds and promoting the independence of older people. It is a time limited service, normally for no more than six weeks, and is considered further at chapter 11. Although the provision of intermediate care services will often satisfy a patient's needs for rehabilitation and recuperation, this will not always be the case. Given the time limited nature of the service, it will frequently be only a first stage of a programme. If at the end of a period a patient has not fully recovered, it may be that he or she can no longer receive rehabilitation support from the intermediate care team. This does not of course mean that NHS responsibility for rehabilitation has come to an end – merely that the specialised input of the intermediate care team is no longer appropriate. A similar situation arises in some areas where the intermediate team is unable to provide a full service to all patients due to

---

38   Para 4 states however that although this NSF focuses on people with neurological conditions, much of the guidance it offers can apply to anyone living with a long-term condition.

excessive demand. Again, in such cases, the duty remains with the NHS, notwithstanding that the intermediate care team is unable to field it.[39]

Respite services

13.49   In *R (T, D & B) v Haringey LBC*[40] the High Court held that the provision of respite care was capable of being a core NHS responsibility, a fact that has been repeatedly emphasised by NHS guidance.

13.50   1995 guidance[41] (now superseded) required the then health authorities to 'arrange and fund an adequate level of such care' and gave three examples of the type of patient who ought to be able to access NHS funded respite services, namely:

- people who have complex or intense health care needs and will require specialist medical or nursing supervision or assessment during a period of respite care;
- people who during a period of respite care require or could benefit from active rehabilitation; and
- people who are receiving a package of palliative care in their own homes but where they or their carer need a period of respite care.

13.51   The above reference to 'active rehabilitation' is of importance in that it is directed towards the needs of people whose condition is chronic rather than acute. By providing such persons with regular periods of respite care where they also receive such services as intensive physiotherapy, speech and occupational therapy, the NHS can prolong their ability to live independently in the community and reduce the pressure on their carers.

13.52   Follow up guidance in 1996[42] advised that NHS eligibility criteria would in general be too restrictive if confined to the above three examples, suggesting that the criteria should cover other contingencies, such as 'where carers have been providing a level of health care which is not reasonably available in a residential setting'. It is likely that all such respite care provided by the NHS should be fully funded and so free at the point of use.

13.53   In 2001 the above guidance was, in England, ostensibly consolidated[43] with the updated guidance advising (at para 25) that although local councils would 'usually have the lead responsibility for arranging and funding respite care' nevertheless 'the NHS also has important responsibilities for respite health care, including people who, during a period of respite care, require or could benefit from rehabilitation (which may include a package of intermediate care)'. The 2001 guidance has now been replaced by the

---

39 See in this respect Department of Health, *Discharge from hospital: pathway, process and practice*, 2003, para 6.1; considered at para 5.10 above.

40 [2005] EWHC 2235 (Admin); (2006) 9 CCLR 58.

41 LAC (95)5: HSG (95)8 *NHS Responsibilities for Meeting Continuing Health Care Needs*: WOC 16/95 and WHC (95)7 in Wales.

42 EL (96)8 para 16.

43 Department of Health guidance LAC (2001)18 *Continuing Care: NHS and Local Councils' responsibilities*.

2007 *National Framework for NHS Continuing Healthcare*[44] and although this document merely mentions 'respite' in the list of the range of services the NHS is expected to arrange and fund, given the genesis of the 2007 guidance, it must be assumed that it in no way detracts from the previous advice on this question.

13.54　In Wales, guidance issued in 2004[45] also provides little in the way of detail as to the nature of the respite care that the NHS should provide; at para 10 it however confirms the responsibility of the NHS for the funding of a 'wide range of services to meet the health care needs, both short and long term, of the population' and that these will, 'where necessary' include 'respite . . . care'.

13.55　The *NSF for Long-term Conditions*[46] addresses respite care in the context of it being a shared obligation of the NHS and social services and highlights the importance of 'appropriate respite care at home or in specialised settings', noting that 'respite care is a key factor in enabling care to be provided at home over a long period'.

Palliative health care

13.56　The World Health Organisation definition of palliative health care (which is accepted by the Department of Health) is:

> The total active care of patients whose disease is not responsive to curative treatment. Control of pain, and other symptoms of psychological, social and spiritual problems is paramount. The goal of palliative care is achievement of the best quality of life for the patients and their families.

13.57　Palliative care must however be distinguished from the care of 'terminally ill people', who are defined by the Department of Health (at EL (93)14 Annex F) as people with an active and progressive disease for which curative treatment is not possible or not appropriate and whose death can reasonably be expected within 12 months.[47]

13.58　The 1995 guidance (now revoked[48]) expressly required health authorities to provide:

44　Department of Health, *The National Framework for NHS Continuing Healthcare and NHS Funded Nursing Care*, 2007, para 79 – which from 1 October 2007 will be covered by directions and LASSA 1970 s7 guidance.

45　WHC (2004)54: NAFWC 41/2004 *NHS Responsibilities for Meeting Continuing NHS Health Care Needs*.

46　Department of Health, March 2005, p47 para 6 – see para 13.46 above.

47　In contrast, for the purposes of social security legislation a person has a terminal illness if it is a 'progressive disease and his death in consequence of that disease can be reasonably be expected within 6 months' – Social Security Contributions and Benefits Act 1992 s66.

48　In England, the much criticised superseding 2001 guidance (see para 14.25 below) made a number of cursory references to the NHS's responsibility for delivering palliative care (eg paras 16, 18, 23, 29 and in annex C) and likewise in Wales, WHC (2004)54: NAFWC 41/2004 makes similar references at paras 10, 14, 25 and annex B para 2. The English guidance has in turn been superseded by *The National Framework for NHS Continuing Healthcare and NHS funded Nursing Care* which makes even fewer references to palliative care, although does make reference to end of life care at para 27.

- palliative health care, on an inpatient basis, fully funded by the NHS in hospital, hospice or in a limited number of cases in nursing homes capable of providing this level of care;
- specialist palliative health care to old people already in nursing homes;
- palliative health care support to people in their own homes or in residential care.

13.59   In relation to the community care overlap between social services and health authorities, EL (93)14 gives the following guidance (at Annex C paras 10–14):

> 10. Under the wider community care reforms, from April 1993, local authorities will be responsible for assessing people's needs for care, including residential care and nursing home places. Where people have health as well as social needs, appropriate NHS staff will be involved in these assessments.
>
> 11. Where assessment reveals that a person is terminally ill and requires specialist in-patient palliative care, it will be for the health authority to arrange that, whether in a voluntary hospice, an NHS facility or an independent sector nursing home capable of providing such care. This applies equally to respite palliative care.
>
> 12. Where it is decided on the basis of assessment that a person's needs make a placement in a residential care or nursing home appropriate, the local authority will generally be responsible for arranging such a placement (although precise responsibilities will have been agreed between local authorities and health authorities).[49] Although not in need of specialist in-patient palliative care at the time of their initial assessment and placement, some people placed in this way may eventually become terminally ill[50] or enter the terminal phase of a long-term condition. Some of these patients may come in time to require specialist palliative care. Health authorities will be responsible for providing such specialist care. Depending on the individual's needs, specialist palliative care could be provided by means of a placement for temporary or permanent specialist in-patient care elsewhere (for which new placement the health authority would bear the cost) or by additional specialist health care to the person in the home where they live (in which case the health authority would fund only the additional care).
>
> 13. There has been some confusion about whether nursing homes which currently attract the 'Terminal Illness' level of Income Support should, therefore, automatically look to health authorities for funding. This is not necessarily the case. Responsibility for funding depends on the care needs as described above.

49 The wording used here is tendentious. Whether a person has a health or a social need is in every case a question of fact and agreement; whether the majority of such persons end up as the responsibility of the NHS or social services cannot be relevant in an individual's case. The Executive Letter guidance is here echoing the wording used in the draft guidance which preceded LAC (95)5; the 1994 draft stated '[t]he expectation will be that the significant majority of people who require continuing care in a nursing home setting are likely to have their needs met through social services'. This draft was the subject of substantial criticism (see eg *Community Care*, 29 September 1994, p24) and in consequence was heavily rewritten with this passage omitted.

50 That is, have (amongst other things) a life expectancy of less than 12 months.

14. HSG (92)50, issued to health authorities and Trusts in December 1992, sets out health authorities' responsibilities for the health care of people placed in residential care and nursing homes under local authority contracts. Broadly, health authorities would be expected to provide specialist palliative care to people in residential care homes as if they were living at home, and in nursing homes to provide any necessary additional specialist palliative health care in addition to general nursing (which will continue to be included in the local authority's contract with the home). Arrangements for this need to be agreed locally between health and local authorities. Local discussion and agreement are the key to seamless and responsive care.

13.60   EL (96)8 (at para 16) reminded authorities that eligibility criteria which applied time limits for palliative care would be inappropriate; such care should be provided by the NHS purely on the basis of clinical need.

13.61   In the opinion of a House of Commons Select Committee,[51] the system for providing palliative care for terminally ill patients is unfair and incompatible with the principle of a national health service, and the committee recommended (at para 47) that the Department of Health develop national criteria for continuing care, including criteria for palliative care, to remove the inequitable anomalies that arise between criteria operated by different SHAs. In its view the anomalies that arise in trying to distinguish between health and social care needs and the associated disputes, 'are especially abhorrent in respect of palliative care, where unseemly arguments about who should pay for different elements of a care package can lead to inexcusable delays and poor practice that is anything but patient-centred'.

13.62   The government response to the committee's report stated its view that 'patients who receive palliative care should meet the local criteria for fully funded NHS continuing care, in which case their personal care should remain the responsibility of the NHS'.[52]

13.63   The committee also noted research by Marie Curie Cancer Care that suggested that the cost of providing palliative health care for people in their own homes was materially less expensive than providing it in a hospital (14 days of such 'home' care costing circa £2,500 as opposed to £4,200 in a hospital).

13.64   The NHS has additional responsibilities for patients 'likely to die in the near future' – and these are considered at para 14.53 below.

51   House of Commons Health Committee Fourth Report of Session 2003–04, *Palliative Care, Volume 1*, HC 454-I, accessible at http://www.publications.parliament.uk/pa/cm200304/cmselect/cmhealth/454/454.pdf.

52   Published 16 September 2004, accessible at http://www.dh.gov.uk/PublicationsAndStatistics/Publications/PublicationsPolicyAndGuidance/PublicationsPolicyAndGuidanceArticle/fs/en?CONTENT_ID=4089264&chk=GVBNjV.

Wheelchairs

13.65 The Department of Health estimates that there are 1.2 million wheelchair users in England, of which over 800,000 are regular users of NHS wheelchair services – with still more needing to use the service for a time limited period only.[53] It appears that the service provided by the NHS has for very many years been far from satisfactory not least due to 'inequitable variations in prescribing, management structures, staffing, criteria, funding, costs and levels of services' and the lack of any national minimum standards.[54] Over the last 20 years there have been a constant stream of critical reports concerning the inadequacies of the NHS wheelchair services[55] and the evidence suggests that the service continues to leave much to be desired.[56]

13.66 Wheelchairs are seen as a facility or service provided by the NHS under section 3 of the 2006 Acts[57] and are the subject of brief Department of Health guidance issued in 1996[58] (when electrically powered indoor/outdoor wheelchairs (EPIOCs) and vouchers became available for severely disabled people through the NHS) and 2004 good practice guidance.[59] Individual can also obtain a powered wheelchair (or a scooter) through the Motability Scheme by surrendering their high rate mobility component of DLA.

13.67 Wheelchairs may be obtained from NHS trusts for temporary use on discharge from hospital,[60] and residential care homes are expected to provide wheelchairs for occasional use[61] – but for regular use they should access the same wheelchair services as disabled people living

---

53 Department of Health/Care Services Improvement Partnership, *Out and about: Wheelchairs as part of a whole-systems approach to independence*, October 2006, p5.

54 See *National standards for wheelchair services: Final Consultation Draft Document*, 2003, accessible at http://www.wheelchairmanagers.nhs.uk/servicestandards.doc.

55 See eg I McColl, *Review of artificial limb and appliance centre services*, DHSS, 1986; *National Prosthetic and Wheelchair Services Report 1993–1996* (the Holderness report), College of Occupational Therapists; Audit Commission, *Fully equipped: the provision of equipment to older or disabled people by the NHS and social services in England and Wales*, 2000; Audit Commission, *Fully equipped 2002: assisting independence*, 2002; Department of Health, *Evaluation of the Powered Wheelchair and Voucher System 2000*, 2002; emPower, *NHS Wheelchair and Seating Services Mapping Project: final report*, Limbless Association, 2004; Prime Minister's Strategy Unit, *Improving the life chances of disabled people*, 2005.

56 See eg N Sharma with J Morrison, *Don't push me around! Disabled children's experiences of wheelchair services in the UK*, 2006, a joint report published by Barnardo's and Whizz-Kidz and endorsed by the UK's four Children's Commissioners.

57 Department of Health/Care Services Improvement Partnership, *Out and about: Wheelchairs as part of a whole-systems approach to independence*, October 2006, p30.

58 HSG (96)34 *Powered indoor/outdoor wheelchairs for severely disabled people* and HSG(96)53 *The wheelchair voucher scheme*.

59 Department of Health, *Improving Services for Wheelchair Users and Carers: Good Practice Guide*, December 2004.

60 It appears that in practice many trusts fail to provide wheelchairs in such situations, relying on separate PCT commissioning (eg from the local Red Cross) or via a joint equipment store (see para 9.113).

61 Department of Health, *Discharge from hospital: pathway, process and practice*, 2003, para 5.3.1.

independently.⁶² It appears, however, that due to a flawed interpretation of NHS hospital discharge guidance in England,⁶³ not infrequently the provision of wheelchairs for nursing home residents is unsatisfactory. The guidance states that such homes should provide 'some standard items of equipment for anyone needing them and for the safety of staff'. Some PCTs have interpreted this as requiring the home to have a pool of wheelchairs so that (in general) residents may not be provided with a permanent wheelchair. In such situations, where there is an inadequate number of chairs or no suitable chair, the resident will be severely disadvantaged. In the absence of special factors this would appear to amount unjustified discrimination in relation to goods and services, since the difference in treatment stems solely from the location of the care – rather than individual need.⁶⁴

13.68   The assessment of need for, and the provision of, wheelchairs (and wheelchair cushions etc) is in practice undertaken by local NHS wheelchair services in England, and in Wales by the Artificial Limb and Appliance Service.⁶⁵ The assessment is undertaken by a specialist, usually an occupational therapist, physiotherapist or consultant who will then identify the most suitable wheelchair. If the disabled person has difficulty using a manual wheelchair the trust can supply an electric model, including one for outdoor use if appropriate.⁶⁶ The NHS in England additionally operates a 'wheelchair voucher scheme' that gives users the option of purchasing from an independent supplier or from the wheelchair service. In either case the user can top up the voucher cost (which covers only the cost of a 'standard' wheelchair to meet the user's needs – ie not an EPIOC) to enable a more expensive model to be acquired. However if the chair is purchased from an independent supplier it is owned by the user who is responsible for its maintenance and repair, whereas if the 'wheelchair services' option is chosen, the trust retains ownership but is also responsible for its maintenance.⁶⁷

13.69   Since 1996 funding has been available for the provision of EPIOCs, although targeted on 'more severely disabled users (including children) who could benefit from them to enjoy enhanced levels of independent mobility inside and outside their home'.⁶⁸ The suggested

62 Department of Health, *Community Equipment Services*, HSC 2001/008: LAC (2001)13, which at para 7 makes clear that although community equipment services may provide wheelchairs for short term loan, the service is not for permanent wheelchair users, 'as these are prescribed and funded by different NHS services'.
63 Department of Health, *Discharge from hospital: pathway, process and practice*, 2003, para 5.3.1.
64 In this respect, see also HSC 2001/17: LAC (2001)26 *Guidance on free nursing care in nursing homes* p8 para 9 which states that PCTs should ensure that care home residents should have access to the full range of specialist NHS support that is available in other care settings including 'aids to mobility'.
65 Which operates from three centres, namely Cardiff, Swansea and Wrexham.
66 HSG (96)34.
67 HSG (96)53.
68 As a general rule, once an individual receives an EPIOC, the manual wheelchair should also be retained as a back up.

(1996) criteria for such wheelchairs being that the severely disabled person is:[69]

- unable to propel a manual chair outdoors;
- able to benefit from the chair through increased mobility leading to improved quality of life;
- able to handle the chair safely.

Research has however suggested that these criteria exclude significant numbers of potential beneficiaries and the availability of EPIOCs[70] is currently being reviewed.

13.70   A 2006 Department of Health report concerning wheelchair provision[71] advised that social services authorities could, in appropriate cases, consider using their powers under Carers (Equal Opportunities) Act 2004 s3 (see para 16.100) to 'request that the NHS provide a certain type of wheelchair (perhaps one more expensive than usual) in order not only to meet the needs of the disabled person, but also to make life easier for the carer'. The 2006 report also suggests that a wheelchair could be provided by social services under the community care legislation[72] (presumably under Chronically Sick and Disabled Persons Act 1970 s2). Wheelchairs have been included in the new 'retail model' proposed for the future provision of equipment.[73]

Incontinence services

13.71   Incontinence services, despite their significant cost,[74] frequently appear to be of poor quality. A 2006 report[75] expressed concern over the reduced availability of specialist nurses, the continued inadequate assessment of incontinence and the over emphasis on the use of pads rather than less expensive preventative measures which gave greater dignity to users.

13.72   Since April 2004 continence supplies in England and Wales should be provided free of charge by PCTs/LHBs in all settings.[76] The English

---

69 NHS Executive, *Powered indoor/outdoor wheelchairs for severely disabled people*, HSG (96)34, May 1996.

70 Department of Health funded research undertaken by the York Health Economics Consortium, *The Evaluation of the Powered Wheelchair and Voucher Scheme Initiatives*, March 2000, accessible at http://www.dh.gov.uk/en/Publicationsandstatistics/Publications/PublicationsPolicyAndGuidance/DH_4009655.

71 Department of Health/Care Services Improvement Partnership, *Out and about: Wheelchairs as part of a whole-systems approach to independence*, October 2006, p30.

72 Ibid, p15 Case Study E.

73 Details can be found at http://www.csed.csip.org.uk/workstreams/transforming-community-equipment–wheelchair-services/community-equipment.html.

74 The annual cost of these services to the NHS in 2004 was estimated to be in the region of £743 million per year: DA Turner, C Shaw, CW McGrowther et al, 'The cost of clinically significant urinary storage symptoms for community dwelling adults in the UK' (2004) 93(9) *BJU International* 1246–1252.

75 Royal College of Physicians, *National Audit of Continence Care For Older People*, November 2006, accessible at http://www.rcplondon.ac.uk/news/news.asp?PR_id=331.

76 Prior to 2001 in England and 2004 in Wales people in nursing homes were not provided with incontinence supplies by the NHS.

2001 guidance[77] stated that 'PCTs are responsible for arranging ... the provision of nursing advice, eg continence advice and stoma care' and at para 29 that it is their responsibility to provide 'continence pads and equipment and nursing aids'. While the 2007 *National Framework for NHS Continuing Healthcare*, which supersedes 2001 English guidance, make no mention of continence services, it appears that the policy intention of the 2001 guidance remains, including that in circular HSC 2001/17: LAC (2001)26[78] which advises as follows:

- ... An overview assessment for continence needs (see Annex E of the single assessment process guidance) should be carried out as part of the initial NHS assessment and RNCC determination of current residents of nursing homes. A subsequent assessment ... should be carried out by a continence adviser or other suitably qualified nurse professional where this is indicated. [The Good Practice Guidance[79]] should ... inform the continence aspects of any comprehensive assessment of needs for people newly entering a nursing home.
- Systems should be established to ensure nursing homes receive the continence supplies required by residents[80] ... The provision of continence products should always follow an assessment of the patient's needs. ...

13.73 Detailed practice guidance has additionally been issued in England concerning the organisation and range of continence services that should be made available.[81]

13.74 The nature and quantity of continence supplies made available will depend upon an individual assessment of need in every case. The evidence suggests[82] that despite the need for pads to be available on the basis of clinical need, almost 75 per cent of PCTs operate a fixed policy which stipulates a maximum number of continence pads that can be provided over a specified period. Such policies are contrary to the guidance, fetter the authorities' discretion and, where individual hardship results, constitute maladministration.

---

77 LAC (2001)18, para 23.
78 Department of Health, *Guidance on free nursing care in nursing homes*, 2001. This guidance too is superseded on 1 October 2007 by new guidance regarding the nursing bands (see para 14.37 below) and although no mention is made of the requirement for an assessment of continence needs of residents, absent an announcement to the contrary it is inconceivable that the policy intention does not remain.
79 Department of Health, *Good Practice in Continence Services*, April 2000.
80 Nursing homes should not need to charge fees for continence products to individuals. These should be paid for in the fees paid by councils for residents they support or through the NHS in the case of self funders.
81 Department of Health, *Good Practice in Continence Services*, April 2000.
82 Royal College of Physicians, *National Audit of Continence Care For Older People*, November 2006, accessible at http://www.rcplondon.ac.uk/news/news.asp?PR_id=331.

Chiropody, speech therapy and physiotherapy

13.75 The NHS is responsible for the provision of such services as physio-therapy, speech and language therapy and chiropody[83] for all people in need of such services regardless of whether they are living independently or in local authority or independent sector care homes. To this list, 2001 guidance[84] in England added occupational therapy, dietetics and podiatry.

13.76 Cutbacks to chiropody services have been widespread over recent years. In many areas toe nail cutting services have been withdrawn and increasingly chiropody services are only available to people with specific conditions such as diabetes.

13.77 As a result of many people in care homes having to pay for chiropody services, guidance has reminded local authorities that residents should not be expected to use their personal expenses allowance for items that have been assessed as necessary to meet their needs by the council or the NHS: the guidance further reminds authorities that the care plans of residents must fully reflect their incontinence and chiropody needs.[85]

Transport

13.78 The 2001 guidance[86] and 2004 Welsh guidance[87] list specialist transport as a service that must be provided by the NHS. The guidance is to be found in HSG 1991(29) which sets out the standards and eligibility for emer-gency and urgent ambulances as well as criteria for establishing which patients are eligible for non-emergency patient transport services (PTS). Until April 2007 such services were only available for travel to hospital settings. However this has been extended to a wider range of settings, to reflect the fact that treatment that used to be provided in hospital is now often provided in more diverse local settings. Under the new arrange-ments PCTs are to assume responsibility from the acute trusts for com-missioning PTS. The consultation document states that it updates and replaces the 1991 guidance.[88]

---

83   LAC (92)24, para 2 and see also LAC (95)5: HSG (95)8 *NHS Responsibilities for Meeting Continuing Health Care Needs*; WOC 16/95 and WHC (95)7 in Wales.

84   LAC (2001)18, paras 23 and 29. The Welsh 2004 guidance NAFWC 41/2004 similarly lists 'therapies, dietetics and podiatry' in annex B para 2. Although the English 2001 guidance is now superseded (see para 14.37) and the new 2007 guidance does not mention these services, absent an announcement to the contrary it is inconceivable that the policy intention (or indeed legal obligation) that the NHS provide this range of services, does not remain.

85   The latest in a number of reminders about this subject is in LAC DH(2007) 04 and NAFWC 19/07.

86   LAC (2001)18, paras 23 and 29. Although the English 2001 guidance is now superseded (see para 14.37) and the new 2007 guidance does not mention transport services, absent an announcement to the contrary it is inconceivable that the policy intention (or indeed legal obligation) that the NHS provide transport in appropriate situations, does not remain.

87   NAFWC 41/20 annex B para 2.

88   Department of Health, *Eligibility Criteria for Patient Transport Services*, November 2006, para 1.

13.79   Patients who are eligible for PTS are those:

- where the patient's medical condition is such that he or she requires the skill of PTS staff on/after the journey or where it would be detrimental to the patients' condition or recovery if he or she were to travel by other means;
- where the patient's medical condition impacts on his or her mobility to such an extent that he or she would not be able to access health care and/or it would be detrimental to the patient's condition or recovery if he or she were to travel by other means;
- who are parents or guardians of children being conveyed to and from hospital.

13.80   Transport can also be provided to escorts or carers where their particular skills are needed such as to accompany a person with physical or mental incapacity, or to act as a translator. This is discretionary.

13.81   The decision about eligibility for transport is taken by a health care professional who is either working for the NHS or working under contract to the NHS. Commissioners have been told to develop a standard approach so that patients do not receive different responses from each site they visit.[89] Although patients cannot be charged for transport if it is required for a health need, the consultation guidance states[90] that PCTs can use it for income generation if the provision of transport is a 'social' need rather than a 'medical' need.

13.82   More detailed information and guidance[91] accompanies the consultation document and covers the use of ambulances, helicopters, transporting patients out of area, care homes, hospices and social service facilities, and transporting private patients.

13.83   In respect of transport of residents to and from (or between) care homes, it states:

> As many such patients are receiving a joint package of health and local authority (social services) care it is reasonable for the PTS costs for these patients to be commissioned by the PCT . It will represent a small contribution to the health care package of jointly funded patients. Historically the NHS would have provided the majority of such services and the local authority funding would not have been used for this purpose. It is therefore considered equitable for the NHS to continue to meet the cost. Care should be exercised however to ensure that these journeys are on medical rather than social grounds.[92]

13.84   It is arguable that this provision should not just extend to joint packages but to those situations where it is considered medically necessary for a resident to move to and from a home or between homes. For instance, if it is the opinion of NHS staff that a self funding resident needs to move to a nursing home, and transport is required.

---

89   Ibid, para 3.
90   Ibid, para 12, which further refers to *NHS income generation – best practice: Revised guidance on income generation in the NHS*, February 2006.
91   Department of Health, *Finance Arrangements for Ambulance Services*, November 2006, chapter 20.
92   Ibid, para 20.54.

NHS specialist or intensive services for people in care homes

13.85 It is a basic tenet of the NHS that all medical and nursing services are provided free at the point of need. Whilst this principle is curtailed in so far as it applies to the needs of residents in nursing homes not funded by the NHS, the limitation only applies to the non-registered nursing[93] needs of such residents.

13.86 The respective responsibilities of the NHS and social services authorities in this area have been the subject of successive guidance. LAC (92)24 advised, at para 2:

> 2. Local authority contracts for independent sector residential care should not include provision of any service which it is the responsibility of the NHS to provide. It will continue to be the responsibility of the NHS to provide where necessary community health services to residents of LA and independent residential care homes on the same basis as to people in their own homes. These services include the provision of district nursing and other specialist nursing services (eg, incontinence advice) as well as the provision, where necessary, of incontinence and nursing aids, physiotherapy, speech and language therapy and chiropody. Where such services are provided they must be free of charge to people in independent sector homes as well as to residents of local authority Part III homes.

13.87 1995 guidance[94] clarified this distinction in the following terms:

> Some people who will be appropriately placed by social services in nursing homes, as their permanent home, may still require some regular access to specialist medical, nursing or other community health services. This will also apply to people who have arranged and are funding their own care. This may include occasional continuing specialist medical advice or treatment, specialist palliative care, specialist nursing care such as incontinence advice, stoma care or diabetic advice or community health services such as physiotherapy, speech therapy and language therapy and chiropody. It should also include specialist medical or nursing equipment (for instance specialist feeding equipment) not available on prescription and normally only available through hospitals . . .

> Assessment procedures and arrangements for purchasing care should take account of such needs and details should be identified in individual care plans. In such cases the NHS can either provide such services directly or contract with the home to provide the additional services required. Such additional services should be free at the point of delivery.

13.88 LAC (92)24 defined what was meant by 'specialist nursing' as 'primarily continence advice and stoma care, but also other specialist nursing such as diabetic liaison and other community health services (primarily physiotherapy, speech and language therapy and chiropody'.

---

93 The NHS is responsible for all nursing care provided by a registered nurse, or nursing care planned, supervised and/or delegated by a registered nurse (even if actually undertaken by a non-registered nurse) – see para 13.96 below.

94 LAC (95)5: HSG (95)8 *NHS Responsibilities for Meeting Continuing Health Care Needs*: WOC 16/95 and WHC (95)7 in Wales.

13.89   In relation to NHS services for care home residents, the 2007 *National Framework for NHS Continuing Healthcare*[95] guidance advises that:

> Additional health services apart from registered nursing may also be funded by the NHS if these are agreed as part of the care plan. The range of services which the NHS is expected to arrange and fund includes but is not limited to:
> - Primary health care
> - Assessment involving doctors and registered nurses
> - Rehabilitation and recovery (where this forms part of an overall package of NHS care as distinct from intermediate care)
> - Respite health care
> - Community health services
> - Specialist health care support
> - Palliative care.

13.90   The list in the superseded 2001 guidance[96] in England[97] was more specific, including in addition the items below. Absent an announcement to the contrary, it is inconceivable that the policy intention (or indeed legal obligation) that the NHS provide these services, does not remain.

> - access to GP and other primary care services (including community nursing);
> - physiotherapy, occupational therapy, speech and language therapy, dietetics and podiatry;
> - continence pads and equipment and nursing aids (see below);
> - the provision of district nursing (in residential care homes) and other nursing services eg continence advice and stoma care;
> - specialist medical and nursing equipment (in nursing homes eg specialist feeding equipment) normally only available through hospitals;
> - and access to hospital care, which should also be arranged whenever it is required.

Specialist medical equipment in care homes

13.91   The joint responsibilities of social services and the NHS for the community equipment services is considered at para 9.113 above. However the issue of 'specialist medical and nursing' equipment can cause problems. In general however, a care home providing nursing only has to provide the general equipment which is a prerequisite for its registration. Thus if a patient is in need of equipment which is not part of the basic registration requirement, it may be argued that this is therefore 'specialist' in the

---

95   Department of Health, *The National Framework for NHS Continuing Healthcare and NHS Funded Nursing Care*, 2007, para 79.

96   LAC (2001)18, paras 23 and 29.

97   The Welsh 2004 guidance NAFWC 41/2004 merely lists the general services that are available in the community (see para 14.92), stating that 'some specific arrangements apply'.

sense that it ought to be funded by the NHS.[98] The Health Service Ombudsman has, for instance, investigated a complaint[99] concerning an elderly nursing home resident who had to be fed by means of a gastric tube. Although the liquid feed was supplied on prescription she was required to pay for the tubes through which the feed was delivered (at £25 per week). The health authority accepted that this was incorrect and refunded the cost of the tubes.

13.92   Guidance has been issued concerning the provision of such equipment through joint community equipment stores[100] (see para 9.113). Department of Health circular HSC 2001/17: LAC (2001)26[101] additionally made the following comments concerning specialist equipment:

> 8. For the majority of care home residents, much of the equipment necessary for their care will be available in the care home. Equipment is also available on prescription from a GP or a prescribing nurse. Details are contained in the Drug Tariff. This covers a range of appliances, including stoma and incontinence appliances, as well as the domiciliary oxygen therapy service.

> 9. Care home residents should have access to the full range of specialist NHS support that is available in other care settings and to people receiving care at home. In addition to equipment that is provided or secured by the care home in accordance with the minimum standards, the NHS should also consider whether there is a need to provide residents with access to dietary advice, as well as to the full range of available community equipment services, including pressure redistributing equipment, aids to mobility, and communication aids, etc that are available in other settings. Specialist equipment needs for individual use should be specified in the assessment and subsequent care plan, together with the arrangements for getting the equipment in place, and any aftercare that may be necessary. Residents should have access to other NHS services, such as the wheelchair service, and staff working for the NHS should be responsible for assessing them.

13.93   LAC 2003 (7): HSC 2003/006[102] states at para 30:

> Where the NHS has determined that the individual requires a particular piece of equipment, it should ensure either that the care home provides it; or provide it on a temporary basis until the care home is able to provide it;

---

98   Para 5.3.1 of the pathways guidance (see para 5.10) states that 'care homes providing nursing care are expected to have, as part of the facilities they provide, some standard items of equipment for anyone needing them and for the safety of staff. These should include hoists, wheelchairs for occasional use, bath and shower seats and fixed items such as grab rails. All other items of equipment to meet the needs of an individual should be, or should have been, provided to them on the same basis as if they were living in a private house, applying the same eligibility criteria'.

99   Case no E.985/94, p61 Selected Investigations April–September 1996.

100   HSC 2001/008: LAC (2001)13 *Community Equipment Services.*

101   Department of Health, *Guidance on free nursing care in nursing homes*, 2001. Although this guidance is to be replaced in October 2007 by new guidance regarding the nursing bands (see para 13.111 below), its advice in this respect must remain valid, not least because the subsequent (extant) guidance *Community Equipment in Care Homes* (cited below) makes frequent reference to this 2001 guidance.

102   Department of Health, *Good Practice in Continence Services*, April 2000.

or provide it to the individual as long as they need it. It would be unreasonable to expect care homes to provide items of equipment , that by the nature of the design size and weight requirements, need to be specially tailored to meet the individual's needs and would not be capable of being used by other care home residents.

13.94 Further non-statutory guidance[103] issued in 2004 concerning equipment in care homes includes the suggestion (p7) that:

> If a significant number of people use a particular item of equipment in a particular care home it is more likely to be for the care home to provide. If it is for a single user as part of a specific agreed care plan, then it is more likely for health or social services to be the provider even though some of these items may not always be called 'specialist'.

NHS payments for registered nursing care in nursing homes

13.95 In 1999 the Royal Commission on long term care published its report *With Respect to Old Age*[104] recommending that personal care and nursing services should be provided free of charge to all persons assessed as being in need of these services (regardless of whether they were living in the community, a care home or a hospital). The government in England felt unable to accept the full recommendations and opted instead to fund only the registered nursing care costs of residents in nursing homes.[105] There had been much concern that the only people who had to pay for their nursing care were people in care homes providing nursing care. In all other situations at home or in residential care the NHS provided the nursing care via the district nursing services.

13.96 The policy proposal was brought into effect in England and Wales via HSCA 2001 s49 which makes it unlawful for a local authority to provide nursing 'by a registered nurse'. Section 49 provides:

> 49(1) Nothing in the enactments relating to the provision of community care services[106] shall authorise or require a local authority, in or in connection with the provision of any such services, to –

---

103 *Community Equipment in Care Homes*, accessible at http://www.icesdoh.org/ doc.asp?ID=28. It states that it does not create new guidance, nor resolve contradictions that may occur from the application or interpretation of existing or future government guidance, nor does it necessarily represent the views of the Department of Health.

104 Royal Commission on Long-Term Care, *With Respect to Old Age: Long-Term Care – Rights and Responsibilities*, Cm 4192, TSO, 1999.

105 Announced in Department of Health, *The NHS Plan*, July 2000, para 15.181 and enacted as HSCA 2001 s49.

106 In *R (T, D and B) v Haringey LBC* [2005] EWHC 2235 (Admin); (2006) 9 CCLR 58 the section 49 prohibition was found only to apply to adults. This arises out of the wording of section 49 which prohibits registered nursing care being provided pursuant to local authorities' community care functions under NHSCCA 1990 s46 which do not include the CA 1989.

> (a) provide for any person, or
> (b) arrange for any person to be provided with,
>   nursing care by a registered nurse.
> (2) In this section 'nursing care by a registered nurse' means any services provided by a registered nurse and involving –
>   (a) the provision of care, or
>   (b) the planning, supervision or delegation of the provision of care, other than any services which, having regard to their nature and the circumstances in which they are provided, do not need to be provided by a registered nurse.

13.97 The legislation came into effect from October 2001 (December 2001 in Wales) for residents who funded their own care, and from April 2003 (April 2004 in Wales) for residents funded by the local authority.

13.98 Guidance (incorporating directions) concerning the impact of section 49 in England was issued in 2001[107] and in 2003[108] (in this section referred to as the 2001 and the 2003 guidance). This guidance has from October 2007 been superseded by new statutory guidance and directions.[109] In England all nursing home residents (regardless of whether self funding or supported by social services) are provided with an assessment by their local PCT, which determines the extent of their nursing care needs (known as the 'registered nursing care contribution – RNCC). Prior to October 2007 these needs were banded[110] into 'high', 'medium' and 'low' and a contribution made by the PCT in relation to each (as at April 2007, these amounted to £139, £87 or £40 per week). Flexibility existed to pay a higher rate than the £139, and also for PCTs to decide on a case by case basis an amount between the low and medium band. In contrast in Wales, the Assembly opted for a much simpler approach – that every nursing home resident would receive the same contribution from the LHB and as at April 2007 it amounted to £114.90 per week.[111] From October 2007 there is just one band in England, which has provisionally been set at £101 per week. [112]

Section 49 and its interface with continuing care

13.99 It could argued that with the introduction of section 49, continuing health care responsibilities came to an end, since the section provided a clear

---

107 HSC (2001)17: LAC (2001)26 *Guidance on Free Nursing Care in Nursing Homes.*
108 HSC 2003/006: LAC (2003)7 *Guidance on NHS Funded Nursing Care.*
109 The guidance is to be found in annex D of Department of Health, *The National Framework for NHS continuing Healthcare and NHS Funded Nursing Care*, 26 June 2007. The directions coming into force on 1 October 2007 are the NHS (Nursing Care in Residential Accommodation) (England) Directions 2007 (see para 3.112).
110 These are detailed in Department of Health, *NHS Funded Nursing Care Practice Guide & Workbook*, August 2001.
111 NAFWC 34/01 *Paying for NHS Funded Nursing Care in Nursing Homes*. Further guidance was issued in 2004 when the provisions in HSCA 2001 s49 came fully into effect in Wales – NAFWC 25/2004: WHC (2004)024.
112 Department of Health, *The National Framework for NHS continuing Healthcare and NHS Funded Nursing Care. Final Regulatory Impact Assessment*, 2007, para 34.

demarcation between the respective responsibilities of the NHS and social services. This is not the case. The obligation under section 49 is entirely separate. As the explanatory note accompanying section 49 states, its purpose is to remove:

> local authorities' functions to purchase nursing care by a registered nurse under community care legislation. This is intended to strengthen the incentives for the NHS to ensure effective rehabilitation after acute illness or injury. It is estimated that around 35,000 people who are currently paying for their nursing care will receive free nursing care through the NHS.

13.100   The payments made by the PCTs/LHBs are in any event recycled social services monies[113] – in that the funds to pay for these contributions have been deducted from social services Formula Spending Share and transferred to PCTs /LHBs.

13.101   The English 2001 guidance appendix 6 was explicit about the distinction between section 49 payments and continuing care:

> *Relationship with Continuing Care*
> Nothing in this guidance changes the duties of HA's to arrange and fully fund services for people whose primary needs are for healthcare rather than for accommodation and personal care.

13.102   The 2003 guidance stressed this even more clearly at paras 18 and 19:

> Regardless of the eventual setting which the individual is likely to be cared for, in carrying out a joint assessment of the individuals' needs, the first consideration should always be to the extent to which that person meets, or does not meet, the criteria for NHS continuing health care.

> This must be done on a case by case basis, looking at *all* the individual's needs – for medical and nursing care as well as therapeutic and personal care. NHS funded nursing care is part of a spectrum of care, where people needs a mixture of nursing and social care. It is different from, and is not a substitute for, fully funded NHS continuing care, where a person's health needs will be beyond the scope of what can be funded through NHS funded nursing care.

13.103   Notwithstanding this guidance, the very existence of the RNCC bands created a conceptual problem in relation to the scope of the NHS's continuing health care responsibilities. This stemmed from an appreciation of status of these 'bands' – namely that they were the creation of the Department of Health, not parliament, and the three bands[114] (high, medium and low) were arbitrary to the extent that the Department of Health had an almost entirely free hand in determining the eligibility criteria for each band of support.

---

113   For details of how the PCT contributions are actually paid, see HSC 2003/006: LAC (2003) 7.
114   These are detailed in Department of Health, *NHS Funded Nursing Care Practice Guide & Workbook*, August 2001.

13.104   A number of commentators suggested that Department of Health in its guidance set the high level of support (ie the 'high' band) above the level defined by the Court of Appeal as the point at which a person could expect full continuing care funding.[115] By so doing, the department had caused very considerable confusion amongst PCTs. Para 3.8 of the guidance[116] describes the 'high band' as follows:

> 3.8 People with high needs for registered nursing care will have complex needs that require frequent mechanical, technical and/or therapeutic interventions. They will need frequent intervention and re-assessment by a registered nurse throughout a 24 hour period, and their physical/mental health state will be unstable and/or unpredictable.

13.105 The patient who was the subject of the complaint to the Health Service Ombudsman in the Leeds case – about a failure by the NHS to provide long term care for a brain-damaged patient – would not have met these criteria, nor would Pamela Coughlan. Indeed the high band accurately described the condition of the Wigan and Bolton nursing home resident whom the Health Service Commissioner considered to be unquestionably entitled to continuing health care funding.

13.106   Concern was expressed not only in relation to the high band. A person assessed as qualifying for the 'medium band', it was suggested, might also qualify for continuing care. Para 3.9 describes the medium band in the following terms:

> 3.9 People whose needs for registered nursing care are judged to be in the medium banding may have multiple care needs. They will require the intervention of a registered nurse on at least a daily basis, and may need access to a nurse at any time. However, their condition (including physical, behavioural and psychosocial needs) is stable and predictable, and likely to remain so if treatment and care regimes continue.

Both Pamela Coughlan and the patient who was the subject of the Leeds case might have had difficulty qualifying for this band.

13.107   In *R (Grogan) v Bexley NHS Care Trust and others*[117] Charles J agreed with the many critics that the RNCC had caused confusion and (at para 61):

> . . . that as a matter of fact registered nursing care falling within the high band (and perhaps the medium bands) falls outside that limit set by *Coughlan*, particularly when it is remembered that the focus of *Coughlan* was on nursing care and the decision of the Court of Appeal was that the care she needed was well outside the limits of what could be lawfully provided by a local authority . . .

115 In *R (Grogan) v Bexley NHS Care Trust and others* [2006] EWHC 44 (Admin); (2006) 9 CCLR 188 at [59], Charles J cited with approval criticisms made (i) in the 3rd edition of this book, (ii) by the Health Service Commissioner, and (iii) by the Select Committee in its Sixth Report of Session 2004–05 (HC 399-i) on NHS Continuing Care.

116 Department of Health, *NHS Funded Nursing Care Practice Guide & Workbook*, August 2001.

117 [2006] EWHC 44 (Admin); (2006) 9 CCLR 188.

13.108 In March 2006 the Department of Health issued 'interim' guidance to address the *Grogan* judgement.[118] The guidance emphasised that the RNCC assessment was only applicable once it has been established that the patient was not eligible for continuing care funding (para 19), stating that 'any suggestion that the description of the RNCC bands operate on the decision to award NHS Continuing Healthcare should be removed from criteria' (para 29). The guidance also made a number of ambiguous statements concerning the high and middle bands of health care – which may or may not reduce their demanding nature. In this context it states (para 26) that 'to the extent that the descriptions of the high band and of the medium band . . . appear to describe a need for nursing care beyond that which could be deemed incidental and ancillary . . . [they] should be disregarded'. This statement has been repeated in annex D of the 2007 guidance pending the change in October 2007 to just one band. It also states that the workbook will be reviewed before the implementation of the single band.

13.109   It appears that there were about 15–20,000 people in high band RNCC at the time of the *Grogan* decision.[119]

Moving to one band of payment in England

13.110 With the removal of the banding system, the above commentary will be academic for new residents. However there are a large number of current cases outstanding regarding either disputes about the level of the RNCC or if indeed the resident should be funded under NHS continuing care, rather than just be given a contribution to his or her nursing care needs.

13.111   The 2007 guidance issued in June 2007 states that '[t]he determination for NHS funded Nursing Care should be integrated into the same framework as eligibility determination and care planning for NHS Continuing Healthcare'. From October 2007 the main decision that is required for a person who needs care in a care home providing nursing care, is whether or not he or she should be fully funded by the NHS (see chapter 14). The making of that decision should provide sufficient information for a decision as to whether the individual requires registered nursing care in a care home. In those cases where the person has not been considered as requiring a continuing care assessment but is still considered as needing registered nursing in a care home providing nursing care, the normal assessment process should be followed, such as the single assessment process, 'to ensure the decisions reached are proportionate, reasoned and recorded'.[120]

118 Department of Health, *NHS Continuing Health Care: Action Following the Grogan Judgment*, 3 March 2006.
119 M Henwood, *Self-funding of long-term care and potential for injustice*, Background Paper prepared for BBC Panorama, 2006, accessible at http://news.bbc.co.uk/1/shared/bsp/hi/pdfs/05_03_06_melaniehenwood.pdf.
120 2007 guidance annex D para 2.

13.112 The 2007 guidance at annex D explains that when the single band is implemented through directions[121] it triggers the PCT's responsibility to fund the care from a registered nurse through a single rate. New residents in homes providing nursing care who do not qualify for NHS continuing health care will receive the single rate unless it is determined that the person no longer has any need for nursing care, leaves nursing home care, becomes eligible for NHS continuing health care, or dies.[122] It follows that for the majority of residents who are currently on the £40 or £87 bands, the single band represents an increase from 1 October 2007. In an accompanying document *The response to consultation* the Department of Health states that 'we recognise there are issues around people currently receiving high band payments and any change in funding will be made on review rather than immediately on 1 October 2007'.[122a] The directions have clarified that there will be transitional protection for those currently on the £139 band. Residents on this band will stay on it until they are assessed. If on assessment they are found not to require NHS continuing health care, but have needs that are higher than the criteria for the current guidance for the middle band (see para 13.106) then the higher payment will remain in place. If the resident is assessed as needing only the middle band applying the old guidance[122b] then they (and the care home) will be informed of this in writing and the payment reduced to the flat rate amount, no sooner than 14 days after the date of the notice.[122c] It is understood that the higher band will continue to be upratedbut will cease if any of the changes of circumstances described above occur. The 2007 guidance at para 86 further states that if an individual on review is found to be eligible for NHS continuing health care under the new system, and his or her needs have not changed, 'it should be considered whether their funding should be backdated to the implementation of the National Framework' (ie, October 2007). This applies to all reviews following the implementation date, so could also affect those who were in the lower bands.

13.113 From 1 October 2007 the 2001 and 2003 guidance will be cancelled, and the nurses workbook is to be reviewed prior to that date (presumably with a view to a new one being published).

---

121 The 2001 and 2003 directions and 2001 and 2003 guidance on NHS funded nursing care are revoked from 1 October 2007.

122 Direction 5 National Health Service (Nursing Care in Residential Accommodation) (England) Directions 2007.

122a At p14. Furthermore, in Department of Health, *The National Framework for NHS continuing Healthcare and NHS Funded Nursing Care. Final Regulatory Impact Assessment*, 2007, para 35 it explains that an allowance in the total cost has been allowed 'for PCTs to continue paying the high band RNCC to all those currently receiving it until they have had chance to review the cases individually'.

122b Given that in response to the Grogan case (see para 13.108) the Department of Health advised against using the descriptors for the middle band as well as the high band, there may well be grounds for challenge against being taken off the high band and placed on the flat rate band. Likewise those who remain on the high band should check carefully against the national framework and decision support tool as to why they do not fulfil the criteria for NHS continuing health care.

122c Direction 4 National Health Service (Nursing Care in Residential Accommodation) (England) Directions 2007.

Payments of the registered nursing care contribution

13.114 NHS payments are made directly to the care home, and not to the residents. In 2001 when the payments were introduced for those funding their own care there was considerable disquiet as in many cases the homes raised their fee levels by the amount the person had been allocated. The residents failed therefore to see the benefit of the NHS payments. Homes now have to be much clearer about the fee levels and, in the case of nursing homes, the information about the total fees payable must relate to the fee before any contribution from the NHS is taken into account.

13.115   The 2003 guidance suggested that where a local authority is funding a resident the preferred option is to use budget sharing arrangements under (what is now) NHSA 2006 s75 (see para 13.122 below), such that the local authority pays the full fee including (on behalf of the PCT) the RNCC contribution.[123] In some areas PCTs have arrangements whereby the local authority makes all the RNCC payments for their area (including for those funding their own care) on behalf of the PCT. These arrangements are likely to continue under the new single band.

Payments during absences

13.116 Although the 2001 guidance is quite clear that payments of the RNCC should not be paid if the resident is in hospital, the 2003 guidance takes a more pragmatic approach. It suggests that in order to secure a place in the home on return from hospital and to avoid residents having to pay any shortfall while they are in hospital, PCTs will want to consider paying a retainer equivalent to the value of the RNCC. It points out that custom and practice has been for local authorities to agree to pay the full fee for a set period of time, and that the NHS and local councils will wish to review their current arrangements.[124] Although the 2007 guidance does not reiterate any of these practical arrangements, there would seem to be no reason why such payments to secure the place in the home should not continue.

Responsible commissioner

13.117 The responsibility for the funding of HSCA 2001 s49 payments to nursing home residents is based on the usual rules of each country for establishing the responsible commissioner (ie in England it is based on the PCT of the GP with whom the person is registered, and in Wales it is based on the LHB where the home is situated.) Cross border protocols have been developed to deal with the differing amounts paid by England and Wales.

---

123 2003 guidance paras 49–56. The Welsh 2004 guidance suggests similar arrangements at appendix 2 paras 2.4–2.10.

124 2003 guidance para 23. There is similar but not identical guidance in Wales: 2004 guidance para 38. The implication is that a retainer can be paid for up to six weeks during a period of hospital admission.

Exceptions have been made in relation to certain specialist providers of respite care. The above provisions are considered further at para 6.52 above.

Registered nursing care contribution reviews

13.118 The guidance states that reviews should take place within three months of admission to a care home and annually thereafter (or more often should the resident's circumstances warrant it).[125]

13.119   If a person disagrees with the level of his or her banding (in England prior to October 2007) or considers that he or she should be fully funded by the NHS, he or she can request a review of the decision.

Budget sharing arrangements

13.120 Historically the ability of the NHS and social services authorities to pool budgets, or transfer resources from one to another, was severely curtailed. In consequence it was argued that innovation had been stifled and 'cost shunting' between authorities encouraged.[126] This situation was relaxed as a consequence of HA 1999 ss29–31, which enabled health bodies and social services to enter into a wide range of 'partnership arrangements'. These provisions are now to be found in NHSA 2006 ss75–76 and 256–257.[127]

13.121   NHSA 2006 ss256–257[128] enable SHAs and PCTs to make payments to local authorities in respect of any local authority function that is 'health-related', and section 76[129] provides a reciprocal power for local authorities to make payments to SHAs or PCTs in relation to 'prescribed functions'. Regulations made under this section have[130] defined 'prescribed functions' widely,[131] excluding only such matters as 'surgery, radiotherapy, termination of pregnancies, endoscopy, [certain] laser treatments and other invasive treatments' (reg 2).

---

125 2001 guidance para 21; Welsh 2004 guidance appendix 3 para 3.19. The 2007 guidance, by integrating the determination of nursing payments into the general framework for NHS continuing health care, also places the same timescales for reviews, namely three months following the initial decision and then at least one a year.

126 Department of Health discussion paper, *Partnership in Action*, September 1998.

127 NHS(W)A 2006 ss33–34 and ss194–196.

128 NHS(W)A 2006 ss194–196 provides LHBs with the same powers.

129 NHS(W)A 2006 s34 provides local authorities with the same powers to make payments to LHBs.

130 NHS (Payments by Local Authorities to NHS Bodies) (Prescribed Functions) Regulations 2000 SI No 618 and NHS (Payments by Local Authorities to Health Authorities) (Prescribed Functions) (Wales) Regulations 2001 SI No 1543 (W108), which regulations continue to be valid by virtue of NHS (Consequential Provisions) Act 2006 s4 and Sch 2 para 1(2).

131 Including services under the NHS Acts 2006 ss2 and 3(1) as well as functions under MHA 1983 ss25A–25H and 117.

Partnerships arrangements (formerly known as section 31[132] agreements)

13.122   NHSA 2006 s75[133] allows NHS bodies and local authorities to pool their resources, delegate functions and transfer resources from one party to another and enable a single provider to provide both health and local authority services. In effect it permits:

- **Pooled fund arrangements:** where authorities pool resources so that they will effectively 'lose their health and local authority identity', allowing staff from either agency to develop packages of care suited to particular individuals irrespective of whether health or local authority money is used.
- **Delegation of functions – lead commissioning:** where PCTs and local authorities delegate functions to one another (including the secondment or transfer of staff). In the case of health and social care this enables one of the partner bodies to commission all mental health or learning disability services locally.
- **Delegation of functions – integrated provision:** this consists of the provision of health and local authority services from a single managed provider. The arrangement can be used in conjunction with lead commissioning and pooled fund arrangements.

13.123   As with the budget sharing regulations above, most NHS functions can be the subject of partnership arrangements (with the same exceptions – see para 13.121 above).[134] Likewise a wide range of social services functions can be the subject of partnership arrangements – including in England (but not Wales) charging for care home accommodation under the National Assistance Act 1948 and for non-accommodation community care services.[135] NHSA 2006 s75(5)[136] provides that any partnership arrangements made under section 75 will not affect the liability of the NHS body or the local authority for the exercise of its functions. Liability remains, therefore, with the body primarily responsible for the discharge of the function (ie the body with this responsibility prior to the partnership arrangement).

13.124   Guidance on these arrangements has been issued as HSC 2000/010: LAC (2000)9 in England.

---

132   Under HA 1999 s31.
133   NHS(W)A 2006 s33.
134   NHS Bodies and Local Authorities Partnership Arrangements Regulations 2000 SI No 617 and National Health Service Bodies and Local Authorities Partnership Arrangements (Wales) Regulations 2000 SI No 2993 (W193), which Regulations continue to be valid by virtue of NHS (Consequential Provisions) Act 2006 s4 and Sch 2 para 1(2).
135   NHS Bodies and Local Authorities Partnership Arrangements (Amendment) (England) Regulations 2003 SI No 629, which regulations continue to be valid by virtue of the NHS (Consequential Provisions) Act 2006 s4 and Sch 2 para 1(2).
136   NHS(W)A 2006 s33(5).

Dowry payments

13.125 Prior to the HA 1999 amendments, budget transfers were only permitted one way – from NHS bodies to local authorities, housing associations and certain other bodies in respect of personal social services, education for disabled people and housing. Detailed guidance[137] and directions[138] were issued in relation to these payments. These provisions permitted various schemes, including an arrangement known as 'dowry' payments.

13.126   Dowry payments were used to facilitate the transfer of patients from long-stay hospitals into the community. They involved a lump-sum payment or annual payment to a local authority taking over the patient's care; the amount of the lump-sum or annual payment and the length of time for which annual payments were to be made being negotiated by the respective authorities. In this respect HSG (95)45 advised (annex para 4.1):

> . . . in respect of people being discharged from long stay institutions, the NHS is responsible for negotiating arrangements with local authorities, including any appropriate transfer of resources which assist the local authority meeting the community care needs of such people and of their successors who may otherwise have entered the institution.

13.127 The relevance of such arrangements (or more precisely the lack of these) was spelt out in LAC (92)17 (annex A para 10) which stated that:

> Where residential care arrangements in the community for a person who was formerly a patient in a long-stay hospital appear to be breaking down . . . then the LA . . . should take the lead in seeing that the appropriate arrangements are secured . . . Where no agreement has been made between the DHA responsible for the hospital care before discharge and the LA about respective responsibilities, the HA should assist the LA . . . and if the resecuring or reprovisioning of care leads the LA to incur additional expenditure, the HA will be expected to use its powers under s28A to assist the LA to fund the care.

Section 64[139] agreements

13.128 Although NHSA 2006 ss256–257[140] are the appropriate statutory provisions by which a health body transfers to a social services authority its responsibility for patients who are capable of being supported through the community care regime, it appears that in the past, a number of health authorities and PCTs have inappropriately sought to use their powers under Health Services and Public Health Act 1968 s64. This improper use was highlighted by the Department of Health in a 2003 report.[141]

13.129   Section 64 of the 1968 Act gives the secretary of state powers to make grants to voluntary and community sector organisations. These can be

---

137 LAC (92)17, HSG (92)43 and HSG (95)45.
138 Directions under NHSA 1977 s28A being contained as annex C to HSG (92)43.
139 Under Health Services and Public Health Services Act 1968 s64.
140 NHS(W)A 2006 ss194–196.
141 *Report of a review group established to examine the use of the power to make grants under Section 64 of the Health Services and Public Health Act 1968*, September 2003, accessible at http://www.dh.gov.uk/assetRoot/04/03/53/66/04035366.pdf.

made nationally (from the 'General Scheme') although most frequently they are made locally, for which the use of section 64 has been delegated to PCTs. There is no requirement to report on the use made of section 64, and, as the Department of Health report makes clear, it does not in fact hold any information about the grants that have been awarded.

13.130   The 2003 report describes how PCTs (and indeed the Department of Health) have been using section 64 inappropriately. Instead of making grants under this provision, they entered into service level agreements with voluntary and community sector organisations. As the report states (para 10), the 'distinction between a grant and a contract for the provision of a service is clear'. The report also explains that the appropriate mechanism for a PCT to enter into a contract for services, is to use its powers under what is now NHSA 2006 s12[142] or to transfer the money to social services via what is now NHSA 2006 ss256–257.[143] The importance of the latter arrangement is that, in order to do so, the PCT (or the Health Authority before it) would have had to have obtained social services' agreement to it discharging the (hitherto) NHS function. In the absence of such an agreement the function remains with the NHS – if for example the voluntary/community sector organisation withdraws from the contract. This has occurred on a number of occasions in the recent past, due to the schemes becoming uneconomic due to the reconfiguration of Supporting People's monies (see para 15.96 below).

142   NHS(W)A 2006 s10.
143   Ibid, ss194–196.

CHAPTER 14

NHS continuing health care responsibilities

continued

Introduction

14.1 This chapter considers the interface between the NHS's responsibilities for social care support under the NHS Acts 2006 and the responsibilities of social services authorities under the community care legislation. At some point individuals, because they have become so unwell, may move across the interface – from the means tested social services system to the 'free at the point of need' NHS system. In crossing the interface one moves from a detailed community care statutory regime into a system regulated by largely aspirational legislation and guidance of questionable quality. In many respects such people are crossing from a system steeped in the principles of the Poor Law to a regime infused with the idealistic principles of the Attlee government – principles that come at a cost that no government has been able or willing to fund fully.

14.2 Governments are not the only bodies who balk at the cost implications of the health/social service divide. For many individuals, entitlement to fully funded NHS health care is of great significance, particularly if living in a care home. As at March 2006 the average weekly care home fee amounted to £570 per week – and of course in some areas, particularly London and the Home Counties, fees are considerably higher.

14.3 June 2007 statistics[1] indicate that as of 31 March 2007 31,000[2] people were being fully funded by the NHS in care homes or in their own home. These figures reveal remarkably wide variations in the proportion of the population who receive such funding in different PCTs: ranging from 0.26 per 10,000 population to 41.75 per 10,000 population. Only 26 primary care trusts (PCTs) (out of 152) have recorded figures that show more than 10 per 10,000 population get continuing health care.[3] The Department of Health estimates that as a result of the new framework (see para 14.37 below) a further 5,500 people are likely to qualify, and has earmarked £220 million for the implementation from April 2008.

14.4 This chapter considers the legal position as of 1 October 2007. The situation has changed since the third edition of this book in that there is now a single national framework in England, accompanied by a 'Decision Support Tool' to help PCT's to decide who should get full funding. Wales has worked to a single framework since 2004 but the wording is materially different to that in England and is considered separately at para 14.92 below. Due to the number of outstanding complaints for reimbursement of care home fees we include details of the pre-October 2007 responsibilities in England, albeit that the relevant guidance has now been cancelled.

---

1   Department of Health, *The National Framework for NHS Continuing Healthcare and NHS funded Nursing Care in England. Final Regulatory Impact Assessment*, 2007.
2   This represents an increase of 6,000 people in the previous year. Since the *Coughlan* case and following the ombudsman's report in 2003 the increases have been marked. In 2002/03 only 18,439 people received fully funded care.
3   Percentage of population figures extrapolated from information supplied by the Department of Health to Age Concern.

14.5   This chapter commences with a brief explanation of the context in which the guidance has developed – the third edition contains a more detailed analysis of the critical reports of the Health Service Ombudsman and the Health Select Committee that have proved to be formative in shaping and developing policy in this area. The chapter then considers the current policy framework in England and Wales and concludes with short descriptions of the health and social needs of individuals whose cases have proved to be important and which can be valuable as comparators.

Historical and legal context of the health and social care divide

14.6   The debate over continuing health care responsibilities is not new. Means, Morbey and Smith[4] chart the organisational tensions that have existed over the health/social care divide since the formation of the NHS. They conclude that these have been characterised by a failure of the NHS to invest in community health services or to transfer significant resources to social services (p85). They describe how the conflict has generally been expressed in debates over what is health care and what is social care.

14.7   Pivotal to an understanding of the health social services divide is the interaction between NHS Act (NHSA) 2006 ss1 and 3[5] (see para 13.6 above) and National Assistance Act (NAA) 1948 s21(1) and (8).

14.8   NAA 1948 s21(1) places a duty on social services authorities to provide residential accommodation for (amongst others) elderly ill and disabled people. However section 21(8) contains a caveat, namely:

> Nothing in this section shall authorise or require a local authority to make any provision authorised or required to be made (whether by that or by any other authority) by or under any enactment not contained in this Part of this Act, or authorised or required to be provided under the [NHS Acts 2006].

14.9   In simple terms section 21(8) means that it is unlawful for social services to provide a service that could be provided by the NHS (but see para 14.14 below). The full implications of this provision however had to wait until 1999 when the Court of Appeal delivered its judgment in *R v North and East Devon Health Authority ex p Coughlan*[6] – discussed in detail below.

14.10   The 1957 Boucher report[7] is an early example of the government's continuing attempts to identify the line between the two statutory regimes. The impetus for the report stemmed from local authority concerns that their residential homes cared for many people who ought to be cared

---

4   R Means, H Morbey and R Smith, *From Community Care to Market Care?* Policy Press, 2002.
5   Which are materially unchanged since 1948: the 1948 and 1946 Acts came into force on the same day – 5 July 1948.
6   *R v North and East Devon Health Authority ex p Coughlan* [2000] 2 WLR 622; (1999) 2 CCLR 285.
7   Cited in Means, Morbey and Smith (note 4 above) p78.

for in hospital. The report resulted in circular guidance outlining the respective responsibilities of the welfare and hospital authorities; welfare authorities were to provide:

- care of the otherwise active resident in a welfare home during minor illness, which may well involve a short period in bed;
- care of the infirm (including the senile) who may need help in dressing, toilet, and so on, and may need to live on the ground floor because they cannot manage stairs, and may spend part of the day in bed (or longer periods in bad weather);
- care of those older persons in a welfare home who have to take to bed and are not expected to live more than a few weeks (or exceptionally months). Who would, if in their own homes, stay there because they cannot benefit from treatment or nursing care beyond help that can be given at home, and whose removal to hospital away from familiar surroundings and attendance would be felt to be inhumane.[8]

14.11   Hospital authorities, however, were to take responsibility for:

- care of the chronic bedfast who may need little or no medical treatment, but who do require prolonged nursing care over months or years;
- convalescent care of older sick people who have completed active treatment, but who are not yet ready for discharge to their own homes or to welfare homes;
- care of the senile confused or disturbed patients who are, owing to their mental condition, unfit to live a normal community life in a welfare home.[9]

14.12   Although the demarcation of the health/social care boundary described in the Boucher report is a long way from the situation today, legally there has been no material diminution in the scope of the NHS's continuing health care responsibilities since that time. There has been no amendment to the primary statutory obligation (albeit that the duty is now to be found in the consolidated 2006 Acts). There has been no ministerial statement, no direction by the secretary of state or any other kind of announcement to the effect that the entitlement to continuing health care has been curtailed. Indeed in 2007 the Care Minister was reported as having accepted that PCTs had 'reneged on their responsibilities for funding continuing care and shunted costs on to councils'.[10]

14.13   The material changes have been in terms of demography, policy and funding arrangements. In relation to the latter two factors, the most significant concerned the availability in 1979 of supplementary benefit payments (later income support) to cover the cost of private nursing home accommodation. This situation led to the closure of many NHS

8   Ministry of Health, *Local authority services for the chronic sick and infirm* Circular 11/50, 1957, as cited by Means, Morbey and Smith (note 4 above) p78.
9   Ministry of Health, *Geriatric services and the care of the chronic sick* HM (57)86, 1957, as cited by Means, Morbey and Smith (note 4 above) p78.
10   *Community Care* 22–28 February 2007 p8.

continuing care wards, with the patients being transferred to privately run nursing homes funded by the social security budget.

14.14   On 1 April 1993 social services authorities became the 'gate keepers' for such community placements. This led to a general, but incorrect, assumption that the NHS no longer had the same responsibility for funding long term care. The fact that social services authorities were (for the first time) empowered to make payments towards the cost of independent nursing home placements also encouraged the view that the NHS was no longer an agency responsible for making similar payments. In fact, the responsibility for the care of persons in need of nursing home accommodation is an overlapping one between the two services.

14.15   The 1980s were characterised by a rapid closure of long term beds[11] and an increase in inheritable wealth. By the early 1990s many individuals found that when they became chronically ill and needed care outside their own home, they had to pay for this in a nursing home – whereas previously such people had received it free in a long stay NHS bed. They and their carers accordingly paid substantial sums to private nursing homes (frequently having to sell their former family home[12]) in situations where previously the care would have been provided without charge by the NHS.

14.16   It is this aspect that came prominently to the fore with the publication by the Health Service Commissioner of a highly critical report into a premature hospital discharge by the Leeds Health Authority in 1994.[13] In spite of considerable health needs the patient was discharged to a nursing home where he had to pay for his care. The ombudsman found:

> This patient was a highly dependent patient in hospital under a contract made with the Infirmary by Leeds Health Authority; and yet, when he no longer needed care in an acute ward but manifestly still needed what the National Health Service is there to provide, they regarded themselves as having no scope for continuing to discharge their responsibilities to him because their policy was to make no provision for continuing care. The policy had the effect of excluding an option whereby he might have the cost of his continuing care met by the NHS. In my opinion the failure to make available long-term care within the NHS for this patient was unreasonable and constitutes a failure in the service provided by the Health Authority. I uphold this complaint . . . I recommend that the Authority review their provision of services for the likes of this man in view of the apparent gap in service available for this particular group of patients. (Para 22)

11   Between 1983 and 1993 there was a 30% (17,000) reduction in the number of long term geriatric and psychogeriatric NHS beds (T Harding *et al, Options for Long Term Care,* HMSO, 1996, p8) and between 1988 and 2001 a loss of 50,600 such beds; see House of Commons Health Committee, *Delayed Discharges: Third Report of Session 2001–02 Volume 1,* HC 617-I, 2002, p35, accessible at http://www.publications.parliament.uk/pa/cm200102/cmselect/cmhealth/617/617.pdf .

12   It is estimated that about 40,000 people sell their homes each year to pay for their care home fees, of which a conservative estimate suggests that between 120 and 640 should have had their fees funded by the NHS – M Henwood, *Self-funding of long-term care and potential for injustice,* background paper prepared for BBC Panorama, 2006, accessible at http://news.bbc.co.uk/1/shared/bsp/hi/pdfs/05_03_06_melaniehenwood.pdf.

13   Health Service Commissioner Second Report for Session 1993–94; Case no E62/93–94: see Table 16 below for a brief description of his condition.

14.17   The ombudsman was so concerned about the situation disclosed by the Leeds complaint that he took the exceptional step of having his report separately published.[14] In response, the government undertook to issue guidance, indicating:

> If in the light of the guidance, some health authorities are found to have reduced their capacity to secure continuing care too far – as clearly happened in the case dealt with by the Health Service Commissioner – then they will have to take action to close the gap.[15]

1995–2007: 1995 guidance, case-law and complaints

1995 Guidance

14.18   In February 1995, as a consequence of the Health Service Ombudsman's 'Leeds report',[16] continuing care guidance was published in England and Wales as a first step towards defining with greater precision the boundaries between the responsibilities of the NHS and social services authorities for continuing care.[17] The guidance required every health authority to prepare and publish local 'continuing health care statements' which spelt out which patients would be entitled to free continuing health care funded by the NHS. As part of this process the government also announced procedures that enabled patients to challenge their discharge from in-patient hospital care.[18]

14.19   Although in 1996 the Department of Health issued follow up guidance to improve the quality of continuing health care statements,[19] the evidence suggests that the 1995 guidance (which was superseded in England by 2001 guidance and now by framework guidance – see below) was misapplied by health authorities and that the Department of Health was inactive in policing individual health authority continuing care statements.[20]

The Coughlan judgment

14.20   In 1999 the Court of Appeal delivered its judgment in *R v North and East Devon Health Authority ex p Coughlan*.[21] It reinforced the finding of the

---

14   Normally only an abbreviated selection of his reports is published twice yearly.
15   Virginia Bottomley, Secretary of State for Health, 4 November 1994.
16   At para 3 it states that the guidance 'addresses a number of concerns raised in the report made last year by the Health Service Ombudsman'.
17   LAC (95)5: HSG (95)8 *NHS Responsibilities for Meeting Continuing Health Care Needs*: WOC 16/95 and WHC (95)7 in Wales.
18   LAC (95)17: HSG (95)39, although this guidance has been cancelled and not replaced. See para 5.53 for detail of how to challenge a decision about hospital discharge.
19   See eg EL (96)8 and EL (96)89 – see note 41.
20   Indeed the evidence suggests the contrary – as the Health Service Ombudsman noted in her Second Report for Session 2002–03 *NHS funding for long term care*, HC 399, 2003, para 21: 'My enquiries so far have revealed one letter (in case E.814/00–01) sent out from a regional office of the Department of Health to health authorities following the 1999 guidance, which could justifiably have been read as a mandate to do the bare minimum'.
21   *R v North and East Devon Health Authority ex p Coughlan* [2000] 2 WLR 622; (1999) 2 CCLR 285.

Health Service Commissioner in the Leeds health authority complaint, that entitlement to NHS continuing care support arose, not merely when a patient's health care needs were complex, but also when they were substantial – the so called 'quality/quantity' criteria (see below).

14.21   The Court of Appeal held that social services could only lawfully fund low level nursing care – low in terms of its quality and quantity. The court expressed this as follows (at [30]):

(d) There can be no precise legal line drawn between those nursing services which are and those which are not capable of being treated as included in such a package of care services.

(e) The distinction between those services which can and cannot be so provided is one of degree which in a borderline case will depend on a careful appraisal of the facts of the individual case. However, as a very general indication as to where the line is to be drawn, it can be said that if the nursing services are:

- merely incidental or ancillary to the provision of the accommodation which a local authority is under a duty to provide to the category of persons to whom section 21 refers; and
- of a nature which it can be expected that an authority whose primary responsibility is to provide social services can be expected to provide, then they can be provided under section 21.

It will be appreciated that the first part of the test is focusing on the overall quantity of the services and the second part on the quality of the services provided.

14.22   Additionally the court emphasised that the setting of a person's care was not determinative of eligibility for continuing health care funding. In its view, 'where the primary need is a health need, then the responsibility is that of the NHS, even when the individual has been placed in a home by a local authority' (at [31]) and 'the fact that a case does not qualify for in-patient treatment in a hospital does not mean that the person concerned should not be a NHS responsibility' (at [41]).

14.23   The continuing care policies of North and East Devon Health Authority were, it appears, not unusual. A 1999 Royal College of Nursing Report '*Rationing by Stealth*' suggested that the continuing care policies of over 90 per cent of health authorities were equally deficient.

Continuing care guidance following the Coughlan judgment

14.24   The *Coughlan* judgment was followed in England by 'interim guidance' HSC 1999/180: LAC (1999)30, that did little more than ask health and local authorities to 'satisfy themselves that their continuing' care policies were in line with the judgment'. Unfortunately it also gave a clear indication that further guidance would be issued 'later this year' (at para 2) and this expectation of this further guidance led to many health authorities taking no decisive action in the wake of the *Coughlan* judgment.[22]

22 In this respect, see the comments of the Health Service Ombudsman in her Second Report for Session 2002–03 *NHS funding for long term care*, HC 399, 2003.

14.25   The Department of Health took two years to issue further guidance (HSC 2001/015: LAC (2001)18). This guidance has been the subject of robust criticism by the High Court[23] and the Health Service Commissioner, most particularly in her special report on continuing NHS healthcare.[24] The need for a special report stemmed from the large number of complaints that the Commissioner had received on this issue (as had been the case with her predecessor in 1994[25]). She was trenchant in her criticism of the Department of Health's failure to provide clear guidance in conformity with the Court of Appeal's judgment in *Coughlan*; commenting (at para 31):

> I do not underestimate the difficulty of setting fair, comprehensive and easily comprehensible criteria . . . But that is all the more reason for the Department to take a strong lead in the matter: developing a very clear, well-defined national framework. One might have hoped that the comments made in the Coughlan case would have prompted the Department to tackle this issue . . . [however] Authorities were left to take their own legal advice about their obligations to provide continuing NHS health care . . . The long awaited further guidance in June 2001 . . . gives no clearer definition than previously of when continuing NHS health care should be provided: if anything it is weaker, since it simply lists factors authorities should 'bear in mind' and details to which they should 'pay attention' without saying how they should be taken into account . . . I fear I would find it even harder now to judge whether criteria were out of line with current guidance. Such an opaque system cannot be fair.

14.26   The ombudsman has since 2003 issued further reports expressing concern about the processes PCTs and strategic health authorities (SHAs) were adopting to remedy their past failures[26] and relating to restitution and the level of interest that should be paid. In addition she has given written and oral evidence to the Health Select Committee.[27]

Pointon and the Health Service Ombudsman's report

14.27   A further individual report of note relates to the home care provided to a man suffering from Alzheimer's disease by his wife and care assistants, known as the Pointon case. The Health Service Ombudsman held that the fact that Mr Pointon was receiving (what was in effect) nursing care from his wife, did not mean he could not qualify for continuing health care; that

---

23   *R (Grogan) v Bexley NHS Care Trust and others* [2006] EWHC 44 (Admin); (2006) 9 CCLR 188 – see para 14.31 below.

24   Health Service Ombudsman's Second Report for Session 2002–03 *NHS funding for long term care*, HC 399, 2003, para 38.

25   While it appears that Sir William Reid as Health Service Ombudsman in 1994 had had about 20 such complaints, Ann Abrahams the current Health Service Ombudsman had had over 3,000 complaints at the time of her 2003 report and over 4,000 at the time of her 2004 report (note 27 below).

26   As a result the ombudsman has issued checklists for PCTs to follow – see para 14.84 below.

27   *NHS funding for long term care – follow-up report*, HC 144, 2004–05; Memorandum by the Health Services Ombudsman for England to the Health Select Committee inquiry into NHS continuing care; *Retrospective Continuing Care Funding and Redress*, HC 386, 2006–07. All available at http://www.ombudsman.org.uk.

the health bodies had failed to take into account his severe psychological problems and the special skills it takes to nurse someone with dementia; that the assessment tools used by the NHS were skewed in favour of physical and acute care; and the fact that Mr Pointon needed care at home – rather than in a nursing care home – was not material to the question of continuing health care responsibility.[28]

14.28   The Pointon report is of considerable importance, being a clear example of entitlement to continuing health care funding where (1) the nature of the health care need was not for acute medical support but for nursing of a quality that could manage his psychologically challenging behaviour and (2) the need arose from someone living in the community and not a residential care setting. Mr Pointon was also receiving care from untrained assistants and his wife, and this too is sometimes used as a reason for refusing entitlement to continuing health care. This (as the following *Haringey* case illustrates) is an irrelevant factor. What is of key importance is what a person needs – not what he or she is receiving.

R (T, D and B) v Haringey LBC

14.29   *R (T, D and B) v Haringey LBC*[29] concerned two people (aged 3 and 19 at the hearing) both of whom had complex medical conditions which required – among other things – a tracheostomy (a tube in the throat) which would be needed for several years. The tubes needed, on occasions, suctioning as regularly as every 15 minutes and in general about three times a night. The tube required replacing each week and if it was not suctioned there was a severe risk of suffocation and death within minutes, or serious brain damage in a shorter time. Although children who have tracheostomies are often discharged from hospital and cared for at home, their parents have to be trained to make the daily routines and cope with the emergencies that may arise. In the *Haringey* case the care was primarily being provided by the children's mother – but nevertheless the court held that it was of a nature that social services could not provide.

14.30   In the opinion of Ouseley J the *Coughlan* criteria applied with equal force to children, regardless of the fact that the social services care regime would have been regulated by the Children Act 1989 and not the NAA 1948 (see para 9.65 above). In his opinion the decisive factors were the 'scale and type of nursing care' and the purpose of the care – in this case it was 'designed to deal with the continuing medical consequences of an operation, which if not met will give rise to urgent or immediate medical needs'. Ouseley J additionally addressed the central dilemma of the case, namely the different public law entitlements provided by the social care statutes and the NHS Acts: the former creating specifically enforceable duties and the latter mere 'target duties' (see para 13.13 above). The judge accepted that in principle there could be an entitlement gap – essentially that a person could cease to be eligible for social care support because his

28   Case no E.22/02/02–03 Funding for Long Term Care (The Pointon Case).
29   [2005] EWHC 2235 (Admin); (2006) 9 CCLR 58.

or her need fell above the limits of what social care could provide (ie the section 21(8) cut off) but have needs below that which the Department of Health/Assembly had specified as necessary to qualify for NHS continuing care support, ie the 'primary health need' requirement.

R (Grogan) v Bexley NHS Care Trust

14.31   The question of the 'gap' in entitlement identified in the *Haringey* judgment was addressed directly in *R (Grogan) v Bexley NHS Care Trust and others*.[30] In essence Charles J held that the section 21(8) 'limits of social care' test was the crucial determinant. The reason for this conclusion was straightforward. The 'limits of social care' test is statutory in origin (ie section 21(8)) and had been authoritatively interpreted by the Court of Appeal in *Coughlan*. On the other hand the 'primary health need' test is a policy construct developed by the secretary of state. While it is the secretary of state's entitlement under the NHS Acts to propound such a policy, she could not (by guidance) undermine the statutory regime. Since both the secretary of state (and the Assembly in Wales) had made unequivocal statements that there must be no gap in entitlement, then in Charles J's opinion the only way of resolving this dilemma (short of statutory amendment) was for the NHS to drop the policy 'bar' to the height set by the Court of Appeal in *Coughlan* when defining the limits of social care support.

14.32   Like the ombudsman Charles J was critical of the Department of Health's 2001 guidance, in particular (at [66]):

i)   the absence of a clear, distinct and early expression of the test and approach to be applied, and thus of the test or approach, against which the relevance and effect of the qualitative and quantitative criteria and factors listed in the Guidance have to be assessed, and

ii)   . . . the absence of an explanation that the Primary Health Need Approach is to be applied to achieve the result that all nursing care (including RNCC) is merely (a) incidental or ancillary to the provision of the accommodation which a local authority is under a duty to provide, and (b) of a nature which prior to the enactment of s49 Health and Social Care Act (HSCA) 2001 it could have been expected that an authority whose primary responsibility is to provide social services could have been expected to provide, and could thus have been lawfully provided by a local authority (see *Coughlan*).

And (at [67]) the lack of:

. . . sensibly drafted guidance as to the provision of Continuing NHS Health Care should inevitably include a clear and distinct expression of the overall test to be applied and thus the test to which the factors identified were relevant.

14.33   In the opinion of Charles J, the guidance used by Bexley NHS Trust failed to explain how relevant factors, such as the quantity and/or quality of a patient's care needs, should be weighted – with the consequence that a

30   [2006] EWHC 44 (Admin); (2006) 9 CCLR 188.

decision-maker was left to 'drift on a sea of factors without guidance as to the test or tests he should apply to assess and weigh (in the words of the criteria) the nature or complexity or intensity or unpredictability and the impact on an individual's health needs in determining the category into which the relevant person falls'.

14.34   The *Grogan* judgment additionally addressed the incongruity between the continuing health care criteria and the registered nursing care contribution (RNCC) criteria (see para 13.99 above). As a consequence of the findings in this case the Department of Health issued interim guidance revising the RNCC banding (see para 13.108 above) and advising health bodies and local authorities to work together to ensure that service users do not fall into a 'gap' between services.[31] The guidance additionally committed the government in England to the introduction of a single national framework for continuing health care entitlement.

Directions and guidance

14.35   Since 1995 the debate concerning continuing health care responsibilities has been dominated by criticism of the relevant Department of Health guidance. The 1995 guidance was shown to be inadequate in *Coughlan* and the replacement 2001 guidance was rejected as wholly unfit for purpose by the Health Service Ombudsman, the High Court, the Health Select Committee and many other commentators. The RNCC guidance too was ruled to be, in effect, unlawful. For the Department of Health to have been so consistently criticised for the quality of its guidance is unusual – possibly unique. It suggests there is an internal problem that is somehow frustrating its normally assured and generally excellent legal analysis. The problem is almost certainly a political one. The NHS has for the last ten years been driven by government targets that focus on the government's priorities which are almost exclusively short term acute health care – primarily the cutting of waiting lists. Diverting resources to fund the long term needs of ill people does not advance this dominant agenda.

14.36   The effect of the *Coughlan* judgment was that entitlement to continuing health care support was more substantial than the government would have liked it to have been. The difficulty could have been resolved by amending the NHS and community care legislation, but this was presumably deemed politically treacherous. The response in 2001 could be viewed as an attempt to blunt the impact of the *Coughlan* judgment – to use guidance in effect to frustrate the law, something that has of course a reasonable pedigree.[32] With the judicial rejection of the 2001 guidance, new guidance has now been issued and a commitment made to divert limited resources into this domain. Whether the 2007 guidance is an

---

31   Issued on 3 March 2006, *Action following the Grogan judgement*. This guidance has now been superseded by the new framework guidance.

32   See eg *R v Secretary of State for Health ex p Pfizer Ltd* (1999) 2 CCLR 270 – considered at para 1.54 above.

adequate response to the *Coughlan* judgment remains to be seen. It is however of concern that at this early stage it appears that Ms Coughlan herself would not appear to qualify for such assistance under the new regime (see para 14.46) below.

The 2007 National Framework

14.37 In June 2007 a new *National Framework for NHS Continuing Healthcare and NHS funded Nursing Care in England*[33] was issued by the Department of Health accompanied by a 'decision support tool'[34] designed to provide a fair and effective way of establishing individual entitlement to continuing health care. In the following section we refer to the two documents as the framework guidance and the 'decision support tool'. With the publication of these two documents the 2001 guidance[35] was cancelled.

14.38   Under the new regime PCTs are responsible for promoting awareness of the policy, as well as ensuring it is properly implemented and applied – which includes maintaining good practice, providing training, identifying and acting on issues in the provision of NHS continuing health care, and informing commissioning arrangements both on a strategic and individual basis.[36] SHAs will continue to have their general overview function of 'ensuring local systems operate effectively and deliver improved performance'.[37]

14.39   Directions have been issued on 30 August 2007 to underpin the national framework, to both the NHS under NHSA 2006 and to social services under Local Authority Social Act (LASSA) 1970 s7.[38] Previous directions are revoked and the new directions come into force on 1 October 2007. The 2007 Responsibilities Directions require PCTs to:

- take reasonable steps to ensure that an assessment for NHS continuing health care is carried out in all cases where there may be a need for such care before an RNCC assessment is undertaken (direction 2(2));
- use the needs checklist (see para 14.55) if the PCT wishes to use an initial screening process to decide if such an assessment is needed, (direction 2(3);
- ensure that a multidisciplinary team undertakes an assessment to

33 Department of Health, *The National Framework for NHS Continuing Healthcare and NHS funded Nursing Care in England*, 2007.
34 Department of Health, *Decision-Support Tool for NHS Continuing Healthcare*, 1 July 2007.
35 HSC 2001/015: LAC (2001)18.
36 Framework guidance para 100.
37 Ibid, para 102.
38 The NHS Continuing Healthcare (Responsibilities) Directions 2007 (described in this chapter as the 2007 Responsibilities Directions). At the same time the Delayed Discharges (Continuing Care) Directions 2007 were issued to NHS bodies regarding their responsibilities to undertake assessments for NHS continuing health care where a person is about to be discharged from hospital – these are discussed at para 5.7. New directions have also been issued in relation to the NHS payments for the registered nursing care contribution in care homes providing nursing which are discussed in para 13.112.

inform a decision as to a person's eligibility for NHS continuing health care and following that assessment ensure the decision support tool (see para 14.60) is completed to inform the decision as to whether the person has a primary health need, and if they have the PCT must decide the person is eligible for NHS continuing health care (directions 2(4 and 5);

- consider, when deciding if the person has a primary health need, whether nursing or other health services are more than incidental or ancillary to accommodation which social services is, or would be but for the person's means[38a] be under a duty to provide or of a nature beyond which a social services authority whose primary responsibility is to provide social services could be expected to provide, and if in totality they have the PCT must decide that the person has a primary health need (direction 2(6))

- inform the person in writing and give reasons for the decision, and if they are not considered eligible for NHS continuing health care inform the perso (or someone acting on their behalf) of the circumstance and manner in which they can apply for a review if they are dissatisfied with the procedure followed or the application of the criterion in relation to the decision(directions 2 (7and 8);

- consult with as far as reasonably practicable with the relevant social services department before making a decision about eligibility for NHS continuing health care and the social services department is required as far as practicable to provide advice and assistance to the PCT and use any information from an assessment pursuant to NHSCCA 1990 s47 to provide such advice and asistance (direction 3)

The 2007 Responsibilities Directions are produced in full in appendix B.

14.40   There are no equivalent directions relating to NHS continuing health care in Wales. The 2007 reforms in England have no direct impact on the regime in Wales which remains subject to principal guidance issued in 2004 which is considered separately at para 14.92 below.

Definition of NHS continuing health care

14.41   The framework guidance states (at para 7) that 'Continuing care' means care provided over an extended period of time to a person aged 18 or over to meet physical or mental health needs which have arisen as the result of disability, accident or illness' and adds that '"NHS Continuing Healthcare" means a package of continuing care arranged and funded solely by the NHS'. The 2007 Responsibilities Directions define it as a 'package of care arranged and funded solely by the health service for a person aged 18 or over to meet physical or mental health needs which have arisen as a result of illness'.

38a The wording of this direction is presumably is to ensure that both aspects of the quantity/quality test are applied in all circumstances regardless of whether social services is under a duty to accommodate the person.

The legal and policy framework and the health/social care divide

The 'primary health need' vs 'limits of social care' assessments

14.42   The framework guidance recognises (at para 16) that words such as 'continuing care', 'NHS Continuing Healthcare' or 'primary health need' do not appear in the legislation. However the framework guidance then goes on (at para 23) to state that the secretary of state has developed the concept of 'primary health need' to assist in deciding what treatment and health services it is appropriate for the NHS to provide 'and to distinguish between those and the services LAs may provide'. This concept of primary health need has been incorporated into the 2007 Responsibilities Directions. The primary health need test is not that adopted by the Court of Appeal in *Coughlan*, where it referred to this approach on only one occasion (para 31) where it noted that the 'Secretary of State accepts that, where the primary need is a health need, then the responsibility is that of the NHS, even when the individual has been placed in a home by a local authority'. The court however immediately went on to suggest that such an approach presented difficulties and ultimately it opted for an altogether different test, namely the quantity/quality test which sets the limits on what social services can provide, and which are now reflected in the 2007 Responsibilities Directions.[38b]

14.43   The framework guidance resolves the differences between these two approaches by stating (in terms) that a 'primary health need' arises where a person has exceeded the limits of the social care responsibility. This acceptance is important and is contained at para 24, which provides:

> There should be no gap in the provision of care, such that people might be in a situation where neither the NHS nor (subject to the person meeting the relevant means test) the relevant LA, separately or together, will fund care. Therefore, the 'primary health need' test should be applied so that a decision of ineligibility for NHS Continuing Healthcare is possible only where, taken as a whole, the nursing or other health services required by the individual:
> i.   are no more than incidental or ancillary to the provision of accommodation which LA Social Services are under a duty to provide; and
> ii.   are not of a nature beyond which a LA whose primary responsibility is to provide Social Services could be expected to provide.

14.44   The framework guidance retains reference to the terms nature, intensity,

---

38b   The Association of Directors of Adult Services (ADASS) and the Local Government Association (LGA) are intending to issue advice to social services departments to ensure they work effectively with the NHS and that they do not take responsibility for care that is outside their powers to provide. This advice will be on the ADASS and LGA websites from 1 October 2007. It is likely that this advice will be widely used by social services staff in conjunction with the national framework.

complexity and unpredictability³⁹ which first appeared in the 1995 guidance. These have been criticised as unnecessarily complicating the assessment process.⁴⁰ The framework guidance attempts (at para 26) to link these four indicators with the quantity/quality test preferred by the Court of Appeal in *Coughlan* and provides a more detailed explanation of each of these characteristics than that in the 2001 guidance.⁴¹ It suggests that use of the decision support tool along with practitioner's own experience and professional judgement 'should therefore enable them to apply the primary health need test in practice in a way which is consistent with the limits of what can lawfully be provided by a LA, in accordance with the *Coughlan* and *Grogan* judgments' (para 28).

14.45   The decision support tool is considered at para 14.60 below, but crucial to its correct application is the way in which its 'user notes' are interpreted, particularly the following (which might be altered as the Department of Health has indicated it may make further changes to the tool) see para 14.65:

> 17. If there are a number of domains with **high** and/or **moderate** needs, **this can also indicate a primary health need.** In this case, the overall need, the interactions between needs in different care domains, and the evidence from risk assessments, should be taken into account in deciding whether a recommendation of eligibility to NHS Continuing Healthcare should be made. It is not possible to equate a number of incidences of one level with a number of incidences of another level, for example 'two moderates equals one high'.

> 18. If need in all domains are recorded as '**low**' or '**no need**', this would indicate ineligibility. This does not, however, mean that these domains should be disregarded, as low needs can add to the overall picture and alter the impact that other needs have on the individual.

14.46 The details of Ms Coughlan's condition are well documented (see Table 16) and were analysed in detail by the Court of Appeal. It concluded that her needs were well outside what social services could provide – of a 'wholly different category'.⁴² It is of concern therefore that the decision support tool does not clearly establish that she would qualify for NHS

39 '[B]eing predictably unpredictable' should never be used as a reason for *not* giving NHS continuing health care –Department of Health, *A National Framework for NHS Continuing Healthcare and NHS-Funded Nursing Care in England: Response to Consultation*, 2007, p13.

40 See eg Law Society, *National Framework for NHS Continuing Healthcare and NHS-funded Nursing Care in England Comments by the Law Society of England and Wales*, 2006, where they were described as 'elusive, overlapping and likely to confuse'.

41 The 2001 guidance (like the earlier 1995 guidance) listed these same four key factors of relevance. These four key factors are alternatives – they are not cumulative. Accordingly a need for substantial general nursing alone is sufficient to qualify a patient for continuing health care funding. Guidance issued by the Department of Health in 1996 (EL (96)8)) was critical of a number of continuing care statements which, rather than being sensitive to the complexity *or* intensity *or* unpredictability of a person's needs, placed too much emphasis on the need for people to meet multiple criteria for NHS-funded care. Follow up guidance (EL (96)89) noted with concern that of the 25 health authority continuing care statements considered, ten required individuals to meet at least two or more criteria.

42 *R v North and East Devon Health Authority ex p Coughlan* [2000] 2 WLR 622; (1999) 2 CCLR 285 at [118].

continuing care funding – indeed unless substantial weight is given to the above advice, it would appear likely that Ms Coughlan would not meet the requirements of the tool.

14.47   This difficulty was raised by a number of respondents to the consultation process preceding the launch of the new regime and in response the Department of Health stated that in the trials 'we have seen that people using the tool have been able to assess people as eligible for NHS Continuing Healthcare whether they have many lower needs or a few higher needs. We think therefore the decision support tool does capture the concept of continuity or totality/volume' (p14). While such comments are encouraging, areas running trials were presumably mindful that their decisions would be scrutinised, and it is possible that in practice the decision support tool may prove to be inadequate in addressing what has been described as a culture of 'ineligibility'[43] within certain health bodies.

Assessment – directions and 2007 framework

14.48   The 2007 Responsibilities Directions require PCTs to take reasonable steps to ensure that an assessment for NHS continuing health care is carried out in all cases where it appears to the trust that there may be a need of such care services; to inform the person of the decision in writing and to make a record of that decision and how to apply for a review if dissatisfied (see para 14.39).[44]

14.49   Additionally, the Delayed Discharges (Continuing Care) Directions 2007 place a duty on NHS bodies to take reasonable steps to undertake an NHS continuing health care assessment before issuing a notification to social services under Community Care (Delayed Discharges etc) Act 2003 s2 (see para 5.31 above). Where appropriate, this assessment should be in consultation with social services, and the NHS body is required to consult with the patient and/or carer and to notify the patient of the decision and of the right to seek a review.

14.50   The framework guidance contains detailed guidance on the assessment process, amplifying the requirements of the 2007 directions: most notably it:

- introduces a fast track pathway tool (see para 14.53 below);
- introduces a checklist to help practitioners identify who will need a full assessment (see para 14.55 below); and
- introduces a decision support tool which NHS bodies and PCTs are required to use by the directions to inform a decision following a multidisciplinary team assessment (see para 14.60 below).

43   See eg L Clements, *An evaluation of the proposed National Framework Document for NHS Continuing Healthcare and NHS-Funded Nursing Care in England, issued for Consultation by the Department of Health on the 19th June 2006*, 2006.

44   The NHS Continuing Healthcare (Responsibilities) Directions 2007 directions 2(1), 2(7) and 2(8).

14.51   It makes a number of helpful statements about the way the full assessment should be carried out:

- Before using the decision support tool, practitioners should ensure
  that they have obtained evidence from all the necessary assessments
  (comprehensive and specialist) (para 29).
- The process of assessment and decision-making should be person-
  centred. This means placing the individual, his or her perception of his
  or her support needs and preferred models of support at the heart of
  the assessment and care-planning process (para 30).
- Assessments should be organised so that the person who is undergoing an assessment and his or her family and/or carers understand
  the process, and receive advice and information to enable them to
  participate in informed decisions about their future care (para 32).
- The individual's informed consent should be obtained before the
  process of determining eligibility for NHS continuing health care
  begins. If there are concerns about capacity this should be determined
  in accordance with the Mental Capacity Act 2005 and the PCT may
  need to consider the appointment of an Independent Mental Capacity
  Advocate, especially when deciding on long term care provision (para
  33). The decision support tool further states that consent should
  include whether the person is happy for other family members or
  individuals to be involved (decision support tool para 7).
- The views and knowledge of family members may be taken into
  account, where consent has been given to seek those views (para 34).
- PCTs and local authorities are reminded that carers providing regular care have a right to an assessment of their needs as a carer (para
  35).
- The decision-making rationale should not marginalise a need because
  it is successfully managed – well managed need is still need (para 37).
- A person carrying out an assessment for NHS continuing health
  care should always consider whether there is further potential for
  rehabilitation and regaining independence (para 40).
- The risks and benefits to the individual of a change of location or
  support (including funding) should be considered carefully before any
  move or change is confirmed. Neither the PCT nor local authority
  should unilaterally withdraw from funding an existing package
  without appropriate reassessment (para 41).
- Assessments in acute settings can sometimes poorly represent the
  individual's capacity to maximise potential. To help avoid this problem,
  but to ensure unnecessary stays on acute wards are avoided, it should
  be considered whether further NHS- funded therapy and/or rehabilitation might make a difference to the potential of the individual in the
  following few months, and if so, transfer the patient to the appropriate
  NHS service (para 49).
- A comprehensive, multidisciplinary assessment of an individual's care
  needs including all relevant specialist and non-specialist assessment,
  should be carried out by a multidisciplinary team (para 53).

- Involving social services colleagues as well as health professionals in the assessment process will streamline the process of care planning. Local authorites should not allow an individual's financial circumstances to affect a decision to participate in a joint assessment (para 54).
- The time between a referral for full consideration of need and communication of the funding decision to the individual and his or her carers or representative where appropriate should not exceed two weeks in most cases. Timescales should be clearly communicated to the person and his or her carers (para 63).
- Furthermore the decision support tool has a space for the individual's assessment of his or her care needs and it must be noted whether the individual, carer or advocate was present during the multi-disciplinary assessment and whether he or she has seen and agreed to the content of the completed decision support tool (p20).

14.52 If this guidance is fully followed it should result in greater transparency in the decision-making process than has been the case in the past, where individuals have sometimes not been aware of an assessment and the decision has not been recorded.[45]

Fast track pathway tool

14.53 The fast track pathway tool has been introduced where individuals with a rapidly deteriorating condition, which may be entering a terminal phase, require fast tracking for immediate provision of NHS continuing health care. This might be where the person wishes to return home to die or to allow appropriate end of life support to be arranged. In such cases the rate of deterioration would bring the patient within the 'primary health needs' requirement and the framework guidance provides for the use of a fast track pathway tool which can be used by a senior clinician such as a ward sister, consultant or GP to outline the reason for the fast tracking decision. Justification for the use of the tool can be supported with a prognosis, 'but strict time limits are not relevant for end of life cases and should not be imposed'.[46]

14.54 The framework guidance reminds PCTs (at para 45) that careful decision-making is essential to avoid undue distress that might result from moving in and out of continuing care within a very short period of time. Although the fast track tool was published with the framework guidance there may be some further changes prior to October 2007 as the analysis of PCT testing has not been completed.

---

45 M Henwood, *Continuing Health Care: Review, revision and restitution*, 2004. This review found thatpoor quality of documentation and of assessment data featured throughout the sites. Sometimes this was simply a reflection of the passage of time, more often it was indicative of a lack of base line assessments, failure to continue any care management, and a casual disregard for the importance of record keeping (p8).
46 Framework guidance para 45.

The NHS continuing health care checklist[47]

14.55   Originally called a screening tool (which is what it is) the checklist has been designed to help practitioners identify people who need a full assessment for NHS continuing health care. The checklist is based on the decision support tool. As with the fast track tool there may be further revisions before October 2007. The 2007 Directions[47a] require that if any PCT or NHS body wishes to use an initial screening process it must complete and use the checklist to inform the decision and inform the person in writing of the outcome of the decision whether to carry out an assessment for NHS continuing health care and inform them (or someone acting for them) of how to request a review.

14.56   The checklist is a relatively brief document that adopts a tick box approach. It replicates the 11 domains of the decision support tool, but only lists the high level descriptors (see para 14.63 below). Assessors are then required to state whether the patient's needs (A) exceed the descriptor, or (B) meet it or (C) clearly do not meet it. Guidance notes with the checklist explain the implications of various scorings – ie that the patient does or does not qualify for a full assessment. These notes indicate that full consideration for NHS continuing health care may be necessary even where a patient does not meet the specified threshold.[48] Since it is highly unlikely that the checklist alone would have identified Ms Coughlan as qualifying for an assessment, it is clearly essential that this particular advice is widely adopted. Given that the screening is likely to be undertaken by a wide range of staff, it is regrettable that no guidance is given as to the reasons why someone not meeting the threshold might still need a full assessment.

14.57   Written reasons must be given for the decision and the individual or his or her carer should be informed of the decision, and advised they can ask for a full assessment if they disagree with the checklist decision, and that this request will be given due consideration.[49] The framework guidance stresses the importance of informing individuals that just because they are eligible for an assessment does not necessarily mean they will be found eligible for NHS continuing health care.[50]

14.58   The checklist can be completed by a range of professionals – the guidance suggests nurse, doctor, other qualified health care professional or social worker. There appears to be no reason therefore why the checklist could not be completed by suitable care home staff at their regular reviews of residents needs. Patients or relatives may want to use it to prompt themselves as to whether a full assessment should be requested.

47 Department of Health, *The NHS Continuing Healthcare Checklist*, 1 July 2007.
47a This requirement is in both the 2007 Responsibilities Directions (direction 2(3)) and the Delayed Discharge (Continuing Care) Directions 2007 (direction 2(4)).
48 Ibid, para 7.
49 Ibid, para 8. This is also repeated at para 51 of the framework guidance where it says that additional information from the individual or carer will be taken into consideration.
50 Framework guidance para 46.

14.59   The framework guidance states that if the checklist is used at the point of discharge from hospital and indicates either a need for a full assessment or an inconclusive result, a decision should be made and recorded to undertake a full consideration of eligibility once all treatment and rehabilitation has been completed. This full consideration should be completed in the appropriate setting, but in the interim the PCT retains responsibility for funding appropriate care.

The decision support tool

14.60   There are severe limitations in using standardised assessment tools to assess whether a patient may or may not qualify for NHS continuing health care. The tools tend to require micro-measurement of various factors which are then combined to produce a determination or presumption for or against qualification. Such tools, while they have their uses, are clearly open to considerable criticism. Most obviously they cannot say where the line between NHS/social services responsibility lies.

14.61   Additionally, standardised assessment tools seek to render empirical a process that has been legally (not scientifically) determined and may depend upon highly subjective factors (eg patient perceptions of pain[51]). The choice of the individual factors to be measured and the range of scores available for these factors is also a subjective process. In the Health Service Ombudsman's report on the Pointon[52] complaint, for instance, she was critical of the tools adopted by the relevant PCT as they were 'skewed in favour of physical and acute care' and did not take into account the patient's significant psychological problems. Criticism has also been levelled at the use of tools, on the ground that they inhibit communication with patients and their carers – and thereby sideline crucial user information from the decision-making process.[53]

14.62   The aim is that the decision support tool is used following a comprehensive multidisciplinary team assessment. It is seen as a way of bringing together and recording the full range of the individual's needs in a 'single practical format'.[54] An individual (or individuals) should be identified to co-ordinate and take responsibility for the whole process until the decision is made and a care plan written.[55]

---

51 See eg Social Security Commissioner's Decision no CDLA 902 2004, 18 June 2004 which at para 15 found that 'medical professionals who are expert in pain do not recognise a direct link between clinical findings and pain [accordingly authorities state that] . . . there is no direct causal link between disease or injury and pain, the only direct evidence of pain can come from the claimant'.

52 Case no E.22/02/02–03 Funding for Long Term Care (The Pointon Case).

53 See eg G Huby, J Stewart, A Tierney and W Rogers, 'Planning older people's discharge from acute hospital care: linking risk management and patient participation in decision-making' (2004) 6(2) *Health, Risk and Society* 115–132 who found that standardised assessment tools inhibited communication because they did not afford older people the opportunity to put any results into context for staff – cited in Social Care Institute for Excellence, *Using qualitative research in systematic reviews: Older people's views of hospital discharge*, February 2006, p36.

54 Decision support tool para 3.

55 Framework guidance para 53.

Table 15:   Division of levels of need in the different care domains

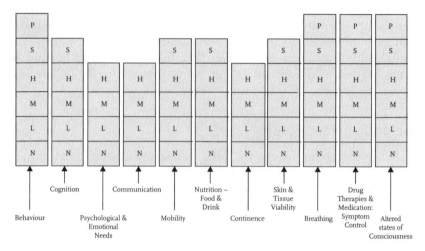

14.63   There are 11 care domains which all have to be completed and there is space in each domain for the reasons why a particular level ('No Need'; 'Low'; 'Moderate'; 'High'; 'Severe'; or, Priority;) is appropriate. A table (reproduced above as Table 15) summarises the domains, from which it can be seen that not all have a 'Priority' or 'Severe' category.

14.64   A clear recommendation for NHS continuing health care would be expected if a person has a priority need in any one of the four domains that carry this level or a total of two or more incidences in the severe category. As stated above it is then up to individual's judgement if people have lower needs than this level. Paras 17 and 18 of the guidance for the decision support tool, which are crucial in the way they are interpreted, are reproduced in full at para 14.45 above.

14.65   The tool is not supposed to determine eligibility directly and the indicative guidelines are not to be viewed prescriptively. Professional judgement should be exercised in all cases. Once the multi-disciplinary team have reached agreement, they make their recommendations about eligibility to the PCT.[56] The decision support tool must include the individual's assessment of his or her care needs (or carers' or advocates' summary where appropriate) and a note of whether he or she was invited to attend the assessment and whether he or she has seen and agreed the content of the decision support tool.[57] The Department of Health has 'reserved the right' to make some further alterations to the decision support tool before October 2007.

The funding decision

14.66   The final decision on funding is for the PCT. The framework guidance recognises that many PCTs use panels but cautions against their use as a gate keeping function or as a financial monitor. Para 63 states:

56   Ibid, paras 58 and 59.
57   Decision support tool p20.

Only in exceptional circumstances and for clearly articulated reasons, should the multidisciplinary team's recommendation not be followed. A decision to overturn the recommendation should never be made by one person acting unilaterally. Because the final eligibility decision should be independent of budgetary constraints, finance officers should not be part of a decision- making panel.

Care planning for NHS continuing health care

14.67 The framework guidance contains more detail than the 2001 guidance concerning case management once an eligibility decision has been made. It reminds PCTs that NHS commissioning includes an ongoing case management role in addition to regular reviews.[58] Although the PCT is not bound by the views of the local authority as to what services the individual needs, their contribution to the assessment will be important in identifying the individual's needs and the options for meeting them.[59] It states that NHS payments cannot be made as direct payments or for individual budgets but then goes on to say that PCTs can commission to maximise continuity of care, ie to maintain an existing package already in place.[60] Unfortunately no guidance is offered on how this should be done. The subject of NHS continuing health care and direct payments is considered separately at para 12.78 above.

Palliative care and end of life care

14.68 We have noted above (at para 13.57) that palliative care and end of life care have different meanings. The framework guidance unhelpfully mentions palliative care in the section called 'care planning for other care packages', although as noted at para 13.62 above the government, in response to criticism by the Health Select Committee, has suggested that patients who receive palliative care should meet the criteria for fully funded NHS continuing care. The care domain on drug therapies and medication relating to symptom control within the decision support tool would indicate that palliative care would normally fall within the severe or priority categories.

14.69 The 2001 guidance was clearer in this respect, stipulating (at para 18) that the NHS is responsible for the continuing health care funding of patients who require palliative care and whose prognosis is that they are likely to die in the near future. It states that such patients:

> . . . should be able to choose to remain in NHS funded accommodation (including in a nursing home), or to return home with the appropriate support. Patients may also require episodes of palliative care to deal with complex situations (including respite palliative care). The number of episodes required will be unpredictable and applications of time limits for this care are not appropriate;

The framework guidance likewise imposes no time limits.

---

58 Framework guidance para 74.
59 Ibid, para 75.
60 Ibid, para 77.

14.70   Many people at the end of their lives do not receive palliative care from specialist palliative care teams, and do not have their pain managed. Para 27 of the framework guidance mentions rapidly deteriorating conditions and the fact that this would be a primary health need, which along with the fast track pathway tool (see para 14.53) might suggest that those reaching the end of their life may no longer have to rely on the vagaries of whether they get palliative care in order to qualify for NHS continuing health care funding. There will be an end of life care strategy published by the end of 2007.[61]

14.71   A House of Commons Select Committee[62] has expressed concern about the patchy nature of PCT acceptance of responsibility for patients who require palliative care, and whose prognosis is that they are likely to die in the near future. The committee cited the 2001 Department of Health guidance that 'eligibility should be based on need, and not on an anticipated time to death (which is notoriously hard to predict)' and referred to the 'worrying picture' of different time limits employed across SHAs, noting (at para 46) that while the guidance states that time limits should not be applied:

> . . . in practice it does still seem to happen. This process cannot be activated unless you are within the last six weeks of life or eight weeks or 11 weeks, or whatever it might be . . . therefore, that is a barrier to some effective discharges.

14.72   In its response to the committee report[63] the government outlined plans as to how it proposes to make the option of dying at home a reality – not least by requiring PCTs to accept responsibility for 'unscheduled care' (ie 24 hour care and support at home).

14.73   The 2004 Welsh guidance (para 14(iv)) mirrors the English 2001 guidance: however it contains an explanatory note which suggests that 'near future' may be taken to mean around six to eight weeks and that if the patient improves and is later diagnosed as being likely to live for some time longer, then he or she may cease to qualify under this ground.

Reviews

14.74   The framework guidance states that cases should be reviewed three months following the initial assessment (including those who did not receive a full assessment following the application of the checklist) and at least yearly thereafter.[64] When reviewing the NHS funded nursing care, potential eligibility for NHS continuing health care should always be considered.

14.75   The Department of Health seeks in the framework guidance to restrict

---

61 Department of Health press releases 27 July 2006 and 26 January 2007, 'Better end of life care for patients – Government announces strategy to improve end of life care'.

62 House of Commons Health Committee Fourth Report of Session 2003–04 on Palliative Care, Volume 1, HC 454-I, accessible at http://www.publications. parliament.uk/pa/cm200304/cmselect/cmhealth/454/454.pdf.

63 Secretary of State for Health, *Government Response to House of Commons Health Committee Report on Palliative Care: Fourth Report of Session 2003–04*, Cm 6327, 2004.

64 Framework guidance para 82.

successful claims for NHS continuing health care being back dated prior to October 2007, stating at para 86:

> Assuming that the old decision was properly taken (ie the criteria at the time were lawful, the criteria were properly applied, there were sound reasons for the decision taken and the process was properly documented) that should not entitle the person to be reimbursed from the date they were previously refused NHS Continuing Healthcare. However if their needs have not changed, it should be considered whether their funding should be back-dated to the implementation date of the National Framework.

Dispute resolution

14.76　The 2007 Responsibilities Directions, which detail the procedure for reviewing NHS continuing health care decisions, are similar to the 2004 directions in relation to SHAs' responsibilities for such reviews. The review process has been little altered. The full text of the 2007 Responsibilities Directions is at appendix B.

14.77　　　The process consists of two stages: local resolution (which the framework guidance states normally takes the form of a PCT review panel), followed by a further review by a SHA panel. Since it is the local resolution process that often causes the greatest difficulty for complainants (particularly the delay in convening a PCT panel) it is to be regretted that the opportunity has not been taken to impose time limits on the local resolution stage. The 2007 Responsibilities Directions make a half-hearted attempt to ensure a more speedy process by stating that a person may apply to a SHA for a review where he or she 'has been unable to resolve the matter through any local dispute resolution procedure where the use of such a procedure would not have caused undue delay' (direction 4 (3)).

14.78　　　Once local resolution has been exhausted the case should be referred to the SHA's independent review panel (IRP) which will consider the case and make recommendations to the PCT. The key tasks of the panel are to assess whether the PCT has correctly applied the *National Framework for NHS Continuing Healthcare or NHS funded nursing care*, and has followed the processes set out in the guidance.[65]

14.79　　　The framework guidance (at paras 92 et seq) gives key principles that should be followed by the IRP regarding evidence gathering, involvement of the individual/carer and giving them opportunity to input at all stages, recording of the panel and clear and evidence based written decisions. Annex E of the framework guidance outlines the purpose and scope of the review panel.

14.80　　　The review procedure does not apply if individuals or their families wish to challenge the content of the eligibility criteria, the type or location of any NHS funded care, the content of any alternative package, or their treatment by any of the services they are receiving. This should be dealt with through the complaints procedure.

14.81　　　Individuals must be informed of their right to use the review procedure and advocates should be provided where this supports the

---

65　Ibid para 91.

individual through the review process. There should be a designated individual in each SHA to maintain the review procedure, and each SHA needs to identify clear time frames for the process which should be made explicit especially to individuals and carers.[66] While the review procedure is being conducted the PCT should continue to fund appropriate care. 'Any existing care package, whether hospital care or community health services, should not be withdrawn under any circumstance until the outcome of the review is known.'[67]

14.82   The chair of the IRP should be selected by open recruitment. The appointment of representatives of PCTs and local councils will be on the basis of nomination of those organisations. Panels are open for key parties to put their views in writing or to attend. An individual may have a representative to speak on his or her behalf if he or she chooses. If the IRP needs independent clinical advice such arrangements should avoid any obvious conflict of interest between the individual clinicians giving the advice and the organisation from which the individual has been receiving care. If a SHA decides in very exceptional circumstances to reject an IRP recommendation, it should put in writing to the individual and the chairman of the panel its reasons for so doing. In all cases the SHA must communicate in writing to the individual the outcome of the review with reasons.

14.83   If the individual is still aggrieved the case should be referred to the Healthcare Commission (although this may change in 2009 when the various regulatory commissions are due to merge).

14.84   Based on the Health Service Ombudsman's experience of many hundreds of NHS continuing health care cases since 2003, she has issued checklists on the procedures for SHAs and PCTs to follow as minimum acceptable practice.[68]

Reviews of cases prior to October 2007 and the 2001 guidance

14.85   In any case where a person wishes to have a review of a NHS continuing health care decision made prior to 1 October 2007, it will be necessary to be aware of the 2001 guidance and the eligibility criteria that applied in the SHA areas where the decision was made.

14.86   The 2001 guidance placed the responsibility for developing local criteria on the then 28 SHAs. Annex C to the 2001 guidance listed a number of

---

66 This aspect of the guidance is different from the 2001 guidance regarding reviews which stated '[e]ach Health authority should aim to ensure that the review procedure is completed within two week of the request being received. This period starts once any action to resolve the case informally has been completed, and should be extended only in exceptional circumstances.' Likewise the 2007 Responsibilities Directions merely state at 4(7) that notice about the decision must be given as soon as reasonably practicable.

67 Framework guidance annex E para 8.

68 Health Service Commissioner, *Continuing care: Health Service Ombudsman's investigation tool checklists for retrospective continuing care funding complaints*, 2005, available at http://www.ombudsman.org.uk/make_a_complaint/health/continuing_care_templates.html.

key issues that had to be considered in the framing of continuing health care eligibility criteria, stating:

1. The eligibility criteria or application of rigorous time limits for the availability of services by a health authority should not require a local council to provide services beyond those they can provide under [NAA 1948 s21] . . .

2. The nature or complexity or intensity or unpredictability of the individual's health care needs (and any combination of these needs) requires regular supervision by a member of the NHS multidisciplinary team, such as the consultant, palliative care, therapy or other NHS member of the team.

3. The individual's needs require the routine use of specialist health care equipment under supervision of NHS staff.

4. The individual has a rapidly deteriorating or unstable medical, physical or mental health condition and requires regular supervision by a member of the NHS multidisciplinary team, such as the consultant, palliative care, therapy or other NHS member of the team.

5. The individual is in the final stages of a terminal illness and is likely to die in the near future.

6. A need for care or supervision from a registered nurse and/or a GP is not, by itself, sufficient reason to receive continuing NHS health care.

7. The location of care should not be the sole or main determinant of eligibility. Continuing NHS health care may be provided in an NHS hospital, a nursing home, hospice or the individual's own home.

14.87 Most SHA guidance followed this framework, in particular following the ombudsman's 2003 report, although as stated above the *Grogan* case found fatal flaws in the local guidance being used at the time. The stumbling block for many people was the way the guidance was interpreted, the idiosyncrasy of local assessment tools, and the processes in place by which decisions were made.

14.88 Reviews of cases where the period is prior to 2004 are dealt with by the Health Service Ombudsman. Cases which cover the period after 2004 are dealt with by the Healthcare Commission. The Department of Health has issued a letter[69] aiming to close requests for reviews of eligibility decisions made before April 2004 or which involve a period of time falling mainly before April 2004 not previously challenged. Such cases should be raised by 30 November 2007. Unless there are exceptional circumstances new cases involving decisions made prior to April 2004 will be returned with an explanation of why they cannot be examined.

Redress

14.89 The protracted nature of many of the reviews that have been undertaken since 2003 and the backdating of NHS continuing health care responsibilities has raised the issue about the financial losses that have been suffered by complainants. In 2007 a special report was issued by the Parliamentary Ombudsman and the Health Service Ombudsman. The Parliamentary Ombudsman found that there was maladministration in

---

69 Closing the continuing care retrospective review process. Dear colleague letter 31 July 2007.

the Department of Health's decision making and communication of its approach to recompense for wrongly denied continuing care funding. The department had advised the NHS to pay recompense based on the principle of restitution for only those monies paid out in care fees. This approach discouraged PCTs from considering full redress, including, for example, redress for claimed financial loss for premature sale of a property or inconvenience and distress that individuals had suffered in making unnecessary difficult decisions about how to fund care.

14.90   In the same report the Health Service Ombudsman found no maladministration on the part of an NHS trust, in a case where a house had been sold when it need not have been if the NHS continuing health care decision had been correctly made, since this was due to the Department of Health's 'unclear and inconsistent' guidance. In this case the local government ombudsman had already considered the complaint that no deferred payment (see para 8.76 above) had been offered to the family – since this would have avoided the necessity of selling the property pending the outcome of the NHS challenge.[70] As a result of the 2007 special report the Department of Health has issued guidance to remind PCTs of their responsibilities concerning maladministration and redress; to remind them that they are empowered to make ex gratia payments where appropriate; to advise them how to calculate interest payments for redress; and to remind them about the powers of local authorities regarding deferred payment agreements.[71]

14.91   The court has also scrutinised the question of interest and found that the award of interest should be 'tailor made to each case'.[72] It agreed that no account should be taken of payments made to the claimant by third parties (such as the benefits paid by the Department for Work and Pensions) in deciding the rate of interest payable. The court changed its provisional decision that the applicant should receive interest at the retail price index rate and ordered that he should receive interest at the (higher) court rate.

Wales 2004 guidance

14.92 With the introduction of the framework guidance in England the situation in Wales is materially different. In August 2004 the Welsh Assembly issued revised continuing health care guidance[73] together with guidance as to how the new criteria should be implemented.[74] The guidance is very similar to the 2001 English guidance. The implementation guidance gives detail on the process. So for instance there is guidance (para 5.3) on how

---

70 *Retrospective Continuing Care Funding and Redress*, February 2007. Available at www.ombudsman.org.uk/improving_services/special_reports/hsc/care07/report.html.

71 Department of Health, *NHS Continuing Healthcare; Continuing Care Redress*, March 2007.

72 *R v Kemp and Denbighshire Health Board* [2006] EWHC 1339 (Admin).

73 WHC (2004)54: NAFWC 41/2004, accessible at http://new.wales.gov.uk/publications/circular/circulars04/NAFWC412004?lang=en.

74 *Continuing NHS Health Care: Framework for implementation in Wales 2004*, accessible at http://www.wales.nhs.uk/documents/ACF3BF8.pdf.

to decide whether an individual should have a full assessment for continuing NHS health care, and that the decision on what level and type of assessment should be recorded and justified on the case notes. The implementation guidance has a specific chapter on information to patients and carers (chapter 8). Local health boards are responsible for review panels with a similar system to that in England.

14.93   In October 2006 the Assembly issued a revision note to address the findings in *Grogan*.[75] The advice note accepts there is a need for the Assembly to 'clarify and remove the potential for confusion' in respect of the 2004 guidance and implementation framework. The note (at annex B) gives interim guidance – stating that 'fully revised guidance will be produced to incorporate the implications of the *Grogan* judgment as well as the Mental Capacity Act' although no timescale is provided. The main points in the guidance note are:

- An individual will qualify for NHS continuing care if his or her assessed needs for health care (including nursing services provided by a registered nurse under Health and Social Care Act (HSCA) 2001 s49) are of a quality or quantity beyond that of the community care services which may be provided by a local authority under NAA 1948 s21 (annex B para 1(b)).
- The assessment of individual entitlement to NHS continuing care must include consideration, not only of the nature, complexity, predictability, intensity of the person's care needs, but also of the amount of the health care inputs – the assessment must 'consider both the quality and quantity of health care required' (annex B para 2).
- The reference in para 14.1 of the 2004 guidance to regular input from an NHS member of the multi-disciplinary team as normally referring to weekly or more often does not exclude the scope for less frequent NHS input where there has been clear and appropriate delegation of that input (annex B para 4).
- Para 24 of the 2004 guidance is rebalanced, by making it clear that although 'a need for care from a registered nurse and/or GP alone may not of itself be sufficient reason for receiving continuing NHS health care' this does not mean that the totality of such a package could not qualify a patient for NHS continuing care (annex B para 5).
- Where a person is assessed as having a need for nursing or other health services that is in excess of the *Coughlan* quality/quantity threshold, he or she will be eligible for continuing NHS health care (annex B para 7).

14.94   The Ombudsman in Wales (see para 27.146) has also voiced his concern about the 2004 guidance, particularly its failure to 'clearly introduce a single set of criteria upon which all applications for continuing care made in Wales will be determined'.[76]

75 Welsh Assembly, *Further advice to the NHS and Local Authorities on Continuing NHS Health Care*, WHC (2006) 046: NAFWC 32/2006.
76 The Public Services Ombudsman for Wales, Annual Report 2004/05, p70, accessible at http://www.wales.nhs.uk/documents/Ombudsmanannualreport04–05.pdf.

14.95   The fact that fully revised guidance has been promised suggests that at some stage the Welsh Assembly may issue guidance based on the experience of the reception of the English framework guidance.

Patients covered by NHS continuing health care guidance

14.96   The framework guidance applies only to adults and states that '[t]he actual services provided as part of that package should be seen in the wider context of best practice and services development for each client group'.

Children

14.97   In relation to children the framework guidance states at para 70:

> This guidance does not cover under 18s (children). Whilst similar principles and values apply there are different legislative drivers for younger people's services in this area including their need for education.

14.98   The Department of Health's response to the consultation process further states 'Guidance on this topic [ie children] is currently under consideration'.[77]

14.99   In *R (T, D and B) v Haringey LBC*[78] the High Court indicated that it considered the *Coughlan* principles applied to children as to adults. The *Haringey* case was unusual in that the applicant was arguing that the children were not the responsibility of the NHS and accordingly there was not necessarily full argument on the question. It is at least arguable that social services have no power whatsoever to fund any nursing home provision for disabled children. It appears that in no legislation concerning local authority responsibilities for children are they permitted to fund any nursing care. This is different for adults (as the court noted in *Coughlan*) since NAA 1948 s26(1B) did make limited reference to nursing care (now in NAA 1948 s26(1A) and (1C)).

14.100   The framework guidance addresses the question of children receiving continuing care who reach adulthood in the following way:

> . . . a child in receipt of Children's Continuing Care should be reassessed for their eligibility for Adult NHS Continuing Healthcare, and that until they have been assessed, the current package of care should be maintained. It is therefore in the child/young person's and the PCT and LA's interests to monitor those recipients of continuing care who are aged 16 or 17, to ensure continuity of care provision (not necessarily funding) once the individual reaches 18. The transition from childhood to adulthood is thus a trigger for a full review.

14.101   The 2004 Welsh guidance (para 4) states that it covers all persons, regardless of age or illness/disability.

77   Department of Health, *A National Framework for NHS Continuing Healthcare and NHS-Funded Nursing Care in England: Response to Consultation*, 2007, p6.
78   [2005] EWHC 2235 (Admin); (2006) 9 CCLR 58.

Learning disability services and NHS continuing health care

14.102 Circular guidance HSG (92)43 and LAC (92)17 has referred to the historically anomalous position of people with learning difficulties; essentially that although their needs are primarily social, historically the NHS has provided for people with learning difficulties and therefore the NHS has received the funding for the continuing care needs of such people. Thus the 1992 guidance states that:

> . . . it is well recognised that many people (ie people with learning difficulties) traditionally cared for in long-stay hospitals are predominantly in need of social care, and should be cared for in the community. In order to support in the community ex long-stay patients and people who might in earlier times have been cared for in long-stay hospitals, health finance may be spent on social services rather than on health services.

14.103 Until the large scale closure of the large NHS hospitals specifically catering for people with learning disabilities, one fifth of people with severe or profound learning disabilities received their care services from the NHS.[79] 'Even today, close to 3,000 people with learning disabilities live as inpatients in NHS residential accommodation, or 'NHS campuses'.[80] The 1992 guidance advocates, therefore, not only that the NHS transfer monies to social services for the present support of such persons (and their successors[81]) but also that it should develop new and innovative services to meet the social (as opposed to health) needs of such persons. The framework guidance deals with this situation thus:

> There may be other circumstances, aside from a PCT's responsibilities for NHS Continuing Healthcare and under the Mental Health Act 1983, when the NHS will be expected to take responsibility for a person's long term care. An example might be people with learning disabilities, where there may be an existing commitment to fund ongoing care to individuals following the closure of long stay hospitals or campuses. These responsibilities arise independently of the PCT's responsibility to provide continuing care and there should not be any assumption that these responsibilities equate to eligibility for continuing care or vice versa.[82]

14.104 Many people with learning disabilities will qualify directly for NHS continuing health care funding on the general ground that as a consequence of the nature or complexity or intensity or unpredictability of their health care needs, the care they require is neither incidental or ancillary to the provision of social services nor of a nature such that an authority whose primary responsibility is to provide social services can be expected to provide it – ie the *Coughlan* criteria. In this respect, particular regard should also be given to the comments of the Health Service Ombudsman in the Pointon complaint[83] that health bodies must take into

---

79 LAC (92)15.
80 Department of Health white paper, *Our health, our care, our say: a new direction for community services*, Cm 6737, 2006, para 4.90.
81 HSG (92)43: LAC (92)17.
82 Framework guidance para 69.
83 Case no E.22/02/02–03 Funding for Long Term Care (The Pointon Case): see para 14.27.

account a person's psychological problems and the special skills it takes to care for such people.

14.105   Although not specifically stated in the framework guidance, the response to the consultation comments that the intention in the new framework is 'to ensure that the needs of people with mental health problems and learning disabilities can be properly assessed under the proposed framework, and – in particular – that it is made as clear as it possibly could be, that NHS Continuing Healthcare can apply to people with mental health problems or learning disabilities as well as to people with physical disability or organic disease' (p13).

14.106   The framework guidance anticipates the new *Bournewood* provisions in the Mental Health Act (MHA) 2007 (see para 18.44 above) whereby individuals who lack capacity may be deprived of their liberty in a care home or hospital. It argues that this does not affect the assessment of whether a person is eligible for NHS continuing health care.[84]

Mental health services and NHS continuing health care

14.107   The joint nature of the duty under MHA 1983 s 117 (see para 21.27 below) has created tensions, since it is arguable that a patient could fall within the entitlement criteria for both regimes. To a large extent it is immaterial to the individual as in either case care is free, but the question is of considerable budgetary relevance to local authorities and local health bodies since section 117 services are a joint responsibility (see para 21.34 below). The framework guidance seems to have missed this point, stating merely that because section 117 services are free and constitute a free standing duty 'it is not therefore necessary to assess eligibility for NHS Continuing Healthcare if all the services in question are to be provided as after-care under section 117'. It goes on to state:

> However, a person in receipt of after-care services under section 117 may also have needs for continuing care which are not related to their mental disorder and which may not fall within the scope of section 117. An obvious example would be a person who was already receiving continuing care in relation to physical health problems before being detained under the 1983 Act and whose physical health problems remain on discharge. Where such needs exist, it may be necessary to carry out a consideration for NHS Continuing Healthcare.[85]

14.108   The inter-relationship between section 117 services and NHS continuing health care is considered further at para 21.43 below.

Continuing health care in community settings

14.109   In *Coughlan* the court held that 'the fact that the resident at a nursing home does not require in-patient treatment in a hospital does not mean that his or her care should not be the responsibility of the NHS' (at [42])

---

84   Framework guidance para 68.
85   Ibid, paras 66 and 67.

and that where the primary need is a health need, the responsibility is that of the NHS, even when the individual has been placed in a home by a local authority (at [31]).

14.110   This finding accorded with 1992 guidance[86] which stated that where a patient's need is primarily for health care, any placement (in a nursing home or elsewhere) must be fully funded by the health authority. The 2001 guidance made this point explicit, stating that:

> The location of care should not be the sole or main determinant of eligibility. Continuing NHS health care may be provided in an NHS hospital, a nursing home, hospice or the individual's own home.

14.111 In a 2003 complaint investigated by the Health Service Commissioner[87] she criticised an authority whose continuing health care statement had the effect of requiring 'on-site medical provision' (ie hospital based) in order to qualify for full NHS funding. The Pointon case (see para 14.27) likewise further clarified the position that NHS continuing health care could be provided in people's own homes and that the fact that Mr Pointon's care was provided by non-health staff did not preclude his needs from being health needs. The framework guidance expands on the 2001 guidance thus:

> NHS Continuing Healthcare may be provided by PCTs in any setting (including, but not limited to, a care home, hospice or the person's own home). Eligibility for NHS Continuing Healthcare is therefore not determined or influenced by either the setting where the care is provided nor by the characteristics of the person who delivers the care.

Social services responsibilities

14.112 When NHS continuing health care is provided at home it can bring into sharp relief the difference between the legislative frameworks under which the NHS and social services operate.[88] This was at the heart of the *Haringey* case (para 14.29 above) where social services had assessed a child as needing four nights a week of nursing care to give her mother a rest, but the PCT accepting responsibility for providing the nursing care, disagreed with the level of care social services considered necessary. In this case the mother and child were left to cope with the reduced service the PCT was prepared to provide.

14.113   However it is arguable that the duties of social services in the case of care at home do not end if a person is entitled to NHS continuing health care at home. The statutory prohibition in NAA 1948 s21(8) applies to residential accommodation provided under section 21(1) and 'other services . . . provided in connection with the accommodation' under section 21(5). Where those services are 'authorised or required to be provided' under, materially, the National Health Service Acts 2006, the local authority cannot lawfully provide them.

86 LAC (92)24 annex A para 7.
87 Berkshire Health Authority Case no E.814/00–01; Second Report for Session 2002–03 *NHS funding for long term care*, HC 399, 2003.
88 For a fuller explanation of the arguments put forward in this section see L Clements and P Bowen, 'NHS Continuing Care and independent living' (2007) 10 CCLR 343–351.

14.114   What is sometimes overlooked, is that the exclusionary effect of NAA 1948 s21(8) is limited to people in residential accommodation and to services provided 'in connection with' such accommodation. It does not exclude the following services:

- Services provided by local authorities under the NHS Acts 2006,[89] including non-accommodation services to prevent people becoming ill. Such services are deemed to be 'community care services'.[90] The Court of Appeal in *Coughlan* does not appear to have heard argument concerning the community care duties of social services authorities under the NHS Acts 2006, because these duties are limited to the provision of non-residential care services[91] and Ms Coughlan was not seeking such support.

- Services provided under NAA 1948 s29 and Chronically Sick and Disabled Persons Act (CSDPA) 1970 s2. These might be provided either to (a) individuals living at home, in respect of whom NAA 1948 s21(8) has no application, or (b) to those living in residential accommodation, where the services cannot properly be described as provided 'in connection with' the residential accommodation within the meaning of NAA 1948 s21(5) (for example, educational opportunities provided on another site).

14.115   Where services are more properly considered as falling within NAA 1948 s29 (which includes services under CSDPA 1970 s2) the corresponding provision to NAA 1948 s21(8) is NAA 1948 s29(6)(b) (see para 9.37 above). However, this provision only prohibits social services from providing services 'required' to be provided under the NHS Acts, as opposed to those that are 'authorised or required' to be so provided in section 21(8). This excludes only those services which must, as a matter of law, be provided under the NHS Acts 2006 ('required'), not those which could as a matter of law be provided either by the NHS or by a local authority but which, as a matter of *policy*, the secretary of state has decided should be provided by the NHS as NHS continuing care ('authorised'). Thus, for example, any adaptations necessary to enable a person to live at home could be provided either by the NHS under the NHS Acts or by a local authority under NAA 1948 s29 and CSDPA 1970 s2, and the fact that the individual qualifies for NHS continuing care would not displace the local authority's duty to provide such services if they are not met by the NHS.

14.116   It follows therefore that social services can provide all manner of community care services for the support of a person living in the community who is entitled to NHS continuing health care support apart from those services which, as a matter of law, can only be provided by the NHS (for example, registered nursing pursuant to HSCA 2001 s49).[92]

89 NHSA 2006 s 254 and Sch 20; NHS(W)A 2006 s 192 and Sch 15 – see para 9.137 above.
90 NHS and Community Care Act 1990 s46(3).
91 NHSA 2006 Sch 20 para 2(11); NHS(W)A 2006 Sch 15 para 2(11).
92 In this respect it should be noted that NHSA 2006 Sch 20 para 3 and NHS(W)A 2006 Sch 15 para 3 oblige social services authorities (and not the NHS) to provide a home help service for households where such help is required owing to the presence of a person who (amongst other things) is suffering from illness. Under the current

14.117   The framework guidance attempts to clarify this point at para 18:

> LAs also have the function of providing services under section 29 of the National Assistance Act 1948 (which includes functions under section 2 of the Chronically Sick and Disabled Persons Act 1970). Section 29(6)(b) of the National Assistance Act 1948 only prohibits LAs from providing services under section 29 which are 'required' to be provided under the National Health Service Act 2006 so excludes only those services which can, as a matter of law, be provided under the National Health Service Act 2006.

14.118 And at para 76 the framework guidance further advises:

> The LA is, however, not prevented from providing services, as it sees fit. Indeed in some cases, there may have to be individual arrangements reached between LAs and PCTs with respect to the provision of services. This may be particularly relevant where the person is to be cared for in a community setting.

14.119 In consequence the framework guidance acknowledges that notwithstanding a determination of entitlement to NHS continuing health care support, social services still have a role since such a person may still appear to be 'in need' of community care services and as a consequence the duty to assess under the National Health Service and Community Care Act (NHSCCA) 1990 is triggered.[93] As we note at para 3.76 above the Department of Health has reminded all local authorities that even where an individual is being wholly funded by the NHS, a duty to assess under the 1990 Act will generally subsist.

Impact on social security benefits

14.120 Department for Work and Pensions guidance[94] exists concerning the impact on benefits of a decision that a person qualifies for NHS continuing health care support. Residents will generally be treated as hospital inpatients for benefit purposes, from the date the PCT made a formal entitlement decision – provided the care home concerned is a 'similar institution to a hospital' – and payments made to refund patients for the period during which they were wrongly charged for their care do not retrospectively turn these claimants into hospital inpatients for that period (ie provided the resident notifies the Department for Work and Pensions of the funding, there should not be any overpayment).

Department of Health directions concerning what is 'required' to be provided under NHSA 2006 Sch 20 para 2 and NHS(W)A 2006 Sch 15 para 2 it is the duty of social services authorities to make domiciliary care arrangements for the purpose of preventing mental disorder, as well as for persons, who are or who have been, suffering from mental disorder – see LAC (93)10 appendix 3 para 3(2) (which by virtue of NHS (Consequential Provisions) Act 2006 s 4 and Sch 2 para 1(2) continues to apply with equal effect to the consequent provisions in the NHS Acts 2006).

93   *R v Bristol City Council ex p Penfold* (1998) 1 CCLR 315: see para 3.73 above.
94   Continuing Care – NHS Responsibilities. Memo DMG Vol 3 08/04, 26 May 2004. The Department of Work and Pensions advice on this is available on the Department of Health website in the continuing NHS care section.

14.121   As a consequence of changes to the rules governing entitlement to benefits while a hospital inpatient (ie now the only benefits affected are attendance allowance and disability living allowance in hospital or in care homes if the person is fully funded by the NHS) there are fewer problems about what happens to benefits if a retrospective NHS continuing health care payment is made.

14.122   A tribunal of Social Security Commissioners[95] has held that persons with severe learning disabilities who had been placed by the NHS in independent care homes were maintained in 'hospital' and so barred from receiving DLA. The prohibition applies where a local authority has taken responsibility for a person's placement (ie under NAA 1948 s21) when his or her nursing needs were such that the NHS should have accepted NHS continuing health care responsibility. The tribunal further explained the implications of this finding as follows:

> Of course, if no care is provided by the National Health Service or if the only care is provided at the claimant's home, regulation 8[96] does not bite because the claimant is not 'maintained . . . in a hospital or similar institution under the NHS Act of 1977'; but, if some nursing services are provided by the National Health Service to a claimant in a care home and if the claimant's nursing needs are more than merely incidental and ancillary to other care needs, regulation 8 does bite.

Decided cases as comparators

14.123   Given the widespread criticism of central government guidance it is frequently instructive to use the cases determined by the courts and Health Service Ombudsman as comparators when seeking to determine eligibility for NHS continuing care funding. Both the ombudsman and the government in England have found such an approach useful. For example Virginia Bottomley, Secretary of State for Health in 1994 specifically referred to the care needs of the patient at the centre of the Leeds complaint as a benchmark for funding,[97] and the Health Service Commissioner compared the nursing care needs for the patient in the complaint concerning Wigan and Bolton Health Authority to those of Pamela Coughlan.[98] Table 16 below provides a resume of the care needs of some of the patients whose cases have been reported.

14.124   The framework guidance seeks to dissuade PCTs from using cases as comparators stating (at para 61):

> PCTs should be aware of cases which have indicated circumstances where a finding of eligibility for NHS Continuing Healthcare should

---

95   CDLA 3161 2003 (27 July 2005).

96   Social Security (Disability Living Allowance) Regulations 1991 SI No 2890.

97   Department of Health press release of 4 November 1994 and the Department of Health in its guidance EL (96)8 at para 16.

98   See eg the comments of the Health Service Commissioner in her 2003 report concerning Wigan and Bolton Health Authority and Bolton Hospitals NHS Trust Case no E.420/00–01, Second Report for Session 2002–03 *NHS funding for long term care*, HC 399, 2003.

have been made, and where the same outcome would be expected if the same facts were being considered in an assessment for NHS Continuing Healthcare under the National Framework (e.g. *Coughlan*, and those in the Health Service Ombudsman's report NHS funding for long term care of older and disabled people). However, they should be wary of trying to extrapolate generalisations about eligibility for NHS Continuing Healthcare from the limited information they may have about those cases. There is no substitute for a careful and detailed assessment of the needs of the individual whose eligibility is in question.[99]

14.125 This is questionable guidance, given the reliance placed on these cases by the court, the ombudsman and the government. The argument that PCTs should be wary because of the limited information they may have about these cases is particularly disingenuous in relation to Ms Coughlan for whom we have detailed information about her health care needs and for whom it is highly questionable whether the new regime would establish entitlement to NHS continuing health care. It is at least arguable that the reason why the Department of Health is cautious about the use of comparators is that they might thereby expose the shortcomings of the 2007 framework.

Table 16: Resumé of patients involved in continuing care disputes

R v North and East Devon Health Authority ex p Coughlan

Miss Coughlan was grievously injured in a road traffic accident in 1971. She is tetraplegic; doubly incontinent, requiring regular catheterisation; partially paralysed in the respiratory tract, with consequent difficulty in breathing; and subject not only to the attendant problems of immobility but to recurrent headaches caused by an associated neurological condition (para 3 of judgment).

Leeds Ombudsman Report Case no E.62/93–94, January 1994

A man suffered a brain haemorrhage and was admitted to a neurosurgical ward. . . . He received surgery but did not fully recover. He was incontinent, unable to walk, communicate or feed himself. He also had a kidney tumour, cataracts and occasional epileptic fits, for which he received drug treatment. After 20 months in hospital he was in a stable condition but still required full time nursing care. His condition had reached the stage where active treatment was no longer required but he was still in need of substantial nursing care, which could not be provided at home and which would continue to be needed for the rest of his life (para 22 of report).

The importance of this assessment was emphasised in NHS guidance EL (96)8 which (at para 16) criticised continuing care statements which
Continued

---

99 Framework guidance para 61.

placed an 'over-reliance on the needs of a patient for specialist medical supervision in determining eligibility for continuing in-patient care' and specifically referred to the fact that this was not considered by the ombudsman in the Leeds case as an acceptable basis for withdrawing NHS support'.

Wigan and Bolton Health Authority and Bolton Hospitals NHS Trust Case no E.420/00–01[100]

Mrs N had suffered several strokes, as a result of which she had no speech or comprehension and was unable to swallow, requiring feeding by PEG tube (a tube which allows feeding directly into the stomach). Mrs N was being treated as an in-patient in the Trust's stroke unit and was discharged to a nursing home (para 1 p24).

The Health Services Commissioner concluded (para 30, p32): 'I cannot see that any authority could reasonably conclude that her need for nursing care was merely incidental or ancillary to the provision of accommodation or of a nature one could expect Social Services to provide (paragraph 15). It seems clear to me that she, like Miss Coughlan, needed services of a wholly different kind.'(In essence the ombudsman had found the decision *Wednesbury* unreasonable.)

Dorset Health Authority and Dorset HealthCare NHS Trust Case no E.208/ 99–00[101]

Mr X suffered from Alzheimer's disease and was admitted to a nursing home (p11 para 1), allegedly receiving services very similar to Miss Coughlan's (p20 para 23).

The Health Services Commissioner concluded (at para 26, p21): 'I ... recommend that the ... Authority should, with colleague organisations, determine whether there were any patients (including Mr X senior) who were wrongly refused funding for continuing care, and make the necessary arrangements for reimbursing the costs they incurred unnecessarily ... Mr X senior suffered a degenerative condition, so he was more likely to be eligible for funding as time went by.'

Berkshire Health Authority Case no E.814/00–01[102]

Mrs Z, a 90-year-old admitted to a hospital suffering with vascular dementia (para 1 p35) and in need of 'all help with daily living, except feeding' and resistant to help and needing supervision if she was to take the medication she needed (para 12 p38).

Continued

---

100   From the Health Service Ombudsman's Second Report for Session 2002–03 *NHS funding for long term care*, HC 399, 2003.
101   Ibid.
102   Ibid.

The Health Services Commissioner concluded (at para 39, p46): 'It is certainly very possible (but not entirely certain) that, if appropriate criteria had been applied, Mrs Z would have qualified for fully funded care'.

Birmingham Health Authority Case no E.1626/01–02[103]

Mrs R, a 90-year-old admitted to hospital following a severe stroke, which had left her immobile, incontinent, and confused (and unlikely that her condition would change) (para 1, p49).

The Health Services Commissioner concluded (at para 23, p54): 'Had Mrs R been assessed against criteria which were in line with the then guidance and the Coughlan judgment, she might (though it is not possible to be certain) have been deemed eligible for NHS funding for her nursing home care'.

Complaint against the former Shropshire Health Authority Case no E.5/02–03[104]

Mrs F has Alzheimer's Disease and in June 2000 was assessed by a consultant psychiatrist as needing specialist elderly mentally ill (EMI) care. A nursing assessment in November 2000 noted that she required full assistance with all her personal tasks including washing, dressing, feeding and toileting. She was also doubly incontinent, was dependent upon others for her safety, and could only mobilise with assistance.
The ombudsman was advised by her independent clinical assessor that Mrs F required significant nursing care and it was debatable whether that could properly be regarded as merely incidental or ancillary to the accommodation which Mrs F also needed. The ombudsman upheld the complaint.

Complaint against the former Shropshire Health Authority Case no E.2119/ 01[105]

Mr C suffered a severe stroke and the clinical assessment found that he was unable to manage any aspect of personal care independently. The notes recorded that he had an in-dwelling urinary catheter, occasional faecal incontinence (largely avoided by regular toileting by hoist transfer to commode/toilet); that he required to be fed soft pureed diet with thickened oral fluids; that he had a PEG Gastrostomy tube in place, used to administer additional fluids overnight if necessary; that a hoist was used for all transfers; that all pressure areas remained intact with repositioning two hourly; that communication was by eye contact and head movement; that he could not speak.

Continued

---

103 Ibid.
104 Health Service Ombudsman's Fifth Report for the Session 2002–03, HC 787, 2003.
105 Ibid.

The ombudsman's specialist assessor concluded that from the information provided Mr C's needs were primarily health needs.

Complaint against Cambridgeshire Health Authority and PCT (the 'Pointon' case)[106]

Mr P is severely disabled with dementia and unable to look after himself. His wife cared for him at home. She took a break one week in five but had to pay more than £400 for the substitute care assistant, because the NHS would not pay, because Mrs P was not a qualified nurse (and could not therefore be offering nursing care). It was held that the fact that Mr P was receiving (what was in effect) nursing care from his wife, did not mean he could not qualify for continuing health care; that the health bodies had failed to take into account his severe psychological problems and the special skills it takes to nurse someone with dementia; that the assessment tools used by the NHS were skewed in favour of physical and acute care; the fact that Mr P needed care at home – rather than in a nursing care home – was not material to the question of continuing health care responsibility.

R (T, D and B) v Haringey LBC[107]

Two sisters (aged 3 and 19 at the hearing) both of whom had complex medical conditions which required – among other things – a tracheostomy (a tube in the throat) which would be needed for several years. The tubes needed suctioning about three times a night. The tube required replacing about once a week and if the young person was not suctioned or if the tube became unstuck she would suffocate and die within minutes, or suffer serious brain damage in a shorter time. Although children who have tracheostomies are often discharged from hospital and cared for at home, their parents have to be trained by the hospital to make the daily routines and cope with the emergencies that may arise.

106   Case no E.22/02/02–03 Funding for Long Term Care (The Pointon Case).
107   [2005] EWHC 2235 (Admin); (2006) 9 CCLR 58.

CHAPTER 15

Housing and community care

continued

Introduction

15.1   Appropriate housing has been described as 'the basic requirement – the foundation – of community care'.[1] Such a view recognises not merely the increased acknowledgment of the right to 'independent living' (see para 000 above) but also the practical everyday benefits that suitable housing can provide for people in need of community care services. As the Audit Commission has noted:[2]

> . . . it is not simply the provision of a roof over people's heads that makes housing's contribution so important, it is the personal support to help vulnerable people cope with everyday living – for example, negotiating the complexities of rent payments or resolving problems with water, gas and electricity suppliers – that makes the difference between life in the community and institutionalisation.[3]

15.2   This chapter is concerned with the general obligations on housing authorities in relation to matters that impinge upon community care support services – including those that may arise in eviction proceedings; in relation to the provision of disabled facilities grants and accommodation for homeless people who have community care needs. It additionally considers the discreet questions of services provided under the 'Supporting People' initiative and the 'Adult Placement' regulatory regime.

15.3   Since appropriate accommodation is a fundamental theme in relation to almost all community care services, many aspects of the housing contribution to community care are also considered elsewhere in this book, most notably the provision of residential care accommodation (which may comprise nothing more than a simple tenancy), which is considered at para 7.51 and home adaptations under the Chronically Sick and Disabled Persons Act (CSDPA) 1970 s2(1)(e) are considered at para 9.93 above.

Responsibilities of housing authorities

15.4   Housing authorities, in meeting their responsibilities under Housing Act (HA) 1985 s8 to consider housing conditions and provision in their area are required, by CSDPA 1970 s3, to have specific regard to the special needs of chronically sick and disabled persons, including the provision or adaptation of existing accommodation for their own disabled tenants. In

---

1   P Arnold et al, *Community Care: The housing dimension*, Joseph Rowntree Foundation, 1993; and see also P Arnold and D Page, *Housing and Community Care*, University of Humberside, 1992.
2   Audit Commission, *Home Alone: The housing aspects of community care*, 1998, para 7.
3   A recent survey of Directors of Adult Services revealed that over half of those responding had taken on responsibility for housing services, and suggests that the importance of housing in the well-being of a community is now being recognised more clearly (*Community Care*, 4 April 2007).

this respect 2006 good practice guidance[4] issued to housing authorities stresses the importance of aspiring 'for the social inclusion of all its citizens' and the general need 'to design in access and accept a corporate responsibility for countering disabling environments'. The promotion of independent living is clearly as much a goal for housing authorities as it is for social services authorities (see para 4.44 above).

15.5   Housing authorities must, in the framing of their allocation schemes – which determine who is to have priority for housing – give reasonable preference to people who need to move on medical or welfare grounds including grounds relating to a disability.[5] In *R (Ireneschild) v Lambeth LBC*[6] the High Court considered the relationship between a housing needs assessment undertaken by the Housing Department (to ascertain the applicant's priority for rehousing) and a community care assessment considering that person's need for accommodation under National Assistance Act (NAA) 1948 s21. In the opinion of Lloyd Jones J the two assessments had 'entirely different' foci. The fact that the housing assessment indicated an urgent need for rehousing did not mean that section 21 accommodation had to be provided. However the housing needs assessment was a material (and possibly a 'compelling') consideration to be taken into account in the community care assessment. This finding was approved by the Court of Appeal.

Eviction

15.6   The community care needs of disadvantaged people will not infrequently come to the notice of the courts by way of possession proceedings founded upon their failure to pay rent or their behaviour. In such cases the courts have power to adjourn to enable an urgent assessment of needs to be carried out. Such an assessment will inevitably involve the social services department liaising with the housing authority under National Health Service and Community Care Act (NHSCCA) 1990 s47(3) (see para 3.130 above). The courts have wide powers to adjourn possession proceedings in secure and assured tenancy cases,[7] however, in assured shorthold cases judges will need to rely on the power they have to adjourn under CPR 3.1 and 3. 2 in furtherance of the over-riding objective in CPR 1.1 to enable the court to deal with the case 'justly'. Where the application for possession is brought by a housing department a failure to liaise with the social services department and the absence of a full

---

4   *Delivering Housing Adaptations for Disabled People A good practice guide*, June 2006, issued by the Department for Communities and Local Government in conjunction with the Departments for Education and Skills and for Health.
5   HA 1996 s 167(2)(d) as amended by HA 2004 s223; see also Housing Act 2004 (Commencement No 2) (England) Order 2005 SI No 1120.
6   [2006] EWHC 2354 (Admin); (2006) 9 CCLR 686; [2007] EWCA Civ 234 at [64].
7   HA 1985 s85 and HA 1988 s9.

assessment will be relevant to the question of 'reasonableness' – if not maladministration.[8]

15.7   In determining whether it is reasonable to make a possession order on the grounds of nuisance, relevant factors will include whether or not the defendant's behaviour (if stemming from a disability) is amenable to treatment and, if so, whether he of she has agreed to this treatment, as well as the person's likely fate in the event of an eviction order being made.[9] Disability Discrimination Act (DDA) 1995 s22(3)(c)[10] introduces an additional factor in any such proceedings, in that it makes it unlawful for a landlord to discriminate against a disabled tenant by (amongst other things) eviction. It will not however be discrimination if the eviction 'is necessary in order not to endanger the health or safety of any person' (section 24(3)(a)). *North Devon Homes Ltd v Brazier*[11] concerned an application to evict a tenant with mental health problems who was causing 'annoyance, nuisance and inconvenience' to her neighbours. The court held that the tenant's 'bizarre and unwelcome behaviour' was attributable to her mental illness. In its view, it followed (by virtue of section 22(3)(c)) that an eviction would amount to less favourable treatment on grounds of her disability and in the circumstances of the case, it could not be justified. The court however noted[12] that:

> . . . unlawfulness under the 1995 Act would not necessarily be determinative of the application under the Housing Act . . . The 'Act does not bar evictions: only those which are not justified by the specific circumstances set out in Section 24. The respondent, having adopted a proper review of the situation in accordance with the express terms of the Act, may conclude in the future that the health and safety of her neighbours are prejudiced and thus steps should be taken to evict the appellant. But this situation has not arisen.

15.8   However in *Manchester City Council v Romano*[13] the Court of Appeal held that where possession proceedings involved a disabled tenant and the reason for the proceedings related to the tenant's disability, then provided the landlord believed that it was justified in taking action in order not to endanger the health or safety of neighbours and it was reasonable in all the circumstances for the landlords to hold that opinion, the eviction would not be unlawful within the meaning of the DDA 1995. In the court's view 'health' had to be given a wide meaning to include 'physical, mental and social well-being and not merely the absence of disease or infirmity'.[14] In

---

8   See eg complaint no 05/C/04684 against Kirklees MC, 28 February 2007 where a failure to make proper enquiries before taking legal action was held to constitute maladministration and Complaint no 03/A/14278 against Southend-on-Sea BC, 27 June 2005 where the authority instituted possession proceedings based on arrears that had arisen due to the authority's failure to take into account the claimant's mental illness when processing his housing benefit claims.

9   *Croydon LBC v Moody* (1999) 2 CCLR 92.

10 See also *Clark v TDG Ltd (T/A Novacold)* [1999] 2 All ER 977; (1998) 48 BMLR 1, CA.

11 [2003] EWHC 574 (QB); (2003) 6 CCLR 245.

12 Ibid, at [22].

13 [2004] EWCA Civ 834; [2005] 1 WLR 2775 .

14 Ibid, at [69] adopting the World Health Organisation definition.

Knowsley Housing Trust v McMullen[15] a neighbour's health and safety was held to be endangered by the disabled person's behaviour when his general social well-being was put at risk.

15.9   Where a person is evicted because of his or her disability related conduct, the social services authority will have a duty to that person under the community care legislation. However in *R v Kensington and Chelsea RLBC ex p Kujtim*[16] the Court of Appeal held that the duty to provide accommodation under NAA 1948 s21 can be treated as discharged if the applicant 'either unreasonably refuses to accept the accommodation provided or if, following its provision, by his conduct he manifests a persistent and unequivocal refusal to observe the reasonable requirements of the local authority in relation to the occupation of such accommodation' (see para 4.36 above).

Collaboration and joint working

15.10   Housing and social services authorities are under a variety of statutory duties to co-operate fully in the community care planning and assessment processes – most obviously under NHSCCA 1990 s47(3) (see para 3.130 above). The duty to co-operate has been reinforced by joint guidance issued by the Departments of Health and the Environment in 1992,[17] which includes the following advice:

> 16. Social services authorities and housing should construct an individual's care plan with the objective of preserving or restoring non-institutional living as far as possible, and of securing the most appropriate and cost-effective package of care, housing and other services that meets the person's future needs. For some people the most appropriate package of care will be in a nursing or residential home, but in many cases this will be achieved by bringing in domiciliary support and making any necessary adaptations to the individual's existing home. The balance between these should be considered carefully. For example, where expensive or disruptive adaptations or improvements are being considered it may be more cost-effective to provide domiciliary care and support together with more minor works. In other cases adaptations or improvements (eg to help people bathe or cook by themselves) may reduce or obviate the need for domiciliary support . . .

> 19. The new proposals will require effective relationships to be established and built upon between all parties involved. The aim should be to provide a seamless service for clients, with a mutual recognition of all authorities' responsibilities. This will require all the relevant agencies, including housing, health and social services authorities, to put an emphasis on discussion, understanding and agreement in the planning of services, rather than unilateral decision making. Joint working will be important to maximise the use of existing resources. Administrative systems will need to be developed, perhaps including joint planning structures, in order to

15 [2006] EWCA Civ 539; [2006] HLR 43.
16 [1999] 4 All ER 161; (1999) 2 CCLR 340 at 354I.
17 *Housing and Community Care* LAC (92)12/DOE Circular 10/92.

monitor and plan effective use of services. Authorities may wish to set up pilot projects. In taking forward their role in community care, housing authorities in particular should have regard to the points made in the annex to this circular [which amongst other things expands upon what 'joint working' is likely to entail].

15.11 A duty on housing authorities to co-operate with social services is mirrored by the duty under HA 1996 s213 which requires social services to co-operate 'to the extent that is reasonable in the circumstances where its assistance is sought by a housing authority in relation to the discharge of its duties under the 1996 Act'. Section 213A of the 1996 Act further requires that housing authorities have arrangements in place that enable them to notify (with the person's agreement) social services of the essential facts of that person's homelessness where it considers that he or she is not eligible for assistance under their homelessness duties.

15.12 Similar advice is given in relation to the process of housing renewal, with central government guidance[18] to local authorities stressing the need for integrated working with all agencies:[19]

> 2.11 Housing, Social Service Departments and the National Health Service (NHS) are delivering increasingly integrated services for vulnerable households that recognise the benefits of enabling people to stay in their own homes wherever possible. Poor housing can be a barrier for older and disabled people, contributing to immobility, social exclusion, ill health and depression. Renewal policies can contribute by facilitating hospital discharge and preventing hospitalisation, and by enabling people to live in secure, safe, well-maintained, warm and suitable housing.

Joint working

15.13 Homelessness Act 2002 s3 requires all housing authorities to have a homelessness strategy that seeks to prevent homelessness, to secure that sufficient accommodation is available for people in their district who are or may become homeless, and that there is satisfactory provision of support for people who are or are at risk of homelessness. The social services authority must assist with the development of these strategies and the 2006 Homelessness Code of Guidance for Local Authorities[20] stresses the need for housing authorities to:

> 8. .... ensure that all organisations, within all sectors, whose work can help to prevent homelessness and/or meet the needs of homeless people in their district are involved in the strategy. This will need to include not just housing providers (such as housing associations and private landlords) but

18 Office of Deputy Prime Minister circular 05/2003 *Housing Renewal*.

19 As a result of the Regulatory Reform (Housing Assistance) (England and Wales) Order 2002 SI No 1860 (RRO) (see para 15.66 below) local authorities have a new wide-ranging power to provide assistance for housing renewal, and much of the former prescriptive legislation concerning renewal grants has been repealed (with the exception of DFGs).

20 Department of Communities and Local Government, July 2006. Under HA 1996 s182(1), social services authorities in England are required to have regard to the guidance when exercising their functions relating to homelessness and the prevention of homelessness.

also other statutory bodies such as social services, the probation service, the health service and the wide range of organisations in the private and voluntary sectors whose work helps prevent homelessness or meet the needs of people who have experienced homelessness.

9. Housing authorities will also need to give careful consideration to the scope for joint working between social services and the many other key players in the district who are working to meet the needs of people who are homeless or have experienced homelessness.

15.14　At para 5.6 it gives examples of the collaborative working envisaged, for instance:

- establishment of a multi-agency forum for key practitioners and providers to share knowledge, information, ideas and complementary practices;
- clear links between the homelessness strategy and other key strategies such as Supporting People, and the NHS Local Delivery Plan;
- protocols for the referral of clients between services and sharing information between services – for example a joint protocol between hospital-based social workers and housing officers to address the housing needs of patients to be discharged from hospital;
- joint consideration of the needs of homeless people by housing and social services authorities under Part 7, the Children Act 1989 and community care legislation;
- establishment of formal links with other services – for example with those provided by voluntary and community sector organisations.

15.15　At para 5.14 it specifically refers to local authority powers under Local Government Act (LGA) 2000 s2 (see para 1.67 above) suggesting that these provide substantial opportunity for 'cross-boundary partnership working with other authorities and partners, such as the health and social services sectors'. In relation to health care, this will be of particular relevance in the context of hospital discharge, and the 2003 hospital discharge guidance[21] states that 'it is vital all hospitals consider the housing situation of patients to ensure that people are not discharged to inappropriate places, homeless or become homeless as a result of their stay in hospital'.

Housing homeless persons overlap

15.16　The obligation to house homeless persons originated as NAA 1948 s21(1)(b), being a power to provide temporary accommodation for persons who were homeless in circumstances that could not have been foreseen. The power was repealed by the Housing (Homeless Persons) Act 1977, although the relic duty to provide residential accommodation for persons 'in urgent need' remains under NAA 1948 s21(1)(a) (see para 7.30).

21　*Discharge from hospital: pathway, process and practice*, 2003, para A5.5.1 (see para 5.10 above), accessible at http:/www.dh.gov.uk/en/Publicationsandstatistics/Publications/ PublicationsPolicyAndGuidance/DH_4003252.

Likewise in relation to the needs of 'children in need' the Children Act 1989 empowers social services authorities to provide ordinary housing in appropriate circumstances (see para 24.53 below).

15.17 Disabled, elderly or ill people may however also come within the scope of the homelessness provisions of HA 1996 Part VII since it provides that:

a) a person is homeless for the purposes of the Act if he or she has no accommodation which it would be reasonable for him or her to occupy[22] (HA 1996 s175(3)); and

b) a person is considered in priority need if he or she 'is vulnerable as a result of old age, mental illness or handicap or physical disability or other special reason, or is a person with whom such a person resides or might reasonably be expected to reside' (HA 1996 s189(1)(c)).[23]

15.18 The relationship between the housing authority homelessness obligations under HA 1996 Part VII and the community care obligations of social services authorities is considered at paras 3–4 (in particular) of the annex to LAC (92)12:

3. Housing authorities should bear in mind their duties under the homelessness legislation to secure accommodation for applicant households who are unintentionally homeless and in priority need. Section 59(1) of the Housing Act 1985[24] defines priority need categories as including families with dependent children, households containing a pregnant woman, or people who are vulnerable through old age, mental illness or handicap or other special reasons.

4. Paragraph 6.11 of the Homelessness Code of Guidance (Third Edition) sets out the procedures to be followed in the case of those recently discharged, or about to be discharged, from psychiatric or learning difficulty (mental handicap) hospitals. In such cases, if the housing authority sees the need, they should establish whether the local social services authority has been involved and give consideration to referring cases for assessment if this seems appropriate.

15.19 This advice has been given statutory effect via Homelessness Act 2002 s1(2) which requires social services authorities to assist housing authorities in the formulation of their homelessness strategies. This obligation is explained in the 2006 Homelessness Code of Guidance as follows:

1.6. In non-unitary districts, where the social services authority and the housing authority are different authorities, section 1(2) of the 2002 Act requires the social services authority to give the housing authority such assistance as may be reasonably required in carrying out a homelessness review and formulating and publishing a homelessness strategy. **Since a number of people who are homeless or at risk of homelessness will require**

---

22 HA 1996 s175(3); which section 176 qualifies by stipulating that accommodation shall be treated as available for a person's occupation only if it is available for occupation by him or her together with any other person who normally resides with him or her as a member of the family, or any other person who might reasonably be expected to reside with him or her.

23 As a cautionary note, see *Ortiz v City of Westminster* (1995) 27 HLR 364.

24 Now HA 1996 s189(1).

social services support, it is unlikely that it would be possible for a housing authority to formulate an effective homelessness strategy without assistance from the social services authority. It will be necessary therefore in all cases for housing authorities to seek assistance from the social services authority.[25] In unitary authorities the authority will need to ensure that the social services department assists the housing department in carrying out a homelessness review and formulating and publishing a homelessness strategy.

15.20   Para 10.13 of the 2006 Code advises that the critical test of vulnerability for applicant is:[26]

> . . . whether, when homeless, the applicant would be less able to fend for him/herself than an ordinary homeless person so that he or she would suffer injury or detriment, in circumstances where a less vulnerable person would be able to cope without harmful effects.

15.21   It then provides guidance in relation to the specific classes of people deemed to be 'vulnerable' including:

Old age

> 10.15. Old age alone is not sufficient for the applicant to be deemed vulnerable. However, it may be that as a result of old age the applicant would be less able to fend for him or herself as provided in paragraph 10.13 above. All applications from people aged over 60 need to be considered carefully, particularly where the applicant is leaving tied accommodation. However, housing authorities should not use 60 (or any other age) as a fixed age beyond which vulnerability occurs automatically (or below which it can be ruled out); each case will need to be considered in the light of the individual circumstances.

Mental illness or learning disability or physical disability

> 10.16. Housing authorities should have regard to any advice from medical professionals, social services or current providers of care and support. In cases where there is doubt as to the extent of any vulnerability authorities may also consider seeking a clinical opinion. However, the final decision on the question of vulnerability will rest with the housing authority. In considering whether such applicants are vulnerable, authorities will need to take account of all relevant factors including:
> i)   the nature and extent of the illness and/or disability which may render the applicant vulnerable;
> ii)   the relationship between the illness and/or disability and the individual's housing difficulties; and
> iii) the relationship between the illness and/or disability and other factors such as drug/alcohol misuse, offending behaviour, challenging behaviours, age and personality disorder.

> 10.17. Assessment of vulnerability due to mental health will require close co-operation between housing authorities, social services authorities and mental health agencies. Housing authorities should consider carrying out joint assessments or using a trained mental health practitioner as part of

---

25 Emphasis as in the original Code.
26 See *R v Camden LBC ex p Pereira* (1998) 31 HLR 317 and *Osmani v Camden LBC* [2004] EWCA Civ 1706; [2005] HLR 22.

an assessment team. Mental Health NHS Trusts and local authorities have an express duty to implement a specifically tailored care programme (the Care Programme Approach – CPA) for all patients considered for discharge from psychiatric hospitals and all new patients accepted by the specialist psychiatric services (see Effective care co-ordination in mental health services: modernising the care programme approach, DH, 1999). People discharged from psychiatric hospitals and local authority hostels for people with mental health problems are likely to be vulnerable. Effective, timely, liaison between housing, social services and NHS Trusts will be essential in such cases but authorities will also need to be sensitive to direct approaches from former patients who have been discharged and may be homeless.

10.18. Learning or physical disabilities or long-term acute illnesses, such as those defined by the Disability Discrimination Act 1995, which impinge on the applicant's housing situation and give rise to vulnerability may be readily discernible, but advice from health or social services staff should be sought, wherever necessary.

10.31. Housing authorities must keep an open mind and should avoid blanket policies that assume that particular groups of applicants will, or will not, be vulnerable for any 'other special reason'. Where a housing authority considers that an applicant may be vulnerable, it will be important to make an in-depth assessment of the circumstances of the case. Guidance on certain categories of applicants who may be vulnerable as a result of any 'other special reason' is given below. The list below is not exhaustive and housing authorities must ensure that they give proper consideration to every application on the basis of the individual circumstances. In addition, housing authorities will need to be aware that an applicant may be considered vulnerable for any 'other special reason' because of a combination of factors which taken alone may not necessarily lead to a decision that they are vulnerable (e.g. drug and alcohol problems, common mental health problems, a history of sleeping rough, no previous experience of managing a tenancy).

10.32. Chronically sick people, including people with AIDS and HIV-related illnesses. People in this group may be vulnerable not only because their illness has progressed to the point of physical or mental disability (when they are likely to fall within one of the specified categories of priority need) but also because the manifestations or effects of their illness, or common attitudes to it, make it very difficult for them to find and maintain stable or suitable accommodation. Whilst this may be particularly true of people with AIDS, it could also apply in the case of people infected with HIV (who may not have any overt signs or symptoms) if the nature of their infection is known.

Disabled facilities grants

15.22　Disabled facilities grants (DFGs) are grants paid towards the cost of building works which are necessary in order to meet the needs of a disabled occupant. The housing authority is responsible for the administration and payment of the grant, although the original application may be instigated (and referred to it) by a social services authority after a community care assessment. Grants are subject to a means test for disabled adults (see para 15.77 below).

15.23　The relevant guidance recognises that the obligation to facilitate adaptations for disabled people extends beyond the mere detail of the relevant statutory regime, since the underlying purpose is 'to modify disabling environments in order to restore or enable independent living, privacy, confidence and dignity for individuals and their families'.[27] While the precise extent of the 'right to independent living' is uncertain (see para 4.44 above), it is undoubtedly the case that a gross failure by a public authority to discharge its responsibilities in this respect will engage article 8 of the European Convention on Human Rights ('the Convention').

15.24　*R (Bernard) v Enfield LBC*[28] concerned a disabled applicant and her family, who through the local authority's failure to assess her community care needs properly, and then to provide the necessary adaptations, had been forced to live in 'deplorable conditions' for over 20 months. The court considered that the council's failure to act on its assessments had the effect of condemning the applicant and her family to live in conditions which made it virtually impossible for them to have any meaningful private or family life and accordingly found a violation of article 8 of the Convention.

Statutory regime

15.25　The relevant statutory provision regulating the availability of DFGs is Housing Grants, Construction and Regeneration Act (HGCRA) 1996 Part I. Section 23 of the 1996 Act provides:

> *Disabled facilities grants: purposes for which grant must or may be given.*
> 23. – (1) The purposes for which an application for a grant must be approved, subject to the provisions of this Chapter, are the following –
>> (a) facilitating access by the disabled occupant to and from –
>>> (i) the dwelling, qualifying houseboat or caravan, or
>>> (ii) the building in which the dwelling or, as the case may be, flat is situated;
>> (b) making –
>>> (i) the dwelling, qualifying houseboat or caravan, or
>>> (ii) the building, safe for the disabled occupant and other persons residing with him;
>> (c) facilitating access by the disabled occupant to a room used or usable as the principal family room;
>> (d) facilitating access by the disabled occupant to, or providing for the disabled occupant, a room used or usable for sleeping;
>> (e) facilitating access by the disabled occupant to, or providing for the disabled occupant, a room in which there is a lavatory, or facilitating the use by the disabled occupant of such a facility;

27　*Delivering Housing Adaptations for Disabled People: A Good Practice Guide*, June 2006, jointly issued by the Department for Communities and Local Government, Department for Education and Skills and the Department of Health, at para 1.6.
28　[2002] EWHC 2282 (Admin); (2002) 5 CCLR 577.

(f) facilitating access by the disabled occupant to, or providing for the disabled occupant, a room in which there is a bath or shower (or both), or facilitating the use by the disabled occupant of such a facility;

(g) facilitating access by the disabled occupant to, or providing for the disabled occupant, a room in which there is a washhand basin, or facilitating the use by the disabled occupant of such a facility;

(h) facilitating the preparation and cooking of food by the disabled occupant;

(i) improving any heating system in the dwelling, qualifying houseboat or caravan to meet the needs of the disabled occupant or, if there is no existing heating system there or any such system is unsuitable for use by the disabled occupant, providing a heating system suitable to meet his needs;

(j) facilitating the use by the disabled occupant of a source of power, light or heat by altering the position of one or more means of access to or control of that source or by providing additional means of control;

(k) facilitating access and movement by the disabled occupant around the dwelling, qualifying houseboat or caravan in order to enable him to care for a person who is normally resident there and is in need of such care;

(l) such other purposes as may be specified by order of the Secretary of State.

. . .

(3) If in the opinion of the local housing authority the relevant works are more or less extensive than is necessary to achieve any of the purposes set out in subsection (1), they may, with the consent of the applicant, treat the application as varied so that the relevant works are limited to or, as the case may be, include such works as seem to the authority to be necessary for that purpose.

15.26   The provisions of the 1996 Act are fleshed out by regulations,[29] principally the Housing Renewal Grants Regulations 1996 (updated annually in both England and Wales) and separate regulations dealing with such matters as the maximum amount of the grant,[30] the prescribed forms to be used for the process and so on.

15.27   DFGs are only available where a disabled person has been assessed as needing the relevant adaptations. It follows that there is a clear overlap with the responsibilities owed by social services authorities to disabled people who are assessed as needing assistance with adaptations under CSDPA 1970 s2 . Since the duty under the CSDPA 1970 only arises where the authority is satisfied that its assistance is necessary, it is arguable that this duty does not in general arise (if at all) until after a DRG application has been determined.[31]

---

29   Issued under HGCRA 1996 ss3(3) and (4), 30, 31(5) and 146(1) and (2).

30   See eg Disabled Facilities Grants and Home Repair Assistance (Maximum Amounts) (Amendment No 2) Order 2001 SI No 4036.

31   See *R (Fay) v Essex CC* [2004] EWHC 879 (Admin) at [28], but see also para 9.97 above.

NHS powers

15.28 NHS bodies have extensive statutory powers to transfer monies to social services (discussed at para 000 above) and the guidance advises that these can be used to facilitate housing adaptation, particularly if in so doing it 'releases beds by expediting discharge' (para 5.26). It cautions, however, that patients 'should not be discharged without either an adaptation in place or appropriate interim arrangements already in place' (para 5.24).

Guidance

15.29 Detailed 'non-statutory' good practice guidance on the scheme has been issued by the Department for Communities and Local Government[32] as *Delivering Housing Adaptations for Disabled People: A Good Practice Guide* (June 2006): this is referred to in this section as the 'practice guidance', and references to paragraphs in the following section are references to paragraphs of this guidance unless otherwise stated. In Wales relatively brief guidance was issued in 2002 as NAFWC 20/02 *Housing Renewal Guidance*.[33]

15.30 As has been noted above (para 9.96), there is considerable overlap between the duties of the housing authority to process these grants, and the duties owed by social services authorities to facilitate such adaptations. Unfortunately this complex inter-play of duties has not been simplified by the existence of separate guidance from the Department of Health on the social services responsibilities, as LAC (90)7.[34]

Reform

15.31 The government in England is consulting on the future development of the grant scheme[35] following on from the findings of an independent (2005) study by Bristol University.[36] In Wales a similar review is underway following an internal 2005 review.[37]

32 *Delivering Housing Adaptations for Disabled People: A Good Practice Guide*, June 2006, para 1.14 explains that it replaces the previous guidance contained in annex I of Department of Environment Circular 17/96 annex I and states that it should be read in conjunction with Office of Deputy Prime Minister circular 05/2003 (and, in particular, chapter 4 of that circular) which is primarily concerned with the impact of the RRO – see para 15.66 below.

33 The guidance is primarily concerned with the implementation of the RRO (see para 15.66 below) and only contains relatively brief advice concerning DFGs, which largely replicates previous advice in annex I of WOC 59/96.

34 LAC (90)7 was issued jointly as Department of the Environment Circular 10/90. While DoE Circular 10/90 has been withdrawn LAC (90)7 remains in force (see DoE 4/98 and LASSL (99)21).

35 Department for Communities and Local Government, *Disabled Facilities Grant Programme: The Government's proposals to improve programme delivery*, January 2007, para 31a.

36 Office of the Deputy Prime Minister, *Reviewing the Disabled Facilities Grant Programme*, Housing Research Summary 223, October 2005.

37 *Review of housing adaptations including Disabled facilities grants – Wales*, report by Chris Jones (on secondment to the Assembly) for the Housing Directorate, Welsh Assembly Government, March 2005.

Eligibility

Disability

15.32 The grant is only payable in respect of disabled occupants; ie, persons who are 'substantially and permanently handicapped' within the meaning of NAA 1948 s29 (see para 9.19). It is not therefore available for persons whose need arises solely through age or temporary illness.[38]

Main residence

15.33 HGCRA 1996 ss21(2)(b) and 22(2)(b) provide that DFGs are only available to disabled people who live (or intend to live) in the accommodation as their only or main residence (see annex B paras 42–47 of the practice guidance).

15.34 Where a disabled child has parents who are separated and the child lives for part of the time with both parents, arrangements may need to be made to provide for adaptations at both locations. A mandatory DFG is, however, only available at the 'main residence' of the disabled occupant (annex B para 50 of the practice guidance). It follows that if a community care assessment determines that adaptations are required at the other location, this may trigger a duty under CSDPA 1970 to facilitate those adaptations – see para 9.96.

Tenants

15.35 All disabled owner-occupiers, tenants (both council, housing association and private) and licensees[39] are eligible to apply for disabled facilities grants as are landlords on behalf of disabled tenants. The practice guidance advises:[40]

> 3.21 Access to assistance in the provision of adaptations should not depend upon the tenure of the disabled person. A local authority may determine that it will fund adaptations in property within its own ownership other than through the DFG mechanism. However, this should not result in a worse service to their occupants than that received by applicants who live in other tenures. This applies both to the level of support received and the time taken to provide a service.

15.36 Accordingly any material difference in treatment of council and non-council tenants will constitute maladministration.[41] In such cases the local government ombudsman has held that 'any delay beyond six months'

---

38 Housing authorities have a general power under article 3 of the RRO to give discretionary assistance in such cases, in any form (eg grant, loan or equity release) for adaptations. This power replaces the previous 'discretionary' grant schemes that operated prior to the RRO – see para 15.66 below.

39 HGCRA 1996 s19(5) extends eligibility for a DFG to a range of licensees, eg secure or introductory tenants who are licensees, agricultural workers, and service employees such as publicans.

40 *Delivering Housing Adaptations for Disabled People: A Good Practice Guide*, para 3.21.

41 See the report and further report on complaint no 99/B/00012 against North Warwickshire DC, 15 May 2000 and 30 November 2000 respectively.

(from the social services referral to the execution of the works) will generally be considered unjustified and constitute maladministration.[42]

15.37   The local government ombudsman has highlighted a problem with the DFG scheme in that it only applies to existing tenants (HGCRA 1996 s24(2)).[43] Accordingly where it is proposed that a disabled person move to a new tenancy and that tenancy be adapted prior to the move, in order to obtain the grant it will be necessary to take on the new tenancy. During this period the applicant will bear the cost of two tenancies. It follows that there is a need for such works to be done as quickly as possible and without any unnecessary delays.[44]

15.38   Where the tenant is the applicant for the DFG the consent of the landlord of the property will be required. The practice guidance advises that the authority should make every effort to secure this approval 'and in appropriate circumstances authorities should be prepared to assure the landlord that if requested by him they will 'make good' when a tenant no longer requires the adaptation' (para 6.3).

Caravans, mobile homes and houseboats

15.39   The DFG scheme was extended in 2003[45] to persons living in mobile homes and houseboats. However only mobile home owners living in a 'qualifying park home' were covered, ie people on a protected site within the meaning of the Mobile Homes Act 1983. As a result of representations made concerning the discriminatory effect of this measure (Gypsies living on local authority sites did not come within the scope of the provision) the scheme was amended by HA 2004 s224 which substituted references to 'park homes' in the 1996 Act with the term 'caravans' and likewise the references to 'pitch' with references to 'land'.

15.40   Section 19(1)(c) of the 1996 Act now provides that DFGs are available where 'the applicant is an occupier (alone or jointly with others) of a qualifying houseboat or a caravan and, in the case of a caravan, that at the time the application was made the caravan was stationed on land within the authority's area'.[46]

Five years' occupancy requirement

15.41   Grants are payable subject to a requirement that the disabled person lives (or intends to live) in the accommodation as his or her only or main residence throughout the grant condition period 'or for such shorter period as his health and other relevant circumstances permit'.[47] HGCRA

---

42   Complaint no 02/C/08679 against Bolsover DC, 30 September 2003.
43   In *R v Bradford MDC ex p Pickering* (2001) 33 HLR 38, Munby J held that a purchaser under an (uncompleted) rental purchase agreement had a sufficient 'owner's interest' for the purposes the grant.
44   Complaint no 00/C/19154 against Birmingham, 19 March 2002.
45   By virtue of an amendment to HCGRA 1996 s23 via RRO art 2.
46   Although this provision came into effect on 18 January 2005, the 2006 practice guidance on DFGs still persists in using the term 'park home'.
47   HCGRA 1996 ss21(2)(b) and 22(2)(b).

1996 s44(3)(a) provides that 'the "grant condition period" means the period of five years, or such other period as the Secretary of State may by order specify or as may be imposed by the local housing authority with the consent of the Secretary of State, beginning with the certified date' and section 44(3)(b) states that 'the 'certified date' means the date certified by the local housing authority as the date on which the execution of the eligible works is completed to its satisfaction.

15.42 In this context, the practice guidance advises as follows:

> 6.7 Where it appears to the person carrying out the assessment, or the person evaluating the application for grant, that the applicant may not continue to occupy the adapted property for a period of five years or more they should consider the circumstances. If the reason for suspecting this is a prognosis of a deteriorating condition or possible imminent death of the applicant, this should not be a reason for withholding or delaying grant approval. This is the case whether or not the prognosis is known to the disabled person, their family or carer.

> 5.22 Assessment and recommendation should seek sensitively to provide for the progress of the illness which may be difficult to predict. A relatively limited period in which a particular adaptation is appropriate should not be regarded as a sufficient reason for delaying or withholding its provision.

15.43 However para 29 of annex B to the practice guidance qualifies this advice, stating that 'where an applicant's prognosis implies that degeneration in the short term will occur, then this should be taken into account when considering the eligible works'.

Maximum grant

15.44 The maximum mandatory grant is currently £25,000 in England[48] and £30,000 in Wales,[49] although local authorities are empowered to make higher awards (see para 15.66). Special rules apply for minor adaptations under £1,000 (see para 15.45). In England the government has announced[50] its intention to increase 'immediately' the maximum to £30,000 and has undertaken to keep the figure under review 'with the aim of increasing to £50,000 in stages' if its other reform proposals in this regard prove effective. Where an adaptation is assessed as costing more than the grant maximum, various options exist to cover the excess, including the housing authority providing additional sums by exercising its discretionary powers (see para 15.66 below) and/or the social services authority paying for the excess (see para 9.102 below).

---

48 Disabled Facilities Grants and Home Repair Assistance (Maximum Amounts) (Amendment No 2) (England) Order 2001 SI No 4036, although it is anticipated that the grant will rise.

49 Disabled Facilities Grants and Home Repair Assistance (Maximum Amounts) (Amendment) (Wales) Order 2002 SI No 837 (W99).

50 Department for Communities and Local Government, *Disabled Facilities Grant Programme: The Government's proposals to improve programme delivery*, January 2007, para 31a.

Adaptations under £1,000

15.45 Community Care (Delayed Discharges etc) Act (CC(DD)A 2003 ss15 and 16 provide for the making of minor adaptations to be exempt from any charge in England and Wales (respectively). Regulations have been issued in England[51] which, the good practice guidance[52] explains, require that any community care equipment and minor adaptations for:

> . . . the purposes of assisting with nursing at home or aiding daily living which a person has been assessed to need, and for which he or she is eligible, should be provided free of charge provided the cost is £1,000 or less.

15.46 The relevant guidance to the CC(DD)A 2003 advises that 'all community equipment for older people (eg aids and minor adaptations) will be provided within seven days'.[53] A further proposal to improve the delivery of adaptations involves redesignating stair lifts such that they will in the future be deemed community equipment and be delivered as 'minor adaptations'. However as stair lifts normally cost more than £1,000 to install, it is suggested that charges could be applied 'in accordance with the means test as set out in Fairer Charging for Care Services'.[54]

Role of the housing authority

15.47 The housing authority is responsible for the administration of the disabled facilities grant, through all stages from initial enquiry (or referral by the social services authority) to post-completion approval. This requirement stems from HGCRA 1996 s24(3):

> A local housing authority shall not approve an application for a grant unless they are satisfied –
> (a) that the relevant works are necessary and appropriate to meet the needs of the disabled occupant, and
> (b) that it is reasonable and practicable to carry out the relevant works having regard to the age and condition of –
> (i) the dwelling, qualifying houseboat or caravan, or
> (ii) the building.
> In considering the matters mentioned in paragraph (a) a local housing authority which is not itself a social services authority shall consult the social services authority.

---

51 Community Care (Delayed Discharges etc) Act (Qualifying Services) (England) Regulations 2003 SI No 1196.
52 Para 2.26.
53 Department of Health, *Discharge from hospital: pathway, process and practice*, 2003, para 2.3 – see para 5.10 above.
54 Department for Communities and Local Government, *Disabled Facilities Grant Programme: The Government's proposals to improve programme delivery*, January 2007, para 108. However, as the means test for DFGs (see para 15.78) does not have an upper capital limit and most local authorities apply a capital limit for fairer charging (see para 10.26) this could mean that some people will no longer be able to access a grant for a stair lift.

15.48 Although the HGCRA 1996 specifically requires housing authorities to consult with social services authorities over whether the proposed works are necessary and appropriate, it is nevertheless for housing authorities to decide in any particular case whether or not to approve a grant; they are not bound to follow the social services authority's advice (annex B para 34 of the guidance).

Reasonable and practicable

15.49 HGCRA 1996 s24(3)(b) charges the housing authority with the duty of deciding whether it is reasonable and practicable to carry out the proposed adaptation works. In making its assessment, a housing authority is specifically required to have regard to the age and condition of the dwelling or building. While section 24(4) permits grants to be made even where on completion of the works the property would remain unfit for human habitation, the guidance advises as to the alternatives that should be investigated by the housing and social services departments if the final 'unfitness' of the property is considered to render the proposed works unreasonable and impractical (annex B para 36 of the practice guidance).[55] In determining whether the work is reasonable and practicable, the guidance refers to other relevant considerations, including the architectural and structural characteristics of the property, conservation considerations, the practicalities of carrying out work on properties with difficult or limited access (such as steep flights of steps or narrow doorways etc) and the impact on other occupants of the proposed works[56] (annex B para 37 of the practice guidance).

More suitable alternative accommodation

15.50 On occasions a housing authority may have misgivings about approving a DFG on the basis that it would be more cost effective if the disabled person moved to different accommodation. It is unclear as to whether the existence of such an alternative would constitute lawful reasons for refusing a grant – if the proposed adaptations were in every other respect 'reasonable and practicable' and 'necessary and appropriate'. Much would no doubt turn on the context of the individual case and the extent to which 'what is reasonable' would encompass a consideration of other alternatives which might appear 'more reasonable'.

---

55 Including urging the disabled person to seek other assistance (if available) to make the property fit; considering whether a reduced level of adaptations to the property would be viable; and considering rehousing in more suitable accommodation: in which respect the guidance advises that this 'would make sense if major expenditure on adaptations could be avoided and a suitably adapted house was available'.

56 That is, if the works would lead to substantial disruption to other tenants (eg the noise of an air-compressor, in *R v Kirklees MBC ex p Daykin* (1998) 1 CCLR 512, or alternatively be of indirect benefit to neighbours as in *R v Kirklees MBC ex p Good* (1998) 1 CCLR 506.

15.51   The practice guidance, however, advises that 'where major adaptations are required and it is difficult to provide a cost-effective solution in a client's existing home, then the possibility of moving elsewhere, either into a local authority or Registered Social Landlord (RSL) dwelling, or a more suitable dwelling in the private sector should be considered' (para 6.15). Without addressing the question of what would occur if the applicant was unwilling to consider this option, it considers the process that would need to be followed if he or she were willing to consider a move. These would include 'close liaison with local authority or RSL housing management staff' and the use of the authority's powers under the Regulatory Reform (Housing Assistance) (England and Wales) Order 2002 (see para 15.66 below) if a move to another private sector home is a possibility – including helping with the purchase and adaptation of a new property either within or outside the authority's area.

Necessary and appropriate

15.52   In deciding whether the proposed works are necessary and appropriate to meet the needs of the disabled occupant, HGCRA 1996 s24 requires housing authorities, which are not themselves social services authorities, to consult the relevant social services authority on the adaptation needs of disabled people.

15.53   The consideration of what 'meets' the assessed needs of a disabled person may include consideration of any alternative way of meeting the need. Thus in *R v Kirklees MBC ex p Daykin*[57] (a case concerning CSDPA 1970 s2) the disabled person was assessed as needing to be able to get into and out of his council flat. Collins J held that it was reasonable for the authority to decide that this need could either be met by the provision of a stair lift, or by rehousing, and for it to take into account the respective costs of both options, in deciding which was to be preferred.

15.54   *R (B) v Calderdale MBC*[58] the Court of Appeal considered the interplay between HGCRA 1996 s23 and s24(3), commenting as follows:

> 28. . . . What . . . the local authority has . . . failed to do . . . [is] to segregate the s24(3) question from the s23(1) question, and to answer it in the light of the fact that the claimant has established his grant-eligibility in principle under [section 23(1)]. The council must now decide whether it is satisfied that a loft conversion is necessary and appropriate to meet D's particular needs, which include the need not to harm his brother. This is a matter for the council's considered judgment. Unless it is so satisfied it cannot pay the grant.
>
> 29. One has no wish to be critical of non-lawyers who have to apply this difficult and sensitive legislation not in the calm of a courtroom but in the course of a pressured day's work in the office. But one straightforward guideline is that s23(1) and s24(3) should be applied sequentially. A lot of the difficulty in the present case arose from decision-makers running the two together. S23(1) is a gateway provision. S24(3) is a control for those applications which get through the gateway. In a suitable case, no doubt, it

57   (1998) 1 CCLR 512.
58   [2004] EWCA Civ 134; [2004] 1 WLR 2017.

may be legitimate to decide that, even assuming that the application passes the s23(1) threshold, the work cannot be regarded as necessary or as appropriate. But that too is sequential reasoning. What is not permissible is to decide the s23(1) issue by reference to the s24(3) criteria.

Grant-eligible works

Mandatory grants

15.55 Section 23(1) details the purposes for which mandatory grants may be awarded – principally to facilitate access and provision. As detailed above, these are primarily for the purpose of:

- facilitating a disabled person's access to:
  - the dwelling;
  - a room usable as the principal family room, or for sleeping in;
  - a WC, bath, shower, etc (or the provision of a room for these facilities);
- facilitating the preparation of food by the disabled person;
- improving/providing a heating system to meet the disabled person's needs;
- facilitating the disabled person's use of a source of power;
- facilitating access and movement around the home to enable the disabled person to care for someone dependent upon him or her;
- making the dwelling safe for the disabled person and others residing with him or her.

15.56 The duty is not a 'resource' dependent duty (see para 1.24 above); thus in *R v Birmingham CC ex p Taj Mohammed*[59] Dyson J held that housing authorities were not entitled to take resources into account when deciding whether or not to approve a DFG. The work will generally be within a dwelling but may in certain situations be elsewhere, for instance, in the common parts of a building containing flats (annex B para 31 of the guidance). Currently the works eligible for grant support can be conveniently grouped as follows although it appears likely that these may be extended to cover new situations, such as providing increased space for disabled children to play, and ensuring access to the garden for a disabled person.[60]

Making the dwelling safe

15.57 Section 23(1)(b) allows a grant to be given for adaptations to make a property safe for the disabled person and other persons residing with him or her. Annex B para 18 of the practice guidance explains that works under this heading may include 'adaptations designed to minimise the risk of

---

59 (1998) 1 CCLR 441.
60 Department for Communities and Local Government, *Disabled Facilities Grant Programme: The Government's proposals to improve programme delivery*, January 2007, paras 89–93.

danger where a disabled person has behavioural problems which causes him to act in a boisterous or violent manner damaging the house, himself and perhaps other people'. It may also include enhanced alarm systems for people with hearing difficulties (annex B para 19 of the practice guidance).

15.58   In *R (B) v Calderdale MBC*[61] Sedley LJ (at [24]) considered that a grant to make a dwelling safe (under HGCRA 1996 s23(1)(b)) required that:

> . . . the proposed works must be such as to minimise the material risk, that is to say to reduce it so far as is reasonably practicable, assuming that it cannot be eliminated.

Facilitating access and provision

15.59   Annex B para 16 of the practice guidance explains that this includes works which remove or help overcome any obstacles which prevent the disabled person from moving freely into and around the dwelling and enjoying the use of the dwelling and the facilities or amenities within it. In particular this includes works which enable the disabled person to prepare and cook food as well as facilitating access to and from the dwelling and to the following:

- the principal family room;
- a room used for sleeping (or providing such a room);
- a room in which there is a lavatory, a bath or shower and a washbasin (or providing such a room).

Room usable for sleeping

15.60   Annex B para 21 of the practice guidance advises that the building of a new room 'usable for sleeping' should only be grant funded if the housing authority is satisfied that the adaptation of an existing room (or access to that room) is not a suitable option. It states, however, that where the disabled person shares a bedroom, grant funding may be given to provide a room of sufficient size 'so that the normal sleeping arrangements can be maintained'.

Bathroom

15.61   The practice guidance explains (annex B para 22) that the Act separates the provision of a lavatory and washing, bathing and showering facilities, in order to clarify that a grant support is available to ensure that the disabled person has access to each of these facilities (as well as facilitating their use). The fundamental importance of being able properly to manage bathing/washing with dignity has been emphasised by the ombudsman[62] – see para 4.71 above.

---

61   [2004] EWCA Civ 134; [2004] 1 WLR 2017.
62   Complaint nos 02/C/8679, 02/C/8681 and 02/C/10389 against Bolsover DC, 30 September 2003.

Facilitating preparation and cooking of food

15.62 Eligible works under this heading include the rearrangement or enlargement of a kitchen to ease manoeuvrability of a wheelchair, and specially modified or designed storage units, gas, electricity and plumbing installations to enable the disabled person to use these facilities independently (annex B paras 23–24). The practice guidance advises, however, that a full adaptation of a kitchen would not generally be appropriate where most of the cooking and preparation is done by another household member.

Heating, lighting and power

15.63 The guidance (annex B paras 25–26) advises that although grant support may be made in order to provide (or improve, or replace) a heating system, this should only extend to rooms normally used by the disabled person and central heating should only be funded 'where the wellbeing and mobility of the disabled person would be otherwise adversely affected'. Works in relation to lighting and power may include the relocation of power points and the provision of suitably adapted controls.

Dependent residents

15.64 Grant support is available to cover work which improves a disabled person's access and movement around a dwelling in order to care for another person who normally resides there (HGCRA 1996 s23(1)(k)). The practice guidance makes it clear that the dependent being cared for need not be a disabled person and need not be a relation (annex B para 27).

Sensory impaired disabled people

15.65 Mandatory grants are available to meet the adaptation needs of disabled people whose needs 'are less obvious such as those with sight or hearing impairment' (annex B para 28). The guidance gives the following example:

> . . . partially sighted people may require an enhanced form of lighting of a particular kind in the dwelling to enable them to carry out every day tasks and activities in the home. Such works may be required to facilitate access into and around the home and for such purposes as the preparation and cooking of food, to improve the ability to use sources of power or to provide greater safety of the disabled occupant. Works for these purposes qualify for mandatory grant under section 23(1). Where safety is an issue, the works could qualify under subsection (1)(b).

Discretionary grants

15.66 Prior to July 2003, the HGCRA 1996 provided for discretionary grants (under section 23(2)) to be made in certain situations. Although this provision has been repealed, it has been replaced with a wide ranging power under article 3 of the Regulatory Reform (Housing Assistance) (England and Wales) Order 2002 (RRO) which enables housing authorities to give discretionary assistance, in any form, for adaptations or other housing purposes. The financial assistance can also be provided indirectly to the disabled person through a third party and may be paid in addition, or as an alternative to the grant, and there is no restriction on the amount of assistance that may be given. Guidance on the RRO was issued by the Office of Deputy Prime Minister as Circular 05/2003.[63]

15.67   Para 2.24 of the DFG practice guidance[64] gives examples of the type of assistance that can be provided under the RRO powers:

- to provide small-scale adaptations to either fulfil needs not covered by mandatory DFGs or, by avoiding the procedural complexities of mandatory DFGs, to deliver a much quicker remedy for urgent adaptations;
- to provide top-up assistance to mandatory DFG where the local authority takes the view that the amount of assistance available under DFG is insufficient to meet the needs of the disabled person and their family; and
- to assist with the acquisition of other accommodation (whether within or outside the authority's area) where the authority is satisfied that this will benefit the occupant at least as much as improving or adapting his existing accommodation.

15.68   Para 6.18 of the practice guidance advises that the RRO powers could additionally be used where an authority considered that the statutory means test was 'biting particularly harshly in a particular case'.

15.69   Assistance provided under the RRO may be in any form deemed appropriate by the authority – for instance as an outright grant or as a loan or by way of an equity release. In this context the guidance advises:

> 6.22 The greater funding flexibility now opened up by the new RRO powers is also encouraging local housing authorities to consider alternatives to supporting disabled persons through grant assistance. For example, Houseproud[65] is a partnership between a number of local authorities and the Home Improvement Trust to provide advice and financial help to disabled people for housing adaptations and repairs. This is done by the provision of affordable loans and for those over 75 an equity release policy is available. Again such policies do not affect a persons right to mandatory DFG and a loan of this type can be used as an additional form of assistance if the applicant for a DFG is assessed as having to make a contribution towards the costs of the works.
>
> 6.23 More generally local authorities should consider whether any adaptations assistance provided under the RRO powers always needs to be in the form of grant. For example, assistance to fund works in excess of [the maximum grant] or to help with the applicants assessed contribution could be met through some form of loan or equity release scheme.

---

63 Office of Deputy Prime Minister circular 05/2003 *Housing Renewal.*
64 *Delivering Housing Adaptations for Disabled People: A Good Practice Guide,* June 2006, jointly issued by the Department for Communities and Local Government, Department for Education and Skills and the Department of Health.
65 See http://www.houseproud.org.uk.

15.70   Similar considerations will apply where the top-up grant support is paid under CSDPA 1970 s2 – see para 9.102 below.

Ineligibility for grant and the social services overlap

15.71   Cases arise where the social services authority assesses a need for an adaptation, but the housing authority refuses or is unable to approve the grant. This may occur because the works in question do not come under the mandatory scheme, or because the housing authority does not consider the proposed works to be reasonable or practicable or because the applicant fails the means test. In addition it may be that the proposed works will cost significantly more than the maximum grant (see para 15.44 above). In such situations the failure of the DFG application does not absolve the social services authority of its duty to meet an assessed need under CSDPA 1970 s2 (a point emphasised at para 2.6 of the practice guidance). The practice guidance states at para 6.19 that 'social services funding streams can also be legitimately utilised to increase the overall resource to fund an adaptation' since 'by definition, adaptations increase independence'. This advice is further and amplified at para 2.8 in the following terms:

> Social Service authorities may discharge their duties by the direct provision of equipment or adaptations, by providing loan finance to a disabled person to enable them to purchase these facilities, or by providing a grant to cover or contribute to the costs of provision. They may make charges for their services, where appropriate, using their powers under section 17 of the *Health and Social Services and Social Security Adjudications Act 1983*. They have a duty to ensure that the assistance required by disabled people is secured. This includes those cases where the help needed goes beyond what is available through DFG, or where a DFG is not available for any reason, or where a disabled person cannot raise their assessed contribution.

15.72   The social services authority obligations under CSDPA 1970 s2 in relation to adaptations and other facilities are considered at para 9.93 above.

15.73   In *R (BG) v Medway Council*[66] the High Court held that it was not unreasonable for an authority to impose conditions on a grant that it made under CSDPA 1970 s2 to cover the shortfall in the moneys awarded under a DFG. The 'top-up' loan in question was to be secured by way of a 20-year legal charge on the home – which would not be repayable, unless the disabled person ceased to reside at the property during the 20-year period, and any amount repayable would be subject to interest. The authority however undertook that in the event of repayment being required it would have regard to the family's personal and financial circumstances and would not act unreasonably by insisting on repayment immediately or on terms that would result in financial hardship.

66   [2005] EWHC 1932 (Admin); (2005) 8 CCLR 448.

Fixtures and fittings

15.74   While DFGs are available to cover (among other things) adaptations to the fabric of a building, questions do arise as to whether items such as specialist equipment come within the scheme. The 2006 practice guidance is largely silent upon this question, whereas the previous (now revoked) guidance[67] gave some steer as to how the line should be drawn. Since that guidance suggests a workable approach to such problems, its advice would appear to remain pertinent notwithstanding that it no longer has any formal authority. It advises:

> 7.6.1 Under arrangements agreed between the Secretaries of State for Health and the Environment, help with equipment which can be easily installed and removed with little or no modification to the dwelling, is normally the responsibility of the social services authority under its responsibilities under the 1970 Act with larger adaptations requiring structural modification of a dwelling normally coming within the scope of a disabled facilities grant. However, it is for housing authorities and social services authorities between them to decide how the particular adaptation needs of a disabled person should be funded. In taking such decisions authorities should not forget that the needs of the disabled occupant are paramount within the framework of what can be offered.

> 7.6.2 Close cooperation between the respective authorities is vital to ensure that those requiring help in paying for works for essential adaptations to meet their special needs, are given the most efficient and effective support.

15.75   Additional advice in the (revoked) guidance, at Annex I states:

> 7. It is for housing authorities and social services authorities between them to decide how particular adaptations should be funded either through CSDPA 1970 or through a DFG.

> 8. However, since DFGs were introduced in 1990 under the Local Government and Housing Act 1989, it has been common practice that equipment which can be installed and removed fairly easily with little or no structural modification of the dwelling is normally the responsibility of the social services authority.

> 9. For larger items such as *stairlifts* and *through floor lifts* which require such structural works to the property, help is normally provided by housing authorities through DFG. However, some routine installations may not involve structural work. To ensure that such adaptations are progressed quickly, the respective authorities should jointly agree a standard line on the installation of lifts which will apply unless there are exceptional circumstances. Authorities will wish to include arrangements for routine servicing, maintenance, removal and possible re-use.

Equipment service costs

15.76   The practice guidance advises (para 8.1) that where items of equipment have been installed (such as stair and through-floor lifts, ceiling hoists etc)

---

67   Department of the Environment guidance circular 17/96.

which will need 'regular servicing and provision made for repair in cases of failure' then it is:

> ... good practice for these arrangements, covering the likely service life of the equipment, to be secured by the local authority at the time of installation. The cost of securing services by way of extended guarantee or service contract, when met by a single payment on commissioning, should be included in the calculation of any grant payable.

Means testing of disabled facilities grants

15.77 HGCRA 1996 s30 provides that eligibility for a DFG is subject to a means test. Only the financial circumstances of the disabled occupant,[68] his or her spouse or civil partner[69] or co-habiting partner are assessed and not other members of the household. If the DFG is required in order to enable a spouse or civil partner to return to his or her home and that person's absence is likely to exceed 52 weeks, his or her financial circumstances alone may be relevant.[70] Applications for a disabled person under the age of 19 made on or after 31 December 2005 no longer require a means test.

15.78 The details of the means test are determined by regulations[71] and are relatively complex, although in many instances the calculation adopts housing benefit principles; thus the value of a person's savings is determined in the same way as for housing benefit and a tariff income of £1 per £250 (per £500 if aged over 60) is applied to any capital in excess of £6,000 (there is no upper capital limit). Unlike housing benefit, however, there are no deductions for 'non-dependents'. There is also an extra premium to reflect housing costs.[72]

15.79 The net income of each assessed person is taken into account, although for grant purposes the income of those on income support or income-based jobseeker's allowance/joint jobseeker's allowance is deemed to be nil.

15.80 Various allowances and premiums are included in the calculation (relating to such matters as dependent children, lone parenthood, disability and old age) as are certain income disregards (eg housing/council tax benefit, disability living allowance/attendance allowance and between £5 and £25 per week of earnings).

15.81 Where the total income equals or is below the applicable allowances and premiums (the 'threshold'), the applicant will be entitled to a grant equivalent to the full cost of the approved works, or the maximum DFG

---

68 The disabled occupant may or may not be the applicant.
69 It is at least arguable that estranged spouses living in the premises may not, however, be members of the same 'household' – see *R (Fay) v Essex CC* [2004] EWHC 879 (Admin) at [15].
70 Housing Renewal Grant Regulations 1996 SI No 2890 reg 9(2)(b) and see also local government ombudsman complaint no 05/B/06334 against Stafford BC, 20 July 2006.
71 The Housing Renewal Grants Regulations which are subject to annual amendment in England and separately in Wales.
72 For more detail and regularly updated information on the DFG means test see *Disability Rights Handbook*, 32nd edn, Disability Alliance, 2007.

sum whichever is less. However where the total income exceeds the threshold, the grant is reduced pro rata based on a notional 'loan generation factor' – which represents the payments that would have to be made on a loan taken out for the sum repayable over ten years (for an owner occupier) or five years for a tenant.

15.82   There are proposals to replace the existing DFG means test to one more broadly based on local authority fairer charging policies. Since April 2007 individual budget pilot areas (see para 12.72) are able to use the local authority charging policy for assessing the amount to be paid towards an adaptation.

Timescales and grant deferment

15.83   HGCRA 1996 s34 requires housing authorities to approve or refuse a grant application as soon as reasonably practicable and in any event not later than six months after the date of application. By section 36 the actual payment of the grant may be delayed until a date not more than 12 months following the date of the application.

15.84   Section 36 provides the only statutory flexibility local authorities have in the managing of the cost implications of the grant: a grant, as noted above, payable as a consequence of a non-resource dependent duty.[73] Notwithstanding the mandatory nature of this obligation, local authorities routinely adopt all manner of extra-statutory impediments to frustrate the expeditious processing of grant applications. Since the statutory clock only starts ticking once a completed application has been submitted to the housing authority, a common tactic is to delay the pre-application assessment process, by creating inappropriate administrative hurdles[74] and by delaying the preliminary assessments, for instance by claiming a shortage of assessors.[75] Disappointingly, the government, and to a degree the local government ombudsman, have been less than robust in challenging such behaviour – appearing to sympathise more with local authority cash flow difficulties than compliance with the law or the often dreadful circumstances endured by disabled people as they wait for vital works.

---

73   *R v Birmingham CC ex p Taj Mohammed* (1998) 1 CCLR 441 – (see para 15.56 above).

74   See eg complaint no 02/C/04897 against Morpeth BC and Northumberland CC, 27 November 2003 where the ombudsman criticised a process which required an applicant to queue twice – once for the social services input and then again for the housing authority determination.

75   For very many years local authorities have claimed that a shortage of occupational therapists (OTs) has rendered it impossible for them to undertake timely assessments. In complaint no 90/C/0336, 3 October 1991 the local government ombudsman, in holding that a wait of nine months for an OT assessment amounted to maladministration, observed that if insufficient OTs were available, authorities should find other way of assessing the needs. This advice is reinforced by the practice guidance which encourages (at para 5.11) the use of 'other staff' to carry out assessments for minor adaptations – such as 'Care Managers and those undertaking assessment for Home Care services' who may be well placed to carry out assessments for minor adaptations.

15.85   A government assurance that it was to strengthen its advice to local authorities to ensure that grants were only delayed in 'exceptional circumstances' has not been honoured – nor has its view that 'waiting times for any adaptation of more than 250 working days, from the point of initial inquiry to completion, are unacceptable'[76] been given any substance in guidance. Indeed the previous Department of Environment guidance[77] which contained a number of specific and important statements concerning delay – for instance that 'local authorities should not use pre-application tests as a way of delaying applications or avoiding their statutory duty to process applications within six months'[78] and that the power to defer payment for up to 12 months from the date of application 'should be used only in exceptional circumstances and not where the applicant would suffer undue hardship'[79] – has been revoked and replaced by the decidedly anodyne 2006 non-statutory practice guidance (see para 15.29 above) in which neither of the above statements are to be found.

15.86   While it is surprising that the courts have not yet been called upon to consider the legality of the widespread use by local authorities of rationing mechanisms, this may be due to cases of this nature being settled at an early stage by local authorities. In *Qazi v Waltham Forest LBC*[80] Richards J dismissed a private law claim which alleged that the authority had deliberately delayed the processing of grant applications and failed to explain clearly the status of applications – namely that they were not 'pending applications' (to which the mandatory timescales in the Act applied) but merely 'enquiries'. While the judgment addressed the specific private law issues in the case, the judge observed that 'it is plainly arguable that the scheme operated by the defendant was unlawful' and that:

> Notwithstanding the difficulties that the 1989 Act[81] created for local authorities, with their limited resources, I confess to a degree of surprise that systems of this kind received approval in principle, as I am told, from the Local Government Commissioner. Had an application been made at the time to challenge the system by way of judicial review, there must be a good chance that it would have been successful or at the very least that leave would have been granted.

15.87   Where hardship is being caused by the delayed processing of a grant, social services authorities should be pressed to facilitate the works via their parallel duties under CSDPA 1970 s2 (see above) and, if it be the case, requiring that the works be completed urgently and without the delay occasioned by at full community care assessment (see para 4.76).

---

76 HC Debates col 696, 27 January 2003, Parliamentary Under-Secretary of State, Office of the Deputy Prime Minister (Mr Tony McNulty).
77 Department of the Environment guidance circular 17/96.
78 Ibid, annex I para 45.
79 Ibid, para 7.5.4.
80 (1999) 32 HLR. 689, a case based upon an allegation of misfeasance in public office and negligent misstatement.
81 The case concerned the Local Government and Housing Act 1989 under which DFGs were payable at the time. The material parts of the Act are now found in the 1996 Act, which repealed the 1989 provisions.

Priority cases

15.88   The practice guidance accepts that in processing DFG applications local authorities will prioritise some applications over others. It advises (at para 4.8) that although most such schemes depend upon an assessment of medical risk these should now be 'broadened to reflect the social model of disability' and (at para 5.21) that particular attention need be paid to people with deteriorating conditions where the response 'should be as fast as possible' with consideration being given 'to expedited procedures and interim solutions where some measure of delay is inevitable'.

15.89   In order to meet their statutory duties local authorities must inevitably undertake a strategic assessment of need and then set aside an adequate budget to ensure that the need is met. An inevitable corollary of this duty is, as stated in the guidance (paras 3.13–3.14), that 'budgets, cashflow and workload arrangements should ensure that there is equity in outcomes regardless of when in the year the first approach is made'.

15.90   The guidance advises that the measurement of the target time for the completion of assessment should begin at the point at which a priority is assigned and that this must be done within two working days of the receipt of an enquiry or referral (para 4.9) and that the applicant must be advised of this and given an explanation of (among other things) the local authority's criteria for its priorities and the likely timescale for the completion of the assessment.

15.91   Any social welfare system of this nature must endeavour to prioritise those whose needs are most urgent while ensuring that all potential applicants are dealt with expeditiously and in accordance with the law. Inevitably there is potential for conflict, since a clear prioritisation process is only one part of a fair and legal scheme. A poorly resourced system might have an admirable prioritisation process – but in practice might only progress the applications of those in most urgent need. Although the local government ombudsman has long accepted (and indeed advocated for) local authority DFG prioritisation procedures,[82] this approach was questioned by the High Court (as noted above – see para 15.86) in *Qazi v Waltham Forest LBC*.[83] However this may be explained by reference to the fact that (a) prior to 2000 the ombudsman may have been less firm with recalcitrant local authorities than was appropriate – an approach that may now be changing – and (b) that provided all grants are processed expeditiously, such an arrangement is to be encouraged. The problem is, however, that there is substantial evidence to suggest that the focus on prioritisation arrangements has led to a neglect of the severe and widespread problem of chronic delay for non-priority applicants – whose need may still be very substantial.

---

82   See eg complaint no 04/C/12312 against West Lancashire DC, 9 June 2005, complaint no 02/C/04897 against Morpeth BC and Northumberland CC, 27 November 2003; and complaint no 04/C/12312 against West Lancashire DC, 9 June 2005.

83   (1999) 32 HLR. 689, a case based upon an allegation of misfeasance in public office and negligent misstatement.

15.92   It appears that the local government ombudsmen are now turning their attention to the issue of chronic delay and the importance of having reasonable time targets for the completion of works. In a 2002 complaint, for example, the ombudsman stated that she 'does not accept that lack of resources is an acceptable reason for excessive delays in helping people whose need have been clearly assessed and accepted' and that she 'would generally regard any delay beyond six months as unjustified'.[84] Likewise in a 2006 report[85] the ombudsman states:

> It seems to me that eight months is an unreasonable length of time for a disabled person to have to wait for a request for adaptations to be properly assessed; and then to wait a further six months for the relatively minor adaptations recommended to be carried out . . . In my view, a process taking 14 months should have taken no longer than six months to complete.

15.93   The practice guidance advises that in the setting of target times for the processing of DFGs local authorities should estimate the complete process (ie including the period prior to the formal application). It then provides a table (Table 17 below) to illustrate 'a possible approach to time targeting, setting out possible target times for each stage from the initial enquiry about services, which may or may not result in a DFG, to completion of adaptations work' (at para 9.3).

Interim arrangements

15.94   In many, if not most, cases there will be a delay between the identification of a need for adaptations and the completion of the works. Local authorities have an obligation, not only to process the DFG application with expedition, but also to ameliorate – to the extent that they are able – the hardship experienced by the disabled person (and all others affected) by any delay and by the works, if they are extensive and if they severely disrupt ordinary living arrangements. In this respect the practice guidance advises that (para 5.40):

> It is not acceptable that the disabled person and carers should be left for a period of weeks or months without such interim help when the timescale for the provision of an adaptation is foreseen to be lengthy. In addition to the problems an absence of interim measures may cause for the disabled person and for carers, it may result in additional costs for Health and Social Care authorities.

15.95   In relation to the disruption caused by building works the advice is as follows:

> 5.43 . . . where the period of significant disruption is expected to be only a few days then the disabled person may be able to stay with friends or family, or take a holiday. The social services and the housing authority should consider meeting all or part of the costs arising from such arrangements.

84 Complaint nos 02/C/8679, 02/C/8681 and 02/C/10389 against Bolsover DC, 30 September 2003.
85 Complaint no 05/B/00246 against Croydon LBC, 24 July 2006, para 37.

5.44 Where more prolonged disruption is unavoidable then a temporary move to other accommodation should be considered. An RSL or the local authority housing service may have appropriate stock available. Arranging such a temporary move is a complex and difficult business in which practical and financial support should be available where the disabled person requests it.

Table 17: Disabled Facilities Grants			
INDICATIVE TIME TARGETS (working days)	**Priority ranking in Assessment**		
	High	Medium	Low
Referral to allocation/response (including screening, prioritisation and preliminary test of resources form issued)	2	2	2
(NB where complex needs are identified some time may elapse before the need for adaptation is clarified and the process proceeds)			
Assessment carried out within:	3	15	40
Recommendation and report prepared and forwarded	2	5	5
Notice to disabled person of recommendation and application form issued	2	2	2
Home visits to assist in completion of form, measure up and consult on proposals	5	15	30
Preparation of schedule and drawings	10	20	30
Second home visit to confirm proposals	5	15	30
Issue specification to contractors, concurrently seek confirmation of title, etc	3	5	5
Await return of tenders, concurrently seek completion of full test of resources	30	30	30
Evaluate tenders, calculate and check DFG, issue confirmation of DFG	3	5	5
Date to start not exceeding	10	30	60
Time on site will depend upon the size and complexity of works but allow 5 days per £5,000 value for general building work, less when value includes major items of equipment such as stairlifts:			
For average DFG of £5,000:	5	5	5
Inspection on completion	1	2	5
Secure guarantees and documentation, advise on repair and maintenance, consult disabled person on satisfaction, consider any remaining needs	2	5	10
TOTALS	**83**	**151**	**259**

Supporting People programme

15.96 In 2003, in an effort to streamline the housing benefit scheme, the costs attributable to various housing support services required by vulnerable people, were transferred to a separate budget – the 'Supporting People programme'. People who need these support services ceased to be eligible for enhanced rates of housing benefit, but sought instead assistance with the costs from the authority that administers these monies (the 'administering authority'[86]). Unlike the housing benefit scheme, Supporting People extends in theory (and sometimes in practice) to owner occupiers. The system in England and Wales is very similar, with the grant payments to administering authorities being made by the Department of Communities and Local Government in England and by the National Assembly in Wales. Administering authorities are responsible for entering into contracts with providers of housing-related support on behalf of their partners in the programme – eg health trusts, probation services and the housing/social services authorities as the case may be. In 2004 in England, it was estimated that there were 37,000 individual contracts with over 6,000 programme providers supporting over 1.2 million vulnerable people.[87]

15.97 The services funded under the programme are not 'community care services', and accordingly are subject to a distinct assessment and charging regime. Although the programme does not affect the responsibility of social services authorities to meet the assessed needs of service users, the funds it makes available do enable local authorities to provide a greater breadth of housing related solutions in any particular case. Thus instead of providing a person with a care home or home help service, the local authority could utilise the Supporting People's monies to fund a warden service[88] in a sheltered housing scheme or provide support for a person with learning disabilities or mental health problems in moving into more independent living (for instance by providing help in making rent payments and ensuring windows are locked at night and that other housing related obligations are discharged).

15.98 Research studies concerning the programme have generally concluded that it has been successful, but suffered from poor financial forecasting in its early years which has resulted in budget and operational uncertainty at local level.[89]

Statutory and administrative regime

15.99 The statutory basis of the Supporting People programme is LGA 2000 s93. Section 93 authorises the secretary of state and the National Assembly in Wales to pay grants to local authorities towards expenditure incurred by

---

86 This is generally the local social services authority although separate provisions apply to 'excellent' authorities – namely authorities accorded 3 or 4 stars by the Audit Commission in its Comprehensive Performance Assessment.
87 Office of Deputy Prime Minister, *What is Supporting People*, 2004.
88 This might be a 'floating' warden service, where wardens visit a number of different homes or as an on-site warden.
89 See eg Audit Commission, *Supporting People*, 2005; Robson Rhodes, *Review of the Supporting People Programme: Independent Report undertaken for the Office of the Deputy Prime Minister*, 2004; and L Watson, M Tarpey, K Alexander and C Humphreys, *Supporting People: Real change? Planning housing and support for marginal groups*, Joseph Rowntree Foundation, 2003.

them 'in providing, or contributing to the provision of, such welfare services' as the secretary of state/National Assembly determine or 'in connection with any such welfare services'. Section 93 empowers the secretary of state/National Assembly to issue guidance and directions and to set terms and conditions for the award of grant support.

15.100   The key documentation governing the programme in England[90] can be accessed at the Supporting People website.[91] The regulations, directions and guidance listed below, distinguish between 'excellent' authorities (for which they provide only a light regulatory touch) and 'non-excellent authorities'. The principal materials are as follows:

- the Supporting People (England) Directions – new directions are issued each year which revoke their predecessors;
- the Supporting People Programme Grant and Grant Conditions – these are updated annually;
- the Supporting People Grant (England) Guidance 2007 ('the 2007 guidance');[92] and
- the Local Authorities (Charges for Specified Welfare Services) (England) Regulations 2003.[93]

Services under the Supporting People programme

15.101 The directions and guidance detail the services that can be funded under the scheme – and those that cannot. The English scheme as at June 2007 is described below.

Eligible services

15.102 Eligible services were defined in Schedule 1 to the 2007 grant conditions: such a service must fulfil the following criteria:

1.   It must be a housing-related support service

15.103 A 'housing-related service' is one whose purpose is to develop or sustain an individual's capacity to live independently in accommodation.

15.104   The 2007 guidance makes it clear that such services cannot be general health, social services, or statutory personal care services, but rather a service whose aim is to support more independent living arrangements

---

90   In Wales there are currently two grant schemes – Supporting People Revenue Grant (SPRG) (paid by the Welsh Assembly Government), and Supporting People Grant (SPG) (paid by local authorities). The key documents can be accessed at http:// new.wales.gov.uk/topics/housingandcommunity/housing/supportingpeople/ support/?lang=en. The principal guidance is *Guidance to Local Authorities on the Arrangements for the Implementation and Administration of Supporting People in Wales,* February 2003.
91   http://www.spkweb.org.uk.
92   The guidance is issued under LGA 2000 s93(8) which provides that a local authority must have regard to any guidance issued by the secretary of state 'with respect to the administration and application of grants under this section which are paid to them'.
93   SI No 907.

(para 8) and at para 9 suggests that where there is doubt as to whether a service is eligible it may be helpful to ask the following questions:

- Would this person be unable to move to more independent housing, or be at risk of losing their home and moving to less independent care, if this housing related support was not provided?
- Is the primary purpose of the service to enable the person to live in more independent accommodation than they otherwise might, or to prevent the loss of this independent accommodation?

For example, the service may provide help with life skills such as cooking or budgeting, which are an integral part of living independently in accommodation; or an elderly person may need the general support of a visiting support worker to give them the confidence to sustain their own home.

2. It must be provided as part of an agreed package of support services

15.105 In this respect the 2007 guidance at para 17 explains:

> This means that services of an ad hoc nature providing general advice (such as occasional advice on housing management issues provided on demand, or drop in services for the public) are not eligible services. The exception to this are 'occasional welfare services' which are provided on an ad hoc basis and directly enable an aspect of an agreed package of support to be delivered . . .

> *Occasional welfare services*
> The scheme aims not to be overly prescriptive, and accordingly services that do not fit exactly within the detailed definitions may still be eligible for grant support. Para 1(3) of the 2007 Grant Conditions for instance, allows for payments to be made with respect to '*occasional welfare services*'. As the 2007 Guidance explains (paras 13–14) these are 'services that it may be necessary from time to time to provide in order for the main package of support to be delivered to the service recipient'. The Guidance suggests that examples of such services might be:
> - the provision from time to time of services in a domestic violence refuge to enable a woman to take part in support meetings or to seek new accommodation; and
> - arrangements for tidying the garden for an elderly person perhaps to allow support workers to access the property to deliver support.

> *Handyperson services*
> Para 1(4) of the 2007 Grant Conditions empowers payments to be made for services which are provided for the purpose of carrying out of maintenance and minor repairs to a vulnerable person's home through a Handyperson scheme where:
> (a) such services are not provided to the service recipient under the terms of a tenancy agreement or lease, and
> (b) any one task or group of connected tasks will take a single handy person no more than 16 hours to complete.

Adult Placement Services
Para 1(5) of the 2007 Grant Conditions empowers payments to be made for a housing-related support service which is provided by an Adult Support Scheme (as defined in the Adult Support Scheme (England) Regulations 2004[94]).

Payments made in respect of tenancy deposits
Para 1(6) of the 2007 Grant Conditions empowers payments to be made in respect of the whole or a part of a tenancy deposit – if paid in conjunction with a housing related support service and the Administering Authority ensures that reasonable procedures are in place to secure the return of the deposit on termination of the tenancy.

3.   It must be provided to people 'with vulnerabilities' in need of support services

15.106 Services under the programme are for people who are vulnerable and as a consequence in need of support services. The 2007 guidance (para 17) states that service users with 'any of the following vulnerabilities' are potentially eligible for support:[95]

- previous homelessness or rough sleeping
- previous imprisonment, or at risk of re-offending
- mental health problems
- learning difficulties
- being at risk of domestic violence
- teenage pregnancy
- older vulnerable people
- young people at risk
- drug and alcohol problems
- physical and sensory disability
- having HIV or AIDS
- being a refugee
- a previous history of repeated and unplanned loss of tenancy
- travellers
- asylum seekers
- families at risk.

4.   It must represent best value

15.107 Condition 5 of the 2007 grant conditions requires that the service arrangements must be 'in the view of the Administering Authority, value for money, strategically relevant and good quality'.

---

94   See para 15.112 below.
95   The list is 'not exhaustive, therefore the decision to offer support to any client group should be based upon local eligibility criteria, needs and priorities', 2007 guidance p11 fn 2.

15.108   Where an administering authority proposes to terminate or amend a contract with a provider organisation – for instance because the service it delivers is not considered to represent value for money or be strategically relevant or of adequate quality – then it will of course need to consult appropriately on the proposed course of action and take full account of the impact the change may have on existing service users, to whom the authority may owe separate obligations under the community care legislation.[96]

Excluded services

15.109 Certain services are explicitly excluded from the programme, and these are detailed in the 2007 grant conditions as including:

- services provided at a residential care establishment registered under the Care Standards Act 2000;
- provided by a person required to be registered under the Care Standards Act 2000 ('registered provider of care') in his or her capacity as a registered provider of care;
  Although the 2007 guidance provides no explanation for this exclusion, the previous guidance (2003 guidance at para 59) explained that:

  > some registered care providers also provide services that are not required to be delivered by a registered care provider. Such additional or separate services are eligible, but not the services for which registration is required;

- nursing or personal care services (as defined in the Care Standards Act 2000);
- services that are provided in satisfaction of a statutory duty;
  Although the 2007 guidance provides no explanation for this exclusion, the previous guidance (2003 guidance at para 59) explained that although Supporting People monies are not to be used for support services that local authorities have a statutory duty to provide:

  > housing-related support services may be provided under one contract to a range of people, some of whom may have a statutory right to receive support while others do not. As long as administrative arrangements allow for the separation of Supporting People grant from payment from other funding sources, there should be no impediment to funding such a mix of clients within a single service;

- building works (including any adaptation, improvement or repair in relation to a building) other than handyman services (detailed above) and advice and assistance in obtaining grants for such building works or personal support services during such works;
- provision of equipment (for example stair-lifts or specialist adaptations) unless the equipment is used to deliver the particular service in question.

---

96 See eg *R (DG, MM, WG, SM and CG) v Worcestershire CC* [2005] EWHC 2332 (Admin); (2006) 9 CCLR 21 and [2006] EWHC 2613 (Admin).

- psychological therapy or programmes of therapeutic counselling;
  Although the 2007 guidance provides no explanation for this exclusion, the previous guidance (2003 guidance at para 59) explained that:

  > providing housing-related support is an activity of advice and counselling, but what is excluded here is specialist counselling. An example of a counselling activity that would be ineligible might be counselling as part of a drug or alcohol rehabilitation project delivered by specialist accredited therapeutic counsellors. The intention of Supporting People is to enable or sustain independent living, and the elements of counselling have this as its specific purpose can be funded through the Supporting People grant. This is not to say that an individual should not benefit from a package of support, care and counselling – simply that it is only the housing-related support element of this package that should be funded by Supporting People;

- services to enforce specific requirements imposed by a court of law;
- general housing management services.

Charging for Supporting People services

15.110 LGA 2003 s93, the Local Authorities (Charges for Specified Welfare Services) (England) Regulations 2003, the 2007 directions and 2007 grant conditions authorise and require local authorities to develop charging schemes for recipients of Supporting People monies. Annex B para 7 to the 2007 Grant Conditions and paras 36–40 of the 2007 guidance set out principal requirements for any charging scheme including that:

- charges may not be levied by service providers other than those specifically provided for in the agreement with the administering authority;
- they are transparent and fair;
- people receiving housing benefit and people in 'short-term services' are exempt from charging: a 'short-term service' is defined[97] as a service which:
  - (a) aims to bring about independent living within two years (disregarding practical delays in securing move-on accommodation) following resolution of a specific need or needs which the supported living arrangement aims to remedy, or following completion of a time-limited programme of support of under two years intended duration; or
  - (b) aims to increase the capacity for independent living (even if fully independent living may not be likely) through a package of time-limited housing related support, which package has an intended duration of under two years.

  A service is not short term if provided by a Home Improvement Agency, or is provided through a Handyperson scheme (see para 15.105) or aims to maintain a limited degree of independent living which is not expected to increase, and may diminish over time, as part of a permanent or open-ended arrangement;

---

97   2007 grant conditions para 5.

- there is a procedure for reducing or waiving the charges.

15.111 If the person is not exempt from charging he or she can apply for an assessment under the local fairer charging policy. Authorities were told in 2003 when Supporting People was introduced that they must avoid a 'cliff edge' whereby people who are just above the limits for housing benefit would be charged the full cost of services.[98] Where there is a package of both Supporting People services and domiciliary care, authorities should use their fairer charging policy (see para 10.13). Even though there is no obligation on authorities to use their fairer charging policies, the grant conditions ensure that they must have some procedure for reducing or waiving charges.

Adult placements

15.112 Adult placements are frequently likened to fostering arrangements. They involve an adult placement scheme (often, but not always, a local authority run scheme) placing a vulnerable and disabled adult in the care (and frequently the home) of an approved adult placement carer. Most commonly the disabled person has learning disabilities but the scheme is not limited in this respect and can provide for people with physical disabilities, mental health issues, or drug/alcohol problems.

15.113 The purpose of such an arrangement is to enable the person to live as independently and to have as normal a life in the community as is possible. Placements may be long term or as a transitional arrangement. Before any placement the disabled person must have been assessed under the community care legislation and the placement must be deemed an appropriate care plan to meet the person's assessed needs.

15.114 Adult placement carers are self employed and can care for a maximum, at any one time, of three adults (two in Wales).

Statutory and regulatory regime

15.115 Adult placement schemes are governed by regulations in England[99] and Wales[100] made under the Care Standards Act 2000.[101] The English regulations provide for the registration and inspection of such schemes by the Commission for Social Care Inspection whereas in Wales this is the responsibility of the National Assembly. In both cases the regulations provide for the regulation and conduct of such schemes – including such

98 Supporting People guidance 2003 para 43, available at http://www.spkweb.org.uk/NR/rdonlyres/C69EF825-A562–4FD9–8DA5-E07306BD2E4D/0/Statutory_Guidance.doc.

99 Adult Placement Schemes (England) Regulations 2004 SI No 2071 and Care Standards Act 2000 (Extension of the Application of Part 2 to Adult Placement Schemes) (England) Regulations 2004 SI No 1972.

100 Adult Placement Schemes (Wales) Regulations 2004 SI No 1756 (W188).

101 The regulatory powers authorised by Care Standards Act 2000 ss11(4), 12(2), 14(1)(d), 15(3), 16(1) and (3), 22(1), (2)(a) to (d), (f) to (j), (5)(a) and (b), (7)(a) to (h) and (j), 25(1), 31(7), 33, 34(1), 35, 42(1) and (5) and 118(5), (6) and (7).

matters as the fitness of the persons carrying on and managing a scheme and the terms and conditions upon which a person can be placed, the monitoring and review of such placements and so on. The changes made by the 2004 Regulations have had implications for matters relating to 'ordinary residence' and for charging. Prior to 2004 it was the placement that had to be registered and now it is the scheme that is registered. This means that residents in adult placements no longer necessarily come under NAA 1948 s24. See chapter 6 for more details about 'ordinary residence'. Likewise, as individual placements are no longer registered, they do not fall to be charged and assessed under the residential charging rules, but can claim benefits and are charged as if in their own home (see below).

15.116   The English and Welsh regulations (regulation 2 in each case) define an 'adult placement carer' in much the same way – the English definition being:

> ... a person who, under the terms of a carer agreement entered into with a person who carries on an adult placement scheme, provides, or intends to provide, care or support (which may include accommodation in the carer's home) for service users.

15.117   The Welsh definition however is limited to the provision of personal care whereas (as clear from the above) the English requires either personal care or 'support'.

15.118   Although both the English and Welsh definitions of an 'adult placement scheme' (regulation 2 in each case) exclude arrangements for care provided by a relative, the Welsh definition is narrower, in that it is limited to schemes 'under which arrangements are made or proposed to be made for not more than two adults to be accommodated and provided with personal care in the home [of the carer]'. The English definition envisages a broader range of activities, namely schemes:

> ... carried on (whether or not for profit) by a local authority or other person for the purposes of –
> (a) recruiting and training adult placement carers;
> (b) making arrangements for the placing of service users with adult placement carers; and
> (c) supporting and monitoring placements.

15.119   National Minimum Standards for Adult Placement Schemes have been published in England and Wales (both in 2004) in accordance with Care Standards Act 2000 s23 and which form the basis on which the Commission for Social Care Inspection/Care Standards Inspectorate for Wales discharge their regulatory responsibilities.

Charging

15.120   The way people are charged for adult placement has undergone a number of changes over the years. With the changes in 2004, the adult placement itself ceased to have to be registered, and it is now the *scheme* that is registered. So prior to 2004 users were charged in the same way as other residents of registered care homes. Now that only the scheme is registered those in adult placement are able to claim housing benefit for the housing element and they are charged in the same way as people living in their own home for any care provided either via supporting people services (see para 15.110 above) or domiciliary care services (see para 10.13).

Supported living

15.121 Supported living is a generic term that has come to describe arrangements whereby a local authority seeks to change the status of a service user from that of a resident in a residential care home to that of a person living independently albeit under a 'supported living' (sometimes referred to as 'supported housing and care') arrangement.

15.122 Local authorities have a number of reasons for promoting such schemes in addition to the laudable goal of maximising user independence. Two such reasons concern government targets and local finances. A number of performance indicators are designed to reward authorities who have a high ratio of their service users living independently and the social security system places a greater burden on local finances for service users living in residential care home accommodation than it does for those living 'independently'. A key factor for targets and the financing of care packages centres on the question of whether a person is resident in a registered care home. It follows that authorities can improve local finances and their 'performance ratings' simply by changing the status of someone's accommodation – for instance by encouraging the home to 'deregister' (see para 17.13 below).

15.123 Such a change may result in no greater independence for the service user and in certain situations it may result in less security and indeed an inferior support package. It follows that local authority activity to promote 'supported living' packages is not necessarily synonymous with the promotion of independent living. Indeed in the past, local authorities gained considerably in financial terms by encouraging homes to deregister and then refinance the arrangement using what was then known as transitional housing benefit (now 'Supporting People' funding – see para 15.96 above). A number of such arrangements were effected with considerable haste and have since been called into question by the regulatory bodies (see para 17.13 below). Recent changes to the Supporting People programme are undermining the economic viability of some of the packages engineered to maximise the use of this funding stream. This factor can leave a service user in a precarious situation, and subject to a reassessment of his or her needs – ostensibly because of changes to the council's eligibility criteria regime, but in reality because an opportunistic funding arrangement has come unstuck. In such cases a charge of maladministration could be levelled – namely that by speculating on a short term financial gain the authority has jeopardised the security of the service user's long term care arrangements.

15.124   Since supported living is a generic concept, many aspects of the arrangement are considered elsewhere in this book. Some of the key elements, however, include:

1) **Non-residential care**

The service user lives in a non-residential care home setting. In the past this has involved deregistration of care homes and this issue is addressed at para 17.13 below. It follows that the local authority social services support provided under the arrangement will be delivered as a domiciliary care package – most probably under CSDPA 1970 s2 (see para 9.62 above).

2) **Tenancy rights**

Frequently the former care home resident is granted an assured tenancy of the property he or she occupies, in order to attract housing benefit for the rental component and Supporting People funding for housing related support (see para 15.96 below). On occasions there may be questions as to whether the service user has sufficient mental capacity to enter into a tenancy[102] (see chapter 18).

3) **Mixed funding streams**

A wide range of fund streams may be attracted by such an arrangement, in addition to social security and disability related benefits for the service user, including independent living fund support and in appropriate cases funding via NHS Act 2006 ss256–257[103] in cases where the NHS and social services agree to joint funding arrangement (see para 13.122 above).

The mix of benefits and grants that are attracted by supported living arrangements has the benefit in many cases of increasing the overall amount of funding available for an individual package (and decreasing the local authority contribution). It has dangers however, since some of the funding streams are insecure – in that the grant rules may change (as they are changing with the supported living grant (see para 15.96 above) and even the qualifying criteria for social security benefits may change. The *Turnbull decision*[104] is such a case, concerning the rules of entitlement to enhanced sums of housing benefit (EHB) – on which many supported living schemes depend. In this case, the Social Security Commissioner ruled that tenants in a supported living arrangement with a private landlord[105] could not in general qualify for EHB, but only the local reference rent (LRR). In this case the EHB claimed was £238.92 per week but the LRR was only £45.00 per week.

---

102   It appears that if the landlord is aware of the incapacity (to enter into a tenancy) at the time the tenancy is entered into, this has the effect of creating a valid (but voidable) contract – voidable by the tenant – and so housing benefit is payable for such an arrangement. See decision of Social Security Commissioner Mesher, CH/2121/2006, 13 November 2006 analysed in *Social Care Law Today*, Issue 47, May 2007.
103   NHS(W)A 2006 ss194–196 provide LHBs with the same powers.
104   The decision of the Social Security Commissioner Charles Turnbull, CH/423/2006, 19 June 2006 (generally known as the 'Turnbull decision').
105   The decision does not apply where the landlords is a 'Registered Social Landlord'.

4) **Ordinary residence**

Determination of a person's ordinary residence is considered at chapter 6 above. Particular difficulties can arise where a supported living arrangement involves a service user placed outside the area of the funding authority. If the initial placement is in a registered care home, the service user's ordinary residence is deemed by NAA 1948 s24(5) to be that of the placing authority and not the host authority and accordingly the placing authority retains financial responsibility. If however the care home deregisters or the service user moves into ordinary (ie non-registered) accommodation, in principle the ordinary residence changes and crystallises with the host authority.

An area of uncertainty concerns ordinary residence disputes relating to adult placement schemes. Until 2004 the ordinary residence rules for placements were aligned with the residential rules and accordingly the placing authority retained responsibility even if the placement was in the area of another authority. With the change in registration requirements for adult placement schemes it appears that the host authorities will in most cases be the responsible authority for ordinary residence funding purposes. Anecdotal evidence suggests that many authorities have continued to honour their previous arrangements but some have given notice to the host authority that they propose to cease funding. Clearly the situation has potential to create funding inequalities and a perverse incentive for authorities to place out of area.

CHAPTER 16

Carers

continued

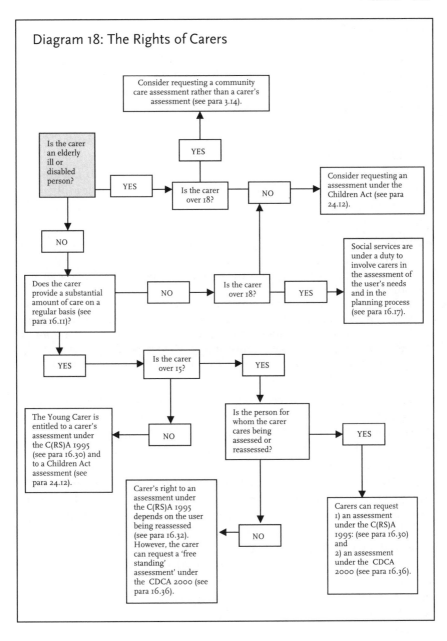

Diagram 18: The Rights of Carers

Is the carer an elderly ill or disabled person?

YES → Is the carer over 18?

YES → Consider requesting a community care assessment rather than a carer's assessment (see para 3.14).

NO → Consider requesting an assessment under the Children Act (see para 24.12).

NO → Does the carer provide a substantial amount of care on a regular basis (see para 16.11)?

NO → Is the carer over 18?

YES → Social services are under a duty to involve carers in the assessment of the user's needs and in the planning process (see para 16.17).

YES → Is the carer over 15?

YES → Is the person for whom the carer cares being assessed or reassessed?

NO → The Young Carer is entitled to a carer's assessment under the C(RS)A 1995 (see para 16.30) and to a Children Act assessment (see para 24.12).

YES → Carers can request 1) an assessment under the C(RS)A 1995: (see para 16.30) and 2) an assessment under the CDCA 2000 (see para 16.36).

NO → Carer's right to an assessment under the C(RS)A 1995 depends on the user being reassessed (see para 16.32). However, the carer can request a 'free standing' assessment' under the CDCA 2000 (see para 16.36).

Introduction

16.1   There are six million 'carers' in Britain (one in eight people, one in six households) of which 855,000 provide care for more than 50 hours a week. Over half of all carers are in full or part-time work whereas only a quarter are retired. Carers are most commonly aged between 45 and 64; 58 per cent are women; nine out of ten care for a relative and half of all carers look after someone aged over 75.[1] The task of providing care has subjected over half of all carers to a health related problem.

16.2   A key objective of the community care reforms was to ensure that 'service providers made practical support for carers a high priority'.[2] The 1989 white paper[3] emphasised the crucial role played by carers in the provision of community care:

> The reality is that most care is provided by family, friends and neighbours. The majority of carers take on these responsibilities willingly, but the Government recognises that many need help to be able to manage what can become a heavy burden. Their lives can be made much easier if the right support is there at the right time, and a key responsibility of statutory service providers should be to do all they can to assist and support carers. Helping carers to maintain their valuable contribution to the spectrum of care is both right and a sound investment. Help may take the form of providing advice and support as well as practical services such as day, domiciliary and respite care.[4]

16.3   Since 1986 carers have attracted significant legislative attention. Initially as a passing reference in the Disabled Persons (Services, Consultation and Representation) Act (DP(SCR)A) 1986 and then through a series of carer specific statutes, originating as private members' bills – the Carers (Recognition and Services) Act (C(RS)A) 1995, the Carers and Disabled Children Act (CDCA) 2000 and the Carers (Equal Opportunities) Act (C(EO)A) 2004. Since 2004 the rights of carers are, increasingly, being addressed in general statutes whose focus is wider than carers caring for disabled, elderly or ill people: relevant examples of this trend being the Work and Families Act 2006 and the Childcare Act 2006, both of which are considered below.

16.4   Prior to the enactment of the C(EO)A 2004 the carers Acts had been directly concerned with sustaining the caring role: ensuring that the services received by the disabled person were sufficient to enable the carer to maintain a caring role. The 2004 Act adopts a different approach as it seeks to address the social exclusion experienced by many carers (in effect 'by association' with disabled people). The evidence suggests, for example, that:

- carers lose an average of £9,000 per annum by taking on significant caring responsibilities;[5]

---

1   *Caring about Carers: A National Strategy for Carers* LASSL (99)2.
2   *Caring for People*, Cm 849, HMSO, 1989, para 1.11.
3   Ibid.
4   Ibid, para 2.3.
5   *The True Cost of Caring, Caring Costs*, Carers National Association, 1996.

- over half of all carers have a caring related health condition;[6]
- carers represent one of the most socially excluded groups of people – for whom the government's inclusion policy appears (to date) to have failed.[7]

16.5   As a consequence, government action is now directed towards challenging the isolation and relative deprivation of carers by maximising their economic potential – primarily by enabling them to remain in or to rejoin the workforce. Cutting across these enlightened policy objectives, however, are the deepening financial difficulties of local authorities and the consequent tightening of eligibility criteria. Commenting on this dilemma, the Commission for Social Care Inspection (CSCI) has observed:[8]

> . . . there are major tensions for councils in their policies to support carers. They are charged with improving efficiency and targeting resources effectively and are consequently restricting eligibility to services. But at the same time they are looking to support carers, recognising the risk that without support many carers own health and well-being may suffer and they, too, will need help in their own right. The danger, as ever, is that carers are only seen as a 'resource' and some carers continue to be socially excluded and barred from the opportunities others would expect.

Statutory overview

16.6   Of the three Acts that deal directly with the needs of carers, the C(RS)A 1995 contains the core statutory responsibilities. It introduced the concept of a 'carer's assessment'. The CDCA 2000 extended the rights of carers, to include the right to support services, and for these services to be made available by way of direct payments and 'vouchers'. The C(EO)A 2004 extended the obligations in relation to assessments, by: (1) introducing a statutory obligation on social services to inform carers of their rights, and (2) by requiring that carer's assessments consider whether the carer works or wishes to work and/or is undertaking, or wishes to undertake, education, training or any leisure activity.

Guidance

16.7   Guidance has been issued in relation to three carers Acts. Policy and practice guidance was issued concerning the C(RS)A 1995 in England[9] and Wales[10] (in identical terms). A number of volumes of guidance were

---

6   Carers UK, *Missed Opportunities: the impact of new rights for carers*, June 2003.
7   *Breaking the Cycle: Taking stock of progress and priorities for the future. A report by the Social Exclusion Unit*, Office of the Deputy Prime Minister, September 2004, para 6.17.
8   CSCI, *The state of social care in England 2005–06*, 2006.
9   *Carers (Recognition and Services) Act 1995: Policy Guidance and Practice Guidance* LAC (96)7.
10 *Carers (Recognition and Services) Act 1995 Guidance* WOC 16/96: WHC (96)21.

issued concerning the CDCA 2000, both in England and in Wales.[11] The policy guidance for the CDCA 2000 has, in England, been consolidated (see below) but the English practice guidance[12] remains of considerable relevance.[13] In addition guidance has been issued in both England and Wales (in very similar terms) concerning the carer's assessment process.

16.8   In 2004 combined policy guidance was issued by the Department of Health concerning both the CDCA 2000 and the C(EO)A 2004. In addition, and most importantly, practice guidance on the C(EO)A 2004 was issued by the Social Care Institute for Excellence (SCIE).[14] In Wales no guidance on this Act has as yet been issued, although in anticipation of the implementation of the Act an additional annex (12) to the Unified Assessment Process was issued to strengthen the practice obligations in Wales to provide separate carer's assessments.

Carer – definition

16.9   There is no single definition of a 'carer' although its use in this text excludes persons who are under a contract of employment to provide the care. National Health Service and Community Care Act (NHSCCA) 1990 s46(3) defines a private carer (for the purposes of strategic planning – see above) as:

> . . . a person who is not employed to provide the care in question by any body in the exercise of its function under any enactment.

16.10   Such a definition includes non-resident carers and makes no stipulation as to the age of the carer or the quantity or quality of care provided. In general any reference to a 'carer' (unless the context shows otherwise) must therefore be to such a heterogeneous group; indeed the 1990 policy guidance makes clear that the term may encompass 'families, friends and neighbours'.[15] The common denominator for such carers is that they all provide some 'service', even though this might be, for instance, in the form of advocacy or emotional support, rather than a personal care service of the kind delivered by a social services authority.

11 Comprising in England (1) *Carers and Disabled Children Act 2000: Carers and people with parental responsibility for disabled children: Policy Guidance*; (2) *Carers and Disabled Children Act 2000: Carers and people with parental responsibility for disabled children: Practice Guidance*; (3) *Practitioners Guide to Carers' Assessments under the Carers and Disabled Children Act 2000*; (4) *Carers and Disabled Children Act 2000: Direct payments for young people: Policy Guidance and Practice Guidance*; (5) *Carers and Disabled Children Act 2000: Practice Guidance on the provisions of the Act as they affect Disabled 16 and 17 year old young people*; and in Wales (1) *Guidance 2000 Act*; and (2) *Practitioners Guide to Carers' Assessment.*

12 Department of Health, *Carers and Disabled Children Act 2000: Practice Guidance*, 2001.

13 The English practice guidance is similar (but slightly more extensive) than the Welsh policy guidance – namely Welsh Assembly, *Guidance 2000 Act*, 2001.

14 *SCIE practice guide 5: Implementing the Carers (Equal Opportunities) Act 2004.* The guidance is updated (most recently in October 2005). It has the status of Department of Health practice guidance: see statement by Liam Byrne, Parliamentary under Secretary of State for Care Services, HC Debates col 722W, 11 July 2005.

15 1990 policy guidance para 3.28.

Defining 'substantial' and 'regular'

16.11 The carers Acts do not define what is meant by the words 'substantial' or 'regular' The Department of Health has elsewhere given advice on the interpretation of the word 'substantial' and advised that it should be given a 'wide interpretation' which takes 'full account of individual circumstances'.[16]

16.12 The English practice guidance issued under the CDCA 2000[17] states:

> It is not only the time spent each week caring that has an impact on carers. For some, such as those caring for adults with learning disabilities, the caring role can have the additional impact of being a life long commitment. For others, such as those caring for adults with severe mental health problems, caring can be a sporadic or cyclical responsibility. The carer may not be physically or practically caring at all at certain times, but still be anxious and stressed waiting for, or actively seeking to prevent, the next crisis. In addition, caring responsibilities may conflict with other family responsibilities, such as parenting or holding down a job. Any assessment of the carer's need for support has to look at the impact of the whole caring situation.

> The term 'substantial and regular' is not defined in this guidance. In any given situation, the test that a practitioner should apply will relate to the impact of the caring role on the individual carer. In particular the practitioner will need to address the following questions.
> • Is the caring role sustainable?
> • How great is the risk of the caring role becoming unsustainable?

16.13 It follows that what is 'substantial' has both a subjective and objective element and is primarily concerned with the impact that the caring role has on the individual carer.

16.14 It appears that the word 'regular' adds little to the qualifying requirements, since 'regular' should be distinguished from 'frequent': merely connoting an event which recurs or is repeated at fixed times or uniform intervals.[18] The practice guidance to the C(RS)A 1995[19] points out that:

> Some users with mental health or substance misuse problems or with conditions such as neurological disorders, dementia, cancer or HIV/AIDS will have care needs which vary over time but may present regular and substantial burdens for carers.

---

16 LAC (93)10 appendix 4 para 8: see para 9.35 above.
17 At paras 67–68 and the Welsh policy guidance to the 2000 Act at para 4.11. Very similar wording is to be found at paras 48–49 of the combined policy guidance under the 2000 and 2004 Acts.
18 *Shorter Oxford English Dictionary.*
19 LAC (96)7 para 7; WOC 16/96 and WHC (96)21 in Wales.

Defining 'intending to provide'

16.15   A carer may be entitled to a carer's assessment even if not presently fulfilling a caring role, provided the authority is satisfied that he or she is intending to provide a substantial amount of care on a regular basis. The intent underlying this provision was explained by the policy guidance to the C(RS)A 1995 (at para 16):

> By including carers both providing or intending to provide care, the Act covers those carers who are about to take on substantial and regular caring tasks for someone who has just become, or is becoming, disabled through accident or physical or mental ill health. Local and health authorities will need to ensure that hospital discharge procedures take account of the provisions of the Act and that carers are involved once planning discharge starts.

16.16   The provision (although not restricted to such cases) is of particular relevance to the carers of people who are about to be discharged from hospital. The English guidance on the hospital discharge process, *Discharge from hospital: pathway, process and practice,* contains substantial advice concerning the involvement of carers, and is considered at para 5.15 above.

Disputes as to whether a carer provides 'substantial' amounts of care

16.17   In practice, there should be little need for an authority to dispute whether a carer is providing regular and substantial care. Since all carers, regardless of whether or not they provide regular and substantial amount of care, are entitled to have their views taken into account during the community care assessment process (see paras 3.20 and 3.87 above), a carer seeking a separate assessment might be best accommodated by providing this, given that there is no statutory definition as to what that assessment comprises (see para 16.47). Additionally, while authorities are under a duty to undertake assessments of carers who provide regular and substantial care, they have a power to assess carers even if their caring responsibilities are not deemed 'substantial' (under Local Government Act 2000 s2 if needs be – see para 1.67 above).

16.18   Not infrequently a local authority will be unable to decide upon the extent of a carer's responsibilities without undertaking such an assessment. Where there is uncertainty an assessment should take place. The local government ombudsman has been highly critical of a local authority that refused to undertake a carer's assessment in such circumstances, commenting:[20]

> It should also have been obvious to the Council that a carer's assessment was necessary in order to see (a) how much support [the carer] could reasonably be expected to provide for his brother without placing his own health at unacceptable risk; and (b) what practical help could be provided to [the carer] with respite from his caring responsibilities.

20   Complaint no 02/C/08690 against Sheffield City Council, 9 August 2004.

Employed and volunteer carers

16.19 The carers Acts do not give rights to persons who provide the care by virtue of a contract of employment or as volunteers for a voluntary organisation.[21] This restriction does not exclude carers who are in receipt of carer's allowance[22] or similar social security benefits, but care assistants employed by a home care service (whether private or public) will be excluded as may be foster carers of disabled children.

16.20 If a disabled person uses a community care direct payment (see para 12.34 below) to employ his or her (previously unpaid) carer, this might disentitle that person to an assessment and services under the carers legislation. If, however, the carer provides additional (and substantial) care over and above that to which the payment relates, the entitlement to an assessment/services would remain, since the restriction only relates to carers who provide 'the care in question . . . by virtue of a contract of employment'.

Carer's assessment rights

16.21 While the views of all carers are relevant when social services or the NHS are making decisions about the needs of those for whom they care, certain carers (those who 'provide or intend to provide a substantial amount of care on a regular basis') are entitled to additional assistance from social services departments.

16.22 All carers, however, have the right to have their views taken into account by social services when considering how best to make provision for those for whom they care.

16.23 Community Care Directions 2004, direction 2 requires that when undertaking a community care assessment, social services must:

- consider whether the person has any carers and, if so, also consult them if the authority 'thinks it appropriate'; and
- take all reasonable steps to reach agreement with the person and, where they think it appropriate, any carers of that person, on the community care services which they are considering providing to meet his or her needs.

16.24 The 1990 policy guidance[23] sets out the way social services authorities should deal with all carers, ie, regardless of whether the care they provide is either regular or substantial. Paragraph 3.25 emphasises that assessments and care plans must take account of 'user's and the carer's own

---

21 C(RS)A 1995 s1(3) and CDCA 2000 s1(3).
22 A taxable, non-contributory benefit for people aged 16 or over caring for more than 35 hours a week for someone who is getting attendance allowance or the middle/higher rate care component of disability living allowance.
23 *Community Care in the Next Decade and Beyond*, HMSO, 1990.

preferences', and (at para 3.16) that they 'must feel that the process is aimed at meeting their wishes'.[24] It continues:

Role of carers in the assessment

3.27 Service users and carers should be informed of the result of the assessment and of any services to be provided. In the case of carers, due regard should be had to confidentiality, particularly where the carer is not a close relative. Where care needs are relatively straightforward the most appropriate way of conveying decisions can best be determined taking individual circumstances into account. A written statement will normally be needed if a continuing service is to be provided. Written statements should always be supplied on request.

3.28 Most support for vulnerable people is provided by families, friends and neighbours. The assessment will need to take account of the support that is available from such carers. They should feel that the overall provision of care is a shared responsibility between them and the statutory authorities and that the relationship between them is one of mutual support. The preferences of carers should be taken into account and their willingness to continue caring should not be assumed. Both service users and carers should therefore be consulted – separately, if either of them wishes – since their views may not coincide. The care plan should be the result of a constructive dialogue between service user, carer, social services staff and those of any other agency involved.

Carers' own needs

3.29 Carers who feel they need community care services in their own right can ask for a separate assessment. This could arise if the care plan of the person for whom they care does not, in their view, adequately address the carer's own needs.

16.25 This advice is reiterated in 1993 Department of Health guidance – that the views and interests of carers who do not come within this category (ie who do not provide substantial or regular care) should be taken into account when an assessment is undertaken.[25]

The assessment rights of 'regular' and 'substantial' carers

16.26 As noted above, carers who provide (or intend to provide) a substantial amount of care on a regular basis have additional rights during the assessment process, most particularly the right to a separate carer's assessment. These additional rights are considered in the context, first of the DP(SCR)A 1986 and second in the context of the three primary Acts, namely the C(RS)A 1995, the CDCA 2000 and the C(EO)A 2004.

24 And any failure to take into account user and carer preferences will normally render invalid any assessment, *R v North Yorkshire CC ex p Hargreaves* (1997) 1 CCLR 104.
25 *Empowerment, Assessment, Care Management and the Skilled Worker*, HMSO, 1993. The report uses the term 'significant others' as a separate category from 'carer'; although neither term is defined, the report accepts the importance of involving 'members of the user's networks to negotiate and sustain arrangements which integrate resources from the statutory and independent sectors with the help given through family and/or neighbourhood networks'.

Carer's assessments and the Disabled Persons (Services, Consultation and Representation) Act 1986

16.27 DP(SCR)A 1986 s8(1)[26] provides that where:

(a) a disabled person is living at home and receiving a substantial amount of care on a regular basis from another person (who is not a person employed to provide such care by any body in the exercise of its functions under any enactment), and

(b) it falls to a local authority to decide whether the disabled person's needs call for the provision by them of any services for him under any of the welfare enactments,

the local authority shall, in deciding that question, have regard to the ability of that person to continue to provide such care on a regular basis.

16.28 Although the 1986 Act gives less substantial rights to carers than the C(RS)A 1995 and the CDCA 2000 it nevertheless remains of importance in certain situations. Most obviously the obligation it imposes (to have regard to the ability of such carers) exists in all cases and does not have to be triggered by a request from the carer. Guidance on the 1986 Act is given in circular LAC (87)6. It is an obligation that exists even if the carer declines an assessment under the C(RS)A 1995 or CDCA 2000 and a refusal to be assessed in such cases should not be 'used as a reason to exclude the carer from assisting with care planning'.[27]

16.29 A number of the terms used in DP(SCR)A 1986 s8 are also to be found in the C(RS)A 1995 and the CDCA 2000 (such as 'regular', 'substantial' and 'ability') and these are considered below.

Carer's assessments and the Carers (Recognition and Services) Act 1995

16.30 The C(RS)A 1995 originated as a private member's bill[28] aimed at securing for carers recognition of their central importance as providers of community care services. This recognition is provided by requiring the social services authority (if so requested) to carry out a separate assessment of the carer at the same time as it assesses the person for whom the care is provided. The right of a carer to an 'assessment' under the C(RS)A 1995 is to be contrasted with the situation under the DP(SCR)A 1986 which merely requires the social services authority to 'have regard to' the carer's ability. The C(RS)A 1995 is however misnamed, in that there is only one service it provides for carers, namely an assessment.[29]

---

26 This subsection of the Act came into force on 1 April 1987; subsections (2) and (3) are still not in force.

27 *Community Care Directions 2004 Guidance* LAC(2004)24 para 2.2.

28 Sponsored by Malcolm Wicks MP.

29 Local Authority Social Services Act 1970 Sch 1 was amended to include the assessment under C(RS)A 1995 s1 as a social services authority function.

16.31   Section 1(1) of the Act is aimed at carers (of whatever age) who care for adults and section 1(2) at carers (of whatever age)[30] who care for disabled children.

16.32   Carers, in order to be eligible for an assessment under the Act, must, in addition to the substantial/regular and unpaid requirements:

1) request the assessment (considered further at para 16.41 below); and

2) have their assessment in conjunction with the service user's assessment.

16.33   It follows that there is no free-standing right to a carer's assessment under the C(RS)A 1995: such an assessment must coincide with the disabled person's community care or Children Act (CA) 1989 assessment. This had the potential to cause problems – if for instance the disabled person refused an assessment. Such difficulties have however been resolved by the CDCA 2000 which makes provision for free-standing assessments in such cases (see below).

16.34   In many respects the C(RS)A 1995 and CDCA 2000 have created a unified assessment duty and in this text we consider the carer's assessment process in this context. In a number of respects the C(RS)A 1995 however remains the primary provision for carers – not least for carers under the age of 16, whose needs are not addressed by the CDCA 2000.

Carer's assessments and the Carers and Disabled Children Act 2000

16.35   In 1999 the Department of Health published its national strategy for carers[31] in which it acknowledged that the then legislation prevented carers receiving help in their own right. It undertook 'when Parliamentary time allowed' to rectify this situation, and to ensure that:

> Individual carers . . . have greater flexibility and choice . . . [via] . . . direct payments or credit scheme arrangements to enable them – with the consent of the person needing care – to arrange for services to be given to them in a way that was useful and at a time and a form that was appropriate.

16.36   These undertakings were discharged with the enactment of the CDCA 2000. The Act has the same restrictions as the C(RS)A 1995 in relation to substantial/regular (para 16.11 above) and paid carers (para 16.19 above) and by section 1 entitles qualifying carers aged 16 or over who care for another person aged 18 or over to an assessment of their need for services (under section 2). The right to an assessment exists even where the person cared for has refused a community care assessment or community care services following the assessment. Section 2 provides for services for such carers (see para 16.86), section 3 provides for respite vouchers (see para

---

30 It would include young carers, for example, if caring for disabled siblings etc.

31 Department of Health, *Caring about Carers: A national strategy for carers*, 1999. LASSL (99)2, chapter 6 paras 12–14.

16.92) and section 6 provides for an assessment of the needs of people with parental responsibility for disabled children.

16.37 The CDCA 2000 uses much of the same terminology as the C(RS)A 1995 and in many respects duplicates its provisions (for instance CDCA 2000 s6 and C(RS)A 1995 s1(2)). Given the substantial overlap, the following review of the carer's assessment duty combines analysis of these two Acts and the impact that the C(EO)A 2004 has had upon then both.

The carer's assessment duty

Preliminary questions

Referral protocols

16.38 The English policy guidance to the CDCA 2000[32] attempted to deal with the problem of how a local authority could determine whether a carer was actually providing regular and substantial care if the disabled person had refused to co-operate or agree to an assessment, and advised that 'referral protocols' be developed. Paragraph 21 of the practice guidance explained that:

> Such a form would record that in the opinion of a professional, GP, voluntary sector worker, carers' group representative etc that the carer being referred was a substantial and regular carer within the terms of the Act and local eligibility criteria.

16.39 Paragraph 21 additionally contains a simple pro forma example. It is difficult to understand the logic for such a bureaucratic approach to the problem. A radical solution might be simply to trust carers who ask for assistance in such situations and who confirm that their caring role is both regular and substantial (see also para 16.11 above).

Boundary problems

16.40 The English practice guidance to the CDCA 2000[33] gives guidance on boundary problems where the carer lives some distance away from the user. It advises that in general it will be the disabled person's home authority (not the carer's) which will be responsible for the assessment and the provision of any services under the Act.

The carer must request the assessment

16.41 The local authority duty to undertake a carer's assessment under the C(RS)A 1995 and/or CDCA 2000 is only triggered once a carer has requested that one take place. This is in contrast to a community care assessment which is triggered not by a request but 'by the appearance of

---

32 At paras 11–13: the Welsh guidance only makes brief reference to this issue, at para 3.3.3.
33 At paras 24–27; para 4.3 of the Welsh guidance.

need' (see para 3.69 above). The evidence[34] suggested that many carers were not being made aware of their assessment rights by local authorities and accordingly CEOA 2004 s1 (through amendment to the C(RS)A 1995 and CDCA 2000[35]) now places a duty on social services authorities to inform carers of their right to request a carer's assessment. This duty arises when the social services department is either:

a)   carrying out a community care or Children Act assessment of a disabled person; or is

b)   contemplating undertaking such an assessment.[36]

16.42   There duty does not arise, however, if the carer has recently been informed of the right in another context,[37] for instance a carer's assessment has recently been undertaken or the carer has had a shortened assessment as part of a hospital discharge of the person for whom he or she cares.[38]

16.43   The guidance requires that authorities should make the information available in 'minority languages and a variety of formats'.[39] It encourages authorities to build upon the statutory duty to advise of the right to an assessment by providing more extensive information services for carers.[40]

Delegation of carers' assessments

16.44   The duty to assess under the carers Acts is a social services function which cannot be delegated unless (and unusually) the authority has entered into a formal partnership arrangement with an NHS body under NHS Act 2006 s75.[41] The general position is explained by the combined policy guidance under the CDCA 2000 and C(EO)A 2004 (at para 45):

> A local authority may contract with another body to carry out part of the assessment process on its behalf, for example interviewing the carer, researching possible assistance, preparing a report and even making a recommendation. However, as an assessment is a statutory function of the local authority it will have to make the final decision about whether or not to provide services itself. It is not enough for the local authority to simply check on a complete or partial basis the outcomes of another organisation's assessments.

34   A research study by Carers UK, *Missed Opportunities: The impact of new rights for carers*, 2003 suggested that almost half of qualifying carers were not advised of their right to an assessment when the person they care for is being assessed. This evidence was reinforced by a Department of Health (Social Services Inspectorate) study *Independence Matters*, December 2003, para 5.25, p33 which confirmed that carers 'were not consistently offered a separate assessment of their needs' and see also para 19 of the combined policy guidance under the 2000 and 2004 Acts.

35   By amending C(RS)A 1995 s1 (by inserting a new section 2B) and by amending CDCA 2000 s6 (by inserting a new section 6A).

36   But has not as yet completed one (eg because the disabled person is refusing to co-operate with the assessment).

37   CDCA 2000 s6A.

38   Community Care (Delayed Discharges etc) Act 2003 s4(3) – see para 5.37 above.

39   Para 20 of the combined policy guidance under the 2000 and 2004 Acts.

40   See eg L Clements, *Carers and their rights: The law relating to carers*, 2nd edn, Carers UK, 2007, para 4.4.

41   NHS (Wales) Act 2006 s33.

The setting and format of the assessment

16.45 Guidance under both the C(RS)A 1995 and CDCA 2000 has emphasised the importance of carers having the opportunity to have their assessments in private – ie away from the disabled person, if the carer so chooses. The guidance states that 'the assessment should listen to what [carers] are saying and offer an opportunity for private discussion in which carers can candidly express their views',[42] The CDCA 2000 guidance takes this right further by advising that in order that the carer have an opportunity to opt for a confidential meeting, the assessor is advised to make arrangements for the assessment 'over the phone, and away from the home or while the cared for person is out'.[43]

Advocacy/support

16.46 The guidance advises that carers should be made aware that they can have a friend or advocate present at their assessment.[44]

The carer's assessment process

16.47 A carer's assessment differs markedly from a community care assessment. Under NHSCCA 1990 s47(1) the object of a user's assessment is to identify that person's need for community care services. The object of a C(RS)A 1995 carer's assessment is to identify his or her 'ability to provide and to continue to provide care' (section 1(1) and (2)) and this is the primary focus of the carer's assessment process. Additionally, however, the assessment may reveal a need by the carer for services in his or her own right. In such cases these can be provided either: (1) under CDCA 2000 s2 if the carer is 16 or older caring for someone aged 18 or over; or (2) under CA 1989 s17 in the case of a young carer aged under 16 or someone with parental responsibility for a disabled child. The process by which such an assessment provides benefits to the carer is outlined in the example below.

The carer's assessment process – general outline

When a community care assessment (or Children Act assessment of a disabled child) is being undertaken and there is a carer providing or intending to providing on a regular basis a substantial amount of care, he or she may request an assessment. The process should then proceed as follows:

Continued

---

42 Practice guidance LAC (96)7 and WOC 16/96 and WHC (96)21 in Wales. For adult carers at paras 9–11 and for young carers at para 16.
43 *Carers and Disabled Children Act 2000: Practice Guidance* para 59 and the Welsh Assembly policy guidance *Guidance 2000 Act* para 3.11.
44 *Carers and Disabled Children Act 2000: Practice Guidance* para 60 and the Welsh Assembly policy guidance *Guidance 2000 Act* para 3.1.

1. The information about the 'presenting needs' of the disabled person should be gathered in the normal way – ie all those needs that he or she (and those close to him or her) identifies as well as those identified by the assessor (see para 3.89 above).
2. Before the assessor decides which of these various needs 'call for the provision' of services by the local authority, the carer should have his or her assessment.
3. The carer's assessment analyses the sustainability of the caring role – primarily whether the carer is willing and able to carry on caring and/or providing the same level of care. The risks to sustainability can include health risks to the carer, his or her wishes to remain in work or return to work or undertake training, education or leisure activities etc.
4. Once the assessor has completed the carer's assessment, he or she will then be in a position to decide what services should be provided to the disabled person and (if needs be) what services might be provided to the carer (ie services under the CDCA 2000 or the CA 1989).
5. The assessor should then draw up a care plan explaining how the disabled person's needs will be met (ie by identifying the services the local authority will provide) and how the carer's needs will be met (either by providing additional services to the disabled person, eg respite care) or (more unusually) by providing services to the carer.

16.48   The C(RS)A 1995 and CDCA 2000 enable the secretary of state to issue directions as to the manner in which a carer's assessment is to be carried out.[45] To date no such direction has been issued.

16.49   The policy guidance accompanying the C(RS)A 1995 gives limited and general advice on the form such assessments should take (at paras 21–25), whereas slightly more detail is provided in the practice guidance[46] including:

> 9.1 The assessment is not a test for the carer. It should not be prescriptive but recognise the carer's knowledge and expertise. The assessment should listen to what they are saying and offer an opportunity for private discussion in which carers can candidly express their views.

16.50   Guidance under the CDCA 2000 provides significantly more assistance in detailing the key attributes and approach of a carer's assessment.[47] The practice guidance, for instance, stresses that an 'assessment is not a process for its own sake' and should 'not be a bureaucratic process based on

---

45 C(RS)A 1995 s1(4) and CDCA 2000 ss1(4) and 6(3); mirroring NHSCCA 1990 s47(4).
46 For adult carers at paras 9–11 and for young carers at para 16.
47 Department of Health, *Practitioners Guide to Carers' Assessments under the Carers and Disabled Children Act 2000*, 2001 and Welsh Assembly, *Practitioners Guide to Carers' Assessment*, 2001.

ticking boxes'[48] and that the presumption is that assessments will be 'face-to-face'.[49]

16.51 Specific guidance exists in both England and Wales[50] concerning the assessment process, emphasising that it should 'focus on outcomes the carer would want to see help them in their caring roles and maintain their health and well-being'.[51]

Carer's assessment – key issues

16.52 The law requires that carer's assessments address two distinct questions, namely:

1) The sustainability of the caring relationship. The assessment must assess the carer's 'ability to provide and to continue to provide care' for the person cared for.[52]

2) The work education and leisure needs of the carer. The assessment must specifically consider whether the carer (a) works or wishes to work; and (b) is undertaking, or wishes to undertake, education, training or any leisure activity.[53]

Sustainability

16.53 The C(RS)A 1995 requires an assessment of the carer's 'ability to provide and to continue to provide care'. As noted above the practice guidance to the CDCA 2000 advised that:[54]

> In any given situation, the test that a practitioner should apply will relate to the impact of the caring role on the individual carer. In particular the practitioner will need to address the following questions.
> • Is the caring role sustainable?
> • How great is the risk of the caring role becoming unsustainable?

16.54 The English practice guidance to the CDCA 2000 suggests that in determining what is 'sustainable', four crucial dimensions of the carer's experience should be considered, namely:

* autonomy,
* health and safety,
* managing daily routines, and
* involvement.

---

48 *Carers and Disabled Children Act 2000: practice guidance* para 47.
49 Ibid, para 61.
50 Department of Health, *Practitioners Guide to Carers' Assessments under the Carers and Disabled Children Act 2000,* 2001 and Welsh Assembly, *Practitioners Guide to Carers' Assessment,* 2001.
51 *Practitioners Guide to Carers' Assessments under the Carers and Disabled Children Act 2000* para 29 and para 3.6 of the Welsh guidance.
52 C(RS)A 1995 s1.
53 C(EO)A 2004 s2.
54 *Carers and Disabled Children Act 2000: Practice Guidance* para 68.

16.55   These four domains derive from community care assessment guidance.[55] The following section considers each of these domains.

Autonomy/choice

16.56   Coercion and compulsion have no place in the language that describes caring relationships. While parents have responsibilities towards their children and spouses are liable to maintain each other, the law recognises that it is impossible to compel one individual to provide care for another. Good practice therefore dictates that carers should have the right to choose the nature and the extent of their caring responsibilities. Ultimately if a failure of care occurs, the state has a positive obligation to provide support.

16.57   The practice guidance to the CDCA 2000[56] explains that the concept of autonomy (in the context of caring relationships):

> . . . describes the carer's freedom to choose the nature of the tasks they will perform and how much time they will give to their caring role. It is dependent on recognition of their role and an agreed sense of shared responsibility between the local councils and the carer/s.

16.58   The practice guidance to the C(RS)A 1995[57] described the proposition in the following terms:

> In assessing the carer's ability to care or continue to care, care managers should not assume a willingness by the carer to continue caring, or continue to provide the same level of support. They will wish to bear in mind the distinction between caring about someone and caring for them. Many carers continue to care deeply about a person even though their ability to care for them may change.

16.59   The choice available to carers should relate not only to the quantity of care they provide but also the quality or type of the caring roles they are prepared to assume. As the practice guidance to the C(RS)A 1995[58] explains:

> . . . it is important that care managers do not make assumptions about carers' willingness to undertake the range of caring tasks, particularly those related to intimate personal care. This is highlighted in a discussion of spouse carers[59] which emphasises the difficulties faced by some husbands or wives when their ability to cope with changed behaviour or personality and/or tasks involving physical intimacy is taken for granted . . .

---

55   Department of Health, *Fair Access to Care Services Guidance on Eligibility Criteria*, 2002, para 40 and see also Welsh Assembly, *Creating a Unified and Fair System for Assessing and Managing Care*, 2002, para 2.36: see para 3.158 above.

56   *Carers and Disabled Children Act 2000: Practice Guidance* para 69.

57   LAC (96)7 para 9.8; WOC 16/96 and WHC (96)21 in Wales. For adult carers at paras 9–11 and for young carers at para 16.

58   LAC (96)7 para 9.3; WOC 16/96 and WHC (96)21 in Wales. For adult carers at paras 9–11.

59   K Atkin, 'Similarities and differences between informal carers' in *Carers: Research and Practice*, HMSO, 1992.

16.60 The practice guidance to the CDCA 2000[60] describes 'an extensive loss of autonomy' as a 'critical risk' for a carer – ie one that demands a response by the local authority. Such a situation would arise where the carer believed that he or she was essentially trapped, having no choice over the caring commitments and that no adequate support or respite was available. Such an extensive loss of autonomy would require a response from the social services department to the extent that it enabled the carer to recover a belief that he or she had 'freedom to choose the nature of the tasks they will perform and how much time they will give to their caring role'.[61]

Health and safety

16.61 The practice guidance to the CDCA 2000 (para 69) describes the import-ance of assessments addressing the health and safety impacts on carers, in the following terms:

> Here the issues of risk to the carer's own health of maintaining their caring role at its current level must be looked at in view of their own age and other commitments. For example, cover may need to be provided in such a way as to allow the carer to attend medical and dental appointments as and when they need. Suitable equipment may need to be installed to aid the carer in providing intimate support to the person they care for. Issues may need to be discussed around the safety of the carer from harm caused by the person cared for. Harm can be caused intentionally or unintentionally.

16.62 There is substantial evidence to suggest significant caring responsibili-ties can be harmful. A Princess Royal Trust for Carers' report[62] found that:

- 85% of carers had found that caring had an adverse impact on their health, with particularly high-risk groups including those who looked after people with serious or mental and physical illnesses, and long-term carers;
- caring had been to the detriment of the mental well-being of almost 90% of carers;
- over 40% said their physical well-being had been affected by caring.

16.63 A similar study by Carers UK[63] found that:

- 55% of carers reported they had significant health problems;
- 43% reported they had sought medical treatment for depression, stress or anxiety since becoming a carer (these problems were particularly apparent in young carers and carers looking after mentally ill people).

---

60 *Carers and Disabled Children Act 2000: Practice Guidance* para 70 – and see Table 19 below.
61 Ibid, para 69.
62 Princess Royal Trust for Carers, *Carers Speak Out Project: Report on findings and recommendations*, October 2002.
63 Carers UK, *Missed Opportunities: the impact of new rights for carers*, June 2003.

16.64   The practice guidance to the CDCA 2000[64] describes 'the development of major health problems' as a 'critical risk' for a carer, ie one that demands a response by the local authority. Such a situation would arise not merely when a carer had been diagnosed as suffering from a serious illness, but also where a link had been established between an illness and the carer's caring responsibilities (ie chronic stress and anxiety in a carer who already had high blood pressure or a history of stress related illnesses).

16.65   In addition to addressing the negative impact that caring may have on a carer's health, a local authority may have a general duty of care to a carer – a question that is considered separately at para 17.37 below.

Managing daily routines and 'involvement'

16.66   Carer's assessments should address the extent to which caring responsibilities interfere with the ability of carers 'to manage their daily routines' as well as the extent to which they inhibit the freedom of carers 'to maintain relationships, employment, interests and other commitments alongside their caring responsibilities'.[65] In this context the practice guidance to the CDCA 2000[66] states that a critical risk includes 'an inability to look after one's own domestic needs and other daily routines; a risk to employment or other responsibilities; a risk to significant social support systems or relationships'.

16.67   This categorisation of 'critical' is of importance, being an explicit statement by the Department of Health that a risk to a carer's employment or a 'significant relationship' is one that demands action from the statutory authorities. Thus if a carer feels compelled to give up full time work, or is at risk of losing a significant relationship because of his or her caring responsibilities, this risk should result in a positive intervention by the local authority to secure support services and ensure that the caring responsibilities do not jeopardise the employment or the relationship.[67]

Employment, training education and leisure activities

16.68   The above categorisation of a risk to employment or other responsibilities as a 'critical risk' has been reinforced by further specific guidance and more recently by statute. In respect of the former, the practice guidance to the CDCA 2000 develops the theme in the following terms:

> 35. Carers should be supported to stay in work, or to return to work, where this is what they want to do. The local council should therefore:
> - identify links with partner agencies to ensure carers assessed have access to good quality information on training and other support to build confidence prior to returning to work

---

64   *Carers and Disabled Children Act 2000: Practice Guidance* para 70 – and see Table 19 below.
65   Ibid, para 69.
66   Ibid, para 70 – and see Table 19 below.
67   *SCIE practice guide 5: Implementing the Carers (Equal Opportunities) Act 2004*, p5, citing L Clements, *Carers and their rights: The law relating to carers*, Carers UK, 2005. Carers UK approves the assertion that 'identification of a critical risk in a Carers' Act assessment triggers a local authority obligation to make an appropriate response to address this risk'.

- make sure that the Welfare to Work Joint Investment Plan cross-refers to the multi-agency carers' strategy and state where the local council's policy on carers and employment is addressed
- audit services to identify how well they support carers through providing flexible and reliable packages of care which allow carers to continue to work
- remember that if involvement in employment is or will be at risk this constitutes a critical risk to the sustainability of the caring role . . .

16.69 Statutory reinforcement to this right has come via C(EO)A 2004 s2, which places a duty on local authorities when undertaking a carer's assessment specifically to consider whether the carer:

i) works or wishes to work;
ii) is undertaking, or wishes to undertake, education, training or any leisure activity.

16.70 During the reading of the bill (that became the 2004 Act), the minister expressed the government's intention in relation to this provision, stating:[68]

> We want carers who wish to work to have the right to work. For those carers who wish to take part in education, we want that to be built in to the care plans that are put together for the person for whom they are caring. We want them to have the opportunity to engage in leisure activities, to the extent that I feel that it would be appropriate that if a carer wanted to take part in a physical fitness or aerobics class in the evening, the care plan should be adapted to ensure that the person could be cared for while the carer went out to engage in such activity.

16.71 Relying heavily on the obligations created by the C(EO)A 2004, the Welsh Ombudsman[69] has held it be maladministration for a local authority to assert that 'childcare was the responsibility of the parents, whether or not children have a disability' and for the authority to fail to provide appropriate support to a parent of a disabled child who wished to pursue his university studies. In the ombudsman's opinion there was an obligation on the local authority to ensure that the parent was not 'disadvantaged in pursuit of education/training any more than other parents'.

Carers' employment rights

16.72 An extended analysis of the employment rights of carers is outside the scope of this book, but in summary, they include the following:

Emergency leave employment rights

16.73 Carers have limited rights to take (unpaid) time off work to care for a dependant. This right is found in Employment Rights Act 1996 s57A(1)[70] which provides:

---

68 Parliamentary Under-Secretary of State for Health (Dr Stephen Ladyman): Standing Committee C, col 7, 10 March 2004 .
69 Public Service Ombudsman (Wales) Complaint no B2004/0707/S/370 against Swansea City Council, 22 February 2007 – see in particular paras 78, 133 and 137.
70 Inserted by Employment Relations Act 1999 s8 and Sch 4 Part II.

57A. – (1) An employee is entitled to be permitted by his employer to take a reasonable amount of time off during the employee's working hours in order to take action which is necessary –

(a) to provide assistance on an occasion when a dependant falls ill, gives birth or is injured or assaulted

(b) to make arrangements for the provision of care for a dependant who is ill or injured,

(c) in consequence of the death of a dependant,

(d) because of the unexpected disruption or termination of arrangements for the care of a dependant, or

(e) to deal with an incident which involves a child of the employee and which occurs unexpectedly in a period during which an educational establishment which the child attends is responsible for him.

16.74   'Dependant' is defined widely in relation to persons who live in the same household[71] and there is a general obligation upon carers who take such time off work, to tell the employer the reason for the absence as soon as practicable and how long the absence is likely to last.[72] In relation to the situations detailed in subsections (a)–(c) above, the event which requires the carer to take time off need not be 'unexpected'. Any time off work claimed as a result of this statutory provision is to be taken as unpaid leave.

Flexible working rights

16.75   Parents with children under six, or disabled children under 18, who have worked for their employer for at least 26 weeks have the right to apply for flexible working arrangements.[73] The right has been extended by Work and Families Act 2006 s12[74] to cover other carers. The procedure for requesting flexible working rights is governed by detailed regulations[75] which require that the employee submits a carefully considered application.[76] The employer is then required to follow a set procedure to ensure the request is considered seriously: a refusal is only permitted where there is a recognised business ground for doing so.

---

71 Employment Rights Act 1996 s57A(3).
72 Ibid, s57A(2).
73 Employment Act 2002 s47 (which amended the Employment Rights Act 1996 primarily by way of the insertion of a new Part 8A into that Act) and see generally the Department of Trade and Industry guidance *Flexible Working: The right to request and the duty to consider*, 2003.
74 Amending Employment Rights Act 1996 s80F.
75 Flexible Working (Eligibility, Complaints and Remedies) Regulations 2002 SI No 3236 as amended by Flexible Working (Eligibility, Complaints and Remedies) (Amendment) Regulations 2006 SI No 3314 and Flexible Working (Eligibility, Complaints and Remedies) (Amendment) Regulations 2007 SI No 1184.
76 The Department for Employment and Learning has produced a leaflet which provides a detailed explanation of the process, its timescales and the application form – *ER 36 Flexible working: a guide for employers and employees*, and ACAS has produced two guidance notes: (1) *Advice leaflet – The right to apply for flexible working, A short guide for employers, working parents and carers* and (2) a more detailed guidance note, *Flexible working and work-life balance*.

16.76 The Regulations[77] define a 'carer' for the purposes of the 2006 Act as an employee who is or expects to be caring who:

i) is married to, or the partner (including a civil partner) of the employee; or

ii) is a relative of the employee; or

iii) falls into neither category i) nor ii), but lives at the same address as the employee.

16.77 Relative is defined widely[78] and the regulations do not require in addition a level of care that has to be provided by such a carer, in order to qualify for the permissive right (to request flexible working rights). In the government's view 'defining a level of care would be extremely complex'; would be 'unlikely to make matters any clearer'; and might deter some people from applying for flexible working if they felt that the definition did not cover their exact circumstances.[79]

16.78 It has been argued that an unjustified refusal to allow a woman flexible working rights may amount to unlawful sex discrimination since such a practice would disadvantage women more than men, because more women than men take primary responsibility for child care and are disadvantaged by having to work longer hours and (in relation to women caring for adults) more women of working age are carers of adults than men.[80]

Unpaid parental leave[81]

16.79 People who have been employed by their employer for over 12 months and who have responsibility for a child born on or after 15 December 1999 are entitled to unpaid parental leave of up to 13 weeks for children under five or 18 weeks for a disabled child. The leave can usually be taken for up to four weeks a year. In the case of a disabled child the leave can be taken as a day or multiples of a day or, for children under five, in weekly blocks.

Equal Treatment Framework Directive 2000/78/EC

16.80 The Equal Treatment Directive makes unlawful, direct or indirect discrimination on grounds of (amongst other things) disability. In many respects the provision reinforces the existing requirements of the Disability Discrimination Act 1995. However in one respect, it may go

77 Flexible Working (Eligibility, Complaints and Remedies) Regulations 2002 reg 3B.
78 Ibid, reg 2 (as amended).
79 Department of Trade and Industry, *Draft Flexible Working: Regulations Summary of Responses and Government Response to the 2006 Consultation*, 2006.
80 See C Palmer, 'New rights at work for parents and carers from April 2007' April 2007 *Legal Action* 33–35 at 35.
81 These derive from the Maternity and Parental Leave etc Regulations 1999 SI No 3312 and Maternity and Parental Leave (Amendment) Regulations 2001 SI No 4010 in exercise of powers under the Employment Rights Act 1996 as amended by the Employment Relations Act 1999 implementing (among other things) the provisions of Council Directive 92/85/EEC and the Framework Agreement on Parental Leave annexed to Council Directive 96/34/EC.

further. It is arguable that the Directive makes it unlawful to discriminate against a person on the ground of disability – even if the person is not disabled – provided the reason for the differential treatment is a disability related reason.

16.81   In *Coleman v Law*[82] the applicant claimed that she was discriminated against by her employers because she took time off to care for her disabled son. She argued that this contravenes the Directive since it amounts to discrimination on grounds of disability. In July 2006 the case was referred to the European Court of Justice for a ruling as to whether the Directive protects employees who though they are not themselves disabled are treated less favourably on the ground of their association with a person who is disabled

Eligibility criteria and carer's assessments

16.82 The practice guidance to the CDCA 2000 (para 70) requires local authorities to grade the 'extent of risk to the sustainability of the caring role' into one of four categories, namely 'critical, substantial, moderate and low' and provides descriptors for these four bands in a table, which is reproduced as below. The grading system is a formal determination of:

> . . . the degree to which a carer's ability to sustain that role is compromised or threatened either in the present or in the foreseeable future by the absence of appropriate support.

16.83 Although the grading system is modelled on that which regulates community care assessments the consequences of a categorisation are different. If a disabled person is assessed as having a 'critical' need, this means that the local authority is under a duty to make services available to meet that need. However a categorisation of critical in relation to the caring relationship does not mean that the local authority is under a duty to make services available to the carer – since there is no duty under the CDCA 2000 to provide services (merely a 'power').

16.84   However, as a matter of public law, the categorising of a risk to the sustainability of a caring role as 'critical' brings with it an obligation on the authority to secure support services and ensure that this state of affairs does not continue (or come to pass). Although in such a situation the local authority is not obliged to provide the carer with services, it is obliged to act. It has the choice therefore of providing the necessary support either to the carer by way of a service under the CDCA 2000 or by way of additional support to the disabled person by provision of a community care service. The bottom line, however, is that the identification of a critical risk in a carer's assessment triggers a local authority obligation to make an appropriate response to address this risk. [83]

---

82 Case C-303/06; London Employment Tribunal case no 2303745/2005.
83 *SCIE practice guide 5: Implementing the Carers (Equal Opportunities) Act 2004*, p5, citing L Clements, *Carers and their rights: The law relating to carers*, Carers UK, 2005. Carers UK approves the assertion that 'identification of a critical risk in a Carers' Act assessment triggers a local authority obligation to make an appropriate response to address this risk'.

Table 19: Carers: Eligibilty Criteria

CRITICAL

Critical risk to sustainability of the caring role arises when:
- their life may be threatened;
- major health problems have developed or will develop;
- there is, or will be, an extensive loss of autonomy for the carer in decisions about the nature of tasks they will perform and how much time they will give to their caring role;
- there is, or will be, an inability to look after their own domestic needs and other daily routines while sustaining their caring role;
- involvement in employment or other responsibilities is, or will be, at risk;
- many significant social support systems and relationships are, or will be, at risk.

SUBSTANTIAL

Substantial risk to sustainability of the caring role arises when:
- significant health problems have developed or will develop;
- there is, or will be, some significant loss of autonomy for the carer in decisions about the nature of tasks they will perform and how much time they will give to their caring role;
- there is, or will be, an inability to look after some of their own domestic needs and other daily routines while sustaining their caring role;
- involvement in some significant aspects of employment or other responsibilities is, or will be, at risk;
- some significant social support systems and relationships are, or will be, at risk.

MODERATE

Moderate risk to sustainability of the caring role arises when:
- there is, or will be, some loss of autonomy for the carer in decisions about the nature of tasks they will perform and how much time they will give to their caring role;
- there is, or will be, some inability to look after their own domestic needs and other daily routines while sustaining their caring role;
- several social support systems and relationships are, or will be, at risk.

LOW

Low risk to sustainability of the caring role arises when:
- there is, or will be, some inability to carry out one or two domestic tasks while sustaining their caring role;
- one or two social support systems and relationships are, or will be, at risk.

16.85   As noted above, the four domains of carers' need are aligned with those that apply when disabled people are being assessed against the FACS criteria (see para 16.55 above). Noting this common approach, Department of Health guidance[84] stresses that there can be 'no place for artificial divides in the assessment process' (ie between carers' needs and those of disabled people).

Support services for carers

16.86   Although a carer's assessment may have many outcomes, its legislative purpose is to provide information that enables the social services department to decide what additional services or support should be provided:

- to the disabled person;[85] and/or
- to the carer.[86]

16.87   If these services are provided to the disabled person, they will be provided under the community care or Children Act legislation. However if the services are required by the carer, ordinarily they will be provided either under CDCA 2000 s2 or under the CA 1989.

Respite/short break care

16.88   In general terms respite (or short break) care services are services provided to a disabled person which enable the carer to take a break from his or her caring responsibilities. In other words, respite care support is legally a community care service[87] or service under the CA 1989 and not a service provided under the CDCA 2000. This state of affairs has been explained in the following terms:[88]

> People who care may be assessed as needing a break from their caring role. This need will be clearly recorded on their own assessment documentation.
>
> The person they care for will then be assessed for the additional support that they will need to allow their usual carer to take a break. This need will be recorded on their assessment documentation. The additional service remains a community care service delivered to the cared for person, not a carer service under this Act.

---

84   Department of Health, *Practitioners Guide to Carers' Assessments under the Carers and Disabled Children Act 2000*, 2001, para 8.
85   These services can be provided either under the community care legislation – generally where the disabled person is over 18 – or under CA 1989 s17 if the disabled person is under 18.
86   Services can be provided to carers aged 16 or over caring for someone 18 or over under CDCA 2000 s2 or under CA 1989 s17 if the disabled person is under 18.
87   Eg as 'practical assistance in the home' (eg a 'sitting service') under Chronically Sick and Disabled Persons Act 1970 s2 or as a short period in residential care under National Assistance Act 1948 s21.
88   Department of Health, 'Questions and Answers' briefing to the 2000 Act, question 7.

16.89 Although respite care will be recorded as a service on the disabled person's care plan (eg 'a sitting service') there is no reason why the 'break' that the carer enjoys as a consequence should not be recorded as a 'service to the carer': ie the carer's care plan recording that he or she has been given a 'break', and for auditing purposes the CSCI requires authorities to record the number of 'breaks services' that they have provided for carers.[89]

16.90 Since respite care services are technically (ie as a matter of law) community care services rather than services provided under the carers Acts, it follows that once a disabled person has been assessed as needing respite care, the local authority is legally obliged to provide services to meet this need.[90]

16.91 The importance of timely respite care/short break services has been repeatedly highlighted by research, guidance and case-law. By way of example, guidance to the C(RS)A 1995[91] referred to research that suggested that 'some of the most cost effective care packages were where carers continued to perform caring tasks but were given sufficient support and respite to enhance their well being and maintain their own health'.[92]

Respite care and voucher schemes

16.92 CDCA 2000 ss3 and 7 provide for local authority social services departments to run short break voucher schemes. Voucher schemes are designed to offer flexibility in the timing of carers' breaks and choice in the way services are delivered to disabled people while their usual carer is taking a break. Regulations[93] made under CDCA 2000 s3 and guidance[94] have been issued in England: the essential details of English scheme being:

- All voucher schemes must now be in accordance with these regulations.
- Vouchers may be expressed in terms of money or a period of time, but a time voucher must specify the service for which the voucher may be redeemed and may specify the supplier of services authorised by the local authority to supply that service.
- Community care time vouchers may be issued:
  - to a person cared for, or
  - a carer, provided the person cared for either consents to this or is unable to consent through lack of capacity.
- Children Act vouchers may be issued to a parent-carer.

---

89 CSCI PAF Guidance Book PAF C62 adopting the definition that applied in the Carers Grant Guidance.
90 See eg *R (Hughes) v Liverpool City Council* [2005] EWHC 428 (Admin); (2005) 8 CCLR 243 at [33]–[34].
91 LAC (96)7 para 9.3 (WOC 16/96 and WHC (96)21 in Wales): this advice is repeated in relation to adult carers at paras 9–11 and for young carers at para 16.
92 D Challis et al, *Care Management and Health Care of Older People*, Canterbury, 1995.
93 Carers and Disabled Children (Vouchers) (England) Regulations 2003 SI No 1216.
94 Department of Health, *Carers and Disabled Children's Act 2000 – Vouchers for short-term breaks – Policy and Practice Guidance*, 2003.

- Money vouchers may only be issued in the case of a community care voucher to a person cared for, or in the case of Children Act vouchers to a parent-carer.
- Vouchers must not be issued to persons who are proscribed under the direct payment regulations (see para 12.27 above).
- All vouchers must be redeemed within the financial year during which they are is issued; a voucher is redeemed on the day on which the service that is secured against the value of the voucher is delivered.
- A voucher shall only be redeemable for services supplied by (a) the local authority that issued the voucher; or (b) a relevant supplier of services.
- Where the voucher holder indicates he or she wants to use a supplier with whom the local authority does not have a contract the authority must enter into a contract with this supplier provided the preferred supplier agrees and complies with the authority's usual terms and conditions
- If the service user ceases to be ordinarily resident in the issuing authority's area without the full value of any vouchers held in relation to him or her being redeemed, any vouchers which remain unredeemed on the day on which that person ceases to be so ordinarily resident must be returned to the issuing authority.
- Where a voucher holder wishes the supplier to provide additional or more expensive services, this may occur if a third party agrees to pay to the supplier the difference between the cost which will be met by the voucher and the actual cost of the service supplied ('third party' means someone other than the service user, the parent-carer, or the issuing authority).
- A voucher must not be used to secure residential accommodation:
  - for a period in excess of 28 consecutive days; and
  - in any period of 12 months for periods which exceed 120 days in total.

Carers' services under the Carers and Disabled Children Act 2000

16.93   CDCA 2000 s2 enables social services departments to provide services to carers following a carer's assessment. The Act does not define what is a carer's service other than to stipulate that a carer's service can be anything that could 'help the carer care for the person cared for'.[95] In general a service to a carer under the CDCA 2000 cannot involve any intimate care of the person for whom he or she cares. This question is considered separately below (para 16.107).

16.94   The guidance gives examples of the type of services that could be provided to carers, including:

---

95   CDCA 2000 s2(2)(b).

Examples in the CDCA 2000 practice guidance

- Trips (such as holidays or on special events);
- driving lessons;
- travel assistance (including for instance help with taxi fares);
- training;
- laundry;
- gardening;
- help with housework.

Examples given in the combined policy guidance under the CDCA 2000 and C(EO)A 2004

- Driving lessons, moving and handling classes, a mobile phone, taxis to work to maximise the carer's time, or a short holiday for the carer to enable them to have time to themselves (para 65).

Examples given in the C(EO)A 2004 practice guidance

- A computer for a carer who could not access computer services from the local library because he felt unable to leave the person he cared for;
- repairs/insurance costs for a car, where transport is crucial to the caring role;
- entry phone with audio/video system where the carer lives in a two storey house and has mobility problems;
- £500 contribution to a flight for a grandmother to come from another country and care for a woman with MS.

16.95 The range of services capable of being provided under section 2 is potentially very wide, given that anything that promotes a carer's sense of personal well-being is likely to help him or her 'care for the person cared for'. The reference in the guidance to 'best value' and the fact that there is no 'duty' to provide the services, means that in practice the provision of such services may depend upon the authority being satisfied that they are a cost effective means of sustaining the caring relationship.

Direct payments

16.96 Health and Social Care Act 2001 s57 enables carers to receive direct payments in lieu of services (see generally para 12.9 above). Thus if a carer is assessed as needing a service such as driving lessons or relaxation therapy and the authority decides that it will provide this support, the carer has the right to have the assistance provided as a direct payment.

NHS responsibilities for carers

16.97 Neither the C(RS)A 1995 nor the CDCA 2000 place any obligation on the NHS to address the support needs of carers. The policy guidance to the C(RS)A 1995 advised (at para 29) that local authorities should 'review with

NHS commissioning agencies and NHS providers how they might best be involved in the carer's assessment', and that:

> 30. Primary care staff, including GPs and community nurses through their contact with users and carers, are in a good position to notice signs of stress, difficulty or rapidly deteriorating health particularly in carers. The provisions of the Act will help primary care staff to meet the medical and nursing needs of their patients who are carers. When making a referral for a user's assessment they should be able to inform the carer that they may also have a right to request an assessment and will be well-placed to encourage patients whom they consider will benefit most to take up the opportunity. Social services departments should make sure that primary care staff have relevant information about social services criteria and know who to contact to make a referral. GPs nurses and other members of multi-disciplinary teams may be able to assist in an assessment of a carer's ability to provide and continue to provide care.

16.98   Concern about the failure of the NHS to address directly the needs of carers prompted the Health Minister in 2003[96] to remind primary care trusts (PCTs) and other health providers of government policy regarding the 'critical role carers play'. The guidance she referred to stated:

> Carers organisations have highlighted the limited inclusion of carers issues in health service planning as representative of a lack of recognition of their vital role. NHS organisations are reminded that in line with the 1999 National Carers Strategy ('Caring for Carers'), they should be actively working in partnership with social services to consult, inform and support carers.[97]

16.99   The Carers (Equal Opportunities) Bill (in 2004) sought to legislate on this question and contained provisions: (1) requiring the NHS to co-operate with social services in relation to the provision of support for carers and (2) requiring the NHS to promote the health and welfare of carers. Although the first provision is present in the final Act the second is not. Howell Francis MP agreed to withdraw the clause requiring the NHS to promote the health and welfare of carers upon the minister undertaking to issue directions requiring PCTs to include provision for carers in their local development plans (under Health Act 1999 s28).[98] Unfortunately the government then changed its mind. The minister apologised for 'having inadvertently misled Members', and stated:

> We can better deliver on the promise to ensure that PCTs will have to consult and take into account the health needs of carers through developmental support rather than through directing them through secondary legislation. I assure the House that although we will not proceed with the directions we will pursue alternatives.[99]

To date this undertaking has not been discharged.[100]

96   *Hansard* HC Debates col 663W, 6 May 2003.
97   Department of Health, *Chief Executive's Bulletin*, 28 March to 3 April 2003, para 8.
98   See the comments of the Parliamentary Under-Secretary of State for Health (Dr Stephen Ladyman), Standing Committee C col 14, 10 March 2004.
99   Parliamentary Under-Secretary of State for Health (Dr Stephen Ladyman), *Hansard* HC Debates col 586, 14 May 2004.
100 In June 2004 the government stated that it was still considering how best to take the

The duty to co-operate under the Carers (Equal Opportunities) Act 2004

16.100 CEOA 2004 s3 reinforces the general duty of the NHS and local authorities to co-operate under NHS Act 2006 s82 (see para 13.25 above). It provides:

- that a local authority may request another authority or health body[101] to assist it in planning the provision of services to carers and persons being cared for. The other body is then required to give 'due consideration' to such a request; and
- that where a local authority forms the view that a carer's ability to provide care might be enhanced by the provision of services by another authority or health body it may request that other body to provide the service, to which request the other body must give due consideration.

16.101 In the light of this new statutory obligation the combined policy guidance under the CDCA 2000 and the C(EO)A 2004 advises (at para 33) that social services and their local NHS partners:

> . . . develop a multi-agency carers strategy . . . [and] . . . ensure that agreed protocols are in place for support from partner organisations in providing support to carers. This sort of process may also help to embed carers' needs in other local strategies, for example, welfare to work, joint investment plans, hospital discharge plans and life-long learning strategies.

and explains (at para 36) that:

> . . . due consideration means . . . an NHS organisation could not refuse to consider any request made to them in relation to the provision of lifting and handling support for carers . . . In demonstrating that due consideration has been given, it would be reasonable to expect public authorities to document the decision taken in relation to requests, along with the reasons for that decision.

16.102 A 2006 Department of Health report[102] has given as an example of this power, the possibility of a social services authority requesting 'that the

---

commitment forward, but that it would require 'the local NHS to demonstrate to their strategic health authorities that they are effectively taking account of the needs of carers in their planning processes. If strategic health authorities are not satisfied that that is the case or if the Department of Health has specific examples of how the process is not working, we will intervene. I can reassure my noble friend about that.'Parliamentary Under-Secretary of State, Department of Health (Lord Warner), HL Debates col 1493, 25 June 2004.

101 Being either 'another local authority, an education authority, a housing authority or a Special Health Authority, a Local Health Board, a Primary Care Trust, an NHS Trust or NHS foundation trust'.

102 Department of Health/Care Services Improvement Partnership, *Out and about: Wheelchairs as part of a whole-systems approach to independence*, October 2006, p30.

NHS provide a certain type of wheelchair (perhaps one more expensive than usual) in order not only to meet the needs of the disabled person, but also to make life easier for the carer'.

Hospital discharge

16.103 The guidance relating to hospital discharge arrangements contains substantial reference to the importance of ensuring that carers' needs and concerns are addressed, and is considered separately at para 5.15 above.

NHS continuing care

16.104 At para 14.113 above we consider the residual duties of social services authorities in cases where it has been determined that a person is entitled to NHS continuing care. If this analysis is correct, it means that such a determination does not disentitle a person to support under the community care regime and as a consequence any qualifying carer to an assessment under the carers Acts. Without explaining the legal basis of its opinion, the Department of Health has also advised[103] that carers do not lose their entitlement to an assessment when the person for whom they care is entitled to NHS continuing care.

Carer's grant

16.105 As part of the 1999 National Strategy for Carers[104] the government announced the creation of a special grant for carers which was to be paid to local authorities 'for the enhancement of services to allow carers to take a break from caring'. A similar initiative followed in Wales.[105] The grant could be used to pay for respite care services to enable carers to have a break from their caring responsibilities or to provide services for carers under CDCA 2000 s2.[106]

16.106   Research suggests that the grant has been effective in promoting flexible breaks for carers.[107] In England it amounted to £185 million in 2005/06.[108] Although no longer ring fenced[109] in England, local authorities

---

103 Department of Health, *The National Framework for NHS Continuing Healthcare and NHS Funded Nursing Care*, 2007, para 35.

104 http://www.carers.gov.uk/pdfs/care.pdf.

105 See The Carers Strategy in Wales – Implementation Plan 2006.

106 Department of Health, *Carers Grant Guidance 2004/05*, 2004, para 5, accessible at http://www.carers.gov.uk/carersgrant04_05.pdf.

107 Kings Fund, *Analysis of local authority plans and progress reports to assess the effectiveness of the Carers Special Grant in promoting flexible breaks for carers*, 2001.

108 See Department of Health, *Determination of a Grant under s31 of the Local Government Act 2003 of the Carers Grant for 2005/2006*, 2006. In Wales the grant amounted to £23m in 2004/05.

109 Department of Health, *Carers Grant Guidance 2004/05*, 2004.

will continue to be monitored by the CSCI on the extent to which they are providing such respite care services.[110]

Carer/service user conflict

16.107 Department of Health guidance[111] and other publications[112] give general advice as to appropriate local authority responses where there is (or may be) conflict between carers and the persons for whom they care. CDCA 2000 s2(3) contains however a provision designed to get around the problem of a disabled person who refuses services that would be of benefit to his or her carer. It states that a service, although provided to the carer:

(a) may take the form of a service delivered to the person cared for if it is one which, if provided to him instead of to the carer, could fall within community care services and they both agree it is to be so delivered; but

(b) if a service is delivered to the person cared for it may not, except in prescribed circumstances, include anything of an intimate nature.

16.108 This arrangement is explained by the English practice guidance to the CDCA 2000 by reference to an example, which is reproduced below.

Jim is a substantial and regular carer for his mother Elsie who is frail and in the early stages of dementia. She is often incontinent. Elsie lives round the corner from Jim. Jim does all his mother's laundry.

There are various ways the local council may be able to help Jim:

a) Elsie is eligible for community care support. If Elsie agrees to be assessed by social services, then a cleaning and laundry service could be provided as a **community care service** and delivered to her. Elsie would be the person financially assessed for any charges.

b) If Elsie refuses to be assessed by social services (although she would be eligible for community care services) Jim could ask for a carers' assessment. The local council could agree to provide, as a carer's service, a cleaning and laundry service at Elsie's house. The local council would need to be satisfied that Elsie is prepared to tolerate the visits from these services. It turns out that so long as they don't bother her, Elsie will tolerate them. Social services arrange to pick the laundry up when Jim is at Elsie's home. This is a **carer's service**

Continued

---

110 Commenting on this change the minister (Stephen Ladyman) stated '[although] the carers grant . . . ring fence will be removed for next year . . . it is still a targeted grant. A very explicit memo explains to councils what the carers grant is intended to do, and we will back that up with inspections of councils to ensure that carers are still being cared for': see *Hansard* HC Debates col 1063, 6 February 2004.

111 LAC (2004)24 *Guidance accompanying the Community Care Directions 2004*, paras 2.3–2.5.

112 See eg L Clements, *Carers and their rights: The law relating to carers* (2nd edn, Carers UK, 2007), chapter 9.

> **provided for the carer (Jim), delivered to the cared for person (Elsie).**
> Jim would be liable for any charge as the service is provided to help
> him in his caring role. Jim and the care manager hope that Elsie will
> get used to people other than Jim coming round and may sub-
> sequently change her mind about being assessed and helped by
> social services.
>
> c) If Jim decides that the easiest way for him to cope with all this extra
>   laundry is for him to have a new washing machine installed at his
>   own home, he could then discuss with the care manager the provi-
>   sion of a direct payment so that he can buy one. This would then be
>   **a carers' service provided for the carer (Jim), delivered to the carer
>   (Jim).** Jim would again be the person financially assessed in relation
>   to any charges.

16.109 Accordingly certain care services, that would otherwise be construed as
community care services, may be deemed to be services under the CDCA
2000. Such services can only be delivered to the carer, if:

- they could be a community care service;
- both the disabled person and the carer agree to them being provided to
  the carer; and
- the services are not of an intimate nature (except in prescribed
  circumstances).

16.110 In respect of these services the English policy guidance to the CDCA 2000
(at para 25) states:

> Cared for people may not be forced to accept services they do not wish to
> receive. However, in some circumstances they may accept a level of contact
> with social services that helps the person who cares for them. A cared for
> person who has refused an assessment may agree to the delivery of a non-
> intimate sitting service provided as a carer's service to give their usual carer
> a short break.

16.111 Regulations[113] define the meaning of 'intimate care' – stipulating that a
service is deemed to be of an 'intimate' nature if it involves physical
contact such as 'lifting, washing, grooming, feeding, dressing, bathing or
toileting the person cared for'. Such service cannot be provided to the
cared for person under CDCA 2000 s2(3) except in 'prescribed circumstances'. The Regulations[114] clarify the scope of 'prescribed circumstances'
as where (essentially):

- a) the person cared for agrees to the intimate care; or
- b) in an emergency (which is likely to cause the cared for person
      serious personal harm) either:

---

113 Carers (Services) and Direct Payments (Amendment) (England) Regulations 2001 SI
     No 441 reg 2(1) and in Wales the Carers (Services) and Direct Payments
     (Amendment) (Wales) Regulations 2001 SI No 2186 (W150).
114 Ibid, reg 2(2) and see also para 28 of the 2001 policy guidance (para 2.3 of the Welsh
     guidance).

- the cared for person is unable to consent; or
- he or she does not consent but the intimate care is necessary to alleviate the imminent risk of serious personal harm.

Young carers

16.112 Carers who are under the age of 18 are generally referred to as 'young carers'. The C(RS)A 1995 and C(EO)A 2004 apply to all carers irrespective of their age. In addition to the benefit of a carer's assessment under the C(RS)A 1995, young carers may be entitled to services in their own right, under the Children Act (CA) 1989. In general it will be more appropriate for a young carer to be assessed under the 1989 Act. In this respect the combined policy guidance under the CDCA 2000 and C(EO)A 2004 states (at para 10):

> Children (anyone aged under 18) who are carers should be routinely assessed under the Children Act 1989. As a matter of law they could be assessed under the 1995 Act but that would not be expected, nor would it be in line with the Children Act 1989 guidance. Nevertheless, whichever of these Acts they were assessed under, the new obligation to consider a young carer's wish to work or undertake education, training or leisure would still apply . . .

16.113 While the CA 1989 will be the general assessment route for young carers, this will not always be the case. The obligations under the C(RS)A 1995 specifically encompass the needs of young carers because it is recognised that some adult services have, in the past, failed this group. The C(RS)A 1995 obliges adult services to ensure that children and young people looking after an adult are not left with unreasonable caring responsibilities.

Young carers and the Carers (Recognition and Services) Act 1995

16.114 Young carers, if they are providing or intending to provide a substantial amount of care on a regular basis, are entitled to an assessment under the C(RS)A 1995. Although this is primarily directed at establishing their ability to provide and continue to provide care (the continuation of which will generally be inappropriate), it must additionally address (by virtue of C(EO)A 2004 s2) not only their desire to work (for example if a 15-year-old wanted to take up a paper round[115]) but also whether they wish to undertake, education, training or any leisure activity.

---

115   Para 10 of the combined policy guidance under the 2000 and 2004 Acts.

Young carers and the Children Act 1989

16.115 There is no legislation which specifically refers to young carers. Guidance concerning young carers has, however, been issued by the Department of Health[116] and the Social Services Inspectorate in England (SSI).[117] The SSI guidance adopts a definition of a 'young carer' as 'a child or young person who is carrying out significant caring tasks and assuming a level of responsibility for another person, which would usually be taken by an adult'. Such duties as are owed to young carers by a social services authority are primarily contained in the CA 1989 as clarified by guidance issued by the Department of Health[118]/Welsh Assembly.[119]

16.116   For a child to benefit from help under the CA 1989, it is necessary for him or her to come within the definition of a 'child in need'. CA 1989 s17(10) defines a child to be 'in need' if:

(a) he is unlikely to achieve or maintain, or to have the opportunity of achieving or maintaining, a reasonable standard of health or development without the provision for him of services by a local authority . . .; or

(b) his health or development is likely to be significantly impaired, or further impaired, without the provision for him of such services; or

(c) he is disabled.

16.117 The policy guidance under the C(RS)A 1995 (at para 14) refers to, and adopts the SSI guidance,[120] stating:

> . . . many young people carry out a level of caring responsibilities which prevents them from enjoying normal social opportunities and from achieving full school attendance. Many young carers with significant caring responsibilities should therefore be seen as children in need.[121]

16.118 A key determinant therefore is whether the young carer's caring responsibilities are 'significant'. In this respect the practice guidance to the C(RS)A 1995 (at para 15.2) stressed that young carers should not be expected to carry out 'inappropriate' levels of caring. It follows that when undertaking a community care assessment of a disabled or ill parent, the local authority must ensure that support mechanisms are put in place to prevent a young carer undertaking unreasonable caring responsibilities –

---

116 Department of Health, Social Services Inspectorate, *Young Carers: Making a Start*, 1998.

117 Guidance letter CI (95)12.

118 Principally the *Framework for the Assessment of Children in Need and their Families*, TSO, 2000, and two volumes of guidance issued under the CA 1989 of relevance to young carers – Volume 2: *Family Support* and Volume 6: *Children with Disabilities* (both HMSO, 1991).

119 Department of Health, *Framework for the Assessment of Children in Need and their Families*, TSO, 2000.

120 Guidance letter CI (95)12 annex A para 1.1.

121 See also para 2.4 of Volume 2: *Family Support* (note 118 above) which emphasises that 'the definition of "need" in the Act is deliberately wide to reinforce the emphasis on preventive support and services to families'.

or indeed suffering in any other inappropriate way. The general duties under Children CA 1989 s17 are considered at para 24.42 below.

16.119 The policy guidance concerning the assessment of young carers issued by the Department of Health and the Welsh Assembly[122] states (among other things):

Assessing the Needs of Young Carers

3.61 A group of children whose needs are increasingly more clearly recognised are young carers for example those who assume important caring responsibilities for parents and siblings. Some children care for parents who are disabled, physically or mentally ill, others for parents dependent on alcohol or involved in drug misuse . . .

3.62 An assessment of family circumstances is essential. Young carers should not be expected to carry inappropriate levels of caring which have an adverse impact on their development and life chances. It should not be assumed that children should take on similar levels of caring responsibilities as adults. Services should be provided to parents to enhance their ability to fulfil their parenting responsibilities. There may be differences of view between children and parents about appropriate levels of care. Such differences may be out in the open or concealed. The resolution of such tensions will require good quality joint work between adult and children's social services as well as co-operation from schools and health care workers. This work should include direct work with the young carer to understand his or her perspective and opinions. The young person who is a primary carer of his or her parent or sibling may have a good understanding of the family's functioning and needs which should be incorporated into the assessment.

3.63 Young carers can receive help from both local and health authorities. Where a child is providing a substantial amount of care on a regular basis for a parent, the child will be entitled to an assessment of their ability to care under section 1(1) of the *Carers (Recognition and Services) Act 1995* and the local authority must take that assessment into account in deciding what community care services to provide for the parent. Many young carers are not aware that they can ask for such an assessment. In addition, consideration must be given as to whether a young carer is a child in need under the Children Act 1989. The central issue is whether a child's welfare or development might suffer if support is not provided to the child or family. As part of the *National Strategy for Carers*,[123] local authorities should take steps to identify children with additional family burdens. Services should be provided to promote the health and development of young carers while not undermining the parent.

16.120 As a result of amendments made by the CA 2004,[124] any assessment of a young carer must, among other things:

---

122 Department of Health, *Framework for the Assessment of Children in Need and their Families*, 2004 and Welsh Assembly, *Framework for the Assessment of Children in Need and their Families*, 2001; the cited extract appears at para 3.65 of the Welsh guidance.
123 Department of Health, *Caring about Carers: A National Strategy for Carers*, 1999.
124 CA 1989 s17(4A) (inserted by CA 2004 s53).

a)   ascertain the child's wishes and feelings regarding the provision of such services as the local authority is proposing to make available; and

b)   give due consideration (having regard to his or her age and understanding) to such wishes and feelings of the child as they have been able to ascertain.

Parent carers

16.121   People with parental responsibility for a disabled child (ie a person aged under 18) are entitled (if their caring role is substantial) to an assessment under C(RS)A 1995 s1(2)and under CDCA 2000 s6. It is self-evident that most parent carers provide a 'substantial amount of care on a regular basis'. Neither the C(RS)A 1995 nor the CDCA 2000 include a stipulation (found in social security law) that the care provided to the disabled child must (for instance) be 'substantially in excess of the normal requirements of persons of his age'.[125]

16.122   Parent carers have a right to a separate assessment under the 1995 and 2000 Acts in addition to their needs being fully addressed in their child's Children Act assessment. In general, however, this should not be necessary, provided the local authority fully addresses the parent's employment, training, education, leisure and other needs. As the combined policy guidance under the CDCA 2000 and C(EO)A 2004 advises (at para 71):

> Following the passage of the 2004 Act, the assessment should take account of the parent's ability to provide or continue to provide care for the child and consideration of whether they work, or undertake any education, training or leisure activity or wish to do so. This means that local authorities have a duty to ask carers about these activities and take their wishes into account when planning the care package.

16.123   It will however be maladministration for a local authority not to undertake such a separate assessment or to suggest this is merely a 'good will gesture' – when clearly it is a statutory responsibility.[126]

16.124   If a local authority is failing to implement its duties to parent carers (for instance in order to enable them to remain in work/rejoin the work force and /or take part in leisure training or education activities), parent carers may have to insist on having a separate assessment under the C(RS)A 1995 and CDCA 2000. In *R (LH and MH) v Lambeth LBC*[127] the local authority accepted that the applicant's son's behaviour was having an adverse affect on her health, emotionally, mentally and physically: that she was 'depressed and at the end of her tether, crying all the time and only just coping'. However the care plan for the son failed to explain how his mother's needs would be addressed. The court declared that the

---

125   See eg Social Security Contributions and Benefits Act 1992 s72(6).
126   Public Service Ombudsman (Wales) Complaint no B2004/0707/S/370 against Swansea City Council, 22 February 2007, para 131.
127   [2006] EWHC 1190 (Admin); (2006) 9 CCLR 622.

authority was in breach of its assessment obligations under the CA 1989 (to the child) and under the C(RS)A 1995 and the CDCA 2000 (for the mother).

16.125 Parent carers (like all other qualifying carers) have the right to have their employment, training, education and leisure aspirations addressed. It is the government's view that all 'carers who wish to work have the right to work' (see para 16.68 above). The English practice guidance to the CDCA 2000 highlights the importance of providing such assistance, stating (at para 36):

> People with parental responsibility for disabled children will also benefit from joining or re-joining the workforce. Such carers often face difficulties re-entering the workforce because of lack of suitable child-care services. Many parents of disabled children would like to return to work and, if they were able to do so, would benefit socially and emotionally as well as financially.

16.126 The policy guidance to the C(EO)A 2004 amplifies this point, stating:

> ... the assessment should take account of the parent's ability to provide or continue to provide care for the child and consideration of whether they work, or undertake any education, training or leisure activity or wish to do so. This means that local authorities have a duty to ask carers about these activities and take their wishes into account when planning the care package. For example, the package may provide the possibility of freeing some leisure time for the carer and for other children in the family through a structured playtime with the disabled child, while social services provides services to run the house. The local authority must take assessments carried out under section 6 of the 2000 Act into account when deciding what services, if any, to provide under section 17 of the Children Act 1989.

16.127 The Childcare Act 2006 requires English and Welsh councils (sections 6 and 22) to secure, 'so far as is reasonably practicable', sufficient child care to meet the requirements of parents in their area who require child care in order to work or to undertake training or education to prepare for work. In relation to disabled children, the obligation extends to child care facilities up to 1 September after their 18th birthday. In determining whether the provision of child care is sufficient, councils must have regard to (among other things) the needs of parents for child care that is eligible for the child care element of the working tax credit, and for child care that is suitable for disabled children.

16.128 The duty under the Childcare Act 2006 to assess the adequacy of child care provision came into force in April 2007 and the duty to secure sufficient child care is expected to come into force in April 2008.

Carers of mental health service users

16.129 People with mental health problems are entitled to a community care assessment, in common with other disabled people. In some cases, however, they are entitled to additional assistance, under the 'Care

Programme Approach' (CPA), (considered separately at para 21.7 below). The rights of persons subject to the CPA have been detailed in English and Welsh *National Service Frameworks for Mental Health*[128] and their carers identified as entitled to certain specified rights. The English framework states:

> Standard 6 – Caring about carers
> All individuals who provide regular and substantial care for a person on CPA should:
> - have an assessment of their caring, physical and mental health needs,
> - repeated on at least an annual basis,
> - have their own written care plan, which is given to them and implemented in discussion with them.

16.130 The rights under Standard 6 are in addition to the basic rights to which all carers of people with a mental health problem are entitled. Thus if the person cared for is not receiving care from the specialist psychiatric services, his or her carer will be entitled to an assessment under the C(RS)A 1995 and the CDCA 2000 (if providing or intending to provide regular and substantial care).

16.131   The rationale behind Standard 6 is explained in the following terms:[129]

> Carers play a vital role in helping to look after service users of mental health services, particularly those with severe mental illness. Providing help, advice and services to carers can be one of the best ways of helping people with mental health problems. While caring can be rewarding, the strains and responsibilities of caring can also have an impact on carers' own mental and physical health. These needs must be addressed by health and social services.

16.132 Standard 6 contains detailed guidance on what action should be taken to support the carer.[130] It requires social services to draw up a care plan and agree it with the carer and at the same time to take into account his or her health needs. The plan should be in writing and reviewed at least annually and its contents should be communicated to the GP and primary care team. The carer's care plan should include:

- information about the mental health needs of the person for whom he or she is caring, including information about medication and any side-effects which can be predicted, and support services available;
- action to meet defined contingencies;
- information on what to do and who to contact in a crisis;
- what will be provided to meet the carer's own mental and physical health needs, and how it will be provided;

---

128 Department of Health, *A National Service Framework for Mental Health: Modern Standards and Service Models*, 1999. In Wales the equivalent NSF is Welsh Assembly, *Raising the Standard: The Revised Adult Mental Health National Service Framework and an Action Plan for Wales*, 2005, para 1.4 of which states that the relevant Standard (Standard 2) concerning carer participation is under 'review'.
129 Ibid, p69
130 Ibid, p72.

- action needed to secure advice on income, housing, educational and employment matters;
- arrangements for short term breaks;
- arrangements for social support, including access to carers' support groups;
- information about appeals or complaints procedures.

CHAPTER 17

Care standards, regulation and health and safety

Introduction

17.1   This chapter provides a brief summary of the care home and domiciliary care regulatory framework, focusing on the issues of relevance to the provision of community care services. For detailed analysis and guidance on the registration regime, reference should be made to a specialist text on the subject[1] and the websites of the Commission for Social Care Inspection (CSCI) in England and the Care and Social Services Inspectorate Wales (CSSIW).

17.2   We address a number of associated regulatory questions elsewhere in this text. For example in relation to the protection for vulnerable adults, at chapter 25, and complaints relating to local authority care home funded placements are considered at para 27.24 and para 27.83 below.

17.3   The extent to which regulatory requirements impinge upon any particular care package depends in part on the nature of the package. Thus if a local authority directly provides or commissions services, these will generally have to be delivered by service providers registered under the Care Standards Act (CSA) 2000 and subject to the full regulatory regime. However if the care is delivered via an adult placement scheme, although still governed by the 2000 Act, the arrangement will be subject to lighter regulatory control. If the local authority meets the assessed need by way of a direct payment or individual budget, then in general the arrangement will be entirely outside the registration arrangements.

The regulation of care homes

17.4   The regulation of care homes in England and Wales is governed by the CSA 2000. The Act repealed the Registered Homes Act (RHA) 1984 which had previously been the principal statute regulating residential care homes and nursing homes (as they were then termed). The Act is augmented by a plethora of regulations and 'National Minimum Standards'.[2]

17.5   In April 2002 responsibility for the registration and inspection of services provided by care homes became the responsibility of the National Care Standards Commission (NCSC) in England and the Care Standards Inspectorate for Wales (CSIW) in Wales. Previously registration and inspection had been a local authority responsibility (for independent residential care homes) and a health authority responsibility (for nursing homes). In addition the new regulatory bodies assumed responsibility for (among other things) the inspection and registration of local authority care homes and domiciliary care agencies.

17.6   In April 2004 the functions of the NCSC were transferred to the CSCI as a result of the enactment of Health and Social Care (Community

---

1   See eg R Jones, *Care Standards Manual*, Sweet & Maxwell, 2004 and P Ridout, *Care Standards: A Practical Guide*, Jordans, 2003.

2   The principal regulations in England are the Care Homes Regulations 2001 SI No 3965 and in Wales the Care Homes (Wales) Regulations 2002 SI No 324 (W37).

Health and Standards) Act 2003 s102. In April 2007 the functions of the CSIW were transferred to the CSSIW – an 'operationally distinct division of the Department of Public Services and Performance in the Welsh Assembly Government'.

17.7 The CSCI/CSSIW have extensive enforcement powers and operate a complaints procedure through which service users and family members can lodge complaints about registered services (see para 27.83 below).

17.8 It is a criminal offence for any person to carry on, or manage, a care home without being registered.[3] CSA 2000 s3 defines a care home as follows:

> 3. – (1) For the purposes of this Act, an establishment is a care home if it provides accommodation, together with nursing or personal care, for any of the following persons.
> (2) They are –
> (a) persons who are or have been ill;[4]
> (b) persons who have or have had a mental disorder;[5]
> (c) persons who are disabled[6] or infirm;
> (d) persons who are or have been dependent on alcohol or drugs.
> (3) But an establishment is not a care home if it is –
> (a) a hospital;
> (b) an independent clinic; or
> (c) a children's home,
> or if it is of a description excepted by regulations.

Personal care

17.9 Establishments that cater for such persons as are listed in CSA 2000 s3(2) by the provision of accommodation 'together with nursing or personal care' must be registered with the CSCI/CSSIW. Under RHA 1984 s1, 'board' was required in addition to 'personal care', however under the 2000 Act this is no longer the case. Personal care is not defined, although CSA 2000 s121(3) states that the expression 'does not include any pre-scribed activity' and section 121(9) that the care that is provided must include 'assistance with bodily functions [eg toileting, eating] where such assistance is required'.

17.10 The CSA 2000 does not define 'personal care'[7] and it remains to be determined whether in that Act it bears the same meaning as that given to

---

3　CSA 2000 s1.
4　Under CSA 2000 s121(1), 'illness' includes injury.
5　Under CSA 2000 s121(1), 'mental disorder' means mental illness, arrested or incomplete development of mind, psychopathic disorder, and any other disorder or disability of mind.
6　CSA 2000 s121(2) provides that, for the purposes of the Act, a person is disabled if (i) his or her sight, hearing or speech is substantially impaired; (ii) he or she has a mental disorder; or (iii) he or she is physically substantially disabled by any illness, any impairment present since birth, or otherwise.
7　CSA 2000 s121(3) states that the expression 'does not include any prescribed activity' and section 121(9) states that '[a]n establishment is not a care home for the purposes of this Act unless the care which it provides includes assistance with bodily functions where such assistance is required'.

the same phrase in the RHA 1984, although it would appear that parliament intended it to be so construed.[8] In *Harrison v Cornwall CC*[9] the Court of Appeal considered that the concept of 'personal care' was wider than the mere provision of assistance with bodily functions and embraced 'care in many forms, emotional or psychiatric as well as physical'.[10] The Department of Health[11] and Welsh Assembly[12] guidance on the 2000 Act however define personal care as care requiring:

- assistance with bodily functions such as feeding, bathing, and toileting;
- care which falls just short of assistance with bodily functions, but still involving physical and intimate touching, including activities such as helping a person get out of a bath and helping them to get dressed.

17.11 The guidance has been the subject of criticism[13] and it has been suggested that its definition of personal care is considerably narrower than that under the RHA 1984. In other contexts the phrase 'bodily functions' has been held not to include 'general counselling and support'[14] but physical contact is not necessarily essential.[15] It may include reading to or guiding a person with a severe visual impairment,[16] or the provision of any similar assistance in relation to the 'operation of the senses', for instance the provision of an interpreter to a severely deaf person.[17]

17.12 The mere fact that accommodation and care services are provided by separate legal entities (as may happen in 'supported housing' for instance) does not in itself mean that the unit is not a care home. The CSA 2000 speaks of an 'establishment' providing the accommodation 'together with' care services.

17.13 In *Alternative Futures Ltd v National Care Standards Commission*[18] the Care Standards Tribunal held that whether an establishment was a 'care home' for the purposes of the CSA 2000 was, in borderline cases, a difficult question for which no single factor could be considered

---

8 See eg, the statement of the Minister of State, Department of Health (Mr John Hutton) HC Standing Committee G, 4 July 2000: 'I remind the Committee that the proposed requirements are the same as those in the Registered Homes Act 1984, which were clarified by the *Harrison v Cornwall County Council* judgment with which the Committee is familiar . . . we intend that the homes that are currently required to register under the 1984 Act should be required to register under the Bill'.

9 (1991) 11 BMLR 21; (1991) 90 LGR 81.

10 RHA 1984 s20, however, defined personal care as meaning care which includes assistance with bodily functions 'where such assistance is required' and the words in quotation marks do not appear in the 2000 Act.

11 *Supported Housing and Care Homes Guidance on Regulation*, August 2002, para 8.

12 *Clarification of the Registration Requirements for Supported Housing and Extra Care Schemes under the Care Standards Act 2000 Guidance*, August 2002, para 16.

13 See eg, the criticisms voiced at paras 59 and 78 in *Alternative Futures Ltd v National Care Standards Commission* [2002] 101–111 NC, (2004) 7 CCLR 171.

14 *R v North Cornwall DC ex p Singer* (1993) *Times* 12 January 1994.

15 *Mallinson v Secretary of State for Social Security* [1994] 1 WLR 630.

16 Ibid.

17 *Secretary of State for Social Security v Fairey (aka Halliday)* [1997] 1 WLR 799.

18 (2004) 7 CCLR 171.

determinative. Thus the fact that the care and accommodation are provided by separate companies was not conclusive (especially if these services remained closely co-ordinated) nor was the level of personal care provided,[19] nor was the provision of tenancies to the residents, nor the fact that the residents had 'person centred' care plans.

17.14 In the tribunal's view an important factor was that of choice – that it was necessary for the provider to demonstrate that service users were genuinely able to choose who provided their personal care.

17.15 The tribunal's decision was the subject of an unsuccessful judicial review by some of the care home residents. In the High Court[20] Mitting J upheld the decision but questioned whether the reliance on user choice was a relevant question, commenting that 'it was unnecessary for it to go on to consider, let alone hold to be decisive, the absence of choice by residents when entering into the new arrangements'.[21] The Court of Appeal[22] concurred. It agreed that 'establishment' need not have a technical meaning and could include a situation where different agencies provided the accommodation and care services – and that there was nothing in principle to exclude the provision of accommodation by way of a tenancy.[23] In the court's view:

> The crucial consideration is whether the establishment provides the accommodation together with nursing or personal care. That is essentially a question of fact which does not arise in the present case as the appellants accepted for the purposes of the appeal that Housing and Futures, together with each house, were an establishment. The establishment of a lessor and lessee relationship can be an indicator of a situation where an establishment does not provide both the accommodation and the care, but cannot be determinative.[24]

17.16 2005 guidance has been issued by the CSCI as a result of the *Alternative Futures* litigation.[25]

Care homes providing nursing

17.17 Under the RHA 1984 quite separate regimes existed for the registration and inspection of residential care homes and nursing homes – albeit that it was possible to have 'dual registration'. Under the CSA 2000 (and the

19 As the tribunal noted, 'the level of personal care is not on its own the determining factor. We agree . . . that s 121(9) must not be read to mean that where bodily assistance is provided or required then registration as a care home is required.'
20 *R (Moore) v Care Standards Tribunal and National Care Standards Commission* [2004] EWHC 2481 (Admin); (2005) 8 CCLR 91.
21 Ibid, at [34].
22 *Moore v Care Standards Tribunal and Commission for Social Care Inspection* [2005] EWCA Civ 627; [2005] 1 WLR 2979; (2005) 8 CCLR 354.
23 The existence of tenancies was contested in the appeal although the court expressed reservations about the possibility of tenancies in the present case – see ibid, at [10]–[11].
24 Ibid, at [21].
25 CSCI, *Interim Policy and Guidance: Guidance to CSCI staff regarding Court of Appeal judgment: Andrew Moore and others v Care Standards Tribunal and Commission for Social Care Inspection*, 29 June 2005.

regulations thereto) the CSCI/CSSIW has power when issuing a certificate of registration to impose conditions, including the categories of person the home can accommodate – for instance authorising the accommodation of people requiring nursing care.[26] The current terminology therefore for what formerly was called a nursing home is a 'care home with nursing'. It is of course legally possible for nursing to be provided at a care home that is not registered to provide nursing (by, for instance, the NHS district nursing services providing this care).[27]

Registration criteria

17.18   As with the RHA 1984, where different persons are responsible for the carrying on and management of a care home they must both be registered.[28] The CSA 2000 sets out a broad range of regulation making powers covering, among other matters, the management, staff, premises and conduct of social care and independent health care establishments and agencies. The Regulations[29] list and describe in some detail the requirements that must be satisfied in order for an establishment to be registered and to retain its registration. These include:

- that the registered provider and manager be 'fit' to carry on the running of the home (together with an explanation as to what this entails – regs 7–10);[30]
- that the care home is conducted so as to promote and make proper provision for the health and welfare of service users (including where appropriate their treatment, education and supervision – regs 12–13);
- that accommodation should not be provided until (in so far as it is practicable) the service user has been assessed by a suitably trained person; and the registered person has obtained a copy of the assessment; and there has been appropriate consultation regarding the assessment with the service user or his or her representative; and the home has confirmed in writing to the service user that having regard to the assessment it is suitable for the purpose of meeting his or her needs in respect of his or her health and welfare; and that the assessment of the service user's needs is kept under review; and revised as and when necessary (reg 14);
- that after consultation with the service user or his or her representative (in so far as it is practicable) a written plan be prepared as to how the service user's health and welfare needs are to be met and this

---

26 National Care Standards Commission (Registration) Regulations 2001 SI No 3969 reg 9(f).
27 *R (Goldsmith) v Wandsworth LBC* [2004] EWCA Civ 1170; (2004) 7 CCLR 472.
28 Care Homes Regulations 2001 reg 2 describes the person carrying on the home (ie the person in ultimate control) as the 'registered provider': this of course can now include a local authority.
29 Principally the Care Homes Regulations 2001.
30 For a consideration of what is meant by 'fit' for the purposes of regulation 9, see *National Care Standards Commission v Jones* [2004] EWHC 918 (Admin).

plan to be available to the service user[31] and kept under review (reg 15);

- that facilities and services are provided in accordance with the care home's written statement (under reg 4). These include such matters as telephone facilities, furniture, laundry, kitchen equipment, wholesome and nutritious food, the maintenance of satisfactory standards of hygiene, secure deposit arrangement for money and valuables, arrangements for social, recreational religious and community activities (reg 16).

17.19　Additionally the regulations address such issues as the proper keeping of records; the adequacy of staffing arrangements; staff training and procedures for their concerns to be registered; and complaints procedures for service users.

17.20　All care homes are liable to a minimum of two inspections a year by the CSCI/CSSIW; such inspections may be unannounced.[32]

National minimum standards

17.21　CSA 2000 s23 gives power to the Secretary of State/Welsh Assembly to publish 'national minimum standards' which the CSCI/CSSIW must take into account when making their decisions. The status of such standards is further considered at para 1.61 above. These standards form the basis for judgments made by the CSCI/CSSIW regarding registration and the imposition of conditions for registration, variation of any conditions and enforcement of compliance with the CSA 2000 and associated regulations, including proceedings for cancellation of registration or prosecution.

17.22　Both the Department of Health and the Welsh Assembly have now published a series of national minimum standards, which in effect flesh out the basic requirement of the regulations. Although not legally binding they must be taken into account by the CSCI/CSSIW when making decisions about whether or not the regulations have been complied with (eg whether to approve a registration or to cancel a registration). The standards are revised from time to time. As at July 2007, national minimum standards had been approved in England in respect of the following categories:

- care homes for older people;
- adult placements;
- care homes for adults 18–65;
- domiciliary care;
- nurses' agencies.

31　A failure by a local authority to provide a care home with a copy of the service user's care plan will constitute maladministration: complaint no 99/B/3078 against Kent CC, March 2001 para 97.

32　National Care Standards Commission (Fees and Frequency of Inspections) Regulations 2001 SI No 3980 reg 6.

17.23   The CSCI previously discharged registration functions in relation to children's services. As a result of the Education and Inspections Act 2006 these functions were (in effect) transferred in April 2007 to the Office for Standards in Education, Children's Services and Skills (Ofsted).

Complaints

17.24   The Care Homes Regulations[33] require that care homes have appropriate complaints procedures: that complaints are investigated within 28 days; and all residents are made aware of their right to take their complaint to the CSCI/CSSIW. In addition residents placed in their home by a local authority will generally have access to that authority's complaints process. The right of residents to complain is considered further at para 12.83 below.

Domiciliary care agencies

17.25   The CSA 2000 brought domiciliary care agencies (including those run by local authorities) within the CSCI/CSSIW regulatory framework.[34] CSA 2000 s4 defines a 'domiciliary care agency' as:

> An undertaking[35] which consists of or includes arranging the provision of personal care in their own homes for persons who by reason of illness, infirmity or disability are unable to provide it for themselves without assistance.

17.26   The registration and inspection regimes for such undertakings are in broad measure the same as for care homes and are detailed in regulations.[36]

17.27   The requirement to register as a domiciliary agency is limited to undertakings that provide care to persons who are 'unable to provide [the personal care] for themselves'. Although, therefore, the provision of 'personal care' (see para 17.9 above) is a necessary requirement for registration, this is qualified by the requirement that it only becomes registrable when the service users are unable to provide it for themselves – accordingly, it has a narrower meaning than for the registration of care homes. As the minister noted during the debate on the bill:

> I hope that it is clear from the words 'unable to provide it for themselves without assistance' that personal care in this context has a narrower meaning than in the context of a care home. It will clearly include assistance with bodily functions and physical care, which falls short of assistance such as helping a person to get dressed. However, it could not extend to encouragement and emotional support, as that is not a form of personal care that a person could be said to be unable to provide for

33   Care Homes Regulations 2001 reg 22; Care Homes (Wales) Regulations 2002 reg 23.
34   By CSA 2000 s11 it is a criminal offence for a person to carry on or manage a domiciliary care agency without being registered in respect of it.
35   Widely defined in CSA 2000 s121(2).
36   Domiciliary Care Agencies Regulations 2002 SI No 3214.

themselves. Within the normal meaning of the words, a person cannot be said to be either able or unable to provide themselves with emotional support.[37]

Adult placement schemes

17.28 Adult placement schemes are regulated by the CSA 2000. Initially they were regulated as care homes, however since 2004 they are subject to a separate regime, which is considered further at para 15.112 below.

Health and safety issues

17.29 A detailed consideration of general health and safety issues that arise out of the delivery of care services is beyond the scope of this text. Specialist guidance (in relation to care home services) has been issued by the Health and Safety Executive in its booklet HS(G)104, *Health and Safety in Residential Care Homes*.[38] The guidance details the main heads of legal responsibility to employees and residents under the Health and Safety at Work Act 1974 as well as in tort and contract. The guidance gives practical advice on the handling and reporting of incidents; occupational health; training; the working environment; kitchen, laundry and outdoor safety; as well as covering other issues such as violence to staff.

Manual handling

17.30 Of increasing and particular concern, however, is the question of the avoidance of procedures that involve manual handling. This question arises not only in residential care settings, but also in general domiciliary and community care situations. HS(G)104 emphasises the importance of proper manual handling arrangements, thus:

> 89. Almost four of every ten accidents reported in the health care sector arise from manual handling. In residential care homes there will be a range of manual handling tasks from the simple lifting of provisions to complicated lifts involving residents. Sprains and strains of backs and limbs are often sustained from manual handling. Injuries may also occur as a result of cumulative damage often sustained over a considerable period, which can result in physical impairment, or even permanent disability.

17.31 Because of the general prevalence of such injuries throughout all types of work environment, European Directive 90/269/EEC required all member states to take specific legislative action to reduce such injuries at work. In consequence, the Manual Handling Operations Regulations 1992[39]

---

37 Minister of State, Department of Health (Mr John Hutton) HC Standing Committee G, 4 July 2000.
38 Obtainable from HSE Books, PO Box 1999, Sudbury, Suffolk, CO10 6FS. Tel: 01787 881165.
39 SI No 2793.

were issued and more recently the Management of Health and Safety at Work Regulations 1999.[40] Detailed guidance on the 1992 Regulations has been issued by the Health and Safety Executive under reference L23. Regulation 4 of the 1992 Regulations (as amended) provides that:

4(1) Each employer shall:
  (a) so far as is reasonably practicable, avoid the need for his employees to undertake any manual handling operations at work which involve a risk of their being injured;
  (b) where it is not reasonably practicable to avoid the need for his employees to undertake any manual handling operations at work which involve a risk of their being injured –
    (i)   make suitable and sufficient assessment of all manual handling operations to be undertaken by them, having regard to the factors which are specified in column 1 of Schedule 1 to these Regulations and considering the questions which are specified in the corresponding entry in column 2 of that Schedule,
    (ii) take appropriate steps to reduce the risk of injury to those employees arising out of their undertaking any such manual handling operations to the lowest level reasonably practicable,
    (iii) take appropriate steps to provide any of those employees who are undertaking any such manual handling operations with general indications and, where it is reasonably practicable to do so, precise information on–
      (aa) the weight of each load, and
      (bb) the heaviest side of any load whose centre of gravity is not positioned centrally.
  (2) Any assessment such as is referred to in paragraph (1)(b)(i) of this regulation shall be reviewed by the employer who made it if –
  (a) there is reason to suspect that it is no longer valid; or
  (b) there has been a significant change in the manual handling operations to which it relates;
     and where as a result of any such review changes to the assessment are required, the relevant employer shall make them.
  (3) In determining for the purposes of this regulation whether manual handling operations at work involve a risk of injury and in determining the appropriate steps to reduce that risk regard shall be had in particular to –
  (a) the physical suitability of the employee to carry out the operations;
  (b) the clothing, footwear or other personal effects he is wearing;
  (c) his knowledge and training;
  (d) the results of any relevant risk assessment carried out pursuant to regulation 3 of the Management of Health and Safety at Work Regulations 1999;
  (e) whether the employee is within a group of employees identified by that assessment as being especially at risk; and
  (f) the results of any health surveillance provided pursuant to regulation 6 of the Management of Health and Safety Regulations 1999.

---

40 SI No 3242.

17.32   As the guidance L23 states, regulation 4 establishes a clear hierarchy of measures which an employer is required to adopt, namely:

a)   avoid hazardous manual operations so far as is reasonably practicable;

b)   assess any hazardous manual handling operations that cannot be avoided;

c)   reduce the risk of injury so far as is reasonably practicable.

17.33   The very detailed guidance given by the Health and Safety Executive is of great practical importance, analysing the appropriate use of hoists and other possible lifting mechanisms when moving patients. What the regulations do not do, however, is prohibit the lifting of patients. Frequently it appears that social services authorities and health authorities are adopting an extremely restrictive interpretation of the regulations which has the end result that a patient does not receive a service (such as a bath) because it involves some element of manual handling.

17.34   In *R (A and B) v East Sussex CC*[41] Munby J was asked to give general guidance concerning how local authorities should seek to resolve the relative interests of disabled people – to be lifted safely and with dignity – and their paid carers – to avoid risks of injury from manual handling. By the time of the hearing the local authority had accepted that its previous inflexible 'no manual handling' policy was unlawful and had revised it. Nevertheless a dispute remained as to the application of the new policy to the needs of the applicants – two young women with profound physical and learning disabilities. The judge reviewed:

- the relevant legislation (as detailed above); and
- the relevant guidance/advice publications, and considered that in the context of the handling of incapacitated people in their own homes, the most relevant was *Handling home care: Achieving safe, efficient and positive outcomes for care workers and clients* Health and Safety Executive, HSG 225, 2001; and
- the relevant domestic case law, in particular *King v Sussex Ambulance NHS Trust*[42] which concerned an injury sustained by an ambulance man in carrying an elderly person down the stairs of a cottage. In Munby J's view the case established a principle:

> that an employee whose job is to lift people (the ambulance man) may have to accept a greater degree of risk than one who is employed to move inanimate objects (the furniture remover) and that what is reasonable (and ... practicable) has to be evaluated having regard to the social utility of the operation and a pubic authority's duties to the public and to the particular member of the public who has called for the authority's help. At the same time one has to recognise, of course, that none of this can justify exposing an employee to ... 'unacceptable risk'.

41   [2003] EWHC 167 (Admin); (2003) 6 CCLR 194.
42   [2002] EWCA Civ 953; (2002) 68 BMLR 177.

From this analysis the judge concluded that there may be situations where 'some manual handling is on any view an inherent – an inescapable – feature of the very task for which this who care . . . are employed';

- the relevant human rights instruments and Strasbourg case law, including the European Convention on Human Rights, the Charter of Fundamental Rights of the European Union, *Price v UK*[43] which case he considered established that profoundly disabled people were entitled to an 'enhanced degree of protection' under the Convention, and *Botta v Italy*[44] which he considered endorsed the principle recognised in article 26 of the Charter, namely 'the rights of persons with disabilities to benefit from measures designed to ensure their independence, social and occupational integration and participation in the life of the community'.[45]

17.35   Munby J did not make a definitive decision as to what degree of manual handling was required in the particular case. He gave general guidance, however, as to how the balance of interest should be struck. In his view this was not a 'situation in which the disabled person's rights "trump" those of the carer, though equally . . . the carer's rights do not "trump" those of the disabled person'. There is no doubt but that such cases raise extremely challenging issues, and in difficult cases the resolution may require the installation of specialist (and expensive) equipment beyond that which has generally been sanctioned by local authorities and health bodies.

17.36   The judge gave guidance on how the assessment should be conducted and how the disabled person's wishes, feelings and preferences should be ascertained. At the end of this process, a decision had to be made:

> Once the balance has been struck, if it comes down in favour of manual handling, then the employer must take appropriate assessments and take all appropriate steps to minimise the risks that exist.

Unpaid carers

17.37   In those cases where authorities are using the regulations as a reason for refusing to provide a service, they are often willing to admit that in consequence the task is carried out by a carer instead. Although such a person is not an employee for the purposes of the regulations and other health and safety at work legislation, he or she is someone to whom the authority prima facie owes a duty of care (respect for, and the support of, carers being at the heart of the community care reforms). If an authority fully conversant with the good practice and knowledge engendered by the regulations stands by and allows a carer to carry out tasks it believes to be

43   (2001) 34 EHRR 1285.
44   (1998) 26 EHRR 241.
45   [2003] EWHC 167 (Admin); (2003) 6 CCLR 194 at 220D.

unduly hazardous for its own employees, then it may well be liable in negligence for any injuries that result (unless, perhaps, it has taken steps to inform and/or train the carer in safe lifting techniques etc).

17.38   Such health risks are foreseeable: well publicised research has shown that over 50 per cent of unpaid carers have suffered a physical injury such as a strained back since they began to care. In addition, the research reveals that caring also subjects carers to other health related problems, with over half receiving treatment for stress-related illness since becoming carers.[46]

46 M Henwood, *Ignored and Invisible? Carers Experience of the NHS,* Carers National Association, 1998: cited in *Caring about Carers: A National Strategy for Carers* LASSL (99)2; and see also para 16.61 above.

CHAPTER 18

Mental capacity

Introduction

18.1   Not infrequently questions are raised as to the extent of a community care service user's mental capacity to make decisions, and people with impaired mental capacity come within the definition of a 'disabled person' (see para 9.33 above) for the purposes of the primary community care statutes. In this chapter we accordingly provide a brief guide to key principles and procedures that regulate this branch of the law. We do not seek, however, to emulate the many and excellent and extensive guides concerning the law of mental capacity, to which reference should be made for a more detailed understanding of the law in this field. We additionally consider issues of capacity elsewhere in this text, for instance, in relation to the community care assessment process (see para 3.111 above), hospital discharges (see para 5.18 above), direct payments (see para 12.15 above), access to personal information (see para 26.17 above) and so on.

Overview

18.2   The law regulating mental capacity has been developed by many centuries of court decisions which have established various principles to be applied in individual cases. The law, like this chapter, can be divided into two broad sections: (1) the legal rules that are used to determine whether an individual has sufficient mental capacity to make a particular decision, and (2) where it is determined that he or she does not, the rules that are applied when a decision has to be made on his or her behalf.

18.3   The present state of our domestic law concerning the decision making powers of third parties on behalf of people who lack the necessary mental capacity is complex and some of the principles applied are still evolving – indeed evolving speedily in certain situations. In an effort to rationalise and codify these principles, in 1995 the Law Commission recommended[1] a wholesale reform of the law; its proposals covered a number of areas including adult abuse and decision making. In 1997 the government issued a consultation paper *Who Decides? Making Decisions on Behalf of Mentally Incapacitated Adults*[2] and in 1999 it published its conclusions as '*Making Decisions*'.[3] In June 2004 the government published the final bill which became the Mental Capacity Act (MCA) 2005. The Act came into force in October 2007. The Act is primarily concerned with 'decision making' and does not directly address the adult abuse provisions proposed by the Law Commission: this omission remains a significant problem and is considered separately at chapter 25.

---

1   Law Com no 231, February 1995.
2   Lord Chancellor's Department, Cm 3803, December 1997.
3   Lord Chancellor's Department, Cm 4465, October 1999.

18.4   MCA 2005 s42 provides for the publication of a code of practice ('the Code') and reference to this Code[4] is made in the section that follows. It is very informative and readable and provides an excellent starting point for the understanding of the law in this field. Section 42 of the Act sets out categories of people who are placed under a duty 'to have regard' to the Code, namely:

- People working in a professional capacity (for example, a doctor who is assessing a person's or a social worker who is arranging for a person lacking capacity to move into a supported living arrangement);
- People who are receiving payment for work in acting in relation to the person without capacity (for example, a care assistant working in a residential care home for people with learning disabilities);
- Anyone who is an attorney of a Lasting Power of Attorney, a deputy appointed by the Court of Protection, an Independent Mental Capacity Advocate or who is carrying out research approved in accordance with the Act.

18.5   The Code states (at p2) that these people:

> . . . must be aware of the Code of Practice when acting or making decisions on behalf of someone who lacks capacity to make a decision for themselves, and they should be able to explain how they have had regard to the Code when acting or making decisions.

18.6   It also suggests (at p2) that other people will also be expected to follow the guidance in the Code, since the Act applies to '*everyone*' who looks after, or cares for, someone who lacks capacity' including carers or family carers and the Code will help them to understand the Act and apply it. It adds at p5 that:

> . . . failure to comply with the Code can be used in evidence before a court or tribunal in any civil or criminal proceedings, if the court or tribunal considers it to be relevant to those proceedings. For example, if a court or tribunal believes that anyone making decisions for someone who lacks capacity has not acted in the best interests of the person they care for, the court can use the person's failure to comply with the Code as evidence. That's why it's important that anyone working with or caring for a person who lacks capacity to make specific decisions should become familiar with the Code.

18.7   In order to understand properly the legal principles underpinning the concept of mental capacity and decision making, a number of principles and concepts need to be considered. Some of these are of particular importance since they appear to have been the subject of widespread misconception: for instance that 'best interests' does not necessarily mean 'what is objectively best for the person' or that 'next of kin' do not have enhanced rights or that ultimately whether or not a person has sufficient capacity to make a decision is a legal not a medical decision.

---

4   Department of Constitutional Affairs, *Mental Capacity Act 2005 Code of Practice*, 2007, accessible at http://www.dca.gov.uk/menincap/legis.htm#codeofpractice.

The determination of capacity

18.8   In seeking to determine whether or not a person has sufficient mental capacity to make a particular decision, it is useful to bear in mind the following principles/concepts:

1) Presumption of capacity.
2) A functional question – what is it that has to be decided?
3) Understanding the consequences of acting/not acting.
4) An ability to rationalise/weigh up the information.
5) An appreciation that there is a problem – upon which advice is required.
6) Ultimately a legal not a medical question.

Presumption of capacity

18.9   MCA 2005 s1(2) creates, for adults, a presumption of capacity, that 'a person must be assumed to have capacity unless it is established that he lacks capacity'. The fact that (for instance) a person has been diagnosed as having advanced dementia or has been described as having severe learning disabilities or has been detained under the Mental Health Act (MHA) 1983 does not affect this presumption.[5] In the absence of proof to the contrary, such a person is assumed to retain his or her capacity to make informed decisions. The standard of proof is 'the balance of probabilities'. Where, however, an adult has been found to lack capacity to make an informed decision concerning a particular question, he or she is then presumed to continue to lack capacity in relation to that matter until it is established that capacity has been regained.

18.10   The presumption of capacity only applies to adults. In relation to children the test remains that propounded by the House of Lords in *Gillick v West Norfolk and Wisbech AHA*.[6] In simple terms this held that the parents' right to make certain decisions on their child's behalf ends when the child achieves sufficient intelligence and understanding to make his or her own decision. The court cited with approval comments of Lord Denning,[7] namely:

> . . . the legal right of a parent to the custody of a child ends at the 18th birthday: and even up till then, it is a dwindling right which the courts will hesitate to enforce against the wishes of the child, and the more so the older he is. It starts with a right of control and ends with little more than advice.

---

5   The MHA 1983 is not primarily concerned with the needs of vulnerable adults: the central provisions of the 1983 Act concern the detention and treatment of 'mentally disordered' persons. Part VII of the Act, however, concerns the power of the Court of Protection to manage the affairs of persons deemed 'incapable, by virtue of mental disorder, of managing and administering' their property (section 94(2)).

6   [1986] AC 112; [1985] 3 WLR 830 and see also *R (Axon) v Secretary of State for Health* [2006] EWHC 372 (Admin); [2006] 2 WLR 1130.

7   In *Hewer v Bryant* [1970] 1 QB 357, p369.

Functional test

18.11 Whether, as a matter of law, a person has sufficient mental capacity to make a decision depends upon the decision that has to be made. Thus a person may have sufficient mental capacity to enter into an agreement to buy a CD but insufficient to purchase a house. In the former case the issue is straightforward whereas in the latter the size and implications of the transaction (including the legal responsibilities of a home owner) demand a greater comprehension. MCA 2005 s2(1) provides therefore that (for the purposes of the Act):

> . . . a person lacks capacity in relation to a matter if at the material time he is unable to make a decision for himself in relation to the matter because of an impairment of, or a disturbance in the functioning of, the mind or brain.

18.12 The 'matter' specific nature of the test means that it is not normally sufficient (for instance) that a person is incapable of handling money without clarifying exactly how much money: accordingly someone may not have the capacity to manage an inheritance of £250,000 but may be quite capable of handing a small weekly allowance. Likewise a person might have sufficient mental capacity to manage a direct payment – which enabled him or her to retain a home care agency to provide the care – but insufficient capacity to be an employer (see para 12.17 above).

Understanding the consequences

18.13 While a person may be unable to make a decision about a matter because of (for instance) its size and complexity, it is also necessary to have regard to the potential consequences of the decision. Ultimately a person can decide to take action which may result in his or her death – for instance to require the ventilator that is keeping him or her alive to be switched off (as occurred in *B v NHS Hospital Trust*[8]). To make a life and death decision, however, one requires considerably more mental capacity than to decide, for instance, what clothes to wear or television programme to watch. Accordingly a gravely ill person who is unable to care for him/herself, will require more capacity to discharge him/herself from hospital (where no home care may immediately be available) than a person for whom a premature hospital discharge had no such risks. Ultimately, however, if a person understands the consequences of the decision and is capable of 'weighing up' the risks (see below), he or she can decide to take the action regardless of whether the professionals concerned think it sensible. In this respect MCA 2005 s1(4) specifically states that a person is not to be treated as unable to make a decision merely because the decision is an unwise one.

8   [2002] EWHC 429 (Fam); [2002] 2 All ER 449.

Ability to rationalise

18.14   Infrequently a person may understand the consequences of a decision, but because of a mental block (for instance an extreme phobia or incontrollable obsessional and compulsive disorder) be mentally powerless to act on that understanding. *Re MB (Caesarean Section)*,[9] for instance, concerned a patient whose life was believed to be in severe danger unless she delivered her baby by caesarean section. MB understood the danger, but refused the operation because she had an absolute phobia of needles and was incapable of agreeing to anything that might involve her being injected. The Court of Appeal held that this inability to apply any rationality to the information meant that she lacked capacity to decide on the treatment in question. MCA 2005 s3(1) adopts the court's approach and provides:

> . . . a person is unable to make a decision for himself if he is unable –
> (a) to understand the information relevant to the decision,
> (b) to retain that information,
> (c) to use or weigh that information as part of the process of making the decision, or
> (d) to communicate his decision (whether by talking, using sign language or any other means).

18.15   Section 3(1) requires, therefore, the ability to understand and retain relevant information for sufficiently long to make the decision. Thus if a person has a short term memory problem, as long as the relevant information is understood at the time the decision is made, the fact that it is then forgotten may not mean there is a lack of capacity (see also in this respect section 3(3)). Information need only be retained if it is relevant. Accordingly a person with dementia who is demanding to be discharged from hospital may lack capacity to make this decision if unable to remember that the reason for the admission was his or her severely neglected state. The requirement that the information be used or weighed as part of the decision-making process is the element that was of particular relevance in the *MB* proceedings.

18.16   Section 3(1)(d) raises an additional ground, namely the problem that arises where a person is incapable of communicating intelligibly (or at all) and a decision has to be taken on his or her behalf. A person may suffer from 'locked in syndrome' for instance – namely he or she appears to be in a coma and incapacitated, but in fact is aware of what is going on but completely unable to communicate, even by blinking an eye. Alternatively the person may be able to communicate, but what is said or done may make no sense to anyone involved in his or her care In such cases (provided all practicable steps to help the person communicate have been taken without success – section 1(3)) he or she may be deemed to lack capacity. Obviously what is practicable will depend on the urgency of the

---

9   [1997] 2 FLR 426; [1997] FCR 541; (1998) 38 BMLR 175.

situation and in general an act should not be taken in such cases unless it is necessary (section 1(6)).

Understanding there is a problem

18.17 The legal test of capacity thus focuses on the issue of understanding and not the ability to make prudent or wise decisions,[10] or indeed the ability to comprehend personally the fine detail of the choice or question in issue. In many situations the fact that a person is aware that he or she has a problem, may be sufficient to establish capacity to make that decision.

18.18 *White v Fell*[11] concerned the capacity of a disabled person to agree settlement terms in court proceedings. Boreham J considered that the assessment of capacity should be construed in a common sense way and observed:

> I have no doubt that the plaintiff is quite incapable of managing unaided a large sum of money such as the sort of sum that would be appropriate compensation for her injuries. That, however, is not conclusive. Few people have the capacity to manage all their affairs unaided . . . It may be that she would have chosen, and would choose now, not to take advice, but that is not the question. The question is: is she capable of doing so? To have that capacity she requires first the insight and understanding of the fact that she has a problem in respect of which she needs advice . . . Secondly, having identified the problem, it will be necessary for her to seek an appropriate adviser and to instruct him with sufficient clarity to enable him to understand the problem and to advise her appropriately . . . Finally, she needs sufficient mental capacity to understand and to make decisions based upon, or otherwise give effect to, such advice as she may receive.

18.19 In the judge's opinion it followed that:

> . . . the court should only take over the individual's function of decision making when it is shown on the balance of probabilities that such person does not have the capacity sufficiently to understand, absorb and retain information (including advice) relevant to the matters in question sufficiently to enable him or her to make decisions based upon such information.

18.20 In many situations a person may be aware that he or she does not understand something – for instance that he or she is having difficulty adding up or remembering the value of certain coins. The fact that he or she is aware of the problem is an indication that he or she has capacity – because he or she can then seek help. If the person has a learning disability, this might mean that an advocate could help him or her to learn what can and cannot be purchased with certain coins or who to ask when having to make payments. Such a state of affairs is indeed little different to many

---

10 *Masterman-Lister v Jewell* [2002] EWCA Civ 1889; [2003] WLR 1511; (2004) 7 CCLR 5 at[46].

11 12 November 1987, unreported, cited in *Masterman-Lister v Jewell* [2002] EWCA Civ 1889; [2003] 1 WLR 1511; (2004) 7 CCLR 5 at [18]–[20].

normally intelligent people not understanding (for example) the terms of a consumer credit agreement.

Ultimately a legal not a medical test

18.21   Where in court proceedings the extent of a person's mental capacity is in issue, medical evidence will generally be sought: ultimately however the decision is a legal one.[12] In this respect, the senior judge of the Court of Protection has observed that[13] 'although the court attaches a great deal of weight to the evidence of a registered medical practitioner on questions of incapacity, it does not automatically prefer medical opinion to lay opinion'.

18.22   *Re K (Enduring Powers of Attorney)*[14] illustrates the medical/legal distinction in this area. The case concerned a refusal by the Court of Protection to register an enduring power of attorney. A short interval after the power was signed, the attorney applied for its registration, which was refused on the basis that the short period between the signing and the registration suggested that the person lacked mental capacity at the time the document was signed. Allowing the appeal Hoffmann J held that there was no logical reason why a person who understood that something needed to be done, but who lacked the requisite understanding to do it personally, should not confer on another the power to do what needs to be done.[15] Accordingly a person may have insufficient mental capacity to manage his or her affairs, but sufficient capacity to delegate this function to an attorney.

18.23   It follows that medical evidence may be of limited value unless it is demonstrated that the expert is aware of the relevant legal test for capacity: what exactly it is that the person is required to comprehend. The courts have given guidance on a large range of capacity decisions (eg the capacity to make a will; to revoke a will; to have sexual relations; to vote; to make a gift; to litigate; to consent to medical treatment – and so on) and guidance on the relevant criteria has been given by the British Medical Association and the Law Society.[16]

18.24   By way of example, in *Banks v Goodfellow*[17] the court held that in order to be able to make a will a person must:

- be able to understand the nature of the act of making a will;
- know which persons he or she should consider as possible beneficiaries;

---

12 *Masterman-Lister v Jewell* [2002] EWCA Civ 1889; [2003] WLR 1511; (2004) 7 CCLR 5 at [34] and *Richmond v Richmond* (1914) 111 LT 273, p274.
13 D Lush, *Elderly Clients*, Jordans, 1996, p38.
14 [1988] Ch 310.
15 ibid, pp315B–C; see also Chadwick LJ in *Masterman-Lister v Jewell* [2002] EWCA Civ 1889; [2003] WLR 1511; (2004) 7 CCLR 5 at [83].
16 *Assessment of Mental Capacity: Guidance to Doctors and Lawyers*, 2004. A joint publication by the British Medical Association (BMA) and Law Society, published by and available from the BMA.
17 (1870) LR 5 QB 549.

- be able to understand the extent of the property of which he or she is disposing;
- not be subject to any disorder of the mind as shall 'poison his affections, pervert his sense of right or prevent the exercise of his natural faculties'; and
- have the mental capacity to arrive at a 'rational, fair and just' testament.[18]

Best interests

18.25 Where a decision needs to be made in respect of a person who lacks the requisite mental capacity, the law requires that the decision be based upon the concept of 'best interests'. This is an unfortunate phrase since in common usage it connotes simply 'what's best for the person' – ie an objective analysis. However the legal concept is altogether more complex and subjective: starting from the position of making the decision that the person would have made if he or she had capacity. The courts' thinking on best interests is still developing and it is unclear whether, when making a best interests decision, primacy should be given to the subjective question 'what the person would have done' or the objective assessment of 'what is best for them'. This will vary with the different contexts, although it is arguable that the court's approach differs depending upon the nature of the mental impairment. In relation to people with significant learning disabilities the court has tended to adopt the objective approach (ie a balance sheet assessment of adding up the benefits and disbenefits of a particular intervention – see para 25.64 below). For people who have had full mental development which has then become impaired (for instance through dementia, a stroke or an acquired brain injury), the courts tend to weight their decisions in favour of the 'doing what they would have done' approach.

18.26 In general the issue of best interests only arises if the adult lacks capacity – however in rare cases it may be of relevance where the person is 'deprived of the capacity to make the relevant decision, or disabled from making a free choice, or incapacitated or disabled from giving or expressing a real and genuine consent' (see para 25.59 below).

18.27 The 'best interests' to be served by the intervention are, of course, those of the incapacitated person's alone. Thus in *Re Y (Mental Incapacity: Bone Marrow Transplant)*[19] the court held that the fact that the donation of bone marrow by a mentally incompetent woman to her sister would save the sister's life, was not relevant unless as a result of that donation the best interests of the donor were served.

---

18 See, in this context, *Sharp and Bryson v Adam, Adam, Hall and Hancock* [2005] EWHC 1806 (Ch).
19 [1997] 2 WLR 556.
20 [1990] 2 AC 1; [1989] 2 WLR 1025; a case concerning the circumstances when medical treatment could be lawfully given without consent.

18.28   In *Re F (Mental Patient: Sterilisation)*[20] the House of Lords identified the importance of 'best interests' as an essential ingredient of the principle of necessity. In order to advance the justification of necessity, the court required the presence of two factors:

> ... not only (1) must there be a necessity to act when it is not practicable to communicate with the assisted person, but also (2) the action taken must be such as a reasonable person would in all the circumstances take, acting in the best interests of the assisted person.[21]

18.29   In *Re MB (Caesarean Section)*[22] the Court of Appeal held that a patient's best interests were not confined to his or her medical best interests and in *Re A (Medical Treatment: Male Sterilisation)*[23] the High Court considered that they could encompass medical, emotional and all other welfare issues.

18.30   MCA 2005 s4(1)–(7) provides:

Best interests

(1) In determining for the purposes of this Act what is in a person's best interests, the person making the determination must not make it merely on the basis of –
   (a) the person's age or appearance, or
   (b) a condition of his, or an aspect of his behaviour, which might lead others to make unjustified assumptions about what might be in his best interests.
(2) The person making the determination must consider all the relevant circumstances and, in particular, take the following steps.
(3) He must consider –
   (a) whether it is likely that the person will at some time have capacity in relation to the matter in question, and
   (b) if it appears likely that he will, when that is likely to be.
(4) He must, so far as reasonably practicable, permit and encourage the person to participate, or to improve his ability to participate, as fully as possible in any act done for him and any decision affecting him.
(5) Where the determination relates to life-sustaining treatment he must not, in considering whether the treatment is in the best interests of the person concerned, be motivated by a desire to bring about his death.
(6) He must consider, so far as is reasonably ascertainable –
   (a) the person's past and present wishes and feelings (and, in particular, any relevant written statement made by him when he had capacity),
   (b) the beliefs and values that would be likely to influence his decision if he had capacity, and
   (c) the other factors that he would be likely to consider if he were able to do so.
(7) He must take into account, if it is practicable and appropriate to consult them, the views of –
   (a) anyone named by the person as someone to be consulted on the matter in question or on matters of that kind,

---

21   Per Lord Goff at [75].
22   [1997] 2 FLR 426; [1997] FCR 541; (1998) 38 BMLR 175.
23   (2000) 53 BMLR 66, p72.

(b) anyone engaged in caring for the person or interested in his welfare,

(c) any donee of a lasting power of attorney granted by the person, and

(d) any deputy appointed for the person by the court,

as to what would be in the person's best interests and, in particular, as to the matters mentioned in subsection (6).

18.31 The Act does not, therefore, define best interests – for instance in terms of explaining whether the principle of 'doing what the person would have done (had they capacity)' trumps the principle of 'doing what is objectively considered best for them'. It merely lays down a process, at the end of which the decision maker is presumed to be able to form a reasonable belief as to what decision would be in the person's best interests. In doing this the decision-maker will (following the key steps in section 4) need to consider:

1) Whether the decision is really necessary – or if it could be put off. This may be of particular relevance for a person thought likely to recover capacity in the near future – for instance someone who has had a stroke, but is recovering or someone with fluctuating capacity. In such cases it might be in the person's best interest to delay any decision.

2) The present views of the incapacitated person – these are of great importance even if they are not ultimately determinative.

3) The person's past views – these are of primary relevance when ascertaining 'what they would have done' had they not lost capacity.

4) The views of significant others. In this analysis the Act gives no precedence to relatives. The aim is to ascertain from the relevant third parties (a) what they think the person would have done' had he or she not lost capacity as well as what they objectively think would be the best decision for that person.

'Necessity' and 'section 5 acts'

18.32 MCA 2005 s5 endeavours to convert the common law principle of necessity into statutory language. It does this by stipulating that if:

1) a person (eg a carer) 'acts in connection with the care or treatment of' someone believed to lack capacity; and

2) the person (eg a carer) has formed a reasonable belief as to:

   a) the person's lack of capacity and

   b) best interests,

3) then the person (eg the carer) will not be liable for the action – provided it is something that the incapacitated person could have consented to had he or she capacity.

18.33 Accordingly if a consultant in a hospital casualty ward is confronted by an unconscious patient who is haemorrhaging she might have a reasonable belief that (a) the person lacks capacity to consent to medical treatment; and (b) that to operate would be in the person's best interests. Since people can consent to medical treatment, in such a case the consultant could not be sued/prosecuted for assault. However if she was negligent in her treatment, section 5 would provide no defence because negligence is not something to which one can consent. Such acts are known as 'section 5 acts'. The explanatory notes to the bill explain that such acts may be performed by a range of people on any one day. The key requirements are that the person acts in connection with the care or treatment of another person and that the person carrying out the act has formed a reasonable belief as to the incapacitated person's lack of capacity and best interests.

18.34   The Code of Practice (at para 6.5) suggests that the following actions might be covered by section 5:

Personal care
- helping with washing, dressing or personal hygiene
- helping with eating and drinking
- helping with communication
- helping with mobility (moving around)
- helping someone take part in education, social or leisure activities
- going into a person's home to drop off shopping or to see if they are alright
- doing the shopping or buying necessary goods with the person's money
- arranging household services (for example, arranging repairs or maintenance for gas and electricity supplies)
- providing services that help around the home (such as homecare or meals on wheels)
- undertaking actions related to community care services (for example, day care, residential accommodation or nursing care) . . . [24]
- helping someone to move home (including moving property and clearing the former home).

Healthcare and treatment
- carrying out diagnostic examinations and tests (to identify an illness, condition or other problem)
- providing professional medical, dental and similar treatment
- giving medication
- taking someone to hospital for assessment or treatment
- providing nursing care (whether in hospital or in the community)
- carrying out any other necessary medical procedures (for example, taking a blood sample) or therapies (for example, physiotherapy or chiropody)
- providing care in an emergency.

---

24 In certain situations these changes may require external sanction – for instance the commissioning of a report by an Independent Mental Capacity Advocate – see para 18.67.

Paying for goods and services

18.35   Section 5 will also sanction the use of the money of incapacitated adults to pay for necessary goods and services when this is believed to be in the person's best interests. In such situations there will be no requirement for a lasting power of attorney or other Court of Protection order. What is 'necessary' for an individual depends in part upon his or her wealth and expectations, as the Code advises:

> 6.58 'Necessary' means something that is suitable to the person's condition in life (their place in society, rather than any mental or physical condition) and their actual requirements when the goods or services are provided (section 7(2)). The aim is to make sure that people can enjoy a similar standard of living and way of life to those they had before lacking capacity. For example, if a person who now lacks capacity previously chose to buy expensive designer clothes, these are still necessary goods – as long as they can still afford them. But they would not be necessary for a person who always wore cheap clothes, no matter how wealthy they were.

Restraint

18.36   Section 6 places limitations on certain section 5 acts: materially in relation to 'restraint', which is defined as the use or threat of force where the incapacitated person is resisting, and secondly on any restriction of liberty of movement (eg pulling someone away from the road, putting a seat belt on someone in a car or administering sedatives in order to undertake treatment).

18.37   Restraint can only be used when:

1) the person restraining reasonably believes it is necessary to prevent harm to the incapacitated person; and
2) it is proportionate both to:
   a) the likelihood of the harm and
   b) the seriousness of the harm; and
3) if it would not constitute detention under article 5(1) of the European Convention on Human Rights ('the Convention'). This requirement (under section 6(5)) will be repealed when MHA 2007 s50 Sch 9 Part 10 comes into force, which is expected to take place in 2008.

18.38   The Code of Practice (paras 6.40–6.53) contains an analysis of the principles involved when assessing the extent and reasonableness of any restraint including:

> 6.44 Anybody considering using restraint must have objective reasons to justify that restraint is necessary. They must be able to show that the person being cared for is likely to suffer harm unless proportionate restraint is used. A carer or professional must not use restraint just so that they can do something more easily. If restraint is necessary to prevent harm to the person who lacks capacity, it must be the minimum amount of force for the shortest time possible.

6.42   Healthcare and social care staff should also refer to:
- professional and other guidance on restraint or physical intervention, such as that issued by the Department of Health[25] or Welsh Assembly Government,[26] and
- limitations imposed by regulations and standards, such as the national minimum standards for care services.

Deprivation of liberty and the *Bournewood* gap

18.39   Although the Act permits reasonable restraint, it does not (pending amendment – see below) permit action which would amount to a deprivation of liberty for the purposes of article 5(1) of the Convention.

18.40   *HL v UK*[27] concerned a challenge in the European Court of Human Rights to a decision of the House of Lords, known as the *Bournewood* case.[28] The European Court held that the lack of any procedural protection for 'informally detained' patients violated article 5(1) and it rejected the UK's argument that such people were not 'detained', stating:

> . . . the right to liberty is too important in a democratic society for a person to lose the benefit of Convention protection for the single reason that he may have given himself up to be taken into detention . . . especially when it is not disputed that that person is legally incapable of consenting to, or disagreeing with, the proposed action.

18.41   In the Strasbourg Court's opinion, he was detained because he was 'under continuous supervision and control and was not free to leave'. Furthermore it was 'not determinative whether the ward was "locked" or "lockable"', and a person could be detained 'even during a period when he was in an open ward with regular unescorted access to the unsecured hospital grounds and unescorted leave outside the hospital'.

18.42   The Code of Practice gives the following advice concerning the distinction between restriction and deprivation of liberty:

> 6.52   It is difficult to define the difference between actions that amount to a restriction of someone's liberty and those that result in a deprivation of liberty. In recent legal cases, the European Court of Human Rights said that the difference was 'one of degree or intensity, not one of nature or substance'.[29] There must therefore be particular factors in the specific situation of the person concerned which provide the 'degree' or 'intensity' to result in a deprivation of liberty. In practice, this can relate to:
> - the type of care being provided
> - how long the situation lasts

---

25   For guidance on using restraint with people with learning disabilities and autistic spectrum disorder, see *Guidance for restrictive physical interventions* (published by the Department of Health and Department for Education and Skills and available at http://www.dh.gov.uk/assetRoot/04/06/84/61/04068461.pdf).

26   In Wales, the relevant guidance is the Welsh Assembly Government's *Framework for restrictive physical intervention policy and practice* (available at http://www.childrenfirst.wales.gov.uk/content/framework/phys-int-e.pdf).

27   (2005) 40 EHRR 32.

28   *R v Bournewood Community and Mental Health NHS Trust ex p L* [1998] 3 WLR 107; (1997) 1 CCLR 390.

29   *HL v UK* (2005) 40 EHRR 32 at [89].

- its effects, or
- the way in a particular situation came about.[30]

18.43   *JE v DE and Surrey CC*[31] concerned an elderly man (DE) with dementia placed by the council in a care home. The court, having concluded that he lacked capacity to decide where he should live, had to consider whether he was detained. The evidence was that he repeatedly expressed the wish to go home and that his wife was told that if she tried to take him home the police would be called. Legally this was an idle threat in that her husband was not formally detained under the MHA 1983. After considering these factors the court held that he had been deprived of his liberty noting (at [115] et seq):

> But the crucial question in this case . . . is not so much whether . . . DE's freedom or liberty was or is curtailed *within* the institutional setting. The fundamental issue in this case, in my judgment, is whether . . . DE has been and is deprived of his liberty to leave the Y home. And when I refer to leaving . . . I do not mean leaving for the purpose of some trip or outing approved by SCC or by those managing the institution; I mean leaving in the sense of removing himself permanently in order to live where and with whom he chooses, specifically removing himself to live at home with JE.

> After all . . . prisoners detained in an open prison may be subject to virtually no physical restraint within the prison, may be allowed to have extensive social and other contact with the outside world and may even be allowed to leave the prison from time to time, yet they are indubitably 'deprived of their liberty.' And the reason why this is so is because . . . they 'are not permitted to leave the place where they are detained and go anywhere they like and at any time they want.' . . .

> I agree, therefore . . . the crucial issue here [is] . . . whether DE . . . is or is not, 'free to leave'. And I agree . . . that DE . . . is not 'free to leave', and was and is, in that sense, completely under the control of SCC, because . . . it was and is SCC who decides the essential matters of where DE can live, whether he can leave and whether he can be with JE.

Mental Health Act 2007 reforms

18.44   MHA 2007 Part 2 chapter 2 will amend the MCA 2005 to authorise detention of people who lack capacity in certain situations. The amendments are likely to come into effect in late 2008 or 2009. The effect of the amendment is to create an alternative and complex detention procedure to that under the MHA 1983. In theory the procedure only applies to compliant, mentally incapacitated people for whom detention is required in order to protect them from harm. Such people can be detained under the MCA 2005 when, either an authorising authority has issued a

---

30 In *HL v UK* the European Court said that 'the key factor in the present case [is] that the health care professionals treating and managing the applicant exercised complete and effective control over his care and movements'. They found 'the concrete situation was that the applicant was under continuous supervision and control and was not free to leave'.

31 [2006] EWHC 3459 (Fam); (2007) 10 CCLR 149.

standard or urgent authorisation, or the Court of Protection has authorised detention as a condition on a person welfare order.

18.45   The amendments provide a procedure to decide whether a person should be deprived of his or her liberty under the Act and, if the situation is urgent,[32] the amendments also empower the Court of Protection to authorise a person's detention pending such a decision being made.

18.46   The MCA 2005 amendments create two new Schedules to the Act:

- Schedule A1, which sets out the detailed procedures and requirements relating to standard and urgent authorisations of deprivation of liberty in hospitals or care homes.
- Schedule 1A, which details who cannot be detained under the MCA 2005 procedures – primarily people subject to the MHA 1983 procedures.

Lasting powers of attorney

18.47   MCA 2005 ss9–14 replace enduring powers of attorney (EPAs) with a new statutory power – the lasting power of attorney (LPA). EPAs derive from the Enduring Powers of Attorney Act 1985 which enabled people (known as 'donors'), while they had sufficient capacity, to appoint an attorney whose powers would endure even if the donor then ceased to have capacity. Such attorneys are only authorised to make decisions concerning property and affairs. The attorney is under a duty to apply to the Office of the Public Guardian as soon as he or she has reason to believe that the donor is (or is becoming) mentally incapable. Before applying, the attorney must give notice of the intention to apply for registration of the EPA, to the donor, the donor's relatives and any 'co-attorney'. At least three relatives must receive the notice (and the Act states the priority of relative). People served with these notices have the power to object to registration. Failing an objection, the registration takes effect (within about 5–12 weeks).

18.48   Although no new EPAs can be created once the LPA provisions come into effect (expected to be October 2007) this rule will not affect EPAs created before that date. It appears, therefore that for many years to come such attorneys will be being registered with the Office of the Public Guardian and will continue to be part of the decision making process.

18.49   LPAs, however, unlike an EPA, will have the potential to make decisions concerning personal welfare matters (including health care and consent to medical treatment) as well as to property and affairs. A separate form must be completed to create a financial LPA and a personal welfare LPA and (if desired) different attorneys may be appointed to take these different types of decision.[33]

---

32 To enable life sustaining treatment or treatment believed necessary to prevent a serious deterioration in the person's condition.

33 It is anticipated that the forms to be used to create and register LPAs will be available on the Office of the Public Guardian's website.

18.50   Financial LPAs can be used both before and after the donor loses capacity, according to the donor's wishes. However, personal welfare LPAs can only be used when the donor lacks capacity to make a particular personal welfare decision. LPAs, unlike EPAs, will have to be registered before the power is used, even if the donor has capacity, unlike EPA which are only registered once the attorney has reason to believe that the donor is (or is becoming) mentally incapable.

18.51   It is proposed that all LPAs will have to contain a certificate from a 'third party' confirming that there has been no undue pressure put on the donor and that he or she has capacity. In addition, before it can be registered five people named by the donor will have to be notified (and given the right to object). If the donor does not wish anyone notified, then there will need to be two certificates from 'worthy' persons. It is proposed that separate forms will be used to appoint a financial LPA and social welfare LPA and that existing financial EPAs will continue to be valid.

Personal welfare lasting powers of attorney

18.52   The Code (at para 7.21) provides advice concerning the scope of personal welfare LPAs:

> LPAs can be used to appoint attorneys to make decisions about personal welfare, which can include healthcare and medical treatment decisions. Personal welfare LPAs might include decisions about:
> - where the donor should live and who they should live with
> - the donor's day-to-day care, including diet and dress
> - who the donor may have contact with
> - consenting to or refusing medical examination and treatment on the donor's behalf
> - arrangements needed for the donor to be given medical, dental or optical treatment
> - assessments for and provision of community care services
> - whether the donor should take part in social activities, leisure activities, education or training
> - the donor's personal correspondence and papers
> - rights of access to personal information about the donor, or
> - complaints about the donor's care or treatment.

18.53   The Code (at para 7.27) explains that even where an LPA includes health care decisions, attorneys do not have the right to consent to or refuse treatment in situations where:

- **the donor has capacity to make the particular healthcare decision (section 11(7)(a))**
  An attorney has no decision-making power if the donor can make their own treatment decisions.
- **the donor has made an advance decision to refuse the proposed treatment (section 11(7)(b))**
  An attorney cannot consent to treatment if the donor has made a

valid and applicable advance decision to refuse a specific treatment (see chapter 9). But if the donor made an LPA after the advance decision, and gave the attorney the right to consent to or refuse the treatment, the attorney can choose not to follow the advance decision.

- **a decision relates to life-sustaining treatment (section 11(7)(c))**
  An attorney has no power to consent to or refuse life-sustaining treatment, unless the LPA document expressly authorises this . . .
- **the donor is detained under the Mental Health Act (section 28)**
  An attorney cannot consent to or refuse treatment for a mental disorder for a patient detained under the Mental Health Act 1983.

Property and affairs lasting powers of attorney

18.54   A property and affairs LPA can limit the powers of the attorney to certain acts, although if unrestricted, a general property and affairs LPA would cover actions such as those listed below (extracted from para 7.36 of the Code):

- buying or selling property
- opening, closing or operating any bank, building society or other account
- giving access to the donor's financial information
- claiming, receiving and using (on the donor's behalf) all benefits, pensions, allowances and rebates (unless the Department for Work and Pensions has already appointed someone and everyone is happy for this to continue)
- receiving any income, inheritance or other entitlement on behalf of the donor
- dealing with the donor's tax affairs
- paying the donor's mortgage, rent and household expenses
- insuring, maintaining and repairing the donor's property
- investing the donor's savings
- making limited gifts on the donor's behalf
- paying for private medical care and residential care or nursing home fees
- applying for any entitlement to funding for NHS care, social care or adaptations
- using the donor's money to buy a vehicle or any equipment or other help they need
- repaying interest and capital on any loan taken out by the donor.

Court of Protection powers and deputies

18.55   MCA 2005 ss45–61 abolishes the former Court of Protection and creates a new one, which is to be part of the High Court: it is intended that the new court will have a regional presence initially (in addition to London, in Birmingham, Bristol, Cardiff, Manchester/Preston and Newcastle). Sections 15–21 detail the powers of the new Court of Protection – which will include the power to make declarations – as discussed below. It will additionally be able to appoint a deputy (rather than a 'receiver') to make substitute decisions about personal welfare matters as well as issues concerning the property and affairs of persons lacking capacity.

18.56   Section 20 sets a number of limitations on the powers of deputies. They cannot make decisions prohibiting a person from having contact with the adult lacking capacity or to direct a person responsible for the health care of the person lacking capacity to allow a different person to take over the health care: such decisions must be made by the court.

Social security appointees

18.57   Social security claimants are able to nominate a person to collect their benefits for them when they are unable, due to illness or other circumstances, to collect the benefits personally. In such cases the person collecting the benefit is simply acting as an 'agent' for the claimant. Such agency arrangements can however only occur in respect of claimants who have the requisite mental capacity to manage their social security monies.

18.58   Social Security (Claims and Payments) Regulations 1987[34] reg 33 allows for an appointee to be appointed where the claimant is 'unable for the time being to act'. Guidance suggests that persons are unable to act if they 'do not have the mental ability to understand and control their own affairs, for example because of senility or mentally illness'.

18.59   The Department for Work and Pensions is the responsible authority for the appointment, supervision and revocation of appointeeships. The appointee is personally responsible for ensuring that the social security monies are applied in the patient's interests.[35]

18.60   Standard 35 of the *National Minimum Standards for Care Homes for Older People*[36] states that the registered manager of a care home may only be appointed as agent for a service user where no other individual is available. In such cases the manager must ensure that the registration authority is notified of this arrangement and that records are kept of all incoming and outgoing payments. Additionally, if the manager is an appointee for social security purposes the relevant social security office must be notified. Age Concern has stated that 'although the home

---

34   SI No 1968.
35   See CIS/12022/96 which concerned an appointee's failure to notify the DSS about an increase in the disabled person's savings; the consequent over payment was held to be recoverable from the appointee in addition to the claimant.
36   Department of Health, March 2001 issued under CSA 2000 s23(1).

proprietor may be prepared to manage an individual's financial affairs, large groups of homes may have a specific Finance Department, it should be remembered that no available guidance recommends this. It should therefore be considered only as a last resort, and all the parties involved must ensure that the appropriate safeguards are observed.'[37]

18.61   Concern has also been expressed about the lack of protection for people who are the subject of an appointeeship order,[38] including the lack of any adequate appeal provision. At present all that an individual can do in such cases is to request that the secretary of state exercise his or her discretion to revoke such an order. It is arguable that this state of affairs conflicts with article 6(1) of the Convention.

Advance decisions to refuse treatment

18.62   MCA 2005 ss24–26 put on a limited statutory basis 'living wills'. This, however, only covers advance decisions (ADs) to refuse treatment. These can only be made by persons 18 or over who have capacity. The Act does not impose any particular formalities concerning the format of ADs to refuse treatment or the procedures involved in making an AD, except for decisions relating to life-sustaining treatment. Although ADs concerning the refusal of other types of treatment may be written or oral, para 9.19 of the Code provides a checklist of information that it would be helpful to find in any written statement, namely:

- full details of the person making the advance decision, including date of birth, home address and any distinguishing features (in case health-care professionals need to identify an unconscious person, for example)
- the name and address of the person's GP and whether they have a copy of the document
- a statement that the document should be used if the person ever lacks capacity to make treatment decisions
- a clear statement of the decision, the treatment to be refused and the circumstances in which the decision will apply
- the date the document was written (or reviewed)
- the person's signature (or the signature of someone the person has asked to sign on their behalf and in their presence)
- the signature of the person witnessing the signature, if there is one (or a statement directing somebody to sign on the person's behalf).

---

37 *Residents Money*, Age Concern, 1996.
38 See eg Parliamentary Ombudsman annual report Session 2002–2003 (5th report) case reference C1560/02.

Advance decisions to refuse life-sustaining treatment

18.63 MCA 2005 s25 imposes strict formalities concerning ADs refusing life-sustaining treatment. Paragraph 9.24 of the Code of Practice lists the requirements for a valid AD refusing life-sustaining treatment:

- They must be put in writing. If the person is unable to write, someone else should write it down for them. For example, a family member can write down the decision on their behalf, or a healthcare professional can record it in the person's healthcare notes.
- The person must sign the advance decision. If they are unable to sign, they can direct someone to sign on their behalf in their presence.
- The person making the decision must sign in the presence of a witness to the signature. The witness must then sign the document in the presence of the person making the advance decision. If the person making the advance decision is unable to sign, the witness can witness them directing someone else to sign on their behalf. The witness must then sign to indicate that they have witnessed the nominated person signing the document in front of the person making the advance decision.
- The advance decision must include a clear, specific written statement from the person making the advance decision that the advance decision is to apply to the specific treatment even if life is at risk.
- If this statement is made at a different time or in a separate document to the advance decision, the person making the advance decision (or someone they have directed to sign) must sign it in the presence of a witness, who must also sign it.

18.64 Section 4(10) defines life sustaining treatment as treatment which a person providing health care regards as necessary to sustain life. The Code at para 9.25 explains that whether a treatment is 'life sustaining' or not depends not only on the type of treatment, but also on the particular circumstances in which it may be prescribed – for example 'in some situations antibiotics may be life-sustaining, but in others they can be used to treat conditions that do not threaten life'.

18.65 An AD may not refuse measures that are necessary to keep a patient comfortable, sometimes called basic or essential care – eg warmth, shelter, action to keep a person clean. The Code explains at para 9.28 that this also includes the offer 'of food and water by mouth' – but that an AD 'can refuse artificial nutrition and hydration'.

18.66 An AD will not apply where the person who created it has not lost his or her capacity to make the decision;[39] or if it is defective, eg the person lacked capacity when he or she created it;[40] or it relates to life sustaining

---

39 See eg *Re C (Adult Refusal of Medical Treatment)* [1994] 1 WLR 290.
40 See eg *NHS Trust v T* [2004] EWHC 1279 (Fam); [2005] 1 All ER 387; (2005) 8 CCLR 38.

treatment and does not comply with the above detailed formalities; or there is evidence to believe that the person may have changed his or her mind since creating it;[41] or the treatment in issue is not covered (or was not anticipated) by the AD.[42]

Independent mental capacity advocate service

18.67   The role of the independent mental capacity advocate (IMCA) service and the powers and duties of individual advocates stem from MCA 2005 ss35–41, and are fleshed out in regulations[43] and are the subject of detailed guidance in chapter 10 of the Code of Practice. In addition, guidance for Commissioners on the independent mental capacity advocate service has been published by Turning Point.[44] It is the responsibility of local authorities in England and local health boards in Wales to commission and fund the service.

18.68   The IMCA's role is to support and represent the person who lacks capacity, and when acting in this role the IMCA has the right to see relevant health care and social care records.[45] The local authority/NHS is obliged to take into account the IMCA's comments and findings as part of their decision-making process. An IMCA must be independent of the decision-maker and must support and represent the incapacitated person to identify and promote his or her best interests.

18.69   MCA 2005 ss35–41 require (save in cases of emergency)[46] that an IMCA must be instructed, and then consulted, for people lacking capacity who have no one else to support them (ie no family or friends)[47] (other than paid staff), whenever:

---

41   MCA 2005 s25(2)(c): 'has done anything else clearly inconsistent with the advance decision remaining his fixed decision' – and see eg *HE v A Hospital NHS Trust* [2003] EWHC 1017 (Fam); [2003] 2 FLR 408.

42   MCA 2005 s25(4) lists various examples, namely that treatment is not the treatment specified in the AD, or any circumstances specified in the AD are absent, or there are reasonable grounds for believing that circumstances exist which the person creating the AD did not anticipate at the time of the AD and which would have affected the decision.

43   Mental Capacity Act 2005 (Independent Mental Capacity Advocate) (General) Regulations 2006 SI No 1832; Mental Capacity Act 2005 (Independent Mental Capacity Advocate) (Expansion of Role) Regulations 2006 SI No 2883; Mental Capacity Act 2005 (Independent Mental Capacity Advocate) (Wales) Regulations 2007 SI No 852 (W77).

44   *Guidance for Commissioners on the Independent Mental Capacity Advocate Service*, Turning Point, 2006.

45   MCA 2005 s35(6)(b).

46   MCA 2005 ss37(4) and 39(4)(b). In such cases the Code of Practice (para 10.24) requires that where the decision concerned a move of accommodation, the local authority must appoint an IMCA as soon as possible afterwards. In relation to serious medical treatment, para 10.46 of the Code states that an IMCA will be required for any serious treatment that follows the emergency treatment.

47   A financial LPA or a financial attorney does not count, when deciding whether there is support available to the person lacking capacity – MHA 2007 Sch 9 (which amends MCA 2005 ss38–39).

- an NHS body is proposing to provide (or withhold) serious medical treatment,[48] or
- an NHS body or local authority is proposing to arrange accommodation (or a change of accommodation) in hospital or a care home, and
  - the person will stay in hospital longer than 28 days, or
  - the person will stay in the care home for more than eight weeks.

18.70 The Code of Practice explains (at paras 10.51–10.58) that the obligation to instruct an IMCA in relation to a change of accommodation decision arises where accommodation is provided or arranged by the NHS, or the local authority or under MHA 1983 s117. This includes placements:

- by the NHS of a person in a hospital or a decision to move the person to another hospital for any period in excess of 28 days; or
- by the NHS and/or a local authority in a care home or its equivalent[49] for what is likely to be longer than eight weeks.

18.71 The local authority obligation only arises, however, where it has assessed the person under NHS and Community Care Act 1990 s47(1) and has decided it has a duty to accommodate the person under the community care legislation. The role of the IMCA in such an accommodation decision may be of some complexity where the person is in hospital but ordinarily resident in another authority. Presumably, in order to make the decision, the IMCA will need to have some knowledge of alternatives available in that other area as well as contacting the care management professionals in the other area.

18.72 In addition to the mandatory grounds for the appointment of an IMCA, Regulations[50] provide that one may be instructed to support someone who lacks capacity to make decisions concerning:

- care reviews, where no one else is available to be consulted;[51]
- adult protection cases, whether or not family, friends or others are involved.[52]

18.73 Where, after providing his or her report, an IMCA disagrees with the NHS or local authority decision and this cannot be resolved by discussion,

---

48 Para 10.45 of the Code states that it is impossible to set out all types of procedures that may amount to 'serious medical treatment', but by way of illustration suggests chemotherapy, ECT, sterilisation, major surgery (such as open-heart surgery or brain/neuro-surgery), major amputations, treatments which will result in permanent loss of hearing or sight, the withholding or stopping artificial nutrition and hydration, and termination of pregnancy.

49 Which para 10.11 of the Code states would include a care home, nursing home, ordinary and sheltered housing, housing association or other registered social housing or private sector housing provided by a local authority or hostel accommodation.

50 Mental Capacity Act 2005 (Independent Mental Capacity Advocate) (Expansion of Role) Regulations 2006 regs 3 and 4.

51 Code of Practice para 10.62.

52 Ibid, para 10.66.

the IMCA is empowered to make a formal complaint challenging a decision.[53]

18.74   The Code makes clear (at paras 10.37–10.39) that an IMCA can pursue a complaint as far as the relevant ombudsman if needed. In particularly serious or urgent cases, an IMCA may seek permission to refer a case to the Court of Protection or even for a judicial review, having first sought the assistance of the Official Solicitor.

---

53   Mental Capacity Act 2005 (Independent Mental Capacity Advocate) (General) Regulations 2006 reg 7 provides that the IMCA 'has the same rights to challenge the decision as he would have if he were a person (other than an IMCA) engaged in caring for P or interested in his welfare'.

Learning disability: policy and services

Introduction

19.1   It is estimated that there are about 210,000 people with severe learning disabilities in England, and about 1.2 million with a mild or moderate disability. Annual health and social services expenditure on services for adults with learning disabilities amounts to approximately £3 billion.[1]

19.2   People with learning disabilities come within the definition of a 'disabled person' (see para 9.33 above) for the purposes of the primary community care statutes (ie National Assistance Act (NAA) 1948 and Chronically Sick and Disabled Persons Act (CSDPA) 1970 s21) as well as the Disability Discrimination Act (DDA) 1995. It follows that they have an equal right to services under these statutes and that any difference in treatment, based upon a categorisation of 'learning disability', will require justification under the 1995 Act.

19.3   The service provision needs of people with learning disabilities are such that in a number of situations policy and practice guidance singles them out for specific mention. This can be seen, for instance, in relation to the obligations on the NHS to fund long term support arrangements (see para 14.102) and in relation to the 'less dependent residents' provisions that apply to some people with learning disabilities receiving services under NAA 1948 s21 (see para 8.111).

19.4   In 2001 the Department of Health[2] published the white paper *Valuing People: A New Strategy for Learning Disability for the 21st Century*[3] which promised a number of new policy initiatives[4] concerning the rights of people with learning disabilities and undertook to ensure that four key principles would underpin all new proposals: 'Rights, Independence, Choice and Inclusion'.

19.5   In large measure the white paper sought to ensure that existing schemes (such as the Quality Protects programme,[5] the Schools Access

---

1   Department of Health, *Valuing People: A New Strategy for Learning Disability for the 21st Century*, Cm 5086, March 2001, p2.
2   No equivalent paper has been published in Wales. There is however an emerging programme being developed by the Learning Disability Implementation Advisory Group (whose reports can be accessed at http://www.ldiag.org.uk); see also in this respect the report *Fulfilling the Promises*, 2001, produced by All Wales People First and obtainable from Mencap Cymru, 31 Lambourne Crescent, Cardiff Business Park, Llanishen, Cardiff CF14 5GF.
3   Cm 5086, March 2001.
4   Including a new Learning Disability Development Fund of £50 million per annum to support (among other things) the modernisation of day centres, enabling people to move from long stay hospitals into the community, developing supported living schemes and specialist local services for people with severe challenging behaviour and developing integrated facilities for children with severe disabilities and complex needs. Additionally an Implementation Support Fund of £2.3 million a year to fund advocacy programmes, a national information centre and help line.
5   The programme seeks to tackle the social exclusion of children looked after by councils; children in the child protection system; and other children in need – details at http://www.doh.gov.uk/qualityprotects.

Initiative and the Connexions Service[6]) were sensitive to the needs of people with learning disabilities.[7] It additionally committed the government to take measures to increase the potential for people with learning disabilities to benefit from direct payments, and to improve their access to advocacy services. In relation to direct payments the subsequent guidance has emphasised the policy aim of increasing take up from this client group (see para 12.19), and much of the research concerning 'individual budgets' (see para 12.72 above) has focused on its potential for people with learning disabilities.

19.6   The white paper proposed the development within each local authority area of learning disability partnership boards whose responsibility it would be to implement the adult aspects of the programme. Policy guidance in 2001[8] outlined the composition and responsibilities of these boards. This has since been followed up by more detailed practice guidance on implementation.[9]

Wales

19.7   In Wales the Assembly is still in the process of formulating its policy in this area. The Welsh Office's 1983 *All Wales Strategy for the development of Services for Mentally Handicapped People* remains the underpinning policy, as updated in 1994 by 'Revised Guidance'.[10] In 1999 a Learning Disability Implementation Advisory Group (LDIAG) was charged with the preparation of a draft framework of services designed to promote the interests of people with learning disabilities along similar lines to that proposed by the Department of Health's white paper *Valuing People*. A 2001 report from the Advisory Group *Fulfilling the Promises*[11] was adopted in principle by the Assembly and a new LDIAG commissioned to take the policy forwards. The Assembly in 2004 issued policy guidance which at present is the key policy document. As with *Valuing People* it advocates such matters as 'person-centred' approaches to individual planning, adequate advocacy support, joint working-partnership in planning and community living.[12] In 2006 the LDIAG published (for consultation) its proposals for

6   The Connexions service offers a range of guidance and support for 13 to 19-year-olds to help make the transition to adult life a smooth one.

7   This aims to make mainstream schools more accessible to children with disabilities and special educational needs – details at http://www.teachernet.gov.uk/management/sen/schools/accessibility/sai.

8   *Valuing People: a New Strategy for Learning Disability for the 21stCentury: Implementation Guidance*HSC 2001/016: LAC(2001)23 (policy guidance for the purposes of Local Authority Social Services Act 1970 s7 (see para 1.46 above).

9   See Department of Health, *Planning with People Towards Person Centred Approaches – Guidance For Partnership Boards*, 2001.

10   Neither the original 1983 Strategy nor the 1994 guidance is accessible on the internet.

11   LDIAG, *Fulfilling the Promises*, 2001, accessible at http://www.allwalespeople1st.co.uk/downloads/fulfillingthepromises.pdf.

12   Welsh Assembly, *Section 7 Guidance on Service Principles and Service Responses for Adults and Older Persons with a Learning Disability*, 2004.

future development of this area.[13] The Assembly's response to the consultation is presently pending.[14]

Definition and IQ

19.8   *Valuing People* does not attempt an exhaustive definition of what constitutes a learning disability, but at para 1.5 states that it includes the presence of:

- A significantly reduced ability to understand new or complex information, to learn new skills (impaired intelligence), with;
- A reduced ability to cope independently (impaired social functioning);
- which started before adulthood, with a lasting effect on development.

19.9   At para 1.6 it goes on to caution against over reliance on IQ scores. Not infrequently however, some local authorities do define learning disability in such terms – typically having a score of less than 70 or 75. There has been substantial criticism of such an approach[15] and reliance on this fact alone could not be considered a rational way of approaching the community care assessment duty.

19.10   Although the Department of Health's definition includes many people with (amongst other conditions) autism, it would not cover someone with a higher level autistic spectrum disorder who may be of average or even above average intelligence – such as some people with Asperger's Syndrome.[16] This does not however mean that such a person is not 'disabled' within the meaning of the community care legislation or the Children Act (CA) 1989 or indeed the DDA 1995.[17] The definition of 'disabled' under NAA 1948 s29 and CA 1989 s17(11) includes persons with a 'mental disorder of any kind' which under Mental Health Act (MHA) 1983 s1 is defined as including, not just the specified disorders (mental illness, arrested or incomplete development of the mind and a psychopathic disorder) but also 'any other disorder or disability of mind'. It follows that a person with (say) Asperger's Syndrome who had an above average IQ would still be entitled to community care services if an assessment revealed an eligible need.

---

13 LDIAG,*Proposed statement on policy and practice for adults with a learning disability*, 2006.
14 As at July 2007.
15 There is an extensive literature on this question, but see eg D Francis *et al*, 'Defining learning and language disabilities' (1996) 27 *Language, Speech, and Hearing Services in Schools* 132–143; and L Siegel, 'IQ is irrelevant to the definition of learning disabilities' (1989) 22(8) *The Journal of Learning Disabilities* 469–478, 486.
16 *Valuing People* para 1.6.
17 See eg *Dunham v Ashford Windows* [2005] IRLR 608, EAT.

Person-centred planning

19.11 A key phrase emerging from the white paper is that of a 'person-centred approach' to the needs of people with learning disabilities to enable them 'to have as much choice and control as possible over their lives'.

19.12 The need for such an approach is explained in at para 4.1 of the white paper in the following terms:

> People with learning disabilities currently have little control over their own lives, though almost all, including the most severely disabled, are capable of making choices and expressing their views and preferences. The current problems are:
>
> - Services have been too slow to recognise that people with learning disabilities have rights like other citizens;
> - Provision of advocacy services is patchy;
> - People with learning disabilities have little involvement in decision making;
> - Few people with learning disabilities receive direct payments;
> - People with learning disabilities and their families are not central to the planning process;
> - Not enough effort to communicate with people with learning disabilities in accessible ways.

19.13 Follow-up 2001 practice guidance[18] stipulated that the development of a person-centred approach in organisational cultures and practice was a priority for partnership boards who were required to produce a framework for implementation of this approach by April 2002. The guidance defined 'person centred planning' as:[19]

> . . . a *process* for continual listening and learning, focussed on what is important to someone now and for the future, and acting upon this in alliance with family and friends. This listening and learning is used to understand a person's capacities and choices. Person centred planning is a basis for problem solving and negotiation to mobilise the resources necessary to pursue the person's aspirations. These resources may be obtained from a person's personal network, from service agencies or from a range of non-specialist and non-service sources.

19.14 Although it has now become common to refer to the care plans for people with learning disabilities as 'person centred plans', this is a mis-nomer. As the 2001 guidance explains:[20]

> Person centred planning is not the same as assessment and care planning under section 47 of the NHS and Community Care Act (1990). Assessment and care planning should, however be undertaken using person centred *approaches* and is greatly assisted by person centred planning undertaken independently of it. Where services are required, formal assessment might

---

18 Department of Health, *Planning with People Towards Person Centred Approaches – Guidance For Partnership Boards*, 2001.
19 Ibid, p2.
20 Ibid, p4.

well be triggered by person centred planning. [Neither is it] the same as reviews of service provision. Person centred planning should, however, make a significant contribution to reviews, ensuring that they are based on what matters to a person from their own perspective.

Service reconfigurations

19.15 The white paper[21] sought to address the severe social exclusion experienced by many people with learning disabilities by endeavouring (among other things) to bring about service reconfigurations including (para 4.19) a requirement that local bodies make 'significant progress' in relation to the reduction of the use of large day centres. In the government's opinion (at para 1.18) some of these offered little more than 'warehousing'. Authorities were to replace these services with flexible and individual support, the white paper stating:

> 7.25 These problems will be addressed through a five year programme to support local councils in modernising their day services. Our aim will be to ensure that the resources currently committed to day centres are focused on providing people with learning disabilities with new opportunities to lead full and purposeful lives. Securing the active involvement of people with learning disabilities and their families in redesigning services will be essential to the success of the programme. The Government recognises that, for many families, day centres have provided essential respite from the day to day demands of caring. The services that replace them must result in improvements for both users and their families. The needs of people with profound or complex disabilities will be carefully considered as part of the modernisation programme.

Exclusions from services

19.16 The local government ombudsman has criticised councils that have excluded disabled people from services because of their challenging behaviour – where that behaviour was part and parcel of their condition (see para 4.34 above). In so doing the ombudsman has cited[22] with approval the following reference in the white paper:

> Excluding people with learning disabilities from services if they are found to be difficult to handle or present with challenging behaviour represents a major source of stress for carers, who may be left unsupported to cope with their son or daughter at home. This practice is unacceptable and families must not be left to cope unaided. No service should be withdrawn on these grounds without identifying alternative options and putting a suitable alternative service in place where possible. Decisions to exclude a person with learning disabilities from a service should always be referred to the Learning Disability Partnership Board, which will be responsible for the provision of alternative services in such cases . . .[23]

21 *Valuing People* para 7.21.
22 Complaint no 03/C/16371 against Stockton-on-Tees BC, 18 January 2005 para 13.
23 *Valuing People* para 5.7 and see also HSC 2001/016: LAC (2001)23 paras 37 and 38.

19.17   A 2004 ombudsman's complaint[24] concerned a young man with challenging behaviour associated with his autism. The council, largely for resource reasons, placed him in insufficiently supportive accommodation on his transition from schooling. His mother was strongly opposed to the placement, but her views were not properly heeded. In the ombudsman's view the council ignored her objections 'and attempted to force on the family its [placement] decision'. In so doing 'it ignored both the principles of the White Paper "Valuing People" and the impracticality of trying to integrate [the young man] successfully into a placement his mother (to whom he is very close) did not accept'.

19.18   The council, because of its failure to undertake a proper assessment, underestimated how extreme his response to change could be and failed to take into account how severely challenging his behaviour became when he was under stress. His behaviour became so violent that he was eventually detained under MHA 1983 s3 and remained in a locked psychiatric ward for 18 months. The ombudsman concluded that this was because 'the Council failed to fund an appropriate alternative placement'. In her opinion, although the 'decision to detain him was lawful, [he] was only in this situation because of the failure by the Council to make proper provision to meet his needs'. She considered that there was 'no excuse for the Council's failure to anticipate the level of violence and destructive behaviour of which [he was] capable when faced with sudden change or social situations that he finds difficult or frightening'. The report recommended a total of £30,000 compensation be paid.

Advocacy and learning disability services

19.19   Independent advocacy services exist in most parts of England and Wales and have many different names and functions.[25] Broadly, however, they can be divided into the following two general categories:

Citizen advocacy

19.20   Citizen advocacy involves 'developing a longer term relationship with the disabled person'.[26] It is a form of advocacy where 'an ordinary citizen develops a relationship with another person who risks social exclusion or other unfair treatment because of a handicap. As the relationship develops, the advocate chooses ways to understand, respond to, and represent the other person's interests as if they were the advocate's own.'[27]

---

24   Complaint no 02/C/17068 against Bolton MBC, 30 November 2004.
25   For a review of the role of advocacy see R Henderson and M Pochin, *A Right Result?* Policy Press, 2001.
26   See eg A Dunning, *Citizen Advocacy with Older People: a Code of Good Practice*, CPA, 1995.
27   See B Sang and J O'Brien, *Advocacy: the United Kingdom and American experiences*, King's Fund Project paper no 51, 1984, p27.

Crisis advocacy

19.21   Crisis advocacy is generally concerned with short tem interventions, most commonly in relation to a dispute or complaint. The following sections are primarily concerned with the provision of this form of advocacy support.

19.22   While the white paper[28] acknowledged that effective advocacy, including self-advocacy, had the ability to transform the lives of people with learning disabilities, it cautioned that:

> . . . both citizen advocacy and self-advocacy are unevenly developed across the country. Barriers to future development include: insecure funding; limited support for local groups; and potential for conflicts of interest with statutory agencies who provide funding. This must change.

19.23   In order to address the problem it committed the government to the (long term) aim of 'developing a range of independent advocacy services available in each area so that people with learning disabilities can choose the one which best meets their needs' (para 4.9) and to establish 'a National Citizen Advocacy Network and to promote self-advocacy, both in partnership with the voluntary sector'; the aim being to ensure the establishment of at least one citizen advocacy group in each local authority area. Advocacy arrangements were accordingly made a high priority for the new learning disability partnership boards.[29] In its 2005 review[30] the Department of Health referred to its continuing (indirect) funding of advocacy services[31] although it expressed concern (at para 4.1.7) that much local authority 'advocacy funding is short-term, which makes it difficult for advocacy organisations to plan for the future' and recommended that 'councils and other funders need to find ways of providing more secure funding'.

19.24   The Mental Capacity Act 2005 makes specific provision for an independent mental capacity advocacy service (IMCA), which provides assistance when certain significant decisions are being made concerning adults who lack sufficient mental capacity to make the decisions themselves. The role of the IMCA is considered at para 18.67 above.

---

28 *Valuing People* para 4.7.
29 See LAC (2001)23 para 27
30 Department of Health, *The story so far . . . Valuing People*, 2005.
31 Ibid, para 2.4.4, that through its Learning Disability Development Fund £40 million (2005/06) is provided which 'has made a real difference' in particular 'for advocacy and person centred planning'.

CHAPTER 20

Older people: policy and services

Introduction

20.1   Today a fifth of the population of the UK is over 60, and the proportion is growing – particularly in relation to people aged over 80. It is estimated that between 1995 and 2025 the numbers of people over 80 will increase by 50 per cent and the number of people over 90 will double. At present almost 45 per cent of both the NHS's and social services' budgets are spent on people over the age of 65.[1] About 600,000 such older people receive domiciliary services from the local authority and about 480,000 are in care homes (about 1 in 20 of all elderly people).[2] In terms of social services care home expenditure alone, this equates to approximately £8.2 billion per annum with over £1.5 billion being recouped in charges.[3]

20.2   In response to the social and health care challenges posed by an ageing population, the government in England published in 2001 a *National Service Framework for Older People* (NSF).[4] The NSF sets out eight key standards, providing in each case guidance on the local action required to ensure these are implemented – with detailed timescales and 'milestones to ensure progress, with performance measures to support performance improvement'. The eight standards are as follows:

1. *Rooting out age discrimination*
    NHS services will be provided, regardless of age, on the basis of clinical need alone. Social care services will not use age in their eligibility criteria or policies, to restrict access to available services.

2. *Person-centred care*
    NHS and social care services treat older people as individuals and enable them to make choices about their own care. This is achieved through the single assessment process, integrated commissioning arrangements and integrated provision of services, including community equipment and continence services.

3. *Intermediate care*
    Older people will have access to a new range of intermediate care services at home or in designated care settings, to promote their independence by providing enhanced services from the NHS and councils to prevent unnecessary hospital admission and effective rehabilitation services to enable early discharge from hospital and to prevent premature or unnecessary admission to long-term residential care.

---

1   Commission for Healthcare Audit and Inspection, *Living well in later life: A review of progress against the National Service Framework for Older People*, 2006, p5.
2   Royal Commission on Long Term Care report *With Respect to old age*, Cm 4192, TSO, 1999.
3   Information Centre, *Personal Social Services Expenditure and Unit Costs England, 2005–06*, 2007.
4   See para 1.61 above: in Wales the equivalent initiative is *The Strategy for Older People in Wales*, 2003.

4. *General hospital care*
   Older people's care in hospital is delivered through appropriate specialist care and by hospital staff who have the right set of skills to meet their needs.

5. *Stroke*
   The NHS will take action to prevent strokes, working in partnership with other agencies where appropriate. People who are thought to have had a stroke have access to diagnostic services, are treated appropriately by a specialist stroke service, and subsequently, with their carers, participate in a multidisciplinary programme of secondary prevention and rehabilitation.

6. *Falls*
   The NHS, working in partnership with councils, takes action to prevent falls and reduce resultant fractures or other injuries in their populations of older people. Older people who have fallen receive effective treatment and, with their carers, receive advice on prevention through a specialised falls service.

7. *Mental health in older people*
   Older people who have mental health problems have access to integrated mental health services, provided by the NHS and councils to ensure effective diagnosis, treatment and support, for them and for their carers.

8. *The promotion of health and active life in older age*
   The health and well-being of older people is promoted through a co-ordinated programme of action led by the NHS with support from councils.

Older people and the single assessment process

20.3 Key Standard 2 (above) of the 2001 NSF committed the government to improve the assessment process for older people – particularly to reduce the number of times they had to tell their story to different professionals and be subject to multiple assessments within the NHS and social care, stating at para 2.29:

> All older people should receive good assessment which is matched to their individual circumstances. Some older people will benefit from a fuller assessment across a number of areas or domains . . . and some may need more detailed assessment of one, or a few, specialist areas. The single assessment process should be designed to identify all of their needs. For the older person, it will also mean far less duplication and worry – the fuller assessment can be carried out by one front-line professional and where other professionals need to be involved to provide specialist assessment this will be arranged for the older person, to provide a seamless service.

20.4 Although in theory the single assessment process (SAP) is operational throughout England, the evidence suggests that the assessment process for older people still leaves much to be desired. In 2006, for instance, a joint report by the Commission for Social Care Inspection, the Healthcare Commission and the Audit Commission expressed the need for a 'change of culture' of the assessment process, and the need to move away from:

> . . . services being service-led to being person centred, so that older people have a central role not only in designing their care with the combination and type of service that most suits them, but also in planning the range of services that are available to all older people.[5]

20.5   Guidance[6] on the SAP has been issued to health and social services bodies and requires that they have fully integrated commissioning arrangements and integrated provision of services including community services and continence services.

20.6   Apart from the insistence on a joint health/social services assessment process, the SAP guidance is in many respects a gloss on the Fair Access to Care Services (FACS) guidance and reference should be made to chapter 3 where this guidance is further considered. Such assessments cannot in fact be 'unified' in the legal sense, unless the agencies have entered into formal partnership arrangements under NHS Act (NHSA) 2006 s75[7] (see para 13.122 above).

Wales

20.7   In Wales the Unified and Fair System for Assessing and Managing Care (UFSAMC) 2002 policy guidance[8] (see para 3.26 above) constitutes the equivalent guidance (ie effectively a combined FACS and SAP document).

Commissioner for Older People (Wales)

20.8   The Commissioner for Older People (Wales) Act 2006 empowers the Welsh Assembly to create a post of Commissioner for Older People and to clarify his or her role through regulations.[9] The Assembly considers that the Commissioner's role will be to ensure that the interests of older people in Wales, who are aged 60 or more, are safeguarded and promoted.

SAP and the care programme approach

20.9   Severe misgivings have been expressed about the quality of older persons' mental health services compared to the equivalent services provided for young persons: that the 'division between mental health services for adults of working age and older people has resulted in the development of an unfair system'.[10]

---

5   Commission for Healthcare Audit and Inspection, *Living well in later life: A review of progress against the National Service Framework for Older People*, 2006, p9.

6   In particular HSC 2002/001: LAC (2002)1 *Guidance on the Single Assessment Process for Older People*, January 2002. The guidance is also considered at para 3.31 above.

7   NHS (Wales) Act (NHS(W)A) 2006 s33.

8   Welsh Assembly, *The Unified and Fair System for Assessing and Managing Care*, 2002.

9   Commissioner for Older People in Wales Regulations 2007 SI No 398 (W44).

10 Commission for Healthcare Audit and Inspection, *Living well in later life: A review of progress against the National Service Framework for Older People*, 2006, p7.

20.10   The Department of Health has issued a clarification note[11] concerning the interface between these two assessment regimes (the care programme approach (CPA) process is considered at para 21.7 below). The guidance advises:

- The CPA should be applied to older people with severe mental illness due to schizophrenia or other psychoses. The assessment of their needs should be based on the SAP for older people.
- SAP, plus critical aspects of CPA, should be applied to other older people with severe functional or organic mental health problems, who were they younger would be provided for under CPA.
- When individuals subject to CPA reach old age, switches to SAP are not inevitable, and should only be made in the best interests of individuals and the continuity of their care.

Advocacy and older people

20.11   Increasing attention is being given to the important role that advocacy services can fulfil in ensuring that the needs of older people are properly addressed. In this respect the SAP guidance advises:[12]

Agencies should consider at the earliest opportunity whether older people might need, or benefit, from the assistance of advocates, interpreters and translators, and specific communication equipment, during the assessment process and subsequent aspects of care planning and service delivery. Where such a need exists, councils should either arrange for this support or facilitate access to it.

As emphasised in the NSF for Older People, the contribution of trained bi- or multi-lingual co-workers can be important in this regard. It is the Department of Health's view that translation and interpretation is best provided by accredited professionals. The role of an advocate is a specialism in its own right, and should ideally be provided by professionals who are independent of both statutory agencies and the older person.

Community care services for older people

20.12   As noted above (para I.19), the community care legislation divides service users into three discreet (but largely artificial) categories: namely older people; disabled people; and ill people. Not infrequently an individual will straddle all three categories – for instance an older person with dementia. However for some people, the need for services arises not because of illness or disability, but merely because the ageing process has made them frail – for instance through muscle wastage. Although such persons are entitled to accommodation services under National Assistance Act (NAA)

---

11 Department of Health, *Care Management for Older People with Serious Mental Health Problems*, 2002.

12 HSC 2002/001: LAC (2002)1 *Guidance on the Single Assessment Process for Older People*, January 2002, annex pp19–20.

1948, s21 (see para 7.11), they are not eligible for domiciliary or community based services under NAA 1948 s29 or Chronically Sick and Disabled Persons Act (CSDPA) 1970 s2 – because they do not fall within the definition of a disabled person for the purposes of these sections (see para 9.20). Such persons are however entitled to care services under Health Services and Public Health Act (HSPHA) 1968 s45.

Care services under Health Services and Public Health Act 1968 s45

20.13   Section 45 of the 1968 Act provides:

(1)   A local authority may with the approval of the Secretary of State, and to such extent as he may direct, shall make arrangements for promoting the welfare of old people.

20.14   Section 45 is drafted to the same pattern as NAA 1948 s29 (see para 9.37 above), in that it does not require the provision of any services but leaves to the secretary of state the power to specify in directions what services may and what services must be provided.

20.15   The only (and current) directions that have been issued are contained in DHSS circular 19/71 (see below). The circular explains (at para 3) that the purpose of HSPHA 1968 s45 is to enable authorities to make approved arrangements for the elderly who are not substantially and permanently handicapped, and thus to promote the welfare of the elderly generally and so far as possible to prevent or postpone personal deterioration or breakdown.

Client group

Old people

20.16   HSPHA 1968 s45 services are specific to old people. The phrase 'old people' is not defined, and probably needs no definition. If a person requires domiciliary services for any reason other than the fact that age has made him or her frail, other statutory provisions exist to enable that service to be provided.[13]

20.17   The circular guidance suggested however that in the early days of the power (ie, post April 1971):

... it might prove desirable to start by identifying the needs of certain groups of the elderly who seem likely to be particularly vulnerable, eg, (a) elderly people, especially the more elderly, who are housebound or living alone or recently bereaved or about to be discharged from hospital, and (b) other persons over, say, 75 living in the community, particularly where there are high concentrations of very elderly people in particular districts.[14]

---

13   That is, under NAA 1948 s29, CSDPA 1970 s2, NHSA 2006 Sch 20, NHS(W)A 2006 Sch 15 or Mental Health Act 1983 s 117.
14   DHSS circular 19/71 para 7.

Ordinarily resident

20.18   Neither the Act nor the directions restrict HSPHA 1968 s45 services to persons 'ordinarily resident' in the local authority's area. This again is not strictly necessary, in that the directions have been limited to authorising (but not directing) the provision of such services. Accordingly social services authorities are entitled to reach a general policy decision (without fettering their individual discretion) to limit the use of their powers to elderly persons ordinarily resident within their area.

Services under Health Services and Public Health Act 1968 s45

20.19   The statutory framework for the provision of services under HSPHA 1968 s45 is similar to that under NAA 1948 s29. As with NAA 1948 s29, section 45 leaves to the secretary of state the power to determine the type of domiciliary services which can be provided. Section 45 services are subject to three basic limitations, namely:

1) that the purpose of the service must be the promotion of the welfare of elderly people;[15]
2) by virtue of section 45(4)(a) that the direct payment of money to 'old people' is not permitted (except if a payment for their 'work in accordance with the arrangements'). As noted, however, this restriction is now academic as a consequence of the direct payments legislation (see chapter 12 above); and
3) by virtue of section 45(4)(b) that no accommodation or services can be provided under section 45 if the accommodation or services could be provided under the NHS Acts 2006.[16]

20.20   The Secretary of State's only direction in respect of HSPHA 1968 s45 services was issued in DHSS circular 19/71 para 4, in March 1971. Although the wording of section 45 would allow the directions to place social services authorities under a duty to provide certain services, the directions merely empower the provision of the specified services, without creating any obligation.

20.21   The directions give social services authorities the discretion to provide[17] the services specified below. Authorities may provide services over and above those actually specified in the directions if they first obtain the secretary of state's specific approval.[18] Given the wide powers now available under Local Government Act 2000 s2 (see para 1.67 above), such a provision would now appear to be redundant.

---

15   The wording of HSPHA 1968 s45 is such that the service need not be provided *to* the disabled person; ie, a service provided to a carer may be 'an arrangement which promotes the welfare of an elderly person'.
16   See para 14.115 above.
17   The local authority may provide the services alone, or by employing independent or private providers – see HSPHA 1968 s45(3) and DHSS circular 19/71 paras 5(b), 7 and 11 et seq.
18   DHSS circular 19/71 para 4.

'Meals and recreation in the home or elsewhere'

20.22   The guidance suggests that:

> ... many of the elderly who are mobile or who can be transported will require social centres providing meals and opportunities for occupation as well as companionship and recreation. For the housebound and the frailer elderly meals-on-wheels will also need to be developed.[19]

20.23   The services available under this direction include the provision of 'recreation'. This would include day centres, outings, the provision of a television in the home and so on. District councils are empowered to provide similar services by virtue of Health and Social Services and Social Security Adjudications Act (HASSASSAA) 1983 Sch 9 (see para 20.33 below). The equivalent services for disabled people (under CSDPA 1970 s2(1)(g) and (c) respectively) are considered at paras 9.122 and 9.77, and for people who are, or have been, ill, under the NHS Acts 2006, at para 9.160.

Information on elderly services

20.24   'To inform the elderly of services available to them and to identify elderly people in need of services.' The guidance cautions against attempts to develop a comprehensive register of elderly people.[20] It emphasises however that:

> ... good services together with wide and continuing publicity about them are a pre-requisite of any scheme for finding out needs. The elderly and those who know of them cannot be expected to come forward if they do not know of any reason for doing so.[21]

20.25   The more specific duty to inform under CSDPA 1970 s1 is considered at para 2.38 above.

Travel assistance to participate in section 45 services

20.26   'To provide facilities or assistance in travelling to and from the home for the purpose of participating in services provided by the authority or similar services.' The equivalent duty under the CSDPA 1970 is dealt with at para 9.85.

Assistance in finding boarding accommodation

20.27   'To assist in finding suitable households for boarding elderly persons.' Social services authorities are given the power to provide this service (and those detailed in paras 20.28 and 20.29 below) to meet the needs of elderly people, similar to the powers approved for disabled people under NAA 1948 s29 in LAC (93)10 appendix 2 para 3 (see para 9.53).

---

19   Ibid, para 10.
20   Ibid, para 6(a).
21   Ibid, para 6(b).

Social work support and advice

20.28 'To provide visiting and advisory services and social work support.' The guidance suggests that social visiting services should be given high priority and that they should be co-ordinated by local authorities but largely undertaken by voluntary workers or others after suitable preparatory training.[22]

Home help and home adaptations

20.29 'To provide practical assistance in the home, including assistance in the carrying out of any additional facilities designed to secure the greater safety, comfort or convenience.' The guidance states that 'home-help, including laundry services and other aids to independent living, should probably be high on any priority list'.[23] The equivalent (and more substantial) duties to provide such services under CSDPA 1970 s2 and under NHSA 2006 Sch 20 para 3 (home helps only) are dealt with at paras 9.70 and 9.161 respectively.

Subsidy of warden costs

20.30 'To contribute towards the cost of employing a warden on welfare functions in warden-assisted housing schemes.' Social services authorities are given the power to provide this service to meet the needs of elderly people, similar to the powers approved for disabled people under NAA 1948 s29 in LAC (93)10 appendix 2 para 3 (see para 9.54).

Warden services

20.31 'To provide warden services for occupiers of private housing.' Social services authorities are given the power to provide this service to meet the needs of elderly people, similar to the powers approved for disabled people under NAA 1948 s29 in LAC (93)10 appendix 2 para 3 (see para 9.55).

Excluded groups

20.32 The effect of Immigration and Asylum Act 1999 s117, by amending section 45, is to exclude from services older people who are asylum seekers and are in need of community care services solely on account of being 'destitute'[24] (see para 22.14 above).

---

22 Ibid, para 10; and see also para 9.41 where the equivalent service under NAA 1948 s29 is considered.
23 Ibid, para 10.
24 Section 45(4A) as inserted by Immigration and Asylum Act 1999 s117.

Care services under Health and Social Services and Social Security Adjudications Act 1983 Sch 9

20.33 HASSASSAA 1983 s29 and Sch 9 Part II make provision for district councils to provide 'meals and recreation for old people'. Schedule 9 para 1 states:

> A district council or Welsh county council or county borough council shall have power to make such arrangements as they may from time to time determine for providing meals and recreation for old people in their homes or elsewhere and may employ as their agent for the purpose of this paragraph any voluntary organisation whose activities consist in or include the provision of meals or recreation for old people.

20.34 In order to achieve these objectives Sch 9 para 2 empowers such authorities to contribute to the funds of voluntary organisations, and to permit them to use their premises or furniture, vehicles or equipment (gift or loan or otherwise). Paragraph 3 provides the secretary of state with regulation making powers – which have not as yet been exercised.

20.35 It appears that these powers are generally exercised by district councils in collaboration with social services authorities in respect of supported accommodation arrangements. The partnership arrangements under NHSA 2006 s75[25] (see para 13.122) enable payments to be made by health bodies to district councils in relation to such arrangements.[26]

---

25 NHS(W)A 2006 s33.
26 Health Act 1999 s31(8).

Mental health: policy and services

Introduction

21.1   At any one time, approximately one in six people of working age have a mental health problem (most often anxiety or depression) and one in 250 will have a psychotic illness such as schizophrenia or bipolar affective disorder (manic depression).[1]

21.2   People who have a mental disorder of any description are entitled to the full range of community care services: including accommodation under the National Assistance Act (NAA) 1948, and non-accommodation services under NAA 1948 s29, Chronically Sick and Disabled Persons Act (CSDPA) 1970 s2, and the NHS Acts 2006. The definition of 'disabled' under NAA 1948 s29 and Children Act (CA) 1989 s17(11) includes persons with a 'mental disorder' of any description which under Mental Health Act (MHA) 1983 s1 includes not just the specified disorders (mental illness, arrested or incomplete development of the mind and a psychopathic disorder) but also 'any other disorder or disability of mind'. It follows that a person with even a transient mental health problem is entitled to a community care assessment and services if the assessment reveals an eligible need. Certain persons with mental health difficulties are entitled to distinct community care services under MHA 1983 s117 and this service regime is considered at para 21.19 below.

National Service Framework for Mental Health

21.3   In order to address the social and mental health needs of working age adults up to 65, in 1999 the government in England published a *National Service Framework (NSF) for Mental Health*.[2] The role and status of NSF's is considered further at para 1.61 above.

21.4   The English NSF sets out seven key standards, providing in each case detailed guidance on the local action required to ensure these are implemented – with timescales and 'milestones to ensure progress, with performance measures to support performance improvement'. In Wales an equivalent NSF was published in 2002 and updated in 2005.[3] The seven English standards are as follows:

1   Department of Health, *A National Service Framework for Mental Health: Modern Standards and Service Models*, 1999, p1.
2   Ibid.
3   Welsh Assembly, *Raising the Standard: The Revised Adult Mental Health National Service Framework and an Action Plan for Wales*, 2005. The Welsh NSF has eight standards, namely (1) promoting social inclusion; (2) empowerment and support of service users and carers; (3) promotion of opportunities for a normal pattern of daily life; (4) providing and commissioning equitable, accessible services; (5 and 6) delivering responsive, comprehensive services; (7) effective client assessment and care pathways; and (8) ensuring a well staffed, skilled and supported workforce.

1. *Mental health promotion*
   Health and social services should:
   - promote mental health for all, working with individuals and communities
   - combat discrimination against individuals and groups with mental health problems, and promote their social inclusion.

2. *Primary care and access to services*
   Any service user who contacts their primary health care team with a common mental health problem should:
   - have their mental health needs identified and assessed
   - be offered effective treatments, including referral to specialist services for further assessment, treatment and care if they require it.

3. *Primary care and access to services*
   Any individual with a common mental health problem should:
   - be able to make contact round the clock with the local services necessary to meet their needs and receive adequate care
   - be able to use *NHS Direct*, as it develops, for first-level advice and referral on to specialist helplines or to local services.

4. *Effective services for people with severe mental illness*
   All mental health service users on the Care Programme Approach (CPA) should:
   - receive care which optimises engagement , prevents or anticipates crisis, and reduces risk
   - have a copy of a written care plan which:
     - includes the action to be taken in a crisis by service users, their carers, and their care co-ordinators
     - advises the GP how they should respond if the service user needs additional help
     - is regularly reviewed by the care co-ordinator
   - be able to access services 24 hours a day, 365 days a year.

5. *Effective services for people with severe mental illness*
   Each service user who is assessed as requiring a period of care away from their home should have:
   - timely access to an appropriate hospital bed or alternative bed or place, which is:
     - in the least restrictive environment consistent with the need to protect them and the public
     - as close to home as possible
   - a copy of a written after care plan agreed on discharge, which sets out the care and rehabilitation to be provided , identifies the care co-ordinator, and specifies the action to be taken in a crisis.

6. *Caring about carers*
   All individuals who provide regular and substantial care for a person on CPA should:
   - have an assessment of their caring, physical and mental health needs, repeated on at least an annual basis

- have their own written care plan, which is given to them and implemented in discussion with them.

7. *Preventing suicide*

Local health and social care communities should prevent suicides by:
- promoting mental health for all, working with individuals and communities (Standard one)
- delivering high quality primary mental health care (Standard two)
- ensuring that anyone with a mental health problem can contact local services via the primary care team, a helpline or an A&E department (Standard three)
- ensuring that individuals with severe and enduring mental illness have a care plan which meets their specific needs, including access to services round the clock (Standard four)
- providing safe hospital accommodation for individuals who need it (Standard five)
- enabling individuals caring for someone with severe mental illness to receive the support which they need to continue to care (Standard six).

and in addition:
- supporting local prison staff in preventing suicides among prisoners
- ensuring that staff are competent to assess the risk of suicide among individuals at greatest risk
- developing local systems for suicide audit to learn lessons and take any necessary action.

Assessment and care planning for mental health service users

21.5   Standard 2 of the NSF concerns the right of mental health service users to a needs' assessment and standard 3 entitles them to 'round the clock' access to the local services necessary to meet their needs and to receive adequate care. Standard 4 elaborates upon the rights of mental health service users to be assessed using the care programme approach (CPA, considered at para 21.7 below).

21.6   As noted above, people with mental health problems are eligible to receive community care services and, if under 18, services under the CA 1989. In addition, however, 'adults of working age in contact with the secondary mental health system'[4] are entitled to an integrated health and social care assessment under what is generally referred to as the 'care programme approach'.

4   Department of Health, *Effective care co-ordination in mental health services: Modernising the care programme approach – a policy booklet*, 1999, para 17.

The care programme approach

21.7   The CPA was introduced by the joint health/social services circular HC (90)23: LASSL (90)11. Health authorities were given lead responsibility for implementing the policy although there was an obligation on health and social services authorities to reach formal and detailed inter-agency agreements to ensure its full implementation.[5] The Department of Health has consistently stressed the importance it attaches to the CPA[6] and has issued updating guidance[7] culminating with the current 1999 guidance[8] (referred to below as the '1999 CPA guidance').

21.8   Equivalent guidance was issued in Wales in 2003[9] and updated in 2004.[10] The guidance retains the CPA in Wales on broadly similar lines to that in England, although it seeks to integrate such assessments within the unified assessment process (see para 3.26 above).

21.9   The CPA applies to all patients receiving care from the specialist psychiatric services[11] – ie regardless of whether or not the patient has been detained under the MHA 1983. The four main elements of the CPA are:[12]

- Systematic arrangements for assessing the health and social needs of people accepted into specialist mental health services;
- The formation of a care plan which identifies the health and social care required from a variety of providers;
- The appointment of a key worker to keep in close touch with the service user and to monitor and co-ordinate care; and
- Regular review and, where necessary, agreed changes to the care plan.

21.10 Although the CPA is specifically directed at 'the most needy of service users who require a complex care planning response',[13] it is also intended that all service users in contact with specialist psychiatric services are dealt with under the programme, albeit that in respect of such persons a less intensive/bureaucratic response is required from the relevant services. As the 1999 CPA guidance explains (para 18):

5   Department of Health, *Social Services Departments and the Care Programme Approach: An SSI Inspection Report*, 1995, para 4.3.11.

6   Department of Health, *Care Management and Assessment: Managers' Guide*, HMSO, 1991, p93; *Health of the Nation: Key Area Handbook: Mental Illness*, 1993, appendix 9.3; 1995, chapters 9 and 11.

7   Department of Health, *Guidance on the Discharge of Mentally Disordered People and their Continuing Care in the Community* HSG (94)27: LASSL (94)4; Department of Health, *Audit Pack for Monitoring the Care Programme Approach*, 1996.

8   Department of Health, *Effective care co-ordination in mental health services: modernising the care programme approach – a policy booklet*, 1999.

9   Welsh Assembly, *Mental Health Policy Wales Implementation Guidance: The Care Programme Approach for Mental Health Service Users*, 2003.

10 Welsh Assembly, *Adult Mental health Services: Stronger in Partnership*, 2004.

11 HSG (96)6 *The spectrum of care a summary of comprehensive local services for people with mental health problems 24 hour nursed beds for people with severe and enduring mental illness an audit pack for the care programme approach*.

12 1999 CPA guidance para 4.

13 Ibid, para 18.

The key principles of the CPA are applicable to all service users, even those who require only a uni-disciplinary intervention. They have the right to a thorough assessment of their needs, the development of a care plan and a review of that care by the professionals involved in their care. Indeed, this is good professional practice.

21.11   The guidance accordingly separates service users into two categories, those that require a 'standard CPA' and those that require a more intensive or 'enhanced CPA'.

Standard CPA

21.12   The 1999 CPA guidance at para 57 suggests that the characteristics of people on standard CPA will include some of the following:

- they require the support or intervention of one agency or discipline or they require only low key support from more than one agency or discipline;
- they are more able to self-manage their mental health problems;
- they have an active informal support network;
- they pose little danger to themselves or others;
- they are more likely to maintain appropriate contact with services.

21.13   The guidance explains the nature of the standard CPA as follows:

19. It is important to stress, however, that where the service user has standard needs and has contact with only one professional, that professional will in effect be the person who coordinates their care and any clinical or practice notes will constitute the care plan and record of review. Service users should be given the opportunity to sign the agreed care plan and then receive a copy. It is not necessary to engage in further bureaucracy for the care of such people. As a minimum, service providers must ensure that central records are maintained on all those in contact with services and that care planning and review take place regularly.

Enhanced CPA

21.14   The enhanced CPA is described by the 1999 guidance as being appropriate to service users who have some of the following characteristics (para 58):

- they have multiple care needs, including housing, employment etc, requiring inter-agency co-ordination;
- they are only willing to co-operate with one professional or agency but they have multiple care needs;
- they may be in contact with a number of agencies (including the Criminal Justice System);
- they are likely to require more frequent and intensive interventions, perhaps with medication management;
- they are more likely to have mental health problems co-existing with other problems such as substance misuse;

- they are more likely to be at risk of harming themselves or others;
- they are more likely to disengage with services.

CPA and the code of practice guidance to the Mental Health Act 1983

21.15 MHA 1983 s118 requires the secretary of state to prepare a code of practice for the guidance of the relevant professionals on the application of the Act. The current code was published in 1999[14] and has been held to be – in effect – strong policy guidance (see para 1.56 above) that should be followed unless in an individual case there is a good reason for departing from it.[15] At chapter 27 of the code, the objectives and requirements of the CPA are outlined as follows:

> 27.2 These objectives apply to all patients receiving treatment and care from the specialist psychiatric services, whether or not they are admitted to hospital and whether or not they are detained under the Act. They are embodied in the Care Programme Approach (CPA) set out in Circular HC(90)23/LASSL(90)11, and in the Welsh Office Mental Illness Strategy (WHC(95)40[16]). The key elements of the CPA are:
> - systematic arrangements for assessing people's health and social care needs;
> - the formulation of a care plan which addresses those needs;
> - the appointment of a key worker to keep in close touch with the patient and monitor care;
> - regular review and if need be, agreed changes to the care plan.
>
> 27.4 NHS Managers and Directors of Social Services should ensure that all staff are aware of the CPA and related provisions. Further guidance on the discharge of mentally disordered people and their continuing care in the community is given in HSG(94)27/LASSL(94)4 and WHC(95)7 and WHC(96)26. The relationship between the CPA, section 117 after-care and local authority arrangements for care management is more fully explained in *Building Bridges-A Guide to arrangements for inter-agency working for the care and protection of severely mentally ill people (Department of Health 1995).*
>
> 27.5 Before the decision is taken to discharge or grant leave to a patient, it is the responsibility of the rmo to ensure, in consultation with the other professionals concerned, that the patient's needs for health and social care are fully assessed and the care plan addresses them. If the patient is being given leave for only a short period a less comprehensive review may suffice but the arrangements for the patient's care should still be properly recorded.
>
> 27.6 The RMO is also responsible for ensuring that:
> - a proper assessment is made of risks to the patient or other people;
> - in the case of offender patients, the circumstances of any victim and their families are taken into account;

---

14 Department of Health and Welsh Office, *Code of Practice Mental Health Act*, 1999.
15 *Munjaz v Mersey Care NHS Trust and others* [2003] EWCA Civ 1036; [2003] 3 WLR 1505; (2003) 74 BMLR 178.
16 WHC (95)40 was in fact a draft document and the correct reference should have been to WC 19/96.

- consideration is given to whether the patient meets the criteria for after-care under supervision, or under guardianship (see Chapter 13 and 28); and
- consideration is given to whether the patient should be placed on the supervision register established in accordance with HSG(94)5.

Mental Health Review Tribunals and managers' hearings

27.7 The courts have ruled[17] that in order to fulfil their obligations under section 117 health authorities and local authority social services authorities must take reasonable steps to identify appropriate after-care facilities for a patient before his or her actual discharge from hospital. In view of this, some discussion of after-care needs, including social services and other relevant professionals and agencies, should take place before a patient has a Mental Health Review Tribunal or managers hearing, so that suitable after-care arrangements can be implemented in the event of his or her being discharged (see para 22.12).

Who should be involved

27.8 Those who should be involved in consideration of the patient's after-care needs include:

- the patient, if he or she wishes and/or a nominated representative;
- the patient's RMO;
- a nurse involved in caring for the patient in hospital;
- a social worker/care manager specialising in mental health work;
- the GP and primary care team;
- a community psychiatric/mental health nurse;
- a representative of relevant voluntary organisations;
- in the case of a restricted patient, the probation service;
- subject to the patient's consent, any informal carer who will be involved in looking after him or her outside hospital;
- subject to the patient's consent, his or her nearest relative;
- a representative of housing authorities, if accommodation is an issue.

27.9 It is important that those who are involved are able to take decisions regarding their own and as far as possible their agency's involvement. If approval for plans needs to be obtained from more senior levels (for example, for funding) it is important that this causes no delay to the implementation of the care plan.

Considerations for after-care

27.10 Those concerned must consider the following issues:

a. the patient's own wishes and needs, and those of any dependents;
b. the views of any relevant relative, friend or supporter of the patient;
c. the need for agreement with authorities and agencies in the area where the patient is to live;
d. in the case of offender patients, the circumstances of any victim and their families should be taken into account when deciding where the patient should live;
e. the possible involvement of other agencies, eg probation, voluntary organisations;
f. the establishing of a care plan, based on proper assessment and clearly identified needs, including:

---

17   *R v Ealing District Health Authority ex p Fox* [1993] 1 WLR 373, QBD.

- day time activities or employment,
- appropriate accommodation,
- out-patient treatment,
- counselling, and personal support,
- assistance in welfare rights and managing finances,
- a contingency plan should the patient relapse.

g. the appointment of a key worker (see para 27.2) from either of the statutory agencies to monitor the care plan's implementation, liaise and co-ordinate where necessary and report to the senior officer in their agency any problems that arise which cannot be resolved through discussion;

h. the identification of any unmet need.

27.11 The professionals concerned should establish an agreed outline of the patient's needs, taking into account his or her social and cultural background, and agree a time-scale for the implementation of the various aspects of the plan. All key people with specific responsibilities with regard to the patient should be properly identified. Once plans are agreed it is essential that any changes are discussed with others involved with the patient before being implemented. The plan should be recorded in writing.

27.12 The care plan should be regularly reviewed. It will be the responsibility of the key worker to arrange reviews of the plan until it is agreed that it is no longer necessary. The senior officer in the key worker's agency responsible for after-care arrangements should ensure that all aspects of the procedure are followed.

CPA and community care assessments under National Health Service and Community Care Act 1990 s47

21.16 The relationship between the administrative obligation on joint NHS/ social services teams to prepare CPA assessments and the social services statutory duty to undertake community care assessments under National Health Service and Community Care Act 1990 (NHSCCA) 1990 s47 was considered in *R (HP and KP) v Islington LBC*.[18] The case concerned a patient being cared for at home by his family. He was assessed by the psychiatric services as suffering from a form of depression and at risk of severe neglect and 'vulnerable to deterioration in his mental state particularly if he stops taking his medication'. He was however considered not to have a 'severe and enduring mental illness' and deemed ineligible for CPA support. In view of this finding the local authority determined that he was not eligible for 'community care provision'. In quashing this decision, Munby J held that the authority had misunderstood the relationship between the CPA and the duty to assess under section 47(1). The fact that the patient lacked a 'severe and enduring mental illness . . . was not determinative of whether he nonetheless had a need for generic health or social services community care'.[19] Accordingly, in the judge's opinion:

---

18 [2004] EWHC 7 (Admin); (2005) 82 BMLR 113.
19 Ibid, at [37].

In my judgment, Islington's demonstrable and serious error in its whole approach to the fundamental underlying questions must, in the circumstances, invalidate both parts of the process.[20] In my judgment there has never been a proper and comprehensive Community Care assessment of Mr P, only a CPA assessment. The process in relation to the Community Care assessment must start again.

21.17   It will be maladministration to fail to undertake an expeditious community care assessment in circumstances where a compulsorily detained patient cannot be discharged until it has been completed.[21]

CPA and the single assessment process

21.18   Guidance on the interface between the CPA and the single assessment process (SAP) is provided in a 2002 Department of Health clarification note[22] and is considered further at para 20.9 above.

Services under Mental Health Act 1983 s117

21.19   Most non-accommodation services that authorities provide for people with a mental health difficulty are delivered under CSDPA 1970 s2. These services are available to persons 'who suffer from a mental disorder of any description'.[23] Likewise, most accommodation services that authorities provide for people with a mental health difficulty are delivered under NAA 1948 s21.

21.20   Only a small minority of people who receive community care services are entitled to their services under MHA 1983 s117. For such people, however, as section 117 creates specifically enforceable individual rights to a virtually unlimited range of services (including where appropriate, the provision of accommodation – see para 21.31 below), the availability of these services under other Acts is in reality academic. From a service user's perspective, the receipt of services under MHA 1983 s117 has the added advantage that social services authorities are not empowered to charge for them (see para 21.41).

21.21   MHA 1983 s117 (as amended) reads as follows:

(1) This section applies to persons who are detained under section 3 above, or admitted to a hospital in pursuance of a hospital order made under section 37 above, or transferred to a hospital in pursuance of a hospital direction made under s45A above or a transfer direction made under section 47 or 48 above, and then cease to be detained and (whether or not immediately after so ceasing) leave hospital.

---

20 The first being to undertake a 'needs assessment' and the second to arrive at a 'service provision decision' – see ibid, at [38].

21 Complaint no 04/B/01280 against York City Council, 31 January 2006.

22 Department of Health, *Care Management for Older People with Serious Mental Health Problems*, 2002.

23 In addition services are also available under the NHS Acts 2006 for (among others) persons who are, or have been, suffering from an illness (see para 9.156 above).

(2) It shall be the duty of the Primary Care Trust or Health Authority[24] and of the local social services authority to provide, in co-operation with relevant voluntary agencies, after-care services for any person to whom this section applies until such time as the Primary Care Trust or Health Authority and the local social services authority are satisfied that the person concerned is no longer in need of such services but they shall not be so satisfied in the case of a patient who is subject to after-care under supervision at any time while he so remains subject.

(2A) It shall be the duty of the Primary Care Trust or Health Authority to secure that at all times while a patient is subject to after-care under supervision –

  (a) a person who is a registered medical practitioner approved for the purposes of section 12 above by the Secretary of State as having special experience in the diagnosis or treatment of mental disorder is in charge of the medical treatment provided for the patient as part of the after-care services provided for him under this section; and

  (b) a person professionally concerned with any of the after-care services so provided is supervising him with a view to securing that he receives the after-care services so provided.

(2B) Section 32 above shall apply for the purposes of this section as it applies for the purposes of Part II of this Act.

(3) In this section 'the Primary Care Trust or Health Authority' means the Primary Care Trust or Health Authority and 'the local Social services authority' means the local social services authority for the area in which the person concerned is resident or to which he is sent on discharge by the hospital in which he was detained.

Reasons for detention

Section 3

21.22 Persons are detained under MHA 1983 s3 when admitted for treatment (as opposed to being detained under MHA 1983 s2 (admission for assessment, whether or not accompanied by any treatment).

---

24 Although the section has been amended (as a result of the demise of health authorities in England and Wales) to insert 'Primary Care Trusts' (National Health Service Reform and Health Care Professions Act 2002 Sch 2(2) para 56), no equivalent amendment has occurred in Wales to insert the term 'Local Health Boards'. It appears however that this is not strictly necessary, as a result of a combination of the Health Authorities (Transfer of Functions, Staff, Property, Rights and Liabilities and Abolition) (Wales) Order 2003 SI No 813 (W98) – which transfers all functions of health authorities in Wales to the Assembly – and the Local Health Boards (Functions) (Wales) Regulations 2003 SI No 150 (W20) which provide (subject to exceptions) that functions that were exercised by health authorities and were transferred to the Assembly by SI 2003 No 813 are to be exercised by local health boards.

Section 37

21.23   Persons may only be detained under MHA 1983 s37 by order of a criminal court after being convicted of an offence (punishable by imprisonment) in criminal proceedings and the court being satisfied (amongst other things) that at the time of conviction the offender was suffering from a specific mental disorder.

Section 45A[25]

21.24   Under MHA 1983 s45A, and subject to certain restrictions, the Crown Court may, when sentencing a person who suffers from a psychopathic disorder to a term of imprisonment, direct that he or she be detained in a specified hospital.

Section 47

21.25   Persons may only be detained under MHA 1983 s47 if they are serving a sentence of imprisonment (in a prison) and the secretary of state is satisfied (among other things) that they are suffering from a specific mental disorder (ie, mental illness, psychopathic disorder, mental impairment or severe mental impairment) and should in consequences be removed and detained in a hospital.

Section 48

21.26   Detention under MHA 1983 s48 arises in the same circumstances as under MHA 1983 s47, except that section 48 applies to persons who, although detained, are not serving a sentence of imprisonment (eg, they are on remand pending trial, are civil prisoners or being detained under the Immigration Act 1971), and the person must be suffering from a mental illness of severe mental impairment.

The nature of the section 117 duty

21.27   The duty to provide after-care services under MHA 1983 s117 crystallises when the person 'ceases to be detained'. The nature of the duty under section 117, and the meaning of the phrase 'ceases to be detained' has been considered in a number of diverse fact cases, including by the Court of Appeal in *R (K) v Camden and Islington Health Authority*[26] and the House of Lords in *R (IH) v SSHD and others*.[27] From these decisions, it appears that the section 117 duty:

1) only arises on the patient's discharge from hospital although the NHS body has the power to take preparatory steps prior to discharge.[28] In *R*

---

25   Inserted by Crime (Sentences) Act 1997.
26   [2001] EWCA Civ 240; [2001] 3 WLR 553; (2001) 4 CCLR 170.
27   [2003] UKHL 59; [2003] 3 WLR 1278; (2004) 7 CCLR 147.
28   *R (K) v Camden and Islington Health Authority* [2001] EWCA Civ 240; [2001] 3 WLR 553; (2001) 4 CCLR 170 at [20].

(B) v Camden LBC and others[29] Stanley Burnton J held that no express duty to take steps to secure after-care services arose until the health/social services authorities were informed of the discharge of a detainee (see para 3.67 above);

2) in so far as it relates to the provision of ordinary social care services, there is a specific duty (see para 1.25) to ensure that these services are made available;[30]

3) in so far as it relates to the provision of personal/professional services (most notably by the NHS in the form of securing a psychiatrist prepared to accept responsibility for the patient on discharge into the community), the duty is merely to 'use its best endeavours to procure' the services it deems necessary (or those specified by a mental health review tribunal).[31]

21.28 MHA 1983 s117 services are also available to patients on MHA 1983 s17 leave.[32] Section 17 provides that a 'responsible medical officer' can authorise leave of absence to patients detained under Part II of the Act (ie under non-criminal detention). This entitlement arises because MHA 1983 s117 services are provided to a person who is detained under (among others) section 3 'and then ceases to be detained and (whether or not immediately after so ceasing) leave hospital'. A person can therefore be entitled to services under MHA 1983 s117 even though still formally detained under section 3, since the crucial question is whether or not he or she is physically detained in a hospital rather than legally 'liable to be detained' under MHA 1983 s3.

District or area of residence

21.29 MHA 1983 s117(3) provides that services under that section are the responsibility of the social services/health body for the area in which 'the person concerned is resident or to which he is sent on discharge by the hospital in which he was detained'. The question of ordinary residence under section 117 is considered further at para 21.29 above.

Services

21.30 Section 117 places no restriction upon the type of services that can be provided.[33] All that is required is that the person concerned must need these services. 'After-care' services under MHA 1983 s117 include therefore all the traditional community care services such as advice, guidance and counselling; occupational, social, cultural or recreational activities as

---

29 [2005] EWHC 1366 (Admin). (2005) 8 CCLR 422 at [66]–[67].
30 *R v Ealing District Health Authority ex p Fox* [1993] 1 WLR 373, QBD.
31 *R (IH) v SSHD and others* [2003] UKHL 59; [2003] 3 WLR 1278; (2004) 7 CCLR 147 at [29].
32 This entitlement, which is noted in the Code of Practice to the 1983 Act (para 20.7 asserts that the 'duty to provide after-care under MHA 1983 s117 includes patients on leave of absence') was confirmed by Sullivan J, in *R v Richmond LBC and others ex p Watson and others* (1999) 2 CCLR 402; see also para 21.36 below.
33 In co-operation with the relevant voluntary agencies – MHA 1983 s117(2).

well as day centre and drop-in centre provision; domiciliary care[34] as well as laundry and other such services; residential care accommodation and so on.

21.31   Only limited guidance on the nature and extent of section 117 services has been issued. The Code of Practice at para 27.1 notes, however that:

> . . . a central purpose of all treatment and care is to equip patients to cope with life outside hospital and function there successfully without danger to themselves or other people.

and at para 27.10(f) it suggests that the user's care plan should identify various needs, including:

- day time activities or employment
- appropriate accommodation
- out-patient treatment
- counselling and personal support
- assistance in welfare rights and managing finances
- a contingency plan should the patient relapse.

21.32 Guidance on the Mental Health (Patients in the Community) Act 1995 (see below) suggests that MHA 1983 s117 services may include[35] 'appropriate daytime activities, accommodation, treatment, personal and practical support, 24-hour emergency cover and assistance in welfare rights and financial advice' as well as 'support for informal carers'.

21.33   In *Clunis v Camden and Islington Health Authority*,[36] Beldam LJ considered that the services available under section 117:

> . . . would normally include social work, support in helping the ex-patient with problems of employment, accommodation or family relationships, the provision of domiciliary services and the use of day centre and residential facilities.[37]

A joint health/social services duty

21.34 In *R v Mental Health Review Tribunal ex p Hall*[38] the Divisional Court held that the duty to provide after-care services under MHA 1983 s117(2) was jointly shared by the health and social services authority in which the patient was resident at the time he or she was detained. It is therefore up to individual health bodies and social services authorities to decide among themselves how they will discharge these joint responsibilities. Although the Department of Health has advised health and social services authorities to develop local policies clarifying their respective responsibilities,[39] it appears that in practice this is something that has been neglected.

---

34 Including, for instance, such services as are detailed in CSDPA 1970 s2.
35 LAC (96)8: HSG (96)11 para 18.
36 [1998] 1 WLR 902, (1997) 1 CCLR 215 at 225G.
37 In *R (B) v Lambeth* [2006] EWHC 2362 (Admin); (2007) 10 CCLR 84 the court reaffirmed the view that the section 117 duty includes the provision of accommodation.
38 [2000] 1 WLR 1323; (1999) 2 CCLR 383.
39 Department of Health, *After-care under the Mental Health Act 1983: section 117 after-care services* HSC 2000/003: LAC (2000)3.

21.35   Many patients entitled to section 117 services have health care needs which could also qualify them for NHS continuing health care funding and the interface between these responsibilities is considered at para 21.43 below.

The duration of the duty

21.36   The services provided under MHA 1983 s117 must continue to be supplied until the authorities are satisfied that the former patient is no longer in need of them. In *R v Richmond LBC and others, ex p Watson and others*[40] (a case concerning the lawfulness of charging for services under MHA 1983 s117 – see para 21.41 below), Sullivan J held that after-care provision under section 117 does not have to continue indefinitely, although it must continue until such time as the health body and the local authority are satisfied that the individual is no longer in need of such services.

21.37   In his judgment he considered the following question: 'What are the local authorities' duties under MHA 1983 s117 towards a person, who because of old age, illness or other circumstances, has been provided with residential accommodation under NAA 1948 s21, then becomes mentally unwell, is detained under MHA 1983 s3, is discharged from hospital and returns to his or her former accommodation as part of their after-care package?' He held:

> I can see no reason why such a person should be in any worse position than the patient who has not previously been provided with accommodation under s21. On leaving hospital, the local authority will owe them a duty under s117. There may be cases where, in due course there will be no more need for after care services for the person's mental condition' but he or she will still need social services provision for other needs, for example, physical disability. Such cases will have to be examined individually on their facts, through the assessment process provided for by s47. In a case ... where the illness is dementia, it is difficult to see how such a situation could arise.

21.38   The issue was also considered by the local government ombudsman in a complaint against Clwyd.[41] The facts were that the resident had been detained under MHA 1983 s3 from which she was discharged and eventually moved to an elderly mentally ill nursing home. Steps were then taken by the local authority to assess her liability for residential care charges and in due course the authority placed a charge on her home.

21.39   After the resident's daughter questioned the authority's power to levy such charges, the hospital consultant met with the relevant social worker and purported to discharge the section 117 after-care: neither the resident or her daughter were aware of the discharge meeting or decision.

---

40 (1999) 2 CCLR 402.
41 Dated 19 September 1997, see (1998) 1 CCLR 546; and see also Report no 98/B/0341 from the English local government ombudsman against Wiltshire where a similar finding was made coupled with a recommendation that the cases of other people who might have had to pay for services inappropriately also be reviewed.

21.40   The ombudsman considered all these matters, but in particular the decision to discharge the MHA 1983 s117 arrangements. In his decision he held:

1) The council had a duty to provide after-care services at no cost to the resident from the moment she was discharged from hospital until such time as it was satisfied that she was no longer in need of such services.

2) In deciding that she no longer needed after-care under MHA 1983 s117 the council had failed to address the relevant question which was whether she needed and whether she continued to need after-care services. The ombudsman concluded that if the council had asked itself the relevant question, it would have had to conclude that she was in need of the specialist care provided at a home for the elderly mentally infirm.

3) The ombudsman concluded that the council's maladministration had been exacerbated by a number of factors including its failure to take account of the daughter's views before ceasing to provide after-care services under MHA 1983 s117.

Charging for Mental Health Act 1983 s117 services

21.41   In *R v Manchester City Council ex p Stennett and others*[42] the House of Lords held that it was unlawful for local authorities to charge for services under MHA 1983 s117. Although the judgment confirmed the consistent view of the Department of Health,[43] many local authorities had hitherto been charging for such services and accordingly a substantial number of claims were then made for reimbursement – many of which came to the notice of the local government ombudsman. Accordingly in July 2003 a special report was issued by the three English local government ombudsmen,[44] the key advice therein being summarised as follows:[45]

> That, in general, social services authorities (SSAs) should not carry out retrospective assessments purporting to remove a person from section 117 aftercare as from an earlier date.
> - That SSAs should review any retrospective assessments that have so far been made.
> - That, for the next 12 months at least, complaints made about previous assessments to end section 117 aftercare should not be rejected by SSAs as out of time.
> - That where previous assessments to end section 117 aftercare were not properly made, then restitution will generally be appropriate until a proper assessment is devised.

---

42 [2002] UKHL 34; [2002] 3 WLR 584; (2002) 5 CCLR 500.

43 See eg LAC (2000)3 *After-care under the Mental Health Act 1983: section 117 after-care services.*

44 July 2003: the report contains copies of the key reports: Clwyd, 19 September 1997, (1997) 1 CCLR 546; Wiltshire County Council, 14 December 1999, (2000) 3 CCLR 60; and Leicestershire, 25 October 2001; C00/B/08307.

45 July 2003 guidance (see note 44 above) para 5.

- That people who have paid for section 117 aftercare should receive financial restitution with interest.
- That SSAs should now put mechanisms in place to identify those persons improperly charged, or improperly deprived of financial assistance, and establish arrangements for reimbursing them or their estates.
- That no generally applicable cut-off date should be used when calculating repayments. Cases where such cut-off dates have been applied should be reviewed.

21.42 While it is clearly established that service users cannot be charged for section 117 services, it is less clear whether a resident receiving section 117 support can 'top-up' the care home fees to purchase a service more expensive than the assessed need requires. This question is considered further at para 7.116 above.

Section 117 and NHS continuing health care

21.43 We consider at chapter 14 above the responsibilities of the NHS for the care of people who are so unwell that they are entitled to NHS continuing health care funding. Many of these individuals may have mental health problems. Where such a person was formerly detained under MHA 1983 s3 or one of the criminal provisions, the question arises as to whether his or her entitlement to services derives from section 117 or under the NHS continuing health care regime.

21.44 While the Assembly in Wales has suggested that in certain situations the NHS continuing health care funding responsibility may 'trump' the section 117 duty, the Department of Health has indicated otherwise, stating:[46]

> Under section 117, PCTs and LAs have a duty to provide after-care services for individuals who have been detained under certain provisions of the Mental Health Act 1983 until such time as they are satisfied that the person is no longer in need of such services. Section 117 is a free-standing duty and PCTs and LAs have been advised to have in place local policies detailing their respective responsibilities.[47]

21.45 The Department of Health is certainly correct in stating that section 117 is a freestanding service provision obligation. This in itself does not mean that the NHS continuing health care obligation is irrelevant. The duty to provide services under NAA 1948 s29 is a freestanding obligation but in certain situations it is trumped by the overlapping duty under CSDPA 1970 s2.

21.46 At present there is no decided case-law to determine the issue but the following considerations would need to be addressed in order to decide this point.

---

46 Department of Health, *The National Framework for NHS Continuing Healthcare and NHS funded Nursing Care in England. Final Regulatory Impact Assessment*, 2007, para 65.
47 Department of Health, *After-care under the Mental Health Act 1983: section 117 after-care services* HSC 2000/003: LAC (2000)3.

1) To what extent is the NHS continuing health care obligation seen to trump other service provision duties? This was seen to occur in *Cough-lan*[48] in relation to the duty under NAA 1948 s21 and in *R (T, D and B) v Haringey LBC*[49] in relation to the CA 1989 s17 duty – where Ouseley J thought that this was a principle of general application (see para 14.29 above). Since section 117 services are but one example of the community care services listed in NHSCCA 1990 s46(3) (see para 3.134 above), this might suggest that it should be subject to such a general principle.

2) What liability is triggered as a result of an after-care meeting preceding a patient's discharge? It seems unlikely that it is to provide all services that are required by the patient – since the guidance suggests that this does not include care provided by an unpaid carer and likewise it would probably not generally include ordinary housing services. If this is the case, it might be argued that the duty is to provide those services which would not otherwise arise – ie the shortfall. If this is the case, it could be argued that the NHS continuing health care obligation arises before the section 117 obligation.

3) Is it relevant that the Health and Social Care Act 2001 s49 restriction treats section 117 services in the same way as it does other community care provisions (see para 13.96 above)? If section 117 creates an entirely separate regime outside the usual NHS/social services formalities, it is arguable that section 49 would not have included explicit reference to such services.

4) Is it anomalous that the NHS can have less responsibility in financial terms for a patient who has been forcibly detained in a psychiatric unit than for one who has not?

5) What is the weight to be given to the Welsh Assembly Continuing Care Guidance[50] which states (at p6 para 14(iii)) that an individual will qualify for NHS continuing health care if (among other things) he or she is 'detained in accordance with Section 17 of the Mental Health Act'? Patients on section 17 leave come within the ambit of section 117.[51]

6) Is the comment of Otton LJ in *Richmond BC v Watson, Stennett and others*[52] determinative? In his opinion the section 117 duty was one that 'reduces the opportunity of [health and social services] authorities to try to pass the buck and as a result [make] no proper provision'. In his opinion 'the language of section 117 ensures a seamless provision . . . permitting cross-funding of community care services between the two authorities'.

21.47   While the above analysis suggests that the demarcation of responsibilities under the two regimes is by no means clear, it would suggest that section

---

48   *R v North and East Devon Health Authority ex p Coughlan* [2000] 2 WLR 622; (1999) 2 CCLR 285.
49   [2005] EWHC 2235 (Admin); (2006) 9 CCLR 58.
50   WHC (2004)54: NAFWC 41/2004 – see para 14.92 above.
51   See Code of Practice to the 1983 Act para 20.7 and *R v Richmond LBC and others ex p Watson and others* (1999) 2 CCLR 402.
52   [2000] 3 WLR 1127; (2000) 3 CCLR 1136.

117 creates a distinct funding regime to that of NHS continuing health care (so long as the section 117 responsibility endures). If such a conclusion is correct, it does not answer the question of how the NHS and social services should apportion their respective liabilities. Arguably the division could logically be determined by social services taking responsibility for those individuals who were primarily in need of social support and the NHS taking responsibility for those whose primary need was for health care – ie the same as under the NHS continuing health care provisions.

Guardianship under Mental Health Act 1983 s7

21.48   MHA 1983 ss7–9 provide for the making of guardianship orders and for the powers of guardians, and are considered further at para 25.77 below. The 1983 Act does not however authorise or require the provision of any services in connection with the guardianship. Accordingly where residential or domiciliary care services are provided for a person the subject of a guardianship order, these services are made available under other statutory provisions (ie NAA 1948 s21, CSDPA 1970 s2, MHA 1983 s117 etc). Whether or not a charge can be levied for such a service will depend upon whether charging is permitted under the statute in question.

21.49   The Northern Irish charging rules prohibit charges being levied for accommodation provided to residents subject to guardianship[53] and the Department of Health has expressed the opinion[54] that the right to free services under MHA 1983 s117 also applies to guardianship, although it is doubtful that it is still of this view. Nevertheless an argument exists that charges might in certain situations be unconscionable. Persons subject to guardianship may have no choice but to live at a specified address, and while this may not amount to detention (see para 18.39 above) it is clearly a significant restriction on their liberty and engages article 8 of the European Convention on Human Rights (right to respect for private life and home – see para 27.225 below). If the state is requiring them to live in more expensive accommodation (a registered care or nursing home rather than

53   Department of Health, Social Services and Public Safety (Northern Ireland), *Charging for Residential Accommodation Guide (CRAG)*, 2006, provides at para 1.005A that: 'Trusts should not charge for after-care services, which can include residential care, provided under Article 18 of the Mental Health (NI) Order 1986."After-care" includes the provision of accommodation for persons who are subject of a guardianship order that requires them to reside at a place other than a hospital. Therefore the Health and Personal Social Services (Assessment of Resources) Regulations (Northern Ireland) 1993 do not apply and the Trust cannot charge a person for the residential accommodation in which he resides whilst subject to guardianship under the 1986 Order.'

54   In a letter of 18 January 1995 to Oldham Social Services. The letter states that 'until recently it had been assumed that local authorities could use an implied power to charge based upon s111 Local Government Act 1972, if they wished to charge for any services where they had no express power to charge. Following the decision in *R v Richmond LBC ex p McCarthy* [1992] 2 AC 48, it is now clear that this is not the case . . .'

rented accommodation), the added requirement that they pay the additional cost could again be articulate in the language of article 8.

21.50   Some support for this line of reasoning is provided by the comments of Lord Steyn in *R v Manchester City Council ex p Stennett and others*[55] where he referred with approval (at [14]) to the observations by Buxton LJ in the Court of Appeal[56] that not charging service users under s117 was not anomalous since they constituted:

> . . . an identifiable and exceptionally vulnerable class. To their inherent vulnerability they add the burden, and the responsibility for the medical and social service authorities, of having been compulsorily detained. It is entirely proper that special provision should be made for them to receive after-care, and it would be surprising, rather than the reverse, if they were required to pay for what is essentially a health-related form of care and treatment.

21.51   Lord Steyn then referred to the situation of patients discharged into residential care under section 117 and observed (at [15]) that in relation to such accommodation and care, it:

> . . . can hardly be said that the mentally ill patient freely chooses such accommodation. Charging them in these circumstances may be surprising. Moreover, under section 73 of the 1983 Act in respect of restricted patients . . . the tribunal is empowered to impose conditions of discharge upon the patient with which the patient is obliged to comply, eg in respect of residence and treatment . . . Plainly in such cases the patients do not voluntarily avail themselves of the after-care services. If the argument of the authorities is accepted that there is a power to charge these patients such a view of the law would not be testimony to our society attaching a high value to the need to care after the exceptionally vulnerable.

21.52   In a number of respects it could be argued that this analysis has force for patients required to reside in a care home under conditions of a guardianship order.

Mental Health (Patients in the Community) Act 1995

21.53   The 1995 Act introduced the possibility of 'after-care under supervision', generally referred to as supervised discharge. Its purpose has been described in the following terms:[57]

> After-care under supervision is an arrangement by which a patient who has been detained in hospital for treatment under the provisions of the Act may be subject to formal supervision after he or she is discharged. Its purpose is to help ensure that the patient receives the after-care services to be provided under section 117 of the Act. It is available for patients suffering from any of the four forms of mental disorder in the Act but is primarily intended for those with severe mental illness.

---

55 [2002] UKHL 34; [2002] 3 WLR 584; (2002) 5 CCLR 500.
56 *Richmond BC v Watson, Stennett and others* [2000] 3 WLR 1127; (2000) 3 CCLR 276.
57 Code of Practice to the Mental Health Act, April 1999, para 28.2.

21.54 For such a supervised discharge to take place, it must be shown:

a) that unless after-care services under section 117 are provided there will be:
   i) a substantial risk of serious harm to the health or safety of the patient or the safety of others; or
   ii) a risk that the patient will be seriously exploited; and
b) in any event that placing the patient under supervised discharge is likely to help ensure that he or she will receive the relevant after-care services.

21.55 Guidance on the 1995 Act has been issued in the form of circular LAC (96)8: HSG (96)11,[58] which includes the following:

> 18. The arrangements for after-care under supervision will need to be drawn up as part of the normal discharge planning process, following the principles of the Care Programme Approach in England and WHC (95)40[59] in Wales and in accordance with the formal consultation requirements in the Act (see below). Chapter 27 of the Code is also relevant. The professional team providing care in the community will need to consider and plan the services to be provided, including as may be appropriate daytime activities, accommodation, treatment, personal and practical support, 24-hour emergency cover and assistance in welfare rights and financial advice. They will also need to consider how often the patient is likely to need particular services. Support for informal carers should not be overlooked as the care plan may be to some degree dependent on their role.
>
> 19. The Act defines requirements which may be imposed when a patient is subject to supervised discharge. These are:
> • that the patient should live in a particular place;
> • that the patient should attend a particular place at set times for medical treatment, occupation, education or training;
> • that the supervisor, or a person authorised by the supervisor, should be allowed access to the patient at his or her place of residence (see paragraph 51 below).
> The reasons for imposing requirements should be explained to the patient, and details of them should be included in the care plan. A requirement to attend for medical treatment does not carry with it any power to impose medication or other treatment against the patient's wishes.

Mental Health Act 1983 reform

21.56 The MHA 2007 will, when it comes into force, make important changes to the detention and treatment provisions of the MHA 1983 and the Mental Capacity Act 2005 (considered at para 18.44 above). The Act retains the obligation to provide services under section 117 and the powers of guardianship (although these are amended). The impact will be wide ranging and is beyond the scope of this edition. It is expected that the Act will come into force during 2008.

---

58 WHC (96)11 in Wales.
59 WHC (95)40 was in fact a draft document and the correct reference should have been to WC 19/96.

CHAPTER 22

Asylum seekers and persons who are destitute

Background

22.1   This chapter deals with the community care support available to asylum seekers and to other overseas nationals in the UK who, for whatever reason, are unable to access social welfare assistance (public housing support and welfare benefits). Constant legislative change over the course of the last decade and the consequent case-law has made the subject exceedingly complex and on occasions brought the higher courts to the point of exasperation. In order, therefore, to make the subject comprehensible it is necessary to commence with a review of the relevant history and of the key definitions.

Definitions – 'asylum seeker'

22.2   In loose terms an asylum seeker is someone who has applied for asylum in the UK and whose application remains pending (either before the secretary of state or at appeal). The statutory definition, however, is set out in Immigration and Asylum Act (IAA) 1999 s94(1) which defines an 'asylum seeker' as:

> . . . a person who is not under 18 and has made a claim for asylum which has been recorded by the Secretary of State but which has not been determined.

22.3   Section 94 also clarifies the meaning of a claim for asylum, namely:

> . . . a claim that it would be contrary to the United Kingdom's obligations under the Refugee Convention, or under Article 3 of the Human Rights Convention, for the claimant to be removed from, or required to leave, the United Kingdom.

22.4   Asylum seekers within this definition are, in general, entitled to accommodation and financial support while in the UK.

Historical background

22.5   Until 6 February 1996 asylum seekers were entitled to means tested benefits and housing through homeless provisions.[1] From 6 February 1996 applicants who applied for asylum 'in country' rather than 'at port' (ie those who claimed after they had entered the UK rather than on their arrival) were excluded from social welfare benefits and homelessness assistance. This change was brought about by virtue of Asylum and Immigration Act 1996 ss9 and 11. Subsequently IAA 1999 s115 extended the disentitlement of benefits from late-claiming asylum seekers to almost all those subject to immigration control.

22.6   The 1999 Act envisaged that the majority of asylum seekers would become the responsibility of a new designated body and set up a new

---

1   Housing Act 1996 Part VII.

organisation, known as the National Asylum Support Service (NASS)[2] (see para 22.11). However, persons who had made a claim for asylum on arrival ('at port') in the UK on or before the introduction of the IAA 1999 continued to be entitled to means tested benefits.[3] These people (known as the '2000 Transitional Protected' cases) retained their entitlement to benefits until the first negative decision on their asylum claim[4] (after which time they fell to be supported by NASS).

22.7 As a consequence of the 1996 removal of benefit entitlement from in-country asylum applicants, a number of asylum seekers became destitute and sought assistance under National Assistance Act (NAA) 1948 s21(1)(a) on the basis that they came within the 'any other circumstance' category (see para 7.11 above) and were thus entitled to residential accommodation from the local authority. In *R v Hammersmith LBC ex p M*[5] their claims succeeded, albeit that the Court of Appeal stressed that section 21 was not a 'safety net' provision 'on which anyone who is short of money and/or short of accommodation can rely'.[6]

22.8 The *Hammersmith* judgment caused not inconsiderable financial problems for a number of local authorities. A 1998 government white paper described the position thus:[7]

> The Court of Appeal judgment . . . meant that, without warning or preparation, local authority social services departments were presented with a burden which is quite inappropriate, which has become increasingly intolerable and which is unsustainable in the long term, especially in London, where the pressure on accommodation and disruption to other services has been particularly acute.

22.9 The *Hammersmith* judgment has come to be seen as a landmark decision, since when many aspects of asylum and immigration law have become inextricably intertwined with community care law. As the case-law has developed, parliament has responded with new Acts and regulations such that the system is today complex to a degree bordering on the Kafkaesque and so lacking in any obvious logic that it has prompted judicial exasperation – as occurred, for example, in *R (A and others) v Croydon LBC*,[8] where Laws LJ observed:

---

2   In March 2007 asylum cases were transferred to a new regime known as New Asylum Modelor 'NAM'. NAMwas designed to be a more efficient and streamlined approach to processing and deciding asylum claims. A key feature of NAM is that asylum claims are dealt with by one single named case owner. In addition to changes to the asylum process, NASS as an organisation ceased to exist and the NAM case owners will now deal with all asylum support decisions. A legacy team has been put in place to deal with NASS cases prior to NAM.

3   Social Security (Immigration and Asylum) Consequential Amendment Regulations 2000 SI No 636 reg 12(4).

4   Ibid, regs 2 and 12 .

5   This being a consolidated appeal, comprising *R v Hammersmith LBC ex p M; R v Lambeth LBC ex p P and X and R v Westminster City Council ex p A* (1997) 1 CCLR 85.

6   (1997) 1 CCLR 85 at 94K.

7   Home Office, *Fairer, Faster and Firmer – A Modern Approach to Immigration and Asylum*, Cm 4018, 1998,para 8.14, cited by Lord Hoffman in *Westminster CC v NASS* [2002] UKHL 38; [2002] 1 WLR 2956; (2002) 5 CCLR 511 at 519C.

8   [2007] EWCA Civ 266 at [55]; (2007) *Times* 11 May.

In the course of this judgment we have used the term 'paper chase', and have done so advisedly. This important area of the law governs the use of scarce public resources in a difficult and sensitive field. We have already referred . . . to the pressing and uneven burden borne by some local authorities. One part of the overall scheme has had to be litigated in the House of Lords. Now this part, closely related, has had to be litigated in this court. No doubt there are great pressures on the legislators. But the distribution of responsibility which is at the core of this case could surely have been provided much more clearly and simply.

22.10   This chapter treads a difficult line. It seeks to focus on the rights to community care support of people who are non-UK nationals and either seeking asylum or unlawfully in the UK or for some other reason have restricted rights to such services. It is difficult however to focus on this question without straying occasionally into the more general area of immigration law. Of necessity, however, we have had to limit these incursions severely, and a reader wishing to understand these issues in further detail should refer to a specialist text on the subject.[9]

Asylum seekers

National Asylum Support Service and New Asylum Model

22.11   Following the *Hammersmith* judgment, the government announced its intention to amend the NAA 1948[10] to:

> . . . make clear that social services departments should not carry the burden of looking after healthy and able bodied asylum seekers. This role will fall to the new national support machinery.

22.12   In consequence amendments were made to the community care legislation[11] (including NAA 1948 s21) by IAA 1999 s116, which inserted into NAA 1948 s21 a new subsection (1A), namely:

> (1A)   A person [subject to immigration control, including asylum seekers] may not be provided with residential accommodation under subsection (1)(a) if his need for care and attention has arisen solely –
> (a)   because he is destitute; or
> (b)   because of the physical effects, or anticipated physical effects, of his being destitute.

22.13   Support for 'able bodied' asylum seekers was to be provided for by NASS, established under IAA 1999 Part VI. NASS (now superseded by the New Asylum Model (NAM)[12]) made provision for the support of all destitute asylum seekers and their dependants. On arrival in the UK,

---

9   See eg S Wilman, S Knafler and S Pierce, *Support for Asylum Seekers: a guide to legal and welfare rights*, 2nd edn, Legal Action Group, 2004; and Joint Council for Welfare Immigrants, *Immigration Nationality & Refugee Handbook*, 2006.
10   Home Office, *Fairer, Faster and Firmer – A Modern Approach to Immigration and Asylum*, Cm 4018, 1998, para 8.23.
11   See also para 7.8 above.
12   See note 2 above.

asylum seekers are entitled to 'Initial' or 'Emergency' accommodation provided under IAA 1999 s98 until a decision is reached on the person's claim for 'full asylum support' under IAA 1999 s95. Full NAM support can include accommodation and financial support but, unlike community care services, accommodation under NAM is almost always provided away from London and the South East (in accordance with the government's policy to disperse those reliant on this support away from these areas).

Destitution

22.14   Destitution is a key concept in the determination of entitlement to NAM support and is defined in IAA 1999 s95(3) as follows:

> For the purposes of this section, a person is destitute if –
> (a) he does not have adequate accommodation or any means of obtaining it (whether or not his other essential living needs are met); or
> (b) he has adequate accommodation or the means of obtaining it, but cannot meet his other essential living needs.

22.15   The Asylum Support Regulations 2000[13] set out what NASS (now NAM) caseworkers must consider when assessing whether an applicant is destitute. The whole family's circumstances must be considered in assessing whether any individual member is destitute (regulations 6 and 12), and when assessing an applicant's resources account must be taken of any other support which the person might reasonably be expected to have during the prescribed period (regulation 6(4)). The prescribed period is 14 days' essential living needs. Where other support is available, NAM support can be denied; a point of importance in situations where an asylum seeker might be seeking community care support.

'Destitution plus'

22.16   The 1999 amendment to section 21 did not achieve its objective of relieving social services authorities from the bulk of their obligations to asylum seekers. As Lord Hoffman noted in *Westminster CC v NASS*[14] (hereafter the 2002 *Westminster* case):

> 29. What may have escaped notice in the aftermath of *Ex p M*[15] was that the 1996 Act had brought into the scope of section 21 of the 1948 Act two distinct classes of asylum seekers who would not have been entitled to Part III accommodation if the 1996 Act had not excluded them from the normal

---

13   SI No 704. This contains the detailed rules concerning NASS, and the Border and Immigration Agency (formerly the Home Office Immigration and Nationality Directorate) has produced NASS Policy Bulletins which set out the internal guidance that NASS caseworkers should follow.
14   [2002] UKHL 38; [2002] 1 WLR 2956; (2002) 5 CCLR 511 at 519E.
15   This being a consolidated appeal, comprising *R v Hammersmith LBC ex p M; R v Lambeth LBC ex p P and X and R v Westminster City Council ex p A* (1997) 1 CCLR 85.

social security system. The first class were the able bodied asylum seekers who qualified solely because, being destitute, they were already or were likely to become in need of care and attention. This was the class highlighted in *Ex p M*. I shall call them 'the able bodied destitute', who came within section 21 solely because they were destitute. The second class were asylum seekers who had some infirmity which required the local social services to provide them with care and attention, but who would not ordinarily have needed to be provided with accommodation under section 21 because it was available in other ways, for example, under the homelessness legislation. They would not have come within the section 21 duty because they would not have satisfied the third condition which I have quoted from the judgment of Hale LJ in *Wahid's* case[16] . . .

22.17   The problem highlighted by Lord Hoffman was that use of the word 'solely' in amended NAA 1948 s21(1A) had the effect of only excluding the 'able bodied' destitute. The second class (which he referred to as the 'infirm destitute') were able to claim assistance from social services authorities under NAA 1948 s21, not 'solely' because of their destitution, but additionally because of their infirmity. And since they had access to such assistance they were excluded from the NASS scheme by virtue of the above mentioned stipulation in the Asylum Support Regulations 2000. Lord Hoffman accordingly held:[17]

> The present case has been argued throughout on the footing that [the applicant] has a need for care and attention which has not arisen solely because she is destitute but also (and largely) because she is ill. It is also common ground that she has no access to any accommodation in which she can receive care and attention other than by virtue of section 21 or under Part VI of the 1999 Act. The first question for your Lordships is whether in those circumstances she comes prima facie within section 21(1)(a) and, if so, the second is whether she is excluded by section 21(1A). In my opinion, the answers to these questions are yes and no respectively. The third question is whether the existence of a duty under section 21 excludes [the applicant] from consideration for asylum support. Again, in agreement with the Court of Appeal, I think that the answer is yes.

22.18   In the 2002 *Westminster* case, regard was had to two earlier cases, *R v Wandsworth LBC ex p O* and *R v Leicester City Council ex p Bhikha*[18] in which the local authorities argued that the insertion of subsection (1A) into section 21 made the claimants ineligible under that section. In the leading judgment Simon Brown LJ[19] adopted the applicants' construction of section 21, namely:

> . . . that if an applicant's need for care and attention is to any material extent made more acute by some circumstance other than the mere lack of accommodation and funds, then, despite being subject to immigration control, he qualifies for assistance.

16 Namely that 'the care and attention which is needed must not be available otherwise than by the provision of accommodation under section 21': *R (Wahid) v Tower Hamlets LBC* [2002] EWCA Civ 287; (2002) 5 CCLR 239 at 247H – see para 7.17 above.
17 [2002] UKHL 38; [2002] 1 WLR 2956; (2002) 5 CCLR 511 at [49].
18 [2000] 1 WLR 2539; (2000) 3 CCLR 237.
19 Ibid at 2548D–2549B.

22.19 In this respect, Simon Brown LJ observed that:

> The word 'solely' in the new section is a strong one and its purpose there seems to me evident. Assistance under the Act of 1948 is, it need hardly be emphasised, the last refuge for the destitute. If there are to be immigrant beggars on our streets, then let them at least not be old, ill or disabled.

22.20 It follows that an applicant, in order to cross the NAA 1948 s21(1A) threshold, must establish that he or she is a person whose need for care and attention does not arise solely because of destitution or its physical, or anticipated physical effects. This requirement is commonly referred to as the 'destitution plus test'.

22.21 The *ex p O and ex p Bhikha* decisions were followed in R *(Mani)* v *Lambeth LBC.*[20] The question in *Mani* was whether a local authority has a duty to provide residential accommodation for a destitute asylum seeker who suffers a disability which, of itself, gives rise to a need for care and attention which falls short of calling for the provision of residential accommodation. The decision of the court was that it did.

22.22 This line of case-law, culminating in the 2002 *Westminster* case, established that where an asylum seeker does satisfy the destitution plus test, the responsibility for financially supporting and accommodating that person lies with the local authority, rather than with NASS (now NAM).

22.23 In order to qualify for support under NAA 1948 s21, asylum seekers must therefore satisfy the following criteria:

1) That they are not excluded from support under section 21 by virtue of Nationality, Immigration and Asylum Act (NIAA) 2002 Sch 3 (see para 22.20 above). For asylum seekers this is straightforward as they are not excluded from community care provisions under Schedule 3.

2) That they pass the 'destitution plus test' under section 21(1A). As outlined above, this proviso has been interpreted[21] to mean that their need for care and attention is to any material extent made more acute by some factor other than destitution or the effects or anticipated physical effects of destitution.

3) That they do not have support otherwise available in accordance with NAA 1948 s21(1). When considering whether an asylum seeker has support otherwise available, regard should not be given to any support the person may receive from NAM. In R *(AW)* v *Croydon LBC* and R *(A, D and Y)* v *Hackney LBC and SSHD*[22] it was held that:

> ... where a person is assessed as in need of care and attention under Section 21 (1) and (1A), there is a duty on the local authority to exercise its powers or perform its duties to the extent necessary to avoid a breach of convention rights. It is not open to a local authority to refuse to provide support which it would otherwise be required to provide, on the ground

20 [2002] EWHC 735 (Admin); (2002) 5 CCLR 486.
21 R v *Wandsworth LBC ex p O and R v Leicester City Council ex p Bhikha* [2000] 1 WLR 2539; (2000) 3 CCLR 237.
22 [2005] EWHC 2950 (Admin); (2006) 9 CCLR 252 at [56].

that accommodation could be provided by the Secretary of State under Section 4, which would prevent a breach of convention rights.[23]

22.24   Since the 2002 *Westminster* case the courts have been asked to consider what illness or level of infirmity would satisfy the destitution plus test. Accordingly in *R (M) v Slough BC*[24] the Court of Appeal held that an HIV positive asylum seeker had to be accommodated by the authority: that he satisfied the 'destitution plus' test even though he was not suffering symptoms and his condition was stable. It has been suggested[25] that the *Slough* judgment should not necessarily be interpreted as entitling all HIV positive applicants to 'destitution plus' status, and that in contested cases medical evidence may prove vital.

22.25   'Destitution plus' status may also arise through mental health difficulties.[26] In *R (PB) v Haringey LBC*[27] the court considered that if the applicant's depression arose from factors other than just destitution,[28] it cannot be said that destitution and its physical effects are the sole cause.

Nationality, Immigration and Asylum Act 2002

22.26   The NIAA 2002 was a response, in part, to the failure of the IAA 1999 to deter sufficient numbers of unlawful immigrants and asylum seekers from entering the UK. In addition it sought to deal with what the government termed 'entitlement shopping' – namely 'individuals who move to the UK for the sole or main purpose of accessing residential accommodation and other services in preference to similar services in the EEA[29] country of origin'.[30]

22.27   NIAA 2002 s54 and Sch 3 prohibit local authorities from providing community care services in general, services under CA 1989 s17 (except for unaccompanied minors) and services under Local Government Act (LGA 2000) s2 for:

- individuals with refugee status in other EEA countries,
- citizens of other EEA countries,
- failed asylum seekers who have not co-operated with removal directions, and

23   This approach was confirmed in *Binomugisha v Southwark LBC* [2006] EWHC 2254 (Admin) and although these cases refer to support under IAA 1999 s4 (see para 22.35), the principle is equally applicable to support under IAA 1999 s95.
24   [2006] EWCA Civ 655; (2006) 9 CCLR 438.
25   See *Social Care Law Today*, Issue 40, July 2006, Arden Publishing.
26   Where entitlement to Mental Health Act (MHA) 1983 s117 support exists, there is no prohibition in the provision of such community care support.
27   [2006] EWHC 2255 (Admin); (2007) 10 CCLR 99 at [49]–[50].
28   PB's anxieties were largely attributable to her fragile mental health and her concern about her children who were subject to care proceedings.
29   European Economic Area – this consists of the EU countries together with Iceland, Liechtenstein, Norway and Switzerland.
30   Department of Health, *Section 54 of the Nationality, Immigration and Asylum Act 2002 and community care and other social services for adults from the EEA living in the UK: Note of Clarification* para 4, accessible at http://www.dh.gov.uk/prod_consum_dh/ idcplg?IdcService=GET_FILE&dID=4171&Rendition=Web.

- individuals who are unlawfully in the UK and who are not asylum seekers.

The exclusions do not apply however to services under MHA 1983 s117.

22.28 The NIAA 2002 does not change the law concerning social services responsibilities to asylum seekers (whose claims have not been determined), although it did materially change the obligations of NASS (now NAM) to asylum seekers who failed to make their asylum claim 'as soon as reasonably practicable' after their arrival in the UK[31] and to failed asylum seekers, as follows.

Late claims and Nationality, Immigration and Asylum Act 2002 s55

22.29 In order to qualify for NAM support, asylum seekers are expected to show that they claimed asylum 'as soon as reasonably practicable' after their arrival in the UK. Failure to do so can result in support being refused (NIAA 2002 s55(1)). Applicants cannot be excluded under section 55 if they have dependent children under the age of 18 (section 55(b) and (c)) or if to do so would result in a breach of their human rights (section 55(5)(a)).

The human rights exemption

22.30 In *R (Adam, Limbuela and Tesema) v SSHD*[32] the House of Lords sought to identify the point at which deprivation becomes so grave that the state is obliged to intervene and provide support. The Lords held that an asylum seeker would be at risk of suffering degrading treatment (contrary to article 3 of the European Convention on Human Rights ('the Convention')) if he, with 'no alternative sources of support, unable to support himself, is, by the deliberate action of the state, denied shelter, food or the most basic necessities of life'.[33] The state therefore had a duty to provide support when:[34]

> ... it appears on a fair and objective assessment of all relevant facts and circumstances that an individual applicant faces an imminent prospect of serious suffering caused or materially aggravated by denial of shelter, food or the most basic necessities of life. Many factors may affect that judgment, including age, gender, mental and physical health and condition, any facilities or sources of support available to the applicant, the weather and time of year and the period for which the applicant has already suffered or is likely to continue to suffer privation.

22.31 While it was not possible to 'formulate any simple test applicable in all cases' the court considered that the potential breach of article 3 would require that a person be supported if the person was:

---

31 NIAA 2002 s55. See *R (Q and Others) v SSHD* [2003] EWCA Civ 364; [2003] 3 WLR 365; (2003) 6 CCLR 136.
32 [2005] UKHL 66; [2005] 3 WLR 1014; (2006) 9 CCLR 30.
33 Ibid, at [7]
34 Ibid, at [8].

. . . obliged to sleep in the street, save perhaps for a short and foreseeably finite period, or was seriously hungry, or unable to satisfy the most basic requirements of hygiene.

22.32   Baroness Hale in her judgment (at [78]) did come close to providing a simple test – essentially arguing that 'cashlessness + rooflessness = inhuman and degrading treatment'.[35]

22.33   The current position is, therefore, that on receiving a section 55 'refusal of support decision' an asylum seeker must show that he or she or a dependant is facing an imminent prospect of serious suffering caused, or materially aggravated, by denial of shelter, food or the most basic necessities of life, and that a failure to support will result in a breach of their rights under article 3. They must be able to point to evidence that they have sought charitable support and that this is either not available or has been exhausted.

22.34   The prohibition in NIAA 2002 s54 against social services providing care services (ie relating to certain EEA citizens of other EEA countries, non-co-operating failed asylum seekers and other persons unlawfully in the UK – see para 22.27 above) is also qualified by the requirement that any failure to provide assistance must not constitute a breach of the person's rights under the Convention.

Failed asylum seekers

New Asylum Model

22.35   Asylum seekers whose applications for asylum have been refused and finally determined (ie appeal rights exhausted) are required to leave the UK. However, there are some failed asylum seekers who are destitute and unable to leave the UK immediately due to circumstances beyond their control. In such cases they can be provided with support under IAA 1999 s4 (as amended by NIAA 2002 s49). Section 4 support (commonly known as 'hard case support') was intended as a limited and temporary form of support for people who are expected to leave the UK within a short period of time. Many failed asylum seekers, however, find themselves supported under section 4 for indefinite periods.

22.36   In order to obtain support, the applicant must show that he or she is destitute. The definition of destitution for section 4 purposes is the same as in IAA 1999 s95(3).

22.37   Hard case support is circumscribed by the term 'facilities for the accommodation of a person'. What can be provided under section 4 must be linked to the accommodation being provided. Current interpretation by the secretary of state enables only food to be 'linked to the accommodation'. There is thus no provision within the relevant regulations for sup-

---

35   See in this regard the commentary in A Mackenzie, 'Case analysis: R. v Secretary of State for the Home Department Ex p. Adam, Limbuela and Tesema' [2006] EHRLR 67–73.

port to be provided as cash.[36] This inevitably causes problems, in particular in terms of clothing and travel.[37] It is of course possible, in the case of a failed asylum seeker with a child, for a request to be made to the local authority for an assessment and services under CA 1989 s17 (see para 24.12 below)[38] for items that section 4 cannot provide.

22.38   Failed asylum seekers requesting support under section 4 must meet the eligibility criteria in the relevant regulations.[39] Arguably the most important of these criteria, and certainly the one that local authorities and practitioners come across most frequently, is the requirement that the applicant must be taking all reasonable steps to leave the UK (regulation 3(2)(a)). Where a failed asylum seeker with children who does not qualify for section 95 support refuses to comply with this requirement (ie where he or she is not taking all reasonable steps to leave the UK) and support is refused, the local authority may become involved if the family becomes destitute. In *R (Grant) v Lambeth LBC*[40] the Court of Appeal held, however, that the local authority can discharge its CA 1989 duties by accommodating the child under section 20 of the Act, rather than providing support under section 17 (see para 24.42 below). In the court's opinion the consequences of support being provided this way (eg by the child, effectively, being taken into care) are not imputable to the state (and hence not a violation of article 8 of the Convention) because they result from the choice of the unlawfully present person – see *R (Kimani) v Lambeth LBC*.[41]

22.39   It may be that in certain situations section 17 services are appropriate or required – for instance where no section 4 support is available or where an application is pending for such support.[42]

Community care provisions

22.40 As with asylum seekers, failed asylum seekers who satisfy the 'destitution plus' test are the responsibility of local authority social services departments under NAA 1948 s21. In *R (AW) v Croydon LBC*[43] it was held that vulnerable failed asylum seekers whose human rights call for accommodation are to have that accommodation provided by local authorities, and not by NASS.[44] For social care purposes the law divides failed asylum seekers into two distinct categories.

---

36 Immigration and Asylum (Provision of Accommodation to Failed Asylum Seekers) Regulations 2005 SI No 930.

37 See *R (AW (Kenya)) v SSHD* [2006] EWHC 3147 (Admin). The Immigration, Asylum and Nationality Act 2006 contains draft regulations 4(10)–(11).

38 NIAA 2002 Sch 3 does not prevent services being provided to a child.

39 Immigration and Asylum (Provision of Accommodation to Failed Asylum Seekers) Regulations 2005 reg 3.

40 [2004] EWCA Civ 1711; [2005] 1 WLR 1781.

41 [2003] EWCA Civ 1150; [2004] 1 WLR 272; (2003) 6 CCLR 484.

42 *R (Grant) v Lambeth LBC* [2004] EWCA Civ 1711; [2005] 1 WLR 1781.

43 [2005] EWHC 2950 (Admin); (2006) 9 CCLR 252.

44 IAA 1999 s4 provides that the availability of NAA 1948 s21 accommodation prevents NASS from providing accommodation – see para 22.35 above.

22.41   The first category is comprised of those asylum seekers who claimed asylum as soon as they arrived in the UK ('at port'). They will normally have been granted temporary admission to enter the UK which means they are in the UK lawfully.[45] As they are lawfully present, they remain entitled to local authority support until such time as formal steps to remove them from the UK are not complied with. If a failed asylum seeker fails to comply with removal directions (by which in this context we mean directions given to a carrier such as a ship or aeroplane) at any time, they are excluded from community care services by virtue of NIAA 2002 Sch 3.

22.42   Failed asylum seekers who did not claim at port are in the UK in breach of immigration law.[46] As they are deemed not to have entered the UK, they can only receive community care assistance if support is necessary to avoid a breach of their Convention rights, namely article 3. In consequence failed asylum seekers who claimed asylum 'at port' remain eligible for section 21 accommodation even after their claim for asylum has been refused, whereas those who did not claim 'at port' cease to be eligible for section 21 accommodation once their claims for asylum have been finally determined, unless support is required to prevent a breach of their Convention rights.

Duties owed to children

Children of asylum seekers

22.43   As noted above, IAA 1999 s95 empowers the Home Secretary (through what is now NAM) to provide support for adult asylum seekers who are destitute or likely to become destitute. However, by IAA 1999 s122, there is a duty on NAM to support destitute asylum seekers with dependent children, and in particular, under section 122(3), to make available 'adequate accommodation for the child'. In *R (A) v NASS and Waltham Forest LBC*[47] the court held that the accommodation of asylum seeking families with disabled children was the sole responsibility of NASS, although in discharging this duty NASS could seek assistance from a local authority under IAA 1999 s100 (and in such cases the authority must assist so far as is 'reasonable in the circumstances').

22.44   In *R (O) v Haringey LBC and SSHD*[48] the facts were reversed in that it was the mother who was disabled, not the children. In that case the Court of Appeal held that the local authority owed the mother a duty under NAA 1948 s21, but this did not extend to accommodating her children for whom NASS was responsible under IAA 1999 s122(5).[49] On a practical

45   NIAA 2002 s11.
46   Ibid.
47   [2003] EWCA Civ 1473; [2004] 1 WLR 752; (2003) 6 CCLR 538 – see also *R (O) v Haringey LBC* [2003] EWHC 2798 (Admin) where it was held that the NASS had responsibility even where there were disabled adult family members.
48   [2004] EWCA Civ 535; (2004) 7 CCLR 310.
49   They are to be treated as 'destitute' by virtue of Asylum Support Regulations 2000 regs 6 and 12 even though living with their mother.

level the court suggested that the local authority should accommodate the whole family, with NASS making a financial contribution to cover the cost of accommodating the children.

Children of failed asylum seekers

22.45 IAA 1999 s122 only applies to asylum seekers. The case of failed asylum seekers is materially different since there no free-standing obligation or power enabling NAM (formerly NASS) to accommodate or fund the child of a failed asylum seeker.

22.46 This has the result that, where the local authority is supporting an adult failed asylum seeker under NAA 1948 s21 it also falls to the local authority to support the children under CA 1989 s17. This is because a person who has ceased to be an asylum seeker is not entitled to be considered for support under IAA 1999 s95 and therefore the provisions under s122 do not apply. The power to accommodate dependents of a failed asylum seeker is found in section 4(2) and this power only exists where there is a power to accommodate the adult failed asylum seeker. Unlike with asylum seekers, the local social services authority in this situation is not precluded from providing support under CA 1989 s17.

Unaccompanied asylum seeking children

22.47 The Border and Immigration Agency (formerly the Home Office and Nationality Directorate) defines an unaccompanied asylum seeking child as:

> . . . an individual who is under 18 and applying for asylum in his/her own right; and is separated from both parents and not being cared for by an adult who by law or custom has responsibility to do so.[50]

22.48 CA 1989 s 20(1) provides that the local authority shall:

> . . . provide accommodation for a child in need who requires it as a result of there being no-one with parental responsibility for him; being lost or abandoned or the person caring for him has been prevented (whether or not permanently and for whatever reason) from providing him with suitable accommodation or care.

22.49 The duty of the local authority under section 20 applies in relation to a child in need 'within their area' (see para 6.33 above). The duty for accommodating and supporting unaccompanied asylum seeking children therefore falls to the local authority within whose area the child is residing or has just arrived.

22.50 If the local authority disputes the claimed age of the applicant, it has the power to conduct a detailed age assessment.[51] On reaching 18 (or 21 if the child has been granted leave to remain in the UK – typically

---

50 *Planning Better Outcomes and Support for Unaccompanied Asylum Seeking Children*, IND Consultation Paper, February 2007.
51 *B v Merton LBC* [2003] EWHC 1689 (Admin); [2003] 4 All ER 280; (2003) 6 CCLR 457.

discretionary leave) the local authority's duty is the same as for any other person leaving care, and the grant of leave entitles the person to access public funds (see para 24.22 below).[52] However, if the child is still an asylum seeker, the local authority continues to have responsibility for the accommodation and subsistence of that person but NAM takes over financial responsibility and reimburses the costs of the local authority. This protects unaccompanied asylum seeking children from dispersal.

EEA nationals

22.51   The European Economic Area (EEA) consists of 30 countries, made up of the European Union states[53] together with Norway, Iceland and Liechtenstein.

22.52   Under the Treaty of Rome 1959 (and subsequent treaties and legislation) citizens of these states enjoy various rights of free movement within the territory of the EEA. These rights are set out in various European directives and regulations.[54]

22.53   Free movement benefits not only citizens of the member states but also certain of their family members (whatever the nationality of the family member) and confers rights of residence and various associated rights and entitlements (eg to social assistance and benefits entitlements). These rights vary, however, according to the nationality and economic status of the citizen in question. The most extensive rights are enjoyed by nationals of the 18 states who were members of the EEA prior to 1 May 2004 (the so-called pre-enlargement states) as well as nationals of Cyprus and Malta.[55] More limited rights are in general enjoyed by nationals of eight of the countries that joined the European Union on 1 May 2004 (the so-called A8 countries[56]), as well as of nationals of the two countries that joined on 1 January 2007 (Romania and Bulgaria, known as the A2 countries).

22.54   The restrictions affect access to the labour market for nationals of these countries and have consequential limitations on their access to social assistance (welfare benefits and housing assistance). The restrictions are far more extensive for A2 nationals than for A8 nationals.

---

52 Provided an application for extension of leave is submitted prior to current leave expiring, leave continues by virtue of Immigration Act 1971 s3C until a final decision is made on the application.

53 The full list of EEA states is Austria, Belgium, Denmark, Finland, France, Germany, Greece, Holland, Ireland, Italy, Luxembourg, Portugal, Spain, Sweden, the UK, Norway, Iceland, Liechtenstein, Cyprus, Malta, Czech Republic, Estonia, Hungary, Latvia, Lithuania, Poland, Slovakia, Slovenia, Bulgaria and Romania.

54 Of which the most important are EC/1612/68 and EC/2004/38.

55 Rights of free movement also apply to citizens of Switzerland.

56 Czech Republic, Estonia, Hungary, Latvia, Lithuania, Poland, Slovakia and Slovenia.

EEA nationals from the pre-enlargement states, Cyprus and Malta

22.55 The key concept in EEA law for the purposes of this text is that of the 'qualified person' as defined in the Immigration (European Economic Area) Regulations 2006.[57] An EEA national from a pre-enlargement state or from Cyprus or Malta is qualified if he or she is:

- a worker;[58]
- a work seeker;
- a self employed person or a service provider;
- a student;
- economically self-sufficient.

22.56 A qualified EEA national has an entitlement to reside in the UK 'without the requirement for leave to remain under the Immigration Act 1971 for as long as he remains a qualified person'.[59]

22.57 Such persons are said to enjoy 'full free movement rights' and have unrestricted access to the UK labour market.

22.58 Qualified EEA nationals are not excluded from social welfare assistance (housing and welfare benefits) under IAA 1999 s115 and thus should not normally need to access community care provisions. However, EEA nationals who are not qualified have no access to social assistance provisions (with the exception of contributory benefits). The consequence is that on facing destitution, these EEA nationals frequently turn to the local social services authority for assistance.

22.59 As previously noted, the prohibition in NIAA 2002 s54 against social services providing care services does not apply where a failure to provide assistance would constitute a breach of the person's Convention rights. This applies equally where failure to provide services would breach a person's rights under a European Union (EU) Treaty. The Department of Health considers that the EU exception will mean that:

> EEA nationals who work or have worked in the UK, their families, self-employed and former self-employed EEA nationals, and students should be provided with social care services by councils if they are eligible for such care in order to protect their freedom of movement. They are entitled on the same basis as UK nationals.[60]

22.60 However, in the case of an EEA citizen (or a person with refugee status in an EEA state or other persons unlawfully in the UK[61]), the local authority

---

57 SI No 1003.
58 This definition includes workers temporarily unfit for work through illness or accident or pregnancy and childbirth.
59 *Barnet LBC v Ismail and Abdi* [2006] EWCA Civ 383; [2006] 1 WLR 2771 clarified that an EEA national who is not a qualified person does not have a right to reside and is subject to immigration control.
60 *Note of Clarification*(note 30 above) para 13.
61 Although for this group (unlike for EEA citizens or persons with refugee status in an EEA state) there is no power to make travel arrangements under the Withholding and Withdrawal of Support (Travel Assistance and Temporary Accommodation) Regulations 2002 SI No 3078.

can discharge any duty under community care provisions by offering an assisted return back to the EEA national's home country.[62] Where there is a dependant child, the local authority may arrange for the person and the child to be accommodated pending their removal from the UK.[63] If however the person does not take reasonable steps to leave the UK and in consequence becomes destitute, the local authority only has a duty to the child which it can accommodate under Children Act (CA) 1989 s20. As noted above (para 22.38) such consequences are not (in the courts' opinion) imputable to the state (and hence not a violation of article 8 of the Convention) because they result from the choice of the unlawfully present person – see *R (Kimani) v Lambeth LBC.*[64]

A8 nationals

22.61   Nationals of the 'A8' countries are subject to a Worker Registration Scheme (WRS) introduced in May 2004. A8 nationals, though able to take any employment, are required under this scheme to register their employment with the Home Office.[65]

22.62   As a general rule, A8 nationals are treated as 'qualified persons' if, during their first year of employment, they have registered under the Home Office's WRS.[66] These A8 nationals are entitled to 'in-work' benefits (tax credits, child benefit, housing and council tax benefit) during their 12 month WRS period. Upon completion of 12 months' employment in accordance with the WRS scheme, an A8 national ceases to be subject to the WRS and acquires equal rights to nationals of the pre-enlargement states. Such persons are commonly referred to as having acquired 'full rights of free movement'.

A2 nationals

22.63   Nationals of the 'A2' countries (Bulgaria and Romania) are subject to a separate scheme which came into effect on 1 January 2007, known as the Worker Authorisation Scheme. The restrictions imposed on A2 nationals under this scheme are more extensive than those imposed on A8 nationals under the WRS.

---

62 Ibid, Sch 3.
63 Ibid, reg 3.
64 [2003] EWCA Civ 1150; [2004] 1 WLR 272; (2003) 6 CCLR 484.
65 It should be noted that there are certain categories of A8 nationals not required to register under the WRS. Details are beyond the scope of this text, however for further details, see Joint Council for the Welfare of Immigrants, *Immigration Nationality & Refugee Handbook*, 2006.
66 In accordance with the Accession (Immigration and Worker Registration) Regulations 2004 SI No 1219 and the Immigration (European Economic Area) and Accession (Amendment) Regulations 2004 SI No 1236. These Regulations derogate from articles 1–6 of the European Directive EC/1612/68 by introducing restrictions on rights of entry and residence and on access to the labour market.

22.64   In general A2 workers are required to obtain work authorisation from the Home Office before taking up employment.[67] Like A8 nationals, A2 nationals are entitled to 'in-work benefits' during their 12 month period of authorised work and acquire full movement rights after 12 months' lawful employment.

Domestic violence

22.65   A difficult situation can arise in relation to foreign spouses of British or settled persons where the foreign spouse has suffered domestic violence and as a consequence needs social services support and accommodation. More commonly than not the foreign spouse is the wife and she has fled before being granted indefinite leave to remain[68] or after her spouse visa has expired.

22.66   Provided the foreign national spouse is in the UK on a spouse visa, she will have express permission to work but there will be a prohibition on recourse to public funds. When the violence causes the spouse to flee, she may turn to the local authority social services department for assistance. Frequently there are children, meaning that the wife's ability to work is impaired (not least that she will not be able to claim tax credits for her child care costs) or she may have been prevented from learning sufficient English to be able to communicate effectively enough to work.

22.67   A spouse in the UK on a visa is not precluded from support by NIAA 2002 Sch 3. Unfortunately, many women who have experienced domestic violence have also had their husbands refuse to put in an extension application, such that they are then in the UK unlawfully, having overstayed. 'Overstayers' are precluded from community care provisions unless support is required to prevent a breach of their Convention rights. If they have children, Schedule 3 does not prevent services being provided for children and so support can be offered under CA 1989 s17. However, as outlined in para 22.60, the local authority can discharge its duty under section 17 by offering an assisted return unless this would lead to a Convention breach. However if the parent is precluded from support, she cannot benefit from section 17 assistance. Accommodation is provided on the basis that it is in the child's best interest to remain with the parent.

22.68   Where there are no children the position is more complicated as domestic violence itself does not satisfy the destitution plus test for services under NAA 1948 s21. The destitution is said to result from the domestic violence but the domestic violence is not a need for care and attention over and above destitution. In such a situation, in *R (Khan) v Oxfordshire CC*[69] it was decided that domestic violence was the cause of destitution only and the need for care and attention arose solely from the

---

67 The details of the scheme are involved and beyond the scope of this text, however for further details, see Joint Council for the Welfare of Immigrants, *Immigration Nationality & Refugee Handbook*, 2006.

68 A grant of indefinite leave to remain attracts full recourse to public funds.

69 [2004] EWCA Civ 309; (2004) 7 CCLR 215: see also para 1.72 above.

destitution. However, the court considered that in some circumstances, in addition to causing destitution, domestic violence could make the need for care and attention more acute. When faced with such a case, careful consideration should be given to establish whether there are any additional circumstances which create a section 21 need. Examples might include physical or mental injury caused by the domestic violence.

Drug, alcohol and HIV/ AIDS services

Introduction

23.1   This chapter considers the community care responsibilities for people with HIV/AIDS and for those who misuse drugs and alcohol. The analysis takes the form of an overview, since the needs of these distinct groups are frequently addressed by specialist agencies or within the mainstream NHS.

23.2   We commence by reviewing the community care responsibilities for drug and alcohol misusers, and at para 23.43 the obligations towards people with HIV/AIDS.

Drug and alcohol misusers and community care

23.3   It is thought that about four million people in England and Wales use at least one illicit drug each year, of which about one million use one of the most dangerous drugs (such as heroin and crack).[1] Approximately 350,000 such users are 'problematic drug users'[2] and it is this group that is considered responsible for 99 per cent of the social and economic costs associated with drug misuse – which are thought to be in the region of £18 billion a year. In 2003/04 over 125,000 people were provided with structured drug treatment services.[3]

23.4   In England 23 per cent of the population (aged 16–64) are believed to drink hazardously or harmfully (about 7.1 million people) and a further 1.1 million people are dependent on alcohol.[4] It is estimated[5] that about £1.7 billion is spent each year dealing with alcohol-related illness, with over 30,000 hospital admissions annually for alcohol dependence syndrome. In terms of specific services, the NHS spends about £95 million each year providing treatment at almost 475 specialised alcohol treatment services in England. The government estimates that the social and economic costs associated with alcohol misuse amount to approximately £20 billion a year.[6]

1   Home Office, *Updated Drug Strategy*, 2002.
2   Royal Society for the Encouragement of Arts, Manufactures & Commerce, *Drugs – facing facts*, 2007, p52, estimates that there were 287,670 problematic drug users in England in 2001 (citing M Frisher et al, 'Prevalence of problematic and injecting drug users for Drug Action Team areas in England' (2006) 28(1) *Journal of Public Health* 3–9) and estimates the UK total to be 360,811.55, citing (N Singleton, R Murray, L Tinsley, *Measuring different aspects of problem drug use: methodological developments*, Home Office Online report 16/06, 2006).
3   Department of Health and Home Office, *Models of Care: for treatment of adult drug misusers*, July 2006, para 2.3.
4   Department of Health, *Alcohol Needs Assessment Research Project (ANARP)*, 2005.
5   Cabinet Office, *Alcohol Harm Reduction Strategy for England*, 2004, para 5.2.
6   Ibid, p12.

Drug and alcohol misuse policy framework

23.5 In 1998 the government published a strategy paper *Tackling Drugs To Build A Better Britain*[7] in order to co-ordinate its 'combating misuse' policies. The policy was reviewed and revised in 2002 and most recently in 2006 when an updated strategy was published. The current programme targets those considered to have a serious drug problem, particularly the 50 per cent who are not in treatment. It aims to double the number of people in treatment by (among other things) increasing the availability of services, with (in 2005) the expenditure on treatment services of £573 million. The government is pledged to increase this expenditure significantly. There is evidence that the increased emphasis on service provision is having a positive impact[8] with, for instance, the average waiting time for treatments falling from over 9 weeks in 2001 to 2.3 weeks in June 2005.[9]

23.6 The service provision strategy in England is co-ordinated via the National Treatment Agency for Substance Misuse (NTA), a special health authority created in 2001[10] to improve the availability, capacity and effectiveness of treatment for drug misuse in England. The NTA issues policy and practice guidance and distributes funding (via its nine regional offices) to the 147 drug action teams (DATs) which cover each English local authority. DATs are local consortiums that include representatives of all the local agencies involved in tackling the misuse of drugs, including primary care trusts, the local authority, police, and probation. It is the responsibility of DATs to provide drug misusers with access to advice and information, needle exchanges, and counselling.

23.7 A number of similar alcohol misuse policy initiatives have occurred in parallel with these programmes, most recently the 2004 *Alcohol Harm Reduction Strategy for England*[11] and the 2006 Department of Health guidance *Models of care for alcohol misusers* (hereafter referred to as the *Models of care (alcohol misuse)*).[12] These are considered further below.

Wales

23.8 The following sections provide an overview of substance misuse policies in England. It will be seen that there are two similar policy documents, one directed at alcohol misuse and the other at drug misuse, and both entitled 'Models of Care'.[13] In Wales a combined policy document exists that closely mirrors these two documents (and which adopts similar

7 Department of Health, *Tackling Drugs to Build a Better Britain The Government's Ten-Year Strategy for Tackling Drugs Misuse*, Cm 3945, TSO, 1998.
8 See eg Audit Commission, *Drug Misuse 2004: Reducing the Local Impact*, 2004.
9 Department of Health and Home Office, *Models of Care: for treatment of adult drug misusers*, July 2006, para 2.2.
10 National Treatment Agency (Establishment and Constitution) Order 2001 SI No 713.
11 Cabinet Office, *Alcohol Harm Reduction Strategy for England*, 2004.
12 Department of Health National Treatment Agency for Substance Misuse, *Models of care for alcohol misusers*, 2006.
13 Department of Health and Home Office, *Models of Care: for treatment of adult drug misusers*, 2006 and Department of Health National Treatment Agency for Substance Misuse, *Models of care for alcohol misusers*, 2006.

terminology including the differing levels of assessment and tiers of service response). The guidance, *Substance Misuse Treatment Framework for Wales*,[14] comprises six separate chapters, namely: (1) Service Framework for Residential Rehabilitation; (2) Service Framework for Residential Rehabilitation; (3) Service Framework for Community Prescribing; (4) Service Framework for Inpatient Treatment; (5) Service Framework to Meet the Needs of People with Co-occurring Substance Misuse and Mental Health Problems; and (6) Needle Exchange Service Framework.

23.9   Given the similarity between the Welsh and English policy initiatives, the following analysis is limited to the English guidance.

Community care provision for drug and alcohol misusers

23.10   The white paper *Health of the Nation*[15] and the policy guidance confirm that an important objective of the community care reforms was to ensure that community care services were available to those whose need for them arose by reason of alcohol or drug misuse. The 1990 policy guidance (at para 8.4) emphasised the point thus:

> The Government attaches a high priority[16] to tackling the problems associated with the misuse of alcohol and drugs, and to ensuring the provision of a comprehensive network of services for alcohol and drug misusers.

23.11   In similar vein, guidance on the housing/community care interface LAC (92)12 stated:

> Housing authorities will need to be aware that for some clients, such as alcohol and drug misusers, their care plan may include a planned progression from some form of residential care to a more independent lifestyle, possibly away from their original area of residence.[17]

23.12   The principal social services circular guidance concerning services for drug and alcohol misusers remains LAC (93)2, which stresses the special circumstances surrounding the provision of services for this client group, and in particular comments:

> 12. Addressing the needs of people with alcohol and drug problems will present a particular challenge to LAs. The aim must be to respond effectively and to offer a programme of care that will help the misuser make positive changes to his or her life. LAs will need to bear in mind that people who misuse alcohol and drugs may:
> • present to LAs with problems other than alcohol and/or drug misuse. LAs will need to ensure that the possibility of alcohol and drug misuse is covered in essential procedures;

---

14 Welsh Assembly, *Substance Misuse Treatment Framework for Wales*, 2004.
15 Department of Health, *The Health of the Nation*, Cm 1523, HMSO, 1991 – see eg paras D.17–D.18.
16 The point is also made in the white paper *Tackling Drugs Together*, Cm 2846, 1995, para B.55.
17 At para 2 of the annex to the circular.

- have particularly complex needs including urgent workplace or family crises or difficulties with child care, which may not have been revealed to LA services;
- move between areas frequently, and a significant proportion will have no settled residence or be living away from their area of ordinary residence;
- self-refer to agencies which are not in their home area, both because of their transient lifestyle and for therapeutic reasons, and many will need urgent help;
- avoid contact with statutory services; drug misusers in particular may be reluctant to become involved with statutory agencies because of the illegal nature of their drug-related activities;
- need to be provided with services several times before they succeed in controlling their alcohol or drug misuse;
- require residential treatment and rehabilitation as a positive treatment choice;
- sometimes behave unpredictably and may not fit easily into assessment and care management systems designed to meet the needs of other client groups.

Assessment procedures

23.13 The key guidance in relation to drug treatment strategies *Models of care (drug misuse)*[18] advises the relevant professionals to adopt three broad levels of assessment, each of which incorporates a risk assessment that addresses (at para 4.5):

- Risk of suicide or self-harm;
- Risks associated with substance use (such as overdose);
- Risk of harm to others (including harm to treatment staff, harm to children and domestic violence);
- Risk of harm from others (including domestic violence);
- Risk of self-neglect.

23.14 The three levels of assessment are:

1) **Screening assessment** (at para 4.1). These are brief assessments that seek to establish whether there is a drug and alcohol problem, what other related problems exist, and whether there is an immediate risk for the client. The assessment will identify whether there is a need to refer on to drug treatment services and the urgency of the referral.

2) **Triage**[19] **assessment** (at para 4.2). These are usually undertaken when the misuser makes contact with the specialist drug treatment services. The assessment seeks to determine the seriousness and urgency of the problems, the most appropriate treatment and the person's motivation to engage in treatment, current risk factors and the urgency of need to

---

18 Department of Health and Home Office, *Models of Care: for treatment of adult drug misusers*, July 2006.

19 A process for sorting people based on their need for or likely benefit from treatment (from the French 'trier' – to sort).

access treatment. The assessment will generally include 'an initial care plan' (para 4.3).

3) **Comprehensive assessment** (at para 4.4). These are targeted at drug misusers with 'more complex needs and those who will require structured drug treatment interventions'. Comprehensive assessments will be an ongoing process rather than a single event and may have input from various professionals, such as doctors (for prescribing expertise) and psychologists.

23.15   The *Models of care (alcohol misuse)*[20] guidance adopts the same terminology and requires the same three broad levels of assessment, which (with the necessary changes) require the same content and level of analysis.

23.16   Circular LAC (93)2 makes a number of important points concerning the need for authorities to adopt flexible assessment procedures in relation to people who misuse alcohol or drugs, and the related need in many cases to develop a close working relationship with the probation services.

> 13. People with serious and urgent alcohol and/or drug problems are likely to need a rapid response because of crises and to capture fluctuating motivation. Serious deterioration which may carry social, legal and care implications may ensue if there is delay before assessment or if assessment procedures are prolonged.
>
> *Eligibility for assessment*
> 14. LAs should ensure that any criteria they may develop governing eligibility for assessment are sensitive to the circumstances of alcohol and drug misusers. As with all other user groups, the LA should have criteria for determining the level of assessment that is appropriate to the severity or complexity of the need. LAs should ensure that:
> *   arrangements have been agreed with all the agencies in their area to which misusers are likely to present for help, which will enable those agencies to initiate assessment procedures where in their view they are indicated;
> *   arrangements are in place to facilitate the assessment of a person by another authority where that person is ordinarily resident in that other authority's area, for example by agreeing with another LA to undertake an assessment on that authority's behalf;
> *   individuals who are of no settled residence are not excluded from assessment by means of eligibility criteria which require duration of residence. The Department proposes to issue guidance to LAs in 1993 about the resolution of disputes and the procedures to be adopted in the last resort where disputes cannot be resolved between the authorities concerned.[21] Disputes about ordinary residence should not prevent people receiving the care they need.
>
> *Adapting assessment to the special needs of alcohol and drug misusers*
> 15. LAs will need to ensure that their assessment systems take full account of the different ways in which alcohol and drug misusers present for services, their different characteristics and their particular needs:

---

20 Department of Health National Treatment Agency for Substance Misuse, *Models of care for alcohol misusers*, 2006, paras 2.3 et seq.
21 This was effected via LAC (93)7 Part II – see para 6.9 above.

- standard LA assessment procedures and documentation should include consideration of substance misuse.
- LA staff will need to be able to identify the indications of substance misuse so that specialist agencies can be involved where appropriate.

Rapid assessment procedures ('fast-track' assessment)

16. There are a range of organisations and professionals who deal frequently with alcohol and drug misusers. A great many of the services, including virtually all residential services, are provided by the independent sector. There is, therefore, within the independent sector, a substantial reservoir of experienced professionals with skills to undertake assessment in this field. LAs should consider involving independent sector agencies in the assessment process. Practice guidance issued by the Department of Health Social Services Inspectorate[22] emphasises the importance of training to equip those people within LAs who undertake assessment with the necessary knowledge and skills. Policy guidance issued by the Department, 'Community Care in the Next Decade and Beyond'[23] states that where a specialist service – for example a drug and alcohol service – is provided by an independent agency under arrangements with a social services department, it will be possible to include assessment of needs in relation to such services in contract arrangements. In these circumstances LAs will need to ensure that the specialist agency is aware of other potential needs for which LAs have a responsibility.

17. Residential placements should not normally take place without a comprehensive needs assessment. Where assessment is contracted to an independent specialist agency, decisions to commit resources and ultimate responsibility for the assessment remains with the LA.

18. Because many alcohol and drug misusers present or are referred to services outside their area of ordinary residence LAs are encouraged to work together to identify systems so that they can feel confident about committing resources on the basis of an assessment undertaken in another LA. This may be facilitated by the development of standard and agreed assessment procedures and forms and networks of named responsible officers within LAs.

19. The Department is encouraging local authority associations to work with the independent sector to establish rapid assessment procedures for alcohol and drug misusers and good practice guidance in out of area referrals which they can commend to local authorities.

20. Individual LAs and independent service providers should, together, ensure that rapid assessment procedures meet the needs of alcohol and drug misusers. In order to do so LAs and providers may want to determine the pattern of referrals of their residents/clients in order to establish contact and set up appropriate arrangements where regular flows exist. LAs and independent sector service providers will together wish to have regard to the Department's study examining good practice in care management and assessment for alcohol and drug misusers which will be available to local authorities shortly.

---

22 *Care Management and Assessment: A Practitioners' Guide*, 1991, see para 3.24 above.
23 Referred to in this text as the 1990 policy guidance; see para 3.24 above.

Emergency action

21. LAs need to be aware that alcohol and drug misusers may sometimes be in such urgent need that residential care will need to be provided immediately. 'The Care Management and Assessment' practice guidance issued by the Department of Health covers the arrangements for urgent admission to both residential and nursing home care.[24]

22. LAs may contract with a provider to offer an emergency direct access service for people in urgent need, with assessment and a decision about longer term treatment following as soon as practicable. LAs may wish to contract with a voluntary organisation to provide direct access to residential care without assessment in these circumstances. In such cases of urgent need the area of ordinary residence of the person should not be a consideration.[25]

Out of area referrals

23. Because of the transient lifestyles of a significant proportion of drug and alcohol misusers LAs will be involved in negotiations about area of ordinary residence for people with alcohol and drug misuse problems to a greater extent than for others. Where people are ordinarily resident in the area of the LA undertaking the assessment, there may be therapeutic benefit in referring people to a residential service away from the area in which they are experiencing their alcohol and drug problems. LAs are reminded that the statutory direction on choice[26] of residential accommodation advises that people assessed as needing residential care should be able to exercise choice over the place where they receive that care. LAs should ensure that resources can be identified for out of area placements.

24. LAs should ensure that there are arrangements in place for responding to the following types of out of area referrals:
  *   where people are ordinarily resident outside the area of the LA undertaking the assessment, there will be a need to liaise with the LA in the area of ordinary residence to establish responsibility for funding the care package.
  *   where people are ordinarily resident outside the area of the LA but are in urgent need of residential care[27].
  *   here it is impossible to identify a person's area of ordinary residence; in these circumstances the LA where they present for services should assume responsibility for arranging and providing the necessary services.[28]

Probation service

25. Some alcohol and/or drug misusing clients of the Probation Service will continue to seek access to residential and non-residential care, and LAs should liaise with probation services to ensure that these needs can be considered within the community care arrangements. Attention should be given to establishing joint assessment or common assessment procedures, such as those LAs have developed with other client groups. LAs will also

24 Practice guidance, 1991, para 4.45 for nursing homes and para 4.97 for residential homes.
25 NAA 1948 s24(3).
26 NAA 1948 (Choice of Accommodation) Directions 1992; see para 7.90 and Appendix B.
27 NAA 1948 s24(3)(b).
28 Ibid, ss24(3)(a) and 32.

need to be aware that there may be requests for resources to provide residential and non-residential care for persons whose alcohol or drug misuse comes to light through offending, appearance in court and/or involvement with probation services. LAs are reminded that the Criminal Justice Act 1991 which came into force on 1 October 1992 emphasises that it is preferable for offenders who misuse alcohol or drugs to be dealt with in the community rather than in custody.[29]

23.17   In this respect, the strategy paper, *Tackling Drugs To Build A Better Britain*[30] also highlighted the crucial role of inter-disciplinary working (particularly between health, social services, housing, education and employment services).

The provision and commissioning of services

23.18   Although the statutory responsibility for the provision of heath and social care services for drug and alcohol misusers rest with the NHS and social services authorities, in practice the assessment and service provision functions are discharged by DATs.

23.19   Every DAT should have access to a range of services to cater for the assessed needs of misusers. These services are detailed in *Models of care (drug misuse)*.[31] Although the precise nature of the guidance is unclear, its predecessor guidance stated that it was to have a 'similar status to a national service framework'.[32] The guidance anticipates that a person may receive a number of different forms of treatment at the same time – for example someone may be receiving counselling as well as medication, or a sequence of treatment, for example as a hospital inpatient for a detoxification programme, followed by a residential rehabilitation service.

23.20   *Models of care (drug misuse)* provides general advice on the care planning process (at chapter 5), outlining the format and contents of care plans. More detailed guidance on the care process has also been issued.[33] *Models of care (drug misuse)* envisages care plans as being not merely descriptive of the care package that is to be provided, but also an 'agreement on a plan of action between the client and service provider' (para 5.3.2). Care plans should be 'brief and readily understood by all parties involved' and explicitly identify the roles of specific individuals and services in the delivery of the care plan. Considerable emphasis is placed on the need to sustain and retain the service user during the early phases of treatment and for there to be a key worker in this context (paras 5.3.3–5.3.4).

---

29   See Powers of Criminal Courts Act 1973 Sch 1A.
30   Cm 3945, 1998, p23.
31   Department of Health and Home Office, *Models of Care: for treatment of adult drug misusers*, July 2006.
32   Department of Health, *Models of Care: for treatment of adult drug misusers. Framework for developing local systems of effective drug misuse treatment in England*, 2002, para 2.1.
33   National Treatment Agency for Substance Misuse, *Care planning practice guide*, 2006.

23.21   Care plans should address four key domains, in order to identify goals by which progress can be measured. The domains are:

- drug and alcohol misuse;
- health (physical and psychological);
- offending;
- social functioning (including housing, employment and relationships).

23.22   *Models of care (drug misuse)* requires that DATs ensure that users have access to four 'tiers' of service. The 2006 guidance requires 'far greater emphasis' to be given to reducing drug-related harm (para 3.2.1) and seeks to expand the commissioning of Tier 4 services (specialist residential services) which it considers to be 'crucial' and to have been (in comparative terms) neglected. A 2007 report[34] makes the same point:

> One major weakness in the existing array of treatment options is in the provision of services involving residential care. Residential rehabilitation has been found to be generally more effective than treatment in the community where 'effective' is taken to mean enabling people to become drug-free.[35] . . . In recent years, as the treatment system has developed, the residential rehabilitation sector has been neglected in favour of maintenance prescribing and other services at the Tier 3 level, delivered in the community. At present it can accommodate no more than 5 per cent of all the people in drugs treatment.

and

> Moreover, even if there were a system in place for making referrals to residential rehabilitation, as often as not the funding is not there to pay for them. Drug rehabilitation has tended to come, like other forms of residential care, out of the community care budgets of local authorities' social services departments and it therefore competes with all the other demands on these overstretched budgets.

23.23   *Models of care (drug misuse)* advises that in commissioning care packages, greater emphasis should be given to 'effective and well-co-ordinated' drug-related after-care provision and that Supporting People funding should be considered in tandem with other funding streams (para 3.7).

23.24   *Models of care (drug misuse)* at pp20 et seq describes the four tiers of intervention that must be commissioned and provided locally. It recommends that these be in a range of settings and that local systems should 'allow for some flexibility in how interventions are provided, with the crucial factors being the patterns of local need and whether a service provider is competent to provide a particular drug treatment intervention' (para 3.8). The four tiers are summarised as follows:

---

34 Royal Society for the Encouragement of Arts, Manufactures & Commerce, *Drugs – facing facts*, 2007, pp199–200.
35 M Gossop, 'Developments in the treatment of drug problems' in P Bean and T Nemitz (eds), *Drug treatment: what works?* Routledge, 2004.

Tier 1 Drug-related information and advice, screening and referral to specialised drug treatment services.

This level of support will usually be provided in general health care settings (where the main focus is not drug treatment, eg liver units, antenatal wards, Accident and Emergency and pharmacies), as well in social services, education or criminal justice settings. As a minimum, commissioners must ensure that the following services are available:
- drug treatment screening and assessment;
- referral to specialised drug treatment;
- drug advice and information;
- partnership or 'shared care' working with specialised drug treatment services to provide specific drug treatment interventions for drug misusers.

Tier 2 Assessment, referral to structured drug treatment, brief psychosocial interventions, harm reduction interventions (including needle exchange) and after-care.

This level of support will generally be provided by specialised drug treatment services or in hospital – however they may be provided in outreach services, in primary care settings, in pharmacies, criminal justice settings and so on.

As a minimum commissioners must ensure that the following services are available:
- triage assessment and referral for structured drug treatment;
- drug interventions;
- interventions to reduce harm and risk due to blood-borne viruses including dedicated needle exchanges;
- interventions to minimise the risk of overdose and diversion of prescribed drugs;
- brief psychosocial interventions for drug and alcohol misuse;
- brief interventions for specific target groups including high-risk and other priority groups;
- drug-related support for clients seeking abstinence;
- drug-related after-care support for those who have left care-planned structured treatment;
- liaison and support for generic providers of Tier 1 interventions;
- outreach services to engage clients into treatment and to re-engage people who have dropped out of treatment;
- a range of the above interventions for drug-misusing offenders.

Tier 3 Community-based specialised drug assessment and co-ordinated care planned treatment and drug specialist liaison.

This level of support will generally be provided by the same range of providers as Tier 2 interventions above.

As a minimum commissioners must ensure that the following services are available:
- comprehensive drug misuse assessment;
- care planning, co-ordination and review for all in structured treatment, often with regular keyworking sessions as standard practice;
- community care assessment and case management for drug misusers;

- harm reduction activities as integral to care-planned treatment;
- a range of prescribing interventions[36] as part of a package of care including: prescribing for stabilisation and oral opioid maintenance prescribing; community based detoxification; injectable maintenance prescribing, and a range of prescribing interventions to prevent relapse and ameliorate drug and alcohol-related conditions;
- a range of structured evidence-based psychosocial interventions to assist individuals to make changes in drug and alcohol using behaviour;
- structured day programmes and care-planned day care;
- liaison services for acute medical and psychiatric health services (eg pregnancy, mental health and hepatitis services);
- liaison services for social care services (eg social services (child protection and community care teams), housing, homelessness);
- a range of the above interventions for drug-misusing offenders.

Tier 4 Specialised drug treatment (including inpatient drug detoxification and stabilisation) 'care planned and care coordinated to ensure continuity of care and aftercare'.

This level of support will generally be provided in specialist settings such as residential substance misuse units or wards, specialist inpatient detoxification beds or specialist addiction units attached to residential rehabilitation units, step programmes, residential rehabilitation or halfway houses which may be located away from their area of residence and drug misusing networks.

As a minimum commissioners must ensure that the following services are available:
- inpatient specialist drug and alcohol assessment, stabilisation, and detoxification/assisted withdrawal services;
- a range of drug and alcohol residential rehabilitation units to suit the needs of different service users;
- a range of drug halfway houses or supportive accommodation for drug misusers;
- residential drug and alcohol crisis intervention units (in larger urban areas);
- inpatient detoxification/assisted withdrawal provision, directly attached to residential rehabilitation units for suitable individuals;
- provision for special groups for which a need is identified (eg for drug-using pregnant women, drug users with liver problems, drug users with severe and enduring mental illness);
- a range of the above interventions for drug-misusing offenders.

23.25   *Models of care (alcohol misuse)*[37] adopts a similar four tiered service provision response requirement, which are, in brief:

Tier 1 The provision of alcohol-related information and advice; screening; simple brief interventions; and referral. At this stage the intervention is aimed at identifying hazardous, harmful and dependent drinkers;

36 In compliance with Department of Health, *Drug Misuse and Dependence – Guidelines on Clinical Management*, 1999, known as 'the clinical guidelines'.
37 Department of Health National Treatment Agency for Substance Misuse, *Models of care for alcohol misusers*, 2006, pp20–23.

providing information on sensible drinking; simple brief interventions to reduce alcohol-related harm; and referral of those with alcohol dependence or harm for more intensive interventions.

Tier 2 Open access, non-care-planned, alcohol-specific interventions: at this stage interventions include the provision of open access facilities and outreach services that provide alcohol-specific advice, information and support; extended brief interventions to help alcohol misusers reduce alcohol-related harm; and assessment and referral of those with more serious alcohol-related problems for care-planned treatment.

Tier 3 Community-based, structured, care-planned alcohol treatment: at this stage interventions include providing community-based specialised alcohol misuse assessments, and alcohol treatment that is care co-ordinated and care-planned.

Tier 4 Specialist inpatient treatment and residential rehabilitation: at this stage interventions include the provision of residential, specialised alcohol treatment services which are care-planned and co-ordinated to ensure continuity of care and after-care.

Service user failure

23.26   Drug and alcohol services can be expensive, and the guidance (LAC (93)2 para 11) states, 'there is a comparatively rapid turnover' of such service users in residential accommodation due in part to the relatively high 'failure rate' experienced by people trying to rid themselves of an addiction. The NTA endorse this advice – that relapses are to be expected and planned for, stating that 'most drug misusers relapse and need to return to treatment a number of times before getting their habit under control'. It notes, however that 'around 50 per cent of those who do complete a comprehensive treatment programme are still drug-free after five years'.[38]

23.27   The importance of this factor was also stressed in *Purchasing Effective Treatment and Care for Drug Misusers*[39] which stated (at para 1.7):

Drug misusers suffer relapses, and may need several periods of treatment before they achieve the ultimate aim of 'abstinence'. 'Instant' cures are relatively rare, partly because drug misuse is closely associated with many other problems. These include unemployment, family break up, homelessness and crime. Tackling drug misuse effectively may therefore involve a range of interventions by several agencies, for people at different stages of their drug misusing careers. If these are not properly co-ordinated resources will be wasted.

23.28   *Models of care (drug misuse)* refers to US evidence (at para 3.9.1) that suggests that:

. . . an average time in treatment for someone with a heroin or crack dependence problem is five to seven years, with some heroin users requiring indefinite maintenance on substitute opioids. Evidence also tells us that service users gain cumulative benefit from a series of treatment

---

38   NTA 'background' briefing statement at http://www.nta.nhs.uk.
39   March 1997.

episodes. However, the biggest improvements in client outcomes are likely to be made in the first six years of treatment.

23.29   In similar vein *Models of care (alcohol misuse)*[40] advises that alcohol dependence is recognised to be a commonly recurring condition and that individuals:

> . . . may require a number of episodes of treatment before they reach their goals, which in relation to their drinking behaviour are likely to be either lower-risk drinking or abstinence. Some more 'entrenched' or recurrent alcohol misusers with severe dependence, and who may have other problems, may not reach their drinking goals or other goals in a particular episode of care. Treatment interventions may, in some cases, need to be carried out over extended periods, or individuals may benefit from multiple treatment episodes.

NHS obligations

23.30   The effects of alcohol/drug misuse can be life-threatening and frequently require specialist medical and nursing interventions. The NHS has a clear responsibility in this field, although it is, in relation to such matters as rehabilitation and recovery, an overlapping responsibility with social services authorities. LAC (93)2 confirms[41] that 'the new community care arrangements do not affect health authorities' responsibilities for funding the healthcare element of any alcohol and drug service. LAs will need to consider and draw up agreements with health authorities covering arrangements for funding treatment and rehabilitation services for people with alcohol and/or drug problems.'

23.31   The white paper *Tackling Drugs Together*,[42] in referring to the role of health care services stated:[43]

> The Government's aim is to provide a comprehensive range and choice of local services to help drug misusers give up drugs and maintain abstinence. Such services also promote better health and reduce the risks of drug misuse, including infections associated with sharing injecting equipment such as HIV and hepatitis. These services include residential detoxification and rehabilitation, community drug dependency services, needle and syringe exchange schemes, advice and counselling, and after-care and support services. Facilities are provided by both statutory and independent agencies. General practitioners are also encouraged to address the needs of drug misusers. Guidelines on clinical management, *Drug Misuse and Dependence*[44] were issued to all doctors in 1991. Guidelines for the clinical management of substance misusers in police custody[45] were issued in March 1995.

40   Department of Health National Treatment Agency for Substance Misuse, *Models of care for alcohol misusers*, 2006, para 2.5.
41   At para 7.
42   Cm 2846, HMSO, 1995.
43   At para B.49.
44   Department of Health, HMSO, 1991.
45   Department of Health, *Substance Misuse Detainees in Police Custody: Guidelines on Clinical Management*, 1995.

23.32   EL (95)114 required health authorities to review and report on their arrangements for 'shared care' of drug misusers. The outcome of this review and advice on general health authority commissioning is contained in *Purchasing Effective Treatment and Care for Drug Misusers*, appendix C to which lists a number of specific health services that ought to be available for drug misusers. These include hospital drug detoxification units,[46] providing urgent assessment and acute care as well as support, counselling and rehabilitation; methodone reduction programmes; hospital outpatient and community-based clinics; general counselling as well as GP training and encouragement to 'identify drug misuse, promote harm minimisation and where appropriate refer to specialist services'. The publication expressed particular concern about failures of co-ordination between health and local authorities such that there were 'long waits for detoxification', noting that this may mean that drug misusers lose their motivation to continue with treatment (para 8.5).

23.33   The above guidance has now been augmented by 2005 guidance on the commissioning of in-patient and residential rehabilitation drug and alcohol treatment interventions.[47]

Social services obligations

Accommodation

23.34   The duty to provide residential care or nursing home accommodation under National Assistance Act (NAA) 1948 s21 specifically includes a duty towards persons who are 'alcoholic or drug-dependent'.[48] The duties under NAA 1948 s21 are considered in detail in chapter 7. Specific guidance has been issued concerning the commissioning of residential services.[49]

23.35   The role of residential care facilities is the subject of guidance in LAC (93)2, which states:

> 10. Residential services are an important component of overall service provision for alcohol and drug misusers and have developed as a national network. There are many LAs without such an alcohol or drug service in their area. Residential services offer a number of different treatment approaches, and LAs will need to ensure that people are referred to a service best suited to their needs. LAs can obtain information about the network of residential service provision in publications from two national voluntary organisations, Alcohol Concern and SCODA.[50]

---

46 Or through specialist nursing home facilities.
47 Department of Health and Home Office, *Initial Guide for the Commissioning of In-Patient and Residential Rehabilitation Drug and Alcohol Treatment Interventions as part of Treatment Systems*, 2005.
48 LAC (93)10 appendix 1 para 2(6).
49 Department of Health and Home Office, *Initial Guide for the Commissioning of In-Patient and Residential Rehabilitation Drug and Alcohol Treatment Interventions as part of Treatment Systems*, 2005.
50 Standing Conference on Drug Abuse, Waterbridge House, 32–36 Loman Street, London SE1 0EE. Tel: 020 7928 9500.

11. The length of treatment programmes in a residential setting varies between three and eighteen months. The comparatively rapid turnover of alcohol and drug clients in residential care mean that places will begin to become vacant on a relatively large scale after 1 April 1993. LAs will need to address issues of assessment and care management for these people now so that they are ready from 1 April 1993 to provide new applicants with the care they need.[51]

23.36   A Social Services Inspectorate report *Residential Care for People with Drug/ Alcohol Problems*, 1994, made the following general comments concerning the accommodation needs of such people:

- Drug/alcohol misusers often have a range of problems which may contribute to, or be exacerbated by, substance misuse; residential care is only one part of a continuum of services.
- Residential care may be the preferred option most appropriate to meet individual need for one of the following reasons:
- the service user may need 'time out' from an environment which is not conducive to cessation of drug/alcohol misuse;
- the service user many have a number of complex and inter-related problems which can be addressed only in a residential environment.
- A primary and major need of people, in other client groups, requiring residential care is usually for supervised accommodation; for drug/ alcohol misusers, accommodation is often only one of a range of needs which require intensive support.
- The characteristics and needs of drug/alcohol misusers are different in some ways from those of other client groups who require residential care because they are unable, or do not feel able, to live independently in their home environment. Many drug/alcohol misusers are in their early adult years and residential care is required as an appropriate temporary environment in which to provide intensive therapeutic care as well as physical and social care. Residential care is rarely provided for drug/alcohol misusers as a permanent home.

Non-accommodation obligations

23.37   Services under NHS Act (NHSA) 2006 Sch 20 and NHS (Wales) Act (NHS(W)A) 2006 Sch 15 are specifically available for persons who are 'alcoholic or drug-dependent' and these services are considered at para 9.137 above.

23.38   The description of possible arrangements which can be made under NHSA 2006 Sch 20 (NHS(W)A 2006 Sch 15) is so widely drafted as to be capable of encompassing virtually all the traditional domiciliary and community care services. The inclusion in the directions (appendix 3 to LAC(93)10) of a separate category of potential service 'specifically for persons who are alcoholic or drug-dependent', is clearly designed to ensure that authorities are empowered to provide all the relevant services which may be required by alcohol or drug misusers. The 1990 policy guidance (at

51   LAC (93)2 was issued in January 1993.

para 8.6) states that the range of services local authorities will need to consider 'include prevention and harm minimisation, advice and counselling, day care and residential rehabilitation'.[52]

23.39   *Purchasing Effective Treatment and Care for Drug Misusers* gives commissioning advice on various community and residential based services, including outreach programmes and structured day care.[53] It however emphasised the central part played by counselling (both structured and general) in all drug misuse treatments (para 8.6) and the 'evidence that residential rehabilitation programmes can effectively help many drug misusers, particularly with chaotic lifestyles and severe problems related to their misuse' (para 8.5).

Dual diagnosis

23.40   Between a third to a half of people with severe mental health problems have substance misuse related problems.[54] In order to avoid such persons being 'shuttled between services, with a corresponding loss of continuity of care', attempts have been made to ensure that specialist mental health services and specialist substance abuse services co-operate closely.

23.41   The key 'good practice guideline' in this domain is a Department of Health publication *Mental Health Policy Implementation Guide Dual Diagnosis Good Practice Guide,* 2002, which has been augmented by 2006 guidance[55] concerning the assessment and clinical management of such patients who are in psychiatric inpatient or day care settings. The 2002 guidance seeks to better integrate working between the specialist agencies – rather than create a separate organisation for 'dual diagnosis' users. In relation to the policy that should inform specialist units working in these fields, it summarises the key points of its advice thus:

- Mainstream mental health services have a responsibility to address the needs of people with a dual diagnosis.
- Where they exist, specialist teams of dual diagnosis workers should provide support to mainstream mental health services.
- All staff in assertive outreach must be trained and equipped to work with dual diagnosis.
- Adequate numbers of staff in crisis resolution and early intervention teams, CMHTs and inpatient settings must also be so trained.
- They must be able to link up with each other and with specialist advice and support, including from drug and alcohol agencies.

---

52   SCODA, *New Options: Changing residential and social care for drug users,* 1997 (see note 50 above).

53   See also SCODA, *Structured Day Programmes: new options in community care for drug misusers,* 1996 .

54   Department of Health, *Mental Health Policy Implementation Guide Dual Diagnosis Good Practice Guide,* 2002, para 1.3.1.

55   Department of Health, *Dual diagnosis in mental health inpatient and day hospital settings. Guidance on the assessment and management of patients in mental health inpatient and day hospital settings who have mental ill-health and substance use problems,* 2006.

- All local health and social care economies must map need including for those in prison.
- Project teams must be set up and must agree a local plan to meet need which must contain an agreed local focused definition, care pathways/care coordination protocols and clinical governance guidelines.
- All clients must be on the CPA and must have a full risk assessment regardless of their location within services.
- LITs should take the lead in implementing these guidelines ensuring that commissioning is coordinated across PCTs and DATs.

23.42   It summarises the key points of its advice, concerning assessment and treatment approaches in the following terms:

- Assessment of substance misuse forms an integral part of standard assessment procedures for mental health problems.
- Services need to develop routine screening procedures and, where substance misuse is identified, the nature and severity of that misuse and its associated risks should be assessed.
- An awareness of specific groups for whom these dual conditions generate specific needs must inform the assessment process.
- Treatments should be staged according to an individual's readiness for change and engagement with services.
- Staff should avoid prematurely pushing clients towards abstinence but adopt a harm reduction approach.
- An optimistic and longitudinal perspective regarding the substance misuse problem and its treatment are necessary.
- A flexible and adaptive therapeutic response is important for the integrated management of these dual conditions.
- Attention must be paid to social networks of clients, to meaningful daytime activity and to sound pharmacological management.

People with HIV/AIDS

23.43   It appears that about 63,500 adults were living with HIV in the UK at the end of 2005, of whom 20,100 (32 per cent) were unaware of their infection. In 2005, there were about 7,450 new diagnoses of HIV. While the number of new HIV diagnoses is increasing (almost doubling in the five years to 2005), the number of AIDS diagnoses and deaths in HIV-infected individuals has declined (largely due to effective drug combination therapy introduced in 1996), with 730 reports of AIDS and 503 deaths during 2005.[56]

23.44   In contrast to the requirements of people who abuse alcohol or drugs, the needs of people with HIV or AIDS are not specifically mentioned in the community care legislation or directions. However people with HIV/AIDS are potential (or actual) community care users and therefore

---

56   Office for National Statistics, *HIV and AIDS*, 2007, at http://www.statistics.gov.uk/cci/nugget.asp?id=654.

entitled to an assessment and, where appropriate, services. In general residential care or nursing home accommodation will be provided by social services departments under NAA 1948 s21 (see chapter 7 above) and by health authorities under the continuing care obligations (see Chapter 14 above).

23.45 　In relation to non-accommodation services, the social services obligation under Chronically Sick and Disabled Persons Act (CSDPA) 1970 s2 is owed to people who are already 'substantially and permanently handicapped'. These services are therefore only likely to be available for people who have developed the AIDS symptoms. In contrast the social services duties under NHSA 2006 Sch 20 (NHS(W)A 2006 Sch 15) are owed to people who have an illness (whether or not it is has already resulted in them becoming permanently and substantially handicapped) or people who are recovering from an illness or in order to prevent illness. These services, which are of primary relevance to people with HIV who have not yet developed the AIDS symptoms, are considered in detail at para 9.137 above.

23.46 　The Department of Health[57] has published guidance and issued a number of circulars concerning the social care needs of people with HIV infection and AIDS; these include:

1) *HIV infection – The working interface between voluntary organisations and social services departments*, 1992.
2) *Children and HIV – Guidance for local authorities*, 1992.
3) *The health and social care of people with HIV infection and AIDS – Findings and good practice recommendations from research funded by the DoH 1986–1992*, 1993.
4) *Women and HIV*, 1993.
5) *Inspection of local authority services for people affected by HIV/AIDS: Overview*, 1994.
6) *Implementing Caring for People: Caring for People with HIV and AIDS*, 1994.
7) *Support grant for social services for people with HIV/AIDS* LAC (DH) (2007)5.
8) *Better prevention: Better services: Better sexual health: The national strategy for sexual health and HIV Implementation action plan*, June 2002.

57　There does not appear to be any community care specific AIDS/HIV guidance issued by the Welsh Assembly.

Children Act 1989 duties to children in need

Introduction

24.1   Read and others[1] highlight the lack of accurate data on the prevalence of disability in children in Britain but suggest that a re-analysis of the census data for 1985–89 indicates that there were then about 327,000 disabled children under the age of 16. Adopting the Disability Discrimination Act (DDA) 1995 definition of disability, they consider that the population of disabled children might now number 700,000. Their analysis highlights however the recent and significant increases in numbers identified as having autistic spectrum and attention deficit disorders as well as low birthweight babies and those with severe and complex disorders who are surviving and being cared for at home.

24.2   This chapter reviews the social care service provision entitlements of disabled children, although frequently this is done by cross reference to other chapters where the particular issue is capable of being addressed in a context that is not age specific. The community care rights of disabled parents are considered at para 16.121 above.

Disabled children and the Children Act 1989

24.3   The Children Act (CA) 1989 is widely regarded as a statute that both radically reformed and simplified child care law in England and Wales. While this is undoubtedly the case for child protection proceedings, this was not so in relation to the provision of services for disabled children. In this respect the Act complicated matters, creating new rights and duties which apply alongside and overlap those of the pre-existing legislation. As a consequence disabled children and their carers have rights to child and family support services under the CA 1989 and under the community care and carers' legislation.[2] In general, however, it will be appropriate for disabled children to be assessed under the CA 1989 regime – even if the services that are subsequently provided derive from another statute.

Disabled child – definition

24.4   CA 1989 s17(1) places a general duty on social services authorities to safeguard and promote the interests of children 'in need' and in further-ance of this duty they are empowered to provide a wide range of services.

24.5   CA 1989 s17(10) provides that a child shall be taken to be 'in need' if:

(a) he is unlikely to achieve or maintain, or to have the opportunity of achieving or maintaining, a reasonable standard of health or

---

1   J Read, L Clements and D Ruebain, *Disabled Children and the Law*, Jessica Kingsley Publishers, 2006, pp30–31.
2   Disabled children have rights to services under the community care legislation (eg NHS Act 2006 Sch 20 para 3 – see para 3.39 above). As a consequence they are entitled to be assessed under National Health Service Community Care Act (NHSCCA) 1990 s47.

development without the provision for him of services by a local authority . . .; or

(b) his health or development is likely to be significantly impaired, or further impaired, without the provision for him of such services; or

(c) he is disabled.

24.6 The definition of a disabled child (which closely follows the definition of a disabled adult in National Assistance Act (NAA) 1948 s29) is contained in CA 1989 s17(11), namely:

> For the purposes of this Part, a child is disabled if he is blind, deaf or dumb or suffers from mental disorder of any kind or is substantially and permanently handicapped by illness, injury or congenital deformity or such other disability as may be prescribed; and in this Part –
>
> 'development' means physical, intellectual, emotional, social or behavioural development; and
>
> 'health' means physical or mental health.

24.7 As noted above (see para 9.33), by including reference to a 'mental disorder of any kind' the legislation defines disability in broad terms. Mental Health Act 1983 s1 defines 'mental disorder' as including, not just the specified disorders (mental illness, arrested or incomplete development of the mind and a psychopathic disorder) but also 'any other disorder or disability of mind'. It follows that a child with (for instance) Asperger's Syndrome who has above average IQ would still be defined as a disabled child for the purposes of the CA 1989 and entitled to services under that Act (and the Chronically Sick and Disabled Persons Act (CSDPA) 1970) if an assessment revealed an eligible need. Likewise children with hyperactive and attention deficit disorders (sometimes referred to as Attention Deficit Hyperactivity Disorder (ADHD) and Attention Deficit Disorder (ADD)) should – if professionally diagnosed as having such a disorder – be considered to be within the definition. Even if there is no such diagnosis, such children could fall within the ambit of section 17(10)(a) and/or (b). In the context of community care these subsections are also of relevance to young carers (considered at para 6.112 above).

24.8 Many children's services departments discharge their various responsibilities through specialist social work teams – for instance a 'child protection team', a 'disabled children's team' and so on. Not infrequently a disabled children's' team will have terms of reference that exclude certain children, for instance those with 'high functioning' (ie a high IQ) Asperger's Syndrome or those with ADHD or ADD. Authorities are, in general, free to make these organisational arrangements provided they ensure that the needs of such children are given equal attention (albeit by a different section) and do not fall between the terms of reference of the various teams. It would be maladministration (and potentially unlawful action under the DDA 1995) if organisational arrangements of this nature resulted in such children's needs being neglected.

24.9 Having identified the potential recipients of assistance under section 17, the Act then follows a similar route to the community care legislation, namely that access to support services is in general dependent upon a needs assessment.

Disabled children's register

24.10   Social services departments are obliged to keep a register of children with disabilities,[3] as part of their duty to safeguard and promote the interests of disabled children. Volume 6 of the *Children Act Guidance (Children with Disabilities)* makes the following comments on the role of registers:

> 4.2   ... There is no duty on parents to agree to registration (which is a voluntary procedure) and services are not dependent upon registration. Registration can contribute positively to coherent planning of service provision for children with disabilities under the Children Act ...

> 4.3 [Social Services Departments] SSD's ... will need to liaise with their education and health counterparts to achieve an understanding of disability which permits early identification; which facilitates joint working; which encourages parents to agree to registration and which is meaningful in terms of planning services for the children in question and children in general. The creation of a joint register of children with disabilities between health, education and social services would greatly facilitate collaboration in identification and a co-ordinated provision of services under the Act ...

> 4.4   Whichever agency is the first to identify a child as having a disability whether it is the [local education authority] LEA, SSD or child health services they should initiate discussions with the parents about services or procedures which might be beneficial to the child and family. This should include an explanation of what other agencies can provide and information about the register. The registration of children with disabilities will be effective and productive only if parents and children are regarded as partners in the assessment process and as experts in their own right, from whom professionals may have much to learn.

24.11   CA 2004 s12 provides for the creation of a more substantial information database – potentially in relation to all children in need, and not merely disabled children.[4]

The assessment of children in need

24.12   There is no explicit duty to assess under the CA 1989 equivalent to that found in NHS and Community Care Act (NHSCCA) 1990 s47. However, in *R (G) v Barnet LBC and others*[5] Lord Hope expressed the view that there was a specific law obligation to assess under the Act, observing:

3   CA 1989 Sch 2 para 2; and see also Department of Health, *The Children Act 1989 Guidance and Regulations Volume 6, 'Children with Disabilities'*, HMSO, 1991, para 4.2.
4   See Information Sharing Index (England) Regulations 2006 SI No 983.
5   [2003] UKHL 57; [2003] 3 WLR 1194; (2003) 6 CCLR 500. Lord Scott (also part of the majority) was of the opinion that at the very least it was 'implicit in this provision that the local authority will assess the actual needs of a child in need whenever it appears necessary to do so' – at [117].

77. My noble and learned friend Lord Nicholls has said that, on the respondents' approach to the construction of section 17(1), it follows that a local authority is not under a duty to assess the needs of a child in need under section 17(1) and that this would go far to stultify the purpose of Part III of the Act. I . . . am unable to agree that this conclusion follows from the respondents' argument. Section 17(2) provides that, for the purpose of facilitating the discharge of the general duty under that section, every local authority shall have the specific duties and powers set out in Part I of Schedule 2. The duty of the local authority to take reasonable steps to identify the extent to which there are children in need in their area is to be found in paragraph 1 of the Schedule. That will involve assessing the needs of each child who is found to be in need in their area as paragraph 3 makes clear.

24.13 The assessment obligation is strongly reinforced by policy guidance and, given the alternative rights of disabled children to an assessment under the community care legislation (see para 24.55 below), the CA 1989 assessment obligation must in most cases be tantamount to a public law duty.

24.14 The original CA 1989 policy guidance[6] concerning assessments' states as follows:

2.7 Good practice requires that the assessment of need should be undertaken in an open way and should involve those caring for the child, the child and other significant persons. Families with a child in need, whether the need results from family difficulties or the child's circumstances, have the right to receive sympathetic support and sensitive intervention in their family's life . . .

2.8 In making an assessment, the local authority should take account of the particular needs of the child – that is in relation to health, development, disability, education, religious persuasion, racial origin, cultural and linguistic background, the degree (if any) to which these needs are being met by existing services to the family or the child and which agencies' services are best suited to the child's needs.

Guidance on assessment

24.15 The two key guidance documents in England concerning the CA 1989 assessment process are the 2000 *Framework for Assessing Children in Need and their Families* policy guidance and practice guidance[7] issued by the Department of Health.[8] Very similar policy and practice guidance has been

---

6   Department of Health, *The Children Act 1989 Guidance to the Children Act 1989 Volume 2, 'Family Support'*, HMSO, 1991, para 2.7.
7   The practice guidance contains detailed material on the way in which the framework should be applied to disabled children and their families.
8   Department of Health, Department for Education and Employment and Home Office, *Framework for Assessing Children in Need and their Families* (policy guidance), TSO, 2000. Department of Health, *Assessing Children in Need and their Families: Practice Guidance*, TSO, 2000.

issued in Wales and the following section refers to the English framework guidance.[9]

24.16   The guidance requires assessors to look at the needs of disabled children in the context of the whole family and local community. The policy guidance consists of three domains and within each there are a number of dimensions to be explored.

1. Domain A: Child's Developmental Needs
    - health
    - education
    - emotional and behavioural development
    - identity
    - family and social relationships
    - social presentation
    - self-care skills.

2. Domain B: Parenting Capacity
    - basic care
    - ensuring safety
    - stimulation
    - guidance and boundaries
    - stability.

3. Domain C: Family and Environmental Factors
    - family history and functioning
    - housing
    - employment
    - income
    - family's social integration
    - community resources
    - involving disabled children in the assessment process.

24.17   The practice guidance takes the view that practitioners need to start by assuming that disabled children have the same basic needs as all children, but because they are living with impairments some may require additional support, assistance and intervention (at para 3.6). Considerable emphasis is placed upon social factors which restrict and disable. The guidance demands that the needs, capacities and opinions of all family members, including the disabled child, are taken into account.

24.18   The English policy guidance describes the social services response to an initial contact or a referral requesting help as 'critically important' (para 3.3) and lays down a timetable for the assessment process, in the following terms:

> 3.8   There is an expectation that **within one working day** of a referral being received or new information coming to or from within a social services department about an open case, there will be a decision about what response is required. A referral is defined as a request for services to be

---

9   Welsh Assembly, *Framework for Assessing Children in Need and their Families*, TSO, 2001; Welsh Assembly, *Assessing Children in Need and their Families: Practice Guidance*, 2001.

provided by the social services department. The response may include no action, but that is itself a decision and should be made promptly and recorded. The referrer should be informed of the decision and its rationale, as well as the parents or caregivers and the child, if appropriate.

3.9 A decision to gather more information constitutes an initial assessment. An initial assessment is defined as a brief assessment of each child referred to social services with a request for services to be provided. This should be undertaken **within a maximum of 7 working days** but could be very brief depending on the child's circumstances. It should address the dimensions of the Assessment Framework, determining whether the child is in need, the nature of any services required, from where and within what timescales, and whether a further, more detailed core assessment should be undertaken. An initial assessment is deemed to have commenced at the point of referral to the social services department or when new information on an open case indicates an initial assessment should be repeated. All staff responding to referrals and undertaking initial assessments should address the dimensions which constitute the Assessment Framework . . .

3.10 Depending on the child's circumstances, an initial assessment may include some or all of the following:
- interviews with child and family members, as appropriate;
- involvement of other agencies in gathering and providing information, as appropriate;
- consultation with supervisor/manager;
- record of initial analysis;
- decisions on further action/no action;
- record of decisions/rationale with family/agencies;
- informing other agencies of the decisions;
- statement to the family of decisions made and, if a child is in need, the plan for providing support.

As part of any initial assessment, the child should be seen. This includes observation and talking with the child in an age appropriate manner . . .

3.11 **A core assessment** is defined as an in-depth assessment which addresses the central or most important aspects of the needs of a child and the capacity of his or her parents or caregivers to respond appropriately to these needs within the wider family and community context. While this assessment is led by social services, it will invariably involve other agencies or independent professionals, who will either provide information they hold about the child or parents, contribute specialist knowledge or advice to social services or undertake specialist assessments. Specific assessments of the child and/or family members may have already been undertaken prior to referral to the social services department. The findings from these should inform this assessment. At the conclusion of this phase of assessment, there should be an analysis of the findings which will provide an understanding of the child's circumstances and inform planning, case objectives and the nature of service provision. The timescale for completion of the core assessment is a **maximum of 35 working days**. A core assessment is deemed to have commenced at the point the initial assessment ended, or a strategy discussion decided to initiate enquiries under s47, or new information obtained on an open case indicates a core assessment should be undertaken. Where specialist assessments have been commissioned by social services from other agencies or independent professionals, it is recognised that they will not necessarily be completed within the 35 working day period. Appropriate services should be provided whilst awaiting the completion of the specialist assessment.

24.19   In *R (AB & SB) v Nottingham City Council*[10] Richards J described the assessment process detailed in the policy guidance in the following terms:

> There should be a systematic assessment of needs which takes into account the three domains (child's developmental needs, parenting capacity, family and environmental factors) and involves collaboration between all relevant agencies so as to achieve a full understanding of the child in his or her family and community context. It is important, moreover, to be clear about the three-stage process: identification of needs, production of a care plan, and provision of the identified services. It seems to me that where an authority follows a path that does not involve the preparation of a core assessment as such, it must nevertheless adopt a similarly systematic approach with a view to achievement of the same objectives. Failure to do so without good cause will constitute an impermissible departure from the guidance.

24.20   The *Nottingham* case concerned a child with learning disabilities and behavioural problems for whom the local authority had sought an anti-social behaviour order under the Crime and Disorder Act 1998. It was argued on his behalf that no such order could be made where the authority had failed properly to assess the child's needs under the 1989 Act.[11]

24.21   Although the policy guidance accepts that in some situations there may not have to be a core assessment, this is unlikely to be the case in relation to disabled children. However, where an authority is considering reducing services (for instance respite care) it will be maladministration to take such a step without first undertaking such an assessment.[12]

Children (Leaving Care) Act 2000

24.22   The Children (Leaving Care) Act 2000 implemented proposals first detailed in the consultation document *Me, Survive, Out There? – New Arrangements for Young People Living in and Leaving Care* published in July 1999. The consultation document set out detailed proposals for improving the life chances of young people living in and leaving local authority care. Essentially the Act gives practical effect to the 'Quality Protects' policy by endeavouring to ensure that local authorities provide the same level of support as children who have not been in care might in general expect

---

10 [2001] EWHC 235 (Admin); (2001) 4 CCLR 294 at 306G–I. See also *R (J) v Newham LBC* [2001] EWHC (Admin) 992; (2002) 5 CCLR 302 where a similar mandatory order to undertake a CA 1989 assessment was made.

11 See also *R (M) v Sheffield Magistrates' Court* [2004] EWHC 1830 (Admin); [2005] 1 FLR 81 where it was held that a conflict of interest would arise when a local authority sought an anti-social behaviour order in relation to a child in its care, and accordingly special safeguards should apply in such proceedings, and see also *R (K) v Manchester City Council* [2006] EWHC 3164 (Admin); (2007) 10 CCLR 87.

12 Complaint no 05/B/00611 against Northamptonshire CC, 30 November 2006.

from their parents. Guidance under the Act has been issued in both England and Wales.[13]

24.23 The main purpose of the Act is to help young people who have been looked after by a local authority move from care into living independently in as stable a fashion as possible. It seeks to promote this aim by amending key provisions of the CA 1989 to place specific duties on social services authorities[14] in respect of 'eligible' and 'relevant' children.

24.24 'Eligible' children are those shortly to stop being 'looked after' as they approach 18.[15] The local authority has a duty to assess and meet the care and support needs of children in care aged 16 and 17 who have been looked after for 13 weeks, either continuously or in aggregate (but excluding certain respite care periods). Local authorities are required to:

1) Undertake an assessment of young people's needs with a view to determining what advice, assistance and support it would be appropriate to provide:
   a) while the local authority is still looking after them; and
   b) after the local authority has ceased to look after them,
   and then to prepare a pathway plan for them.[16] The assessment should be completed not more than three months after the child reaches the age of 16.[17]

2) Prepare a written statement describing the manner in which their needs would be assessed. The content of these statements is specified in the regulations[18] and must include, for instance, the complaints process, the name of the person responsible for conducting the assessment and so on.

3) Appoint a personal adviser who is responsible for (among other things) the co-ordination of services – including ensuring that the person leaving care makes use of such services.[19] In *R (J) v Caerphilly CBC*[20] the High Court held that it was essential that the personal adviser was independent of the authority and was not the person responsible for the preparation of the assessment or the pathway plan.

24.25 'Relevant' children are aged 16 and 17 who would have been 'eligible' before they ceased being 'looked after'.[21] The local authority duties include:

1) to 'keep in touch' with such care leavers, until aged 21 and beyond in some cases;

2) to prepare 'Pathway Plans'. These plans take over from the child's

13 Department for Education and Skills, *Children (Leaving Care) Act 2000 Regulations and Guidance*, 2001 and Welsh Assembly, *Children Leaving Care Act Guidance*, 2001.
14 The responsible local authority is the one who last looked after the child, even if the child has since moved into the area of another authority.
15 CA 1989 Sch 2 para 19B(2).
16 Ibid, para 19B(4).
17 Children (Leaving Care) (England) Regulations 2001 SI No 2874 reg 7; Children (Leaving Care) (Wales) Regulations 2001 SI No 2189 (W151).
18 Children (Leaving Care) (England) Regulations 2001 reg 5.
19 Ibid, reg 12.
20 [2005] EWHC 586 (Admin); (2005) 8 CCLR 255 at [30].
21 CA 1989 s23A.

existing care plan and run at least until the age of 21, covering education, training, career plans and support needs. Such plans will be subject to review every six months. The guidance[22] identifies these plans as
'pivotal to the process whereby children and young people map out
their future'.[23]

24.26   In *R (P) v Newham LBC*[24] a local authority was held to have acted unlawfully by failing to provide a personal pathway plan before the severely
disabled child in care turned 19 years, in breach of CA 1989 Sch 2 para
19B(4) and the Children (Leaving Care) (England) Regulations 2001.[25] It
was irrelevant that the local authority had started an alternative process
which it believed to be more appropriate – namely a transitional plan. As
Ouseley J observed, 'whatever the merits of that process may be and however well it may be done, it is not one which meets the requirements of the
statute'.

The child's perspective

24.27   The policy guidance requires social services departments to 'develop clear
assessment procedures for children in need . . . which take account of the
child's and family's needs and preferences, racial and ethnic origins, their
culture, religion and any special needs relating to the circumstances of
individual families'.[26] The importance of involving children in the assessment process is emphasised in the policy guidance at para 3.41 which
stresses that:

> . . . direct work with children is an essential part of assessment, as well as
> recognising their rights to be involved and consulted about matters which
> affect their lives. This applies all children, including disabled children.
> Communicating with some disabled children requires more preparation,
> sometimes more time and on occasions specialist expertise, and
> consultation with those closest to the child. For example, for children with
> communication difficulties it may be necessary to use alternatives to
> speech such as signs, symbols facial expression, eye pointing, objects if
> reference or drawing.

24.28   A failure properly to involve a disabled child in his or her assessment
(even if there are profound communication or behavioural problems[27])
may well result in a court holding the procedure unlawful.[28] *CD v Anglesey
CC*,[29] for example, concerned a 15-year-old wheelchair user with quadri-
plegic cerebral palsy. Her mother was unwell and felt unable to care for

---

22   Department for Education and Skills,*Children (Leaving Care) Act 2000 Regulations and
     Guidance*, 2001 para 20 p40 and Welsh Assembly, *Children Leaving Care Act Guidance*,
     2001, para 7.2.
23   See also *R (J) v Caerphilly CBC* [2005] EWHC 586 (Admin); (2005) 8 CCLR 255.
24   [2004] EWHC 2210 (Admin); (2004) 7 CCLR 553.
25   See note 17 above.
26   Department of Health, *The Children Act 1989 Guidance and Regulations Volume 6*,
     'Children with Disabilities', HMSO, 1991, para 5.1.
27   *R (J) v Caerphilly CBC* [2005] EWHC 586 (Admin); (2005) 8 CCLR 255.
28   *R v North Yorkshire CC ex p Hargreaves* (1994) 1 CCLR 105.
29   [2004] EWHC 1635 (Admin); (2004) 7 CCLR 589.

her daughter full-time, even with substantial social services funded support. Accordingly, when aged five, a respite placement was found for her daughter and legally therefore she became a 'looked after child' under CA 1989 s20.

24.29 The daughter developed a very strong bond with her respite foster carers even though, as she grew older, their home became increasingly unsuitable. The authority decided that the placement should end and that she should return to live with her mother, who opposed this alteration and sought a judicial review (acting as her daughter's litigation friend).

24.30 The authority failed to assist with adaptations to the foster carers' home and (against the advice of an independent social worker it had commissioned) decided that they should be deregistered.

24.31 Legally, the daughter was a child in need, under CA 1989 s17(1), to whom the authority owed a duty to promote her welfare and, so far as is consistent with that duty, to promote her upbringing by her family, by providing a range and level of services appropriate to her needs. As a disabled child, by virtue of section 17(2) and Schedule 2(6) the authority was obliged to provide services designed to minimise the effect upon her of her disabilities and to give her the opportunity to lead a life which was as normal as possible. As a 'looked after' child, by section 23(8), the local authority was obliged (so far as reasonably practicable) to secure that the accommodation was not unsuitable for her particular needs. In addition under section 20(6) there was a duty to ascertain her wishes regarding such provision and give due consideration to them having regard to her age and understanding.

24.32 The court held the local authority's actions to be unlawful. In particular it had failed to give due consideration to the child's wishes, had failed to take account of her mother's inability to provide full time care when formulating a care plan, and had acted unlawfully in deregistering the child's foster carers on the pretext that their home was unsuitable without giving due consideration to the child's needs.

Disabled children's services and the service provision decision

24.33 As with community care assessments (see para 3.134 above), entitlement to services under the CA 1989 depends upon the assessment disclosing sufficient evidence to prompt a service response. However, unlike the community care assessment process the guidance lays down no standard procedure for establishing who is and who is not eligible for support services. It is in this respect that the policy and practice guidance are particularly weak. The policy guidance fails because it is, in reality, dominated by the notion of child protection: accordingly its advice on responses to identified needs (at chapter 4) leans heavily in the direction of family interventions. The practice guidance, although specifically directed at the needs of disabled children, is also disappointing when it comes to service responses and is silent on the assessment of eligibility.

24.34   It is difficult to envisage how a consistent policy of responding to assessed needs can be implemented without some agreement as to what constitutes eligible needs. Unfortunately the guidance lays down no clear guidelines – indeed it has even been suggested that use of eligibility criteria in relation to children's services may be inappropriate: Lord Laming for example in his Victoria Climbié Inquiry Report said as follows:[30]

> 1.53 The use of eligibility criteria to restrict access to services is not found either in legislation or in guidance, and its ill-founded application is not something I support. Only after a child and his or her home circumstances have been assessed can such criteria be justified in determining the suitability of a referral, the degree of risk, and the urgency of the response.

> 1.54 Local government in this country should be at the forefront of organisations serving the public. Sadly, little I heard persuades me that this is so. Many of the procedures that I heard about seemed to me to be self-serving – supporting the needs of the organisation, rather than the public they are set up to serve.

24.35   Lord Laming is presumably concerned, not so much about the notion of deciding who should and who should not receive support services, but rather about the use of inappropriate and rigid criteria to make this determination. In practice, authorities have to decide and in so doing require – whatever one might like to call it – a formula or scale by which they can prioritise those in most need and devote resources to those for whom the resources can have the most positive impact.

24.36   Local authorities do, in practice, have such prioritisation procedures for disabled children's services, although they are not infrequently inadequate, poorly publicised and formulated with little or no consultation. It appears that in many cases, access to support services is measured largely by assessing the imminence of family breakdown. Thus if it is imminent or has occurred, resources can be accessed, but not otherwise. Clearly such criteria cater for the needs of children suffering abuse or neglect but are likely to be inappropriate for many families with disabled children or young carers. In practice such policies deny support to families until such time as they fall into (or are at severe risk of falling into) the child protection regime: effectively therefore they cater, not for CA 1989 Part III (provision of services for children and their families) but for Part VI (child protection).

24.37   Once all the relevant evidence concerning the needs of the child and his or her family has been identified, the authority must make a rational decision as to which (if any) of these needs require to be met by the provision of support services. The decision will have to take into account the consequences of not providing services – be it harm or impaired development of the child (development including physical, intellectual, emotional, social and behavioural – s17(11)) as well as the consequences for the family – in terms of their needs (for instance to work, or undertake education, training and leisure activities – see para 16.53) and also their

---

30   Lord Laming, *The Victoria Climbié Inquiry: Report of an Inquiry*, Cm 5730, TSO, 2003.

ability to sustain the caring relationship. If the family support cannot be sustained without services (including respite provision) the child is likely to suffer significant harm.

24.38　　In *R (Spink) v Wandsworth BC*[31] the Court of Appeal held that in deciding whether services were required, a local authority could (in the somewhat unusual facts of the case) take into consideration the financial situation of the parents.

24.39　　Following an assessment, a wide spectrum of services can be made available to disabled children. These services may be home, community or institutionally based and may derive from a variety of legislative provisions, although the primary statutes are the CSDPA 1970 and the CA 1989.

Services for disabled children under the Chronically Sick and Disabled Persons Act 1970

24.40　As noted at para 9.131 above, by virtue of CSDPA 1970 s28A, services under section 2 of the 1970 Act are available to disabled children. The range of services under the 1970 Act is considered at paras 9.70–9.123 above. In *R v Bexley LBC ex p B*[32] the court held that if there was a choice of providing services under the 1970 Act or under CA 1989 s17, then the duty under the 1970 Act effectively trumped the 1989 duty (see para 9.133 above) – not least because the duty under the 1970 Act is a specific law duty whereas the duty under section 17 is almost certainly a target duty (see para 1.24).

24.41　　It follows that once an authority is satisfied that it is necessary to provide a service under the 1970 Act, then it is under a specifically enforceable duty to do so.

Services for disabled children under the Children Act 1989

24.42　Once a child has been accepted as being 'in need', and that need identified by an assessment or otherwise, the CA 1989 specifies that a range of support services be made available. Section 17(1) provides:

> It shall be the general duty of every local authority (in addition to the other duties imposed on them by this Part) –
> (a) to safeguard and promote the welfare of children within their area who are in need; and
> (b) so far as is consistent with that duty, to promote the upbringing of such children by their families,
> by providing a range of services appropriate to those children's needs.

24.43　Section 17(2) refers to additional specific duties under Part I of Schedule 2 to the Act, which comprise:

31　[2005] EWCA Civ 302; [2005] 1 WLR 2884; (2005) 8 CCLR 272.
32　(2000) 3 CCLR 15.

Paragraph 6: provision for disabled children
Every local authority shall provide services designed –
(a) to minimise the effect on disabled children within their area of their disabilities; and
(b) to give such children the opportunity to lead lives which are as normal as possible.

Paragraph 8 (Provision for children living with their families)
Every local authority shall make such provision as they consider appropriate for the following services to be available with respect to children in need within their area while they are living with their families –
(a) advice, guidance and counselling;
(b) occupational, social, cultural or recreational activities;
(c) home help (which may include laundry facilities);
(d) facilities for, or assistance with, travelling to and from home for the purpose of taking advantage of any other service provided under this Act or of any similar service;
(e) assistance to enable the child concerned and his family to have a holiday.

24.44   The guidance to the CA 1989 conveniently summarises the breadth of powers available to social services authorities in such cases:[33]

> This general duty is supported by other specific duties and powers such as the facilitation of 'the provision by others, including in particular voluntary organisations of services' (section 17(5) and Schedule 2). These provisions encourage SSDs to provide day and domiciliary services, guidance and counselling, respite care and a range of other services as a means of supporting children in need (including children with disabilities) within their families. The Act recognises that sometimes a child can only be helped by providing services for other members of his family (section 17(3)) 'if it [the service] is provided with a view to safeguarding or promoting the child's welfare' . . . The SSD may make such arrangements as they see fit for any person to provide services and support 'may include giving assistance in kind, or in exceptional circumstances in cash' (section 17(6)[34]). However, where it is the SSD's view that a child's welfare is adequately provided for and no unmet need exists, they need not act.

24.45   In *R (G) v Barnet LBC and others*[35] (which involved a number of consolidated appeals) the House of Lords had to determine (among other things) whether the obligation to provide services under the 1989 Act was a target or specific law duty. The case was unusual in that the CA 1989 service sought by the appellants was the provision of housing. In a split 3:2 judgment, the majority held that although there was an obligation under the CA 1989 to provide accommodation (once it had been identified in an assessment as a 'need'), this was a target duty rather than a specific law duty (see para 1.24 above). The thrust of the judgment in relation to the target nature of the section 17 duty was applied in *R (T, D and B) v*

33 Department of Health, *The Children Act 1989 Guidance and Regulations Volume 6*, 'Children with Disabilities', HMSO, 1991, para 3.3.
34 Subsequent to this guidance the CA 1989 was amended to insert an additional right to direct payments – see para 12.9 below.
35 [2003] UKHL 57; [2003] 3 WLR 1194; (2003) 6 CCLR 500.

Haringey LBC[36] where the court held that the service provision arrangements under Schedule 2(5) to the Act were also target in nature: that the section 17(1) duty:

> ... left substantial matters to the discretion of the local authority ... which could not lead to an enforceable duty towards an affected individual.

24.46   The *Barnet LBC* decision is not an easy one to understand and has been the subject of considerable criticism. It can also lead to absurd outcomes – not least that disabled children in certain situations have inferior rights to social care support than do disabled adults. In practice however the judgment is likely to have only a limited legal impact on the rights of disabled children to services. This arises, principally, from the fact that most of the support services required by disabled children and their families will derive from the broad list of services specified in CSDPA 1970 s2.

24.47   In a few situations the service may not be capable of being met by the 1970 Act – for instance respite care to be delivered in a residential setting. It is possible that this might still come within the ambit of section 2(1)(f), namely 'holidays', or section 2(1)(c) 'recreational facilities outside his home' but if this is not the case such a service would need to be provided under CA 1989 s17 (in this respect see para 24.51 below). However in such cases, it is still not clear that the local authority could rely on the target nature of the obligation as a reason for not providing the services. Most obviously such a decision could be challenged if the authority made resource considerations determinative (see para 3.192). However two additional factors may be relevant in such cases.

24.48   The first arises from a conceptual appreciation of the assessment process. As we have noted above (see para 4.24), the process is 'needs led'. If one took, for example, the need of a family for respite (and the concomitant need of the disabled child for a family that did not break down under the pressure of not having respite), there would of course be many ways of meeting that need. One could be some arrangement in the home (for instance a sitting service under the 1970 Act) and another would be for the child to spend a short period out of the home in residential respite. If the local authority refused to provide the latter service on the ground that it was merely in discharge of a target duty, it would not obviate the requirement to meet the assessed need where there was an alternative way of meeting it under an Act that gave rise to a specific duty – as for instance under the 1970 Act.

24.49   The second qualification arises from the direct payment regulations (see para 12.9 below). Section 17A of the 1989 Act read in conjunction with the regulations strongly suggests that once an authority has decided that services need to be provided under section 17 for a disabled child then (subject to the usual restrictions – see para 12.9 above) the authority is under a specifically enforceable duty to make direct payments in lieu of the services. As noted at para 12.35 above, such payments can cover periodic residential respite placements.

---

36   [2005] EWHC 2235 (Admin); (2006) 9 CCLR 58; and also applied in *Blackburn-Smith v Lambeth LBC* [2007] EWHC 767 (Admin).

24.50   Not infrequently however, the service difficulty encountered is that of a dearth of service providers available to meet an assessed need – for instance a need for respite or short break care. In such situations it may be that the parents of the disabled child could make the necessary arrangements themselves if they had direct payments – for instance by arranging for one of their acquaintances or relations to provide the service (see para 12.29 above where this is further considered).

Residential respite care

24.51   In most cases, a local authority will be able to provide respite/short break support for disabled children and their families by providing sitting services under CSDPA 1970 s2(1)(a). Not infrequently however, what will be needed will be for the child to have a short period away from the family home, and in such cases questions arise as to whether this service is provided under section 20 or section 17 of the 1989 Act. If provided under section 20 the child is a 'looked after' child and the accommodation provision is subject to significant regulatory obligations.[37] In general, however, a child provided with respite care accommodation (even if for more than 24 hours) is provided with the service under section 17.[38]

24.52   The government in England has confirmed its view that children who receive short break/respite care should not be routinely classified as 'looked after' under section 20, stating:[39]

> Children in short breaks should only be given looked after status where that is in their best interests. 'Looked after' status should not be an automatic response to the use of [respite care] . . . children should only be placed away from home overnight after the local authority has carried out an in-depth assessment of the needs of the child and family, including ascertaining the wishes and feelings of the child. Following the assessment, they should determine whether the child and family should receive services and, if so, which services will be appropriate and the relevant legal status. However, local authorities and families have told us that there is confusion about the legal status of some of these placements and the requirements for assessment which surround these arrangements. To address this we will:
> * Issue statutory guidance (within the revised Children Act 1989 guidance) specifically on the issues of support/short break care to clarify the applicable regulations for different settings and arrangements. The guidance will set out the circumstances in which it would be expected that the child would be looked after.

---

37 See eg the Arrangements for Placement of Children (General) Regulations 1991 SI No 890 and the Placement of Children (Wales) Regulations 2007 SI No 310 (W27).

38 See Adoption and Children Act 2002 s116 which amended CA 1989 s22(1) to state specifically that a child is not a looked after child if provided with accommodation under section 17; see also Carers and Disabled Children Act 2000 s7 which inserted section 17B into the CA 1989 explicitly dealing with section 17 respite care (and allowing vouchers in lieu of direct service provision).

39 Department for Education and Skills white paper, *Care Matters: Time for Change*, Cm 7137, TSO, 2007, para 2.33.

Housing and residential care services

24.53 In *R v Tower Hamlets LBC ex p Bradford*[40] the court considered the housing and community care needs of a family which included a severely disabled mother and an 11-year-old son with special educational needs. Although the family members experienced particularly unpleasant harassment from their neighbours, their 'housing points' were insufficient to make them an 'overriding priority' for rehousing. A judicial review challenging this decision was adjourned on grounds that the authority undertook various assessments, including under CA 1989 Part III. When considering its duty to provide accommodation under the Act, the authority effectively confined its attention to CA 1989 s20, the cross-heading to which section states 'provision of accommodation for children: general'. This section (which is in effect what, prior to 1989, used to be called 'voluntary care') only arises where there is no one with parental responsibility, or where the child is lost or abandoned or where the parents are prevented from providing suitable accommodation or care. Since these factors were not present, the authority declined to provide accommodation under Part III of the Act. Dyson J held that the authority had fundamentally misunderstood its accommodation powers under the Act; in that any housing would be provided under CA 1989 s17 (and not CA 1989 s20). Section 17 enables authorities to provide an almost unlimited range of services including, in appropriate cases, housing.

24.54 Subsequent to the *ex p Bradford* decision, considerable controversy arose concerning the extent of the housing obligation under CA 1989 s17, culminating in the House of Lords judgment in *R (G) v Barnet LBC and others*,[41] where the majority concluded that there was only a target duty under CA 1989 s17 to provide this service. The position has now been put beyond doubt, by the amending of section 17(6)[42] expressly to include the provision of 'accommodation' as one of the general services that may be provided (and section 22 amended so as to exclude children provided with accommodation under section 17). Guidance on these amendments has been provided in England in LAC (2003)13.

NHS services for disabled children

24.55 Disabled children are entitled to a variety of social care support services under the NHS Acts 2006. As noted above (para 9.141) these include home help and laundry services for which social services authorities are responsible under NHS Act 2006 Sch 20. Since such services are 'community care services' (for the purposes of NHSCCA 1990 s46(3)) it follows that disabled children are entitled to have their needs assessed under the 1990 Act in addition to the CA 1989.

40 (1998) 1 CCLR 294.
41 [2003] UKHL 57; [2003] 3 WLR 1194; (2003) 6 CCLR 500.
42 Effected by Adoption and Children Act 2002 s116.

24.56   Disabled children are additionally entitled to NHS continuing health care in certain situations and this issue is addressed further at para 14.97 above.

24.57   The NHS (like all local authority departments) is subject to the 2004 guidance *The National Service Framework for Children, Young People and Maternity Services* (NSF) (see para 1.61 above).[43] The *Standard for Hospital Services*[44] includes the following statement:

> 4.52   Disabled children have the same right to high quality services as any other child, though evidence suggests many are excluded from mainstream services . . . As more disabled children with complex needs survive for longer, they make up an increasing part of the work of children's hospital services. Hospitals need to recognise and meet the very particular needs of this group of patients and involve them and their parents in the planning of services.

> 4.55   There should be a multi-agency plan, developed and agreed with the disabled young person and their parents, and updated as needed . . . It should say who does what – GP, hospital, social services, therapy services, school, and respite setting.

and continues:[45]

> Children and young people should receive care that is integrated and co-ordinated around their particular needs, and the needs of their family. They, and their parents, should be treated with respect, and should be given support and information to enable them to understand and cope with the illness or injury, and the treatment needed. They should be encouraged to be active partners in decisions about their health and care, and, where possible, be able to exercise choice.

> Children, young people and their parents will participate in designing NHS and social care services that are readily accessible, respectful, empowering, follow best practice in obtaining consent and provide effective response to their needs.

24.58   The standard amplifies the above requirement (at para 3.16), stating:

> 3.16 Staff working with children and young people should have training in the necessary communication skills to enable them to work effectively with children, young people and parents, and to support them to be active partners in decision making. Ideally, this should include:
> - How to listen to and communicate with children, young people, parents and carers, and the need to understand the extent and the limits of children's comprehension at various stages of development.

43 Department for Education and Skills and Department of Health, *National Service Framework for Children, Young People and Maternity Services*, TSO, 2004. The NSF aims to set standards for services for all children, including those who are disabled, across the next decade: it is probably best understood as setting benchmarks for what children and families ought to be able to expect in the way of best practice and service provision.

44 Department of Health, *Getting the right start: National Service Framework for Children Standard for Hospital Services*, 'Hospital Standard Part One Child-Centred Services', 2004.

45 Ibid, p13.

- Recognition of the role of parents in looking after their children in hospital
- Providing information that is factual, objective, and non-directive, about a child's condition, likely prognosis, treatment options, and likely outcomes.
- Giving bad news in a sensitive non-hurried fashion, with time offered for further consultation away from the ward environment.
- Enabling a child and family to exercise choice, taking account of age and competence to understand the implications.

The transition into adulthood[46]

24.59 The CA 2004 requires English social services authorities to divide their functions into adult services and children's services departments and many Welsh authorities also have similar departmental divisions. While there may be good policy reasons for this division there is no significant justification for it in relation to the service provision entitlements of disabled children. Although in general services for disabled children under the CA 1989 cease to be available when they reach the age of 18,[47] their entitlement to services under CSDPA 1970 s2 and under NHSA 2006 Sch 20 para 3 remain.

24.60 There are of course dangers in separating adult and child care services and these often surface when care responsibilities are being transferred from the child to the adult social work team. All too often at this stage the quality of the service deteriorates significantly or the child is effectively lost to the system and ceases to receive any continuing care. Such a transfer of responsibility often occurs when the young person's special education provision is also coming to an end.

24.61 For the past 20 years there have been continuous expressions of grave concern over the failure of social services authorities to manage the transition of disabled children into adulthood – and these continue. A 2007 report,[48] for instance, called for 'urgent action' to tackle the 'considerable difficulties' faces by disabled young people and their families in the transition from children's to adult services and noted that for some the process was considered to be a 'nightmare'. The Department of Health has issued policy guidance[49] requiring social services authorities to have 'adequate arrangements' in place 'to ensure that all young people with long-term social care needs have been assessed and, where eligible,

---

46 For a detailed consideration of these issues, see J Read, L Clements and D Ruebain, *Disabled Children, the Law and Good Practice*, Jessica Kingsley Publishers, 2006.
47 Subject to important exceptions, notably as a consequence of the Children (Leaving Care) Act 2000.
48 Commission for Social Care Inspection, *Growing Up Matters: Better transition planning for young people with complex needs*, 2007.
49 Department of Health, *Guidance on the Statutory Chief Officer Post of Director of Adult Social Services issued under s7(1) Local Authority Social Services Act 1970*, 2006.

receive a service which meets their needs throughout their transition to becoming adults'.[50]

24.62   Statutory provisions exist which endeavour to ensure that there is a smooth hand-over of responsibility from the education section of an authority (responsible for special education provision) to the social services section. Disabled Persons (Services, Consultation and Representation) Act 1986 ss5 and 6 require education authorities to consult social services authorities to establish whether a child over the age of 14 who has been 'statemented' under Education Act 1996 Part IV, is likely to require support from the social services department when he or she leaves school. This duty has been reinforced by Education (Special Educational Needs) (England) (Consolidation) Regulations 2001 reg 21[51] which requires the contribution of social services departments and others to a transitional plan which the education department is required to prepare on the annual review of a statement made when the student attains the age of 14. The essential aim of such a plan is to ensure a smooth transition for the young person into adult life.

24.63   The CA 1989 guidance also stresses the social services' obligation to ensure such a smooth transition, stating:[52]

> The SSD's provision of services to children with disabilities should involve an initial assessment of need, a continuing process of reassessment and review of the plan for the child. Continuity should not be broken for reasons which concern organisational or administrative convenience rather than the welfare of the child or young person. A smooth transition, when the young person reaches 18 . . . should be the objective.

24.64   Paragraph 55 of the FACS (2002) policy guidance (see para 3.26 above) additionally states:

> Councils should have in place arrangements to identify individuals who, as they move from youth to adulthood and then into older age, may need different kinds of service. In these situations, councils may wish to re-assess their needs, but in responding should note that marked changes in the type, level and location of support are usually not in service users' best interests.

24.65   The *Special Educational Needs Code of Practice 2001* issued by the Department for Education and Skills in 2002[53] provides detailed guidance on the education and social services departments' responsibilities in developing and progressing the transitional plan of disabled pupils (paras 9.51–9.64).

---

50 In similar vein the NSF Complex Disability Exemplar provides a detailed outline of what 'Standard 4 – Growing up into adulthood, smooth transition to adult services' demands in terms of good professional practice: Department of Health and Department for Education and Skills, *The National Service Framework for Children, Young People and Maternity Services Complex Disability Exemplar*, 2005, pp50–55.

51 SI No 3455; Education (Special Educational Needs) (Wales) Regulations 2002 SI No 152 (W20) reg 21.

52 Department of Health, *The Children Act 1989 Guidance and Regulations Volume 6*, '*Children with Disabilities*', HMSO, 1991, para 5.4.

53 In Wales the equivalent (and very similar) code is Welsh Assembly, *Special Educational Needs Code of Practice for Wales*, 2002, paras 9.51 *et seq*.

24.66   Many children with learning disabilities experience particularly acute problems in negotiating the transfer from child care to adult care services. Accordingly the white paper *Valuing People* identifies young people moving from children's to adult services as a priority group who should have benefited from a person-centred approach by 2003.[54] The local government ombudsman has also expressed concern about acute shortfalls in service provision at the transition stage. She has reiterated that assessed needs must be met – regardless of the age of the service user – and that local authorities may not 'use available services as a starting point and just fit the people into them'.[55] In a complaint concerning this problem she illustrated her concerns by citing the following comments – made by professionals and parents – that 'once they become 18 it seems they have no interest in looking after them' and 'you hit adult services, it's like hitting a brick wall'.[56]

24.67   A 2003 complaint against East Sussex[57] concerned a young man with learning disabilities due to leave college. His parents wanted him to move to an independent residential provider for his post college needs (as many of his co-pupils were moving to this provider). The local authority assessed his needs and concluded (1) that this provider would meet his needs and (2) that there was no suitable alternative local provision available. The provider however indicated that the council should make a speedy decision as other students were also seeking the place identified. The council's internal policies required that the placement be approved by a series of funding panels which met throughout the year. The funding panel initially refused funding and placed the request on a 'service pending list'. As a consequence the placement ceased to be available and although the council made temporary arrangements, the young man's placement in the independent facility was delayed by two years. In finding maladministration (and recommending over £30,000 compensation) the ombudsman held:

> . . . clearly the Council's Social Services budget is under heavy pressure . . . however, the Council knew of [the disabled person's] needs, has accepted its duty to fund the provision and was happy that the provision offered by [the independent provider] was suitable. Therefore it was unacceptable for it not to have made specific budgetary provision that would enable it to respond more quickly once a placement was offered.

54 Circular HSC 2001/016: LAC(2001)23 para 33.
55 Complaint no 03/C/16371 against Stockton-on-Tees BC, 18 January 2005, citing *Valuing People*, para 4.17.
56 Complaint no 03/C/16371 against Stockton-on-Tees BC, 18 January 2005 paras 53 and 54.
57 Complaint no 00/B/18600 against East Sussex CC, 29 January 2003: and see also the not dissimilar report on complaint no 02/C/17068 against Bolton MBC, 30 November 2004 where the ombudsman found that the service user was not in any way properly prepared for his return to the community on leaving school and that 'there is overwhelming evidence that' the council's reluctance to fund the parents' preferred option was because of the impact this would have 'on the Social Services agency budget'.

Charging for children's services

Charging for domiciliary and community based services

24.68   As with most statutory adult care services, local authorities are empowered to charge for the services they provide under the CA 1989. The Act's charging provisions differ in a number of respects from those for adult service users (see chapter 10 above), most obviously in the fact that it is generally the carer's (ie, the parent's[58]) means which are assessed rather than the service user's.

24.69   CA 1989 s29(1) empowers the authority to recover 'such charge as they consider appropriate'. This is subject to the following restrictions:

- that no person can be charged while in receipt of income support, or of any element of child tax credit (other than the family element) or working tax credit or of an income-based jobseeker's allowance (section 29(3)); and
- that where the authority is satisfied that a person's means are insufficient for it to be reasonably practicable for him or her to pay the charge, the authority cannot require him or her to pay more than he or she can reasonably be expected to pay (section 29(2)). This provision follows closely the wording found in Health and Social Services and Social Security Adjudications Act 1983 s17, and reference should be made to paras 10.9 et seq where the issues of charge reduction or waiver are considered in detail.

24.70   The persons who can be charged are specified in CA 1989 s29(4), namely:

(a)   where the service is provided for a child under sixteen, each of his parents;

(b)   where it is provided for a child who has reached the age of sixteen, the child himself; and

(c)   where it is provided for a member of the child's family, that member.

24.71   As with charges for adult non-accommodation services, authorities are empowered to recover outstanding charges 'summarily as a civil debt',[59] and where a service is assessed as being required, the authority must provide it even if the liable person refuses to pay the assessed charge. In practice few authorities do make charges for such services.

Charging for services under the Chronically Sick and Disabled Persons Act 1970

24.72   Local authorities are empowered to charge for services provided under CSDPA 1970 s2 on the same basis that they are empowered to charge for domiciliary services under CA 1989 s17. This question is considered further at para 10.60 above. In general few authorities do make charges for such services.

---

58   CA 1989 s17(8) states that for charging purposes the local authority can take into account the means of the parent and child.

59   CA 1989 s29(5).

Charging for accommodation services under the Children Act 1989

24.73 CA 1989 Sch 2 Part III empowers (but does not oblige) local authorities to charge for the cost of accommodating children. The rules are the same as for non-accommodation services, save only that (in addition):

- the local authority cannot charge a sum greater than 'they would normally be prepared to pay if they had placed a similar child with local authority foster parents'; and
- provision is made for the local authority to serve what is known as a 'contribution notice' which it is able to enforce through the magistrates' court if necessary; which court can also arbitrate on any dispute as to the reasonableness of such a notice.

Safeguarding adults from abuse

continued

Introduction

25.1　The law regulating the protection from abuse of vulnerable adults in England and Wales derives from a complex mishmash of legislation, guidance and ad hoc court interventions. Since 2000 the courts have developed a procedure of 'declaratory relief' in an effort to fill the statutory void – as Sedley J expressed it 'to speak where Parliament, although the more appropriate forum, was silent'.[1] Unlike the Scottish Parliament, which has introduced legislation,[2] the government in England and Wales has so far resisted calls to introduce specific adult protection legislation[3] albeit that it is still 'considering' the case for legislation.[4]

25.2　It could be argued that the current statutory and policy framework, if effectively administered, should be adequate to protect people who are in situations where they might be abused, since most forms of abuse contravene criminal law (eg amounting to theft or assault). Indeed it has been argued that having a different system for protection against abuse, creates its own problems by undermining the requirement that abusers should be punished under the criminal code, and accordingly that:

> Appropriate use of adult protection procedures should ensure that, just as any other citizen, a vulnerable adult has access to the criminal justice system. Otherwise, practice that results in only 'welfare' based responses to adult abuse decriminalises acts that in any other walk of life would be deemed a criminal offence and serves to justify oppressive and discriminatory responses on the part of organisations and practitioners.[5]

25.3　Concern has also been expressed about the use of the term 'vulnerable adults' since it directs attention at the individual and locates 'the cause of the abuse within the victim, rather than in placing the responsibility with the actions or omissions of others'.[6] The Scottish legislation has moved away from this term and uses 'adults at risk' to describe those who come under the ambit of the Adult Support and Protection (Scotland) Act 2007.

25.4　While it is clear that the introduction of the legislation and guidance described in this chapter (and initiatives such as the Dignity in Care

---

1　*Re F (Adult: Court's Jurisdiction)* [2000] 3 WLR 1740; (2000) 3 CCLR 210.
2　Adult Support and Protection (Scotland) Act 2007 (placing a duty on councils to investigate in cases where an adult may be at risk, powers to enter premises where abuse of adults is thought to be taking place, creating banning orders to remove perpetrators from those settings, and establishing statutory adult protection committees).
3　For instance the Law Commission in 1995 called for the enactment of 'a new set of modern and acceptable emergency protective powers': Law Com no 231 *Mental Incapacity*, HMSO, 1995. See also Action on Elder Abuse at http://www.elderabuse.org.uk/Mainpages/Campaigns.htm.
4　HC Hansard col 2173W, 21 June 2007.
5　D Galpin and J Parker, 'Adult protection in mental health and inpatient settings' (2007) 9(2) *Journal of Adult Protection* 6.
6　Association of Directors of Social Services, *Safeguarding adults*, October 2005.

campaign[7]) are aimed at improving the protection of adults, it is legitimate to question the extent of the Westminster government's commitment to tackling adult abuse. As we note above, through its *Fair Access to Care* guidance[8] (see para 3.148) it explicitly permits services to be limited to people whose needs are 'critical', but only describes 'serious' abuse and neglect as falling within that band (abuse and neglect is merely described as a substantial need). The policy suggests therefore that the government only has zero tolerance of 'serious abuse'.[9]

25.5   Definitions of abuse are varied but the most often quoted (and adopted by the World Health Organisation) is that developed by Action on Elder Abuse:[10]

> A single or repeated act or lack of appropriate action occurring within any relationship where there is an expectation of trust, which causes harm or distress to an older person.

25.6   On the basis of this definition a 2006 study of mistreatment[11] of older people found that about 1 in 40 people in the UK[12] aged 66 and over had been mistreated in their own homes (in the preceding year). When this prevalence of mistreatment (including both abuse and neglect) was broadened to include neighbours and acquaintances the prevalence increased to 1 in 25.[13] The study estimated that only about 3 per cent of cases were picked up by adult protection services.[14]

25.7   The study was undertaken as a result of concern expressed by the Health Select Committee in its inquiry into elder abuse as to the lack of up-to-date data on the prevalence of abuse. The committee made a number of recommendations to improve the current regulatory regime,

---

7   Launched on 14 November 2006 with the aim to stimulate a national debate around dignity in care and create a care system where there is zero tolerance of abuse and disrespect of older people.
8   At para 16.
9   The Welsh Assembly Government guidance,*Creating a Unified and Fair System for Assessing and Managing Care*, 2002, in contrast treats all abuse as critical (para 5.16).
10 World Health Organisation,*Toronto declaration of global prevention of elder abuse*, 2002.
11 M O'Keeffe et al,*UK Study of Abuse and Neglect of Older People*, National Centre for Social Research and King's College London – prepared for Comic Relief and Department of Health, June 2007.
12 Equating to about 227,000 people. For methodological reasons the study considers that it is likely to have underestimated the prevalence of abuse.
13 This is broadly in line with prevalence studies in other countries. Most commonly reported (1.1%) was neglect followed by financial abuse (0.7%). The prevalence of psychological and physical abuse was 0.4% and sexual abuse (including harassment) 0.2%. 6% of those reporting mistreatment in the past year reported two different types of mistreatment. Highest among those reported as mistreating a person were partners 51% and other family members 49%. 13% reported being mistreated by a care worker and 5% a close friend. In the case of partners there was a sharp rise in neglect for those aged 85 or over, suggesting that the neglect may not be deliberate but due to the decreasing health of the partner 'as the consequence of two people with increasing disabilities trying to support each other – and increasingly failing' (at para 7.9).
14 At para 7.6.

although it did not suggest that there should be specific adult protection legislation.[15]

25.8   The study did not directly consider the prevalence of abuse of residents in institutional settings although the evidence suggests that this is problematical: not least the 2006/07 reports into abuse in Cornwall[16] and Sutton and Merton.[17] In these cases, it appears that although the procedures for reporting abuse were known by staff, they were largely unaware of what constituted abuse. Evidence suggests that adults in mental health settings are also at risk of abuse.[18] A 2006 report, for instance, identified widespread evidence of possible sexual abuse in mental health settings, including details of 122 allegations between November 2003 and September 2005 including rape, exposure and invasive touching by both other patients and staff members.[19]

25.9   The context of protecting adults against abuse is wide ranging and generally outside the normal parameters of community care law. This chapter addresses those issues most closely associated with the subject of this text and does not therefore deal with the wider legal framework such as consumer protection issues regarding rogue traders and the more general criminal offences.

25.10   This chapter first considers the statutory measures that exist to protect adults against abuse, and then reviews the policy framework that exists to address suspected or actual abuse. It does not include the protection measures in place for children.

Measures to protect adults from abuse

The human rights context

25.11   Human Rights Act 1998 s6 places a duty on public authorities to comply with the European Convention on Human Rights; article 3 of which (see para 27.214) obliges states, not merely to refrain from subjecting anyone to degrading treatment, but also to take positive measures to ensure that no one is treated in this way. Accordingly in *Z and others v UK*[20] the European Court of Human Rights found that there had been a violation of article 3 because a local authority 'had been aware of the serious ill-treatment . . . over a period of years . . . and failed to take any effective

15 Health Select Committee, *Elder Abuse – Second Report*, March 2004.

16 Commission for Social Care Inspection and Healthcare Commission, *Joint Investigation into the Provision of Services for People with Learning Disabilities at Cornwall Partnership NHS Trust*, 2006.

17 Healthcare Commission, *Investigation into the Provision of Services for People with Learning Disabilities provided by Sutton and Merton Primary Care Trust*, 2007. See also para 7.133.

18 See eg Commission for Health Improvement, *Investigation into matters arising from care on Rowan Ward Manchester Mental Health and Social Care Trust*, 2003.

19 National Patient Safety Agency, *With safety in Mind: Mental Health Services and patient safety*, 2006.

20 (2001) 34 EHRR 3.

steps to bring it to an end'. In the court's opinion article 3 (in conjunction with article 1) required states:

> . . . to take measures designed to ensure that individuals . . . are not subjected to . . . degrading treatment . . . [which measures should] . . . provide effective protection, in particular, of children and other vulnerable persons and include reasonable steps to prevent ill-treatment of which the authorities had or ought to have had knowledge.

25.12   The case law on article 3 has established that the courts and social services are obliged to use their powers to protect, not merely children, but also vulnerable adults[21] from abuse. Additionally, where credible evidence exists that an individual has suffered abuse while in the care of a public authority, a positive obligation arises under article 3 for an independent and open investigation to be convened.[22]

25.13   The Human Rights Act 1998 gives new impetus to the challenge posed by the widespread emotional, physical and sexual abuse of vulnerable adults,[23] not only by providing a cause of action in cases of abuse (see para 25.55 below) but also by providing a framework which can further the development of a culture where abuse is not tolerated. As Trevor Philips, Chair of the Commission for Equality and Human Rights, has pointed out:

> But our ultimate aim in creating a human rights culture is to reduce the need to resort to legislation retrospectively, after a human rights abuse has taken place. If we are successful, human rights principles, as basic principles of decency and dignity, will be embedded into public authorities' approach to service delivery; they will become, to use Cherie Blair's phrase 'models of good practice'. This is part of what we mean by an active human rights culture.[24]

Legislation to protect adults from abuse

25.14   The relevant legislation falls into four broad groups:

- that which bars certain individuals from working with vulnerable people;
- that which involves setting up protocols and procedures to prevent abuse;
- that which imposes duties to act in a person's best interests and restricts the actions they can take in relation to people who lack capacity;
- that which might act as a deterrent by criminalising certain actions in relation to vulnerable adults.

21   *Re F (Adult: Court's jurisdiction)* [2000] 3 WLR 1740; (2000) 3 CCLR 210.
22   *Assenov v Bulgaria* (1998)28 EHRR 652; see also *Labita v Italy* 6 April 2000, unreported.
23   Home Office, *Setting the Boundaries: Reforming the law on sex offences*, 2000, para 0.17.
24   Trevor Philips, speech to Human Rights Lawyers, 18 June 2007, at http://www.cehr.org.uk/news/docview.rhtm/454004.

Preventing certain people from working with vulnerable adults

25.15 Care Standards Act (CSA) 2000 Part 7 provides for the establishment of a set of controls to prevent unsuitable persons from working with vulnerable adults in England and Wales. The controls revolve around the establishment of a list of persons who have been found to be unsuitable to work with vulnerable adults (the 'POVA' list). The scheme originally extended to persons working for, or providing care homes and domiciliary care agencies including those provided by local authorities. Adult placement schemes have since been added.[25] The scheme does not include nurses and NHS staff, although nursing agencies are included to the extent that they supply care workers to registered providers of care homes and domiciliary agencies.[26]

25.16 Initially, pre-employment POVA checks including Criminal Records Bureau (CRB) checks were required before an employee could work with vulnerable adults in such situations. However due to administrative delays in obtaining such checks the regulations were amended to enable a 'POVA First' check to be made in situations where the provider would otherwise be unable to meet its statutory staffing levels. In essence if the individual does not appear on the POVA list, he or she can be employed in advance of a full CRB disclosure. Stringent supervision of the employee in the interim must however be provided.[27]

25.17 Police Act 1997 s115 provides for enhanced disclosure (such as non-conviction information held by the police) where a certificate is required in relation to workers whose work involves the caring for, training, supervising or being in sole charge of children or persons aged 18 or over who are vulnerable adults.[28] The Court of Appeal has held[29] that the principle of confidentiality is not absolute in such situations and it is not unreasonable for the police to disclose to a third party as part of an enhanced disclosure that allegations (which were discontinued) of indecent exposure had been made against a social worker with no convictions. In the court's opinion Police Act 1997 s115 created a presumption in such cases in favour of disclosure unless there was good reason to the contrary:

> This was obviously required by Parliament because it was important (for the protection of children and vulnerable adults) that the information should be disclosed even if it only might be true. If it might be true, the person who was proposing to employ the claimant should be entitled to take it into account before the decision was made as to whether or not to employ the claimant. This was the policy of the legislation in order to serve a pressing social need. In my judgement it imposes too heavy an obligation

25 Care Standards Act 2000 (Extension of Protection of Vulnerable Adults Scheme) Regulations 2004 SI No 2070.
26 Practice guidance *Protection of Vulnerable Adults Scheme*, para 27.
27 Ibid, para 38.
28 Vulnerable adult is defined inthe Police Act 1997 (Enhanced Criminal Record Certificates) (Protection of Vulnerable Adults) Regulations 2002 SI No 446.
29 *R (X) v Chief Constable of West Midlands Police* [2004] EWCA (Civ) 1068; [2005] 1 WLR 65.

on the Chief Constable to require him to give an opportunity for a person to make representations prior to the Chief Constable performing his statutory duty of disclosure.

25.18 Providers of care registered under the CSA 2000 (including employment agencies and businesses providing care workers) have a duty to refer any worker (paid or voluntary) to the secretary of state, if they have been suspended, dismissed or placed in a non-caring position, because of misconduct that harmed a vulnerable adult or placed him or her at risk.[30] The Commission for Social Care Inspection has the power to refer a care worker (if he or she has not already been referred) if it considers that he or she has been guilty of such misconduct.

25.19 Once the reference has been made to the secretary of state, the person is placed on the list provisionally and given the opportunity to make representations. A decision is then made either to include or remove the person from the list. There is no right to appeal a provisional listing, however once confirmed a right of appeal lies directly to the secretary of state or to the Care Standards Tribunal.[31] A worker who has been on the list for ten years can apply to be removed from the list.

25.20 The High Court has held that the procedure for placing workers on the POVA list is incompatible with the European Convention on Human Rights: in breach of articles 6 and 8. Of concern to the court was the restriction on care workers applying to the Care Standards Tribunal: in particular the requirement to obtain leave and that applications can only be made after being on the list for nine months.[32]

Safeguarding Vulnerable Groups Act 2006

25.21 The Safeguarding Vulnerable Groups Act (SVGA) 2006 introduces a new vetting and barring scheme for those who work with children and vulnerable adults in either a paid or volunteer capacity. The scheme is due to come into force in autumn 2008 and will replace the POCA (the equivalent barring list for children) and POVA schemes. The scheme will cover health (including the NHS) and social care services.

25.22 Individuals will be placed on these lists (barred) either automatically – if they are convicted or cautioned for certain offences – or following a decision by the Independent Safeguarding Authority taking into account other offences or cautions, or relevant information.

25.23 All barring decisions will be taken by the new Independent Safeguarding Authority that will be set up under the SVGA 2006. The Independent Safeguarding Authority, referred to in the Act as the Independent Barring Board, will be a new non-departmental public body whose role is to take decisions as to who should be included in the lists of people barred from working with children and/or vulnerable adults.

30 CSA 2000 ss82 and 83.
31 Ibid, s86.
32 *Wright, Jummun, Quinn, Gambier v Secretary of State of Health* [2006] EWHC 2886 (Admin); [2007] 1 All ER 825; (2007) 10 CCLR 34; the case is due to go to the Appeal Court.

25.24 Regulations will be made prior to the implementation of the Act which will be accompanied by detailed guidance. Consultation has taken place concerning:

- The period allowed for an individual to prepare for and make representations. This includes getting access to legal or other advice, gathering evidence etc.
- The minimum period before an individual is able to apply for permission to apply for a review of his case. The Independent Safeguarding Authority will not grant permission unless it is satisfied that the individual no longer poses a risk to children or vulnerable adults.
- How an individual's age should be taken into account in relation to the length of the minimum no-review period.
- A proposed list of offences that will result in an automatic bar under the new scheme.

Care Standards Act 2000 – protocols and procedures

25.25 The National Minimum Standards (NMS) under the CSA 2000 have a number of standards that relate to the prevention of abuse. Standard 18 of the NMS for care homes for older people, for example, states:

> The registered person ensures that service users are safeguarded from physical, financial or material, psychological or sexual abuse, neglect, discriminatory abuse or self harm, inhuman or degrading treatment, through deliberate intent, negligence or ignorance, in accordance with written policies.

25.26 More detailed standards on the safeguarding of residents money and financial affairs are also contained within standard 18.

25.27 Similar guidance for domiciliary care agencies is contained in standard 14 with a separate standard (13) for handling of service users' money, dealing with the payment of bills, collection of pensions, shopping, acceptance of gifts etc.[33] The local government ombudsman has criticised the lack of financial monitoring where withdrawals of money were not always recorded, and there was little evidence of the shopping that the carer was supposed to have done.[34]

25.28 A 2007 report by the Commission for Social Care Inspection on financial systems and safeguards to support people with their money found that 88 per cent of care homes for older people and 74 per cent of home care agencies met the standards. Standards not met included receipts not being kept, poor financial record keeping, lack of procedures or staff unaware of procedures, pooled accounts, people having poor access to their money or failing to encourage financial independence, lack of choice about purchases made, unsafe storage of money and valuables.[35]

---

33 These standards derive from Care Homes Regulations 2001 SI No 3965 regs 13 and 16, and Domiciliary Care Regulations 2002 SI No 3214 reg 14.
34 Complaint no 00/C/10708 against Sheffield City Council, 21 June 2001.
35 CSCI, *In Safe Keeping*, May 2007.

25.29   In addition the NMS requires that providers must have policies to respond to allegations of abuse.

Safeguarding provisions in relation to people who lack capacity

25.30   The Law Commission's 1995 reform proposals for the law concerning mental capacity called for the enactment of a 'new set of modern and acceptable emergency protective powers' to protect vulnerable adults from abuse. The Mental Capacity Act (MCA) 2005, although a direct outcome of the Law Commission study, lacks any direct adult protection measures. The Act is outlined at para in chapter 18 above and contains various provisions that may prove to be of value in this regard, including:

- the principles (section 1) requiring acts to be done in the incapacitated person's best interests (section 4);
- the powers of the new office of public guardian to investigate cases of abuse (considered at para 25.49 below);
- the power to appoint deputies (which could include local authorities) to take social welfare decisions in addition to financial decisions to ensure that the incapacitated person is adequately protected. The role of deputies is considered at para 18.55 above;
- the creation of a new criminal offence of ill-treating or wilfully neglecting people lacking capacity (see para 25.33 below).

Criminal offences

25.31   While it is debatable how far the possibility of being charged with a criminal offence deters people from abusing adults, over the last few years there has been an increase in the number of offences which are specific to adults who are in vulnerable situations or may be vulnerable to abuse. These include:

Mental Health Act 1983 s127

25.32   Section 127 makes it an offence for (among other things) any individual to ill-treat or wilfully neglect a mentally disordered patient who is subject to his or her guardianship or otherwise in his or her custody or care. While this is potentially a wide ranging provision, it is limited procedurally since proceedings can only be instigated by or with the permission of the Director of Prosecutions.

Mental Capacity Act 2005 s44

25.33   Section 44 makes it an offence for anyone caring for or who is an attorney under a lasting power of attorney or enduring power of attorney, or is a deputy for a person who lacks capacity, to ill treat or wilfully neglect that person. The provision is limited to people who lack capacity (and accordingly narrower in scope than section 127 above) but is not restricted by an requirement to obtain leave before charges are laid.

Fraud Act 2006 s4

25.34 Section 4 concerns 'fraud by abuse of position' and makes it an offence for a person who occupies a position where he or she is required to safeguard (or not act against) the financial interests of another person, to dishonestly abuse that position, with the intent of self-benefit or to benefit others.

Sexual Offences Act 2003 ss30–41

25.35 The Sexual Offences Act 2003 contains a range of provisions relating to people with mental disorder (bearing the same meaning as in the Mental Health Act (MHA) 1983). Sections 30–33 create offences that rely on the inability of the person to refuse the sexual activity on account of lack of capacity or where the person is unable to communicate refusal. Sections 34–37 relate to situations where the person suffering from a mental disorder is induced, threatened or deceived into sexual activity where the perpetrator knows or could reasonably be expected to know that the person suffered a mental disorder. Sections 38–41 relate to care workers where the assumption is that the worker must have known or reasonably expected to have known that the person had a mental disorder and do not rely on the inability of the victim to refuse.

Domestic Violence, Crime and Victims Act 2004 s5

25.36 Section 5 makes it an offence to cause or allow the death of a child or vulnerable adult and is designed to address the evidential problem of proving who in a household was actually responsible for causing or allowing the death to occur. In such circumstances a person is guilty of an offence if there was significant risk of serious physical harm, and the person either caused the victim's death, or was or ought to have been aware of the risk and failed to take steps to protect the victim, and the act occurred in circumstances that the person foresaw or ought to have foreseen. The definition of household includes people who do not live in the property but whose visits are sufficiently frequent for them to be counted as such.

Vulnerable witnesses

25.37 Many victims of crime, whose mental capacity is impaired, experience considerable difficulties in delivering their evidence. The report *Speaking Up For Justice*[36] made a number of recommendations aimed at encouraging and supporting vulnerable or intimidated witnesses to give their best evidence in criminal cases. Many of its provisions were enacted

36 Home Office, 1998.

in Youth Justice and Criminal Evidence Act 1999 Part 2, including the right of vulnerable witnesses to have the assistance of an intermediary when being interviewed or giving evidence (section 29). Home Office guidance has been issued concerning the procedures.[37]

Safeguarding adults if abuse has occurred

Local authority guidance

25.38   In 2000 guidance was issued by both the Department of Health (*No Secrets*)[38] and the Welsh Assembly (*In Safe Hands*)[39] concerning the procedures local authorities should adopt to monitor and respond to concerns about adult abuse. The guidance is process orientated and contains no new powers to enable local authorities to protect the victims of abuse, concentrating instead upon such issues as:

- The clarification of the roles and responsibilities of the relevant agencies (eg social services, the police, NHS bodies);
- The development of multi disciplinary procedures for responding to concerns and referrals, including joint protocols on such issues as information sharing;
- Contract monitoring with independent providers;
- Improvements to information for service users, carers and members of the public;
- The development of monitoring systems and training strategies.

25.39   These processes, valuable as they may be, sometimes just serve to show how powerless social services are when faced with cases of abuse where there is not enough evidence to prosecute. The new Directors of Adult Services are expected to ensure a 'clear organisational focus on safeguarding adults in vulnerable situations' but this does not appear to add much in the way of teeth to the guidance.[40]

25.40   Although multi-agency policies and procedures for addressing abuse now exist in all local authorities, the Health Committee inquiry into elder abuse found there is considerable diversity in the way they are arranged and the resources allocated to fulfil the work.[41] The local government

---

37   Home Office, *Achieving Best Evidence in Criminal Proceedings: Guidance for vulnerable or intimidated witnesses (including children)*, 2002, accessible athttp://www.cps.gov.uk/publications/prosecution/bestevidencevol1.html and see also K Stone, 'Voice Box' *Community Care*, 20–26 November 2003 p421.

38   Department of Health and Home Office, *No Secrets: Guidance on developing and implementing multi-agency policies and procedures to protect vulnerable adults from abuse*, 2000.

39   National Assembly for Wales, *In Safe Hands*, 2000.

40   Department of Health, *Best Practice on the role of the Director of Adult Services*, 2006.

41   There is indeed evidence to suggest that even the guidance has not been effectively implemented by social services– D Mathew et al, 'The response to No Secrets' (2002) 4(1) *Journal of Adult Protection* 4.

ombudsman has, for instance, found maladministration where a local authority, in spite of having developed inter-agency procedures, failed to investigate properly an allegation of sexual assault on a young service user with learning difficulties while she was in respite care. In this case the Primary Care Trust did not inform social services for two weeks after the incident was alleged to have occurred, neither agency informed the police, and the service user was not interviewed until over a month after the incident. The council's guidelines stressed that such allegations should be investigated as a matter of urgency. The council then failed to provide a proper care plan to address any new needs that had resulted as a result of the alleged incident and the changes in her behaviour.[42]

25.41   A major criticism of the *No Secrets* (*In Safe Hands*) guidance is that it only extends to people described as vulnerable adults, defined as those who are or may be in need of community care services and who are unable to protect themselves from significant harm or exploitation. The Health Committee recommended that this definition should be broadened to include 'those individuals who do not require community care services, for example older people living in their own homes without support of health and social services, and those who can take care of themselves'. [43]

25.42   The Association of Directors of Social Services (ADSS), in its national framework for good practice in adult protection work,[44] uses the term 'Safeguarding Adults' and has moved away from definitions of vulnerability and describes the procedures as a multi-agency response which is made to every adult who is or may be eligible for community care services and whose independence and well-being is at risk due to abuse or neglect. 'This definition specifically includes those people who are assessed as being able to purchase all or part of their community care services, as well as those who are eligible for community care services but whose need – in relation to safeguarding – is for access to mainstream services such as the police. It goes on to state:

> Whilst these particular adults are the specific focus of 'Safeguarding Adults' policy and procedure, this does not negate the public duty of those carrying out this work to protect the human rights of **all** citizens, including those who are the subject of concern but are not covered by these procedures, or those who are not subject to the initial concern.

25.43   The ADSS framework sets standards and details the responsibilities of Safeguarding Adult Teams in relation to joint planning and capability, prevention of abuse and neglect and responding to abuse and neglect which give clear time frames, and access and involvement.

---

42 Complaint no 03/B/18884 against Bromley LCA, 9 December 2004.
43 House of Commons Health Committee. *Elder Abuse*, HC 111-I, 2004, para 14; and see also *The Government's response to the recommendations and conclusions of the Health Select Committee's inquiry into elder abuse*, Cm 6270, 2004.
44 ADSS, *Safeguarding Adults*, 2005. This document is described as being 'arguably the most important policy document since *No Secrets*' by the authors of the report into the prevalence of abuse (see para 25.6).

The role of regulators

25.44   Concern exists over the role of social and health care regulators in investigating allegations of abuse. Where abuse is suspected in an institutional setting, such as an independent care home, it might appear logical that the regulatory and inspection authority – namely the Commission for Social Care Inspection in England (CSCI) and in Wales the Care and Social Services Inspectorate Wales – should undertake the investigation. These bodies have, after all, the power of entry and the power to close failing care homes. The CSCI however does not consider itself to be the appropriate agency, stating that 'the responsibility for investigation of individual cases within safeguarding adults procedures rests primarily with other partners including the local authority'.[45] Given the severe limitations on the powers of local authorities, the failure of the government to accord the CSCI such an investigatory role means that many vulnerable residents are left unprotected.

25.45   In February 2007 a new protocol was published between the CSCI, the ADSS and the Association of Chief Police Officers 'demonstrating CSCI's commitment to working with other agencies to ensure that people within regulated services are appropriately safeguarded'.[46] It identifies three levels of engagement by the CSCI in response to a safeguarding alert:

- Where there is serious risk to a person's life, health or well-being the CSCI will not suspend its own statutory enforcement powers pending the outcome of another (eg criminal) process. While it will aim to co-ordinate any regulatory activity, the CSCI will however give primary consideration to its statutory responsibilities.
- Where a safeguarding adults referral received by a local council suggests breaches of regulations and certain criteria are met (eg in relation to the scale of the abuse, the involvement of registered persons and the regulatory history of the service) the CSCI may decide to conduct inquiries as part of the multi-agency strategy.
- Where there are no indications of serious risk, the outcome of any investigations by partner agencies will inform CSCI's decision-making about further regulatory action.

25.46   The protocol contains further details about information sharing, and responding to alerts about possible abuse.

25.47   Two reports by the Healthcare Commission on major and long standing incidents of abuse in healthcare settings[47] have led to an audit being undertaken of 200 NHS and private services.

45   P Snell, Chief Inspector, CSCI, *The role of regulation and inspection in protecting vulnerable adults*, 30 November 2006, accessible at http://www.csci.org.uk/docs/snell_301106.doc.

46   CSCI, *Safeguarding Adults Protocol and Guidance*, 2007, accessible at http://www.csci.org.uk/professional/care_providers/all_services/guidance/safeguarding_adults_protocol.aspx.

47   *Investigation into services for people with learning disabilities at Cornwall Partnership NHS Trust*, June 2006 and *Investigation into the service for people with learning disabilities provided by Sutton and Merton Primary Care Trust*, January 2007.

Whistle blowing

25.48 The Public Interest Disclosure Act 1998 should in theory give workers, who raise concerns about abuse and malpractice, protection from dismissal and victimisation. Covering all areas of employment, it can be of particular use where care workers are concerned about abusive practices experienced by service users within their organisation. The Harold Shipman report expressed concerns that others in the NHS did not come forward when they had some worries about the deaths where Dr Shipman was involved. It quotes a survey by Unison that 50 per cent of its members in the NHS did not know whether their trust had a whistleblowing policy and 30 per cent considered that their trust would not want to be told about a major problem. The Shipman report suggested a number of amendments to the Public Interest Disclosure Act 1998 and other recommendations aimed at encouraging employees to raise their concerns.[48] In its response to this report the government has proposed that all organisations providing services to the NHS should have a written policy setting out the procedures to be followed by staff wishing to raise concerns. It did not however consider it necessary to amend the 1998 Act, given the other measures that were being taken.[49]

The role of the Office of the Public Guardian

25.49 The MCA 2005 creates a new Public Guardian[50] supported by the Office of the Public Guardian, who is responsible for the administration of the registers of lasting powers of attorney, enduring powers of attorney and court appointed deputies (see para 18.55 above). However the Public Guardian is only responsible for supervising deputies, and it intended that the level of supervision will be based on a risk assessment. The Public Guardian can receive reports from attorneys and deputies but will normally only investigate attorneys if representations have been made about the way they are carrying out their duties.[51]

25.50 In relation to the powers of the Office of the Public Guardian and the 'Court of Protection Visitors' the Code of Practice comments:

> 14.10 The role of a Court of Protection Visitor is to provide independent advice to the court and the guardian . . . There are two types of visitor: General Visitors and Special Visitors. Special visitors are registered medical practitioners with relevant expertise. The court or Public Guardian can send whichever type of visitor is most appropriate to visit and interview a person who may lack capacity. Visitors can also interview attorneys or deputies and inspect any relevant healthcare or social care records. Attorneys and deputies must co-operate with the visitors and provide them with all relevant information. If attorneys or deputies do not co-operate, the

---

48 *The Shipman Inquiry* Fifth Report chapter 11, 2004.
49 *Safeguarding patients. The Government's response to the recommendations of the Shipman Inquiry's Fifth Report*, Cm 7015, February 2007, para 5.33.
50 MCA 2005 s57.
51 Ibid, s58.

court can cancel their appointment, where it thinks that they have not acted in the person's best interests.

14.11 Court of Protection Visitors have an important part to play in investigating possible abuse. But their role is much wider than this. They can also check on the general wellbeing of the person who lacks capacity, and they can give support to attorneys and deputies who need help to carry out their duties.

25.51 The absence of specific provisions in the Act to address financial and other abuse has been the subject of considerable adverse comment. In the second draft Code of Practice (2006) it was suggested (at para 13.19) that the Office of the Public Guardian could 'itself investigate cases where there are allegations of financial abuse on the part of the attorney or the deputy'. However in the final code this has been watered down, and states:

14.19 Many people who lack capacity are likely to get care or support from a range of agencies. Even when an attorney or deputy is acting on behalf of a person who lacks capacity, the other carers still have a responsibility to the person to provide care and act in the person's best interests. Anybody who is caring for a person who lacks capacity, whether in a paid or unpaid role, who is worried about how attorneys or deputies carry out their duties should contact the Public Guardian.

14.20 The OPG will not always be the most appropriate organisation to investigate all complaints. It may investigate a case jointly with:
- healthcare or social care professionals
- social services
- NHS bodies
- the Commission for Social Care Inspection in England or the Care and Social Services Inspectorate for Wales (CSSIW)[52]
- the Healthcare Commission in England or the Healthcare Inspectorate for Wales, and
- in some cases, the police.

14.21 The OPG will usually refer concerns about personal welfare LPAs or personal welfare deputies to the relevant agency. In certain circumstances it will alert the police about a case. When it makes a referral, the OPG will make sure that the relevant agency keeps it informed of the action it takes. It will also make sure that the court has all the information it needs to take possible action against the attorney or deputy.

25.52 The current Public Guardianship Office has a financial investigations unit which in 2005/06 concluded 78 investigations and as a consequence recovered £1.1 million of client funds. It appears that referrals came primarily from social services authorities and families, but whistleblowers, Lord Chancellor's visitors and solicitors also made use of the unit.[53] It is assumed that this unit will continue to work in conjunction with other protection agencies after October 2007.

52 In April 2007, the Care Standards Inspectorate for Wales (CSIW) and the Social Services Inspectorate for Wales (SSIW) came together to form the Care and Social Services Inspectorate for Wales.
53 Public Guardianship Office, *Annual Report and Accounts 2006/07*, accessible at http://www.guardianship.gov.uk/downloads/PGO_Annual_Report_2006–07.pdf.

The role of independent mental capacity advocates

25.53   MCA 2005 ss35–41 place a duty on local authorities and NHS bodies to provide an independent mental capacity advocate (IMCA) service. The role and scope of the IMCA service is detailed in regulations[54] and subject to guidance in the MCA Code of Practice. The regulations[55] provide for the appointment of an IMCA to assist when an NHS body or local authority is contemplating taking adult protection measures, whether or not family, friends or others are involved.[56]

25.54   Guidance accompanying the regulations suggests that local authorities and NHS bodies should draw up a policy statement outlining who would most benefit from the safeguard of an IMCA, and that this should be widely distributed.[57] The guidance reminds councils and NHS bodies that if a person meets the qualifying criteria it would be unlawful for them not to consider exercising their power to instruct an IMCA.[58]

Declaratory relief and the role of the High Court

25.55   Since the enactment of the Human Rights Act 1998, the higher courts have dynamically developed a number of latent common law doctrines and mechanisms in an effort to provide legal protection for vulnerable adults. The MCA 2005 preserves the current right of concerned parties to apply to the court for a declaration of 'best interests' – presently known as 'declaratory relief. The new Court of Protection has the full powers of the High Court to make declarations on financial or welfare matters affecting people who lack capacity to make decisions. It also enables a concerned party to apply to be appointed an incapacitated person's 'deputy', and it can remove deputies and attorneys who are acting inappropriately.[59] While it is likely that the new Court of Protection will assume the 'declaratory relief' jurisdiction developed by the High Court since 2000, it will be limited to cases of people lacking sufficient mental capacity. As noted at para 25.59 below, the High Court has also developed its jurisdiction in relation to people who, although considered to have mental capacity, are otherwise vulnerable and in need of protection. In relation to this group, the High Court Family Division will (presumably) retain its jurisdiction.

---

54   Mental Capacity Act 2005 (Independent Mental Capacity Advocate) (General) Regulations 2006 SI No 1832; Mental Capacity Act 2005 (Independent Mental Capacity Advocate) (Expansion of Role) Regulations 2006 SI No 2883; Mental Capacity Act 2005 (Independent Mental Capacity Advocate) (Wales) Regulations 2007 SI No 852 (W77).
55   Mental Capacity Act 2005 (Independent Mental Capacity Advocate) (Expansion of Role) Regulations 2006 regs 3 and 4.
56   See Code of Practice para 10.66.
57   Department of Health, *Adult Protection Care Reviews and IMCAs*, January 2007.
58   Ibid, para 10.
59   MCA 2005 s45.

25.56   The High Court's declaratory relief procedure for vulnerable adults first found full expression in *Re F (Adult: Court's jurisdiction).*[60] The case concerned a young adult who lacked sufficient mental capacity to make informed decisions as to where she should live or who posed a risk to her safety. As a minor she had been neglected and exposed to abuse while in the care of her parents and had accordingly been made a ward of court and placed in specialist accommodation. The wardship came to an end on her 18th birthday and the authority feared that without some form of fresh court order her mother would seek her return home where she would be at risk of further abuse. As Dame Butler-Sloss observed:[61]

> There is an obvious gap in the framework of care for mentally incapacitated adults. If the court cannot act ... this vulnerable young woman would be left at serious risk.

25.57   To fill this gap, the court's solution was for it to 'grow' and 'shape'[62] the common law principle of 'necessity'; or as Sedley LJ expressed it, 'to speak where Parliament ... was silent'.[63] In the court's judgment, therefore, where a serious justiciable issue arose as to the best interests of an adult without the mental capacity, then the High Court was able to grant declarations (in the exercise of its inherent jurisdiction) as to what would be in that person's best interests.[64]

25.58   The courts have in subsequent judgments developed the principles established by *Re F* and in so doing, have clarified the scope and availability of the declaratory jurisdiction.[65] The key requirements can be summarised as follows.

Mental incapacity/vulnerability

25.59   Much of the early case-law suggested that the court can only deploy its declaratory relief jurisdiction once it has been established that the person in question is incapable (by reason of mental incapacity) of making the relevant decision – see for instance *Newham LBC v BS and S.*[66] In *A Local Authority v MA, NA and SA,*[67] however, Munby J held that incapacity was not essential. In his view the court could exercise its inherent jurisdiction:

> ... in relation to a vulnerable adult who, even if not incapacitated by mental disorder or mental illness, is, or is reasonably believed to be, either (i) under constraint or (ii) subject to coercion or undue influence or (iii) for some other reason deprived of the capacity to make the relevant decision, or disabled from making a free choice, or incapacitated or disabled from giving or expressing a real and genuine consent.

60 [2000] 3 WLR 1740; (2000) 3 CCLR 210.
61 Ibid at 219J.
62 Ibid, per Sedley LJ at 227B.
63 Ibid at 226B.
64 Ibid at 218 C–E.
65 Proceedings should be commenced in the High Court under CPR Part 8 – *M v B, A and S* [2005] EWHC 1681 (Fam); [2006] 1 FLR 117.
66 [2003] EWHC 1909 (Fam); (2004) 7 CCLR 132.
67 [2005] EWHC 2942 (Fam); [2006] 1 FLR 867 at [55].

25.60 In many respects this development follows the Law Commission's 1995 proposals in their original Mental Incapacity Bill which suggested (at clause 36) that the adult protection powers could be used where the person was (among other things) 'unable to protect himself against significant harm or serious exploitation'.[68] In coming to this conclusion Munby J cited an extensive case-law,[69] including *Re G (An Adult) (Mental Capacity: Court's Jurisdiction)*[70] where the court held that G lacked capacity because of her 'father's ability to overbear [her] decision-making' ability. As a consequence G was placed by the court under a 'protective regime, which limited the father's access to' her – as a result she recovered her capacity to make decisions. The problem, of course, was that if the court's power ceased when she recovered capacity, then she would fall under her father's power again – and so be caught in a rotating door. As Bennett J stated:

> If the restrictions were lifted . . . it is probable that the situation would revert to what it was prior to March 2004. G's mental health would deteriorate to such an extent that she would again become incapacitated to take decisions about the matters referred to. Such a reversion would be disastrous for G.

25.61 In the circumstances the court held that incapacity was not an essential requirement for it to exercise its inherent jurisdiction.

A serious justiciable issue

25.62 A 'serious justiciable issue' must exist which requires resolution. The courts have not sought to define precisely what is meant by this phrase. It will exist when the facts 'demonstrate a situation in which the doctrine of necessity might arise';[71] it is not the same as the threshold test for care proceedings under Children Act (CA) 1989 s31[72] and can arise even where there is no evidence of ill-treatment.

What is the question that needs to be determined?

25.63 In *Newham LBC v BS and S*[73] a question arose as to whether the 'significant issue' that had to be determined was (a) if abuse had occurred; or (b) where the incapacitated person should live. The local authority applied for a declaration, basing its application on evidence that the disabled person's father drank excessively and had assaulted her. The court rejected this evidence, but nevertheless considered that an order should be made. In this respect Wall J held:

68 The Law Commission's proposals are replicated in the Care of Older and Incapacitated People (Human Rights) Bill (2006) Part III – accessible at http://www.publications.parliament.uk/pa/cm200506/cmbills/112/2006112.pdf.
69 [2005] EWHC 2942 (Fam); [2006] 1 FLR 867 at [59]–[60].
70 [2004] EWHC 2222 (Fam).
71 *Re F (Adult: Court's jurisdiction)* [2000] 3 WLR 1740; (2000) 3 CCLR 210 per Butler Sloss LJ.
72 *Re S (Adult Patient) (Inherent Jurisdiction: Family Life)* [2002] EWHC 2278 (Fam); [2003] 1 FLR 292, per Munby J.
73 [2003] EWHC 1909 (Fam); (2004) 7 CCLR 132.

I agree that there must be good reason for local authority intervention in a case such as the present. Equally, if there are disputed issues of fact which go to the question of [the father's ability] and suitability to care for S, the court may need to resolve them, if their resolution is necessary to the decision as to what is in S's best interests. Findings of fact against [the father] . . . would plainly reflect upon his capacity properly to care for S. But it does not follow, in my judgment, that the proceedings must be dismissed simply because the factual basis upon which the local authority instituted them turns out to be mistaken, or because it cannot be established on the balance of probabilities. What matters (assuming always that mental incapacity is made out) is which outcome will be in S's best interests. There will plainly be cases which are very fact specific. There will be others in which the principal concern is the future, and the relative suitability of the plans which each party can put forward for both the short and the long term care of the mentally incapable adult. The instant case, in my judgment, is one of the cases in the latter category.

Best interests and the 'balance sheet' assessment

25.64   The meaning of best interests is considered at para 18.25. However, when exercising their declaratory powers, the courts have required a 'balance sheet' to be drawn up listing the potential benefits and 'dis-benefits' that may flow from an intervention. This approach was identified by the Court of Appeal in *Re A (Medical Treatment: Male Sterilisation)*,[74] in the following terms:

> The . . . judge . . . should draw up a balance sheet. The first entry should be of any factor or factors of actual benefit . . . Then on the other sheet the judge should write any counter-balancing disbenefits to the applicant . . . Then the judge should enter on each sheet the potential gains and losses in each instance making some estimate of the extent of the possibility that the gain or loss might accrue. At the end of that exercise the judge should be better placed to strike a balance between the sum of the certain and possible gains against the sum of the certain and possible losses. Obviously only if the account is in relatively significant credit will the judge conclude that the application is likely to advance the best interests of the claimant.

25.65   In the *Newham LBC* proceedings Wall J considered that the benefits of the daughter remaining with her father included his love for, and strong sense of duty towards her and the fact that he had adequately provided for her in the recent past. The benefits of her moving to an independent residential care placement included the fact that her father (due to his age and poor health) would progressively find it difficult to care for her; that she could have contact with her siblings (who were not prepared to visit her at her father's house); the proposed care home would provide her with an opportunity for social contact with people of her own age group. In addition the court considered that the professional evidence was 'crucial': the social and health professionals were of the opinion that the care home placement was the better option. In the judge's opinion there-

74   [2000] 1 FLR 549, p560F–H.

fore, the balance sheet came down firmly in favour of the care home placement.

The proportionality of interventions

25.66 The 'benefits/disbenefits' assessment process will almost always relate to an issue of fundamental relevance to a disabled person's private and family life and their home – and thus require an examination of the proportionality of the proposed action from the perspective of article 8 of the Convention. In this context, it would appear that there are certain presumptions – for instance that the state interference will be the least restrictive and presumably that there should be no 'order' unless strictly necessary.[75]

25.67 In declaratory relief proceedings – to date – the courts have not adopted such an approach. Thus in *Re S (Adult Patient) (Inherent Jurisdiction: Family Life)*,[76] although the court held that the assessment exercise is not predicated on any formal presumptions (for instance of the type to be found in CA 1989 Part I), nevertheless:

> . . . whilst there was no presumption that mentally incapacitated adults would be better off if they lived with a family, rather than an institution, the burden was on a local authority to establish, if it sought to do so, that it was the more appropriate person to look after the mentally incapacitated adult than his own family.

25.68 Likewise in *Re A (Medical Treatment: Male Sterilisation)*[77] as noted above, it was held that intervention could be sanctioned even if the ledger was only 'in relatively significant credit'.

25.69 In analogous proceedings, however, the article 8 rights of parties have not been viewed as neutral. *Re Connor*[78] (a case heard by the Court of Appeal in Northern Ireland) concerned a 55-year-old woman who had cognitive impairment as a result of long-term alcohol abuse. For a number of years she had been receiving psychiatric treatment. As a consequence of injuries she sustained while living in the community with her cohabitee, Mr Connor, she became subject to a further guardianship order. Shortly after the order was made she and Mr Connor married.

25.70 The health trust (her guardian) placed restrictions upon how often Mrs Connor could live with her husband – although these restrictions were gradually relaxed. At the time of the hearing her home leave was stipulated as being four consecutive nights a week (Thursday to Sunday).

25.71 Mrs Connor challenged the proportionality of these restrictions under article 8(1) of the Convention. She argued that the trust had, not only to demonstrate the necessity of the restrictions imposed, but also

---

75 In this context, see the approach to a not dissimilar balancing exercise taken by Munby J, in *R (A and B) v East Sussex CC (No 2)* [2003] EWHC 167 (Admin); (2003) 6 CCLR 194 at 226–232.

76 [2002] EWHC 2278 (Fam); [2003] 1 FLR 292.

77 [2000] 1 FLR 549.

78 [2004] NICA 45; (2005) 8 CCLR 328.

to undertake an explicit analysis of her situation 'through the prism of the European Convention'.[79] The first instance judge disagreed, stating that:

> While that 'right' [under article 8(1)] may not be specifically mentioned in the reports, it is clear that the Trust were actively considering the relationship between the applicant and her husband and the question of overnight stays. In those circumstances the Trust were dealing with the substance of the issue in the context of where and with whom the applicant should reside.

25.72   The Northern Ireland Court of Appeal rejected this approach, holding:

> 29. There is no evidence that the trust ever recognised, much less addressed, the interference with the appellant's article 8 rights. In none of the documents generated by the trust's consideration of her case can any reference to article 8 be found. [The trust's barrister] claims that what the trust officers were embarked upon in considering Mrs Connor's case was 'in essence' an article 8 exercise. We cannot accept that argument. The consideration of whether an interference with a convention right can be justified involves quite a different approach from an assessment at large of what is best for the person affected. The trust's consideration of Mrs Connor's case clearly partakes of the latter of these.

Ex parte applications

25.73   Such applications to the court may, in appropriate cases, be made to the court without other parties being notified – for instance in situations of urgency such as *B BC v S and S*[80] where a nursing home was no longer willing or able to cope with the elderly resident, but his wife was known to be implacably opposed to a temporary placement in hospital.

The range of potential declarations

25.74   In the *Newham LBC* decision, Wall J made a declaration authorising the local authority to continue with the care home arrangement (with defined contact between the father and daughter). Additionally he declared that the authority was to consult her father about any future medical treatment/care arrangements she might require and that she be provided with an independent advocate.

25.75   Declarations can also be sought concerning future situations, provided they are rooted in a serious 'justiciable issue' and are not overly hypothetical.[81] In *Re S (Adult Patient) (Inherent Jurisdiction: Family Life)*[82] the local authority was concerned that it might have to return to the court – repeatedly – for additional declarations, given the difficult relationship that existed between it and the incapacitated person's father. The authority

---

79   [Ibid, at [19].
80   [2006] EWHC 2584 (Fam); (2006) 9 CCLR 596.
81   See eg *R v Portsmouth Hospitals NHS Trust ex p Glass* (1999) 2 FLR 905; (1999) 50 BMLR 269 where the court held a future treatment decision to be too hypothetical.
82   [2002] EWHC 2278 (Fam); [2003] 1 FLR 292.

accordingly asked the court to declare that it had – in effect – proxy decision making power on a range of social welfare questions. Munby J held as follows:

> The court has jurisdiction to grant whatever relief in declaratory form is necessary to safeguard and promote the incapable adult's welfare and interests. If the court thinks that his interests will be best served by a judicial identification of some third party (the local authority) as the most appropriate person to be responsible not merely for his care but also for taking the kind of decisions to which I have already referred . . . then, in my judgment, there can be no objection whatever to the court so declaring. Indeed were the court not to do so in an appropriate case, it would, as it seems to me, be failing in its duties under both the common law and the Convention . . .
>
> Moreover, some such mechanism is essential if those caring for the incapable are to be allowed to get on with their task without the need for endless reference to the court something which . . . would serve neither the public interest nor the interests of the mentally incapacitated.
>
> So, subject always to being satisfied that this really is in the best interests of the mentally incapacitated person, the court has, and in my judgment always has had, power to declare that some specified person is to be, in relation to specified matters, what is, in effect, a surrogate decision-maker for the incapable adult.

25.76 Munby J took matters further in *Sunderland City Council v PS and CA*[83] where he confirmed that the court's inherent jurisdiction permitted it to authorise the detention of an adult lacking capacity and also to appoint a receiver (ie without the local authority having to apply separately to the Court of Protection for such authority).

Guardianship

25.77 MHA 1983 s7 provides for the making of a guardianship order in relation to mentally disordered people (aged 16 or over) where 'it is necessary in the interests of the welfare of the patient or for the protection of other persons that'[84] such an order be made. It follows that mental incapacity is not a necessary pre-requisite for the making of a guardianship order.

25.78 Under MHA 1983 s8 the guardian (normally the social services department) has three limited powers, namely:

1) the power to require the patient to reside at a place specified;
2) the power to require the patient to attend at places for medical treatment, occupation, education or training and;
3) the power to require access to the patient to be given.

83 [2007] EWHC 623 (Fam).
84 MHA 1983 s7(2)(b).

25.79   Mental disorder is currently[85] defined (by MHA 1983 s1) as:

- mental illness;
- psychopathic disorder;
- mental impairment;
- severe mental impairment.

25.80   A mental impairment is defined as 'a state of arrested or incomplete development of mind which . . . is associated with abnormally aggressive or seriously irresponsible conduct'.

25.81   Where therefore the person has a learning disability, guardianship is not available unless the disability is associated with 'abnormally aggressive or seriously irresponsible conduct'.[86] In *Re F (Mental Health Act: Guardianship)*[87] the Court of Appeal approved the Law Commission's interpretation of this requirement – that 'unless the meaning of these words is distorted, the vast majority of those with a learning disability (mental handicap) will be excluded from guardianship'.[88]

25.82   In *Lewis v Gibson and MH*[89] it was held that there is no requirement that a local authority seek 'declaratory relief' (see above) in preference to a guardianship order, although when seeking to displace a nearest relative as a component of a guardianship application, it was essential (for the purposes of articles 6 and 8) that the patient be served and his or her capacity to act ascertained.

85   MHA 2007 ss1–3 amend the definition: the amendments are expected to come into force during 2008.
86   MHA 1983 ss7(2)(a) and 1(2).
87   [2000] 1 FLR 192; (1999) 2 CCLR 445.
88   Law Com no 231 *Mental Incapacity*, 1995, para 2.21.
89   [2005] EWCA Civ 587; (2005) 8 CCLR 399.

CHAPTER 26

Access to personal information, data protection and confidentiality

Introduction

26.1   This chapter considers the rights of access to personal information and the right to have one's personal information kept confidential. Clearly there is potential for these two rights to be incompatible, and this chapter explores how the law seeks to resolve such conflict.

26.2   Crucial to any analysis of the law of confidentiality is an appreciation that the right is not an 'absolute' one. It is qualified, and like all qualified rights requires a balance to be struck between competing interests and principles. In certain situations therefore the state is entitled to interfere with a person's 'privacy' provided the interference pursues a legitimate aim (for instance the protection of the person or another) and the interference is not disproportionate. In terms, therefore, an understanding of the law requires an understanding of article 8 of the European Convention on Human Rights ('the Convention') – the right (among other things) to respect for one's private life. At times, the right can only be 'respected' by a disclosure of confidential information – for instance where a vulnerable person lacking capacity has been abused and the police need to be informed of this fact. In other situations the striking of a balance may require a limited disclosure. The local government ombudsman has held, for example, that while the confidential nature of risk assessments means that councils are not obliged to share them with service providers, this does not mean that they are under no duty to share information about (for instance) a service user's history of challenging behaviour.[1]

The legal framework

26.3   The striking of the balance has not been eased by the legal framework that has developed to regulate this important function. In essence there are three domains of the law that bear upon such decisions, namely:

- the Data Protection Act (DPA)1998;
- the Human Rights Act (HRA) 1998; and
- the common law.

26.4   The relevant provisions of the DPA 1998, the HRA 1998 and the common law are reviewed below. However the interplay between them was considered in *R (S) v Plymouth City Council*.[2] The case concerned 'C', a 27-year-old man with learning and behavioural difficulties who had been assessed as lacking mental capacity to consent to the disclosure of his file to his mother (his nearest relative for the purposes of Mental Health Act 1983 s11). The local authority obtained a guardianship order in relation to C, since it believed that it was not in his best interests to live with his mother. The mother expressed concerns about the guardianship order, and in order to decide whether or not to object to its continuation, she

1   Complaint no 04/C/16195 against Birmingham City Council, 23 March 2006.
2   [2002] EWCA Civ 388; [2002] 1 WLR 2583; (2002) 5 CCLR 251.

asked to see the relevant papers in his social services and health care files. The local authority refused, initially asserting that it could not disclose the information because it was confidential. Subsequently it shifted its position, accepting that it had power to disclose, but that this could not occur without very good reasons (and it considered that no such reasons existed). The Court of Appeal disagreed with this approach. Reviewing the DPA 1998 it noted that although all the information that the mother was seeking was 'sensitive personal data' within the meaning of DPA 1998 s2(e), this did not mean that it could not be disclosed to third parties – since the Act permitted this in various situations, including:[3]

> . . . where it is necessary in order to protect the vital interests of the data subject or another person in a case where consent cannot be given by or on behalf of the data (Sched 3, para 3); or for the purpose of, or in connection with, any legal proceedings (including prospective legal proceedings) or for the purpose of obtaining legal advice, or where it is otherwise necessary for the purposes of establishing, exercising or defending legal rights (para 6); or where it is necessary for the administration of justice, or for the exercise of any functions conferred on any person by or under an enactment. (para 7)

26.5 In the circumstances therefore it considered that the Act provided little assistance and that the final decision on the disclosure of the confidential information[4] depended upon a careful analysis of the relevant common law and HRA 1998 principles – which required that 'a balance be struck between the public and private interests in maintaining the confidentiality of this information and the public and private interests in permitting, indeed requiring, its disclosure for certain purposes'.

26.6 Following a detailed analysis the court concluded as follows:

> 48. Hence both the common law and the Convention require that a balance be struck between the various interests involved. These are the confidentiality of the information sought; the proper administration of justice; the mother's right of access to legal advice to enable her to decide whether or not to exercise a right which is likely to lead to legal proceedings against her if she does so; the rights of both C and his mother to respect for their family life and adequate involvement in decision-making processes about it; C's right to respect for his private life; and the protection of C's health and welfare. In some cases there might also be an interest in the protection of other people, but that has not been seriously suggested here.

> 49. C's interest in protecting the confidentiality of personal information about himself must not be under-estimated. It is all too easy for professionals and parents to regard children and incapacitated adults as having no independent interests of their own: as objects rather than subjects. But we are not concerned here with the publication of information to the whole wide world. There is a clear distinction between

3 Ibid, at [27].
4 The court was of the view that it was overly simplistic to consider that all the information in the file was confidential, commenting (at [33]) 'some of it may not be confidential at all: straightforward descriptions of everyday life are not normally thought confidential'.

disclosure to the media with a view to publication to all and sundry and disclosure in confidence to those with a proper interest in having the information in question. We are concerned here only with the latter. The issue is only whether the circle should be widened from those professionals with whom this information has already been shared (possibly without much conscious thought being given to the balance of interests involved) to include the person who is probably closest to him in fact as well as in law and who has a statutory role in his future and to those professionally advising her. C also has an interest in having his own wishes and feelings respected. It would be different in this case if he had the capacity to give or withhold consent to the disclosure: any objection from him would have to be weighed in the balance against the other interests, although as *W v Egdell*[5] shows, it would not be decisive. C also has an interest in being protected from a risk of harm to his health or welfare which would stem from disclosure; but it is important not to confuse a possible risk of harm to his health or welfare from being discharged from guardianship with a possible risk of harm from disclosing the information sought. As *Re D*[6] shows, he also has an interest in decisions about his future being properly informed.

50. That balance would not lead in every case to the disclosure of all the information a relative might possibly want, still less to a fishing exercise amongst the local authority's files. But in most cases it would lead to the disclosure of the basic statutory guardianship documentation. In this case it must also lead to the particular disclosure sought. There is no suggestion that C has any objection to his mother and her advisers being properly informed about his health and welfare. There is no suggestion of any risk to his health and welfare arising from this. The mother and her advisers have sought access to the information which her own psychiatric and social work experts need in order properly to advise her. That limits both the context and the content of disclosure in a way which strikes a proper balance between the competing interests.

26.7   In such cases, public bodies should analyse precisely why they are asserting 'confidentiality' and ask themselves whether this does indeed promote the best interests of the third party: is confidentiality being claimed to protect themselves rather than the disabled person? In its guidance on protecting vulnerable adults, *No Secrets*[7] the Department of Health emphasised this point (at para 5.8), stating 'principles of confidentiality designed to safeguard and promote the interests of service users and patients should not be confused with those designed to protect the management interests of an organisation. These have a legitimate role but must never be allowed to conflict with the interests of service users and parents.'

5   [1990] 2 WLR 471, CA – see para 26.40 below .
6   *Re D (Minors) (Adoption Reports: Confidentiality)* [1995] 3 WLR 483, HL.
7   Department of Health and Home Office, *No Secrets: Guidance on developing and implementing multi-agency policies and procedures to protect vulnerable adults from abuse*, 2000; in Wales, National Assembly for Wales, *In Safe Hands*, 2000, para 9.5 – see para 25.38 above.

Data Protection Act 1998

26.8   The DPA 1998 covers all social services and health records. It is not an easy Act and where possible courts tend to try and articulate the law using other reference points – principally the common law and article 8 of the Convention (as did the Court of Appeal in the *Plymouth City Council* case). Indeed a former Lord Chancellor has observed that:[8]

> The problem about the Data Protection Act is that it is almost incomprehensible. It is very difficult to understand. The precise limits of it are problematic. There are constant difficulties about what information you are allowed to share between departments for instance. I just think it needs to be looked at again at some stage to make it more simple.

26.9   Legal guidance on the Act has been issued by the Information Commissioner,[9] in addition to which specific NHS[10] and social services guidance has been issued by the Department of Health. In the following section, paragraph references are to the social services guidance LASSL (2000)2 ('the guidance')[11] unless the context indicates otherwise.

26.10   The 1998 Act applies to all 'accessible public records', no matter when they were compiled and includes electronic and manual data. An accessible public record is a record which contains any personal information held by the health body or social services department for the purposes of their health/social services functions, irrespective of when the information was recorded (DPA 1998 s68). The information held may include factual material as well as 'any expressions of opinion, and the intentions of the authority in relation to the individual' (guidance para 5.4).

26.11   The Act applies eight basic principles to the disclosure of information. These essentially require data to be processed fairly, legally, accurately and that the information be retained no longer than necessary; they restrict the transfer of data as well as unnecessary reprocessing of data, and require organisations holding such information to take appropriate measures to restrict unauthorised access to it.

26.12   Where joint records are held, for example by social services and an NHS trust in a community mental health team, a request for access to that information can be made to either body (para 5.2), the guidance stating that:

> Authorities and their partners in joint record holding will therefore need to have procedures in place to ensure that the data subject is aware that he/

---

8   Lord Falconer as quoted in P Wintour, 'Fees pledge on information act' (2004) *Guardian* 18 October.

9   Formerly called the Data Protection Commissioner: the guidance *Data Protection Act 1998 – Legal Guidance* is accessible at http://www.ico.gov.uk.

10 See eg Department of Health, *Guidance for Access to Health Records Requests under the Data Protection Act 1998*, 2003 and Department of Health, *Confidentiality NHS Code of Practice*, 2003.

11 Department of Health, *Data Protection Act 1998 – Guidance to Social Services*, 2000. Virtually identical guidance has been issued in Wales – Welsh Assembly, *Data Protection Act 1998 – Guidance to social services*, 2000.

she is not obliged to apply to all partners for access and to inform each other that access has been given.

26.13 The Act gives a right of access by individuals to any personal information held by the authority about them. Where the information concerns other individuals (for instance a local authority file on an entire family) one member is not in general entitled to see information about another member without that person's consent (guidance paras 5.5–5.7). The Act permits the disclosure of information notwithstanding that it has been provided by a third party and that party has not consented to the disclosure, although in deciding whether to agree to disclosure regard is to be had to various factors, including the duty of confidence to the third party; the steps taken to obtain his or her consent (and whether he or she is capable of giving such consent); as well as the reasons for any refusal given by the third party (DPA 1998 s7(4); guidance para 5.7).

Access to information by or on behalf of children

26.14 The guidance (at paras 5.8 et seq) makes clear that where a person under 18 seeks access to his or her records the authority must decide whether or not he or she has 'sufficient understanding to do so' which means 'does he or she understand the nature of the request'. If the requisite capacity exists then the request for access should be complied with. If however insufficient understanding exists, the request may be made by a person with parental responsibility who can make the request on the child's behalf. Disclosure to parents in such cases should only occur after the authority has satisfied itself:

a)   that the child lacks capacity to make a valid application, or has capacity and has authorised the parent to make the application; and

b)   (where the child does not have capacity) that the request made by the parent on the child's behalf is in that child's interest (guidance para 5.9).

26.15 The advice accurately reflects the statutory and common law position. The definition of parental responsibility in Children Act 1989 s3(1) includes the right of parents to consent on the child's behalf to a wide range of matters, including medical treatment. However Family Law Reform Act 1969 s8 makes clear that a child of 16 or 17 has the same capacity to consent to medical treatment as an adult[12] and in *Gillick v West Norfolk and Wisbech Area Health Authority*[13] the House of Lords had to consider whether the parental right to make decisions on a child's behalf ended at an earlier moment – namely when the child achieved sufficient intelligence and understanding to make its own decision. The court held that it did, and cited with approval comments of Lord Denning,[14] namely:

12   See eg *Re W (A Minor) (Medical Treatment)* [1992] 3 WLR 758.
13   [1985] 3 WLR 830.
14   In *Hewer v Bryant* [1970] 1 QB 357, p369.

... the legal right of a parent to the custody of a child ends at the 18th birthday: and even up till then, it is a dwindling right which the courts will hesitate to enforce against the wishes of the child, and the more so the older he is. It starts with a right of control and ends with little more than advice.

Requests made through another person (an agent)

26.16 Individuals with sufficient mental capacity are entitled to make their request for information via an agent. Paragraph 5.13 of the guidance states that agents should provide evidence (normally in writing) of their authority and confirm their identity and relationship to the individual, and authorities (if satisfied that the agent is duly authorised) must treat the request as if it had been made by the individual concerned. Paragraph 5.14 accepts that some persons with profoundly physical impairments may not be able to give written consent to their agents and that in such cases the local authority should give the individual as much assistance as possible and ultimately need not always insist on permission in writing.

Access to information on behalf of an adult lacking mental capacity

26.17 A general outline of the law concerning adults who lack mental capacity is contained at chapter 18 above.

26.18 The DPA 1998 makes no special provisions about requests for access made on behalf of an adult who lacks sufficient understanding to make the request in his or her own name. The guidance however states (at para 5.11) that:

> ... if a person lacks capacity to manage their affairs, a person acting under an order of the Court of Protection or acting within the terms of a registered Enduring Power of Attorney can request access on her or his behalf.

26.19 Although the wording in this respect is an improvement on the draft guidance,[15] the failure of the Act to deal with this issue and the inadequacy of the guidance on this point has been the subject of considerable criticism. However, these defects in the DPA 1998 are ameliorated to a degree by the approach the courts have taken in relation to the powers available under the common law and consequent upon the implementation of the HRA 1998 (as evidenced above in *R (S) v Plymouth City Council*.[16]

26.20 The Code of Practice to the Mental Capacity Act (MCA) 2005 (see para 18.4 above) at chapter 16 contains much useful information on the principles applicable to disclosure and should be read in full. It considers and gives examples of the situations where local authorities and health bodies are empowered to disclose information to third parties, even when these

---

15 LASSL (99)16 para 2.12, which stated such requests could 'only' be made by such persons.

16 [2002] EWCA Civ 388; [2002] 1 WLR 2583; (2002) 5 CCLR 251.

persons are not doing so as an enduring power of attorney, lasting power of attorney or deputy for the person lacking capacity, and includes:

> 16.19 Healthcare and social care staff may disclose information about somebody who lacks capacity only when it is in the best interests of the person concerned to do so, or when there is some other, lawful reason for them to do so.

> 16.20 The Act's requirement to consult relevant people when working out the best interests of a person who lacks capacity will encourage people to share the information that makes a consultation meaningful. But people who release information should be sure that they are acting lawfully and that they can justify releasing the information. They need to balance the person's right to privacy with what is in their best interests or the wider public interest . . .

> 16.21 Sometimes it will be fairly obvious that staff should disclose information. For example, a doctor would need to tell a new care worker about what drugs a person needs or what allergies the person has. This is clearly in the person's best interests.

> 16.22 Other information may need to be disclosed as part of the process of working out someone's best interests. A social worker might decide to reveal information about someone's past when discussing their best interests with a close family member. But staff should always bear in mind that the Act requires them to consider the wishes and feelings of the person who lacks capacity.

> 16.23 In both these cases, staff should only disclose as much information as is relevant to the decision to be made.

26.21   In 1991 practice guidance the Department of Health advised that advocates should in general be given access to relevant information concerning the person for whom they advocate and are enabled to consult with appropriate individuals in order to establish the best interests of that person.[17]

26.22   MCA 2005 s35(6) entitles independent mental capacity advocates (see para 18.67 above) to (at all reasonable times) examine and take copies of, (i) any health record, (ii) any record of, or held by, a local authority and compiled in connection with a social services function, and (iii) any record held by a person registered under Part 2 of the Care Standards Act 2000 (see para 17.18 above) which the person holding the record considers may be relevant to the independent mental capacity advocate's investigation.

26.23   The local government ombudsman has also suggested that 'confidentiality' should not be used as a reason for not disclosing relevant information in such cases. In criticising a council for not sharing information with the parents of a 24-year-old man with serious learning difficulties, she commented:

> I accept that this would not be regular practice when the Council is looking after an adult: the privacy of the individual demands that the parents be kept at some distance. But [the user] had such a high level of dependency

---

17 *Care Management and Assessment Practitioners Guide*, HMSO, 1991, para 3.28.

that the Council should have been willing to reconsider its approach to parental involvement in this case.[18]

Access procedures

26.24 DPA 1998 s7(2)(a) requires all requests for access to information to be in writing and section 7(8) requires the information to be disclosed 'promptly' and in any event within 40 days. All information must be disclosed, unless subject to any of the exceptions detailed below (most notably where the data includes information about another person).

26.25 The information should not be altered in any way (guidance para 5.20) and should be the information which the authority held at the time of the request. Any amendment or deletion made between the time of request and supply should however be noted (if the changes would have occurred regardless of the request) (para 5.21). The Act contains procedures by which applicants can apply to have inaccurate information corrected.[19]

26.26 DPA 1998 s8(2) stipulates that the information should generally be provided in the form of a permanent copy although a copy need not be provided if is not possible, or would involve disproportionate effort or the applicant has agreed otherwise.

26.27 The 40-day time period for disclosure is subject to certain restrictions, namely:

1) *Sufficient description of information sought.* The applicant must provide the authority with sufficient information to enable it to identify the person about whom the information is sought and where that information is likely to be held. Authorities are permitted to provide a standard request form for this purpose but are not permitted to insist on its use (para 5.16).

2) *Payment of the appropriate fee.* Authorities are permitted to charge a fee for the provision of information, which must not however exceed the statutory maximum of £10, including the cost of supplying copies (special rules apply for access to manual health records for which the maximum fee is currently £50[20]). The guidance requires authorities to advise applicants promptly of the need to pay a fee (if one is charged) and advises that procedures should exist for waiving the fee where the applicant's means or any other circumstances dictate such a course (para 5.17). Since the 40-day period only commences when the fee has been paid it may be appropriate to include payment in the initial letter of request (see appendix C below for a precedent letter of request).

The guidance advises (at para 2.18) that where authorities do not have the requested information, applicants should be informed as quickly as possible, and a decision then made as to whether the fee should be returned. In so deciding it should consider the applicant's circumstances, the effort

---

18 Complaint no 97/C/4618 against Cheshire, 1999.
19 DPA 1998 s14 and see also paras 5.31 et seq of the guidance.
20 Data Protection (Subject Access) (Fees and Miscellaneous Provisions) (Amendment) Regulations 2001 SI No 3223.

involved in discovering that there was no data, and its own policy on charging.

3) *Repeated requests.* Section 8(3) provides that access can be refused where the authority has previously complied with an identical or similar request from the applicant, unless a reasonable interval separates the requests.[21]

26.28   Not infrequently social services authorities suggest that the individual first view the data (eg files) in the presence of a social worker, before providing such copies as are required. It is doubtful whether it is lawful for an authority to refuse to copy a file to an individual without his or her prior attendance to view it in the company of a social worker, since this imposes an extra non-statutory hurdle to access. Attendance at a social services office may be physically difficult for many service users and may be particularly daunting for the unassertive. If, however, the prior attendance requirement is put forward as good practice, to explain confusing or unclear aspects of the information and how it has been recorded, then, provided this does not significantly delay the provision of copies and provided proper consideration is given to difficulties service users may have in attending, such a requirement may be sustainable.

Third party information

26.29   DPA 1998 s7(4) states that where an authority is unable to comply with a request for information without disclosing information relating to another individual (who can be identified from that information), it is not obliged to comply with the request, unless, either:

a)   the other individual has consented to the disclosure, or
b)   it is reasonable in all the circumstances to comply with the request without the consent.

26.30   In deciding whether or not it is reasonable to make a disclosure without the third party's consent, section 7(6) requires the authority to have particular regard to the following factors:

a)   any duty of confidentiality owed to that other individual;
b)   any steps taken [by the authority] with a view to seeking the consent of the other individual;
c)   whether the other individual is capable of giving consent;
d)   any express refusal of consent by the other individual.

26.31   The guidance makes the following observations:

2.25   Section 7(6) is likely to be of particular relevance when a request is received for access to very old files and the possibility of tracing any third party is remote.

2.26   An authority should set itself a sensible timescale, within the 40 days allowed, in which to seek any third party consent. The 40 day period does

21   Para 5.19 of the guidance gives advice on what amounts to a 'reasonable interval'.

not commence until the authority has received the written request, the appropriate fee, and if necessary, the further information required to satisfy itself as to the identity of the person making the request, and to locate the information sought.

2.27 If consent is not given by a third party within 40 days, an authority should give as much information as possible without identifying the third party (see DPA, section 7(5)). An authority should explain why some of the information requested has not been given. Where consent is or cannot be given and the authority considers it reasonable to comply with the request without consent then the authority may be required to justify its actions

. . .

2.28 Where the authority is satisfied that the data subject will not be able to identify the other individual (the third party source) from the information, taking into account any other information which the authority reasonably believes is likely to be in or to come into the possession of the [applicant] then the authority must provide the information.

26.32 In addition to the above factors, the statutory exemptions detailed below also apply to decisions about disclosure, most importantly where it is considered that disclosure could result in serious harm to the other individual. Indeed, if the third party is a social worker, access cannot be refused unless the 'serious harm test' applies (para 2.37).

Statutory exemptions from disclosure

26.33 DPA 1998 Part IV provides that authorities do not have to disclose information in certain situations. The principal grounds of relevance for the purposes of community care are (in summary):

1) *The prevention or detection of crime (DPA 1998 s29)*. Where the authority considers that disclosure would be likely to prejudice criminal investigations, or crime prevention, it is exempt from the duty to disclose, although the guidance (para 3.37) advises that this only applies where there is a 'substantial chance' rather than a 'mere risk'.

2) *Information about physical or mental health conditions (DPA 1998 s30(1))*. Social services are prohibited from disclosing any information without first consulting an appropriate health professional[22] (normally this will be the person responsible for the person's current clinical care, eg a GP or psychiatrist) in connection with the matters to which the information relates. The relevant exemption order in relation to health information specifically permits the refusal of disclosure to the extent to which it would be likely to cause serious harm to the physical or mental health or condition of the data subject or any other person.[23]

3) *Where disclosure is prevented by another enactment*. This category includes such examples as adoption records and reports, parental

---

22 As defined in the relevant order, namely the Data Protection (Subject Access Modification) (Health) Order 2000 SI No 413.
23 Ibid, art 5.

order records and reports under Human Fertilisation and Embryology Act 1990 s30.[24]

4) *Specific social services exemptions.* Information held for the purposes of social work is exempt from disclosure if it would be likely to prejudice the carrying out of social work, by causing serious harm to the physical or mental health (or condition) of the applicant or another person.[25]

26.34 If any of these exemptions are to be relied upon, the applicant must be notified as soon as practicable and in writing, even where the decision has also been given in person; reasons should also be given (para 5.39).

Appeals procedure

26.35 If disclosure is refused the applicant may apply either to the Data Protection Commissioner or to the courts; the choice of remedy is up to the applicant.

Caldicott Guardians – information management and sharing

26.36 Considerable concern has been expressed about the way the NHS and other statutory bodies respect the confidential information they store. As a result of this concern, in 1996 a review was commissioned by the Chief Medical Officer of England into the use of patient-identifiable information by the NHS in England and Wales with the aim of ensuring that confidentiality was not being compromised. The review was chaired by Dame Fiona Caldicott.

26.37 Her subsequent report[26] made a number of recommendations, including the need to raise awareness of confidentiality and information security requirements among all staff within the NHS; the need to track all dataflows within the NHS; the need for protocols to protect the exchange of patient-identifiable information between NHS and non-NHS bodies; and the appointment of a senior person, in every health organisation, to act as a guardian, responsible for safeguarding the confidentiality of patient information. This latter person has come to be known as a 'Caldicott Guardian' and the government has endeavoured to implement the recommendations of the report in a series of initiatives. Initially these were restricted to the NHS although recently the process has been extended to cover all English social services departments.[27]

24 These exemptions are listed in the Data Protection (Miscellaneous Subject Access Exemptions) Order 2000 SI No 419 (as amended by the Data Protection (Miscellaneous Subject Access Exemptions) (Amendment) Order 2000 SI No 1865).
25 Data Protection (Subject Access Modification) (Social Work) Order 2000 SI No 415.
26 The Caldicott Committee, *Report on the review of patient-identifiable information,* December 1997.
27 Department of Health, *Implementing the Caldicott standard in social care* HSC 2002/ 003: LAC (2002)2.

The common law and the Human Rights Act 1998

26.38 As has been noted above, the DPA 1998 is only one part of our domestic legal framework that seeks to both protect confidentiality and promote the right of access to personal information. The common law and the HRA 1998 also play an important role in this respect, particularly in clarifying the principles that are relevant when the exercise of discretion to (or not to) disclose is being considered.

The common law

26.39 The common law has long recognised the concept of a person's right to confidentiality,[28] a right that arises 'when confidential information comes to the knowledge of the person (the confidant) in circumstances where he has notice or is held to have agreed that the information is confidential with the effect that it would be just in all the circumstances that he should be precluded from disclosing the information to others'.[29] The common law of confidentiality is based upon a presumption against disclosure to third parties.[30]

26.40 *W v Egdell*[31] concerned a doctor who disclosed a medical report commissioned from him by solicitors acting for a patient who was held in a secure hospital having killed a number of people. The patient applied to a tribunal with the eventual purpose of being discharged from detention. The doctor considered that the patient still posed a danger and although he stated this in his report, the solicitors decided not to disclose it. The doctor was so concerned about the potential risk, that he gave a copy of the report to the hospital, which then copied it to the tribunal. The patient sued the doctor for breach of confidence.

26.41 In his judgment Bingham LJ accepted that the doctor owed a duty of confidence:

> He could not lawfully sell the contents of his report to a newspaper. Nor could he, without a breach of the law as well as professional etiquette, discuss the case in a learned article, or in his memoirs, or in gossiping with friends, unless he took the appropriate steps to conceal the identity of W.

26.42 However the Court of Appeal concluded that the 'public interest' justified Dr Egdell's limited disclosure – his limited breach of the obligation of confidentiality.

26.43 In *Woolgar v Chief Constable of Sussex Police and the UKCC*[32] the Court of Appeal considered the extent of the 'public interest' defence and concluded that the disclosure of confidential information to a regulatory body (the UK Central Council for Nursing, Midwifery and Health Visiting) to

---

28 *Prince Albert v Strange* (1849) 1 Mac & G 25.
29 *Attorney-General v Guardian Newspapers* [1988] 3 WLR 776 per Lord Goff.
30 *R v Mid Glamorgan FHSA ex p Martin* [1995] 1 WLR 110.
31 [1990] 2 WLR 471.
32 [2000] 1 WLR 25 and see also *R v Chief Constable of North Wales ex p AB* [1997] 3 WLR 724; (2000) 3 CCLR 25.

assist them in their investigation of a matter which might affect the safety of patients, was sufficiently serious as to justify this action. The court came to a similar conclusion in *Maddock v Devon CC*[33] which concerned the disclosure of confidential information from the applicant's social services file to a university at which the applicant had obtained a place to study to become a social worker: the essence of the information being that she was potentially unsuited to that role.

The Human Rights Act 1998

26.44   In *A Health Authority v X*[34] the court had to determine whether it was permissible to order the disclosure of personal health records held by a GP practice to a health authority (investigating various alleged irregularities in the way the practice had been run). The court held that since the proposed disclosure of the records did amount to an interference with that patient's rights under article 8 of the Convention, it could only be justified where:

1) the authority reasonably required them for its regulatory or administrative functions; and
2) there was a compelling public interest in their disclosure; and
3) there was in place effective and adequate safeguards against abuse including safeguards of the particular patient's confidentiality and anonymity.

26.45   HRA 1998 s6 requires public authorities to act in conformity with Convention rights, including article 8, which protects privacy. In a number of cases the European Court of Human Rights has confirmed that article 8 is concerned both with the duty on the state to protect individuals from the unreasonable disclosure of publicly held confidential information[35] as well as with the right of individuals to access such information.

26.46   In *Gaskin v UK*[36] the applicant sought access to his social services records. The request was refused in part on the ground that some of the information had originally been given in confidence and certain of the informants had not consented to their material being disclosed. The information was important to Mr Gaskin as he had spent almost all his life in care and he wanted it in order to understand his early childhood: essentially for his own sense of identity. His was a legitimate claim, as indeed was the refusal to divulge the information, which had been given to the local authority in confidence. The court concluded that article 8 required a balancing of the conflicting interests in such a situation; and that this required an independent adjudication system to decide whether the papers should be disclosed. As no such system existed, it found a violation of article 8.

---

33   Lawtel, 15 September 2003.
34   [2001] 2 FLR 673; upheld on appeal [2001] EWCA Civ 2014; [2002] 2 All ER 780; [2002] 1 FLR 1045.
35   See eg *Z v Finland* (1997) 25 EHRR 371 and *MS v Sweden* (1997) 3 BHRC 248.
36   (1989) 12 EHRR 36. See also *MG v UK* (2003) 36 EHRR 3; (2002) 5 CCLR 525.

26.47   It has been suggested that a useful checklist for determining whether a disclosure of confidential health care information is legally justified would include the following factors:[37]

1) Is the information in question of a confidential nature? For example, anonymised patient information is less likely to be given legal protection against disclosure.

2) Was the information imparted to the clinician on the understanding that it would not be disclosed, or only disclosed for limited reasons such as for diagnosis treatment and care? Most patients tell their doctors about themselves on the understanding that it will be communicated on a need-to-know basis to others involved in their care.

3) Has guidance issued by the relevant regulatory body (such as the General Medical Council) been complied with?

4) Is there a legal requirement that information be disclosed? There are some legislative provisions requiring disclosure of medical records to health service, government or other bodies.

5) Is the legislation proportionate to any legitimate objective being sought?

6) Is access reasonably required to permit the body to carry out its legal functions? If there is another way to access the information that is needed, or if anonymised information would suffice, then the courts would be unlikely to sanction unconsented disclosure of patient records.

7) Are there adequate safeguards against abuse? The body seeking access to the records must be able to show that it would protect any information coming into its hands against further unauthorised disclosure.

---

37 Association of Community Health Councils for England and Wales Briefing Paper April 2002: arguably this checklist is of relevance – with the necessary modifications – for other professionally held information.

Remedies

continued

Introduction

27.1   Frequently the most effective way of resolving a community care dispute will be through informal contact with the local authority or NHS body or an MP or a local councillor; indeed contact with the local media can also be a very effective way of remedying a problem. The law however provides six principal procedures by which a failure in the provision of community care services may be challenged. These are:

1) a complaint via the local authority complaints procedures;
2) a complaint via the NHS complaints procedures;
3) a complaint via the relevant ombudsman;
4) an application to the High Court for judicial review;
5) an application to the Secretary of State for Health or the Welsh Assembly to use their default powers;
6) an ordinary court application under Human Rights Act (HRA) 1998 s7.

27.2   Other procedures or remedies may be available in certain specific cases. Mentally disordered people and their carers continue to have direct access to the Mental Health Commission, and individuals continue to have access to their elected representatives for assistance in any particular case.[1] In addition, where judicial review proceedings fail to provide an adequate remedy, there remains the option of an application to the European Court of Human Rights.

27.3   A complainant will generally be expected to give the local authority or NHS body the opportunity to remedy the problem before the court, ombudsman or secretary of state concerned will be prepared to consider a complaint. In certain situations the ombudsman or court will accept an application without the complaints process being utilised: these circumstances are discussed in the relevant sections below.

Local authority complaints procedures

27.4   Health and Social Care (Community Health and Standards) Act (HSC(CHS)A) 2003 s114 authorises the secretary of state in England and the Assembly in Wales to make regulations concerning the handling of social services complaints (including complaints concerning jointly provided health and social care services[2]). These powers have been exercised with regulations issued in both England[3] and Wales.[4] In the following section the English Regulations are referred to as 'the regulations' and the equivalent Welsh Regulations cited in the footnotes.

27.5   In addition, policy guidance under Local Authority Social Services Act (LASSA) 1970 has been issued in both England and Wales and in the

---

1   1990 policy guidance para 6.34.
2   HSC(CHS)A 2003 s113 contains similar powers in relation to health care complaints – see para 27.71 below.
3   Local Authority Social Services Complaints (England) Regulations 2006 SI No 1681.
4   Social Services Complaints Procedure (Wales) Regulations 2005 SI No 3366 (W263).

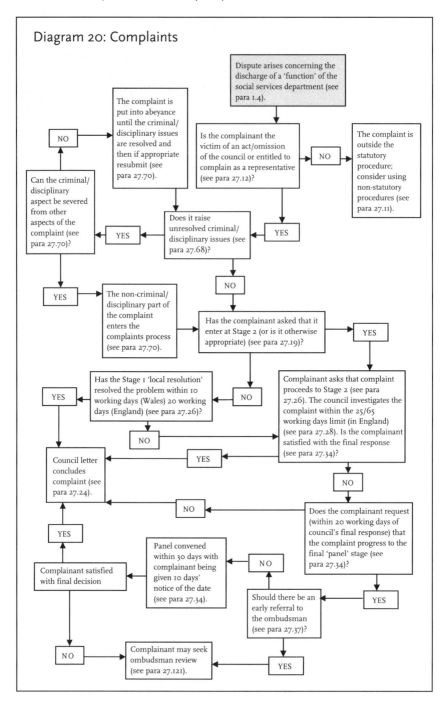

Diagram 20: Complaints

Dispute arises concerning the discharge of a 'function' of the social services department (see para 1.4).

The complaint is put into abeyance until the criminal/disciplinary issues are resolved and then if appropriate resubmit (see para 27.70).

Is the complainant the victim of an act/omission of the council or entitled to complain as a representative (see para 27.12)?

The complaint is outside the statutory procedure; consider using non-statutory procedures (see para 27.11).

NO

NO

Can the criminal/disciplinary aspect be severed from other aspects of the complaint (see para 27.70)?

Does it raise unresolved criminal/disciplinary issues (see para 27.68)?

YES

YES

YES

NO

YES

The non-criminal/disciplinary part of the complaint enters the complaints process (see para 27.70).

Has the complainant asked that it enter at Stage 2 (or is it otherwise appropriate) (see para 27.19)?

YES

Has the Stage 1 'local resolution' resolved the problem within 10 working days (Wales) 20 working days (England) (see para 27.26)?

YES

NO

Complainant asks that complaint proceeds to Stage 2 (see para 27.26). The council investigates the complaint within the 25/65 working days limit (in England) (see para 27.28). Is the complainant satisfied with the final response (see para 27.34)?

NO

YES

Council letter concludes complaint (see para 27.24).

NO

NO

YES

Does the complainant request (within 20 working days of council's final response) that the complaint progress to the final 'panel' stage (see para 27.34)?

Panel convened within 30 days with complainant being given 10 days' notice of the date (see para 27.34).

NO

Complainant satisfied with final decision

Should there be an early referral to the ombudsman (see para 27.37)?

YES

NO

Complainant may seek ombudsman review (see para 27.121).

YES

following section the English guidance[5] is referred to as 'the guidance' and the equivalent Welsh guidance[6] cited in the footnotes.

27.6   The guidance[7] defines a complaint as 'an expression of dissatisfaction or disquiet about the actions, decisions or apparent failings of a local authority's adult's social services provision which requires a response'. It gives the following examples of matters to which complaints may relate[8]:

- an unwelcome or disputed decision;
- concern about the quality or appropriateness of a service;
- delay in decision making or provision of services;
- delivery or non-delivery of services including complaints procedures;
- quantity, frequency, change or cost of a service;
- attitude or behaviour of staff;
- application of eligibility and assessment criteria;
- the impact on an individual of the application of a local authority policy; and
- assessment, care management and review.

What can be complained about?

27.7   Regulation 4[9] provides that complaints must concern 'the discharge of, or the failure to discharge a relevant function'. Regulation 2[10] defines a relevant function as:

(a) a social services function within the meaning of section 1A of the Local Authority Social Services Act 1970;[11] or

(b) a function which is discharged by a local authority under arrangements made between a local authority and an NHS body under [what is now NHS Act (NHSA) 2006 ss75–76 and ss256–257[12]].

27.8   The process covers therefore any complaint concerning the way social services' services have been delivered (or not delivered) and any failures in relation to the assessment of care planning process. The regulations[13] exempt various matters, namely where:

- the same complaint has already been dealt with at all stages of the procedure;
- the same complaint has already been investigated by a local commissioner;

---

5   Department of Health, *Learning From Complaints Social Services Complaints Procedure for Adults*, 2006.

6   Welsh Assembly, *Listening and Learning: A guide to handling complaints and representations in local authority social services in Wales*, 2006.

7   At para 2.1.1 (Welsh guidance para 4.1.2).

8   At para 2.2.2 (Welsh guidance para 4.1.5).

9   The equivalent provision (although with different phrasing) is found at regulation 10 of the Welsh Regulations.

10 Welsh Regulations reg 2.

11 Which includes the list of functions set out in LASSA 1970 Sch 1.

12 NHS (Wales) Act 2006 ss33–34 and 194–196.

13 English Regulations reg 5 and a more limited list of exemptions is at Welsh Regulations reg 11.

- the complaint is unclear, or it is frivolous or vexatious;
- matters should be dealt with under other proceedings such as:
  - disciplinary proceedings;
  - grievance procedure;
  - complaints from staff about personnel issues;
  - complaints that should be considered under the local authority's corporate complaints procedure;
  - services for which an alternative statutory appeals process already exists;
  - criminal investigation where court action is pending;
  - the making of a decision to detain under the Mental Health Act (MHA) 1983 (although not the process of assessment leading up to that decision).

27.9   Also exempted are complaints where the complainant 'has stated in writing that he intends to take legal proceedings'.[14] The guidance (at para 2.3.3) however advises that authorities may wish to apply this restriction:

> . . . only in instances where the complainant has commenced legal action or where the complainant is certain that the complaint cannot be resolved through the complaints procedure, and that he intends to take legal proceedings in relation to the substance of the complaint.

Who can complain?

27.10   Regulation 4[15] states that in order to be eligible to make a complaint under the statutory procedure (ie concerning the discharge of, or the failure to discharge a relevant function) the individual must be someone in respect of whom the relevant function is being, or has been, discharged, or in respect of whom there has been a failure to discharge a relevant function. Provision is also made, however for complaints to be made in a representative capacity (see below).

27.11   The guidance (at paras 7.8.1 et seq) advises that where a complaint does not fall within the statutory procedure, the authority may investigate in any event. The local government ombudsman has made the same point where, though accepting that the complainant was not a qualifying individual, she held that it was nevertheless important that her 'complaints were still given full and proper consideration in a way which equated to the standard of service a complaint would have received under the council's formal complaints procedure'.[16]

---

14 English Regulations reg 5; Welsh Regulations reg 12.
15 An equivalent, but differently worded, provision is at Welsh Regulations reg 11.
16 The complaint in fact concerned the CA 1989 complaint procedures, but is nevertheless of no less relevance: see report no 94/C/2959 against Nottingham City Council, 28 November 1994. See also complaint no 97/C/1614 against Bury MBC, 1999 where the ombudsman accepted that part of the complaint lay outside the statutory complaints process but nevertheless warranted investigation, and commented 'it is hard to identify any aspect of the Council's handling of Mr Redfern's complaints which was in the proper manner or in full accordance with the statutory complaints procedure and/or the Council's own written complaints procedure'.

Representatives

27.12 Regulation 4[17] provides that a representative may make a complaint on behalf of an otherwise eligible complainant if the representative is acting on behalf of that person and he or she is either (i) unable to make the complaint him/herself, or (ii) has asked the representative to act on his or her behalf, or (iii) is under the age of 18.

27.13 The guidance advises[18] that if the complaints manager considers the representative to be unsuitable, he or she should 'notify the representative accordingly in writing, explaining why no further action is being taken'. Research highlights the importance of service users being supported in making complaints and that 'fear of the consequences' was by far the most commonly cited reason for service users not making formal complaints – fear of retaliatory action by the authority (for instance the withdrawal of discretionary services).[19] Given these difficulties, authorities should be slow to question the good faith or 'standing' of a representative, particularly if the issue raised is one of importance.

27.14 Both the English and Welsh guidance emphasise the importance of advocacy,[20] with the English guidance being the more overt – requiring authorities to facilitate 'independent and confidential advocacy', which it deems particularly important in relation to 'complainants whose first language is not English and those with communication difficulties', particularly those 'who are vulnerable, or who find it difficult to make their views heard'.

Time limits

27.15 The English Regulations (reg 5) require that complaints be made within 12 months. The Welsh Regulations however impose no time limits. It is unclear whether the difference will in practice prove fundamental. The Welsh guidance accepts (at para 4.3.3) that on occasions a delay in making a complaint may make it unrealistic to investigate – giving as examples where relevant staff have left the organisation, or died or where 'records of the issues complained about are not available'. In consequence it advises that in such cases authorities may decline to deal with the matter through the complaints procedures. The English guidance however (at paras 3.3.2–3.3.3) advises that it might not be appropriate to apply the time limit where 'it would not be reasonable to expect the complainant to have made the complaint earlier and it would still be possible to consider the complaint in a way that would be effective and fair to those involved' and gives as possible examples (among others) 'if a service user was particularly vulnerable and did not complain due to fear of reprisal' or 'where there is likely to be sufficient access to information or individuals involved at the time, to enable an effective and fair investigation to be carried out'.

17 An equivalent, but differently worded, provision is at Welsh Regulations reg 11.
18 At para 2.5.2 (Welsh guidance para 4.4.5).
19 K Simons, *I'm Not Complaining, but . . .*, Joseph Rowntree Foundation, 1995.
20 English guidance para 3.4; Welsh guidance para 6.4.

Complaints manager

27.16   Authorities must designate an officer to manage[21] the complaints process. The Welsh Regulations specifically require that the designated officer should be a senior officer. The local government ombudsman has stated that such a system can only function properly if the designated officer is of sufficient seniority to run the complaints system and to ensure that complaints are dealt with, not only within the statutory times, but also with sufficient commitment[22] and has commented as follows:

> In my view the Council's procedures for dealing with complaints are seriously flawed. There seems to be no officer of sufficient seniority to run the complaints system and to ensure that complaints are dealt with, not only within the statutory times, but also with sufficient commitment.[23]

Freezing or deferring decisions

27.17   The guidance envisages complaints managers having the power to defer or freeze decisions which are being challenged – for instance a proposed change to a care plan or a decision to change a placement.[24] Guidance is given on how this power should be exercised, who should be consulted and the need to ensure that decisions do not have a significant effect upon the mental or physical wellbeing of an individual.

The structure of the complaints system

27.18   The structure and key timescales of the complaints system are outlined in the regulations. They require that the basic structure of all such complaints procedures be made up of three distinct stages:

Stage 1   Local resolution
Stage 2   Investigation
Stage 3   Review panel

27.19   While authorities have no discretion in respect of the basic framework of the process, the regulations give a certain discretion in the way the process is managed. By way of example, not infrequently the possibility for local resolution may be limited and no useful purpose served by having a stage 1 process. The Welsh guidance is explicit on this point, namely (at para 6.5.5) that from the outset 'the complainant can decide at any time to dispense with local resolution and move things on to the next stage'. The English guidance however states (at para 3.5.1) that if the 'authority or the complainant believes that it would not be appropriate to consider the complaint at Stage 1, they should discuss this together. Where both parties agree, the complaint can move directly to Stage 2.' It is difficult to see

---

21   English Regulations reg 16; Welsh Regulations reg 5.
22   Complaint no 92/A/3725 against Haringey LBC.
23   Report no 94/C/2659 against Nottingham City Council.
24   English guidance paras 6.5 et seq; Welsh guidance paras 6.3 et seq.

why the English guidance is phrased in this way since it would appear that 'local resolution' can only work if both parties agree that it should. The Welsh Ombudsman has been highly critical of an authority that refused to allow a complainant to go directly to stage 2 of the complaints process (and then closed the investigation at stage 1 without the agreement of the complainant).[25]

27.20   Inevitably there will be certain types of complaint which raise particular problems requiring that they be subject to different procedures (such as complaints which involve an NHS-social services overlap of responsibilities or those which concern the discharge by a private operator of a community care function, or complaints which raise disciplinary questions). These are discussed below under the heading of 'special cases'.

Stage 1: Local resolution

27.21   Regulation 5 requires that authorities within 20 working days of receiving a complaint (or, where that is not possible, as soon as reasonably practicable) take all reasonable steps to resolve the complaint informally; notify the complainant of the outcome of this process, stating: (1) the extent to which it is considered well-founded (and giving reasons for its findings); (2) the action to be taken (if the complaint is well-founded); and (3) the right to seek a formal investigation (under stage 2). Although the Welsh Regulations (reg 10) impose a shorter time scale for the local resolution stage (ten days), the English guidance also advises that the expectation is that most complaints will be concluded within ten days (para 3.5.3).

27.22   Complaints should be recorded and complainants advised of the possibility of advocacy support.[26] They should be given clear information about how the complaints procedures operate and how to contact the complaints manager.[27] The provision of a leaflet with this information does not obviate the need to advise complainants (in correspondence at the appropriate times) of their rights at subsequent stages (ie of the right to seek a panel hearing if dissatisfied with a stage 2 report).[28] It will also be maladministration to fail to make it clear to a complainant at which particular stage of the process the complaint is currently being considered.[29]

27.23   The local government ombudsman has been critical of councils who have arbitrarily decided that a complaint is not a complaint but an 'issue' or some such other grumble which it could then ignore.[30] Although in general the ombudsman has considered offers of mediation to be 'positive' she has held them to be premature if made before basic facts have been established.[31]

---

25   Complaint no B2004/0707/S/370 against Swansea City Council, 22 February 2007, para 138.
26   English guidance para 3.2.1; Welsh guidance paras 3.6.7 and 6.2.
27   English guidance para 3.2.3; Welsh guidance para 6.5.1.
28   Complaint no 97/A/2464 against Waltham Forest LBC, 1998.
29   Complaint no 96/B/4438 against Devon CC, 1998.
30   Local Government Ombudsman, *Annual Report 1997/98* p10.
31   Complaint no 02/C/16768 against Bradford MDC, 4 November 2003.

27.24   At the conclusion of the stage 1 process the authority must write to the complainant confirming the extent to which it considers the complaint to be well-founded, its reasons for so deciding, and advising of the right to seek a formal investigation under stage 2.[32] If the complainant is dissatisfied he or she has 20 working days from the expiry of the stage 1 time limit or the date the local authority response was sent in which to request consideration at stage 2.[33]

Stage 2: the investigation stage

27.25   This stage involves the formal investigation of the complaint. The mere fact that a complaint has progressed to stage 2 does not absolve the authority from its duty to try and resolve the problem.[34]

27.26   Where a complainant seeks a formal investigation the authority must as soon as reasonably practicable ensure that it records the complaint in writing, invites the complainant's comments on it, investigates the complaint, and keeps the complainant informed of the progress of the investigation.[35]

27.27   The guidance explains[36] that the complaints manager should at this stage appoint an investigating officer to lead the investigation of the complaint with a view to preparing a report. The investigating officer may be employed by the authority or be wholly independent but in any event should not be in direct line management of the service or person about whom the complaint is being made. The complaints manager should ensure that the complainant understands how the investigation will be conducted and is informed of progress throughout, and a copy of the complaint should be sent to any person who is involved in the complaint (unless doing so would prejudice consideration of the complaint).

27.28   The stage 2 investigation should be completed and the response sent to the complainant within 25 working days from the date on which the claimant's request for an investigation was received. However if this is impractical the regulations allow for further extensions, with in England an overall maximum of 65 working days whereas in Wales, if the initial 25-day period if not possible the regulations merely require that is completed as reasonably practicable thereafter.[37] Possible reasons for an extension of the 25-day period, given in the guidance, include:

- where the complaint involves several agencies or all or some of the matters concerned are the subject of a concurrent investigation (such as a disciplinary process);
- if the complaint is particularly complicated; or
- if a key witness is unavailable for part of the time.

32   English Regulations reg 7; Welsh Regulations reg 18.
33   English guidance paras 3.5.6–3.5.7.
34   Complaint no 98/C/3591 against Liverpool, 1999.
35   English Regulations reg 9; Welsh Regulations reg 19.
36   English guidance paras 3.6.3 et seq; Welsh guidance paras 7.2.1 et seq.
37   English Regulations reg 10; Welsh Regulations reg 20, amplified in English guidance para 3.6.7 and Welsh guidance para 7.5.

27.29 Where it is not possible to complete the investigation within 25 working days the guidance requires that the complaints manager agree any extensions and that if possible these are also agreed with the complainant.[38] This presupposes that they are communicated to the complainant before the period expires with a letter explaining the reason for the delay and the date by which the complainant should receive a response.[39]

27.30 While it has been suggested that a breach of the time limits alone may justify an application for judicial review,[40] it would have to be an extreme case for such action to serve any useful purpose (given the inherent delay involved in such proceedings). In general, authorities should be reminded of the time limits and asked to explain any failure to comply with them; provided the investigation is being conducted diligently, it is unlikely to be criticised either by the courts or the ombudsman.

27.31 The English guidance envisages a role for an independent person in certain complaints where there are significant concerns about the vulnerability of the complainant and the seriousness of the complaint (whereas the Welsh guidance limits their role to complaints under the Children Act (CA) 1989).[41]

27.32 Once the investigation has been completed, the report (plus that of any independent person) is then submitted to a senior officer in the authority for a final decision ('adjudication'). Before doing this, the complaints manager or investigating officer should give the complainant the opportunity to comment upon the draft report[42] (particularly in relation to any contra-allegations that may have been made[43]). The report sent to the senior officer should[44] include 'all relevant information'; be clear about what the findings and outcomes are against each point of complaint; distinguish between fact, feelings and opinion; contain details of findings, conclusions and recommended actions;[45] recommend how to remedy any injustice to the complainant; and be written in plain language, avoiding jargon, so that everyone can understand it. The local government ombudsman expects councils 'to act urgently to rectify' problems highlighted at the conclusion of stage 2 (for instance a service provision deficit).[46]

27.33 The senior officer of the authority is then required to respond to each point of the complaint and state what action (if any) is to be taken (with

---

38 English guidance para 3.6.9; Welsh guidance para 7.5.5.
39 See complaint no 98/C/1088 against Bolton MBC in which the local government ombudsman acknowledged the difficulty of local authorities investigating complaints within the (then) timescale of 28 days but stressed the need for councils to endeavour to meet the timescales and provide full explanations when this proved impossible.
40 See R Gordon, *Community Care Assessments*, Longman, 1993 p50.
41 English guidance para 3.7.1; Welsh guidance para 7.3.
42 Complaint no 97/C/4618 against Cheshire, 1999.
43 Report no 98/C/1294 against Calderdale MBC.
44 English guidance para 3.8.1; Welsh guidance para 7.6.3.
45 In this regard see also complaint no 97/C/4618 against Cheshire, 1999 where it was stated that in general the investigator's report should distinguish between fact and conclusion, and 'all matters put forward as issues by the complainant should be dealt with: if they are considered unfounded or insignificant, the report should explain this'.
46 Complaint no 03/C/16371 against Stockton-on-Tees BC, 18 January 2005, para 91.

timescales for implementation).[47] This (together with the investigation report and any report from an independent person) is then sent to the complainant who must additionally be advised of the right to seek a review panel hearing if dissatisfied and that this must be requested within 20 working days.[48]

Stage 3: the review stage

27.34   In England regulation 11 requires that on receipt of a request by the complainant within the specified 20-day period, the authority is required to establish a review panel: the complaints manager has overall responsibility for this phase (para 3.16.1). The panel must be convened within 30 days of this request (reg 12) and must consist of three people, none of whom may be officers of the authority (or spouses or civil partners of officers) and at least two of whom (including the chair person) must be independent (ie neither members of the local authority nor spouses or civil partners of members). The guidance suggests (para 3.14.7) that the third member of the panel may be either a further independent person or an elected member.

Wales

27.35   In Wales the stage 3 process is similar, with similar timescales save only that the panel stage is conducted by an independent panel appointed and administered by the Assembly. Regulation 21 of the Welsh Regulations requires that the Assembly maintain two lists of suitable panel members, one list being of persons with social services experience and the other being of lay persons with no such experience.

27.36   The Welsh guidance explains (at paras 8.2.1 et seq) that with the authority's determination under the stage 2 process, complainants must also be notified of their right to have their complaint reviewed by an independent panel (together with its contact details[49]) and that this request must be made within 20 working days from the date of the letter at the end of stage 2. The process then follows much the same route as the English system, save only that it is the secretariat that is responsible for the convening and administration of the panel hearings and the local authority complaints officer's duty to liaise with the secretariat.

Early referral to the local government ombudsman

27.37   The English guidance (but not the Welsh) envisages the possibility that in a small number of cases the complaints manager may decide not to convene a review panel but instead refer the complaint to the local govern-

---

47   English Regulations reg 10; Welsh Regulations reg 20, amplified at English guidance para 3.9.1 and Welsh guidance para 7.7.3.
48   English Regulations reg 11; Welsh Regulations reg 22.
49   The Independent Complaints Secretariat, Business Services Centre, Mamhilad House, Mamhilad Park Estate, Pontypool, Torfaen NP4 0XS.

ment ombudsman.[50] It suggests that this may arise where the facts indicate that 'reasonable, appropriate consideration of the complaint has been undertaken at Stage 2 and that further consideration by the review panel would not produce a demonstrably different outcome'. If such a course is envisaged the complaints manager is required to discuss the possibility of such a referral with the complainant. This step can only be taken once stage 2 has been concluded and the complainant has received the authority's final position on the complaints.

27.38   Before taking this decision the complaints manager should ensure that there has been a complete adjudication at stage 2; that the stage 2 report is 'very robust'; that all significant complaints have been upheld; that the authority is already providing a clear action plan for delivery; and/or that the authority has agreed to meet the majority or all of the desired outcomes presented by the complainant.

27.39   In effect it appears that the process is giving power to the complaints manager not to convene a panel where it is believed that nothing further could be achieved. The implication is that the ombudsman in such cases may decline to accept the complaint for the same reason – namely that any maladministration has been remedied and there are no outstanding issues. Such a power is open to misuse, and evidence suggests that unless it is used sparingly it will be used inappropriately.[51]

Panel hearings

27.40   Complainants are entitled to make written submissions to the panel before the meeting and to make oral submissions at the meeting. They are entitled to be accompanied by another person who is entitled to be present throughout the meeting and to speak on their behalf although the guidance advises (para 3.11.3) that 'ideally, no party should feel the need to be represented by lawyers' as 'the presence of lawyers can work against the spirit of openness and problem solving'.[52] Equity dictates that if the applicant is not entitled to have legal representation at a panel hearing, then the same applies to the local authority. The local ombudsman has criticised the presence of a local authority's solicitor at a hearing, stating:

---

50 English guidance annex 3.

51 The previous NHS complaints procedures gave a similar (but wider) discretion to trusts not to convene panels and the Health Service Ombudsman was highly critical of the way this power was used by a number of trusts: see the comments in this regard in the 3rd edition of this book and complaint nos E.859/96–97 and E918/96–97 in the Health Service Commissioner's *Annual Report 1996–97*; the general comments at p iii of the Health Service Commissioner's *Report of Selected Investigations April–September 1996* and generally in his *Annual Report 1996–97*.

52 The regulations are silent on this question and the guidance uses the words 'should not' rather than 'cannot' (para 3.17.1); in certain instances legal representation may be desirable (as indeed occurred at the panel hearing the subject matter of the judicial review in *R v Avon CC ex p M* (1999) 2 CCLR 185); if there is no lawyer present for the complainant, natural justice requires that this is also the case for the authority (see note 53 below, where the ombudsman came to such a conclusion).

> I find it hard to see how a solicitor employed by the Council could be
> seen as an 'unbiased observer' and consider the way he joined at the
> outset in the in camera deliberations of the Panel to be unwise at the
> very least.[53]

27.41   The panel hearing must follow the rules of natural justice. If the complainant and/or his or her representative attend the hearing, the panel
members should not talk to (or have lunch with) one party in the absence
of the other.[54] The panel is however entitled to set reasonable time limits
on the oral submissions to be made by the parties, provided these are used
as 'guidelines rather than guillotines'.[55]

27.42   The guidance advises on the need to avoid undue stress being put on
participants: suggesting for instance (para 3.12.1) the desirability of limiting the total number of local authority representatives attending; conducting hearings in the presence of all the relevant parties with equity of
access; ensuring arrangements are made for people with any special
communication or mobility needs, and so on.

27.43   The guidance contains advice on the administration of panels (ie the
need for local authorities to provide proper support, facilities and training)
and requires that the relevant papers be sent to all attendees as soon as
these have been agreed by the chair and no later than ten working days
before the date of the panel (para 3.16.5). The guidance advises that these
should normally include:

- information on Stage 1 (as relevant);
- the Stage 2 investigation report(s);
- the local authority's adjudication;
- any policy, practice or guidance information relevant to the complaint;
  and
- any comments that the complainant has submitted to the Panel . . .
- information on the local practice around Panels, such as start time,
  conduct, roles and responsibilities.

27.44   There is a need for panel members to read these key papers before the
hearing. If on reading these the panel requires further information (for
instance, a copy of a relevant assessment or details of the authority's
eligibility criteria), it should endeavour to obtain this before the hearing.
Likewise any possible conflict on legal interpretation should be resolved
before any hearing, as the panel is not qualified to make such determinations: ultimately, if the conflict persists, it will have little option other
than to accept the local authority's view on such issues. A problem that
has been identified on a number of occasions relates to the complainant's
access to his or her social services file. The law allows 40 days for files to
be prepared (see para 26.24 above), whereas the directions require that a
panel meet within 28 days; the local government ombudsman has noted
this problem and a possible solution, namely that 'information should

---

53 Complaint no 92/C/1042 against Cleveland CC.
54 Complaint no 96/B/4438 against Devon, 1998.
55 Complaint no 96/B/4438.

be given about rights of access and timescales at the first stage of the procedure'.[56]

27.45 The guidance advises that the role of the panel is to consider whether the local authority dealt adequately with the complaint in the stage 2 investigation. It is the panel's job to re-examine the previous decision; it is the 'body entrusted with the basic fact-finding exercise under the complaints procedure'.[57] The guidance cautions, however, against panels reinvestigating the complaint or considering any substantively new complaints that have not been first considered at stage 2 (para 3.11.2). It advises that the panel should discharge its role by:

- listening to all parties;
- obtaining any further information and advice that may help resolve the complaint to all parties' satisfaction;
- focusing on achieving resolution for the complainant by addressing his clearly defined complaints and desired outcomes;
- reaching findings on each of the complaints being reviewed;
- making recommendations that provide practical remedies and creative solutions to complex situations;
- supporting local solutions where the opportunity for resolution between the complainant and the local authority exists;
- identifying any consequent injustice to the complainant, where complaints are upheld, and to recommend appropriate redress; and
- recommending any service improvements for action by the authority.

27.46 The local government ombudsman has made a number of criticisms about the conduct of panel hearings, including:

- a failure to ensure that key witnesses attended the panel hearing;[58]
- the panel interviewing witnesses at an adjourned hearing, in the absence of the complainant;[59]
- the failure of the local authority to ensure that the panel had clerical assistance: 'the job entrusted to Panels is complex and stressful enough and they need adequate administrative support to be able to perform efficiently and effectively';[60]
- the introduction of new material by the local authority, at the hearing;[61]
- the need for independent advocates to assist complainants when the

---

56 Complaint no 93/A/3007 against Hounslow LBC, 10 October 1995; and see also complaint no 97/A/1082 where the need for local authority files to be made available, promptly, for inspection be complainants was emphasised.
57 *R v Avon CC ex p M* (1999) 2 CCLR 185.
58 Complaint no 97/B/2441 against Hampshire, 1999.
59 Ibid.
60 Ibid.
61 See eg complaint no 96/B/4438 against Devon, 1998 and Complaint no 99/A/00988 against Southwark LBC, 2001 where the local authority produced a chronology at a panel hearing which it had not previously disclosed to the complainant. However, it will amount to serious maladministration for the local authority to suggest that evidence put forward by a complainant at a panel hearing is 'new material' when it is not: complaint no 97/C/1614 against Bury MBC, 1999.

complaint is serious or particularly distressing (for instance involving bereavement);[62]

- the presence of a senior social services officer throughout a panel hearing as this may have 'inhibited junior staff from saying all they felt to be pertinent';[63]
- the interviewing of several members of staff, at different levels of seniority, simultaneously;[64]
- failing to give clear reasons for its recommendations;[65]
- failing to provide sufficient training.[66]

27.47 The guidance (at para 3.23) provides the following table (Table 21) to explain the relevant timescales:

Table 21: Complaints Panel Timetable

Action	Time
Complainant requests Review Panel	Within 20 working days after receipt of the Stage 2 report or expiry of the time limit
Complaints Manager acknowledges request	Within 2 working days
Complaints Manager appoints Chair and confirms attendees and content of Panel papers with Chair	Within 10 working days of the complainant's request for Review Panel
Local authority agrees the other Panellists and date for Review Panel	Within 30 working days of the complainant's request for Review Panel
Local authority circulates Panel papers	Within 10 working days of the date for the Panel
Review Panel produces its written report (including any recommendations)	Within 5 working days after the Panel has met
Relevant Director issues his response	Within 15 working days from receipt of the Panel's report

27.48 Regulation 13 requires that within five days of the hearing, the panel must reach a decision in writing and forward this to the complainant and the local authority. The guidance (at para 3.21.2) requires that the panel's findings 'explain simply and clearly any recommendations and the

---

62 Complaint no 97/C/4618 against Cheshire, 1999.
63 Ibid.
64 Ibid.
65 Complaint no 99/B/3078 against Kent, 2001, para 106.
66 Complaint no 01/C/09018 against Wolverhampton CC, 2002, where the ombudsman found it 'most disturbing' that the chairperson had not understood the 'extent of his responsibility as an independent Chair' and 'did not know he had the power to reject an investigation report, to ask for a fresh investigation, or even ask for additional investigation of specific matters', concluding that such a process was 'very far from the robust and "arms length" complaints procedure that the legislation requires' and that the failure to provide the panel with 'proper support, guidance and training to enable them to carry out their responsibilities properly' was maladministration.

reasons for them'. If a panel member disagrees with the majority recommendation, the decision letter should also record that member's view, and the reasons for it.

27.49 A panel's recommendations can fall into four broad categories, namely:

1) recommendations of a factual nature;
2) recommendations concerning compensation;
3) recommendations of a policy nature;
4) recommendations of a legal nature.

Factual recommendations

27.50 The panel is, as stated above, the basic fact-finding body in the complaints process. Its task is to weigh up the evidence, evaluate witnesses, consider all the relevant facts, ignore irrelevant factors and apply these considerations reasonably in order to reach its recommendations. The panel should concentrate on resolving the complaint and endeavour to ensure (if appropriate) that any issues of wider significance arising out of the complaint are made known to the senior management of the authority: the guidance at para 3.11.1 identifies as one of its roles to recommend any service improvements for action by the authority.

27.51 A panel's recommendations may be wide-ranging. The local government ombudsman has, for instance, commented favourably on a panel's decision which (among other things) recommended that the local authority prepare a report 'in a year's time or earlier if appropriate, on what action had been taken [on the broad policy implications arising out of their findings]; and that a copy of the report be sent to the complainants'.[67]

27.52 The local government ombudsman expects local authorities to act on practical recommendations made by panels, and has noted that 'it is no use having a complaints procedure which provides for a thorough investigation but where no one acts upon its recommendations'.[68]

Compensation

27.53 One of the defects of many local authority complaints procedures is their disinclination to award compensation. Historically this stemmed from a belief that this was not permitted by law. However as a result of pressure from the ombudsman[69] the government has legislated to put this point beyond doubt. Local Government Act (LGA) 2000 s92 provides that:

> (1) Where a relevant authority consider –
>   (a) that action taken by or on behalf of the authority in the exercise of their functions amounts to, or may amount to, maladministration, and
>   (b) that a person has been, or may have been, adversely affected by that action,
>   the authority may, if they think appropriate, make a payment to, or provide some other benefit for, that person.

67 Complaint no 93/A/3007 against Hounslow LBC, 10 October 1995.
68 Local Government Ombudsman, *Digest of Cases 1996* p112; and see also similar criticism at p112 of the *Digest of Cases 1998*.
69 *Annual Report 1998/99* p7.

(2) Any function which is conferred on the Greater London Authority under this section is to be exercisable by the Mayor of London and the London Assembly acting jointly on behalf of the Authority.

(3) In this section –

'action' includes failure to act,

'relevant authority' has the same meaning as in Part III of this Act.

27.54   The guidance at paras 6.3 et seq addresses the question of redress and advises that it should be appropriate and proportionate to the injustice; put complainants in the position they would have been in except for the fault; consider financial compensation, where restitution to the previous position is not possible; and take into account complainants' views as well as their own actions (such as delay on their part). The guidance differentiates between compensation and quantifiable loss and refers on this question to advice given by the local government ombudsman.

27.55   The local government ombudsman has stressed that the possibility of compensation should be an element in a good complaints procedure[70] and expressed irritation with authorities who do not, in appropriate cases, offer to pay complainants compensation (or some other appropriate recompense) as part of their settlement.[71] The ombudsman is showing an increasing willingness to be robust on compensation claims and express strong views about the inadequacy of council proposals: for instance that an offer of £4,000 to compensate a child for three years of council incompetence was 'derisory'.[72] The local government ombudsman has issued good practice guidance (in the following section referred to as the 'LGO guidance') aimed at promoting greater consistency in the remedies recommended by local authorities[73] and stressed that appropriate redress is particularly important in relation to complaints panel recommendations.[74]

27.56   The LGO guidance notes that an appropriate remedy may require a number of separate elements, including recommendations as to specific action that should be taken and as to an apology. As a general principle the remedy needs to be 'appropriate and proportionate to the injustice; it should, as far as possible, put the complainant in the position he or she would have been in but for the maladministration' and where 'this cannot be achieved because of the passage of time or of events which have occurred . . . financial compensation may be the only available approach'.[75]

27.57   On the question of compensation, the LGO guidance states that 'financial compensation may be appropriate, for example, if the council

---

70   *Guidance on Good Practice 1: Devising a Complaints System*, February 1992, appendix 2.

71   Local Government Ombudsman, *Annual Report 1996/97* p11.

72   Complaint no 05/C/14043 against Birmingham CC, 2007, 13 March 2007, and see also Complaint no 05/C/11921 against Trafford MBC, 26 July 2007 which recommended that over £100,000 be paid for a service failure.

73   *Guidance on good practice 6: Remedies*, February 2005 (replacing the previous guidance of September 1996) accessible at http://www.lgo.org.uk/pdf/remedies.pdf.

74   Local Government Ombudsman, *Annual Report 1998/99* p11. This is particularly so if the complaint concerns a failure to provide adequate (or any services), see complaint no 00/B/09315 against Hertfordshire, 29 January 2002.

75   LGO guidance p3.

has taken the appropriate action but has delayed in doing so and the delay has caused injustice; or if there is no practical action which would provide a full and appropriate remedy; or if the complainant has sustained loss and suffering'. It suggests that the calculation of what is appropriate may include consideration of:

- The effect of the complainant's own action.
- Reimbursement to the complainant of any money which is owing but unpaid (ie unpaid housing benefit).
- Quantifiable loss; ie 'paying for the additional help the parents procured for a child with special educational needs because the council delayed in drawing up a statutory statement or providing the help'.
- Loss of a non-monetary benefit; ie 'a council tenant has been unable to use one of the rooms in his or her flat for a period because of lack of repair'.
- Loss of value; where something owned by the complainant has lost value.
- Lost opportunity; 'compensation for a lost opportunity may sometimes be a fairly small sum, because it is only the loss or opportunity which is certain and the actual outcome which would have obtained cannot be known'.
- Distress 'including stress, anxiety, frustration, uncertainty, worry, inconvenience or outrage'. 'This element may be a moderate sum of no more than a few hundred pounds or less but in cases where the distress has been severe and/or prolonged, a more substantial sum may be justified.' The LGO guidance suggests that generally it 'could range from £50 (for example, for a period of uncertainty about the date or outcome of an assessment) to thousands of pounds in cases where, for example, allegations of abuse made against a complainant have not been investigated properly, or action requested by a complainant to prevent children from being abused has not happened'.[76]
- Professional fees in pursuing the dispute; while the LGO guidance advises that complainants usually do not need a solicitor or other professional to help them make a complaint, it may sometimes be appropriate. In such cases the recommendation may be for a contribution to costs rather than reimbursement of the whole of the expenditure.[77]
- Time and trouble in pursuing the complaint (but this should not be confused with the question of distress (as above). The LGO guidance suggests that this element need not always be included (for instance where minor failings in the complaints process have occurred) but in general complaints concerning social services complaints may be 'higher than the range of £50 to £250' to reflect the difficulty which

---

76 Ibid, p48.
77 However where an accountant acting under an enduring power of attorney pursued a complaint, the ombudsman held that he was entitled to be paid at his professional rate, and recommended over £16,000 for this item alone: complaint no 00/C/03176 against Nottingham County and City Councils, 2002, 22 January 2002.

a complainant with physical or mental health problems, or who is vulnerable for any other reason, may have in pursuing a complaint.[78]

- Offsetting compensation; in circumstances where the complainant owes money to the council (eg rent arrears) 'it would usually be appropriate for the compensation to be offset against the debt'.
- Interest.
- Formula; the guidance advises that 'sometimes it may be appropriate to express a remedy, not as a sum of money, but as a formula which sets out how the council should itself calculate the requisite sum of money. Where relevant, this needs to include reference to any continuing problem so that the formula is designed to encompass the future as well as the past.'

Policy recommendations

27.58   Panels will need to know (preferably before any hearing) the status of any policy matters relevant to the hearing (eg, eligibility criteria or charging policies and whether they are in draft form, approved or in the process of revision). Panels should be wary of making any recommendations which would be contrary to such general policies if they have been formulated and approved by the elected members (and especially if this was after the policies were the subject of proper consultation). The risk in such cases is of course that the panel might thereby usurp the democratic role of the council.

27.59   The local government ombudsman's guidance on good practice suggests, however, that in suitable cases the panel's recommendation can include advice that the authority review its practices, procedures or policies or give consideration to particular suggestions for improvements that have come to its notice.

Legal recommendations

27.60   Where there is a straightforward disagreement between the complainant and the local authority about the law, it is doubtful that the panel can do anything other than accept the authority's interpretation. While in such cases a complainant can use the complaints process, it is difficult to see that it can produce anything of value; the appropriate remedy in such a case would appear to be by way of a judicial review or a request for clarification from the Department of Health or Assembly (possibly through the medium of a request for the exercise of their default powers (see para 27.201).

27.61   The panel is required to give reasons for its recommendation (direction 8(3)). The extent of this obligation is discussed below (in that the same obligation rests with the local authority when deciding its response to the recommendations).

---

78   LGO guidance p49.

Local authority response to panel recommendations

27.62 The authority is obliged (by regulation 14) to send its response to the panel's recommendations to the complainant (and other participants as necessary) within 15 working days of receiving the panel's report as well as advising of the right to approach the local government ombudsman if dissatisfied. The guidance (at para 3.22.1) advises that the adult services director should explain in the response how the local authority will respond to the panel's recommendations and what action will be taken, and that if there is deviation from the panel's recommendations, the reasons for this should be fully explained.

27.63 While a local authority is not bound to accept a panel's recommendation, it will in practice have to have extremely cogent reasons for deciding differently. Sedley J held in *R v Islington LBC ex p Rixon*[79] that 'a failure to comply with a review panel's recommendations is not by itself a breach of law; but the greater the departure, the greater the need for cogent articulated reasons if the court is not to infer that the panel's recommendations have been overlooked'.

27.64 The case of *R v Avon CC ex p M*[80] concerned the failure of a social services department to comply with the findings of its complaints review panel. Henry J held:

> I would be reluctant to hold (and do not) that in no circumstances whatsoever could the Social Services Committee have overruled the Review Panel's recommendation in the exercise of their legal right and duty to consider it. Caution normally requires the Court not to say 'never' in any obiter dictum pronouncement. But I have no hesitation in finding that they could not overrule that decision without a substantial reason and without having given that recommendation the weight it required. It was a decision taken by a body entrusted with the basic fact-finding exercise under the complaints procedure. It was arrived at after a convincing examination of the evidence, particularly the expert evidence. The evidence before them had, as to the practicalities, been largely one way. The Panel had directed themselves properly, in law, and had arrived at a decision in line with the strength of the evidence before them. They had given clear reasons and they had raised the crucial factual question with the parties before arriving at their conclusion . . . It seems to me that anybody required, at law, to give their reasons for reconsidering and changing such a decision must have good reasons for doing so, and must show that they gave that decision sufficient weight and, in my judgment, it failed to do. Their decision must be quashed.

27.65 The case was, however, distinguished by Dyson J in *R v North Yorkshire CC ex p Hargreaves*,[81] where he stated:

> All that Henry J was saying was that where a panel has given a carefully reasoned decision adverse to the local authority on the subject of a complaint and the local authority rejects the panel's recommendation without itself giving a rational reason for doing so, then there is a

79 (1998) 1 CCLR 119.
80 (1999) 2 CCLR 185.
81 (1994) 30 September, CO/878/94, unreported.

strong prima facie case for quashing the local authority's decision as unlawful.

27.66   The local authority is (like the panel) required to give reasons for its decision. Such reasons must be 'proper, adequate and intelligible' and must deal with the substantial points raised by the complainant.[82] An unparticularised assertion that 'on the evidence' the panel makes certain findings and 'recommends . . .' will be considered inadequate.[83]

Special cases

27.67   Certain complaints will inevitably require a different investigative or review procedure by virtue of their particular facts or the nature of the subject matter.

Disciplinary or grievance procedures

27.68   The guidance (at para 7.2.1) stresses the importance of keeping complaints procedures separate from grievance procedures (which concern staff issues, such as conditions of service) and disciplinary procedures.

27.69   Where serious allegations are made, senior staff will need to be involved at the outset. Where such allegations suggest that a criminal offence may have been committed the police must be notified immediately.[84]

27.70   The complaints procedures do not cover disciplinary matters[85] and the guidance[86] advises that where complaints include a grievance or disciplinary element, the authority should if possible run the complaints and grievance/disciplinary procedures concurrently: that the fact that disciplinary procedures have commenced is not in itself a reason to stop the complaints process in all cases (unless to do so would compromise or prejudice the concurrent investigation). If an authority decides to suspend (or delay) the commencement of the complaints investigation, it should start or resume once the concurrent investigation is discontinued or completed.

NHS overlap

27.71   The NHS complaints procedures remain separate from those applied by social services authorities, notwithstanding a policy intention by the English and Welsh governments to unify the two systems.[87] Not

---

82   *Westminster City Council v Great Portland Estates plc* [1985] 1 AC 661, p673, HL and *In re Poyser and Mills' Arbitration* [1964] 2 QB 467, p478.

83   *R v Secretary of State for Transport ex p Cumbria CC* [1983] RTR 129, QBD.

84   Department of Health and Home Office, *No Secrets: Guidance on developing and implementing multi-agency policies and procedures to protect vulnerable adults from abuse*, 2000, para 2.8; National Assembly for Wales, *In Safe Hands*, 2000, para 7.8.

85   English Regulations reg 5; Welsh Regulations reg 12.

86   English guidance paras 7.3 et seq; Welsh guidance paras 5.1 et seq.

87   See eg Department of Health, *Making Experiences Count: The proposed new arrangements for handling health and social care complaints – Detailed policy background*, 2007; Welsh guidance para 5.4.2.

infrequently, however, a complaint will concern a matter which is an overlapping responsibility of both agencies.

27.72 Where this occurs the Welsh guidance urges co-operation,[88] whereas the English Regulations and guidance require a more focused response,[89] stating that 'people who use services should not have to worry about who to approach with complaints about different aspects of the service that they receive. Instead, the complaint can be made in its entirety to any one of the bodies involved.'

27.73 The English Regulations[90] require that where the complaint consists of elements relating to both social services functions and services provided by an NHS body, the local authority should, within ten working days, ask the complainant if he wishes details of the NHS complaint to be sent to the relevant NHS body. If the complainant agrees, the local authority should send the NHS complaint to the NHS body as soon as reasonably practicable. It should also advise the complainant which parts of the complaint the local authority is considering. The regulations additionally place a duty on local authorities and NHS bodies to co-operate with each other and to agree which of the two bodies will take the lead in handling the complaint, in order to provide a co-ordinated response.

27.74 The guidance (at para 7.5.4) states that 'ideally, both responses should be completed simultaneously and reports delivered to the complainant together. In order to facilitate this, the two bodies should aim to work to the shorter of their respective complaints procedure timescales.'

27.75 In 2007 the local government ombudsman published a special report[91] on the problems caused by the lack of a unified system to enable joint investigations into complaints that straddle (amongst other bodies) health and social services, and criticised authorities that insist on complainants having to make separate NHS/social services complainants when they concern the same facts.[92] It has been held to be maladministration for an authority not to have in place procedures to ensure that where a complaint raises matters that are outside the authority's remit, the complainant is directed to the appropriate body.[93]

27.76 A 2006 local government ombudsman complaint concerned excessive delays in the assessment of a disabled person for adaptations to his home, and a defective investigation in response to his complaint about the delay. The council had entered into a partnership with the NHS care trust and delegated (among other things) its statutory obligations (under Chronically Sick and Disabled Persons Act (CSDPA) 1970 s2) to the trust – which

---

88 Welsh guidance paras 5.4 et seq.
89 English Regulations reg 15; English guidance paras 7.5 et seq.
90 Ibid.
91 Local Government Ombudsman, *Special Report: Handling complaints about local partnerships*, 2007.
92 See complaint no 97/A/4002 against Bexley LBC – where the ombudsman also stated (at para 134) that it was unreasonable to expect complainants to have to pursue separate complaints against each authority; and complaint no 99/C/1276 against Northumberland CC where she approved a joint NHS/social services investigation (at para 61).
93 Complaint no 02/B/03622 against Harrow LBC, 22 June 2004.

included the duty to assess a need for adaptations. When the disabled person complained about the delay, the local authority passed the complaint to the care trust to address under stage 1. Although the local government ombudsman saw sense in this, he reminded the authority that it retained responsibility for the complaints process (as it related to a social services function) and was under a duty to monitor the progress of the complaint and to ensure that the relevant timescales were met.[94]

Overlap with other local authority functions

27.77   The statutory procedures for social services complaints (described above) are not applicable to complaints concerning education or housing (or indeed any other local authority function). It follows that the local authorities have greater latitude in the arrangements they make for such complaints. Good administration requires, however, that any complaints process must incorporate the principles outlined in the local ombudsman's guidance on the operation of complaints procedures.[95]

27.78   Not infrequently it may be unclear whether a complaint relates to a housing or social services function: for instance a dispute concerning adaptations funded via a disabled facilities grant – or the provision of a house identified as needed in a care plan. The local ombudsman has considered a number of such cases. In a complaint against Kirklees Metropolitan Council[96] she concluded:

> There was confusion within the Council as to whether [the] complaint should be considered by the Housing or Social Services Department. From [the complainants'] point of view this was irrelevant, they simply wanted the complaint to be considered thoroughly and promptly. The Council should have been able to do that. Although officers say they made internal changes as a result of the complaint no remedy was offered to [the complainants] for the Council's acknowledged failings.

27.79   Likewise in a complaint against Sunderland City Council[97] she concluded:

> I consider that [the complainant's] complaint about the failure to rehouse his family should also have been dealt with under the Social Services Statutory Complaints Procedure as the application arose out of a stated need in a Care Plan. The failure to consider the complaint under the statutory procedure was maladministration. This has caused injustice as it denied [the complainant] the opportunity of having his complaints properly addresses at an earlier date.

---

94   Complaint no 05/C/07195 against Northumberland CC, 18 April 2006, para 34.
95   Local Government Ombudsman, *Good Practice 1: Devising a Complaints System*, February 1992; see also complaint no 94/C/2959 against Nottingham City Council, 28 November 1994; complaint no 97/C/1614 against Bury MBC, 1999, where the ombudsman accepted that part of the complaint lay outside the statutory complaints process but nevertheless warranted investigation, and commented 'it is hard to identify any aspect of the Council's handling of Mr Redfern's complaints which was in the proper manner or in full accordance with the statutory complaints procedure and/or the Council's own written complaints procedure'.
96   Complaint no 01/C/00627 against Kirklees MC, 28 January 2003, para 68.
97   Complaint nos 00/C/12118 and 00/C/12621 against Sunderland City Council, 21 August 2002, para 252.

27.80 The English and Welsh complaints guidance urges authorities to develop a 'seamless service' for complaints which straddle more than one departmental function. The English guidance advises[98] that:

> 7.8.2 Building links with the local authority's other complaints procedures can be an essential way to develop the overall corporate obligation of the local authority to provide a high quality service. Local authorities are encouraged to offer a complete single response to complainants where possible, for example where a complainant has complaints relating to both a local authority's housing and social services functions.
>
> 7.8.3 The Complaints Manager responsible for social services should liaise with other staff as relevant. These members of staff should agree who will take the lead, to make sure that the complainant is kept informed and, wherever possible, gets a single reply that covers all aspects of his complaint.

Children procedures

27.81 In England complaints concerning the discharge by an authority of any of its functions under CA 1989 Part III (services for children 'in need', including disabled children – see para 24.5) are dealt with under a similar but separate procedure.[99] The most significant differences between the two systems is that (1) at the equivalent second stage of the children's complaints procedure an independent person must be involved[100] and (2) that all looked after children or children in need involved in the complaints process are entitled to an advocate.[101]

27.82 In Wales the community care and children's complaints systems are essentially unified, all such complaints being dealt with under virtually the same procedures and subject to the same guidance, albeit that the children's process is regulated by a separate set of regulations.[102]

Independent and private sector providers

27.83 The Care Homes Regulations[103] require that care homes have appropriate complaints procedures: that complaints are investigated within 28 days; and all residents are made aware of their right to take their complaint to the Commission for Social Care Inspection (CSCI) in England or the Care and Social Services Inspectorate Wales (CSSIW) (see chapter 17).

27.84 As a general rule, residents will only have access to the local authority complaints procedures in relation to acts or omissions by a care home if

---

98 Very similar advice is given in the Welsh guidance at paras 5.7.1–5.7.2.

99 CA 1989 Representations Procedure (England) Regulations 2006 SI No 1738 and the statutory guidance, namely Department for Education and Skills, *Getting the Best from Complaints Social Care Complaints and Representations for Children, Young People and Others*, 2006.

100 CA 1989 Representations Procedure (England) Regulations 2006 reg 17(2).

101 CA 1989 ss24D and 26A, and the Advocacy Services and Representations Procedure (Children) (Amendment) Regulations 2004 SI No 719.

102 Representations Procedure (Children) (Wales) Regulations 2005 SI No 3365 (W262).

103 Care Homes Regulations 2001 SI No 3965 reg 22; Care Homes (Wales) Regulations 2002 SI No 324 (W37) reg 23.

the authority is responsible for their placement or care plan. The guidance explains[104] that if the complaints manager receives such a complaint, he or she should normally direct it to the service provider, unless the authority was responsible for the original assessment of need that led to a placement and associated funding. It follows that some service users may have two ongoing complaints, one to a care home, for example, about its failure to comply with the national minimum standards (see para 17.21) and one to the local authority concerning its failure to commission suitable services.

27.85 The guidance advises (at para 7.6.7) that where an authority receives a complaint concerning a care home it should, within five working days, ask the complainant if he or she wishes details of the complaint to be sent to the registered person – and if he or she does, then the complaint should be forwarded as soon as reasonably practicable. At the same time, however, details of the complaint should also be sent to the authority's care management team and the contract monitoring team.

27.86 Paragraph 7.6.8 deals with complaints which concern both social services functions and services provided under the Care Standards Act 2000, advising that:

> . . . the local authority should cooperate with the provider to ensure that the complainant receives a coordinated response dealing with all aspects of the complaint. The local authority should, within 10 working days, ask the complainant if he wishes details of the Care Standards element of the complaint to be sent to the registered person. If the complainant agrees, the local authority should send the Care Standards element of the complaint to the registered person as soon as reasonably practicable. It should inform the complainant when it has done this as well as which element of the complaint the local authority is considering.

27.87 The primary role of the CSCI and the CSSSIW is as the regulator in social care to ensure compliance with the regulations and associated national minimum standards. As the English guidance explains:

> 7.7.4 The regulator is not a complaints agency and has no statutory duties or powers for the investigation of complaints about either care services or local authority social services. It can only consider matters relating to the provider's compliance with regulations and National Minimum Standards. It should also not be seen as a mediator between care service providers and those commissioning or using a service.

> 7.7.5 Where the regulator receives information indicating a concern, complaint or allegation about a care service, it undertakes an assessment of that information and the accumulated evidence about the care service to determine the nature of its response. In the case of concerns and complaints, the regulator normally refers the matter to the care service provider and/or commissioning agency (where applicable). This highlights the importance of complaints procedures for both care services and local authorities. [105]

---

104 English guidance paras 7.6 *et seq*; Welsh guidance paras 5.9 *et seq*.
105 In this respect, see the local government ombudsman's report concerning complaint no 97/A/4002 against Bexley LBC.

NHS complaints

27.88 Considerable concern has been expressed about the performance of the NHS complaints process.[106] Following on from the 1994 Wilson Committee report *Being Heard,* major changes were introduced in 1996, with the possibility of a quasi-independent 'panel' hearing. However this new system failed to gain public confidence – particularly the process of accessing a panel hearing and the actual hearings themselves. Accordingly the government undertook a further evaluation/consultation exercise in 2001.[107] The proposals for change were then published as *NHS Complaints Reform – Making Things Right*[108] and enacted as chapter 9 of the HSC(CHS)A 2003.

27.89 It remains to be seen whether these latest changes (which came into effect in 2005) will lead to any significant improvement. Evidence suggests that for many the process of complaining about the NHS (and the support available to complainants) continues to be poor – with a major problem being the defensive or dismissive way some complaints are handled.[109] The Health Service Ombudsman has also issued a critical report on the operation of the complaints scheme[110] and (at para 23) identified five key weaknesses:

- complaints systems are fragmented within the NHS, between the NHS and private health care systems, and between health and social care;
- the complaints system is not centred on the patient's needs;
- there is a lack of capacity and competence among staff to deliver a quality service;
- the right leadership, culture and governance are not in place;
- just remedies are not being secured for justified complaints.

Patient advice and liaison service

27.90 *The NHS Plan,* 2000, announced the commitment to establish a patient advice and liaison service (PALS) in every English NHS trust by 2002.[111] PALS are a non-statutory advice service that 'do not replace existing specialist advocacy services, such as mental health and learning disability advocacy. Rather, they are complementary to existing services. Providing

---

106 For an analysis of the fragmented nature of the current health service complaints process see S Kerrison and A Pollock, 'Complaints as accountability? The case of health care in the United Kingdom' [2001] PL 115–133.

107 See Department of Health, *NHS Complaints Procedure National Evaluation* and *Reforming the NHS Complaints Procedure – a Listening Document,* both published on 3 September 2001, accessible at http://www.dh.gov.uk/assetRoot/04/05/89/33/04058933.pdf and http://www.dh.gov.uk/assetRoot/04/08/05/27/04080527.pdf respectively.

108 2003, accessible at http://www.dh.gov.uk/assetRoot/04/06/90/09/04069009.pdf.

109 L Phelps and A Williams, *The Pain of Complaining – CAB/ICAS Evidence of NHS Complaints Procedure,* Citizens Advice, 2005.

110 2nd Report – Session 2004–2005 *Making things better? A report on reform of the NHS complaints procedure in England,* HC 413, TSO, 2005.

111 Department of Health, *The NHS Plan,* Cm 4818-I, TSO, July 2000, para 10.17.

information and on the spot help for patients, their families and carers, they are powerful lever for change and improvement.'[112] PALS are regulated by a Department of Health standards and evaluation framework[113] and their core functions include:

- being accessible to patients, their carers, friends and families;
- providing on the spot help in every trust with the power to negotiate immediate solutions or speedy resolutions of problems. PALS will listen and provide the relevant information and support to help resolve service users' concerns quickly and efficiently. They will liaise with staff and managers, and, where appropriate, with other PALS services, health and related organisations, to facilitate a resolution;
- acting as a gateway to appropriate independent advice and advocacy services, including the independent complaints advocacy services;
- providing accurate information to patients, carers and families.

Independent complaints advocacy service

27.91   NHSA 2006 s248[114] obliges the secretary of state to 'arrange, to such extent as he considers necessary to meet all reasonable requirements' for the provision of independent complaints advocacy services (ICAS) to assist individuals making complaints against the NHS. ICAS replaced the service previously provided by community health councils (CHCs) in England. The service is provided on a regional basis by independent agencies who have been awarded contracts to deliver the service by the Department of Health. Patients who want to complain about NHS services can approach ICAS directly (or be directed there by the PALS). Complaints managers at trust level are also expected to advise patients of the availability of this service and assist them in making contact. Further information on the service can be accessed from the Department of Health website.[115]

27.92   In Wales CHCs continue to exist, and provide support and advocacy assistance to complainants: there is one CHC for every local health board.

NHS complaints process

27.93   Social Care (Community Health and Standards) Act 2003 s113 gives the secretary of state in England and the Assembly in Wales power to make regulations concerning the structure of the NHS complaints procedure. Regulations (amended) have been issued in England placing responsibility on individual NHS bodies for the first 'local resolution' stage of the

---

112   See Department of Health website 'Patient Advice and Liasion Services'.
113   PALS Core National Standards and Evaluation Framework, 2003, accessible at http://www.dh.gov.uk/en/Publicationsandstatistics/Publications/PublicationsPolicyAndGuidance/DH_4119314.
114   Previously Health and Social Care Act 2001 s12.
115   http://www.dh.gov.uk/en/Policyandguidance/Organisationpolicy/Complaintspolicy/NHScomplaintsprocedure/DH_4087428.

complaints procedure and the Healthcare Commission[116] for the second 'independent review' stage.[117] These amended regulations are referred to in the subsequent sections as 'the regulations'.

27.94   In Wales, directions[118] have been issued, establishing a similar process. The first stage is the responsibility of individual NHS bodies and an Independent Review Secretariat is responsible for the second 'independent review' stage.[119] In England the Department of Health has issued guidance as *Guidance to support implementation of the National Health Service (Complaints) Regulations,* 2004 and in Wales the Assembly has issued guidance as *Complaints in the NHS: A Guide to handling complaints in Wales,* 2003.

27.95   Separate regulations govern the procedures for primary care providers (eg GP, dentists), notably the National Health Service (General Medical Services Contracts) Regulations 2004,[120] Part 6 of which requires that such providers operate a similar complaints procedure.

27.96   The following outline is of the procedure in England, which, as noted above, is similar to that operating in Wales.

Complaints personnel

27.97   Every NHS body must appoint a 'complaints manager' with responsibility for ensuring that complaints are properly investigated (reg 5) and in addition it must appoint a member of its board of directors to take overall responsibility for the scheme (reg 4). The complaints manager need not be an employee of the particular NHS body and may fulfil the complaints function for more than one trust.[121] The system must be (reg 3(2)):

> . . . accessible and such as to ensure that complaints are dealt with speedily and efficiently, and that complainants are treated courteously and sympathetically and as far as possible involved in decisions about how their complaints are handled and considered.

Who may complain (reg 8)

27.98   Complaints may be made by a patient or anyone 'who is affected by or likely to be affected by the action, omission or decision of the NHS body which is the subject of the complaint'. Where a complaint is made by a

---

116   The correct title of the Healthcare Commission is the Commission for Healthcare Audit and Inspection.

117   National Health Service (Complaints) Regulations 2004 SI No 1768 as amended by the National Health Service (Complaints) Amendment Regulations 2006 SI No 2084.

118   Welsh Assembly, *Directions to NHS Trusts and Local Health Boards on Hospital Complaints Procedures* and *Directions to Local Health Boards on Dealing with Complaints about Family Health Service Practitioners, Providers of Personal Medical Services and Personal Dental Services other than Personal Dental Services provided by NHS Trusts,* 27 March 2003, accompanied by guidance *Complaints in the NHS – A Guide to Handling Complaints in Wales.*

119   By direction 2, ibid, a 'unit, which is part of Powys Local Health Board, established to administer the second stage of the NHS complaints procedure'.

120   SI No 291.

121   Regulation 5(3) as amended by National Health Service (Complaints) Amendment Regulations 2006 reg 5.

representative on behalf of a patient who has died or lacks the physical or mental capacity to make the complaint in person, then he or she must 'in the opinion of the complaints manager' have a sufficient interest in the patient's welfare and be 'a suitable person to act as representative'.

27.99 Complaints on behalf of a child must be made by:

> . . . a parent, guardian or other adult person who has care of the child and where the child is in the care of a local authority or a voluntary organisation, the representative must be a person authorised by the local authority or the voluntary organisation.

Time limits (reg 10)

27.100 Complaints must be made within six months of the date of the incident in question or six months of the date on which the issue came to the notice of the complainant. Complaints can be made outside these time limits where the complaints manager is of the opinion that:

(a) having regard to all the circumstances, the complainant had good reasons for not making the complaint within that period; and

(b) notwithstanding the time that has elapsed it is still possible to investigate the complaint effectively and efficiently.

27.101 Para 3.37 of the Department of Health guidance advises that:

> The discretion to vary the time limit should be used flexibly and with sensitivity. An example of where discretion might be exercised would be where the complainant has suffered such distress or trauma as to prevent him/her from making their complaint at an earlier stage.

Complaints – subject matter (regs 6 and 7)

27.102 A complaint by or on behalf of a patient may in general terms concern anything done that is reasonably connected with the exercise by the particular NHS body of a NHS function. Regulation 7 contains various exclusions, primarily relating to complaints made by bodies providing services to the NHS or employees or misplaced complaints (eg complaints concerning another NHS body, or relating to a request for information under the Data Protection Act 1998 or the Freedom of Information Act 2000). The most material exclusions for patients concern complaints:

- which are being or have been investigated under the regulations[122] or by the Health Service Commissioner;
- where the complainant has stated in writing that he or she intends to take legal proceedings; and
- about which the NHS body 'is taking or is proposing to take disciplinary proceedings in relation to the substance of the complaint against a person who is the subject of the complaint'.

---

122 Regulation 7(j) as amended by National Health Service (Complaints) Amendment Regulations 2006 reg 6.

Local authority overlap

27.103   Regulations 3A and 3B[123] provide that where it appears to a complaints manager that part of a complaint falls to be considered by the local authority under the social services complaints procedures, he or she must ask the complainant (within ten working days) whether he or she wishes the local authority part of the complaint to be sent to the local authority and, if the complainant agrees, it should then be sent as soon as reasonably practicable. In such cases the manger must make it clear which part of the complaint will be handled under the NHS procedures, and the NHS and social services authority must co-operate 'with a view to the complainant receiving a coordinated response to his complaint'. Where however the complaints manager considers that the complaint falls entirely within the social services complaints process, he or she must ask the complainant (within five working days) whether he or she wishes that material to be sent to the local authority to which it relates and, if the complainant agrees, it should be sent as soon as reasonably practicable and the complaint shall then be deemed to have been introduced under the social services complaints regulations.

Stage 1

27.104   Complaints may be made orally or in writing (including electronically) and must be recorded by the complaints manager. When made orally 'the complaints manager must make a written record of the complaint' (reg 9). Regulation 11 requires the complaints manager to acknowledge the complaint (in writing) within two days of its receipt and, if made orally, the acknowledgement must include a written record of the complaint. The complaints manager must send a copy of the complaint and his or her acknowledgement to any person who is the subject of the complaint. The letter of acknowledgement must also include information about the right to advocacy assistance under NHSA 2006 s248.[124]

27.105   The complaints manger must investigate the complaint, 'to the extent necessary and in the manner which appears to him most appropriate to resolve it speedily and efficiently'. The regulations provide for conciliation and mediation (where agreed by the complainant – regulation 12) and require the complaints manager to keep the complainant informed about the progress of the investigation. Regulation 13 requires that a written response is provided (generally signed by the chief executive of the NHS body) summarising the nature and substance of the complaint, describing the investigation and summarising its conclusions: this is to be provided within 20 working days of the date on which the complaint was made – unless impractical, in which case it is to be done 'as soon as reasonably

---

123   Inserted by National Health Service (Complaints) Amendment Regulations 2006 reg 4.

124   In Wales, the complainant must be informed of the right to seek assistance from the local Community Health Council – see *Complaints in the NHS: A Guide to handling complaints in Wales*, 2003, para 1.41.

practicable'. The response should be copied to any person identified in the complaint as the subject of the complaint and must advise of the right to have the complaint referred to the Healthcare Commission (or in Wales to the Independent Review Secretariat).

Stage 2

27.106 An independent review stage exists in both England and Wales. The English procedure is the responsibility of the Healthcare Commission whereas in Wales it is administered by the Independent Review Secretariat.[125] The two procedures are similar and the following section describes the English process.

27.107   The Healthcare Commission has issued brief guidance on the operation of the second stage review[126] and its website provides general guidance as to the procedures it adopts.[127]

27.108   If the complainant is dissatisfied with the outcome of the first stage process (or the complaints manager has declined to investigate it), the complainant can ask the Healthcare Commission to investigate (special rules relate to NHS foundation trusts[128]). The request must be made 'within two months of, or as soon as reasonably practicable after' the first stage response (reg 14). It may be made orally or in writing (including electronically – details are on the Commission's website). The Healthcare Commission must acknowledge the request, and then decide (reg 16(2)) whether to:

- take no further action (in which case the complainant must be advised of his or her right to complaint to the Health Service Ombudsman);
- refer the complaint back to the NHS body with recommendations as to what action might be taken to resolve it;
- investigate the complaint further itself, either by convening a panel or 'otherwise';
- consider the subject matter of the complaint as part of or in conjunction with any other investigation which it is conducting or proposes to conduct;
- refer the complaint to a health regulatory body;
- refer the complaint to the Health Service Ombudsman.

27.109 On receiving a complaint, the Healthcare Commission sends an acknowledgement to the complainant and to the health care provider and then designates a case manager who undertakes an initial review. This will consider whether there are outstanding issues not addressed at the first

---

125   Which is administered by Powys Local Health Board – see note 119 above.
126   *Reforming the NHS complaints procedure,*accessible at http://
       www.healthcarecommission.org.uk/_db/_documents/04008195.pdf.
127   See http://www.healthcarecommission.org.uk/contactus/complaints.cfm and
       Spotlight on Complaints: A report on second-stage complaints about the NHS in England,
       January 2007, accessible at http://www.healthcarecommission.org.uk/_db/
       _documents/spotlight_on_complaints.pdf.
128   National Health Service (Complaints) Regulations 2004 reg 15 as amended by
       National Health Service (Complaints) Amendment Regulations 2006 reg 9.

stage and whether the complaint is eligible for further review. The investigation undertaken by the provider will then be considered (and additional information obtained if necessary) and independent clinical advice will be sought in appropriate cases. At this stage one of the following decisions is then made about all or each part of a complaint:

- that the complaint is not eligible because it does not meet the Healthcare Commission's criteria;
- that no further action be taken;
- to refer the complaint back to the healthcare provider or NHS body for further action;
- to refer the complaint to another body for further action or investigation, eg the General Medical Council or the Health Service Ombudsman;
- to refer the complaint for action by another section of the Healthcare Commission;
- to carry out a full investigation of the complaint;
- to refer the complaint for a panel hearing.

27.110 A 2007 Healthcare Commission report[129] indicates that approximately 33 per cent of cases are referred back to the healthcare provider for further action; 12 per cent of cases are resolved or withdrawn; 26 per cent are rejected for jurisdictional reasons; 19 per cent are not upheld or no further action is taken on them; 8 per cent are upheld in full or in part and 2 per cent are referred on to the Health Service Ombudsman.

27.111 If the complainant is unhappy with the outcome of the initial review, the remedy is to complain to the Health Service Ombudsman.

Reference back

27.112 Where the Healthcare Commission refers a complaint back to the healthcare provider or NHS body for further action it will generally recommend that the provider/NHS body take action to resolve the complaint including:

- giving more information to the complainant;
- carrying out further investigation;
- taking remedial action, eg offering treatment that may rectify a problem, improving procedures, following disciplinary procedures, arranging for an independent person to mediate between the complainant and the healthcare provider.

Healthcare Commission investigation

27.113 Regulation 17 provides that where the Healthcare Commission decides to investigate the complaint itself, it must within ten working days advise the complainant of its proposed terms of reference for the investigation.

---

129 *Spotlight on Complaints: A report on second-stage complaints about the NHS in England,* January 2007, accessible at http://www.healthcarecommission.org.uk/_db/ _documents/spotlight_on_complaints.pdf.

CHAI's guidance explains that where it decides to undertake its own investigation, its case manager will give the complainant and respondent an opportunity to comment on the draft terms of reference.

27.114   Depending upon the type of complaint, independent expert advice will be sought (eg medical or legal advice or advice from someone who can give a patient or public interest perspective). The case manager may also decide to interview people connected with the complaint including the complainant, the respondent and witnesses.

27.115   Regulation 19 requires the Healthcare Commission to complete its report as soon as reasonably practicable and that the report contain a reasoned response provided to the complainant together with advice of the right to take the matter to the Health Service Ombudsman if dissatisfied. In this context, the Healthcare Commission's guidance[130] indicates that it aims to complete investigations within six months of the date it decides to investigate and explains that the complainant and respondent will be sent a draft copy of the report for comment on factual accuracy. The report is then finalised and copied to:

- the complainant;
- the patient, if he or she is different from the complainant;
- the person complained against;
- the Chief Executive of the relevant NHS organisation;
- any experts consulted;
- the strategic health authority.

Panels

27.116   Regulation 18 requires the Healthcare Commission to maintain a list of people who are suitable to be members of an independent lay panel (employees and members of NHS bodies are excluded from membership). Individual panels consist of three such persons – one of whom is designated by the Healthcare Commission as the chair.

27.117   The Healthcare Commission's guidance[131] states that the case manager and chair will agree the terms of reference for the panel following comments from the complainant and the respondent. At that stage a panel co-ordinator assumes responsibility for organising the panel and producing the report of the outcomes. As with investigation reports, all parties involved with the panel are given the opportunity to check the draft report for factual accuracy before it is finalised. The report is copied to the same parties as listed above (in relation to investigation reports). CHAI aims to complete the panel process within four months of the date of the request (including the distribution of the panel report).

Further complaint

27.118   If a complainant is unhappy with the outcome of the panel hearing, the remedy lies with a complaint to the Health Service Ombudsman.

130   See http://www.healthcarecommission.org.uk/contactus/complaints.cfm.
131   Ibid.

Reform

27.119 As noted above, the NHS complaint process has been the subject of almost continual change since 1996 and both the Department of Health and the Welsh Assembly[132] are seeking its further reform with the aim of aligning or ultimately combining the NHS and social services systems. In June 2007 the Department of Health issued for consultation a proposal to advance this objective.[133]

Challenging discharge and continuing care decisions

27.120 The procedures for challenging hospital discharge and NHS continuing health care decisions are considered separately at paras 5.53 and 14.76 above.

Local government ombudsman procedures

27.121 The Commissioners for Local Administration in England and Wales (generally known as the local government ombudsmen) were established by (and in England[134] remain governed by) LGA 1974 Part III. In Wales the system has been amended as a result of the Public Services Ombudsman (Wales) Act 2005, such that the Public Services Ombudsman now fulfils the role of local government ombudsman, health service ombudsman and central government ombudsman – and his role is considered briefly at para 27.151 below.

27.122 By virtue of LGA 1974 s25 the local government ombudsmen in England are empowered to investigate (among other things) any local authority. Section 26 stipulates that all complaints must be in writing and made by members of the public who claim to have sustained injustice in consequence of maladministration in connection with action taken by or on behalf of an authority. Complaints no longer have to be introduced by a local councillor, although this remains advisable where possible.

27.123 The ombudsmen in England operate from three regional offices, namely London,[135] Coventry[136] and York.[137] Their website[138] contains copies of the complaint forms (which can also be obtained from Citizen's Advice Bureaux), previous relevant reports, publications and key addresses. Full

---

132 See eg Welsh Assembly, *Listening and Learning: A guide to handling complaints and representations in local authority social services in Wales*, 2006,para 5.4.2.

133 Department of Health, *Making Experiences Count: The proposed new arrangements for handling health and social care complaints – Detailed policy background*, 2007.

134 The local government ombudsman is governed by the provisions of LGA 2000 Part III and the Commission for Local Administration in Wales and Local Commissioner in Wales (Functions and Expenses) Regulations 2001 SI No 2275 (W165).

135 10th Floor, Millbank Tower, Millbank, London SW1P 4QP, tel: 020 7217 4620.

136 The Oaks, No 2, Westwood Way, Westwood Business Park, Coventry CV4 8JB, tel: 024 7682 0000.

137 Beverley House, 17 Shipton Road, York YO30 5FZ, tel: 01904 380200.

138 http://www.lgo.org.uk.

copies of all the local ombudsman's reports in England can be obtained from the London office, and for a modest annual fee a subscription can be taken out to receive all copies of social services complaints reports (generally dispatched by email).

27.124   Although only 8 per cent of the local government ombudsman's complaints concern social services,[139] concern has been expressed that while other areas (eg housing (32 per cent) and planning (23 per cent)) are showing improvement – a 'major concern now is the provision about social care, about which we are receiving an increasing number of justified complaints'.[140]

27.125   In *R v Commissioner for Local Administration ex p Eastleigh BC*[141] Lord Donaldson MR commented:

> Maladministration is not defined in the 1974 Act, but its meaning was considered in *R v Local Comr for Administration for the North and East Area of England, ex p Bradford MCC* [1979] 2 All ER 881. All three judges (Lord Denning MR, Eveleigh LJ and Sir David Cairns) expressed themselves differently, but in substance each was saying the same thing, namely that administration and maladministration, in the context of a local authority, is concerned with the *manner* in which decisions by the authority are reached and the *manner* in which they are or are not implemented.

27.126   The Health Service Ombudsman in his annual report for 1993/94 (para 1.4) commented on the nature of maladministration in the following terms:

> The terms given by Mr Richard Crossman in 1966 were 'bias, neglect, inattention, delay, incompetence, ineptitude, perversity, turpitude, arbitrariness and so on'. I have added:
> - rudeness (though that is a matter of degree);
> - unwillingness to treat the complainant as a person with rights; refusal to answer reasonable questions;
> - neglecting to inform a complainant on request of his or her rights or entitlement;
> - knowingly giving advice which is misleading or inadequate;
> - ignoring valid advice or overruling considerations which would produce an uncomfortable result for the overruler;
> - offering no redress or manifestly disproportionate redress;
> - showing bias whether because of colour, sex or any other grounds;
> - omission to notify those who thereby lose a right of appeal;
> - refusal to inform adequately of the right of appeal;
> - faulty procedures; failure by management to monitor compliance with adequate procedures;
> - cavalier disregard of guidance which is intended to be followed in the interest of equitable treatment of those who use the service;
> - partiality; and
> - failure to mitigate the effects of rigid adherence to the letter of the law where that produces manifestly inequitable treatment.

139   *Annual report 2004/05* p20.
140   *Annual report 2004/05* p24.
141   [1988] 3 WLR 113, CA.

27.127 Complaints must in general be made to the local government ombuds-man (or the local councillor) within 12 months from the date on which the person aggrieved first had notice of the matters alleged in the complaint, although the local ombudsman has an overall discretion to extend time if he or she considers it reasonable to do so (LGA 1974 s26(4)).

27.128 The local government ombudsman cannot investigate a complaint unless it has first been drawn to the attention of the local authority in question, and that authority has been afforded an opportunity to investi-gate and reply to the complaint (LGA 1974 s26(5)).

27.129 Unless the local government ombudsman is satisfied that in the par-ticular circumstances it is not reasonable to expect the aggrieved person to resort to such a remedy, complaints cannot be entertained where there exists an alternative remedy, for instance a right of appeal to a tribunal or to a minister of the Crown or a remedy by way of court proceedings. However, in general, it appears that relatively few complaints are rejected by the local ombudsman on these grounds (5 per cent in 1998/99). The ombudsman has stated that he will investigate a complaint before the statutory complaints process has been exhausted 'where there has been a breakdown of trust between the complainant and the authority, or where both sides agree that there is no point in completing a process which is unlikely to satisfy the complainant'.[142] In addition he has indicated that 'in general' judicial review is not considered to provide a remedy 'that is reasonable for most complainants to resort to'.[143]

27.130 Only about 1 per cent of all complaints result in the local government ombudsman preparing a final report; the most significant reasons for a complaint not resulting in a report being: (1) it discloses no maladminis-tration (in about 30 per cent of cases); (2) the complaint is premature (in about 25 per cent of cases); (3) a local settlement results (in about 15 per cent of cases); and (4) the complaint is outside the ombudsman's jurisdic-tion (in about 13 per cent of cases). [144]

27.131 The ombudsman receives an increasing (although relatively small) number of complaints concerning the actions of social services author-ities. In 2002/03 they amounted to 7 per cent of all complaints,[145] 1,201 in all (of which 593 concerned services for adults, 489 services for children, 14 registered homes and 105 'other'). Only 20 full investigation reports (concerning social services) were produced by the ombudsman during that period.[146]

27.132 LGA 1974 s26(5) requires complainants to bring complaints to the notice of the local authority before the local ombudsman will consider them. In general the ombudsman requires complainants to use the authority's complaints procedures before he or she will be prepared to investigate the matter. However, if the complaint is not investigated

---

142 J White, 'Community care and the local government ombudsman for England' (2006) 9 CCLR 8, p8.
143 Ibid, p9.
144 Percentages extracted from the *Annual Report 2004/05*.
145 The total number of complaints (ie including all categories) amounted to 18,376.
146 *Annual Report 2002/03*.

properly by the authority (for instance, if there was an unjustified breach of the timescales or a serious breach of the rules of natural justice), the local ombudsman may be prepared to accept the complaint even though it has not traversed the local authority's entire complaints process.

27.133   In his annual report for 1992/93 the ombudsman commented on his general approach in this area:

> The recommendations of a statutory complaints panel to a director of social services are not binding. In assessing complaints that have been through the procedure and have then been rejected, I have looked at the investigation process; if it has been satisfactory, I have often adopted the recommendations of the panel and attempted to settle the matter. In this way I have been able to avoid the need for a further lengthy and costly investigation by my office.

27.134   As complaints to the local government ombudsman are only (in general) accepted if no effective legal remedy is available, the judicial review and ombudsman procedures are distinct and not 'alternative options'.[147] In *R v Commissioner for Local Administration ex p PH*[148] an applicant commenced judicial review proceedings against a local authority on the grounds that it had delayed undertaking a special educational needs assessment. As a consequence such an assessment took place. Subsequently she complained to the ombudsman seeking compensation for the effect of the council's delay. The ombudsman decided, under LGA 1974 s26(6), that the complaint was outside his jurisdiction because the complainant had already sought a judicial review of the council's actions. In upholding the ombudsman's decision, Turner J held:

> It can hardly have been the intention of Parliament to have provided two remedies, one substantive by way of judicial review and one compensatory by was of the Local Commissioner . . . where a party has ventilated a grievance by way of judicial review it was not contemplated that they should enjoy and alternative, let alone an additional right by way of complaint to a local commissioner.

27.135   Prior judicial review proceedings will not, however, always be a bar to a subsequent ombudsman investigation. In *R (Goldsmith) v Wandsworth LBC*[149] the Court of Appeal quashed a local authority decision to require a resident to move to a nursing home (from her residential care home of many years). In order to avoid the contested move (pending the court decision) the resident's daughter had paid a private agency to provide her mother's nursing needs. On the Court of Appeal ruling that the local authority's decision making was irrational, the daughter complained to the ombudsman seeking to recover her expenditure on the nursing costs

---

147 Ombudsman decisions are, however, susceptible to judicial review; see eg *R v Parliamentary Commissioner ex p Dyer*[1994] 1 WLR 621 and *R v Parliamentary Commissioner ex p Bachin* (1999) EGCS 78.

148 [1999] COD 382, as cited in the *Annual Report 1998/99*, p7.

149 [2004] EWCA Civ 1170; (2004) 7 CCLR 472 – see also para 3.221 above.

amounting to over £27,000 plus interest. The ombudsman upheld her complaint and recommended the compensation be paid in that sum.[150]

27.136　The fact that lawyers are involved and threatening legal action does not of itself make the ombudsman process unavailable. A 2001 report concerned a council that delayed the provision of (assessed) services until threatened with a judicial review. A subsequent complaint concerning the delay was upheld and a compensation recommendation made by the ombudsman.[151]

27.137　There are many advantages to a complainant in using the local ombudsman procedures. They are free to the complainant, they can result in the award of significant sums in compensation, and the authority is required to publicise the ombudsman's report (LGA 1974 s30). The ombudsman has access to all the relevant files and other records, can require the authority to furnish additional information and has the same powers as the High Court in respect of the attendance and examination of witnesses and the production of documents (LGA 1974 s29). Complaints to the local government ombudsman are not subject to such short time limits as in judicial review.

27.138　The ombudsman is concerned with the factual basis of local authority decisions – whereas in judicial review the court is largely confined to a review of the decision's legality. The ombudsman is capable of undertaking a very detailed review of the relevant documentation, of interviewing all the participants to a decision (eg the director of social services, councillors as well as the staff in actual contact with service user/carers). This analysis frequently sees through protestations by an authority that its decision was not 'resource led'. Examples of this type of review can be found at paras 3.186, 4.29 and 24.67 above.

27.139　The disadvantages include the apparent reluctance of the local ombudsman to accept many complaints, the fact that only about 1 per cent of all complaints actually result in a final report, the length of time taken to complete the investigations (although this has shown recent improvement, with more than half of all complaints being resolved within 52 weeks[152]) and the fact that in general ombudsman's recommendations are not binding on local authorities.[153]

27.140　Each year a very few such recommendations are not accepted by local authorities. Trafford Metropolitan Borough Council is a recent example of such a recalcitrant authority, having refused to comply with recommendations made in a 2006 report[154] concerning its decision to require the repayment of an improvement grant made to an elderly woman with significant mental health problems. In the face of such a refusal, all that the ombudsman can do is issue a further critical report drawing attention

---

150　Complaint no 05/B/02414 against Wandsworth, 27 September 2006.
151　Complaint no 99/B/04621 against Cambridgeshire, 29 January 2001.
152　*Annual Report 2002/03* p5.
153　It may however be *Wednesbury* unreasonable (see para 27.172 below) for a public body to reject such a finding: *R (Bradley and others) v Secretary of State Work and Pensions* [2007] EWHC 242 (Admin).
154　Complaint no 04/C/17057 against Trafford MBC, 30 November 2006.

to the failure. In the Trafford case this was done in 2007[155] in trenchant terms. Clearly when such a deadlock occurs (and it is not limited to English cases[156]) it is profoundly unsatisfactory for the complainant and evidence of the limitations of the process (compared to that of judicial review).

Compensation/other recommendations

27.141 The local government ombudsman will often recommend action in addition to an apology and compensation. By way of example, a 2006 complaint against Blackpool Borough Council[157] included a recommendation that (among other things) the council should:

- offer Mrs Lloyd an appropriate form of tribute or memorial to her aunt (whose death had prompted the complaint) and bring that into effect within six months;
- formally adopt at member level a policy that ensures that risks to individual service users will be assessed as an integral part of the response to both individual complaints and a known failure in home care services;
- ensure that there are adequate resources available to the contracts unit so that it can fulfil its role in monitoring contract performance;
- review complaint procedures and staff training to ensure the development of an appropriate customer care culture which recognises the difficulty and fears that vulnerable service users may have in making complaints.

27.142 Likewise in a 2006 complaint against Leeds City Council[158] he recommended (among other things) that the council pay for a two week UK summer holiday for the family.

Overlap with the Health Service Ombudsman

27.143 The local government ombudsman in England has expressed concern about the difficulty in investigating complaints that allege maladministration by both health and social services authorities, stating that 'it is becoming increasingly difficult to identify whether a complaint should be pursued though the social services authority on the one hand, or the health authority on the other'.[159] A consultation document issued by the Cabinet Office in 2005[160] proposed reforms that would (among other things) address this problem by enabling the various ombudsmen to

155 Further report concerning complaint no 04/C/17057, 15 May 2007.
156 See eg the comments of the Public Service Ombudsman for Wales in his *Annual Report 2006/07* (p22) concerning the failure of Gwynedd Council.
157 Complaint no 03/C/17141 against Blackpool BC, 23 February 2006.
158 Complaint no 04/C/16622 against Leeds CC, 4 May 2006, para 38.
159 J White, 'Community care and the local government ombudsman for England' (2006) 9 CCLR 8, p9.
160 Cabinet Office consultation paper, *Reform of public sector ombudsmen services in England*, 2005.

'consult with each other and work together on cases and issues that are relevant to more than one of them'.

27.144   In July 2007 the local government ombudsman published a special report[161] addressing this issue in which it was noted that a regulatory reform order due to come into force on 1 August 2007 would remove the limitations on the ombudsmen's ability to carry out joint investigations and issue joint reports.

Health Service Ombudsman

27.145 The Health Service Commissioner (generally called the NHS (or Health Service) Ombudsman) has wide powers to investigate complaints concerning GPs, trusts and health authorities, including clinical practice. These powers derive from the Health Service Commissioners Act 1993 (as amended[162]) and provide (at section 3) for the commissioner to investigate complaints made:

> . . . by or on behalf of a person that he has sustained injustice or hardship in consequence of –
> (a) a failure in a service provided by a health service body,
> (b) a failure of such a body to provide a service which it was a function of the body to provide, or
> (c) maladministration connected with any other action taken by or on behalf of such a body,

27.146 Until 2006 the Health Service Ombudsman was responsible for health care complaints in both England and Wales. However as a result of the Public Services Ombudsman (Wales) Act 2005 her remit no longer extends beyond England, and in Wales the Public Services Ombudsman now discharges this function (in addition to the role of local government ombudsman and central government ombudsman). His role is considered briefly at para 27.151 below. The Health Service Ombudsman also fulfils the role of central government (or parliamentary) ombudsman and is based in London.[163]

27.147   Health Service Commissioners Act 1993 s5 contained a general inhibition on the investigation of matters of clinical judgment. This was repealed by Health Service Commissioners (Amendment) Act 1996 s6. Accordingly the potential scope of the Health Service Ombudsman's powers is wide. There are however limits, not least that she should restrict her investigations to the complaints that have been made and not (for instance) widen the scope of the investigation because she is concerned about separate or issues.[164]

---

161 Local Government Ombudsman, *Special Report: Handling complaints about local partnerships*, 2007.
162 By the Health Service Commissioners (Amendment) Act 1996 and HSC(CHS)A 2003 Part 2 chapter 9.
163 The Health Service Commissioner for England, Millbank Tower, Millbank, London SW1P 4QP, tel: 0845 0154033.
164 *Cavanagh and others v Health Service Commissioner* [2005] EWCA Civ 1578; [2006] 1 WLR 1229.

27.148   In general the Health Service Ombudsman cannot consider a complaint until the relevant NHS complaints procedures have been exhausted. A previous NHS ombudsman has however stated that:[165]

> In considering whether to investigate, I consider, case by case, what is the most appropriate way to resolve the particular complaint. If there is still scope for it to be done locally, then I shall continue to favour that. If, however, there is evidence of a breakdown of trust between the complainant and the NHS body, or if I believe that further local action would not satisfy the complainant, I may use my discretion to investigate the substance of the complaint when the matter first comes to me, even though it has not gone through all the possible stages of the NHS procedure.

27.149   Complaints must concern issues of maladministration and be made within one year of the date when the action complained about occurred. Details of the complaints procedures and past reports are accessible at the ombudsman's website.[166]

27.150   The Health Service Ombudsman has issued a number of highly influential reports concerning the provision of NHS continuing care and these are considered separately at para 14.25 above.

Public Services Ombudsman for Wales

27.151   The Office of Public Services Ombudsman for Wales came into being in April 2006, replacing the previous offices of the Local Government Ombudsman for Wales, Health Service Ombudsman for Wales, Welsh Administration Ombudsman and the Social Housing Ombudsman for Wales. These changes took effect as a consequence of the enactment of the Public Services Ombudsman (Wales) Act 2005. The ombudsman's office is on the outskirts of Bridgend in South Wales.[167]

27.152   In the Public Services Ombudsman's first year of operation, he received 1,698 complaints and of those that concerned public bodies, 16 per cent were NHS complaints and 10 per cent concerned social services. The procedure for making complaints is similar to that for the separate ombudsman in England.

Judicial review

27.153   Judicial review is a procedure by which the High Court reviews the lawfulness of decisions made by public bodies, such as the departments of state, local authorities and NHS bodies. Since applications for a judicial review must generally be made promptly and in any event within three

---

165   Health Service Commissioner, *Annual Report 1997/98* chapter 3.
166   http://www.ombudsman.org.uk.
167   Public Services Ombudsman for Wales, 1 Ffordd yr Hen Gae, Pencoed, CF35 5LJ, tel: 01656 641 150, website: http://www.ombudsman-wales.org.uk.

months of when the claim first arose,[168] it is vital that lawyers expert in this process be retained, if possible, and any action be commenced at the earliest opportunity.

27.154 In general this will require either legal aid funding (and obtaining this can take not inconsiderable time) or access to significant resources – although there is nothing to stop an individual seeking to take a judicial review without lawyers.[169] One difficulty with such a course, however, concerns the risk, if unsuccessful, of having to pay the costs of the other party. In certain situations the court is prepared to consider limiting the sum an unsuccessful party may have to pay by making what is known as a protective costs order. In *Refugee Legal Centre v SSHD*[170] Brooke LJ considered that such an order was appropriate for various reasons, including the fact that it was on behalf of an organisation which was on the face of it 'looking after the interests of vulnerable people against all the resources of the state'; that it concerned an allegation of 'systemic unfairness' which if not challenged by the Refugee Legal Centre would necessitate (to establish the 'systemic' nature) perhaps ten or more individual cases – which in turn would mean ten or more 'different legal aid certificates, perhaps ten different solicitors' firms, and counsel and solicitors' and so on.

27.155 Judicial review is primarily concerned with process rather than substance. It follows that for many community care disputes of a factual nature, it has severe limitations as a remedy. As Collins J observed in *Gunter v South Western Staffordshire PCT*:[171]

> Judicial review is an unsatisfactory means of dealing with cases . . . where there are judgments to be made and factual issues may be in dispute. At best, it can identify failures to have regard to material considerations and a need for a reconsideration. Very rarely if ever will it result in mandatory orders to the body which has the responsibility to reach the relevant decision.

27.156 In general the law allows private individuals or businesses to behave unreasonably or make capricious decisions; public bodies however have no such freedom. They must act reasonably in reaching decisions, and (since October 2000) must not act in any way which is incompatible with the European Convention on Human Rights.[172] If they fail to act in such a way, and significant injustice results, the High Court may be prepared to quash the decision and require that it be considered again without the contaminant of unfairness.

27.157 What is 'reasonable' depends upon the nature of the decision and the context in which it is to be made. It will invariably require that in reaching

---

168 CPR 54.5.
169 The procedure is detailed in CPR Part 54, accessible at http://www.justice.gov.uk/ civil/procrules_fin/contents/parts/part54.htm#rule54_5, and a useful guide to the process is J Manning, *Judicial Review Proceedings: a practitioner's guide*, 2nd edn, Legal Action Group, 2004. There are not inconsiderable court fees, although these can be reduced or waived.
170 [2004] EWCA Civ 1239.
171 [2005] EWHC 1894 (Admin); (2006) 9 CCLR 121 at [19].
172 HRA 1998 s6.

a decision all relevant matters be considered; that all irrelevant matters are disregarded; that the body correctly applies the relevant law (including that it has the power to make the decision). In certain situations reasonableness may require that prior to making a decision, consultation take place with persons who are likely to be affected. Likewise reasonableness may require that a particular decision making procedure be followed, if affected parties have a 'legitimate expectation' that this will occur. Even if a public body adheres to all these principles, its ultimate decision will be capable of judicial challenge if it bears no sensible relationship to the material facts on which it was based (if it in essence 'defies logic') or if the decision amounts to an abuse of power.

27.158   The High Court, through the use of judicial review, seeks to improve the way public bodies make decisions and thus contribute to a fairer and more open administrative system. It does not seek to usurp the powers of these bodies. It follows therefore that the court will only get involved if the aggrieved party acts swiftly and produces significant evidence, not only of a 'flawed' decision making process but also that as a consequence a real risk of injustice may result.

27.159   While decisions made by private or voluntary providers (such as independent nursing homes or voluntary sector day centres, etc) are not susceptible to judicial review (unless adopted by a responsible public body), they may constitute a breach of private law rights (eg, a breach of a contract with a nursing home).

Complaint to local authority monitoring officer

27.160   Where judicial review proceedings are contemplated, it is often advisable, as a preliminary step, to make a formal complaint to the local authority monitoring officer requesting that the impugned decision be reviewed. This may be in the form of (and constitute) the letter before action in appropriate cases. In general, the monitoring officer will be the senior legal officer of the authority.

27.161   The duties of the monitoring officer are set out in Local Government and Housing Act 1989 s5.[173] Section 5(2) provides that if it at any time it appears to the monitoring officer that 'any proposal, decision or omission by the authority' (or any officer or committee of the authority) is likely to contravene 'any enactment or rule of law or of any code of practice made or approved by or under any enactment' then the monitoring officer must investigate this and prepare a report on the issue in question. Formerly this obligation also applied to allegations that the authority's actions amounted to maladministration. The situation now, however, is that in such cases the monitoring officer has a power to investigate (which presumably it would be wise to do if the evidence provided were substantial) but not a duty – until such time as the local government ombudsman/ Public Service Ombudsman has 'conducted an investigation' in relation to

173 As amended by LGA 2003 s113.

the alleged maladministration.[174] Given that the duty to investigate and prepare a report is triggered by the monitoring officer receiving credible evidence that the law or a 'rule of law' has been (or will be) contravened, letters seeking the involvement of the monitoring officer should (if it be the case) be phrased in these terms.

27.162   The monitoring officers' functions were extended by the LGA 2000 to include consideration of allegations of misconduct against members and former members of the local authority who have been investigated by the authority's ethical standards officer (LGA 2000 ss59, 60 and 64). Under LGA 2000 s66 the secretary of state has power to make regulations to determine the way in which such matters should be dealt with.

Sufficient standing

27.163 In order to apply for judicial review, an applicant must have a sufficient interest in the matter to which the application relates.

27.164   In *R v Gloucestershire CC ex p RADAR*[175] Carnwath J considered an application by the Royal Association for Disability and Rehabilitation (RADAR) for judicial review of a decision made by Gloucestershire County Council relating to a general procedure which the council had adopted for the reassessment of the community care needs of disabled people. Having considered the relevant authorities (such as *R v Foreign Secretary ex p World Development Movement*[176]) he held:

> ... the general principle, that the Authority is obliged to go through a process of reassessment in respect of all those affected by the 1994 decision [consequent on the decision in *R v Gloucestershire CC ex p Mahfood*][177] is one which can, in my view, properly and conveniently be asserted by a body such as RADAR. It cannot be in anyone's interests that it should be left to each individual separately to assert that right. No doubt other individual test cases can be bought, but there is always a risk that if the particular individual loses his direct interest, either because his circumstances change or because the Authority carry out a reassessment, then the proceedings will prove abortive. In my view, RADAR has a sufficient interest to entitle it to a declaration as to the position as I have outlined it.

27.165 Carnwath J, however, went on to suggest that it would 'be very rare that it would be appropriate for a coercive order such as an order for mandamus, to be granted to a body like RADAR'.

An alternative remedy?

27.166 Judicial review is not available where the applicant has failed to pursue an equally convenient, expeditious and effective remedy. This will mean that, in the absence of cogent reasons, an applicant should first utilise the complaints procedures or seek to invoke an available 'default' remedy (see

---

174 Local Government and Housing Act s2A.
175 (1998) 1 CCLR 476.
176 [1995] 1 WLR 386, QBD.
177 (1997) 1 CCLR 7.

para 27.201 below). As a general rule disputes which are primarily factual are best suited to the complaints process and disputes which concern the interpretation of directions or guidance may be suited to resolution via the default procedures.[178]

27.167   The court may be prepared to entertain a judicial review, notwithstanding that the applicant has not attempted to use the complaints or default procedures, if it can be shown that there are substantial reasons for believing that these remedies are not 'equally convenient, expeditious and effective'. Frequently this will be the case where:

- the matter in issue is a clear-cut dispute of a legal definition;
- what is in issue is a blanket practice or fixed policy;
- there is an urgent need for the service (ie, a requirement for 'interim relief') or it can be otherwise shown that the complaints procedure would be incapable of adequately resolving the dispute.[179]

27.168   In *R v Gloucestershire CC ex p RADAR*[180] it was unsuccessfully argued that an application for judicial review could not be made until the alternative remedy of a local authority complaint under LASSA 1970 s7B had been pursued. Carnwath J held that in certain cases such a remedy might be appropriate, especially:

> . . . where individual relief is being sought. However, in relation to a general issue of principle as to the authority's obligations in law . . . I do not think that can be regarded as a suitable or alternative remedy to the procedure of judicial review.[181]

27.169   Likewise, in *R v Devon CC ex p Baker and others*[182] such an argument (not only that an alternative remedy via the complaints procedure existed, but also that under LASSA 1970 s7D the applicants should first have asked the secretary of state to use her default powers, see para 27.201), was rejected on the grounds that:

> . . . as the issue is entirely one in law in a developing field which is peculiarly appropriate for decisions by the Court rather than by the Secretary of State, I would hold that the Applicants in the Durham case were not precluded from making their application for Judicial Review by the availability of another remedy; the case is one which it is proper for this Court to entertain.[183]

27.170   In *Cowl and others v Plymouth CC*[184] the Court of Appeal spoke of the heavy obligation on lawyers in such disputes to resort to litigation only where it

---

178   *R v Westminster CC ex p P and others* (1998) 1 CCLR 486 and see also *R v Kirklees MBC ex p Good* (1998) 1 CCLR 506.
179   See R Gordon, *Community Care Assessments*, Longman, 1993, pp61 et seq.
180   (1998) 1 CCLR 506.
181   See also *R v Hampshire CC ex p Ellerton* [1985] 1 WLR 749, and *R v Kent CC ex p Bruce* (1996) *Times* 8 February.
182   [1995] 1 All ER 73.
183   Per Dillon LJ at p87; and see also *R v Brent LBC ex p Sawyers* [1994] 1 FLR 203, CA.
184   [2001] EWCA Civ 1935; [2002] 1 WLR 803; (2002) 5 CCLR 42 at [27]. Views reiterated by Maurice Kay J in *R (Dudley, Whitbread and others) v East Sussex CC* [2003] EWHC 1093 (Admin).

is unavoidable and in *R v Barking and Dagenham LBC ex p Lloyd*[185] the Court of Appeal held that it was not an appropriate organ to prescribe the degree of detail that should go into a care plan or the amount of consultation to be carried out with a patient's advisers. However speaking in a personal capacity, Collins J has stated that he is 'not persuaded that in general alternative dispute resolution (ADR) is appropriate in public law'.[186]

Grounds for judicial review

27.171 As noted above, judicial review generally concerns a challenge to the decision-making process (ie the procedure followed in coming to the decision) rather than to the decision itself. In such 'procedural' challenges, applicants are required to show some substantial flaw in the process by which the public body reached its decision. In certain cases, however, the court will entertain a 'substantive' challenge to the actual decision itself; for instance on the basis that (given the process followed) the impugned decision is so absurd that in reaching it, the local authority must 'have taken leave of [its] senses'.[187]

27.172   The principles underlying judicial review are sophisticated and multi-faceted and are continually being refined and developed by the judiciary. Thus, when in *Kruse v Johnson*[188] the High Court indicated that it would be prepared to set aside local authority decisions which were 'manifestly unjust, partial, made in bad faith or so gratuitous and oppressive that no reasonable person could think them justified', it was merely outlining the type of situation which might provoke judicial intervention, not making any definitive statement of the potential grounds for review. Likewise, 50 years later, in *Associated Provincial Picture Houses v Wednesbury Corporation*[189] when Lord Greene described what are now the classic '*Wednesbury*' principles, he was again only sketching out examples of administrative behaviour which might attract judicial censure, not seeking to compile an exhaustive list. In his judgment he instanced the following behaviour as being potentially justiciable:

- contravention of the law;
- a fettering of a discretion;
- unreasonableness in the sense of bad faith or dishonesty;
- failing to consider 'matters which he is bound to consider';
- failing to exclude matters which are irrelevant;

---

185 [2001] EWCA Civ 533; (2001) 4 CCLR 196, p205G; see also the comments of Munby J in *R (P and others) v Essex CC (and others)* [2004] EWHC 2027 (Admin) where he stressed that judicial review 'exists to adjudicate upon specific challenges to discrete decisions' and not to monitor and regulate the performance of public authorities.
186 Collins J, 'Community Care and the Administrative Court' (2006) 9 CCLR 5.
187 *R v Secretary of State for the Environment ex p Nottinghamshire CC* [1986] AC 240, p247, HL.
188 [1898] 2 QB 91.
189 [1948] 1 KB 223.

- reaching a decision that is 'so absurd that no sensible person could even dream that it lay within the powers of the authority'.

27.173 With the enactment of the HRA 1998, the courts have accepted that their traditional approach to administrative scrutiny may no longer be sufficient. In *R (Daly) v SSHD*,[190] Lord Steyn contrasted the traditional *Wednesbury* approach with the requirements of 'proportionality' – when a decision potentially engaged considerations of fundamental human rights. In his view there was considerable overlap between the two approaches and in most cases the same decision would be reached whichever approach was adopted. However in at least three ways, the procedures differed, such that in certain situations they were liable to 'yield different results':

> First, the doctrine of proportionality may require the reviewing court to assess the balance which the decision maker has struck, not merely whether it is within the range of rational or reasonable decisions. Secondly, the proportionality test may go further than the traditional grounds of review inasmuch as it may require attention to be directed to the relative weight accorded to interests and considerations. Thirdly, even the heightened scrutiny test developed in *R v Ministry of Defence, Ex p Smith* [1996] QB 517, 554 is not necessarily appropriate to the protection of human rights. It will be recalled that in *Smith* the Court of Appeal reluctantly felt compelled to reject a limitation on homosexuals in the army. The challenge based on article 8 of the Convention for the Protection of Human Rights and Fundamental Freedoms (the right to respect for private and family life) foundered on the threshold required even by the anxious scrutiny test. The European Court of Human Rights came to the opposite conclusion: *Smith and Grady v United Kingdom* (1999) 29 EHRR 493. The court concluded, at p 543, para 138:
>
> > 'the threshold at which the High Court and the Court of Appeal could find the Ministry of Defence policy irrational was placed so high that it effectively excluded any consideration by the domestic courts of the question of whether the interference with the applicants' rights answered a pressing social need or was proportionate to the national security and public order aims pursued, principles which lie at the heart of the court's analysis of complaints under article 8 of the Convention.'

27.174 The following sub-headings list some of the main principles which are used by the courts today, to test the validity of public law decisions. As indicated above, the labelling of these principles is not a taxonomic science, but merely an attempt to illustrate some of the more obvious characteristics of the jurisprudence in this field.

Illegality

27.175 A judicial review challenge on the grounds of illegality is based upon the notion that a 'decision-maker must understand correctly the law that regulates his decision-making power and give effect to it'.[191] Professor de

---

190 [2001] UKHL 26; [2001] 2 WLR 1622 at [27]–[28].
191 *Council of Civil Service Unions v Minister for the Civil Service* [1985] AC 374, p410, HL .

Smith[192] separates administrative decisions which are flawed for illegality into those which are either beyond the power which authorises the making of the decision, or those which pursue an objective other than that for which the power to make the decision was conferred. Illegality may present itself in a number of guises, for instance action by an authority which although within its power, has an ulterior and improper motive.[193] such as action designed to frustrate the purpose of a statute. Common examples are outlined below.

Ultra vires[194]

27.176 Social services and NHS bodies are statutory creatures and only able to act in accordance with the powers they have been given by statute (although as noted at para 1.67 above social services authorities' powers are now particularly wide). Accordingly it is unlawful for a public body to act beyond its powers (ultra vires).

27.177 By way of example, certain actions are well established as being in general outside social services authority powers; for instance the provision of nursing care by a registered nurse (see para 13.96 above) or the provision of residential accommodation to people entitled to NHS continuing care (see para 14.21 above).

Misdirection of law

27.178 A decision may be challenged by way of judicial review if the authority can be shown to have misunderstood the relevant law in reaching its decision,[195] although the mere existence of a mistake of law does not vitiate the impugned decision unless it 'is a relevant error of law, ie, an error in the actual making of the decision which affected the decision itself'.

27.179 Given the confusing and complex nature of community care law, there is clearly wide scope for local authority decisions to be challenged on this ground; for instance, in *R v Tower Hamlets LBC ex p Bradford*[196] the court held that the authority had fundamentally misunderstood its powers under CA 1989 Part III and so quashed the decision it had reached.

27.180 An authority may make an error of law by misunderstanding the nature of its statutory obligation; it may, for instance, consider its obligation to be discretionary when it is in fact mandatory.

Decision not made in accordance with the facts

27.181 The decision made by the authority must be in accordance with (and supported by) the evidence. Authorities cannot simply 'go through the motions' by paying lip service to the evidence but in reality having no

---

192 De Smith, Woolf and Jowell, *Judicial Review of Administrative Action*, 5th edn, Sweet & Maxwell, 1995.
193 Ibid, p330 note 69.
194 Action which is outside the public body's legal powers.
195 *R v Hull University Visitor ex p Page* [1993] AC 682, pp701–702, HL.
196 (1998) 1 CCLR 294; see para 24.53 above.

regard to the individual merits of the case.[197] Accordingly in *R v Avon CC ex p M*[198] Henry J overruled a decision by the social services authority which directly conflicted with a recommendation made by the panel. In so doing, he stated:

> The evidence before [the panel] had, as to the practicalities, been largely one way. The panel had directed themselves properly at law, and had arrived at a decision in line with the strength of the evidence before them . . . the strength, coherence and apparent persuasiveness of that decision had to be addressed head-on if it were to be set aside and not followed. These difficulties were not faced either by the Respondent's officers in their paper to the Social Services committee or by the Social Services committee themselves. Not to face them was either unintentional perversity on their part or showed a wrong appreciation of the legal standing of that decision. It seems to me that you do not properly reconsider a decision when, on the evidence, it is not seen that the decision was given the weight it deserved.

Relevant and irrelevant considerations

27.182 A basic tenet of the *Wednesbury* decision is that a decision-maker must take into account all relevant considerations before making the decision and must ignore the irrelevant. Whether or not a consideration is 'relevant' is initially a question for the decision maker and as a general rule courts will only intervene if the failure to take it into account is either perverse or 'one which, on the true construction of the relevant statute, Parliament must have expressly or impliedly identified as being required to be considered'.[199]

27.183   In *R v Avon CC ex p M* the court found that the authority, in deciding which residential placement to support, had ignored the applicant's psychological needs. In so doing it failed to take account of a relevant (and in the court's view a 'crucial') consideration. In addition, the authority had decided that the applicant's preferred home should not be funded because (among other reasons) such a funding decision would 'set a precedent'. In this context the judge held that this was a misleading consideration; essentially whether or not the decision set a precedent was irrelevant. The same principle applies to the local ombudsman's decision[200] on a complaint against East Sussex County Council. The complaint concerned a panel's refusal to recommend the payment of compensation for benefits a service user lost as a result of wrong advice he received from the social services department. The ombudsman held that the refusal was based upon an irrelevant consideration (namely that it was the Benefits Agency, not the local authority, which was responsible for the payment of such benefits).

---

197 *Hemns v Wheller* [1948] 2 KB 61 and *Sagnata Investments v Norwich Corporation* [1971] 2 QB 614, CA.

198 (1999) 2 CCLR 185.

199 See *R (Ireneschild) v Lambeth LBC* [2007] EWCA Civ 234 at [41] where this quotation from *CREEDNZ v Governor-General* [1981] 1 NZLR 172 first adopted in *In re Findlay* [1985] AC 318 was cited with approval.

200 Complaint no 93/A/3738 against East Sussex CC.

Fettering of discretion

27.184 While an authority 'charged with exercising an administrative discretion is entitled to promulgate a policy or guidelines as an indication of a norm which is intended to be followed',[201] it is not entitled to fetter its discretion by approaching a decision with a pre-determined policy as to how all cases falling within a particular class will be treated. Accordingly in *R v Ealing LBC ex p Leaman*[202] Mann J held that where a disabled person had applied to a local authority under CSDPA 1970 s2(1)(f) for financial assistance in taking a privately arranged holiday, it was an error of law for the authority to decline to consider the application on the ground that it would only grant such assistance for holidays which it itself had arranged or sponsored (as the Act specifically allows for the support of holidays 'provided under arrangements made by the authority or otherwise'). On this principle, it would also be unlawful for an authority to have a fixed policy that it will not fund home help which consists solely of cleaning a house or ironing, etc (as no such limitation is imposed by CSDPA 1970 s2(1)(a)); likewise fixed policies by health or local authorities in relation to drug rehabilitation, which either confine such rehabilitation solely to funding detoxification (as opposed to harm minimisation or stabilisation) or where there is a fixed policy only to fund detoxification for a fixed and limited period, would again amount to a fettering of discretion (given again, that no such limitations are imposed by the primary legislation).[203]

27.185 In *R v North West Lancashire Health Authority ex p A*[204] the Court of Appeal held that the respondent's policy of not providing treatment for gender reassignment 'save in cases of overriding clinical need' was 'nonsense' since the authority considered that there was no effective treatment for the condition, and accordingly an 'overriding clinical need' could not arise. Auld, LJ held:

> ... the stance of the authority, coupled with the near uniformity of its reasons for rejecting each of the respondent's requests for funding was not a genuine application of a policy subject to individually determined exceptions of the sort considered acceptable by Lord Scarman in *Findlay*.[205] It is similar to the over-rigid application of the near 'blanket policy' questioned by Judge J in *R v Warwickshire County Council ex p Collymore* [1995] ELR 217, at 224 *et seq*
>
> > 'which while in theory admitting exceptions, may not, in reality result in the proper consideration of each individual case on its merits'.

27.186 The court also made reference to *R v Bexley LBC ex p Jones*[206] where Leggatt LJ held:

---

201 See *R v Eastleigh BC ex p Betts* [1983] 2 AC 613, HL.
202 (1984) *Times* 10 February.
203 National Assistance Act 1948 s21, subject to the directions in LAC (93) 10 Appendix 1 para 2(6) and under National Health Service Act 1977 Sch 8 para 2, subject to the secretary of state's directions in LAC (93) (10) Appendix 3 para 3(3)(g).
204 (1999) *Times*, 24 August.
205 *In re Findlay* [1985] 1 AC 316.
206 [1995] ELR 42, p55.

It is . . . legitimate for a statutory body . . . to adopt a policy designed to ensure a rational and consistent approach to the exercise of a statutory discretion in particular types of case. But it can only do so provided that the policy fairly admits of exceptions to it. In my judgment, the respondents effectively disabled themselves from considering individual cases and there has been no convincing evidence that at any material time they had an exceptions procedure worth the name. There is no indication that there was a genuine willingness to consider individual cases.

Unlawful delegation or dictation

27.187   Decision makers cannot avoid their duties by allowing themselves to be dictated to by, or simply accepting the decision of, another body.[207] Decision makers may not delegate their decisions to others unless they have specific power to do so and have done so properly. In the context of community care, for example, local authorities cannot ordinarily delegate their duty to undertake community care assessments (see para 3.44 above) or assessments of carers (see para 16.44 above).

Procedural impropriety

27.188   Procedural impropriety embraces a number of issues of natural justice.

The duty to act fairly

27.189   Decision makers must act fairly, must not be biased, must allow a party time to prepare his or her case, must ensure that a party has a proper opportunity to be heard, and in appropriate situations, must give reasons for their decisions.

27.190   In *R (Montgomery) v Hertfordshire CC*,[208] for instance, the court held that the local authority had acted unlawfully because it had:

> . . . failed manifestly and flagrantly to comply with the fundamental principles of fairness. They had given no notice of their action, they did not explain the grounds of their action, they have not explained the basis of future fears based upon the past complaints and they have not given the claimant any opportunity before this decision was taken to respond to any such matters with effective representations.

Legitimate expectation and the abuse of power

27.191   The courts, initially, developed the notion of 'legitimate expectation' as a facet of 'procedural impropriety' or the requirement of administrative fairness. The courts are now extending the doctrine's reach to encompass substantive challenges. The basic principle, however, requires that if a public authority has committed itself to acting in a certain way it should meet that commitment in the absence of a good reason not to do so.[209] Put

---

207   J Manning, *Judicial Review Proceedings*, 2nd edn, Legal Action Group, 2004, para 6.78.
208   [2005] EWHC 2026 (Admin) at [34].
209   *R (Goldsmith) v Wandsworth LBC* (2004) EWCA Civ 1170; (2004) 7 CCLR 472.

another way, it requires that no decision should be taken which will adversely affect an individual, without that person being given an opportunity to make representations as to why the particular benefit or advantage should not be withdrawn.[210]

27.192   In *R v North and East Devon Health Authority ex p Coughlan*[211] the Court of Appeal reviewed the development of the doctrine which it considered had 'emerged as a distinct application of the concept of abuse of power in relation to substantive as well as procedural benefits'. The court continued:

> Legitimate expectation may play different parts in different aspects of public law. The limits to its role have yet to be finally determined by the courts. Its application is still being developed on a case by case basis. Even where it reflects procedural expectations, for example concerning consultation, it may be affected by an overriding public interest. It may operate as an aspect of good administration, qualifying the intrinsic rationality of policy choices. And without injury to the *Wednesbury* doctrine it may furnish a proper basis for the application of the new established concept of abuse of power.[212]

and

> . . . in relation to this category of legitimate expectation, we do not consider it necessary to explain the modern doctrine in *Wednesbury* terms, helpful though this is in terms of received jurisprudence . . . We would prefer to regard the *Wednesbury* categories themselves as the major instances (not necessarily the sole ones . . .) of how public power may be misused. Once it is recognised that conduct which is an abuse of power is contrary to law its existence must be for the court to determine.[213]

27.193 An example of legitimate expectation is found in *R (Theophilus) v Lewisham LBC*.[214] The claimant accepted a place to study law at a college in Dublin, after the authority informed her that she would receive student support if she studied anywhere in the European Union. The authority subsequently informed her that it had made an error and she was not entitled to support under the Education (Student Support) Regulations 2001.[215] This was correct, but the local authority continued to have power to fund the placement under LGA 2000 s2 (see para 1.67 above). On the basis of the legitimate expectation, created by the promise of grant support, the authority was held obliged to use its powers under the 2000 Act.

27.194   An authority may be released of its obligation to meet a person's legitimate expectation where the circumstances have changed after it gave its undertaking – *R (Lindley) v Tameside MBC*.[216]

---

210   *Council of Civil Service Unions v Minister for the Civil Service* [1985] AC 374, HL.
211   [2000] 2 WLR 622; (1999) 2 CCLR 285, CA.
212   Ibid, p311.
213   Ibid, p315.
214   [2002] EWHC 1371 (Admin); [2002] 3 All ER 851.
215   SI No 951.
216   [2006] EWHC 2296 (Admin).

The duty to consult

27.195 The principle of procedural propriety also appears, in certain situations, as a duty to consult. In *R v Devon CC and Durham CC ex p Baker*[217] it was stated that the duty:

> . . . encompasses those cases in which it is held that a particular procedure, not otherwise required by law in the protection of an interest, must be followed consequent upon some specific promise or practice. Fairness requires that the public authority be held to it.

27.196 In this case, the court quashed a decision by Durham County Council to close various residential care homes because the authority had not properly consulted (see para 7.135 above). The court approved an earlier judgment[218] where the duty to consult was formulated as consisting of four parts, the requirements being:

> First that the consultation must be at a time when proposals are still at a formative stage. Second that the proposer must give sufficient reasons for any proposal to permit of intelligent consideration and response. Third . . . that adequate time must be given for consideration and response and, finally, fourth, that the product of consultation must be conscientiously taken into account in finalising any statutory proposals.[219]

27.197 In general consultations should conform to the Cabinet Office's code of practice[220] which states that 12 weeks should be 'standard minimum period' for a consultation exercise. It also states that the:

> Timing of consultation should be built into the planning process for a policy (including legislation) or service from the start so that it has the best prospect of improving the proposals concerned, and so that sufficient time is left for it at each stage.

27.198 The courts have shown increasing impatience with cases alleging a lack of adequate consultation preceding decisions to close care homes (see para 7.138) and noted that this is always likely to be an imperfect art – particularly when service users have limited mental capacity. In *R (Grabham) v Northamptonshire CC*,[221] for example, Black J observed:

> It was inevitable, in my view, that consulting adults with learning disabilities would be a challenging process. Perfection will never be achieved in such an exercise. However the council give every appearance of having gone about it responsibly and they succeeded to a tolerable extent. I do not think that it can validly be argued that such flaws as there were invalidated the consultation.

217 [1995] 1 All ER 73, QBD.
218 *R v Brent LBC ex p Gunning* (1986) 84 LGR 168.
219 [1995] 1 All ER 89, p91.
220 Cabinet Office, *Code of Practice on Written Consultation*, 2000, accessible at http://archive.cabinetoffice.gov.uk/servicefirst/2000/consult/code/_consultation.pdf.
221 [2006] EWHC 3292 (Admin) at [64].

The duty to act in accordance with mandatory or directory requirements

27.199 A further requirement of the duty to act fairly is that the decision-maker must comply with procedures laid down by parliament. This is sometimes known as the duty to act in accordance with 'mandatory or directory requirements'. In *R v North Yorkshire CC ex p Hargreaves*[222] it was accepted that the respondent authority, in assessing the applicant's sister's needs, failed to take into account the preferences of the sister, contrary to the mandatory (or directory) requirements set out in the 1990 policy guidance.[223] As the guidance was made under LASSA 1970 s7(1) requiring authorities to act 'under' such guidance, a failure to do so rendered the decision unlawful. Dyson J held that the requirements of the 1990 policy guidance were mandatory and that the decision should, therefore, be quashed. See also *Secretary of State for Trade and Industry v Langridge*[224] where guidance was given on the principles to be applied in deciding whether a particular duty is mandatory or directory.

The duty to give reasons

27.200 Although there is no general duty on authorities to give reasons for their decisions, where the relevant statute, regulation or direction stipulates that reasons should be given, then the reasons must be 'proper, adequate and intelligible' and must deal with the substantial points raised by the complainant. An unparticularised assertion that 'on the evidence' the decision maker makes certain findings 'and recommends . . .' will be considered, in general, to be inadequate.[225] In the absence of an express provision requiring the giving of reasons, they may nevertheless be required, if, for instance, the decision would otherwise be unintelligible, or would contravene the minimum standards of fairness.[226]

Default procedures

27.201 LASSA 1970 s7D[227] provides:

(1) If the Secretary of State is satisfied that any local authority have failed without reasonable excuse, to comply with any of their duties which are social services functions[228] (other than a duty imposed by or under the Children Act 1989,[229] section 1 or 2(4) of the Adoption (Intercountry Aspects) Act 1999 or the Adoption and Children Act 2002), he may

---

222 (1994) 30 September, QBD, CO/878/94.
223 Paras 3.16 and 3.25; and see also *R v Islington LBC ex p Rixon* (1998) 1 CCLR 119.
224 [1991] 2 WLR 1343.
225 See paras 27.46 and 27.66 above.
226 *R v Secretary of State for Home Department ex p Doody* [1993] 3 WLR 154, HL.
227 Inserted by National Health Service and Community Care Act 1990 s50 and replacing an equivalent provision under National Assistance Act 1948 s36(1).
228 A function set out in LASSA 1970 Sch 1 other than a duty imposed by or under the CA 1989.
229 An equivalent default power is found in CA 1989 s84.

make an order declaring that authority to be in default with respect to the duty in question.

(2) An order under subsection (1) may contain such directions for the purpose of ensuring that the duty is complied with within such period as may be specified in the order as appear to the Secretary of State to be necessary.

(3) Any such direction shall, on the application of the Secretary of State, be enforceable by mandamus.

27.202 On the face of it, a person aggrieved by a local authority decision may seek redress by making formal request to the secretary of state that he or she use this default power to remedy the particular injustice. In reality such executive powers are rarely if ever exercised. The power under LASSA 1970 s7D is no exception; it appears that it has never been used, and it is highly unlikely that, in anything but the most extreme of situations, it would be so exercised. The power can only be used where the authority has failed to exercise a 'duty' (rather than a 'power'); it only arises if the local authority has 'no reasonable excuse' for its failure; the secretary of state has to be 'satisfied' about the lack of any reasonable excuse; and even then he or she has wide discretion whether or not to take any such action.

27.203 In LASSL (96)12[230] the Department of Health set out its policy on responding to correspondence received from the public (as well as from MPs and corporate bodies). In general the department copies the correspondence to the relevant authority, but (at para 10):

> ... where the letter seems strongly to suggest that SSD policy or practice may be inconsistent in some significant respect with the law or Departmental guidance we will normally expect to reply substantively ourselves, but will refer the letter to the SSD for their observations before doing so.

27.204 In practice such an exchange, where the local authority is required to explain its position to the department, can prove to be an effective lever. There is some evidence that this action has, in the past at least, led to a resolution of various problems.[231]

27.205 In *R v Kent CC ex p Bruce*[232] it was held that the secretary of state was not a 'tribunal of fact' and in considering whether to exercise the default procedure 'must properly be concerned with whether the local authority had misdirected itself in law or formed an irrational view of the facts'. In *R v Devon CC ex p Baker and others*[233] an argument that the existence of the default procedure constituted an alternative remedy which thereby excluded the use of judicial review was, in this particular case, rejected (see para 7.135 above).

230 LASSL 96(12) *Correspondence on Social Services Matters*, 21 January 1997.
231 See eg pp5 et seq of *Putting Teeth into the Act*, a report produced by RADAR on attempts made between 1970–81 to enforce CSDPA 1970 s2.
232 (1986) *Times* 8 February.
233 [1985] 1 All ER 73.

27.206   In *R v Westminster CC ex p P and others*[234] four destitute asylum seekers challenged the policy of various London boroughs to accommodate them outside London. Simon Brown LJ, in rejecting the application (on grounds that there was an alternative remedy) held as follows:

> For my part I have reached the clear conclusion that the more 'convenient, expeditious and effective' course here is indeed that of applying to the Secretary of State to exercise his default powers under s7D. This is par excellence an area of administration in which the Secretary of State rather than the courts should be closely involved. In the first place it is the Secretary of State who funds the housing of asylum seekers under s21 of the 1948 Act. Secondly, it is the proper construction and application of his own Directions and Guidance which lie at the heart of the dispute. Thirdly, it was at the Secretary of State's insistence that the appeal form the Court of Appeal's decision in *R v Westminster CC ex p M*,[235] which was to be heard by the House of Lords last month, was adjourned, specifically because the Government are currently conducting a review of the treatment of asylum seekers and did not wish to risk a final judgment depriving asylum seekers of all protection until a decision had been made as to what (if any) alternative arrangements should be made.

The European Convention on Human Rights

27.207 The following section makes reference to the case law of the European Court of Human Rights: all judgments of the court are accessible on the Council of Europe website.[236]

27.208   HRA 1998 s6, in general terms, makes it unlawful for a public body to act in such a way as to violate a person's 'convention rights'.[237] Section 6(3)(b) of the Act extends the definition of public authority to cover bodies which, although not public authorities, who exercise functions of a 'public nature'. It was assumed at the time the Act came into force that this would mean that independent providers of community care services would be covered by the definition (for instance care homes accommodating frail elderly residents at public expense or day centres run by charities under a contract with the local authority). However the courts have consistently applied a restrictive interpretation to the concept of 'public authority' such that independent providers of this kind are generally excluded from the reach of the Act.

27.209   In *YL v Birmingham City Council and others*[238] the House of Lords held (applying its earlier decision in *Parish of Aston Cantlow v Wallbank* (2003)[239]) that for the purposes of section 6 there are two types of 'public authority' – namely 'core' and 'hybrid' authorities. Core authorities (eg local author-

234   (1998) 1 CCLR 486 and see also *R v Kirklees MBC ex p Good* (1998) 1 CCLR 506.
235   *R v Westminster CC ex p M* (1997) 1 CCLR 85.
236   http://cmiskp.echr.coe.int/tkp197/search.asp?skin=hudoc-en.
237   An 'act' for the purposes of s6 includes 'a failure to act' – HRA 1998 s6(6).
238   [2007] UKHL 27; [2007] 3 WLR 112; (2007) 10 CCLR 505.
239   [2003] UKHL 37: [2003] 3 WLR 283 : [2003] 3 All ER 1213.

ities and government departments) are classic public bodies who are unable to rely on the convention in court proceedings (ie they cannot be victims of a convention violation[240]) whereas hybrid authorities can. In the majority Lords opinion (Lord Bingham and Baroness Hale dissenting) a private care home providing accommodation for elderly residents under a contract with a local authority was not even a hybrid public body exercising 'functions of a public nature' for the purposes of the 1998 Act. It considered that the arrangement of care and accommodation for those unable to arrange it themselves was an inherently public function – but not the actual provision of that care. In a joint response to the judgment[241] the Disability Rights Commission, JUSTICE, Liberty, the British Institute of Human Rights, Help the Aged, and Age Concern England observed:

> Whilst the decision of the House of Lords does not affect the responsibility of local authorities to protect the human rights of those they place in residential care, this will be of little comfort to those, like YL, who are placed by authorities in care homes run by the private or voluntary sector. Residents and their families should be able to challenge human rights abuses 'at source'. This decision means that instead, complaints must be taken all the way to the local authority. This will almost certainly be a disincentive for those already frightened by the prospect of 'speaking out' against poor treatment. In practical terms, an individual's rights in these circumstances will be of lesser value than if they existed against the care home itself. In some cases – notably in home closure situations – a remedy against the local authority will be worthless.
>
> In addition, any contractual term imposed on the care home to observe residents' Convention rights is not an adequate substitute for potential liability of the care home under the HRA. Where behaviour is incompatible with a Convention right, such treatment needs to be seen in those terms and not merely as a matter of private law. A finding that the HRA has been breached would send a strong signal to all care homes that such behaviour is a violation of fundamental human rights and cannot be tolerated in a democratic society. Crucially, it would also help to encourage the development of a positive culture in which respect for fundamental rights is placed at the heart of care home service provision. A court action in contract law would not have the same impact. In any event, despite guidelines on procurement, there is no guarantee that contractual terms relating to HRA compliance will be in place in every case where a breach may occur, nor that any existing contract terms will be enforceable by the care home resident as a matter of contract law.

27.210　Where a violation of such a 'convention right' by a public body is alleged to have occurred, an individual can institute court proceedings (HRA 1998 s7) for (among other things) compensation (HRA 1998 s8). In *R (Bernard) v Enfield LBC*[242] the court considered that the appropriate level of damages for violations of the 1998 Act was that which would have been

---

240　For further discussion on the issue of 'victimhood' see Harlow C [2000] PL Autumn 2000 490 and see also Oliver. D (2000) The Frontiers of the State: Public Authorities and Public Functions under the Human Rights Act [2000] PL 476.
241　Accessible at www.bihr.org/downloads/YL_Response_of_Interveners.pdf
242　[2002] EWHC 2282 (Admin); (2002) 5 CCLR 577.

awarded by the local government ombudsman. However in *Anufrijeva and others v Southwark LBC*[243] the Court of Appeal cautioned against such an approach, without however disagreeing with the damages awarded in the *Enfield* case (a total of £10,000 – see below). In *Anufrijeva* the Court of Appeal suggested[244] that permission ought not to be given at the leave stage to proceed by way of judicial review unless the claimant satisfied the court that a complaint to the ombudsman was not more appropriate. Speaking in a personal capacity[245] Collins J has expressed doubt as to whether this could in fact be correct since LGA 1974 s26(6)(c) states that the local government ombudsman cannot act in respect of 'any action in respect of which the person aggrieved has or had a remedy by way of proceedings in any court of law'.

Convention rights

27.211 The Convention rights of most relevance in the context of community care law are articles 2, 3 5, 6, 8 and 14 of the European Convention on Human Rights. These articles are considered elsewhere in this text (see for instance paras 3.194, 4.48, 4.71, 18.39 and 25.11 above) and what follows is merely a brief summary of the general scope of the rights. For a detailed analysis of their nature reference should be made to one of the many specialist texts on this subject.[246]

Article 2: the right to life

27.212 Article 2, although primarily negative in nature (ie requiring the state to refrain from arbitrarily killing people[247]), has been held to place a positive obligation on the state to protect life.[248] Cases are likely to occur concerning actions by health and social services authorities which might be harmful, such as the closure of dementia wards or residential care homes, as well as decisions not to provide treatment for people with serious illness, such as the decision in *R v Cambridge Health Authority ex p B*[249] considered at para 13.13 above).

27.213 Violations of the obligations under article 2 have been found in cases such as the failure to protect a vulnerable prisoner from a dangerous

---

243 [2003] EWCA Civ 1406; [2004] 2 WLR 603; (2003) 6 CCLR 415 at [53]. See also *R (Greenfield) v SSHD* [2005] UKHL 14; [2005] 1 WLR 673 where the House of Lords endorsed the approach in *Anufrijeva*, and *Andrews v Reading BC* [2004] EWHC 970 (Admin); [2004] 2 All ER(D) 319 where however Collins J held that where a claim under the HRA 1998 does not depend upon proving maladministration, then *Anufrijeva* does not prevent the claim being issued in the county or High Court.

244 *R (Anufrijeva) v Southwark LBC* [2003] EWCA Civ 1406; [2004] 2 WLR 603; (2003) 6 CCLR 415 at [81].

245 Collins J, 'Community care and the Administrative Court' (2006) 9 CCLR 5.

246 See eg L Clements and J Read, *Disabled People and European Human Rights*, Policy Press, 2003.

247 *McCann v UK* (1995) 21 EHRR 97.

248 *Osman v UK* (1998) EHRR 245, p305 – and see generally L Clements and J Read, *Disabled People and the Right to Life*, Routledge, 2007.

249 [1995] 1 WLR 898, CA.

cellmate.[250] The court has accepted that positive obligations require special measures to be taken to protect potentially suicidal patients[251] and may require individuals to be warned if exposed to any serious environmental or health risks.[252] The Commission has likewise considered the extent of the state's obligation to reduce the risks of a vaccination programme[253] or to fund a health service.[254] There are however limits to the obligation under article 2; it cannot for instance be construed to provide a right for an incapacitated adult to have another assist her in dying (*Pretty v United Kingdom*[255]).

Article 3: degrading treatment

27.214   As with article 2, article 3 is also primarily negative in its scope – requiring states to refrain from subjecting anyone to torture, inhuman and degrading treatment. It too, however, has been held to place a positive obligation on the state to take reasonable measures to ensure no one is subjected to such treatment.

27.215   The court has emphasised that for treatment to be 'degrading' it must reach a minimum threshold of severity,[256] although it has indicated that this may be significantly lower for disabled[257] and elderly people.[258] Arbitrary and gross acts of discrimination may exceptionally be considered to violate article 3, even in the absence of actual physical or mental harm.[259] The negative obligations under article 3 are engaged by detention conditions,[260] corporal punishment[261] and poor prison conditions.[262] Extradition may violate article 3 if the expelled person is thereby put at risk of degrading treatment: even (exceptionally) if solely a consequence of inadequate medical treatment in the receiving country.[263]

27.216   As noted above (para 25.11) article 3 has been construed as creating a positive obligation on states to ensure that no one suffers from degrading treatment, and in this respect eligibility criteria cannot exclude services from persons at 'significant risk of harm' (see para 3.195 above). The case-law on article 3 has established that the courts and social services are obliged to use their powers to protect children[264] and vulnerable

250   *Edwards v UK* (2002) 35 EHRR 19.
251   *Keenan v UK* (2001) 33 EHRR 38.
252   *LCB v UK* (1998) 27 EHRR 212.
253   *Association X v UK* DR 14/31.
254   *Osman v UK* (1998) 29 EHRR 245.
255   (2002) 35 EHRR 1; and see also domestic proceedings at [2001] UKHL 61; [2001] 3 WLR 1598.
256   *Costello-Roberts v UK* (1993) 19 EHRR 112.
257   *Price v UK* (2001) 34 EHRR 1285; (2002) 5 CCLR 306.
258   See *Papon v France* [2001] Crim LR 917, an inadmissibility decision.
259   See *Cyprus v Turkey* (2002) 35 EHRR 30 and *Patel v UK (the East African Asians case)* (1981) 3 EHRR 76.
260· *McGlinchley v United Kingdom* (2003) 37 EHRR 41.
261   *Campbell and Cosans v UK* (1982) 2 EHRR 293.
262   *Napier v Scottish Ministers* (2001) *Times* 15 November and see also *Price v UK* (2001) 34 EHRR 1285; (2002) 5 CCLR 306.
263   *D v UK* (1997) 24 EHRR 423.
264   *Z and others v UK* (2002) 34 EHRR 97.

adults[265] from abuse. Where credible evidence exists that an individual has suffered abuse while in the care of a public authority, a positive obligation arises under article 3 for an independent and open investigation to be convened.[266]

27.217   *Price v UK*[267] concerned a Thalidomide impaired applicant who in the course of debt recovery proceedings refused to answer questions put to her and was committed to prison for seven days for contempt of court. She alleged that she suffered degrading treatment as a result of the prison's inadequate facilities, but the UK government argued that any discomfort she experienced had not reached the minimum level of severity required by article 3. The court however considered that the threshold depended 'on all the circumstances of the case, such as the duration of the treatment, its physical and mental effects and, in some cases, the sex, age and state of health of the victim', and after a thorough review it concluded:

> . . . that to detain a severely disabled person in conditions where she is dangerously cold, risks developing sores because her bed is too hard or unreachable, and is unable to go to the toilet or keep clean without the greatest of difficulty, constitutes degrading treatment contrary to Article 3.

27.218 Of particular interest was the concurring opinion of Judge Greve, in which she stated:

> It is obvious that restraining any non-disabled person to the applicant's level of ability to move and assist herself, for even a limited period of time, would amount to inhuman and degrading treatment – possibly torture. In a civilised country like the United Kingdom, society considers it not only appropriate but a basic humane concern to try to ameliorate and compensate for the disabilities faced by a person in the applicant's situation. In my opinion, these compensatory measures come to form part of the disabled person's bodily integrity.

Article 5: detention

27.219 Article 5(1) places a total prohibition upon a state's power to detain people except in six clearly defined instances, including under article 5(1)(e) 'the lawful detention of persons for the prevention of the spreading of infectious diseases, of persons of unsound mind, alcoholics or drug addicts or vagrants'. A substantial body of case-law exists concerning the Convention requirements that must be satisfied before a mental health service user can be legally detained, and the MHA 1983 was largely a response to a number of adverse Strasbourg judgements.[268] Increasingly the court is requiring detention under this ground to be accompanied by a suitably therapeutic environment.[269]

---

265 *In re F (Adult: Court's jurisdiction)* [2000] 3 WLR 1740; (2000) 3 CCLR 210.
266 *Assenov v Bulgaria* (1998) 28 EHRR 652; see also *Labita v Italy* (2000) 6 April, unreported.
267 (2001) 34 EHRR 1285; (2002) 5 CCLR 306.
268 See eg *X v UK* (1981) 4 EHRR 188; *Ashingdane v UK* (1985) 7 EHRR 528 and *Winterwerp v Netherlands* (1979) 2 EHRR 387.
269 *Aerts v Belgium* (1998) 29 EHRR 50.

27.220   In *Winterwerp v Netherlands*[270] and a series of subsequent cases,[271] the court has laid down a number of factors which must be satisfied before the detention of a person of unsound mind is lawful within the meaning of the Convention, including:

1. The mental disorder must be reliably established by objective medical expertise.
2. The nature or degree of the disorder must be sufficiently extreme to justify the detention.
3. The detention should only last as long as the medical disorder (and its required severity) persists.
4. If the detention is potentially indefinite, then there must be a system of periodic reviews by a tribunal that has power to discharge.
5. The detention must be in a hospital, clinic or other appropriate institution authorised for the detention of such persons.[272]

27.221   Anyone detained for the purposes of article 5 must be so detained 'in accordance with a procedure prescribed by law'. *HL v UK*[273] concerned a challenge in the European Court of Human Rights to a decision of the House of Lords, known as the *Bournewood* case.[274] The European Court held that the lack of any procedural protection for 'informally detained' patients violated article 5(1) and it rejected the UK's argument that such people were not 'detained', stating:

> . . . the right to liberty is too important in a democratic society for a person to lose the benefit of Convention protection for the single reason that he may have given himself up to be taken into detention . . . especially when it is not disputed that that person is legally incapable of consenting to, or disagreeing with, the proposed action.

27.222   In the Strasbourg Court's opinion, he was detained because he was 'under continuous supervision and control and was not free to leave':[275] it was 'not determinative whether the ward was "locked" or "lockable"': a person could be detained, 'even during a period when he was in an open ward with regular unescorted access to the unsecured hospital grounds and unescorted leave outside the hospital'.

Article 6: fair hearing

27.223   Article 6(1) entrenches the right of parties to a fair hearing when their civil rights are affected (or when charged with a criminal offence). It requires

270   (1979) 2 EHRR 387.
271   See eg *X v UK* (1981) 4 EHRR 188 and *Ashingdane v UK* (1985) 7 EHRR 528.
272   *Ashingdane v UK* (1985) 7 EHRR 528 at [44] and see *Aerts v Belgium* (1998) 29 EHRR 50 where the court found a violation of article 5(1) in relation to the detention of the applicant in the psychiatric wing of a prison which was not an 'appropriate establishment' in view of the lack of qualified personnel.
273   (2005) 40 EHRR 32.
274   *R v Bournewood Community and Mental Health NHS Trust ex p L* [1998] 3 WLR 107; (1997) 1 CCLR 390.
275   See also in this respect, *JE v DE and Surrey CC* [2006] EWHC 3459 (Fam); (2007) 10 CCLR 149 where Munby J considered the crucial question to be whether or not the individual was objectively 'free to leave'.

hearings to be before 'independent and impartial' tribunals and to be held within a 'reasonable time' which may require 'exceptional diligence' to ensure early listing.[276] A difficulty experienced with the application of article 6(1) concerns the way the European Court of Human Rights has interpreted the phrase 'civil rights'. Put simply it covers the laws of a particular country which are neither criminal nor administrative/public law rights. In general civil rights are 'private law' rights, concerned with such matters as employment, property and commercial law. A 'civil' dispute must generally be something that could be the subject of proceedings in the county court, or before the relevant social security or planning or employment tribunal. Thus a dispute concerning a child's education is not considered a civil dispute[277] (although it engages a Convention right – article 2 of the first protocol), whereas a dispute about social security benefits is considered civil.[278]

27.224   The right to a fair hearing may require the state to take positive action to ensure legal or advocacy assistance is available to a party under a disability. As the court observed in *Airey v Ireland*:[279]

> . . . the fulfilment of a duty under the Convention on occasion necessitates some positive action on the part of the State; in such circumstances, the State cannot simply remain passive . . . The obligation to secure an effective right of access to the courts falls into this category of duty.

Article 8: private life, family and home

27.225 The court has consistently defined article 8 as positive in nature.[280] This arises out of the presence of the word 'respect': rather than obliging states 'not to interfere' with private and family life, article 8(1) provides that 'everyone has the right to respect for his private and family life, his home and his correspondence'. The demonstration of 'respect' is inherently positive in nature.

27.226   While family life, the home and correspondence have been given their everyday meanings, the concept of 'private life' has acquired an altogether more expansive interpretation, including a 'person's physical and psychological integrity' for which respect is due in order to 'ensure the development, without outside interference, of the personality of each individual in his relations with other human beings'.[281] Thus issues of sexual rights,[282] environmental pollution,[283] physical barriers to movement,[284] access to files[285]

---

276 *H v UK* (1988) 10 EHRR 95; see also *P and D v UK* [1996] EHRLR 526.
277 *R v Alperton Community School and others ex p B and others* [2001] EWHC 229 (Admin).
278 *Schuler-Zgraggen v Switzerland* (1995) 16 EHRR 405.
279 (1979) 2 EHRR 305.
280 *Marckx v Belgium* (1979) 2 EHRR 330.
281 *Botta v Italy* (1998) 26 EHRR 241.
282 *Norris v Ireland* (1988) 13 EHRR 186.
283 *Hatton v UK* (2001) 34 EHRR 1.
284 *Botta v Italy* (1998) 26 EHRR 241.
285 *Gaskin v UK* (1989) 12 EHRR 36.

and information about one's illness[286] have been held to come within its reach.

27.227   Article 8 is a 'qualified right' in that state interference with the right is permitted, but only where the interference is 'lawful' and is done in a proportionate way in pursuance of a legitimate aim. Although article 8(2) provides an exhaustive list of six legitimate aims, these are so widely drawn (including, for example, action which protects the rights and freedoms of others, action for economic reasons, or to protect morals or to prevent crime) that in general the court will have little difficulty in finding any 'interference' with article 8(1) pursues a legitimate aim.

27.228   It is however in respect of the second limb of the test that public bodies have most difficulty. They must establish that what they did, not only had a legitimate aim, but also that it was 'proportionate'. Although there is substantial jurisprudence concerning the of concept of 'proportionality', the key principles of most relevance in a social welfare context concern the need for the action to be 'the least restrictive interference' commensurate with the legitimate aim pursued, and also that overall the action be 'balanced'.

27.229   In *Gaskin v UK*[287] the applicant sought access to his social services records. The request was refused in part on the ground that some of the information had originally been given in confidence and the law at that time did not permit disclosure of information where such third parties had not provided their consent to the disclosure. The information was important to Mr Gaskin as he had spent almost all his life in care and he wanted it for identity purposes. His was a legitimate claim, as indeed was the refusal to divulge the information, which had been given to the local authority in confidence.

27.230   The court considered that the refusal to disclose pursued a legitimate aim (that of protecting the rights and freedoms of others) but was disproportionate. It was not the 'least restrictive interference'. The court considered that some of the 'third party' material could be disclosed without prejudicing the rights of others – for instance if the person who had given the information had since died, or could not be traced, or if anyone reading the information would be unable to identity its author. It also considered that the blanket refusal was not 'balanced' since it meant that in such cases Mr Gaskin's claim always failed – and the concept of 'balance' requires that in certain situations the balance of interest might come down in favour of the person seeking disclosure. It was as a consequence of the *Gaskin* judgment that the changes in the Data Protection Act 1998 to accessing social services files were introduced (see para 26.8 above).

27.231   For many disabled people, their home is (in one form or another) in an institutional setting. Provided the stay has been for a reasonable length of time,[288] the care home or hospital ward etc will be deemed the person's

---

286   *McGinley and Egan v UK* (1998) 27 EHRR 1; and *LCB v UK* (1998) 27 EHRR 212.
287   (1989) 12 EHRR 36.
288   In *O'Rourke v UK* (2001) 26 June, App no 39022/97, the court doubted that occupation of a hotel room for one month was sufficient and continuous enough to make it his 'home' for the purposes of article 8.

'home' for the purposes of article 8. Accordingly any attempt to move the resident will have to be justified as being proportionate. *R v North and East Devon Health Authority ex p Coughlan*[289] concerned an attempt by a health authority to move the applicant from her specialist NHS unit where she had lived for six years. Having regard to all the circumstances (which included the health authority's desire to close the facility for budgetary reasons) the court considered that the authority had failed to establish that such an interference with the applicant's article 8 right was justified.

27.232   *R (Bernard) v Enfield LBC*[290] concerned a disabled applicant and her family who through the local authority's failure to assess her community care needs properly, and then provide the necessary services, had been forced to live in 'deplorable conditions' for over 20 months. Although the court held that this level of suffering had not attained the threshold required by article 3, it considered that the council's failure to act on its assessments had the effect of condemning the applicant and her family to live in conditions which made it virtually impossible for them to have any meaningful private or family life – and on the facts found a violation of article 8.

Article 14: discrimination

27.233 Article 14 can only be invoked in relation to one of the substantive rights set out in articles 2–12 of the Convention and the protocols. Article 14 requires that in the delivery of the substantive rights, there be no discrimination. Discrimination is permissible under article 14, if it is established that the measure has an objective and reasonable justification and is 'proportionate'.

27.234   Thus a violation of article 14 can only occur in combination with another article;[291] for instance the inferior inheritance rights of illegitimate children in Belgium (compared to legitimate children) were held to violate article 14 in conjunction with article 8[292] (right to family life). The court has been particularly forthright on the issue of sex discrimination, holding that '[t]he advancement of the equality of the sexes is today a major goal in the Member-States of the Council of Europe and very weighty reasons would have to be put forward before such a difference of treatment could be regarded as compatible with the Convention'.[293]

European Court of Human Rights

27.235 A complaint can only be made to the European Court of Human Rights once all domestic remedies have been exhausted. The complainant must

---

289 [2000] 2 WLR 622; (1999) 2 CCLR 285.
290 [2002] EWHC 2282 (Admin); (2002) 5 CCLR 577.
291 It may be that major improvement in this field will more likely flow from EU law, ie the Amsterdam Treaty amendments.
292 *Marckx v Belgium* (1979) 2 EHRR 330.
293 *Schuler-Zgraggen v Switzerland* (1995)16 EHRR 405.

be an individual who claims to have suffered as a result of the measure in issue, and the complaint must be made within six months of the exhaustion of the last domestic remedy. The complaint must allege a violation of at least one of the principal articles of the Convention (or the first protocol thereto).[294]

---

294 For detailed consideration of the law and procedures, see P Leach, *Taking a Case to the European Court of Human Rights*, Oxford University Press, 2005.

APPENDICES

Legislation

Statutory extracts in appendix A are reproduced as amended, up to date to August 2007. © *Crown Copyright.*

NATIONAL ASSISTANCE ACT 1948 (EXTRACTS)

PART III: LOCAL AUTHORITY SERVICES

Provision of accommodation

Duty of local authorities to provide accommodation

21(1) Subject to and in accordance with the provisions of this Part of this Act, a local authority may with the approval of the Secretary of State, and to such extent as he may direct shall, make arrangements for providing—

(a) residential accommodation for persons aged eighteen or over who by reason of age, illness, disability or any other circumstances are in need of care and attention which is not otherwise available to them; and

(aa) residential accommodation for expectant and nursing mothers who are in need of care and attention which is not otherwise available to them.

(b) [*Repealed.*]

(1A) A person to whom section 115 of the Immigration and Asylum Act 1999 (exclusion from benefits) applies may not be provided with residential accommodation under subsection (1)(a) if his need for care and attention has arisen solely—

(a) because he is destitute; or

(b) because of the physical effects, or anticipated physical effects, of his being destitute.

(1B) Subsections (3) and (5) to (8) of section 95 of the Immigration and Asylum Act 1999, and paragraph 2 of Schedule 8 to that Act, apply for the purposes of subsection (1A) as they apply for the purposes of that section, but for the references in subsections (5) and (7) of that section and in that paragraph to the Secretary of State substitute references to a local authority.

(2) In making any such arrangements a local authority shall have regard to the welfare of all persons for whom accommodation is provided, and in particular to the need for providing accommodation of different descriptions suited to different descriptions of such persons as are mentioned in the last foregoing subsection.

(2A) In determining for the purposes of paragraph (a) or (aa) of subsection(1) of this section whether care and attention are otherwise available to a person, a local authority shall disregard so much of the person's resources as may be specified in, or determined in accordance with, regulations made by the Secretary of State for the purposes of this subsection.

(2B) In subsection (2A) of this section the reference to a person's resources is a reference to his resources within the meaning of regulations made for the purposes of that subsection.

(3) [*Repealed.*]

(4) Subject to the provisions of section 26 of this Act accommodation provided by a local authority in the exercise of their functions under this section shall be provided in premises managed by the authority or, to such extent as may be determined in accordance with the arrangements under this section, in such premises managed by another local authority as may be agreed between the two authorities and on such terms, including terms as to the reimbursement of expenditure incurred by the said other authority, as may be so agreed.

(5) References in this Act to accommodation provided under this part thereof shall be construed as references to accommodation provided in accordance with this and the five next following sections, and as including references to board and other services, amenities and requisites provided in connection with the accommodation except where in the opinion of the authority managing the premises their provision is unnecessary.

(6) References in this Act to a local authority providing accommodation shall be construed, in any case where a local authority agree with another local authority for the provision of accommodation in premises managed by the said other authority, as references to the first-mentioned local authority.

(7) Without prejudice to the generality of the foregoing provisions of this section, a local authority may—

(a) provide, in such cases as they may consider appropriate, for the conveyance of persons to and from premises in which accommodation is provided for them under this Part of the Act;

(b) make arrangements for the provision on the premises in which the accommodation is being provided of such other services as appear to the authority to be required.

(8) Nothing in this section shall authorise or require a local authority to make any provision authorised or required to be made (whether by that or by any other authority) by or under any enactment not contained in this Part of this Act or authorised or required to be provided under the National Health Service Act 2006 or the National Health Service (Wales) Act 2006.

Charges to be made for accommodation (England and Wales)

22(1) Subject to section 26 of this Act, where a person is provided with accommodation under this Part of this Act the local authority providing the accommodation shall recover from him the amount of the payment which he is liable to make in accordance with the following provisions of this section.

(2) Subject to the following provisions of this section, the payment which a person is liable to make for any such accommodation shall be in accordance with a standard rate fixed for that accommodation by the authority managing the premises in which it is provided and that standard rate shall represent the full cost to the authority of providing that accommodation.

(3) Where a person for whom accommodation in premises managed by any local authority is provided, or proposed to be provided, under this Part of this Act satisfies the local authority that he is unable to pay therefore at the standard rate, the authority shall assess his ability to pay, and accordingly determine at what lower rate he shall be liable to pay for the accommodation:

(4) In assessing for the purposes of the last foregoing subsection a person's ability to pay, a local authority shall assume that he will need for his personal requirements such sum per week as may be prescribed by the Minister, or such other sum as in special circumstances the authority may consider appropriate.

(4A) Regulations made for the purposes of subsection (4) of this section may prescribe different sums for different circumstances.

(5) In assessing as aforesaid a person's ability to pay, a local authority shall give effect to regulations made by the Secretary of State for the purposes of this subsection except that, until the first such regulations come into force, a local

authority shall give effect to Part III of Schedule 1 to the Supplementary Benefits Act 1976, as it had effect immediately before the amendments made by Schedule 2 to the Social Security Act 1980.

(5A) If they think fit, an authority managing premises in which accommodation is provided for a person shall have power on each occasion when they provide accommodation for him, irrespective of his means, to limit to such amount as appears to them reasonable for him to pay the payments required from him for his accommodation during a period commencing when they begin to provide the accommodation for him and ending not more than eight weeks after that.

(6) [*Repealed.*]

(7) [*Repealed.*]

(8) Where accommodation is provided by a local authority in premises managed by another local authority, the payment therefore under this section shall be made to the authority managing the premises and not to the authority providing accommodation, but the authority managing the premises shall account for the payment to the authority providing the accommodation.

(8A) This section shall have effect subject to any regulations under section 15 of the Community Care (Delayed Discharges etc) Act 2003 (power to require certain community care services and services for carers to be provided free of charge).

(9) [*Repealed.*]

Management of premises in which accommodation provided

23(1) Subject to the provisions of this Part of this Act, a local authority may make rules as to the conduct of premises under their management in which accommodation is provided under this Part of this Act and as to the preservation of order in the premises.

(2) Rules under this section may provide that where by reason of any change in a person's circumstances he is no longer qualified to receive accommodation under this Part of this Act or where a person has otherwise become unsuitable therefore he may be required by the local authority managing the premises to leave the premises in which the accommodation is provided.

(3) Rules under this section may provide for the waiving of part of the payments due under the last foregoing section where in compliance with the rules persons for whom accommodation is provided assist in the running of the premises.

Authority liable for provision of accommodation

24(1) The local authority empowered under this Part of this Act to provide residential accommodation for any person shall subject to the following provisions of this Part of this Act be the authority in whose area the person is ordinarily resident.

(2) [*Repealed.*]

(3) Where a person in the area of a local authority—
(a) is a person with no settled residence, or
(b) not being ordinarily resident in the area of the local authority, is in urgent need of residential accommodation under this Part of this Act,
the authority shall have the like power to provide residential accommodation for him as if he were ordinarily resident in their area.

(4) Subject to and in accordance with the arrangements under section twenty-one of this Act, a local authority shall have power, as respects a person ordinarily resident in the area of another local authority, with the consent of that other authority to provide residential accommodation for him in any case where the authority would have a duty to provide such accommodation if he were ordinarily resident in their area.

(5) Where a person is provided with residential accommodation under this Part of this Act, he shall be deemed for the purposes of this Act to continue to be ordinarily resident in the area in which he was ordinarily resident immediately before the residential accommodation was provided for him.

(6) For the purposes of the provision of residential accommodation under this Part of this Act, a patient in a hospital vested in the Secretary of State, a Primary Care Trust, an NHS trust or an NHS Foundation trust shall be deemed to be ordinarily resident in the area, if any, in which he was ordinarily resident immediately before he was admitted as a patient to the hospital, whether or not he in fact continues to be ordinarily resident in that area.

(7) In subsection (6) above 'NHS trust' means a National Health Service trust established under the National Health Service Act 2006, the National Health Service (Wales) Act 2006] or under the National Health Service (Scotland) Act 1978, and 'Primary Care Trust' means a Primary Care Trust established under section 18 of the National Health Service Act 2006.

25   [*Repealed.*]

Provision of accommodation in premises maintained by voluntary organisations (England and Wales)

26(1)   Subject to subsections (1A) and (1C) below, arrangements under section 21 of this Act may include arrangements made with a voluntary organisation or with any other person who is not a local authority where—

(a) that organisation or person manages premises which provide for reward accommodation falling within subsection (1)(a) or (aa) of that section, and

(b) the arrangements are for the provision of such accommodation in those premises.

(1A) Arrangements must not be made by virtue of this section for the provision of accommodation together with nursing or personal care for persons such as are mentioned in section 3(2) of the Care Standards Act 2000 (care homes) unless—

(a) the accommodation is to be provided, under the arrangements, in a care home (within the meaning of that Act) which is managed by the organisation or person in question; and

(b) that organisation or person is registered under Part II of that Act in respect of the home.

(1C) Subject to subsection (1D) below, no arrangements may be made by virtue of this section for the provision of accommodation together with nursingwithout the consent of such Primary Care Trust or Local Health Board as may be determined in accordance with regulations.

(1D) Subsection (1C) above does not apply to the making by an authority of temporary arrangements for the accommodation of any person as a matter of urgency; but, as soon as practicable after any such temporary arrangements have been made, the authority shall seek the consent required by subsection (1C) above to the making of appropriate arrangements for the accommodation of the person concerned.

(1E) [*Repealed.*]

(2) Any arrangements made by virtue of this section shall provide for the making by the local authority to the other party thereto of payments in respect of the accommodation provided at such rates as may be determined by or under the arrangements and subject to subsection (3A) below the local authority shall recover from each person for whom accommodation is provided under the arrangements the amount of the refund which he is liable to make in accordance with the following provisions of this section.

(3) Subject to subsection (3A) below A person for whom accommodation is provided under any such arrangements shall, in lieu of being liable to make

payment therefore in accordance with section twenty-two of this Act, refund to the local authority any payments made in respect of him under the last foregoing subsection:

Provided that where a person for whom accommodation is provided, or proposed to be provided, under any such arrangements satisfies the local authority that he is unable to make a refund at the full rate determined under that subsection, subsections (3) to (5) of section twenty-two of this Act shall, with the necessary modifications, apply as they apply where a person satisfies the local authority of his inability to pay at the standard rate as mentioned in the said subsection (3).

(3A) Where accommodation in any premises is provided for any person under arrangements made by virtue of this section and the local authority, the person concerned and the voluntary organisation or other person managing the premises (in this subsection referred to as 'the provider') agree that this subsection shall apply—

    (a) so long as the person concerned makes the payments for which he is liable under paragraph (b) below, he shall not be liable to make any refund under subsection (3) above and the local authority shall not be liable to make any payment under subsection (2) above in respect of the accommodation provided for him;

    (b) the person concerned shall be liable to pay to the provider such sums as he would otherwise (under subsection (3) above) be liable to pay by way of refund to the local authority; and

    (c) the local authority shall be liable to pay to the provider the difference between the sums paid by virtue of paragraph (b) above and the payments which, but for paragraph (a) above, the authority would be liable to pay under subsection (2) above.

(4) Subsections (5A), (7) and (9) of the said section 22 shall, with the necessary modifications, apply for the purposes of the last foregoing subsection as they apply for the purposes of the said section 22.

(4A) Section 21(5) of this Act shall have effect as respects accommodation provided under arrangements made by virtue of this section with the substitution for the reference to the authority managing the premises of a reference to the authority making the arrangements.

(5) Where in any premises accommodation is being provided under this section in accordance with arrangements made by any local authority, any person authorised in that behalf by the authority may at all reasonable times enter and inspect the premises.

(6) [*Repealed.*]

(7) In this section the expression 'voluntary organisation' includes any association which is a housing association for the purposes of the Housing Act, 1936, or the Housing (Scotland) Acts, 1925 to 1946 and 'exempt body' means an authority or body constituted by an Act of Parliament or incorporated by Royal Charter.

27 [*Repealed.*]

28 [*Repealed.*]

29. Welfare arrangements for blind, deaf, dumb and crippled persons, etc.

(1) A local authority may, with the approval of the Secretary of State, and to such extent as he may direct in relation to persons ordinarily resident in the area of the local authority shall make arrangements for promoting the welfare of persons to whom this section applies, that is to say persons aged eighteen or over who are blind, deaf or dumb, or who suffer from mental disorder of any description and other persons aged eighteen or over who are substantially and permanently handicapped by illness, injury, or congenital deformity or such other disabilities as may be prescribed by the Minister.

(2) [*Repealed.*]

(3)   [*Repealed.*]

(4)   Without prejudice to the generality of the provisions of subsection(1) of this section, arrangements may be made thereunder—

   (a)   for informing persons to whom arrangements under that subsection relate of the services available for them thereunder;

   (b)   for giving such persons instruction in their own homes or elsewhere in methods of overcoming the effects of their disabilities;

   (c)   for providing workshops where such persons may be engaged (whether under a contract of service or otherwise) in suitable work, and hostels where persons engaged in the workshops, and other persons to whom arrangements under subsection(1) of this section relate and for whom work or training is being provided in pursuance of the Disabled Persons (Employment) Act, 1944, or the Employment and Training Act 1973 may live;

   (d)   for providing persons to whom arrangements under subsection(1) of this section relate with suitable work (whether under a contract of service or otherwise) in their own homes or elsewhere;

   (e)   for helping such persons in disposing of the produce of their work;

   (f)   for providing such persons with recreational facilities in their own homes or elsewhere;

   (g)   for compiling and maintaining classified registers of the persons to whom arrangements under subsection(1) of this section relate.

(4A)   Where accommodation in a hostel is provided under paragraph (c) of subsection (4) of this section—

   (a)   if the hostel is managed by a local authority, section 22 of this Act shall apply as it applies where accommodation is provided under section 21;

   (b)   if the accommodation is provided in a hostel managed by a person other than a local authority under arrangements made with that person, subsections (2) to (4A) of section 26 of this Act shall apply as they apply where accommodation is provided under arrangements made by virtue of that section; and

   (c)   sections 32 and 43 of this Act shall apply as they apply where accommodation is provided under sections 21 to 26;

   and in this subsection references to 'accommodation' include references to board and other services, amenities and requisites provided in connection with the accommodation, except where in the opinion of the authority managing the premises or, in the case mentioned in paragraph (b) above, the authority making the arrangements their provision is unnecessary.

(5)   [*Repealed.*]

(6)   Nothing in the foregoing provisions of this section shall authorise or require—

   (a)   the payment of money to persons to whom this section applies, other than persons for whom work is provided under arrangements made by virtue of paragraph (c) or paragraph (d) of subsection (4) of this section or who are engaged in work which they are enabled to perform in consequence of anything done in pursuance of arrangements made under this section; or

   (b)   the provision of any accommodation or services required to be provided under the National Health Service Act 2006 or the National Health Service (Wales) Act 2006.

(7)   A person engaged in work in a workshop provided under paragraph (c) of subsection (4) of this section, or a person in receipt of a superannuation allowance granted on his retirement from engagement in any such workshop, shall be deemed for the purposes of this Act to continue to be ordinarily resident in the area in which he was ordinarily resident immediately before he was accepted for work in that workshop; and for the purposes of this

subsection a course of training in such a workshop shall be deemed to be work in that workshop.

Voluntary organisations for disabled persons' welfare

30(1) A local authority may, in accordance with arrangements made under section 29 of this Act, employ as their agent for the purposes of that section any voluntary organisation for the time being registered in accordance with this Act being an organisation having for its sole or principal object or among its principal objects the promotion of the welfare of persons to whom the last foregoing section applies any voluntary organisation or any person carrying on, professionally or by way of trade or business, activities which consist of or include the provision of services for any of the persons to whom section 29 above applies, being an organisation or person appearing to the authority to be capable of providing the service to which the arrangements apply.

(2) [*Repealed.*]

(3) [*Repealed.*]

Research

30A Without prejudice to any powers conferred on them by any other Act, —

(a) the Secretary of State may promote research into any matter relating to the functions of local authorities under this Part of this Act, and, in particular, may participate with or assist other persons in conducting such research; and

(b) a local authority may conduct or assist other persons in conducting research into any matter relating to the functions of local authorities under this Part of this Act.

31 [*Repealed.*]

FINANCIAL ADJUSTMENTS BETWEEN LOCAL AUTHORITIES

Adjustments between authority providing accommodation, etc and authority of area of residence

32(1) Any expenditure which apart from this section would fall to be borne by a local authority—

(a) in the provision under this Part of this Act of accommodation for a person ordinarily resident in the area of another local authority, or

(b) in the provision under section 29 of this Act of services for a person ordinarily so resident, or

(c) in providing under paragraph (*a*) of subsection (7) of section 22 of this Act for the conveyance of a person ordinarily resident as aforesaid,

shall be recoverable from the said other local authority.

(2) For the purposes of paragraph (a) of the last foregoing subsection it shall be assumed that the expenditure incurred by a local authority in providing accommodation for any person is, as respects accommodation provided in premises managed by a local authority, at the rate for the time being fixed for that accommodation under subsection (2) of section twenty-two of this Act, and, as respects accommodation provided pursuant to an arrangement made under section twenty-six of this Act, at the rate referred to in subsection (2) of that section.

(3) Any question arising under this Part of this Act as to the ordinary residence of a person shall be determined by the Minister.

LOCAL AND CENTRAL AUTHORITIES

Local Authorities for purposes of Part III

33(1) In this Part of this Act the expression 'local authority' means a council which is a local authority for the purposes of the Local Authority Social Services Act

1970 in England or Wales, and a council constituted under section 2 of the Local Government etc. (Scotland) Act 1994 in Scotland.

(2)   [*Repealed.*]

HEALTH SERVICES AND PUBLIC HEALTH ACT 1968

Promotion by local authorities, of the welfare of old people

45(1) A local authority may with the approval of the Secretary of State, and to such extent as he may direct shall, make arrangements for promoting the welfare of old people.

(2)   [*Repealed.*]

(3)   A local authority may employ as their agent for the purposes of this section any voluntary organisation having for its sole or principal object, or among its principal objects, the promotion of the welfare of old people any voluntary organisation or any person carrying on, professionally or by way of trade or business, activities which consist of or include the provision of services for old people, being an organisation or person appearing to the authority to be capable of promoting the welfare of old people.

(4)   No arrangements under this section shall provide—

   (a) for the payment of money to old people except in so far as the arrangements may provide for the remuneration of old people engaged in suitable work in accordance with the arrangements;

   (b) for making available any accommodation or services required to be provided under the National Health Service Act 2006 or the National Health Service (Wales) Act 2006.

(4A) No arrangements under this section may be given effect to in relation to a person to whom section 115 of the Immigration and Asylum Act 1999 (exclusion from benefits) applies solely—

   (a) because he is destitute; or

   (b) because of the physical effects, or anticipated physical effects, of his being destitute.

(4B) Subsections (3) and (5) to (8) of section 95 of the Immigration and Asylum Act 1999, and paragraph 2 of Schedule 8 to that Act, apply for the purposes of subsection (4A) as they apply for the purposes of that section, but for the references in subsections (5) and (7) of that section and in that paragraph to the Secretary of State substitute references to a local authority.

(5)   The National Assistance Act 1948 shall have effect as if the following references included a reference to this section, that is to say,—

   (a) the reference, in section 32, to section 29 of that Act;

   (b) the references, in sections 35, 36,45, 52 . . . to Part III of that Act;

   (c) the references, in sections 54, 56 and 59, to that Act.

(6)   [*Repealed.*]

(7)   [*Repealed.*]

(8)   [*Repealed.*]

(9)   The Health Visiting and Social Work (Training) Act 1962 shall have effect in relation to functions of local authorities under this section as it does in relation to functions of local authorities under Part III of the National Assistance Act 1948.

(10) Section 31(1) of the National Assistance Act 1948 (which empowers local authorities to make arrangements for the provision of meals and recreation for old people) shall cease to have effect except as respects the councils of county districts.

(11) In this section 'local authority'(except where used in the expression 'public or local authority') means the council of a county, other than a metropolitan

county or of a county borough, metropolitan district or London borough or the Common Council of the City of London, and 'voluntary organisation' means a body the activities of which are carried on otherwise than for profit but does not include any public or local authority.

(12) [*Repealed.*]

CHRONICALLY SICK AND DISABLED PERSONS ACT 1970 (EXTRACTS)

Information as to need for and existence of welfare services

1(1) It shall be the duty of every local authority having functions under section 29 of the National Assistance Act 1948 to inform themselves of the number of persons to whom that section applies within their area and of the need for the making by the authority of arrangements under that section for such persons.

(2) Every such local authority—

(a) shall cause to be published from time to time at such times and in such manner as they consider appropriate general information as to the services provided under arrangements made by the authority under the said section 29 which are for the time being available in their area; and

(b) shall ensure that any such person as aforesaid who uses any of those services is informed of any other service provided by the authority (whether under any such arrangements or not) which in the opinion of the authority is relevant to his needs and of any service provided by any other authority or organisation which in the opinion of the authority is so relevant and of which particulars are in the authority's possession.

(3) This section shall come into operation on such date as the Secretary of State may by order made by statutory instrument appoint.

Provision of welfare services

2(1) Where a local authority having functions under section 29 of the National Assistance Act 1948 are satisfied in the case of any person to whom that section applies who is ordinarily resident in their area that it is necessary in order to meet the needs of that person for that authority to make arrangements for all or any of the following matters, namely—

(a) the provision of practical assistance for that person in his home;

(b) the provision for that person of, or assistance to that person in obtaining, wireless, television, library or similar recreational facilities;

(c) the provision for that person of lectures, games, outings or other recreational facilities outside his home or assistance to that person in taking advantage of educational facilities available to him;

(d) the provision for that person of facilities for, or assistance in, travelling to and from his home for the purpose of participating in any services provided under arrangements made by the authority under the said section 29 or, with the approval of the authority, in any services provided otherwise than as aforesaid which are similar to services which could be provided under such arrangements;

(e) the provision of assistance for that person in arranging for the carrying out of any works of adaptation in his home or the provision of any additional facilities designed to secure his greater safety, comfort or convenience;

(f) facilitating the taking of holidays by that person, whether at holiday homes or otherwise and whether provided under arrangements made by the authority or otherwise;

(g) the provision of meals for that person whether in his home or elsewhere;

(h) the provision for that person of, or assistance to that person in obtaining, a telephone and any special equipment necessary to enable him to use a telephone,

then, subject to the provisions of section 35(2) of that Act (which requires local authorities to exercise their functions under Part III of that Act in accordance with the provisions of any regulations made for the purpose) and to the provisions of section 7(1) of the Local Authority Social Services Act 1970 (which requires local authorities in the exercise of certain functions, including functions under the said section 29, to act under the general guidance of the Secretary of State) and to the provisions of section 7A of that Act (which requires local authorities to exercise their social services functions in accordance with directions given by the Secretary of State) it shall be the duty of that authority to make those arrangements in exercise of their functions under the said section 29.

(2) [*Repealed.*]

LOCAL AUTHORITY SOCIAL SERVICES ACT 1970 (EXTRACTS)

The director of social services

6(A1) A local authority in England shall appoint an officer, to be known as the director of adult social services, for the purposes of their social services functions, other than those for which the authority's director of children's services is responsible under section 18 of the Children Act 2004.

(1) A local authority in Wales shall appoint an officer, to be known as the director of social services, for the purposes of their social services functions.

(2) Two or more local authorities may, if they consider that the same person can efficiently discharge, for both or all of them, the functions of director of [adult social services or (as the case may be)] social services, concur in the appointment of a person as director of adult social services or (as the case may be) social services for both or all of those authorities.

(3) [*Repealed.*]
(4) [*Repealed.*]
(5) [*Repealed.*]
(6) A local authority which have appointed, or concurred in the appointment of, a director of social services, shall secure the provision of adequate staff for assisting him in the exercise of his functions.
(7) [*Repealed.*]
(8) [*Repealed.*]

Local authorities to exercise social services functions under guidance of Secretary of State[1]

7(1) Local authorities shall, in the exercise of their social services functions, including the exercise of any discretion conferred by any relevant enactment, act under the general guidance of the Secretary of State.

(2) [*Repealed.*]
(3) [*Repealed.*]

---

1 See further, the National Health Service Act 2006, s77(11)(a), (12) and National Health Service (Wales) Act 2006, s35(11)(a), (12) which provide, respectively, that in connection with the exercise by a body designated as Care Trust or an NHS Trust of any relevant social services functions under LA delegation arrangements this section shall apply to the body as if it were a local authority within the meaning of this Act.

Directions by the Secretary of State as to exercise of social services functions[2]

7A(1) Without prejudice to section 7 of this Act, every local authority shall exercise their social services functions in accordance with such directions as may be given to them under this section by the Secretary of State.

(2) Directions under this section—

(a) shall be given in writing; and

(b) may be given to a particular authority, or to authorities of a particular class, or to authorities generally.

7B [*Repealed.*]

Inquiries

7C(1) The Secretary of State may cause an inquiry to be held in any case where, whether on representations made to him or otherwise, he considers it advisable to do so in connection with the exercise by any local authority of any of their social services functions (except in so far as those functions relate to persons under the age of eighteen).

(2) Subsections (2) to (5) of section 250 of the Local Government Act 1972 (powers in relation to local inquiries) shall apply in relation to an inquiry under this section as they apply in relation to an inquiry under that section.

Default powers of Secretary of State as respects social services functions of local authorities

7D(1) If the Secretary of State is satisfied that any local authority have failed, without reasonable excuse to comply with any of their duties which are social services functions (other than a duty imposed by or under the Children Act 1989, section 1 or 2(4) of the Adoption (Intercountry Aspects) Act 1999 or the Adoption and Children Act 2002), he may make an order declaring that authority to be in default with respect to the duty in question.

(2) An order under subsection(1) may contain such directions for the purpose of ensuring that the duty is complied with within such period as may be specified in the order as appear to the Secretary of State to be necessary.

(3) Any such direction shall, on the application of the Secretary of State, be enforceable by mandamus.

Grants to local authorities in respect of social services for the mentally ill

7E The Secretary of State may, with the approval of the Treasury, make grants out of money provided by Parliament towards any expenses of local authorities incurred in connection with the exercise of their social services functions in relation to persons suffering from mental illness.

MENTAL HEALTH ACT 1983

After-care

117(1) This section applies to persons who are detained under section 3 above, or admitted to a hospital in pursuance of a hospital order made under section 37 above, or transferred to a hospital in pursuance of a hospital direction made under section 45A above or a transfer direction made under section 47 or 48 above, and then cease to be detained and (whether or not immediately after so ceasing) leave hospital.

---

2 See further, the National Health Service Act 2006, s77(11)(b), (12) and National Health Service (Wales) Act 2006, s35(11)(b), (12) which provide, respectively, that in connection with the exercise by a body designated as Care Trust or an NHS Trust of any relevant social services functions under LA delegation arrangements this section shall apply to the body as if it were a local authority within the meaning of this Act.

(2)   It shall be the duty of the Primary Care Trust or Local Health Board and of the local social services authority to provide, in co-operation with relevant voluntary agencies, after-care services for any person to whom this section applies until such time as the Primary Care Trust or Local Health Board and the local social services authority are satisfied that the person concerned is no longer in need of such services; but they shall not be so satisfied in the case of a *community patient while he remains such a patient.*[3]

(2A) [*Repealed.*][4]

(2B) Section 32 above shall apply for the purposes of this section as it applies for the purposes of Part II of this Act.

(3)   In this section 'the Primary Care Trust or Local Health Board' means the Primary Care Trust or Local Health Board, and 'the local social services authority' means the local social services authority, for the area in which the person concerned is resident or to which he is sent on discharge by the hospital in which he was detained.

HEALTH AND SOCIAL SERVICES AND SOCIAL SECURITY ADJUDICATIONS ACT 1983 (EXTRACTS)

Charges for local authority services in England and Wales

17(1) Subject to subsection (3) below, an authority providing a service to which this section applies may recover such charge (if any) for it as they consider reasonable.

(2)   This section applies to services provided under the following enactments—

(a)   section 29 of the National Assistance Act 1948 (welfare arrangements for blind, deaf, dumb and crippled persons etc.);

(b)   section 45(1) of the Health Services and Public Health Act 1968 (welfare of old people);

(c)   Schedule 8 to the National Health Service Act 1977 (care of mothers and young children, prevention of illness and care and aftercare and home help and laundry facilities);

(d)   section 8 of the Residential Homes Act 1980 (meals and recreation for old people); and

(e)   paragraph 1 of Part II of Schedule 9 to this Act

(f)   section 2 of the Carers and Disabled Children Act 2000

other than the provision of services for which payment may be required under section 22 or 26 of the National Assistance Act 1948.

(3)   If a person—

(a)   avails himself of a service to which this section applies, and

(b)   satisfies the authority providing the service that his means are insufficient for it to be reasonably practicable for him to pay for the service the amount which he would otherwise be obliged to pay for it,

the authority shall not require him to pay more for it than it appears to them that it is reasonably practicable for him to pay.

(4)   Any charge under this section may, without prejudice to any other method of recovery, be recovered summarily as a civil debt.

---

3 Words in italics inserted by the Mental Health Act 2007 s32(4), Sch 3, paras 1, 24. See s53, Sch 10, paras 1 and 5 for transitional provisions.

4 Repealed, from a date to be appointed, by the Mental Health Act 2007 s55, Sch 11, Pt 5. See s53, Sch 10, paras 1 and 5 for transitional provisions.

Recovery of sums due to local authority where persons in residential accommodation have disposed of assets

21(1) Subject to the following provisions of this section where—

    (a) a person avails himself of Part III accommodation; and

    (b) that person knowingly and with the intention of avoiding charges for the accommodation—

        (i) has transferred any asset to which this section applies to some other person or persons not more than six months before the date on which he begins to reside in such accommodation; or

        (ii) transfers any such asset to some other person or persons while residing in the accommodation; and

    (c) either—

        (i) the consideration for the transfer is less than the value of the asset; or

        (ii) there is no consideration for the transfer,

the person or persons to whom the asset is transferred by the person availing himself of the accommodation shall be liable to pay to the local authority providing the accommodation or arranging for its provision the difference between the amount assessed as due to be paid for the accommodation by the person availing himself of it and the amount which the local authority receive from him for it.

(2) This section applies to cash and any other asset which falls to be taken into account for the purpose of assessing under section 22 of the National Assistance Act 1948 the ability to pay for the accommodation of the person availing himself of it.

(3) Subsection(1) above shall have effect in relation to a transfer by a person who leaves Part III accommodation and subsequently resumes residence in such accommodation as if the period of six months mentioned in paragraph (b)(i) were a period of six months before the date on which he resumed residence in such accommodation.

(3A) If the Secretary of State so directs, subsection(1) above shall not apply in such cases as may be specified in the direction.

(4) Where a person has transferred an asset to which this section applies to more than one person, the liability of each of the persons to whom it was transferred shall be in proportion to the benefit accruing to him from the transfer.

(5) A person's liability under this section shall not exceed the benefit accruing to him from the transfer.

(6) Subject to subsection (7) below, the value of any asset to which this section applies, other than cash, which has been transferred shall be taken to be the amount of the consideration which would have been realised for it if it had been sold on the open market by a willing seller at the time of the transfer.

(7) For the purpose of calculating the value of an asset under subsection (6) above there shall be deducted from the amount of the consideration—

    (a) the amount of any incumbrance on the asset; and

    (b) a reasonable amount in respect of the expenses of the sale.

(8) In this Part of this Act 'Part III accommodation' means accommodation provided under sections 21 to 26 of the National Assistance Act 1948, and, in the application of this Part of this Act to Scotland, means accommodation provided under the Social Work (Scotland) Act 1968 or section 7 (functions of local authorities) of the Mental Health (Scotland) Act 1984,.

Arrears of contributions charged on interest in land in England and Wales

22(1) Subject to subsection (2) below, where a person who avails himself of Part III accommodation provided by a local authority in England, Wales or Scotland—

(a) fails to pay any sum assessed as due to be paid by him for the accommodation; and

(b) has a beneficial interest in land in England or Wales, the local authority may create a charge in their favour on his interest in the land.

(2) In the case of a person who has interests in more than one parcel of land the charge under this section shall be upon his interest in such one of the parcels as the local authority may determine.

(2A) In determining whether to exercise their power under subsection(1) above and in making any determination under subsection (2) above, the local authority shall comply with any directions given to them by the Secretary of State as to the exercise of those functions.

(3) Any interest in the proceeds of sale of land held upon trust for sale is to be treated, subject to subsection (8) below, as an interest in land for the purposes of this section.

(4) Subject to subsection (5) below, a charge under this section shall be in respect of any amount assessed as due to be paid which is outstanding from time to time.

(5) The charge on the interest of an equitable joint tenant in land shall be in respect of an amount not exceeding the value of the interest that he would enjoy in the land if the joint tenancy were severed but the creation of such a charge shall not sever the joint tenancy.

(6) On the death of an equitable joint tenant in land whose interest in the land is subject to a charge under this section—

(a) if there are surviving joint tenants, their interests in the land; and

(b) if the land vests in one person, or one person is entitled to have it vested in him, his interest in it, shall become subject to a charge for an amount not exceeding the amount of the charge to which the interest of the deceased joint tenant was subject by virtue of subsection (5) above.

(7) A charge under this section shall be created by a declaration in writing made by the local authority.

(8) Any such charge, other than a charge on the interest of an equitable joint tenant in land, shall in the case of unregistered land be a land charge of Class B within the meaning of section 2 of the Land Charges Act 1972 and in the case of registered land be a registrable charge taking effect as a charge by way of legal mortgage.

Interest on sums charged on or secured over interest in land

24(1) Any sum charged on or secured over an interest in land under this Part of this Act shall bear interest from the day after that on which the person for whom the local authority provided the accommodation dies.

(2) The rate of interest shall be such reasonable rate as the Secretary of State may direct or, if no such direction is given, as the local authority may determine.

PART II: MEALS AND RECREATION FOR OLD PEOPLE

1 A district council or Welsh county council or county borough council shall have power to make such arrangements as they may from time to time determine for providing meals and recreation for old people in their homes or elsewhere and may employ as their agent for the purpose of this paragraph any voluntary organisation whose activities consist in or include the provision of meals or recreation for old people.

2 A district council or Welsh county council or county borough council may assist any such organisation as is referred to in paragraph 1 above to provide meals or recreation for old people—

(a) by contributing to the funds of the organisation;

(b) by permitting them to use premises belonging to the council on such terms as may be agreed; and

    (c) by making available furniture, vehicles or equipment (whether by way of gift or loan or otherwise) and the services of any staff who are employed by the council in connection with the premises or other things which they permit the organisation to use.

3(1) District councils or Welsh county councils or county borough councils shall exercise their functions under this Part of this Schedule (including any discretion conferred on them under it) in accordance with the provisions of any regulations of the Secretary of State made for the purposes of this paragraph; and without prejudice to the generality of this paragraph, regulations under this paragraph—

    (a) may provide for conferring on officers of the Secretary of State authorised under the regulations such powers of inspection as may be prescribed in relation to the exercise of functions under this Part of this Schedule by or by arrangement with or on behalf of district councils or Welsh county councils or county borough councils; and

    (b) may make provision with respect to the qualifications of officers employed by district councils or Welsh county councils or county borough councils for the purposes of this Part of this Schedule or by voluntary organisations acting under arrangements with or on behalf of district councils or Welsh county councils or county borough councils for those purposes.

(2) The power to make regulations under this paragraph shall be exercisable by statutory instrument which shall be subject to annulment in pursuance of a resolution of either House of Parliament.

4 In this Part of this Schedule—

'functions' includes powers and duties; and

'voluntary organisation' means a body the activities of which are carried on otherwise than for profit, but does not include any public or local authority.

DISABLED PERSONS (SERVICES, CONSULTATION AND REPRESENTATION) ACT 1986 (EXTRACTS)

PART I: REPRESENTATION AND ASSESSMENT

Services under s2 of the 1970 Act: duty to consider needs of disabled persons

4 When requested to do so by—

    (a) a disabled person,

    (b) his authorised representative, or

    (c) any person who provides care for him in the circumstances mentioned in section 8,

a local authority shall decide whether the needs of the disabled person call for the provision by the authority of any services in accordance with section 2(1) of the 1970 Act (provision of welfare services).

Duty of local authority to take into account abilities of carer

8(1) Where—

    (a) a disabled person is living at home and receiving a substantial amount of care on a regular basis from another person (who is not a person employed to provide such care by any body in the exercise of its functions under any enactment), and

    (b) it falls to a local authority to decide whether the disabled person's needs call for the provision by them of any services for him under any of the welfare enactments,

the local authority shall, in deciding that question, have regard to the ability of that other person to continue to provide such care on a regular basis.

(2)   Where that other person is unable to communicate, or (as the case may be) be communicated with, orally or in writing (or in each of those ways) by reason of any mental or physical incapacity, the local authority shall provide such services as, in their opinion, are necessary to ensure that any such incapacity does not prevent the authority from being properly informed as to the ability of that person to continue to provide care as mentioned in subsection (1).

(3)   Section 3(7) shall apply for the purposes of subsection (2) above as it applies for the purposes of section 3(6), but as if any reference to the disabled person or his authorised representative were a reference to the person mentioned in subsection (2).

PART IV: SUPPLEMENTAL

Interpretation

16(1) In this Act—

'the 1948 Act' means National Assistance Act 1948;
'the 1968 Act' means the Social Work (Scotland) Act 1968;
'the 1970 Act' means the Chronically Sick and Disabled Persons Act 1970;

'the 1977 Act' means the National Health Service Act 1977;
'the 1978 Act' means the National Health Service (Scotland) Act 1978;
'the 1980 Act' means the Education (Scotland) Act 1980;
'the 1983 Act' means the Mental Health Act 1983;
'the 1984 Act' means the Mental Health (Scotland) Act 1984;
'the 2003 Act' means the Mental Health (Care and Treatment) (Scotland) Act 2003;
'the 2006 Act' means the National Health Service Act 2006;
'authorised representative' has the meaning given by section 1(1) above;
'disabled person'—
(a) in relation to England and Wales, means—
    (i)   in the case of a person aged eighteen or over, a person to whom section 29 of the 1948 Act applies, and
    (ii) in the case of a person under the age of eighteen, a person who is disabled within the meaning of Part III of the Children Act 1989; and
(b) in relation to Scotland, means—
    (i)   in the case of a person aged eighteen or over, one chronically sick or disabled or one suffering from mental disorder (being, in either case, a relevant person for the purposes of section 12 of the Social Work (Scotland) Act 1968; and
    (ii) in any other case, a disabled child ('disabled child' being construed in accordance with Chapter 1 of Part II of the Children (Scotland) Act 1995);
'guardian'(except in section 1(6))—
(a) in relation to England and Wales, means a person appointed by deed or will or by order of a court of competent jurisdiction to be the guardian of a child; and
(b) in relation to Scotland, means a person appointed by deed or will or by order of a court of competent jurisdiction to be the tutor, curator or guardian of a child;
'Health Board' means a Health Board within the meaning of the 1978 Act;
'hospital'-
(a) in relation to England and Wales, means—
    (i)   a health service hospital within the meaning of the 1977 Act, or
    (ii) any accommodation provided by any person pursuant to arrangements made under section 23(1) of that Act (voluntary organisations and other bodies) and used as a hospital; and

(b) in relation to Scotland, means a health service hospital within the meaning of the 1978 Act;

'local authority' (except in section 2(7))—

(a) in relation to England and Wales, means a council which is a local authority for the purposes of the Local Authority Social Services Act 1970 or, so long as an order under section 12 of that Act is in force, the Council of the Isles of Scilly; and

(b) in relation to Scotland, means a council constituted under section 2 of the Local Government etc. (Scotland) Act 1994 on whom functions are imposed by section 1 of the 1968 Act or any of the enactments mentioned in section 5(1B) of that Act;

'Local Health Board' means a Local Health Board established under section 11 of the National Health Services (Wales) Act 2006;

'mental disorder'—

(a) in relation to England and Wales, has the meaning given by section 1 of the 1983 Act; and

(b) in relation to Scotland, has the meaning given by section 328 of the 2003 Act;

'modifications' includes additions, omissions and amendments;

'parent'—

(a) in relation to England and Wales, means, in the case of a child who is illegitimate, his mother, to the exclusion of his father; and

(b) in relation to Scotland, means, in the case of a child whose father is not married to the mother, his mother, to the exclusion of his father;

'parental responsibility' has the same meaning as in the Children Act 1989;

'Primary Care Trust' means a Primary Care Trust established under section 18 of the National Health Service Act 2006;

'services' includes facilities;

'Special Health Authority' means a Special Health Authority established under section 28 of the 2006 Act or section 22 of the National Health Service (Wales) Act 2006;

'special hospital' means a special hospital within the meaning of the 2003 Act;

'State hospital' means a State hospital within the meaning of the 1984 Act;

'statutory services'—

(a) in relation to England and Wales, means services under any arrangements which a local authority are required to make by virtue of any of the welfare enactments, and

(b) in relation to Scotland, means services which a local authority find it necessary to provide themselves or by arrangement with another local authority, or with any voluntary or other body, in connection with the performance of the local authority's functions under the welfare enactments;

'Strategic Health Authority' means a Strategic Health Authority established under section 13 of the 2006 Act;

'voluntary organisation' means a body the activities of which are carried on otherwise than for profit, but does not include any public or local authority;

'the welfare enactments' means Part III of the 1948 Act, section 2 of the 1970 Act and—

(a) in relation to England and Wales, Schedule 20 to the 2006 Act and Schedule 15 to the National Health Service (Wales) Act 2006 and Part III of the Children Act 1989, and

(b) in relation to Scotland, section 27 of the National Health Service (Scotland) Act 1947, the 1968 Act, sections 7 and 8 of the 1984 Act and Chapter 1 of Part II of the Children (Scotland) Act 1995.

(2) In this Act any reference to a child who is looked after by a local authority has the same meaning as in the Children Act 1989.

(2A) In this Act as it applies in relation to Scotland, any reference to a child who is looked after by a local authority shall be construed in accordance with section 17(6) of the Children (Scotland) Act 1995.

CHILDREN ACT 1989 (EXTRACTS)

PART III: LOCAL AUTHORITY SUPPORT FOR CHILDREN AND FAMILIES

Provision of services for children and their families

Provision of services for children in need, their families and others

17(1) It shall be the general duty of every local authority (in addition to the other duties imposed on them by this Part)—

    (a) to safeguard and promote the welfare of children within their area who are in need; and

    (b) so far as is consistent with that duty, to promote the upbringing of such children by their families,

by providing a range and level of services appropriate to those children's needs.

(2) For the purpose principally of facilitating the discharge of their general duty under this section, every local authority shall have the specific duties and powers set out in Part 1 of Schedule 2.

(3) Any service provided by an authority in the exercise of functions conferred on them by this section may be provided for the family of a particular child in need or for any member of his family, if it is provided with a view to safeguarding or promoting the child's welfare.

(4) The Secretary of State may by order amend any provision of Part I of Schedule 2 or add any further duty or power to those for the time being mentioned there.

(4A) Before determining what (if any) services to provide for a particular child in need in the exercise of functions conferred on them by this section, a local authority shall, so far as is reasonably practicable and consistent with the child's welfare—

    (a) ascertain the child's wishes and feelings regarding the provision of those services; and

    (b) give due consideration (having regard to his age and understanding) to such wishes and feelings of the child as they have been able to ascertain.

(5) Every local authority—

    (a) shall facilitate the provision by others (including in particular voluntary organisations) of services which the authority have power to provide by virtue of this section, or section 18, 20, 23, 23B to 23D, 24A or 24B; and

    (b) may make such arrangements as they see fit for any person to act on their behalf in the provision of any such service.

(6) The services provided by a local authority in the exercise of functions conferred on them by this section may include providing accommodation and giving assistance in kind or, in exceptional circumstances, in cash.

(7) Assistance may be unconditional or subject to conditions as to the repayment of the assistance or of its value (in whole or in part).

(8) Before giving any assistance or imposing any conditions, a local authority shall have regard to the means of the child concerned and of each of his parents.

(9) No person shall be liable to make any repayment of assistance or of its value at any time when he is in receipt of income support, working families tax credit or disabled person's tax credit under the Part VII of the Social Security Contributions and Benefits Act 1992, of any element of child tax credit other

than the family element, of working tax credit, *of an income-based jobseeker's allowance or of an income-related employment and support allowance.*[5]

(10) For the purposes of this Part a child shall be taken to be in need if—
   (a) he is unlikely to achieve or maintain, or to have the opportunity of achieving or maintaining, a reasonable standard of health or development without the provision for him of services by a local authority under this Part;
   (b) his health or development is likely to be significantly impaired, or further impaired, without the provision for him of such services; or
   (c) he is disabled,
   and 'family', in relation to such a child, includes any person who has parental responsibility for the child and any other person with whom he has been living.

(11) For the purposes of this Part, a child is disabled if he is blind, deaf or dumb or suffers from mental disorder of any kind or is substantially and permanently handicapped by illness, injury or congenital deformity or such other disability as may be prescribed; and in this Part—
   'development' means physical, intellectual, emotional, social or behavioural development; and
   'health' means physical or mental health.

(12) The Treasury may by regulations prescribe circumstances in which a person is to be treated for the purposes of this Part (or for such of those purposes as are prescribed) as in receipt of any element of child tax credit other than the family element or of working tax credit.

Direct payments

17A(1) The Secretary of State may by regulations make provision for and in connection with requiring or authorising the responsible authority in the case of a person of a prescribed description who falls within subsection (2) to make, with that person's consent, such payments to him as they may determine in accordance with the regulations in respect of his securing the provision of the service mentioned in that subsection.

(2) A person falls within this subsection if he is—
   (a) a person with parental responsibility for a disabled child,
   (b) a disabled person with parental responsibility for a child, or
   (c) a disabled child aged 16 or 17,
   and a local authority ('the responsible authority') have decided for the purposes of section 17 that the child's needs (or, if he is such a disabled child, his needs) call for the provision by them of a service in exercise of functions conferred on them under that section.

(3) Subsections (3) to (5) and (7) of section 57 of the 2001 Act shall apply, with any necessary modifications, in relation to regulations under this section as they apply in relation to regulations under that section.

(4) Regulations under this section shall provide that, where payments are made under the regulations to a person falling within subsection (5)—
   (a) the payments shall be made at the rate mentioned in subsection (4)(a) of section 57 of the 2001 Act (as applied by subsection (3)); and
   (b) subsection (4)(b) of that section shall not apply.

(5) A person falls within this subsection if he is—
   (a) a person falling within subsection (2)(a) or (b) and the child in question is aged 16 or 17, or
   (b) a person who is in receipt of income support under Part 7 of the Social Security Contributions and Benefits Act 1992 (c 4), of any element of

---

5 Words in italics inserted by the Welfare Reform Act (WRA) 2007, s 28(1), Sch 3, para 6(1), (2). Not yet in force: see WRA 2007 s70(2).

child tax credit other than the family element, of working tax credit, *of an income-based jobseeker's allowance or of an income-related employment and support allowance.*[6]

(6)   In this section—

'the 2001 Act' means the Health and Social Care Act 2001;

'disabled' in relation to an adult has the same meaning as that given by section 17(11) in relation to a child;

'prescribed' means specified in or determined in accordance with regulations under this section (and has the same meaning in the provisions of the 2001 Act mentioned in subsection (3) as they apply by virtue of that subsection).

Vouchers for persons with parental responsibility for disabled children

17B(1)   The Secretary of State may by regulations make provision for the issue by a local authority of vouchers to a person with parental responsibility for a disabled child.

(2)   'Voucher' means a document whereby, if the local authority agrees with the person with parental responsibility that it would help him care for the child if the person with parental responsibility had a break from caring, that person may secure the temporary provision of services for the child under section 17.

(3)   The regulations may, in particular, provide—

(a)   for the value of a voucher to be expressed in terms of money, or of the delivery of a service for a period of time, or both;

(b)   for the person who supplies a service against a voucher, or for the arrangement under which it is supplied, to be approved by the local authority;

(c)   for a maximum period during which a service (or a service of a prescribed description) can be provided against a voucher.

Day care for pre-school and other children

18(1)   Every local authority shall provide such day care for children in need within their area who are—

(a)   aged five or under; and

(b)   not yet attending schools,

as is appropriate.

(2)   A local authority (in Wales)[7] may provide day care for children within their area who satisfy the conditions mentioned in subsection (1)(a) and (b) even though they are not in need.

(3)   A local authority may provide facilities (including training, advice, guidance and counselling) for those—

(a)   caring for children in day care; or

(b)   who at any time accompany such children while they are in day care.

(4)   In this section 'day care' means any form of care or supervised activity provided for children during the day (whether or not it is provided on a regular basis).

(5)   Every local authority shall provide for children in need within their area who are attending any school such care or supervised activities as is appropriate—

(a)   outside school hours; or

(b)   during school holidays.

(6)   A local authority (in Wales)[8] may provide such care or supervised activities for children within their area who are attending any school even though those children are not in need.

---

6   Words in italics inserted by the Welfare Reform Act (WRA) 2007, s 28(1), Sch 3, para 6(1), (3). Not yet in force: see WRA 2007 s70(2).

7   Words 'in Wales' inserted by the Childcare Act 2006, s 103(1), Sch 2, para 4(a). For appointment see Childcare Act 2006, ss 109(2), 110(1), (5)(c).

8   Words 'in Wales' inserted by the Childcare Act 2006, s 103(1), Sch 2, para 4(a). For appointment see Childcare Act 2006, ss 109(2), 110(1), (5)(c).

(7) In this section 'supervised activity' means an activity supervised by a responsible person.

Review of provision for day care, child minding, etc
19 [*Repealed.*]

Provision of accommodation for children: general
20(1) Every local authority shall provide accommodation for any child in need within their area who appears to them to require accommodation as a result of—
  (a) there being no person who has parental responsibility for him;
  (b) his being lost or having been abandoned; or
  (c) the person who has been caring for him being prevented (whether or not permanently, and for whatever reason) from providing him with suitable accommodation or care.

(2) Where a local authority provide accommodation under subsection(1) for a child who is ordinarily resident in the area of another local authority, that other local authority may take over the provision of accommodation for the child within—
  (a) three months of being notified in writing that the child is being provided with accommodation; or
  (b) such other longer period as may be prescribed.

(3) Every local authority shall provide accommodation for any child in need within their area who has reached the age of sixteen and whose welfare the authority consider is likely to be seriously prejudiced if they do not provide him with accommodation.

(4) A local authority may provide accommodation for any child within their area (even though a person who has parental responsibility for him is able to provide him with accommodation) if they consider that to do so would safeguard or promote the child's welfare.

(5) A local authority may provide accommodation for any person who has reached the age of sixteen but is under twenty-one in any community home which takes children who have reached the age of sixteen if they consider that to do so would safeguard or promote his welfare.

(6) Before providing accommodation under this section, a local authority shall, so far as is reasonably practicable and consistent with the child's welfare—
  (a) ascertain the child's wishes and feelings regarding the provision of accommodation; and
  (b) give due consideration (having regard to his age and understanding) to such wishes and feelings of the child as they have been able to ascertain.

(7) A local authority may not provide accommodation under this section for any child if any person who—
  (a) has parental responsibility for him; and
  (b) is willing and able to—
    (i) provide accommodation for him; or
    (ii) arrange for accommodation to be provided for him,
  objects.

(8) Any person who has parental responsibility for a child may at any time remove the child from accommodation provided by or on behalf of the local authority under this section.

(9) Subsections (7) and (8) do not apply while any person—
  (a) in whose favour a residence order is in force with respect to the child;
  (aa) who is a special guardian of the child; or
  (b) who has care of the child by virtue of an order made in the exercise of the High Court's inherent jurisdiction with respect to children,
  agrees to the child being looked after in accommodation provided by or on behalf of the local authority.

(10) Where there is more than one such person as is mentioned in subsection (9), all of them must agree.

(11) Subsections (7) and (8) do not apply where a child who has reached the age of sixteen agrees to being provided with accommodation under this section.

Provision of accommodation for children in police protection or detention or on remand, etc

21(1) Every local authority shall make provision for the reception and accommodation of children who are removed or kept away from home under Part V.

(2) Every local authority shall receive, and provide accommodation for, children—

(a) in police protection whom they are requested to receive under section 46(3)(f);

(b) whom they are requested to receive under section 38(6) of the Police and Criminal Evidence Act 1984;

(c) who are—

(i) on remand (within the meaning of the section) under paragraph 7(5) of Schedule 7 to the Powers of Criminal Courts (Sentencing) Act 2000 or section 23(1) of the Children and Young Persons Act 1969; or

(ii) the subject of a supervision order imposing a local authority residence requirement under paragraph 5 of Schedule 6 to that Act of 2000,

or a foster parent residence requirement under paragraph 5A of that Schedule,

and with respect to whom they are the designated authority.

(3) Where a child has been—

(a) removed under Part V; or

(b) detained under section 38 of the Police and Criminal Evidence Act 1984,

and he is not being provided with accommodation by a local authority or in a hospital vested in the Secretary of State or a Primary Care Trust, or otherwise made available pursuant to arrangements made by a Local Health Board or a Primary Care Trust, any reasonable expenses of accommodating him shall be recoverable from the local authority in whose area he is ordinarily resident.

Duties of local authorities in relation to children looked after by them

General duty of local authority in relation to children looked after by them

22(1) In this Act, any reference to a child who is looked after by a local authority is a reference to a child who is—

(a) in their care; or

(b) provided with accommodation by the authority in the exercise of any functions (in particular those under this Act) which are social services functions within the meaning of the Local Authority Social Services Act 1970 , apart from functions under sections 17, 23B and 24B.

(2) In subsection(1) 'accommodation' means accommodation which is provided for a continuous period of more than 24 hours.

(3) It shall be the duty of a local authority looking after any child—

(a) to safeguard and promote his welfare; and

(b) to make such use of services available for children cared for by their own parents as appears to the authority reasonable in his case.

(3A) The duty of a local authority under subsection (3)(a) to safeguard and promote the welfare of a child looked after by them includes in particular a duty to promote the child's educational achievement.

(4) Before making any decision with respect to a child whom they are looking after, or proposing to look after, a local authority shall, so far as is reasonably practicable, ascertain the wishes and feelings of—

(a) the child;

(b) his parents;

(c) any person who is not a parent of his but who has parental responsibility for him; and

(d) any other person whose wishes and feelings the authority consider to be relevant,

regarding the matter to be decided.

(5) In making any such decision a local authority shall give due consideration—

(a) having regard to his age and understanding, to such wishes and feelings of the child as they have been able to ascertain;

(b) to such wishes and feelings of any person mentioned in subsection (4)(b) to (d) as they have been able to ascertain; and

(c) to the child's religious persuasion, racial origin and cultural and linguistic background.

(6) If it appears to a local authority that it is necessary, for the purpose of protecting members of the public from serious injury, to exercise their powers with respect to a child whom they are looking after in a manner which may not be consistent with their duties under this section, they may do so.

(7) If the Secretary of State considers it necessary, for the purpose of protecting members of the public from serious injury, to give directions to a local authority with respect to the exercise of their powers with respect to a child whom they are looking after, he may give such directions to the authority.

(8) Where any such directions are given to an authority they shall comply with them even though doing so is inconsistent with their duties under this section.

Provision of accommodation and maintenance by local authority for children whom they are looking after

23(1) It shall be the duty of any local authority looking after a child—

(a) when he is in their care, to provide accommodation for him; and

(b) to maintain him in other respects apart from providing accommodation for him.

(2) A local authority shall provide accommodation and maintenance for any child whom they are looking after by—

(a) placing him (subject to subsection (5) and any regulations made by the Secretary of State) with—

(i) a family;

(ii) a relative of his; or

(iii) any other suitable person,

on such terms as to payment by the authority and otherwise as the authority may determine (subject to section 49 of the Children Act 2004);

(aa) maintaining him in an appropriate children's home; or

(f) making such other arrangements as—

(i) seem appropriate to them; and

(ii) comply with any regulations made by the Secretary of State.

(2A) Where under subsection (2)(aa) a local authority maintains a child in a home provided, equipped and maintained by the Secretary of State under section 82(5), it shall do so on such terms as the Secretary of State may from time to time determine.

(3) Any person with whom a child has been placed under subsection (2)(a) is referred to in this Act as a local authority foster parent unless he falls within subsection (4).

(4) A person falls within this subsection if he is—

(a) a parent of the child;

(b) a person who is not a parent of the child but who has parental responsibility for him; or

(c) where the child is in care and there was a residence order in force with respect to him immediately before the care order was made, a person in whose favour the residence order was made.

(5) Where a child is in the care of a local authority, the authority may only allow him to live with a person who falls within subsection (4) in accordance with regulations made by the Secretary of State.

(5A) For the purposes of subsection (5) a child shall be regarded as living with a person if he stays with that person for a continuous period of more than 24 hours

(6) Subject to any regulations made by the Secretary of State for the purposes of this subsection, any local authority looking after a child shall make arrangements to enable him to live with—
(a) a person falling within subsection (4); or
(b) a relative, friend or other person connected with him,
unless that would not be reasonably practicable or consistent with his welfare.

(7) Where a local authority provide accommodation for a child whom they are looking after, they shall, subject to the provisions of this Part and so far as is reasonably practicable and consistent with his welfare, secure that—
(a) the accommodation is near his home; and
(b) where the authority are also providing accommodation for a sibling of his, they are accommodated together.

(8) Where a local authority provide accommodation for a child whom they are looking after and who is disabled, they shall, so far as is reasonably practicable, secure that the accommodation is not unsuitable to his particular needs.

(9) Part II of Schedule 2 shall have effect for the purposes of making further provision as to children looked after by local authorities and in particular as to the regulations that may be made under subsections (2)(a) and (f) and (5).

(10) In this Act—
'appropriate children's home' means a children's home in respect of which a person is registered under Part II of the Care Standards Act 2000; and
'children's home' has the same meaning as in that Act.

Advice and assistance for certain children and young persons

The responsible authority and relevant children

23A(1) The responsible local authority shall have the functions set out in section 23B in respect of a relevant child.

(2) In subsection(1) 'relevant child' means (subject to subsection (3)) a child who—
(a) is not being looked after by any local authority;
(b) was, before last ceasing to be looked after, an eligible child for the purposes of paragraph 19B of Schedule 2; and
(c) is aged sixteen or seventeen.

(3) The Secretary of State may prescribe—
(a) additional categories of relevant children; and
(b) categories of children who are not to be relevant children despite falling within subsection (2).

(4) In subsection(1) the 'responsible local authority' is the one which last looked after the child.

(5) If under subsection (3)(a) the Secretary of State prescribes a category of relevant children which includes children who do not fall within subsection (2)(b) (for example, because they were being looked after by a local authority in Scotland), he may in the regulations also provide for which local authority is to be the responsible local authority for those children.

Additional functions of the responsible authority in respect of relevant children

23B(1) It is the duty of each local authority to take reasonable steps to keep in touch with a relevant child for whom they are the responsible authority, whether he is within their area or not.

(2) It is the duty of each local authority to appoint a personal adviser for each relevant child (if they have not already done so under paragraph 19C of Schedule 2).

(3) It is the duty of each local authority, in relation to any relevant child who does not already have a pathway plan prepared for the purposes of paragraph 19B of Schedule 2—

(a) to carry out an assessment of his needs with a view to determining what advice, assistance and support it would be appropriate for them to provide him under this Part; and

(b) to prepare a pathway plan for him.

(4) The local authority may carry out such an assessment at the same time as any assessment of his needs is made under any enactment referred to in sub-paragraphs (a) to (c) of paragraph 3 of Schedule 2, or under any other enactment.

(5) The Secretary of State may by regulations make provision as to assessments for the purposes of subsection (3).

(6) The regulations may in particular make provision about—

(a) who is to be consulted in relation to an assessment;

(b) the way in which an assessment is to be carried out, by whom and when;

(c) the recording of the results of an assessment;

(d) the considerations to which the local authority are to have regard in carrying out an assessment.

(7) The authority shall keep the pathway plan under regular review.

(8) The responsible local authority shall safeguard and promote the child's welfare and, unless they are satisfied that his welfare does not require it, support him by—

(a) maintaining him;

(b) providing him with or maintaining him in suitable accommodation; and

(c) providing support of such other descriptions as may be prescribed.

(9) Support under subsection (8) may be in cash.

(10) The Secretary of State may by regulations make provision about the meaning of 'suitable accommodation' and in particular about the suitability of landlords or other providers of accommodation.

(11) If the local authority have lost touch with a relevant child, despite taking reasonable steps to keep in touch, they must without delay—

(a) consider how to re-establish contact; and

(b) take reasonable steps to do so,

and while the child is still a relevant child must continue to take such steps until they succeed.

(12) Subsections (7) to (9) of section 17 apply in relation to support given under this section as they apply in relation to assistance given under that section.

(13) Subsections (4) and (5) of section 22 apply in relation to any decision by a local authority for the purposes of this section as they apply in relation to the decisions referred to in that section.

Continuing functions in respect of former relevant children

23C(1) Each local authority shall have the duties provided for in this section towards—

(a) a person who has been a relevant child for the purposes of section 23A (and would be one if he were under eighteen), and in relation to whom they were the last responsible authority; and

(b) a person who was being looked after by them when he attained the age of eighteen, and immediately before ceasing to be looked after was an eligible child,

and in this section such a person is referred to as a 'former relevant child'.

(2) It is the duty of the local authority to take reasonable steps—
  (a) to keep in touch with a former relevant child whether he is within their area or not; and
  (b) if they lose touch with him, to re-establish contact.

(3) It is the duty of the local authority—
  (a) to continue the appointment of a personal adviser for a former relevant child; and
  (b) to continue to keep his pathway plan under regular review.

(4) It is the duty of the local authority to give a former relevant child—
  (a) assistance of the kind referred to in section 24B(1), to the extent that his welfare requires it;
  (b) assistance of the kind referred to in section 24B(2), to the extent that his welfare and his educational or training needs require it;
  (c) other assistance, to the extent that his welfare requires it.

(5) The assistance given under subsection (4)(c) may be in kind or, in exceptional circumstances, in cash.

(6) Subject to subsection (7), the duties set out in subsections (2), (3) and (4) subsist until the former relevant child reaches the age of twenty-one.

(7) If the former relevant child's pathway plan sets out a programme of education or training which extends beyond his twenty-first birthday—
  (a) the duty set out in subsection (4)(b) continues to subsist for so long as the former relevant child continues to pursue that programme; and
  (b) the duties set out in subsections (2) and (3) continue to subsist concurrently with that duty.

(8) For the purposes of subsection (7)(a) there shall be disregarded any interruption in a former relevant child's pursuance of a programme of education or training if the local authority are satisfied that he will resume it as soon as is reasonably practicable.

(9) Section 24B(5) applies in relation to a person being given assistance under subsection (4)(b) as it applies in relation to a person to whom section 24B(3) applies.

(10) Subsections (7) to (9) of section 17 apply in relation to assistance given under this section as they apply in relation to assistance given under that section.

Personal advisers

23D(1) The Secretary of State may by regulations require local authorities to appoint a personal adviser for children or young persons of a prescribed description who have reached the age of sixteen but not the age of twenty-one who are not—
  (a) children who are relevant children for the purposes of section 23A;
  (b) the young persons referred to in section 23C; or
  (c) the children referred to in paragraph 19C of Schedule 2.

(2) Personal advisers appointed under or by virtue of this Part shall (in addition to any other functions) have such functions as the Secretary of State prescribes.

Pathway plans

23E(1) In this Part, a reference to a 'pathway plan' is to a plan setting out—
  (a) in the case of a plan prepared under paragraph 19B of Schedule 2—
    (i) the advice, assistance and support which the local authority intend to provide a child under this Part, both while they are looking after him and later; and
    (ii) when they might cease to look after him; and

(b) in the case of a plan prepared under section 23B, the advice, assistance and support which the local authority intend to provide under this Part, and dealing with such other matters (if any) as may be prescribed.

(2) The Secretary of State may by regulations make provision about pathway plans and their review.

Persons qualifying for advice and assistance

24(1) In this Part 'a person qualifying for advice and assistance' means a person to whom subsection (1A) or (1B) applies—

(1A) This subsection applies to a person—

(a) who has reached the age of sixteen but not the age of twenty-one;

(b) with respect to whom a special guardianship order is in force (or, if he has reached the age of eighteen, was in force when he reached that age); and

(c) who was, immediately before the making of that order, looked after by a local authority.

(1B) This subsection applies to a person to whom subsection (1A) does not apply, and who—

(a) is under twenty-one; and

(b) at any time after reaching the age of sixteen but while still a child was, but is no longer, looked after, accommodated or fostered.

(2) In subsection (1B)(1)(b), 'looked after, accommodated or fostered' means—

(a) looked after by a local authority;

(b) accommodated by or on behalf of a voluntary organisation;

(c) accommodated in a private children's home;

(d) accommodated for a consecutive period of at least three months—

(i) by any Local Health Board, Special Health Authority, Primary Care Trust or local education authority, or

(ii) in any care home or independent hospital or in any accommodation provided by a National Health Service trust or NHS Foundation Trust; or

(e) privately fostered.

(3) Subsection (2)(d) applies even if the period of three months mentioned there began before the child reached the age of sixteen.

(4) In the case of a person qualifying for advice and assistance by virtue of subsection (2)(a), it is the duty of the local authority which last looked after him to take such steps as they think appropriate to contact him at such times as they think appropriate with a view to discharging their functions under sections 24A and 24B.

(5) In each of sections 24A and 24B, the local authority under the duty or having the power mentioned there ('the relevant authority') is—

(za) in the case of a person to whom subsection (1A) applies, a local authority determined in accordance with regulations made by the Secretary of State;

(a) in the case of a person qualifying for advice and assistance by virtue of subsection (2)(a), the local authority which last looked after him; or

(b) in the case of any other person qualifying for advice and assistance, the local authority within whose area the person is (if he has asked for help of a kind which can be given under section 24A or 24B).

Advice and assistance

24A(1) The relevant authority shall consider whether the conditions in subsection (2) are satisfied in relation to a person qualifying for advice and assistance.

(2) The conditions are that—

(a) he needs help of a kind which they can give under this section or section 24B; and

(b) in the case of a person to whom section 24(1A) applies, or to whom section 24(1B) applies and who was not being looked after by any local authority, they are satisfied that the person by whom he was being looked after does not have the necessary facilities for advising or befriending him.

(3) If the conditions are satisfied—
(a) they shall advise and befriend him if he was being looked after by a local authority or was accommodated by or on behalf of a voluntary organisation; and
(b) in any other case they may do so.

(4) Where as a result of this section a local authority are under a duty, or are empowered, to advise and befriend a person, they may also give him assistance.

(5) The assistance may be in kind and, in exceptional circumstances, assistance may be given—
(a) by providing accommodation, if in the circumstances assistance may not be given in respect of the accommodation under section 24B, or
(b) in cash.

(6) Subsections (7) to (9) of section 17 apply in relation to assistance given under this section or section 24B as they apply in relation to assistance given under that section.

Employment, education and training

24B(1) The relevant local authority may give assistance to any person who qualifies for advice and assistance by virtue of section 24(1A) or section 24(2)(a) by contributing to expenses incurred by him in living near the place where he is, or will be, employed or seeking employment.

(2) The relevant local authority may give assistance to a person to whom subsection (3) applies by—
(a) contributing to expenses incurred by the person in question in living near the place where he is, or will be, receiving education or training; or
(b) making a grant to enable him to meet expenses connected with his education or training.

(3) This subsection applies to any person who—
(a) is under twenty-four; and
(b) qualifies for advice and assistance by virtue of section 24(1A) or section 24(2)(a), or would have done so if he were under 21

(4) Where a local authority are assisting a person under subsection (2) they may disregard any interruption in his attendance on the course if he resumes it as soon as is reasonably practicable.

(5) Where the local authority are satisfied that a person to whom subsection (3) applies who is in full-time further or higher education needs accommodation during a vacation because his term-time accommodation is not available to him then, they shall give him assistance by—
(a) providing him with suitable accommodation during the vacation; or
(b) paying him enough to enable him to secure such accommodation himself.

(6) The Secretary of State may prescribe the meaning of 'full-time', 'further education', 'higher education' and 'vacation' for the purposes of subsection (5).

Information

24C(1) Where it appears to a local authority that a person—
(a) with whom they are under a duty to keep in touch under section 23B, 23C or 24; or
(b) whom they have been advising and befriending under section 24A; or
(c) to whom they have been giving assistance under section 24B,

proposes to live, or is living, in the area of another local authority, they must inform that other authority.

(2) Where a child who is accommodated—

   (a) by a voluntary organisation or in a private children's home;

   (b) by any Local Health Board, Special Health Authority, Primary Care Trust or local education authority; or

   (c) in any care home or independent hospital or any accommodation provided by a National Health Service trust or NHS Foundation Trust,

   ceases to be so accommodated, after reaching the age of sixteen, the organisation, authority or (as the case may be) person carrying on the home shall inform the local authority within whose area the child proposes to live.

(3) Subsection (2) only applies, by virtue of paragraph (b) or (c), if the accommodation has been provided for a consecutive period of at least three months.

Representations: sections 23A to 24B

24D(1) Every local authority shall establish a procedure for considering representations (including complaints) made to them by—

   (a) a relevant child for the purposes of section 23A or a young person falling within section 23C;

   (b) a person qualifying for advice and assistance; or

   (c) a person falling within section 24B(2),

   about the discharge of their functions under this Part in relation to him.

(1A) Regulations may be made by the Secretary of State imposing time limits on the making of representations under subsection (1).

(2) In considering representations under subsection (1), a local authority shall comply with regulations (if any) made by the Secretary of State for the purposes of this subsection.

Use of accommodation for restricting liberty

25(1) Subject to the following provisions of this section, a child who is being looked after by a local authority may not be placed, and, if placed, may not be kept, in accommodation provided for the purpose of restricting liberty ('secure accommodation') unless it appears—

   (a) that—

      (i) he has a history of absconding and is likely to abscond from any other description of accommodation; and

      (ii) if he absconds, he is likely to suffer significant harm; or

   (b) that if he is kept in any other description of accommodation he is likely to injure himself or other persons.

(2) The Secretary of State may by regulations—

   (a) specify a maximum period—

      (i) beyond which a child may not be kept in secure accommodation without the authority of the court; and

      (ii) for which the court may authorise a child to be kept in secure accommodation;

   (b) empower the court from time to time to authorise a child to be kept in secure accommodation for such further period as the regulations may specify; and

   (c) provide that applications to the court under this section shall be ade only by local authorities.

(3) It shall be the duty of a court hearing an application under this section to determine whether any relevant criteria for keeping a child in secure accommodation are satisfied in his case.

(4) If a court determines that any such criteria are satisfied, it shall make an order authorising the child to be kept in secure accommodation and specifying the maximum period for which he may be so kept.

(5)   On any adjournment of the hearing of an application under this section, a court may make an interim order permitting the child to be kept during the period of the adjournment in secure accommodation.

(6)   No court shall exercise the powers conferred by this section in respect of a child who is not legally represented in that court unless, having been informed of his right to apply for representation funded by the Legal Services Commission as part of the Community Legal Service or Criminal Defence Service and having had the opportunity to do so, he refused or failed to apply.

(7)   The Secretary of State may by regulations provide that—

(a)   this section shall or shall not apply to any description of children specified in the regulations;

(b)   this section shall have effect in relation to children of a description specified in the regulations subject to such modifications as may be so specified;

(c)   such other provisions as may be so specified shall have effect for the purpose of determining whether a child of a description specified in the regulations may be placed or kept in secure accommodation.

(8)   The giving of an authorisation under this section shall not prejudice any power of any court in England and Wales or Scotland to give directions relating to the child to whom the authorisation relates.

(9)   This section is subject to section 20(8).

Review of cases and inquiries into representations

26(1)   The Secretary of State may make regulations requiring the case of each child who is being looked after by a local authority to be reviewed in accordance with the provisions of the regulations.

(2)   The regulations may, in particular, make provision—

(a)   as to the manner in which each case is to be reviewed;

(b)   as to the considerations to which the local authority are to have regard in reviewing each case;

(c)   as to the time when each case is first to be reviewed and the frequency of subsequent reviews;

(d)   requiring the authority, before conducting any review, to seek the views of—

(i)   the child;

(ii)   his parents;

(iii)   any person who is not a parent of his but who has parental responsibility for him; and

(iv)   any other person whose views the authority consider to be relevant,

including, in particular, the views of those persons in relation to any particular matter which is to be considered in the course of the review;

(e)   requiring the authority, in the case of a child who is in their care—

(i)   to keep the section 31A plan for the child under review and, if they are of the opinion that some change is required, to revise the plan, or make a new plan, accordingly,

to consider, whether an application should be made to discharge the care order;

(f)   requiring the authority, in the case of a child in accommodation provided by the authority—

(i)   if there is no plan for the future care of the child, to prepare one,

(ii)   if there is such a plan for the child, to keep it under review and, if they are of the opinion that some change is required, to revise the plan or make a new plan, accordingly,

(iii)   to consider, whether the accommodation accords with the requirements of this Part;

(g) requiring the authority to inform the child, so far as is reasonably practicable, of any steps he may take under this Act;

(h) requiring the authority to make arrangements, including arrangements with such other bodies providing services as it considers appropriate, to implement any decision which they propose to make in the course, or as a result, of the review;

(i) requiring the authority to notify details of the result of the review and of any decision taken by them in consequence of the review to—

(i) the child;

(ii) his parents;

(iii) any person who is not a parent of his but who has parental responsibility for him; and

(iv) any other person whom they consider ought to be notified;

(j) requiring the authority to monitor the arrangements which they have made with a view to ensuring that they comply with the regulations.

(k) for the authority to appoint a person in respect of each case to carry out in the prescribed manner the functions mentioned in subsection (2A) and any prescribed function.

(2A) The functions referred to in subsection (2)(k) are—

(a) participating in the review of the case in question,

(b) monitoring the performance of the authority's functions in respect of the review,

(c) referring the case to an officer of the Children and Family Court Advisory and Support Service or a Welsh family proceedings officer, if the person appointed under subsection (2)(k) considers it appropriate to do so.

(2B) A person appointed under subsection (2)(k) must be a person of a prescribed description.

(2C) In relation to children whose cases are referred to officers under subsection (2A)(c), the Lord Chancellor may by regulations—

(a) extend any functions of the officers in respect of family proceedings (within the meaning of section 12 of the Criminal Justice and Court Services Act 2000) to other proceedings,

(b) require any functions of the officers to be performed in the manner prescribed by the regulations.

(2D) The power to make regulations in subsection (2C) is exercisable in relation to functions of Welsh family proceedings officers only with the consent of the National Assembly for Wales.

(3) Every local authority shall establish a procedure for considering any representations (including any complaint) made to them by—

(a) any child who is being looked after by them or who is not being looked after by them but is in need;

(b) a parent of his;

(c) any person who is not a parent of his but who has parental responsibility for him;

(d) any local authority foster parent;

(e) such other person as the authority consider has a sufficient interest in the child's welfare to warrant his representations being considered by them,

about the discharge by the authority of any of their functions under this Part in relation to the child.

(3A) The following are qualifying functions for the purposes of subsection (3)—

(a) functions under this Part,

(b) such functions under Part 4 or 5 as are specified by the Secretary of State in regulations.

(3B) The duty under subsection (3) extends to representations (including complaints) made to the authority by—

(a) any person mentioned in section 3(1) of the Adoption and Children Act 2002 (persons for whose needs provision is made by the Adoption Service) and any other person to whom arrangements for the provision of adoption support services (within the meaning of that Act) extend,

(b) such other person as the authority consider has sufficient interest in a child who is or may be adopted to warrant his representations being considered by them,

about the discharge by the authority of such functions under the Adoption and Children Act 2002 as are specified by the Secretary of State in regulations.

(3C) The duty under subsection (3) extends to any representations (including complaints) which are made to the authority by—

(a) a child with respect to whom a special guardianship order is in force,

(b) a special guardian or a parent of such a child,

(c) any other person the authority consider has a sufficient interest in the welfare of such a child to warrant his representations being considered by them, or

(d) any person who has applied for an assessment under section 14F(3) or (4),

about the discharge by the authority of such functions under section 14F as may be specified by the Secretary of State in regulations.

(4) The procedure shall ensure that at least one person who is not a member or officer of the authority takes part in—

(a) the consideration; and

(b) any discussions which are held by the authority about the action (if any) to be taken in relation to the child in the light of the consideration,

But this subsection is subject to subsection (5A).

(4A) Regulations may be made by the Secretary of State imposing time limits on the making of representations under this section.

(5) In carrying out any consideration of representations under this section a local authority shall comply with any regulations made by the Secretary of State for the purpose of regulating the procedure to be followed.

(5A) Regulations under subsection (5) may provide that subsection (4) does not apply in relation to any consideration or discussion which takes place as part of a procedure for which provision is made by the regulations for the purpose of resolving informally the matters raised in the representations.

(6) The Secretary of State may make regulations requiring local authorities to monitor the arrangements that they have made with a view to ensuring that they comply with any regulations made for the purposes of subsection (5).

(7) Where any representation has been considered under the procedure established by a local authority under this section, the authority shall—

(a) have due regard to the findings of those considering the representation; and

(b) take such steps as are reasonably practicable to notify (in writing)—

(i) the person making the representation;

(ii) the child (if the authority consider that he has sufficient understanding); and

(iii) such other persons (if any) as appear to the authority to be likely to be affected,

of the authority's decision in the matter and their reasons for taking that decision and of any action which they have taken, or propose to take.

(8) Every local authority shall give such publicity to their procedure for considering representations under this section as they consider appropriate.

26ZA[*Repealed.*]

Representations: further consideration (Wales)

26ZB(1) The Secretary of State may by regulations make provision for the further consideration of representations which have been considered by a local authority in Wales under section 24D or section 26.

(2) The regulations may in particular make provision—

(a) for the further consideration of a representation by an independent panel established under the regulations;

(b) about the procedure to be followed on the further consideration of a representation;

(c) for the making of recommendations about the action to be taken as the result of a representation;

(d) about the making of reports about a representation;

(e) about the action to be taken by the local authority concerned as a result of the further consideration of a representation;

(f) for a representation to be referred back to the local authority concerned for reconsideration by the authority.

(3) The regulations may require—

(a) the making of a payment, in relation to the further consideration of a representation under this section, by any local authority in respect of whose functions the representation is made;

(b) any such payment to be—

(i) made to such person or body as may be specified in the regulations;

(ii) of such amount as may be specified in, or calculated or determined under, the regulations; and

(c) for an independent panel to review the amount chargeable under paragraph (a) in any particular case and, if the panel thinks fit, to substitute a lesser amount.

(4) The regulations may also—

(a) provide for different parts or aspects of a representation to be treated differently;

(b) require the production of information or documents in order to enable a representation to be properly considered;

(c) authorise the disclosure of information or documents relevant to a representation to a person or body who is further considering a representation under the regulations;

and any such disclosure may be authorised notwithstanding any rule of common law that would otherwise prohibit or restrict the disclosure.

Advocacy services

26A(1) Every local authority shall make arrangements for the provision of assistance to—

(a) persons who make or intend to make representations under section 24D; and

(b) children who make or intend to make representations under section 26.

(2) The assistance provided under the arrangements shall include assistance by way of representation.

(2A) he duty under subsection(1) includes a duty to make arrangements for the provision of assistance where representations under section 24D or 26 are further considered under section 26ZB.

(3) The arrangements—

(a) shall secure that a person may not provide assistance if he is a person who is prevented from doing so by regulations made by the Secretary of State; and

(b) shall comply with any other provision made by the regulations in relation to the arrangements.

(4) The Secretary of State may make regulations requiring local authorities to

monitor the steps that they have taken with a view to ensuring that they comply with regulations made for the purposes of subsection (3).

(5)   Every local authority shall give such publicity to their arrangements for the provision of assistance under this section as they consider appropriate.

Co-operation between authorities

27(1) Where it appears to a local authority that any authority mentioned in sub-section (3) could, by taking any specified action, help in the exercise of any of their functions under this Part, they may request the help of that other authority specifying the action in question.

(2)   An authority whose help is so requested shall comply with the request if it is compatible with their own statutory or other duties and obligations and does not unduly prejudice the discharge of any of their functions.

(3)   The authorities are—
       (a) any local authority;
       (b) any local education authority;
       (c) any local housing authority;
       (d) any Local Health Board, Special Health Authority, Primary Care Trust, National Health Service trust or NHS Foundation Trust; and
       (e) any person authorised by the Secretary of State for the purposes of this section.

(4)   [*Repealed.*]

Consultation with local education authorities

28(1) Where—
       (a) a child is being looked after by a local authority; and
       (b) the authority propose to provide accommodation for him in an establish-ment at which education is provided for children who are accommodated there, they shall, so far as is reasonably practicable, consult the appropriate local education authority before doing so.

(2)   Where any such proposal is carried out, the local authority shall, as soon as is reasonably practicable, inform the appropriate local education authority of the arrangements that have been made for the child's accommodation.

(3)   Where the child ceases to be accommodated as mentioned in subsection (1)(b), the local authority shall inform the appropriate local education authority.

(4)   In this section 'the appropriate local education authority' means—
       (a) the local education authority within whose area the local authority's area falls; or,
       (b) where the child has special educational needs and a statement of his needs is maintained under Part IV of the Education Act 1996, the local education authority who maintain the statement.

Recoupment of cost of providing services, etc

29(1) Where a local authority provide any service under section 17 or 18, other than advice, guidance or counselling, they may recover from a person specified in subsection (4) such charge for the service as they consider reasonable.

(2)   Where the authority are satisfied that that person's means are insufficient for it to be reasonably practicable for him to pay the charge, they shall not require him to pay more than he can reasonably be expected to pay.

(3)   No person shall be liable to pay any charge under subsection(1) for a service provided under section 17 or section 18(1) or (5) at any time when he is in receipt of income support under Part VII of the Social Security Contributions and Benefits Act 1992, of any element of child tax credit other than the family element, of working tax credit, of an income-based jobseeker's allowance or of an income-related employment and support allowance.

(3A) No person shall be liable to pay any charge under subsection(1) for a service provided under section 18(2) or (6) at any time when he is in receipt of income support under Part VII of the Social Security Contributions and Benefits Act 1992, of an income-based jobseeker's allowance or of an income-related employment and support allowance.

(3B) No person shall be liable to pay any charge under subsection(1) for a service provided under section 18(2) or (6) at any time when—
  (a) he is in receipt of guarantee state pension credit under section 1(3)(a) of the State Pension Credit Act 2002, or
  (b) he is a member of a couple (within the meaning of that Act) the other member of which is in receipt of guarantee state pension credit.

(4) The persons are—
  (a) where the service is provided for a child under sixteen, each of his parents;
  (b) where it is provided for a child who has reached the age of sixteen, the child himself; and
  (c) where it is provided for a member of the child's family, that member.

(5) Any charge under subsection(1) may, without prejudice to any other method of recovery, be recovered summarily as a civil debt.

(6) Part III of Schedule 2 makes provision in connection with contributions towards the maintenance of children who are being looked after by local authorities and consists of the re-enactment with modifications of provisions in Part V of the Child Care Act 1980.

(7) Where a local authority provide any accommodation under section 20(1) for a child who was (immediately before they began to look after him) ordinarily resident within the area of another local authority, they may recover from that other authority any reasonable expenses incurred by them in providing the accommodation and maintaining him.

(8) Where a local authority provide accommodation under section 21(1) or (2)(a) or (b) for a child who is ordinarily resident within the area of another local authority and they are not maintaining him in—
  (a) a community home provided by them;
  (b) a controlled community home; or
  (c) a hospital vested in the Secretary of State or a Primary Care Trust or any other hospital made available pursuant to arrangements made by a Strategic Health Authority, a Local Health Board or a Primary Care Trust,
  they may recover from that other authority any reasonable expenses incurred by them in providing the accommodation and maintaining him.

(9) Except where subsection (10) applies, Where a local authority comply with any request under section 27(2) in relation to a child or other person who is not ordinarily resident within their area, they may recover from the local authority in whose area the child or person is ordinarily resident any reasonable expenses incurred by them in respect of that person.

(10) Where a local authority ('authority A') comply with any request under section 27(2) from another local authority ('authority B') in relation to a child or other person—
  (a) whose responsible authority is authority B for the purposes of section 23B or 23C; or
  (b) whom authority B are advising or befriending or to whom they are giving assistance by virtue of section 24(5)(a),
  authority A may recover from authority B any reasonable expenses incurred by them in respect of that person.

NHS AND COMMUNITY CARE ACT 1990 (EXTRACTS)

PART III: COMMUNITY CARE: ENGLAND AND WALES

General provisions concerning community care services

Local authority plans for community care services

46(1) Each local authority—

   (a) shall, within such period after the day appointed for the coming into force of this section as the Secretary of State may direct, prepare and publish a plan for the provision of community care services in their area;

   (b) shall keep the plan prepared by them under paragraph (a) above and any further plans prepared by them under this section under review; and

   (c) shall, at such intervals as the Secretary of State may direct, prepare and publish modifications to the current plan, or if the case requires, a new plan.

(2) In carrying out any of their functions under paragraphs (a) to (c) of subsection(1) above, a local authority shall consult—

   (a) any Health Authority and Local Health Board the whole or any part of whose area lies within the area of the local authority;

   (b) [*Repealed.*]

   (c) in so far as any proposed plan, review or modifications of a plan may affect or be affected by the provision or availability of housing and the local authority is not itself a local housing authority, within the meaning of the Housing Act 1985, every such local housing authority whose area is within the area of the local authority;

   (d) such voluntary organisations as appear to the authority to represent the interests of persons who use or are likely to use any community care services within the area of the authority or the interests of private carers who, within that area, provide care to persons for whom, in the exercise of their social services functions, the local authority have a power or a duty to provide a service.

   (e) such voluntary housing agencies and other bodies as appear to the local authority to provide housing or community care services in their area; and

   (f) such other persons as the Secretary of State may direct.

(3) In this section—

   'local authority' means the council of a county, a county borough, a metropolitan district or a London borough or the Common Council of the City of London; 'community care services' means services which a local authority may provide or arrange to be provided under any of the following provisions—

   (a) Part III of the National Assistance Act 1948;

   (b) section 45 of the Health Services and Public Health Act 1968;

   (c) section 21 of and Schedule 8 to the National Health Service Act 1977; and

   (d) section 117 of the Mental Health Act 1983; and

   'private carer' means a person who is not employed to provide the care in question by any body in the exercise of its functions under any enactment.

Assessment of needs for community care services

47(1) Subject to subsections (5) and (6) below, where it appears to a local authority that any person for whom they may provide or arrange for the provision of community care services may be in need of any such services, the authority—

   (a) shall carry out an assessment of his needs for those services; and

   (b) having regard to the results of that assessment, shall then decide whether his needs call for the provision by them of any such services.

(2) If at any time during the assessment of the needs of any person under subsection (1)(a) above it appears to a local authority that he is a disabled person, the authority—

    (a) shall proceed to make such a decision as to the services he requires as is mentioned in section 4 of the Disabled Persons (Services, Consultation and Representation) Act 1986 without his requesting them to do so under that section; and

    (b) shall inform him that they will be doing so and of his rights under that Act.

(3) If at any time during the assessment of the needs of any person under subsection (1)(a) above, it appears to a local authority—

    (a) that there may be a need for the provision to that person by such Primary Care Trust or Health Authority as may be determined in accordance with regulations of any services under the National Health Service Act 2006 or the National Health Service (Wales) Act 2006, or

    (b) that there may be a need for the provision to him of any services which fall within the functions of a local housing authority (within the meaning of the Housing Act 1985) which is not the local authority carrying out the assessment,

the local authority shall notify that Primary Care Trust, Health Authority or local housing authority and invite them to assist, to such extent as is reasonable in the circumstances, in the making of the assessment; and, in making their decision as to the provision of the services needed for the person in question, the local authority shall take into account any services which are likely to be made available for him by that Primary Care Trust, Health Authority or local housing authority.

(4) The Secretary of State may give directions as to the manner in which an assessment under this section is to be carried out or the form it is to take but, subject to any such directions and to subsection (7) below, it shall be carried out in such manner and take such form as the local authority consider appropriate.

(5) Nothing in this section shall prevent a local authority from temporarily providing or arranging for the provision of community care services for any person without carrying out a prior assessment of his needs in accordance with the preceding provisions of this section if, in the opinion of the authority, the condition of that person is such that he requires those services as a matter of urgency.

(6) If, by virtue of subsection (5) above, community care services have been provided temporarily for any person as a matter of urgency, then, as soon as practicable thereafter, an assessment of his needs shall be made in accordance with the preceding provisions of this section.

(7) This section is without prejudice to section 3 of the Disabled Persons (Services, Consultation and Representation) Act 1986.

(8) In this section—

    'disabled person' has the same meaning as in that Act; and

    'local authority' and 'community care services' have the same meanings as in section 46 above.

CARERS (RECOGNITION AND SERVICES) ACT 1995

Assessment of ability of carers to provide care: England and Wales

1(1) Subject to subsection (3) below, in any case where—

    (a) a local authority carry out an assessment under section 47(1)(a) of the National Health Service and Community Care Act 1990 of the needs of a person ('the relevant person') for community care services, and

(b) an individual ('the carer') provides or intends to provide a substantial amount of care on a regular basis for the relevant person,

the carer may request the local authority, before they make their decision as to whether the needs of the relevant person call for the provision of any services, to carry out an assessment of his ability to provide and to continue to provide care for the relevant person; and if he makes such a request, the local authority shall carry out such an assessment and shall take into account the results of that assessment in making that decision.

(2) Subject to subsection (3) below, in any case where—

(a) a local authority assess the needs of a disabled child for the purposes of Part III of the Children Act 1989 or section 2 of the Chronically Sick and Disabled Persons Act 1970, and

(b) an individual ('the carer') provides or intends to provide a substantial amount of care on a regular basis for the disabled child,

the carer may request the local authority, before they make their decision as to whether the needs of the disabled child call for the provision of any services, to carry out an assessment of his ability to provide and to continue to provide care for the disabled child; and if he makes such a request, the local authority shall carry out such an assessment and shall take into account the results of that assessment in making that decision.

(2A) For the purposes of an assessment under subsection(1) or (2), the local authority may take into account, so far as it considers it to be material, an assessment under section 1 or 6 of the Carers and Disabled Children Act 2000.

(2B) In any case where—

(a) a local authority are carrying out an assessment mentioned in paragraph (a) of either subsection(1) or subsection (2) above in relation to the relevant person or (as the case may be) a disabled child, and

(b) it appears to the local authority that an individual may be entitled to request (but has not requested) an assessment under the subsection in question of his ability to provide and to continue to provide care for the relevant person or the disabled child,

the local authority must inform the individual that he may be so entitled before they make their decision as to the needs of the relevant person or the disabled child.

(2C) An assessment under subsection(1) or (2) above must include consideration of whether the carer—

(a) works or wishes to work,

(b) is undertaking, or wishes to undertake, education, training or any leisure activity.

(3) No request may be made under subsection(1) or (2) above by an individual who provides or will provide the care in question—

(a) by virtue of a contract of employment or other contract with any person; or

(b) as a volunteer for a voluntary organisation.

(4) The Secretary of State may give directions as to the manner in which an assessment under subsection(1) or (2) above is to be carried out or the form it is to take but, subject to any such directions, it shall be carried out in such manner and take such form as the local authority consider appropriate.

(5) Section 8 of the Disabled Persons (Services, Consultation and Representation) Act 1986 (duty of local authority to take into account ability of carers) shall not apply in any case where—

(a) an assessment is made under subsection(1) above in respect of an individual who provides the care in question for a disabled person; or

(b) an assessment is made under subsection (2) above.

(6) In this section—

'community care services' has the meaning given by section 46(3) of the National Health Service and Community Care Act 1990;

'child' means a person under the age of eighteen;

'disabled child' means a child who is disabled within the meaning of Part III of the Children Act 1989;

'disabled person' means a person to whom section 29 of the National Assistance Act 1948 applies;

'local authority' has the meaning given by section 46(3) of the National Health Service and Community Care Act 1990; and

'voluntary organisation' has the same meaning as in the National Assistance Act 1948.

(7) [*Repealed.*]

HOUSING GRANTS, CONSTRUCTION AND REGENERATION ACT 1996

Grants: purposes for which grant must or may be given

23(1) The purposes for which an application for a grant must be approved, subject to the provisions of this Chapter, are the following—

(a) facilitating access by the disabled occupant to and from—
   (i) the dwelling, qualifying houseboat or [caravan], or
   (ii) the dwelling or the building in which the dwelling or, as the case may be, flat is situated;

(b) making—
   (i) the dwelling, qualifying houseboat or caravan, or
   (ii) the building,
Safe for the disabled occupant and other persons residing with him;

(c) facilitating access by the disabled occupant to a room used or usable as the principal family room;

(d) facilitating access by the disabled occupant to, or providing for the disabled occupant, a room used or usable for sleeping;

(e) facilitating access by the disabled occupant to, or providing for the disabled occupant, a room in which there is a lavatory, or facilitating the use by the disabled occupant of such a facility;

(f) facilitating access by the disabled occupant to, or providing for the disabled occupant, a room in which there is a bath or shower (or both), or facilitating the use by the disabled occupant of such a facility;

(g) facilitating access by the disabled occupant to, or providing for the disabled occupant, a room in which there is a washhand basin, or facilitating the use by the disabled occupant of such a facility;

(h) facilitating the preparation and cooking of food by the disabled occupant;
   (i) improving any heating system in the dwelling, qualifying houseboat or caravan to meet the needs of the disabled occupant or, if there is no existing heating system in the dwelling or any such system is unsuitable for use by the disabled occupant, providing a heating system there suitable to meet his needs;

(j) facilitating the use by the disabled occupant of a source of power, light or heat by altering the position of one or more means of access to or control of that source or by providing additional means of control;

(k) facilitating access and movement by the disabled occupant around the dwelling, qualifying houseboat or caravan in order to enable him to care for a person who is normally resident there and is in need of such care;

(l) such other purposes as may be specified by order of the Secretary of State.

(2) [*Repealed.*]

(3)   If in the opinion of the local housing authority the relevant works are more or less extensive than is necessary to achieve any of the purposes set out in subsection (1), they may, with the consent of the applicant, treat the application as varied so that the relevant works are limited to or, as the case may be, include such works as seem to the authority to be necessary for that purpose.

Grants: approval of application

24(1)   The local housing authority shall approve an application for a grant for purposes within section 23(1) subject to the following provisions.

(2)   Where an authority entertain an owner's application for a grant made by a person who proposes to acquire a qualifying owner's interest, they shall not approve the application until they are satisfied that he has done so.

(3)   A local housing authority shall not approve an application for a grant unless they are satisfied—
  (a) that the relevant works are necessary and appropriate to meet the needs of the disabled occupant, and
  (b) that it is reasonable and practicable to carry out the relevant works having regard to the age and condition of —
    (i)   the dwelling, qualifying houseboat or caravan, or
    (ii) the building.
  In considering the matters mentioned in paragraph (a) a local housing authority which is not itself a social services authority shall consult the social services authority.

(4)   [*Repealed.*]

(5)   A local housing authority shall not approve a common parts application for a grant unless they are satisfied that the applicant has a power or is under a duty to carry out the relevant works.

CARERS AND DISABLED CHILDREN ACT 2000 (EXTRACTS)

Right of carers to assessment

1(1)   If an individual aged 16 or over ('the carer')—
  (a) provides or intends to provide a substantial amount of care on a regular basis for another individual aged 18 or over ('the person cared for'); and
  (b) asks a local authority to carry out an assessment of his ability to provide and to continue to provide care for the person cared for,
  the local authority must carry out such an assessment if it is satisfied that the person cared for is someone for whom it may provide or arrange for the provision of community care services.

(2)   For the purposes of such an assessment, the local authority may take into account, so far as it considers it to be material, an assessment under section 1(1) of the Carers (Recognition and Services) Act 1995.

(3)   Subsection(1) does not apply if the individual provides or will provide the care in question—
  (a) by virtue of a contract of employment or other contract with any person; or
  (b) as a volunteer for a voluntary organisation.

(3A) An assessment under subsection(1) must include consideration of whether the carer—
  (a) works or wishes to work,
  (b) is undertaking, or wishes to undertake, education, training or any leisure activity.

(4) The Secretary of State (or, in relation to Wales, the National Assembly for Wales) may give directions as to the manner in which an assessment under subsection(1) is to be carried out or the form it is to take.

(5) Subject to any such directions, it is to be carried out in such manner, and is to take such form, as the local authority considers appropriate.

(6) In this section, 'voluntary organisation' has the same meaning as in the National Assistance Act 1948.

Services for carers

2(1) The local authority must consider the assessment and decide—

(a) whether the carer has needs in relation to the care which he provides or intends to provide;

(b) if so, whether they could be satisfied (wholly or partly) by services which the local authority may provide; and

(c) if they could be so satisfied, whether or not to provide services to the carer.

(2) The services referred to are any services which—

(a) the local authority sees fit to provide; and

(b) will in the local authority's view help the carer care for the person cared for, and may take the form of physical help or other forms of support.

(3) A service, although provided to the carer—

(a) may take the form of a service delivered to the person cared for if it is one which, if provided to him instead of to the carer, could fall within community care services and they both agree it is to be so delivered; but

(b) if a service is delivered to the person cared for it may not, except in prescribed circumstances, include anything of an intimate nature.

(4) Regulations may make provision about what is, or is not, of an intimate nature for the purposes of subsection (3).

Vouchers

3(1) Regulations may make provision for the issue of vouchers by local authorities.

(2) 'Voucher' means a document whereby, if the local authority agrees with the carer that it would help him care for the person cared for if the carer had a break from caring, the person cared for may secure that services in lieu of the care which would otherwise have been provided to him by the carer are delivered temporarily to him by another person by way of community care services.

(3) The regulations may, in particular, provide—

(a) for the value of a voucher to be expressed in terms of money, or of the delivery of a service for a period of time, or both;

(b) for the person who supplies a service against a voucher, or for the arrangement under which it is supplied, to be approved by the local authority;

(c) for vouchers to be issued to the carer or to the person cared for;

(d) for a maximum period during which a service (or a service of a prescribed description) can be provided against a voucher.

Assessments and services for both carer and person cared for

4(1) In section 1 of the Carers (Recognition and Services) Act 1995 (which provides for carers to be assessed as to their ability to care in connection with an assessment of the needs of the individual cared for), after subsection (2) insert—

(2A) For the purposes of an assessment under subsection(1) or (2), the local authority may take into account, so far as it considers it to be material, an assessment under section 1 or 6 of the Carers and Disabled Children Act 2000.'

(2)   Subsection (4) applies if the local authority—
   (a) is either providing services under this Act to the carer, or is providing community care services to or in respect of the person cared for (but not both); and
   (b) proposes to provide another service to (or in respect of) the one who is not receiving any such service,
   and the new service, or any service already being provided, is one which could be provided either under this Act, or by way of community care services.

(3)   Subsection (4) also applies if—
   (a) the local authority is not providing services to the carer (under this Act) or to the person cared for (by way of community care services), but proposes to provide services to each of them following an assessment under section 1 and under section 47 of the National Health Service and Community Care Act 1990; or
   (b) the local authority is providing services both to the carer (under this Act) and to the person cared for (by way of community care services), and proposes to provide to either of them a new service,
   and (in a paragraph (a) case) any of the services, or (in a paragraph (b) case) the new service, is one which could be provided either under this Act, or by way of community care services.

(4)   In the case of each such service, the local authority must decide whether the service is, or is in future, to be provided under this Act, or by way of community care services (and hence whether it is, or is in future, to be provided to the carer, or to the person cared for).

(5)   The local authority's decision under subsection (4) is to be made without regard to the means of the carer or of the person cared for.

5   [*Repealed.*]

Assessments: persons with parental responsibility for disabled children

6(1) If a person with parental responsibility for a disabled child—
   (a) provides or intends to provide a substantial amount of care on a regular basis for the child; and
   (b) asks a local authority to carry out an assessment of his ability to provide and to continue to provide care for the child,
   the local authority must carry out such an assessment if it is satisfied that the child and his family are persons for whom it may provide or arrange for the provision of services under section 17 of the Children Act 1989 ('the 1989 Act').

(2)   For the purposes of such an assessment, the local authority may take into account, so far as it considers it to be material, an assessment under section 1(2) of the Carers (Recognition and Services) Act 1995.

(2A) An assessment under subsection(1) must include consideration of whether the person with parental responsibility for the child—
   (a) works or wishes to work,
   (b) is undertaking, or wishes to undertake, education, training or any leisure activity.

(3)   The Secretary of State (or, in relation to Wales, the National Assembly for Wales) may give directions as to the manner in which an assessment under subsection(1) is to be carried out or the form it is to take.

(4)   Subject to any such directions, it is to be carried out in such manner, and is to take such form, as the local authority considers appropriate.

(5)   The local authority must take the assessment into account when deciding what, if any, services to provide under section 17 of the 1989 Act.

(6)   Terms used in this section have the same meaning as in Part III of the 1989 Act.

Duty to inform carers of right to assessment

6A(1) Subsection (2) applies if it appears to a local authority that it would be required to carry out a carer's assessment on being asked to do so by—

(a) the carer, or

(b) a person with parental responsibility for a disabled child ('the responsible person').

(2) The local authority must inform the carer or, as appropriate, the responsible person that he may be entitled to a carer's assessment (but this is subject to subsections (3) and (4)).

(3) Subsection (2) does not apply in relation to the carer if the local authority has previously—

(a) carried out a carer's assessment for him in relation to the person cared for,

(b) informed him that he may be entitled to a carer's assessment in relation to the person cared for, or

(c) carried out an assessment of him under section 4(3) of the Community Care (Delayed Discharges, etc) Act 2003 in relation to the person cared for.

(4) Subsection (2) does not apply in relation to the responsible person if the local authority has previously carried out a carer's assessment for him in relation to the disabled child or informed him that he may be entitled to a carer's assessment in relation to the disabled child.

(5) In this section 'carer's assessment' means—

(a) in the case of the carer, an assessment under section 1 of his ability to provide and to continue to provide care for the person cared for,

(b) in the case of the responsible person, an assessment under section 6 of his ability to provide and to continue to provide care for the disabled child.

LOCAL GOVERNMENT ACT 2000 (EXTRACTS)

Promotion of well-being

2(1) Every local authority are to have power to do anything which they consider is likely to achieve any one or more of the following objects—

(a) the promotion or improvement of the economic well-being of their area,

(b) the promotion or improvement of the social well-being of their area, and

(c) the promotion or improvement of the environmental well-being of their area.

(2) The power under subsection(1) may be exercised in relation to or for the benefit of—

(a) the whole or any part of a local authority's area, or

(b) all or any persons resident or present in a local authority's area.

(3) In determining whether or how to exercise the power under subsection (1), a local authority must have regard to their strategy under section 4.

(4) The power under subsection(1) includes power for a local authority to—

(a) incur expenditure,

(b) give financial assistance to any person,

(c) enter into arrangements or agreements with any person,

(d) co-operate with, or facilitate or co-ordinate the activities of, any person,

(e) exercise on behalf of any person any functions of that person, and

(f) provide staff, goods, services or accommodation to any person.

(5) The power under subsection(1) includes power for a local authority to do anything in relation to, or for the benefit of, any person or area situated outside their area if they consider that it is likely to achieve any one or more of the objects in that subsection.

(6)   Nothing in subsection (4) or (5) affects the generality of the power under subsection (1).

Limits on power to promote well-being

3(1)   The power under section 2(1) does not enable a local authority to do anything which they are unable to do by virtue of any prohibition, restriction or limitation on their powers which is contained in any enactment (whenever passed or made).

(2)   The power under section 2(1) does not enable a local authority to raise money (whether by precepts, borrowing or otherwise).

(3)   The Secretary of State may by order make provision preventing local authorities from doing, by virtue of section 2(1), anything which is specified, or is of a description specified, in the order.

(3A)   The power under subsection (3) may be exercised in relation to—
    (a)   all local authorities,
    (b)   particular local authorities, or
    (c)   particular descriptions of local authority.

(4)   Subject to subsection 4A, before making an order under subsection (3), the Secretary of State must consult such representatives of local government and such other persons (if any) as he considers appropriate.

(4A)   Subsection (4) does not apply to an order under this section which is made only for the purpose of amending an earlier order under this section—
    (a)   so as to extend the earlier order, or any provision of the earlier order, to a particular authority or to authorities of a particular description, or
    (b)   so that the earlier order, or any provision of the earlier order, ceases to apply to a particular authority or to authorities of a particular description.

(5)   Before exercising the power under section 2(1), a local authority must have regard to any guidance for the time being issued by the Secretary of State about the exercise of that power.

(6)   Before issuing any guidance under subsection (5), the Secretary of State must consult such representatives of local government and such other persons (if any) as he considers appropriate.

(7)   In its application to Wales, this section has effect as if for any reference to the Secretary of State there were substituted a reference to the National Assembly for Wales.

(8)   In this section 'enactment' includes an enactment comprised in subordinate legislation (within the meaning of the Interpretation Act 1978).

Payments in cases of maladministration, etc

92(1)   Where a relevant authority consider—
    (a)   that action taken by or on behalf of the authority in the exercise of their functions amounts to, or may amount to, maladministration, and
    (b)   that a person has been, or may have been, adversely affected by that action,
the authority may, if they think appropriate, make a payment to, or provide some other benefit for, that person.

(2)   Any function which is conferred on the Greater London Authority under this section is to be exercisable by the Mayor of London and the London Assembly acting jointly on behalf of the Authority.

(3)   In this section—
'action' includes failure to act,
'relevant authority' has the same meaning as in Part III of this Act.

HEALTH AND SOCIAL CARE ACT 2001

Direct payments

57(1) Regulations may make provision for and in connection with requiring or authorising the responsible authority in the case of a person of a prescribed description who falls within subsection (2) to make, with that person's consent, such payments to him as they may determine in accordance with the regulations in respect of his securing the provision of the service mentioned in paragraph (a) or (b) of that subsection.

(2) A person falls within this subsection if a local authority ('the responsible authority') have decided—

    (a) under section 47 of the 1990 Act (assessment by local authorities of needs for community care services) that his needs call for the provision by them of a particular community care service (within the meaning of section 46 of that Act), or

    (b) under section 2(1) of the Carers and Disabled Children Act 2000 (services for carers) to provide him with a particular service under that Act.

(3) Regulations under this section may, in particular, make provision—

    (a) specifying circumstances in which the responsible authority are not required or authorised to make any payments under the regulations to a person, whether those circumstances relate to the person in question or to the particular service mentioned in paragraph (a) or (b) of subsection (2);

    (b) for any payments required or authorised by the regulations to be made to a person by the responsible authority ('direct payments') to be made to that person ('the payee') as gross payments or alternatively as net payments;

    (c) for the responsible authority to make for the purposes of subsection (4) or (5) such determination as to—

        (i) the payee's means, and

        (ii) the amount (if any) which it would be reasonably practicable for him to pay to the authority by way of reimbursement or contribution,

    as may be prescribed;

    (d) as to the conditions falling to be complied with by the payee which must or may be imposed by the responsible authority in relation to the direct payments (and any conditions which may not be so imposed);

    (e) specifying circumstances in which the responsible authority—

        (i) may or must terminate the making of direct payments,

        (ii) may require repayment (whether by the payee or otherwise) of the whole or part of the direct payments;

    (f) for any sum falling to be paid or repaid to the responsible authority by virtue of any condition or other requirement imposed in pursuance of the regulations to be recoverable as a debt due to the authority;

    (g) displacing functions or obligations of the responsible authority with respect to the provision of the service mentioned in subsection (2)(a) or (b) only to such extent, and subject to such conditions, as may be prescribed;

    (h) authorising direct payments to be made to any prescribed person on behalf of the payee.

(4) For the purposes of subsection (3)(b) 'gross payments' means payments—

    (a) which are made at such a rate as the authority estimate to be equivalent to the reasonable cost of securing the provision of the service concerned; but

    (b) which may be made subject to the condition that the payee pays to the responsible authority, by way of reimbursement, an amount or amounts determined under the regulations.

(5) For the purposes of subsection (3)(b) 'net payments' means payments—
    (a) which are made on the basis that the payee will himself pay an amount or amounts determined under the regulations by way of contribution towards the cost of securing the provision of the service concerned; and
    (b) which are accordingly made at such a rate below that mentioned in subsection (4)(a) as reflects any such contribution by the payee.
(6) Regulations under this section shall provide that, where direct payments are made in respect of a service which, apart from the regulations, would be provided under section 117 of the Mental Health Act 1983 (c. 20)(after-care)—
    (a) the payments shall be made at the rate mentioned in subsection (4)(a); and
    (b) subsection (4)(b) shall not apply.
(7) Regulations made for the purposes of subsection (3)(a) may provide that direct payments shall not be made in respect of the provision of residential accommodation for any person for a period in excess of a prescribed period.
(8) In this section 'prescribed' means specified in or determined in accordance with regulations under this section.

CARERS (EQUAL OPPORTUNITIES) ACT 2004

Duty to inform carers of right to assessment

1(1) In section 1 of the Carers (Recognition and Services) Act 1995 (assessment of ability of carers to provide care), after subsection (2A) there is inserted—
"(2B) In any case where—
    (a) a local authority are carrying out an assessment mentioned in paragraph (a) of either subsection(1) or subsection (2) above in relation to the relevant person or (as the case may be) a disabled child, and
    (b) it appears to the local authority that an individual may be entitled to request (but has not requested) an assessment under the subsection in question of his ability to provide and to continue to provide care for the relevant person or the disabled child,
the local authority must inform the individual that he may be so entitled before they make their decision as to the needs of the relevant person or the disabled child.'
(2) After section 6 of the Carers and Disabled Children Act 2000 (c. 16) there is inserted—
"**6A Duty to inform carers of right to assessment**
(1) Subsection (2) applies if it appears to a local authority that it would be required to carry out a carer's assessment on being asked to do so by—
    (a) the carer, or
    (b) a person with parental responsibility for a disabled child ('the responsible person').
(2) The local authority must inform the carer or, as appropriate, the responsible person that he may be entitled to a carer's assessment (but this is subject to subsections (3) and (4)).
(3) Subsection (2) does not apply in relation to the carer if the local authority has previously—
    (a) carried out a carer's assessment for him in relation to the person cared for,
    (b) informed him that he may be entitled to a carer's assessment in relation to the person cared for, or
    (c) carried out an assessment of him under section 4(3) of the Community Care (Delayed Discharges etc.) Act 2003 in relation to the person cared for.

(4) Subsection (2) does not apply in relation to the responsible person if the local authority has previously carried out a carer's assessment for him in relation to the disabled child or informed him that he may be entitled to a carer's assessment in relation to the disabled child.

(5) In this section 'carer's assessment' means—

    (a) in the case of the carer, an assessment under section 1 of his ability to provide and to continue to provide care for the person cared for,

    (b) in the case of the responsible person, an assessment under section 6 of his ability to provide and to continue to provide care for the disabled child.'

Assessment of carers

2(1) In section 1 of the Carers (Recognition and Services) Act 1995 (assessment of ability of carers to provide care), after subsection (2B)(inserted by section 1) there is inserted—

"(2C) An assessment under subsection(1) or (2) above must include consideration of whether the carer—

    (a) works or wishes to work,

    (b) is undertaking, or wishes to undertake, education, training or any leisure activity.'

(2) In section 1 of the Carers and Disabled Children Act 2000 (c. 16)(right of carer to assessment), after subsection (3) there is inserted—

"(3A) An assessment under subsection(1) must include consideration of whether the carer—

    (a) works or wishes to work,

    (b) is undertaking, or wishes to undertake, education, training or any leisure activity.'

(3) In section 6 of that Act (assessment of person with parental responsibility caring for disabled child), after subsection (2) there is inserted—

"(2A) An assessment under subsection(1) must include consideration of whether the person with parental responsibility for the child—

(a) works or wishes to work,

(b) is undertaking, or wishes to undertake, education, training or any leisure activity.'

Co-operation between authorities

3(1) If a local authority requests an authority mentioned in subsection (5) to assist it in planning the provision of services to persons—

    (a) entitled to an assessment under any of the provisions mentioned in subsection (4), or

    (b) for whom those persons provide, or intend to provide, a substantial amount of care on a regular basis,

the authority mentioned in subsection (5) must give due consideration to the request.

(2) Subsection (3) applies if—

    (a) under a provision mentioned in subsection (4) a local authority is assessing, or has assessed, the ability of a person ('the carer') to provide and to continue to provide care for another person ('the person cared for'), and

    (b) the local authority forms the view that the carer's ability to provide and to continue to provide care for the person cared for might be enhanced by the provision of services (whether for the carer or the person cared for) by an authority mentioned in subsection (5).

(3) If the local authority requests such an authority to provide any such services the authority or person must give due consideration to the request.

(4) The provisions are—

    (a) section 1 of the Carers (Recognition and Services) Act 1995 (c. 12), and

    (b) sections 1 and 6 of the Carers and Disabled Children Act 2000 (c. 16).

(5)   The authorities are—
   (a)   any other local authority,
   (b)   any local education authority,
   (c)   any local housing authority, and
   (d)   any Special Health Authority, Local Health Board, Primary Care Trust, National Health Service Trust or NHS foundation trust.
(6)   Subsections(1) and (3) do not apply in relation to any action which could be the subject of a request by the local authority to the authority mentioned in subsection (5) under section 27 of the Children Act 1989 (c. 41).
(7)   In this section—
   'local authority' has the same meaning as in section 46 of the National Health Service and Community Care Act 1990 (c. 19),
   'local education authority' has the same meaning as in the Education Act 1996 (c. 56), and
   'local housing authority' has the same meaning as in the Housing Act 1985 (c. 68).

NHS ACT 2006 (EXTRACTS)

PART 1: PROMOTION AND PROVISION OF THE HEALTH SERVICE IN ENGLAND
The Secretary of State and the health service in England

Secretary of State's duty to promote health service
1(1)   The Secretary of State must continue the promotion in England of a comprehensive health service designed to secure improvement—
   (a)   in the physical and mental health of the people of England, and
   (b)   in the prevention, diagnosis and treatment of illness.
(2)   The Secretary of State must for that purpose provide or secure the provision of services in accordance with this Act.
(3)   The services so provided must be free of charge except in so far as the making and recovery of charges is expressly provided for by or under any enactment, whenever passed.

General power to provide services

Secretary of State's general power
2(1)   The Secretary of State may—
   (a)   provide such services as he considers appropriate for the purpose of discharging any duty imposed on him by this Act, and
   (b)   do anything else which is calculated to facilitate, or is conducive or incidental to, the discharge of such a duty.
(2)   Subsection(1) does not affect—
   (a)   the Secretary of State's powers apart from this section,
   (b)   Chapter 1 of Part 7 (pharmaceutical services).

Secretary of State's duty as to provision of certain services
3(1)   The Secretary of State must provide throughout England, to such extent as he considers necessary to meet all reasonable requirements—
   (a)   hospital accommodation,
   (b)   other accommodation for the purpose of any service provided under this Act,
   (c)   medical, dental, ophthalmic, nursing and ambulance services,
   (d)   such other services or facilities for the care of pregnant women, women who are breastfeeding and young children as he considers are appropriate as part of the health service,

(e) such other services or facilities for the prevention of illness, the care of persons suffering from illness and the after-care of persons who have suffered from illness as he considers are appropriate as part of the health service,

(f) such other services or facilities as are required for the diagnosis and treatment of illness.

(2) For the purposes of the duty in subsection (1), services provided under—

(a) section 83(2)(primary medical services), section 99(2)(primary dental services) or section 115(4)(primary ophthalmic services)', or

(b) a general medical services contract, a general dental services contract or a general ophthalmic services contract,

must be regarded as provided by the Secretary of State.

(3) This section does not affect Chapter 1 of Part 7 (pharmaceutical services).

Provision of services otherwise than by the Secretary of State

Secretary of State's arrangements with other bodies

12(1) The Secretary of State may arrange with any person or body to provide, or assist in providing, any service under this Act.

(2) Arrangements may be made under subsection(1) with voluntary organisations.

(3) The Secretary of State may make available any facilities provided by him for any service under this Act—

(a) to any person or body carrying out any arrangements under subsection (1), or

(b) to any voluntary organisation eligible for assistance under section 64 or section 65 of the Health Services and Public Health Act 1968 (c. 46).

(4) Where facilities are made available under subsection (3), the Secretary of State may make available the services of any person employed in connection with the facilities by—

(a) the Secretary of State,

(b) a Strategic Health Authority,

(c) a Primary Care Trust,

(d) a Special Health Authority, or

(e) a Local Health Board.

(5) Powers under this section may be exercised on such terms as may be agreed, including terms as to the making of payments by or to the Secretary of State.

(6) Goods or materials may be made available either temporarily or permanently.

(7) Any power to supply goods or materials under this section includes—

(a) a power to purchase and store them, and

(b) a power to arrange with third parties for the supply of goods or materials by those third parties.

PART II: HEALTH SERVICE BODIES

Co-operation between NHS bodies

72 It is the duty of NHS bodies to co-operate with each other in exercising their functions.

Co-operation between NHS bodies and local authorities

82 In exercising their respective functions NHS bodies (on the one hand) and local authorities (on the other) must co-operate with one another in order to secure and advance the health and welfare of the people of England and Wales.

---

9 Not yet in force in relation to primary Ophthalmic Services.

Local social service authorities

254(1) Subject to paragraphs (d) and (e) of section 3(1), the services described in Schedule 20 in relation to—

(a) care of mothers,

(b) prevention, care and after-care,

(c) home help and laundry facilities,

are functions exercisable by local social services authorities.

(2) A local social services authority which provides premises, furniture or equipment for any of the purposes of this Act may permit the use of the premises, furniture or equipment by—

(a) any other local social services authority,

(b) any of the bodies established under this Act, or

(c) a local education authority.

(3) The permission may be on such terms (including terms with respect to the services of any staff employed by the authority giving permission) as may be agreed.

(4) A local social services authority may provide (or improve or furnish) residential accommodation for officers—

(a) employed by it for the purposes of any of its functions as a local social services authority, or

(b) employed by a voluntary organisation for the purposes of any services provided under this section and Schedule 20.

(5) In this section and Schedule 20 'equipment' includes any machinery, apparatus or appliance, whether fixed or not, and any vehicle.

Power of Primary Care Trusts to make payments towards expenditure on community services

256(1) A Primary Care Trust may make payments to—

(a) a local social services authority towards expenditure incurred or to be incurred by it in connection with any social services functions (within the meaning of the Local Authority Social Services Act 1970 (c. 42)), other than functions under section 3 of the Disabled Persons (Employment) Act 1958 (c. 33),

(b) a district council, or a Welsh county council or county borough council, towards expenditure incurred or to be incurred by it in connection with its functions under Part 2 of Schedule 9 to the Health and Social Services and Social Security Adjudications Act 1983 (c. 41)(meals and recreation for old people),

(c) an authority which is a local education authority for the purposes of the Education Act 1996 (c. 56), towards expenditure incurred or to be incurred by it in connection with its functions under the Education Acts (within the meaning of that Act), in so far as it performs those functions for the benefit of disabled persons,

(d) a local housing authority within the meaning of the Housing Act 1985 (c. 68), towards expenditure incurred or to be incurred by it in connection with its functions under Part 2 of that Act (provision of housing), or

(e) any of the bodies mentioned in subsection (2), in respect of expenditure incurred or to be incurred by it in connection with the provision of housing accommodation.

(2) The bodies are—

(a) a registered social landlord within the meaning of the Housing Act 1985 (see section 5(4) and (5) of that Act),

(b) the Commission for the New Towns,

(c) a new town development corporation,

(d) an urban development corporation established under the Local Government, Planning and Land Act 1980,

(e) the Housing Corporation.

(3) A Primary Care Trust may make payments to a local authority towards expenditure incurred or to be incurred by the authority in connection with the performance of any of the authority's functions which, in the opinion of the Primary Care Trust—

(a) have an effect on the health of any individuals,

(b) have an effect on, or are affected by, any NHS functions, or

(c) are connected with any NHS functions.

(4) 'NHS functions' means functions exercised by an NHS body.

(5) A payment under this section may be made in respect of expenditure of a capital or of a revenue nature or in respect of both kinds of expenditure.

(6) The Secretary of State may by directions prescribe conditions relating to payments under this section or section 257.

(7) The conditions include, in particular, conditions requiring, in such circumstances as may be specified—

(a) repayment of the whole or part of a payment under this section, or

(b) in respect of property acquired with a payment under this section, payment of an amount representing the whole or part of an increase in the value of the property which has occurred since its acquisition.

(8) No payment may be made under this section in respect of any expenditure unless the conditions relating to it conform with the conditions prescribed under subsection (6) for payments of that description.

(9) 'A disabled person' is a person who has a physical or mental impairment which has a substantial and long-term adverse effect on his ability to carry out normal day-to-day activities or who has such other disability as may be prescribed.

Payments in respect of voluntary organisations under section 256

257(1) This section applies where the expenditure in respect of which a payment under section 256 is proposed to be made is expenditure in connection with services to be provided by a voluntary organisation.

(2) Where this section applies, the Primary Care Trust may make payments to the voluntary organisation towards the expenditure incurred or to be incurred by the organisation in connection with the provision of those services, instead of or in addition to making payments under section 256(1) or (3).

(3) Where this section applies—

(a) a body falling within any of paragraphs (a) to (d) of section 256(1) which has received payments under the paragraph, and

(b) a local authority which has received payments under section 256(3),

may make out of the sums paid to it payments to the voluntary organisation towards expenditure incurred or to be incurred by the organisation in connection with the provision of those services.

(4) No payment may be made under subsection (2) or (3) except subject to conditions which conform with the conditions prescribed for payments of that description under section 256(6).

SCHEDULE 20: FURTHER PROVISION ABOUT LOCAL SOCIAL SERVICES AUTHORITIES

Care of mothers and young children

1 A local social services authority may, with the Secretary of State's approval, and to such extent as he may direct must, make arrangements for the care of pregnant women and women who are breast feeding (other than for the provision of residential accommodation for them).

Prevention, care and after-care

2(1) A local social services authority may, with the Secretary of State's approval, and to such extent as he may direct must, make the arrangements mentioned in sub-paragraph (2).

(2) The arrangements are for the purpose of the prevention of illness, for the care of persons suffering from illness and for the after-care of persons who have been suffering from illness and in particular for—

  (a) the provision, for persons whose care is undertaken with a view to preventing them from becoming ill, persons suffering from illness and persons who have been suffering from illness, of centres or other facilities for training them or keeping them suitably occupied and the equipment and maintenance of such centres,

  (b) the provision, for the benefit of such persons as are mentioned in paragraph (a), of ancillary or supplemental services, and

  (c) the exercise of the functions of the local social services authority in respect of persons suffering from mental disorder who are received into guardianship under Part 2 or 3 of the Mental Health Act 1983 (c. 20)(whether the guardianship of the authority or of other persons).

(3) A local social services authority may not, and is not under a duty to, make under this paragraph arrangements to provide facilities for any of the purposes mentioned in section 15(1) of the Disabled Persons (Employment) Act 1944 (c. 10).

(4) No arrangements under this paragraph may provide for the payment of money to persons for whose benefit they are made, except in so far as they fall within sub-paragraph (5).

(5) Arrangements fall within this sub-paragraph if—

  (a) they provide for the remuneration of such persons engaged in suitable work in accordance with the arrangements of such amounts as the local social services authority considers appropriate in respect of their occasional personal expenses, and

  (b) it appears to the authority that no such payment would otherwise be made.

(6) No arrangements under this paragraph may be given effect to in relation to a person to whom section 115 of the Immigration and Asylum Act 1999 (c. 33)(exclusion from benefits) applies solely—

  (a) because he is destitute, or

  (b) because of the physical effects, or anticipated physical effects, of his being destitute.

(7) Section 95(2) to (7) of that Act apply for the purposes of sub-paragraph (6); and for that purpose a reference to the Secretary of State in section 95(4) or (5) is a reference to a local social services authority.

(8) The Secretary of State may make regulations as to the conduct of premises in which facilities are provided in pursuance of arrangements made under this paragraph for persons—

  (a) who are or have been suffering from mental disorder within the meaning of the Mental Health Act 1983, or

  (b) whose care is undertaken with a view to preventing them from becoming sufferers from mental disorder.

(9) 'Facilities' means facilities for training such persons or keeping them suitably occupied.

(10) This paragraph does not apply in relation to persons under the age of 18.

(11) No authority is authorised or may be required under this paragraph to provide residential accommodation for any person.

Home help and laundry facilities

3(1) Each local social services authority—

    (a) must provide or arrange for the provision of, on such a scale as is adequate for the needs of its area, of home help for households where such help is required owing to the presence of a person to whom sub-paragraph (2) applies, and

    (b) may provide or arrange for the provision of laundry facilities for households for which home help is being, or can be, provided under paragraph (a).

(2) This sub-paragraph applies to any person who—

    (a) is suffering from illness,

    (b) is pregnant or has recently given birth,

    (c) is aged, or

    (d) handicapped as a result of having suffered from illness or by congenital deformity.

Research

4(1) A local social services authority may conduct or assist other persons in conducting research into matters relating to the functions of local social services authorities under this Schedule.

(2) Sub-paragraph(1) does not affect any powers conferred by any other Act.

Regulations and directions

SECRETARY OF STATE'S APPROVALS AND DIRECTIONS UNDER SECTION 21(1) OF THE NATIONAL ASSISTANCE ACT 1948

(LAC(93)10 Appendix 1)

The Secretary of State for Health, in exercise of the powers conferred on her by section 21(1) of the National Assistance Act 1948, hereby makes the following Approvals and Directions –

Commencement, interpretation and extent

1(1) These Approvals and Directions shall come into force on 1st April 1993.

(2) In these Approvals and Directions, unless the context otherwise requires, 'the Act' means the National Assistance Act 1948.

(3) The Interpretation Act 1978 applies to these Approvals and Direction as it applies to an Act of Parliament.

(4) These Approvals and Directions shall apply only to England and Wales.

Residential accommodation for persons in need of care and attention

2(1) The Secretary of State hereby –

(a) approves the making by local authorities of arrangements under section 21(1)(a) of the Act in relation to persons with no settled residence and, to such extent as the authority may consider desirable, in relation to persons who are ordinarily resident in the area of another local authority, with the consent of that other authority; and

(b) directs local authorities to make arrangements under section 21(1)(a) of the Act in relation to persons who are ordinarily resident in their area and other persons who are in urgent need thereof, to provide residential accommodation for persons aged 18 or over who by reason of age, illness, disability or any other circumstance are in need of care and

attention not otherwise available to them.

(2) Without prejudice to the generality of sub-paragraph (1), the Secretary of State hereby directs local authorities to make arrangements under section 21(1)(a) of the Act to provide temporary accommodation for persons who are in urgent need thereof in circumstances where the need for that accommodation could not reasonably have been foreseen.

(3) Without prejudice to the generality of sub-paragraph (1), the Secretary of State hereby directs local authorities to make arrangements under section 21(1)(a) of the Act to provide accommodation –

(a) in relation to persons who are or have been suffering from mental disorder, or

(b) for the purposes of the prevention of mental disorder, for persons who are ordinarily resident in their area and for persons with no settled residence who are in the authority's area.

(4) Without prejudice to the generality of sub-paragraph (1) and subject to section 24(4) of the Act, the Secretary of State hereby approves the making by local authorities of arrangements under section 21(1)(a) of the Act to provide 861

residential accommodation –

    (a) in relation to persons who are or have been suffering from mental disorder;

or

    (b) for the purposes of the prevention of mental disorder, for persons who are ordinarily resident in the area of another local authority but who following discharge from hospital have become resident in the authority's area.

(5)   Without prejudice to the generality of sub-paragraph (1), the Secretary of State hereby approves the making by local authorities of arrangements under section 21(1)(a) of the Act to provide accommodation to meet the needs of persons for –

    (a) the prevention of illness;

    (b) the care of those suffering from illness; and

    (c) the aftercare of those so suffering.

(6)   Without prejudice to the generality of sub-paragraph (1), the Secretary of State hereby approves the making by local authorities of arrangements under section 21(1)(a) of the Act specifically for persons who are alcoholic or drug dependent.

Residential accommodation for expectant and nursing mothers

3 The Secretary of State hereby approves the making by local authorities of arrangements under section 21(1)(aa) of the Act to provide residential accommodation (in particular mother and baby homes) for expectant and nursing mothers (of any age) who are in need of care and attention which is not otherwise available to them.

Arrangements to provide services for residents

4 The Secretary of State hereby directs local authorities to make arrangements in relation to persons provided with accommodation under section 21(1) of the Act for all or any of the following purposes –

    (a) for the welfare of all persons for whom accommodation is provided;

    (b) for the supervision of the hygiene of the accommodation so provided;

    (c) to enable persons for whom accommodation is provided to obtain –

        (i) medical attention,

        (ii) nursing attention during illnesses of a kind which are ordinarily nursed at home, and

        (iii) the benefit of any services provided by the National Health Service of which they may from time to time be in need,

    but nothing in this paragraph shall require a local authority to make any provision authorised or required to be provided under the National Health Service Act 1977;

    (d) for the provision of board and such other services, amenities and requisites provided in connection with the accommodation, except where in the opinion of the authority managing the premises their provision is unnecessary;

    (e) to review regularly the provision made under the arrangements and to make such improvements as the authority considers necessary.

Arrangements for the conveyance of residents

5 The Secretary of State hereby approves the making by local authorities of arrangements under section 21(1) of the Act to provide, in such cases as the authority considers appropriate, for the conveyance of persons to and from premises in which accommodation is provided for them under Part III of the Act.

Duties in respect of residents in transferred accommodation

6(1) Where a person is provided with accommodation pursuant to section 21(1) of the Act, and –

(a) the residential accommodation is local authority accommodation provided pursuant to section 21(4) of the 1948 Act; and

(b) the local authority transfer the management of the residential accommodation to a voluntary organisation who –

(i) manages it as a residential care home within the meaning of Part I of the Registered Homes Act 1984, and

(ii) is registered under that Part or is not required to be so registered by virtue of being an exempt body; and

(c) the person is accommodated in the residential accommodation immediately before and after the transfer, while that person remains accommodated in that residential accommodation, the local authority shall remain under a duty to make arrangements to provide accommodation for him after any transfer to which paragraph (b) of this subparagraph refers.

(2) For the purposes of paragraph (c) of sub-paragraph (1), a person shall be regarded as accommodated in residential accommodation if –

(a) he is temporarily absent from such accommodation (including circumstances in which he is in hospital or on holiday);

(b) before 1st April 1993, that accommodation was provided under paragraph 2(1) of Schedule 8 to the National Health Service Act 1977.

(3) Where immediately before these Approvals and Directions come into force a local authority was under a duty to provide a person with accommodation by virtue of –

(a) the Secretary of State's former Directions under section 21(1) of the National Assistance Act 1948 contained in Annex 1 of Department of Health Circular LAC(91)12; or

(b) the Secretary of State's former Directions under paragraph 2 of Schedule 8 to the National Health Service Act 1977 contained in Annex 2 of Department of Health Circular LAC(91)12,

while that person remains accommodated in that residential accommodation, the local authority shall remain under a duty to make arrangements to provide that person with accommodation from the date on which these Directions come into force.

Powers to make arrangements with other local authorities and voluntary organisations, etc

7 For the avoidance of doubt, these Approvals and Directions are without prejudice to any of the powers conferred on local authorities by section 21(4) and section 26(1) of the Act (arrangements with voluntary organisations, etc).
Dated 17/2/1993

SECRETARY OF STATE'S APPROVALS AND DIRECTIONS UNDER SECTION 29(1) OF THE NATIONAL ASSISTANCE ACT 1948

(LAC(93)10 Appendix 2)

The Secretary of State for Health, in exercise of the powers conferred on her by section 29(1) of the National Assistance Act 1948, hereby makes the following Approvals and Directions –

Commencement, interpretation and extent

1(1) These Approvals and Directions shall come into force on 1st April 1993.

(2) In these Approvals and Directions, unless the context otherwise requires, 'the Act' means the National Assistance Act 1948.

(3)   The Interpretation Act 1978 applies to these Approvals and Directions as it applies to an Act of Parliament.

(4)   These Approvals and Directions shall apply only to England and Wales.

Powers and duties to make welfare arrangements

2(1)   The Secretary of State hereby approves the making by local authorities of arrangements under section 29(1) of the Act for all persons to whom that subsection applies and directs local authorities to make arrangements under section 29(1) of the Act in relation to persons who are ordinarily resident in their area for all or any of the following purposes –

(a)   to provide a social work service and such advice and support as may be needed for people in their own homes or elsewhere;

(b)   to provide, whether at centres or elsewhere, facilities for social rehabilitation and adjustment to disability including assistance in overcoming limitations of mobility or communication;

(c)   to provide, whether at centres or elsewhere, facilities for occupational, social, cultural and recreational activities and, where appropriate, the making of payments to persons for work undertaken by them.

(2)   The Secretary of State hereby directs local authorities to make the arrangements referred to in section 29(4)(g) of the Act (compiling and maintaining registers) in relation to persons who are ordinarily resident in their area.

(3)   The Secretary of State hereby approves the making by local authorities of arrangements under section 29(1) of the Act for all persons to whom that subsection applies for the following purposes –

(a)   to provide holiday homes;

(b)   to provide free or subsidised travel for all or any persons who do not otherwise qualify for travel concessions, but only in respect of travel arrangements for which concessions are available;

(c)   to assist a person in finding accommodation which will enable him to take advantage of any arrangements made under section 29(1) of the Act;

(d)   to contribute to the cost of employing a warden on welfare functions in warden assisted housing schemes;

(e)   to provide warden services for occupiers of private housing.

(4)   Save as is otherwise provided for under this paragraph, the Secretary of State hereby approves the making by local authorities of all or any of the arrangements referred to in section 29(4) of the Act (welfare arrangements, etc.) for all persons to whom section 29(1) applies.

Welfare arrangements with another local authority

3 The Secretary of State hereby approves the making by local authorities of arrangements under section 29(1) of the Act, where appropriate, with another local authority for the provision of any of the services referred to in these Approvals and Directions.

Welfare arrangements with voluntary organisations and otherwise

4 For the avoidance of doubt, these Approvals and Directions are without prejudice to the powers conferred on local authorities by section 30(1) of the Act (voluntary organisations for disabled persons' welfare).

Dated 17/3/1993

SECRETARY OF STATE'S APPROVALS AND DIRECTIONS UNDER PARAGRAPHS 1 AND 2 OF SCHEDULE 8 TO THE NATIONAL HEALTH SERVICE ACT 1977

(LAC(93)10 Appendix 3)

The Secretary of State for Health, in exercise of the powers conferred on her by paragraphs 1(1) and 2(1) of Schedule 8 to the National Health Service Act 1977, hereby makes the following Approvals and Directions –

Commencement, interpretation and extent

1(1) These Approvals and Directions shall come into force on 1st April 1993.

(2)   In these Approvals and Directions, unless the context otherwise requires, 'the Act' means the National Health Service Act 1977.

(3)   The Interpretation Act 1978 applies to these Approvals and Directions as it applies to an Act of Parliament.

(4)   For the avoidance of doubt, these Approvals and Directions apply only to England and Wales.

Services for expectant and nursing mothers

2 The Secretary of state hereby approves the making of arrangements under paragraph 1(1) of Schedule 8 to the Act for the care of expectant and nursing mothers (of any age) other than the provision of residential accommodation for them (services for the purpose of the prevention of illness etc.).

3(1) The Secretary of State hereby approves the making by local authorities of arrangements under paragraph 2(1) of Schedule 8 to the Act for the purpose of the prevention of illness, and the care of persons suffering from illness and for the aftercare of persons who have been so suffering and in particular for –

(a)   the provision, for persons whose care is undertaken with a view to preventing them becoming ill, persons suffering from illness and persons who have been so suffering, of centres or other facilities for training them or keeping them suitably occupied and the equipment and maintenance of such centres;

(b)   the provision, for the benefit of such persons as are mentioned in paragraph (a) above, of ancillary or supplemental services.

(2)   The Secretary of State hereby directs local authorities to make arrangements under paragraph 2(1) of Schedule 8 to the Act for the purposes of the prevention of mental disorder, or in relation to persons who are or who have been suffering from mental disorder –

(a)   for the provision of centres (including training centres and day centres) or other facilities (including domiciliary facilities), whether in premises managed by the local authority or otherwise, for training or occupation of such persons;

(b)   for the appointment of sufficient social workers in their area to act as approved social workers for the purposes of the Mental Health Act 1983;

(c)   for the exercise of the functions of the authority in respect of persons suffering from mental disorder who are received into guardianship under Part II or III of the Mental Health Act 1983 (whether the guardianship of the local social services authority or of other persons);

(d)   for the provision of social work and related services to help in the identification, diagnosis, assessment and social treatment of mental disorder and to provide social work support and other domiciliary and care services to people living in their homes and elsewhere.

(3)   Without prejudice to the generality of sub-paragraph (1), the Secretary of State hereby approves the making by local authorities of arrangements under paragraph 2(1) of Schedule 8 to the Act for the provision of –

    (a)   meals to be served at the centres or other facilities referred to in sub-paragraphs (1)(a) and (2)(a) above and meals-on-wheels for house-bound people not provided for –

        (i)   under section 45(1) of the Health Services and Public Health Act 1968(a), or

        (ii)   by a district council under paragraph 1 of Part II of Schedule 9 to the Health and Social Services and Social Security Adjudications Act 1983;

    (b)   remuneration for persons engaged in suitable work at the centres or other facilities referred to in sub-paragraphs (1)(a) and (2)(a) above, subject to paragraph 2(2)(a) of Schedule 8 to the Act;

    (c)   social services (including advice and support) for the purposes of preventing the impairment of physical or mental health of adults in families where such impairment is likely, and for the purposes of preventing the break-up of such families, or for assisting in their rehabilitation;

    (d)   night-sitter services;

    (e)   recuperative holidays;

    (f)   facilities for social and recreational activities;

    (g)   services specifically for persons who are alcoholic or drug-dependent.

Services made available by another local authority etc.

4 For the purposes of any arrangements made under these Approvals and Directions, the Secretary of State hereby approves the use by local authorities of services or facilities made available by another authority, voluntary body or person on such conditions as may be agreed, but in making such arrangements, a local authority shall have regard to the importance of services being provided as near to a person's home as is practicable.

Dated 17/3/1993
Signed on behalf of the Secretary of State for Health

NATIONAL ASSISTANCE ACT 1948 (CHOICE OF ACCOMMODATION) DIRECTIONS 1992

The Secretary of State in exercise of the powers conferred by section 7A of the Local Authority Social Services Act 1970 and of all other powers enabling her in that behalf hereby makes the following Directions –

Citation, commencement and extent

1(1)   These Directions may be cited as the National Assistance Act 1948 (Choice of Accommodation) Directions 1992 and shall come into force on 1st April 1993.

(2)   These Directions extend only to England.

Local authorities to provide preferred accommodation

2   Where a local authority have assessed a person under section 47 of the National Health Service and Community Care Act 1990 (assessment) and have decided that accommodation should be provided pursuant to section 21 of the National Assistance Act 1948 (provision of residential accommodation) the local authority shall, subject to paragraph 3 of these Directions, make arrangements for accommodation pursuant to section 21 for that person at the place of his choice within England and Wales (in these Directions called 'preferred accommodation') if he has indicated that he wishes to be accommodated in preferred accommodation.

3 Subject to paragraph 4 of these Directions the local authority shall only be required to make or continue to make arrangements for a person to be accommodated in his preferred accommodation if –

(a) the preferred accommodation appears to the authority to be suitable in relation to his needs as assessed by them;

(b) the cost of making arrangements for him at his preferred accommodation would not require the authority to pay more than they would usually expect to pay having regard to his assessed needs;

(c) the preferred accommodation is available;

(d) the persons in charge of the preferred accommodation provide it subject to the authority's usual terms and conditions, having regard to the nature of the accommodation, for providing accommodation for such a person under Part III of the National Assistance Act 1948.

GUIDANCE ON NATIONAL ASSISTANCE ACT 1948 (CHOICE OF ACCOMMODATION) DIRECTIONS 1992

NATIONAL ASSISTANCE (RESIDENTIAL ACCOMMODATION) (ADDITIONAL PAYMENTS AND ASSESSMENT OF RESOURCES) (AMENDMENT) (ENGLAND) REGULATIONS 2001

(LAC (2004) 20)

1 Summary

1.1 If, after an assessment of need, made in accordance with the General Principles of Assessment in LAC(2002)13 *Fair Access to Care Services*[1] and, where applicable, in accordance with a specific assessment framework[2] and discussion with the individual and their carers, a council decides to provide residential accommodation under section 21 of the National Assistance Act 1948 either permanently or temporarily (intermediate care or short term break or any interim care arrangement), it will make a placement on behalf of the individual in suitable accommodation. Nearly all placements under section 21 of the National Assistance Act 1948 are made in registered care homes. However, some adults are placed under section 21 of the National Assistance Act 1948 in unregistered settings where they need neither nursing care or personal care. While the detail of this guidance applies to registered care homes, the principles apply to adults placed in unregistered settings.

1. When the term 'residential care' is used in this guidance, it covers placements made on both a long-term and a temporary (which includes short-term care) basis to care homes, whether they provide nursing care or not.

1.3 If the individual concerned expresses a preference for particular accommodation ('preferred accommodation') within England and Wales, the council must arrange for care in that accommodation, provided:

- The accommodation is suitable in relation to the individual's assessed needs (see paragraphs 2.5.1 to 2.5.3)

1 http://www.dh.gov.uk/PublicationsAndStatistics/LettersAndCirculars/fs/en.
2 Such as in HSC(2002)001 and LAC(2002)1 Single Assessment Process for Older People at http://www.dh.gov.uk/PublicationsAndStatistics/LettersAndCirculars/LocalAuthorityCirculars/CircularsLast12Months/LocalAuthorityCircularsArticle/fs/en?CONTENT_ID=4003997&chk=IrtVRa

- To do so would not cost the council more than what it would usually expect to pay for accommodation for someone with the individual's assessed needs see paragraphs 2.5.4 to 2.5.8). This is referred to throughout this guidance as the usual cost.
- The accommodation is available (see paragraphs 2.5.9 and 2.5.15)
- The provider of the accommodation is willing to provide accommodation subject to the council's usual terms and conditions for such accommodation (see paragraphs 2.5.16 to 2.5.17)

1.4   If an individual requests it, the council must also arrange for care in accommodation more expensive than it would usually fund provided a third party or, in certain circumstances, the resident, is willing and able to pay the difference between the cost the council would usually expect to pay and the actual cost of the accommodation (to 'top up'). These are the only circumstances where either a third party or the resident may be asked to top up (see paragraph 3).

2   Preferred accommodation

2.1   As with all aspects of service provision, there should be a general presumption in favour of individuals being able to exercise reasonable choice over the service they receive. The limitations on councils' obligation to provide preferred accommodation set out in the Directions and the Regulations are not intended to deny individuals reasonable freedom of choice but to ensure that councils are able to fulfil their obligations for the quality of service provided and for value for money. The terms of the Directions and the Regulations are explained more fully below. Where, for any reason, a council decides not to arrange a place for someone in their preferred accommodation it must have a clear and reasonable justification for that decision which relates to the criteria of the Directions and is not in breach of the Regulations.

2.2   Arrangements under section 26(3A) of the National Assistance Act 1948 require the agreement of all parties. Individuals should not be refused their preferred accommodation without a full explanation from councils, in writing, of their reasons for doing so

2.3   The location of the preferred accommodation need not be limited by the boundaries of the funding council. Councils are obliged to cater for placements falling within the Directions or the Regulations in any permitted care home within England or Wales. Any extension to this beyond England and Wales is subject to any future regulations governing cross-border placements (but see LAC(93)18 in respect of placements involving Scotland and the Department of Health/Welsh Assembly protocol on NHS funded nursing care for cross border placements).

2.4   Funding councils may refer to their own usual costs when making placements in another council's area. However, because costs vary from area to area, if in order to meet a resident's assessed need it is necessary to place an individual in another area at a higher rate than the funding council's usual costs, the placing council should meet the additional cost itself.

2.5   The Directions state that a council must arrange for care in an individual's preferred accommodation subject to four considerations:

   (a) Suitability of accommodation

   2.5.1   Suitability will depend on the council's assessment of individual need. Each case must be considered on its merits.

   2.5.2   Accommodation provided in a care home will not necessarily be suitable for the individual's needs simply because it satisfies registration standards. On the other hand, accommodation will not necessarily be

---

3   http://www.dh.gov.uk/PolicyAndGuidance/OrganisationPolicy/TertiaryCare/ NHSFundedNursingCare/fs/en

unsuitable simply because it fails to conform to the council's preferred model of provision, or to meet to the letter a standard service specification laid down by the council.

2.5.3 The Directions and Regulations do not affect Section 26(1A) of the National Assistance Act 1948 as amended by the Care Standards Act 2000. Arrangements should not be made for the provision of accommodation together with nursing or personal care in a care home unless the accommodation to be provided is managed by an organisation or person who is registered under Part II of the Care Standards Act 2000. Similarly, the Directions and the Regulations do not require a council to contract with any accommodation where for any other reason it is prevented by law from doing so.

(b) Cost

2.5.4 One of the conditions associated with the provision of preferred accommodation is that such accommodation should not require the council to pay more than they would usually expect to pay, having regard to assessed needs (the 'usual cost'). This cost should be set by councils at the start of a financial or other planning period, or in response to significant changes in the cost of providing care, to be sufficient to meet the assessed care needs of supported residents in residential accommodation. A council should set more than one usual cost where the cost of providing residential accommodation to specific groups is different. In setting and reviewing their usual costs, councils should have due regard to the actual costs of providing care and other local factors. Councils should also have due regard to Best Value requirements under the Local Government Act 1999.

2.5.5 Individual residents should not be asked to pay more towards their accommodation because of market inadequacies or commissioning failures. Where an individual has not expressed a preference for more expensive accommodation, but there are not, for whatever reason, sufficient places available at a given time at the council's usual costs to meet the assessed care needs of supported residents, the council should make a placement in more expensive accommodation. In these circumstances, neither the resident nor a third party should be asked to contribute more than the resident would normally be expected to contribute and councils should make up the cost difference between the resident's assessed contribution and the accommodation's fees. Only when an individual has expressed a preference for more expensive accommodation than a council would usually expect to pay, can a third party or the resident be asked for a top up (see paragraph 3.1). Costs of accommodation should be compared on the basis of gross costs before income from charging. Given the different amounts that councils will recover from individuals by ways of charges, it would not be appropriate for a council to determine a usual net cost that it would expect to pay.

2.5.6 For the cost of placements in other councils' areas see paragraph 2.3.

2.5.7 Councils should not set arbitrary ceilings on the amount they expect to pay for an individual's residential care. Residents and third parties should not routinely be required to make up the difference between what the council will pay and the actual fees of a home. Councils have a statutory duty to provide residents with the level of service they could expect if the possibility of resident and third party contributions did not exist

2.5.8 Costs can vary according to the type of care provided. For example, the cost a council might usually expect to pay for short-term care might be different from its usual cost for long-term care. There are also a number of situations where there may be higher costs incurred in providing residential care, be it long or short-term. Examples include specialist care for specific user groups with high levels of need or where necessary to prepare special diets and provide additional facilities for medical or cultural reasons. Councils should be prepared to meet these higher costs in order to ensure an individual's needs are appropriately met.

(c) Availability

2.5.9   Generally, good commissioning by councils should ensure there is sufficient capacity so individuals should not have to wait for their assessed (that is, eligible) needs to be met. However, waiting is occasionally inevitable, particularly when individuals have expressed a preference towards a particular care home where there are no current vacancies. Where individuals may need to wait at home or elsewhere, their access to the most appropriate (and possibly, preferred) service should be based solely on their assessed need, and councils should ensure that in the interim adequate alternative services are provided. Waiting for the preferred care home should not mean that the person's care needs are not met in the interim or that they wait in a setting unsuitable for their assessed needs, and this includes an acute hospital bed, until the most suitable or preferred accommodation becomes available. In view of the Community Care (Delayed Discharges etc.) Act 2003, councils should have contingency arrangements in place, that address the likelihood that an individual's preferred accommodation will not always be readily available. These arrangements should meet the needs of the individual and sustain or improve their level of independence. For some, the appropriate interim arrangement could be an enhanced care package at home.

2.5.10 Councils should give individuals an indication of the likely duration of the interim arrangement. Councils should place the individual on the waiting list of the preferred accommodation and aim to move them into that accommodation as soon as possible. Information about how the waiting list is handled should be clear and the individual should be kept informed of progress. If the duration of the interim arrangement exceeds a reasonable time period, eg 12 weeks, the individual should be reassessed to ensure that the interim and preferred accommodation, are still able to meet the individual's assessed needs and to prevent any unnecessary moves between care homes that are unable to meet the individual's assessed needs. As part of this reassessment, individuals should also be asked if their preference is now to remain in the interim accommodation or whether they wish to continue waiting for their original preferred accommodation (see paragraph 2.5.14 for guidance on individuals who choose to remain in the interim accommodation).

2.5.11 Councils should ensure that while waiting in temporary residential accommodation, if an individual has to contribute towards their care costs it is in accordance with the National Assistance (Assessment of Resources) Regulations 1992. Individuals who are waiting in these

---

4 in accordance with the principles set out in Building Capacity and Partnership in Care – An Agreement between the statutory and independent social care, health care and housing sectors at www.dh.gov.uk/PublicationsAndStatistics/Publications/ PublicationsPolicyAndGuidance/PublicationsPolicyAndGuidanceArticle/fs/ en?CONTENT_ID=4006241&chk=BPcEi1

5 5www.legislation.hmso.gov.uk/acts/acts2003/20030005.htm

circumstances should not be asked to pay more than their assessed financial contribution to meet the costs of these residential care services which have been arranged by the council to temporarily meet their assessed needs and councils should make up the cost difference between the resident's assessed contribution and the accommodation's fees. Only when an individual has expressed a preference for more expensive accommodation than a council would usually expect to pay, can a third party or the resident be asked for a top up (see paragraph 3.1).

2.5.12 Councils should take all reasonable steps to gain an individual's agreement to an interim care home or care package. Councils should make reasonable efforts to take account of the individual's desires and preferences. In doing this, councils should ascertain all relevant facts and take into account all the circumstances relevant to the person, and ensure that the individual (and their family or carers) understands the consequences of failing to come to an agreement. Where patients have been assessed as no longer requiring NHS continuing inpatient care, they do not have the right to occupy indefinitely an NHS bed. If an individual continues to unreasonably refuse the interim care home or care package, the council is entitled to consider that it has fulfilled its statutory duty to assess and offer services, and may then inform the individual, in writing, they will need to make their own arrangements. This position also applies to the unreasonable refusal of a permanent care home, not just the interim care home or care package. If at a later date further contact is made with social services regarding the individual, the council should re-open the care planning process, if it is satisfied that the individual's needs remain such to justify the provision of services and there is no longer reason to think that the individual will persist in refusing such services unreasonably. Councils should refer to Annex A of LAC(2003)21 – The Community Care (Delayed Discharges etc) Act 2003 Guidance for Implementation. Councils may wish to take their own legal advice in such circumstances.

2.5.13 In all but a very small number of cases where an individual is being placed under Part II of the Mental Health Act 1983, individuals have the right to refuse to enter a care home. This includes patients who are awaiting discharge from hospital. In such cases the social services department should work with the person, his or her family and carers, and NHS partners, (and potentially housing partners), to explore alternative options, including a package of health and social care in the person's own home or suitable alternative accommodation.

2.5.14 In some cases, individuals who move into a care home for an interim period may choose to remain there, even if a place in their original preferred accommodation becomes available. If the care home is able to accept the individual on a long-term basis, they should be taken off the waiting list of their original preferred accommodation. If the cost of the interim care home is higher than the usual cost the council would expect to pay for their assessed need, upon making the choice to remain in that home, a third party or the resident could be approached for the total difference between the two rates. This should be clearly explained to individuals before they enter the home. See paragraph 3.2 for fuller details.

6 www.dh.gov.uk/PolicyAndGuidance/OrganisationPolicy/TertiaryCare/Delayed-Discharge/DelayedDischargeArticle/fs/en?CONTENT_ID=4067273&chk=x2raIF

2.5.15 The Directions only apply to individuals whose care is being arranged by a council under Part 3 of the National Assistance Act 1948. For example, where hospital patients need to move to a different type of care, and social services are not involved, this is a matter for the NHS and the individual patient and the Directions do not apply. For good practice on handling these situations, see the Hospital Discharge Workbook[7]

(d) Terms and conditions

2.5.16 In order to ensure that they are able to exercise proper control over the use of their funds, councils need to be able to impose certain contractual conditions, for example, in relation to payment regimes, review, access, monitoring, audit, record keeping, information sharing, insurance, sub-contracting, etc.

2.5.17 The contractual conditions required of preferred accommodation should be broadly the same as those councils would impose on any other similar operation. Stricter conditions should never be used as a way of avoiding or deterring a placement. As with suitability, account should be taken of the nature and location of the accommodation. There may be occasions where it would be unreasonable for a council not to adapt its standard conditions and others where it would be unreasonable to expect it to do so. For example, councils should take into account the fact that care homes in other areas, or those that take residents from many areas, may have geared themselves to the normal requirements of other councils. Councils should be flexible in such circumstances and avoid adding to the administrative burden of care homes.

3   More expensive accommodation

3.1   The guidance set out in paragraphs 3.2 to 3.5.11, applies only where a resident explicitly chooses to enter accommodation other than that which the council offers them, and where that preferred accommodation is more expensive than the council would usually expect to pay.

3..2   In certain circumstances, councils can make placements in more expensive accommodation than they would usually expect to pay for, provided a resident or a third party is able and willing to make up the difference (to 'top up'). Residents that are subject to the 12 week property disregard or have agreed a deferred payments agreement with the council may make top-ups from specified resources on their own behalf. These are the only situations where the resident may top up. The most common arrangement is that a third party is providing the top-up. A third party in this case might be a relative, a friend, or any other source. For liable relatives see paragraph 3.5.10.

3.3   When setting its usual cost(s) a council should be able to demonstrate that this cost is sufficient to allow it to meet assessed care needs and to provide residents with the level of care services that they could reasonably expect to receive if the possibility of resident and third party contributions did not exist.

3.4   Councils should not seek resident or third party contributions in cases where the council itself decides to offer someone a place in more expensive accommodation in order to meet assessed needs, or for other reasons. Where there are no placements at the council's usual rate, councils should not leave individuals to make their own arrangements having determined that they need to enter residential accommodation and do not have care and attention otherwise available to them. In these instances, councils should

7 at www.publications.doh.gov.uk/hospitaldischarge/index.htm

make suitable alternative arrangements and seek no contribution from the individual other than their contribution as assessed under the National Assistance (Assessment of Resources) Regulations 1992. Councils must never encourage or otherwise imply that care home providers can or should seek further contributions from individuals in order to meet assessed needs.

3.5 This paragraph deals with considerations that apply where either residents or third parties are making further contributions to costs over and above the resident's assessed contribution under the National Assistance (Assessment of Resources) Regulations 1992.

(a) Responsibility for costs of accommodation

3.5.1 When making arrangements for residential care for an individual under the National Assistance Act 1948, a council is responsible for the full cost of that accommodation. Therefore, where a council places someone in more expensive accommodation, it must contract to pay the accommodation's fees in full. The resident's or the third party's contribution will be treated as part of the resident's income for charging purposes and the council will be able to recover it in that way. However, under a deferred payments agreement, where the resident is topping up against the value of their home, their top-up contribution is added to their deferred contribution.

3.5.2 Councils will be aware that under section 26(3A) of the National Assistance Act 1948 (as inserted by the NHS and Community Care Act 1990), it is open to them to agree with both the resident and the person in charge of their accommodation that, instead of paying a contribution to the council, the resident may pay the same amount direct to the accommodation, with the council paying the difference. In such a case, the third party would also pay the accommodation direct on behalf of the resident. However, it should be noted that even where there is such an agreement for the resident to make payments direct to the accommodation, the council continues to be liable to pay the full costs of the accommodation should either the resident or relative fail to pay the required amount.

3.5.3 Where top-ups are required from a resident or third party, the resident will therefore need to demonstrate that either they or the third party is able and willing to pay the difference between the council's usual rate and the accommodation's actual fees.

3.5.4 In order to safeguard both residents and councils from entering into top-up arrangements that are likely to fail, the resident or the third party must reasonably be expected to be able to continue to make top-up payments for the duration of the arrangements. Councils should, therefore, assure themselves that residents or third parties will have the resources to continue to make the required top-up payments. Councils should seek similar assurances when residents top-up against the value of their home when the home is subject to a deferred payments agreement. When the home is eventually sold, it should be possible for the resident or their estate to pay back the deferred contribution including the resident top-ups.

(b) The amount of the resident or third party top-up

3.5.5 The amount of resident or third party top-up payments should be the difference between the actual fee for the accommodation and the amount that otherwise the council would usually have expected to pay for someone with the individual's assessed needs. In determining the precise amounts in individual cases, the council will take account of the guidance give in paragraphs 2.5.4 to 2.5.8 above.

3.5.6 The amount of the resident or third party top-up should be calculated on gross costs; that is, the difference between the preferred accommodation's fees and the fees that a council would usually expect to pay. The fact that a resident might not have been able to meet the full cost of the accommodation that the council would otherwise have arranged does not affect their ability to benefit from the additional top-up payments.

(c) Price increases

3.5.7 Arrangements between the council, resident and third party will need to be reviewed from time to time to take account of changes to accommodation fees. There will also be changes to the council's usual cost, which should be reasonable and set in accordance with paragraphs 2.5.4 to 2.5.8. However, fees and usual costs may not change at the same rate, and residents and third parties should be told that there cannot be a guarantee that any increases in the accommodation's fees will automatically be shared evenly between the council and/or the resident or third party, should the particular accommodation's fees rise more quickly than the costs the council would usually expect to pay for similar individuals. A council may find it useful to agree with the resident (or third party) that the resident's (or third party's) contribution will be reviewed on a regular basis on the understanding that clear explanations for proposed increases are given. It is also important that individuals know when, and in what circumstances, the fees for their accommodation will be reviewed.

(d) Responsibilities of residents and third parties

3.5.8 Councils should make clear to residents and third parties, in writing, the basis on which arrangements are to be made when they seek to exercise their right to more expensive preferred accommodation. It should be clear from the outset to the resident, third party and person providing the accommodation that:

- failure to keep up top-up payments may result in the resident having to move to other accommodation unless, after an assessment of need, it is shown that assessed needs can only be met in the current accommodation. In these circumstances, councils should make up the cost difference between the resident's assessed contribution and the accommodation's fees. Where a resident's top-ups are being made against the value of property subject to a deferred payments agreement, a council will have assured itself from the outset that top-up payments are viable and recoverable when the home is sold;

- an increase in the resident's income will not necessarily lessen the need for a top-up contribution, since the resident's own income will be subject to means testing by the council in the normal way;

- a rise in the accommodation's fees will not automatically be shared equally between council, resident (if making a top-up), and third party.

(e) Suitability and Conditions

3.5.9 With reference to paragraphs 2.5.1 to 2.5.3 and 2.5.16 to 2.5.17 above, the criteria of suitability and willingness to provide on the basis of normal conditions should be applied in the same way as for other preferred accommodation. An exception to this is that it would be reasonable to expect providers entering this kind of arrangement to agree to do so on the basis that the council has the right, subject to notice, to terminate the contract should the resident's or third party's top-up payments cease to be adequate.

(f) Liable relatives

3.5.10 Liable relatives who are making maintenance contributions cannot act as third parties for the care of the relative to whose care they are already contributing under section 42 of the National Assistance Act 1948. This limitation does not apply to top-up arrangements agreed prior to 1 October 2001 with liable relatives. Neither does the limitation apply to liable relatives who are not making contributions under section 42 of the 1948 Act.

4 Individuals already resident in residential care

4.1 Individuals already placed by a council in residential accommodation, and those already in residential accommodation as self-funders but who, because of diminishing resources, are on the verge of needing council support, have the same rights under these Directions as those who have yet to be placed by the council. Any such individual who wishes to move to different or more expensive accommodation may seek to do so on the same basis as anyone about to enter residential care for the first time. Should a self-funder who is resident in a care home that is more expensive than a council would usually expect to pay later become the responsibility of the council due to diminishing funds, this may result in the resident having to move to other accommodation, unless, after an assessment of need, it is shown that assessed needs can only be met in the current accommodation. In these circumstances, neither the resident nor a third party should be asked for a top-up payment and councils should make up the cost difference between the resident's assessed contribution and the accommodation's fees.

5 Individuals who are unable to make their own choices

5.1 There will be cases in which prospective residents lack capacity to express a preference for themselves. It would be reasonable to expect councils to act on the preferences expressed by their advocate, carer or legal guardian in the same way that they would on the resident's own wishes, unless that would in the council's opinion be against the best interests of the resident.

6 Effect on contracting

6.1 Any block contract or other form of contract that a council may have with a provider should not serve to limit choice. An individual should not be limited to care homes that hold such contracts with the funding council, or cares homes that are run by councils. It would not be reasonable for a council to use as a test for the suitability of accommodation, its presence or absence from a previously compiled list of preferred suppliers. The Directions and Regulations do not, however, prevent an authority having a list of preferred providers with which it will contract where a potential resident expresses no preference for particular accommodation, nor from recommending such providers to prospective residents.

7 Information

7.1 Individuals, and/or those who represent them, need information on the options open to them if they are to be able to exercise genuine choice. They should be given fair and balanced information with which to make the best choice of accommodation for them. Councils should explain to individuals their rights under the Directions and the Regulations. Councils should also consider providing material in a range of forms including written leaflets in local community languages, Braille, on audio tape and in accessible language e.g. easy words, short sentences, large print and pictures (for those with learning disabilities). Councils should supply copies of the Directions and this guidance if requested in appropriate forms. They should work with local Primary Care Trusts (PCTs) and local hospitals to provide clear information to hospital patients as early as possible in their stay about what the council will be able to provide should they require short or long-term residential care at the end of their hospital stay. Individuals should be told explicitly that:

- they are free to choose any accommodation that is likely to meet their needs subject to the constraints set out in the Directions and the Regulations.
- they may allow the council to make a placement decision on their behalf; and
- they may choose from a preferred list (if the authority operates such a system).

7.2   Councils should ensure that individuals are informed that they have a choice of accommodation irrespective of whether they express a preference for particular accommodation. Individuals should also be told what will happen if the preferred accommodation is not available. Councils may also wish to cover the matters described in paragraph 2.5.12. Wherever possible, the individual should be encouraged to have a relative, carer or advocate present during the conversation. A written record of the conversation should be kept, in particular, recording any decisions taken or preferences expressed by the individual. This record should be shared with the individual.

8   Complaints

8.1   Complaints about the application of the Directions and the Regulations and decisions taken in individual cases will fall within the scope of councils' statutory complaints procedure. As in all aspects of their activity, councils should ensure that prospective residents are aware of and understand the existence of the complaints procedure and their rights under it.

Department of Health

14 October 2004

THE COMMUNITY CARE ASSESSMENT DIRECTIONS 2004

The Secretary of State for Health, in exercise of the powers conferred on him by section 47(4) of the National Health Service and Community Care Act 1990 hereby makes the following Directions:

Commencement, application and interpretation

1(1)   These Directions come into force on 1 September 2004 and apply to every local authority in England.

(2)   In these Directions—
'the Act' means the National Health Service and Community Care Act 1990;
'community care services' has the same meaning as in section 46(3) of the Act;
'local authority' has the same meaning as in section 46(3) of the Act.

Manner and form of assessment of needs for community care services

2(1)   In assessing the needs of a person under section 47(1) of the Act a local authority must comply with paragraphs (2) to (4).

(2)   The local authority must consult the person, consider whether the person has any carers and, where they think it appropriate, consult those carers.

(3)   The local authority must take all reasonable steps to reach agreement with the person and, where they think it appropriate, any carers of that person, on the community care services which they are considering providing to him to meet his needs.

(4)   The local authority must provide information to the person and, where they think it appropriate, any carers of that person, about the amount of the

payment (if any) which the person will be liable to make in respect of the community care services which they are considering providing to him.

Signed by authority of the Secretary of State

26 August 2004

Craig Muir, Member of the Senior Civil Service

Department of Health

THE NHS CONTINUING HEALTHCARE (RESPONSIBILITIES) DIRECTIONS 2007

The Secretary of State for Health makes the following Directions in exercise of the powers conferred on him by sections 8, 272(7) and (8) and 273(1) of the National Health Service Act 2006 and section 7A of the Local Authority Social Services Act 1970.

Commencement, application and interpretation

1(1) These Directions come into force on 1 October 2007 and apply to every Strategic Health Authority, Primary Care Trust and social services authority in England.

(2) In these Directions—

'appropriate Strategic Health Authority' means—

(a) in relation to a Primary Care Trust, the Strategic Health Authority in whose area the Primary Care Trust is situated(c);

(b) in relation to an English NHS trust, the Strategic Health Authority which is the appropriate Strategic Health Authority for the purposes of the National Health Service (Functions of Strategic Health Authorities and Primary Care Trusts and Administration Arrangements) (England) Regulations 2002;

'care home' has the same meaning as in section 3 of the Care Standards Act 2000;

'the criterion' means the criterion in direction 2(5)(b) of having a primary health need;

'Decision Support Tool' means the Decision Support Tool for NHS Continuing Healthcare issued by the Secretary of State as amended from time to time;

'Delayed Discharges Directions' means the Delayed Discharges (Continuing Care) Directions 2007;

'English NHS trust' means an NHS trust all or most of whose hospitals, establishments and facilities are situated in England;

'health care profession' means a profession (whether or not regulated by, or by virtue of any enactment) which is concerned (wholly or partly) with the physical or mental health of individuals;

'multi-disciplinary team' means a team consisting of at least two professionals from different health care or social care professions;

'National Framework Guidance' means the National Framework for NHS Continuing Healthcare and NHS-funded Nursing Care issued by the Secretary of State and dated 26 June 2007;

'Needs Checklist' means the NHS Continuing Healthcare Needs Checklist issued by the Secretary of State as amended from time to time;

'NHS Continuing Healthcare' means a package of care arranged and funded solely by the health service for a person aged 18 or over to meet physical or mental health needs which have arisen as a result of illness;

'relevant social services authority' means the social services authority appearing to the Primary Care Trust to be the authority in whose area the patient is ordinarily resident;

'social care profession' means the profession of being a social worker within the meaning of section 55(2)(a) of the Care Standards Act 2000;

'social services authority' means a local authority for the purposes of the Local Authority Social Services Act 1970 and the Council of the Isles of Scilly.

(3) In these Directions—
   (a) except in direction 4, references to the 'standing chairman' include a reserve standing chairman appointed under direction 4(1)(b); and
   (b) references to the area in which a Primary Care Trust is situated are to be construed in accordance with direction 9.

Duties of Primary Care Trusts: determining eligibility for NHS Continuing Healthcare

2(1) In exercising their functions under sections 2 and 3 of the National Health Service Act 2006 insofar as they relate to NHS Continuing Healthcare, Primary Care Trusts must comply with paragraphs (2) to (8).

(2) Subject to paragraph (9), a Primary Care Trust must take reasonable steps to ensure that an assessment for NHS Continuing Healthcare is carried out—
   (a) in all cases where it appears to the Trust that there may be a need for such care or for a variation in the provision of such care; and
   (b) before any assessment is carried out pursuant to direction 2(1) of the National Health Service (Nursing Care in Residential Accommodation) (England) Directions 2007.

(3) If a Primary Care Trust wishes to use an initial screening process to decide whether to undertake an assessment of a person's eligibility for NHS Continuing Healthcare it must—
   (a) complete and use the Needs Checklist to inform that decision;
   (b) inform that person in writing of the decision as to whether to carry out an assessment of his eligibility for NHS Continuing Healthcare (including the matters referred to in paragraph (8)); and
   (c) make a record of the decision.

(4) A Primary Care Trust must ensure that a multi-disciplinary team undertakes an assessment that is to be used to inform a decision as to a person's eligibility for NHS Continuing Healthcare.

(5) Following an assessment by a multi-disciplinary team in accordance with paragraph (4), a Primary Care Trust must—
   (a) ensure that the Decision Support Tool is completed; and
   (b) use the completed Decision Support Tool to inform the decision as to whether that person has a primary health need, and if that person does have a primary health need, the Primary Care Trust must decide that the person is eligible for NHS Continuing Healthcare.

(6) In deciding whether a person has a primary health need in accordance with paragraph (5), a Primary Care Trust must consider whether the nursing or other health services required by that person are—
   (a) where that person is, or is to be, accommodated in a care home, more than incidental or ancillary to the provision of accommodation which a social services authority is, or would be but for a person's means, under a duty to provide; or
   (b) of a nature beyond which a social services authority whose primary responsibility is to provide social services could be expected to provide,
   and if it decides that the nursing or other health services required do, when considered in their totality, fall within paragraph (a) or (b), it must decide that the person has a primary health need.

(7) Subject to paragraph (9), where an assessment for NHS Continuing Healthcare has been carried out in respect of any person, the Primary Care Trust shall—

(a) notify the person assessed in writing of the decision made about his eligibility for NHS Continuing Healthcare, the reasons for that decision and the matters referred to in paragraph (8); and

(b) make a record of the decision.

(8) Subject to paragraph (9), where a Primary Care Trust has decided that a person is not eligible for NHS Continuing Healthcare pursuant to paragraph (3) or (5), it must inform the person (or where relevant someone acting on that person's behalf) of the circumstances and manner in which he may apply for a review of the decision if he is dissatisfied with—

(a) the procedure followed by a Primary Care Trust in reaching that decision; or

(b) the application by a Primary Care Trust of the criterion in relation to such a decision.

(9) This direction does not apply in a case in which a Primary Care Trust is obliged to comply with direction 2(2) to (9) of the Delayed Discharges Directions.

Duties of Primary Care Trusts and social services authorities: joint working

3(1) A Primary Care Trust shall, so far as is reasonably practicable, consult with the relevant social services authority before making a decision about a person's eligibility for NHS Continuing Healthcare.

(2) The relevant social services authority shall, so far as is reasonably practicable, provide advice and assistance to the Primary Care Trust who has consulted it pursuant to paragraph (1).

(3) Nothing in this direction affects a social services authority's duty to carry out an assessment of a person's needs for community care services pursuant to section 47 of the National Health Service and Community Care Act 1990, and if it has carried out such an assessment, it shall, so far as reasonably practicable, use the information obtained as a result of that assessment to comply with its duty under paragraph (2).

(4) Any dispute between a Primary Care Trust and the relevant social services authority about—

(a) a decision as to eligibility for NHS Continuing Healthcare; or

(b) where a person is not eligible for NHS Continuing Healthcare, the contribution of a Primary Care Trust or social services authority to a joint package of care for that person,

shall be resolved in accordance with a dispute resolution procedure agreed between the two bodies concerned.

Review of decisions

4(1) Each Strategic Health Authority must—

(a) appoint a person ('the standing chairman') to act as chairman of any panel to which a matter is referred under paragraph (4);

(b) appoint a person or persons ('a reserve standing chairman') to act as chairman of such a panel in the event referred to in paragraph (4)(a); and

(c) establish a list consisting of the following persons—

(i) at least one person ('a PCT member') appointed by the Strategic Health Authority in respect of each Primary Care Trust situated within the Authority's area; and

(ii) at least one person ('a social services authority member') appointed by the Strategic Health Authority in respect of each social services authority all or part of whose area is situated within the Authority's area.

(2) The appointments of the standing chairman, a reserve standing chairman, the PCT members and the social services authority members are subject to direction 5.

(3) Where a person, or someone acting on a person's behalf—
    (a) is dissatisfied about—
        (i) the procedure followed by a Primary Care Trust or an English NHS trust in reaching a decision as to the person's eligibility for NHS Continuing Healthcare pursuant to direction 2(3) or (5) of these Directions or direction 2(4) or (6) of the Delayed Discharges Directions; or
        (ii) the application by a Primary Care Trust or an English NHS trust of the criterion referred to in direction 2(5)(b) of these Directions or direction 2(6)(b) of the Delayed Discharges Directions, in relation to such a decision; and
    (b) has been unable to resolve the matter through any local dispute resolution procedure where use of such a procedure would not have caused undue delay,
he may apply in writing to the appropriate Strategic Health Authority for a review of the decision.

(4) Following receipt of an application for a review under paragraph (3), a Strategic Health Authority must notify the standing chairman in writing that the application has been received, and may refer the matter for a decision to a panel of members ('a review panel') consisting of—
    (a) the standing chairman or, in the event of his being unavailable to deal with the matter within the relevant timescale, a reserve standing chairman;
    (b) one PCT member drawn from the list established under paragraph (1)(c) who has been appointed in respect of a Primary Care Trust other than—
        (i) where a decision of a Primary Care Trust is the subject of the review, that Primary Care Trust; and
        (ii) where a decision of an English NHS trust is the subject of the review, the Primary Care Trust in whose area all or most of the hospitals, establishments or facilities of that NHS trust are situated; and
    (c) one local authority member drawn from that list who has been appointed in respect of a local authority other than one covering all or part of the area of the Primary Care Trust whose decision is the subject of the review.

(5) The procedure and operation of the review panel are to be a matter for the standing chairman or a reserve standing chairman (as the case may be), having regard to any guidance issued by the Secretary of State or the Strategic Health Authority, in particular the National Framework Guidance.

(6) The Strategic Health Authority must pay to the standing chairman, a reserve standing chairman, the PCT members and the social services authority members such expenses as appear to it to be reasonable.

(7) The Strategic Health Authority must give notice in writing of the review panel's decision and the reasons for it to the applicant and, as the case may be, the Primary Care Trust or English NHS trust whose decision has been the subject of the review. Such notice must be given as soon as reasonably practicable.

Appointment and tenure of office

5(1) Subject to direction 6 (disqualification for appointment), the PCT members and social services authority members must be appointed by the Strategic Health Authority, following nomination by the Primary Care Trust or, as the case may be, the social services authority.

(2) A Primary Care Trust or social services authority shall, when requested to do so by a Strategic Health Authority, provide its nomination pursuant to paragraph (1) as soon as is reasonably practicable.

(3) Subject to direction 8 (termination of tenure of office), the term of office of the standing chairman, the PCT members and the social services authority

members is to be such period, not exceeding three years, as the Strategic Health Authority specifies on making the appointment.

(4) Subject to direction 6 (disqualification for appointment), the standing chairman, the PCT members and the social services authority members are to be eligible for reappointment on the termination of their office.

Disqualification for appointment

6(1) A person is disqualified for appointment as standing chairman if he is—

(a) the chairman, a member, a director or employee of a health service body; or

(b) an elected member or employee of a social services authority or a county borough council.

(2) A person is disqualified for appointment as a PCT member or social services authority member if he is—

(a) the chairman, chief executive, a non-executive director or a non-officer member of a health service body; or

(b) an elected member of a social services authority or a county borough council.

(3) Subject to direction 7 (cessation of disqualification), a person is disqualified for appointment as a standing chairman, PCT member or social services authority member if—

(a) he has within the previous 5 years been convicted in the United Kingdom of any offence, or convicted elsewhere for an offence which, if committed in any part of the United Kingdom would constitute a criminal offence in that part, and in either case has had passed on him a sentence of imprisonment (whether suspended or not) for a period of not less than three months without the option of a fine, and which has not been quashed on appeal;

(b) he has been dismissed, otherwise than by reason of redundancy or retirement, from any paid employment with a health service body or social services authority;

(c) he is a person whose tenure of office as the chairman or as a member or director of a health service body has been terminated on the grounds that—

(i) it was not in the interests of, or conducive to the good management of, that body that he should continue to hold office,

(ii) it was not in the interests of the health service that he should continue to hold office,

(iii) he failed, without reasonable cause, to attend any meeting of that body for a period of 3 months or more, or

(iv) he failed to declare a pecuniary interest or withdraw from consideration of any matter in respect of which he had a pecuniary interest; or

(d) he has been—

(i) removed from the office of charity trustee or trustee for a charity by an order made by the Charity Commissioners or the High Court on the grounds of any misconduct or mismanagement in the administration of the charity for which he was responsible or to which he was privy, or which he by his conduct contributed to or facilitated; or

(ii) removed under section 7 of the Law Reform (Miscellaneous Provisions) (Scotland) Act 1990 (powers of Court of Session to deal with management of charities), from being concerned in the management or control of any body.

(4) For the purposes of paragraph (3)(a), the date of conviction is deemed to be the date on which the ordinary period allowed for making an appeal or application with respect to the conviction expires or, if such an appeal or

application is made, the date on which the appeal or application is finally disposed of or abandoned or fails by reason of its not being prosecuted.

(5)   For the purposes of paragraph (3)(b), a person is not to be treated as having been in paid employment by reason only of his having been the chairman or a member of, and in the case of an NHS trust, a member of the board of directors of, the health service body in question.

(6)   In paragraphs (1) to (3) 'health service body' means—
  (a) a Strategic Health Authority;
  (b) a Special Health Authority;
  (c) an NHS trust;
  (d) an NHS foundation trust;
  (e) a Primary Care Trust; or
  (f) a Local Health Board.

Cessation of disqualification

7(1) Subject to paragraph (2), where a person is disqualified under direction 6(3)(b), he may, after the second anniversary of the day on which he was dismissed, apply in writing to the Strategic Health Authority to remove the disqualification, and the Authority may decide that the disqualification is removed.

(2)   Where the Strategic Health Authority refuses an application to remove a disqualification, no further application may be made by that person until the second anniversary of the day of the refusal and this paragraph applies to any subsequent application.

(3)   Where a person is disqualified under direction 6(3)(c) the disqualification is to cease on the second anniversary of the termination of his tenure of office, or such longer period as may be specified on the termination, but the Strategic Health Authority may, on application being made to him by that person, reduce the period of disqualification.

Termination of tenure of office

8(1) The standing chairman, PCT members or social services authority members may resign their office at any time during their term of office by giving notice in writing to the Chief Executive of the Strategic Health Authority.

(2)   Subject to paragraph (3), where the Strategic Health Authority is of the opinion that it is not in the interests of the health service that the standing chairman or a PCT member or social services authority member should continue to hold office, it may forthwith terminate his tenure of office by giving him notice in writing to that effect.

(3)   The tenure of office of a PCT member or social services authority member must not be terminated under paragraph (2) unless the body responsible for nominating that member has been consulted.

(4)   Where a person has been appointed to be the standing chairman or a PCT member or social services authority member—
  (a) if he becomes disqualified for appointment under direction 6, the Strategic Health Authority must forthwith notify him in writing of such disqualification; or
  (b) if it comes to the notice of the Strategic Health Authority that, at the time of his appointment, he was so disqualified, the Authority must forthwith declare that the person in question was not duly appointed and notify him in writing to that effect.

(5)   Upon receipt of any notification referred to in paragraph (4), the person's tenure of office, if any, shall be terminated and he must cease forthwith to act as a standing chairman, a PCT member or a social services authority member.

Arrangements for Primary Care Trusts situated in more than one Strategic Health Authority

9(1) Subject to paragraph (2), for the purposes of these Directions, a Primary Care Trust is situated in the area of a Strategic Health Authority if all or part of its area is situated within the area of that Strategic Health Authority.

(2) Where a Primary Care Trust is situated within the area of more than one Strategic Health Authority, the Authorities concerned must enter into arrangements for the purpose of ensuring that only one such Authority exercises the functions in these Directions in respect of that Primary Care Trust.

Revocations and transitional provisions

10(1) Subject to paragraph (2), the Continuing Care (National Health Service Responsibilities) Directions 2004 and the Continuing Care (National Health Service Responsibilities) Modification Directions 2006 are revoked.

(2) Where a Strategic Health Authority has—
  (a) before the relevant date, received an application pursuant to direction 4(3) of the Continuing Care Directions 2004 in respect of which a decision has not yet been made; or
  (b) on or after the relevant date received an application requesting a review of a decision as to eligibility for NHS Continuing Healthcare taken before the relevant date,
paragraph (3) shall apply.

(3) Where this paragraph applies—
  (a) the Strategic Health Authority shall organise the review of a matter falling within paragraph (2) in accordance with—
    (i) the Continuing Care Directions 2004; or
    (ii) these Directions, where consideration of the matter by a review panel has not yet commenced; and
  (b) the Strategic Health Authority shall ensure that the review panel applies the eligibility criteria that were in place at the date on which the decision on eligibility was made pursuant to direction 2(2) of the Continuing Care Directions 2004.

(4) Where, before the relevant date, a Strategic Health Authority has, pursuant to directions 4 and 5 of the Continuing Care Directions 2004—
  (a) appointed a standing chairman,
  (b) appointed a reserve standing chairman; and
  (c) established a list of persons pursuant to directions,
those appointments or that list (as the case may be) shall satisfy the requirements of directions 4 and 5 of these Directions, save that the term of office of the standing chairman, the PCT members and the social services authority members shall not in total exceed the three years specified in direction 5(3).

(5) In this direction—
  (a) 'Continuing Care Directions 2004' means the Continuing Care (National Health Service Responsibilities) Directions 2004 as modified by the Continuing Care (National Health Service Responsibilities) Modification Directions 2006; and
  (b) 'relevant date' means 1 October 2007.

Signed by authority of the Secretary of State
30 August 2007

Member of the Senior Civil Service
Department of Health

Precedents

PRECEDENT 1: COMMUNITY CARE ASSESSMENT REQUEST

To: Director of Social Services / Health Authority / NHS Trust etc
[*address*]

From: *Applicant's name*
[*address*]

Date:

Dear Director of Social Services

Community Care Assessment: Mr Albert Smith [*address*]

I am the [*solicitor/carer/agent/advocate*] for the above named who has asked that I assist him in obtaining an assessment of his needs for community care services under National Health Service and Community Care Act 1990 s47.

Mr Smith is [*insert*] years of age being born on [*insert if known*] and is a [*disabled/elderly/ill*] person, in that he
[*here detail as precisely as possible the impairments which have resulted in the applicant needing community care services*].

The help that Mr Smith currently envisages as being necessary, is

[*here detail if possible the services which are required*].

I understand that your care manager will wish to contact Mr Smith in order to investigate this complaint. He suggests that this be done by [*here give a telephone contact number and the time/days the client or carer etc are normally available or some other convenient way that contact can be made*]

Yours sincerely

PRECEDENT 2: ACCESS TO INFORMATION LETTER

To: Director of Social Services / PCT/ LHB/ NHS Trust etc
[*address*]

From: Applicant's name
[*address*]

Date:

Reference:

Access to personal information: Data Protection Act 1998 s7

I formally request that you give me access to the personal information held by your authority relating to my personal circumstances, by copying the relevant information to [*me*] [*my agent, namely . . .*] at [*insert address*].

The information I require to be disclosed is all personal information which your authority holds which relates to myself. [*If possible describe as precisely as possible the information that is sought, including for instance where the information is likely to be located, the nature of the information and the dates between which it was collected*].

I understand that I am entitled to receive this information within 40 days.

If you need further information from me, or a fee,[1] please let me know as soon as possible. If you do not normally handle these requests for your organisation, please pass this letter to your Data Protection Officer or another appropriate officer.

Please confirm receipt of this request.

Signed:

---

1 The 40-day period runs from the date of receipt of the request and any necessary fee. Accordingly, provision should be expedited if the fee is actually enclosed.

PRECEDENT 3: FORMAL COMPLAINT LETTER

To: Director of Social Services
[*address*]

From: Applicant's name
[*address*]

Date:

Dear Director of Adult Social Services

Formal complaint

I ask that you treat this letter as a formal complaint concerning the discharge by your authority of its functions in respect of [*myself*] [*the person for whom I care ~ Mr/ Mrs/Ms etc. . .*]. I require the complaint to be investigated at the earliest opportunity

My complaint is:
[*here set out as precisely as possible*

(a) what it is that is being complained about
(b) the names of the key social workers who the complaints investigator will need to speak to;
(c) the dates of the relevant acts / omissions;
If possible also enclose copies of any relevant papers]
What I want to achieve by making this complaint is

[*here set out as precisely as possible what you want to be the result of your complaint: ie, an apology, a changed service provision, an alteration to practice, compensation, etc*]

I understand that your Complaints Manager will wish to contact me in order to investigate this complaint. I suggest that this be done by [*here give a telephone contact number and the time/days you are normally available or some other convenient way you can be contacted*]

Signed:

PRECEDENT 4: INDEPENDENT LIVING TRUST DEED

> This sample trust deed is reproduced by kind permission of Kiran Dattani Pitt on
> behalf of Values into Action, Oxford House, Derbyshire Street, London E2 6HG
> and is extracted from 'Trusting Independence: a practical guide to independent
> living trust by Andrew Holman and Catherine Bewley (2001).

The following deed is laid out with the information that should be inserted in
brackets like this [xxx]. Where words are underlined in the original deed they are
underlined below. Words in CAPITALS in the deed are IN CAPITALS BELOW.
Words in (brackets in the deed) are in brackets below. Comment and explanations
on why statements are in the deed *are in italics.*

TRUST DEED.

THIS DECLARATION OF TRUST is made the [xxx] day of [xxxx] 200X by
[NAME OF A TRUSTEE] of [address of trustee] [*followed by NAMES and addresses of
all other trustees*] hereinafter together to be called 'the Trustees'.

WHEREAS

(1) The Trustees wish to provide care and support for [NAME of person benefiting
from trust] of [address of person] who has a learning disability by means of an
Independent Living Scheme

*This sets out your main purpose. It says who the fund is for, why they need a fund and the
main purpose. Independent living scheme (ILS) covers a wide area of activity and it is
useful not to be too precise.*

(2) To that end an Account has been opened at [name of bank] of [Address of bank]
under the name of the [NAME of person] Trust

*A separate account is needed just for the trust fund. The accounts may need to be checked
by an accountant at the end of the year. Some authorities may require a full audit, the
cost of which should be added into the charge.*

(3) Further sums will be credited to the said Account by the [PAYING AUTHOR-
ITY] of [address of authority]

*This just states where money comes from, it is useful because it also states where money
goes back to if the ILS finishes and some money is left over.*

(4) The money in the said Account and any accretions thereto are hereinafter called
'the Trust fund'

(5) The Trustees wish to declare the trusts on which they hold the Trust Fund and
the income thereof

*This includes the use of any interest which is just added into the main fund and used for
the same purpose.*

NOW THIS DEED WITNESSES as follows

1. As from the date of this deed the Trustees shall hold the Trust Fund and the
income thereof upon trust to apply the Trust Fund and the income thereof for the
care and support of the said XXX by making such payments as they in their
absolute discretion shall think fit in order to maintain the said XXX in an
Independent Living Scheme.

*This sets out the purpose of the trust i.e. the care and support of XXX. The trustees should
spend the money to support XXX in an independent living scheme. This leaves the detail
of the scheme open and, therefore, a great deal of leeway in how money is spent Such*

flexibility can be important in more imaginative schemes when less traditional answers are used which can still be seen as maintaining XXX in an ILS.

2. The Trustees shall hold the Trust Fund and the income thereof upon the said trusts until the death of the said XXX or until he shall cease to be maintained in an Independent Living Scheme whichever shall first occur

This states the reasons for ending the trust. There may be other contractual arrangements with an authority that dictate when a scheme fails and payments would finish thus also finishing the trust.

3. Subject to the provisions of clause 2 hereof and to the payment or all outgoings and obligations of the Trustees the Trust Fund and the income thereof shall be held by the Trustees on trust for the said XXX

The money shall be used for the payment of any bills the trust has and on behalf on the person XXX.

4. The power of appointing a new Trustee or new Trustees shall be vested in the Trustees or the survivor of them

Trustees have the responsibility of appointing new trustees to replace any member that drops out.

5. The number of Trustees shall not be less than two individuals at any time and if at any time the number of Trustees shall fall below two immediate steps shall be taken to appoint a new or additional Trustee or Trustees so as to constitute at least two persons as Trustees

A minimum number of trustees should be set.

6..A Trustee shall be entitled to exoneration and indemnity from the Trust Fund for any liability loss or expense incurred under this deed or for any judgment recovered against and paid by such Trustee other than liability loss expense or judgment arising out of his or her own wilful and individual fraud, wrongdoing or neglect.

The trustees do not have any other liabilities unless they deliberately or neglectfully misuse the money for other purposes.

IN WITNESS etc.

Index